SECOND EDITION

JAVA, JAVA, JAVA™!

Object-Oriented Problem Solving

Ralph Morelli

Trinity College

Alan Apt Series

Prentice
Hall

Prentice Hall
Upper Saddle River, New Jersey 07458

Library of Cataloging-in-Publication Data

Morelli, R. (Ralph)
    Java, Java, Java : object oriented problem solving/by Ralph Morelli.—2nd ed.
      p.   cm.
    ISBN 0-13-033370-0
    1. Object-oriented programming (Computer science) 2. Java (Computer
program language) I. Title.
    QA76.64 .M64 2002
    005.13'3—dc21   2001050018

Vice President and Editorial Director: *Marcia Horton*
Publisher: *Alan Apt*
Associate Editor: *Toni D. Holm*
Editorial Assistant: *Patrick Lindner*
Vice President and Director of Production
    and Manufacturing, ESM: *David W. Riccardi*
Executive Managing Editor: *Vince O'Brien*
Assistant Managing Editor: *Camille Trentacoste*
Developmental Editor: *Jerry Ralya*
Production Editor: *Fran Daniele*
Director of Creative Services: *Paul Belfanti*
Creative Director: *Carole Anson*
Art Director: *Heather Scott*
Art Editor: *Xiahong Zhu*
Design Technical Support: *John Christiana*
Manufacturing Manager: *Trudy Pisciotti*
Manufacturing Buyer: *Lynda Castillo*
Marketing Assistant: *Barrie Rheinhold*

© 2003 by Prentice-Hall, Inc.
Upper Saddle River, New Jersey 07458

Printed in the United States of America
10 9 8 7 6 5 4 3

ISBN 0-13-033370-0

Pearson Education Ltd., *London*
Pearson Education Australia Pty. Ltd., *Sydney*
Pearson Education Singapore, Pte. Ltd.
Pearson Education North Asia Ltd., *Hong Kong*
Pearson Education Canada, Inc., *Toronto*
Pearson Educacíon de Mexico, S.A. de C.V.
Pearson Education—Japan, *Tokyo*
Pearson Education Malaysia, Pte. Ltd.
Pearson Education, *Upper Saddle River, New Jersey*

To My Parents, Ralph and Ann Morelli ●————————————————————

Feature Walk Through

Focus on Problem Solving and Program Design

A problem-solving and program development process is introduced to students in Chapter 1 and is used consistently throughout the rest of the book in **Case Studies** and other examples.

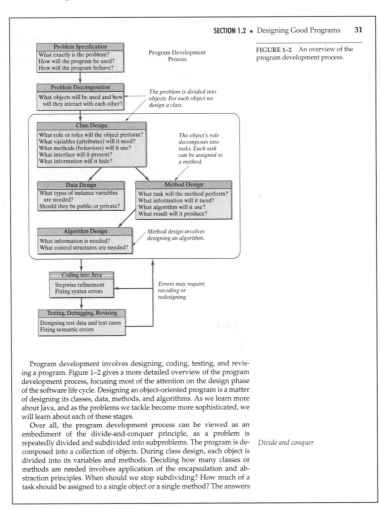

FIGURE 1–2 An overview of the program development process.

Program Development Process

Problem Specification
What exactly is the problem?
How will the program be used?
How will the program behave?

Problem Decomposition
What objects will be used and how will they interact with each other?

The problem is divided into objects. For each object we design a class.

Class Design
What role or roles will the object perform?
What variables (attributes) will it need?
What methods (behaviors) will it use?
What interface will it present?
What information will it hide?

The object's role decomposes into tasks. Each task can be assigned to a method.

Data Design
What types of instance variables are needed?
Should they be public or private?

Method Design
What task will the method perform?
What information will it need?
What algorithm will it use?
What result will it produce?

Algorithm Design
What information is needed?
What control structures are needed?

Method design involves designing an algorithm.

Coding into Java
Stepwise refinement
Fixing syntax errors

Errors may require recoding or redesigning.

Testing, Debugging, Revising
Designing test data and test cases
Fixing semantic errors

Program development involves designing, coding, testing, and revising a program. Figure 1–2 gives a more detailed overview of the program development process, focusing most of the attention on the design phase of the software life cycle. Designing an object-oriented program is a matter of designing its classes, data, methods, and algorithms. As we learn more about Java, and as the problems we tackle become more sophisticated, we will learn about each of these stages.

Over all, the program development process can be viewed as an embodiment of the divide-and-conquer principle, as a problem is repeatedly divided and subdivided into subproblems. The program is decomposed into a collection of objects. During class design, each object is divided into its variables and methods. Deciding how many classes or methods are needed involves application of the encapsulation and abstraction principles. When should we stop subdividing? How much of a task should be assigned to a single object or a single method? The answers

Divide and conquer

- It begins with a clear problem statement, and proceeds through problem decomposition, method and algorithm design, and Java coding.
- **Margin notes** throughout the text ask students questions that remind them of how to apply problem-solving process.
- **Hands-On Learning** sections: Each chapter concludes with these sections which ask students to put the problem-solving process into practice and provide lab activities for courses with such a component.

True Object-Oriented Programming and Object-Oriented Design

Students are introduced to the fundamentals of designing objects and methods before they learn most of the basic language features, helping them to understand the object-oriented concepts without overwhelming them with language details.

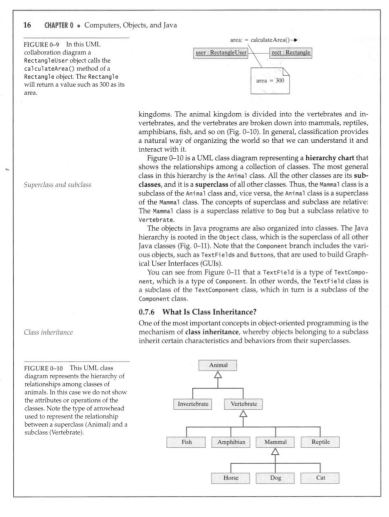

FIGURE 0–9 In this UML collaboration diagram a `RectangleUser` object calls the `calculateArea()` method of a `Rectangle` object. The `Rectangle` will return a value such as 300 as its area.

kingdoms. The animal kingdom is divided into the vertebrates and invertebrates, and the vertebrates are broken down into mammals, reptiles, amphibians, fish, and so on (Fig. 0–10). In general, classification provides a natural way of organizing the world so that we can understand it and interact with it.

Figure 0–10 is a UML class diagram representing a **hierarchy chart** that shows the relationships among a collection of classes. The most general class in this hierarchy is the `Animal` class. All the other classes are its **subclasses**, and it is a **superclass** of all other classes. Thus, the `Mammal` class is a subclass of the `Animal` class and, vice versa, the `Animal` class is a superclass of the `Mammal` class. The concepts of superclass and subclass are relative: The `Mammal` class is a superclass relative to `Dog` but a subclass relative to `Vertebrate`.

Superclass and subclass

The objects in Java programs are also organized into classes. The Java hierarchy is rooted in the `Object` class, which is the superclass of all other Java classes (Fig. 0–11). Note that the `Component` branch includes the various objects, such as `TextFields` and `Buttons`, that are used to build Graphical User Interfaces (GUIs).

You can see from Figure 0–11 that a `TextField` is a type of `TextComponent`, which is a type of `Component`. In other words, the `TextField` class is a subclass of the `TextComponent` class, which in turn is a subclass of the `Component` class.

0.7.6 What Is Class Inheritance?

One of the most important concepts in object-oriented programming is the mechanism of **class inheritance**, whereby objects belonging to a subclass inherit certain characteristics and behaviors from their superclasses.

Class inheritance

FIGURE 0–10 This UML class diagram represents the hierarchy of relationships among classes of animals. In this case we do not show the attributes or operations of the classes. Note the type of arrowhead used to represent the relationship between a superclass (Animal) and a subclass (Vertebrate).

- ● **NEW! Coverage of Unified Modeling Language (UML):** the knowledge of UML, an industry standard, will benefit students in their careers and also makes it easier to teach object-oriented concepts such as information hiding, inheritance, and polymorphism.

- ● **UML diagrams:** help illustrate object-oriented concepts and focus on object-oriented design.

- ● **New exercises:** in Chapters 0–5 and programming exercises in Chapters 6–16 emphasize the use of UML and object-oriented design concepts.

- ● **CyberPet example:** introduced in Chapter 2, as a way of anthropomorphizing the basic features of objects, the CyberPet class is used throughout as a running example to motivate and illustrate important concepts.

Excellent Coverage of GUIs

Coverage of GUIs and applets captures students' interest and introduces them to more real-world examples—encouraging them to study and develop programs that resemble those in the book.

- ● GUIs and applets are introduced in Chapter 4, and new GUI elements are introduced in almost every chapter. Chapters 9 and 10 focus entirely on Java's GUI elements.

Superior Pedagogy

- **Programming, Debugging and Effective Design Tips:** The book features nearly 400 tips to reinforce useful programming and design information in a nutshell.

- **Self-Study Exercises:** More than 200 such exercises with answers help students check their understanding of key topics.

- **Optional Feature Boxes** throughout provide a discussion of real-world application.

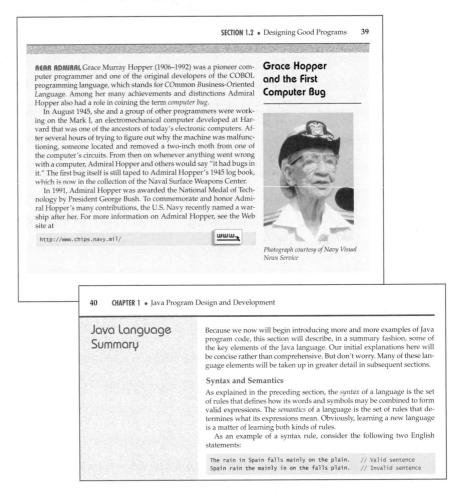

REAR ADMIRAL Grace Murray Hopper (1906–1992) was a pioneer computer programmer and one of the original developers of the COBOL programming language, which stands for *COmmon Business-Oriented Language*. Among her many achievements and distinctions Admiral Hopper also had a role in coining the term *computer bug*.

In August 1945, she and a group of other programmers were working on the Mark I, an electromechanical computer developed at Harvard that was one of the ancestors of today's electronic computers. After several hours of trying to figure out why the machine was malfunctioning, someone located and removed a two-inch moth from one of the computer's circuits. From then on whenever anything went wrong with a computer, Admiral Hopper and others would say "it had bugs in it." The first bug itself is still taped to Admiral Hopper's 1945 log book, which is now in the collection of the Naval Surface Weapons Center.

In 1991, Admiral Hopper was awarded the National Medal of Technology by President George Bush. To commemorate and honor Admiral Hopper's many contributions, the U.S. Navy recently named a warship after her. For more information on Admiral Hopper, see the Web site at

`http://www.chips.navy.mil/`

Grace Hopper and the First Computer Bug

Photograph courtesy of Navy Visual News Service

Java Language Summary

Because we now will begin introducing more and more examples of Java program code, this section will describe, in a summary fashion, some of the key elements of the Java language. Our initial explanations here will be concise rather than comprehensive. But don't worry. Many of these language elements will be taken up in greater detail in subsequent sections.

Syntax and Semantics

As explained in the preceding section, the *syntax* of a language is the set of rules that defines how its words and symbols may be combined to form valid expressions. The *semantics* of a language is the set of rules that determines what its expressions mean. Obviously, learning a new language is a matter of learning both kinds of rules.

As an example of a syntax rule, consider the following two English statements:

```
The rain in Spain falls mainly on the plain.    // Valid sentence
Spain rain the mainly in on the falls plain.    // Invalid sentence
```

Excellent Java Language Reference Material

- **Java Language Summaries:** These sections review and summarize Java's essential syntax and semantics.

- **From the Library sections:**
  Each chapter includes a section that introduces one or more of the library classes from the Java API. These sections introduce tools needed to write programs, explain useful but optional topics, or outline basic GUI components used in program examples.

Substantial Teaching and Learning Package

- **CD-ROM with every text:** This includes Java applications and source code for all the examples in the text; Java™ 2 SDK, Standard Edition, Version 1.3; and Forte™ for Java™ Release 3.0, Community Edition IDE for all platforms.

- **Companion Website:** Designed specifically to accompany the Morelli text, the Companion Website includes an on-line Study Guide with immediate feedback, Java applications and source code for all the examples in the text, an extensive set of PowerPoint slides, and a C++ to Java resource for instructors migrating from C++ — all written by the author!

- **Instructor's Resource CD-ROM** (0-13-033527-4): This contains solutions to all text exercises, Java applications and source code for all the examples in the text, a test bank with fill-in-the-blank, true/false, and multiple-choice questions, an extensive set of PowerPoint® slides, Adobe® Acrobat® files of figures and tables from the text, and additional lab exercises.

- **Course Management Systems: CourseCompass, Blackboard and WebCT:** With these easy-to-use tools, you can create sophisticated Web-based educational programs to enhance an on-campus course or to construct an entirely online course for distance learning. Instructors with little or no experience can use a point-and-click navigational system to design their own online course components, including course calendars, quizzes, assignments, lectures, and self-paced study help.

Value-Added Packages

- **Borland's JBuilder 5 Personal Edition Software** This compiler is available free of charge with the Morelli text. To order this option, which includes Morelli text and CD use ISBN 0-13-066713-7.

- **Durney's The Essential Java Class Reference for Programmers**
  This supplementary book clearly and concisely shows students how to use key class libraries and provides exactly the information they need to write effective, error-free programs. It is available at a 50% discount when packaged with the Morelli text. To order this option, use ISBN 0-13-093385-6.To order just the Durney Reference text use ISBN: 0-13-093385-6.

Preface

Who Should Use This Book?

The topics covered and the approach taken in this book are suitable for a typical Introduction to Computer Science (CS1) course or for a slightly more advanced Java as a Second Language course. The book is also useful to professional programmers making the transition to Java and object-oriented programming.

The book takes an "objects first" approach to programming and problem solving. It assumes no previous programming experience and requires no prior knowledge of Java or object-oriented programming.

What's New in the Second Edition?

The second edition has the following substantive changes:

- **Unified Modeling Language (UML).** UML diagrams have been incorporated throughout the text to help illustrate object-oriented concepts and to describe the design of the Java programs we develop. Some of the UML diagrams replace diagrams used in the first edition, but many new diagrams have been introduced as well.

  UML is rapidly developing into an industry standard for designing object-oriented programs. So it will be useful for students to be familiar with it. But the main reason for incorporating UML is a pedagogical one: It makes it easier to present and teach object-oriented concepts such as information hiding, inheritance, and polymorphism.

- **Emphasis on Object-Oriented Design.** The second edition places somewhat more emphasis on object-oriented design, mostly through the way examples are developed. Many of the programming examples were rewritten to focus on the design before getting into the Java coding details. This approach was greatly aided by the use of UML diagrams.

- **Organizational Changes.** Based on suggestions from reviewers and users of the first edition, several chapters were reorganized. The first two chapters were extensively revised. Chapter 0 now provides a more detailed overview of object orientation and introduces the main features of UML. This should help orient the student before getting into the discussion of Java's implementation of object-oriented concepts. To underscore the importance of design versus coding, Chapter 1 has been reorganized to focus on program design and development before introducing any Java code. It also includes a concise overview of some of the basic Java language features. Thus, the student has been presented with a good bit of overview material before we begin looking at specific Java examples.

In terms of the organization of Java language elements, discussion of the `switch` statement was moved to Chapter 3, where it is covered along with the other selection-control structures. Chapter 11 "Exceptions" was reorganized so that it can more easily be used much earlier in the course.

Why Start with Objects?

Java, Java, Java takes an "objects early" approach to teaching Java, with the assumption that teaching beginners the "big picture" early gives them more time to master the principles of object-oriented programming.

The first time I taught Java in our CS1 course, I followed the same approach I had been taking in teaching C and C++—namely, start with the basic language features and structured programming concepts and then, somewhere around midterm, introduce object orientation. This approach was familiar, for it was one taken in most of the textbooks then available in both Java and C++.

One problem with this approach was that many students failed to get the big picture. They could understand loops, if-else constructs, and arithmetic expressions, but they had difficulty decomposing a programming problem into a well-organized Java program. Also, it seemed that this procedural approach failed to take advantage of the strengths of Java's object orientation. Why teach an object-oriented language if you're going to treat it like C or Pascal?

I was reminded of a similar situation that existed when Pascal was the predominant CS1 language. Back then the main hurdle for beginners was *procedural abstraction*—learning the basic mechanisms of procedure call and parameter passing and learning how to **design** programs as a collection of procedures. *Oh! Pascal!*, my favorite introductory text, was typical of a "procedures early" approach. It covered procedures and parameters in Chapter 2, right after covering the assignment and I/O constructs in Chapter 1. It then covered program design and organization in Chapter 3. It didn't get into loops, if-else, and other structured programming concepts until Chapter 4 and beyond.

Presently, the main hurdle for beginners is *object abstraction*. Beginning programmers must be able to see a program as a collection of interacting objects and must learn how to decompose programming problems into well-designed objects. Object orientation subsumes both procedural abstraction and structured programming concepts from the Pascal days. Teaching "objects early" takes a top-down approach to these three important concepts. The sooner you begin to introduce objects and classes, the better the chances that students will master the important principles of object orientation.

Object orientation (OO) is a fundamental problem-solving and design concept, not just another language detail that should be relegated to the middle or the end of the book (or course). If OO concepts are introduced late, it is much too easy to skip over them when push comes to shove in the course.

Java is a good language for introducing object orientation. Its object model is better organized than C++. In C++, it is easy to "work around" or completely ignore OO features and treat the language like C. In Java, there are good opportunities for motivating the discussion of object orientation. For example, it's almost impossible to discuss applets without discussing inheritance and polymorphism. Thus, rather than using contrived examples of OO concepts, instructors can use some of Java's basic features—applets, the class library, GUI components—to motivate these discussions in a natural way.

Key Features

In addition to its "objects early" approach, this book has several other important features.

- **Unified Modeling Language (UML) Diagrams.** More than 225 UML diagrams have been incorporated throughout the text to explain object-oriented concepts and to focus on object-oriented design. The advantages of using UML are several. First, UML diagrams provide a concise visual means of describing the main features of classes and objects. In one glance you can see an object's attributes and methods, whether they are private or public, and how the class or object relates to other classes. Second, UML diagrams provide simple graphical models for important object-oriented concepts such as inheritance and polymorphism. A picture is worth 1,000 words, so in addition to the descriptions provided in words, the UML diagrams should help students learn these important concepts. Third, for the purposes for which it is used in this book, UML is relatively easy and intuitive to understand. The basic notation is introduced in Chapter 0 through simple, accessible examples. Finally, UML is rapidly becoming an industry standard. So gaining familiarity with UML in this book will make other books on Java or object-oriented design more accessible.

- **The CyberPet Example.** Throughout the text a CyberPet class is used as a running example to motivate and illustrate important concepts. The CyberPet is introduced in Chapter 2, as a way of "anthropomorphizing" the basic features of objects. Thus, individual CyberPets belong to a class (definition), have a certain state (instance variables), and are capable of certain behaviors like eating and sleeping (instance methods). Method calls are used to command the CyberPets to eat and sleep. In Chapter 3 the emphasis is on defining and using methods and parameters to promote communication with CyberPets. In subsequent chapters, concepts such as inheritance, randomness, animation, and threads are illustrated in terms of the CyberPet. Some of the lab and programming exercises are also centered around extending the behavior and sophistication of the CyberPet.

- **Applets and GUIs.** Applets and GUIs are first introduced in Chapter 4 and then used throughout the rest of the text. Clearly, applets are a "turn-on" for introductory students and can be used as a good motivating factor. Plus, *event-driven programming* and Graphical User Interfaces (GUIs) are what students ought now to be learning in CS1. We are long past the days when command-line interfaces were the norm in applications programming. Another nice thing about Java applets is that they are fundamentally object oriented. To understand them fully, students need to understand basic OO concepts. That's why applets are not introduced until Chapter 4, where they provide an excellent way to motivate the discussion of inheritance and polymorphism.

- **Companion Web Site.** The text is designed to be used in conjunction with a companion Web site that includes many useful resources, including the Java code and Java documentation (in HTML) for all the examples in the text, additional lab and programming assignments, online quizzes that can be scored automatically, and PowerPoint class notes.

- **Problem-Solving Approach.** A pedagogical, problem-solving approach is taken throughout the text. There are a total of 13 fully developed case studies, as well as numerous other examples that illustrate the problem-solving process. Marginal notes in the text repeatedly emphasize the basic elements of object-oriented problem solving: What objects do we need? What methods and data do we need? What algorithm should we use? And so on.

- **Self-Study Exercises.** The book contains more than 200 self-study exercises, with answers provided at the back of each chapter.

- **End-of-Chapter Exercises.** Over 400 end-of-chapter exercises are provided, including "Challenge" exercises at the end of most sets. The answers are provided in an Instructor's Manual, which is available to adopters.

- **Programming, Debugging, and Design Tips.** The book contains nearly 400 separately identified "tips" (Programming Tips, Debugging Tips, Effective Design Principles, and Java Language Rules) that provide useful programming and design information in a nutshell.

- **Hands-On Learning Sections.** Each chapter concludes with a laboratory exercise, so the text can easily be used to support lab-based CS1 courses. For CS1 courses that are not lab based, these sections can still be read as preparation for a programming assignment, or as an in-class demo, or as some other form of hands-on exercise. For each lab in the text, the companion Web site contains additional resources and handouts, as well as a repository of alternative lab assignments.

- **"From the Library" Sections.** Each chapter includes a section that introduces one or more of the library classes from the Java API (Application Programming Interface). In the early chapters, these sections provide a way of introducing tools, such as I/O classes and methods, needed to write simple programs. In subsequent chapters, some of these sections introduce useful but optional topics, such as the NumberFormat class used to format numeric output. Others introduce basic GUI (Graphical User Interface) components that are used in program examples and the laboratory sections.

- **"Object-Oriented Design" Sections.** Each chapter includes a section on object-oriented design, which is used to underscore and amplify important principles such as inheritance, polymorphism, and information hiding. For instructors wishing to emphasize object-oriented design, Table 1 provides a list of sections that should be covered.

- **"Java Language Summary".** Those chapters that introduce language features contain "Java Language Summary" sections that summarize the features' essential syntax and semantics.

TABLE 1 An overview of object-oriented sections.

Topic	Section
What Is Object Orientation?	Chapter 0.7
Overview of UML	Chapter 0.8
Object-Oriented Design Process	Chapter 1.2
Objects: Defining, Creating, Using	Chapter 2
Methods: Communicating with Objects	Chapter 3
Inheritance: The `toString()` Method	Chapter 3, OOD
Inheritance and Polymorphism in Applets	Chapter 4.2-4.4
Inheritance and Polymorphism: `ToggleButton`	Chapter 4, OOD
Information Hiding	Chapter 5, OOD
Structured Programming Concepts	Chapter 6, OOD
Abstract Classes: `Cipher`	Chapter 7, OOD
Polymorphism: Polymorphic Sorting	Chapter 8, OOD
Model-View-Controller Architecture	Chapter 9, OOD
Inheritance and Polymorphism: Spider/Fly Classes	Chapter 13.6
Generic Client/Server Classes	Chapter 15.7
Abstract Data Types: `List` Class	Chapter 16, OOD

Organization of the Text

The book is organized into three main parts. The first part (Chapters 0 through 4) introduces the basic concepts of object orientation, including objects, classes, methods, parameter passing, information hiding, inheritance, and polymorphism. Although the primary focus in these chapters is on object orientation rather than on Java language details, each of these chapters has a "Java Language Summary" section that summarizes the language elements introduced.

In Chapters 1 to 3, students are given the basic building blocks for constructing a Java program from scratch. Although the programs at this stage have limited functionality in terms of control structures and data types, the priority is placed on how objects are constructed and how they interact with each other through method calls and parameter passing.

The second part (Chapters 5 through 8) focuses on the remaining language elements, including data types and operators (Chapter 5), control structures (Chapter 6), strings (Chapter 7), and arrays (Chapter 8). Once the basic structure and framework of an object-oriented program are understood, it is relatively easy to introduce these language features.

Part Three (Chapters 9 through 16) covers a variety of advanced topics, including Graphical User Interfaces (Chapter 9), graphics (Chapter 10), exceptions (Chapter 11), recursion (Chapter 12), threads (Chapter 13), files (Chapter 14), sockets (Chapter 15), and data structures (Chapter 16). Topics from these chapters can be used selectively depending on instructor and student interest.

Table 2 provides an example syllabus from my one-semester CS1 course. Our semester is 13 weeks (plus one reading week during which classes do not meet).

Note that the advanced topic chapters needn't be covered in order. Recursion (Chapter 12) could be introduced at the same time or even before loops (Chapter 6). The recursion chapter includes examples using strings, arrays, and drawing algorithms (fractals), as well as some

TABLE 2   A one-semester course.

Weeks	Topics	Chapters
1	Object Orientation, UML	Chapter 0
	Program Design and Development	Chapter 1
2–4	Objects and Class Definitions	Chapter 2
	Methods and Parameters	Chapter 3
	Selection Structure (if-else)	
5	Applet Programming	Chapter 4
	Inheritance	
6	Data Types and Operators	Chapter 5
7–8	Control Structures (Loops)	Chapter 6
	Structured Programming	
9	String Processing (loops)	Chapter 7
10	Array Processing	Chapter 8
11	Recursion	Chapter 12
12	Advanced Topic (GUIs)	Chapter 9
13	Advanced Topic (Exceptions)	Chapter 11
	Advanced Topic (Threads)	Chapter 13

standard numerical algorithms (factorial). Another way to teach recursion would be to incorporate it into the discussion of strings (Chapter 7), arrays (Chapter 8), and graphics (Chapter 10), thereby treating iteration and recursion in parallel.

Exceptions (Chapter 11) could also be covered earlier. The examples in the first few sections of this chapter use simple arithmetic operations and the basic for loop. If these language elements are introduced separately, then exceptions could be covered right after Chapter 3.

Some of the examples in the advanced chapters use applets (Chapter 4) and GUIs (Chapter 9), so these chapters should ideally be covered before Chapters 10 (graphics), 13 (threads), 14 (files), and 15 (sockets and networking). However, Chapter 16 (data structures) and sections of the other advanced topic chapters can be covered independently of applets and GUIs. Figure 1 shows the major chapter dependencies in the book.

FIGURE 1   Chapter dependencies.

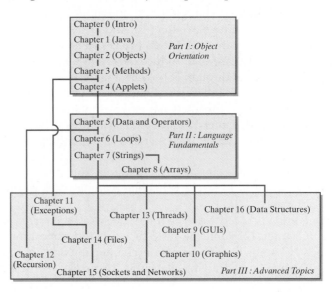

Acknowledgments

First, I would like to thank the reviewers and technical reviewers, whose comments often suggested important additions and revisions. For the first edition these include Pedro Larios (Metrowerks), Laird Dornin (Sun Microsystems), Katherine Lowrie (Trilogy Inc.), Robert Holloway (University of Wisconsin at Madison), Deborah Trytten (University of Oklahoma), Alan Miller (Golden Gate University), Haklin Kimm (University of Tennessee), and Jim Roberts (Carnegie Mellon University).

For the second edition the reviewers include Jim Buffenbarger (Idaho State University), Dianne Wolff (Western Virginia Community College), Hamid Namati (University of North Carolina at Greensboro), Kelli Davis (Cape Fear Community College, North Carolina), Le Gruenwald (University of Oklahoma), Haklin Kimm (East Stroudsburg University), Dave Barrington (University of Massachusetts at Amherst), and John Ellis (University of Wyoming). The following UML experts deserve thanks for their many helpful suggestions regarding the use of UML in the book: William Tepfenhart (Monmouth University), Rolf Kamp (AT&T), Scott Henninger (Univerity of Maryland), and Michael Huhns (University of South Carolina).

At Prentice Hall, my appreciation goes to Sandi Hakansan for encouraging me to send the manuscript to Prentice Hall; to Alan Apt for taking on this project and for being a source of guidance and encouragement throughout; to Ana Arias Terry for her cheerful and professional management of the project; to Rose Kernan for guiding the project through a very tough production phase; and to Eric Unhjem and Toni Holm for their help and support. I especially want to thank my development editor, Jerry Ralya, whose careful work and many suggestions helped shape and improve the final result of both editions in immeasurable ways.

I want to thank a number of Trinity College students who helped track down typos and other errors in earlier drafts of the text. These include Christian Allen, Jeff Green, Ryan Carmody, and Michael Wilson. I especially want to thank Jamie Mazur, whose feedback on the manuscript and enthusiasm for the objects-first approach and whose role in developing the solutions manual were much appreciated. My thanks to the following list of individuals who helped identify errors in the first edition: Ashton Hobbs, Elissa Lowe, Peter Casey, Bernd Bruegge, David Mix Barrington, Rommy Mayerowitz, Jason Smart, Colleen Kubont, Jonathan Amery, Shakira Ramos, Jennifer Chen, Robert Gaspar, Yolanda McManus, and Jim Parry.

Thanks to my colleague Joe Palladino in the Engineering Department, who served as the LaTeX meister throughout the project; to Chuck Liang in the Computer Science Department for interesting Java examples; and to my good Hawaii friend and limerick meister, Lanning Lee.

To my Trinity computer science colleagues, Madalene Spezialetti and Ralph Walde, thanks for their generous support and advice, especially during the early stages of this project. They're the ones who pulled me back over the rail when I went overboard with the "objects first" juggernaut. They also helped rescue CyberPet from its germ as a (lame!) horse. With their conjurings and refinements it evolved through a dog, a parrot, and then a "net pet," before settling, rather nicely we think, as CyberPet. They also have my gratitude for being willing to subject our students to

earlier (incomplete) drafts of the manuscript in their sections of our intro course. Madalene's suggestion to emphasize basic language features
early led eventually to the book's "Java Language Summary" sections.
She also took the first pass at drafting material that appears in Chapter
0 and 1. Although that material has been rewritten (and whatever flaws
it has are entirely mine), it still bears the stamp of her influence. Their
criticisms and suggestions have improved the text in immeasurable and
significant ways, and the gentleness, subtleness, and humor with which
they delivered their suggestions have helped sustain our friendship.

Finally, thanks to my wife, Choong Lan How, for her love and encouragement, and for her careful reading of the first three chapters; to my
daughter Alicia for her feedback on artistic matters; and to my daughter
Meisha for her tremendous help in producing the solutions manual and
the on-line study guide.

Brief Contents

Contents

2   Objects: Defining, Creating, and Using   67

3   Methods: Communicating with Objects   115

8 Arrays and Array Processing   377

9   Graphical User Interfaces   439

12 Recursive Problem Solving   595

13 Threads and Concurrent Programming   635

JAVA, JAVA, JAVA™!

Object-Oriented Problem Solving

Photograph courtesy of Nick Koudis, PhotoDisc, Inc.

0

Computers, Objects, and Java

OBJECTIVES

After studying this chapter, you will

- Be familiar with the notion of programming.
- Understand why Java is a good introductory programming language.
- Know some of the principles of the object-oriented programming approach.
- Understand basic computer terminology that will be used in the rest of the book.
- Recognize Unified Modeling Language (UML) diagrams.

OUTLINE

0.1   Welcome

Welcome to *Java, Java, Java*. This book introduces you to object-oriented programming using the Java language. Three important questions come to mind: Why study programming? Why study Java? What is object-oriented programming? This first chapter will address these questions and will provide a brief introduction to computers.

0.2   Why Study Programming?

A **computer program** is a set of instructions that directs the computer's behavior. *Computer programming* is the art and science of designing and writing programs. Years ago it was widely believed that entrance into the computer age would require practically everyone to learn how to program. But this is no longer true. Today's computers come with so much easy-to-use software that knowing how to use a computer no longer requires programming skills.

Another reason to study programming might be to gain entry into computer science. However, although programming is one of its primary tools, computer science is a broad and varied discipline, which ranges from engineering subjects, such as processor design, to mathematical subjects, such as performance analysis. So there are many computer scientists who do little or no programming as part of their everyday work. If you plan to major or minor in computer science, you will certainly learn to program, but good careers in the computing field are available to programmers and nonprogrammers alike.

One of the best reasons to study programming is because it is a creative and enjoyable problem-solving activity. This book will teach you to develop well-designed solutions to a range of interesting problems. One of the best things about programming is that you can actually see and experience your solutions as running programs. As many students have indicated, there's really nothing like the kick you get from seeing your program solving a problem you've been struggling with. Designing and building well-written programs provides a powerful sense of accomplishment and satisfaction. What's more, Java is a language that makes programming even more fun, because once they're finished, many Java programs can be posted on the World Wide Web (WWW) for all the world to see!

0.3   Why Java?

Java is a relatively young programming language. It was initially designed by Sun Microsystems in 1991 as a language for embedding programs into electronic consumer devices, such as microwave ovens and home security systems. However, the tremendous popularity of the *Internet* and the *World Wide Web (WWW)* led Sun to recast Java as a language for embedding programs into Web-based applications. As you probably know, the Internet is a global computer network, and the WWW is that portion of the network that provides multimedia access to a vast range of information. Java has become one of the most important languages for Web and Internet applications.

Java was initially named "Oak" after a tree outside the office of its developer, James Gosling. When it was discovered that there was already a programming language named Oak, the name "Java" was suggested by members of its development team during a visit to a local coffee shop.

Java has also generated significant interest in the business community, where it is seen as having commercial potential. In addition to being a useful tool for helping businesses promote their products and services over the Internet, Java is also a good language for distributing software and providing services to employees and clients on private corporate networks or *intranets*.

Because of its original intended role as a language for programming microprocessors embedded in consumer appliances, Java has been designed with a number of interesting features:

- Java is a *simple* language. While it uses many of the same language constructs as C and C++, Java is designed to be simple enough so that fluency in the language should come relatively easily compared to learning C or C++.
- Java is **object oriented**. Object-oriented languages divide programs into separate modules, called **objects**, that encapsulate the program's various attributes and actions. Thus, object-oriented programming (OOP) and object-oriented design (OOD) refer to a particular way of organizing programs, one which is rapidly emerging as the preferred approach for building complex software systems. Java is a pure OO language, whereas C++ is a hybrid language, allowing non-OO constructs to be used. Java comes with an excellent collection of libraries that can be used to build object-oriented programs.
- Java is *robust*, meaning that errors in Java programs don't cause system crashes as often as errors in other programming languages. Certain features of the language enable many potential errors to be detected before a program is run, and its excellent *exception handling* capability allows it to "catch" errors while a program is running.
- Java is *platform independent*. A platform, in this context, is just a particular kind of computer system, such as a Macintosh or a Windows system. Java's trademark is "Write once, run anywhere." This means that a Java program can be run without changes on different kinds of computers. This is not true for any other high-level programming language, and this is one reason that Java is suited for WWW applications.
- Java is a *distributed* language, which means that its programs can be designed to run on computer networks. It contains features and code libraries that make it particularly easy to build applications for the Internet and the WWW. This is one of the reasons why Java is so well suited for supporting applications on corporate networks.
- Java is a *secure* language. Designed to be used on networks, Java contains features that protect against *untrusted code*—code that might introduce a virus or corrupt your system in some way. For example, Web-based Java programs are severely constrained in the actions they can take once they are downloaded into your browser.

Despite this list of attractive features, perhaps the best reason for choosing Java as an introductory programming language is its potential for bringing fun and excitement into learning how to program. In what other language can a beginning programmer write a computer game or a graphically based application that can be distributed on a Web page to just about

FIGURE 0–1   An image from the CyberPet applet.

any computer in the world? The simplicity of Java's design and its easily accessible libraries bring such accomplishments within reach of the most neophyte programmers.

For example, one of the projects we will work on throughout the text is the CyberPet program, which we begin designing in Chapter 2. Cyber-Pet starts out as a very simple simulation of a pet that responds to commands like "eat" and "sleep." As we learn more sophisticated programming techniques, we gradually build more complexity into the simulation. For example, we learn how to add graphical images to the program in Chapter 4. In Chapter 6 we learn how to animate the CyberPet's eating behavior. In Chapter 8 we add randomness to the CyberPet's behavior, so that it disobeys our commands from time to time. Finally, in Chapter 13 we learn how to introduce multiple CyberPets of different kinds that behave in a completely autonomous fashion (see Fig. 0–1). To get a look at where we're headed you might want to play with CyberPet by visiting the author's companion Web site at

```
http://starbase.trincoll.edu/~jjjava/cyberpet/
```

0.4   What Is a Computer?

A *computer* is a machine that performs calculations and processes information. A computer works under the control of a computer program, a set of instructions that tell a computer what to do. *Hardware* refers to the electronic and mechanical components of a computer. *Software* refers to the programs that control the hardware.

A *general-purpose computer* of the sort that we will be programming stores its control programs in its memory and so is capable of changing its control program and, hence, changing what it does. This is in contrast to a *special-purpose computer,* such as the one that resides in your microwave oven or the one that controls your digital watch or calculator. These types of computers contain control programs that are fixed and cannot be changed.

A computer's hardware is organized into several main subsystems or components (Fig. 0–2).

FIGURE 0–2   A block diagram of the main functional components in a computer system. The arrows indicate the flow of information between various components.

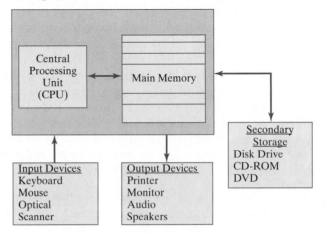

- The *output devices* provide a means by which information held in the computer can be displayed in some human-sensible form. Common output devices include printers, monitors, and audio speakers.

- The *input devices* bring data and information into the computer. Some of the more common input devices are the keyboard, mouse, microphone, and scanner.

- The *primary memory* or *main memory* of a computer is used to store both data and programs. This type of memory is built entirely out of electronic components—integrated circuit chips—which makes it extremely fast. A computer's main memory is *volatile*, which means that any information stored in it is lost when the computer's power is turned off. In a sense, main memory acts as the computer's scratch pad, storing both programs and data temporarily while a program is running.

- The *secondary storage* devices are used for long-term or permanent storage of relatively large amounts of information. These devices include magnetic disks, compact disks (CDs), digital video disks (DVDs), and magnetic tapes. All of these devices are *nonvolatile*, meaning that they retain information when the computer's power is turned off. Compared to a computer's primary memory, these devices are relatively slow, because their access devices all require some form of mechanical motion to retrieve and store data.

- The *central processing unit (CPU)* is the computer's main engine. The CPU is the computer's *microprocessor*, such as the Intel Pentium processor, which serves as the foundation for most Windows PCs, or the PowerPC processor, which serves as the foundation for Macintosh computers. The CPU is designed to perform the *fetch-execute cycle*, whereby it *Fetch-execute cycle* repeatedly fetches the next machine instruction from memory and executes it. Under the direction of computer programs (software), the CPU issues signals that control the other components that make up the computer system. One portion of the CPU, known as the *arithmetic-logic unit (ALU)*, performs all calculations, such as addition and subtraction, and all logical comparisons, such as when one piece of data is compared to another to determine if they are equal.

There are two main types of software:

- *Application software* refers to programs designed to provide a particular task or service, such as word processors, computer games, spreadsheet programs, and Web browsers.

- *System software* includes programs that perform the basic operations that make a computer usable. For example, an important piece of system software is the *operating system*, which contains programs that manage the data stored on the computer's disks. An operating system assists application software in performing very primitive tasks, such as memory management and input/output.

Processors Then and Now

Photograph courtesy of Roger Duboisson, The Stock Market

TO GIVE you some idea of how rapidly computer hardware technology has advanced, let's compare the first digital processor with one of today's models.

The *ENIAC* (which stood for Electronic Numerical Integrator and Calculator) was developed in 1946 at the University of Pennsylvania. ENIAC occupied more than 640 square feet of floor space and weighed nearly 30 tons. Instead of the *integrated circuits* used in today's computers, ENIAC's digital technology was based on over 17,000 vacuum tubes. At a speed of 100,000 pulses per second, ENIAC ran more than 500 times faster than other computing machines of that day and age. Its main application was for computing ballistic trajectories for the U.S. Army. It could perform around 300 multiplications in a second. To program the ENIAC, you would have to manipulate hundreds of cables and switches. It took two or three days for a team of several programmers, most of whom were young women, to set up a single program that would then run for a few seconds.

The Pentium IV processor is Intel's most advanced and powerful processor for desktop computers. The chip contains 42 million transistors and runs at speeds over 1 GHz (1 gigahertz or 1 billion cycles per second). The Pentium processor is small enough to fit completely within the confines of the fingernail on your pinky finger. It executes millions of instructions per second. It supports a huge range of multimedia applications, including three-dimensional graphics, streaming audio and video, and speech recognition applications. To program the Pentium, you can choose from a wide range of high-level programming languages, including the Java language.

Another important thing that the operating system does is to serve as an interface between the user and the hardware. The operating system determines how the user will interact with the system, or conversely, how the system will look and feel to the user. For example, in *command-line* systems, such as Unix and DOS (short for Disk Operating System), a program is run by typing its name on the command line. By contrast, in graphically based systems, such as Windows and Macintosh, a program is run by clicking on its icon with the mouse. Thus, this "point-and-click" interface has a totally different "look and feel" but does the same thing.

0.5 The Internet and the World Wide Web

Most personal computers contain software that enables them to be connected to *networks* of various sizes. Networks allow many individual users to share costly computer resources, such as a high-speed printer or a large disk drive or *file server* that is used to store and distribute both data and programs to the computers on the network.

Client/server mode

File servers are just one example of *client/server computing*, a computing model made possible by networks. According to this model, certain computers on the network are set up as *servers*, which provide certain well-defined services to *client* computers. For example, one computer in a network may be set up as the *mail server*, with the responsibility of sending, receiving, and storing mail for all users on the network. Users may use client application software, such as Eudora or Pine, to access their mail on the server. Similarly, another server may be set up as a *Web server*, with the responsibility of storing and serving up Web pages for all the users on the network. Users can run Web browsers, another type of client software, to access Web pages on the server. Java is particularly well suited for these types of networked or distributed applications, where part of the application software resides on a server and part resides on the client computer.

Networks can range in size from *local area networks (LANs)*, which connect computers and peripherals over a relatively small area, such as within a lab or a building, through *wide area networks (WANs)*, which can span large geographic areas, such as cities and nations.

The *Internet* (with a capital *I*) is a network of networks whose geographical area covers the entire globe. The *World Wide Web (WWW)* is another example of distributed, client/server computing. The WWW is not a separate physical network. Rather it is a subset of the Internet that uses the *HyperText Transfer Protocol (HTTP)*. A *protocol* is a set of rules and conventions that govern how communication takes place between two computers. HTTP is a multimedia protocol. It supports the transmission of text, graphics, sound, and other forms of information. Certain computers within a network run special software that enables them to play the role of HTTP (or Web) servers. They store Web documents and are capable of handling requests for documents from client browser applications. The servers and clients can be located anywhere on the Internet.

The documents stored on Web servers are encoded in a special text-based language known as *HyperText Markup Language*, or *HTML*. Web browsers, such as Netscape's Navigator and Microsoft's Internet Explorer, are designed to interpret documents coded in this language. The language itself is very simple. Its basic elements are known as *tags*, which consist of certain keywords or other text contained within angle brackets, $<$ and $>$. For example, if you wanted to italicize text on a Web page, you would enclose it between the $<I>$ and $</I>$ tags. Thus, the following HTML code

```
<I>Italic font</I> can be used for <I>emphasis</I>.
```

would be displayed by the Web browser as

Italic font can be used for *emphasis*.

When you use a Web browser to surf the Internet, you repeatedly instruct your browser to go to a certain location and retrieve a page that is encoded in HTML. For example, if you typed the following *URL (Uniform Resource Locator)*

```
http://www.prenhall.com/morelli/index.html
```

into your browser, the browser would send a message to the Web server www located in the prenhall.com domain—the prenhall portion of this address specifies Prentice Hall and the com portion specifies the commercial

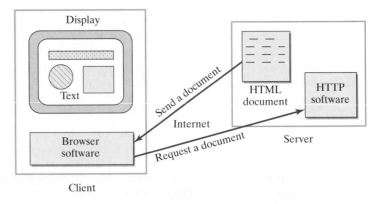

domain of the Internet—requesting that the document named `index.html` in the `morelli` home directory be retrieved and sent back to your computer (Fig. 0–3). The beauty of the Web is that it is possible to embed text, sound, video, and graphics within an HTML document, making it possible to download a wide range of multimedia resources through this (relatively) simple mechanism.

The Web has enormous potential to change business, entertainment, commerce, and education. The fact that it is possible to download computer games and other application software from the Web will completely change the way new software is purchased and distributed. Similarly, as noted earlier, many businesses have begun to organize their information systems into intranets—private networks that have implemented the HTTP protocol. Currently, one of the big areas of development on the Web is commerce. As soon as consumers gain confidence that credit card information can be securely transmitted over the Web (as it can over a telephone), the Web will explode as a marketing medium as powerful, perhaps, as television is today. Because Java has been designed to support secure, distributed, networked applications, it is ideally suited to be used as the language for these types of applications.

0.6 Programming Languages

Most computer programs today are written in a **high-level language**, such as Java, C, C++, or FORTRAN. A programming language is considered high level if its statements resemble English-language statements. For example, all of the languages just mentioned have some form of an "if" statement, which says, "if some condition holds, then take some action."

Computer scientists have invented hundreds of high-level programming languages, although relatively few of these have been put to practical use. Some of the widely used languages have special features that make them suitable for one type of programming application or another. COBOL (COmmon Business-Oriented Language), for example, is still widely used in commercial applications. FORTRAN (FORmula TRANslator) is still preferred by some engineers and scientists. C and C++ are still the primary languages used by systems programmers.

In addition to having features that make them suitable for certain types of applications, high-level languages use symbols and notation that make them easily readable by humans. For example, arithmetic operations in

Java make use of familiar operators such as "+" and "−" and "/", so that arithmetic expressions look more or less the way they do in algebra. So, to take the average of two numbers, you might use the expression

```
(a + b) / 2
```

The problem is that computers cannot directly understand such expressions. In order for a computer to run a program, the program must first be translated into the computer's *machine language*, which is the *instruction set* understood by its CPU or microprocessor. Each type of microprocessor has its own particular machine language. That's why when you buy software it runs either on a Macintosh, which uses the PowerPC chip, or on a Windows machine, which uses the Pentium chip, but not on both. When a program can run on just one type of chip, it is known as *platform dependent*.

Platform independence

In general, machine languages are based on the *binary code*, a two-valued system that is well suited for electronic devices. In a binary representation scheme everything is represented as a sequence of 1's and 0's, which corresponds closely to the computer's electronic "on" and "off" states. For example, the number 13 would be represented as 1101. Similarly, a particular address in the computer's memory might be represented as 01100011, and an instruction in the computer's instruction set might be represented as 001100.

The instructions that make up a computer's machine language are very simple and basic. In most cases, a single instruction carries out a single machine operation. For example, a typical machine language might include instructions for ADD, SUBTRACT, DIVIDE, and MULTIPLY, but it wouldn't contain an instruction for AVERAGE. Therefore, the process of averaging two numbers would have to be broken down into two or more steps. A machine language instruction itself might have something similar to the following format, in which an *opcode* is followed by several *operands*, which refer to locations in the computer's primary memory. The following instruction says ADD the number in LOCATION1 to the number in LOCATION2 and store the result in LOCATION3:

Opcode	Operand 1	Operand 2	Operand 3
011110	110110	111100	111101
(ADD)	(LOCATION 1)	(LOCATION 2)	(LOCATION 3)

Given the primitive nature of machine language, an expression like the preceding one, (a + b)/2, would have to be translated into a sequence of several machine language instructions that, in binary code, might look as follows:

```
011110110110111100111101
000101000100010001001101
001000010001010101111011
```

In the early days of computing, before high-level languages were developed, computers had to be programmed directly in their machine languages, an extremely tedious and error-prone process. Imagine how

FIGURE 0–4 Translator software translates high-level *source code* to machine language *object code*.

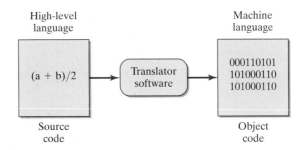

difficult it would be to detect an error that consisted of putting a 0 in the preceding program where a 1 should occur!

Fortunately, we no longer have to worry about machine languages, because special programs can be used to translate a high-level or **source code** program into machine language or **object code**. In general, a program that translates source code to object code is known as a *translator* (Fig. 0–4). Thus, with suitable translation software for Java or C++ we can write programs as if the computer could understand Java or C++ directly.

Source code translators come in two varieties. An **interpreter** translates a single line of source code directly into machine language and executes the code—which means runs it on the computer—before going on to the next line of source code. A **compiler** translates the entire source code program into executable object code. The object code can then be run directly without further translation.

There are advantages and disadvantages to both approaches. Interpreted programs generally run less efficiently than compiled programs, because they must translate and execute each line of the program at the same time. Once compiled, an object program is just executed without any need for further translation. It is also much easier to optimize compiled code to make it run more efficiently. But interpreters are generally easier to write and provide somewhat better error messages when things go wrong. Some languages, such as BASIC, LISP, and Perl, are mostly used in interpreted form, although compilers are also available for these languages. Programs written in COBOL, FORTRAN, C, C++, and Pascal are compiled. As we will see in Chapter 1, Java programs use both compilation and interpretation in their translation process.

0.7 What Is Object-Oriented Programming?

Java is an object-oriented (OO) language, and this book takes an object-oriented approach to programming. So before beginning our discussion of Java, it is important that you understand some of the underlying concepts. We need to talk about what an object is and what a class is, how objects interact with each other, and how objects use messages to communicate with each other.

0.7.1 Basic Object-Oriented Programming Metaphor: Interacting Objects

A Java program, and any object-oriented program, is a collection of interacting objects that models some collection of real-world objects.

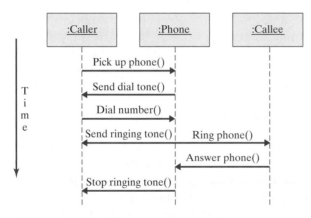

FIGURE 0–5   This *UML sequence diagram* represents the objects and actions involved in a phone call. The objects are represented by labeled rectangles. In this example the labels represent the *type* of object (a caller) rather than the name of an object (Alice). The actions are represented as arrows, which symbolize *messages* that are passed between objects.

For example, let's create a simple model of the task of calling someone on the telephone. The immediate objects involved are the *caller*, the *callee*, and the *telephone*. The interaction among these objects begins something like this: The caller picks up the phone and receives a dial tone. The caller dials the callee's number. The callee's phone rings and the caller's phone plays a corresponding tone. The callee answers the phone. The *actions* involved in this activity are such things as *pick up the phone*, *answer the phone*, *send a dial tone*, and so on.

Figure 0–5 provides an abstract model of this activity in a notation called **Unified Modeling Language (UML)**. We will be using UML diagrams throughout the book to illustrate object-oriented concepts. The diagram represents our model of phone calling. It has symbols representing each of the important objects and actions and shows how they interact.

A **model** is an abstract representation of some real object or situation. By **abstract** we mean that the model does not attempt to represent every single feature of the object or situation. Instead it presents a simplification of the real situation by focusing just on certain features that are deemed appropriate for the problem the model purports to solve. For instance, in our model of the phone call, we did not represent the wires that connect the phones, the electronic signals passing over wires, and so forth. So a model is a simplification of some real-world situation.   *Model*

0.7.2   What Is a Java Object?

In the real world, objects have **attributes** (or *characteristics*) and **behaviors** (or *actions*). For example, in addition to physical attributes, such as height, weight, hair color, and so on, a person has abstract characteristics, such as a name and phone number. Notice that all of these attributes are themselves objects, some of them physical (hair color) and some abstract (name, phone number). A telephone has a receiver, buttons, a dial tone, and lots of other attributes. In terms of behaviors, a person can walk and talk, but can also dial a phone number, listen for a dial tone, and so on. Among other things, a telephone's actions include sending a dial tone, and ringing. Note that in our model we chose to ignore certain attributes and actions of the objects involved. This is this idea of *abstraction* again.   *Abstraction*

In general, we also talk about an object's attributes as making up its *state*. An object's state is the particular set of values that its attributes have at any given time. For example, the caller's state in our phone   *An object's state* example would include her name and phone number ("Alice," "111-222-3333"), as would the callee's ("Bob," "222-111-4444"). The phone's state might include attributes such as whether it is ringing and whether it has a dial tone. Obviously, a phone's state changes during a phone call, but the caller's and callee's states do not change, at least not in our abstract model.

In Java and in other object-oriented programming languages, an **object** is a module that encapsulates certain **variables** and **methods**, which correspond respectively to the object's attributes (or characteristics) and behaviors (or actions). In general, when we are talking about an object in the abstract or as represented in a UML diagram, we will use the terms *attribute* (or *characteristic*) and *behavior* (or *action*) to describe its features. But when talking about a piece of Java code we will use the terms *variable* and *method*.

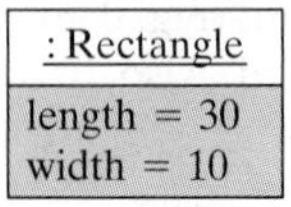

To take an example, let's focus on a simple object, say, a geometric rectangle. What attributes does a rectangle have? Well, a rectangle has a length and width. And a rectangle also has a certain area and perimeter. Notice that we can calculate a rectangle's area by multiplying its length times its width. But we can't calculate its length or width from its area or from any other values. Therefore, a rectangle's length and width are more fundamental than its area. So we can best represent a rectangle's *state* in terms of these two fundamental attributes: length and width.

But what if we want to know a rectangle's area? Well, we can calculate it from its length and width. And we can treat this calculation as one of the rectangle's behaviors. Just as a person can tell us his or her name, a rectangle can calculate its area.

Figure 0–6 is a UML *object diagram* that represents a model of the type of rectangle we just described. Note that we have given specific values to the rectangle's attributes. In this case, the rectangle's length is 30 and its width is 10. If we asked this rectangle to calculate its area, the result would be 300 (30 × 10).

One of the things to notice about our model of a rectangle is that it *encapsulates* the knowledge and expertise needed to represent a rectangle. In addition to having a length and width, the rectangle knows how to calculate its area. This is an appropriate way to organize information and behavior in an object-oriented program. In other types of programming languages we wouldn't group things in this way. This approach corresponds fairly well with how the real world is organized. A car mechanic encapsulates the knowledge and behavior needed for fixing cars. A tax accountant encapsulates the knowledge and behavior needed for doing taxes. Like our rectangle, both are experts in their respective domains.

0.7.3 What Is a Java Class?

A **class** is a blueprint or a template that defines the characteristics and behaviors of all objects of a certain type. We say that an object is an **instance** of a class. In terms of our rectangle example, individual rectangles have different lengths and widths and areas, but all rectangles have a length, width, and an area. So a class is an *abstraction* that contains the attributes and behaviors common to all objects of a given type.

A class is like an abstract concept. In the real world we rely on these kinds of abstractions all the time. They are important elements in our

Objects, variables, methods

: Rectangle
length = 30
width = 10

FIGURE 0–6 A *UML object diagram*. To represent an object in UML we use a rectangle with up to three partitions. The first gives the object's label—here giving the object's *type* rather than its name. The second shows the object's *attributes* and their *values*. The third, not shown in this case, gives the object's *behaviors*. When talking about objects in Java, we will use the term *variables* (for attributes) and *methods* (for behaviors or actions).

Encapsulation

Class and instance

Abstraction

thinking and our language. Thus, our word *person* is a reference to an abstract concept that encapsulates the attributes and behaviors common to all persons. And our word *rectangle* stands for the abstract concept of a rectangle that encompasses the attributes and behaviors common to all rectangles.

Figure 0–7 is a *UML class diagram* that represents the rectangle class. It has the same basic structure as the UML object diagram in Figure 0–6, but note that its attributes have no values. Thus, it represents what all rectangles have in common, without representing any particular rectangle. In this sense a class is an abstraction of what is common to all the objects it represents.

Rectangle
− length : double
+ width : double
+ calculateArea() : double

FIGURE 0–7 A *UML class diagram.* Like an object symbol, a class is represented by a rectangle with up to three partitions. The first gives the name of the class. The second gives the attributes, and the third gives the behaviors. Note that unlike in the object diagram (Fig. 0–6), the name is not underlined. Also, in this case we specify what types of data (double) these variables are. In Java, `double` data are real numbers.

0.7.4   What Is a Message?

In the object-oriented framework, objects interact with each other by sending messages back and forth. This also is based loosely on how objects interact in the real world. If I want my spouse to pass me the salt, I say "Please pass me the salt," and she invariably complies. More abstractly, if my car's oil pressure sensor detects that the engine's oil pressure is too low, it sends an "Oil pressure warning" message to some controller, which in turn sends a "Turn on" message to the warning light on my dashboard. Figure 0–8 is a UML sequence diagram depicting the messages passing between the sensor, the controller, and the dashboard light.

So a **message** represents the passing of information between objects. In Java, passing a message is done by *calling a method.* For example, if we want to know a rectangle's area, we would call its `calculateArea()` method. This would cause the rectangle to engage in its area-calculating behavior, which would involve multiplying its length times width and returning the product. Figure 0–9 is a *UML collaboration diagram* that depicts a method call between a `RectangleUser` named `user` and a `Rectangle` named `rect`. In this case the area returned would be 300, given a length of 30 and a width of 10. Thus, calling a method is like giving an order or making a request. It's like ordering your dog to sit, which leads to its sitting (assuming it is better behaved than my dog). Or it's like asking your friend to pass the salt.

Messages are method calls

0.7.5   What Is a Class Hierarchy?

Classifying means grouping things together based on their similarities. The ability to classify is an important element in our thinking and a natural part of our attempt to understand the world. For example, biologists group organisms into five major classes, including the animal and plant

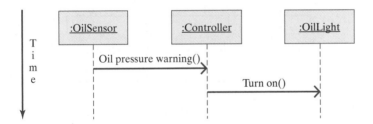

FIGURE 0–8 This UML sequence diagram depicts an interaction between your engine's oil pressure sensor and the oil warning light on your dashboard, with a controller as a mediator.

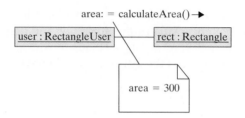

kingdoms. The animal kingdom is divided into the vertebrates and invertebrates, and the vertebrates are broken down into mammals, reptiles,
amphibians, fish, and so on (Fig. 0–10). In general, classification provides
a natural way of organizing the world so that we can understand it and
interact with it.

Figure 0–10 is a UML class diagram representing a **hierarchy chart** that
shows the relationships among a collection of classes. The most general
class in this hierarchy is the `Animal` class. All the other classes are its **subclasses**, and it is a **superclass** of all other classes. Thus, the `Mammal` class is a
subclass of the `Animal` class and, vice versa, the `Animal` class is a superclass
of the `Mammal` class. The concepts of superclass and subclass are relative:
The `Mammal` class is a superclass relative to `Dog` but a subclass relative to
`Vertebrate`.

Superclass and subclass

The objects in Java programs are also organized into classes. The Java
hierarchy is rooted in the `Object` class, which is the superclass of all other
Java classes (Fig. 0–11). Note that the `Component` branch includes the various objects, such as `TextFields` and `Buttons`, that are used to build Graphical User Interfaces (GUIs).

You can see from Figure 0–11 that a `TextField` is a type of `TextCompo-
nent`, which is a type of `Component`. In other words, the `TextField` class is
a subclass of the `TextComponent` class, which in turn is a subclass of the
`Component` class.

0.7.6   What Is Class Inheritance?

Class inheritance

One of the most important concepts in object-oriented programming is the
mechanism of **class inheritance**, whereby objects belonging to a subclass
inherit certain characteristics and behaviors from their superclasses.

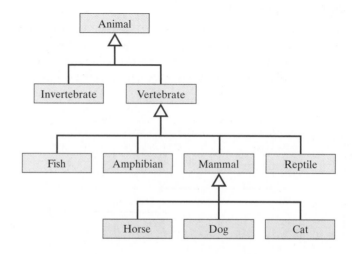

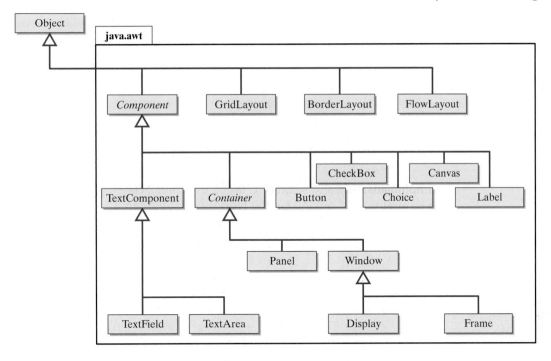

FIGURE 0–11   Part of the Java class hierarchy rooted at Object. The classes shown are part of the `java.awt` package, a collection of classes that make up Java's *Abstract Windowing Toolkit*.

This concept also has its analogue in the natural world. For example, we know that mammals (the subclass) have all of the characteristics possessed by animals (the superclass). In general we can say that members of a subclass *inherit* all of the characteristics of members of the superclass. The inheritance relationship extends throughout the class hierarchy. So characteristics and behaviors of a given class are inherited by all the classes that occur below it in the hierarchy. Thus, dogs and cats (subclasses) have all the characteristics and behaviors of animals (superclass).

In object-oriented systems the concept of inheritance is used to allow one class to be defined in terms of another. This is a way of extending the existing functionality of a collection of classes without having to write things from scratch. It's a way to *reuse* existing code and to *avoid reinventing the wheel*. It allows object-oriented systems to be *extensible*—that is, systems can be extended to new behaviors—with a minimum amount of additional programming.

Extensibility

For example, suppose we have a system of geometric objects in which we have already defined a `Rectangle` class. If we now want to define a `Square`, we can define it as an *extension* or *specialization* of a `Rectangle`. After all, a square is just a rectangle in which both the length and width have the same value. Figure 0–12 provides an illustration of this concept. A `Square` is a specialization of a `Rectangle` in which its only dimension is the length of a side. Thus, to define a `Square` in terms of a `Rectangle` we need only ensure that `side = length = width`. This will guarantee that

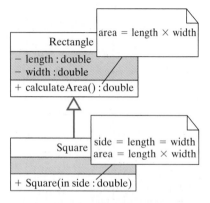

FIGURE 0–12   In this UML class diagram a Square is defined as an extension of a Rectangle. A Square is a special type of Rectangle in which length = width = side. Because a Square is a Rectangle, it can use the inherited calculateArea() method to compute its area.

Overriding behavior

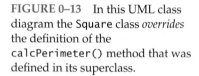

the calculateArea() method, which multiplies length times width, gives us the correct result for either a Rectangle or a Square. In this sense, the Square *inherits* the calculateArea() method from the Rectangle class.

Thus, inheritance in object-oriented languages provides a powerful mechanism for reusing code and for extending the functionality of existing code. In this example we are reusing code, the calculateArea() method, defined in the superclass. But we can also use this mechanism to define very generic superclasses, in which we partially define certain generic behaviors but leave most of their behavior undefined so that it can be specialized in the subclass.

For example, a subclass can *override* a behavior inherited from the superclass. This also has its analogue in the natural world. Thus, all dogs have a keen sense of smell, but bloodhounds have been specially bred to have an extremely well-developed sense of smell.

We can create the same sort of specialization when we design objects. For example, suppose our Rectangle class has a method, calcPerimeter(), to calculate its perimeter (Fig. 0–13). The formula for calculating the perimeter of a rectangle is $P = 2 \times length + 2 \times width$. But for a square we know that length equals width, so that this formula can be simplified to $P = 4 \times length$. This formula is somewhat more efficient to compute than the other: It involves only one multiplication whereas the original formula involved two multiplications and one addition. Even though this is only a minor improvement in efficiency, if we desire this kind of improvement, we could easily achieve it by *overriding* the calcPerimeter() method in the Square class. Actually, this improvement in efficiency is not really that different from the sort of improvement in smelling efficiency that one finds in bloodhounds.

0.7.7   What Is an Interface?

In the real world an interface is a system of devices, or mechanisms, or behaviors that enables two entities to interact with each other. For example, a vending machine has a system of buttons, labels, and coin slots that enable a person to purchase a soda or a candy bar. A diplomat engages in a certain agreed-upon pattern of behavior (known as a *protocol*) when interacting with his or her counterpart from another country.

A Java **interface** is a class that contains only methods, no variables. Because it has no attributes, it most closely resembles a protocol, with its methods constituting the agreed-upon behavior used by the interacting

FIGURE 0–13   In this UML class diagram the Square class *overrides* the definition of the calcPerimeter() method that was defined in its superclass.

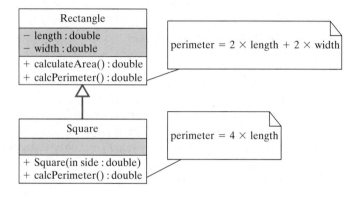

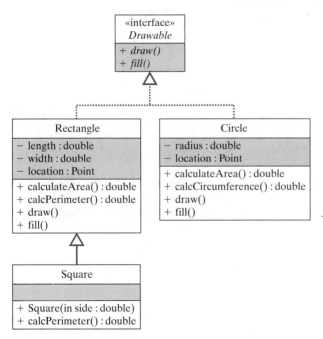

FIGURE 0–14 This UML class diagram illustrates how we represent a Java *interface*. The fact that *draw()* and *fill()* are italicized in Drawable means they are abstract. They merely outline the behaviors of drawing and filling. These methods are given specific behaviors in the Rectangle and Circle classes. Like two diplomats using a protocol, participating in the Drawable interface is a matter of implementing these methods by taking specific, but appropriate, drawing actions.

diplomats. Whereas an object encapsulates both attributes and behavior, an interface just encapsulates behavior. Thus, unlike an object, an interface has no state. It consists entirely of behavior. Yet many objects might wish to share this behavior, which is what makes the interface useful.

For example, suppose we were designing a set of geometric objects, such as rectangles, squares, and circles, and we wanted to give these objects the ability to draw themselves. One way to do this would be to define an interface named Drawable that encapsulates those methods required to draw geometric shapes. For example, the interface might consist of two methods: *draw()*, which draws an outline of the shape, and *fill()*, which paints the shape's interior. The interface would provide a generic definition of these methods but would leave it up to each shape to provide its own implementation of these two methods (Fig. 0–14). In this way each shape could be drawn in an appropriate way. Thus, in order for any shape to participate in a drawing program all it needs to do is implement the Drawable interface. This is its way of agreeing to abide by the behaviors specified in the interface.

0.7.8 What Is Polymorphism?

Another powerful mechanism in object-oriented programming is the concept of **polymorphism**. The word means *many forms* (*poly* = many, *morph* = shapes) and refers to the ability of the same method to elicit different behaviors depending upon the object that executes it. In order to appreciate the importance of this mechanism, we will first have to learn more details of the Java language. But we can provide an inkling of how this works by means of a simple example.

Polymorphism

Consider how different kinds of animals move. A dog walks by moving its legs. A fish swims by pushing water with its fins. A snake crawls along the ground by wriggling its entire body. Thus, the moving behavior of

FIGURE 0–15   In this UML class diagram the move() method is an example of a *polymorphic* method. It is defined abstractly in the Animal class and given a different implementation in each of the specific Animal subclasses.

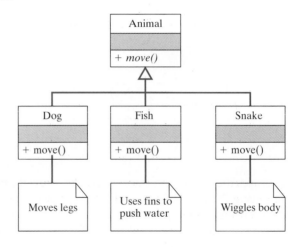

animals is polymorphic because it takes a different form depending on the type of animal.

One way we might represent this situation is to view moving, at the level of the animal class, as an abstract method—that is, one that has no specific behavior associated with it. You can't tell how an animal moves unless you know what kind of animal it is. So it is only in the animal subclasses where moving behavior can be specified. Figure 0–15 provides a UML representation of this situation. The Animal class contains the abstract move() method, which is given a specific implementation in each of Animal's subclasses.

0.7.9   Principles of Object-Oriented Design

In general a good object-oriented program *simulates* or *models* the interaction of objects in the real world. The closer the simulation, the better the program. As we have discussed, an object-oriented program is composed of many objects communicating with each other. The process of designing an object-oriented program to solve some problem or other involves several important principles:

- **Divide-and-Conquer Principle.** Generally, the first step in designing a program is to divide the overall problem into a number of objects that will interact with each other to solve the problem. Thus, an object-oriented program employs a *division of labor* much as we do in organizing many of our real-world tasks. This *divide-and-conquer* approach is an important problem-solving strategy as well as an important element in designing object-oriented programs.
- **Encapsulation Principle.** Once the objects are identified, the next step involves deciding, for each object, what attributes it has and what actions it will take. The goal here is to *encapsulate* within each object the expertise needed to carry out its role in the program. This aspect of object-oriented design also resembles the way we approach real-world problems. If you have a kidney problem, you would go to a urologist, who encapsulates the expertise needed to diagnose and treat your problem. Each object is designed to be a self-contained *module* with a clear responsibility and the tools (attributes and actions) necessary to carry out its role. In addition to knowing how to perform its role, each

object has the requisite information (attributes) and knows exactly what information it needs to obtain from its collaborators.

- **Interface Principle.** In order for objects to work cooperatively and efficiently, we have to clarify exactly how they should interact, or *interface*, with one another. An object's interface should be designed to protect its integrity and to constrain the way the object can be used by other objects. Think of the different interfaces presented by a digital and analog clock. In one case, time is displayed in discrete units, and buttons are used to set the time in hours and minutes. In the other, the time is displayed by hands on a clock face, and time is set by turning a small wheel. In both cases the clock's interface determines how it can be used.
- **Information Hiding Principle.** The details of each object's performance should be hidden from other objects. This also will help objects work together cooperatively and efficiently. In terms of the clock analogy again, in order to use a clock we needn't know how its timekeeping mechanism works. That level of detail is hidden from us. Objects should employ a similar form of *information hiding* in their design.
- **Generality Principle.** As long as we are designing an object to solve a problem, we should design it in as general a way as possible. We design objects not for a particular task but rather for a particular *kind* of task. We might call this the *generality principle*. If they are designed well, objects can be used in any number of programs that require their services. For example, the Java class library contains objects that specialize in performing certain kinds of input and output operations. Rather than having to write our own routine to print a message on the console, we can use a library object to handle our printing tasks.
- **Extensibility Principle.** One of the strengths of the object-oriented approach is the *extensibility* of objects. This also has its analogue in the everyday world. If a company needs sales agents who specialize in hardware orders, it would be more economical to extend the skills of some of the current sales agents instead of training a novice from scratch. In the same way, in the object-oriented approach, an object whose role is to input data might be specialized to input numeric data.
- **Abstraction Principle.** Taken together, these principles describe object-oriented programming and problem solving. Taken individually, each of the preceding principles provides a manifestation of the more general principle of *abstraction*. Abstraction is the ability to group large quantities of information together into a single *chunk*. The term *chunk* was coined by George Miller in his 1956 article "The Magic Number Seven, Plus or Minus Two," in which he claimed that humans have the ability to manage only seven (plus or minus two) chunks of information at one time. Therefore, we manage large quantities of information by forming abstractions. For example, it is easier to remember a long string of digits if we chunk the digits. So a phone number gets organized into three chunks (200-990-1179), rather than one chunk consisting of 10 digits (2009901179).

The process of abstraction takes many forms and is involved in several of the preceding principles. Organizing a complex set of attributes and actions into a single object and then dealing with the module as a whole is a form of abstraction. Dividing a problem into its component objects is a form of abstraction, similar in nature to dividing a phone number into its components. Designing an object with a particular public interface forces the user to deal with the object in terms of the abstractions defined by the interface. Finally, in terms of program design, a good abstraction is extensible and achieves the right degree of generality.

0.8   Summary of UML Elements

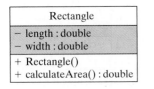

FIGURE 0–16   A basic UML class diagram.

You have already seen 11 examples of *Unified Modeling Language (UML)* diagrams used to illustrate various features of object-oriented design. We will be using such diagrams throughout the text both to help illustrate object-oriented concepts and to describe the design of the various Java programs we develop. In this section we provide a brief overview of some of the key elements of UML.

UML resulted from a unification of several object-modeling notations, hence, the name *Unified Modeling Language*. It is used for designing and analyzing object-oriented programs, and it is rapidly becoming an industry standard. UML is a broad and complex language. We will use only a small part of it in this text. (For more information on UML, see www.omg.org and www.rational.com, or see the list of references in Appendix G.)

0.8.1   Class Diagrams

A **class diagram** is used to describe a class or to describe the structure of a program in terms of the relationships between the classes and interfaces involved. We will frequently use class diagrams to describe classes in the Java library.

Classes are drawn as rectangles, which may be divided into one, two, or three partitions (Fig. 0–16). The top partition contains the class's name. The middle partition contains its variables. And the third partition contains its methods. The symbols that precede the names of the variables and methods are *visibility indicators* and there are three types, as shown in Table 0.1. Generally speaking, a class's private elements are hidden from other objects, whereas its public and protected elements can be used by other objects.

We will usually not include every detail of a class in the class diagram, especially when describing a Java library class. Sometimes we will show only a class's methods or only its variables. Sometimes, particularly when we are describing a class hierarchy, as in Figure 0–11, we will use a one-partition class symbol containing only the name of the class and we will show none of its elements.

A Java *interface* is drawn similarly to a class except that it usually has just two partitions because an interface does not contain variables (Fig. 0–17). Words written in double angle brackets are known as *stereotypes*, and are used to modify the elements in the class diagram. In this example we use a stereotype to identify Drawable as an <<interface>>. Note also that when a method's name is shown in italic font, as the draw() and fill() methods are, that means that the method is abstract. This same convention applies to class names. An italicized class name indicates an abstract class.

TABLE 0.1   Visibility Indicators

Visibility Indicator	Interpretation
+	Public
–	Private
#	Protected

FIGURE 0–17   A basic Java interface. Elements whose labels are italicized are abstract.

0.8.1.1 Associations

Class diagrams are also used to depict the relationships between classes. Two of the most important relations are *class inheritance* and *interface implementation*. As shown earlier in Figure 0–14, a solid line with a closed arrowhead is used to represent the superclass/subclass relationship. Thus, a `Square` is a subclass of `Rectangle`. The arrowhead always points to the superclass whose attributes are inherited by the subclass. A dotted line with a closed arrowhead represents that a class implements an interface. Thus, in Figure 0–14, both `Rectangle` and `Circle` implement the `Drawable` interface.

The other sorts of relationships between classes are known as **associations**, and they come in a wide variety. For this reason, associations are usually labeled. For example, Figure 0–18 shows an association in which a `RectangleUser` uses one or more `Rectangles`. The name of the association is always capitalized. The names of each class's *role* occurs on the association line near the respective class symbols. The triangle near the association name shows the direction in which you should read the association. So in this case a `RectangleUser` *uses* a `Rectangle`. The `RectangleUser`'s role is that of a *user*, and the `Rectangle`'s role is that of *usee*. The numbers on the association are *multiplicity indicators*. In this case, one `RectangleUser` uses one or more `Rectangles`. The main varieties are shown in Table 0.2.

When a *navigation arrow* is used to represent an association, as in Figure 0–18, the arrowhead indicates the direction in which the association is navigated. In this case it indicates that the `RectangleUser` class has a reference—the variable `rect`—to the `Rectangle` class but not vice versa. So the `RectangleUser` can send messages to—invoke methods of—the `Rectangle` class but not vice versa.

0.8.1.2 Aggregations

An **aggregation** is an association in which one object contains many others. The container class has a diamond on its end of the association. Thus, in Figure 0–19, a single `Panel` contains zero or more `Components`.

0.8.2 Packages

A **package** in Java is a collection of related classes. Packages are the primary organizing category for the Java class library. Sometimes we will organize the classes in a class diagram into their respective packages, especially when describing classes in the Java class library. Earlier, in Figure 0–11, we showed an example of this notation for a portion of Java's `java.awt` package, a collection of Graphical User Interface (GUI) components.

0.8.3 Object Diagrams

Objects can appear in class diagrams as well as in other UML diagrams. As we noted earlier, for the most part, objects are symbolized in the same way as classes, by one-, two-, or three-partition rectangles. The difference is that names for object symbols are underlined and their names can consist of two parts, `objectName:className`. When an object's name is not important, we frequently use just the object's class name to identify it. Note that when an object is represented we sometimes show the state of some

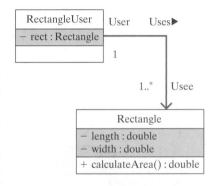

FIGURE 0–18   This UML class diagram shows an association between a `RectangleUser` and one or more `Rectangles`. The association is represented by a labeled line.

TABLE 0.2   Multiplicity Indicators

Multiplicity Indicator	Interpretation
1	*One*
0..2	*Zero to two*
0..*	*Zero or more*
*	*Zero or more*
1..*	*One or more*

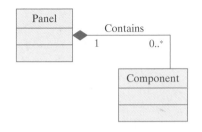

FIGURE 0–19   This class diagram shows an aggregation, a special type of association in which one object contains many others. In this case a `Panel` contains 0 or more `Components`.

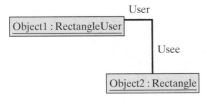

FIGURE 0–20   An *object diagram* is a class diagram that contains nothing but objects.

or all of its variables. The example shown in Figure 0–20 is called an **object diagram** because it consists entirely of interrelated objects (and no classes).

0.8.4   Collaboration Diagrams

Collaboration diagrams are used to describe the collaborations between a set of objects. The associations between objects are called *links*, but they are symbolized in the same way as associations between classes. They can be labeled just as if they were class associations.

An important element of collaboration diagrams is that they show the details of the interactions between objects. A number of interactions can occur over a given link, and each interaction involves a *method call*. A method call is the Java mechanism for passing messages between objects. For example, in Figure 0–9, we showed the interaction by which a Rect-angleUser object calls a Rectangle's calculateArea() method to calculate its area. In that example, the value that's returned by the method, which is assumed to be 300, is stored in a variable named area. As we develop more sophisticated programs, the number of messages that get passed back and forth over a link will increase.

0.8.5   Sequence Diagrams

A **sequence diagram** shows the sequence of interactions that takes place, over time, among a group of objects. Such diagrams are used mainly to help design an object-oriented program. They identify the objects involved and the types of messages that pass back and forth between them. Several of the examples used earlier in this chapter are sequence diagrams (see Figs. 0–5 and 0–8).

CHAPTER SUMMARY

Technical Terms

abstract	computer program	object diagram
aggregation	hierarchy chart	object-oriented
association	high-level language	package
attribute	instance	polymorphism
behavior	interface	sequence diagram
class	interpreter	source code
class diagram	method	subclass
class inheritance	message	superclass
collaboration	model	Unified Modeling
diagram	object	Language (UML)
compiler	object code	variable

Summary of Important Points

- A Java program is a set of interacting objects. This is the basic metaphor of *object-oriented programming*. The main principles of the object-oriented programming approach are as follows:
  - Divide and Conquer: Successful problem solving involves breaking a complex problem into objects.
  - Encapsulation and Modularity: Each object should be assigned a clear role.
  - Public Interface: Each object should present a clear public interface that determines how other objects will use it.
  - Information Hiding: Each object should shield its users from unnecessary details of how it performs its role.
  - Generality: Objects should be designed to be as general as possible.
  - Extensibility: Objects should be designed so that their functionality can be extended to carry out more specialized tasks.
- *Abstraction* is the ability to group a large quantity of information into a single chunk so it can be managed as a single entity. Abstraction is an overarching principle of the OOP approach.
- A computer system generally consists of input/output devices, primary and secondary memory, and a central processing unit. A computer can only run programs in its own *machine language*, which is based on the *binary code*. Special programs known as *compilers* and *interpreters* translate *source code* programs written in a *high-level language*, such as Java, into machine language *object code* programs.
- *Application software* refers to programs designed to provide a particular task or service; *systems software* assists the user in using application software.
- The *client/server* model is a form of *distributed computing* in which part of the software for a task is stored on a *server* and part on *client* computers.
- HyperText Markup Language (HTML) is the language used to encode WWW documents.

EXERCISES

EXERCISE 0.1   Fill in the blanks in each of the following statements.

a. Dividing a problem or a task into parts is an example of the _____ principle.

b. Designing a class so that it shields certain parts of an object from other objects is an example of the _____ principle.

c. The fact that Java programs can run without change on a wide variety of different kinds of computers is an example of _____ .

d. The fact that social security numbers are divided into three parts is an example of the _____ principle.

e. To say that a program is robust means that _____ .

f. An _____ is a separate module that encapsulates a Java program's attributes and actions.

EXERCISE 0.2 Explain the difference between each of the following pairs of concepts.

a. *hardware* and *software*
b. *systems* and *application* software
c. *compiler* and *interpreter*
d. *machine language* and *high-level language*
e. *general-purpose* and *special-purpose* computer
f. *primary* and *secondary* memory
g. the *CPU* and the *ALU*
h. the *Internet* and the *WWW*
i. a *client* and a *server*
j. *HTTP* and *HTML*
k. *source* and *object* code

EXERCISE 0.3 Fill in the blanks in each of the following statements.

a. A _____ is a set of instructions that directs a computer's behavior.
b. A disk drive would be an example of a _____ device.
c. A mouse is an example of an _____ device.
d. A monitor is an example of an _____ device.
e. The computer's _____ functions like a scratch pad.
f. Java is an example of a _____ programming language.
g. The Internet is a network of _____ .
h. The protocol used by the World Wide Web is the _____ protocol.
i. Web documents are written in _____ code.
j. A _____ is a networked computer that is used to store data for other computers on the network.

EXERCISE 0.4 Identify the component of computer hardware that is responsible for the following functions.

a. The *fetch-execute cycle*
b. arithmetic operations
c. executing instructions
d. storing programs while they are executing
e. storing programs and data when the computer is off

EXERCISE 0.5 Explain why a typical piece of software, such as a word processor, cannot run on both a Macintosh and a Windows machine.

EXERCISE 0.6 What advantages do you see in platform independence? What are the disadvantages?

EXERCISE 0.7 In what sense is a person's name an *abstraction*? In what sense is any word of the English language an abstraction?

EXERCISE 0.8 Analyze the process of writing a research paper in terms of the divide-and-conquer and encapsulation principles.

EXERCISE 0.9 Analyze your car in terms of object-oriented design principles. In other words, pick one of your car's systems, such as the braking system, and analyze it in terms of the divide-and-conquer, encapsulation, information-hiding, and interface principles.

EXERCISE 0.10 Suppose your car's radiator is broken. Consider the process of getting it fixed in terms of the object-oriented programming principles. In other words, describe how divide-and-conquer and encapsulation strategies are used in this process. Describe various forms of information hiding and interfacing involved in this process.

UML EXERCISES

EXERCISE 0.11   Draw a UML object diagram to depict a relationship between two objects, a telephone and a user.

EXERCISE 0.12   Draw a UML object diagram to depict a relationship between two objects, a dog and its owner.

EXERCISE 0.13   Modify the diagram in the previous exercise to show that the pet owner is named "Bill" and the pet is named "Lily."

EXERCISE 0.14   Modify the diagram in the previous exercise to represent the following exchange between Bill and Lily: Bill says "Speak" and Lily says "Arf."

EXERCISE 0.15   Draw a UML diagram to represent a relationship between a customer and the customer's savings account. Have the customer deposit $50 into the account.

Photograph courtesy of Hisham F. Ibrahim, PhotoDisc, Inc.

1

Java Program Design and Development

OBJECTIVES

After studying this chapter, you will

- Know the basic steps involved in the program development process.
- Understand the difference between a Java application and a Java applet.
- Understand how a Java program is translated into machine language.
- Know how to edit, compile, and run Java programs.
- Understand some of the basic elements of the Java language.
- Know how to use simple output operations in a Java program.
- Be able to distinguish between syntax and semantic errors in a program.

OUTLINE

1.1   Introduction

This chapter introduces some of the basic concepts and techniques involved in Java program design and development. We begin by identifying the main steps involved in designing an object-oriented program. The steps are illustrated by designing a program that represents a simple rectangle. Following the design phase, we then focus on the steps involved in coding a Java program, including the process of editing, compiling, and running a program. Because Java programs come in two varieties, applications and applets, we describe how the coding process differs for these two varieties.

Next we begin to familiarize ourselves with Java's extensive class library by studying its `PrintStream` and `System` classes. These classes contain objects and methods that enable us to print output from a program. By the end of the chapter you will be able to design and write a Java application that "sings" your favorite song. Finally, the lab project for this chapter involves editing, compiling, and running a Java applet. Once you get the applet running, you will perform several experiments designed to illustrate the different kinds of errors that can occur in a program.

1.2   Designing Good Programs

Programming is not simply a question of keyboarding Java code. Rather, it involves a considerable amount of planning and designing. Badly designed programs hardly ever work correctly. Even though it is tempting for novice programmers to start entering code almost immediately, one of the first rules of programming is

> PROGRAMMING TIP: The sooner you begin to type code, the longer the program will take to finish. Careful design of the program must precede coding of the program. This is particularly true of object-oriented programs.

In other words, the more thought and care you put into designing a program, the more likely you are to end up with one that works correctly. The following subsections provide a brief overview of the program development process.

1.2.1   The Software Life Cycle

The **software life cycle** refers to the different phases involved in the design and development of a computer program. *Software engineers*, those who have studied this process, have developed many models of the software development process. One of the simplest models is known as the **waterfall model** (Fig. 1–1). In this model, each phase of development is completed before the next phase is begun. Thus, the specification phase is completed before the design phase is begun, and the design phase is completed before implementation is begun.

Our depiction of the software life cycle, and our presentation of examples in the book, will focus on four phases of the overall life cycle: *specification, design, implementation,* and *testing*. In a real-world application there are additional phases, such as concept exploration and systems analysis, preceding these four, and system installation and system maintenance following these four.

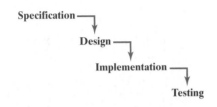

FIGURE 1–1   The waterfall model of software development.

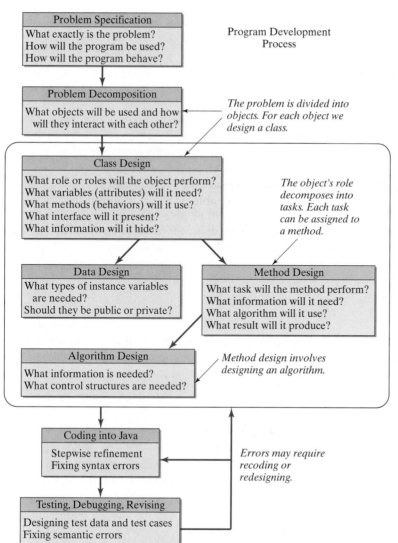

Program Development
Process

FIGURE 1–2   An overview of the program development process.

Program development involves designing, coding, testing, and revising a program. Figure 1–2 gives a more detailed overview of the program development process, focusing most of the attention on the design phase of the software life cycle. Designing an object-oriented program is a matter of designing its classes, data, methods, and algorithms. As we learn more about Java, and as the problems we tackle become more sophisticated, we will learn about each of these stages.

Over all, the program development process can be viewed as an embodiment of the divide-and-conquer principle, as a problem is repeatedly divided and subdivided into subproblems. The program is decomposed into a collection of objects. During class design, each object is divided into its variables and methods. Deciding how many classes or methods are needed involves application of the encapsulation and abstraction principles. When should we stop subdividing? How much of a task should be assigned to a single object or a single method? The answers

Divide and conquer

to these and similar questions are not easy. Good answers require the kind of good judgment that comes through experience. Here again, as we learn more about object-oriented programming, we'll learn more about how to apply these principles.

Problem Specification

The first step in the program development process is making sure you understand the problem. Thus, we begin by developing a detailed *problem specification*, which should address three basic questions:

- What exactly is the problem to be solved?
- How will the program be used?
- How will the program behave?

In the real world, the problem specification is often arrived at through an extended process of negotiation between the customer and the developer. In an introductory programming course, the specification is usually given in the laboratory or programming assignment itself.

To help make these ideas a little clearer, let's design a solution to a very simple problem.

> **Problem Specification.** Design a class that will represent a simple geometric rectangle with a given length and width. The definition of this class should make it possible to create rectangles of various dimensions and to calculate their areas.

1.2.2 Problem Decomposition

Most problems are too big and too complex to be solved in one fell swoop. So the next step in the design process is to divide the problem into parts that make the solution more manageable. This *divide-and-conquer* approach should be applied repeatedly. In the object-oriented approach, a problem is divided into objects, where each object will handle one specific aspect of the program's overall job. In effect, each object will become an expert or specialist in some aspect of the program's overall behavior.

Note that there is some ambiguity here about how far we should go in decomposing a given program. This ambiguity is inherent in the design process. How much we should decompose the program before its parts become "simple to solve" depends on the problem we're trying to solve and on the problem solver.

One useful design guideline for trying to decide what objects are needed is the following:

EFFECTIVE DESIGN: Looking for Nouns.   Choosing a program's objects is often a matter of looking for nouns in the problem specification.

Again, there's some ambiguity involved in this guideline. For example, the key noun in our current problem is *rectangle*, so our solution will involve an object that serves as a model for a rectangle. The main task of this Java object will be simply to represent a geometric rectangle. But what about the nouns *length* and *width* in the problem specification? Do we need objects to represent them as well? In some object-oriented languages (for

- Class Name: Rectangle
- Role: To represent a geometric rectangle
- Attributes (Information)
  - Length: A variable to store the rectangle's length (private)
  - Width: A variable to store the rectangle's width (private)
- Behaviors
  - Rectangle(): A method to set a rectangle's length and width
  - calculateArea(): A method to calculate a rectangle's area

FIGURE 1–3 Design specification for the Rectangle class.

example, Smalltalk) everything is an object. So if we were using Smalltalk, we would use objects to represent the rectangle's length and width. Java, however, distinguishes between objects and primitive data elements, such as simple numbers and characters. For this problem we will use data elements for the length and width. So, for this simple problem we need just one type of object—a rectangle—whose primary role will be to represent a geometric rectangle.

Don't worry too much if our design decisions seem somewhat mysterious at this stage. A good understanding of object-oriented design can come only after much design experience. But we have to start somewhere.

1.2.3   Object Design

Once we have decomposed a problem into a set of cooperating objects, designing a Java program is primarily a matter of designing and creating the objects themselves. In our example, this means we must now design the features of our rectangle object. For each object, we must answer the following basic design questions:

- What role will the object perform in the program?
- What data or information will it need?
- What actions will it take?
- What interface will it present to other objects?
- What information will it hide from other objects?

For our rectangle object, the answers to these questions are shown in Figure 1–3. Note that although we talk about "designing an object," we're really designing a *class of objects*. The following discussion shows how we arrived at these decisions.

The role of the Rectangle object is to model a geometric rectangle. Because a rectangle is defined in terms of its length and width, our Rectangle object will need some way to store these two pieces of information. An **instance variable** is a memory location that belongs to an object. Variables are used to store the information that an object needs to perform its role. They correspond to what we have been calling its attributes. Deciding on these variables provides the answer to the question, "What information does the object need?"

Next we decide what actions a Rectangle object will take. As specified in Figure 1–3, each Rectangle object should provide some means of setting its dimensions and calculating its area. These are the actions or behaviors it will perform or carry out as part of its role of representing a rectangle.

What is the object's role?

What information will the object need?

What actions will the object take?

Another useful design guideline is the following:

EFFECTIVE DESIGN: Looking for Verbs. Choosing the behavior of an object is often a matter of looking for verbs in the problem specification.

For this problem, the key verbs are *create* and *calculate-area* and that is why we have identified both as the actions that our Rectangle object will perform.

Each of the actions we have identified will be encapsulated in a Java method. A **method** is a named section of code that can be invoked or called upon to perform a particular action. In the object-oriented approach, **method invocation** is the means by which interaction occurs among objects. Calling a method is like sending a message between objects. For example, when we create a rectangle we call the Rectangle() method, which is known as a **constructor**, to set its dimensions. When we want to find out a rectangle's area, we can invoke its "calculate area" method, which will give us this information.

What interface will it present, and what information will it hide?

In designing an object, we must decide which methods should be made available to other objects. This determines what interface the object should present and what information it should hide from other objects. In general, those methods that will be used to communicate with an object are designated as part of the object's *interface*. Except for its interface, all other information maintained by each rectangle should be kept "hidden" from other objects. For example, it is not necessary for other objects to know how a rectangle represents its length and width. The fact that length and width are stored in variables named length and width, rather than len and wid, is irrelevant to other objects.

EFFECTIVE DESIGN: Object Interface. An object's interface should consist of just those methods needed to communicate with or to use the object.

EFFECTIVE DESIGN: Information Hiding. An object should hide most of the details of its implementation.

Taken together, these various design decisions lead to the specification shown in Figure 1–4. As our discussion has illustrated, we arrived at the decisions by asking and answering the right questions. Figure 1–4 is an example of a UML *class diagram*. In UML, a class is represented as a rectangle divided into three parts. The first part contains the name of the class. The second contains its *attributes*, and the third part contains its *operations*. In most classes the attributes are private. This is represented by a minus sign (−). In this example, the operations are public, which is represented by the plus sign (+). The figure shows that the Rectangle class has two hidden (or private) variables for storing data and two visible (or public) methods that represent the operations that it can perform.

Rectangle
− length : double
− width : double
+ Rectangle(in l : double, in w : double)
+ calculateArea() : double

FIGURE 1–4 A UML class diagram representing the Rectangle class. Rectangle objects have two private (−) attributes, a length and a width, both of type double. They have two public (+) operations, a Rectangle() constructor method that creates a new rectangle given values (l and w) for its length and width, and a calculateArea() method that calculates the rectangle's area.

1.2.4 Data, Methods, and Algorithms

Once we have developed a specification for the rectangle object, the next step is to design its parts. There are two basic questions involved:

- What type of data will be used to represent the information needed by the rectangle?
- How will each method carry out its appointed task?

Like other programming languages, Java provides a wide range of different types of data, some simple and some complex. So deciding what type of data to use can often require considerable thought, depending on the complexity of the problem at hand. Obviously a rectangle's length and width should be represented by some kind of numeric data. So let's use Java's double type, which will enable us to represent real number values such as 15.6 and 12.5.

What type of data will be used?

In designing a method you have to decide what the method will do. In order to carry out its task, a method will need certain information, which it may store in variables. Plus it will have to carry out a sequence of individual actions to perform the task. And, finally, you must decide what result the method will produce. Thus, as in designing objects, it is important to ask the right questions:

How will each method carry out its task?

- What specific task will the method perform?
- What information will it need to perform its task?
- What algorithm will the method use?
- What result will the method produce?

An **algorithm** is a step-by-step description of the solution to a problem. For example, the algorithm for calculating the area of a rectangle consists of a one-step process: "Multiply length times width." Obviously, the only information it needs to perform this task are the two numbers that represent the rectangle's length and the width. Just as obviously, the result that it produces will be the product of length times width—that is, the rectangle's area. So this is a very simple method to design: Given a rectangle's length and width, multiply them together to obtain the rectangle's area. A summary of our design is shown in Figure 1–5.

Not all methods are so simple to design, and not all algorithms are so trivial. Even when programming a simple arithmetic problem, the steps involved in its algorithm will not always be as obvious as they are when doing the calculation by hand. For example, suppose the problem were to calculate the sum of a list of numbers. If we were telling our classmate how to do this problem, we might just say, "add up all the numbers and report their total." But this description is far too vague to be used in a program. By contrast, here's an algorithm that a program could use:

Algorithm design

1. Initialize the sum to 0.
2. If there are no more numbers to total, go to step 5.
3. Add the next number to the sum.
4. Go to step 2.
5. Report the sum.

- Method Name: calculateArea()
- Task: To calculate the area of a rectangle
- Information Needed (variables)
  - Length: A variable to store the rectangle's length (private)
  - Width: A variable to store the rectangle's width (private)
- Algorithm
  1. area = length × width

FIGURE 1–5 Design specification for the calculateArea() method.

Pseudocode

Note that each step in this algorithm is simple and easy to follow. It would be relatively easy to translate it into Java. Because English is somewhat imprecise as an algorithmic language, programmers frequently write algorithms in the programming language itself or in **pseudocode**, a hybrid language that combines English and programming language structures without being too fussy about programming language syntax. For example, the preceding algorithm might be expressed in pseudocode as follows:

```
sum = 0
while (more numbers remain)
    add next number to sum
print the sum
```

This pseudocode makes use of the while structure, a standard looping structure found in most programming languages. It is, therefore, even easier to translate into Java.

Of course, it is unlikely that an experienced programmer would take the trouble to write out pseudocode for such a simple algorithm. But many programming problems are quite complex and require careful design to minimize the number of errors that the program contains. In such a situation pseudocode could be useful.

Another important part of designing an algorithm is *tracing* it on some sample data. For example, we might test the list-summing algorithm by tracing it on the list of numbers shown in the margin.

Initially, the sum starts out at 0 and the list of numbers contains 54, 30, and 20. On each iteration through the algorithm, the sum increases by the amount of the next number, and the list diminishes in size. The algorithm stops with the correct total left under the sum column. While this trace didn't turn up any errors, it is frequently possible to find flaws in an algorithm by tracing it in this way.

Sum	List of Numbers
0	54 30 20
54	30 20
84	20
104	-

1.2.5   Coding into Java

Once a sufficiently detailed design has been developed, it is time to start generating Java code. The wrong way to do this would be to keyboard the entire program and then compile and run it. This generally leads to dozens of errors that can be both demoralizing and difficult to fix.

Stepwise refinement

The right way to code is to use the principle of **stepwise refinement**. The program is coded in small stages, and after each stage the code is compiled and tested. In this way, small errors are caught before moving on to the next stage. This approach will be demonstrated in the laboratory section of this chapter.

The code for the Rectangle class is shown in Figure 1–6. Even though we have not yet begun learning the details of the Java language, you can easily pick out the key parts of this program: the instance variables length and width of type double, which are used to store the rectangle's dimensions; the calculateArea() method, which computes the rectangle's area; the public methods that make up its interface; and the private portions that are hidden from other objects. The specific language details needed to understand each of these elements will be covered in the next chapter.

```
public class Rectangle
{

    private double length;        // Instance variables
    private double width;

    public Rectangle(double 1, double w)   // Constructor method
    {
        length = 1;
        width = w;
    }  // Rectangle constructor

    public double calculateArea()          // Access method
    {
        return length * width;
    }  // calculateArea()

}  // Rectangle class
```

FIGURE 1–6   The Rectangle class definition.

Syntax and Semantics

Writing Java code requires that you know its syntax and semantics. A language's **syntax** is the set of rules that determines whether a particular statement is correctly formulated. For example, the following Java statement contains a *syntax error*:

Syntax

```
sum = 0
```

because it does not end with a semicolon.

Similarly, the programmer must know the **semantics** of the language— that is, the meaning of each statement. In a programming language, a statement's meaning is determined by what effect it will have on the program. For example, in the preceding algorithm, to initialize the sum to 0, an assignment statement is used to store the value 0 into the memory location named sum. Thus, we say that the statement

Semantics

```
sum = 0;
```

assigns 0 to the memory location sum, where it will be stored until it is needed by some other part of the program.

Learning Java's syntax and semantics is a major part of learning to program. This aspect of learning to program is a lot like learning a foreign language. The more quickly you become fluent in the new language (Java), the better you will be at expressing solutions to interesting programming problems. The longer you struggle with the rules and conventions of Java, the more difficult it will be to talk about problems in a common language. Also, computers are a lot more fussy about correct language than humans, and even the smallest syntax or semantic error can cause tremendous frustration. So, try to be very precise in acquiring an understanding of Java's syntax and semantics.

1.2.6 Testing, Debugging, and Revising

Coding, testing, and revising a program is an iterative process, one that recycles through the different stages as necessary (Fig. 1–2). The process should develop in small incremental stages, where the solution becomes more refined at each step. However, no matter how much care you take, things can still go wrong during the coding process.

Syntax errors

Any *syntax errors* in the code will be detected by the Java compiler. Syntax errors are relatively easy to fix once you understand the error messages provided by the compiler. As long as a program contains syntax errors, the programmer must correct them and recompile the program (Fig. 1–2). If the compiler fails to detect any errors, it will produce an executable version of the program, which can then be run.

When a program is run, the computer carries out the steps specified in the program and produces results. However, just because a program runs does not mean that its actions and results are correct. A running program can contain *semantic errors*, or *logical errors*. A semantic error is caused by an error in the logical design of the program causing it to behave incorrectly, producing incorrect results.

Semantic errors

Unlike syntax errors, semantic errors cannot be detected automatically. For example, suppose that a program contains the following statement for calculating the area of a rectangle:

```
return length + width;
```

Because we are adding length and width instead of multiplying them, the resulting area will be incorrect. Because there is nothing syntactically wrong with the expression length + width, the compiler won't detect an error in this statement. The error resides in the program's logic and meaning. The programmer should have written length * width. Nevertheless, the computer will still execute this statement and compute the incorrect area. But you shouldn't believe the results!

Semantic errors are sometimes very hard to detect, and they can only be discovered by *testing* the program. Because program testing can only detect the presence of errors, not their absence, it is important to do as much testing as possible. The fact that a program *appears* to run correctly might just mean that it has not been adequately tested.

When semantic errors are detected, they must be found and fixed. This phase of programming is known as *debugging*, and when subtle errors occur it can be the most frustrating part of the whole program development process. The various lab exercises presented in this textbook will provide hints and suggestions on how to track down *bugs* in your code. One point to remember when you are debugging the subtlest of bugs is that no matter how convinced you are that your code is correct and that the bug must be caused by some kind of error in the computer, the error is almost certainly caused by your code!

Lanning's Limerick

There are some vain hackers so smug,
They can't see their code has a bug.
They curse the computer,
And some blame the tutor,
When the problem's a hole that they dug.

REAR ADMIRAL Grace Murray Hopper (1906–1992) was a pioneer computer programmer and one of the original developers of the COBOL programming language, which stands for *COmmon Business-Oriented Language*. Among her many achievements and distinctions Admiral Hopper also had a role in coining the term *computer bug*.

In August 1945, she and a group of other programmers were working on the Mark I, an electromechanical computer developed at Harvard that was one of the ancestors of today's electronic computers. After several hours of trying to figure out why the machine was malfunctioning, someone located and removed a two-inch moth from one of the computer's circuits. From then on whenever anything went wrong with a computer, Admiral Hopper and others would say "it had bugs in it." The first bug itself is still taped to Admiral Hopper's 1945 log book, which is now in the collection of the Naval Surface Weapons Center.

In 1991, Admiral Hopper was awarded the National Medal of Technology by President George Bush. To commemorate and honor Admiral Hopper's many contributions, the U.S. Navy recently named a warship after her. For more information on Admiral Hopper, see the Web site at

```
http://www.chips.navy.mil/
```

Grace Hopper and the First Computer Bug

Photograph courtesy of Navy Visual News Service

1.2.7 Writing Readable Programs

Becoming a proficient programmer goes beyond simply writing a program that produces correct output. It also involves developing good *programming style*, which covers, among other things, how readable and understandable your code is, both to yourself and to others. Our goal is to develop a programming style that satisfies the following principles:

Programming style

- **Readability.** Programs should be easy to read and understand. Comments should be used to document and explain the program's code.

- **Clarity.** Programs should employ well-known constructs and standard conventions and should avoid programming tricks and unnecessarily obscure or convoluted code.

- **Flexibility.** Programs should be designed and written so that they are easy to maintain and change.

Java Language Summary

Because we now will begin introducing more and more examples of Java program code, this section will describe, in a summary fashion, some of the key elements of the Java language. Our initial explanations here will be concise rather than comprehensive. But don't worry. Many of these language elements will be taken up in greater detail in subsequent sections.

Syntax and Semantics

As explained in the preceding section, the *syntax* of a language is the set of rules that defines how its words and symbols may be combined to form valid expressions. The *semantics* of a language is the set of rules that determines what its expressions mean. Obviously, learning a new language is a matter of learning both kinds of rules.

As an example of a syntax rule, consider the following two English statements:

```
The rain in Spain falls mainly on the plain.    // Valid sentence
Spain rain the mainly in on the falls plain.    // Invalid sentence
```

The first sentence follows the rules of English syntax (grammar), and it means that it rains a lot on the Spanish plain. The second sentence does not follow English syntax, and, as a result, it is rendered meaningless. Unlike in English, in a programming language, the relationship between syntax and semantics is very strict. If you break even the lightest syntax rule—for example, if you forget to put a semicolon at the end of a Java statement—the program won't work at all. It becomes completely meaningless.

Program Layout

Java is said to be a *free-form* language, which means that white space—blank spaces and blank lines—may occur anywhere in a Java program. Program expressions and statements may occur one per line, several per line, or one per several lines. The fact that the rules governing program layout are so lax makes it all the more important that elements of good programming *style* be used to make programs easy to read. Ample use of spacing between program elements helps to make programs more readable and more attractive.

Java Class Definition

A Java program is expressed as a class definition, which is how an object is defined. An application program is a class that contains a `main()` method. Figure 1–7 illustrates the key elements of a class definition.

In Figure 1–7 the *single-line comments*, which begin with double slashes, (`//`), serve to identify the important components of the program. The program consists of a class definition, which has two parts: a *class header* and a *class body*. The purpose of the header is to identify a class's name (`Example`), its accessibility (`public` as opposed to `private`), and its *pedigree*. The `Example` class is a *subclass of* (extends) the `Object` class, which is the root class of the entire Java class hierarchy.

The class's body, which is enclosed within curly brackets (`{}`), contains the elements that make up the objects of the class. There are generally two kinds of elements: *instance variables* (`num`), which store various kinds

Comments

Class header

Class body

```
public class Example extends Object       // Class header
{                                          // Start of class body
    private double num = 5.0;              // Instance variable

    public void print()                    // Method definition header
    {                                      // Start of method body
        System.out.println(num);           //   Output statement
    } // print()                           // End of print method body

    public static void main(String args[]) // Method definition header
    {                                      // Start of method body
        Example example;          //   Reference variable declaration
        example = new Example();  //   Object instantiation statement
        example.print();          //   Method call
    } // main()                   // End of method body
} // Example                      // End of class body
```

FIGURE 1–7 A Java application program is a class definition that contains a main() method.

of data, and *methods* (print()), which represent the object's actions or behaviors. An Example object has only one piece of data, the floating point (double) number 5.0, and its only action is to print() the number's value.

Method Definition

A **method** is a named section of code that can be called on or *invoked* to carry out an action or an operation. A method definition consists of two parts: the method's header and its body. The method header identifies certain important properties of the method, including its name (print), its accessibility (public or private or protected), the type of data it returns as a result (void), and its list of *parameters*, which in this case is an empty list (). By contrast, the main() method has a String variable in its parameter list. Methods that don't generate a result, such as the methods in this program, have a result type of void.

Defining a method

Method header

The program's **executable statements** are all contained within methods. For example, the print() method contains one statement System.out.println(num), which simply prints the object's number. This statement is an example of a *method call statement*. It calls the println() method, which is a member of the System.out object.

Object Instantiation

In order to get a Java program to take any action—print a string, add two numbers, and so on—you must define objects (classes) that have methods containing the particular actions you want to take. However, defining objects and methods is just the preliminary step. In order to use an object's methods, you must create an instance of the object (**object instantiation**) and then call or invoke the desired methods. An example of object instantiation is shown in the main() method.

```
Example example;          //   Reference variable declaration
example = new Example();  //   Object instantiation statement
example.print();          //   Method call
```

Here, a *reference variable* (example) is declared. The variable serves as the name of the new *instance* that is created. And then the instance is used to print a number (example.print()).

The Example class illustrates some of the key elements and key terminology of a Java program. This program consists of just two objects: the Example object, named example, and the System.out object that is used for printing. Most Java programs will consist of many objects, some predefined, such as System.out, and some programmer defined, such as Example. Once an object has been designed, the basic steps involved in coding it are as follows:

1. Define the object's class.
2. Instantiate one or more instances.
3. Use the instances to do the tasks needed for the program.

Keywords

Java has 47 predefined words or *keywords* (Table 1.1). An important restriction on keywords is that they cannot be used as the names of methods, variables, or classes.

TABLE 1.1   Java keywords.

abstract	default	if	private	throw
boolean	do	implements	protected	throws
break	double	import	public	transient
byte	else	instanceof	return	try
case	extends	int	short	void
catch	final	interface	static	volatile
char	finally	long	super	while
class	float	native	switch	
const	for	new	synchronized	
continue	goto	package	this	

Identifiers

An **identifier** is a name for a class, a method, or a variable. It has the following syntax:

> **JAVA LANGUAGE RULE**   Identifier.   An **identifier** must begin with a letter (A to Z, a to z) and may be followed by any number of letters or digits (0 to 9) or underscores (_). An identifier may not be identical to a Java keyword.

Remember that Java is *case sensitive*, so two distinct identifiers may contain the same letters—for example, thisVar and ThisVar—with the only difference being the use of capitalized letters.

Primitive Data Types

Every piece of data in a Java program is classified according to its *type*. Broadly speaking, there are two types of data in Java: *objects* and **primitive data types**. Java's primitive types are summarized in Table 1.2. Each data type is listed with its keyword and its size in bits. A *bit* is a single binary digit—a 0 or a 1. The values shown as examples in this table are known as **literal values** because the symbols used to represent them are literally the values themselves. Thus, 127 is a literal int value, and 'A' is a literal char value.

TABLE 1.2 Java primitive data types. Except for the boolean type, the size of the primitive types is defined in the Java Language Specification.

Type	Keyword	Size in Bits	Examples
boolean	boolean	–	true or false
character	char	16	`A', `5', `+'
byte	byte	8	–128 to +127
integer	short	16	–32768 to +32767
integer	int	32	–2147483648 to +2147483647
integer	long	64	*really big integers*
real number	float	32	21.3 , –0.45 , 1.67e28
real number	double	64	21.3 , –0.45 , 1.67e28

Aside from the primitive types, everything in Java is an object. So a Rectangle instance is an object. A String is also considered an object in Java. Examples of literal String values would include any string of characters enclosed within double quotes—such as "Hello World".

Variables

A **variable** is a named storage location that can store a value of a particular type. In the Example class, the *instance* variable num stores a value of type double. In the main() method, the variable example stores a reference to an Example object.

These two variables have different *scope* within the program. An *instance variable*, such as num, is defined at the class level and can be used throughout the class. A *local variable*, such as example, can only be used within the method in which it is defined.

Local and class scope

Expressions and Operators

An *expression* is used to specify or produce a value within a Java program, and all expressions have a type. For example, recalling that the num variable is declared as a double within the Example class, all of the following are examples of double expressions:

```
57.4        // A literal double value
num         // A variable (with the double value 5.0)
num + 2.0   // Adding 2 to a double gives 7.0, a double value
num = 45.9  // This assignment expression has the value 45.9
```

As these examples show, technically speaking a literal value (57.4) and a variable (num) are considered expressions in Java. The last two examples are what we normally consider expressions, because they involve familiar **operators**. In this case the plus sign (+) is used to perform addition. The value of the expression num + 2.0 is, in this case, 7.0. In the last example, the equal sign (=) is used as an *assignment operator* in Java, not as the equality operator. So the last example should not be interpreted as "num equals 45.9." Rather it should be interpreted as "num is assigned the value 45.9."

An **assignment expression** is somewhat special. All four of these expressions are said to *have a value* or *evaluate to a value*. The assignment expression has a value of 45.9, because it is assigning 45.9 to num. But the assignment expression also has the side effect of *storing* the value 45.9 in the variable num. No matter what value was previously stored there, after the assignment expression is evaluated, num will contain the value 45.9.

In Java, we use the == symbol to represent equality. Thus, the expression num == 0 should be interpreted as "num is equal to 0," which is either true or false. In other words, equality expressions have a boolean value.

> **JAVA LANGUAGE RULE** Equality and Assignment. Be careful not to confuse = and ==. The symbol = is the *assignment operator*. It assigns the value on its right-hand side to the variable on its left-hand side. The symbol == is the *equality operator*. It evaluates whether the expressions on its left- and right-hand sides have the same value and returns either true or false.

A **method invocation** is another kind of expression. For example, the following expressions are method invocations that produce values of type double, which represent the areas of their respective rectangles:

```
rectangle1.calculateArea()  // Produces 300.0
rectangle2.calculateArea()  // Produces 500.0
```

Statements

The **flow of control**, or *sequence of execution*, in a Java program is controlled by *statements*. A **block** or a **compound statement** is a sequence of statements contained within braces. Thus, the body of a method definition is considered a block of statements. In general, statements are separated from each other by *separators* or *punctuators*, which include the semicolon (;) and braces ({}).

A **declaration statement** declares a variable of a particular type. Java distinguishes between **instance variables**, which are declared at the class level, and *local variables*, which are declared within method bodies or, more generally, within a statement block.

An **executable statement** is a statement that takes some kind of action that affects the state of the program. Here are some simple examples:

```
num = 5.0;                  // Assignment statement assigns a value
                            // to a variable
System.out.println(num);    // A print statement prints a value
return;                     // A return statement exits from a method
```

The first example is an *assignment statement*, which assigns the value 5.0 to the variable num. That means the value 5.0 is stored in the memory location named num. The second is a print statement, which causes a certain value to be printed by the program. The last is a return statement, which is a way of exiting from within a Java method. We will discuss all of these kinds of statements in greater detail as we go. For now, just note that all statements end with a semicolon.

1.3   Editing, Compiling, and Running a Java Program

In this section we discuss the nuts and bolts of the *coding* process—that is, the process of editing, compiling, and running a Java program. We assume here that the program has already been designed. Because Java programs come in two different varieties, applications and applets, the process differs slightly for each variety. So we begin by describing two very simple Java programs.

1.3.1   Java Applications and Applets

A Java **application** is a stand-alone program. A Java **applet** is a program that runs within the context of a Web browser. An application is "stand-alone" in the sense that it does not depend on a browser for its execution.

Perhaps the simplest example of a Java application program might be the traditional HelloWorld program—"traditional" because practically every introductory programming text begins with it. The HelloWorld program (Fig. 1–8) just displays the message "Hello world!" on the console.

As this program illustrates, Java programs are contained within a *class* definition, which consists of a *header* that contains the name of the program plus a *body* that contains a collection of data elements and methods enclosed within braces.

Every Java application must contain a `main()` method, which is where execution of the program begins. The `main()` method in this case contains just one executable statement:

```
System.out.println("Hello world!");
```

When the `HelloWorld` program is run, this statement causes the message "Hello world!" to be displayed on the console or monitor.

The `HelloWorld` program contains two examples of Java comments. Text contained within /* and */ is considered a *multiline* comment. A *single-line* comment begins with double slashes (//), which turn the rest of the line into a comment.

JAVA LANGUAGE RULE   Comments. Double slashes (//) can be used to turn any line or remainder of a line into a *single-line comment*, which is ignored by the compiler. Text contained within /* and */ is considered to be a multiline comment.

Comments are used to document the program and make it more readable. One good use for comments is to annotate closing braces so it is easier

```
/*
 * The HelloWorld application program
 */
public class HelloWorld               // Class header
{                                     // Start of class body
    public static void main(String argv[])   // Main method
    {
        System.out.println("Hello world!");
    }  // End of main
}  // End of HelloWorld
```

FIGURE 1–8   The `HelloWorld` application program.

FIGURE 1–9 The `HelloWorld` applet program.

```
/*
 * HelloWorld applet program
 */
import java.applet.Applet;    // Import the Applet class
import java.awt.Graphics;     //    and the Graphics class

public class HelloWorld extends Applet            // Class header
{                                                  // Start of body
    public void paint(Graphics g)                 // The paint method
    {
        g.drawString("HelloWorld",10,10);
    } // End of paint
} // End of HelloWorld
```

to tell where certain blocks of code begin and end. In this program, comments are used to mark the end of the `main()` method, as well as the end of the `HelloWorld` class itself.

An **applet** is a Java program that is embedded within a Web page and executed by a Web browser. Figure 1–9 shows a Java applet named `HelloWorld`.

This applet does more or less the same thing as the application program: It displays the "HelloWorld" message. As in the case of the application, the program consists of a class definition. It contains a single method, in this case the `paint()` method, which contains a single executable statement:

```
g.drawString("HelloWorld",10,10);
```

This statement displays the "HelloWorld" message. But in this case the message is *painted* on a window within the Web browser.

Because they are intended to run within a Web browser, and because they use a *Graphical User Interface (GUI)*, Java applets are a little more complicated to write than Java applications—at least Java applications, such as the `HelloWorld` application, that don't use a GUI. For example, the `HelloWorld` applet begins with two `import` statements. These statements refer to code from the Java class libraries. The Java class libraries are organized into *packages*, which have names like `java.awt` and `java.applet`. The `java.applet` package contains classes used to create an applet and to enable the applet to communicate with its environment. The `java.awt` package contains classes that define `Buttons`, `TextFields`, and other objects that are used to create graphical interfaces.

Library packages

Because an applet lives within the browser's environment, we have to be able to interact with it the same way we interact with the browser—by clicking on buttons, opening windows, and so on. Fortunately, Java supplies an entire library of classes to support applet and GUI programming.

1.3.2 Java Development Environments

A Java programming environment typically consists of several programs that perform different tasks required to edit, compile, and run a Java program. The following description will be based on the *Java Development Kit (JDK)*, a collection of software development tools available free from the Sun Microsystems Java Web site `http://java.sun.com`. Versions of JDK are

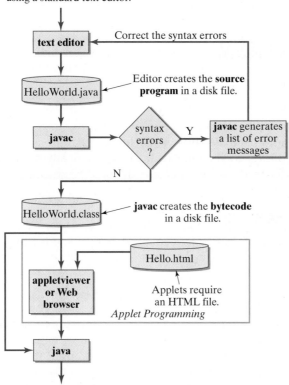

User types program into a file
using a standard text editor.

FIGURE 1–10   Editing, compiling,
and running HelloWorld.java.

The Java Virtual Machine
loads the class file into
memory and interprets and
runs the bytecode.

available for Unix, Windows, and Macintosh computers. (For more details about the JDK, see Appendix B.)

In some cases the individual programs that make up the JDK have been integrated into a single program development environment. For example, Metrowerk's Codewarrior, Borland's JBuilder, and Sun's Forte each provide an *integrated development environment (IDE)* for Java for Macintosh, Windows, or Sun Solaris computers.

The process of creating and running a Java program requires three steps: *editing, compiling,* and *running,* as illustrated in Figure 1–10. The discussion that follows here assumes that you are using the JDK as your development environment. If you are using some other environment, it will be necessary to read the documentation provided with the software to determine exactly how to edit, compile, and run Java programs in that environment.

Step 1. Editing a Program

Any text editor may be used to edit the program, and the process consists merely of typing the program and making corrections as needed. Two popular Unix editors are vi and emacs. On Macintosh systems, popular editors include SimpleText and BBEdit. On Windows systems, an editor such as WinEdit may be used. The program must be saved in a text file named *ClassName.java* where *ClassName* is the name of the Java class contained in the file.

> **JAVA LANGUAGE RULE**   **File Names.** If a file contains a public class named ClassName, then it must be saved in a text file named Class-Name.java. Otherwise an error will result.

For example, in the case of our HelloWorld programs, either the applet or the application, the file must be named HelloWorld.java. Also, because Java is *case sensitive*, which means that Java pays attention to whether a letter is typed uppercase or lowercase, it would be an error if the file were named helloworld.java or Helloworld.java.

> **JAVA LANGUAGE RULE**   **Case Sensitivity.** Java is *case sensitive*, which means that it treats helloWorld and Helloworld as different names.

Step 2. Compiling a Program

Recall that before you can run a Java source program you have to translate it (or compile it) into the computer's machine language. There is no difference between compiling an applet and an application. Compilation translates Java language statements that make up the *source program* into Java *bytecode*, the intermediate code understood by the *Java Virtual Machine (JVM)*. To run a Java program, whether an applet or an application, the JVM is then used to interpret and execute the bytecode.

Platform independence

Java bytecode is said to be *platform independent*, which means that it can run on any hardware or software platform that supports the JVM. All of the major operating systems—Unix, Linux, MacOS, Windows—and both of the major browsers—Netscape Navigator, Internet Explorer—have incorporated the JVM into their software and can, therefore, run Java programs.

The Java Development Kit (JDK) Java compiler is named javac. In some environments—such as within Unix or at the DOS command prompt within Windows—HelloWorld.java would be compiled by keyboarding the following command at the system prompt:

```
javac HelloWorld.java
```

If the HelloWorld.java program does not contain errors, the result of this command is the creation of a Java bytecode file named HelloWorld.class—a file that has the same prefix as the source file but the suffix .class. If javac detects errors in the Java code, a list of error messages will be printed.

If you are using some other development environment besides JDK, you would follow the instructions provided for how to compile your program in that environment. If the compilation works, the .class file will be created.

Step 3. Running a Java Application Program

In order to run a program on any computer, the program's *executable code* must be loaded into the computer's main memory. For Java environments, this means that the program's `.class` file must be loaded into the computer's memory, where it is then interpreted by the Java Virtual Machine. On Unix systems or within DOS on Windows systems, a Java application program would be run by typing

```
java HelloWorld
```

at the command prompt. This command loads the JVM, which will then load and interpret the application's bytecode (`HelloWorld.class`). The "HelloWorld" string will be displayed on the command line.

On Macintosh systems, or within an IDE, which do not typically have a command line interface, you would select the compile and run commands from a menu. Once the code is compiled, the run command will cause the JVM to be loaded and the bytecode to be interpreted. The "HelloWorld!" output would appear in a text-based window that automatically pops up on your computer screen. In any case, regardless of the system you use, running the `HelloWorld` application program will cause the "HelloWorld" message to be displayed on some kind of standard output device (Fig. 1–11).

To run a Java applet one must use either a Web browser or the JDK's `appletviewer`, a stripped-down Web browser for running applets. The Web browser (or appletviewer) uses an **HTML (HyperText Markup Language)** document to locate the applet's bytecode files on the Internet. The HTML file must contain an `<applet>` tag, as shown in Figure 1–12. (See Appendix B for more details about the appletviewer and the `<applet>` tag.)

If the applet tag is correctly specified, the Web browser (or appletviewer) will locate the Java bytecode file on the Web (or on your system's hard drive). It will then load the JVM, which will load the applet's code into memory and interpret and execute it.

The code in Figure 1–12 would be placed in a file named with an `.html` suffix to indicate that it is an HTML file. The name of the file in this case is not important, but let's suppose we give it the name `Hello.html`. What is important is that the `<applet>` tag be specified correctly, designating the name of the Java bytecode that should be executed (`HelloWorld.class`). It is also necessary that the HTML file be stored in the same directory or folder as the class file. (There are ways to get around this, but we'll deal with those later.)

FIGURE 1–11   Running the `HelloWorld.java` application program.

```
<html>
...
<applet code="HelloWorld.class" width= 200 height=200 >
</applet>
...
</html>
```

FIGURE 1–12   An example of an HTML file containing an `<applet>` tag. This specification will run the Java program named `HelloWorld.class`.

Given the correctly coded HTML file, `Hello.html`, the `appletviewer` can be used to load and run the applet by typing the following command on the command line:

```
appletviewer Hello.html
```

If you are using a Web browser to run the applet, you would use the browser's menu to load `Hello.html` into the browser, either across the Internet by supplying its *URL (Uniform Resource Locator)* or from your local disk by supplying its file name. In any case, the appletviewer or the browser will load the program's bytecode into the computer's main memory and then verify, interpret, and execute the program. The result, as shown in Figure 1–13, is that the "Hello world!" message will be displayed within the browser or appletviewer window.

FIGURE 1–13 Running the `HelloWorld.java` applet.

From the Java Library

System **and** PrintStream

http://java.sun.com/products /jdk/1.3/docs/api/

JAVA COMES with a library of classes that can be used to perform common tasks. The Java class library is organized into a set of packages, where each **package** contains a collection of related classes. Throughout the book we will identify library classes and explain how to use them. In this section we introduce the `System` and `PrintStream` classes, which are used for printing a program's output.

Java programs need to be able to accept input and to display output. For Java applets, input and output, which we abbreviate as I/O, are usually handled through the applet's *Graphical User Interface (GUI)*, which will be covered in Chapter 4. For application programs the type of input and output required can vary. Many applications also handle I/O through a GUI. For some applications, input is accepted from the keyboard and output is displayed on the computer console. For others, input and output might occur across a network connection or might involve files on the disk drive.

In Java, any source or destination for I/O is considered a *stream* of bytes or characters. To perform output, we insert bytes or characters into the stream. To perform input, we extract bytes or characters from the stream. Even characters entered at a keyboard, if considered as a sequence of keystrokes, can be represented as a stream.

There are no I/O statements in the Java language. Instead, I/O is handled through methods that belong to classes contained in the `java.io` package. We have already used the output method `println()` in our `HelloWorld` application:

```
System.out.println("HelloWorld");
```

This statement prints the message "HelloWorld" on the Java console. Let's now examine this statement more carefully to see how it makes use of the Java I/O classes.

The `java.io.PrintStream` class is Java's printing expert, so to speak. It contains `print()` and `println()` methods that can be used to print all of the various types of data we find in a Java program. A partial definition of `PrintStream` is shown in Figure 1–14. Note that in this case the `PrintStream` class has no attributes, just operations or methods.

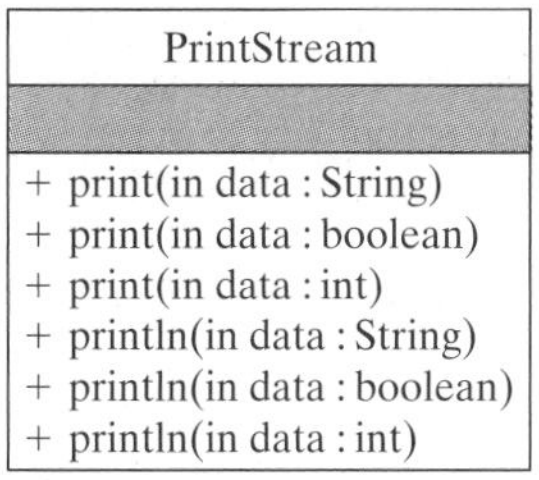

Because the various `print()` and `println()` methods belong to the `PrintStream` class, we can only use them by finding a `PrintStream` object and "telling" it to print data for us. As shown in Figure 1–15, Java's `java.lang.System` class contains three predefined streams, including two `PrintStreams`. This class has public (+) attributes. None of its public methods are shown here. As its name implies, the `System` class is part of the `java.lang` package. This package contains classes fundamental to the design of the Java language.

Both the `System.out` and `System.err` objects can be used to write output to the console. As its name suggests, the `err` stream is used primarily for error messages, whereas the `out` stream is used for other printed output. Similarly, as its name suggests, the `System.in` object can be used to handle input, which will be covered in Chapter 2.

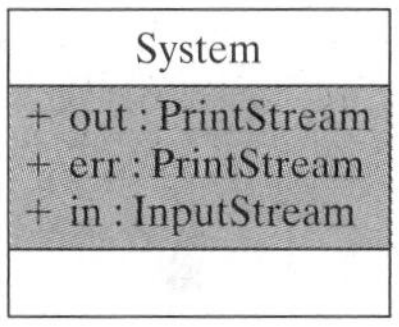

The only difference between the `print()` and `println()` methods is that `println()` will also print a carriage return and line feed after printing its data, thereby allowing subsequent output to be printed on a new line. For example, the following statements

```
System.out.print("hello");          // Ask out to print "hello"
System.out.println("hello again");  // Ask out to print "hello again"
System.out.println("goodbye");      // Ask out to print "goodbye"
```

would produce the following output:

```
hellohello again
goodbye
```

Now that we know how to use Java's printing expert, let's use it to "sing" a version of "Old MacDonald Had a Farm." As you might guess, this program will simply consist of a sequence of `System.out.println()` statements each of which prints a line of the verse. The complete Java application program is shown in Figure 1–16.

```java
public class OldMacDonald
{
    public static void main(String argv[])    // Main method
    {
        System.out.println("Old MacDonald had a farm");
        System.out.println("E I E I O.");
        System.out.println("And on his farm he had a duck.");
        System.out.println("E I E I O.");
        System.out.println("With a quack quack here.");
        System.out.println("And a quack quack there.");
        System.out.println("Here a quack, there a quack,");
        System.out.println("Everywhere a quack quack.");
        System.out.println("Old MacDonald had a farm");
        System.out.println("E I E I O.");
    }  // End of main
}  // End of OldMacDonald
```

PrintStream
+ print(in data : String)
+ print(in data : boolean)
+ print(in data : int)
+ println(in data : String)
+ println(in data : boolean)
+ println(in data : int)

FIGURE 1–14 A UML class diagram of the `PrintStream` class.

System
+ out : PrintStream
+ err : PrintStream
+ in : InputStream

FIGURE 1–15 The `System` class.

FIGURE 1–16 The `OldMacDonald.java` class.

This example illustrates the importance of using the Java class library. If there's a particular task we want to perform, one of the first things we should ask is whether there is already an "expert" in Java's class library that performs that task. If so, we can use methods provided by the expert to perform that particular task.

EFFECTIVE DESIGN: Using the Java Library.   Learning how to use classes and objects from the Java class library is an important element of object-oriented programming.

SELF-STUDY EXERCISES

EXERCISE 1.1   One good way to learn how to write programs is to modify existing programs. Modify the `OldMacDonald` class to "sing" one more verse of the song.

EXERCISE 1.2   Write a Java class that prints the following design:

```
**********
*  **  **  *
*    **    *
*  *    *  *
*  ****   *
**********
```

1.4   Qualified Names in Java

Dot notation

You may be wondering about the meaning of names such as `java.io.-PrintStream` and `System.out.print()`, when they occur in a Java program. These are examples of *qualified names*. They use *dot notation* to clarify or disambiguate the name of something.

Just as in our natural language, the meaning of a name within a Java program depends on the context. For example, the expression `System.out.-print()` refers to the `print()` method, which belongs to the `System.out` object. If we were using this expression from within `System.out`, you wouldn't need to qualify the name in this way. You could just refer to `print()` and it would be clear from the context which method you meant.

This is no different than using someone's first name ("Kim") when there's only one Kim around, but using a full name ("Kim Smith") when the first name alone would be too vague or ambiguous.

One thing that complicates the use of qualified names is that they are used to refer to different kinds of things within a Java program. But this is no different, really, than in our natural language, where names ("George Washington") can refer to people, bridges, universities, and so on.

Here again, just as in our natural language, Java uses the context to understand the meaning of the name. For example, the expression `java.lang.System` refers to the `System` class in the `java.lang` package, whereas the expression `System.out.print()` refers to a method in the `System.out` object.

How can you tell these apart? Java can tell them apart because the first one occurs as part of an `import` statement, so it must be referring to something that belongs to a package. The second expression would only be valid in a context where a method invocation is allowed. You will have to learn a bit more about the Java language before you'll be able to completely understand these names. But here are some naming rules to get you started.

> **JAVA LANGUAGE RULE** Library Class Names. By convention, class names in Java begin with an uppercase letter. When referenced as part of a package, the class name is the last part of the name. For example, `java.lang.System` refers to the `System` class in the `java.lang` package.

> **JAVA LANGUAGE RULE** Dot Notation. Names expressed in Java's *dot notation* depend for their meaning on the context in which they are used. In qualified names—that is, names of the form X.Y.Z—the last item in the name (Z) is the referent. The items that precede it (X.Y.) are used to qualify the referent.

The fact that names are context dependent in this way certainly complicates the task of learning what's what in a Java program. Part of learning to use Java's built-in classes is learning where a particular object or method is defined. It is a syntax error if the Java compiler can't find the object or method that you are referencing.

> **DEBUGGING TIP:** Not Found Error. If Java cannot find the item you are referring to, it will report an "X not found" error, where X is the class, method, variable, or package being referred to.

IN THE LABORATORY: Editing, Compiling, and Running an Applet

The purpose of this first laboratory project is to give you some hands-on experience editing and compiling a Java program. This will not only familiarize you with the software that will be used in your course but will also elaborate on some of the concepts introduced in this chapter. The objectives of this exercise are

- To familiarize you with the process of editing, compiling, and running a Java applet.
- To introduce the *stepwise refinement* coding style.
- To provide some examples of both syntax and semantic errors.

Don't worry that you won't understand all of the Java code in the applet. We'll eventually get to language details in subsequent chapters.

As shown in Figure 1–17, this applet plays a silly game with the user. Every time the user clicks on the button labeled "Click Me Not!" the applet button's label changes to "Click Me!" and vice versa. If you want to try this applet, its URL is

FIGURE 1–17   An applet that toggles its button label.

```
http://starbase.trincoll.edu/~jjjava/sourcecode2E/ch01/firstapplet/clickme.html
```

Program Walkthrough: Program Style and Documentation

FirstApplet's complete source code is shown in Figure 1–18. The program begins with a *comment block*, which presents important information about the program, including the name of the file that contains it, the name of the author, and a brief description of what the program does.

```java
/**
 * File: FirstApplet.java
 * Author: Java Java Java
 * Description: This applet plays the click-me-not game with the user.
 */

import java.awt.*;
import java.applet.Applet;
import java.awt.event.*;

/*
 * The FirstApplet class plays the click-me-not game with the user.
 * @author Java Java Java
 */

public class FirstApplet extends Applet implements ActionListener
{
    private Button clickMe;                      // Declare the button

    /**
     * The init() method initializes the applet.
     */
    public void init()
    {
        clickMe = new Button("Click Me Not!");   // Create the button
        clickMe.addActionListener(this);         // Activate the button
        add(clickMe);                            // Add it to the applet
    }  // init()

    /**
     * The actionPerformed() method is called whenever the button is clicked.
     */
    public void actionPerformed (ActionEvent e)
    {
        if (clickMe.getLabel().equals("Click Me!"))
            clickMe.setLabel("Click Me Not!");
        else
            clickMe.setLabel("Click Me!");
    }  // actionPerformed()
}  // End of FirstApplet
```

FIGURE 1–18   FirstApplet, a Java applet that plays a silly game.

> **JAVA LANGUAGE RULE** Comments. A *multiline comment* begins with "/*" and ends with "*/" and may extend over several lines. It is ignored by the compiler. A multiline comment that begins with "/**" and ends with "*/" is called a *documentation comment*. These kinds of comments can be processed by special software provided by Java that will automatically generate documentation for the class.

> PROGRAMMING TIP: Use of Comments.   A well-written program should begin with a comment block that provides the name of the program, its author, and a description of what the program does.

In addition to the comment block at the beginning of `FirstApplet` and several other comment blocks in the program, there are also several single-line comments used to clarify the code (Fig. 1–18). Commenting your code in this way is an important part of program development. Appendix A lays out the style and documentation guidelines that are followed in this book. In subsequent laboratory projects, as our programs become more sophisticated, we will introduce additional documentation requirements.

Students invariably hate putting comments in their programs. After all, it seems somewhat anticlimactic, having to go back and document your program after you have finished designing, writing, and testing it. The way to avoid the sense of anticlimax is to "document as you go" rather than leaving it to the end. In many cases, your design document can serve as the basis for the comments in your program. One of the main reasons for commenting code is so that you, or someone else, will be able to understand the code the next time you have to modify it. Students who go on to be professional programmers often write back with reports that they now understand how important program documentation is. As a Limerick-writing friend put it:

Lanning's Limerick

All hard-headed coders say "Phooey,
Putting comments in code is just hooey!"
But when they are asked,
To reread what they hacked,
They discover their programs are screwy.

Program Walkthrough: The `import` Declaration

The next portion of the program contains the three `import` statements:

```
import java.applet.Applet;
import java.awt.*;
import java.awt.event.*;
```

The `import` statement is a convenience that allows you to refer to library classes by their short names rather than by their fully qualified names. For example, the first import statement tells the compiler that in this program we will refer to the `java.applet.Applet` class simply as `Applet`. This allows us to write a statement like

```
public class FirstApplet extends Applet
```

instead of being required to use the full name for the `Applet` class

```
public class FirstApplet extends java.applet.Applet
```

But either will work. The expression java.awt.* uses the asterisk ("*") as a *wildcard character* that matches any public class name in the java.awt package. This allows you to refer to all public classes in the java.awt package—for example, java.awt.Button and java.awt.TextArea—by their short names. The third statement matches all the class names in the java.awt.event package, which allows the program to refer to java.awt.event.ActionListener by its short name.

Program Walkthrough: Class Definition

The next element in the program is the *header* of the class definition:

```
public class FirstApplet extends Applet implements ActionListener
```

This is a more complex class header than the one we used for the HelloWorld class. But this applet is a more sophisticated program because it interacts with the user. Don't worry at this point if its operations seem a bit magical.

The class header serves the purpose of naming the class FirstApplet, designating its accessibility public, specifying that it is an Applet, and declaring that it implements ActionListener, an interface that allows it to respond to the user's mouse clicks. The header begins the definition of the class, which extends all the way to the last line of the program—the line marked with the //End of FirstApplet comment.

The body of a class definition is a *block*, as is the body of a method. Note how the statements in the block are indented and how the braces are aligned and commented. These style conventions serve to make the program more readable.

PROGRAMMING TIP: Use of Indentation. The code within a block should be indented, and the block's opening and closing braces should be aligned. A comment should be used to mark the end of a block of code.

Following the header is a *variable declaration*:

```
private Button clickMe;      // The button
```

As we will see in more detail in the next chapter, *variables* are memory locations that can store values. In this case, the Applet object is storing a reference to a Button object.

PROGRAMMING TIP: Choice of Variable Names. Names chosen for variables, methods, and classes should be descriptive of the element's purpose and should be written in a distinctive style to distinguish them from other elements of the program. For variable and method names, our convention is to start the name with a lowercase letter and use uppercase letters to distinguish words within the name—for example, clickMe. Class names begin with an uppercase letter (FirstApplet).

Program Walkthrough: Method Definition

The next element of the program is the init() method:

```java
public void init()
{
    clickMe = new Button("Click Me Not!");    // Create the button
    clickMe.addActionListener(this);          // Activate the button
    add(clickMe);                             // Add it to the applet
}  // init()
```

The init() method is called once, automatically, whenever an applet is loaded into the Java Virtual Machine. Its purpose is to *initialize* the applet's interface and any variables used in the applet's processing. As the method's comments indicate, the method creates (new) a Button and adds it to the applet, which causes it to appear on the screen when the applet is run.

The actionPerformed() method is the last element in the program:

```java
public void actionPerformed (ActionEvent e)
{
    if (clickMe.getLabel().equals("Click Me!"))
        clickMe.setLabel("Click Me Not!");
    else
        clickMe.setLabel("Click Me!");
}  // actionPerformed()
```

This method is called automatically whenever the applet's button is clicked. Its purpose is to "perform action" when a button-click event takes place. In this case the action it takes is to toggle the button's label from "Click Me!" to "Click Me Not!" or vice versa.

LAB EXERCISE 1: EDITING, COMPILING, AND RUNNING

Using whatever programming environment you have available in your computing lab, edit, compile, and run the FirstApplet program. However, don't just keyboard the whole program and then compile it. Instead, use the stepwise refinement approach as outlined here.

• **Stepwise Refinement: Stage 1.** Begin by keyboarding the entire comment block at the beginning of the program, the import statements, and the following class definition:

```java
public class FirstApplet extends Applet implements ActionListener
{
    public void actionPerformed (ActionEvent e)
    {
    }  // actionPerformed
}  // End of FirstApplet
```

This is an example of a stub class. A **stub class** has the basic outline for a class but no real content. In this case the definition must contain a stub definition of the actionPerformed() method, which is part of the

ActionListener interface. After entering this, compile and run the program. It should compile correctly, but it won't do anything because it doesn't contain any executable code.

- **Stepwise Refinement: Stage 2.** Keyboard the declarations given at the beginning of the class definition and the stub method definition for the init() method. A **stub method** contains a correctly defined *method header* but an incomplete *method body*. The idea is that you will fill in the details of the body later. Your program should then contain the following code:

```java
import java.awt.*;
import java.applet.Applet;
import java.awt.event.*;

public class FirstApplet extends Applet implements ActionListener
{
    private Button clickMe;              // The button

    public void init()
    {
    } // init()

    public void actionPerformed (ActionEvent e)
    {
    } // actionPerformed
} // End of FirstApplet
```

Recompile the program and run it again. It should compile correctly, but it still won't really do anything. But you've accomplished a lot, because you've now correctly coded the basic structure of the program.

- **Stepwise Refinement: Stage 3.** Complete the coding of the init() method by keyboarding all of the executable statements contained within its body. Then recompile and run the program. Now when the program runs you should see a Button on the applet. Note that if any errors occur as you are coding this portion of the program, you know that they must be located in the init() method, because you haven't touched the rest of the program. You've now successfully implemented the applet's user interface.

- **Stepwise Refinement: Stage 4.** Complete the coding of the actionPerformed() method by keyboarding all of the statements in its method body. Then recompile and run the applet. It should now have its full functionality. Every time you click on the button, it should toggle its label. Cool, eh!?

Hopefully, going through this exercise has illustrated some of the advantages of the stepwise refinement approach to writing Java code.

PROGRAMMING TIP: Stepwise Refinement. *Stepwise refinement* is a coding and testing strategy that employs the divide-and-conquer principle. Keyboard and test small segments of the program in a step-by-step fashion. In addition to breaking up the task into more manageable subtasks, this approach helps to *localize* any problems that arise.

LAB EXERCISE 2: GENERATING SYNTAX ERRORS

In this exercise you will make modifications to `FirstApplet`, which will introduce syntax errors into your program. The main purpose here is to give you a first look at how your programming environment reports error messages. You'll also learn some of the most fundamental rules of Java syntax.

For each of the following items, make the editing change and then re-compile the program. Make note of any error messages that are generated by the compiler. Try to understand what the message is telling you, and try to learn from the error, so it will be less likely to occur next time. After you have finished with that error, restore the code to its original form and move on to the next item.

- **Java Language Rule. Every Java statement must end with a semi-colon.** Delete the semicolon at the end of one of the lines in the program. Repeat this experiment for different lines and note the error messages. Are they always the same? Sometimes the compiler can tell that you've forgotten a semicolon, but sometimes a missing semicolon causes the compiler to lose its place.
- **Java Language Rule. Variables must be declared before they can be used.** Turn the line in which the `Button` is declared into a comment by typing double slashes "`//`" at the beginning of the line. The compiler will now skip that line. Because you haven't removed the line from the source code, you can easily put it back in the program by removing the double slashes.
- **Java Language Rule. Java names are case sensitive.** Change the spelling of `clickMe` to `ClickMe` in the declaration statement but nowhere else in the program.

LAB EXERCISE 3: GENERATING SEMANTIC ERRORS

Recall that semantic errors cannot be detected by the compiler. They are errors in the logic of the program that cause it to do something it is not really supposed to do. For each of the following errors, try to think about what will happen before you run the program. Then try to describe the logic error being committed. Ask yourself what kind of test you might perform to detect the error (if you didn't already know where it was).

- **Button, button, who's got the button?** Comment out the line (by beginning it with double slashes) that contains the `add(clickMe);` statement. This is a pretty easy error to detect.
- **What's the difference?** Put a space before the exclamation point in "Click Me!" in the `actionPerformed()` method. This error is a little more subtle than the first one. How would you detect this error?

That's enough! Feel free to make up your own experiments and play around some more with the program.

CHAPTER SUMMARY

Technical Terms

algorithm	identifier	software life cycle
applet	instance variable	stepwise refinement
application	(field)	stub class
assignment	literal value	stub method
expression	method	syntax
block (compound	method invocation	variable
statement)	object instantiation	waterfall model
declaration statement	operator	
executable statement	package	
flow of control	primitive data type	
HyperText Markup	pseudocode	
Language (HTML)	semantics	

Summary of Important Points

- A Java *applet* is a program that runs within the context of a Java-enabled browser. A Java *application* runs in stand-alone mode. Java applets are identified in HTML documents by using the `<applet>` tag.

- Java programs are first *compiled* into *bytecode* and then *interpreted* by the *Java Virtual Machine*.

- A Java source program must be stored in a file that has a `.java` extension. A Java bytecode file has the same name as the source file but a `.class` extension. It is an error in Java if the name of the source file is not identical to the name of the public Java *class* defined within the file. Java is *case sensitive*.

- Good program design requires that each *object* and *method* have a well-defined role and clear definition of what information is needed for the task and what results will be produced.

- An *algorithm* is a step-by-step process that solves some problem. *Pseudocode* is a hybrid language that combines English and programming language constructs.

- Coding Java should follow the *stepwise refinement* process and should make ample use of *stub methods*.

- A *syntax error* results when a statement violates one of Java's syntax rules. Syntax errors are detected by the compiler. A *semantic error* or *logic error* is an error in the program's design and cannot be detected by the compiler.

- Testing a program can only reveal the presence of bugs, not their absence. No matter how convinced you are that a bug is not your program's fault, you're almost certainly wrong! Good program design is important; the sooner you start coding, the longer the program will take to finish.

- Good programs should be designed for *readability*, *clarity*, and *flexibility*.

- The expression `System.out.print("hello")` uses Java *dot notation* to invoke the `print()` method of the `System.out` object. Dot notation takes the form *reference.elementName*.

SOLUTION 1.1   The definition of the `OldMacDonald` class is:

```
public class OldMacDonald
{
    public static void main(String argv[])    // Main method
    {
        System.out.println("Old MacDonald had a farm");
        System.out.println("E I E I O.");
        System.out.println("And on his farm he had a duck.");
        System.out.println("E I E I O.");
        System.out.println("With a quack quack here.");
        System.out.println("And a quack quack there.");
        System.out.println("Here a quack, there a quack,");
        System.out.println("Everywhere a quack quack.");
        System.out.println("Old MacDonald had a farm");
        System.out.println("E I E I O.");

        System.out.println("Old MacDonald had a farm");
        System.out.println("E I E I O.");
        System.out.println("And on his farm he had a pig.");
        System.out.println("E I E I O.");
        System.out.println("With an oink oink here.");
        System.out.println("And an oink oink  there.");
        System.out.println("Here an oink, there an oink,");
        System.out.println("Everywhere an oink oink.");
        System.out.println("Old MacDonald had a farm");
        System.out.println("E I E I O.");
    }  // End of main
}  // End of OldMacDonald
```

SOLUTION 1.2   The definition of the `Pattern` class is:

```
public class Pattern
{
    public static void main(String argv[])     // Main method
    {
        System.out.println("**********");
        System.out.println("* **  ** *");
        System.out.println("*    **   *");
        System.out.println("* *     * *");
        System.out.println("*  ****  *");
        System.out.println("**********");
    }  // End of main
}  // End of Pattern
```

EXERCISES

EXERCISE 1.1   Fill in the blanks in each of the following statements.

a. A Java class definition contains an object's _____ and _____.
b. A stub class is one that contains a proper _____ but an empty _____.

EXERCISE 1.2   Explain the difference between each of the following pairs of concepts.

a. *Application* and *applet*.
b. *Single-line* and *multiline* comment.
c. *Compiling* and *running* a program.
d. *Source code* file and *bytecode* file.
e. *Syntax* and *semantics*.
f. *Syntax error* and *semantic error*.
g. *Data* and *methods*.
h. *Variable* and *method*.
i. *Algorithm* and *method*.
j. *Pseudocode* and *Java code*.
k. *Method definition* and *method invocation*.

EXERCISE 1.3   For each of the following, identify it as either a syntax error or a semantic error. Justify your answers.

a. You write your class header as `public Class MyClass`.
b. You define the `init()` header as `public vid init()`.
c. You print a string of five asterisks by `System.out.println("***");`.
d. You forget the semicolon at the end of a `println()` statement.
e. You calculate the sum of two numbers as `N — M`.

EXERCISE 1.4   Suppose you have a Java program stored in a file named `Test.java`. Describe the compilation and execution process for this program, naming any other files that would be created.

EXERCISE 1.5   Suppose *N* is 15. What numbers would be output by the following pseudocode algorithm? Suppose *N* is 6. What would be output by the algorithm in that case?

```
0. Print N.
1. If N equals 1, stop.
2. If N is even, divide it by 2.
3. If N is odd, triple it and add 1.
4. Go to step 0.
```

EXERCISE 1.6   Suppose *N* is 5 and *M* is 3. What value would be reported by the following pseudocode algorithm? In general, what quantity does this algorithm calculate?

```
0. Write 0 on a piece of paper.
1. If M equals 0, report what's on the paper and stop.
2. Add N to the quantity written on the paper.
3. Subtract 1 from M.
4. Go to step 1.
```

EXERCISE 1.7   Puzzle Problem: You are given two different length strings that have the characteristic that they both take exactly one hour to burn. However, neither string burns at a constant rate. Some sections of the strings burn very fast; other sections burn very slowly. All you have to work with is a box of matches and the two strings. Describe an algorithm that uses the strings and the matches to calculate when exactly 45 minutes have elapsed.

EXERCISE 1.8   Puzzle Problem: A polar bear that lives right at the North Pole can walk due south for one hour, due east for one hour, and due north for one hour, and end up right back where it started. Is it possible to do this anywhere else on earth? Explain.

EXERCISE 1.9   Puzzle Problem: Lewis Carroll, the author of *Alice in Wonderland*, used the following puzzle to entertain his guests: A captive queen weighing 195 pounds, her son weighing 90 pounds, and her daughter weighing 165 pounds, were trapped in a very high tower. Outside their window was a pulley and rope with a basket fastened on each end. They managed to escape by using the baskets and a 75-pound weight they found in the tower. How did they do it? The problem is anytime the difference in weight between the two baskets is more than 15 pounds, someone might get killed. Describe an algorithm that gets them down safely.

EXERCISE 1.10   Puzzle Problem: Here's another Carroll favorite: A farmer needs to cross a river with his fox, goose, and a bag of corn. There's a rowboat that will hold the farmer and one other passenger. The problem is that the fox will eat the goose, if they are left alone, and the goose will eat the corn, if they are left alone. Write an algorithm that describes how he got across without losing any of his possessions.

EXERCISE 1.11   Puzzle Problem: Have you heard this one? A farmer lent the mechanic next door a 40-pound weight. Unfortunately, the mechanic dropped the weight and it broke into four pieces. The good news is that, according to the mechanic, it is still possible to use the four pieces to weigh any quantity between one and 40 pounds on a balance scale. How much did each of the four pieces weigh? (*Hint*: You can weigh a 4-pound object on a balance by putting a 5-pound weight on one side and a 1-pound weight on the other.)

EXERCISE 1.12   Suppose your little sister asks you to help her calculate her homework average in her science course by showing how to use a pocket calculator. Describe an algorithm that she can use to find the average of 10 homework grades.

EXERCISE 1.13   A Caesar cipher is a secret code in which each letter of the alphabet is shifted by N letters to the right, with the letters at the end of the alphabet wrapping around to the beginning. For example, if N is 1, when we shift each letter to the right *daze* would be written as *ebaf*. Note that the z has wrapped around to the beginning of the alphabet. Describe an algorithm that can be used to create a Caesar encoded message with a shift of 5.

EXERCISE 1.14   Suppose you received the message, "sxccohv duh ixq," which you know to be a Caesar cipher. Figure out what it says and then describe an algorithm that will always find what the message said regardless of the size of the shift that was used.

EXERCISE 1.15   Suppose you're talking to your little brother on the phone and he wants you to calculate his homework average. All you have to work with is a piece of chalk and a very small chalkboard—big enough to write one four-digit number. What's more, although your little brother knows how to read numbers, he doesn't know how to count very well so he can't tell you how many grades there are. All he can do is read the numbers to you. Describe an algorithm that will calculate the correct average under these conditions.

EXERCISE 1.16   Write a *header* for a public applet named `SampleApplet`.

EXERCISE 1.17   Write a *header* for a public method named `getName`.

EXERCISE 1.18   Design a class to represent a geometric square with a given length of side, such that it is capable of calculating the area and the perimeter of the square. Use the design specification we created for the `Rectangle` class as a model.

EXERCISE 1.19   Write a *stub definition* for a public class named `Square`.

EXERCISE 1.20   Complete the definition of the `Square` class using the definition of `Rectangle` (Fig. 1–6) as a model.

EXERCISE 1.21   Modify the `OldMacDonald` class to "sing" either "Mary Had a Little Lamb" or your favorite nursery rhyme.

EXERCISE 1.22   Define a Java class, called `Patterns`, modeled after `OldMacDonald`, that will print the following patterns of asterisks, one after the other heading down the page:

```
*****       *****    *****
 ****       *   *    *  * *
  ***       *   *     *  *
   **       *   *    *  * *
    *       *****    *****
```

EXERCISE 1.23   Write a Java class that prints your initials as block letters, for example,

```
******  *         *
*       *  **      **
*       *  * *    *  *
******  *  *  *    *
**      *   *      *
* *     *   *      *
*  *    *   *      *
*   *   *   *      *
```

EXERCISE 1.24   Challenge: Define a class that represents a `Temperature` object. It should store the current temperature in an instance variable of type `double`, and it should have two `public` methods, `setTemp(double t)`, which assigns `t` to the instance variable, and `getTemp()`, which `returns` the value of the instance variable. Use the `Rectangle` class as a model.

EXERCISE 1.25   Challenge: Define a class named `TaxWhiz` that computes the sales tax for a purchase. It should store the current tax rate as an instance variable. Following the model of the `Rectangle` class, you can initialize the rate using a `TaxWhiz()` method. This class should have one `public` method, `calcTax(double purchase)`, which `returns` a `double`, whose value is purchases times the tax rate. For example, if the tax rate is 4 percent, 0.04, and the purchase is $100, then `calcTax()` should return 4.0.

UML EXERCISES

EXERCISE 1.26   Modify the UML diagram of the `Rectangle` class to contain a method for calculating a rectangle's perimeter. Like the `calculateArea()` method, this method should return a `double`.

EXERCISE 1.27   Draw a UML class diagram representing the following class: The name of the class is `Circle`. It has one attribute, a `radius` that is represented by a `double` value. It has one operation, `calculateArea()`, which returns a `double`. Its attributes should be designated as private and its method as public.

EXERCISE 1.28   Draw a UML diagram of the `FirstApplet` class (Fig. 1–18) showing all of its attributes and operations.

EXERCISE 1.29   To represent a triangle we need attributes for each of its three sides and operations to create a triangle, calculate its area, and calculate its perimeter. Draw a UML diagram to represent this triangle.

EXERCISE 1.30   Try to give the Java class definition for the class described in the UML diagram shown in Figure 1–19.

Person
− name : String   − phone : String
+ printName()   + printPhone()

FIGURE 1–19   The `Person` class.

2

Objects: Defining, Creating, and Using

OBJECTIVES

After studying this chapter, you will

- Be familiar with the relationship between classes and objects in a Java program.
- Be able to understand and write simple programs in Java.
- Understand some of the basic principles of object-oriented programming.

OUTLINE

2.1 Introduction

This chapter introduces some more of the basic principles of object-oriented programming. We begin by doing a detailed walkthrough of the Rectangle class we designed in Chapter 1. We focus on the basic Java language elements involved. By the end of this section, you should know how to identify the key elements that make up a Java program.

We then present a detailed example of the programming development process by designing CyberPet, a Java class that simulates a pet that responds to eat and sleep commands. Finally, the lab project for this chapter involves the design, implementation, and testing of a simple class. By completing the lab project, you will have written a complete Java application program from scratch.

2.2 Class Definition

The class as template

To program in Java the main thing you do is write class definitions for the various objects that will make up the program. A class definition *encapsulates* its objects' data and behavior. Once a class has been defined, it serves as a *template*, or blueprint, for creating individual *objects* or **instances** of the class.

Variables and methods

A class definition contains two types of elements: variables and methods. *Variables* are used to store the object's information. *Methods* are used to process the information. To design an object you need to answer five basic questions:

1. What role will the object perform in the program?
2. What data or information will it need?
3. What actions will it take?
4. What interface will it present to other objects?
5. What information will it hide from other objects?

Rectangle
− length : double
− width : double
+ Rectangle(in l : double, in w : double)
+ calculateArea() : double

FIGURE 2–1   The Rectangle class.

2.2.1 The Rectangle Class

Instance variables

Recall our definition of the Rectangle class from Chapter 1, which is summarized in the UML diagram in Figure 2–1. A Rectangle has two attributes, length and width. Each of these variables stores a certain kind of real number known as a double. The Rectangle class contains two methods. The Rectangle() constructor method assigns initial values (l and w) to its length and width variables. The calculateArea() method calculates a rectangle's area—that is, its length times its width.

The instance variables length and width are designated as private (−), but the Rectangle() and calculateArea() methods are designated as public (+). These designations follow two important object-oriented design conventions:

Private vs. public access

EFFECTIVE DESIGN: Private Variables.   Instance variables are usually declared private. This causes them to be *hidden* from other objects. The private elements of an object cannot be directly accessed by other objects.

```
public class Rectangle
{
    private double length;     // Instance variables
    private double width;

    public Rectangle(double l, double w)  // Constructor method
    {
        length = l;
        width = w;
    } // Rectangle constructor

    public double calculateArea()          // Access method
    {
        return length * width;
    } // calculateArea()

} // Rectangle class
```

FIGURE 2–2 The Rectangle class definition.

EFFECTIVE DESIGN: Public Methods. An object's `public` methods can be used by other objects to interact with the object. They make up the object's **interface**.

The reason for these design conventions will become apparent shortly. Figure 2–2 shows the Java class definition that corresponds to the design given in the UML diagram. It contains two private instance variables, `length` and `width`, both of type `double`. It also contains two `public` methods, `Rectangle()` and `calculateArea()`. Thus, in a Java class definition, access to a class element, such as a variable or a method, is controlled by labeling it with either the `private` or `public` *access modifier*.

Access modifier

Note also that the `Rectangle` class itself is declared `public`. This lets other classes have access to the class and to its public variables and methods. Java provides mechanisms that determine the accessibility of classes and their elements.

JAVA LANGUAGE RULE **Class Access.** A `public` class is accessible to any other class, if its containing package is accessible. Otherwise, a class is accessible only to the other classes in its package. Whether a package is accessible or not is determined by the Java runtime system.

As this rule suggests, Java classes are organized into *packages*. When you define a class, you can declare what package it belongs to using the statement

```
package MyPackage;
```

The package declaration is optional, and if it is omitted, Java will place the class in a default, unnamed package. The class definitions in this book will usually omit the package declaration, which is the usual convention when developing small programs. Java runtime systems are required to have at least one unnamed package that is accessible.

As Figures 2–1 and 2–2 illustrate, a class is like a blueprint. It has form but no content. Thus, a `Rectangle` has private elements (−) and public elements (+). The class definition specifies the type of information (attributes) that each individual `Rectangle` contains, but it doesn't contain any actual values. It defines the methods (operations) that each `Rectangle` can perform, but it doesn't actually use the methods. In short, a class serves as a template, providing a detailed blueprint of the objects (or instances) of that class.

Class as blueprint

2.2.2   The `RectangleUser` Class

Although it is a good representation of a rectangle, the `Rectangle` class is not a complete Java application program, because it does not have a `main()` method. Let's define a second class to serve as a *user interface*. This second class, call it `RectangleUser`, will create and use one or more `Rectangles`. Thus, this particular Java program will involve interaction between two classes of objects: a `RectangleUser` and one or more `Rectangles` (Fig. 2–3). Note how our design for this program employs the divide-and-conquer principle. One type of object, `Rectangle`, represents a geometric rectangle and the other, `RectangleUser`, serves as a user of rectangles.

The `RectangleUser` class will contain a `main()` method, in which we will create and interact with some `Rectangle` objects. Its outline takes the following form:

```
public class RectangleUser
{
    public static void main(String argv[])
    {
    }
}
```

By convention, the header of the `main()` method must be specified exactly as shown here. In the next section, we will describe the Java statements that go into the `main()` method.

2.2.3   Object Instantiation: Creating `Rectangle` Instances

Figure 2–4 shows the complete definition of the `RectangleUser` class, which serves as a very simple user interface. It creates two `Rectangle` objects, named `rectangle1` and `rectangle2`. It then asks each object to cal-

FIGURE 2–3   This UML class diagram represents an *association* between the `RectangleUser` and `Rectangle` classes. An object of the `RectangleUser` class will *use* one or more objects of the `Rectangle` class.

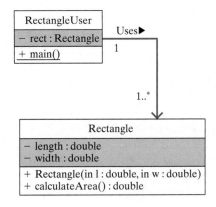

```
public class RectangleUser
{
    public static void main(String argv[])
    {
        Rectangle rectangle1 = new Rectangle(30,10);
        Rectangle rectangle2 = new Rectangle(25,20);
        System.out.println("rectangle1 area" +
                             rectangle1.calculateArea());
        System.out.println("rectangle2 area" +
                             rectangle2.calculateArea());
    } // main()
} // RectangleUser
```

FIGURE 2–4 The RectangleUser class.

culate its area, and it displays the areas on the console. We can run the RectangleUser class to create and use Rectangles.

Let's now discuss the statements that make up RectangleUser's main() method. The following statements use the Rectangle() constructor method to create, or *instantiate*, two *instances* of the Rectangle class:

An object is an instance of a class

```
Rectangle rectangle1 = new Rectangle(30,10);
Rectangle rectangle2 = new Rectangle(25,20);
```

The rectangle1 object is an *instance* of the Rectangle class. In this statement it is given 30 and 10 as the initial values of its length and width, respectively. In the same way, when rectangle2 is created, it is passed 25 and 20 as its length and width. Figure 2–5 gives a conceptual view of these two objects. Each object has its own private instance variables, which hold its essential data, and its own copies of the methods (not shown here) that were defined in the class definition. Each object can be referred to by a unique name (rectangle1 and rectangle2).

rectangle1 : Rectangle
length : double = 30.0
width : double = 10.0

rectangle2 : Rectangle
length : double = 25.0
width : double = 20.0

2.2.4 Interacting with Rectangles

Once we have created Rectangle instances and given them their initial length and width, we can ask each rectangle to calculate and tell us its area:

FIGURE 2–5 Two rectangles. Notice that their instance variables have different values.

```
rectangle1.calculateArea()
rectangle2.calculateArea()
```

These two expressions are examples of *method calls*. A *method* is a named chunk of code, and calling a method is a means of executing its code. The first method call gets the area of rectangle1, and the second gets the area of rectangle2. Recall that as we defined the calculateArea() method in the Rectangle class, it returns a rectangle's length times its width. So the first of these statements will return 300 (30 * 10). The second statement will return 500 (25 * 20).

Method call

DEBUGGING TIP: Method Call versus Method Definition. Don't confuse method calls with method definitions. The definition specifies the method's actions. The method call takes those actions.

If we want to display a rectangle's area, we can embed these method calls within a println() statement

```
System.out.println("rectangle1 area" + rectangle1.calculateArea());
System.out.println("rectangle2 area" + rectangle2.calculateArea());
```

The expression within the parentheses of the println() method concatenates, or joins together, the string rectangle1 area and the value 300 into a single string, which is displayed on the screen. Thus, the output produced by these two statements will be

```
rectangle1 area 300
rectangle2 area 500
```

2.2.5 Define, Create, Use

As our rectangle example illustrates, once a program's classes have been designed, writing a Java program is a matter of three basic steps:

- Define one or more classes (class definition).
- Create objects as instances of the classes (object instantiation).
- Use the objects to do tasks (object use).

The Java class definition determines what information will be stored in each object and what methods each object will perform. Instantiation creates an instance and associates a name with it in the program. The object's methods can then be called as a way of getting the object to perform certain tasks.

SELF-STUDY EXERCISES

EXERCISE 2.1   Identify the following elements in the Rectangle class (Fig. 2–2):
- The name of the class.
- The names of two instance variables.
- The names of two methods.

EXERCISE 2.2   Identify the following elements in the RectangleUser class (Fig. 2–4):
- The names of two Rectangle instances.
- All six method calls in the program.
- Two examples of qualified names.

2.3   CASE STUDY: Simulating a CyberPet

In this section, we will design and write a complete Java application. The program will simulate a CyberPet that responds to simple commands. The program will introduce Java programming fundamentals and object-oriented program design. We will focus on some details of the Java language, with the objective being to understand what the program is doing and how it works without necessarily understanding why it works the way it does. We will get to "why" later in the book.

2.3.1 Designing the CyberPet Class

Problem Specification

Let's design and write a program that simulates a CyberPet. This pet will do two things, eat and sleep, when we tell it to. When we tell it to eat (or sleep), it should simply report that it is eating (or sleeping) by printing a message.

Problem Decomposition

Following the design we used in the Rectangle example, we need two types of objects: one to represent the CyberPet and one to serve as a user interface (Fig. 2–6). The first type of object will be analogous to the Rectangle class—its role will be to represent something—while the second will be analogous to the RectangleUser class—its role will be to provide a user interface. The CyberPet class will represent whether an individual pet is eating or sleeping and will implement methods to define the eat and sleep commands. The TestCyberPet class will create a couple of CyberPet instances and get them to eat and sleep on command.

What objects do we need?

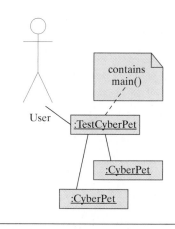

FIGURE 2–6 A TestCyberPet object serves as a *user interface* by mediating the interaction between the user and one or more CyberPet objects.

Class Design: CyberPet

As we saw in the Rectangle example, class definitions can usually be broken down into two parts: (1) the information or attributes that the object needs, and (2) the behavior or actions the object can take. For some types of objects, the information stored in an object's instance variables is sometimes referred to as the object's *state*. For example, a Rectangle's state would be its length and width. Taken together, an object's state and its behavior form a *representation*, or a *model*, of the object.

A consistent model of a pet's state will ensure that a pet is either sleeping or eating, but it cannot be doing both at the same time. One way to model these two mutually exclusive states is to treat them like light switches that can be either on or off. When the eating light is on, the sleeping light must be off, and vice versa.

The Java boolean data type provides a close approximation of a light switch. Each boolean variable can have one of two values, true or false, which are good analogues for a switch's on and off state. Suppose that we represent our pet's state using two boolean variables named isEating and isSleeping. Table 2.1 relates the values of these two instance variables to the pet's overall state. A CyberPet is eating when its isEating variable is true and its isSleeping variable is false. Conversely, a CyberPet is sleeping when its isEating variable is false and its isSleeping variable is true.

What data do we need?

TABLE 2.1 Definition of a pet's state.

State	isEating	isSleeping
eating	true	false
sleeping	false	true

Method Decomposition

What operations will a CyberPet perform? Clearly, we need eat() and sleep() methods, which will be used to represent the CyberPet's basic actions: eating and sleeping. Thus, the eat() method will simply put the pet in the eating state, and the sleep() method will put the pet in the sleeping state. Figure 2–7 summarizes the design of the CyberPet class.

Note that the eat() and sleep() methods are declared public and will thereby form the pet's interface. These will be the methods that other

What methods do we need?

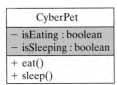

CyberPet
− isEating : boolean
− isSleeping : boolean
+ eat()
+ sleep()

FIGURE 2–7   This UML class diagram summarizes the design of the CyberPet class.

FIGURE 2–8   Definition of the CyberPet class.

objects will use to interact with a CyberPet. Similarly, we have followed the convention of designating that an object's instance variables—the CyberPet's state—be kept hidden from other objects, and so we have designated them as private (−).

2.3.2   Defining the CyberPet Class

Given our design of the CyberPet class, the next step in building our CyberPet simulation is to write the class definition in Java, so this section will focus on details of the Java language. The definition of the CyberPet class is given in Figure 2–8.

```java
public class CyberPet
{ // Data
    private boolean isEating = true;      // CyberPet's state
    private boolean isSleeping = false;

  // Methods
    public void eat()                     // Start eating
    {
        isEating = true;                  // Change the state
        isSleeping = false;
        System.out.println("Pet is eating");
        return;
    } // eat()

    public void sleep()                   // Start sleeping
    {
        isSleeping = true;                // Change the state
        isEating = false;
        System.out.println("Pet is sleeping");
        return;
    } // sleep()
} // CyberPet class
```

The Class Header

A class definition in Java consists of a class header and a class body. A *class header* gives the class a name and specifies how the class can be used. A *class body* contains all the variables and methods that make up the class:

```java
public class CyberPet      // Class header
{                          // Beginning of class body
}                          // End of class body
```

In general, a class header takes the following form:

$$ClassModifiers_{opt} \quad \texttt{class} \quad ClassName \quad Pedigree_{opt}$$

A class header consists of an optional list of *ClassModifiers*, followed by the word class, followed by the name that you want to give your class, followed, optionally, by the class's *Pedigree*. As the *opt* subscript indicates, some of these elements, such as the *ClassModifiers* and the *Pedigree*, are optional. If they are omitted the Java compiler will supply *default* values, but for now we won't worry about this complication.

Our definition of CyberPet uses the access modifier public. An *access modifier* determines whether other objects can have access to the class. By designating CyberPet as public, we allow it to be accessed by any other object. If this modifier were omitted, Java would restrict access to CyberPet to just those classes, if any, defined in the same package. For the most part the classes we define will have public access.

Public access

The word class is a Java **keyword**, which is a term that has special meaning within Java programs. Java has 47 such keywords (see the Java Language Summary from Chapter 1). The name given to our class, Cyber-Pet, is an *identifier*.

> **JAVA LANGUAGE RULE** Identifiers. An **identifier** is a name for a variable, method, or class. It must begin with a letter of the alphabet and may consist of any number of letters, digits, and the special underscore character (_). An identifier cannot be identical to a Java keyword.

Note that CyberPet's header omits *Pedigree*. A class's *pedigree* describes where it fits in the Java class hierarchy. By default, if the pedigree is not specified, Java considers the class a direct subclass of the Object class, as shown in Figure 2–9. (Remember, as a subclass of Object, CyberPet *inherits* certain methods and variables from Object.) Instead of relying on Java's default interpretation, we can make CyberPet's pedigree explicit by changing its header declaration to

```
public class CyberPet extends Object
```

The extends keyword merely specifies that CyberPet is a direct subclass of Object.

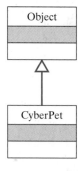

FIGURE 2–9 By default, CyberPet is a subclass of Object.

The Class's Instance Variables

The body of a class follows the header and is contained within curly brackets, {}. As we see both here and in the case of the Rectangle class, the body of a class definition generally consists of two parts: the class's instance variables and the class's methods. In general, a class definition will take the form shown in Figure 2–10.

Variables and methods

```
public class ClassName
{
    // Instance variables that make up the object's state
    VariableDeclaration1
    VariableDeclaration2

    ...

    // Methods that make up the object's behavior
    MethodDefinition1
    MethodDefinition2

    ...
} // End of class
```

FIGURE 2–10 A template for constructing a Java class definition.

Although Java does not impose any particular order on variable and method declarations, in this book we'll define classes using the style shown in Figure 2–10. The class's instance variables go at the beginning of the class definition, followed by method declarations. In Java, instance variables are known technically as *fields*, and their declarations are called **field declarations**. They should be distinguished from other kinds of variables that may be declared within a class—for example, from *local variables* that are declared within methods.

Fields vs. local variables

A declaration for an instance variable, or a *field declaration*, takes the following form:

$$FieldModifiers_{opt} \quad TypeId \quad VariableId \quad Initializer_{opt}$$

Here are some examples of valid field declarations that we have encountered earlier:

```
private double length;
private double width;
private Button clickMe;
```

Each of these declarations contains a *FieldModifier* (`private`), a *TypeId* (`double`, `Button`), and a *VariableId* (`length`, `width`, and so on). None of these declarations has the optional *Initializer*.

Field declaration

A field declaration is a variable declaration that occurs at the class level. It specifies that a certain memory location within the class's objects will store data of type *TypeId* and will be named or referred to as *VariableId*. The *TypeId* must either be one of Java's primitive types, such as `double`, or must be the name of one of the classes in the Java class hierarchy, including those classes which may be defined by your program. The *VariableId* must be a valid Java identifier.

Public/Private Access

A field declaration can have an optional list of *FieldModifiers*, including **access modifiers**, which determine how the field can be accessed. Access to a field can be `public`, `private`, or `protected`. To determine whether a field is accessible, you must first determine whether its containing class is accessible. If the containing class is accessible, then a field that is declared `private` cannot be accessed outside the class in which it is declared. A field that is declared `protected` can only be accessed by subclasses of the class in which it is declared or by other classes that belong to the same package. A field that is declared `public` can be referenced and, hence, modified by any other class. An object's instance variables should almost never be declared `public`.

Private access

> **EFFECTIVE DESIGN: Private Instance Variables.** As a rule, it is good design to declare instance variables `private`, making them hidden from other objects. This will prevent other objects from being able to directly modify the object's state.

Information hiding

If another object had access to an object's instance variables, it could change the object's state, thereby possibly introducing errors. For example, suppose we declared CyberPet's `isEating` and `isSleeping` as `public` and suppose we have a CyberPet named george. In that case, some other object would be able to execute the following statements:

```
george.isEating = true;   // Access OK if isEating is public
george.isSleeping = true; // Access OK if isSleeping is public
```

In this case, both isEating and isSleeping have been set to true, which results in george having an inconsistent state, since a pet cannot be both eating and sleeping at the same time. By restricting access to its instance variables, a CyberPet can guarantee that its state will always be consistent. It does this by requiring other objects to use the eat() and sleep() methods to change a CyberPet's state. So the proper way of getting george to change his state is to use his public methods:

```
george.eat();          // Access OK because eat() is public
```

As long as the eat() and sleep() methods are designed correctly to preserve the consistency of its state, there is no chance that george will end up in an inconsistent state. Thus, by controlling which methods are public and, hence, accessible outside the class, the class definition defines an *interface* that other objects must use to interact with it.

Defining an object's interface

> EFFECTIVE DESIGN: An Object's Interface. An object's interface is defined by designating some elements of an object private and other elements public. This allows carefully controlled access to the object.

Identifier Scope

An identifier's *scope* is simply that portion of the class where it may be used. Fields or instance variables in Java have a scope that extends throughout the entire body of the class definition in which they are declared.

> JAVA LANGUAGE RULE | Class Scope. Fields or instance variables have **class scope**, which means their names can be used anywhere within the class in which they are declared.

Initializer Expressions

Let's now consider the details involved in the field declarations given in the CyberPet class:

```
public class CyberPet
{
    private boolean isEating = true;     // CyberPet's state
    private boolean isSleeping = false;

} // CyberPet
```

Note that both declarations include *Initializer* expressions. Whenever a field is declared, the location assigned to that field is given an initial value. If an *Initializer* is omitted from the declaration, the Java compiler supplies a default value. In the case of boolean variables, the initial value would be false. An *Initializer* can be used to override the default.

Default initialization

JAVA LANGUAGE RULE   Initializer Expression. An **initializer expression** always takes the form

Variable = expression.

The expression on the right of the assignment operator (=) is evaluated and its value is assigned to the variable on the left.

Assignment puts a value into a memory location

The assignment operator (=) means "assign the following value to this location" or "put the following value in this location." It literally takes the value that follows the operator and stores it in that variable's memory location. The value being assigned must have the same type as the variable. It would be a syntax error in Java if we tried to initialize isEating to 0, because isEating is a boolean variable and 0 is an integer value of type int. An int value just won't fit into a boolean memory location; it's too big.

DEBUGGING TIP: Type Error. Assigning a value of one type to a variable of another type will generate a syntax error.

Initializing an object's state

In the CyberPet class, isEating is given an initial value of true, and isSleeping is given an initial value of false. This means that any CyberPet created from this class definition will initially be eating. Assigning initial values to a class's instance variables is one conventional way of setting the initial state of the class's instances.

Figure 2–11 shows the CyberPet class. Recall that a class serves as a template used to define instances of the class. CyberPet contains two fields, isEating and isSleeping, which have been given the initial values specified in the class definition.

To summarize, despite its apparent simplicity, a field declaration actually accomplishes five tasks:

CyberPet
− isEating : boolean = true
− isSleeping : boolean = false
+ eat()
+ sleep()

FIGURE 2–11   Note that in this UML class diagram we have given the instance variables the initial values defined in the class definition.

1. Sets aside a portion of the object's memory that can be used to store a certain type of data.
2. Specifies the type of data that can be stored in that location.
3. Associates a name or *variable identifier* with that location.
4. Determines which objects have access to the variable's name.
5. Assigns an initial value to the location.

The Class's Methods

Method definitions are those parts of classes that contain executable statements—that is, statements that perform some kind of action when the method is invoked. A *method* is a named section of code designed to perform a particular task. By associating a name with the code segment, the program can *call* or *invoke* the method, thereby executing its statements.

Procedural abstraction

Designing and defining methods is a form of abstraction that is sometimes called *procedural abstraction*. By defining a certain sequence of actions (a procedure) as a method, you encapsulate those actions under a single name that can be invoked whenever needed. Instead of having to list the entire sequence again each time you want it performed, you simply call it by name.

A method definition consists of two parts, the method header and the method body. The *method header* declares the name of the method and other general information about the method. The *method body* contains the executable statements that the method performs:

```
public void methodName()    // Method header
{                           // Beginning of method body
}                           // End of method body
```

The Method Header

A method header has the general form shown in the next table. The table also contains several examples of method headers that we have encountered earlier.

MethodModifiers$_{opt}$	ResultType	MethodName	(FormalParameterList)
public static	void	main	(String argv[])
public	void	paint	(Graphics g)
public	void	init	()
		Rectangle	(double l, double w)
public	double	calculateArea	()
public	void	eat	()
public	void	sleep	()

Thus, a method header consists of an optional list of *MethodModifiers*, followed by the method's *ResultType*, followed by the *MethodName*, followed by the method's *FormalParameterList* (which is enclosed in parentheses). The method body follows the method header.

Let's compare the preceding template with the method header used in the definition of the eat() method in the CyberPet class:

```
public void eat()
```

Our definition of the eat() method contains the access modifier public. The rules on scope and method access are the same as the rules on field access: private methods are accessible only within the class itself, protected methods are accessible only to subclasses of the class in which the method is defined and to other classes in the same package, and public methods are accessible to all other classes. A class's public methods make up its *interface*.

EFFECTIVE DESIGN: Object Interface. A class's public methods serve as its interface. Choosing and designing appropriate methods to serve as the interface is an important design consideration.

By controlling which methods are made public, a class definition can control information flow to and from its objects. Generally an object's public methods are those used by other objects to communicate with it. At the

Interface methods vs. helper methods

same time, methods used only to perform internal operations should be hidden by being declared `private`. These methods are sometimes called *utility methods* or *helper methods*.

EFFECTIVE DESIGN: Public versus Private Methods. If a method is intended to be used to communicate with an object, or if it passes information to or from an object, it should be declared `public`. If a method is intended to be used solely for internal operations within the object, it should be declared `private`.

The `eat()` and `sleep()` methods should clearly be declared `public`, because they are used to tell a `CyberPet` when to eat or sleep. Similarly, for the `Rectangle` class, the `calculateArea()` method should be `public` because it retrieves a `Rectangle`'s area.

As in the case of a class's fields, the scope of a method's name extends throughout the class in which the method is defined.

JAVA LANGUAGE RULE   Class Scope. A method has *class scope*, which means it can be called from anywhere within the class in which it is defined.

Methods have a result type

A method's *ResultType* specifies the type of value (`boolean`, `double`, `Object`) that the method returns. Returning a value is the way that a method and, hence, the object to which it belongs can pass information back to the object that called the method. However, some methods, such as our `eat()` and `sleep()` methods, do not return a value. In this case, their *ResultType* is specified as `void`. In this chapter, we will only use methods that do not return values.

JAVA LANGUAGE RULE   Void Methods. Methods that do not return a value should be declared `void`. A `return` statement is optional for **void methods**.

Parameters

The *MethodName* can be any valid Java identifier. The method's name is followed by a *FormalParameterList* enclosed in parentheses. Formal parameters are special variables used to pass information into and out of the method. If no parameters are needed in a particular method, the method's name is just followed by empty parentheses. Because ordering a pet to eat or sleep does not require passing the pet any additional information, `CyberPet`'s `eat()` and `sleep()` methods have an empty parameter list.

SELF-STUDY EXERCISES

EXERCISE 2.3   Add a new declaration to `CyberPet` for a `private boolean` variable named `isDreaming`. Assign the variable an initial value of `false`.

EXERCISE 2.4   Add a new definition to `CyberPet` for a `public` method named `dream`. Assume that this is a `void` method that requires no parameters and that it simply puts the `CyberPet` into the dreaming state.

EXERCISE 2.5 Suppose the CyberPet class had a String instance variable named food and a method named pickFood(), which sets the value of food to either "meat" or "potato." Should this method be declared public or private?

EXERCISE 2.6 Create a (partial) definition of a Square class. Declare appropriate instance variables. Declare stub methods for calculating perimeter and area, and for its constructor. A stub method is a method that has a correctly defined header but an empty body.

The Method Body

The body of a method definition is a block of Java statements enclosed in braces, {}, which will be executed in sequence when the method is called. This method body is taken from the eat() method:

Designing a method is an application of the encapsulation principle.

```
{
    isEating = true;        // Change the state
    isSleeping = false;
    System.out.println("Pet is eating");
    return;
} // eat()
```

The return statement indicates that the method's execution is complete. It causes Java to return control to the object that called the method. When a method does not return any particular result, the return statement may be omitted. If a void method does not contain a return, control will automatically return to the calling object after the last statement of the method has been executed. We'll discuss how method invocation works later in this section.

void methods

The eat() and sleep() methods can be used to command a CyberPet to eat and sleep. Recall that according to our design, a CyberPet is eating when its isSleeping field is false and its isEating field is true. The eat() method effects this change in state by executing the following two **assignment statements**:

```
isEating = true;        // Change the state
isSleeping = false;
```

> **JAVA LANGUAGE RULE** Assignment Statement. A (simple) **assignment statement**, which takes the form
>
> $$VariableName = Expression$$
>
> evaluates the *Expression* on the right of the assignment operator (=) and stores its value in the variable named on the left.

VariableName must be the name of a declared variable. Thus, the first of the preceding statements stores the value true in the isEating variable, and the second statement stores the value false in the isSleeping variable. This puts CyberPet in the eating state. Similarly, the first two statements in the sleep() method (Fig. 2–8) put a CyberPet in the sleeping state by setting isSleeping to true and isEating to false.

The next statement in the eat() method,

```
System.out.println("Pet is eating");
```

displays the message "Pet is eating" on the screen. The purpose of this statement is to give some indication of CyberPet's current state. There are lots of other ways this could be done, including ways that make use of Java's extensive graphics library. However, for now let's keep things simple.

Note the use of the dot (.) notation here. As we saw in Chapter 1, the expression System.out.println() invokes the println() method that belongs to the out object, which is defined in the System class.

> **JAVA LANGUAGE RULE** Qualified Name. A **qualified name** takes the form *reference.elementName*, where *reference* is a reference to some object, and *elementName* is the name of one of the object's variables or methods. The expression is used to refer to the *elementName* contained in *reference*.

Qualified name

Qualified names are context dependent. In some contexts the *reference* can be a simple reference to an object, such as in rectangle1.calculateArea(). In other contexts the reference may refer to a hierarchy of objects, classes, and other entities, such as in System.out.println() or java.awt.Color.red.

Our CyberPet class is finished for now. To summarize, as presently defined, a CyberPet can be in one of two states, eating or sleeping. Its state is modeled by two private instance variables, isEating and isSleeping. These are boolean variables whose values can be either true or false. The CyberPet's interface consists of two methods, eat() and sleep(), which have the effect of changing the pet's state from sleeping to eating or from eating to sleeping. Whenever a pet's state changes, it will output a message on the screen indicating its present state.

SELF-STUDY EXERCISES

EXERCISE 2.7   Complete the definition of the Square class, which you began in the previous exercise, by filling in the bodies of its methods. Model your solution on the Rectangle class.

EXERCISE 2.8   Write a main() method for the Square class, which creates two Square instances, setting their sides to 25 and 15, respectively, and then prints their respective perimeters and areas.

2.3.3   **Creating** CyberPet **Instances**

A class definition is an abstract entity. We now want to use it to create some CyberPet objects or instances. Creating an object consists of two steps:

1. Declaring a *reference variable* or a name for the object.
2. Creating an instance of the object.

Declaring a Reference Variable

A reference variable is associated with an object and can be used to refer to the object. We declare a reference variable the same way we declare any other kind of variable. The reference variable's type is the name of the class whose objects it can refer to. Thus, declaring a reference to an object takes the following form:

> *ClassName VariableName* ;

In other words, to declare a reference to an object, we give the name of the class to which the object belongs, followed by the name of the reference itself, followed by a semicolon. The *ClassName* must be the name of a validly defined class, either a class that is included in Java's class library or one that has been defined by the programmer. The *VariableName* must be a valid Java identifier.

For example, to declare references to CyberPets, we can use the following declarations:

```
CyberPet pet1;
CyberPet pet2;
```

Here both pet1 and pet2 are names or references that can be used to refer to CyberPets. At this point they don't refer to anything, since we haven't yet created any objects for them to name. That will happen during the second part of object creation when we create instances of the CyberPet class.

Declaring vs. creating

DEBUGGING TIP: Declaring a Reference Variable. Don't confuse declaring a reference variable with creating an object.

Object Instantiation: Creating a CyberPet *Instance*

Declaring a reference variable does not by itself create an instance of an object. To *instantiate* a reference variable—that is, to create an object that the variable will refer to—we use the operator, new, in conjunction with a *constructor* method for that object. We saw an example of this when we discussed the Rectangle class. In the case of our CyberPet class, we can use these statements to instantiate pet1 and pet2:

```
pet1 = new CyberPet();
pet2 = new CyberPet();
```

These are assignment statements and work the same way as any other assignment statement. The expression on the right of the assignment operator is evaluated, and its value is assigned to the variable on the left of the operator. However, in this case the term on the right-hand side, CyberPet(), is an invocation of CyberPet's default *constructor* method. Constructor methods (which are covered in Chapter 3) are special methods that are used during object instantiation. If a class does not define a constructor, Java will supply a default, which consists of some very generic code that merely creates an instance of that class. The expression CyberPet() creates an instance of the CyberPet class—an object that has all of the basic features, including the initial state, of a CyberPet.

Constructing a new object

Allocating memory

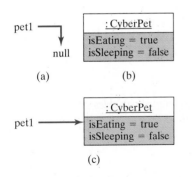

(a)   (b)

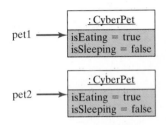

(c)

FIGURE 2–12 Declaring and instantiating a reference variable (pet1) to a CyberPet.

FIGURE 2–13 A conceptual depiction of two CyberPet objects. The references, pet1 and pet2, are variables that point to the objects.

Java data types

The operator, new, allocates a portion of memory for the new object and stores the new object there. It then returns the object's address, so the value of the expression on the right of the assignment operator in the preceding statements is the *address* of the object that was created. This address is stored in the reference variable on the left of the assignment operator.

Consider again the statements

```
CyberPet pet1;
pet1 = new CyberPet();
```

To visualize what happens when an object is created, let's trace through the actions of these statements. The first statement creates a reference variable named pet1 of type CyberPet (Fig. 2–12a). Because pet1 does not yet refer to any object, Java assigns it the initial value null, which is shown in the figure as a grounded arrow.

Next, consider the second statement. This assignment statement will evaluate new CyberPet(), the expression on the right of the "=," and will then assign the result to pet1. First, space is allocated for the new class instance. Then a default constructor is called to create a new CyberPet object. In so doing, the declarations of the CyberPet class are executed, setting aside space for the instance variables isEating and isSleeping and assigning initial values to them. The result is the creation of a CyberPet object (Fig. 2–12b).

Finally, the address where the new object is stored is assigned to pet1 (Fig. 2–12c). Because the value returned is an address, we show it as an arrow in the figure. A reference variable *points to* its object.

When a second CyberPet object is created, the process is just the same, except that the second instance will be stored at a different memory location. Thus, the result of executing the following statements,

```
CyberPet pet1;
CyberPet pet2;
pet1 = new CyberPet();
pet2 = new CyberPet();
```

is shown in Figure 2–13.

JLR

JAVA LANGUAGE RULE *Variable versus Object.* Like the relationship between your name and you, a reference variable refers to an object. They are two different things in the program.

2.3.4 Primitive Types and Reference Types

In Java there are two categories of types, *primitive types* and *reference types*. So far we have encountered two examples of primitive types: boolean, which was used in the CyberPet class, and double, which was used in the Rectangle class. A variable of a primitive type always stores a value of that type and, as we noted, it is an error to try to store some other type of value in that variable. For example, the `isEating` variable can only store the values `true` or `false`.

Reference variables, such as `pet1` and `pet2`, are examples of variables that have reference types. Their types are the classes of the objects to which they can refer. Both `pet1` and `pet2` are of type `CyberPet` because they can refer to instances of the `CyberPet` class.

Rather than storing the object to which it refers, a reference variable actually stores the *address* of the object. Thus, unlike variables of primitive type, which store values of that type, reference variables are said to *refer to* or *point to* their values. If you could open the computer's cabinet and look at what was stored in a primitive variable of type `boolean`, you would see either `true` or `false`. If you opened up the cabinet and looked at the contents of a reference variable, you would find an address of some other location in the computer's memory. If you went to that location, you would then find the object that the variable refers to. Because Java takes care of finding the object for you, whenever you want to refer to an object, you can just use its name, just as you would when referring to an object by name in the natural world.

To summarize, in Figure 2–12c, `pet1` is a reference variable. It stores a reference to a `CyberPet` instance, which is symbolized by the arrow. By contrast, `isEating` and `isSleeping` are primitive variables (within the `CyberPet` object). They simply store their respective values (`true` and `false`).

2.3.5 Using `CyberPets`

Now that we have seen how to create instances of the `CyberPet` class, let's use their reference variables to "order" them to eat and sleep. Our objects, you will recall, are named `pet1` and `pet2`. In other words, we can use the terms `pet1` and `pet2` to refer to these objects, just as you would use the term *Mary* to refer to a person named Mary. In UML, we would represent the two objects as shown in Figure 2–14.

To get `pet1` to eat, we want to call its `eat()` method. This is easily done using Java's dot operator:

```
pet1.eat();
```

In order to call an object's method in this way, the method must be *accessible*. In this case, the `eat()` method is accessible because it was declared `public`. The `eat()` and `sleep()` methods are examples of *mutator methods*—that is, methods that are used to *change* an object's state.

The dot operator can also be used to refer to an object's instance variables, provided they are accessible. For example, we can refer to `isEating` using the dot operator as follows:

```
pet1.isEating = true;    // Access error
```

Although `pet1.isEating` is a valid reference, our use of it here would cause an access error because we declared `isEating` to be `private`. Even though this is a valid reference, the field referenced is inaccessible.

> **DEBUGGING TIP: Access Error.** An attempt to refer to one of an object's private variables or methods will cause a syntax error.

Reference variables point to their objects

pet1 : CyberPet
isEating = true
isSleeping = false

pet2 : CyberPet
isEating = true
isSleeping = false

FIGURE 2–14 Two `CyberPet` objects. In UML, an object's name or reference (`pet1`) is combined with its class name (`CyberPet`) to designate the object (`pet1:CyberPet`).

Mutator method

Access error

2.3.6   Class Design: The TestCyberPet Application

Now that we know how to create and refer to instances of the CyberPet class, let's test that it works properly. In other words, we need to build a user interface for this program. There are a number of ways to design the user interface class. We could design and implement an application program or applet to use CyberPet. Or we could incorporate a main() method right into the definition of CyberPet, thereby turning it into a Java application. Let's explore each of these options.

As we described in Figure 2–6, the TestCyberPet object will serve as an interface between the user and the CyberPet. As a Java application, the TestCyberPet class must contain a main() method (Fig. 2–15). Within main() we will want to create two instances of CyberPet. That way we can test that the class definition serves as a template from which we can create as many instance objects as we wish. Once we have created the instances, we can then write several statements to "command" them to eat and sleep. This will test whether we can successfully use the object's names to refer to their public methods.

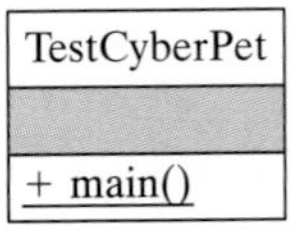

The following pseudocode (pseudocode was discussed briefly in Chapter 1) provides an outline for an appropriate main() method:

1. Declare reference variables pet1 and pet2.
2. Instantiate pet1 and pet2 by creating two *new* objects of type CyberPet.
3. Command pet1 to sleep.
4. Command pet1 to eat.
5. Command pet2 to sleep.

We have already discussed how to do each of these steps, so coding them into Java should be easy. This leads to defining TestCyberPet as shown in Figure 2–16. The header for main() is the same as it was in the RectangleUser program earlier in this chapter. Note that we have inserted two println() statements, one at the beginning of main() and one at the end. These will help visualize what's happening when we run the pro-

```
TestCyberPet
```
```
+ main()
```

FIGURE 2–15   The TestCyberPet class serves as a user interface. CyberPets will be created in its main() method.

FIGURE 2–16   The TestCyberPet class.

```
public class TestCyberPet
{
    public static void main (String argv[])
    {
                                // Execution starts here
        System.out.println("main() is starting");
        CyberPet pet1;              // Declare two references
        CyberPet pet2;
        pet1 = new CyberPet();      // Instantiate the references
        pet2 = new CyberPet();      //   by creating new objects
        pet1.sleep();              // Tell pet1 to sleep.
        pet1.eat();                // Tell pet1 to eat.
        pet2.sleep();              // Tell pet2 to sleep.
        System.out.println("main() is finished");
        return;                    // Return to the system
    } // main()
} // TestCyberPet
```

gram. Recall that the purpose of having a `main()` method in an application is to provide a fixed starting point for the program's execution. Execution of an application begins with the first statement in `main()`'s body. Note also the use of comments to explain what each line of the program is doing. When we become more conversant with Java, these comments will seem trivial and will no longer be needed, but at this stage they still help to clarify the code and make it more readable.

Execution starts in `main()`

When it is run, the `TestCyberPet` application will produce the following output:

```
main() is starting
Pet is sleeping
Pet is eating
Pet is sleeping
main() is finished
```

Unfortunately, the output doesn't distinguish between `pet1` and `pet2`. That's because the `eat()` and `sleep()` methods (Fig. 2–8) just refer to "Pet" and have no way of knowing the pet's name. This is obviously a shortcoming in our design, which we'll have to fix in subsequent versions of `CyberPet`.

2.3.7 Flow of Control: Method Call and Return

A program's **flow of control** is the order in which its statements are executed. In an object-oriented program control passes from one object to another during the program's execution. It's important to have a clear understanding of this process.

In order to understand a Java program, it is necessary to understand the **method call and return** mechanism. We will encounter it repeatedly. A method call causes a program to transfer control to a statement located in another method. Figure 2–17 shows the method call and return structure.

In this example, we have two methods. We make no assumptions about where these methods are in relation to each other. They could be defined in the same class or in different classes. The `method1()` method executes sequentially until it calls `method2()`. This transfers control to the first statement in `method2()`. Execution continues sequentially through the statements in `method2()` until the `return` statement is executed.

> **JAVA LANGUAGE RULE** Return Statement. The `return` statement causes a method to return control to the *calling statement*—that is, to the statement that called the method in the first place.

Recall that if a `void` method does not contain a `return` statement, then control will automatically return to the calling statement after the invoked method executes its last statement.

Default returns

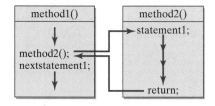

FIGURE 2–17 The method call and return control structure. It's important to realize that `method1()` and `method2()` may be contained in different classes.

2.3.8   Tracing the TestCyberPet Program

In order to help us understand the flow of control in TestCyberPet, we will perform a trace of its execution. In order to simplify our trace, Figure 2–18 shows all of the Java code involved in the program. In addition, it adds line numbers to the program to show the order in which its statements are executed. Keep in mind that there are two source code files involved in this application, TestCyberPet.java and CyberPet.java. The representation in Figure 2–18, which might make it appear as if all of the code is contained in one file, is for illustrative purposes.

Execution of the TestCyberPet program begins with the println() statement on line 1. This has the effect of displaying the message "main() is starting" on the screen. The next two statements, 2 and 3, will create

FIGURE 2–18   A trace showing the order of execution of the TestCyberPet program.

```
     public static void main (String argv[])
     {
                                    // Execution starts here
1        System.out.println("main() is starting");
2        CyberPet pet1;             // Declare two references
3        CyberPet pet2;
4        pet1 = new CyberPet();     // Instantiate the references
7        pet2 = new CyberPet();     //   by creating new objects
10       pet1.sleep();              // Tell pet1 to sleep.
15       pet1.eat();                // Tell pet1 to eat.
20       pet2.sleep();              // Tell pet2 to sleep.
25       System.out.println("main() is finished");
26       return;                    // Return to the system
     } // main()


     public class CyberPet
     {
        // Data
5,8     private boolean isEating = true;   // CyberPet's state
6,9     private boolean isSleeping = false;


        // Methods
        public void eat()          // Start eating
        {
16         isEating = true;        // Change the state
17         isSleeping = false;
18         System.out.println("Pet is eating");
19         return;
        } // eat()


        public void sleep()        // Start sleeping
        {
11,21      isSleeping = true;      // Change the state
12,22      isEating = false;
13,23      System.out.println("Pet is sleeping");
14,24      return;
        } // sleep()

     } // CyberPet class
```

reference variables pet1 and pet2 and give them initial values of null to indicate that they do not yet refer to any object.

In line 4 the program instantiates pet1 by creating an instance of the CyberPet class and associating it with pet1. It does this by transferring to lines 5 and 6, which are contained in the CyberPet class. When lines 5 and 6 are executed, pet1's instance variables (isEating and isSleeping) are created and assigned the initial values true and false, respectively. Thus, initially pet1 is eating. When line 6 has finished executing, control is returned to line 4, where the remaining steps involved in creating a new object are completed. The result of executing lines 4 to 6 is that pet1 refers to a new instance of the CyberPet class. This state of affairs is shown in Figure 2–19.

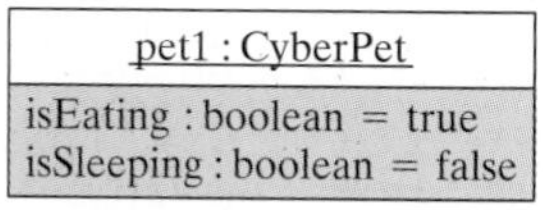

Execution continues with line 7 in main(). Lines 7 to 9 have the same basic effect as lines 4 to 6. They create a new instance of a CyberPet and initialize its state to eating. However, in this case, the new object is associated with pet2. This state of affairs is shown in Figure 2–20.

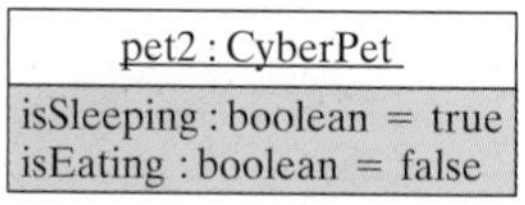

It's important to understand what's going on when lines 5 to 6 (and 8 to 9) are executed. As Figure 2–18 indicates, these are really just the same lines of code executed twice. But this is exactly what we mean when we say that a class definition serves as a template for creating instances of the class. Lines 5 to 6 (and 8 to 9) are used to create instance variables for each instance of the CyberPet class. The first time they are executed (lines 5 to 6), they are used to create and initialize pet1's instance variables. The next time they are executed they are used to create and initialize pet2's instance variables.

After both pet1 and pet2 are created, execution continues on line 10. The statement on line 10 tells pet1 to sleep. When the sleep() method is called, control transfers to line 11, the first line in the sleep() method. Lines 11 and 12 cause pet1's state to change from eating to sleeping. The effect of these statements is to change the values of isEating and isSleeping to false and true, respectively. Thus, after lines 11 and 12 are executed, pet1's state will be as shown in Figure 2–21. Line 13 causes the message "Pet is sleeping" to be displayed on the screen, and line 14 returns control to the main method.

Control resumes on line 15 of main(), where pet1's eat() method is called. This transfers control to line 16, the first line in the eat() method. Lines 16 and 17 have the effect of changing pet1's state back to eating, so that after these statements are executed, pet1 will again have the state shown in Figure 2–19. Line 18 causes the message "Pet is eating" to appear on the screen and line 19 returns control to main().

Control resumes on line 20 of main(), where pet2's sleep() method is called. This transfers control to line 21, the first line in the sleep() method. Lines 21 and 22 have the effect of changing pet2's state from eating to sleeping. After these statements are executed, pet2 will have the state shown in Figure 2–22. Line 23 causes the message "Pet is sleeping" to be output, and line 24 returns control to the main() method.

It's important to see that lines 11 to 14 are executed twice (once as lines 11 to 14, and the second time as lines 21 to 24). They are executed once as pet1's sleep() method and once as pet2()'s sleep method. In the first case, the method changes pet1's instance variables, and in the second case it changes pet2's instance variables. Here again we see clearly the sense in

FIGURE 2–19 The initial state (eating) of pet1, a CyberPet object.

FIGURE 2–20 The initial state (eating) of pet2, a CyberPet object.

Class as a template

Calling a method

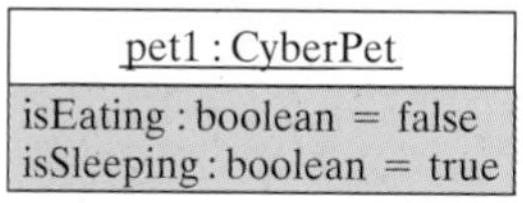

FIGURE 2–21 pet1 is now sleeping.

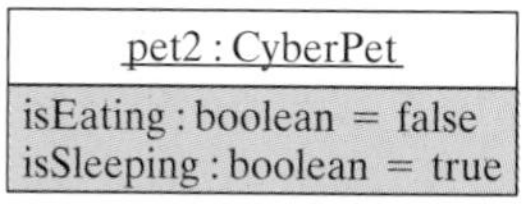

FIGURE 2–22 pet2 is now sleeping.

pet1 vs. pet2

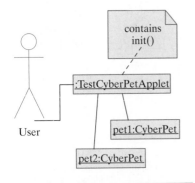

FIGURE 2–23   The TestCyberPetApplet serves as a user interface for the CyberPet simulation.

FIGURE 2–24   The applet's init() method takes the place of the main() method in the Java application.

FIGURE 2–25   The TestCyberPetApplet.

which a class definition—in this case a method within a class definition—serves as a template for the class's instance objects.

The final lines of the program are line 25, which causes the message "main() is finished" to be output, and line 26, which causes the program to terminate and to give control back to the operating system.

2.3.9   Class Design: The TestCyberPetApplet

We can also use a Java applet as a user interface (Fig. 2–23). A Java applet that tests the CyberPet class will closely resemble the application (Fig. 2–24). The main difference is that we replace the application's main() method with an init() method. Recall that the basic outline for the definition of an applet class is as follows:

```
public class TestCyberPetApplet extends Applet
{
} // TestCyberPetApplet
```

The main change we have to make to this is to incorporate an init() method, the method that will be executed as soon as the applet is run. The init() method has the following form:

```
public void init()
{
} // init()
```

Let's simply model our init() method after the main() method from the application program. In other words, let's take all of the statements from within the body of main() and encapsulate them in init()'s body. The only change we will make is to change the word *main* to *init* in each of the println statements (Fig. 2–25).

The TestCyberPetApplet applet is actually a very rudimentary example of a Java applet. It doesn't use any of the Graphical User Interface (GUI) objects, such as buttons or text fields, that characterize an applet

```
import java.applet.*;

public class TestCyberPetApplet extends Applet
{
    public void init()
    {                                    // Execution starts here
        System.out.println("init() is starting");
        CyberPet pet1;                   // Declare two references
        CyberPet pet2;
        pet1 = new CyberPet();           // Instantiate the references
        pet2 = new CyberPet();           //   by creating new objects
        pet1.sleep();                    // Tell pet1 to sleep.
        pet1.eat();                      // Tell pet1 to eat.
        pet2.sleep();                    // Tell pet2 to sleep.
        System.out.println("init() is finished");
        return;                          // Return to the system
    } // init()
} // TestCyberPetApplet
```

interface. Instead it merely produces text output, just like the application. The output generated by the applet will be almost identical to the output produced by the application:

```
init() is starting
Pet is sleeping
Pet is eating
Pet is sleeping
init() is finished
```

(Note that if you run this applet using a Web browser you may have to use the browser's menu to open the Java console. Otherwise you won't be able to see the output. Most browsers assume, rightly so, that a Java applet will have a GUI interface and will not use the Java console window.)

The trace of the `TestCyberPetApplet` applet is nearly identical to the trace of the application program, so we will not go through it in detail. Suffice it to say that execution begins at the first statement in the `init()` method. The two `CyberPet` instances are created in the same way—by using the `CyberPet` class definition as a template—and have the same initial state. Whenever `pet1`'s `sleep()` method is called in `init()`, control transfers to `pet1`, and the statements in its `sleep()` method are executed, and then control returns to `init()`.

Execution begins in `init()`

Again, although this is an incomplete use of Java's applet class, this example does illustrate that we can use an applet to use and test the `CyberPet` class.

2.3.10   Class Design: The `CyberPet` Application

A third way of using and testing the `CyberPet` class is to give it its own `main()` method (Fig. 2–26). We can use the very same definition of `main()` from the preceding `TestCyberPet` application.

It's important to note that `static` methods, such as `main()` in this case, are associated with the class (`CyberPet`), not with any instances of the class. In this way the application is not dependent on the existence of any particular `CyberPet` object. When a `CyberPet` object is created, it does not contain a `main()` method. It just contains the `eat()` and `sleep()` methods. The resulting class definition is shown in Figure 2–27. The `CyberPet` application does exactly the same thing as the `TestCyberPet` application. Its output and trace are left as exercises.

CyberPet
− isEating : boolean − isSleeping : boolean
+ eat() + sleep() + main()

FIGURE 2–26   Any Java class can be turned into an application by giving it a `static main()` method, which is symbolized in UML by underlining the method's name.

OBJECT-ORIENTED DESIGN:
Basic Principles

This completes our discussion of the `CyberPet` class. Before we move on, let's briefly review some of the object-oriented design principles that were employed in this example.

- **Encapsulation.** The `CyberPet` class was designed to encapsulate a certain state and a certain set of actions. It was designed to simulate a pet that could eat, sleep, and respond to the user via the eat and sleep commands. In addition, `CyberPet`'s methods encapsulate the actions that make up their particular tasks.

- **Information Hiding.** `CyberPet`'s state is represented by a pair of `boolean` variables, `isEating` and `isSleeping`, which are declared `private`, thereby

FIGURE 2–27 Including a main() method in the CyberPet class.

```java
public class CyberPet {

    // Data
    private boolean isEating = true;  // CyberPet's state
    private boolean isSleeping = false;

    // Methods
    public void eat()              // Start eating
    {
        isEating = true;           // Change the state
        isSleeping = false;
        System.out.println("Pet is eating");
        return;
    } // eat()

    public void sleep()            // Start sleeping
    {
        isSleeping = true;         // Change the state
        isEating = false;
        System.out.println("Pet is sleeping");
        return;
    } // sleep()

    public static void main (String argv[])
    {
        System.out.println("main() is starting");
                                   // Execution starts here
        CyberPet pet1;             // Declare two references
        CyberPet pet2;
        pet1 = new CyberPet();     // Instantiate the references
        pet2 = new CyberPet();     //   by creating new objects
        pet1.sleep();              // Tell pet1 to sleep.
        pet1.eat();                // Tell pet1 to eat.
        pet2.sleep();              // Tell pet2 to sleep.
        System.out.println("main() is finished");
        return;                    // Return to the system
    } // main()
} // CyberPet class
```

making them inaccessible to other objects. By hiding these variables, we can ensure that other objects cannot change their values. This will help ensure that the CyberPet remains in a valid state—that is, a state in which either isEating or isSleeping, but not both, is true.

- **Clearly Designed Interface.** CyberPet's interface is defined in terms of the public methods eat() and sleep(). These methods constrain the way users can interact with CyberPets and preserve the consistency of a CyberPet's state. Those are the main purposes of a good interface.
- **Generality and Extensibility.** There is nothing in our design of CyberPet that limits its use and its extensibility. Moreover, as we will see later, we can easily extend its functionality both by adding new functionality to the class definition itself (by extending its state to cover

thinking and other behaviors) and by allowing the definition to serve as a superclass in a CyberPet hierarchy (by allowing subclasses to be defined for certain types of pets such as dogs and cats).

Alan Kay and the Smalltalk Language

ALTHOUGH *Simula* was the first programming language to use the concept of an object, the first pure object-oriented language was *Smalltalk*. Smalltalk was first started by Alan Kay in the late 1960s. Kay is an innovative thinker who has had a hand in the development of several advances, such as windowing interfaces and laser printing and the client/server model, that are now commonplace in modern PCs.

One of the abiding themes throughout Kay's career has been the idea that computers should be easy enough for kids to use. In the late 1960s, while still in graduate school, Kay designed a computer model that consisted of a notebook-sized portable computer with a keyboard, screen, mouse, and high-quality graphics interface. He had become convinced that graphics and icons were a far better way to communicate with a computer than the command-line interfaces that were prevalent at the time.

In the early 1970s Kay went to work at the Xerox Palo Alto Research Center (PARC), where he developed a prototype of his system known as the *Dynabook*. Smalltalk was the computer language Kay developed for this project. Smalltalk was designed along a biological model, in which individual entities or "objects" communicate with each other by passing messages back and forth. Another goal of Smalltalk was to enable children to invent their own concepts and build programs with them—hence, the name *Smalltalk*.

Xerox's management was unable to see the potential in Kay's innovations. However, during a visit to Xerox in 1979, Steve Jobs, the founder of Apple Computer, was so impressed by Kay's work that he made it the inspiration of the Macintosh computer, which was first released in 1984.

Kay left Xerox in 1983 and became an Apple Fellow in 1984. In addition to working for Apple, Kay spent considerable time teaching kids how to use computers at his Open School in West Hollywood. In 1996 Kay became a Fellow (an "Imagineer") at the Walt Disney Imagineering's Research and Development Organization, where he continues to explore innovative ways to enhance the educational and entertainment value of computers.

From the Java Library

BufferedReader, String, Integer

AS WE HAVE mentioned before, Java has an extensive class library that contains carefully designed and efficiently programmed class definitions that can be applied to a wide variety of tasks. An important principle of object-oriented design is that one should avoid the temptation to "reinvent the wheel." In other words, when presented with a programming task, one of the first questions you should ask is: Is there a library class that handles this task? Chances are that library code is far more efficient and better designed than code you would have time to write yourself.

EFFECTIVE DESIGN: The Code-Reuse Principle. Before designing and writing your own code, search the Java library to see if it contains a class that solves the problem you're trying to solve.

http://java.sun.com/products /jdk/1.3/docs/api/

As a way of encouraging this approach to program design, each chapter will include a section that features one or more important classes from the Java library. In addition to describing the library class, these sections will contain a simple example showing how the class can be used.

I/O errors

Accepting input is actually one of the more complicated programming tasks because so many things can go wrong during an input operation. For example, an Internet connection can break while downloading a Web page; or a file that is usually readable can be accidently moved or deleted; or the user can type a letter when asked to type a number. In this section we'll describe how to do simple input of `String` and numeric data from the keyboard.

In Java, each program has three I/O streams available to it at startup: `System.in`, `System.out`, and `System.err`. As we saw in the previous chapter, `System.in` is a predefined `InputStream` that is normally associated with the keyboard. However, one limitation of the `java.io.InputStream` class is that it does not contain methods that can be used for simple input. Fortunately, the `java.io.Buffered Reader` class has a `readLine()` method that can be used for simple I/O:

```
public class BufferedReader extends Reader
{
    public BufferedReader(Reader in); // Constructor
    public String readLine();
}
```

Buffers

As its name implies, the `BufferedReader` class contains methods that perform buffered input. A *buffer* is a portion of memory where input is held until it is needed by the program. Using a buffer between, say, the keyboard and the program allows you to use a Backspace key to delete a character. When you hit the Enter key, any characters that you deleted will be ignored when the program retrieves characters from the input buffer.

Note that `BufferedReader`'s constructor takes a `Reader` as a parameter. If you want to perform buffered input from the keyboard, you can just pass a reference to `System.in` to the `BufferedReader()` constructor:

```
BufferedReader input = new BufferedReader
    ( new InputStreamReader (System.in) );
```

This code is rather ugly syntactically, but it does enable us to convert `System.in` into a buffered reader.

Once we have created a `BufferedReader`, here named `input`, we can use the `readLine()` method to read one line of characters from the keyboard and store it in a Java `String` object. A string is just a sequence of characters, such as "Hello World". However, in addition to storing the characters themselves, a Java `String` object keeps track of certain properties of the `String`, such as its length, and includes a number of methods for manipulating `Strings`. The following statement reads one line from the keyboard buffer and stores it in the `String` named `inputString`.

```
String inputString = input.readLine();
```

The readLine() method will read all the characters up to the first Enter keystroke and return a String. Once a line input by the user is stored in a String variable, we can use other library methods to manipulate the input. For example, the following code *prompts* the user for his or her name, grabs the input, stores it in the String variable named inputString, and then prints "Hello" plus whatever the user typed:

```
System.out.print("Hello, input your name please ");
String inputString = input.readLine();
System.out.println("Hello " + inputString ); // Concatenate and print
```

The "+" sign used here is Java's *string concatenation* operator. Suppose the user typed "Kim" for a name. The expression "Hello" + input String will concatenate "Hello" and "Kim" into a single string. Thus, the program will print "Hello Kim". We could also have produced the same output without using the concatenation operator by first printing "Hello" and then printing inputString on the same line:

Concatenating strings

```
System.out.print("Hello, input your name please ");
String inputString = input.readLine();
System.out.print("Hello ");
System.out.println(inputString);
```

Because an input operation is subject to all kinds of unpredictable problems, the readLine method *throws* or raises an IOException if some kind of input error occurs. An *exception* is Java's way of handling runtime anomalies that occur while a program is running. (Exceptions are covered in Chapter 11.) In order to use readLine() in a program, we must either *catch* the exception (handle it) or specify that we are not going to handle it. In the latter case the exception will be handled in some default manner by the Java Virtual Machine. Since the latter option is the simpler one at this point, let's choose not to handle this IOException when using readLine().

I/O exceptions

The simple program in Figure 2–28 illustrates how this is done. Note that in the declaration of the main() method we have specified throws IOException, which says that some kind of IOException may get thrown and not caught during main()'s execution. Should this occur, main() will simply throw the exception to the Java Virtual Machine, where it will be handled, usually by stopping the program and printing an error message.

Java's I/O code is admittedly complicated compared to other aspects of the language. At this point it is not important that you fully understand the concept of a BufferedReader and an InputStreamReader. We will deal with these concepts in detail in Chapter 14. At this point you can simply use the code as we have presented it whenever you need to input values from the keyboard.

FIGURE 2–28   Definition of the
Hello class.

```
import java.io.*;              // Java I/O classes

public class Hello
{                             // Performs screen i/o
    public static void main(String argv[]) throws IOException
    {
        BufferedReader input = new BufferedReader
            (new InputStreamReader(System.in));
        System.out.print("Hello, input your name please ");
        String inputString = input.readLine();
        System.out.println("Hello " + inputString);
    } // main()
} // Hello

OUTPUT: Hello, input your name please Kim
OUTPUT: Hello Kim
```

Reading Numbers from the Keyboard

Converting numeric input

Handling numeric input from the keyboard can also be tricky. One way to handle numeric input is to use readLine() to read in one line of data and then to extract the number from the line. For example, the following line will convert inputString into an int:

```
int number = Integer.parseInt( inputString );
```

Here we are using the parseInt() method of the java.lang.Integer class to convert the inputString into an int. We must do this conversion if we wish to use the number typed at the keyboard in an arithmetic operation.

The Integer wrapper

The Integer class is known as a **wrapper class** (see the "Java Language Summary" in this chapter). Its main function is to convert primitive data of type int into an object that can fit into Java's class hierarchy. Wrapper classes also include many useful methods, such as parseInt(), which converts one type of data to another.

To see why this is so useful, consider a program that computes the average of three exam grades (Fig. 2–29). This program prompts the user for three numbers. On each input operation the user's input is stored in the String variable inputString. Then inputString is converted into an int and stored in one of the three int variables (midterm1, midterm2, finalExam). The statement

```
sum = midterm1 + midterm2 + finalExam;
```

computes the sum of the three grades. And the following statement prints the student's average, which is computed by sum/3 (dividing sum by 3):

```
System.out.print("Your average in this course is " );
System.out.println( sum/3 );
```

I/O problems are more likely to happen when reading numeric data. In the Grader program in Figure 2–29, if the user types 45.9 when Java

```
import java.io.*;    // Java I/O classes

public class Grader
{
    public static void main(String argv[]) throws IOException
    {
        BufferedReader input = new BufferedReader
            (new InputStreamReader(System.in));
        String inputString;

        int midterm1, midterm2, finalExam; // Three exam grades
        float sum;                         // The sum of the 3 grades

        System.out.print("Input your grade on the first midterm: ");
        inputString = input.readLine();
        midterm1 = Integer.parseInt(inputString);
        System.out.println("You input: " + midterm1);
        System.out.print("Input your grade on the second midterm: ");
        inputString = input.readLine();
        midterm2 = Integer.parseInt(inputString);
        System.out.println("You input: " + midterm2);
        System.out.print("Input your grade on the final exam: ");
        inputString = input.readLine();
        finalExam = Integer.parseInt(inputString);
        System.out.println("You input: " + finalExam);
        sum = midterm1 + midterm2 + finalExam;
        System.out.print("Your average in this course is ");
        System.out.println(sum/3);
    } // main()
} // Grader
```

FIGURE 2–29 Definition of the Grader class.

expects to receive an integer, this will cause an error, because 45.9 contains a decimal point. For example, consider what happens when we type nonnumeric data in the Grader program:

```
Input your grade on the first midterm: 65.8
java.lang.NumberFormatException: 65.8
    at java.lang.Integer.parseInt(Integer.java)
    at java.lang.Integer.parseInt(Integer.java)
    at Grader.main(Grader.java:20)
```

Note that the exception that results in this case is a NumberFormatException, not an IOException. The I/O operation happens without error because "65.8" is a valid String and that's what readLine is looking for. The error happens when we try to convert "65.8" into an int in the following statement:

```
midterm1 = Integer.parseInt( inputString );
```

In Chapter 11, we will learn how to handle this kind of exception more gracefully.

JAVA LANGUAGE RULE Default Exception Handling. Java's default exception handling makes it far superior to other languages in the way it handles runtime errors.

SELF-STUDY EXERCISE

EXERCISE 2.9 Suppose that the user of the Grader program had typed in 85, 95, and 90 as her three exam grades. If, as we have done in the program, these input values are converted to ints and then added together using the expression midterm1 + midterm2 + finalExam, we would get 270 as their sum. What would we have gotten if we stored the user's input in three separate String variables, s1, s2, s3, and then performed the following statement?

```
System.out.println(s1 + s2 + s3);  // Concatenation
```

IN THE LABORATORY: The Circle Class

The purpose of this laboratory project is to give you practice designing and implementing a Java class definition. The exercise is patterned after the Java program development described in Chapter 1. The objectives of this project are

- To give practice designing a simple Java class to represent a circle.
- To convert the design into a working Java program.
- To compile, run, and test the Java program.

The following sections provide a step-by-step framework for completing this exercise.

Problem Statement

Design and implement a class to represent a geometric circle, and then test your class definition by implementing a main() method that creates Circle instances and displays their circumferences and areas. Your program should produce the following output on the screen:

```
The diameter of circle1 is 20.0
The area of circle1 is 314.0
The circumference of circle1 is 62.80
The diameter of circle2 is 30.0
The area of circle2 is 706.5
The circumference of circle2 is 94.2
```

Problem Decomposition

This problem can be divided into one class, the Circle class, which will implement the geometric circle. It will contain its own main() method so that it can create and test Circle instances.

Problem Design

Your design should be closely modeled on that of the Rectangle and Square classes discussed earlier. To begin, draw a UML class diagram to describe your design of the Circle class. Then develop a detailed *speci-fication* for the Circle class, which identifies the purpose of the class, its *attributes* (instance variables) and *behavior* (methods). Designate which information will be hidden and which parts of the class will make up its *interface*.

Specification

Type the specification using the same text editor you use for typing the program itself. Enclose the specification within a Java comment block and save it in a file named Circle.java. This file will be the file you use for defining the Circle class. The comment will serve as documentation for the program.

A comment block in Java begins with either "/*" or "/** " and ends with "*/". It can extend over multiple lines. As explained in Appendix A, comments that begin with "/**" are *documentation comments*, which can be automatically turned into documentation for the class by using software that comes with the Java Development Kit (JDK). You would use documentation comments to describe a class's specification. Here's an example format that you can use:

Comments

```
/**
 * Class Name: Circle
 *
 * ... ( the rest of your specification )
 *
 */
```

Implementation

Use the *stepwise refinement* approach, described in Chapter 1, to convert your specification into a Java class definition. That is, write the program in small stages, compiling and running the program after each stage is coded. This will enable you to localize any errors that are made. Remember that Java is *case sensitive* and very fussy about the spelling of *identifiers* and *keywords*.

Stepwise refinement

Note: Rather than typing everything from scratch, another way to write this code is to copy and paste an existing program. You can download the Rectangle source code from the book's companion Web site. Just follow the links on

```
http://starbase.trincoll.edu/~jjjava/sourcecode2E/ch02/rectangle
```

You can then modify it using cut, copy, and paste editing.

Reasonable coding stages for this project would be

- Code the header of the Circle class but leave its body empty. Code the header and an empty body for the main() method, which should be coded exactly as shown in the examples in this chapter.
- Code the declarations for the instance variables as well as the *constructor* method. The constructor method should be closely modeled after Rectangle's constructor.

- Create a `Circle` instance in the `main()` method, so that you can use it to test the constructor. This is where you would use the operator `new` plus the constructor method.

- Write one access method at a time, as well as a method call in `main()` that tests the method. Here is where you would use method calls embedded within `println()` expressions to display the circle's area and perimeter. For example, here's a pair of statements that will output `circle1`'s area:

```
System.out.print("The area of circle1 is ");
System.out.println(circle1.calculateArea());
```

- Complete the documentation for your program. Add comments to your code that will make your program more readable. A good rule might be that you should be able to read your program two years from now and still understand what it does. See Appendix A for guidelines about documentation conventions.

Java Language Summary

This section provides an overview of Java language elements that were introduced in this chapter or elaborates on elements that were introduced in previous chapters.

Class Definition

A class is a template for a Java object. A Java program is expressed as a class definition. An application program is a class definition that contains a `main()` method. Figure 2–30 summarizes the basic elements of a class definition.

FIGURE 2–30   A Java application program is a class definition that contains a `main()` method.

```
public class Greeter extends Object          // Class header
{                                            // Start of class body
    private String greeting = "My name is Joe"; // Instance variable

    public void printGreeting()              // Method definition header
    {                                        // Start of method body
        System.out.println(greeting);        // Output statement
    } // printGreeting()                     // End of method body

    public static void main(String args[])   // Method definition header
    {                                        // Start of method body
        Greeter greeter;                     // Reference variable declaration
        greeter = new Greeter();             // Object instantiation statement
        greeter.printGreeting();             // Method call
    } // main()                              // End of method body
} // Greeter
```

The comments in this program identify each of its main elements. The other features you should note about this definition are

- A class definition consists of a header and a body. The header gives the class a name (Greeter), specifies its accessibility (public), and specifies is pedigree (extends Object). The class body contains definitions of the object's attributes or instance variables (greeting) and behaviors or methods (printGreeting()).
- A static method, such as main(), is associated with the class (not with its instances). By default, when an application is run, the Java runtime system calls the main() method to get the program started.
- A private class element cannot be accessed directly by other objects. Instance variables, such as greeting, are usually designated private. This form of *information hiding* protects the integrity of the object's state.
- Class elements that are designated as public can be accessed by other objects. Some of an object's methods are usually designated public and thereby become part of the object's interface. An object's interface constrains the way other objects can interact with it.
- In order to use an object you must *instantiate* it by declaring a reference for it and creating an instance of it. Then you can use *dot notation* to refer to the object's public methods. In this sample program we create a Greeter object and ask it to print a greeting:

```
Greeter greeter;            // Reference variable declaration
greeter = new Greeter();    // Object instantiation statement
greeter.printGreeting();    // Method call
```

- A variable such as greeter, which is declared within a method, is called a *local variable*. Local variables have *local scope*, which means they can only be used within the method or block in which they are declared. Instance variables and instance methods have *class scope*, which means they can be referred to throughout the class.

Method Definition

An object's methods constitute its behaviors. A method definition is a named section of code within a class that can be called or invoked to perform a behavior. The key elements of a method definition are shown here:

```
public void printGreeting()            // Method definition header
{                                      // Start of method body
    System.out.println(greeting);      //   Output statement
} // printGreeting()                   // End of method body
```

The method header identifies important properties of the method, including its name (printGreeting()), its accessibility (public), its result type (void), and its parameters, if any. The method's body, which is a block of code contained within braces, contains the executable statements that make up the method's actions. In this example, the method just prints a message by calling the println() method in the System.out object.

Access Rules

When a class, field, or method is defined, you can declare it public, protected, or private. Or you can leave its access unspecified, in which case Java's default accessibility will apply.

Java determines accessibility in a top-down manner. Instance variables and methods are contained in classes, which are contained in packages. To determine whether a field or method is accessible, Java starts by determining whether its containing package is accessible, and then whether its containing class is accessible. Access to packages is controlled by the Java runtime system. Access to classes, fields, and methods is defined according to the rules shown in Table 2.2.

TABLE 2.2   Java's accessibility rules.

Type	Declaration	Rule
Package	N/A	Accessibility determined by the system.
Class	`public`	Accessible if its package is accessible.
	by default	Accessible only within its package.
Member (field or method) of an accessible class	`public`	Accessible to all other objects.
	`protected`	Accessible to its subclasses and to other classes in its package.
	`private`	Accessible only within the class.
	by default	Accessible only within the package.

Primitive Data Types

Except for the primitive data types, everything in Java is an object. Java is a *strongly typed* language, which means that every variable and every expression is classified according to its type. A variable's type determines how it can be used. For example, because the CyberPet's isEating variable is a boolean variable, it would be a syntax error to assign the String value "true" to it. You can only assign a boolean value to it.

Java's primitive data types are summarized in Table 2.3 and are taken up in detail in Chapter 5. At this stage the following points are important to note about the primitive types:

- **Integers.** An **integer** is a positive or negative whole number, and Java provides several types based on the number of bits in their representation. A byte uses 8 bits and can represent integer values in the range −128 to +127. An int, which is probably the most widely used integer

TABLE 2.3   Java primitive data types. Except for the boolean type, the size of the primitive types is defined in the Java Language Specification.

Type	Keyword	Size in Bits	Examples
boolean	`boolean`	–	true *or* false
character	`char`	16	'A', '5', '+'
byte	`byte`	8	−128 *to* +127
integer	`short`	16	−32768 *to* +32767
integer	`int`	32	−2147483648 *to* +2147483647
integer	`long`	64	*really big integers*
realnumber	`float`	32	21.3, −0.45, 1.67e28
realnumber	`double`	64	21.3, −0.45, 1.67e28

type, requires 32 bits and can represent integers in the range -2^{31} to $+2^{31} - 1$. When an integer **literal**—an actual value—is used in a Java program, it must observe the following formation rule.

Literal values

JAVA LANGUAGE RULE Literals. An *integer literal* may begin with an optional plus (+) or minus (−) sign followed by one or more digits (0 ... 9). A literal of type long must be terminated with an L or l. All other integer literals are treated as type int.

Thus, the following are examples of valid and invalid integer literals:

```
23   -1   0   50000  987612098774L  // Valid integer literals
50,000   5%  "55" '6'               // Invalid integer literals
```

Integer literals cannot include punctuation of any sort (no commas, dollar signs, and so forth) and cannot be enclosed within quotes, which would turn them into either characters ('5') or Strings ("56").

- **Real Numbers.** Real numbers, or **floating point numbers**, are numbers that contain a fractional part, such as 0.1274 and 3.14. Java provides two types of reals: float, which requires 32 bits, and double, which requires 64 bits. Java also allows real numbers to be expressed in *exponential notation*. Thus, the number 5.041e4 can be used to represent 5.041×10^4 or 50410. The symbol e4 represents 10 raised to the power of 4. This notation can be used to avoid having to write literals such as 0.00000000000000003456 or 34560000000000000000 in a Java program. Real literals can also employ a suffix (F,f,D,d) to distinguish between double and float. If the suffix is omitted, the literal is treated as a double. The following are examples of valid and invalid real literals:

```
23.7   -1.0   50000.336   .14 -1.314e-10F // Valid real literals
50,000.336  $78.99  1.5% "1.9" '1.9'      // Invalid real literals
```

- **Characters.** Characters in Java are represented by the 16-bit char type. Typical characters include letters of the alphabet (A to Z), digits (0 to 9), and symbols of various sorts (+, *). A char literal is always represented as a single character enclosed within *single* quotes. Note that a single character enclosed within *double* quotes is a Java String ("a"). Java characters can also include certain nonprinting characters, such as the newline character (\n) and the tab character (\t). These are called **escape sequences** and may be embedded within strings to add formatting to printed output—for example,

```
This\tstring\thas\ttabs\tbetween\twords\n\n
```

The following are examples of valid and invalid character literals:

```
'A'   'a'   '$'   '8'   '\n'      // Valid character literals
'AB'  '692'  "a"                  // Invalid character literals
```

- **Booleans.** Boolean values are used to represent whether something is true or false. The two boolean values, true and false, are both Java keywords. Note that these values are not enclosed within quotes.

Strings

Strings in Java are full-fledged objects and are treated as such. A String literal is a sequence of one or more characters (char) enclosed within double quotes (quotation marks). The following are valid string literals:

```
"What is your name?"   "There are 3 students"   "F"   "6547"
```

A string composed of digits should not be mistaken for an integer. Thus, the string "6547" is not the same as the integer 6547.

SELF-STUDY EXERCISES

EXERCISE 2.10   Identify the data type of each of the following literal expressions:

a. 44	d. "true"	g. –42
b. 65.98	e. true	h. '6'
c. "42"	f. "$65.98"	

Wrapper Classes

Sometimes it is necessary to convert one type of data to another. And sometimes it is necessary to manipulate a piece of primitive data as if it were an object. In order to facilitate these types of operations, Java supplies a set of **wrapper classes**, which are summarized in Table 2.4.

TABLE 2.4   Java *wrapper classes* for the primitive data types.

Primitive Type	Wrapper Class	Useful Methods
boolean	Boolean	
char	Character	
byte	Byte	
short	Short	
int	Integer	int parseInt(String)
long	Long	
float	Float	
double	Double	double parseDouble(String)

We've already seen one useful application of the Integer.parseInt() method to convert a String that is input from the keyboard into an int. In general, parseInt() converts a String value into an int value:

```
int intValue = Integer.parseInt( "125"); // Converts "125" to 125
```

A similar method in the Double wrapper can be used to convert a String into a double value:

```
double val = Double.parseDouble( "12.5"); // Converts "12.5" to 12.5
```

As we saw in the "From the Java Library" section in this chapter, this type of conversion is necessary to handle numeric input in a program.

Variable Initialization

Variables in a program always store some value or other. Beginning programmers sometimes don't realize this, but there really is no such thing as a memory location with no value in it. If programmer does not know what value is stored in a particular variable, that just means the variable's value is *undetermined*.

In order to minimize data errors caused by uninitialized variables, Java requires that all variables are initialized:

> **JAVA LANGUAGE RULE** Variable Initialization. By default, for instance variables, Java assigns all numeric variables, reals or integers, an initial value of 0, and all `boolean` variables an initial value of `false`. All reference variables, which refer to objects, are given an initial value of `null`. Local variables, those declared within a method, must be initialized by the programmer before they can be used.

The Assignment Statement

One of the most important statements is the *assignment statement*, which is one of the most fundamental ways of assigning a value to a variable. The syntax of the assignment operator is as follows:

> **JAVA LANGUAGE RULE** Assignment Statement. A (simple) **assignment statement**, which takes the form
>
> $$VariableName = Expression$$
>
> evaluates the *Expression* on the right of the assignment operator ($=$) and stores its value in the variable named on the left.

VariableName must be the name of a declared variable, and *Expression* must be a valid expression of the same type as the variable. Recall that an expression in Java can be a literal value ("hello") or a variable `greeting` or method call `calculateArea()` or some kind of operation (5 + 2).

The following would be examples of valid assignments:

```
int m = 5 + 2;                        // m is assigned 7
String s = "hello";                   // s is assigned "hello"
double r = rectangle1.calculateArea(); // r is assigned 300.0
```

The following would be examples of invalid assignments:

```
int m = 52.5;        // Can't assign a double to an int
boolean b= "true";   // Can't assign a String to a boolean
```

Operators

As we have just noted, one type of expression is one that involves one or more of Java's 37 *operators*. For example, the following are examples of integer expressions because they each produce an integer value:

```
25 + 3          // Produces 28
25 * 3          // Produces 75
25 - 3          // Produces 22
25 / 3          // Produces 8
```

Like variables and values, operators are *type dependent*. When used to divide two ints, the (/) operator produces an int result with no decimal places ($25/3 \rightarrow 8$). However, when used to divide two doubles, it produces a double result ($25.0/3.0 \rightarrow 8.333$). We will discuss the subtleties of these rules in Chapter 5.

CHAPTER SUMMARY

Technical Terms

access modifier	flow of control	method call and
assignment	keyword	return
statement	identifier	qualified name
class scope	initializer expression	void method
escape sequence	instance	wrapper class
field declaration	integer	
floating point	interface	
number	literal	

Summary of Important Points

- A Java program is a set of interacting objects. Writing a Java program is a matter of defining a Java *class*, which serves as a *template* for instances of the class. Classes typically contain two kinds of elements, *instance variables* and *methods*. An object's *state* is defined by its instance variables.

- The Java *class hierarchy* organizes all Java classes into a single hierarchy rooted in the Object class. Classes in a hierarchy are related by the *subclass* and *superclass* relationships. The Object class is the superclass of all other classes in the Java hierarchy.

- A *class definition* consists of a *header*, which names the class and describes its use and pedigree, and the *body*, which contains its details. A class's *pedigree* describes where it fits in the Java class hierarchy. By default a class is considered a direct subclass of Object.

- A class definition *encapsulates* the data and methods needed to carry out the class's task. A well-designed class should have a well-defined purpose, should present a well-articulated interface, should hide its implementation details, and should be as general and extensible as possible.

- A boolean variable is a *primitive type* that can have one of two values, true or false.

- Those class elements that are declared public are said to make up the object's *interface*.

- A *keyword* is a term that has special meaning in the Java language.

- An *identifier* must begin with a letter of the alphabet and may consist of any number of letters, digits, and the special underscore character (_). An identifier cannot be identical to a Java keyword.

- A class's instance variables are called *fields*. A *field declaration* reserves memory for the field within the object, associates a name and type with the location, and specifies its accessibility.

- A class's instance variables should generally be hidden by declaring them private.

- The *scope* of an identifier is that portion of the class in which it may be used. A class's fields and methods have *class scope*, which means they can be used anywhere within the class.
- A *method definition* consists of two parts: a *header*, which names the methods and provides other general information about it, and a *body* that contains its executable statements.
- Methods that have a return type must `return` a value of that type. Methods that don't return a value should be declared `void`.
- A method's *formal parameters* are variables that are used to bring information into the method.
- A *qualified name* is one that involves the *dot operator* (.) and is used to refer to an object's methods and instance variables.
- *Declaring* a *reference variable* creates a name for an object but doesn't create the object itself.
- *Instantiating* a reference variable creates an object and assigns the variable as its name or reference.
- Execution of a Java application begins with the first statement in the body of the `main()` method.

SOLUTIONS TO SELF-STUDY EXERCISES

SOLUTION 2.1   For the `Rectangle` class (Fig. 2–2),
- The name of the class: `Rectangle`
- The names of two instance variables: `length, width`
- The names of two methods: `Rectangle(), calculateArea()`

SOLUTION 2.2   For `RectangleUser` class (Fig. 2–4),
- The names of two `Rectangle` instances: `rectangle1, rectangle2`
- All six method calls in the program: `Rectangle(30,10)`, `Rectangle(25,20)`, `rectangle1.calculateArea()`, `rectangle2.calculateArea()`, and the two `System.out.println()` calls
- Two examples of qualified names: `rectangle1.calculateArea()` and `rectangle2.calculateArea()`

SOLUTION 2.3   The definition of the `CyberPet` class is

```
public class CyberPet
{
    private boolean isDreaming = false;
}
```

SOLUTION 2.4   The definition of the `CyberPet` class is

```
public class CyberPet
{
    public void dream()
    {
        isDreaming = true;
        isEating  = false;
        isSleeping = false;
    }
}
```

SOLUTION 2.5   Should the CyberPet's pickFood() method be declared public or private? It depends. If you wish to allow other objects to tell the CyberPet what to eat, it should be public. If the CyberPet is allowed to decide for itself, it should be declared private.

SOLUTION 2.6   Note that in this case the two stub methods return 0. If a method declares a nonvoid return type, it must contain a proper return statement.

```
public class Square
{
    private double side;

    public Square(double s);

    public double calcPerimeter() { return 0 ; }
    public double calcArea()      { return 0 ; }
}
```

SOLUTION 2.7   The definition of the Square class is

```
public class Square
{
    private double side;

    public Square(double s)
    {
        side = s;
    }

    public double calcPerimeter()
    {
        return 4 * side;
    }
    public double calcArea()
    {
        return side * side;
    }
} // Square
```

SOLUTION 2.8   The definition of the main() method is

```
public static void main(String argv[])
{
    Square square1;                  // Declare reference variables
    Square square2;
    square1 = new Square( 25 );  // Create instances
    square2 = new Square( 15 );
    // Statements to test the access methods
    System.out.print("The area of square1 is ");
    System.out.println(square1.calcArea());
    System.out.print("The perimeter of square1 is ");
    System.out.println(square1.calcPerimeter());
    System.out.print("The area of square2 is ");
    System.out.println(square2.calcArea());
    System.out.print("The perimeter of square2 is ");
    System.out.println(square2.calcPerimeter());
} // main()
```

SOLUTION 2.9   If we perform string concatenation on the strings, "85," "95," and "90," we would get a string result "859590." The lesson here is that when you use the plus operator, +, on strings, it performs *string concatenation*. When you use it on numbers, it performs addition. Using the same operator for two completely different operations is an example of *operator overloading*, which we will take up in more detail later on.

SOLUTION 2.10   a. int b. double c. String d. String e. boolean f. String g. int h. char

---

EXERCISE 2.1   Consider the transaction of asking your professor for your grade in your computer science course. Identify the objects in this transaction and the type of messages that would be passed among them.

EXERCISE 2.2   Now suppose the professor in the previous exercise decides to automate the transaction of looking up a student's grade and has asked you to design a program to perform this task. The program should let a student type in his or her name and ID number and should then display his or her grades for the semester, with a final average. Suppose there are five quiz grades, three exams, and two program grades. Identify the objects in this program and the type of messages that would be passed among them. (*Hint*: The grades themselves are just data values, not objects.)

EXERCISE 2.3   Consider the *hierarchy chart* in Figure 0–11. For each of the following pairs of classes, determine if they are related as *subclass/superclass*.

a. BorderLayout/FlowLayout
b. TextArea/TextComponent
c. TextField/Component
d. Button/Component
e. Panel/Object

EXERCISE 2.4   Name all the *subclasses* of the Container class.

EXERCISE 2.5   Based on the hierarchy chart in Figure 0–11, which of the following statements would be true?

a. A Container is an Object.
b. A TextComponent is a Component.
c. A Button is a Component.
d. A Panel is a Container.
e. A TextField is a Component.

EXERCISE 2.6   In the RectangleUser class (Fig. 2–4), give two examples of object instantiation and explain what is being done.

EXERCISE 2.7   Explain the difference between a *method definition* and a *method call*. Give an example of each from the Rectangle, RectangleUser, CyberPet, and TestCyberPet examples discussed in this chapter.

EXERCISE 2.8   In the RectangleUser class (Fig. 2–4), identify three examples of method calls and explain what is being done.

EXERCISE 2.9   Describe how the slogan "define, create, manipulate" applies to the Rectangle and the CyberPet examples.

EXERCISE 2.10   An *identifier* is the name for a _____, _____, or a _____.

EXERCISES

Note: *For programming exercises, **first** draw a UML class diagram describing all classes and their inheritance relationships and/or associations.*

EXERCISE 2.11   Which of the following would be valid *identifiers*?

```
int  74ElmStreet  Big_N      L$&%#  boolean  Boolean  _number
Int  public       Private    Joe    j1       2*K      big numb
```

EXERCISE 2.12   Explain what is meant by *class scope* in terms of the variables and methods of the CyberPet class.

EXERCISE 2.13   Identify the syntax error (if any) in each declaration. Remember that some parts of a field declaration are optional.

a. public boolean isEven ;
b. Private boolean isEven ;
c. private boolean isOdd
d. public boolean is Odd ;
e. string S ;
f. public String boolean ;
g. private boolean even = 0;
h. private String s = helloWorld ;
i. private int payRate = 5.0 ;
j. private double wageRate = 10 ;

EXERCISE 2.14   Write declarations for each of the following instance variables.

a. A private boolean variable named bool that has an initial value of true.
b. A public String variable named str that has an initial value of "hello".
c. A private double variable named payrate that is not assigned an initial value.

EXERCISE 2.15   For each of the following data types, identify what default value Java will give an instance variable of that type if no initializer expression is used when it is declared: boolean, int, String, double, CyberPet.

EXERCISE 2.16   Identify the syntax error (if any) in each method header:

a. public String boolean()
b. private void String ()
c. private void myMethod
d. private myMethod()
e. public static void Main (String argv[])

EXERCISE 2.17   Identify the syntax error (if any) in each assignment statement. Assume that the following variables have been declared:

```
public int m;
public double d;
public boolean b;
public String s;
```

a. m = 86.5 ;   e. s = "1295.98" ;
b. d = 86 ;   f. b = "true" ;
c. d = true ;   g. b = false
d. s = 1295 ;

EXERCISE 2.18   Given the following definition of the NumberAdder class, add statements to its main() method to create two instances of this class, named adder1 and adder2. Then add statements to set adder1's numbers to 10 and 15, and adder2's numbers to 100 and 200. Then add statements to print their respective sums.

```
public class NumberAdder
{
    private double num1;
    private double num2;

    public void setNums(double n1, double n2)
    {
      num1 = n1;
      num2 = n2;
    }
    public double getSum()
    {
      return num1 + num2 ;
    }

    public static void main(String args[])
    {
    }
}
```

EXERCISE 2.19 For the `NumberAdder` class in the previous exercise, what are the names of its instance variables and instance methods? Identify three expressions that occur in the program and explain what they do. Identify two assignment statements and explain what they do.

EXERCISE 2.20 Explain the difference between each of the following pairs of concepts.

a. A *method definition* and a *method invocation*.
b. Declaring a reference variable and creating an instance.
c. Defining a variable and instantiating an object.

EXERCISE 2.21 Look at the following Java program, which uses the `CyberPet` class defined in Figure 2–8. What would the program output be?

```
public class TestCyberPet
{
    public static void main(String argv[])
    {
      CyberPet pet1;
      pet1 = new CyberPet();
      pet1.eat();
      pet1.sleep();
      CyberPet pet2;
      pet2 = new CyberPet();
      pet2.sleep();
      pet2.eat();
      pet1.eat();
    } // main()
} // TestCyberPet
```

EXERCISE 2.22 Write a `main` method that creates two `CyberPet`s named `lilly` and `billy` and then asks each of them to sleep and then eat.

EXERCISE 2.23 Modify `CyberPet` to have a `String` instance variable, `name`. Give `name` an initial value and add a public method `tellMeYourName()` that prints the pet's name. Test your method by invoking it from `main()`.

EXERCISE 2.24   Define a Java class named NumberCruncher that has a single double value as its only instance variable. Then define methods that perform the following operations on its number: get, double, triple, square, and cube. Set the initial value of the number by following the way the length and width variables are set in the Rectangle class.

EXERCISE 2.25   Write a main() method and add it to the NumberCruncher class defined in the previous problem. Use it to create a NumberCruncher instance, with a certain initial value, and then get it to report its double, triple, square, and cube.

EXERCISE 2.26   **Challenge:** Modify your solution to the previous exercise so that it lets the user input the number to be crunched. Follow the example shown in this chapter's "From the Java Library" section.

EXERCISE 2.27   Write a Java class definition for a Cube object. The object should be capable of reporting its surface area and volume. The surface area of a cube is six times the area of any side. The volume is calculated by cubing the side.

EXERCISE 2.28   Write a Java class definition for a CubeUser object that will use the Cube object defined in the previous exercise. This class should create three Cube instances, each with a different side, and then report their respective surface areas and volumes.

EXERCISE 2.29   **Challenge:** Modify your solution to the previous exercise so that it lets the user input the side of the cube. Follow the example shown in this chapter's "From the Java Library" section.

EXERCISE 2.30   **Challenge:** Define a Java class that represents an address book entry, Entry, which consists of a name, address, and phone number, all represented as Strings. For the class's interface, define methods to set and get the values of each of its instance variables. Thus, for the name variable, it should have a setName() and a getName() method.

EXERCISE 2.31   **Challenge:** Write a Java class definition for a Temperature object that is capable of reporting its temperature in either Fahrenheit or Celsius. This class should have one instance variable called temperature and two public methods, one called getFahrenheit(), which returns the temperature in Fahrenheit, and one called getCelsius(), which returns the temperature in Celsius. This method has to convert the stored temperature to Celsius before returning it. An expression for converting Fahrenheit to Celsius is $(5 \times (F - 32)/9)$, where F is the temperature in Fahrenheit.

UML EXERCISES

EXERCISE 2.32   Draw a UML class diagram to represent the following class hierarchy: There are two types of languages, natural languages and programming languages. The natural languages include Chinese, English, French, and German. The programming languages include Java, Smalltalk and C++, which are object-oriented languages, FORTRAN, COBOL, Pascal, and C, which are imperative languages, Lisp and ML, which are functional languages, and Prolog, which is a logic language.

EXERCISE 2.33   Draw a UML class diagram to represent different kinds of automobiles, including trucks, sedans, wagons, SUVs, and the names and manufacturers of some popular models in each category.

EXERCISE 2.34   Draw a UML object diagram of a triangle with attributes for three sides, containing the values 3, 4, and 5.

EXERCISE 2.35 Suppose you are writing a Java program to implement an electronic address book. Your design is to have two classes, one to represent the user interface and one to represent the address book. Draw a UML diagram to depict this relationship. See Figure 2–3.

EXERCISE 2.36 Draw an UML object diagram to depict the relationship between an applet, which serves as a user interface, and three `Triangles`, named `t1`, `t2`, and `t3`.

EXERCISE 2.37 Suppose we add an `isThinking` attribute to the `CyberPet` class with a corresponding new `think()` behavior. Draw a UML class diagram to represent this version of CyberPet.

Photograph courtesy of New Zealand National Archives

3

Methods: Communicating with Objects

OBJECTIVES

After studying this chapter, you will

- Understand the role that methods play in an object-oriented program.
- Know how to use parameters and arguments to pass data to an object.
- Understand how constructor methods are used to instantiate objects.
- Know the difference between passing a value and passing a reference to an object.
- Be able to design your own methods.
- Know how to use the selection control structure.

OUTLINE

3.1   Introduction

In this chapter, we take a look at Java methods and parameters. Methods and parameters are the primary mechanisms for passing information into and out of an object. We will once again focus on the CyberPet simulation that we designed in the previous chapter. In that version, a CyberPet's state is represented by two boolean variables, isEating and isSleeping, and its repertoire of activity consists of responding to two commands, eat() and sleep() (Fig. 2–8).

This version of CyberPet was sufficient to introduce us to Java objects and classes, but it wasn't much of a simulated pet. For one thing, a CyberPet had no name, no color, and so on. And, although our CyberPet had a state, there was no way for it to communicate its state to the rest of the world—we had no means of simply asking a CyberPet, "What are you doing?"

In this chapter, we want to expand CyberPet to make our simulation more realistic. We begin by learning how to pass information to an object. That will enable us to give our CyberPets names. We then consider special methods called constructors, which are used to initialize an object's state when it is created. We also learn how to retrieve information from an object. That will enable us to ask a CyberPet what its name is and what it is doing. Finally, in the lab project for this chapter you will design and implement methods that extend the CyberPet's behavior even more.

3.2   Passing Information to an Object

What data does the object need?

Let's begin by expanding CyberPet to include a String variable that can store the CyberPet's name. Let's name the variable name because that is descriptive of its purpose. The question now is, how should we initialize this variable? If we give it some name as an initial value, say, "Socrates," then every CyberPet instance will have the name "Socrates." That's not a very good design. Instead, let's initialize name to "no name," meaning that the CyberPet has yet to be assigned a name. So, we will add the following declaration to the CyberPet class:

```
private String name = "no name";
```

We declare name to be private, thereby preventing other objects from accessing it directly. This is in keeping with the convention that instance variables should be hidden.

What actions will the class perform?

Now that we have added name to our class, we will need methods to access it. One convention of object-oriented programming is to provide public methods to *set* and *get* the values of some of its private instance variables. Methods that set or reset an object's instance variables are called *mutator methods*. Methods that get or retrieve the value of an instance variable are called *accessor* methods.

It is up to the designer of the class to determine which private variables require accessor and mutator methods. If you were designing a BankAccount class, you might want a public getAccountNumber() method, so that clients could retrieve information about their bank accounts, but you would probably not want a public getAccountPassword() method or a public setAccountBalance() method.

EFFECTIVE DESIGN: Accessor and Mutator Methods.   An **accessor method** is a public method used to *get* the value of an object's instance variable. A **mutator method** is a public method used to *set* the value of an instance variable. Such methods are often named *getVariable()* and *setVariable()*, respectively, where *Variable* is the name of the variable that's being accessed.

In the case of setting and getting the `name` variable, we would name our methods `setName()` and `getName()`. The `setName()` method would be used by other objects to pass a name string to a particular `CyberPet`. The `getName()` method would be used by other objects to retrieve a particular `CyberPet`'s name. The modified `CyberPet` class is summarized in Figure 3–1.

Consider the following definition for the `setName()` method, which has been added to the `CyberPet` class, along with the declaration and initialization of the `name` variable (Fig. 3–2).

```java
public void setName (String str)
{
    name = str;
}
```

CyberPet
− isEating : boolean − isSleeping : boolean − name : String
+ eat() + sleep() + setName(in str : String) + getName() : String

FIGURE 3–1   This version of the CyberPet class has a private `name` variable. The `setName()` method is used to set its value, and the `getName()` method is used to get its value.

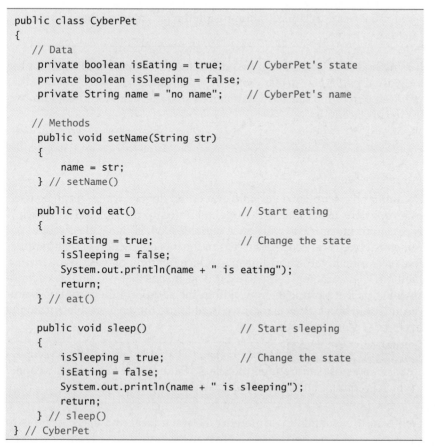

```java
public class CyberPet
{
   // Data
   private boolean isEating = true;     // CyberPet's state
   private boolean isSleeping = false;
   private String name = "no name";     // CyberPet's name

   // Methods
   public void setName(String str)
   {
       name = str;
   } // setName()

   public void eat()                    // Start eating
   {
       isEating = true;                 // Change the state
       isSleeping = false;
       System.out.println(name + " is eating");
       return;
   } // eat()

   public void sleep()                  // Start sleeping
   {
       isSleeping = true;               // Change the state
       isEating = false;
       System.out.println(name + " is sleeping");
       return;
   } // sleep()
} // CyberPet
```

FIGURE 3–2   The CyberPet class with the `setName()` method added.

Recall from Chapter 2 that the general form for a method definition in Java is

*MethodModifiers*_{opt} *ResultType* *MethodName* (*FormalParameterList*)
MethodBody

Parameters

In particular, note the *FormalParameterList* that follows the method's name. Formal parameters, or more simply, parameters, are used to pass information into a method when the method is invoked. Because neither the `eat()` nor `sleep()` method was passed any information, their parameter lists were empty. In both of those cases, simply calling the method was sufficient to tell the `CyberPet` to eat or sleep. No other information was necessary.

Passing information to an object

In the case of the `setName()` method, the situation is quite different. The purpose of this method is to set a `CyberPet`'s name. In order to do this, `setName()` must be given (or passed) a `String` that represents a pet's name. It will then take that string and assign it to its `name` instance variable, thereby setting the `CyberPet`'s name to the string it was passed. The formal parameter is used to hold the string that it is passed while the method is executing.

> **JAVA LANGUAGE RULE** Formal Parameter. A **formal parameter** or more simply, a **parameter**, is a variable that serves as a storage location for information that is passed to a method. To specify a formal parameter, you must provide a type identifier followed by variable identifier, and you must place this declaration inside the parentheses that follow the method's name.

If a method uses more than one parameter, use a comma to separate the individual parameter declarations. For example, if we had a method that required both a first and last name, its parameter list would contain two `String` declarations:

```
(String first, String last)
```

Parameter Scope

Recall that the **scope** of a variable or method defines where it can be used in a program. A parameter's scope is limited to the method in which it is declared. In contrast to instance variables, which have class scope, parameters have **local scope**. The reason for this distinction is that parameters have a relatively short life span. Once the flow of execution leaves a method, its parameters cease to exist. This means that we can only refer to `setName()`'s `str` parameter from within the `setName()` method. For example, it would be a syntax error if we tried to use the `str` variable within the `eat()` or `sleep()` methods.

Local scope

> **JAVA LANGUAGE RULE** Scope. Instance variables have **class scope**, which extends throughout the class. Parameters have **local scope**, which is confined to the method in which they are declared.

Class scope vs. local scope

One way to visualize the difference between local and class scope is to draw boxes around portions of a program to indicate an identifier's scope

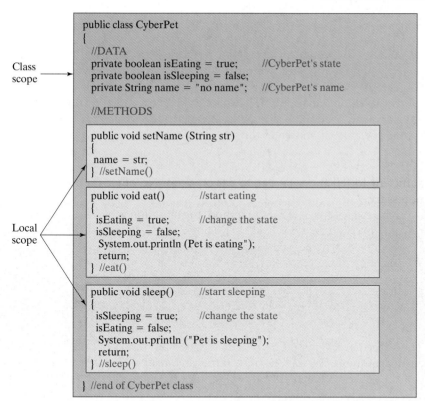

Class scope

Local scope

```
public class CyberPet
{
    //DATA
    private boolean isEating = true;        //CyberPet's state
    private boolean isSleeping = false;
    private String name = "no name";        //CyberPet's name

    //METHODS

    public void setName (String str)
    {
      name = str;
    } //setName()

    public void eat()          //start eating
    {
      isEating = true;         //change the state
      isSleeping = false;
        System.out.println (Pet is eating");
      return;
    } //eat()

    public void sleep()        //start sleeping
    {
      isSleeping = true;       //change the state
      isEating = false;
        System.out.println ("Pet is sleeping");
      return;
    } //sleep()

} //end of CyberPet class
```

FIGURE 3–3 Class scope extends through a class whereas local scope is confined to individual methods.

(Fig. 3–3). For class scope you would draw a box around the entire class. An instance variable or method can be used anywhere within that box. Similarly, draw boxes around each of the methods in the class. The scope of a method's parameters, if it has any, would be confined within these smaller boxes. From within a smaller box you can refer to an instance variable, because the smaller box is completely contained within the class's box. But from within one small box, you cannot refer to anything within one of the other small boxes. This is yet another sense in which both a method and a class encapsulate their elements.

Encapsulation

> DEBUGGING TIP: Scope Error. It would be a syntax error to refer to a method's parameters from outside the method.

3.2.1   Arguments and Parameters

Now that we have incorporated the new method and instance variable into CyberPet, let's create a CyberPet instance and use these new features. Suppose, then, we have the following statement in a Java program:

```
CyberPet pet1 = new CyberPet();
```

If we want to set pet1's name to "Socrates," we need to pass the string "Socrates" to the setName() method. Then setName() will do its task, which is to assign "Socrates" to pet1's name variable. In order to effect this action for pet1, we would use the following method call:

```
pet1.setName("Socrates");
```

Because the definition of `setName()` now includes a single `String` parameter, when we invoke it we must supply a single `String` value (such as "Socrates"). When `setName()` is invoked, its formal parameter (`str`) will be set to the value we supply (to "Socrates"). The value we supply can be any `String`. It needn't be a literal string such as "Socrates". It can also be a `String` variable, as shown in the following example:

```
String s = "Hal";
pet1.setName(s);
```

In this case, the value being passed to `setName()` is "Hal," the value that `s` has at the time the method call is made.

It would be an error to try to pass a value that was not a `String` to `setName()`. For example, each of the following invocations of `setName()` would cause an error:

```
pet1.setName();           // no String supplied
pet1.setName(Socrates) ;  // Socrates is not a String
pet1.setName(10);         // 10 is not a String
```

Parameter vs. argument

The value that is passed to a method when a method is called is known as an **argument**. Even though the terms *argument* and *parameter* are sometimes used interchangeably, it will be useful to observe a distinction. We will use the term **parameter** to refer to the formal parameter—the variable used to pass data to a method—that occurs in the method definition. We use the term *argument* to refer to the actual value that is supplied when the method is invoked.

DEBUGGING TIP: Type Error. It would be a syntax error to use an argument whose type doesn't match the type of its corresponding parameter.

Defining vs. calling a method

Hopefully the distinction between parameter and argument will help drive home the difference between *defining* a method and *invoking* a method. Beginning programmers easily confuse the two. Defining a method is a matter of writing a method definition, such as

```
public void printStr(String s)
{
    System.out.println(s);
}
```

Invoking a method

This method definition defines a method that takes a single `String` parameter, `s`, and simply prints the value of its parameter. On the other hand, invoking a method is a matter of writing a method call statement, such as

```
printStr("HelloWorld");
```

Simple vs. qualified names

This statement calls the `printStr` method and passes it the string "HelloWorld". You might wonder why this method call does not use the dot operator, as have most of our other examples. The rule in Java is that references to methods (or variables) within the same class do not require qualified names (the dot operator) but just the method (or variable) name itself.

> **JAVA LANGUAGE RULE** Qualified Names. Within a class, references to methods or variables are made in terms of simple names. Qualified names, or *dot notation*, are used to refer to methods or variables that belong to other classes.

3.2.2   Passing a String to CyberPet

To get a clearer picture of the interaction that takes place when we invoke setName() and pass it a string, let's write a simple test program to use our new version of CyberPet. As in the previous chapter, we'll call it TestCyberPet. Our first version of this program is shown in Figure 3–4.

```
public class TestCyberPet
{
    public static void main (String argv[])
    {
        CyberPet pet1;              // Declare a CyberPet
        pet1 = new CyberPet();     // Instantiate the references
        pet1.setName("Socrates"); // Set the pet's name
        return;                    // Return to the system
    } // main()
} // TestCyberPet
```

FIGURE 3–4   A program to test the CyberPet class.

The TestCyberPet program simply creates an instance that is referenced by pet1 and then invokes the setName() method to set pet1's name to "Socrates":

```
pet1.setName("Socrates");  // Set the pet's name
```

This interaction between TestCyberPet and CyberPet can be represented in UML as shown in Figure 3–5.

To get a clearer understanding of how a parameter works, it will be instructive to trace through the passing of "Socrates" to a CyberPet. When we make the call setName("Socrates"), this causes Java to assign "Socrates" as the value of setName()'s parameter. If you could look inside pet1 at that point, it would look something like Figure 3–6a. Note that setName()'s parameter points to the String object with the value "Socrates." Note also that pet1's name variable points to the String object with the value "noname." When setName()'s assignment statement is executed, the variable name is also set as a reference to "Socrates" (Fig. 3–6b). After the setName() method completes its execution, pet1's name variable *will* refer to "Socrates." In this way, the parameter, str, has served as a storage container during the execution of the setName() method. After the method call, pet1's state will be as shown in Figure 3–7.

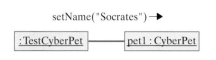

FIGURE 3–5   In this UML collaboration diagram a TestCyberPet object creates a CyberPet and then passes it the name "Socrates" by invoking its setName() method.

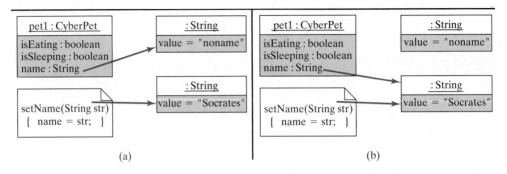

FIGURE 3–6   In (a), `pet1`'s state is shown just after the `setName("Socrates")` method is called. Note that the local parameter, `str`, and the instance variable, `name`, point to different `String` objects. In (b), `pet1`'s state is shown just after `setName()`'s assignment statement is executed. Note that both `str` and `name` point to the same `String` object.

3.2.3   Parameters and the Generality Principle

One of the nice things about parameters is that they allow us to design more general methods. To illustrate this, consider the following badly designed method:

```
public void setNameSocrates()      // Badly designed method!
{
    name = "Socrates";      // Set pet's name to "Socrates"
}
```

Like our `setName()` method, this method could be used to set the name of `pet1` to "Socrates." But it's too narrow in its design. It can't be used to set the pet's name to "Plato" or "Guinevere." In contrast, because it uses a parameter, the `setName()` method can be used to set a pet's name to anything we like. Thus, using parameters enables us to design methods *Generalizing a method* that are more general in what they do, which is an important principle of object-oriented design.

To complete this section, let's modify our `TestCyberPet` application so that it creates two pets with two different names (Fig. 3–8). The revised program will have `pet1` named "Socrates" and `pet2` named "Plato." Figure 3–9 depicts the sequence of messages between `TestCyberPet` and the two `CyberPet` objects.

Recall that output generated by our `CyberPet` class in Chapter 2 couldn't distinguish one pet from another. When we commanded `pet1` to eat, the program would output "Pet is eating." When we commanded `pet2` to eat, it would still display "Pet is eating." Now that our `CyberPets` have individual names, it is relatively simple to fix this problem. Consider the following revised versions of `println()` statements in `eat()` and `sleep()`:

```
System.out.println(name + " is eating");
System.out.println(name + " is sleeping");
```

FIGURE 3–7   `pet1`'s state after setting its name to "Socrates."

---

pet1 : CyberPet

isEating : boolean = true
isSleeping : boolean = false
name : String = "Socrates"

```
public class TestCyberPet
{
    public static void main (String argv[])
    {
        CyberPet pet1;            // Declare CyberPet variables
        CyberPet pet2;
        pet1 = new CyberPet();    // Instantiate the references
        pet1.setName("Socrates"); // Set the pet's name
        pet2 = new CyberPet();
        pet2.setName("Plato");
        pet1.eat();               // Tell pet1 to eat
        pet2.sleep();             // Tell pet2 to sleep
        pet1.sleep();             // Tell pet1 to sleep
        return;                   // Return to the system
    } // main()
} // TestCyberPet
```

FIGURE 3–8 A program to test the CyberPet class.

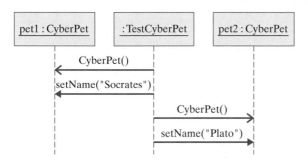

FIGURE 3–9 TestCyberPet uses a constructor to create two CyberPets and uses the setName() method to set one's name to "Socrates" and the other's to "Plato."

These modifications have been incorporated into the revised version of the CyberPet class shown in Figure 3–2. If we now run the test program shown in Figure 3–8, the following (improved) output will be generated:

```
main is starting
Socrates is eating
Plato is sleeping
Socrates is sleeping
main is finished
```

SELF-STUDY EXERCISES

EXERCISE 3.1   Explain the difference between a **method declaration** and a **method invocation**.

EXERCISE 3.2   Explain the difference between a *formal parameter* and an *argument*.

EXERCISE 3.3   Show how you would add an instance variable of type String to the CyberPet class to keep track of what kind of pet this is—for example, "dog," "cat." Write a method named setKind() that sets the pet's kind to a certain value (for example, "mouse").

EXERCISE 3.4   Write a method call statement to set pet1's kind to "mouse" and pet2's kind to "cat."

3.3 Constructor Methods

In the example just finished, we saw how we could define a mutator method, setName(), that assigns a value to a private instance variable. For some instance variables, it would be convenient to be able to set the initial values of these variables each time an object is created.

Constructor names

A **constructor** method is used to create an instance (or object) of a class. A constructor declaration looks just like a method definition except it must have the same name as the class, and it cannot declare a result type. Unlike a class's fields and methods, constructors are not considered members of the class. Therefore, they are not inherited by a class's subclasses. Access to constructors is governed by the access modifiers public and private. Here is a simple constructor for our CyberPet class:

```
public CyberPet()
{
    isSleeping = false;
    isEating = true;
}
```

Constructing an object

This constructor merely sets the initial values of the instance variables, isSleeping and isEating. In our current version of CyberPet these variables are given initial values by using initializer statements when they are first declared:

```
private boolean isSleeping = false;
private boolean isEating = true;
```

Initializing variables

So we now have two ways to initialize a class's instance variables. In the CyberPet class it doesn't really matter which way we do it. However, the constructor provides more flexibility because it allows the pet's state to be initialized at runtime. Of course, it would be somewhat redundant (though permissible) to initialize the same variable twice, once when it is declared and again in the constructor, so we should choose one or the other way to do this. For now, let's stick with initializing the instance variables when they are declared. Later we'll see some other initialization tasks a constructor can do.

EFFECTIVE DESIGN: Constructors.   Constructors provide a flexible way to initialize an object's instance variables when the object is created.

Constructors can't return a value

A constructor cannot return a value and, therefore, its declaration cannot include a return type. Because they cannot return values, constructors cannot be invoked by a regular method invocation. Instead, constructors are invoked as part of an *instance creation expression* when instance objects are created. An instance creation expression involves the keyword new followed by the constructor invocation:

```
CyberPet pet1 = new CyberPet(); // Declare and instantiate pet1
CyberPet pet2 = new CyberPet(); // Declare and instantiate pet2
```

Note here that we have combined variable declaration and instantiation into a single statement, whereas in previous examples we used separate declaration and instantiation statements. Either way is acceptable.

JAVA LANGUAGE RULE Constructors. Constructors cannot return a value. Therefore, no return type should be declared when the constructor is defined.

DEBUGGING TIP: When to Use Return. All method definitions except constructors must declare a return type.

Constructors should be used to perform the necessary initialization operations during object creation. In the case of a CyberPet object, what initializations should be performed? One initialization that would seem appropriate is to initialize the pet's name. In order to do this, we would need a constructor with a single String parameter:

State initialization

```java
public CyberPet(String str)
{
    name = str;
}
```

Now that we have this constructor we can use it when we create instances of CyberPet:

```java
CyberPet pet1 = new CyberPet("Socrates");
CyberPet pet2 = new CyberPet("Plato");
```

The effect of these two statements is the same as if we had used the set-Name() method to set the names of pet1 and pet2. The difference is that we can now set a pet's name when we create it instead of using the setName() method.

Should we keep the preceding constructor and get rid of the setName() method? No. Let's keep both in our class definition. The constructor can only be invoked as part of a new statement when the object is created. The setName() method can be called anytime we want. If we ever want to change a CyberPet's name, we will need to use setName(). So let's keep it in our class definition along with the preceding constructor.

Redundancy and flexibility

EFFECTIVE DESIGN: Using Redundancy. Incorporating some redundancy into a class, such as providing more than one way to set the value of an instance variable, makes the class more widely usable.

SELF-STUDY EXERCISES

EXERCISE 3.5 What's wrong with the following constructor definition?

```java
public void CyberPet(String s)
{
    name = str;
}
```

EXERCISE 3.6 Change the CyberPet(String) constructor so that it uses the setName() method to set the pet's name.

3.3.1 Default Constructors

As we noted in Chapter 2, when a class does not contain a constructor, Java automatically provides a *default constructor*.

> **JAVA LANGUAGE RULE** Default Constructor. If a class contains no constructor declarations, Java will automatically supply a default constructor. The default constructor takes no parameters. If the class is public, the default constructor will also be public and, hence, accessible to other objects.

The default constructor's role is simply to create an instance (an object) of that class. It takes no parameters. In terms of what it does, the default constructor for CyberPet would be equivalent to a public constructor method with an empty body:

```
public CyberPet() { }
```

This explains why the following statement is valid regardless of whether a constructor was explicitly declared in the CyberPet class:

```
CyberPet socrates = new CyberPet();
```

3.3.2 Constructor Overloading and Method Signatures

Flexible design

It is often quite useful to have more than one constructor for a given class. For example, consider the following two CyberPet constructors:

```
public CyberPet() {}           // Constructor #1

public CyberPet(String str)    // Constructor #2
{
    name = str;
}
```

The first is an explicit representation of the default constructor. The second is the constructor we defined earlier to initialize a pet's name.

Method overloading

In Java, as in some other programming languages, when two different methods have the same name, it is known as **method overloading**. In this case, CyberPet is used as the name for two distinct constructor methods. What distinguishes one constructor from another is its *signature*, which consists of its name together with the number and types of formal parameters it takes. Thus, our CyberPet constructors have the following distinct signatures:

```
CyberPet()
CyberPet(String)
```

Both have the same name, but the first takes no parameters whereas the second takes a single String parameter.

Methods are known by their signatures

The same point applies to methods in general. Two methods can have the same name as long as they have distinct signatures. A **method signature** consists of its name, and the number, types, and order of its formal parameters. A class may not contain two methods with the same signature, but it may contain several methods with the same name, provided each has a distinct signature.

> JAVA LANGUAGE RULE   Method Signature. A **method signature** consists of the method's name, plus the number, types, and order of its formal parameters. A class may not contain two methods with the same signature.

There is no limit to the amount of overloading that can be done in designing constructors and methods. The only restriction is that each method have a distinct signature. For example, suppose in addition to the two constructors we have already defined, we want a constructor that would let us set a pet's name and what kind of animal it is. To solve this problem, assume that we declare a String instance variable named kind. Given this new variable, the following constructor will do what we want:

```java
private String kind;      // What kind of pet?

public CyberPet(String nStr, String kStr)
{
    name = nStr;          // Initialize pet's name
    kind = kStr;          // Initialize pet's kind
}
```

This constructor takes two String parameters. The first is nStr, which is meant to be passed a string representing the pet's name. The second is kStr, which is meant to be passed a string representing its kind. In the method itself, the first string is assigned to name and the second to kind. When we call this constructor, we will have to take care to pass a name as the value of the first argument and a kind as the value of the second argument:

```java
CyberPet pet3 = new CyberPet("Buddy", "dog");
CyberPet pet4 = new CyberPet("Petunia", "pig");
```

Passing values

When passing values to a method, Java passes the first argument to the first parameter, the second argument to the second parameter, and so forth. If we mistakenly reversed "Buddy" and "dog" in the first of these statements, we would end up with a CyberPet named "dog" whose kind was "Buddy."

We have now defined three constructor methods for the CyberPet class. Each constructor has the name CyberPet, but each has a distinct signature:

```java
CyberPet()
CyberPet(String)
CyberPet(String, String)
```

3.3.3 Constructor Invocation

A constructor is invoked once to create an object

A constructor method is invoked only once, as part of a new expression, when an instance object is first created. Each of these is a valid invocation of a CyberPet constructor:

```
CyberPet pet1 = new CyberPet();              // Default constructor
pet1.setName("Pet1");                        // So use setName()
CyberPet pet2 = new CyberPet("Pet2");        // Sets the pet's name
CyberPet pet3 = new CyberPet("Pet3", "dog"); // Sets name and kind
```

As the comments indicate, the first constructor is the default constructor, which doesn't set either the name or kind. So we need to call setName() (in line 2) to set the name of pet1. The constructor used for pet2 sets its name, and the constructor used for pet3 sets both name and kind.

The following constructor invocations are invalid because there are no matching constructor definitions:

```
CyberPet pet4 = new CyberPet(true);   // No matching constructors
CyberPet pet5 = new CyberPet("Pet2" , "dog", "sleeping");
```

In the first case, there is no constructor method that takes a boolean parameter, so there's no matching constructor. In the second case, there is no constructor that takes three String arguments. In both cases, the Java compiler would complain that there is no constructor method that matches the invocation.

DEBUGGING TIP: Method Call. The signature of the method call—its name and the number, types, and order of its arguments—must exactly match the signature of the method definition.

3.4 Retrieving Information from an Object

The modifications we've made to the CyberPet class allow us to set a CyberPet's name, but there is no way for us to retrieve a CyberPet's name. We declared CyberPet's name field as private, so we cannot access it directly. Therefore, we will need an accessor method to *get* a CyberPet's name. Consider the following method definition:

```
public String getName()
{
    return name;
}
```

Recall again that the general form of a method declaration is

$$MethodModifiers_{opt} \quad ResultType \quad MethodName \quad (\, FormalParameterList \,)$$
$$MethodBody$$

and note that a method's *ResultType* is specified just in front of the *Method-Name*. The eat(), sleep(), and setName() methods did not return a value. So in each case their result types were declared as void (see Fig. 3–2). In this case, we want getName() to return a String that represents the CyberPet's name. Therefore, its result type is declared String.

Note that this definition of getName() has an empty parameter list. Because we will not be passing it any information, it does not need formal parameters. This is not to say that a method that returns a value cannot have a parameter list. For example, consider the following method, which returns the average of its two `double` parameters:

```
public double average (double n1, double n2)
{
    return (n1 + n2) / 2;   // Return the average of n1 and n2
}
```

Note that this method requires both a formal parameter list and a nonvoid return value.

3.4.1   Invoking a Method That Returns a Value

When we invoke a method that returns a value, the invocation expression takes on, or becomes, the value that is returned. For example, if we execute the statements

Retrieving information

```
pet1.setName("Socrates");
pet1.getName();
```

the expression `pet1.getName()` will take on the value "Socrates" after the `getName()` method is finished executing. We can manipulate this value the same way we manipulate any other `String` in a Java program. We can use `System.out.println()` method to output "Socrates" on the Java console:

```
System.out.println(pet1.getName()); // Prints "Socrates"
```

This is an example of a *nested method call*, in which `pet1.getName()` is *nested* inside the expression `System.out.println()`. To evaluate expressions such as these, proceed from the inside out—that is, from the inner-most nested parentheses. In this case, the method call `pet1.getName()` is being passed as an argument to the `System.out.println()` method. Because the value of `pet1.getName()` is "Socrates," this is the same as if `println()` were being passed the argument "Socrates." Before an argument can be passed to a method, it must first be evaluated. In this case, the argument, `pet1.getName()`, is evaluated by invoking `pet1`'s `getName()` method, which returns the value "Socrates." Thus, the value that gets passed to `println()` is "Socrates".

Nested expressions

Another way that we can use the value produced by the method call `pet1.getName()` is to assign it to a `String` variable:

```
String myString ;
myString = pet1.getName();  // Stores "Socrates" in myString
```

The result of these two statements is that `myString` would now have "Socrates" as its value. Thus, when you invoke a method that returns a value, the method invocation expression— `pet1.getName()`—becomes the value that is returned. So `pet1.getName()` becomes "Socrates" and can be manipulated in the same way that any other `String` can be manipulated.

Evaluating a method call

Evaluating Method Calls. A nonvoid method call is an expression that has a value. Nonvoid methods return a value of a particular type.

Figure 3–10 provides a UML representation of the expanded Cyber-Pet class, and Figure 3–11 shows the complete definition of the revised CyberPet class.

Let's also modify TestCyberPet to make use of the getName() method, as shown in Figure 3–12. Our new version of TestCyberPet now contains the following sequence of statements in its main() method:

```
CyberPet
```
CyberPet
– isEating : boolean
– isSleeping : boolean
– name : String
+ CyberPet()
+ CyberPet(in str : String)
+ setName(in str : String)
+ getName() : String
+ eat()
+ sleep()

FIGURE 3–10   A UML class diagram of the expanded CyberPet class.

```java
public class CyberPet
{
    // Data
    private boolean isEating = true;     // CyberPet's state
    private boolean isSleeping = false;
    private String name = "no name";     // CyberPet's name
    // Methods
    public CyberPet() {}                 // Explicit default constructor

    public CyberPet(String str)          // Constructor method
    {
        name = str;
    }

    public void setName(String str) // Access method
    {
        name = str;
    } // setName()

    public String getName()              // Access method
    {
        return name;                     // Return CyberPet's name
    } // getName()

    public void eat()                    // Start eating
    {
        isEating = true;                 // Change the state
        isSleeping = false;
        System.out.println(name + " is eating");
        return;
    } // eat()

    public void sleep()                  // Start sleeping
    {
        isSleeping = true;               // Change the state
        isEating = false;
        System.out.println(name + " is sleeping");
        return;
    } // sleep()
} // CyberPet
```

FIGURE 3–11   The CyberPet class with the CyberPet(String) constructor and getName() methods added.

```
public class TestCyberPet
{
    public static void main (String argv[])
    {
        CyberPet pet1;                        // Declare CyberPet variables
        CyberPet pet2;
        pet1 = new CyberPet("Socrates");      // Create pet1 named "Socrates"
        System.out.println("pet1's name is ");
        System.out.println(pet1.getName());   // Print pet1's name
        pet2 = new CyberPet("Plato");         // Create pet2 named "Plato"
        System.out.println("pet2's name is ");
        System.out.println(pet2.getName());   // Print pet2's name
        pet1.eat();                           // Tell pet1 to eat
        pet2.sleep();                         // Tell pet2 to sleep
        return;                               // Return to the system
    } // main()
} // TestCyberPet
```

FIGURE 3–12   TestCyberPet now contains statements to get a pet's name.

```
pet1 = new CyberPet("Socrates");      // Create pet1 named "Socrates"
System.out.print("pet1's name is ");
System.out.println(pet1.getName()); // Print pet1's name
pet2 = new CyberPet("Plato");         // Create pet2 named "Plato"
System.out.print("pet2's name is ");
System.out.println(pet2.getName()); // Print pet2's name
```

The first statement sets pet1's name to "Socrates." The second statement produces the message "pet1's name is" on the standard output device. The third statement calls the getName() method to retrieve pet1's name ("Socrates") and then displays it on the screen. Similarly, the next three statements set, retrieve, and output pet2's name. The result of these six statements is that the following output would be printed on the screen:

```
pet1's name is Socrates
pet2's name is Plato
```

SELF-STUDY EXERCISES

EXERCISE 3.7   What would these segments of Java code display on the screen?

```
CyberPet myPet = new CyberPet("Fido");
System.out.println(myPet.getName());

CyberPet myPet2 = new CyberPet("Trigger");
System.out.println(myPet2.getName());
```

EXERCISE 3.8   Write a Java method for the CyberPet class to *get* a CyberPet's kind where kind is an instance variable of type String.

EXERCISE 3.9   Write a method to return a description of a CyberPet—for example, "Fido is a dog."

3.5   Passing a Value and Passing a Reference

The effect of passing arguments to a method differs depending on whether you are passing a value of **primitive type** (such as 5 or true) or a value of **reference type** (such as "Socrates" or pet1). See Section 2.3.4 for a review of the distinction between primitive and reference types. When an argument of primitive type is passed to a method, a copy of the argument is passed to the formal parameter. For example, consider the PrimitiveCall class shown in Figure 3–13. Note that we have an int variable k, which initially stores the value 5, and a method myMethod(), which takes an int parameter n. In this case, when we invoke myMethod(k), k's value (5) is copied into n and stored there during the method.

Passing a primitive value

FIGURE 3–13   Passing a primitive value to a method.

```java
public class PrimitiveCall
{
    public static void myMethod(int n)
    {
        System.out.println("myMethod: n= " + n);
        n = 100;
        System.out.println("myMethod: n= " + n);
    } // myMethod()

    public static void main(String argv[])
    {
        int k = 5;
        System.out.println("main: k= " + k);
        myMethod(k);
        System.out.println("main: k= " + k);
    } // main()
} // PrimitiveCall
```

One implication of passing a copy of a primitive value to a method is that the original value of k in main() cannot be altered from inside the method. Thus, the output generated by PrimitiveCall would be

```
main: k= 5
myMethod: n= 5
myMethod: n= 100
main: k= 5
```

Note that in main(), k's value is printed both before and after myMethod() is called, but that its value remains unaffected even though n's value is changed within the method. This is because myMethod() has just a *copy* of k's value, not k itself. So any changes to the copy within myMethod() leave k unaltered.

JAVA LANGUAGE RULE   *Passing a Primitive Value.* When a value of a primitive type—boolean, int—is passed to a method, a copy of the value is passed. That's why its original value remains unchanged outside the method, even if the copy is changed inside the method.

In contrast to this, when an argument of a reference type is passed to a method, a copy of the reference to the object itself is assigned to the parameter. We saw an example of this in Figure 3–6. For example, in the

```
public class ReferenceCall
{
    public static void myMethod(CyberPet p)
    {
        System.out.println("myMethod: pet name is " + p.getName());
        p.setName("Mary");
        System.out.println("myMethod: pet name is " + p.getName());
    } // myMethod()

    public static void main(String argv[])
    {
        CyberPet pet = new CyberPet();
        pet.setName("Harry");
        System.out.println("main: pet name is " + pet.getName());
        myMethod(pet);
        System.out.println("main: pet name is " + pet.getName());
    }// main()
} // ReferenceCall
```

FIGURE 3–14 Passing a reference value to a method.

case of a String parameter or a CyberPet parameter, the method would be passed a reference directly to the object itself. (The object itself is *not* passed, because it would be too inefficient to copy the entire object with all its data and methods.) However, because a reference is really a pointer to an object, the method will have access to the object and can make changes to the object from within the method.

For example, consider the ReferenceCall class (Fig. 3–14). In this case, myMethod() takes a parameter p of type CyberPet. Because CyberPet is an object, p is a reference variable. So when myMethod(pet) is invoked in main(), a reference to pet is passed to myMethod() (Fig. 3–15a). Note that in myMethod(), we use setName() to change the name of p from "Harry" to "Mary," and that this change persists even after the method returns (Fig. 3–15b). The reason is that during the method's execution, both pet and p refer to the exact same object. The output generated by Reference-Call would be

```
main: pet name is Harry
myMethod: pet name is Harry
myMethod: pet name is Mary
main: pet name is Mary
```

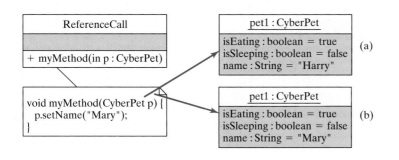

FIGURE 3–15 In (a), when myMethod(pet1) is called, p points to pet1. In (b), myMethod() has changed pet1's name to "Mary." This change will persist when the method returns.

This illustrates that when passing a reference variable to a method, it is possible for the method to change the state of the object associated with the reference variable. In subsequent chapters we will see ways to make use of this feature of reference parameters.

> **JAVA LANGUAGE RULE** Passing a Reference. When a reference to an object is passed to a method, any changes made to the object from within the method will persist when the method is done.

> DEBUGGING TIP: Side Effects. An unintended change to an object is called a **side effect**. Care should be taken in designing methods that the method does not produce unwanted side effects in objects passed as reference parameters.

3.6   Flow of Control: Selection Control Structures

In this section, we will introduce control structures that will enable us to write methods that have more than one execution path. Suppose we want to write a method that will tell us a CyberPet's state (eating or sleeping) at any given time.

What information should the method receive and return?

Like the getName() method, the getState() method should return a String that describes the CyberPet's state. When CyberPet is sleeping, getState() should return "Sleeping," and when the CyberPet is eating, getState() should return "Eating." Because there is no need to pass the CyberPet any information in this case, this method does not require any formal parameters. Following these design decisions, we can devise a preliminary implementation of getState():

```
public String getState()
{
    return "Error in State";
}
```

Stepwise refinement

Recall from the lab exercise in Chapter 1 that a **stub method** consists of a complete header and an incomplete body. If this version of getState() were added to the CyberPet class in this form, it would always return "Error in State" when invoked. Note that the following definition would not be a correct stub for the getState() method, because it does not return a String:

```
public String getState() {}
```

The Java compiler would flag this as an error. The rule is that any method that has a nonvoid result type must contain a return statement.

> **JAVA LANGUAGE RULE** Method Return. A nonvoid method must contain a return statement, and the method's algorithm must ensure that the return statement will, in fact, be executed.

> DEBUGGING TIP: Nonvoid Stub Methods. For nonvoid methods, a *stub method* must return a value of the appropriate type.

3.6.1 The Simple If Statement

Let's now use stepwise refinement to complete the body of this method. *Algorithm design*
In this case, we want getState() to return "Sleeping" when CyberPet is
sleeping (that is, when isSleeping is true) and "Eating" when the CyberPet
is eating (when isEating is true). Consider the definition of getState():

```java
public String getState()
{
    if (isEating)
        return "Eating";        // Exit the method
    if (isSleeping)
        return "Sleeping";      // Exit the method
    return "Error in State";    // Exit the method
}
```

The getState() method makes use of two *if statements* to select between
alternative execution paths or results ("Eating" or "Sleeping"). The first
if statement tests whether isEating is true, and if so returns the String
"Eating" and exits the method. If this path is taken, then the rest of the
statements in the method are not executed. Control returns immediately
to the calling method because the return statement is executed.

If isEating is false, the return statement is not executed and control
drops down to the second if statement, which tests whether isSleeping is
true. If so, it returns the String "Sleeping" and exits the method. If not, control drops down to the last statement in the method, and the String "Error
in State" is returned. Notice that if neither isEating nor isSleeping is true,
then this indeed constitutes an error in the CyberPet's state, because one
or the other (but not both) of these variables must be true in order for the
CyberPet model to be in a consistent state.

The if statement is an example of the **selection** control structure, be- *Selecting a path*
cause it allows the program to select one or the other of two alternative
paths of execution.

> **JAVA LANGUAGE RULE** If Statement. The *if statement* has the following
> syntax:
>
> $$\text{if} \quad (\textit{boolean expression})$$
> $$\textit{statement};$$

The statement contained in the if statement can be any valid Java statement, including a compound statement. A boolean expression is an expression that is either true or false. As we saw in the previous chapter, the simplest possible boolean expression is the boolean literal true
or false. Similarly, a boolean variable, such as isSleeping, which has a
value of either true or false, is another example of a boolean expression.
A third example of a boolean expression would be the equality expression
isSleeping == false.

> **JAVA LANGUAGE RULE** Equality Operator. The == is Java's equality op-
> erator, and the expression isSleeping == false says "isSleeping equals
> false," an expression which itself is either true or false.

DEBUGGING TIP: Equals versus Assigns. A common error is to use the assignment operator (=) where the equality operator (==) is intended.

Given this description of if statement syntax, the following are examples of valid if statements:

```
if (true) System.out.println("Hello");
if (isSleeping == false) System.out.println("not sleeping");
```

For readability, we usually write an if statement with its contained statement indented on the next line:

```
if (true)
    System.out.println("Hello");
if (isSleeping == false)
    System.out.println("not sleeping");
```

The following are all examples of syntax errors involving the if statement:

```
if true                         // Parentheses are missing
    System.out.println("Hello"); //  around the boolean expression

if (isSleeping) return          // Semicolon missing at end

if ("true") return;             // "true" is a String not a boolean

if (true) "Hello";              // "Hello" is a value not a statement
```

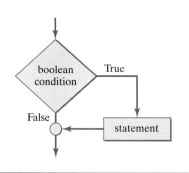

FIGURE 3–16 Flowchart of the if statement. Diamond-shaped symbols at the branch points contain `boolean` expressions. Rectangular symbols can only contain executable statements. Circles act simply as connectors, to connect two or more paths.

If statement semantics

Semantically, the if statement has the following interpretation: First, the **boolean expression** or *boolean condition* is evaluated. If it is true, then the contained *statement* is executed; if it is false, then the contained *statement* is not executed. This is shown in Figure 3–16. The flowchart clearly shows that program flow will take one or the other of the alternative paths coming out of the diamond-shaped boolean condition box. The branch through the rectangular statement box will be taken when the boolean condition is true; otherwise the statement will be skipped.

The flowchart in Figure 3–17 shows the program flow of the entire get-State() method. It is important to note that when a `return` statement is executed in a method, control is returned immediately to the calling method. Thus, if isEating is true, the string "Eating" is returned to the calling method and the getState() method exits at this point. If it is false, then isSleeping should be true (if we have a consistent state) and the string "Sleeping" should be returned and the method exited. Thus, if we have a consistent state—that is, if the pet is either eating or sleeping—then the third `return` statement should never be reached.

As the following example shows, the statement contained in an if statement can be a compound statement:

Compound statement

```
if (isSleeping)
{
    String s = "sleeping";
    System.out.print (name);
    System.out.println (" is sleeping ");
    return s;
}
```

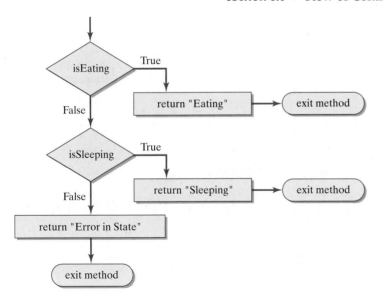

FIGURE 3-17   Flowchart of the `getState()` method.

If `isSleeping` is true, then all four statements in the contained compound statement will be executed. Note here that we are declaring the local variable s in this block. Its scope would extend to the end of the block. Note also that when we use a compound statement, the compound statement itself is not followed by a semicolon because it is already enclosed in braces.

Local scope

A common programming error is to forget the braces around the compound statement. Merely indenting the statements following the if clause doesn't alter the logic of the if statement. For example, the following if statement still has only one statement in its if clause:

```
if (condition1)
    System.out.println("One");
    System.out.println("Two");  // Not part of if's scope
```

This segment will always print "Two" because the second `println()` is not part of the if statement. To include it in the if statement, you must enclose both `println()` statements within braces:

```
if (condition1)
{
    System.out.println("One");
    System.out.println("Two");
}
```

DEBUGGING TIP: Indentation. Indentation can improve the readability of a program but doesn't affect its logic. Braces must be used to group statements in the if clause.

3.6.2 The `if-else` Statement

A second version of the if statement incorporates an *else clause* into the structure. This allows us to execute either of two separate statements (simple or compound) as the result of one boolean expression. For example, the statement

```java
if (isEating)
    System.out.println("Is Eating");
else
    System.out.println("Is NOT Eating");
```

will print "Is Eating" if `isEating` is true. Otherwise, it will print "Is NOT Eating".

> **JAVA LANGUAGE RULE** If-else Statement. The *if-else statement* has the following syntax:
>
> $$if \quad (\textit{boolean expression})$$
> $$\textit{statement1} ;$$
> $$else$$
> $$\textit{statement2} ;$$

If-else syntax

As in the case of the simple if statement, the keyword `if` is followed by a parenthesized *boolean expression*, which is followed by *statement1*, which may be either simple or compound. If *statement1* is a simple statement, then it is followed by a semicolon. The *else clause* follows immediately after *statement1*. It begins with the keyword `else`, which is followed by *statement2*, which can also be either a simple or compound statement. Note that there is no boolean expression following the `else` keyword. In an if-else statement, the boolean expression following the keyword `if` goes with both the if and else clauses.

If-else semantics

Semantically, the if-else statement has the following interpretation: If the *boolean expression* is true, execute *statement1*; otherwise execute *statement2*. This interpretation is shown in Figure 3–18.

3.6.3 The Nested if/else Multiway Selection Structure

The statements that one inserts in place of *statement1* and *statement2* in the if-else statement can be any executable statement, including another if statement or if-else statement. In other words, it is possible to embed one or more if-else statements inside another if-else statement, thereby creating a *nested* control structure. As with most things, making a control structure too complex isn't a good idea, but there is a standard nested if-else control structure that is very useful. It is known as **multiway selection**. As shown in Figure 3–19, the multiway structure is used when you want to select one and only one option from several alternatives.

Suppose we have a CyberPet that can be in one of three states: eating, sleeping, or thinking. In the example shown in Figure 3–19 there are three alternatives plus an error state. Here is the Java code for this example:

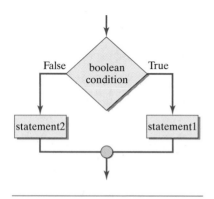

FIGURE 3–18 Flowchart of the `if-else` statement.

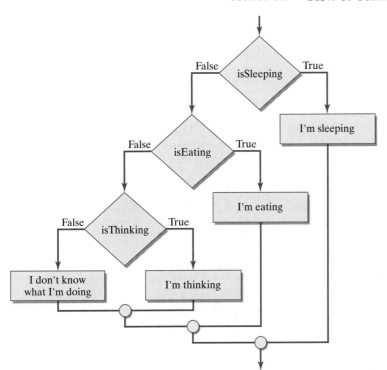

FIGURE 3–19 Flowchart of a nested if-else statement.

```
if (isSleeping)
    System.out.println("I'm sleeping");
else if (isEating)
    System.out.println("I'm eating");
else if (isThinking)
    System.out.println("I'm thinking");
else
    System.out.println("Error: I don't know what I'm doing");
```

Note that the multiway structure has a single entry point and that only one of the four possible alternatives is executed. The CyberPet will print either that it is sleeping, eating, thinking, or that it doesn't know what it is doing.

Multiple alternatives

We will have many occasions to use the if-else structure. Although it does not represent a significant change, we can rewrite our getState() method to make use of the if-else instead of the simple if statement, as follows:

```
public String getState()
{
    if (isEating)
        return "Eating";          // Exit the method
    else
        return "Sleeping";        // Exit the method
}
```

In some respects this version of getState() is simpler. It has only one boolean condition to test, and because isEating must be either true or false, one or the other of "Eating" or "Sleeping" will be returned as the result. There's no longer a need for a `return "Error"` statement at the end of the method, because it would never be reached—`isEating` has to be either true or false. The flowchart for this version of `getState()` is left as an exercise.

3.6.4   The Dangling Else Problem

Dangling else

One of the traditional problems associated with the if-else statement is the **dangling else** problem. This is a problem primarily for the programmer, not the computer. Consider the following nested if-else statement:

```
if (condition1)
    if (condition2)
        System.out.println("One");
else
    System.out.println("Two");
```

From the way this statement is laid out and indented, it looks as if the else clause goes with the first if statement, such that if `condition1` were false, then "Two" would be printed. However, this is *not* what happens. If `condition1` were false, neither "One" nor "Two" would be printed. The rule in Java is this:

> **JAVA LANGUAGE RULE**   Nested if-else. Within a nested if-else statement, an else clause matches with the closest previous unmatched if clause.

According to this rule, the else clause is matched with the second if clause (`condition2`). So if `condition1` were false, nothing would be printed. The flowchart in Figure 3–20 illustrates the proper interpretation of this statement. The proper indentation for this statement should help to clarify its syntactic and semantic structure:

```
if (condition1)
    if (condition2)
        System.out.println("One");
    else
        System.out.println("Two");
```

In this case, the else clause is properly aligned under its matching if clause. Of course, because Java is a free-form language, indentation is simply ignored by the compiler and has no effect on the syntax of a statement. So although indentation makes the code more readable, it doesn't change the way the code is interpreted.

> DEBUGGING TIP: Indentation. Indentation can improve the readability of a program but doesn't affect its logic.

What if we want "Two" to be printed when `condition1` is false? In that case, we would have to use braces to associate the else clause with the first if clause:

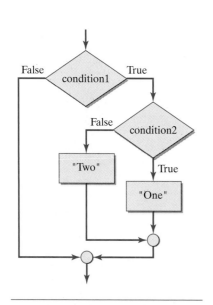

FIGURE 3–20   Proper interpretation of a dangling else statement.

```
if (condition1)
{
    if (condition2)
        System.out.println("One");
}
else
    System.out.println("Two");
```

In this case, the statement associated with condition2 does not contain an else clause; the braces turn it into a simple if statement. Therefore, the else clause now matches the first if clause, which is now the closest previous unmatched if clause.

Whenever there is a chance of ambiguity, it is always best to use braces to clarify the if-else structure. Similarly, take care to use proper indentation when coding if-else statements. Else clauses should be aligned with their corresponding if clauses as in the examples we have discussed. These practices will make the code more readable and may help to avoid subtle errors.

Using indentation and brackets

PROGRAMMING TIP: If-else Statements.   Take care when coding if-else statements to make sure that else clauses are aligned with their corresponding if clauses. Braces may be necessary to achieve the proper logical relationship.

SELF-STUDY EXERCISES

EXERCISE 3.10   Draw a flowchart for the if-else version of the getState() method. Use the figures in this section as a guide. Each if-else structure should be drawn exactly as shown in Figure 3–18. It should have a single entry point that leads directly to the top of a diamond-shaped box that contains a boolean condition. There should be two branches coming out of the condition box. The one going to the right is the true case, and the one going to the left is the false case. Each of these branches should contain one rectangular box, which contains the statements that would be executed in that case. The left and right branches should be connected by a circular symbol that is aligned directly under the diamond box whose conditions it connects. There should be a single exit arrow pointing directly down.

Flowchart symbols

EXERCISE 3.11   Identify the error in the following statements:

```
if (isEating == true)
    System.out.println("Eating");
else ;
    System.out.println("Sleeping");

if (isEating == true)
    System.out.println("Eating")
else
    System.out.println("Sleeping");
```

EXERCISE 3.12 Suppose we had a pet model with three possible states, eating, sleeping, and playing, represented by three boolean variables, isEating, isSleeping, and isPlaying. Write a getState() method that returns a String spelling out the state for this version of the pet model.

EXERCISE 3.13 How does a parameter for a primitive type differ from a parameter for a reference type?

3.6.5 The switch Multiway Selection Structure

Another selection structure to add to our repertoire is the **switch/break structure**. It is meant to provide a shorthand way of coding the following type of multiway selection structure:

```
if (integralVar == integralValue1)
    // some statements
else if (integralVar == integralValue2)
    // some statements
else if (integralVar == integralValue3)
    // some statements
else
    // some statements
```

Note that each of the conditions in this case involves the equality of an integral variable and an integral value. This type of structure occurs so frequently in programs that most languages contain statements specially designed to handle it. In Java, we use a combination of the switch and break statements to implement multiway selection.

The switch is designed to select one of several actions depending on the value of some integral expression:

```
switch (integralExpression)
{
    case integralValue1:
        some statements
    case integralValue2:
        some statements
    case integralValue3:
        some statements
    default:
        some statements
}
```

Integral expression

The *integralExpression* must evaluate to a primitive integral value—that is, a byte, short, int, char, long, or boolean. It may not be a float, double, or a class type. The *integralValues* must be literals or final variables. They serve as labels in the one or more case clauses that make up the switch statement body. The default clause is optional, but it is a good idea to include it.

A switch statement is executed according to the following rules:

1. The *integralExpression* is evaluated.
2. Control passes to the statements following the case label whose value equals the *integralExpression* or, if no cases apply, to the default clause.
3. Beginning at the selected label or at the default, all of the statements up to the end of the switch are executed.

Consider the following example:

```
int m = 2;
switch (m)
{
    case 1:
        System.out.println("m = 1");
    case 2:
        System.out.println("m = 2");
    case 3:
        System.out.println("m = 3");
    default:
        System.out.println("default case");
}
```

In this case, because *m* equals 2, the following output would be produced:

```
m = 2
m = 3
default case
```

Obviously, this output does not match the following if-else multiway selection structure, which would output, simply, m = 2:

```
int m = 2;
if (m == 1)
    System.out.println("m = 1");
else if (m == 2)
    System.out.println("m = 2");
else if (m == 3)
    System.out.println("m = 3");
else
    System.out.println("default case");
```

The reason for this disparity is that the switch executes *all* statements following the label that matches the value of the *integralExpression* (see again Rule 3 on page 142). In order to use the switch as a multiway selection, you must force it to break out of the case clause after executing that clause's statements:

```
int m = 2;
switch (m)
{
    case 1:
        System.out.println("m = 1");
        break;
    case 2:
        System.out.println("m = 2");
        break;
    case 3:
        System.out.println("m = 3");
        break;
    default:
        System.out.println("default case");
}
```

FIGURE 3–21 Flowchart of the multiway switch structure. Note that because of the break statement, one and only one case is executed.

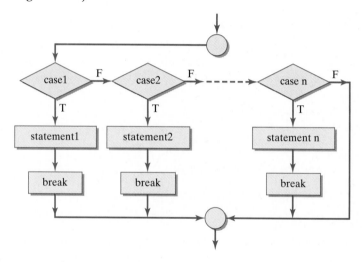

In this example, the break statement causes control to pass to the end of the switch, with the effect being that one and only one case will be executed within the switch. Thus, the output of this code segment will be simply m = 2, matching exactly the behavior of the multiway if-else selection structure (Fig. 3–21).

PROGRAMMING TIP: Multiway Selection. A typical use for the switch statement is to use it together with break to code a multiway selection structure.

JAVA LANGUAGE RULE break. The break statement transfers control out of its enclosing *block*, where a block is any sequence of statements contained within curly brackets { and }.

DEBUGGING TIP: Switch without break. A common error in coding the switch-based multiway selection is forgetting to put a break statement at the end of each clause. This may cause more than one case to be executed.

SELF-STUDY EXERCISES

EXERCISE 3.14 Identify any errors in the following switch structures (if there is no error, specify the output):

```
(a) int k = 0;
    switch (k)
    case 0:
        System.out.println("zero");
        break;
    case 1:
        System.out.println("one");
        break;
    default:
        System.out.println("default");
        break;
```

```
(b) int k = 0;
    switch (k + 1)
    {
        case 0:
            System.out.println("zero");
            break;
        case 1:
            System.out.println("one");
            break;
        default:
            System.out.println("default");
            break;
    }
(c) int k = 6;
    switch (k / 3.0)
    {
        case 2:
            System.out.println("zero");
            break;
        case 3:
            System.out.println("one");
            break;
        default:
            System.out.println("default");
            break;
    }
```

EXERCISE 3.15 Flavors of ice cream are represented as integers where 0 is vanilla, 1 is chocolate, and 2 is strawberry. Write a switch statement that checks an integer variable flavor and prints out the name of the ice cream flavor or prints "Error" in the default case.

EXERCISE 3.16 Modify your solution to the previous exercise to use constants (final variables) to represent the ice cream flavors.

3.7   The Improved CyberPet

The final version (for this chapter) of the CyberPet class has the design summarized in Figure 3–22. It has grown in an incremental fashion from a very simple class into one that contains quite a few elements. Compared to our first version (in Chapter 2), this version of CyberPet presents an interface (to other objects) that is easy and convenient to use. The accessor methods, getName() and getState(), and the mutator method, setName(), provide convenient means to find out the CyberPet's name and state and to set or reset its name. The constructor method provides an easy way to initialize CyberPet instances. At the same time, our use of private instance variables prevents other objects from tampering with a CyberPet's state.

Its complete implementation is shown in Figure 3–23. Note that we have deleted the statements that output the pet's state in the eat() and sleep() methods. Because CyberPet() now has a getState() method, we can print the pet's state in the main() method, as shown in the revised version of TestCyberPet (Fig. 3–24). Note that a single println() statement

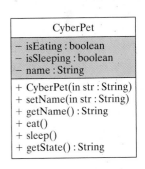

FIGURE 3–22 This version of CyberPet has six methods in its interface.

FIGURE 3–23   The CyberPet class, including the getState() method.

```java
public class CyberPet
{
    private boolean isEating = true;      // CyberPet's state
    private boolean isSleeping = false;
    private String name = "no name";      // CyberPet's name

    public CyberPet (String str)          // Constructor method
    {
        name = str;
    }

    public void setName (String str)      // Access method
    {
        name = str;
    } // setName()

    public String getName()
    {
        return name;                      // Return CyberPet's name
    } // getName()

    public void eat()              // Start eating
    {
        isEating = true;           // Change the state
        isSleeping = false;
        return;
    } // eat()

    public void sleep()            // Start sleeping
    {
        isSleeping = true;         // Change the state
        isEating = false;
        return;
    } // sleep()

    public String getState ()
    {
        if (isEating)
            return "Eating";       // Exit the method
        if (isSleeping)
            return "Sleeping";     // Exit the method
        return "Error in State";   // Exit the method
    } // getState()
} // CyberPet
```

```
public class TestCyberPet
{
    public static void main (String argv[])
    {
        CyberPet pet1;                      // Declare CyberPet variables
        CyberPet pet2;
        pet1 = new CyberPet("Socrates");// Create pet1 named "Socrates"
        pet2 = new CyberPet("Plato");   // Create pet2 named "Plato"
                                        // Print the pets' names and states
        System.out.println(pet1.getName() + " is " + pet1.getState());
        System.out.println(pet2.getName() + " is " + pet2.getState());
        pet1.eat();                     // Tell pet1 to eat
        pet2.sleep();                   // Tell pet2 to sleep
                                        // Print the pets' names and states
        System.out.println(pet1.getName() + " is " + pet1.getState());
        System.out.println(pet2.getName() + " is " + pet2.getState());
        return;                         // Return to the system
    } // main()
} // TestCyberPet
```

FIGURE 3–24 TestCyberPet now contains statements to get a pet's name.

can be used to print both the pet's name and its state by concatenating the results of the calls to the getName() and getState() methods:

```
System.out.println(pet1.getName() + " is " + pet1.getState());
```

Equally important, our design of the CyberPet class makes appropriate use of Java's access modifiers, private and public, to control access to the individual CyberPet objects. By making the CyberPet's instance variables private, we ensure that other objects cannot corrupt its state, thus ensuring its integrity. At the same time, by providing public accessor and mutator methods, we allow other objects to interact with CyberPets in ways that make sense and preserve their integrity. Taken together, the public methods provide other objects with an *interface* that they can use to communicate with individual CyberPet objects.

Information hiding

Public interface

EFFECTIVE DESIGN: Interfaces. Well-designed objects provide a useful public interface and protect the object's private elements from other objects.

Object-oriented design

To reiterate a point made at the outset, object-oriented programming is a process of constructing objects that will interact with each other. Object-oriented programs must ensure that the objects themselves are well designed in terms of their ability to carry out their designated functions. Good design in this sense requires careful selection of instance variables and careful design of methods to ensure that the object can carry out its assigned tasks. However, equal care must be taken to ensure that the interactions that take place among objects are constrained in ways that make sense for that particular program. This aspect of designing objects comes into play in designing the methods—constructor, accessor, and mutator methods—that make up the object's interface.

Intelligent Agents

WOULDN'T IT be nice if we had a CyberPet that could schedule appointments for us, remind us of meetings and commitments, find information for us on the WWW, and manage our e-mail messages for us? Wouldn't it be nice to have a personal assistant CyberPet?

Actually such programs are called *intelligent agents* and intelligent agent technology is becoming an important research area in computer science. An intelligent agent is a program that is capable of acting autonomously to carry out certain tasks. Most agent programs incorporate some kind of machine learning capability, so that their performance improves over time.

As a typical agent activity, suppose I was able to tell my CyberPet to buy me a copy of a certain book that I just heard about. Given a command like "buy me a copy of X," the agent would perform a search of online book sellers and come up with the best deal. Once it had found the best buy, the agent would communicate with a computer-based agent representing the book seller. My agent would make the order and pay for it (assuming I gave it authority to do so), and the book seller's agent would process the order.

As far-fetched as the capability may now seem, this is the direction that research in this area is headed. Researchers are developing agent languages and describing protocols that agents can use to exchange information in a reliable and trustworthy environment. Obviously, you wouldn't want your agent to give your money to a fraudulent book seller, so there are significant problems to solve in this area that go well beyond the problem of simply exchanging information between two agents.

The best way to learn more about this research area is to do a Web search using the search string "Intelligent Agent." There are numerous research groups and companies that provide online descriptions and demos of their products.

From the Java Library

`java.lang.Object`

http://java.sun.com/products
/jdk/1.3/docs/api/

THE MOST general class in Java's class hierarchy is the `java.lang.Object` class. It is the superclass of all classes that occur in Java programs. By default, it is the direct superclass of any class that does not explicitly specify a pedigree in its class definition.

The `public` and `protected` methods contained in `Object` are *inherited* by all of its subclasses—which means by all classes, because every class is a subclass of `Object`. In this section, let's look briefly at how we can use an inherited method and also at how we can *override* it, if it doesn't exactly suit our purposes.

One of the most useful method's in the `Object` class is the `toString()` method:

```
public class Object
{
    public String toString() ;
}
```

The `toString()` method returns a `String` representation of its object. For example, `o1.toString()` will return a `String` that in some sense describes o1.

Because `CyberPet` is a subclass of `Object`, it inherits the `toString()` method (Fig. 3–25). To illustrate the default behavior of `toString()`, let's use it with a `CyberPet` instance:

```java
CyberPet p1 = new CyberPet("Ernie");
CyberPet p2 = new CyberPet("Bert");
System.out.println(p1.toString());
System.out.println(p2.toString());
```

This code segment creates two `CyberPets`, one named "Ernie" and the other named "Bert." The inherited `toString()` method is then invoked on each `CyberPet`, which produces the following output:

```
CyberPet@1dc6077b
CyberPet@1dc60776
```

What this experiment shows is that the default definition of `toString()` returns some kind of internal representation of its object. It looks as if it returns the name of the object's class concatenated with its memory address. This may be useful for some applications. But for most objects we will want to *override* the default definition to make the `toString()` method return a string that is a bit more descriptive.

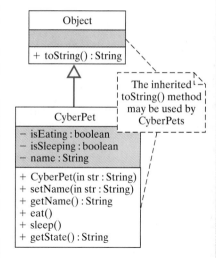

FIGURE 3–25   As a subclass of `Object`, the `CyberPet` class inherits the `toString()` method.

Method Design: toString()

What `String` should the `CyberPet.toString()` method return? Let's have it return a `String` that reports the `CyberPet`'s name and current state. To override a method, you simply define a method with the exact same signature in the subclass. If we override the `toString()` method, we get the design shown in Figure 3–26. In this case, there are two versions of `toString()`, one in the `Object` superclass, and one in the `CyberPet` subclass. If you call `toString()` on an instance of the subclass, its version of the method will be used. In this way, the subclass method *overrides* the superclass version.

Thus, `CyberPet.toString()` will have the following signature:

```java
public String toString();
```

If we were just returning `CyberPet`'s name, the body for this method would consist of a single statement:

```java
return name;
```

However, we also want to return the `CyberPet`'s state. One way to do this might be to use a multiway if-else statement inside the `toString()` method to distinguish between the `CyberPet`'s various states. However, this would duplicate code we've already written in the `getState()` method. Therefore, a better design is simply to invoke the `getState()` method from within the `toString()` method:

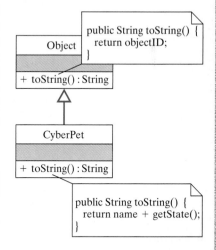

FIGURE 3–26   The `CyberPet` class overrides the `toString()` method, which it inherits from the `Object` class.

```
public String toString()
{
    return name + " is " + getState();
}
```

Simplicity, extensibility, and maintainability

By using the previously defined getState() method in this way, we end up with a simple design that reuses previously designed code. Plus, this design will not require us to recode toString() if we decide to add more states to CyberPet. In that case, we would simply modify the getState() method. Thus, calling an existing method, rather than duplicating its code inside the toString() method, leads to a program that is easier to extend and maintain.

EFFECTIVE DESIGN: Method Abstraction.   Instead of duplicating code at several different places within a program, it is better to encapsulate the code in a method and call the method wherever the code is needed. A single method is easier to maintain and extend, and the resulting program will be shorter and better structured.

If we add the toString() method to CyberPet and then run the program shown in Figure 3–27, we get the following output:

```
Ernie is Eating
Bert is Sleeping
```

FIGURE 3–27   An application to test the overridden toString() method.

```
public class TestPetToString
{
    public static void main(String argv[])
    {
        CyberPet pet1 = new CyberPet("Ernie");
        CyberPet pet2 = new CyberPet("Bert");
        pet2.sleep();
        System.out.println(pet1.toString());
        System.out.println(pet2.toString());
    }//main
} //TestPetToString
```

OBJECT-ORIENTED DESIGN: Inheritance and Polymorphism

Inheritance

This use of Object's toString() method provides our first look at Java's inheritance mechanism and how it promotes the generality and extensibility of the object-oriented approach. As a subclass of Object, our CyberPet class automatically inherits toString() and any other public or protected methods defined in Object. We can simply use these methods as is, insofar as they are useful to us. As we saw in this case, the default version of toString() wasn't very useful. In that case, we can override the method by defining a method in our class with the exact same method signature. The new version of toString() can be customized to do exactly what is most appropriate for the subclass.

One of the great benefits of the object-oriented approach is the ability to define a task, such as toString(), at a very high level in the class hierarchy and let the inheritance mechanism spread that task throughout the rest of the hierarchy. Because toString() is defined in Object, you can invoke this method for any Java object. Moreover, if you override toString() in the classes you define, you will be contributing to its usefulness. Two important lessons from this example are

> **EFFECTIVE DESIGN: Inheritance.** The higher up in the class hierarchy that a method is defined, the more widespread its use can be.

> **EFFECTIVE DESIGN: Overriding** toString()**.** The toString() method is so useful, it should be overridden in almost every Java class.

Obviously there is much more that needs to be explained about Java's inheritance mechanism. Therefore, we will be revisiting this topic again on numerous occasions in subsequent chapters.

Another important concept of object-oriented design is *polymorphism*. The toString() method is an example of a *polymorphic* method. The term *polymorphism* is from the Greek terms *poly*, which means "many," and *morph*, which means "form." The toString() method is polymorphic because it has different behavior when invoked on different objects.

For example, suppose we design a class, Student, as a subclass of Object and define its toString() method to return the student ID number. We would then have the situation shown in Figure 3–28. Given this design, then obj.toString() will return a student ID if obj is an instance of Student, but it will return a name and "eating" or "sleeping" if it is an instance of CyberPet. The following code segment illustrates this point:

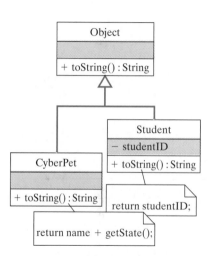

```
Object obj;                        // obj can refer to any Object
obj = new Student("12345");        // obj now refers to a Student
System.out.println(obj.toString()); // Prints "12345"
obj = new CyberPet("Ernie");       // obj now refers to a CyberPet
System.out.println(obj.toString()); // Prints "Ernie is eating"
```

FIGURE 3–28 The toString() method is polymorphic because its behavior depends on the object (Student or CyberPet) on which it is invoked.

Dynamic binding

In this case, the variable obj is used to refer to a Student and then a Cyber-Pet. This is okay because both Students and CyberPets are Objects. When toString() is invoked on obj, Java will figure out what subclass of Object is involved and invoke the appropriate toString() method. The mechanism that Java uses to figure this out is known as **dynamic binding**: The reference to toString() is not bound to an actual method until the expression obj.toString() is executed. That way it can bind to the method that is appropriate for that object.

IN THE LABORATORY: Feeding CyberPet

The purpose of the lab exercise is to familiarize you with Java methods and parameters. You will make several modifications to extend the functionality of the CyberPet class. The objectives of the lab are

- To give practice writing Java methods from scratch.
- To give practice using parameters to pass information to a method.
- To give practice using return values to pass information back from a method.

Problem Statement

Problem specification

Modify the CyberPet and TestCyberPet classes to create a simulation in which pets can eat different kinds of food. The completed program should be capable of producing the following output:

```
pet1's name is Socrates
Socrates is eating an apple
Socrates is sleeping
pet2's name is Cleopatra
Cleopatra is eating beans
Cleopatra is sleeping
...
```

LAB EXERCISE 1: EDITING, COMPILING, AND RUNNING

Download the CyberPet.java and the TestCyberPet.java source files from the companion Web site at

```
http://www.prenhall.com/morelli/
```

Compile and run the program, which corresponds to the program shown in Figures 3–23 and 3–24.

For each of the items that follow, make the editing change and then recompile the program. Make note of any error messages that are generated by the compiler. Try to understand what the message is telling you, and try to learn from the error, so it will be less likely to occur next time. After you have finished with that error, restore the code to its original form and move on to the next item.

CyberPet
− isEating : boolean − isSleeping : boolean − name : String − food : String
+ CyberPet() + CyberPet(in str : String) + setName(in str : String) + getName() : String + eat() + sleep() + eat(in str : String)

FIGURE 3–29 This version of CyberPet contains two eat() methods.

- **Java is case sensitive.** Change the assignment statement in setName() to Name = str with an uppercase "N."
- **Strings require double quotes.** Leave off one of the double quote marks around "Socrates" in the main() method in TestCyberPet.
- **Methods that return a value require a** return **statement.** Comment out the return statement in the getName() method. That is, turn the return statement into a comment line by adding double slashes (//) at the beginning of the line.
- **String concatenation requires an operator.** Delete the plus sign (+) in the System.out.println() expressions in main().
- **Objects must be instantiated.** Comment out the line beginning pet1 = new Pet("Socrates") in main().

LAB EXERCISE 2: MODIFYING THE CyberPet CLASS

Method design

Figure 3–29 provides a design of the modified CyberPet class. It contains a new eat() method that takes a single String parameter representing a type of food—"spinach," "ice cream," and so on. The new method should take the food string that is passed to it and assign it to an instance variable named food. Of course, it should also do everything that the other version of eat() does.

You will have to write the new eat() method. Note that this new method has the same name as an existing method in CyberPet. How will these two methods be distinguished from one another?

Modify the TestCyberPet application program so that it will conduct appropriate tests to make sure your new eat() method is working properly. When you are finished, the output should match the output shown previously in the problem statement. Your test algorithm should tell your CyberPet to eat certain foods.

Be sure to make appropriate use of private and public in your revisions to the CyberPet class.

LAB EXERCISE 3: ORDER OF EXECUTION

Modify your TestCyberPet program so that it produces the following output:

```
pet1 name is Socrates
Socrates is sleeping
Socrates is eating an apple
Socrates is eating a Macintosh
Socrates is eating a Windows/PC
```

LAB EXERCISE 4: GENERATING A TRACE

Add System.out.println() statements to your eat(String) method in order to generate a visible trace of the method call and return mechanism. Use println() to display eat()'s parameter, and the food instance variable both before and after the assignment statement. Try to generate the following output:

Testing and debugging

```
starting the eat method
str parameter = bananas
food instance variable = no food
str parameter = bananas
food instance variable = bananas
exiting the eat method
```

Using println() statements to display the values of variables and to trace program control is a good debugging technique. You will want to use this technique to locate bugs when things go wrong.

Method Declaration

The general form for a method definition is

*MethodModifiers*_{opt}　*ResultType*　*MethodName*　(*FormalParameterList*)　*MethodBody*

where *MethodModifiers* may be one of public, private, or protected. Methods declared private are only accessible from within the class; protected methods are accessible only in subclasses and within classes contained in the same package; and public methods are accessible to all other objects. If

Java Language Summary

a method's accessibility is not explicitly declared, Java's default is to make the method accessible only to other classes in the same package.

Methods with a non void *ResultType* must contain a return statement of the form *return(value)*, where *value* is the same type as *ResultType*; void methods may omit the return statement.

A method's *FormalParameterList* is a list of zero or more parameter declarations, each of which takes the following form:

TypeId1 ParameterId1, TypeId2 ParameterId2, ...

Method Call and Return

A method is invoked (or called) by using its name and by providing arguments for each of its formal parameters. For example, if a method has the signature,

```
public void myMethod(String s, int n);
```

it would be invoked by calling

```
myMethod("hello", 5);
```

The arguments must match the type and order of the parameters. Thus, "hello" is a String and 5 is an int, and they must be provided in that order.

Passing values to a method

When a method is called, the arguments are passed to their corresponding formal parameters. Control is then transferred to the first statement in the method's body. When the method is done executing, control is returned to the calling statement. See Figure 2–17 for an illustration of this.

The program in Figure 3–30 will print "hello", "goodbye", and then "hello friend" on three separate lines. The flow of control follows the sequence given in the program's comments. In the first two method calls,

FIGURE 3–30 A program illustrating method call and return structures.

```
public class MethodCalls
{
    public void method1(String s)
    {
        System.out.println(s);              // 2, 4
    }

    public String method2()
    {
        return "hello";                     // 6
    }

    public static void main(String args[])
    {
        MethodCalls obj = new MethodCalls();
        obj.method1("hello");                        // 1
        obj.method1("goodbye");                      // 3
        System.out.println(obj.method2() + " friend"); // 5
    } // main()
} // MethodCalls
```

when the method is done executing, it may seem as if control returns to the statement following the calling statement (rather than to the calling statement itself, as we have said). Thus, method1() is called on line 1. Control passes to line 2. When the method is done, it looks as if control returns to line 3. However, this is somewhat illusory, even though in this case it makes no practical difference to say that control returns to the statement on line 3.

But don't forget that some methods return a value. That value is used in the calling statement *before* control passes to the next statement. Thus, in the method call on line 5, control passes to line 6. The value "hello" is returned to the statement on line 5, where it is conjoined with "friend" and printed. This clearly illustrates that control always returns to the calling statement of a method call. If there's nothing left for the calling statement to do, control then passes on to the next statement.

Returning a value from a method

The If and If-Else Statements

The *if statement* and *if-else statement* take the following forms:

```
if   ( boolean expression )
          statement
if   ( boolean expression )
          statement
else
          statement2
```

The switch/break Structure

The switch/break combination is an alternative to the nested if-else statement for coding multiway selection. It is particularly well suited for handling menu options. It takes the following form:

```
switch (integralExpression)
{
    case integralValue1:
        // some statements
        break;
    case integralValue2:
        // some statements
        break;
    case integralValue3:
        // some statements
        break;
    default:
        some statements
}
```

An *integralExpression* is one whose type is either byte, short, int, char, long, or boolean. The values used as case values must be constants—either literals or final variables.

The switch statement evaluates its *integralExpression* and then branches to the *case* whose value equals the expression's value. If no such case exists, it branches to the (optional) default case. Once control passes to a case clause, statements are executed in sequence up to the end of the switch statement or until a break is encountered. A break statement transfers control out of its enclosing block. It is used in this structure to transfer control out of the switch statement after one and only one case is executed.

CHAPTER SUMMARY

Technical Terms

accessor method	method definition	reference type
argument	method invocation	scope
boolean expression	method overloading	selection structure
class scope	method signature	side effect
constructor	multiway selection	stub method
dangling else	mutator method	switch/break
dynamic binding	parameter	structure
local scope	primitive type	

Summary of Important Points

- A *formal parameter* is a variable in a method declaration. It always consists of a type followed by a variable identifier. An *argument* is a value that is passed to a method via a formal parameter when the method is invoked. A method's *parameters* constrain the type of information that can be passed to a method.
- **Parameter Passing.** When an argument of primitive type is passed to a method, it cannot be modified within the method. When an argument of reference type is passed to a method, the object it refers to can be modified within the method.
- Except for `void` methods, a *method invocation* or *method call* is an expression which has a value of a certain type. For example, `pet1.getName()` might have the `String` value "Socrates".
- The *signature* of a method consists of its name, and the number, types, and order of its formal parameters. A class may not contain more than one method with the same signature.
- A *constructor* is a method that is invoked when an object is created. If a class does not contain a constructor method, the Java compiler supplies a *default constructor*.
- Restricting access to certain portions of a class is a form of *information hiding*. Generally, instance variables are hidden by declaring them `private`. The class's `public` methods make up its interface.
- The *if statement* executes a statement only if its boolean condition is true. The *if-else statement* executes one or the other of its statements depending on the value of its boolean condition. *Multiway selection* allows one and only one of several choices to be selected depending on the value of its boolean condition.
- The `switch` statement, in conjunction with the `break` statement, is used for coding multiway selection structures.

SOLUTIONS TO SELF-STUDY EXERCISES

SOLUTION 3.1 A *method declaration* defines the method by specifying its name, qualifiers, return type, formal parameters, and its algorithm, thereby associating a name with a segment of executable code. A *method invocation* calls or uses a defined method.

SOLUTION 3.2 A *formal parameter* is a variable in the method declaration, whose purpose is to store a value while the method is running. An *argument* is a value that is passed to a method in place of a formal parameter.

SOLUTION 3.3

```
String kind = "no kind";
public void setKind(String str)
{
    kind = str;
}
```

SOLUTION 3.4

```
pet1.setKind("mouse");
pet2.setKind("cat");
```

SOLUTION 3.5 A constructor cannot have a return type, such as void.

SOLUTION 3.6

```
public CyberPet(String str)
{
    setName(str);
}
```

SOLUTION 3.7

```
Fido
Trigger
```

SOLUTION 3.8

```
public String getKind()
{
    return kind;
}
```

SOLUTION 3.9

```
public String getKind()
{
    return name + " is a " + kind;
}
```

SOLUTION 3.10 See Figure 3–31.

SOLUTION 3.11

```
if (isEating == true)
    System.out.println("Eating") ;
else ;                              // Error (no semicolon here)
    System.out.println("Sleeping");

if (isEating == true)
    System.out.println("Eating")  // Error (missing semicolon here)
else
    System.out.println("Sleeping");
```

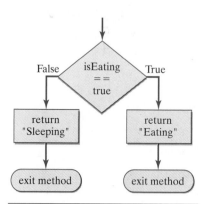

FIGURE 3–31 Flowchart of the if-else version of the getState() method.

SOLUTION 3.12

```java
public String getState()
{
    if (isEating == true)
        return "Eating";
    else if (isSleeping == true)
        return "Sleeping";
    else if (isPlaying == true)
        return "Playing";
    else
        return "Error in state";
}
```

SOLUTION 3.13 When passing an argument for a primitive type, a copy of the argument's value is passed. The actual argument cannot be changed inside the method. When passing a reference to an object, the object can be changed within the method.

SOLUTION 3.14 Identify any errors in the following switch structures (if there is no error, specify the output):

```java
(a) int k = 0;
    switch (k)                 // Syntax error: missing braces
    case 0:
        System.out.println("zero");
        break;
    case 1:
        System.out.println("one");
        break;
    default:
        System.out.println("default");
        break;
(b) int k = 0;
    switch (k + 1)
    {
        case 0:
            System.out.println("zero");
            break;
        case 1:
            System.out.println("one"); // Output "one"
            break;
        default:
            System.out.println("default");
            break;
    }
(c) int k = 6;
    switch (k / 3.0)      // Syntax error: k/3.0 is not integral value
    {
        case 2:
            System.out.println("zero");
            break;
        case 3:
            System.out.println("one");
            break;
        default:
            System.out.println("default");
            break;
    }
```

SOLUTION 3.15   A `switch` statement to print ice cream flavors:

```
switch (flavor)
{
    case 1:
        System.out.println("Vanilla");
        break;
    case 2:
        System.out.println("Chocolate");
        break;
    case 3:
        System.out.println("Strawberry");
        break;
    default:
        System.out.println("Error");
}
```

SOLUTION 3.16

```
public final int VANILLA = 0,
                 CHOCOLATE = 1,
                 STRAWBERRY = 2;
switch (flavor)
{
    case VANILLA:
        System.out.println("Vanilla");
        break;
    case CHOCOLATE:
        System.out.println("Chocolate");
        break;
    case STRAWBERRY:
        System.out.println("Strawberry");
        break;
    default:
        System.out.println("Error");
}
```

EXERCISES

Note: *For programming exercises,* **first** *draw a UML class diagram describing all classes and their inheritance relationships and/or associations.*

EXERCISE 3.1   Fill in the blanks in each of the following sentences:

a. When two different methods have the same name, this is an example of _____ .

b. Methods with the same name are distinguished by their _____ .

c. A method that is invoked when an object is created is known as a _____ method.

d. A method whose purpose is to provide access to an object's instance variables is known as an _____ method.

e. A `boolean` value is an example of a _____ type.

f. A CyberPet variable is an example of a _____ type.

g. A method's parameters have _____ scope.

h. A class's instance variables have _____ scope.

    i. Generally, a class's instance variables should have _____ access.

    j. The methods that make up an object's interface should have _____ access.

    k. A method that returns no value should be declared _____ .

    l. Java's if statement and if-else statement are both examples of _____ control structures.

    m. An expression that evaluates to either true or false is known as a _____ .

    n. In an if-else statement, an else clause matches _____ .

    o. The ability to use a superclass method in a subclass is due to Java's _____ mechanism.

    p. The process of redefining a superclass method in a subclass is known as _____ the method.

EXERCISE 3.2   Explain the difference between the following pairs of concepts:

a. *Parameter* and *argument*.
b. *Method definition* and *method invocation*.
c. *Local scope* and *class scope*.
d. *Primitive type* and *reference type*.
e. *Access method* and *constructor method*.

EXERCISE 3.3   Translate each of the following into Java code:

a. If b1 is true, then print "one" otherwise print "two".
b. If b1 is false and if b2 is true, then print "one" otherwise print "two".
c. If b1 is false and if b2 is true, then print "one", otherwise print "two", or otherwise print "three".

EXERCISE 3.4   Identify and fix the syntax errors in each of the following:

a.

```
if (isWalking == true) ;
    System.out.println("Walking");
else
    System.out.println("Not walking");
```

b.

```
if (isWalking)
    System.out.println("Walking")
else
    System.out.println("Not walking");
```

c.

```
if (isWalking)
    System.out.println("Walking");
else
    System.out.println("Not walking")
```

d.

```
if (isWalking = false)
    System.out.println("Walking");
else
    System.out.println("Not walking");
```

EXERCISE 3.5   For each of the following, suppose that isWalking is true and isTalking is false (first draw a flowchart for each statement and then determine what would be printed by each statement):

a.

```
if (isWalking == false)
    System.out.println("One");
    System.out.println("Two");
```

b.

```
if (isWalking == true)
    System.out.println("One");
    System.out.println("Two");
```

c.

```
if (isWalking == false)
{
    System.out.println("One");
    System.out.println("Two");
}
```

d.

```
if (isWalking == false)
    if (isTalking == true)
        System.out.println("One");
    else
        System.out.println("Two");
else
    System.out.println("Three");
```

EXERCISE 3.6 Show what the output would be if the following version of `main()` were executed:

```
public static void main(String argv[])  // Execution starts here
{
    System.out.println("main() is starting");
    CyberPet pet1;
    pet1  = new CyberPet();
    CyberPet pet2;
    pet2 = new CyberPet();
    pet1.setName("Mary");        // Set pet1's name
    pet2.setName("Peter");       // Set pet2's name
    pet1.eat();                  // Tell pet1 to eat
    pet1.sleep();                // Tell pet1 to sleep
    pet2.sleep();                // Tell pet2 to sleep
    pet2.eat();                  // Tell pet2 to eat
    System.out.println("main() is finished");
    return;                      // Return to the system
}
```

EXERCISE 3.7 Dangling else. For each of the subsequent unindented statements, first draw a flowchart of the statement and then determine its output assuming that isWalking is true and isTalking is false. Then rewrite the statements using proper indentation techniques. Recall that according to the syntax of the if-else statement an else matches the closest previous unmatched if.

a.

```
if (isWalking == true)
if (isTalking == true)
System.out.println("One");
else
System.out.println("Two");
System.out.println("Three");
```

b.

```
if (isWalking == true)
if (isTalking == true)
System.out.println("One");
else {
System.out.println("Two");
System.out.println("Three");
}
```

c.

```
if (isWalking == true) {
if (isTalking == true)
System.out.println("One");
}
else {
System.out.println("Two");
System.out.println("Three");
}
```

d.

```
if (isWalking == true)
if (isTalking == true)
System.out.println("One");
else
System.out.println("Two");
else
System.out.println("Three");
```

EXERCISE 3.8   Determine the output of the following program:

```
public class Mystery
{
    public String myMethod(String s)
    {
        return("Hello" + s);
    }
    public static void main(String argv[])
    {
        Mystery mystery = new Mystery();
        System.out.println( mystery.myMethod(" dolly");
    }
}
```

EXERCISE 3.9   Suppose you have the following method, which contains a boolean parameter and a CyberPet parameter, where CyberPet is defined as shown in Figure 3–23:

```
public void myMethod(CyberPet p, boolean b)
{
    b = false;
    p.sleep();
}
```

Recall the distinction between passing a primitive value and passing a reference to an object. What output would be produced by the following statements?

```
CyberPet pet1 = new CyberPet("Socrates");
boolean isSocrates = true;
System.out.println(pet1.getState());
myMethod(pet1, isSocrates);
if (isSocrates == true)
    System.out.println(" Socrates");
else
    System.out.println(" NOT Socrates");
System.out.println(pet1.getState());
```

EXERCISE 3.10   Write a boolean method—a method that returns a boolean—that takes an int parameter and converts the integers 0 and 1 into false and true, respectively.

EXERCISE 3.11   Define an int method that takes a boolean parameter. If the parameter's value is false, the method should return 0; otherwise it should return 1.

EXERCISE 3.12   Define a void method named hello that takes a single boolean parameter. The method should print "Hello" if its parameter is true; otherwise it should print "Goodbye".

EXERCISE 3.13   Define a method named hello that takes a single boolean parameter. The method should return "Hello" if its parameter is true; otherwise it should return "Goodbye". Note the difference between this method and the one in the previous exercise. This one returns a String. That one was a void method.

EXERCISE 3.14   Write a method named hello that takes a single String parameter. The method should return a String that consists of the word "Hello" concatenated with the value of its parameter. For example, if you call this method with the expression hello("dolly"), it should return "hello dolly". If you call it with hello("young lovers wherever you are"), it should return "hello young lovers wherever you are".

EXERCISE 3.15   Define a void method named day1 that prints "a partridge in a pear tree".

EXERCISE 3.16   Write a Java application program called TwelveDays that prints the Christmas carol "Twelve Days of Christmas." For this version, write a void method named intro() that takes a single String parameter that gives the day of the verse and prints the intro to the song. For example, intro("first") should print, "On the first day of Christmas my true love gave to me". Then write methods day1(), day2(), and so on, each of which prints its version of the verse. Then write a main() method that calls the other methods to print the whole song.

EXERCISE 3.17 Define a void method named `verse` that takes two `String` parameters and returns a verse of the Christmas carol "Twelve Days of Christmas." For example, if you call this method with `verse("first",` `"a partridge in a pear tree")`, it should return, "On the first day of Christmas my true love gave to me, a partridge in a pear tree".

EXERCISE 3.18 Define a void method named `permute`, which takes three `String` parameters and prints out all possible arrangements of the three strings. For example, if you called `permute("a",` `"b",` `"c")`, it would produce the following output: abc, acb, bac, bca, cab, cba, with each permutation on a separate line.

EXERCISE 3.19 Design a method that can produce limericks given a bunch of rhyming words. That is, create a limerick template that will take any five words or phrases and produce a limerick. For example, if you call

```
limerick("Jones","stones","rained","pained","bones");
```

your method might print (something better than)

```
There once a person named Jones
Who had a great liking for stones,
But whenever it rained,
Jones' expression was pained,
Because stones weren't good for the bones.
```

EXERCISE 3.20 Write a constructor method that can be used to set both the name and initial state of a `CyberPet`.

EXERCISE 3.21 Write a constructor method that can be used to set a pet's initial state to something besides its default state. (Hint: Use boolean variables.)

EXERCISE 3.22 Extend the definition of `CyberPet` so that a pet's state can have three possible values: eating, sleeping, and thinking. Modify any existing methods that need to be changed, and add the appropriate access methods for the new state.

EXERCISE 3.23 **Challenge.** Add a *size* instance variable to `CyberPet`, making certain it can be set to either "big" or "small" through a constructor or an access method. Then write an `encounter(CyberPet)` method that allows one `CyberPet` to encounter another. Note that the method should take a `CyberPet` parameter. Depending on the size of the pet, the small pet should be chased by the larger pet or the two should befriend each other. This encounter should be described with a returned `String`. For example, if you create two pets such that `pet1` is big and `pet2` is small, and then you invoke `pet1.encounter(pet2)`, it should return something like "I'm going to eat you."

For each of the following exercises, write a complete Java application program:

EXERCISE 3.24 Define a class named `Donor` that has two instance variables, the donor's name and rating, both `Strings`. The name can be any string, but the rating should be one of the following values: "high," "medium," or "none." Write the following methods for this class: a constructor, `Donor(String,String)`, that allows you to set both the donor's name and rating; and access methods to set and get both the name and rating of a donor.

EXERCISE 3.25 **Challenge.** Define a `CopyMonitor` class that solves the following problem. A company needs a monitor program to keep track of when a particular copy machine needs service. The device has two important (boolean) variables: its toner level (too low or not) and whether it has printed more than 100,000 pages since its last servicing (it either has or has not). The servicing rule that the company uses is that service is needed when either 100,000 pages have been printed or the toner is too low. Your program should contain a method that reports either "service needed" or "service not needed" based on the machine's state. (Pretend that the machine has other methods that keep track of toner level and page count.)

EXERCISE 3.26   Challenge. Design and write an OldMacdonald class that sings several verses of "Old MacDonald Had a Farm." Use methods to generalize the verses. For example, write a method named eieio() to "sing" the "E I E I O" part of the verse. Write another method with the signature hadAnX(String s), which sings the "had a duck" part of the verse, and a method withA(String sound) to sing the "with a quack quack here" part of the verse. Test your class by writing a main() method.

ADDITIONAL EXERCISES

EXERCISE 3.27   Modify the design of the Rectangle class to contain public methods to set and get a rectangle's length and width. Draw a UML class diagram to depict this new design.

EXERCISE 3.28   Draw a UML object diagram to depict an interaction between a user interface object and two rectangles, in which the interface sets the length—setLength()—of each rectangle to a different value.

EXERCISE 3.29   Suppose you have an Object A, with public methods a(), b(), and private method c(). And suppose you have a subclass of A named B with methods named b(), c() and d(). Draw a UML diagram showing the relationship between these two classes. Explain the inheritance relationships between them and identify those methods that would be considered polymorphic.

EXERCISE 3.30   Consider the definition of the class C. Define a subclass of C named B that overrides method m1() so that it returns the difference between m and n instead of their sum.

```
public class C {
    private int m;
    private int n;
    public C(int mIn, int nIn) {
        m = mIn;
        n = nIn;
    }
    public int m1() {
        return m+n;
    }
}
```

4

Applets: Programming for the World Wide Web

OBJECTIVES

After studying this chapter, you will

- Be able to design and implement a Java applet.
- Understand Java's event-handling model.
- Be able to handle button clicks in your programs.
- Have a better appreciation of inheritance and polymorphism.
- Know how to design a simple Graphical User Interface (GUI).

OUTLINE

4.1 Introduction

An **applet** is a Java program embedded within a Web page and run by a *Web browser* such as Netscape Navigator or Internet Explorer. In Lab Exercise 1 (in Chapter 1), we compiled and executed FirstApplet, a playful applet that toggled a button's label each time it was clicked.

GUIs

As we saw in that example, one of the most attractive features of an applet is its **Graphical User Interface (GUI)**. Java applet programming makes it easy to build programs that use graphical components, like windows, menus, and control buttons, to interact with the user. You interact with a Java applet in much the same way as you interact with a Web browser—by using pull-down menus, clicking buttons, and entering text into text fields. And just as with the browser itself, Java applets can handle *multimedia* resources—sound, graphics, and video.

Java applets derive much of their power from two key features of object-oriented programming: *class inheritance* and *method polymorphism*. In this chapter, we will look at these mechanisms.

Event-driven programming

Java applet programming is also *event-driven programming*. A Java applet reacts to events, such as mouse clicks and key presses, that occur in the browser interface. We will, therefore, take a look at Java's *event model* and learn how to write programs that can handle simple events.

We begin by studying a very simple applet, SimpleApplet, which introduces the basic elements of applet programming. We then design and build CyberPetApplet, an applet that provides a GUI interface for our CyberPet simulation. The interface will contain *eat* and *sleep* buttons corresponding to each of the CyberPet's commands and a text field that displays the CyberPet's name and state.

Although this chapter introduces several new Java keywords, it introduces no new statements, control structures, or types of data. Instead, it seeks to provide a good grounding in fundamentals of event-driven GUI programming. Although this chapter focuses on applets, most of the concepts we will study—inheritance, polymorphism, event-driven programming—are also used in the development of Java GUI applications, which are covered in Chapter 9.

Applet
+ getDocumentBase() : URL
+ getParameter(in str : String) : String
+ getImage(in url : URL, in str : String)
+ getAudioClip(in url : URL) : AudioClip
+ play(in url : URL)
+ init()
+ start()
+ stop()

FIGURE 4–1 Partial summary of the Applet class.

4.2 The Applet Class

The java.applet.Applet class is part of Java's class library or **Application Programming Interface (API)**. A UML summary of Applet is shown in Figure 4–1. Because applets run within the context of a browser, most of the Applet's public methods serve to define an interface between the applet and its browser environment. There are methods that get the applet's Web address or URL [getDocumentBase()], methods that enable the applet to play audio files and load images [play(), getImage()], and methods that control the applet's execution [init(), start(), and stop()].

4.2.1 Java's GUI Components

AWT and Swing components

Java's API contains two complete sets of buttons, menus, text fields, checkboxes, and other GUI components: the *Abstract Windowing Toolkit (AWT)* and the *Swing component set*. The AWT has been part of Java since version 1.0. The Swing component set was introduced in version 1.2. Because the AWT model is somewhat simpler than Swing, we will intro-

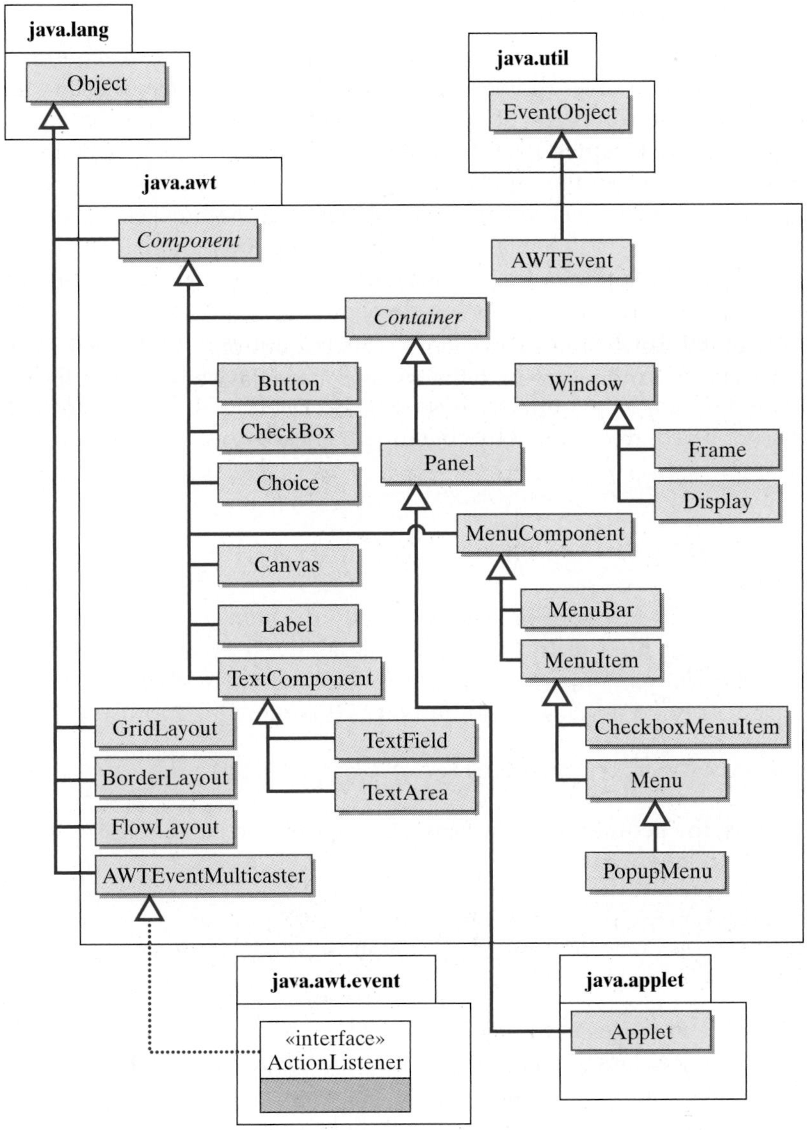

FIGURE 4–2 Part of Java's *Abstract Windowing Toolkit (AWT)* hierarchy.

duce the AWT components in this chapter. However, the Swing components provide greater functionality and address some of the limitations of the AWT. Therefore, in Chapter 9 we'll give a full treatment of the Swing components.

The components in the AWT package (java.awt) are organized into a hierarchy of superclasses and subclasses, part of which is shown in Figure 4–2. As the hierarchy illustrates, an Applet *isa* type of Panel, which *isa* type of Container. As you might expect, a Container *isa* Component that can contain other Components, so an Applet can contain Buttons, TextFields, and other types of Components. Note that the Component class is a subclass of Object and that the Button, Label, Container, and TextField classes are all subclasses of the Component class.

The isa relationship

Inheritance

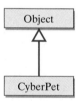

FIGURE 4–3   CyberPet is a direct subclass of the Object class.

4.3   Class Inheritance

Inheritance is the mechanism by which a class of objects can acquire the methods and variables of its superclasses. An object of a subclass is said to inherit the functionality of all of its superclasses. In the *From the Java Library* section of Chapter 3 we showed how all classes in the Java hierarchy inherit the toString() method from the Object class. The lesson there was that an object in a subclass can either use or override any public method defined in any of its superclasses. In this chapter, we want to look at other ways to employ inheritance. In particular, we show that a new class can be defined by *extending* an existing class.

We noted in Chapter 2 that if a class's *pedigree* is not specified in the class definition, the class is assumed to be a direct subclass of Object. This would apply to our definition of CyberPet (Fig. 4–3). We can make CyberPet's pedigree explicit by changing its header declaration to

```
public class CyberPet extends Object { ... }
```

The extends keyword specifies explicitly that CyberPet is a direct subclass of Object.

The extends keyword is used to specify the subclass/superclass relationships that hold in the Java class hierarchy. It is used to define the *isa* relationship among objects in a class hierarchy. Thus, since Applet *isa* subclass of Panel, its class definition takes the following form:

```
public class Applet extends Panel { ... }
```

Similarly, the definitions of the Panel, Container, and Button classes would take the following forms:

```
public class Panel extends Container { ... }
public class Container extends Component { ... }
public class Button extends Component { ... }
```

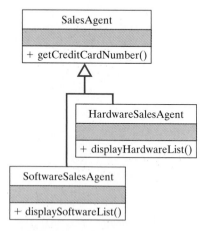

FIGURE 4–4   Subclasses generally specialize the features of their superclasses. In this example, both SoftwareSalesAgent and HardwareSalesAgent inherit the getCreditCardNumber() method.

to reflect their places in the class hierarchy.

Extending a class in this way enables us to create a new class by specializing in an existing class. For example, suppose the Acme Computer Supply Company employs sales agents to help customers order something from Acme's catalog. Suppose now that Acme grows so large it needs to have some sales agents who are experts in software and some who are experts in hardware. To acquire these kinds of experts, it would be good company policy to train some of the existing agents to acquire these new specialties, rather than to train a new person entirely from scratch.

In the same way, if SalesAgent were an existing Java class, we could use it as the basis for definitions of SoftwareSalesAgent and HardwareSales-Agent:

```
public class SoftwareSalesAgent extends SalesAgent { ... }
public class HardwareSalesAgent extends SalesAgent { ... }
```

As subclasses of SalesAgent, these new classes would inherit its public and protected elements (Fig. 4–4). So if SalesAgent had a getCreditCardNumber() method, they could make use of this method. But they could also be given new elements (methods and variables) that would support their new specialties. The `SoftwareSalesAgent` might be given a new method `displaySoftwareList()` to help it describe software products to a customer.

4.3.1 Objects, Assignments, and Types (Optional)

Recall that instance variables for objects are reference variables in Java. The *isa* relationship among classes determines whether an assignment statement involving different types of objects is legal. For example, because a `Panel` *isa* `Container` and a `Container` *isa* `Component` and a `Component` *isa* `Object`, all of the following assignment statements are valid:

```
Panel p = new Panel();
Container cont = p;          // Valid: A Panel is a Container
Component comp = p;          // Valid: A Panel is a Component
Object o = p;                // Valid: A Panel is an Object
```

In other words, it is valid to assign a `Panel` to a `Container`, `Component`, or `Object` because a `Panel` *is* all of these things. In general, it is valid to assign an instance of a subclass to a variable whose type is any of its superclasses.

On the other hand, it is not valid to assign an instance of a superclass to a variable whose type is one of its subclasses:

```
Container c = new Container();
Panel p = c;                 // Invalid: A Container is not a Panel
```

In this case, a `Container` is a more general object than a `Panel` and, therefore, cannot be assigned to a `Panel` variable.

> **JAVA LANGUAGE RULE** Assignment of Objects. An instance of a class can be validly assigned to variables whose type is any of its superclasses, but it cannot be assigned to variables whose type is any of its subclasses.

Actually the situation is somewhat more subtle than just described. In some situations you can *coerce* a reference to an object into a variable of one of its subclasses. For example, consider the following situation:

```
Container c = new Panel();  // c is referring to a Panel
Panel p = (Panel)c;         // We can assign c to p by coercion
```

In this example, the expression `(Panel)` is a *cast operator*. It tells Java that we want to assign the object that *c* references to a `Panel`. Java will allow this assignment because the object that *c* is pointing to really is a `Panel`. On the other hand, Java will not allow the following attempt at coercion:

```
Container c = new Container();  // c is referring to a Container
Panel p = (Panel)c;            // Invalid: We can't change a
                               //    Container into a Panel
```

In this case, *c* is pointing to a `Container`. And there's nothing that we or Java can do to convert a `Container` into a `Panel`. Therefore, this attempted assignment would result in an error message.

SELF-STUDY EXERCISE

EXERCISE 4.1 Given the hierarchy of classes shown in Figure 4–2, which of the following would be valid assignment statements?

```
Panel p = new Container();
Container c1 = new Panel();
Component c2 = new Object();
Component c3 = new Container();
Container c4 = new Component();
```

4.3.2 Defining a `Square` as a Subclass of `Rectangle` (Optional)

To see better how inheritance works in Java, let's define a `Square` as an extension of the `Rectangle` class we defined in Chapter 2. (Before beginning this subsection, you might want to refer back to the discussion of inheritance in Section 0.7.6.) The `Rectangle` class has two instance variables, length and width, and a public method, `calculateArea()`. Its constructor takes two parameters, which are used to pass the initial values for its length and width (Fig. 4–5).

A square is a specialization of a rectangle in which the length and width are equal. Therefore, to construct a square you need only specify one dimension, the length of its side, whereas to construct a rectangle you must specify both its length and width:

```
Square s = new Square(10);
Rectangle r = new Rectangle(10,15);
```

Thus, in Java, the only real difference between the `Square` class and the `Rectangle` class will reside in the way we define their contructor methods. Calculating the area or perimeter of a square can be done exactly the same way as for a rectangle.

Because a square is a specialization of a rectangle, we can define the `Square` class by extending the definition of the `Rectangle` class, as shown in Figure 4–6. Note that the only modification we make to the `Rectangle` class is to declare its length and width variables as protected instead of public. This will allow them be used in the `Square` subclass. The `Square` class will thus inherit length, width, and the `calculateArea()` method. Instead of having its own instance variable for the length of its side the `Square` class will still use length and width to define its dimensions. Our definition just needs to ensure that both dimensions are equal.

To ensure that a square's length and width are equal, we define a `Square()` contructor that inputs the square's side and sets it as the value of its (inherited) length and width variables. Note in Figure 4–6 how the contructor is defined. It takes a single parameter giving the length of the square's side and passes it to the superclass's contructor. The keyword super refers to the name of an object's superclass. Thus, the expression super(side,side) invokes the superclass's contructor, passing it side as the value for both its length and width. This is equivalent to invoking `Rectangle(side,side)`. In

---

Rectangle
– length : double
– width : double
+ Rectangle(in l : double, in w : double)
+ calculateArea() : double

FIGURE 4–5 Note that this version of `Rectangle` has private instance variables; this means the variables cannot be accessed from a subclass.

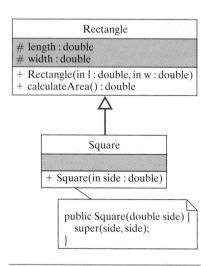

FIGURE 4–6 The `Square` class inherits the `Rectangle`'s protected (#) length and width variables. The `Square()` constructor invokes the superclass constructor, passing it the same value (side) for both its length and width.

```
public class Rectangle
{
    protected double length;        // Instance variables
    protected double width;

    public Rectangle(double l, double w)  // Constructor method
    {   length = l;
        width = w;
    } // Rectangle constructor

    public double calculateArea()            // Access method
    {   return length * width;
    } // calculateArea

} // Rectangle class

public class Square extends Rectangle // Subclass of Rectangle
{
    public Square(double side)
    {   super(side,side);            // Call Rectangle's Constructor
    }
} // Square
```

FIGURE 4–7   The Rectangle and Square classes. Note that Square is a subclass of Rectangle.

effect, we are creating a rectangle whose length equals its width—that is, we are creating a square.

JAVA LANGUAGE RULE   super. The super keyword refers to an object's superclass. The expression super() is used to invoke the superclass's contructor.

The complete definitions of the Rectangle and Square classes are shown in Figure 4–7. The TestSquare class shown in Figure 4–8 illustrates how we can use Square. We instantiate Square by calling its constructor and passing it 100 as the length of its side. The Square() constructor (Fig. 4–7) invokes the superclass constructor, passing it 100 as the value for both its length and width. When we subsequently invoke square.calculate Area(), it will calculate its area as 100×100, as the following output shows:

```
square's area is 10000.0
```

Thus, we have used Java's inheritance mechanism to define an entirely new class, Square, by extending an existing class, Rectangle.

SELF-STUDY EXERCISES

EXERCISE 4.2   Given the definitions of Rectangle and Square (Fig. 4–7), write a public method named calcPerimeter() for the Rectangle class. It

```
public class TestSquare
{
    public static void main(String argv[])
    {
        Square square = new Square (100);
        System.out.println("square's area is " + square.calculateArea());
    }
} // TestSquare
```

FIGURE 4–8   The TestSquare class.

should take no parameters and should return a `double` representing the rectangle's perimeter—the sum of its four sides.

EXERCISE 4.3 Given the definition of the `calcPerimeter()` method from the previous exercise, write Java code that would be added to the `main()` method in `TestSquare` (Fig. 4–8) that prints out `square`'s perimeter.

EXERCISE 4.4 Explain how the inheritance mechanism works in the example from the previous exercise.

4.4 Applet Subclasses

Instantiating vs. extending

Some classes in the Java hierarchy are designed to be *extended* rather than *instantiated* directly. In other words, some classes are designed to be used as the basis for defining subclasses (extended), whereas others are designed to be used as the basis for creating instance objects (instantiated). For example, `CyberPet` and `Rectangle` were designed to be directly instantiated:

Instantiating a `CyberPet`

```
CyberPet pet1 = new CyberPet();        // Create an instance
Rectangle rect1 = new Rectangle();
```

These declarations create `pet1` and `rect1` as objects (or instances) of the `CyberPet` and `Rectangle` class, respectively.

In contrast to these examples, applets cannot be directly instantiated. In other words, you will never see a declaration such as the following:

```
Applet a = new Applet(); // Not the way to do it!
```

You cannot directly create an instance of the `Applet` class. Instead, applets are made by first defining a subclass of `Applet` and then creating an instance of the subclass. In general outline at least, writing Java applets takes the following form:

Extending the `Applet` class

```
public class AppletSubclass extends Applet { ... }// Define a subclass
AppletSubclass myApplet = new AppletSubclass();   // and instantiate it
```

Thus, we first define the `AppletSubclass` as a subclass of `Applet` and then use it as the basis for creating instances.

JLR

JAVA LANGUAGE RULE Creating an Applet. A Java applet is an object that is created by first defining a subclass of `Applet` and then creating an instance of the subclass.

Embedded programs

The reason for doing things this way is somewhat complicated, which is why we have delayed discussing it until now. It has to do with an applet's special status as an *embedded program* —that is, a program that runs within the context of a Web browser. Applets have to be constructed in such a way that they can be instantiated and executed by the browser. *Class inheritance* and *method polymorphism* make this possible. This will become clearer in the next sections.

4.5   A Simple Applet

Let's create a simple applet and examine how it works. The applet shown in Figure 4–9 is a simple variation of the applet described in the Laboratory section of Chapter 1. It consists of a button that is initially labeled "The machine is off". Each time the button is clicked, its label changes from "The machine is off" to "The machine is on", and vice versa.

The Java code for this applet is shown in Figure 4–10. The first three lines of the program contain `import` declarations, which declare the names of library packages used in the program:

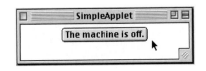

FIGURE 4–9   A simple Java applet. Each time the user clicks on the button, its label changes from "The machine is on" to "The machine is off."

```
import java.applet.*;
import java.awt.*;
import java.awt.event.*;
```

The Java class library is organized into a collection of packages. For example, the `java.applet` package contains definitions of the `Applet` class and other related classes. The `java.awt` package (see Fig. 4–2) contains definitions of Java GUI components, such as the `Button` class. An *import declaration* allows classes defined in the Java class library to be referred to by simple names instead of by their fully qualified names.

Library packages

For example, without using an import declaration, if you wanted to refer to the `Applet` class from within your program, you would have to use its fully qualified name, `java.applet.Applet`. The fully qualified name specifies the package (`java.applet`) that contains the class. By using an import declaration, we can refer to the `Applet` class simply as `Applet`:

```
public class SimpleApplet extends Applet ...
```

Without the import declaration, we would have to use the fully qualified name:

```
public class SimpleApplet extends java.applet.Applet ...
```

Similarly, by including declarations for the `java.awt` and `java.awt. event` packages in our program, we can use simple names to refer to classes contained in these packages, such as the `java.awt.Button` and `java.awt.event.ActionEvent` classes.

The import declarations used in this program (Fig. 4–10) contain the wild card character (*), which allows us to import the names of all the classes in the given package. For example, in this program, we are using simple names for `ActionListener` and `ActionEvent`, both of which are defined in the `java.awt.event` package. If we chose not to use the wild card character, we would have to import both of these names separately:

```
import java.awt.event.ActionListener;
import java.awt.event.ActionEvent;
```

For beginning programmers it is better to use the wild card. That way simple names can be used for all classes defined in a given package. This will lead to fewer "class not found" errors.

FIGURE 4–10 Defining a simple applet.

```java
import java.applet.*;
import java.awt.*;
import java.awt.event.*;

public class SimpleApplet extends Applet implements ActionListener
{
    private Button toggle;          // From java.awt.*

    public void init()
    {
        toggle = new Button ("The machine is off");
        toggle.addActionListener(this);
        add(toggle);
    } // init()

    public void actionPerformed(ActionEvent e)
    {
        String str = toggle.getLabel();   // Get the button's label
        if (str.equals("The machine is on"))      // and change it
            toggle.setLabel("The machine is off");
        else                                      // or
            toggle.setLabel("The machine is on"); // change it back
    } // actionPerformed()
} // SimpleApplet
```

JAVA LANGUAGE RULE Import Declaration. An **import declaration** allows the program to refer to Java library classes by their simple names instead of by their fully qualified names. Its general form is *import packagename.classname*. The wild card character (*) can be used in place of *classname* to import names for all the classes in a package.

DEBUGGING TIP: Not Found Error. A "class not found" or "method not found" error will occur if you use a simple name for a library class or library method without the appropriate import declaration.

4.5.1 Inheriting Functionality

The next line in the program (Fig. 4–10) is the header of the class definition:

```java
public class SimpleApplet extends Applet implements ActionListener
```

Explicit pedigree

Unlike the other examples we have seen, this class header provides an explicit description of SimpleApplet's *pedigree*:

```java
extends Applet implements ActionListener
```

The extends keyword here defines SimpleApplet as a subclass of Applet. In effect, it is saying that SimpleApplet *isa* Applet. This means SimpleApplet inherits the functionality defined in Applet. Whatever an Applet can do, a SimpleApplet can do.

Similarly, the significance of the `implements` keyword here is to define `SimpleApplet` as an implementor of the methods inherited from the `ActionListener` interface. An **interface** is like a class that contains only methods. An interface cannot contain instance variables.

Both `extends` and `implements` are inheritance mechanisms in Java. Together they provide the chief means by which Java programs (applets and applications) can make use of the predefined functionality contained in the Java API. Thus, `SimpleApplet` exhibits two forms of inheritance (Fig. 4–11). It extends the `Applet` class, inheriting its public methods such as `init()` and `play()`, and it implements the `ActionListener` interface by providing its own implementation of the `actionPerformed()` method.

Extending a Superclass

By *extending* `Applet`, `SimpleApplet` acquires several public methods that define its interface with the Web browser, including the `play()` method, which can be used to play audio clips:

```
public void play(URL url);
```

As its signature indicates, `play()` takes an audio file's URL (or address specification) and plays the sounds defined in the file. Our `SimpleApplet` can play an audio file by simply calling this method and passing it the file's URL:

```
play("Hello.au");
```

This is an example of *inheriting functionality*. `SimpleApplet` is able to use any of `Applet`'s public and protected methods *as if they were its own*.

It's important to note that this inheritance mechanism extends all the way up the Java object hierarchy. Thus, `SimpleApplet` inherits functionality from all of its superclasses—from `Applet`, `Panel`, `Container`, `Component`, and `Object` (Fig. 4–12). Thus, the `add()` method, which is defined in the `Container` class, is used to add a `Component` to a `Container`:

```
public Component add(Component comp)
```

The `Component` is passed as the value of its parameter. As we see in the program, because a `SimpleApplet` *isa* `Container`, it can use the `add()` method to add components to itself (see Fig. 4–10).

For example, in `SimpleApplet`'s `init()` method, the following code adds the `toggle` Button to the applet:

```
public void init()
{
    toggle = new Button ("The machine is off");
    ... // Code omitted here
    add(toggle);
} // init()
```

Components that are added to an applet will be displayed when the applet itself is executed (Fig. 4–9).

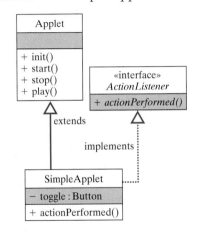

FIGURE 4–11 `SimpleApplet` is a subclass of `Applet` and it implements the `ActionListener` interface. In UML, the names of abstract items (*actionPerformed()* and *ActionListener*) are italicized.

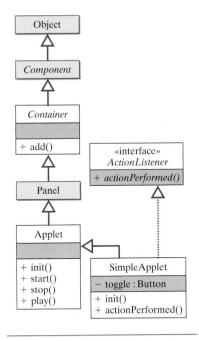

FIGURE 4–12 Hierarchy showing the position of the `SimpleApplet` in the Java class hierarchy. Both of its methods (`init()` and `actionPerformed()`), are inherited.

> **EFFECTIVE DESIGN: The Inheritance Principle.**   An object of a particular subclass can use the `public` and `protected` methods and variables of any of its superclasses. The object *inherits* the functionality contained in its superclasses.

4.5.2   Implementing an Interface

Java interface

A Java **interface** is like a class but it contains only methods and constants (`final` variables). It cannot contain instance variables. The designer of an interface specifies what methods are supported by the classes that *implement* the interface. In the interface definition, the methods are defined abstractly—that is, without specifying the body of the method. The method's body—its implementation—is defined within those classes that implement the method. (You might want to refer back to the discussion of interfaces and polymorphism in Section 0.7.7 and 0.7.8.)

Defining vs. implementing a method

The idea of an `interface` corresponds to what we've been saying all along about the role that methods play in defining an object's interface. The public methods in a Java class are like the buttons on your clothes dryer; they define the dryer's actions or behavior. If you want to tell the dryer to use the permanent press cycle, you press the "Permanent Press" button. If your dryer doesn't contain a "Spin Only" button, then there's no way to tell it to spin the clothes without heat. The dryer's buttons constrain the way you interact with the dryer in much the same way that a class's methods constrain the way you interact with its objects.

Interfaces vs. classes

One use of an `interface` is to define methods that can extend the functionality of a variety of different classes. Defining a class that implements an interface allows the class to attach the methods contained in the interface. This would be something like installing a "Spin Only" button on your dryer. By wiring it up in the correct way, you can add this new functionality to a dryer that previously lacked the ability to spin clothes with the heat turned off. `SimpleApplet`'s use of the `ActionListener` interface is an example of this kind of extension to a class. It adds `actionPerformed()`, a method that enables objects to perform actions in response to events, such as mouse clicks, that happen during the running of the program.

The `ActionListener` interface is defined as follows:

```
public abstract interface ActionListener extends EventListener
{
    public abstract void actionPerformed(ActionEvent e);
}
```

Abstract methods

Instead of using the keyword `class` in its definition, `ActionListener` uses the keyword `interface`. The definition designates `ActionListener` as an *abstract* interface. An **abstract interface** or an `abstract class` is one that contains one or more abstract methods. An **abstract method** is one that lacks an implementation—that is, it does not have a method body. In the `ActionListener` definition, note that the definition of `actionPerformed()` has a semicolon where its body should be.

Declaring this method as `abstract` means that its implementation will be left to the class that *implements* it. Its signature specifies what the method should do. In this case, `actionPerformed()` should take an `Action-Event` object named *e* and perform some kind of action. Of course, the details of the action that's performed are left to the implementor.

SimpleApplet provides the following implementation of `actionPer-formed()`:

```
public void actionPerformed(ActionEvent e)
{
    String str = toggle.getLabel();          // Get the button's label
    if (str.equals("The machine is on"))     // and change it
        toggle.setLabel("The machine is off");
    else                                     // or
        toggle.setLabel("The machine is on");  // change it back
} // actionPerformed()
```

Note that the header in this definition has the same signature as the abstract definition given in the `ActionListener` interface. All we have added to the method is its body, the list of executable statements that specifies, for this program, what action should be performed when a button is clicked. We have, thus, implemented the `actionPerformed()` method in a way that is appropriate to SimpleApplet.

Implementing an abstract method

| JAVA LANGUAGE RULE | Implementing an Interface. Implementing an interface means filling in the details in the method body for each abstract method defined in the `interface`. |

4.5.3 Extending Functionality

In addition to inheriting functionality from its superclasses and interfaces, a subclass, such as SimpleApplet, also extends the functionality of its superclasses and interfaces.

An `Applet` is an executable object that can be run from within a Web browser. Therefore, it contains methods that the browser can invoke to `init()`, `start()`, and `stop()` applets (Fig. 4–11). The `init()` method is a stub method, which is meant to be *overridden* or *redefined* in its subclasses:

Stub methods

```
public class Applet extends Panel  // Partial definition
{   ...
    public void init() { }     // Stub method, trivial body
    ...
}
```

To *override* a stub predefined method, a method with the exact same signature must be defined in the subclass, as in this example of `init()`:

Overriding a method

```
public void init ()
{
    toggle = new Button ("The machine is off");
    toggle.addActionListener(this);
    add(toggle);
} // init()
```

The role of the `init()` method is to *initialize* the applet, which usually consists of initializing its instance variables, creating and initializing its various components, and adding them to the applet. For this program, the only instance variable is `toggle`, a `Button` that is created and then added to the applet.

The first statement in `init()` creates a `Button` labeled "The machine is off". The second statement registers the `toggle` with the object that will respond to its clicks. (We'll explain more about this later.) The third statement adds `toggle` to the applet. These are the only initialization steps necessary for `SimpleApplet`.

Calling `init()` *to start the applet*

The `init()` method is an example of a method you will never invoke in your program. Instead, `init()` is called automatically *by the browser* when the applet is executed. When you run a Java applet from within a browser (or appletviewer), the browser creates an instance of the applet and begins its execution by calling the applet's `init()` method. For example, suppose the browser uses names such as `applet1`, `applet2`, and so on to name the applets it creates. Then the following code segment illustrates how the browser would begin execution of `SimpleApplet`:

```
SimpleApplet applet1 = new SimpleApplet(); // Create an instance
applet1.init();                            //  and initialize it
```

The first statement in this example creates an instance of `SimpleApplet`. The second calls `applet1`'s `init()` method, which creates a `Button` named `toggle` and adds it to `applet1` (Fig. 4–13).

EFFECTIVE DESIGN: The Extensibility Principle. A class definition extends the functionality of its superclass by *overriding* or *redefining* its methods.

A similar mechanism is at work in the case of the `actionPerformed()` method. `SimpleApplet` implements this method by defining its method body. But `actionPerformed()` is another example of a method you will never directly invoke in your programs. Instead, Java automatically invokes `actionPerformed()` whenever a `Button` is clicked (Fig. 4–14). By just implementing `actionPerformed()` with statements that pertain to `toggle`, we can get `SimpleApplet` to take appropriate action whenever `toggle` is clicked.

Calling `actionPerformed()` *to handle events*

4.5.4 Using the Inheritance Hierarchy

Java's default behavior

What if we had forgotten to override the `init()` method? When `applet1.init()` is called by the browser, Java first tries to find it in `SimpleApplet`—that is, in the class to which `applet1` belongs. If Java doesn't find

it there, it searches upward through SimpleApplet's **inheritance hierarchy** until it finds it. First it looks in SimpleApplet's parent class, which is Applet (Fig. 4–12). What Java finds in Applet is the stub version of init(), which it then executes. Of course, because this version of init() is a stub method that does nothing, no components would be created and nothing would be added to the applet. Thus, Java uses an object's inheritance hierarchy to determine which method to run when a method associated with the object is invoked.

To see this mechanism at work again, consider what happens when the add() method is invoked in SimpleApplet's init() method:

```
add(toggle);
```

This method invocation does not include a receiving object, and so it is assumed to pertain to *this* object—that is, to applet1, the SimpleApplet. Thus, Java will look in SimpleApplet for an add() method. Not finding one there, Java will look in SimpleApplet's parent class, Applet. Not finding one there either, Java will continue up SimpleApplet's inheritance hierarchy until it finds an add() method. According to Figure 4–12, the add() method is defined in the Container class. So Java will use the method definition given there, which describes how to add a Component (in this case, toggle) to a Container (in this case, applet1). Thus, in this case, applet1 uses functionality inherited from the Container class to perform the task of adding a component to itself.

> **JAVA LANGUAGE RULE** Inheritance. Java uses an object's *inheritance hierarchy* to resolve method invocations associated with the object. It searches up the object's hierarchy until the method is found.

What if we had forgotten to implement the actionPerformed() method? In this case, SimpleApplet won't compile successfully. It is a syntax error to declare that a class implements some interface without providing an implementation for *all* the methods defined in that interface. Thus, in SimpleApplet, we must provide a full definition of the actionPerformed() method.

> **JAVA LANGUAGE RULE** Implementing an Interface. If a class declares that it implements an interface, all the methods from the interface must be implemented in the class.

This also points out the difference between a *stub method*, such as init(), and an *abstract method*, such as actionPerformed(). A stub method *has* an implementation, but the implementation is trivial—one that will "work" with any of a class's subclasses. By contrast, an abstract method has *no* implementation. Any class that implements such a method must, therefore, define its body or the program simply won't compile.

Stub vs. abstract methods

4.5.5 Polymorphism and Extensibility (Optional)

One question that might occur to you is why we bother to define the `init()` method in the `Applet` class if we're just going to override it in its subclasses. The answer holds the key to understanding how applets work.

Extensible systems

Java applets are an excellent example of an *extensible* system—a system that is designed to work on objects that have yet to be defined. Because any applet—any object that belongs to a subclass of the `Applet` class—has `init()`, `start()`, and `stop()` methods, it can be executed by a Web browser. If the applet redefines these inherited methods, it can customize its performance to suit its purposes. If it fails to redefine these methods, then stub methods, defined in its superclasses, will be used when the browser invokes `applet1.init()` or `applet1.start()`. In either case, the applet will run successfully within the browser's context. If the applet does not redefine inherited methods, then its functionality will be trivial—that is, it won't really do anything. However, if the methods are overridden, the applet can significantly extend what its superclasses do.

By thus designing a system that will process generic `Applet`s—applets that do nothing—we also have a system that will process `SimpleApplet`s and all other subclasses of `Applet`. Java's applet system is *extensible*. By designing certain functionality into the superclass, we can extend a system to its subclasses—indeed, to subclasses that are not yet defined.

> **EFFECTIVE DESIGN: The Extensibility Mechanism.**   Generic functionality designed into a superclass can be extended to its subclasses by *overriding* its stub methods.

Method polymorphism

Like the `toString()` method, which was described in the *Object-Oriented Design* section of Chapter 3, the `init()` method is an example of a **polymorphic method**—that is, a method that has different behavior depending upon the object on which it is called. To illustrate the concept of polymorphism again, let's consider the following example. (This would be a good place to review the discussion of polymorphism in Section 0.7.8.)

Because a browser written in Java must be able to run any applet without knowing the name of its class, it would use a variable of type `Applet` to refer to the applet:

```
Applet applet;
```

Now suppose the browser is running two different applets, `AppletA` and `AppletB`. `AppletA` has the following `init()` method:

```
public void init()
{
    System.out.println("AppletA");
}
```

`AppletB` has the following `init()` method:

```
public void init()
{
    System.out.println("AppletB");
}
```

Now consider the following code segment from our hypothetical browser:

```
Applet applet = new AppletA();
applet.init();              // Prints "AppletA"
applet = new AppletB();
applet.init();              // Prints "AppletB"
```

Thus, the same exact method call—applet.init()—will lead to completely different behavior. It is in this sense that the init() method is said to be polymorphic. Its behavior depends on the type of object (AppletA or AppletB) on which it is called.

Inheritance and polymorphism are important principles of object-oriented design. They can be used to design systems that can easily be extended to accommodate new objects. In this way class libraries, such as the applet package, can be created once and used to build a whole range of objects that inherit and extend the generic features of their superclasses.

Object-oriented design

> **EFFECTIVE DESIGN: Object-Oriented Design.** *Class inheritance* and *polymorphism* can be used to design *extensible* systems—that is, systems that inherit and extend the functionality of their superclasses.

SELF-STUDY EXERCISES

EXERCISE 4.5 The HTML files that contain applets can have tags that supply information to the applet. These are called parameters. The Applet class contains a method named getParameter() (Fig. 4.1) that enables the applet to get a parameter that's defined by name in the applet's HTML file. For example, suppose that SimpleApplet (Fig. 4–10) had an HTML file containing the following HTML code:

```
<html>
 <head><title>Simple Applet</title></head>
 <body>
  <applet code="SimpleApplet.class" width=200 height=200>
    <parameter name="author" value="Java Java Java">
    <parameter name="date" value="February 1999">
  </applet>
 </body>
</html>
```

Add statements to SimpleApplet's init() method to print the values of the "author" and "date" parameters. Just use System.out.println().

EXERCISE 4.6 Define an applet named SmallApplet that simply displays a Button with the label "Click me!" Don't worry about the applet's action-Performed() method.

EXERCISE 4.7 Add a statement to the applet you defined in the previous problem to print your button's label in the init() method.

EXERCISE 4.8 Java's + operator is also polymorphic. Explain.

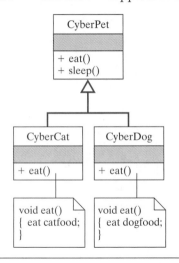

FIGURE 4–15   The polymorphic eat() method.

Events drive the program

Mouse events

Key events

EXERCISE 4.9   As shown in Figure 4–15, define two subclasses of Cyber-Pet named CyberDog and CyberCat, and use polymorphism to give dogs and cats different eating behaviors. Have a CyberDog print "Eating dog-food. Arf!" when its eat() method is called, and have a CyberCat print "Eating a bird. Meow!" when its eat() method is called. Hint: Override the eat() method in each subclass. Don't forget to use super() to put the pets into the eating state.

4.6   Event-Driven Programming

Java applets run under an **event-driven execution** model (Fig. 4–16). According to this model, anything that happens while the computer is running is classified as an event. Every keystroke and mouse click, every time a disk is inserted into a disk drive, every time you close a window on the screen, an event is generated. The computer hardware is designed to encode and classify these events so that they can be handled by the system software—either the operating system (such as Windows, Unix, MacOS) or the browser (such as Navigator, Explorer).

When a regular application program is running, including a Java application, events generated by the hardware are first passed up to the operating system. The operating system handles those events for which it is responsible and passes any events that it doesn't handle to the application program.

For example, if you are running a word processor, whenever you click the mouse on an object that's outside of the word processor's window, that event will be handled by the operating system. Thus, the event generated by clicking in the window of another application (an e-mail program, say) will cause the operating system to transfer control from the word processor to the e-mail program.

On the other hand, if you type a character in the word processor window, that event will be passed up through the operating system to the word processing application, where it is handled appropriately. In modern windowing environments, such as MacOS and Windows, all applications are event driven, which means that all applications are designed to handle those events that fall under their responsibility.

The same sort of thing happens with a Java applet, except that with applets, the Java-enabled browser becomes another level of software resid-

FIGURE 4–16   Java's event model.

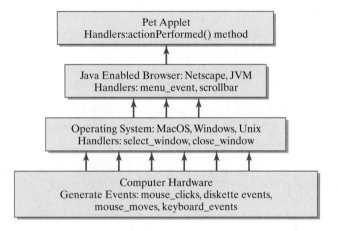

ing between your applet and the computer hardware (Fig. 4–16). Events generated by the hardware are passed up through the operating system to the browser, which handles those events that apply to the browser itself. Events that apply to the applet are passed on to it. When the applet receives an event, it must handle the event in an appropriate way. If you click on your browser's menu bar or on its *reload* button, that event will be handled by the browser itself. If you click on an applet's button, for example, the `toggle` button in `SimpleApplet`, that event will be handled by the applet.

Handling events

4.6.1   The Java Event Model

In Java, all events are represented by a subclass of the `java.util.Event-Object` class. Events that happen as part of an applet's interface, AWT events, are defined as subclasses of `java.awt.AWTEvent`, which is a subclass of `EventObject`. For example, a `Button` can be the source of `ActionEvents` and `MouseEvents`, both of which are generated whenever the user clicks on the `Button`. Similarly, a `TextField` object can be the source of `ActionEvents`, `KeyEvents`, and `TextEvents`, all of which are generated whenever the user types a key inside the `TextField`.

Java's event hierarchy

Figure 4–17 shows Java's `EventObject` hierarchy. Each time an event occurs, some type of `EventObject` is created to represent the event. Among other things, the `EventObject` records the *source* of the event—the object in which the event happened—the time and location of the event, and so on. For example, when the user types a key on the keyboard, a KEYPRESS event and KEYRELEASE event are generated in quick succession. The KeyEvent

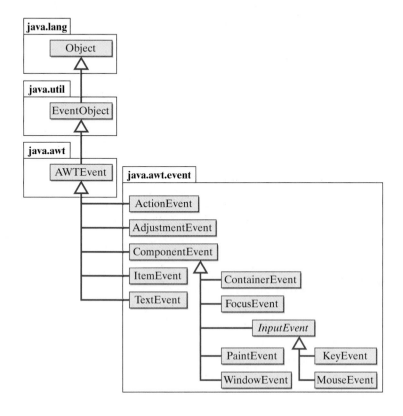

FIGURE 4–17   Java's event hierarchy. Note that classes whose names are *italicized*, such as `InputEvent`, are abstract classes.

objects created in these two cases would record when the event happened, what key was pressed and released, and whether any special keys, such as the Shift key, were also pressed at the same time.

Similarly, when the user moves the mouse in the applet's window, a MOUSEMOVE event is generated to indicate that the mouse has been moved, and a MouseEvent object is created to keep track of the mouse's horizontal and vertical window coordinates.

Multiple events

If you point the mouse at a button on the applet and then click it, this indicates to Java that you wish to take whatever action is associated with the button. The ActionEvent object created for this event will record the source of the mouse click—which button was clicked. A single mouse click on a Button will generate both mouse events and action events. It is possible to handle one or the other or both of these types of events, depending on what the applet is supposed to do. In SimpleApplet, we just handle the action event and simply ignore mouse events. When we study drawing programs later in the book, we'll learn how to handle the lower-level mouse events.

Tracing a button click

Let's trace what happens when the user clicks on the toggle Button in SimpleApplet. A mouse click on toggle will generate an ACTION.EVENT. Java will automatically create a new ActionEvent object with appropriate information about this particular event—what object was clicked, and so on—and pass it to the actionPerformed() method in the object designated as toggle's ActionListener. As its name suggests, an ActionListener is an object that listens for action events. It is the object that you designate in the program to handle that particular type of event. Let's see how we tell Java which object will serve as the action listener.

Button actions

Whenever we create a Button, we must tell Java which object will handle its actions. We do that in the init() method by designating an ActionListener for toggle:

```
toggle.addActionListener(this);
```

The addActionListener() method is defined in the Button class and has the following signature:

```
public void addActionListener(ActionListener l);
```

FIGURE 4–18   By executing `toggle.addActionListener(this)`, `SimpleApplet` sets up a relationship between itself and the button in which it listens for ActionEvents on the button.

It takes a single parameter of type ActionListener. An ActionListener is any object that implements the ActionListener interface. Because SimpleApplet implements ActionListener, *this* instantiation of it—that is, this applet—counts as an ActionListener and can be designated as the listener for clicks on toggle (Fig. 4–18). Note that this is a Java keyword that refers to the current object—the object that executes the this statement.

JAVA LANGUAGE RULE   this. The this keyword is self-referential. It refers to whichever object uses the term. It is similar to saying "me" or "I."

Event objects are passed to listener objects

So any clicks on toggle will generate an ActionEvent that is passed to the actionPerformed() method implemented in SimpleApplet. Let's look at the details of that method:

```
public void actionPerformed(ActionEvent e)
{
    String str = toggle.getLabel();          // Get the button's label
    if (str.equals("The machine is on"))      // and change it
        toggle.setLabel("The machine is off");
    else                                      // or
        toggle.setLabel("The machine is on"); // change it back
} // actionPerformed()
```

The `actionPerformed()` method begins by getting `toggle`'s label, assign-ing it to the local `String` variable `str`. It then checks whether `str` equals "The machine is on" or "The machine is off" and changes `toggle`'s label to its opposite value using the `setLabel()` method. The methods `setLabel()` and `getLabel()` are defined in the `Component` class and inherited by the `Button` class.

The event handler

Inheritance

In this case, because `toggle` is the only object in `SimpleApplet` that gener-ates `ActionEvents`, we know that it must have been clicked in order for ac-tionPerformed() to have been invoked by the browser. Therefore, we can proceed directly to toggling its label from "The machine is off" to "The machine is on," or vice versa. (As we will see, in other cases `actionPer-formed()` may be handling events for several different buttons, in which case we would have to determine which button was clicked before taking action.)

Figure 4–19 summarizes the complex sequence of actions and events that goes into an applet user interface. The applet itself must first be es-tablished as the `ActionListener` for the `Button` that the user will click on. When the user clicks on the button, an ACTION_EVENT is generated and passed to the Java Virtual Machine (JVM). The JVM creates an `ActionEvent` and passes it to the applet, via its `actionPerformed()` method. Within that method the applet will get the button's label and toggle it by invoking the `getLabel()` and `setLabel()` methods in succession.

Figure 4–19 provides a good illustration of the object-oriented program-ming principle of *interacting objects*. In addition to the browser and the JVM we have an `Applet`, a `Button`, and its `String` label ("The machine is off") all working together by sending and receiving messages among themselves.

Interacting objects

The action taken whenever `toggle` is clicked is very simple. However, the Java code required to effect this action is somewhat complicated, and it is important that you understand how it works. Thus, to create a `Button`

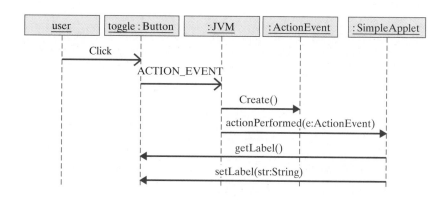

FIGURE 4–19 This UML sequence diagram depicts the sequence of events that takes place when the user clicks on `SimpleApplet`'s `toggle` button.

Creating and handling a button

on an applet and handle its actions appropriately, the following steps must be taken:

1. Declare a subclass of `Applet` that implements the `ActionListener` interface.
2. Declare a `Button` instance variable in the applet.
3. Create a `Button` object in the applet's `init()` method.
4. Use `addActionListener()` in the `init()` method to designate that `this` applet is the listener for the `Button`.
5. Use the `add()` method (in `init()`) to add the `Button` to the applet.
6. Implement an `actionPerformed()` method in the applet with the particular actions that you want performed each time the `Button` is clicked.

As our applets get more sophisticated in their design and behavior we will add steps to this process, but the overall outline of the code will remain more or less as described here.

4.6.2 Tracing an Applet

As we have said, as long as `SimpleApplet` is running, any events that happen within its window will be passed to it. If the event is an `ACTION.EVENT`, such as a click on the `toggle` button, it will be passed to the applet's `actionPerformed()` method, where appropriate action will be taken. In effect, after the applet is initialized, it will do nothing until it is passed an `ActionEvent` that indicates that the user has clicked on `toggle`, in which case it will spring into action and change `toggle`'s label. This behavior will continue until the applet is destroyed.

Browser/applet relationship

Figure 4–20 uses pseudocode to show what happens when `SimpleApplet` is run. As shown there, after creating and initializing an instance of `SimpleApplet` named `applet1`, the browser repeatedly checks whether an `ACTION.EVENT` occurred and, if so, passes the event to `applet1`'s `actionPerformed()` method.

Let's wrap up this section by providing a trace showing the order of execution of `SimpleApplet` for a couple of simple events. Recall from Chapter 1 that an applet is run when the browser opens an HTML document that contains an applet tag specifying the applet's class:

FIGURE 4–20 A summary of what happens when a Java applet is run within a browser.

```
SimpleApplet applet1 = new SimpleApplet();  // Create an applet,
applet1.init();                             //  and call its init()
...                                         // Handle other tasks


repeat  until applet_is_stopped
{...                                         // Handle other tasks
   if (ACTION_EVENT)                         // If an action occurs,
      applet1.actionPerformed(anActionEvent); // pass it to applet
   if (user_quits_browser)                   // If the user quits,
      applet1.destroy();                      // kill the applet
}
```

```
import java.applet.*;
import java.awt.*;
import java.awt.event.*;

public class SimpleApplet extends Applet implements ActionListener
{
     private Button toggle;          // From java.awt.*

     public void init ()
     {
1        toggle = new Button ("The machine is off");
2        toggle.addActionListener(this);
3        add(toggle);
     } // init()

     public void actionPerformed(ActionEvent e)
     {
4,7      String str = toggle.getLabel();       // Get the button's
5,8      if (str.equals("The machine is on"))   // label and change it
9            toggle.setLabel("The machine is off");
         else                                   // or
6            toggle.setLabel("The machine is on");  // change it back
     } // actionPerformed()
} // SimpleApplet
```

FIGURE 4–21   A trace of SimpleApplet showing the order of execution that would result in two consecutive clicks on its toggle button.

```
<html>
 <head><title>Simple Applet</title></head>
 <body>
  <applet code="SimpleApplet.class" width=200 height=200>
    <parameter name="author" value="Java Java Java">
    <parameter name="date" value="February 1999">
  </applet>
 </body>
</html>
```

The applet tag tells the browser which Java class to instantiate and load into memory.

The order of execution of the statements in SimpleApplet is shown in Figure 4–21. Note that the statements in init() are the first to be executed. If an applet contains an init() method—and not all applets do—then its statements will be executed first. Their effect is to create the toggle button with the label "The machine is off." Once the applet is initialized, the browser waits for events to happen, passing all clicks on the toggle button to the actionPerformed() method. The first time toggle is clicked, statements numbered 4 through 6 will be executed, and its label will be changed to "The machine is on." The second time it is clicked, statements 7 through 9 will be executed, and its label is changed back to "The machine is off." Execution will continue in this way until the applet is destroyed.

Tracing SimpleApplet

SELF-STUDY EXERCISES

EXERCISE 4.10   A TextField is a component into which the user can type text. Whenever the user types the Enter key in a TextField, an ActionEvent is generated. Using the `toggle Button` example as a guide, describe how an applet would be programmed to handle this event.

EXERCISE 4.11 What would happen if the line labeled 2 in Figure 4–21 were deleted?

EXERCISE 4.12 What would happen if the line labeled 3 in Figure 4–21 were deleted?

4.7 CASE STUDY: The `CyberPetApplet`

Our CyberPet simulation program from previous chapters represented a CyberPet as an object whose entire state could be specified by its name and by whether it was eating or sleeping. The `CyberPet` class supplied two commands that allowed us to change a `CyberPet`'s state: `eat()`, which put the `CyberPet` in the eating state, and `sleep()`, which put the `CyberPet` in the sleeping state.

Let's now build a Graphical User Interface (GUI) that will support this simulation. The interface should enable us to interact with a single Cyber-Pet object. It should display the CyberPet's state at all times, including its name and whether it is eating or sleeping. The interface should also make it possible for the user to issue "eat" and "sleep" commands, and it should display the CyberPet's new state after each action.

4.7.1 Specifying the Interface

What objects do we need?

As in designing any other Java program, the first question we need to ask is *what objects are needed to perform the program's task?*

One technique used in decomposing a problem is to analyze the problem statement to identify the objects that will make up a solution to the problem. A good general rule to follow is that the nouns in the problem statement are likely candidates for distinct objects in the problem solution.

> EFFECTIVE DESIGN: Problem Decomposition. In order to decompose a problem into its constituents, identify the nouns in the problem statement as likely candidates for objects in the problem solution.

The nouns mentioned in describing our present problem (at the start of Section 4–6) include CyberPet, GUI, commands (eat and sleep), state, and name. Obviously our solution will involve a `CyberPet` object. The GUI is best handled by some kind of applet object. So we will define a subclass of `Applet`. The commands required in our solution suggest that we use `Buttons` to allow the user to issue commands, and the pet's name can be displayed in a `Label` and its state can be displayed in a `TextField`. One reason for choosing a `Label` for its name is that its name is not likely to change and AWT `Labels` are meant to be read-only strings. On the other, because its state is expected to change, we use a `TextField`, which can store different values over time. Fortunately, most of the objects needed for our solution are defined in the Java API.

Problem decomposition

Our plan, then, for designing this solution is as follows. The `CyberPet` will represent the pet and simulate its eating and sleeping. The applet will serve as an interface between the user and the `CyberPet`, as shown in Figure 4–22. It will allow the user to issue commands, such as "eat" and

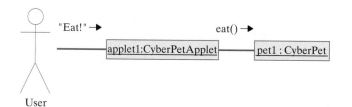

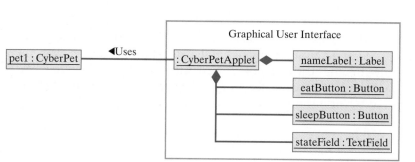

FIGURE 4–22 Relationship between the user, the `CyberPetApplet` object, and a `CyberPet` object.

FIGURE 4–23 This UML collaboration diagram shows the objects that will be interacting in the `CyberPetApplet` program. The black diamond symbol represents the **hasa** relationship. In this case the applet *has* (contains) several `Button`, `TextField`, and `Label` components. Note that all objects except `CyberPet` itself are part of the applet's GUI.

"sleep," and it will pass these along to the `CyberPet`. Of course, as shown in Figure 4–23, the applet itself will contain several other objects—such as `Buttons` and `TextFields`—to help it carry out its tasks. An applet implementation, as we saw in the previous example, will generate a number of other objects—such as `ActionEvents`—to help effect the applet's behavior.

The screenshot in Figure 4–24 shows the appearance of the components used in `CyberPetApplet` objects. It has a `TextField`, which is used to display the `CyberPet`'s current state. It has a `Label`, which is used to display the `CyberPet`'s name. It has two `Buttons`, which are used to give the `CyberPet` commands that will change its state. Whenever the user clicks on the "Eat" `Button`, the applet should display `CyberPet`'s new state in the `TextField`.

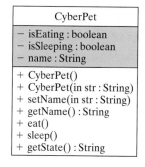

FIGURE 4–24 A screenshot of the pet simulation.

4.7.2 Designing `CyberPetApplet`

The `CyberPetApplet` will provide an interface between the user and the latest version of `CyberPet`. `CyberPet` (Fig. 4–25) contains public methods `eat()` and `sleep()`, which the applet can use to carry out user commands, and it has public methods `getName()` and `getState()`, which can be used by the applet to get the `CyberPet`'s name and state. The applet can then display the pet's name and state on the applet.

Designing an applet is the same as designing any other Java class. We must decide on the applet's overall role, on what information it will need and what methods it will need to carry out its task.

We begin with `CyberPetApplets` place in the Java class hierarchy. As this partial definition shows, `CyberPetApplet` extends the `Applet` class and implements `ActionListener`:

FIGURE 4–25 The `CyberPet` class.

```
import java.awt.*;
import java.applet.*;
import java.awt.event.*;

public class CyberPetApplet extends Applet implements ActionListener
{
} // CyberPetApplet
```

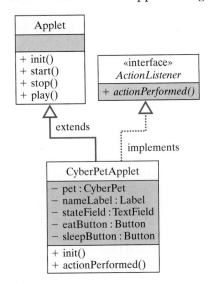

FIGURE 4–26 This UML class diagram shows details of the inheritance relationships of the CyberPetApplet class.

What data do we need?

Declaring vs. instantiating

FIGURE 4–27 Two ways of declaring and instantiating an applet's instance variables: (1) Declare and instantiate in the global portion of the class; (2) declare in the global portion and instantiate in the init() method.

As in the definition of SimpleApplet, the keyword extends signifies that CyberPetApplet is a subclass of Applet. Similarly, the keyword implements signifies that CyberPetApplet will implement the methods defined in the ActionListener interface. This definition sets up the inheritance relationship shown in Figure 4–26.

The next step in defining CyberPetApplet is to define its instance variables. As Figure 4–26 shows, there are instance variables for the various GUI elements, plus an instance variable for the CyberPet. There are two ways to define instance variables. The identifiers for the instance variables can be declared and instantiated in the global portion of the class, immediately after the header (Fig. 4–27 top). Alternatively, the identifiers for the instance variables can be declared in the global portion of the class definition, and their instantiation can be done in the init() method (Fig. 4–27 bottom).

For this applet there is no practical difference between these approaches. Let's adopt the latter method, because it makes clearer the distinction between declaring a variable and instantiating the object that becomes the reference of the variable. Note that all of the instance variables used in this example are declared private, which means they can only be accessed from within the CyberPetApplet class. This is an appropriate

```
public class CyberPetApplet extends Applet          // Top (1)
{
  // Declare and instantiate the instance variables.
    private CyberPet pet1 = new CyberPet("Socrates"); // The CyberPet
    private Label nameLabel = new Label("Name:");     // A Label
    private TextField stateField = new TextField(12); // A TextField
    private Button eatButton = new Button("Eat!");    // Two Buttons
    private Button sleepButton = new Button("Sleep!");
} // CyberPetApplet


public class CyberPetApplet extends Applet          // Bottom (2)
{
  // Declare instance variables.
    private CyberPet pet1;                    // The CyberPet
    private Label nameLabel;                  // Label
    private TextField stateField;             // TextField
    private Button eatButton, sleepButton;    // Buttons

    public void init()
    {
      // Instantiate the instance variables
        pet1 = new CyberPet("Socrates");      // The CyberPet
        nameLabel = new Label("Hi! My name is " + pet1.getName() +
                              " and currently I am : ");
        stateField = new TextField(12);       // TextField
        eatButton = new Button("Eat!");       // Buttons
        eatButton.addActionListener(this);
        sleepButton = new Button("Sleep!");
        sleepButton.addActionListener(this);
    } // init
} // CyberPetApplet
```

design, as there is no obvious need for these variables to be accessible outside of the applet itself.

The instance variables used in CyberPetApplet are of two varieties. First there is a CyberPet variable named pet1. This variable is instantiated by invoking the constructor method we defined in the previous chapter:

What instance variables do we need?

```
CyberPet("Socrates")
```

which has the effect of initializing pet1's state and giving pet1 the name "Socrates." Recall from previous chapters that CyberPet is initially in the eating state.

In addition to the CyberPet variable, there are several GUI objects. These objects are instantiated by invoking their respective constructor methods. Because all of these objects are defined in Java class libraries, such as java.awt, we have to consult the documentation of these libraries to determine the signatures of the various constructor methods. We will provide a more detailed discussion of each of these component classes in Chapter 9, but for now, let's just consider the following three constructor methods:

Object instantiation

```
Label(String)     // Set Label's text to String
Button(String)    // Set Button's label to String
TextField(int)    // Create a TextField of int characters in length
```

Each of the Label, Button, and TextField classes has several different constructors, but we limit ourselves in this example to one constructor for each type of object.

A Label is a component that displays a single line of uneditable text in the applet's window. Typically, a Label is used to label a portion of the applet or to prompt the user in some way. In CyberPetApplet we use a Label to greet the user and display the pet's name. The constructor used in this case takes a single String parameter, whose value is used to set the label's text:

Labels

```
nameLabel = new Label("Hi! My name is " + pet1.getName() +
                    " and currently I am : ");
```

Note the use of string concatenation together with getName() to incorporate pet1's name into the label. The method is used to get the name from pet1.

As we saw in Chapter 2, a Button is a labeled component that is used to trigger some form of action when it is clicked. The Button constructor in this case takes a single String parameter, whose value is used to set the initial value of its label. In this example, we have two buttons, which are instantiated as follows:

Buttons

```
eatButton = new Button("Eat!");
sleepButton = new Button("Sleep!");
```

As their labels suggest, the user will click on the "Eat!" button to tell the pet to eat and on the "Sleep!" button to tell the pet to sleep.

After we instantiate a Button, we need to register it with an Action-Listener as in the following statements:

Algorithm: Handling action events

```
eatButton.addActionListener(this);
sleepButton.addActionListener(this);
```

Note that both buttons will use the same listener, the applet itself, which means we'll have to distinguish which button was actually clicked within the actionPerformed() method.

TextField

A TextField is a component that displays a single line of editable text. The constructor used in this case takes a single int parameter whose value is used to set the width of the text field—that is, how many characters it can display:

```
stateField = new TextField(12);
```

The TextField used in this program will display up to 12 characters, which seems sufficient to display strings such as "eating" and "sleeping." Because stateField is being used to display information and not to input information, we will make it *uneditable*, which will prevent the user from typing in it. We will also display pet1's initial state as its initial value. The following statements will effect these changes:

```
// Initialize the text fields.
stateField.setEditable(false);
stateField.setText(pet1.getState());
```

The setEditable() method is defined in TextComponent, which is the superclass of TextField.

Note that in the second statement the applet gets pet1's state using its getState() method, and passes it to stateField using its setText() method. Here we have three objects interacting: The applet, let's call it applet1, is in control of the activity and mediates the interaction between pet1 and stateField. In more anthropomorphic terms, the applet asks pet1, "What is your state?" and pet1 answers "sleeping." The applet then tells stateField "Use 'sleeping' as your value." Figure 4–28 shows this relationship.

Once the GUI components have been instantiated and initialized they must be added to the applet. To understand this aspect of the program it is necessary again to consider the inheritance relationships involved with the Applet class.

Figure 4–29 shows the complete class diagram for the CyberPetApplet program. It is an expansion of Figure 4–26. In this case we have added

Interacting objects

FIGURE 4–28 This UML sequence diagram shows the interaction over time between the CyberPet, the CyberPetApplet, and the TextField as a result of executing the statement: stateField.setText (pet1.getState()).

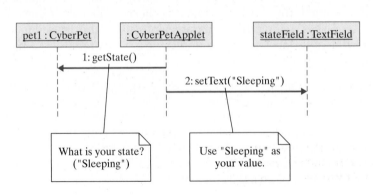

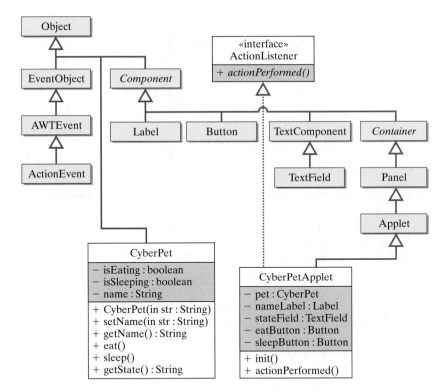

details about `CyberPetApplet`'s internal state. And we also show the relationships of the other classes involved in the program. Note that all GUI elements—`Button`s, `TextField`s, `Label`s, and even `Applet`s—are descendants of the `Component` class. Note also that an `Applet` is a `Container`, which means that it can "contain" other `Component`s. GUI components can be added to an applet by using the `add()` method, which is defined in `Container` and inherited by `CyberPetApplet`. `Component`s are usually added to an applet in its `init()` method, as shown in Figure 4–30.

> **DEBUGGING TIP: Adding Components to an Applet.** If you forget to *add* a component to the applet, it will not appear in the applet's window.

4.7.3 Applet Layout

What does it mean to *add* components to an applet? After all, an applet is an abstract thing, not a physical container. It's not really like dropping marbles into a cup. A `Container` in the Java class library is an *abstraction*, or a *model* of a real container. To model the idea of containment, each container maintains a list of its contents. Each time a component is added to a container, a new entry is made and added to the container's list. The entries on the list refer to the individual components themselves. Thus, it is possible for a container to display all of its components or to tell each of its components to display themselves. Adding the preceding components to `CyberPetApplet` means that `CyberPetApplet` maintains a list of these four components, which it manipulates in various ways as necessary to display the components on the screen.

The abstraction principle

FIGURE 4–30   The init() method.

```
public void init()
{
    /* Instantiate the instance variables.  This
     * creates both the CyberPet, pet1, and the
     * GUI elements that are displayed on the applet
     */
    pet1 = new CyberPet("Socrates");        // CyberPet

    /* Create the GUI components */

    nameLabel = new Label("Hi! My name is " + pet1.getName() +
                          " and currently I am : ");
    stateField = new TextField(12);
    eatButton = new Button("Eat!");         // Buttons
    eatButton.addActionListener(this);      // Assign the listeners
    sleepButton = new Button("Sleep!");
    sleepButton.addActionListener(this);

    /* Initialize the TextField  */

    stateField.setText(pet1.getState());
    stateField.setEditable(false);

    /* Add the components to the applet  */

    add(nameLabel);
    add(stateField);
    add(eatButton);
    add(sleepButton);

    setSize(300,150);        // Set the applet's size to 300 x 150 pixels
} // init
```

Default FlowLayout

This leads to another question. How will these components be arranged on the screen? Obviously screen layout is an important consideration in designing a GUI interface. The geometric relationships between the components can affect the program's usability. By default, components added to a container are arranged in what is known as a FlowLayout—one component after another arranged horizontally across the window starting at the top of the applet's window. If the window is too wide or too narrow, FlowLayout could lead to one or the other of the layouts shown in Figure 4–31.

The actual layout that results from FlowLayout depends on the browser and is quite arbitrary. In Chapter 9, we will learn how to gain more control over applet layout. For now, however, we can use the WIDTH and HEIGHT attributes in the APPLET tag to specify the applet's dimensions:

```
<html>
 <head><title>CyberPet Applet</title></head>
 <body>
  <applet code="CyberPetApplet.class" width=300 height=150>
  </applet>
 </body>
</html>
```

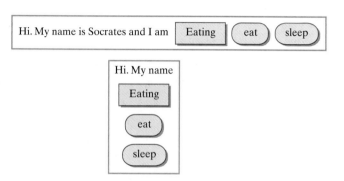

FIGURE 4–31 Possible flow layouts of CyberPetApplet in wide window and narrow windows.

For most browsers, the values used here will produce the layout shown in Figure 4–24. Another way to control the applet's window size is to use the setSize(int w, int h) method to set the applet's width (w) and height (h). This is a method that's defined in the Component class and inherited by the applet. You would place a call to this method in the applet's init() method, as shown in Figure 4–30.

4.7.4 Handling CyberPetApplet Actions

In order to handle events when the user clicks on either eatButton or sleepButton, we must implement the actionPerformed() method. Recall that actionPerformed() is an abstract method inherited from the Action-Listener interface (Fig. 4–29). Our implementation of actionPerformed() will be invoked when either eatButton or sleepButton is clicked. Therefore, it must be able to distinguish when the eatButton is clicked and when the sleepButton is clicked, as in the following implementation:

Handling user actions

```
public void actionPerformed(ActionEvent e)
{
    if (e.getSource() == eatButton)         // If eat button clicked,
        pet1.eat();                         //   tell the pet to eat
    else if (e.getSource() == sleepButton)  // If sleep button clicked,
        pet1.sleep();                       //   tell the pet to sleep

    stateField.setText(pet1.getState());    // Display the pet's state
} // actionPerformed()
```

An if-else statement is used in this case to choose between two alternatives. If the eatButton is clicked— e.getSource() == eatButton— then the pet is told to eat—pet1.eat(). Otherwise, if the sleepButton is clicked—e.getSource() == sleepButton—then the pet is told to sleep—pet1.sleep(). Following one or the other of these actions, the pet's new state is displayed in the applet's state field using the same statement that we used in init():

Which control structure?

```
stateField.setText(pet1.getState());  // Display new state
```

There are a number of points to note about this implementation of actionPerformed(). Most importantly, because it must be able to distinguish between clicks on both the eatButton and sleepButton, we need to use an if-else statement. This approach can be easily generalized to handle as many buttons as we have in an applet:

```
if (e.getSource() == firstButton)
  // Do firstButton's action
else if (e.getSource() == secondButton)
  // Do secondButton's action
else if (e.getSource() == thirdButton)
  // Do thirdButton's action
...
```

Which object caused the event?

Another important point is that we use the ActionEvent's getSource() method to determine which button was clicked. Recall that when a button is clicked, Java will create an ActionEvent containing information about the event, including its source—that is, the object that generated the event. The entire ActionEvent object is then passed to actionPerformed(), where it is referred to as e. As our applets become more sophisticated, we will get other information from e, but in this case we need only use getSource() to determine which button the user clicked.

4.7.5 Running CyberPetApplet

Testing and debugging

The complete listing of the CyberPetApplet.java class is shown in Figure 4–32. The line numbers indicate the order in which statements are executed. No line numbers are shown for the actionPerformed() method, because the order of execution there depends on what particular events take place during the program's execution.

Because so much happens automatically when a Java applet is run, it will be useful to trace CyberPetApplet's execution. As we saw in the SimpleApplet example, when you run an applet within your browser, the applet's class definition is used to create an instance of the applet. The first thing that happens is that the browser calls the applet's init() method to perform any initialization that may be necessary.

Following the call to init(), the browser starts the applet, which continues to run until it is stopped. (The browser uses the Applet's start() and stop() methods for these tasks.) Once an applet is running, the browser will repeatedly pass applet-related events to listener objects. In our example, we have designated the applet itself as the ActionListener for its two buttons. If either of these buttons is clicked, the applet invokes one of pet1's methods to change the pet's state.

OBJECT-ORIENTED DESIGN:
Inheritance and Polymorphism (Optional)

Extending a class

The ability to extend an existing class is one of the most powerful features of object-oriented programming. It allows objects to reuse code defined in the superclasses without having to redefine or recompile the code. Thus, CyberPetApplet uses the public methods defined for Applets, Panels, Containers, Components, and Objects simply by invoking them with a standard method call. By the same token, it can use all of the public and protected

```
import java.applet.*;
import java.awt.*;
import java.awt.event.*;

public class CyberPetApplet extends Applet implements ActionListener
{
    // Declare instance variables
1   private CyberPet pet1;                      // The CyberPet
2   private Label nameLabel;                    // A Label
3   private TextField stateField;               // A TextField
4   private Button eatButton, sleepButton;      // Two Buttons

    public void init()
    {
        /*
         * Instantiate the instance variables.  This creates both the
         * CyberPet, pet1, and the GUI elements that are
           displayed on the applet.
         */
5       pet1 = new CyberPet("Socrates");    // CyberPet

        // Create the GUI components

6       nameLabel = new Label("Hi! My name is " + pet1.getName() +
                              " and currently I am : ");
7       stateField = new TextField(12);
8       eatButton = new Button("Eat!");         // Buttons
9       eatButton.addActionListener(this);  // Assign the listeners.
10      sleepButton = new Button("Sleep!");
11      sleepButton.addActionListener(this);

        // Initialize the TextField

12      stateField.setText(pet1.getState());
13      stateField.setEditable(false);

        // Add the components to the applet.

14      add(nameLabel);
15      add(stateField);
16      add(eatButton);
17      add(sleepButton);

18      setSize(300,150); // Set the applet's size to 300 x 150 pixels
    } // init

    /*
     * The actionPerformed() method is the method that gets called
     * when one of the buttons is pressed
     */
    public void actionPerformed( ActionEvent e)
    {   if (e.getSource() == eatButton)
            pet1.eat();
        else if (e.getSource() == sleepButton)
            pet1.sleep();

        stateField.setText(pet1.getState());
    } //actionPerformed
} // CyberPetApplet
```

FIGURE 4–32 Definition of the CyberPetApplet class.

Tim Berners-Lee, Creator of the WWW

IT'S HARD to believe that the World Wide Web (WWW) was invented by one man. Given the great wealth that the WWW has generated, it's even harder to believe that its inventor has not made any effort to use his invention to enrich himself personally.

In 1989, Tim Berners-Lee was a Fellow at CERN, the European Particle Physics Laboratory, when he conceived of the idea of a multimedia system that could be used by researchers to exchange data, text, images, sounds, and other forms of information that they use in their research.

With a background in system design, real-time communications, and text processing, Berners-Lee wrote the first Web server and the first Web browser, which was called "WorldWideWeb" (no spaces). He later changed the browser's name to "Nexus" to distinguish it from the rapidly emerging multimedia network known as the World Wide Web. His browser was released (for free) on the Internet in 1991, where it was, more or less, an immediate hit. Its success led to the development of other servers and browsers, and the rest, as they say, is history.

Throughout the rapid expansion of the Web, Berners-Lee has devoted himself to trying to preserve the open and public nature of the Web. Between 1991 and 1993, Berners-Lee developed initial specifications for HTTP and HTML, which were refined and discussed in larger public circles as the Web technology spread. In 1994, Berners-Lee joined the Laboratory for Computer Science (LCS) at the Massachusetts Institute of Technology (MIT), where he serves as director of the W3 Consortium. The consortium's goal is to lead the Web to its full potential, ensuring its stability through rapid evolution and revolutionary transformations of its usage. The consortium can be found at

```
http://www.w3.org/
```

instance variables and constants defined in these classes by simply referring to them in its own code. It inherits all of this functionality by virtue of its location in Java's class hierarchy.

If the preexisting code doesn't exactly suit its purposes, `CyberPetApplet` can override (redefine) existing methods or define new methods, as we have done with `init()` and `actionPerformed()`.

`CyberPetApplet` provides one illustration of how inheritance can be used to effect a particular action—such as toggling the label of a `Button`. However,

from a design perspective, our previous example is perhaps not the best way to toggle a button's label. A more object-oriented design would be to define `ToggleButton` as a `Button` subclass that automatically toggles its label whenever it is clicked in addition to carrying out some kind of associated action.

A light switch is a `ToggleButton` in this sense. Whenever you flick a switch, it changes its label from "on" to "off," but it also turns the lights on or off. The action associated with a switch is something that might change from switch to switch—the hall light or the bedroom light—but

Problem decomposition

`ToggleButton` *class*

every light switch toggles its label each time it is clicked. So let's design a `ToggleButton` that behaves like a light switch.

The main idea in our design is that a `ToggleButton` *isa* `Button` that has two labels. An ordinary button just has a single label. Thus, we define `ToggleButton` as a subclass of `Button` with two `String` variables that will serve as its alternate labels (Fig. 4–33). Note that we give it a constructor method that will allow us to provide the initial value of its two label strings. Another important feature of a `ToggleButton` is that it should act as its own `ActionListener` so that it can toggle its label whenever it is clicked. Therefore, it must also implement the `ActionListener` interface.

The complete definition of `ToggleButton` is given in Figure 4–34. Note how we have defined its constructor:

```
public ToggleButton(String l1, String l2) // Constructor method
{
    super(l1);         // Call Button's constructor to set the label
    label1 = l1;       // Set my two labels
    label2 = l2;
    addActionListener(this); // Act as my ActionListener
}
```

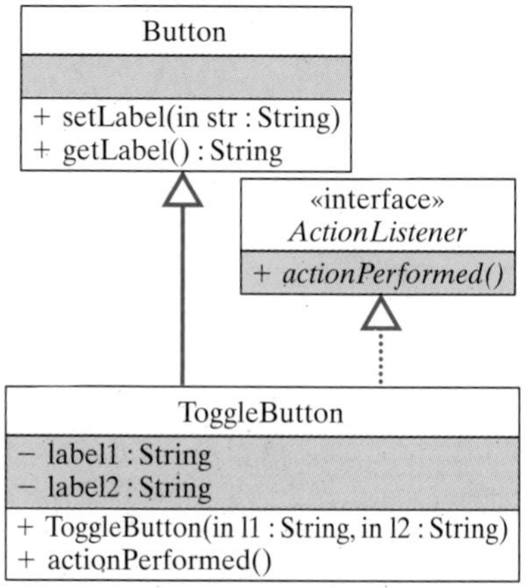

Recall that the `Button` class has a constructor method with the signature `Button(String)`, which allows us to set a `Button`'s label during instantiation. We need to do the same thing with one of `ToggleButton`'s two labels. That is, when we create a `ToggleButton`, we want to initialize its label to one of its two alternative labels (here, "On" or "Off"). Because constructor methods are *not* inherited by the subclass, we need some way to invoke

FIGURE 4–33   A `ToggleButton` *isa* `Button` with two labels.

```
import java.awt.*;
import java.awt.event.*;

public class ToggleButton extends Button implements ActionListener
{
    private String label1;    // Two Labels to toggle between
    private String label2;

    public ToggleButton(String l1, String l2) // Constructor method
    {
        super(l1);                    // Use l1 as the default label
        label1 = l1;
        label2 = l2;
        addActionListener(this);
    }

    public void actionPerformed(ActionEvent e)
    {
        String tempS = label1;  // Swap the labels
        label1 = label2;
        label2 = tempS;
        setLabel(label1);
    } // actionPerformed()
} // ToggleButton
```

FIGURE 4–34   Definition of the `ToggleButton` class.

super

the superclass's constructor. Fortunately, Java supplies the super keyword for just this purpose. super refers to a class's superclass, so when used in super(ll), this is equivalent to calling Button(ll)—that is, it is equivalent to calling Button's constructor method. The only restriction on doing this is that we must call Button's constructor as the very first statement in ToggleButton(). By passing it ll we are making the first string that the user gives us the default label for our ToggleButton. This will be the label that appears on the button when it is first displayed in the applet.

Note also in the ToggleButton() constructor that the ToggleButton is designated as its own ActionListener, so whenever it is clicked, its actionPerformed() method will be invoked.

Swapping algorithm

```
public void actionPerformed(ActionEvent e)
{            // Swap the labels of label1 and label2
                    //    tempS label1 label2
    String tempS = label1;  // 1 off    off     on
    label1 = label2;        // 2 off    on      on
    label2 = tempS;         // 3 off    on      off
    setLabel(label1);       // 4 off-->on or vice versa
} // actionPerformed()
```

The actionPerformed() method exchanges the button's current label for its other label. Swapping two values in memory is a standard programming practice used in lots of different algorithms. In order to do it properly, you must use a third variable to temporarily store one of the two values you are swapping. The comments in actionPerformed() provide a step-by-step trace of the values of the three variables involved.

PROGRAMMING TIP: Swapping Values. It is necessary to use a temporary variable whenever you are swapping two values, of any type, in memory. The temporary variable holds the first value while you overwrite it with the second value.

Swapping values requires a temporary variable

The first statement in actionPerformed() creates a temporary String variable named tempS and assigns it the value of label1. Recall that label1 was the button's initial label. To make this example easier to follow, let's suppose that initially label1 is "off" and that label2 is "on." So after line 1 is executed, both tempS and label1 contain "off" as their value. Line 2 then assigns label2's value to label1. So now both label1 and label2 store "on" as their values. In line 3 we assign tempS's value to label2. Now label2 stores "off" and label1 stores "on," and we have effectively swapped their original values.

Note that the next time we invoke actionPerformed(), label1 and label2 will have their opposite values initially. So swapping them a second time will assign them their initial values again. We can continue toggling their values in this way indefinitely. To complete the method, the last statement in actionPerformed() assigns label1's current value as the new ToggleButton's label.

Multiple event handlers

So a ToggleButton toggles its label between two values. But what about performing an associated action? For this we have to look at ToggleTest, an applet that *uses* a ToggleButton (Fig. 4–35). In its overall structure, this

```
import java.applet.*;
import java.awt.*;
import java.awt.event.*;

public class ToggleTest extends Applet implements ActionListener
{
    private ToggleButton lightSwitch;

    public void init()
    {
        lightSwitch = new ToggleButton ("off","on");
        add(lightSwitch);
        lightSwitch.addActionListener(this);
    } // init()

    public void actionPerformed(ActionEvent e)
    {
        showStatus("The light is " + lightSwitch.getLabel());
    } // actionPerformed()
} // ToggleTest
```

FIGURE 4–35 Definition of the ToggleTest class.

applet is the same as the other applets we have studied in this chapter. It extends the Applet class and implements the ActionListener interface. In this example we use a ToggleButton to simulate a light switch. Note that we assign this applet as an ActionListener for the lightSwitch, so that lightSwitch has two listeners that will respond to its events: the ToggleButton itself, as a result of the actionPerformed() method in its class, and the ToggleTest applet, as a result of actionPerformed() method in this class (Fig. 4–36).

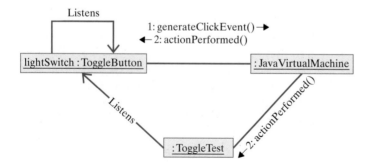

FIGURE 4–36 The ToggleButton has two ActionListeners because both the ToggleTest applet and the ToggleButton itself act as listeners. When the button is clicked, the JVM will call each listener's action-Performed() method. Each listener can then take its own independent action.

The particular action taken by the applet when lightSwitch is clicked is to display the message "The light is on" or "The light is off" in the applet's status bar (Fig. 4–37). But this suffices to illustrate that a ToggleButton both toggles its own label *and* carries out some associated action.

The design of ToggleButton satisfies several of the key design principles of object-oriented programming. It encapsulates ToggleButton's essential behavior within the ToggleButton class itself, and it hides the mechanism by which a ToggleButton manages its labels. It uses inheritance to extend the functionality of the predefined Button class.

FIGURE 4–37 The ToggleTest applet. The button's action is to display "The light is on" or "The light is off" in the applet's status bar.

EFFECTIVE DESIGN: Inheritance.   Inheritance enables you to specialize an object's behavior. A `ToggleButton` does everything that a `Button` does, plus it can toggle its own label.

SELF-STUDY EXERCISES

EXERCISE 4.13   Write a code segment (not a whole method) to swap two boolean variables, b1 and b2.

EXERCISE 4.14   Suppose you are designing an applet that plays a card game, and you want a single button that can be used both to deal the cards and collect the cards. Write a code segment that creates this type of button, adds it to the applet, and designates the applet as its `ActionListener`.

From the Java Library

`java.awt.Image`

www. http://java.sun.com/products /jdk/1.3/docs/api/

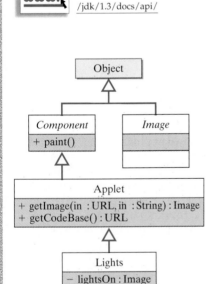

FIGURE 4–38   This UML class diagram shows the classes involved in the `Lights` applet.

JAVA'S AWT makes it especially easy to add images to an applet. Figure 4–38 summarizes the classes and methods involved. The `Applet` class contains the public `getImage()` method, which can be used to load an image into a program given its URL (Uniform Resource Locator).

Images in Java are handled through the `java.awt.Image` class. However, this class is different from the other library classes we've considered because it is an abstract class. Abstract classes cannot be directly instantiated using a constructor. Instead, `Image` instances must be created using a method such as `Applet.getImage()`, which builds the image object from an image stored in a graphics file.

The `Image` class has the following declaration:

```
public abstract class Image extends Object
{
    ... // Details omitted
}
```

Note the use of the `abstract` qualifier in the heading. This means that some of the methods defined in the `Image` class are abstract methods—that is, methods whose implementations (bodies) have not yet been defined.

EFFECTIVE DESIGN: Abstract Class.   An **abstract class** is one that contains one or more abstract methods. An abstract class cannot be directly instantiated and is intended to be subclassed.

The `Lights` applet (Fig. 4–38) declares two `private` instance variables of type `Image` to store the two images that are loaded when the applet runs. The images themselves are in files named `lighton.gif` and `lightoff.gif`, which are stored in the same directory as the applet itself. The images are loaded into the applet using the inherited `getImage()` method:

```
lightOn = getImage(getCodeBase(),"lighton.gif");
lightOff = getImage(getCodeBase(),"lightoff.gif");
```

The inherited `getCodeBase()` method returns the applet's URL (location), which is used as the first argument in `getImage()`. The second argument is the name of the image's GIF file.

```
import java.applet.*;
import java.awt.*;

public class Lights extends Applet
{
    private Image lightOn, lightOff;  // Declare two Image variables

    public void init()
    {
        lightOn = getImage(getCodeBase(),"lighton.gif");
        lightOff = getImage(getCodeBase(),"lightoff.gif");
    } // init()

    public void paint (Graphics g)
    {
        g.drawImage(lightOn, 10, 10, this);
        g.drawImage(lightOff, 70, 10, this);
    } // paint()
} // Lights
```

FIGURE 4–39 Definition of the Lights class.

Figure 4–39 gives the complete implementation of the Lights applet. As shown there, applets that display images or do graphics must override paint(), which is inherited from the Component class (Fig. 4–38). Recall that we also overrode paint() in our very first example of HelloWorld(). The drawImage() method used to display the images is taken from the Graphics class. It has the following signature:

```
drawImage(Image img, int x, int y, ImageObserver observer)
```

The parameters required here are, first, the image to be displayed, followed by the image's coordinates on the applet, followed by the object that "observes" the image. In our case that is the applet itself, which is referred to simply as this. When the applet runs, it appears as shown in Figure 4–40.

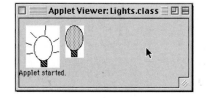

FIGURE 4–40 The Lights applet illustrates how to use Images in an applet.

IN THE LABORATORY: CyberPetApplet

The purpose of this lab exercise is to familiarize you with Java applets. You will make several modifications to extend the functionality of the CyberPetApplet class. The objectives of the lab are

- To introduce the principles of writing a Java applet.
- To introduce some of the basic GUI components.
- To give additional practice using the *if* and *if-else* control structures.
- To introduce a simple graphical object: Image. (optional)

Problem Description

Extend the CyberPet and CyberPetApplet classes by adding a third state to the pet simulation—for example, thinking. The applet GUI should continue to display the CyberPet's name and current state as well as an image that depicts the pet's current state. It should also include command buttons for each of CyberPet's states.

Problem specification

LAB EXERCISE 1: GETTING SET UP

Download the `CyberPet.java` and the `CyberPetApplet` source files from the companion Web site at

```
http://www.prenhall.com/morelli
```

These files correspond to the programs shown in Figures 4–32 and 3–23. Place both of these files into the same directory.

Compile and run `CyberPetApplet` to make sure it runs properly. If you are using JDK, you can compile both `CyberPetApplet.java` and `Cyber-Pet.java` by simply typing

```
javac CyberPetApplet.java
```

at the command line. The compiler will look for `CyberPet.java` in the same directory and will compile it automatically. To run the applet with JDK you will need an HTML file that contains the following applet tag:

```
<APPLET CODE="CyberPetApplet.class" WIDTH=325 HEIGHT=75>
</APPLET>
```

Assuming the HTML file is named `CyberPetApplet.html`, you can run it with the appletviewer by typing

```
appletviewer CyberPetApplet.html
```

LAB EXERCISE 2: RESIZING THE APPLET WINDOW

Controlling the size of the applet's window is important because in this version of the program the applet's components appear in what's called a `FlowLayout`. Under this layout, components are just placed in the applet, one after another, in a row from left to right until there's no more room in the row. Then a new row is started.

The applet tag in `PetApplet.html` should contain `WIDTH` and `HEIGHT` parameters, which control the initial size of the applet. By carefully setting these values, you can exert some control over the applet's layout. Try changing both of these values, one at a time, and observing the effect it has on the appearance of the applet. Through trial and error find appropriate values for the applet's size.

LAB EXERCISE 3: PAYING ATTENTION TO JAVA SYNTAX

Make each of the following changes to `CyberPetApplet.java`, one at a time, then recompile it and note the syntax error that results. Copy the syntax error into your write-up for this lab with a brief note of what caused the error.

- Comment out the first `import` statement in the program.
- Delete the semicolon after `pet1.eat()` in the `actionPerformed()` method.
- Change the spelling of `TextField` to `Textfield` in one of the lines in `init()`.

LAB EXERCISE 4: TRACING THE APPLET

CyberPetApplet inherits a number of methods from its superclasses (Fig. 4–26). The main ones are

- start() is called once when the applet is started by the browser or appletviewer. This method calls init() and paint() automatically and then calls run() to get the applet running.
- run() is called by the start() method. It starts the applet running.
- stop() is called by the browser or appletviewer when the applet is quit.
- init() is called once when an applet starts up to perform any required initializations.
- paint() paints the graphics on the applet. It is called once when the applet starts and then it can be called by repaint() whenever the applet's appearance is changed. This is where you should place any drawing commands.

In addition to the preceding methods, which are inherited from Applet, our applets implement the ActionListener interface, so they also inherit the following method, which must be redefined in the applet:

- actionPerformed() is called automatically whenever one of the Buttons is clicked. It is passed information about the ActionEvent. This is where you should place commands that handle the applet's button clicks.

Of these methods, CyberPetApplet redefines init() and implements actionPerformed(). Definitions for the other methods don't appear in CyberPetApplet.

Place a System.out.println("In method X") statement, where X is the name of the method, in each method of both the CyberPetApplet and CyberPet classes. Run the program and note the output that it produces. Write down the order of execution of the statements in CyberPetApplet and CyberPet for various actions, such as clicking on the eat button or the sleep button.

LAB EXERCISE 5: PAYING ATTENTION TO RUNTIME ERRORS

Make each of the following changes, one at a time, to your program and then rerun it. Make a note of the semantic errors that occur and try to explain each error.

- Comment out the line beginning eatButton = new . . . in the init() method. This is a very common mistake: declaring a variable for an object but failing to create an instance of the object.
- Comment out the statement in init() that adds the eatButton to the applet.
- Delete one of the double quote marks from any pair of quote marks.
- Comment out the last statement in the actionPerformed() method.
- Add the following statement to the beginning of the init() method:

```
Button b1 = new Button ("Local");
```

FIGURE 4–41   A subtle semantic error occurs in this program because the instance `Button b1` is never instantiated.

```java
import java.awt.*;
import java.applet.*;
import java.awt.event.*;

public class SemanticError extends Applet implements ActionListener
{
    private Button b1;    // This class-level b1 is not instantiated

    public void init()
    {                        // Declare and instantiate a local b1
        Button b1 = new Button ("Local"); // This b1 has local scope
        add(b1);                           // Add local b1 to applet
        b1.addActionListener(this);
    } // init()

    public void actionPerformed(ActionEvent e)
    {
        b1.setLabel("Global");  // This refers to the uninstantiated b1
    } // actionPerformed()
} // SemanticError
```

Local scope error

This last semantic error is a very subtle one and is worth additional comment. Consider the example in Figure 4–41. The semantic error in this case is a *scoping* error. There are two variables with the same identifier. The first is the instance variable, whose scope extends throughout the class. It has *class scope*. The second is the local variable declared within the `init()` method, the scope of which is limited to that method. Once the `init()` completes its execution, the local variable ceases to exist. Outside of the `init()` method, any references to b1 will refer to the instance variable. The problem here is that the instance variable was never instantiated. So there is no actual button associated with its name. In the `actionPerformed()` method, the reference to b1 is a reference to the instance variable, but there is no button on the applet that corresponds to this variable, because in the `init()` method, the local variable's button was added to the applet.

> DEBUGGING TIP: Scope Error. Don't declare a component variable in the `init()` method. You won't be able to refer to it in the rest of the program.

LAB EXERCISE 6: ADDING A NEW STATE TO `CyberPet`

Add a third state to the `CyberPet` class and make the appropriate changes in the `CyberPetApplet`. Let's suppose you are adding a *thinking* state. You will need to create an instance variable for `isThinking` and a `think()` method, plus you need to revise the other access methods. All of these revisions would occur in the `CyberPet.java` file. In the `CyberPetApplet.java` file, you would need to add a third button to the applet. If you add a third button, you would need to revise the `actionPerformed()` method to handle clicks on the new button.

LAB EXERCISE 7: ADDING IMAGES
TO `CyberPetApplet` **(OPTIONAL)**

Download the image files provided for this lab. There are three images: `spidereat.gif`, `spidersleep.gif`, and `spiderthink.gif`. Place them in the same directory as your source code (`*.java`) files.

Add images to the applet that correspond to `CyberPet`'s three states. Follow the example shown in Section 4.7.5. There are two modifications that must be made to that example. First, the `paint()` method should draw the image that corresponds to `CyberPet`'s current state:

```java
public void paint(Graphics g)
{
    String petState = pet1.getState();      // Get pet1's state
    if (petState.equals("Eating"))          // Draw an image
        g.drawImage(eatImage, 20, 100, this);
    else if (petState.equals("Sleeping"))
        g.drawImage(sleepImage, 20, 100, this);
    else if (petState.equals("Thinking"))
        g.drawImage(thinkImage, 20, 100, this);
}
```

Finally, it is necessary to `repaint()` the applet after each button click. To do this you would add the following statement at the end of your `actionPerformed()` method:

```java
repaint();    // Call the paint() method
```

The `repaint()` method just calls the applet's `paint()` method. The reason that `paint(Graphics)` is not called directly here is because it requires a `Graphics` parameter, which is not directly available to the `actionPerformed()` method. The `repaint()` method takes care of getting the applet's `Graphics` object and passing it to `paint()`, so the images can be displayed on it.

Java Language Summary

Keywords: `extends`, `super`, `import`, `this`

- The extends keyword is used in a class definition in order to define a subclass of a class. It causes the subclass to *inherit* the superclass's `public` and `protected` instance variables and instance methods. For example, the following definition defines a `Square` as a subclass of `Rectangle`:

`extends`

```java
public class Square extends Rectangle // Rectangle subclass
{
    public Square(double side)
    {
        super(side,side);    // Call Rectangle's Constructor
    }
} // Square
```

- The super keyword refers to an object's superclass. It can be used in an object's constructor to invoke the superclass constructor. When so used, it should be the first statement in the constructor. For example, note in the code segment just preceding this item how the `Rectangle()` constructor is invoked in the `Square()` constructor by using super.

`super`

import

- The import declaration allows classes declared in other (usually library) packages to be referred to by a simple name rather than by their fully qualified name. It takes the form import *package.class*, where *package* is the name of a library package containing the class. For example, if your program declares import java.applet.Applet, it will be able to refer to this class simply as Applet. The wild card character, *, may be used to import all the class definitions in a particular package. For example, the following statement imports definitions of all of the public class names in the Abstract Windowing Toolkit (AWT) package:

```
import java.awt.*;
```

this

- The this keyword is self-referential. Just as "I" refers to the person who utters it, this refers to whatever object uses it. For example, in the following init() method,

```
public class MyApplet extends Applet implements ActionListener
{
    private Button button = new Button("click me!");
    public void init()
    {
        this.add(button);
        button.addActionListener(this);
    } // init()
} MyApplet
```

this refers to whichever MyApplet object executes the statement. That object becomes the listener for button's action events.

Keywords: abstract, interface, protected

abstract

- An abstract class is one that contains one or more abstract methods. An abstract method is one that lacks a method body. It consists entirely of the method header. Classes that extend an abstract class should implement the abstract methods.

interface

- An interface is, essentially, a class that contains only instance methods and constants. It cannot contain instance variables. A class that implements an interface commits itself to defining all the methods contained in the interface. This is a second form of *inheritance*, similar to extending a superclass. For example, applets that need to handle button clicks should implement the ActionListener interface, which consists of one method, the actionPerformed() method. Here's an example:

```
public class MyClass extends Applet implements ActionListener
{
    // Code deleted here

    public void actionPerformed(ActionEvent e)
    {
        // Code to handle button clicks goes here
    } // actionPerformed()
}
```

protected

- Instance variables and instance methods that are declared protected are inherited by subclasses (as well as its public elements). Unlike public elements, protected elements are not accessible by other objects.

Technical Terms

abstract class
abstract interface
abstract method
applet
Application
   Programming
   Interface (API)

event-driven
   execution
Graphical User
   Interface (GUI)
import declaration
inheritance
inheritance hierarchy

interface
polymorphic method

Summary of Important Points

- An *applet* is an embedded program that runs within the context of a Web browser.

- The Java *Application Programming Interface (API)* is a set of predefined classes that can be used to write programs.

- A *Graphical User Interface (GUI)* enables the user to interact with a program via graphical elements such as windows, buttons, and menus. Java's GUI components are defined in the *Abstract Windowing Toolkit (AWT)* package. The import statement allows a Java library class or method to be referred to by its simple name instead of by its fully qualified name.

- The extend keyword is used to define a class's *pedigree*—that is, its place within the Java class hierarchy. A class that *extends* another class is said to be a *subclass* of that class which is its *superclass*. A subclass *inherits* the public and protected methods and fields (instance variables) of its superclasses.

- Methods defined in a class's superclasses can be *overridden* in the subclass by defining a method with the same signature—that is, with the same name and the same number, order, and type of formal parameters.

- Any method that performs some type of operation on different types of objects is said to be *polymorphic*. An applet's init() method is an example, since it is redefined in all Applet subclasses.

- Java applets are *event driven*, which means they are programmed to react to certain events. An Event is an object that records specific information about a particular event, such as a mouse click or a key press. Clicking on a Button in an applet generates an ACTION.EVENT that should be handled by an actionPerformed() method.

- A Label is a GUI component that displays a single line of uneditable text on the applet. A Button is a labeled GUI component that is used to trigger some kind of action when clicked. The setLabel() and getLabel() methods can be used to set and get a Button's label. A TextField is a GUI component that displays a single line of editable text. The setText() and getText() methods can be used to set and get a TextField's text.

- The default layout pattern for Java applets is the FlowLayout.

SOLUTIONS TO SELF-STUDY EXERCISES

SOLUTION 4.1 Given the hierarchy of classes shown in Figure 4–2, which of the following would be valid assignment statements?

```
Panel p = new Container();        // Invalid
Container c1 = new Panel();        // Valid
Component c2 = new Object();       // Invalid
Component c3 = new Container();    // Valid
Container c4 = new Component();    // Invalid
```

SOLUTION 4.2

```
public double calcPerimeter()
{
    return 2 * length + 2 * width;
}
```

SOLUTION 4.3 The following code should be added to main() in TestSquare (Fig. 4–8):

```
System.out.println("square's perimeter is " + square.calcPerimeter());
```

SOLUTION 4.4 Because Square is a subclass of Rectangle, it inherits the calcPerimeter() method, so it can use it in the statement square.calcPerimeter(), just as if it were defined in the Square class.

SOLUTION 4.5 The following code should be added to init():

```
System.out.println("The author of this applet
    is" + getParameter("author"));
System.out.println("The date of this applet
    is " + getParameter("date"));
```

SOLUTION 4.6

```
import java.awt.*;
import java.applet.*;
public class SmallApplet extends Applet
{
    private Button clickme;                   // Declare a variable

    public void init()
    {
        clickme = new Button("Click me!");  // Create the button
        add(clickme);                         // Add it to the applet
    } //init()
} //SmallApplet
```

SOLUTION 4.7 The following statement should be added to init() after the clickme Button has been instantiated:

```
System.out.println(clickme.getLabel());
```

SOLUTION 4.8 The + operator is used to add numbers and to concatenate strings. Thus, it is overloaded. It performs different operations on different types of data.

SOLUTION 4.9 Because implementation of the CyberDog and CyberCat classes are so similar, we show only the CyberDog class here:

```java
public class CyberDog extends CyberPet {

    public CyberDog(String name) {
        super(name); // Call the superclass constructor
    }

    public void eat() {
        super.eat(); // Call the superclass's eat()
        System.out.println("Eating dogfood. Arf!");
    }
} // CyberDog
```

SOLUTION 4.10 You would declare your applet to implement the ActionListener interface and would create a TextField instance in your program. In the init() method, you would use addActionListener() to designate the applet as a listener for the TextField's action events. Then you would implement the actionPerformed() method, giving it instructions on what to do when the user types the Enter key.

SOLUTION 4.11 The applet would ignore the user's clicks on the toggle Button, because no listener was assigned to handle them.

SOLUTION 4.12 The toggle Button would not show up on the screen.

SOLUTION 4.13

```java
boolean temp = b1; // Save b1's value
b1 = b2;           // Change b1 to b2
b2 = temp;         // Change b2 to b1's original value
```

SOLUTION 4.14

```java
private ToggleButton dealer = new ToggleButton("deal","collect");
add( dealer );
dealer.addActionListener( this );
```

EXERCISES

Note: *For programming exercises,* **first** *draw a UML class diagram describing all classes and their inheritance relationships and/or associations.*

EXERCISE 4.1 Fill in the blanks in each of the following sentences:

a. An _____ is an embedded Java program.

b. A method that lacks a body is an _____ method.

c. An _____ is like a class except that it contains only instance methods, no instance variables.

d. Two ways for a class to inherit something in Java is to _____ a class and _____ an interface.

e. Classes and methods not defined in a program must be _____ from the Java class library.

f. Instance variables and instance methods that are declared _____ or _____ are inherited by the subclasses.

g. An object can refer to itself by using the _____ keyword.

h. The Button, TextField, and Component classes are defined in the _____ package.

i. Java applets utilize a form of control known as _____ programming.

j. When the user clicks on an applet's Button, an _____ will automatically be generated.

k. Two kinds of objects that generate ActionEvents are _____ and _____.

l. Buttons, TextFields, Containers, and Labels are all subclasses of _____.

m. The Applet class is a subclass of _____.

n. If an applet intends to handle ActionEvents, it must implement the _____ interface.

o. An applet's init() method is an example of a _____ method, because it does different things depending upon the object that invokes it.

p. When an applet is started, its _____ method is called automatically.

EXERCISE 4.2 Explain the difference between the following pairs of concepts:

a. *Class* and *interface*.
b. *Stub method* and *abstract method*.
c. *Extending a class* and *instantiating an object*.
d. *Defining a method* and *implementing a method*.
e. A protected method and a public method.
f. A protected method and a private method.
g. An ActionEvent and an ActionListener() method.

EXERCISE 4.3 Draw a hierarchy chart to represent the following situation. There are lots of languages in the world. English, French, Chinese, and Korean are examples of natural languages. Java, C, and C++ are examples of formal languages. French and Italian are considered romance languages, while Greek and Latin are considered classical languages.

EXERCISE 4.4 Arrange the Java library classes mentioned in the Chapter Summary into their proper hierarchy, using the Object class as the root of the hierarchy.

EXERCISE 4.5 Look up the documentation for the Button class on Sun's Web site:

```
http://java.sun.com/products/jdk/1.3/docs/api/
```

List the names of all the methods that are inherited by its ToggleButton subclass.

EXERCISE 4.6 Suppose we want to set the text in our applet's TextField. What method should we use and where is this method defined? (*Hint*: Look up the documentation for TextField. If no appropriate method is defined there, see if it is inherited from a superclass.)

EXERCISE 4.7 Does an Applet have an init() method? Explain.

EXERCISE 4.8 Does a Applet have an add() method? Explain.

EXERCISE 4.9 Does a Button have an init() method? Explain.

EXERCISE 4.10 Does a Button have an add() method? Explain.

EXERCISE 4.11 Suppose you type the URL for a "Hello World" applet into your browser. Describe what happens—that is, describe the processing that takes place in order for the applet to display "Hello World" in your browser.

EXERCISE 4.12   Suppose you have an applet containing a Button named button. Describe what happens, in terms of Java's event handling model, when the user clicks on the button.

EXERCISE 4.13   Java's Object class contains a public method, toString(), which returns a string that represents this object. Because every class is a subclass of Object, the toString() method can be used by any object. Show how you would invoke this method for a Button object named button.

EXERCISE 4.14   The applet that follows contains a semantic error in its init() method. The error will cause the actionPerformed() method never to display "Clicked" even though the user clicks on the button in the applet. Why? (*Hint:* Think scope!)

```java
public class SomeApplet extends Applet implements ActionListener
{
    // Declare instance variables
    private Button button;

    public void init()
    {
      // Instantiate the instance variable
      Button button = new Button("Click me");
      add(button);
      button.addActionListener(this);
    } // init()

    public void actionPerformed(ActionEvent e)
    {
      if (e.getSource() == button)
          System.out.println("Clicked");
    } // actionPerformed()
} // SomeApplet
```

EXERCISE 4.15   What would be output by the following applet?

```java
public class SomeApplet extends Applet
{
    // Declare instance variables
    private Button button;
    private TextField field;

    public void init()
    {
      // Instantiate instance variables
      button = new Button("Click me");
      add(button);
      field = new TextField("Field me");
      add(field);
      System.out.println(field.getText() + button.getText());
    } // init()
} // SomeApplet
```

EXERCISE 4.16   Modify the ToggleTest applet so that it displays an image of a light bulb in the "on" or "off" state on alternate clicks of its lightSwitch.

EXERCISE 4.17   Write a simple Java applet that creates a Button, a TextField, and a Label. Add statements to the init() method that use the toString() method to display each object's string representation.

EXERCISE 4.18   Modify the SimpleApplet program so that it contains a second button labeled initially "The Doctor is in." Modify the actionPerformed() method so that every time the user clicks on a button, its label is toggled. The label on the second button should toggle to "The Doctor is out."

EXERCISE 4.19   Modify the SimpleApplet program so that it contains two Buttons, initially labeled "Me first!" and "Me next!" Modify the actionPerformed() method so that every time the user clicks on either one of the buttons, the labels on both buttons are exchanged. (*Hint*: You don't need an if-else statement for this problem.)

EXERCISE 4.20   Modify the SimpleApplet program so that it contains three Buttons, initially labeled "First," "Second," and "Third." Modify the actionPerformed() method so that every time the user clicks on one of the buttons, the labels on the buttons are rotated. Second should get first's label, third should get second's, and first should get third's label.

EXERCISE 4.21   Modify the SimpleApplet program so that it contains a TextField and two Buttons, initially labeled "Left" and "Right." Modify the actionPerformed() method so that every time the user clicks on a button, its label is displayed in the TextField.

EXERCISE 4.22   You can change the size of an applet by using the setSize(int h, int v) method, where *h* and *v* give the horizontal and vertical dimensions of the applet's window in pixels. Write an applet that contains two Buttons, labeled "Big" and "Small." Whenever the user clicks on small, set the applets dimensions to 200×100, and whenever the user clicks on big, set the dimensions to 300×200.

EXERCISE 4.23   Rewrite the size-adjusting applet in the previous exercise so that it uses a single button, whose label is toggled appropriately each time it is clicked. Obviously, when the Button is labeled "Big," clicking it should give the applet its big dimensions.

EXERCISE 4.24   **Challenge:** Design and write an applet that allows the user to change the applet's background color to one of three choices, indicated by buttons. Like all other Java Components, applet's have an associated background color, which can be set by the following commands:

```
setBackground(Color.red);
setBackground(Color.yellow);
```

The setBackground() method is defined in the Component class, and 13 primary colors—black, blue, cyan, darkGray, gray, green, lightGray, magenta, orange, pink, red, white, yellow—are defined in the java.awt.Color class.

EXERCISE 4.25   **Challenge:** Modify CyberPet and CyberPetApplet so that CyberPet can eat two different things—for example, a fly or a beetle. Your interface design should allow the user to set the CyberPet's food type. Whenever the CyberPet is eating, its state should be reported as "Socrates is eating a fly."

ADDITIONAL EXERCISES

EXERCISE 4.26   Given the classes with the following headers

```
public class Animal ...
public class DomesticAnimal extends Animal ...
public class FarmAnimal extends DomesticAnimal...
public class HousePet extends DomesticAnimal...
public class Cow extends FarmAnimal ...
public class Goat extends FarmAnimal ...
public class DairyCow extends Cow ...
```

draw a UML class diagram representing the hierarchy created by these declarations.

EXERCISE 4.27   Given the preceding hierarchy of classes, which of the following are legal assignment statements?

```
DairyCow dc = new FarmAnimal();
FarmAnimal fa = new Goat();
Cow c1 = new DomesticAnimal();
Cow c2 = new DairyCow();
DomesticAnimal dom = new HousePet();
```

EXERCISE 4.28   Following the rectangle-square example, design an `Employee` class with subclasses `HourlyEmployee` and `Manager`, such that each employee has inheritable attributes name of type `String` and id of type `int`, and an inherits method `getName():String` and `setName(String)`. The subclasses should also have the appropriate constructors that allow the employee's ID to be set when an instance is created. Draw a UML diagram showing the details and the relationships among these classes.

EXERCISE 4.29   Extend the design in the previous exercise so that the `Employee` class contains an attribute for `payrate` and a polymorphic method `calcPay()`. This method must be polymorphic because the way an employee's pay is calculated depends on whether the employee is a manager or an hourly employee.

EXERCISE 4.30   Suppose you have a Java interface named `Drawable` that contains the polymorphic method `draw()`. This interface is meant to be used for drawing geometric objects. Design a subclass of `Rectangle` named `DrawableRectangle` that implements the `Drawable` interface and represent your design in a UML diagram.

EXERCISE 4.31   Suppose you have a Java interface named `Scalable` that contains the polymorphic methods `enlarge(double)` and `reduce(double)`. These methods are meant to enlarge or reduce the size of a geometric object by some factor. Modify your design of `DrawableRectangle` so that it also implements the `Scalable` interface.

EXERCISE 4.32   Write an implementation of the `enlarge(double)` method for the `DrawableRectangle` class in the previous exercise.

EXERCISE 4.33   Write an implementation of the `reduce(double)` method for the `DrawableRectangle` class in the previous exercise.

EXERCISE 4.34   Suppose you have a Java applet that contains a `Button` and a `TextField`. Each time the `Button` is clicked, it displays the time in the `TextField` using the `showTime()` method. Draw a UML sequence diagram that depicts this sequence of events.

Photograph courtesy of Craig Brewer, PhotoDisc, Inc.

5

Java Data and Operators

OBJECTIVES

After studying this chapter, you will

- Understand the role that data play in effective program design.
- Be able to use all of Java's primitive types and their operators.
- Appreciate the importance of information hiding.
- Be able to use class constants and class methods in a program.
- Know how to use Java's `Math` and `NumberFormat` classes.
- Be able to perform various kinds of data conversions.

OUTLINE

5.1   Introduction

This chapter has two primary goals. One is to elaborate on Java's *primitive data types*, which were first introduced in Chapter 2. We will cover boolean, integer, character, and real number data types, including the various operations that you can perform on these types. For each type of data we will provide examples of its typical uses.

Our second goal is to introduce various object-oriented design principles, such as information hiding and scalability, and to illustrate the idea that programming is a matter of choosing an appropriate way to represent a problem as well as choosing an appropriate sequence of actions to solve the problem.

To illustrate these principles we will develop two different implementations of the CyberPet class, one based on boolean data, as we did in Chapter 2, and the other based on integer (int) data. Each *model* or *representation* will be designed in such a way that it will function properly with CyberPetApplet, the interface we designed in Chapter 4. In other words, we will change the underlying implementation of the CyberPet class, without changing the interface to it in any way.

5.2   Programming = Representation + Action

Programming is a form of problem solving. Problem solving can be viewed as a two-part process: *representation* and *action*.

Representation means finding a way to look at the problem. This might involve seeing the problem as an example of a known problem or as closely related to a known problem. It might involve seeing that parts of the problem can be broken up into smaller problems that you already know how to solve. In terms of programming problems, representation often means choosing the right kinds of objects and structures.

Action is the process of taking well-defined steps to solve a problem. Given a particular way of representing the problem, what steps must we take to arrive at its solution?

Choosing an appropriate representation is often the key to solving a problem. For example, consider this problem: Can a chessboard, with its top-left and bottom-right squares removed, be completely tiled by dominoes that cover two squares at a time?

One way to solve this problem might be to represent the chessboard and dominoes as shown in Figure 5–1. If we represent the board in this way, then the actions needed to arrive at a solution involve searching for a tiling that completely covers the board. In other words, we can try one way of placing the dominoes on the board. If that doesn't work, we try another way. And so on. This process will be very time consuming, because there are lots of different ways of trying to tile the board. For example, one way would be to find a square with no north or west neighbor and pair that square with either its south or east neighbor. If we repeat this strategy, it will lead to 2^{31} = 2,147,483,000 different possibilities.

An alternative way to represent this problem comes from seeing that the top-left and bottom-right squares of the board are both white. If you remove them, you'll have a board with 62 squares, 32 black and 30 white. To cover the board you'll need 31 dominoes, and each domino must cover one white and one black square. But you can't cover 32 black squares and 30 white squares with 31 dominoes, so the board cannot be tiled.

FIGURE 5–1   Can the chessboard be tiled with dominoes?

Thus, by representing the problem as the total number of black and white squares, the actions required to solve it involve a very simple reasoning process. This representation makes it almost trivial to find the solution. On the other hand, the *brute force* representation presented first—trying all possible combinations—made it almost impossible to solve the problem.

In the remainder of this chapter, we consider two different representations for a CyberPet—boolean and int—and discuss which of the representations provides a better solution to the problem of simulating a CyberPet.

5.3   Boolean Data and Operators

The boolean type is one of Java's primitive types. In the boolean type, there are only two possible values, true and false. The boolean type is derived from the work of George Boole, a British mathematician, who in the 1850s developed a type of algebra to process logical expressions such as *p and q*. Such *boolean expressions* produce a value that is either *true* or *false*. Every modern programming language provides some means of representing boolean expressions.

George Boole

The boolean type has several important uses. As we have seen in the CyberPet example, a boolean variable can be used to represent the presence or absence of a particular characteristic—sleeping or not sleeping. The boolean type is also used to represent the condition in the if statement:

Conditional statement

> if   (*boolean expression*)
>   *statement*;

For this reason, boolean expressions are also called *conditions*. Along these same lines, a boolean variable can be used as a *flag* or a *signal* to "remember" whether or not a certain condition holds. For example, in the following code fragment, we use isDone to mark when a particular process is completed:

Boolean flag

```
boolean isDone = false;   // Initialize the flag
...                       // Do some processing task
isDone = true;            // Set the flag when the task is done
...                       // Do some other stuff
if (isDone)               // Check whether we finished the task
...                       //  If so do something
else
...                       //  Otherwise, do something else
```

Data and operations

5.3.1   Boolean (or Logical) Operations

Like all the other simple data types, the `boolean` type consists of certain data—the values `true` and `false`—and certain actions or operations that can be performed on those data. For the boolean type there are four basic operations, AND (`&&`), OR (`||`), EXCLUSIVE-OR (∧), and NOT (`!`). The effect of these operations can be defined by the *truth table* shown in Table 5.1.

TABLE 5.1   Truth-table definitions of the boolean operators: AND (`&&`), OR (`||`), EXCLUSIVE-OR (∧), and NOT (`!`)

o1	o2	o1 && o2	o1 || o2	o1 ∧ o2	!o1
true	true	true	true	false	false
true	false	false	true	true	false
false	true	false	true	true	true
false	false	false	false	false	true

Binary operator

The boolean AND operation is a **binary** operation—that is, it requires two operands, *o1* and *o2* (column 3 of Table 5.1). If both *o1* and *o2* are true, then (*o1* `&&` *o2*) is true. If either *o1* or *o2* or both *o1* and *o2* are false, then the expression (*o1* `&&` *o2*) is false. The only case in which (*o1* `&&` *o2*) is true is when both *o1* and *o2* are true.

The boolean OR operation (column 4 of Table 5.1) is also a binary operation. If both *o1* and *o2* are false, then (*o1* `||` *o2*) is false. If either *o1* or *o2* or both *o1* and *o2* are true, then the expression (*o1* `||` *o2*) is true. Thus, the only case in which (*o1* `||` *o2*) is false is when both *o1* and *o2* are false.

The boolean EXCLUSIVE-OR operation (column 5 of Table 5.1) is a binary operation, which differs from the OR operator in that it is true when either *o1* or *o2* is true, but it is false when both *o1* and *o2* are true.

Unary operator

The NOT operation (the last column of Table 5.1) is a **unary operator**—it takes only one operand—and it simply reverses the truth value of its operand. Thus, if *o1* is true, *!o1* is false, and vice versa.

5.3.2   Precedence, Associativity, and Commutativity

In order to evaluate complex boolean expressions, it is necessary to understand the order in which boolean operations are carried out by the computer. For example, what is the value of the following expression?

```
true || true && false
```

The value of this expression depends on whether we evaluate the `||` first or the `&&` first. If we evaluate the `||` first, the expression's value will be false; if we evaluate the `&&` first, the expression's value will be true. In the following example, we use parentheses to force one operation to be done before the other:

```
EXPRESSION                    EVALUATION
----------                    ----------
( true || true ) && false     ==> true && false ==> false
true || ( true && false )     ==> true || false ==> true
```

As these evaluations show, we can use parentheses to force one operator or the other to be evaluated first. However, in Java, the && operator
has higher precedence than the || operator. Therefore, the second alter-
native corresponds to the default interpretation that Java would apply
to the unparenthesized expression. In other words, given the expression
true || *true* && *false*, the AND operation would be evaluated before the
OR operation even though the OR operator occurs first (i.e., to the left) in
the unparenthesized expression.

Parentheses supersede

TABLE 5.2   Precedence order of the boolean operators

Precedence Order	Operator	Operation
1	( )	Parentheses
2	!	NOT
4	∧	EXCLUSIVE-OR
3	&&	AND
5	||	OR

As this example illustrates, the boolean operators have a built-in **precedence order** which is used to determine how boolean expressions are to be
evaluated (Table 5.2). A simple method for evaluating an expression is to
parenthesize the expression and then evaluate it. For example, to evaluate
the complex expression

```
true || !false ∧ false && true
```

we would first parenthesize it according to the precedence rules set out in
Table 5.2, which gives the following expression:

```
true || (((!false) ∧ false) && true)
```

We can then evaluate this fully parenthesized expression, step by step,
starting at the innermost parentheses:

```
Step 1. true || ((true ∧ false) && true)
Step 2. true || (true && true)
Step 3. true || true
Step 4. true
```

PROGRAMMING TIP: Parentheses.   Parentheses can (and should) be
used to clarify any expression that appears ambiguous or to override
Java's default precedence rules.

In addition to operator precedence, it is necessary to know about an
operator's *associativity* in order to evaluate boolean expressions of
the form (*op1* || *op2* || *op3*). Should this expression be evaluated as
((*op1* || *op2*) || *op3*) or as (*op1* || (*op2* || *op3*))? The binary boolean opera-
tors all associate from left to right. Thus, the expressions

```
true ∧ true ∧ true       // Same as: (true ∧ true) ∧ true
true && true && true     // Same as: (true && true) && true
true || true || true     // Same as: (true || true) || true
```

would be evaluated as follows:

```
EXPRESSION                      EVALUATION
----------------                -----------------
(true ∧ true)  ∧ true           ==> false ∧ true ==> true
(true && true)  && true         ==> true  && true ==> true
(true || true)  || true         ==> true  || true ==> true
```

Finally, all of the binary boolean operators are *commutative*; that is, *p op q* is equivalent to *q op p*, where *op* is any one of the binary boolean operators.

SELF-STUDY EXERCISE

EXERCISE 5.1   Suppose the following variable declarations are made:

```
boolean A = true, B = true, C = true;
boolean X = false, Y = false, Z = false;
```

Given these declarations, evaluate each of the following expressions (don't forget to take operator precedence and associativity into account):

a. A || B && Z

b. A ∧ X && Z

c. A ∧ X || C

d. !A && !B

e. A && B && X && Y

f. (!X ∧ A) && (B ∧ !Y)

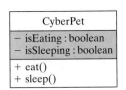

FIGURE 5–2   CyberPet's state is represented using two boolean variables.

5.4   The Boolean-Based CyberPet Model

The CyberPet class we designed in Chapters 2 to 4 (see Figure 3–23) is based on a boolean representation of the pet's state. A CyberPet's state is represented by two private boolean variables: isEating and isSleeping (Fig. 5–2). And changing the pet's state from one mode to the other requires that we assign true to one of these variables and false to the other:

```
private boolean isEating;       // CyberPet's state
private boolean isSleeping;
...
public CyberPet ()              // Constructor method
{
    isEating = true;
    isSleeping = false;
}
```

This representation is simple and easy to understand, but it is somewhat unwieldy and hard to modify. One problem is that each time we wish to add another value to CyberPet's state, we have to add another boolean variable and we have to add assignment statements to each of the methods that affect the state. For example, suppose we want to extend our model to allow for a CyberPet that can also think as well as eat and sleep. Let's suppose that thinking, eating, and sleeping are mutually exclusive for our simple-minded pets.

To add a thinking state to our CyberPet class, we would have to add a new boolean variable, that is,

```
boolean isThinking;
```

and we would have to add a think() method to the class:

```
public void think()  // Change the pet's state to thinking
{
    isSleeping = false;
    isEating = false;
    isThinking = true;
}
```

In addition, we would have to modify several of the existing methods to account for the fact that the value of this new state variable must be set each time the state changes. For example, the default constructor method would have to be modified to

```
public CyberPet()              // Constructor method
{
    isSleeping = false;
    isEating = true;
    isThinking = false;
}
```

and the eat() method would have to be modified to

```
public void eat()
{
    isSleeping = false;        // Change the state
    isEating = true;
    isThinking = false;
}
```

Thus, to add a thinking state to CyberPet, we have to modify every method in the class.

Obviously, using boolean variables to represent a CyberPet's state is not very practical. While the initial model was simple, it is not easily *extensible*. The model is based on the idea that each component of an object's state is represented by a separate boolean variable. This is like adding a new light switch that must be turned on or off each time we wish to extend the model by one new value. If a CyberPet's state is eventually going to have 20 possible values, we would need 20 boolean variables. That's a lot of light switches to manage! We might say that one problem with this rep- *Lack of scalability* resentation is that it doesn't scale. It is not easy to extend the functionality of our model.

> **EFFECTIVE DESIGN: Scalability Principle.** A well-designed model or representation should be easily extensible. It should be easy to add new functionality to the model.

Another problem with the boolean representation is that each change in the state requires modifications in every method in the class. A good design will minimize this ripple effect. Ideally, we want a representation that allows us to add new instance variables and methods without having to modify existing methods. The boolean representation forces us to create methods (that is, modules) that are not complete and self-contained. This is a violation of the modularity principle. *Lack of modularity*

EFFECTIVE DESIGN: Modularity Principle.   A well-designed representation will allow us to design methods that do not require modification each time the model is extended.

Given these limitations to the boolean version of CyberPet, we will develop an alternative model based on an integer representation.

Are We Computers?

GEORGE BOOLE published his seminal work, *An Investigation of the Laws of Thought*, in 1854. His achievement was in developing an algebra for logic—that is, a purely abstract and symbolic system for representing the laws of logic. Boole's was not the first attempt to explore the relationship between the human mind and an abstract system of computation. Back in 1655 Thomas Hobbes had already claimed that all thought was computation.

It is estimated that the human brain contains (10^{12} = 10,000,000,000,000) *neurons*. And each neuron contains something like 10,000 *dendrites*, the fibers that connect one neuron to another. Together the neurons and dendrites make up a web of enormous complexity. Since the 1840s it has been known that the brain is primarily electrical, and by the 1940s scientists had developed a pretty good model of the electrical interactions among neurons. According to this model, neurons emit short bursts of electricity along their *axons*, which function like output channels. The bursts leap over the gap separating axons and dendrites, which function like the neurons' input channels.

In 1943, just before the first digital computers were developed, Warren McCulloch, a neurophysiologist, and Walter Pitts, a mathematician, published a paper titled "A Logical Calculus of the Ideas Imminent in Nervous Activity." In this paper, they showed that all of the boolean operators—AND, OR, NOT, and EXCLUSIVE-OR—could be represented by the behavior of small sets of neurons. For example, they showed that three neurons could be connected together in such a way that the third neuron fired if and only if both of the other two neurons fired. This is exactly analogous to the definition of the boolean AND operator.

A few years later, when the first computers were built, many scientists and philosophers were struck by the similarity between the logic gates and flip-flops that made up the computer's circuits and the neuronal models that McCulloch and Pitts had developed.

The area of neural networks, a branch of artificial intelligence, one of the applied areas of computer science, is based on this insight by McCulloch and Pitts. Researchers in this exciting and rapidly advancing field develop neural network models of various kinds of human thinking and perception.

5.5 Numeric Data and Operators

Java has two kinds of numeric data: integers, which have no fractional part, and real numbers or floating-point numbers, which contain a fractional component. Java has four different kinds of integers, byte, short, int, and long, which are distinguished by the number of *bits* used to represent them. Java has two different kinds of real numbers, float and double, which are also distinguished by the number of bits used to represent them. See Table 5.3.

TABLE 5.3 Java's numeric types

Type	Bits	Range of Values
byte	8	-128 to $+127$
short	16	-32768 to 32767
int	32	-2147483648 to 2147483647
long	64	-2^{63} to $2^{63} - 1$
float	32	$-3.40292347E + 38$ to $+3.40292347E + 38$
double	64	$-1.79769313486231570E + 308$ to $+1.79769313486231570E + 308$

One bit can represent two possible values, 1 and 0, which can be used to stand for true and false, respectively. Two bits can represent four possible values: 00, 01, 10, and 11; three bits can represent eight possible values: 000, 001, 010, 100, 101, 110, 011, 111. And in general, an *n*-bit quantity can represent 2^n different values.

As illustrated in Table 5.3, an integer is a positive or negative whole number. Perhaps the most commonly used integer type in Java is the int type, which is represented in 32 bits. This means that Java can represent 2^{32} different int values, which range from $-2,147,483,648$ to $2,147,483,647$—that is, from -2^{31} to $(2^{31} - 1)$. Similarly, an 8-bit integer, a byte, can represent 2^8 or 256 different values, ranging from -128 to $+127$. A 16-bit integer, a short, can represent 2^{16} different values, which range from -32768 to 32767. And a 64-bit integer, a long, can represent whole number values ranging from -2^{63} to $2^{63} - 1$.

Integer data types

For floating-point numbers, a 32-bit float type can represent 2^{32} different real numbers and a 64-bit double value can represent 2^{64} different real numbers.

EFFECTIVE DESIGN: Platform Independence. In Java, a data type's size (number of bits) is part of its definition and, therefore, remains consistent across all platforms. In C and C++, the size of a data type is dependent on the compiler.

It is worth noting that Java's numeric types are representations or models of whole numbers and real numbers in just the same way as our CyberPet class is a representation or model of a real pet. In all these cases, the representation is an abstraction, which has certain built-in limitations. In designing Java's data types, various trade-offs have been made in order to come up with a practical implementation.

Data types are abstractions

One trade-off is that the set of integers is infinite, but Java's int type can only represent a finite number of values. Similarly, Java cannot represent

Representation trade-offs

Round-off error

the infinite number of values that occur between, say, 1.111 and 1.112. So, certain real numbers cannot be represented at all. For example, one number that cannot be represented exactly is $\frac{1}{10}$. This can cause problems in trying to represent dollars and cents accurately in a program. One possible solution is to use a penny as the basic unit of measurement so that dollar amounts can be represented as whole numbers.

DEBUGGING TIP: Round-off Error. A *round-off error* is the inability to represent certain numeric values exactly.

Another source of problems in dealing with numeric data is due to limits in their *precision*. For example, a decimal number represented as a double value can have at most 17 *significant digits*, and a float can have at most 8. If you tried to store values such as 12345.6789 or 0.123456789 in a float variable, they would be rounded off to 12345.679 and 0.12345679, respectively, causing a possible error.

DEBUGGING TIP: Significant Digits. In using numeric data be sure the data type you choose has enough precision to represent the values your program needs.

SELF-STUDY EXERCISES

EXERCISE 5.2   List all of the binary values that can be represented in 4 bits—that is, all values in the range 0000 to 1111.

EXERCISE 5.3   If a 6-bit representation were used for an integer type, how many different integers could be represented?

EXERCISE 5.4   Give an example of how the size of a data type affects platform dependence.

EXERCISE 5.5   If you were writing a program to process scientific data that had to be accurate to at least 12 significant (decimal) digits, what type of data would you use?

5.5.1   Numeric Operations

Numeric operators

The operations that can be done on numeric data include the standard algebraic operations: *addition* (+), *subtraction* (−), *multiplication* (*), *division* (/), as well as the *modulus* (%) operator. Note that in Java, the multiplication symbol is * and not the ×. The arithmetic operators are binary operators, meaning that they each take two operands. Table 5.4 compares

TABLE 5.4   The standard arithmetic operators in Java

Operation	Operator	Java	Algebra
Addition	+	$x+2$	$x+2$
Subtraction	−	$m-2$	$m-2$
Multiplication	*	$m*2$	$2m$ or $2 \times m$
Division	/	x/y	$x \div y$ or $\frac{x}{y}$
Modulus	%	$x\%y$	x modulo y (for integers x and y)

expressions involving the Java operators with their standard algebraic counterparts.

Although these operations should seem familiar, there are some important differences between their use in algebra and their use in a Java program. Consider the following list of expressions:

```
3 / 2        ==>  value 1     An integer result
3.0 / 2.0    ==>  value 1.5   A floating-point result
3 / 2.0      ==>  value 1.5   A floating-point result
3.0 / 2      ==>  value 1.5   A floating-point result
```

In each of these cases we are dividing the quantity 3 by the quantity 2. However, different results are obtained depending on the *type* of the operands involved. When both operands are integers, as in (3/2), the result must also be an integer. Hence, (3/2) has the value 1, an integer. Because integers cannot have a fractional part, the 0.5 is simply discarded. Integer division (/) always gives an integer result. Thus, the value of (6/2) is 3 and the value of (7/2) is also 3. Because 3.5 is not an integer, the result of dividing 7 by 2 cannot be 3.5. Integer division cannot yield a result that has a fractional part.

Integer division gives an integer result

> **DEBUGGING TIP: Integer Division.** A common source of error among beginning programmers is forgetting that integer division always gives an integer result.

On the other hand, when either operand is a real number, as in the last three cases, the result is a real number. Thus, while the same symbol (/) is used for dividing integers and real numbers, there are really two different operations involved here: *integer division* and *floating-point division*. This use of the same symbol (/) for different operations is called **operator overloading**. It is similar to *method overloading*, which was discussed in Chapter 3.

What if you want to keep the remainder of an integer division? Java provides the modulus operator (%), which takes two operands. The expression (7 % 5) gives the remainder after dividing 7 by 5—2 in this case. In general, the expression (*m* % *n*) (read *m* mod *n*) gives the remainder after *m* is divided by *n*. For example,

Modular arithmetic

```
6 % 4    ==> 6 mod 4 equals 2
4 % 6    ==> 4 mod 6 equals 4
6 % 3    ==> 6 mod 3 equals 0
3 % 6    ==> 3 mod 6 equals 3
```

Numeric Promotion Rules

Because Java is a *strongly typed* language, expressions such as (3/2) have a type associated with them. In cases where one arithmetic operand is an integer and one is a floating-point number, Java *promotes* the integer into a floating-point value and performs a floating-point operation.

Expressions have a type

Promotion is a matter of converting one type to another type. For example, in the expression (5 + 4.0), the value 5 must be promoted to 5.0 before floating-point addition can be performed on (5.0 + 4.0). Generally speaking, automatic promotions such as these are allowed in Java whenever it is possible to perform the promotion *without loss of information*. Because an integer (5) does not have a fractional component, no information will be lost in promoting it to a real number (5.0). On the other hand, you cannot automatically convert a real number (5.4) to an integer (5) because that might lead to loss of information. This leads to the following rule:

> **JAVA LANGUAGE RULE** Integer Promotion. In an operation that contains an integer and a floating-point operand, the integer is *promoted* to a floating-point value *before* the operation is performed.

This rule is actually an instance of a more general rule, for whenever an expression involves operands of different types, some operands must be converted before the expression can be evaluated. Consider the following example:

```
byte n = 125, short m = 32000;
n * m;
```

In this case, *(n * m)* involves two different integer types, `byte` and `short`. Before evaluating this expression Java must first promote the `byte` to a `short` and carry out the operation as the multiplication of two `short`s. Conversion of `short` to `byte` would not be possible because there's no way to represent the value 32000 as a `byte`.

It is important to note that this conversion rule applies regardless of the actual values of the operands. In applying the rule, Java looks at the operand's type, not its value. So even if *m* were assigned a value that could be represented as a byte (for example, 100), the promotion would still go from smaller to larger type. This leads to following the general rule:

Promotion is automatic

> **JAVA LANGUAGE RULE** Type Promotion. In general, when two different types are involved in an operation, the smaller type—the one with fewer bits—is converted to the larger type before the operation is performed. To do otherwise would risk losing information.

Table 5.5 summarizes the actual promotion rules used by Java in evaluating expressions involving mixed operands. Note that the last rule implies that integer expressions involving `byte` or `short` or `int` are performed as `int`. This explains why integer *literals*—such as 56 or −108—are represented as `int` types in Java.

TABLE 5.5 Java promotion rules for mixed arithmetic operators. If two rules apply, choose the one that occurs first in this table.

If either operand is	The other is promoted to
`double`	`double`
`float`	`float`
`long`	`long`
`byte` *or* `short`	`int`

SELF-STUDY EXERCISES

EXERCISE 5.6   Evaluate each of the following integer expressions:

a. 8 / 2   d. 9 % 2   g. 8 % 4
b. 9 / 2   e. 8 % 6   h. 4 % 8
c. 6 / 8   f. 6 % 8

EXERCISE 5.7   Evaluate each of the following expressions, paying special attention to the *type* of the result in each case:

a. 8 / 2.0   c. 6 / 8   e. 8.0 / 6.0
b. 9 / 2.0   d. 0.0 / 2

EXERCISE 5.8   Suppose that the following variable declarations are made:

```
byte m = 3; short n = 4; int p = 5; long q = 6; double r = 7.0;
```

Use type promotion rules to determine the type of expression and then evaluate each of the following expressions:

a. m + n   c. m + n + r   e. r - m
b. p * q   d. p * q * m

5.5.2   Operator Precedence

The built-in precedence order for arithmetic operators is shown in Table 5.6. Parenthesized expressions have highest precedence and are evaluated first. Next come the multiplication, division, and modulus operators, followed by addition and subtraction. When we have an unparenthesized expression that involves both multiplication and addition, the multiplication would be done first, even if it occurs to the right of the plus sign. Operators at the same level in the precedence hierarchy are evaluated from left to right. For example, consider the following expression:

```
9 + 6 - 3 * 6 / 2
```

In this case, the first operation to be applied will be the multiplication (*), followed by division (/), followed by addition (+), and then finally the subtraction (−). We can use parentheses to clarify the order of evaluation. A parenthesized expression is evaluated outward from the innermost set of parentheses:

```
Step 1.   ( (9 + 6) - ((3 * 6) / 2 ) )
Step 2.   ( (9 + 6) - (18 / 2 ) )
Step 3.   ( (9 + 6) - 9 )
Step 4.   ( 15 - 9 )
Step 5.   6
```

TABLE 5.6   Precedence order of the arithmetic operators

Precedence Order	Operator	Operation
1	( )	*Parentheses*
2	* / %	*Multiplication, Division, Modulus*
3	+ −	*Addition, Subtraction*

Parentheses can (and should) always be used to clarify the order of operations in an expression. For example, addition will be performed before multiplication in the following expression:

```
(a + b) * c
```

Another reason to use parentheses is that Java's precedence and promotion rules will sometimes lead to expressions that look fine but contain subtle errors. For example, consider the following expressions:

```
System.out.println(5/3/2.0);    // 0.5
System.out.println(5/(3/2.0));  // 3.33
```

The first gives a result of 0.5, but the use of parentheses in the second gives a result of 3.33. If the second is the expected interpretation, then the parentheses here helped avoid a subtle semantic error.

PROGRAMMING TIP: Parenthesize! To avoid subtle bugs caused by Java's precedence and promotion rules, use parentheses to specify the order of evaluation in an expression.

SELF-STUDY EXERCISE

EXERCISE 5.9 Parenthesize and then evaluate each of the expressions that follow taking care to observe operator precedence rules. Watch for subtle syntax errors.

a. 4 + 5.0 * 6   d. (4 + 5) / 6   g. 9 % 2 * 7 / 3

b. (4 + 5) * 6   e. 4 + 5 % 3   h. 5.0 / 2 * 3

c. 4 + 5 / 6   f. (4 + 5) % 3

5.5.3 Increment and Decrement Operators

Java provides a number of unary operators that are used to increment or decrement an integer variable. For example, the expression k++ uses the *increment operator* ++ to increment the value of the integer variable k. The expression k++ is equivalent to the following Java statements:

```
int k;
k = k + 1 ;  // Add 1 to k and assign the result back to k
```

Preincrement and postincrement

The *unary* ++ operator applies to a single integer operand, in this case to the variable k. It increments k's value by 1 and assigns the result back to k. It may be used either as a *preincrement* or a *postincrement* operator. In the expression k++, the operator *follows* the operand, indicating that it is being used as a *postincrement* operator. This means that the increment operation is done *after* the operand's value is used.

Contrast that with the expression ++k in which the ++ operator *precedes* its operand. In this case, it is used as a *preincrement* operator, which means that the increment operation is done *before* the operand's value is used.

When used in isolation, there is no practical difference between k++ and ++k. Both are equivalent to $k = k + 1$. However, when used in conjunction with other operators, there is a significant difference between preincrement and postincrement. For example, in the following code segment,

```
int j = 0, k = 0;   // Initially both j and k are 0
j = ++k;            // Final values of both j and k are 1
```

the variable k is incremented *before* its value is assigned to j. After execution of the assignment statement, j will equal 1 and k will equal 1. The foregoing sequence is equivalent to

Precedence order

```
int j = 0, k = 0;   // Initially both j and k are 0
k = k + 1;
j = k;              // Final values of both j and k are 1
```

However, in the following example,

```
int i = 0, k = 0; // Initially both i and k are 0
i = k++;           // Final value of i is 0 and k is 1
```

the variable k is incremented *after* its value is assigned to i. After execution of the assignment statement, i will have the value 0 and k will have the value 1. The foregoing sequence is equivalent to

```
int i = 0, k = 0;   // Initially both i and k are 0
i = k;
k = k + 1;          // Final value of i is 0 and k is 1
```

In addition to the increment operator, Java also supplies the *decrement* operator $--$, which can also be used in the predecrement and postdecrement forms. The expression $-- k$ will first decrement k's value by 1 and then use k in any expression in which it is embedded. The expression $k--$ will use the current value of k in the expression in which k is contained and then it will decrement k's value by 1. Table 5.7 summarizes the increment and decrement operators. The unary increment and decrement operators have higher precedence than any of the binary arithmetic operators.

Predecrement and postdecrement

TABLE 5.7   Java's increment and decrement operators

Expression	Operation	Interpretation
$j = ++k$	Preincrement	$k = k+1; j = k;$
$j = k++$	Postincrement	$j = k; k = k+1;$
$j = --k$	Predecrement	$k = k-1; j = k;$
$j = k--$	Postdecrement	$j = k; k = k-1;$

JAVA LANGUAGE RULE   Pre- and Postincrement/Decrement. If an expression like ++k or $--k$ occurs in an expression, k is incremented or decremented *before* its value is used in the rest of the expression. If an expression like k++ or $k--$ occurs in an expression, k is incremented or decremented *after* its value is used in the rest of the expression.

PROGRAMMING TIP: Increment and Decrement Operators. Because of their subtle behavior, be careful in how you use the unary increment and decrement operators. They are most appropriate and useful for incrementing and decrementing loop variables, as we'll see later.

SELF-STUDY EXERCISE

EXERCISE 5.10 What value will j and k have after each of the calculations that follow? Assume that k has the value 0 and j has the value 5 before each operation is done.

a. k = j;   c. k = ++j;   e. k = --j;
b. k = j++;   d. k = j--;

5.5.4 Assignment Operators

In addition to the simple assignment operator (=), Java supplies a number of shortcut assignment operators that allow you to combine an arithmetic operation and an assignment in one operation. These operations can be used with either integer or floating-point operands. For example, the += operator allows you to combine addition and assignment into one expression. The statement

```
k += 3;
```

is equivalent to the statement

```
k = k + 3;
```

Similarly, the statement

```
r += 3.5 + 2.0 * 9.3 ;
```

is equivalent to

```
r = r + (3.5 + 2.0 * 9.3);  // i.e., r = r + 22.1;
```

As these examples illustrate, when using the += operator, the expression on its right-hand side is first evaluated and then *added* to the current value of the variable on its left-hand side.

Table 5.8 lists the other assignment operators that can be used in combination with the arithmetic operators. For each of these operations, the interpretation is the same: Evaluate the expression on the right-hand side

TABLE 5.8 Java's assignment operators

Operator	Operation	Example	Interpretation
=	*Simple assignment*	$m = n;$	$m = n;$
+=	*Addition then assignment*	$m += 3;$	$m = m + 3;$
-=	*Subtraction then assignment*	$m -= 3;$	$m = m - 3;$
*=	*Multiplication then assignment*	$m *= 3;$	$m = m * 3;$
/=	*Division then assignment*	$m /= 3;$	$m = m/3;$
%=	*Remainder then assignment*	$m \% = 3;$	$m = m\%3;$

of the operator and then perform the arithmetic operation (such as addition or multiplication) to the current value of the variable on the left of the operator.

SELF-STUDY EXERCISES

EXERCISE 5.11   What value will j and k have after each of the calculations that follow? Assume that k has the value 10 and that j has the value 5 before each operation is done.

a. `k += j;`   c. `k *= ++j * 2;`   e. `k %= j - 3;`
b. `k -= j++;`   d. `k /= 25 * j--;`

EXERCISE 5.12   Write four different statements that add 1 to the `int` k.

5.5.5   Relational Operators

There are several *relational* operations that can be performed on integers: $<, >, <=, >=, ==$, and $!=$. These correspond to the algebraic operators $<, >, \leq, \geq, =$, and $\neq$. Each of these operators takes two operands (integer or real) and returns a boolean result. They are defined in Table 5.9.

TABLE 5.9   Relational operators

Operator	Operation	Java Expression
$<$	*Less than*	$5 < 10$
$>$	*Greater than*	$10 > 5$
$<=$	*Less than or equal to*	$5 <= 10$
$>=$	*Greater than or equal to*	$10 >= 5$
$==$	*Equal to*	$5 == 5$
$!=$	*Not equal to*	$5 != 4$

Note that several of these relational operators require two symbols in Java. Thus, the familiar equals sign (=) is replaced in Java by ==. This is so *Equals vs. assigns* the equality operator can be distinguished from the assignment operator. Also, less than or equal to ($<=$), greater than or equal to ($>=$), and not equal to ($!=$) require two symbols, instead of the familiar $\leq, \geq$, and $\neq$ from algebra. In each case, the two symbols should be consecutive. It is an error in Java for a space to appear between the $<$ and $=$ in $<=$.

> **DEBUGGING TIP: Equality and Assignment.** A common semantic error among beginning programmers is to use the assignment operator (=) when the equality operator (==) is intended.

Among the relational operators, the inequalities ($<, >, <=$, and $>=$) have higher precedence than the equality operators (== and $!=$). In an expression that involves both kinds of operators, the inequalities would be evaluated first. Otherwise the expression is evaluated from left to right.

Taken as a group the relational operators have lower precedence than the arithmetic operators. Therefore, in evaluating an expression that involves both arithmetic and relational operators, the arithmetic operations are done first. Table 5.10 includes all of the numeric operators introduced so far.

TABLE 5.10   Numeric operator precedence including relations

Precedence Order	Operator	Operation
1	( )	*Parentheses*
2	++ −−	*Increment, decrement*
3	* / %	*Multiplication, division, modulus*
4	+ −	*Addition, subtraction*
5	< > <= >=	*Relational operators*
6	== !=	*Equality operators*

To take an example, let us evaluate the following complex expression:

```
9 + 6 <= 25 * 4 + 2
```

To clarify the implicit operator precedence, we first parenthesize the expression

```
( 9 + 6 ) <= ( (25 * 4 ) + 2 )
```

and then evaluate it step by step:

```
Step 1. ( 9 + 6 ) <= ( (25 * 4 ) + 2 )
Step 2. ( 9 + 6 ) <= ( 100 + 2 )
Step 3. 15 <= 102
Step 4. true
```

The following expression is an example of an ill-formed expression:

```
9 + 6 <= 25 * 4 == 2
```

That the expression is ill formed becomes obvious if we parenthesize it and then attempt to evaluate it:

```
Step 1. ( ( 9 + 6 )  <= ( 25 * 4 ) ) == 2
Step 2. ( 15  <= 100 ) == 2
Step 3. true == 2              // Syntax error results here
```

The problem here is that the expression true == 2 is an attempt to compare an int and a boolean value, which can't be done. As with any other binary operator, the == operator requires that both of its operands be of the same type. This is another example of Java's strong type checking.

Strong typing

SELF-STUDY EXERCISES

EXERCISE 5.13   For each of these questions, what is the value of *m*? Assume that *k* equals 2, *j* equals 3, and *m* equals 10, before each question. Don't forget about precedence.

a. m = j++ + k ;   c. m += j + k;   e. m *= ++j + ++k;
b. m = ++j + k;   d. m *= j++ + k++;

EXERCISE 5.14   Evaluate each of the following expressions, taking care to observe operator precedence rules. If an expression is illegal, mark it illegal and explain why.

a. 4 + 5 == 6 * 2
b. (4 + 5) <= 6 / 3
c. 4 + 5 / 6 >= 10 % 2
d. (4 = 5) / 6

e. 4 + 5 % 3 != 7 - 2
f. (4 + 5) % 3 = 10 -4
g. 9 % 2 * 7 / 3 > 17

5.6 CASE STUDY: Converting Fahrenheit to Celsius

To illustrate some of the issues that arise in using numeric data, let's design an applet that performs temperature conversions from Fahrenheit to Celsius and vice versa.

5.6.1 Problem Decomposition

This problem requires two classes, a `Temperature` class and a `Temperature-Test` class. The `Temperature` class will perform the temperature conversions, and `TemperatureTest` will serve as the user interface (Fig. 5–3).

What objects do we need?

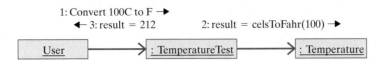

FIGURE 5–3 Interacting objects: The user interacts with the user interface (`TemperatureTest`), which interacts with the `Temperature` object.

5.6.2 Class Design: `Temperature`

The whole purpose of the `Temperature` class is to perform the temperature conversions. In order to do this, it doesn't really need to store any data. When we give it a Celsius value, it will just return the equivalent Fahrenheit value, and vice versa. So this class doesn't need any instance variables. It doesn't have an internal state to represent.

What data do we need?

To perform its tasks, the `Temperature` class will need two public methods: one to convert from Fahrenheit to Celsius and one to convert from Celsius to Fahrenheit. These methods will use the standard conversion formulas: $F = \frac{9}{5}C + 32$ and $C = \frac{5}{9}(F - 32)$.

What methods do we need?

Because we want to be able to handle temperatures that aren't whole numbers (98.6), we should use real-number data for these methods. The `double` type is more widely used than `float`, because Java represents real literals as `double`. Using `double` variables, therefore, cuts down on the number of implicit data conversions that the program has to perform. So both methods should take a `double` parameter and return a `double` result. These considerations lead to the design shown in Figure 5–4.

What type of data do we need?

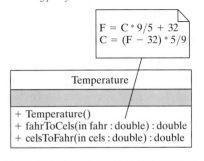

FIGURE 5–4 The `Temperature` class.

> PROGRAMMING TIP: Numeric Types.   Java uses the `int` type for integer literals and `double` for real-number literals. Unless you have some reason to prefer some other type, using these types for your variables and parameters reduces the number of implicit conversions your program would perform.

FIGURE 5–5 The `Temperature` class.

```java
public class Temperature
{
    public Temperature() {}

    public double fahrToCels(double temp)
    {
        return (5.0 * (temp - 32.0) / 9.0);
    }
    public double celsToFahr(double temp)
    {
        return (9.0 * temp / 5.0 + 32.0);
    }
} // Temperature
```

Implementation: `Temperature`

The implementation of the `Temperature` class is shown in Figure 5–5. Note that because `celsToFahr()` uses the `double` value `temp` in its calculation, it uses floating-point literals (9.0, 5.0, and 32.0) in its conversion expression:

```java
private double celsToFahr(double temp)
{   return (9.0 * temp / 5.0 + 32.0);
}
```

This helps to reduce the reliance on Java's built-in promotion rules, which can lead to subtle errors. For example, suppose we had written what looks like an equivalent expression using integer literals:

```java
return (9 / 5 * temp + 32);   // Error: equivalent to (temp + 32)
```

Semantic error

Because 9 divided by 5 gives the integer result 1, this expression is always equivalent to `temp + 32`, which is not the correct conversion formula. This kind of subtle *semantic error* can be avoided if you avoid mixing types wherever possible.

> **PROGRAMMING TIP: Don't Mix Types.** You can reduce the incidence of semantic errors caused by implicit type conversions if, whenever possible, you explicitly change all the literals in an expression to the same type.

5.6.3 Testing and Debugging

Testing strategy

How should this program be tested? As always, you should test the program in a stepwise fashion. As each method is coded, you should test it both in isolation and in combination with the other methods, if appropriate.

Designing test data

Also, you should develop appropriate *test data*. It is not enough to just plug in any values. The values you use should test for certain potential problems. For this program, the following tests are appropriate:

- Test converting 0 degrees C to 32 degrees F.
- Test converting 100 degrees C to 212 degrees F.
- Test converting 212 degrees F to 100 degrees C.
- Test converting 32 degrees F to 0 degrees C.

The first two tests use the `celsToFahr()` method to test the freezing point and boiling point temperatures, two boundary values for this problem. The second pair of tests performs similar checks with the `fahrToCels()` method. One advantage of using these particular values is that we know what results the methods should return.

EFFECTIVE DESIGN: Test Data. Developing appropriate test data is an important part of program design. One type of test data should check the boundaries of the particular calculations you are making.

DEBUGGING TIP: Test, Test, Test! The fact that your program runs correctly on some data is no guarantee of its correctness. The more testing, and the more careful the testing you do, the better.

5.6.4 The `TemperatureTest` Class

The purpose of the `TemperatureTest` class is to serve as a user interface. It will accept a Fahrenheit or Celsius temperature from the user and convert it using the public methods of the `Temperature` class. Its implementation is shown in Figure 5–6.

The `TemperatureTest` program follows an **input-process-output** model for its main algorithm. The user will enter a temperature at the keyboard. The program will convert the temperature from Fahrenheit to Celsius. And the program will output a result. Thus, the input-process-output model has three steps:

Algorithm design

```
Prompt the user and input a value.
Process the input.
Report the result.
```

Note how the program begins with a *prompt* that explains its purpose to the user. It also prompts the user for each input value. A well-designed user interface should provide appropriate prompts to guide the user's actions.

User-interface design

EFFECTIVE DESIGN: User Interface. Prompts should be used to explain a program's purpose to the user and to guide the user's actions, especially when inputting data.

To read the user's keyboard input, the program uses a `BufferedReader` object, which was covered in the "From the Java Library" section of Chapter 2. This object has a `readLine()` method, which can be used to read the user's input into a `String` variable. The `BufferedReader` can be instantiated right in the `main()` method, but because the `readLine()` method can cause an `IOException`, `main()` must declare that it `throws` that exception:

```
import java.io.*;                    // Import the Java I/O classes

public class TemperatureTest
{
    public static void main(String argv[]) throws IOException
    {
        BufferedReader input = new BufferedReader    // Handles console input
            (new InputStreamReader(System.in));
        String inputString;                          // inputString stores the input

        Temperature temperature = new Temperature(); // Create a Temperature object
        double tempIn, tempResult;

        System.out.println("This program will convert Fahrenheit to Celsius and vice versa.");

                   // Convert Fahrenheit to Celsius
        System.out.print("Input a temperature in Fahrenheit > ");  // Prompt for Fahrenheit
        inputString = input.readLine();                            // Get user input
        tempIn = Double.parseDouble(inputString);                  // Convert to double
        tempResult = temperature.fahrToCels(tempIn);               // Convert to Celsius
        System.out.println(tempIn + " F = " + tempResult + " C "); // Report the result

                   // Convert Celsius to Fahrenheit
        System.out.print("Input a temperature in Celsius > ");     // Prompt for Celsius
        inputString = input.readLine();                            // Get user input
        tempIn = Double.parseDouble(inputString);                  // Convert to double
        tempResult = temperature.celsToFahr(tempIn);               // Convert to Fahrenheit
        System.out.println(tempIn + " C = " + tempResult + " F "); // Report the result
    } // main()
} // TemperatureTest
```

FIGURE 5–6   The TemperatureTest class.

```
public static void main(String argv[]) throws IOException
{
    BufferedReader input = new BufferedReader // Handles console input
        (new InputStreamReader (System.in));
    String inputString;                       // Stores the input

    // Code deleted from here

    System.out.print("Input a temperature in Fahrenheit > ");
    inputString = input.readLine();
}
```

5.6.5   Algorithm Design: Data Conversion

Data conversion

One problem that this program faces is that the user's input will be given in the form of String data, but the temperature conversions require double data. Therefore, the program has to convert Strings such as "85.5" into doubles such as 85.5. As we saw in the "Java Language Summary" section of Chapter 2, Java provides *wrapper* classes, such as java.lang.Integer and java.lang.Double, that contain methods for converting one type of data to another. For example, to convert a `String` to an `int`, we can use the `Integer.parseInt()` method:

```
int n = Integer.parseInt("75"); // Converts "75" to 75
```

And to convert a `String` to a `double`, we can use the `Double.parseDouble()` method:

```
double d = Double.parseDouble("75.9");  // Converts "75.9" to 75.9
```

Given the `parseDouble()` method, the algorithm in the main program is now straightforward:

```
                                          // Prompt for Celsius
System.out.print("Input a temperature in Celsius > ");
inputString = input.readLine();           // Get user input
tempIn = Double.parseDouble(inputString); // Convert to double
tempResult = temperature.celsToFahr(tempIn); // Convert to Fahrenheit
                                          // Print the result
System.out.println(tempIn + " C = " + tempResult + " F ");
```

5.6.6 The `TemperatureApplet` Class

Let's now design an applet interface to perform temperature conversions. The `TemperatureApplet` accepts a Fahrenheit or Celsius temperature from the user and converts it using the methods of the `Temperature` class. It will then display the result.

Problem Decomposition

In addition to the `Temperature` object, which will perform the conversions, the applet uses several GUI components to handle the interface tasks (Fig. 5–7). As in `CyberPetApplet` (Chapter 4), `Buttons` are used to let the user control the program: one to convert from Fahrenheit to Celsius, and one to convert in the other direction.

A `TextField` is used to input temperatures from the user. As you know, a `TextField` displays one line of editable text. It has the constructor and methods shown in Figure 5–8. The constructor is used to create a `TextField` of *size* characters in width. The methods are used to read and write the text that's displayed in the `TextField`.

In terms of the applet's control, when the user clicks one of the control buttons, we'll use the `TextField`'s `getText()` method to read the input into the program.

Although it would be possible to use the same `TextField` for both input and output, it would be better to use two different `TextFields`, one for input and one for output, giving us the design shown in Figure 5–9. We'll use the `getText()` method to get the user's input from one, and we'll use the `setText()` method to display the result in the other. We'll use `Labels` to indicate which field is which.

The applet will use an *input-process-output algorithm*. Depending on which button was clicked, it will get the user's input from the input `TextField`, process it, and display the result in the output `TextField`. The applet's `init()` method will instantiate all the GUI components and initialize

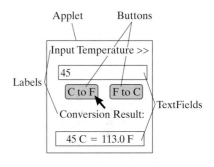

FIGURE 5–7   GUI layout for the `TemperatureApplet`.

What objects do we need?

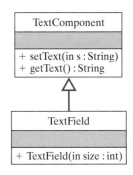

FIGURE 5–8   The `TextField` class inherits `getText()` and `setText()` from its superclass.

What variables and methods do we need?

FIGURE 5–9   In this UML object diagram, multiplicity indicators are used to indicate how many of each type of object is contained in `TemperatureApplet`.

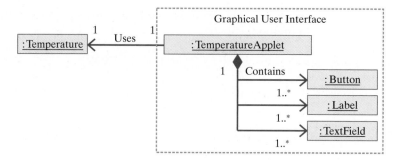

the applet. The `actionPerformed()` method will handle the `Button` actions. Taken together these decisions lead to the design shown in Figure 5–10.

Implementation: `TemperatureApplet`

The implementation of the `TemperatureApplet` class is shown in Figure 5–11. Like our other applet examples, this one extends `Applet` and implements `ActionListener`. Note that all of the instance variables are declared `private` and instantiated in the global section of the class.

Instantiation of each `TextField` object requires that we specify the number of characters that it will hold. This determines how big the `TextField` will be in the applet. We must also remember to `add()` it to the applet in the `init()` method:

TemperatureApplet
− inField : TextField
− resultField : TextField
− prompt1 : Label
− prompt2 : Label
− celsToFahr : Button
− fahrToCels : Button
− temperature : Temperature
+ init()
+ actionPerformed()

FIGURE 5–10   The `TemperatureApplet` class.

```
TextField inField = new TextField(15); // Declare and instantiate
add(tempField);                         // Add to applet -- in init()
```

Instantiation of each `Button` requires that we set the button's label, add it into the applet, and designate its `ActionListener`, which handles its button clicks:

```
                                       // Declare and instantiate
private Button celsToFahr = new Button("C to F");
add(celsToFahr);                       // Add to applet -- in init()
celsToFahr.addActionListener(this); // Add its listener -- in init()
```

What control structures should be used?

The applet's `actionPerformed()` method implements the input-process-output algorithm. It uses an if-else statement to distinguish between the Celsius to Fahrenheit and Fahrenheit to Celsius cases:

```
public void actionPerformed(ActionEvent e)
{
    String inputStr = inField.getText();    // Get user's input
    double userInput = Double.parseDouble(inputStr);
                                            // Convert it to double
    double result = 0;

    if (e.getSource() == celsToFahr) {      // Process and report
        result = temperature.celsToFahr(userInput);
        resultField.setText(inputStr + " C = " + result  + " F");
    } else {
        result = temperature.fahrToCels(userInput);
        resultField.setText(inputStr + " F = " + result  + " C");
    }
} // actionPerformed()
```

```java
import java.applet.*;
import java.awt.*;
import java.awt.event.*;

public class TemperatureApplet extends Applet implements ActionListener
{
    private TextField inField = new TextField(15);  // GUI components
    private TextField resultField = new TextField(15);
    private Label prompt1 = new Label("Input Temperature >>");
    private Label prompt2 = new Label("Conversion Result:");
    private Button celsToFahr = new Button("C to F");
    private Button fahrToCels = new Button("F to C");


                                  // The temperature object
    private Temperature temperature = new Temperature();

    public void init()
    {                       // Set up the user interface
        add(prompt1);         // Input elements
        add(inField);
        add(celsToFahr);      // Control buttons
        add(fahrToCels);
        add(prompt2);         // Output elements
        add(resultField);
                              // Register buttons with listeners
        celsToFahr.addActionListener(this);
        fahrToCels.addActionListener(this);
        setSize(175,200);
    } // init()


    public void actionPerformed(ActionEvent e)
    {
        String inputStr = inField.getText(); // Get user's input
                                         // Convert it to double
        double userInput = Double.parseDouble(inputStr);
        double result = 0;

        if (e.getSource() == celsToFahr) {    // Process and report
          result = temperature.celsToFahr(userInput);
          resultField.setText(inputStr + " C = " + result  + " F ");
        } else {
          result = temperature.fahrToCels(userInput);
          resultField.setText(inputStr + " F = " +  result  + " C ");
        }
    } // actionPerformed()
} // end of TemperatureApplet
```

FIGURE 5–11 Implementation of the TemperatureApplet class.

FIGURE 5–12 This UML sequence diagram shows the events that occur when the user clicks on the "C to F" button after inputting "100" into the input `TextField`. The applet calls the `Temperature` object's `celsToFahr()` method, and it returns the value 212, which is put into the result `TextField`.

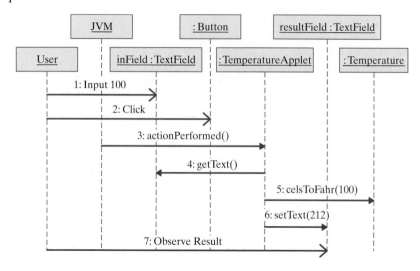

Interacting objects

It is here, in the `actionPerformed()` method, that we can easily see the interaction between the various objects involved in this program (Fig. 5–12). The applet, through its `actionPerformed()` method, is serving as an interface between the user and the `Temperature` object. It takes the user's input from the `TextField`, converts it, and passes it to the `Temperature` object. It gets a result from the `Temperature` object and displays it for the user in the `TextField` object. Figure 5–13 shows the applet's final appearance.

Note the use of the three local variables, `inputStr`, `userInput`, and `result`, to help break the computation into separate steps. The variables serve to carry values over from one step to the next. We use a temporary variable (of the correct type) to store a value produced in one statement and then use that value in the next statement.

FIGURE 5–13 A screenshot of the `TemperatureApplet`.

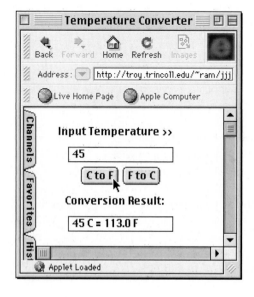

PROGRAMMING TIP: Use of Variables.   Use temporary variables within methods to store intermediate values produced during a calculation. These variables have local scope.

PROGRAMMING TIP: Divide and Conquer.   Use temporary variables to divide a complicated computation into smaller steps.

5.7   An Integer-Based CyberPet Model

Now that we have introduced the int type, let's use it to simplify our representation of the CyberPet class. Recall that the boolean representation forced us to introduce a new boolean variable for each possible value of the CyberPet's state. This caused all kinds of difficulties when we tried to add new states to the class. Many of these problems will go away if we use an integer variable to represent CyberPet's state.

Suppose we declare the CyberPet's state as the following int variable:

```
private int petState;
```

This will lead to the design shown in Figure 5–14. Given that we now represent the pet's state with a single int variable, we can use integer values—for example, 0, 1, 2—to represent the different CyberPet states—0 for eating, 1 for sleeping, 2 for thinking.

5.7.1   Class Constants

Instead of using *integer literals*—0, 1, 2—Java provides a way of creating *named constants* that give names to the state values:

```
public static final int EATING = 0;
public static final int SLEEPING = 1;
public static final int THINKING = 2;
```

A **class constant** is a final static variable that is associated with the class, rather than with its instances.

If a variable is declared static, there is exactly one instance of that variable created no matter how many times its class is instantiated. Even if the class has no instances—even if no individual CyberPet objects are created—the class itself will keep a single copy of its static variables. Because static variables do not depend on the creation of objects (instances), they are called **class variables**.

The final keyword is used to declare a variable that has a constant value throughout the duration of the program. Variables declared final must have an initializer—for example, EATING = 0. Once a final variable has been initialized, any attempt to change its value will cause a syntax error.

Finally, by declaring these constants as public, we make them accessible to objects that use the CyberPet class. There are two ways to reference class constants. They can be accessed through any CyberPet instance, in the same way that we access an instance variable or instance method. Or they can be accessed through the class itself:

CyberPet
– petState : int – name : String
+ CyberPet() + CyberPet(in s : String) + CyberPet(in s : String, in state : int) + CyberPet(in s : String, in state : boolean) + setName(in s : String) + getName() : String + eat() + sleep() + think() + toString() : String + getState() : String

FIGURE 5–14   The revised CyberPet class.

static *keyword*

Class variables

final *keyword*

Using the class as a reference

```
CyberPet socrates = new CyberPet();      // Create an instance
System.out.println(socrates.EATING);     // Refer to a constant

System.out.println(CyberPet.EATING);     // No instance needed
```

Both socrates.EATING and CyberPet.EATING refer to the same value (0).

Being able to refer to class constants before creating an instance allows us to use them in the constructor to set the pet's initial state. For example, our new version of CyberPet (Fig. 5–15) provides four constructor methods, including one with a new signature: CyberPet(String,int). The second parameter here requires an integer that represents the initial value of CyberPet's petState variable. This is one place where we can use a class constant:

```
CyberPet pet3 = new CyberPet ("Ernie", CyberPet.SLEEPING);
```

The Advantage of Class Constants

The notion of associating a constant with a class makes perfect sense. Clearly the proper place for constants such as EATING and SLEEPING is with the class itself and not with any particular CyberPet object, because their values don't depend on the state of any particular CyberPet instance.

Class constants are used extensively in the Java class library. For example, the various built-in colors are represented as constants of the java.awt.Color class—Color.blue and Color.red. The java.awt.Label uses int constants to specify how a label's text should be aligned: Label.CENTER.

Maintainability

Using constants, whether static or not, makes it much easier to modify and maintain a program. As the new version of CyberPet illustrates (Fig. 5–15), constants, such as EATING, are declared at the beginning of the class definition and then used throughout the program instead of literal integer values. If it becomes necessary to change a constant's value, we need only change its initializer. For literals, on the other hand, we would have to change every occurrence of the literal, which could easily lead to errors. So using constants makes program maintenance easier and less prone to error.

EFFECTIVE DESIGN: Maintainability.   Constants should be used instead of literal values in a program. This will make the program easier to modify and maintain.

Programming Style

Note that we have used uppercase characters for the names of the three constants. This is a stylistic convention intended to make our program more readable. It has no effect on the compiler, which only cares about the constant's static final qualifiers. Using uppercase makes constants easily identifiable and easily distinguishable from genuine variables.

PROGRAMMING TIP: Readability.   To make your programs more readable, use uppercase font for constant identifiers.

```
public class CyberPet
{
    public static final int EATING = 0;    // Class constants
    public static final int SLEEPING = 1;
    public static final int THINKING = 2;

    private int petState;    // Instance variables
    private String name;

    public CyberPet() {              // Constructor #1
        name = "no name";
        petState = EATING;
    }
    public CyberPet(String str) {  // Constructor #2
        name = str;
        petState = EATING;
    }
    public CyberPet(String str, int inState) { // Constructor #3
        name = str;
        petState = inState;
    }
    public CyberPet(String str, boolean sleeping) { // Constructor #4
        name = str;
        if (sleeping == true)
            petState = SLEEPING;
        else
            petState = EATING;
    }
    public void   setName(String str) { name = str; } // setName()
    public String getName()  { return name;          } // getName()
    public void   eat()      { petState = EATING;   } // eat()
    public void   sleep()    { petState = SLEEPING; } // sleep()
    public void   think()    { petState = THINKING; } // think()
    public String toString() { return "I am a CyberPet named " + name; }

    public String getState() {
        if (petState == EATING)
            return "Eating";         // Exit the method
        if (petState == SLEEPING)
            return "Sleeping";       // Exit the method
        if (petState == THINKING)
            return "Thinking";
        return "Error in State";     // Exit the method
    } // getState()
} // CyberPet
```

FIGURE 5–15   An integer-based CyberPet model.

5.7.2 The Revised CyberPet Class

Given our new representation for a CyberPet's state, we have to make corresponding changes to its methods (Fig. 5–15). The good news is that several of the methods remained unchanged, including the setName(), getName(), and toString() methods. More good news is that several of the other methods actually became simpler to implement. For example, the constructor methods now require a single assignment statement to set the initial state of a CyberPet:

```
petState = EATING;
```

And several of the access and mutator methods are now so short they can be written on a single line:

```
public String getName()  { return name;        }   // getName()
public void   eat()      { petState = EATING;  }   // eat()
```

The most significant change required in the integer model occurs in the constructor method, CyberPet(String,boolean). In that case, we have to change the method definition as follows:

```
CyberPet(String str, boolean sleeping) {       // Old verion
    name = str;
    isSleeping = sleeping;
    isEating = !isSleeping;
}

CyberPet(String str, int inState) {            // New version
    name = str;
    petState = inState;
}
```

Since we have changed our state representation from boolean to int, we have to change the second parameter in this method from boolean to int.

However, unlike the other changes, this change has implications that extend beyond CyberPet itself. Any program that was using the constructor with the signature CyberPet(String, boolean)—for example, pet1 = new CyberPet("pete", true)—will no longer compile and run, if we remove it from our definition. This is not good. In general, if we make changes to a class, such as CyberPet, we don't want to break the programs that were using that old version of the class. Can anything be done to prevent this situation?

The answer is that instead of removing CyberPet(String,boolean), we should reimplement it as follows:

```
public CyberPet(String str, boolean sleeping) { // Constructor #4
    name = str;
    if (sleeping == true)
        petState = SLEEPING;
    else
        petState = EATING;
}
```

This reimplementation of CyberPet(String,boolean) is compatible with our new state representation, but it can still be used by those programs that were using the old version of CyberPet. It allows the integer-based version of CyberPet to be *backward compatible* with the previous version.

> EFFECTIVE DESIGN: Backward Compatibility.   Modifications to a class should try to preserve its compatibility with other classes that use it.

The problem of backward compatibility is ever present in the software industry, where products are continually revised and upgraded. This goes for the Java language itself, which has gone through versions 1.0, 1.1, 1.2, and 1.3 within the space of a few years. New classes have been added and existing classes have changed. Sun Microsystems warns users when a *deprecated* method or class is being used in a program—that is, one that has been superseded in the new version. But in an effort to maintain compatibility with older versions of Java, it still supports the deprecated element, much as we have done in our modification to CyberPet 1.0!

Backward compatibility

5.7.3   Advantages of the Integer-Based CyberPet

Our new CyberPet is a big improvement over the previous version. For one thing, it uses a much simpler state representation. Maintaining a single integer variable is much simpler than maintaining several boolean variables. Also, the methods used to change the state are much simpler, requiring just a single assignment statement to do their respective tasks.

Simplicity

Moreover, because its methods are more self-contained, our new model is more extensible. For example, note how CyberPet was extended to cover the state of thinking. A class constant was defined:

Extensibility

```
public static final int THINKING = 2;
```

A (thinking) mutator method was defined:

```
public void think() {
    petState = THINKING;
}
```

And a third if statement was added to the getState() method:

```
if (petState == THINKING)
    return "Thinking";
```

These are the only required changes. Most importantly, because of the improved modularity in its method design, a change in one method does not ripple through the entire class, as it did in the boolean version.

Modularity

The integer representation can also be used to model other aspects of a CyberPet's state. For example, the pet's kind could be incorporated into the model as follows:

Generality

```
private int kind;                          // Instance variable

public static final int DOG = 0;     // Class constants
public static final int CAT = 1;
public static final int PARAKEET = 2;
public static final int GERBIL = 3;
                                           // Access and mutator methods
public void setKind(int inKind) { kind = inKind; }
public int  getKind()                { return kind;   }
```

In sum, the integer version of `CyberPet` is much superior to the boolean-based model. Not only does it adopt a simpler state representation, but it also makes the model more extensible. Moreover, the model is general enough to be easily extended without sacrificing backward compatibility. All of these are important design considerations when deciding on an appropriate model for representing a program's objects.

SELF-STUDY EXERCISE

EXERCISE 5.15   To confirm that either the boolean-based CyberPet or the integer-based CyberPet will work the same way, run both models using the `CyberPetApplet` interface you developed in Chapter 4. What does the success of this experiment signify for object-oriented design?

OBJECT-ORIENTED DESIGN: Information Hiding

Preserving the public interface

The fact that the integer-based version of `CyberPet` is *backward compatible* with the previous version is due in large part to the way we have divided up its public and private elements. Because the new version of `CyberPet` still presents the same *public interface*, an object such as `CyberPetApplet` can continue to use `CyberPet` without changing a single line of its own code.

Information hiding

Although we have completely changed the underlying representation of `CyberPet`, the implementation details—its data and algorithms—are hidden from other objects. As long as `CyberPet`'s public interface remains compatible with the old version, changes to its private elements won't cause any inconvenience to those objects that were dependent on the old version. This ability to change the underlying implementation without affecting the outward functionality of a class is one of the great benefits of the information hiding principle.

The lesson to be learned here is that the public parts of a class should be restricted to just those parts that must be accessible to other objects. Everything else should be private. Things work better, in Java programming and in the real world, when objects are designed with the principle of information hiding in mind.

EFFECTIVE DESIGN: Information Hiding.   In designing a class, other objects should be given access just to the information they need and nothing more.

5.8 Character Data and Operators

Another primitive data type in Java is the character type, char. A character in Java is represented by a 16-bit unsigned integer. This means that a total of 2^{16} or 65536 different Unicode characters can be represented, corresponding to the integer values 0 to 65535. The *Unicode* character set is an international standard that has been developed to enable computer languages to represent characters in a wide variety of languages, not just English. Detailed information about this encoding can be obtained at

Unicode

```
http://www.unicode.org/
```

It is customary in programming languages to use unsigned integers to represent characters. This means that all the digits $(0, \ldots, 9)$, alphabetic letters $(a, \ldots, z, A, \ldots, Z)$, punctuation symbols (such as . ; , " " ! _ -), and nonprinting control characters (LINE_FEED, ESCAPE, CARRIAGE_RETURN, ...) that make up the computer's character set are represented in the computer's memory by integers. A more traditional set of characters is the *ASCII (American Standard Code for Information Interchange)* character set. ASCII is based on a 7-bit code and, therefore, defines 2^7 or 128 different characters, corresponding to the integer values 0 to 127. In order to make Unicode backward compatible with ASCII systems, the first 128 Unicode characters are identical to the ASCII characters. Thus, in both the ASCII and Unicode encoding, the printable characters have the integer values shown in Table 5.11.

ASCII code

TABLE 5.11 ASCII codes for selected characters

Code	32	33	34	35	36	37	38	39	40	41	42	43	44	45	46	47
Char	SP	!	"	#	$	%	&	'	(	)	*	+	,	-	.	/

Code	48	49	50	51	52	53	54	55	56	57
Char	0	1	2	3	4	5	6	7	8	9

Code	58	59	60	61	62	63	64
Char	:	;	<	=	>	?	@

Code	65	66	67	68	69	70	71	72	73	74	75	76	77
Char	A	B	C	D	E	F	G	H	I	J	K	L	M

Code	78	79	80	81	82	83	84	85	86	87	88	89	90
Char	N	O	P	Q	R	S	T	U	V	W	X	Y	Z

Code	91	92	93	94	95	96
Char	[	\	]	^	_	`

Code	97	98	99	100	101	102	103	104	105	106	107	108	109
Char	a	b	c	d	e	f	g	h	i	j	k	l	m

Code	110	111	112	113	114	115	116	117	118	119	120	121	122
Char	n	o	p	q	r	s	t	u	v	w	x	y	z

Code	123	124	125	126
Char	{			}	~

5.8.1   Character to Integer Conversions

Is 'A' a character or an integer? The fact that character data are stored as integers in the computer's memory can cause some confusion about whether a given piece of data is a character or an integer. In other words, when is a character, say 'A', treated as the integer (65) instead of as the character 'A'? The rule in Java is that a character literal—'a' or 'A' or '0' or '?'—is always treated as a character, unless we explicitly tell Java to treat it as an integer. So if we display a literal's value

```java
System.out.println('a');
```

the letter 'a' will be displayed. Similarly, if we assign 'a' to a char variable and then display the variable's value,

```java
char ch = 'a';
System.out.println(ch);        // Displays 'a'
```

the letter 'a' will be shown. If, on the other hand, we wish to output a character's integer value, we must use an explicit *cast* operator as follows:

```java
System.out.println((int)'a') ;   // Displays 97
```

A **cast operation**, such as (int), converts one type of data ('a') into another (97). This is known as a **type conversion**. Similarly, if we wish to store a character's integer value in a variable, we can *cast* the char into an int as follows:

```java
int k = (int)'a';        // Converts 'a' to 97
System.out.println(k);   // Displays 97
```

The cast operator

As these examples show, a *cast* is a type conversion operator. Java allows a wide variety of both explicit and implicit type conversions. Certain conversions (for example, promotions) take place when methods are invoked, when assignment statements are executed, when expressions are evaluated, and so on.

Type conversion in Java is governed by several rules and exceptions. In some cases Java allows the programmer to make implicit cast conversions. For example, in the following assignment a char is converted to an int even though no explicit cast operator is used:

```java
char ch;
int k;
k = ch; // convert a char into an int
```

Implicit type conversion

Java permits this conversion because no information will be lost. A character char is represented in 16 bits whereas an int is represented in 32 bits. This is like trying to put a small object into a large box. Space will be left over, but the object will fit inside without being damaged. Similarly, storing a 16-bit char in a 32-bit int will leave the extra 16 bits unused.

Widening conversion

This *widening primitive conversion* changes one primitive type (char) into a wider one (int), where a type's *width* is the number of bits used in its representation.

On the other hand, trying to assign an int value to a char variable leads to a syntax error:

```
char ch;
int k;
ch = k;    // Syntax error: can't assign int to char
```

Trying to assign a 32-bit int to 16-bit char is like trying to fit a big object into an undersized box. The object won't fit unless we shrink it in some way. Java will allow us to assign an int value to a char variable, but only if we perform an explicit cast on it:

```
ch = (char)k; // Explicit cast of int k into char ch
```

The (char) cast operation performs a careful "shrinking" of the int by lopping off the last 16 bits of the int. This can be done without loss of information provided that *k*'s value is in the range 0 to 65535—that is, in the range of values that fit into a char variable. This *narrowing primitive conversion* changes a wider type (32-bit int) to a narrower type (16-bit char). Because of the potential here for information loss, it is up to the programmer to determine that the cast can be performed safely.

Narrowing conversion

JAVA LANGUAGE RULE Type Conversion. Java permits *implicit* type conversions from a narrower type to a wider type. A *cast* operator must be used when converting a wider type into a narrower type.

The cast operator can be used with any primitive type. It applies to the variable or expression that immediately follows it. Thus, parentheses must be used to cast the expression *m + n* into a char:

```
char ch = (char)(m + n);
```

The following statement would cause a syntax error because the cast operator would only be applied to m:

```
char ch = (char)m + n;    // Syntax error: right hand side is an int
```

In the expression on the right-hand side, the character produced by (char)m will be promoted to an int because it is part of an integer operation whose result will still be an int. Therefore, it cannot be assigned to a char without an explicit cast.

SELF-STUDY EXERCISE

EXERCISE 5.16 Suppose that *m* and *n* are integer variables of type int and that *ch1* and *ch2* are character variables of type char. Determine in each of the cases that follow whether the assignment statements are valid. If not, modify the statement to make it valid.

a. m = n;   c. ch2 = n;   e. ch1 = m - n;
b. m = ch1;   d. ch1 = ch2;

5.8.2 Lexical Ordering

Although the actual integer values assigned to the individual characters by ASCII and UNICODE encoding seem somewhat arbitrary, there are a number of important encoding regularities. For example, note that various sequences of digits, '0'...'9', and letters, 'a'...'z' and 'A'...'Z', are represented by sequences of integers (Table 5.11). This makes it possible to represent the concept of *lexical order* among characters in terms of the *less than* relationship among integers. The fact that 'a' comes before 'f' in alphabetical order is represented by the fact that 97 (the integer code for 'a') is less than 102 (the integer code for 'f'). Similarly, the digit '5' comes before the digit '9' in an alphabetical sequence because 53 (the integer code for '5') is less than 57 (the integer code for '9').

This ordering relationship extends throughout the character set. Thus, it is also the case that 'A' comes before 'a' in the lexical ordering because 65 (the integer code for 'A') is less than 97 (the integer code for 'a'). Similarly, the character '[' comes before '}' because its integer code (91) is less than 125, the integer code for '}'.

5.8.3 Relational Operators

char relations

Given the lexical ordering of the char type, the following relational operators can be defined: <, >, <=, >=, ==, !=. Given any two characters, *ch1* and *ch2*, the expression *ch1 < ch2* is true if and only if the integer value of *ch1* is less than the integer value of *ch2*. In this case we say that *ch1 precedes ch2* in lexical order. Similarly, the expression *ch1 > ch2* is true if and only if the integer value of *ch1* is greater than the integer value of *ch2*. In this case we say that *ch1 follows ch2*. And so on for the other relational operators. This means that we can perform comparison operations on any two character operands (Table 5.12).

TABLE 5.12   Relational operations on characters

Operation	Operator	Java	True Expression
Precedes	<	*ch1 < ch2*	$'a' < 'b'$
Follows	>	*ch1 > ch2*	$'c' > 'a'$
Precedes or equals	<=	*ch1 <= ch2*	$'a' <= 'a'$
Follows or equals	>=	*ch2 >= ch1*	$'a' >= 'a'$
Equal to	==	*ch1 == ch2*	$'a' == 'a'$
Not equal to	!=	*ch1 != ch2*	$'a' != 'b'$

5.9   Example: Character Conversions

Another interesting implication of representing the characters as integers is that we can represent various character operations in terms of integer operations. For example, suppose we want to capitalize a lowercase letter. Table 5.11 shows that the entire sequence of lowercase letters ('a' . . . 'z') is displaced by 32 from the sequence of uppercase letters ('A' . . . 'Z'), so we can convert any lowercase letter into its corresponding uppercase letter by subtracting 32 from its integer value, provided we perform an explicit cast on the result. When we perform the cast (char) ('a' - 32), the resulting value is 'A', as the following example shows:

Lowercase to uppercase

```
(char)('a' - 32)                    ==>  'A'
```

Recall that in evaluating 'a' - 32 Java will promote 'a' to an int and then perform the subtraction. Thus, a step-by-step evaluation of the expression would go as follows:

```
Step 1. (char)((int)'a' - 32)   // Promote 'a' to int
Step 2. (char)(97 - 32)         // Subtract
Step 3. (char) (65)             // Cast result to a char
Step 4. 'A'                     // Giving 'A'
```

Similarly, we can convert an uppercase letter into the corresponding lowercase letter by simply adding 32 to its integer code and casting the result back to a char:

Uppercase to lowercase

```
(char)('J' + 32)                ==>  'j'
```

We can group these ideas into a method that performs conversion from lowercase to uppercase:

```
char toUpperCase(char ch) {
    if ((ch >= 'a') && (ch <= 'z'))
        return ch - 32 ;        // Syntax error: can't return an int
    return ch;
}
```

This method takes a single char parameter and returns a char value. It begins by checking if *ch* is a lowercase letter—that is, if *ch* falls between 'a' and 'z' inclusive. If so, it returns the result of subtracting 32 from *ch*. If not, it returns *ch* unchanged. However, the method contains a syntax error that becomes apparent if we trace through its steps. If we invoke it with the expression toUpperCase('b'), then since 'b' is between 'a' and 'z', the method will return 'b' − 32. Because the integer value of 'b' is 98, it will return 98 − 32 or 66, which is the integer code for the character 'B'. However, the method is supposed to return a char, so this last statement will generate the following syntax error:

Type error

```
Incompatible type for return. An explicit cast needed
to convert int to char.
>>      return ch - 32 ;
>>      ^
```

In order to avoid this error, the result must be converted back to char before it can be returned:

```
char toUpperCase (char ch) {
    if ((ch >= 'a') && (ch <= 'z'))
        return (char)(ch - 32);    // Explicit cast required
    return ch;
}
```

Another common type of conversion is to convert a digit to its corresponding integer value. For example, we convert the character '9' to the integer 9 by making use of the fact that the digit '9' is 9 characters beyond the digit '0' in the lexical order. Therefore, subtracting '0' from '9' gives integer 9 as a result:

Digit to integer

```
('9' - '0')  ==> (57 - 48) ==>  9
```

More generally, the expression *ch*– *'0'* will convert any digit, *ch*, to its integer value. We can encapsulate these ideas into a method that converts any digit into its corresponding integer value:

```
int digitToInteger(char ch) {
    if ((ch >= '0') && (ch <= '9'))
        return ch - '0';
    return -1 ;
}
```

This method takes a single `char` parameter and returns an `int`. It first checks that *ch* is a valid digit, and if so, it subtracts the character '0' from it. If not, the method just returns −1, which indicates that the method received an invalid input parameter. Obviously, when an object invokes this method, it should first make sure that the value it passes is in fact a digit.

The Java application program shown in Figure 5–16 illustrates several of the ideas discussed in this section.

5.9.1 Static Methods

Note that the public methods in the `Test` class (Fig. 5–16) are declared `static`. This is due to a restriction in Java applications that prevents `static` methods, such as `main()`, from using nonstatic methods or instance variables. Recall that the modifier `static` means that exactly one copy of the variable or method is created, whether or not the class in which it occurs is instantiated.

FIGURE 5–16   A Java program illustrating character conversions. When run, the program will generate the following outputs, one per line: a, 98, b, A, B, 7.

```
public class Test {
    public static void main(String argv[]) {
        char ch = 'a';            // Local variables
        int k = (int)'b';

        System.out.println(ch);
        System.out.println(k);
                                  // ch = k erroneous assignment
        ch = (char)k;             // so we use an explicit cast
        System.out.println(ch);
        System.out.println(toUpperCase('a'));
        System.out.println(toUpperCase(ch));
        System.out.println(digitToInteger('7'));
    }

    public static char toUpperCase(char ch) {
        if ((ch >= 'a') && (ch <= 'z'))
            return (char)(ch - 32);
        return ch;
    }

    public static int digitToInteger(char ch) {
        if ((ch >= '0') && (ch <= '9'))
            return ch - '0';
        return -1 ;
    }
} // Test
```

The fact that `main()` is `static` means that there is exactly one instance of it no matter how many instances (including none) of its class exist. In order for `main()` to be valid in all cases—even when its class is not instantiated—the methods and variables it uses must also be `static`, so they will exist even if their class is not instantiated.

Static methods

> **JAVA LANGUAGE RULE** Static Methods. Static elements—methods, variables, constants—are associated with the class itself, not with its instances, and may only be used with other static elements.

Methods declared `static` are **class methods**, and they can be invoked through the class (as well as through any instances of the class). For example, the `Test.digitToInteger()` method can be invoked, even if there are no instances of the `Test` class. We have seen several examples of `static` methods already, including those found in the wrapper classes: `Integer.parseInt()`, `Double.parseDouble()`.

THE `java.lang.Math` class provides many common mathematical functions that will prove useful in performing numerical computations. As an element of the `java.lang` package, it is included implicitly in all Java programs. Table 5.13 lists some of the most commonly used Math class methods.

From the Java Library

`java.lang.Math`

http://java.sun.com/products /jdk/1.3/docs/api/

TABLE 5.13 A selection of `Math` class methods

Method	Description	Examples
int abs(int x) *long abs(long x)* *float abs(float x)*	*Absolute value of x*	*if x >= 0 abs(x) is x* *if x < 0 abs(x) is −x*
int ceil(double x)	*Rounds x to the smallest integer not less than x*	*ceil(8.3) is 9* *ceil(−8.3) is −8*
int floor(double x)	*Rounds x to the largest integer not greater than x*	*floor (8.9) is 8* *floor(−8.9) is −9*
double log(double x)	*Natural logarithm of x*	*log (2.718282) is 1.0*
double pow(double x, double y)	*x raised to the y power (x^y)*	*pow(3, 4) is 81.0* *pow(16.0, 0.5) is 4.0*
double random()	*Generates a pseudorandom number in the interval [0,1)*	*random() is 0.5551* *random() is 0.8712*
long round(double x)	*Rounds x to an integer*	*round(26.51) is 27* *round (26.499) is 26*
double sqrt(double x)	*Square root of x*	*sqrt(4.0) is 2.0*

All Math methods are static *class methods* and are, therefore, invoked through the class name. For example, we would calculate 2^4 as Math.pow(2,4), which evaluates to 16. Similarly, we compute the square root of 225.0 as Math.sqrt(225.0), which evaluates to 15.0.

Java's Math class cannot be instantiated and cannot be subclassed. Its basic definition is

```
public final class Math {   // Can't subclass a final class
    private Math() {}        // Can't invoke a  private constructor
    ...
    public static native double sqrt(double a)
          throws ArithmeticException;
}
```

By declaring the Math class public final, we indicate that it can be accessed (public) but it cannot be extended or subclassed (final). By declaring its default constructor to be private, we prevent this class from being instantiated. The idea of a class that cannot be subclassed and cannot be instantiated may seem a little strange at first. The justification for it here is that it provides a way to introduce helpful math functions into the Java language.

Defining the Math class in this way makes it easy to use, because you don't have to create an instance of it. It is also a very efficient design. Because its methods are static elements of the java.lang package, they are loaded into memory at the beginning of your program's execution, and they persist in memory throughout your program's lifetime. Because Math class methods do not have to be loaded into memory each time they are invoked, their execution time will improve dramatically.

EFFECTIVE DESIGN: Static Methods.   A method should be declared static if it is intended to be used whether or not there is an instance of its class.

Rounding to Two Decimal Places

Algorithm design

When dealing with applications that involve monetary values—dollars and cents—it is often necessary to round a calculated result to two decimal places. For example, suppose a program computes the value of a certificate of deposit (CD) to be 75.19999. Before we output this result, we would want to round it to two decimal places—to 75.20. The following algorithm can be used to accomplish this:

```
1. Multiply the number by 100, giving 7519.9999.
2. Add 0.5 to the number giving 7520.4999.
3. Drop the fraction part giving 7520
4. Divide the result by 100, giving 75.20
```

Step 3 of this algorithm can be done using the Math.floor() method. If the number to be rounded is stored in the double variable *R*, then the following expression will round R to two decimal places:

```
R = Math.floor(R * 100.0 + 0.5) / 100.0;
```

Alternatively, we could use the `Math.round()` method (Table 5.13). This method rounds a floating-point value to the nearest integer. For example, `Math.round(65.3333)` rounds to 65 and `Math.round(65.6666)` rounds to 66. The following expression uses it to round to two decimal places:

```
R = Math.round(100.0 * R) / 100.0;
```

It's important here to divide by 100.0 and not by 100. Otherwise the division will give an integer result and we'll lose the two decimal places.

> DEBUGGING TIP: Division. Using the correct type of literal in division operations is necessary to ensure that you get the correct type of result.

ALTHOUGH the `Math.round()` method is useful for rounding numbers, it is not suitable for business applications. Even for rounded values, Java will drop trailing zeroes. So a value such as $10,000.00 would be output as $10000.0. This wouldn't be acceptable for a business report.

Fortunately, Java supplies the `java.text.NumberFormat` class precisely for the task of representing numbers as dollar amounts, percentages, and other formats (Fig. 5–17).

The `NumberFormat` class is an `abstract` class, which means it cannot be directly instantiated. Instead you would use its static `getInstance()` methods to create an instance that can then be used for the desired formatting tasks. (Note that static elements are underlined in UML.)

Once a `NumberFormat` instance has been created, the `format()` method can be used to put a number into a particular format. Methods such as `setMaximumFractionDigits()` and `setMaximumIntegerDigits()` can be used to control the number of digits before and after the decimal point.

For example, the following statements might be used to format a decimal number as a currency string in dollars and cents:

```
NumberFormat dollars = NumberFormat.getCurrencyInstance();
System.out.println(dollars.format(10962.555));
```

These statements would cause the value 10962.555 to be shown as $10,962.56. Similarly, the statements,

```
NumberFormat percent = NumberFormat.getPercentInstance();
percent.setMaximumFractionDigits(2);
System.out.println(percent.format(6.55));
```

would display the value 6.55 as 6.55%.

From the Java Library

`java.text.NumberFormat`

 http://java.sun.com/products /jdk/1.3/docs/api/

NumberFormat
+ getInstance() : NumberFormat
+ getCurrencyInstance() : NumberFormat
+ getPercentInstance() : NumberFormat
+ format(in n : double) : String
+ format(in n : long) : String
+ getMaximumFractionDigits() : int
+ getMaximumIntegerDigits() : int
+ setMaximumFractionDigits(in n : int)
+ setMaximumIntegerDigits(in n : int)

FIGURE 5–17 The `java.text.NumberFormat` class.

5.10 Example: Calculating Compound Interest

Problem statement

To illustrate how we might use the methods of the Math and NumberFormat classes, let's write an application that compares the difference between daily and annual compounding of interest as it applies to a certificate of deposit (CD). How much better will daily compounding be for a given principal, interest, and maturity period?

The formula for compounding interest is shown in Table 5.14. It assumes that interest is compounded annually. For daily compounding, the annual rate must be divided by 365, and the compounding period must be multiplied by 365, giving: $a = p(1 + r/365)^{365n}$.

TABLE 5.14 Formula for calculating compound interest

$a = p(1 + r)^n$ where

- a is the CD's value at the end of the nth year
- p is the principal or original investment amount
- r is the annual interest rate
- n is the number of years or the compounding period

Our program should input a certain principal, interest, and period (in years). It should output the CD's value at the end of the period under both annual and daily compounding.

What objects do we need?

Because this is such a simple calculation, let's use a single class for this problem, the CDInterest class. This class will handle its own I/O.

Class Design: CDInterest

What data and methods do we need?

This is a straightforward input-process-output algorithm. We can make use of double variables to represent the data needed in the interest calculation, all of which would be declared as private instance variables:

```
private double principal;     // The CD's initial principal
private double rate;          // CD's interest rate
private double years;         // Number of years to maturity
private double cdAnnual;      // Annual compounding
private double cdDaily;       // Daily compounding
```

Code reuse

We can use a BufferedReader object to handle keyboard input from the user. Similarly, we can use Double.parseDouble() method again to handle the task of converting the user's String input into double data. Finally, we can use the Math.pow() method to translate the compounding formulas into Java:

```
cdAnnual = principal * Math.pow(1 + rate, years);
cdDaily = principal * Math.pow(1 + rate/365, years*365);
```

Task decomposition

In addition to using these methods, let's divide the program's task into two tasks: (1) inputting the data and (2) calculating and reporting the results. If we tried to handle the entire task in one method, the method would be too long. A method is like a paragraph. If you make it too long, it begins to lose its focus. So it's a good idea to avoid trying to do too much in a single method.

EFFECTIVE DESIGN: Method Length. Methods should be focused on a single task. If you find your methods becoming more than 20 or 30 lines of code, try to divide it into separate methods.

Given these decisions, Figure 5–18 summarizes the design of the CD-Interest class. Its main() method simply creates a CDInterest object and then invokes its getInput() and calcAndReportResult() methods:

```
public static void main( String args[] ) throws IOException {
    CDInterest cd = new CDInterest();    // Create an instance
    cd.getInput();                        // Get user's inputs
    cd.calcAndReportResult();             // Calculate and report
} // main()
```

The implementation of CDInterest is given in Figure 5–19. There are several points to note about this program. First, both main() and getInput() must declare that they throw an IOException. The getInput() method uses the BufferedReader.readLine() method, which could throw an IOException, and main() calls getInput(). (Exceptions and the details behind this requirement will be covered in Chapter 11.)

Second, note how the number formatting is done within the calcAndReportResult() method. The method begins by creating two NumberFormat objects, one for currency amount and one for the interest rate:

```
                                    // Set up formats
NumberFormat dollars = NumberFormat.getCurrencyInstance();
NumberFormat percent = NumberFormat.getPercentInstance();
percent.setMaximumFractionDigits(2);
```

Then when the output is printed, we simply call on these objects to produce the output in the format. For example, a currency amount is output as follows:

```
System.out.println("The original principal is "
                        + dollars.format(principal));
```

The output produced by this program is as follows:

```
******************************* OUTPUT **********************
This program compares daily and annual compounding for a CD.
   Input the CD's initial principal, e.g.  1000.55 > 10000
   Input the CD's interest rate, e.g.  6.5 > 7.768
   Input the number of years to maturity, e.g., 10.5 > 10
The original principal is $10,000.00
The resulting principal compounded daily at 7.77% is $21,743.23
The resulting principal compounded yearly at 7.77% is $21,129.94
******************************* OUTPUT **********************
```

Thus, our tasks of calculating interest and formatting the output have been greatly simplified by using the appropriate classes from the Java class library.

CDInterest
− principal : double
− rate : double
− years : double
− cdAnnual : double
− cdDaily : double
+ getInput()
+ calcAndReportResult()
+ main()

FIGURE 5–18 A class diagram of the CDInterest class.

```java
import java.io.*;                    // Import the Java I/O Classes
import java.text.NumberFormat;      // For formatting as $nn.dd or n%

public class CDInterest {
    private BufferedReader input = new BufferedReader    // Handles console input
                (new InputStreamReader(System.in));
    private String inputString;                    // Stores the input
    private double principal;                      // The CD's initial principal
    private double rate;                           // CD's interest rate
    private double years;                          // Number of years to maturity
    private double cdAnnual;        // Accumulated principal with annual compounding
    private double cdDaily;         // Accumulated principal with daily compounding

    public void getInput() throws IOException {
                                         // Prompt the user and get the input
        System.out.println("This program compares daily and annual compounding for a CD.");

        System.out.print("    Input the CD's initial principal, e.g.  1000.55 > ");
        inputString = input.readLine();
        principal = Double.parseDouble(inputString);

        System.out.print("    Input the CD's interest rate, e.g.  6.5 > ");
        inputString = input.readLine();
        rate = (Double.parseDouble(inputString)) / 100.0;

        System.out.print("    Input the number of years to maturity, e.g., 10.5 > ");
        inputString = input.readLine();
        years = Double.parseDouble(inputString);
    } //getInput()

    public void calcAndReportResult() {
                                     // Calculate and output the result
        NumberFormat dollars = NumberFormat.getCurrencyInstance(); // Set up formats
        NumberFormat percent = NumberFormat.getPercentInstance();
        percent.setMaximumFractionDigits(2);

        cdAnnual = principal * Math.pow(1 + rate, years);        // Calculate interest
        cdDaily = principal * Math.pow(1 + rate/365, years*365);
                                                  // Print the results
        System.out.println("The original principal is " + dollars.format(principal));
        System.out.println("The resulting principal compounded daily at " +
                    percent.format(rate) + " is " + dollars.format(cdDaily));
        System.out.println("The resulting principal compounded yearly at " +
                    percent.format(rate) + " is " + dollars.format(cdAnnual));
    } // calcAndReportResult()

    public static void main( String args[] ) throws IOException {
        CDInterest cd = new CDInterest();
        cd.getInput();
        cd.calcAndReportResult();
    } // main()
} // CD Interest
```

FIGURE 5–19   Java application to calculate compound interest.

5.11   Problem Solving = Representation + Action

Designing classes involves a careful interplay between representation (data) and action (methods). As our comparison of the `boolean` and `int` versions of `CyberPet` shows, the data used to represent an object's state can either complicate or simplify the design of the methods needed to solve a problem.

In writing object-oriented programs, choosing an appropriate data representation is just as important as choosing the correct algorithm. The concept of an object allows us to encapsulate representation and action into a single entity. It is a very natural way to approach problem solving.

If you look closely enough at any problem, you will find this close relationship between representation and action. For example, compare the task of performing multiplication using Arabic numerals—65 * 12 = 380— and the same task using Roman numerals—LXV * XII = DCCLXXX. It's doubtful that our science and technology would be where they are today if our civilization had to rely forever on the Roman way of representing numbers!

IN THE LABORATORY: The Leap-Year Problem

The purpose of this lab is to emphasize the object-oriented design principles discussed in this and previous chapters and to use some of Java's basic language structures, such as if-else, assignment, and arithmetic expressions. The objectives of this project are

- To give practice designing and writing a simple Java program.
- To give practice using if-else and assignment statements.
- To give practice using basic arithmetic and relational operators.

Problem Description

A year is a *leap year* if it is evenly divisible by 4 but not evenly divisible by 100 unless it is also evenly divisible by 400. So 1996 was a leap year. But 1900 was not a leap year because, although it is divisible by 4, it is also divisible by 100 and not by 400. 2000 is a leap year because it is divisible by 400.

Design and write a Java applet that allows the user to enter a year (as an integer) and reports whether the year entered is a leap year or not.

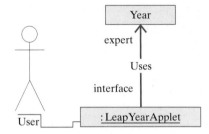

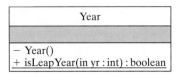

FIGURE 5–20 The LeapYearApplet will serve as a user interface to the Year class.

Year
– Year() + isLeapYear(in yr : int) : boolean

FIGURE 5–21 The Year class is modeled after the Math class. It is a final class with a private constructor and static methods.

Problem Decomposition

One way to decompose this problem is to divide it into two classes, the LeapYearApplet class, which implements the user interface, and the Year class, which contains the expertise needed to decide whether a given value is a leap year or not (Fig. 5–20). LeapYearApplet should get the input from the user (in a TextField), pass it to Year, converting it to whatever form Year requires, and then display the result that Year returns.

Problem Design: Year

The Year class is very simple (Fig. 5–21). Its role is just to wait until it is passed a value and then to determine if that value is a leap year or not. One design we could use here is that of the Temperature class. In that case, public methods were used to convert from Fahrenheit to Celsius.

Another design that would be appropriate here is to model Year after the Math class—that is, as a utility class that provides a useful method but that is not designed to be instantiated at all. Since this latter design is simpler, let's adopt it.

- Purpose: To determine if a year is a leap year
- Modifiers: Final, so it cannot be extended
- Constructor: Private, so no instantiation is possible
- Instance Variables: None (no need to store anything)
- Public Instance Methods: None (no need to have instances)
- Public Static Methods: isLeapYear(int) tests whether its parameter is a leap year using the rule described previously

The isLeapYear() method should be a public method that takes a single int parameter and returns the boolean value true if its parameter is a leap year and false otherwise. In terms of its algorithm, this method should use an if-else control structure to test whether a year is divisible by 400, by 100, and so on. To determine if an integer is *divisible* by another integer, you can use the mod operator (%). For example, if *N* % *100* equals 0, then *N* is divisible by 100. That is, *N* is divisible by 100 if dividing it by 100 leaves a remainder of 0:

```
if (N % 100 == 0) ...
```

You may find it helpful to draw a flowchart for the isLeapYear(). See Chapter 3, especially Self-Study Exercise 3.10, to review the guidelines for drawing flowcharts.

Problem Design: LeapYearApplet

The design of the LeapYearApplet should be similar to that of other applets we've built. It should contain a TextField for user input and a Label for prompting the user. Its interface is shown in Figure 5–22. Note that the interface does not contain a Button. With no button to click, how does the user tell the applet to test whether a year is a leap year or not? The answer is that a TextField generates an action event whenever the user types the Enter key in it. As with button clicks, these events can be handled by an ActionListener. Therefore, after instantiating a TextField, you can simply register it with an appropriate ActionListener:

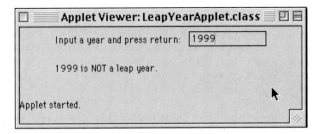

FIGURE 5–22   The LeapYearApplet.

```
inputField = new TextField(10);        // Create a TextField
inputField.addActionListener(this); // Register it with a Listener
```

In this case, the applet's `actionPerformed()` method would handle the TextField's action events just as if it were a `Button`.

The `LeapYearApplet` should implement the `ActionListener.action-Performed()` method to handle `TextField` actions. When the user types Enter, `actionPerformed()` should get the input from the `TextField` and convert it from `String` to `int`. Recall that the `parseInt()` method in the `Integer` class can be used for this purpose:

```
int num = Integer.parseInt(yearField.getText());
```

Here it is assumed that the user's input is in a text field named `yearField`. The integer should then be passed to `Year.isLeapYear()`, which will return a `boolean`. The applet should then report the result.

How should this applet handle the reporting of the result? Perhaps the easiest way is to override `Applet`'s `paint()` method, which was the approach we took in the `HelloWorld` applet in Chapter 1. Recall that `paint()` uses the following kind of statement to display a `String` on an applet:

```
g.drawString("HelloWorld", 10, 50);
```

The *g* in this expression is a reference to `paint()`'s `Graphics` object, which controls any drawing or painting on the applet. The two numbers in the expression are the horizontal and vertical coordinates that specify where "HelloWorld" will be painted on the applet. You will have do some planning and experimenting to determine what values to use for these coordinates.

One important question remains: How will `paint()` know whether to report that the year is or is not a leap year? Perhaps the best way to handle this is to have `actionPerformed()` invoke the `Year.isLeapYear()` method and store its result in an instance variable. Suppose this `boolean` variable is named `yearIsLeapYear`. Then `paint()` could check its value and print the appropriate message:

```
if (yearIsLeapYear)
    g.drawString("That year is a leap year", 10, 50);
```

As members of `LeapYearApplet`, both `actionPerformed()` and `paint()` will have access to `yearIsLeapYear`.

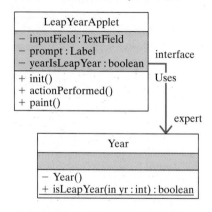

FIGURE 5–23 A UML class diagram summarizing the design of the `LeapYearApplet` and `Year` classes.

Recall also that since we have patterned `Year` after the `Math` class (and `Integer` class), there is no need to instantiate it in order to use its `static` methods. So to test whether a given number is a leap year, we could simply say

```
if (Year.isLeapYear(num)) ...
```

The `isLeapYear()` method is a *class method*—that is, a `static` method that is associated with the class itself. Taken together, the various design decisions we've made are summarized in Figure 5–23.

Implementation

The implementation of this program is left to you as a lab (or programming) exercise.

Java Language Summary

Operator Precedence Order

Java operators are evaluated according to the precedence hierarchy shown in Table 5.15. The lower the precedence number, the earlier an operator is evaluated. So the operators at the top of the table are evaluated before operators that occur below them in the table. Operators at the same precedence level are evaluated according to their *association*, either left to right (L to R) or right to left (R to L).

TABLE 5.15 Java operator precedence and associativity table

Order	Operator	Operation	Association
0	( )	*Parentheses*	
1	++ -- .	*Postincrement, postdecrement, dotOperator*	*L to R*
2	++ -- + - !	*Preincrement, predecrement Unary plus, unary minus, boolean NOT*	*R to L*
3	(type) new	*Type cast, object instantiation*	*R to L*
4	* / %	*Multiplication, division, modulus*	*L to R*
5	+ - +	*Addition, subtraction, string concatenation*	*L to R*
6	< > <= >=	*Relational operators*	*L to R*
7	== !=	*Equality operators*	*L to R*
8	∧	*Boolean XOR*	*L to R*
9	&&	*Boolean AND*	*L to R*
10	||	*Boolean OR*	*L to R*
11	= += -= *= /= %=	*Assignment operators*	*R to L*

Operator Promotion and Casting

Java is a *strongly typed* language, which means that a Java compiler can detect type errors. All expressions have an associated type. In numeric expressions containing values (operands) of different types, Java will generally *promote* the smaller type to a larger type according to Table 5.16.

TABLE 5.16 Java promotion rules for mixed arithmetic operators. If two rules apply, choose the one that occurs first in the table.

If either operand is	The other is promoted to
double	double
float	float
long	long
byte or short	int

Java's promotion rules represent an implicit form of type *casting*—that is, converting one type of data to another. The *cast operator*—*(type)*—is a unary operator that converts the value that follows it to the specified type. In this example, the floating-point (double) value, 95.6, is converted into an int before being assigned to *k*:

```java
int k = (int)95.6;
```

Operator Overloading

Operator symbols are *overloaded* in Java, meaning they may be used for more than one type-dependent operation. For example, the plus sign (+) is used for addition and string concatenation. Table 5.17 lists the operators that apply to each type of data.

TABLE 5.17 Java operators showing operator overloading

Data Types	Operators
Floating-Point Types double float	+ - * / % = += -= *= /= < > <= >= == !=
Integer Types int long byte short	*Same as floating-point types plus* ++ --
char	*Same as integer types*
boolean	&& || == !=
String	+

Keywords: static and final

- Within a class definition, elements that are declared static are called *class elements*—class methods or class variables— and are associated with the class itself, not with its instances. Such elements exist even if no objects of that class exist. They are referenced by qualifying their name with the name of the class. For example, to use the square root method in the java.lang.Math, you would refer to it as Math.sqrt(). *Class elements*
- Within a class definition, any variables that are declared final are called *constants*. They must be given an initial value, which cannot be changed by the program. Constants are frequently declared static as well as final, since then one copy of the constant can be shared by all instances of the class. The following is an example of a *class constant* declaration: *Constants*

```
public class MyClass {
    public static final int MAXWIDTH = 500;
}
```

As with other class elements, the class name can be used as a qualifier in referring to a class constant—MyClass.MAXWIDTH.

CHAPTER SUMMARY

Technical Terms

action	class variable	type conversion
binary operator	input-process-output	unary operator
cast operation	operator overloading	representation
class constant	precedence order	
class method	promotion	

Summary of Important Points

- The way we approach a problem can often help or hinder us in our ability to solve it. Choosing an appropriate *representation* for a problem is often the key to solving it.

- Choosing the wrong type of data to represent a problem can constrain the extensibility of the model. The *scalability principle* states that a well-designed model or representation should be easily *extensible*. The *modularity principle* states that a well-designed model or representation will contain methods that do not have to be modified each time we extend the model.

- In order to evaluate complex expressions, it is necessary to understand the *precedence order* and *associativity* of the operators involved. Parentheses can always be used to override an operator's built-in precedence.

- Java provides several types of integer data, including the 8-bit byte, 16-bit short, 32-bit int, and 64-bit long types. Unless otherwise specified, integer literals are represented as int data in a Java program.

- Java provides two types of floating-point data, the 32-bit float type and the 64-bit double type. Unless otherwise specified, floating-point literals are represented as double data.

- In general, if a data type uses n bits in its representation, then it can represent 2^n different values.

- The fact that Java's primitive types are defined in terms of a specific number of bits is one way that Java promotes *platform independence*.

- It is necessary to distinguish integer operations from floating-point operations even though the same symbols are used. (7/2) is 3, while (7.0/2) is 3.0.

- When revising a class that is used by other classes, it is a good idea to make it *backward compatible*. In revising a class that is used by other classes it is important to preserve as much of the class's *interface* as possible.

- In Java, character data are based on the Unicode character set, which provides $2^{16} = 65{,}536$ different character codes. To provide backward compatibility with the ASCII code, the first 128 characters are the ASCII coded characters.

SOLUTION 5.1
  a. true
      c. true
      e. false
  b. false
      d. false
      f. false

SOLUTION 5.2

```
0000, 0001, 0010, 0011, 0100, 0101, 0110, 0111,
1000, 1001, 1010, 1011, 1100, 1101, 1110, 1111
```

SOLUTION 5.3 In 6 bits, you can represent $2^6 = 64$ different values.

SOLUTION 5.4 Suppose you write a program on a system that uses 32 bits to represent the `int` type, and your program uses numbers like 2,000,000,000. This number cannot be represented properly in 16 bits, so you can't run your program on systems where the `int` type is represented as 16 bits.

SOLUTION 5.5 If you have to represent up to 12 significant digits, you should use `double`, which goes up to 17 digits.

SOLUTION 5.6
  a. 4
     d. 1
     g. 0
  b. 4
     e. 2
     h. 4
  c. 0
     f. 6

SOLUTION 5.7
  a. 4.0
     c. 0
     e. 1.33
  b. 4.5
     d. 0.0

SOLUTION 5.8
  a. 7 `int`
     c. 14.0 `double`
     e. 4.0 `double`
  b. 30 `long`
     d. 90 `long`

SOLUTION 5.9
  a. 34.0
     d. 1
     g. 2
  b. 54
     e. 6
     h. 7.5
  c. 4
     f. 0

SOLUTION 5.10
  a. k==5, j==5
     c. k==6, j==6
     e. k==4, j==4
  b. k==5, j==6
     d. k==5, j==4

SOLUTION 5.11
  a. k==15, j==5
     c. k==120, j==6
     e. k==0, j==5
  b. k==5, j==6
     d. k==0, j==4

SOLUTION 5.12   k = k + 1;   k += 1;   k++;   ++k;

SOLUTION 5.13
  a. m = 5
     c. m = 15
     e. m = 70
  b. m = 6
     d. m = 50

SOLUTION 5.14
  a. false
     d. illegal
     g. false
  b. false
     e. true
  c. true
     f. illegal

SOLUTION 5.15 In the `CyberPet` experiment, the implementation of `CyberPet` is hidden from the user, who interacts only with the `CyberPetApplet` interface. Therefore, it doesn't matter to the user *how* we design `CyberPet`, as long as it works correctly. Of course, as programmers, it does matter to us how `CyberPet` is designed.

SOLUTION 5.16
  a. valid
     d. valid
  b. valid
     e. ch1 = (char)(m-n);
  c. ch2 = (char)n;

EXERCISES

Note: *For programming exercises,* **first** *draw a UML class diagram describing all classes and their inheritance relationships and/or associations.*

EXERCISE 5.1   Explain the difference between the following pairs of terms:

a. *Representation* and *action.*
b. *Binary operator* and *unary operation.*
c. *Class constant* and *class variable.*
d. *Helper method* and *class method.*
e. *Operator overloading* and *method overloading.*
f. *Method call* and *method composition.*
g. *Type conversion* and *type promotion.*

EXERCISE 5.2   Arrange the Java library classes listed in the chapter summary into a hierarchy rooted at the `Object` class.

EXERCISE 5.3   For each of the following data types, list how many bits are used in its representation and how many values can be represented:

a. `int`   b. `char`   c. `byte`   d. `long`   e. `double`

EXERCISE 5.4   Fill in the blanks.

a. Methods and variables that are associated with a class rather than with its instances must be declared _____ .
b. When an operation involves values of two different types, one value must be _____ before the expression can be evaluated.
c. Constants should be declared _____ .
d. Variables that take `true` and `false` as their possible values are known as _____ .

EXERCISE 5.5   Arrange the following data types into a *promotion* hierarchy: `double, float, int, short, long.`

EXERCISE 5.6   Assuming that *o1* is true, *o2* is false, and *o3* is false, evaluate each of the following expressions:

a. `o1 || o2 && o3`   b. `o1 ^ o2`   c. `!o1 && !o2`

EXERCISE 5.7   Arrange the following operators in precedence order:

```
+ - () * / % < ==
```

EXERCISE 5.8   Arrange the following operators into a precedence hierarchy:

```
*,++, %, ==
```

EXERCISE 5.9   Parenthesize and evaluate each of the following expressions (if an expression is invalid, mark it as such):

a. `11 / 3 % 2 == 1`   c. `15 % 3 >= 21 %`   e. `15 / 3 == true`
b. `11 / 2 % 2 > 0`   d. `12.0 / 4.0 >= 12 / 3`

EXERCISE 5.10   What value would *m* have after each of the statements that follow is executed? Assume that *m, k, j* are reinitialized before each statement.

```
int m = 5, k = 0, j = 1;
```

a. `m = ++k + j;`   c. `m %= ++k + ++j;`   e. `m = ++m;`
b. `m += ++k * j;`   d. `m = m - k - j;`

EXERCISE 5.11   What value would *b* have after each of the statements that follow is executed? Assume that *m, k, j* are reinitialized before each statement. It may help to parenthesize the right-hand side of the statements before evaluating them.

```
    boolean b;
    int m = 5, k = 0, j = 1;
```

a. b = m > k + j;
b. b = m * m != m * j;
c. b = m <= 5 && m % 2 == 1;

d. b = m < k || k < j;
e. b = --m == 2 * ++j;

EXERCISE 5.12   For each of the following expressions, if it is valid, determine the value of the variable on the left-hand side (if not, change it to a valid expression):

```
    char c = 'a' ;
    int  m = 95;
```

a. c = c + 5;
b. c = 'A' + 'B';

c. m = c + 5;
d. c = (char) m + 1;

e. m = 'a' - 32;

EXERCISE 5.13   Translate each of the following expressions into Java:

a. Area equals *pi* times the radius squared.
b. Area is assigned *pi* times the radius squared.
c. Volume is assigned *pi* times radius cubed divide by *h*.
d. If *m* and *n* are equal, then *m* is incremented by one; otherwise *n* is incremented.
e. If *m* is greater than *n* times 5, then square *m* and double *n*; otherwise square *n* and double *m*.

EXERCISE 5.14   What would be output by the following code segment?

```
int m = 0, n = 0, j = 0, k = 0;
m = 2 * n++;
System.out.println("m= " + m + " n= " + n);
j += ( --k * 2 );
System.out.println("j= " + j + " k= " + k);
```

Each of the problems that follow asks you to write a method. Of course, as you are developing the method in a stepwise fashion, you should test it. Here's a simple application program that you can use for this purpose:

```
public class MethodTester {
    public static int square(int n) {
        return n * n;
    }

    public static void main(String args[]) {
        System.out.println("5 squared = " + square(5));
    }
}
```

Just replace the square() method with your method. Note that you must declare your method static if you want to call it directly from main() as we do here.

EXERCISE 5.15   Write a method to calculate the sales tax for a sale item. The method should take two double parameters, one for the sales price and the other for the tax rate. It should return a double. For example, calcTax(20.0, 0.05) should return 1.0.

EXERCISE 5.16   Challenge: Suppose you're writing a program that tells what day of the week someone's birthday falls on this year. Write a method that takes an int parameter, representing what day of the year it is, and returns a String like "Monday." For example, for 1999, the first day of the year was on Friday. The thirty-second day of the year (February 1, 1999) was a Monday, so getDayOfWeek(1) should return "Friday" and getDayOfWeek(32) should return "Monday." (*Hint:* If you divide the day of the year by 7, the remainder will always be a number between 0 and 6, which can be made to correspond to days of the week.)

EXERCISE 5.17   Challenge: As part of the birthday program, you'll want a method that takes the month and the day as parameters and returns what day of the year it is. For example, getDay(1,1) should return 1; getDay(2,1) should return 32; and getDay(12,31) should return 365. (*Hint:* If the month is 3, and the day is 5, you have to add the number of days in January plus the number of days in February to 5 to get the result: 31 + 28 + 5 = 64.)

EXERCISE 5.18   Write a Java method that converts a char to lowercase. For example, toLowerCase('A') should return 'a'. Make sure you guard against method calls like toLowerCase('a').

EXERCISE 5.19   Challenge: Write a Java method that shifts a char by *n* places in the alphabet, wrapping around to the start of the alphabet, if necessary. For example, shift('a',2) should return 'c'; shift('y',2) should return 'a'. This method can be used to create a Caesar cipher, in which every letter in a message is shifted by *n* places—hfu ju?

EXERCISE 5.20   Write a method that converts its boolean parameter to a String. For example, boolToString(true) should return "true."

EXERCISE 5.21   Write a Java application that prompts the user for three numbers, which represent the sides of a rectangular cube, and then computes and outputs the volume and the surface area of the cube.

EXERCISE 5.22   Write a Java application that prompts the user for three numbers and then outputs the three numbers in increasing order.

EXERCISE 5.23   Write a Java application that inputs two integers and then determines whether the first is divisible by the second. (*Hint:* Use the modulus operator.)

EXERCISE 5.24   Write a Java application that prints the following table:

N	SQUARE	CUBE
1	1	1
2	4	8
3	9	27
4	16	64
5	25	125

EXERCISE 5.25   Design and write a Java applet that converts kilometers to miles and vice versa. Use a TextField for I/O and Buttons for the various conversion actions.

EXERCISE 5.26   Design and write an (applet) GUI that allows a user to calculate the maturity value of a CD. The user should enter the principal, interest rate, and period, and the applet should then display the maturity value. Make use of the CDInterest program covered in this chapter. Use separate TextFields for the user's inputs and a separate TextField for the result.

EXERCISE 5.27   Design and write an (applet) GUI that lets the user input a birth date (month and day) and reports what day of the week it falls on. Use the `getDayOfWeek()` and `getDay()` methods that you developed in previous exercises.

EXERCISE 5.28   Design and write an (applet) GUI that allows the users to input their exam grades for a course and computes their average and probable letter grade. The applet should contain a single `TextField` for inputting a grade and a single `TextField` for displaying the average and letter grade. The program should keep track internally of how many grades the student has entered. Each time a new grade is entered, it should display the current average and probable letter grade.

ADDITIONAL EXERCISES

EXERCISE 5.29   One of the reviewers of this text has suggested an alternative design for the `Temperature` class (Fig. 5–5). According to this design, the class would contain an instance variable, say, `temperature`, and access methods that operate on it. The access methods would be: `setFahrenheit(double)`, `getFahrenheit():double`, `setCelsius(double)`, and `getCelsius(): double`. One way to implement this design is to store the temperature in the Kelvin scale and then convert from and to Kelvin in the access methods. The formula for converting Kelvin to Celsius is

```
K = C + 273.15
```

Draw a UML class diagram representing this design of the `Temperature` class. Which design is more object oriented, this one or the one used in Figure 5–5?

EXERCISE 5.30   Write an implementation of the `Temperature` class using the design described in the previous exercise.

EXERCISE 5.31   Another way to represent a CyberPet would be to use strings to represent the state—for example, "sleeping" and "eating." Draw a UML class diagram representing this design.

EXERCISE 5.32   Write an implementation of the `CyberPet` class using the design described in the previous exercise.

EXERCISE 5.33   **Challenge:** One possible objection to the integer-based Cyber-Pet is that it does not allow for a pet to be doing more than one thing (eating and thinking) at the same time. Devise a system of integer values that can be used to represent a pet's state that would allow the pet to do more than one thing at a time. Modify the `CyberPet` class to use your scheme and to show that the pet can do more than one thing at a time. *Hint:* Any nonnegative integer value can be computed as sum of unique powers of 2. For example, $13 = 2^3 + 2^2 + 2^0 = 8 + 4 + 1$.

6

Control Structures

OBJECTIVES

After studying this chapter, you will

- Be able to solve problems involving repetition.
- Understand the differences among various loop structures.
- Know the principles used to design effective loops.
- Improve your algorithm design skills.
- Understand the goals and principles of structured programming.

OUTLINE

6.1   Introduction

Suppose you want to write a method that prints the word "Hello" 100 times. One way to code this would be to write 100 `println()` statements into the method body:

```
public void hello100() {
    System.out.println("Hello");
    System.out.println("Hello");
    System.out.println("Hello");
    System.out.println("Hello");
    ...
    System.out.println("Hello");
}
```

This approach is tedious and would be completely impractical if we wanted to print "Hello" 65,535 times or a million times. Another way to handle this problem is illustrated in the following method:

```
public void hello100() {
    for (int k = 0; k < 100; k++)      // For 100 times
        System.out.println("Hello");   //  Print "Hello"
}
```

In this example, `println("Hello")` is executed 100 times by the for statement, a built-in loop control statement.

This chapter introduces Java's looping *control structures*, including the *for*, *while*, and *do-while* statements, all of which are used for repetition. We begin by introducing the idea of a *counting loop*, which is used for performing repetitive tasks when you know beforehand exactly how many iterations are necessary. This type of loop is most often implemented using a for statement.

We then distinguish two kinds of *conditional loops*, which are used for performing repetitive tasks where the number of repetitions depends on some kind of noncounting *bound*. These kinds of loops are usually implemented using Java's while and do-while statements. We give examples of several different kinds of loop bounds and use them to identify several useful principles of loop design. Finally, we introduce some of the key principles of the *structured programming* approach, a disciplined design approach that preceded the object-oriented approach.

6.2   Flow of Control: Repetition Structures

A **repetition structure** is a control structure that repeats a statement or sequence of statements. Many programming tasks require a repetition structure. Consider some examples.

• You're working for the National Security Agency trying to decipher secret messages intercepted from foreign spies, and you want to count the number of times a certain letter, "a," occurs in a document containing N characters. In this case, you would want to employ something like the following (pseudocode) algorithm:

```
initialize totalAs to 0
for each character in the document
    if the character is an 'a'
        add 1 to totalAs
return totalAs as the result
```

- You're working for a caterer who wants to number the invitations to a client's wedding, so you need to print all of the numbers between 1 and 5000, on the invitation cards (it's a big wedding)! In this case, you want to go through each number, 1 to 5000 and simply print it out:

```
for each number, N, from 1 to 5000
    print N on the invitation card
```

- The caterer decides it would be a cute gimmick to give every hundredth guest a door prize, so she wants you to print a special annotation on every hundredth invitation. You decide that every time you come to a number that is divisible by 100, you will also print a special symbol on that card. In this case, you want to go through each number, 1 to 5000, test if it is divisible by 100 and, if so, print the special mark on it:

```
for each number, N, from  1 to 5000
    print N on the card
    if (N % 100 == 0)
        print a special symbol on the card
```

- You are helping the forest service in Alaska keep track of the number of black bear sightings, and you want to compute the average number of sightings per month. Suppose the user enters each month's count at the keyboard, and uses a special number, say, 9999, to signify the end of the sequence. However, 9999 should not be figured into the average. This example differs a bit from the preceding ones, because here you don't know exactly how many numbers the user will input:

```
initialize sumOfBears to 0
initialize numOfMonths to 0
repeat the following steps
    read a number from the keyboard
    if the number is NOT 9999
        add it to the sumOfBears
        add 1 to numOfMonths
until the number read is 9999
divide sumOfBears by numOfMonths giving average
return average as the result
```

We repeat the process of reading numbers and adding them to a running total "until the number read is 9999."

- Student records are stored in a file and you want to calculate Erika Wilson's current GPA. Here we need to perform a repetitive process—searching through the file for Erika Wilson's record—but again we don't know exactly how many times to repeat the process:

```
repeat the following steps
    read a record from the file
until Erika Wilson's record is read
compute Erika Wilson's GPA
return gpa as the result
```

As these examples suggest, two types of loops are used: counting loops and noncounting loops. Counting loops are used whenever you know in advance exactly how many times an action must be performed. Non-counting loops are used when the number of repetitions depends on some condition—for example, the number of data items input from the keyboard or the input of a particular record from a file.

6.3 Counting Loops

The type of loop structure used in the hello100 example and in the fore-going first three examples is a **counting loop** or a *counter-controlled loop*. The exact number of times the loop repeats is known beforehand and can be made dependent on the value of a counter:

```
for (int k = 0; k < 100; k++)
    System.out.println("Hello");
```

In this case, the counter is the variable k, which counts from 0 through 99—that is, it counts 100 times. Note that we start counting from 0 instead of 1. This is a common programming convention for counting loops. Although it doesn't really make any practical difference in this case, later on we will

Zero indexing

use loops to process structures, such as strings and arrays, which use **zero indexing**. This means that such structures count their elements beginning at 0. It's easier to process these structures if our loop counter also starts at 0.

Loop counter

The variable k is called a *counter variable* or a *loop counter*. Although it is certainly possible to name the counter variable anything we like, it is customary to use single letters like i, j, and k as loop counters. The fundamental feature of a counting loop is that we must know beforehand exactly how many iterations the loop will take.

EFFECTIVE DESIGN: Loop Design. A *counting loop* can be used whenever you know exactly how many times a process must be repeated.

6.3.1 The For Structure

Although there are many ways to code a counting loop, Java's *for statement* is ideally suited for this purpose. The for statement has the following syntax:

```
for ( initializer ; loop entry condition ; updater )
    for loop body ;
```

The for statement begins with the keyword for, which is followed by a parenthesized list of three expressions separated by semicolons: an **initializer**, a **loop entry condition**, and an **updater**. Following the parenthesized

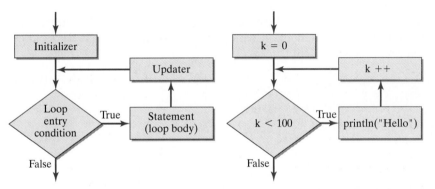

FIGURE 6–1 Flowchart of the for statement.

list is the for **loop body**, which is either a single statement or a sequence of statements contained in curly brackets, {...}.

Figure 6–1 shows how the for statement works. First the initializer is evaluated. In this example, the initializer sets the integer variable k to 0. Then the loop entry condition, which must be a boolean expression, is evaluated. If it is true, the body of the loop is executed; if it is false, the body of the loop is skipped and control passes to the next statement following the for statement. The updater is evaluated after the loop body is executed. After completion of the updater, the loop entry condition is reevaluated and the loop body is either executed again or not, depending on the truth value of the loop entry condition. This process is repeated until the loop entry condition becomes false.

Tracing the order in which the for loop components are evaluated gives this sequence:

```
evaluate initializer
evaluate loop entry condition ==> True
execute for loop body;
evaluate updater
evaluate loop entry condition ==> True
execute for loop body;
evaluate updater
evaluate loop entry condition ==> True
execute for loop body;
evaluate updater
   .
   .
   .
evaluate loop entry condition ==> False
```

As this trace shows, the loop entry condition controls entry to the body of the loop and will, therefore, be the last thing done before the loop terminates.

We have followed the standard convention of declaring the counter variable in the header of the for statement. This restricts the variable's *scope* to the for statement itself. It would be a syntax error to use k outside the scope of the for loop, as in this example:

Loop variable scope

```
for (int k = 0; k < 100; k++)
    System.out.println("Hello");
  System.out.println("k = " + k);    // Syntax error, k is undeclared
```

For some problems it may be necessary to use the loop variable outside the scope of the for statement, in which case the variable should be declared before the for statement:

```
int k = 0;                        // Declare the loop variable here
for (k = 0; k < 100; k++)
    System.out.println("Hello");
System.out.println("k = " + k);  // So it can be used here
```

6.3.2   Loop Bounds

Loop bound

A counting loop starts at some initial value and counts 0 or more iterations until its **loop bound** is reached. In a counting loop, the *loop entry condition* should be a boolean expression that tests whether the loop's bound has been reached. Similarly, in a counting loop, the *updater* should modify the loop counter so that it makes progress toward reaching its bound. Counting loops often increment or decrement their counter by 1, depending on whether the loop is counting forward or backward. The following method contains a countdown loop, which prints 10 9 8 7 6 5 4 3 2 1 BLASTOFF. In this case, progress toward the loop bound is made by decrementing the loop counter:

```
public void countdown() {
    for (int k = 10; k > 0; k--)
        System.out.print(k + " ");
    System.out.println("BLASTOFF");
} // countdown()
```

Unit indexing

Note in this case that we are using **unit indexing** instead of *zero indexing*, because countdowns iterate from 10 down to 1, not from 10 down to 0.

6.3.3   Infinite Loops

If the loop bound is never reached, the loop entry condition will never become false and the loop will repeat forever. This is known as an **infinite loop**. Can you see why each of the following for statements will result in an infinite loop?

Infinite loop

```
for (int k = 0; k < 100; k--)       // Infinite loop
    System.out.println("Hello");

for (int k = 1; k != 100; k+=2)      // Infinite loop
    System.out.println("Hello");

for (int k = 98; k < 100; k = k / 2) // Infinite loop
    System.out.println("Hello");
```

In the first example, k starts out at 0 and is decremented on each iteration, taking on values $-1, -2, -3$, and so on, so k will never reach its loop bound.

In the second example, k starts out at 1 and is incremented by 2 on each iteration, taking on the values 3, 5, 7, and so on. Because all these values are odd, k will never equal 100. A much safer loop bound in this case would be $k <= 100$.

In the third example, *k* starts out at 98 and is halved on each iteration, taking on the values 49, 24, 12, 6, 3, 1, 0, 0, and so on, forever. Thus, it too will be stuck in an infinite loop.

Encountering an unintended infinite loop when developing a program can be very frustrating. If the program is stuck in a loop that generates output, it will be obvious that it is looping, but if no output is being generated, the computer will appear to "freeze," no longer responding to your keyboard or mouse commands. Some programming environments allow you to break out of a looping program by typing a special keyboard command such as CONTROL-C or CTRL-ALT-DELETE or CONTROL-APPLE-ESCAPE, but if that doesn't work you will have to reboot the computer, possibly causing a loss of data. The best way to avoid infinite loops is to determine that the loop's updater expression will eventually reach the loop bound.

Stuck in a loop

> **EFFECTIVE DESIGN: Loop Design.** To guard against infinite loops, make sure that the loop bound will eventually be reached.

6.3.4   Loop Indentation

Note how indentation is used to distinguish the loop body from the heading and from the statement that follows the loop:

```
for (int k = 10; k > 0; k--)        // Loop heading
    System.out.print (k + " ");      //  Indent the body
System.out.println( "BLASTOFF" );    // After the loop
```

Indenting the loop body is a stylistic convention intended to make the code more readable. However, the indentation itself has no effect on how the code is interpreted by Java. Each of the following code segments would still produce the exact same countdown:

```
for (int k = 10; k > 0; k--)
System.out.print (k + " ");
System.out.println("BLASTOFF");


for (int k = 10; k > 0; k--) System.out.print(k + " ");
System.out.println("BLASTOFF");


for
(int k = 10; k > 0; k--)
System.out.print (k + " ");
System.out.println("BLASTOFF");
```

In each case the statement, System.out.println("BLASTOFF"), is not part of the for loop body and is executed only once when the loop terminates.

> **PROGRAMMING TIP: Loop Indentation.** To make loops more readable, indent the loop body to set it off from the heading and to highlight which statement(s) will be repeated.

DEBUGGING TIP: Loop Indentation. Loop indentation has no effect on how Java interprets the loop. The loop body is determined entirely by the syntax of the for statement.

Note that so far the loop body has consisted of a single statement, such as a println() statement. But the loop body may consist of any Java statement, including an if or if-else statement or a compound statement, which contains a sequence of statements enclosed within braces. Consider the following examples. The first example prints the sequence 0, 5, 10, 15, ... 95. Its loop body consists of a single if statement:

```
for (int k = 0; k < 100; k++)    // Print 0 5 10 15 ... 95
    if (k % 5 == 0)              // Loop body is a single if statement
        System.out.println("k= " + k);
```

The next example prints the lowercase letters of the alphabet. In this case, the loop counter is of type char, and it counts the letters of the alphabet. The loop body consists of a single print() statement:

```
for (char k = 'a'; k <= 'z'; k++)    // Print 'a' 'b' 'c' ... 'z'
    System.out.print (k + " ");      // Loop body is a single print()
```

The next example prints the sequence 5, 10, 15, ... 50, but it uses several statements within the loop body:

```
for (int k = 1; k <= 10; k++) {    // Print 5 10 15 20 ... 50
    int m = k * 5;                 // Begin body
    System.out.print (m + " ");
}                                  // End body
```

In this example, the scope of the local variable *m*, declared within the loop body, is limited to the loop body and cannot be used outside of that scope.

JAVA LANGUAGE RULE   Loop Body. The body of a for statement consists of the statement that immediately follows the for loop heading. This statement can be either a simple statement or a **compound statement**— a sequence of statements enclosed within braces, {...}.

Of course, braces can be used in the loop statement even when the loop body consists of a single statement. And some coding styles recommend that braces should always be used for the body of a loop statement. For example, it's always correct to code the for loop as

```
for (int k = 1; k <= 10; k++) {    // Print 1 2 ... 10
    System.out.print (k + " ");    // Begin body
}                                  // End body
```

Another advantage of this coding style is that you can easily place additional statements in the loop body by placing them within the braces.

DEBUGGING TIP: Missing Braces. A common programming error for novices is to forget to use braces to group the statements they intend to put in the loop body. The result will be that only the first statement after the loop heading will be iterated.

SELF-STUDY EXERCISES

EXERCISE 6.1 Identify the syntax error in the following for loop statements.

a. for (int k = 5, k < 100, k++)
       System.out.println(k);

b. for (int k = 0; k < 12 ; k--;)
       System.out.println(k);

EXERCISE 6.2 Identify those statements that result in infinite loops.

a. for (int k = 0; k < 100; k = k)
       System.out.println(k);

b. for (int k = 1; k == 100; k = k + 2)
       System.out.println(k);

c. for (int k = 1; k >= 100; k = k - 2)
       System.out.println(k);

EXERCISE 6.3 Suppose you're helping your little sister learn to count by fours. Write a for loop that prints the following sequence of numbers: 1, 5, 9, 13, 17, 21, 25.

EXERCISE 6.4 What value w ll *j* have when the following loop terminates?

```
for (int i = 0; i < 10; i++) {
    int j;
    j = j + 1;
}
```

6.3.5 Nested Loops

It is possible for the for loop body to contain a **nested** for loop. For example, suppose you are working for Giant Auto Industries, and your boss wants you to print a table that can be used by buyers to figure the cost of buying multiple quantities of a certain part. The cost of individual parts ranges from $1 to $9. The cost of *N* items is simply the unit price times the quantity. Thus, you'll want to print something like the following table of numbers:

```
1  2  3  4  5  6  7  8  9
2  4  6  8  10 12 14 16 18
3  6  9  12 15 18 21 24 27
4  8  12 16 20 24 28 32 36
```

To produce this multiplication table, we could use the following nested for loops:

```
for (int row = 1; row <= 4 ; row++) {  // For each of 4 rows        (1)
    for (int col = 1; col <= 9; col++) // For each of 9 columns      (2)
        System.out.print(col * row + "\t" ); // Print number and tab (3)
    System.out.println();                    // Start a new row      (4)
} // for row
```

Inner and outer loop

Note how indenting is used here to distinguish the levels of nesting and to make the code more readable. In this example, the *outer loop* controls the number of rows in the table, hence, our choice of row as its loop counter. The println() statement is executed after the *inner loop* is done iterating, which allows us to print a new row on each iteration of the outer loop. The inner loop prints the nine values in each row by printing the expression *col*row*. Obviously, the value of this expression depends on both loop variables.

Let's dissect this example a bit. How many times is the for statement on line 2 executed? The inner loop is executed once for each iteration of the outer loop. Thus, it is executed four times, which is the same number of times that line 4 is executed. How many times is the statement on line 3 executed? The body of the inner loop is executed 36 times—9 times for each execution of line 2.

Algorithm design

Sometimes it is useful to use the loop variable of the outer loop as the bound for the inner loop. For example, consider the following pattern:

```
# # # # #
# # # #
# # #
# #
#
```

Note that the number of # symbols in each row varies inversely with the row number. In row 1, we have five symbols; in row 2 we have four; and so on down to row 5, where we have one #.

To produce this kind of two-dimensional pattern, we need two counters: one to count the row number, and one to count the number of # symbols in each row. Because we have to print each row's symbols before moving on to the next row, the outer loop will count row numbers, and the inner loop will count the symbols in each row. But note that the inner loop's bound will depend on the row number. Thus, in row 1 we want five symbols; in row 2 we want four symbols; and so on. If we let row be the row number, then in each row we want to print $6 - row$ symbols. The following table shows the relationship we want:

Row	Bound (6-row)	Number of # Symbols
1	6-1	5
2	6-2	4
3	6-3	3
4	6-4	2
5	6-5	1

If we let j be the counter for the inner loop, then j will be bound by the expression $6 - row$. This leads to the following nested loop structure:

```
for (int row = 1; row <= 5; row++) {      // For each row
    for (int j = 1; j <= 6 - row; j++)    // Print the row
        System.out.print('#');
    System.out.println();                 // And a new row
} // for row
```

Note that the bound of the inner loop varies according to the value of *row*, the loop counter for the outer loop.

6.4 Example: Car Loan

Recall the program from Chapter 5 that calculated the value of a CD (*a*) given its initial principle (*p*), interest rate (*r*), and number of years (*n*), using the formula $a = p(1 + r)^n$. The same formula can be used to figure out how much a car loan will cost for various interest rates over various time periods.

Problem Description

For example, suppose you're planning on buying a car that costs $20,000. You find that you can get a car loan ranging anywhere from 8 to 11 percent, and you can have the loan for periods as short as two years and as long as eight years. Let's use our loop constructs to create a table, showing what the car will actually cost you, including financing. In this case, *a* will represent the total cost of the car, including the financing, and *p* will represent the price tag on the car ($20,000):

	8%	9%	10%	11%
Year 2	$23,469.81	$23,943.82	$24,427.39	$24,920.71
Year 3	$25,424.31	$26,198.42	$26,996.07	$27,817.98
Year 4	$27,541.59	$28,665.32	$29,834.86	$31,052.09
Year 5	$29,835.19	$31,364.50	$32,972.17	$34,662.19
Year 6	$32,319.79	$34,317.85	$36,439.38	$38,692.00
Year 7	$35,011.30	$37,549.30	$40,271.19	$43,190.31
Year 8	$37,926.96	$41,085.02	$44,505.94	$48,211.60

Algorithm Design

The key element in this program is the nested for loop that generates the table. Because the table contains seven rows, the outer loop should iterate seven times, through the values 2, 3, ... 8:

Nested loop design

```
for (int years = 2; years <= 8; years++) // For years 2 through 8
```

The inner loop should iterate through each of the interest rates, 8 through 11:

```
for (int years = 2; years <= 8; years++) { // For years 2 through 8
    for (int rate = 8; rate <= 11; rate++) {
    } // for rate
} // for years
```

The financing calculation should be placed in the body of the inner loop together with a statement to print one cell (not row) of the table. Suppose the variable we use for *a* in the foregoing formula is carPriceWithLoan, and the variable we use for the actual price of the car is `carPrice`. Then our inner loop body is

```
carPriceWithLoan = carPrice * Math.pow(1 + rate/100.0/365.0, years * 365.0);
System.out.print(dollars.format(carPriceWithLoan)  + "\t");
```

Note that the rate is divided by both 100.0 (to make it a percentage) and by 365.0 (for daily compounding), and the year is multiplied by 365.0 before these values are passed to the `Math.pow()` method. It's important here to use 100.0 and not 100 so that the resulting value is a `double` and not the `int` 0.

Implementation

Formatting output

The program must also contain statements to print the row and column headings. Printing the row headings should be done within the (outer) loop, because it must be done for each row. Printing the column headings should be done before the outer loop is entered. Finally, our program should contain code to format the dollar and cents values properly. For this we use the `java.text.NumberFormat` class, as described in Chapter 5. The complete program is shown in Figure 6–2.

```java
import java.text.NumberFormat;   // For formatting $nn.dd or n%

public class CarLoan {

    public static void main(String args[]) {
        double carPrice = 20000;  // Car's actual price
        double carPriceWithLoan;  // Total cost of the car plus financing

        NumberFormat dollars = NumberFormat.getCurrencyInstance(); // Number formatting
        NumberFormat percent = NumberFormat.getPercentInstance();
        percent.setMaximumFractionDigits(2);
                                               // Print the table
        for (int rate = 8; rate <= 11; rate++)         // Print the column heading
            System.out.print("\t" + percent.format(rate/100.0) + "\t" );
        System.out.println();

        for (int years = 2; years <= 8; years++) {     // For years 2 through 8
            System.out.print("Year " + years + "\t");    // Print row heading
            for (int rate = 8; rate <= 11; rate++) {      // Calc and print CD value
                carPriceWithLoan = carPrice * Math.pow(1 + rate / 100.0 / 365.0, years * 365.0);
                System.out.print( dollars.format(carPriceWithLoan)  + "\t");
            } // for rate
            System.out.println();                         // Start a new row
        } // for years
    } // main()
} // CarLoan
```

FIGURE 6–2 The `CarLoan` application.

SELF-STUDY EXERCISE

EXERCISE 6.5   As the engineer hired to design ski jumps, write a nested
for loop to print the following pattern:

```
#
# #
# # #
# # # #
# # # # #
```

6.5   Conditional Loops

Unlike the problems in the previous section, not all loops can be coded as
counting loops. Here's a problem that can't be solved by a counting loop.

Mathematicians, especially number theorists, have found that certain
operations on numbers lead to interesting sequences. For example, the
3N+1 problem is a conjecture in number theory, which says that if N is any
positive integer, then the sequence generated by the following rules will
always terminate at 1.

```
Case            Operation
----            ---------
N is odd        N = 3 * N + 1
N is even       N = N / 2
```

In other words, start with any positive integer, N. If N is odd, multiply
it by 3 and add 1. If N is even, divide it by 2. In either case, assign the
result back to N. The conjecture states that N will eventually equal 1. For
example, if N is initially 26, then the sequence generated is 26, 13, 40, 20,
10, 5, 16, 8, 4, 2, 1.

The 3N+1 problem is an example of a noncounting loop. Because for
any given N we don't know how long the 3N+1 sequence will be, we need
a loop that terminates when the loop variable reaches a *sentinel* value—
when N equals 1. This is an example of a loop that is terminated by a **sentinel bound**. With the exception of infinite loops, all loops are bounded
by some condition, which is why they are sometimes referred to as **conditional loop** structures. The count and sentinel bounds are just special
cases of the conditional loop structure.

Sentinel bound

6.5.1   The While Structure

Consider the following pseudocode algorithm for the 3N+1 problem:

```
Algorithm for computing the 3N+1 sequence
    While N is not equal to 1, do: {
        Print N.
        If N is even, divide it by 2.
        If N is odd, multiply N by 3 and add 1.
    }
    Print N
```

In this structure, the body of the loop prints N and then updates N's value,
using the 3N+1 rules. Suppose N equals 5 when this code segment begins.
It will print the following sequence: 5, 16, 8, 4, 2, 1. Note that the loop body

is entered as long as *N* is not equal to 1. So the loop entry condition in this case is *N != 1*. Conversely, the loop will terminate when *N* equals 1. Also note that in this code segment the loop bound is tested *before* the body of the loop is executed.

We can implement this algorithm using Java's *while statement*:

```
while (N != 1) {                      // While N is not equal to 1
    System.out.print(N + " ");        // Print N
    if (N % 2 == 0)                   // If N is even
        N = N / 2;                    //   divide it by 2
    else                              // If N is odd
        N = 3 * N + 1;                //   multiply N by 3 and add 1
}
System.out.println(N);                // Print N
```

The **while statement** is a loop statement in which the loop entry condition occurs before the loop body. It has the following general form:

```
while ( loop entry condition )
    loop body ;
```

Note that unlike the for statement, the while statement does not contain syntax for the initializer and the updater. These must be coded separately.

Let's make a distinction between a *loop statement*, which is part of the language, and a *loop structure*, which is built by the programmer using the language. For example, the while statement is a construct of the Java language. But as we have seen, it lacks syntax for the initializer and updater, which are important elements of the while loop structure. If we make this distinction, then we can state the following loop-design principle:

EFFECTIVE DESIGN: Loop Structure.   A properly designed *loop structure* must include an *initializer*, a *boundary condition*, and an *updater*. The updater should guarantee that the boundary condition is eventually satisfied, thereby allowing the loop to terminate.

In pseudocode, the *while structure* would take the following form:

```
InitializerStatements;          // Initializer
while (loop entry condition) {  // Bound test
    Statements;                 // Loop body
    UpdaterStatements;          // Updater
}
```

As its form suggests, the while structure is designed so that on some conditions the loop body will never be executed. Because it tests for the loop bound *before* the loop body, it is possible that the loop body is never executed. We might say that it is designed to perform 0 or more iterations.

For example, going back to the 3*N*+1 problem, what if *N* equals 1 initially? In that case, the loop body will be skipped, because the loop entry condition is false to begin with. No iterations will be performed, and the algorithm will simply print the value 1.

Note also that in the while statement the bound test is preceded by initializer statements, and the loop body contains updater statements. The semantics of the while structure are shown in Figure 6–3.

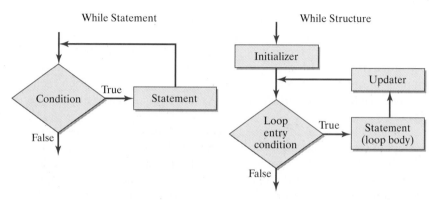

FIGURE 6–3   Flowchart of the while statement and while structure.

The while structure would be an appropriate control structure for the following type of problem:

```
write the homework assignment on the assignment sheet    // Initializer
while there are homework problems on the assignment sheet// Bound test
    do a problem                                         // Loop body
    cross it off the assignment sheet                    // Updater
```

It is possible that the assignment sheet contains no homework problems to begin with. In that case, there's no work for the body of the loop to do and it should be skipped.

SELF-STUDY EXERCISE

EXERCISE 6.6   Here's another number theory problem. Start with any positive integer, N. If N is even, divide it by 2. If N is odd, subtract 1 and then divide it by 2. This will generate a sequence that is guaranteed to terminate at 0. For example, if N is initially 15, then you get the sequence: 15, 7, 3, 1, 0. Write a method that implements this sequence. Use a while statement.

6.5.2   The Do-While Structure

Here's another problem that can't be solved with a counting loop. Your father has been fretting about the bare spots on the front lawn and is considering hiring the ChemSure Lawn Service to fertilize. However, your scientifically minded younger sister wants to reassure him that at the rate the grass is dying, there will be enough to last through the summer. Using techniques she learned in biology, your sister estimates that the grass is dying at the rate of 2 percent per day. How many weeks will it take for half the lawn to disappear?   *Problem description*

One way to solve this problem would be to keep subtracting 2 percent from the current amount of grass until the amount dipped below 50 percent, all the while counting the number of iterations required. Consider the following pseudocode algorithm: *Algorithm design*

```
Algorithm for calculating grass loss
    Repeat the following statements {
        Initialize amtGrass to 100.0
        Initialize nDays to 0
        Repeat the following statements
            amtGrass -= amtGrass * 0.02;
            ++nDays;
        As long as amtGrass > 50.0
    }
    Print nDays / 7
```

We begin by initializing amtGrass to 100.0, representing 100 percent. And we initialize our counter, nDays to 0. Then we repeatedly subtract 2 percent of the amount and increment the counter until the amount drops below 50 percent. In other words, in this case, we repeat the loop body as long as the amount of grass remains above 50 percent of the original. When the loop finishes, we report the number of weeks it took by dividing the number of days by 7.

Limit bound

The loop bound in this case is known as a **limit bound**. The loop will terminate when a certain limit has been reached—in this case, when the amount of grass dips below 50 percent of the original amount. Note that in this case the loop bound is tested *after* the loop body. This is appropriate for this problem, because we know in advance that the loop will iterate at least once. We can implement this algorithm using Java's *do-while statement*:

```java
public int losingGrass(double perCentGrass) {
    double amtGrass = 100.0;              // Initialize amount of grass
    int nDays = 0;                        // Initialize day counter
    do {                                  // Repeat
        amtGrass -= amtGrass * LOSSRATE;  //   Update amount of grass
        ++nDays;                          //   Increment the counter
    } while (amtGrass > perCentGrass);
                                          // As long as enough grass remains
    return nDays / 7;                     // Return the number of weeks
} // losingGrass()
```

The **do-while statement** is a loop statement in which the loop entry condition occurs after the loop body. It has the following general form:

```
do
    loop body ;
while ( loop entry condition ) ;
```

Note, again, that unlike the for statement, the do-while statement does not contain syntax for the initializer and the updater. These must be coded separately.

If we distinguish again between a loop statement and a loop structure, then the *do-while structure* takes the following form:

```
InitializerStatements1;            // Initializer
do {                               // Beginning of loop body
    InitializerStatements2;        //   Another place for initializer
    Statements;                    //   Loop body
    UpdaterStatements              //   Updater
} while (loop entry condition);    // End of body and Bound test
```

Note that initializer statements may be placed before the loop body, at the very beginning of the loop body, or in both places, depending on the particular problem. Like the other loop structures, updater statements occur within the body of the loop. A flowchart of the do-while structure is shown in Figure 6–4.

The do-while structure would be an appropriate control structure for the following type of problem:

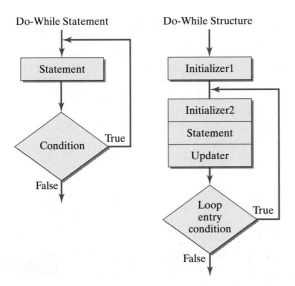

```
do
    dial your friend's telephone number   // Initializer
    if you get a busy signal
        hang up                           // Updater
while there's a busy signal               // Bound test
```

In this case, you want to perform the actions in the body of the loop at least once and possibly more than once (if you continue to receive a busy signal).

EFFECTIVE DESIGN: Do-While Loops.   The *do-while loop* is designed for solving problems in which at least one iteration must occur.

EFFECTIVE DESIGN: While versus Do-While Structures.   For problems where a noncounting loop is required, the *while loop structure* is more general and, therefore, preferable to the *do-while structure*. Use *do-while* only when at least one iteration must occur.

SELF-STUDY EXERCISE

EXERCISE 6.7   For each of the following problems, decide whether a counting loop structure, a while structure, or a do-while structure should be used, and write a pseudocode algorithm.
- Print the names of all visitors to your Web site.
- Validate that a number input by the user is positive.
- Change all the backslashes (\) in a Windows Web page address to the slashes (/) used in a Unix Web page address.
- Find the car with the best MPG ratio among the cars in the *Consumer Reports* database.

6.6   Example: Computing Averages

Algorithm design: what kind of loop?

Suppose you want to compute the average of your exam grades in a course. Grades, represented as real numbers, will be input from the keyboard. To signify the end of the list, we will use a *sentinel value*—9999 or −1 or some other value that won't be confused with a legitimate grade. Because we do not know exactly how many grades will be entered, we will use a noncounting loop in this algorithm. Also, because it's always possible that there will be no grades to average, we will use a while structure. That makes it possible to skip the loop entirely in case there are no grades to average.

Algorithm design

The algorithm should add each grade to a running total, keeping track of the number of grades entered. Thus, this algorithm requires two variables: one to keep track of the running total and the other to keep track of the count. Both should be initialized to 0. After the last grade has been entered, the total should be divided by the count to give the average. In pseudocode, the algorithm for this problem is as follows:

```
initialize runningTotal to 0           // Initialize
initialize count to 0
prompt and read the first grade        // Priming read
while the grade entered is not 9999 {  // Sentinel bound test
    add it to the runningTotal
    add 1 to the count
    prompt and read the next grade     // Update
}
if (count > 0)                         // Guard against divide by 0
    divide runningTotal by count
output the average as the result
```

Priming read

Note that in this problem our loop variable, grade, is read before the loop test is made. This is known as a **priming read**. It is necessary in this case, because the loop test depends on the value that is read. Within the body the updater reads the next value for grade. This is a standard convention for coding while structures that involve input, as this problem does. Note also that we must make sure that count is not 0 before we attempt to compute the average. Otherwise we would create a divide-by-zero error.

Translating the pseudocode algorithm into Java raises several issues. Suppose we store the grades in a double variable named grade. The loop will terminate when grade equals 9999, so its entry condition will be (grade != 9999). Because this condition uses grade, it is crucial that the grade variable be initialized before the bound test is made. This requires a priming read. However, in Java, keyboard input is read as a String, so we will need a second variable, inputString, to store the input, which we must then convert to a double. We can use the Double.parseDouble() method to perform this subtask. This design ensures that the loop will be skipped, if the user happens to enter the sentinel (9999) on the very first prompt:

Initialization step

```
System.out.print("Input a grade (e.g., 85.3) ");
System.out.print("or 9999 to indicate the end of the list >> ");
inputString = input.readLine();       // Initialize: Priming read
grade = Double.parseDouble(inputString);
```

In addition to this initialization, we must initialize the variables used for the running total and the counter.

Within the body of the loop we must add the grade to the running total and increment the counter. Since these variables are not tested in the loop entry condition, they will not affect the loop control. Our loop updater in this case must read the next value from the user, convert it to a `double`, and assign it to `grade`. Placing the updater statement at the end of the loop body will ensure that the loop terminates immediately after the user enters the sentinel value:

Updater step

```
while (grade != 9999) {                    // Sentinel test
    System.out.println("You input " + grade + "\n");
    runningTotal += grade;
    count++;

                               // Update: get the next grade
    System.out.print("Input a grade (e.g., 85.3) ");
    System.out.print("or 9999 to indicate the end of the list >> ");
    inputString = input.readLine();
    grade = Double.parseDouble(inputString);
} // while
```

It's somewhat redundant to repeat the same four statements needed to do the initialization and the updating of the `grade` variable. A better design would be to encapsulate these into a method and then call the method both before and within the loop. The method should take care of prompting the user, reading the input, converting it to `double`, and returning the input value. The method doesn't require a parameter:

Modularity

```
private double getInput() throws IOException {
    System.out.print("Input a grade (e.g., 85.3) ");
    System.out.print("or 9999 to indicate the end of the list >> ");
    String inputString  = input.readLine();
    double grade = Double.parseDouble(inputString);
    System.out.println("You input " + grade + "\n"); // Confirm input
    return grade;
}
```

Note that we've declared this as a `private` method. It will be used to help us perform our task but won't be available to other objects. Also note that because this method performs I/O, it must declare an `IOException`.

This is a much more modular design. In addition to cutting down on redundancy, it makes the program easier to maintain—for example, there's only one method to change if we decide to change the prompt message—and easier to debug—input errors are now localized to the `getInput()` method.

EFFECTIVE DESIGN: Modularity.   Encapsulating code in a method is a good way to avoid redundancy in a program.

DEBUGGING TIP: Localization. Encapsulating code in a method removes the need to have the same exact code at several locations in a program. By localizing the code in this way, you make it easier to modify and debug.

Another advantage of encapsulating the input task in a separate method is that it simplifies the task of calculating the average. This task should also be organized into a separate method:

```java
public double inputAndAverageGrades() throws IOException {
    grade = getInput();                  // Initialize: priming input
    while (grade != 9999) {              // Loop test: sentinel
        runningTotal += grade;
        count++;
        grade = getInput();             // Update: get next input
    } // while

    if (count > 0)                       // Guard against divide-by-zero
        return runningTotal / count;    // Return the average
    else
        return 0;                        // Special (error) return value
}
```

Note that we have declared this as a `public` method. This will be the method you call to calculate your course average. Also, because this method calls `getInput()`, which throws an `IOException`, this method must also declare the exception.

Method decomposition

Because we have decomposed the problem into its subtasks, each subtask is short and simple, making it easier to read and understand.

 EFFECTIVE DESIGN: Method Decomposition. Methods should be designed to have a clear focus. If you find a method becoming too long, you should break its algorithm into subtasks and define a separate method for each subtask.

The complete `Average.java` application is shown in Figure 6–5. Its overall design is similar to application programs we designed in previous chapters. The only instance variable it uses is the `BufferedInput` variable. The other variables are declared locally, within the methods. In this case, declaring them locally makes the algorithms easier to read.

One final point about this program is to note the care taken in the design of the user interface to explain the program to the user, to prompt the user before a value is input, and to confirm the user's input after the program has read it.

 EFFECTIVE DESIGN: User Interface. Whenever you're asking a user for input, the user should know *why* you are asking and *what* you are asking for. Prompts should be used for this purpose. It's also a good idea to confirm that the program has received the correct input.

SELF-STUDY EXERCISES

EXERCISE 6.8 Identify the syntax error in the following while structures:

```java
a. int k = 5;
   while (k < 100) {
       System.out.println(k);
       k++
   }
```

```
import java.io.*;
public class Average {

    private BufferedReader input = new BufferedReader  // Handles console input
        (new InputStreamReader(System.in));

    private double getInput() throws IOException {
        System.out.print("Input a grade (e.g., 85.3) ");
        System.out.print("or 9999 to indicate the end of the list >> ");
        String inputString  = input.readLine();
        double grade = Double.parseDouble(inputString);
        System.out.println("You input " + grade + "\n");  // Confirm user input
        return grade;
    }

    public double inputAndAverageGrades() throws IOException {
        double runningTotal = 0;
        int count = 0;
        double grade = getInput();              // Initialize: priming input
        while (grade != 9999) {                 // Loop test: sentinel
            runningTotal += grade;
            count++;
            grade = getInput();                 // Update: get next input
        } // while

        if (count > 0)                          // Guard against divide-by-zero
            return runningTotal / count;        // Return the average
        else
            return 0;                           // Special (error) return value
    }

    public static void main(String argv[]) throws IOException {
        System.out.println("This program calculates average grade."); // Explain program
        Average avg = new Average();
        double average = avg.inputAndAverageGrades();
        if (average == 0)                                              // Error case
            System.out.println("You didn't enter any grades.");
        else
            System.out.println("Your average is " + average);
    } // main()
} // Average
```

FIGURE 6–5   A program to compute average grade using a `while` structure.

b.
```
int k = 0;
while (k < 12 ;) {
    System.out.println(k);
    k++;
}
```

EXERCISE 6.9 Determine the output and/or identify the error in each of the following while structures:

a.
```
int k = 0;
while (k < 100)
    System.out.println(k);
```

b.
```
while (k < 100) {
    System.out.println(k);
    k++;
}
```

EXERCISE 6.10 Your younger sister is now learning how to count by sixes. Write a while loop that prints the following sequence of numbers: 0, 6, 12, 18, 24, 30, 36.

6.7   Example: Data Validation

One frequent programming task is *data validation*. This task can take different forms depending on the nature of the program. One use for data validation occurs when accepting input from the user.

In the previous program, suppose the user types −10 by mistake when asked to input an exam grade. Obviously this is not a valid exam grade and should not be added to the running total. How should a program handle this task?

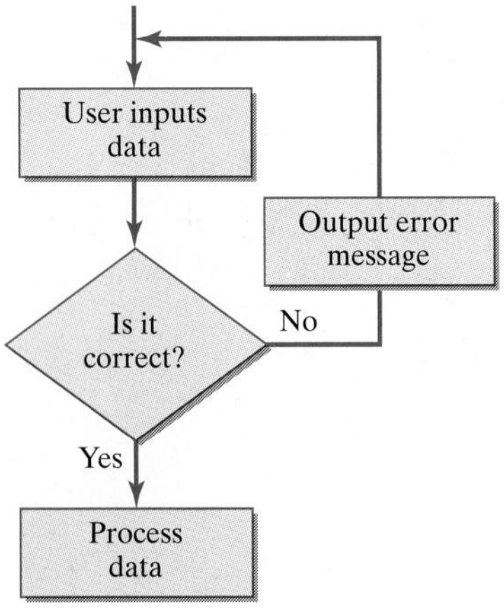

Algorithm Design

Because it is possible that the user may take one or more attempts before getting the input correct, we should use a do-while structure for this problem (Fig. 6–6). The program should first input a number from the user. The number should then be checked for validity. If it is valid, the loop should exit and the program should continue on computing average grade. If it is not valid, the program should print an error message and input the number again. For example, suppose only numbers between 0 and 100 are considered valid. The data validation algorithm would be as follows:

```
do
  Get the next grade                      // Initialize: priming input
  if the grade < 0 or grade > 100 and grade != 9999   // Error case
    print an error message
while the grade < 0 or grade > 100 and grade != 9999  // Sentinel test
                                          // Compute the average
```

Note here that initialization and updating of the loop variable are performed by the same statement. This is acceptable because we must update the value of grade on each iteration *before* checking its validity. Note also that for this problem the loop-entry condition is coded twice: once in the

FIGURE 6–6 Because the user must input at least one value *before* you can check if it is valid, data validation is a good task for a do-while structure.

Algorithm design

Initialization and update step

if statement, so that an appropriate error message can be displayed, and once as the bound test. It is the second occurrence of the condition that will control the loop's behavior.

Let's incorporate the data validation code into the getInput() method we designed in the previous section (Fig. 6–5):

```java
private double getAndValidateGrade() throws IOException {
    double grade = 0;
    do {
        System.out.print("Input a grade (e.g., 85.3) ");
        System.out.print("or 9999 to indicate the end of the list >> ");
        String inputString = input.readLine();
        grade = Double.parseDouble(inputString) ;
        if ((grade != 9999) && ((grade < 0) || (grade > 100)))
                                            // Input error
            System.out.println("Error: grade must be between 0 and 100\n");
        else
                                            // OK input
            System.out.println("You input " + grade + "\n");
    } while ((grade != 9999) && ((grade < 0) || (grade > 100)));
    return grade;
} // getAndValidateGrade()
```

We've changed the name of the method to suggest that it takes care of the entire input and validation task, returning a number between 0 and 100 to the calling method. It, therefore, has a return type of double. The only other change we need to make in the Average program (Fig. 6–5) is to revise the method calls to reflect the new name we have given our input method:

```java
grade = getAndValidateGrade();
```

The revised application, which we've renamed Validate, is shown in Figure 6–7.

SELF-STUDY EXERCISES

EXERCISE 6.11 Identify the syntax error in the following do-while structures:

a.
```java
int k = 0;
do while (k < 100)
{   System.out.println(k);
    k++
}
```
b.
```java
int k = 0;
do {
    System.out.println(k);
    k++;
} while (k < 12)
```

EXERCISE 6.12 Your sister has moved on to counting by sevens. So write a do-while loop that prints the following sequence of numbers: 1, 8, 15, 22, 29, 36, 43.

```java
import java.io.*;

public class Validate {
    private BufferedReader input = new BufferedReader   // Handles console input
        (new InputStreamReader(System.in));

    private double getAndValidateGrade() throws IOException {
        double grade = 0;
        do {
            System.out.print("Input a grade (e.g., 85.3) ");
            System.out.print("or 9999 to indicate the end of the list >> ");
            String inputString = input.readLine();
            grade = Double.parseDouble(inputString) ;
            if ((grade != 9999) && ((grade < 0) || (grade > 100)))
                System.out.println("Error: grade must be between 0 and 100\n");  // Input error
            else
                System.out.println("You input " + grade + "\n");                 // OK input
        } while ((grade != 9999) && ((grade < 0) || (grade > 100)));
        return grade;
    } // getAndValidateGrade()

    public double inputAndAverageGrades() throws IOException {
        double runningTotal = 0;
        int count = 0;
        double grade = getAndValidateGrade();   // Initialize: priming input
        while (grade != 9999) {                  // Loop test: sentinel
            runningTotal += grade;
            count++;
            grade = getAndValidateGrade();       // Update: get next grade
        } // while

        if (count > 0)                           // Guard against divide-by-zero
            return runningTotal / count;         // Return the average
        else
            return 0;                            // Special (error) return value
    } // inputAndAverageGrades()

    public static void main( String argv[] ) throws IOException {
        System.out.println("This program calculates average grade."); // Explain program
        Validate avg = new Validate();
        double average = avg.inputAndAverageGrades();
        if (average == 0)                                        // Error case
            System.out.println("You didn't enter any grades.");
        else
            System.out.println("Your average is " + average );
    } // main()
} // Validate
```

FIGURE 6–7 A program to compute average grade using a while structure. This version validates the user's input.

EXERCISE 6.13 As the owner of Pizza Heaven, every night at the close of business you quickly enter the price of every pizza ordered that day. You take the data from the servers' receipts. Pizzas cost $8, $10, or (the Heavenly Special) $15. You enter the data without dollar signs, and use 99 to indicate you're finished for the day. Write a Java method to input and validate a single pizza data item. If an incorrect price is entered, the program should print an error message and prompt for corrected input. Correct input is used to compute a daily total.

EXERCISE 6.14 Because the pizza prices in the previous exercise are fixed, change the method so you can save time on keyboarding. Instead of entering the price, you'll enter codes of 1, 2, or 3 (corresponding to the $8, $10, and $15 pizzas), and 0 to indicate that you're finished. Validate that the data value entered is correct and then convert it to the corresponding price before returning it.

6.8 CASE STUDY: Animated `CyberPet`

One thing that loops are good for is to create animations. You might remember creating animations as a kid by drawing images on several pieces of paper and then rapidly flipping between the pages to create the illusion of motion. This is the classical motion picture animation technique, still used. A similar effect can be achieved in a computer program. In computer animation the idea is to switch rapidly between two or more images displayed on the screen. In the "From the Java Library" section of Chapter 4 we learned how to incorporate images into an applet. Now let's use our newfound expertise with loops to animate these images.

6.8.1 Problem Description and Specification

In a previous version of `CyberPetApplet`, described in the lab exercise in Chapter 4, we learned how to load and display images in an applet. In that version, the image we used to represent the eating state was just a static image of the pet with its mouth open about to gobble a fly [Figure 6–8(a)]. One way to use animation here is to have the spider chew its prey and then flash a nice smile when it's done. We can do this by using two additional images, one to represent the spider with its mouth closed [Figure 6–8(b)], and the other to represent the happy spider [Figure 6–8(c)]. The animation effect can be achieved by rapidly switching between images *a* and *b* in Figure 6–8. So we want to modify `CyberPetApplet` to incorporate this animation behavior.

6.8.2 Class Design: `CyberPetApplet`

To accomplish this task we must incorporate several additional variables and methods into the `CyberPetApplet` class. Because the proposed changes do not affect the `CyberPet` itself, just our representation of it in the user interface, we don't have to make any changes to the `CyberPet` definition.

We will need one variable for each image that will be used in the program. Let's suppose that we have a two-state version of `CyberPet`—one that alternates between eating and sleeping. We, therefore, need four `Image` variables:

```
private Image eatImg, eat2Img, sleepImg, happyImg;
```

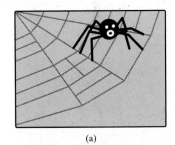

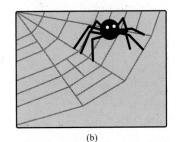

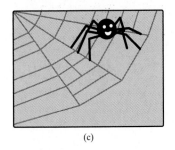

FIGURE 6–8 Animation can be created by alternating rapidly between images (a) and (b), with image (c) being used to represent the pet's state after the fly is eaten.

What variables do we need?

The names we've chosen reflect the images' purposes in the animation. The images themselves must be loaded into the applet during the initialization phase. Thus, the following statements should be added to the init() method:

```
eatImg = getImage(getCodeBase(), "eatImage.gif");
eat2Img = getImage(getCodeBase(), "eat2Image.gif");
sleepImg = getImage(getCodeBase(), "sleepImage.gif");
happyImg = getImage(getCodeBase(), "happyImage.gif");
```

What methods do we need?

In order to process the animation, we will need several new methods. First, the images must be *painted* onto the applet after each action. To paint the image itself, we can use the awt.Graphics.drawImage() method. But we have to paint the right image at the right time. When the pet is sleeping, we have to paint the sleeping image, and when the pet is eating, we have to do the eating animation. In order to coordinate the applet with the pet's state, we must ask the CyberPet to tell us its state:

```
public void paint(Graphics g) {
    String petState = pet1.getState();   // Get the pet's state
   if (petState.equals("Eating"))        // Display appropriate image
       doEatAnimation(g);
   else if (petState.equals("Sleeping"))
       g.drawImage(sleepImg, 20, 100, this);
} // paint()
```

Note how we use the String.equals() method to determine what state the CyberPet is in. Note also how we have encapsulated the animation task itself into a separate method, doEatAnimation(). Because this method will also draw images, it must be passed a reference to the Graphics object, *g*.

6.8.3 Algorithm Design: doEatAnimation()

The algorithm for the doEatAnimation() method will implement the idea we just described: It will rapidly alternate between the eatImg and eat2Img. By doing this several times, the applet will give the illusion of the pet chewing its fly:

```
// Pseudocode for the animation algorithm
 For several iterations
     Display the opened mouth image (eatImg)
     Delay for an instant.
     Display the closed mouth image (eat2Img)
     Delay for an instant.
```

Note that we have incorporated two delays into the algorithm. If we don't do this, the computer will display the images so rapidly that they will go by in one big blur. Therefore, we have to slow down the alternation between the two images.

Algorithm Design: `busyWaiting()` *Algorithm*

Let's design a method that we can call after displaying an image to cause the computer to delay for an instant. One way to do this is to employ a looping technique known as **busy waiting**. In busy waiting the computer just sits in a loop and does nothing:

```
for ( int k = 0; k < N; k++ ) ; // Empty body --- does nothing
```

If we simply place a semicolon after the heading, we create a for loop with an empty body. It will still iterate from 0 to $N - 1$, but it won't do anything. This leads to the following method definition:

```
private void busyWait(int N) {
    for (int k = 0; k < N; k++) ;   // Empty body --- does nothing
}
```

Busy waiting is a rather old-fashioned way of getting an algorithm to delay. A loop that does nothing is actually wasteful of the computer's time. A more modern technique would make use of separate threads to implement the pause, a technique that we will learn in Chapter 13.

> DEBUGGING TIP: Null Loop Statement. A for loop with no body is said to contain a **null statement**. When done unintentionally, by mistakenly putting a semicolon after the loop condition, this code will cause a hard-to-find semantic error. When done intentionally, it should be well documented.

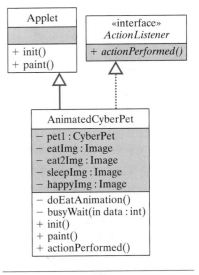

FIGURE 6–9 A UML depiction of the `AnimatedCyberPet` applet.

6.8.4 Implementation

The complete implementation of the `AnimatedCyberPet` applet, whose design is summarized in Figure 6–9, is shown in Figure 6–10. In addition to the various design issues we've discussed, there are several implementation details worth noting about this applet. First, note the use of the named constant, PAUSE, to represent the length of the delay between alternating images. A **named constant** is a `final` variable whose values remain constant throughout the program. Using PAUSE makes the program easier to read and easier to maintain. When we see PAUSE in the program, we immediately know what its purpose is. Also, if we decide to change the PAUSE to, say, 100000, we need only change one line of the program. If we had used a literal, we would have to find and change every occurrence of it in the program.

Named constant

> PROGRAMMING TIP: Named Constants. Avoid using literal values in your programs. Using named constants instead of literal values makes a program much more self-documenting and makes it easier to revise and maintain.

Second, note the use of the `repaint()` method in `actionPerformed()`. This is the conventional way of invoking the `paint()` method, which is never

Polymorphism

```java
import java.applet.*;
import java.awt.*;
import java.awt.event.*;

public class AnimatedCyberPet extends Applet implements ActionListener {
    private final int PAUSE = 2000000;                 // Named constant
                                                       // Instance variables.
    private CyberPet pet1 = new CyberPet("Socrates");  // CyberPet
    private Label nameLabel = new Label("Hi! My name is "  // Label
            + pet1.getName() + " and currently I am : ");
    private TextField stateField = new TextField(12);  // A TextField
    private Button eatButton = new Button("Eat!");     // Two Buttons
    private Button sleepButton = new Button("Sleep!");
    private Image eatImg, eat2Img, sleepImg, happyImg;     // Images for animation

    public void init() {
        eatButton.addActionListener(this);        // Assign the listeners to the buttons.
        sleepButton.addActionListener(this);
        stateField.setText( pet1.getState() ); // Initialize the TextField
        stateField.setEditable(false);
        add(nameLabel);                            // Add the components to the applet.
        add(stateField);
        add(eatButton);
        add(sleepButton);
        eatImg = getImage(getCodeBase(), "eatImage.gif");     // Load the images
        eat2Img = getImage(getCodeBase(), "eat2Image.gif");
        sleepImg = getImage(getCodeBase(), "sleepImage.gif");
        happyImg = getImage(getCodeBase(), "happyImage.gif");
        setSize(300,300);                                  // Set the applet's size
    } // init()

    public void paint(Graphics g) {
        String petState = pet1.getState();
        if (petState.equals("Eating"))
            doEatAnimation(g);
        else if (petState.equals("Sleeping"))
            g.drawImage(sleepImg, 20, 100, this);
    } // paint()

    private void doEatAnimation(Graphics g) {
        for (int k = 0; k < 5; k++) {
            g.drawImage( eatImg ,20, 100, this);
            busyWait(PAUSE);
            g.drawImage(eat2Img, 20, 100, this);
            busyWait(PAUSE);
        }
        g.drawImage(happyImg, 20, 100, this);
    } // doEatAnimation()

    private void busyWait(int N) {
        for (int k = 0; k < N; k++) ;   // Empty for body --- does nothing
    } // busyWait()

    public void actionPerformed(ActionEvent e) {
        if (e.getSource() == eatButton)
            pet1.eat();
        else if (e.getSource() == sleepButton)
            pet1.sleep();
        stateField.setText(pet1.getState());
        repaint();
    } // actionPerformed()
} // AnimatedCyberPet
```

FIGURE 6–10   The AnimatedCyberPet applet.

called directly within a program. The paint() method is another example of a polymorphic method. By overriding its definition in an applet, you enable the system to invoke a paint() method that is appropriate for that particular context. By designing it to work this way, Java can pass it the correct referent to the applet's Graphics context. So the method inherits functionality but allows for extensibility.

Finally, look at the implementation of the doEatAnimation() method. It alternately displays the two eating images, with pauses in between, and when the loop is exited, it displays an image of the happy spider. This implementation is highly platform dependent, because the actual length of the wait depends heavily on the processor's speed. It may be necessary to experiment with how big to make N in order to create a realistic animation. We will remedy this shortcoming when we discuss threads in Chapter 13.

6.9 Principles of Loop Design

Before moving on, it will be useful to summarize the main principles involved in correctly constructing a loop.

- A *counting loop* can be used whenever you know in advance exactly how many iterations are needed. Java's *for statement* is an appropriate structure for coding a counting loop.
- A *while structure* should be used when the problem suggests that the loop body may be skipped entirely. Java's *while statement* is specially designed for the while structure.
- A *do-while structure* should be used only when a loop requires one or more iterations. Java's *do-while statement* is specially designed for the do-while structure.
- The *loop variable* is used to specify the *loop-entry condition*. It must be initialized to an appropriate initial value, and it must be updated on each iteration of the loop.
- A loop's *bound* may be a *count*, a *sentinel*, or, more generally, a *conditional bound*. It must be correctly specified in the loop-entry expression, and progress toward the bound must be made in the *updater*.
- An *infinite loop* may result if the initializer, loop-entry expression, or updater expression is not correctly specified.

The loop types are also summarized in Table 6.1.

TABLE 6.1 A summary of the design decisions required when coding a loop

Use	If	Java Statement
Counting loop	*Number of iterations known in advance*	*for*
While structure	*Number of iterations not known* *Loop may not be entered at all*	*while*
Do-while structure	*Number of iterations not known* *Loop must be entered at least once*	*do-while*

OBJECT-ORIENTED DESIGN:
Structured Programming

Structured programming is the practice of writing programs that are built up from a small set of predefined control structures. As an overall approach to programming, structured programming has largely been superseded by the object-oriented approach. Nevertheless, its design principles are still relevant to the design of the algorithms and methods that make up a program's objects.

The principles of structured programming seem so obvious today that it may be difficult to appreciate their importance. In the 1960s and 1970s, one of the main controls used in programs was the infamous *go to* statement, which could be used to transfer control of a program to any arbitrary location within it, and from there to any other arbitrary location, and so on. This led to incredibly complex and ill-formed programs—so called "spaghetti code"—that were almost impossible to understand and modify.

Spaghetti code

Structured programming evolved in reaction to the unstructured software development practices of the 1960s, which were fraught with budget overruns, costly delays, and failed products. One of the classic research results of that era was a 1966 paper by Boehm and Jacopini that showed that any program using go to's could be represented by an equivalent program that used a sequence of two types of controls: if/else and while structures. Another influential paper by Edgar Dikjstra ("GoTo Statement Considered Harmful") pointed out the various ways in which the go to statement could lead to impossibly complex programs.

The Pascal language, introduced by Nicklaus Wirth in 1971, was designed to promote structured programming techniques and became the language of choice within academic institutions because of its suitability as a teaching language. In Pascal, the go to was replaced with the four structures that control the flow of execution in a program (Fig. 6–11):

• *Sequence*—The statements in a program are executed in sequential order unless their flow is interrupted by one of the following control structures.

FIGURE 6–11 Flowcharts of the four types of control structures. Each small rectangle represents a single executable statement.

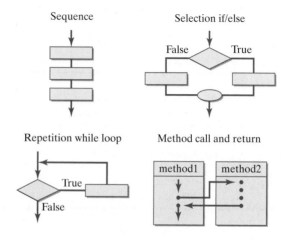

- *Selection*—The if, if/else, and switch statements are *branching* statements that allow choice through the forking of the control path into two or more alternatives.
- *Repetition*—The for, while, and do-while statements are *looping* statements that allow the program to repeat a sequence of statements.
- *Method Call*—Invoking a method transfers control temporarily to a named method. Control returns to the point of invocation when the method is completed.

No matter how large or small a program you write, its flow of control can be constructed as a combination of these four basic types of structures.

Preconditions and Postconditions

The Java language supplies us with a good collection of control structures, and its syntax constrains the way we can use them. One of the features of the four control structures is that each has a single entry point and exit (Fig. 6–11). This is an extremely important property. To grasp its importance, consider the following debugging problem:

```
k = 0;                              // 1. Unstructured code
System.out.println("k= " + k);     // 2. k should equal 0 here
goto label1;                        // 3.
label2:
System.out.println("k= " + k);     // 4. k should equal 1 here
```

In this example a *goto* statement is used to jump to label1, a label that marks a section of code somewhere else in the program. Suppose we're trying to determine how *k* has acquired an erroneous value and that its value is correct in line 2 of this sequence. Given the go to statement on line 3, there's no guarantee that control will ever return to the println() statement on line 4. Thus, in unstructured code it is very difficult to narrow the scope of an error to a fixed segment of code. Because the go to statement can transfer control anywhere in the program, with no guarantee of return, any segment of code can have multiple entry points and multiple exits.

Now contrast the foregoing code with the following well-structured code:

```
k = 0;                              // 1. Structured code
System.out.println("k= " + k);     // 2. k should equal 0 here
someMethod();                       // 3.
System.out.println("k= " + k);     // 4. k should equal 1 here
```

In this case, we can be certain that control will eventually return to line 4. If *k*'s value is erroneous on line 4, we can trace through someMethod() to find the error. Because any segment of a structured program has a single entry and exit, we can use a pair of println() statements in this way to converge on the location of the program bug.

Debugging with println()

An important implication of the single-entry/single-exit property is that we can use **preconditions** and **postconditions** to help us design and debug our code. The previous example provided a simple example: The precondition is that *k* should equal 0 on line 2, and the postcondition is that *k* should equal 1 on line 4. Figure 6–12 shows some additional examples.

FIGURE 6–12 Using pre- and postconditions to document code.

```
•  int k = 0;      // Precondition: k == 0
   k = 5;          // Assignment to k
                   // Postcondition: k == 5

•  int k = 0;                // Precondition: k == 0
   while (k < 100) {         // While loop
       k = 2 * k + 2;
   }
                            // Postcondition: k >= 100

•  /**
    * factorial(n) -- factorial(n) is 1 if n is 0
    *                 factorial(n) is n * n-1 * n-2 * ... * 1 if n > 0
    * Precondition:  n >= 0
    * Postcondition: factorial(n) = 1 if n = 0
    *                             = n * n-1 * n-2 * ... * 1 if n > 0
    */
   public int factorial(int n) {
       if (n == 0)
           return 1;
       else {
           int f = 1;                      // Init a temporary variable
           for (int k = n; k >= 1; k--)    // For n down to 1
               f = f * k;                  //   Accumulate the product
           return f;                       // Return the factorial
       }
   } // factorial()
```

In the first example, we use pre- and postconditions to define the semantics of an assignment statement. No matter what value k has before the assignment, the execution of the assignment (k = 5) will make the postcondition (k == 5) true.

In the second example, the postcondition follows from the semantics of the while loop. Because the loop-entry condition is k < 100, when the loop exits the postcondition (k >= 100) must be true.

The third example shows how pre- and postconditions can be used to design and document methods. The *factorial(n)* is defined for $n \geq 0$ as follows:

```
factorial(n) is 1, if n == 0
factorial(n) is n * n-1 * n-2 * ... * 1, if n > 0
```

In other words, the factorial of N is defined as the cumulative product of multiplying 1 times 2, times 3, and so on up to N. For example, if N is 5, then factorial(5) is 1 * 2 * 3 * 4 * 5 = 120.

Note how the factorial computation is done in the method. The variable *f*, which is used to accumulate the product, is initialized to 1. Then on each iteration of the for loop, *f* is multiplied by *k* and the product is assigned back to *f*. This is similar to the way we accumulate a sum, except in this case we are accumulating a product.

The precondition on the factorial() method represents the condition that must be true in order for the method to work correctly. Factorial is undefined for $n < 0$, so it is important that *n* be greater than or equal to 0 whenever this method is called. Given that the precondition holds, the postcondition gives a precise specification of what must be true when the method is finished.

Design: Defensive Programming

The pre- and postconditions for a method can be used to design defensive code—that is, code that guards against errors. For example, what action should `factorial()` take if its precondition fails to hold? One rather radical approach would be to terminate the program when a precondition fails:

```java
public int factorial(int n) {
    if (n < 0) {                                // Precondition failure
        System.out.println("Error in factorial(), n = " + n);
        System.exit( 0 );
    }
    if (n == 0)
        return 1;
    else {
        int f = 1;                              // Init a temporary variable
        for (int k = n; k >= 1; k--)            // For n down to 1
            f = f * k;                          //    Accumulate the product
        return f;                               // Return the factorial
    }
} // factorial()
```

The `System.exit()` method can be used to terminate the program in an orderly fashion. Note that an error message is printed before exiting.

This error handling strategy would guard against an erroneous value being propagated throughout the program by the `factorial()` method. The failure of the precondition in `factorial()` points to a problem elsewhere in the program, because it is doubtful that the program deliberately passed a negative value to `factorial()`. The discovery of this error should lead to modifications in that part of the program where `factorial()` was invoked—perhaps to some validation of the user's input:

```java
int num = Integer.parseInt(textIn.getText());
if (num >= 0)                      // If factorial() precondition is valid
    factNum = factorial(num);      //    Compute the factorial
else
    System.out.println("Error");   //    Report error in user input
```

This would be the traditional way to handle this kind of error. It incorporates error checking and error handling code right into the program's algorithm. As we will see in Chapter 11, Java's built-in *exception handling* mechanism provides a much more systematic way to handle erroneous or exceptional conditions.

Using Pre- and Postconditions

The use of preconditions and postconditions in the ways we've described can help improve a program's design at several distinct stages of its development:

- Design stage: Using pre- and postconditions in design helps to clarify the design and provides a precise measure of correctness.
- Implementation and testing stage: Test data can be designed to demonstrate that the preconditions and postconditions hold for any method or code segment.
- Documentation stage: Using pre- and postconditions to document the program makes the program more readable and easier to modify and maintain.
- Debugging stage: Using the pre- and postconditions provides precise criteria that can be used to isolate and locate bugs. A method is incorrect if its precondition is true and its postcondition is false. A method is improperly invoked if its precondition is false.

Like other programming skills and techniques, learning how to use pre- and postconditions effectively requires practice. The lab exercise for this chapter and subsequent chapters will require that you provide additional documentation in your programs to identify the pre- and postconditions for each method and for each loop.

Appendix A provides guidelines on how to incorporate pre- and postconditions into your program's documentation. However, it would be a mistake to get in the habit of leaving the identification of pre- and postconditions to the documentation stage. They should be identified during the design stage and should play a role in all aspects of program development.

Effective Program Design

What we're really saying here is that using pre- and postconditions forces you to analyze your program's logic. It is not enough to know that a single isolated statement within a program works correctly at the present time. You have to ask yourself: Will it continue to work if you change some other part of the program? Will other parts of the program continue to work if you revise it? No matter how clever you are, it is not possible to keep an entire model of a good-sized program in your head at one time. It is always necessary to focus on a few essential details and leave aside certain others. Ideally, what you hope is that the details you've left aside for the moment aren't the cause of the current bug you're trying to fix. Using pre- and postconditions can help you determine the correctness of the details you choose to set aside.

EFFECTIVE DESIGN: Pre- and Postconditions.   Pre- and postconditions are an effective way of analyzing the logic of your program's loops and methods. They should be identified at the earliest stages of design and development. They should play a role in the testing and debugging of the program. Finally, they should be included, in a systematic way, in the program's documentation.

PROGRAMMING TIP: Develop your program's documentation at the same time that you develop its code and include the pre- and postconditions in the documentation.

As the programs you write become longer and more complex, the chances that they contain serious errors increase dramatically. There's no real way to avoid this complexity. The only hope is to try to manage it. In addition to analyzing your program's structure, another important aspect of program design is the attempt to reduce its complexity.

EFFECTIVE DESIGN: Reducing Complexity. Design your programs with an aim toward reducing their complexity.

Perhaps the best way to reduce complexity is to build your programs using a small collection of standard structures and techniques. The basic control structures (Fig. 6–11) help reduce the potential complexity of a program by constraining the kinds of branching and looping structures that can be built. The control structures help to manage the complexity of your program's algorithms. In the same way, the following practices can help reduce and manage the complexity in a program.

PROGRAMMING TIP: Standard Techniques. Acquire and use standard programming techniques for standard programming problems. For example, using a temporary variable to swap the values of two variables is a standard technique.

PROGRAMMING TIP: Encapsulation. Use methods wherever appropriate in your own code to encapsulate important sections of code and thereby reduce complexity.

PROGRAMMING TIP: Code Reuse. Instead of reinventing the wheel, use library classes and methods whenever possible. These have been carefully designed by experienced programmers. Library code has been subjected to extensive testing.

Lanning's Limerick

Bad hackers will say without blinking,
That analysis hampers their thinking.
But a task very complex
That's coded by reflex,
Very often will end up just stinking.

SELF-STUDY EXERCISES

EXERCISE 6.15 Identify the pre- and postconditions on *j* and *k* where indicated in the following code segment:

```
int j = 0; k = 5;
do {
    if (k % 5 == 0)  {
                         // Precondition
        j += k;
        k--;
    }
    else k *= k;
} while (j <= k);
                     // Postcondition
```

What Can Be Computed?

DID YOU ever wonder whether there are problems that cannot be solved by a computer, no matter what kind of control structures are used? Well, back in 1939, in his seminal paper titled "On Computable Numbers," Alan Turing proved that indeed there are an infinite number of unsolvable problems. Prior to this, mathematicians and logicians thought all problems could be solved. So Turing's proof was quite a blow!

To help him prove this point, Turing defined an abstract computer, which has come to be known as a Turing machine. A Turing machine has an alphabet of symbols; a read/write head; an infinitely long tape on which the read/write head can write symbols, and from which it can also read symbols; and a control unit, which controls the movement and action of the read/write head. Note that the Turing machine elements correspond to key components of a real computer—although Turing invented this concept a decade before the first computers were developed. The read/write head corresponds to a computer's central processing unit (CPU). The tape corresponds to the computer's memory. And the control unit corresponds to the computer program.

A Turing machine represents a purely abstract concept of computation. It represents the pure idea of an algorithmic solution to a problem. Equipped with this concept, Turing was able to prove that there are unsolvable problems—that is, problems for which no algorithm can arrive at a solution.

One such problem is the *halting problem*. This problem asks whether an algorithm can be devised to determine whether an arbitrary program will eventually halt. If there were such an algorithm, it could be used to detect programs that contain infinite loops, a service that might be really helpful in an introductory computing lab, among other places! But, alas, there can be no such algorithm.

Here's a sketch of a proof by contradiction that the halting problem is unsolvable. (This particular version of the proof was suggested by J. Glenn Brookshear in *Computer Science: An Overview*, Benjamin-Cummings, 1985.)

Suppose you had a program, *P*, that solves the halting problem. That is, whenever *P* is given a self-halting program, suppose it sets a variable *isTerminating* to true, and otherwise it sets *isTerminating* to false. Now let's create a new version of *P*, named *P*′, which is identical to *P* except that right after where *P* sets *isTerminating* to true or false, *P*′ contains the following loop:

```
while (isTerminating == true); // Infinite if isTerminating true
```

In other words, if the input to *P*′ is a self-terminating program, then *P*′ will enter an infinite loop and it won't terminate. Otherwise, if a non-self-terminating program is input to *P*′, *P*′ will skip the loop and will terminate.

Now what if we give a representation of *P*′ to itself. Will it halt? The answer generates a contradiction: If *P*′ is a self-terminating program, then when it is input to itself, it will not terminate. And if *P*′ is not self-terminating, when it is input to itself, it will terminate. Because our assumption that *P* solves the halting problem has led to a contradiction, we have to conclude that it wasn't a very good assumption in the first place. Therefore, there is no program that can solve the halting problem.

The topic of computability is a fundamental part of the computer science curriculum, usually taught in a sophomore- or junior-level course on the theory of computation.

EXERCISE 6.16 Identify the pre- and postconditions for the following method, which computes x^n for $n \geq 0$:

```
public double power(double x, int n) {
    double pow = 1;
    for (int k = 1; k <= n; k++)
        pow = pow * x;
    return pow;
} // power()
```

A java.awt.TextArea is an AWT component for storing and manipulating multiple lines of text (whereas a TextField allows just a single line of text to be input or output). Figure 6–13 shows the pedigree and some of the public methods associated with the java.awt.TextArea class. Note that several important methods are inherited from the TextComponent class.

To create a TextArea you can use one of the following constructors:

```
TextArea()
TextArea(int rows, int cols)
TextArea(String s, int rows, int cols)
```

The first creates an empty TextArea of default size. The second creates a TextArea with a given number of rows and columns. The third creates

From the Java Library

java.awt.TextArea

http://java.sun.com/products /jdk/1.3/docs/api/

FIGURE 6–13 A UML class diagram of the TextArea class.

java.lang

Object

java.awt

Component

TextComponent
- + isEditable() : boolean
- + setEditable(in b : Boolean)
- + getText() : String
- + setText(in s : String)

TextArea
- + TextArea()
- + TextArea(in rows : int, in cols : int)
- + append(in s : String)
- + getColumns() : int
- + setColumns(in cols : int)
- + setRows(in rows : int)

TextField

a `TextArea` containing the text *s* as its initial value and the specified number of rows and columns:

```
TextArea myText = new TextArea("hello", 5, 60);
```

To use a `TextArea` for output only, we want it to be uneditable:

```
myText.setEditable(false);
```

To write text into a `TextArea`, you can use either the `setText()` or `append()` methods:

```
myText.setText("Hello again!\n");
myText.append("Welcome back!\n");
```

The `setText()` method will replace whatever text was in the `TextArea` with "Hello again!" The `append()` method will append "Welcome back!" to the end of the text that was already in the `TextArea`. To extract text from a `TextArea`, you would use `getText()`, which is inherited from `TextComponent`:

```
String str = myText.getText();
```

Using a `TextArea` as an output device is very simple. The program in Figure 6–14 provides an example of how to set up a simple Graphical User Interface (GUI) for performing I/O operations. As Figure 6–14 shows, a `TextField` is used as an input device, and a `Label` is used to prompt the user. A `TextArea` is used as an output device—where the program's results are displayed. In this example, the GUI is used to test the `factorial()` method we defined earlier (Fig. 6–12). As Figure 6–15 summarizes, each time the user types a number and <RETURN> into the `TextField`, the applet checks whether the number is in the appropriate range and then displays its factorial in the `TextArea`. This combined use of a `Label`, a `TextField`, and a `TextArea` is very general and can be used as the basic design for a wide variety of GUIs.

The `FactorialTest` program is shown in Figure 6–16. It instantiates the three components visible in Figure 6–14. These are added to the applet in its `init()` method. Note that the `TextField` must be registered with an `ActionListener` so that the applet can handle the user's input actions.

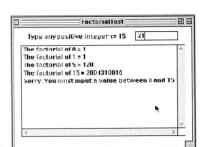

FIGURE 6–14   A Graphical User Interface (GUI) for simple I/O operations.

GUI design

FIGURE 6–15   A UML sequence diagram showing the interactions involved in a basic GUI using a `TextField` for input and a `TextArea` for output. When the user types the RETURN key into the `TextField`, the applet gets the text and passes it (possibly together with a computed result) to the `TextArea`.

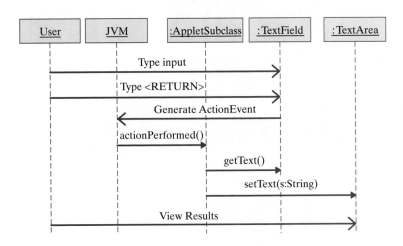

Also, the TextArea is made *uneditable*, which means for this program, it will only be used to display output. Java will just ignore any typing that takes place within it.

There are several other important points worth making about this example. First, note here again we use a named constant, BOUND, instead of using the *literal* value 15 throughout the program. As always, this makes the program easier to read and easier to maintain.

Also note how the error handling is done in this program. In the actionPerformed() method, we check that the user's input is between 0 and BOUND before calling the factorial() method. This validates the user's input and prevents the violation of factorial()'s precondition.

Finally, note how we have simplified the algorithm for factorial(). In the previous version of this method (Fig. 6–12) we explicitly tested for the

```java
import java.awt.*;
import java.awt.event.*;
import java.applet.*;

public class FactorialTest extends Applet implements ActionListener {

    private final int BOUND = 15;                    // Named constant

    private Label prompt = new Label("Type any positive integer <= " + BOUND);
    private TextField input = new TextField(10);     // Input device
    private TextArea display = new TextArea(10,40);  // Output device

    /**
     * Pre:  n >= 0
     * Post: factorial(n) = 1 if n = 0
     *                    = n * n-1 * n-2 * ... * 1, if n > 0
     */
    private int factorial(int n) {
        int f = 1;
        for(int k = n; k >= 1; k--)
            f = f * k;
        return f;
    } // factorial()

    public void init() {
        input.addActionListener(this);        // Register with a Listener
        display.setEditable(false);           // Make TextArea read only
        add(prompt);
        add(input);
        add(display);
    } // init()

    public void actionPerformed(ActionEvent e) {
        int num = Integer.parseInt(input.getText());
        if (num >= 0 && num <= BOUND)
        display.append("The factorial of" + num + " = "
                              + factorial(num) + "\n");
    } // actionPerformed()
} // FactorialTest
```

FIGURE 6–16   Definition of the FactorialTest class.

case of *n == 0* and simply returned 1 as the method's value in that case. However, this case is not strictly necessary. If we initialize our result *f* to 1 and then iterate from *n* down to 1, the method will still return 1 in the case where *n == 0*. In that case, the loop body is skipped entirely because its loop-entry condition is false to begin with.

Cryptography

CRYPTOGRAPHY is the study of secret writing—the study of *encrypting* and *decrypting* secret messages. It is an ancient art and science that's been used throughout history. For example, Caesar used what's come to be known as the *Caesar cipher* to encrypt messages to his generals during the Gaulic campaigns. In a Caesar cipher, a simple integer between 1 and 25 is used as a *secret key*, and a message is encrypted by shifting each letter by the number of letters specified in the key, wrapping around the end of the alphabet, if necessary. For example, if we use a key of 1, then "hello" would be encrypted as "ifmmp." (We will study the Caesar cipher itself in Chapter 7.)

Up until very recently, the best and strongest encryption schemes were owned by the military and government agencies. Today, however, there's a form of *public key encryption* that anybody can use. For example, the popular PGP (Pretty Good Privacy) program is freely distributed on the Web (http://web.mit.edu/network/pgp.html). This approach is based on the idea of breaking up a person's key into a private and public half. Anybody can send secret messages to Alice, by using her public key, but only Alice can decrypt the message using her private key.

The effectiveness of public key encryption depends on the use of very large prime numbers. A *prime number* is a positive integer that is divisible only by itself and 1. A *composite* number is a number that is not prime. Any composite number can be represented as the product of prime numbers. For example, 20 = 2 * 2 * 5, and 65 = 5 * 13. What protects a PGP-encrypted message is the inability of eavesdroppers to factor the large composite numbers that make up the person's key. So prime numbers play a critical role in the development of effective encryption software.

IN THE LABORATORY: Finding Prime Numbers

The purpose of this lab is to provide practice using loop control structures in designing and implementing solutions to programming problems. The objectives are

- To give practice using simple looping constructs.
- To introduce the TextArea component for use in outputting multiple lines of text.

Problem Statement

Suppose that Atlas Computer Security has contacted you about consulting for it to develop public key encryption software. One thing you're going to need in this software is a method that can test whether a number is a prime or not. To help demonstrate your prime number tester, the company wants you to write a Java applet that prompts the user for a positive integer and then displays all of the prime numbers less than or equal to the user's integer. If the company likes your demo, it will probably give you the contract for the encryption software.

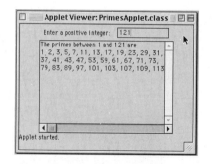

FIGURE 6–17 The user interface for PrimesApplet.

GUI Specifications

The Graphical User Interface (GUI) for this applet needs a component to handle the user's input, and another component to display the prime numbers. A good design for the GUI was described in the previous section and summarized in Figure 6–15. A TextField would be an appropriate input component, because the user needs to input a single integer value. The TextField can also serve as the means by which the user indicates that an action should be taken. Whenever the user types a Return or Enter in the TextField, the program should test the TextField's current value for primality.

The output component should allow the program's output to extend over several lines. This is a perfect job for a TextArea. In addition to these components, we'll need a Label to prompt the user as to what kind of input is expected. Figure 6–17 shows how the GUI will appear to the user.

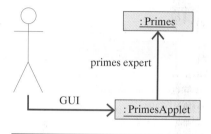

FIGURE 6–18 The PrimesApplet serves as an interface between the user and the Primes object. The Primes object is an expert at computing primes.

Problem Decomposition

There are two tasks involved in the demo program. One is to provide a user interface, a GUI. The other is to provide the expertise needed to determine whether a number is prime. This suggests that we should break this problem up into two objects: a PrimesApplet object, which will manage the interface, and a Primes object, which will contain methods to determine whether a number is prime and to find prime numbers within a certain range (Fig. 6–18).

Problem Design: The PrimesApplet Class

The design of PrimesApplet should be similar to that of other applets we've built. Of course, the applet must create an instance of the Primes class. This is the object it will call upon to test whether numbers are prime.

In terms of its GUI elements, the applet should contain a TextField for user input and a Label for prompting the user. These components should be instantiated in the applet and added to the applet in the init() method. Because it will generate user actions, whenever the user types the Enter key, the TextField should be given an ActionListener. This should also be done in the init() method. (See "In the Laboratory" project in Chapter 5.)

The algorithm used by PrimesApplet is event driven. In the init() method, the applet should be registered as the listener for ActionEvents that occur in the TextField. Then, whenever such an event occurs, Java will call the applet's actionPerformed() method, where the event should

What variables and methods are needed?

Event-driven algorithm

be handled. The `actionPerformed()` method should get the input from the `TextField`, convert it to an integer, and then display all of the prime numbers less than the user's number:

1. Get the user's input from the `TextField`.
2. Convert the input `String` into an `int`.
3. Display in the `TextArea` all the prime numbers less than the user's number.

Step 2 of this algorithm will require us to use the `Integer.parseInt()` method to convert a `String` into an `int`:

```
int num = Integer.parseInt("564"); // Converts "564" to 564
```

Step 3 of this algorithm will require a loop, and it is here where the applet must call on the expertise of the `Primes` object. Because this step will be somewhat complex, it should be encapsulated into a separate method.

Taken together, these design decisions lead to the following specification for the `PrimesApplet` class, which is also summarized in Figure 6–19:

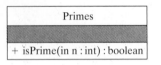

- Purpose: To provide a GUI interface for computing primes.
- Private instance variables: `TextArea`, `TextField`, `Label`.
- Public instance methods: `init()`, `actionPerformed()`.
- Private instance method: `findPrimes(int)` displays in the `TextArea` all of the primes between 1 and its `int` parameter.

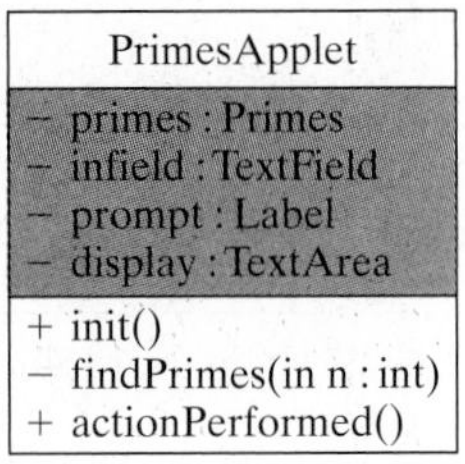

FIGURE 6–19   Design of the `PrimesApplet` class.

Note that the `findPrimes()` method will be a `private` method. This is appropriate, since it is not intended to be used outside of this class.

Problem Design: The `Primes` Class

As our design of the `PrimesApplet` class suggested, the `Primes` class should have a public method that can be used to test whether a number is prime. A *prime* is any positive integer that is divisible only by itself and 1. Let's call this method `isPrime()`. This should be a `boolean` method that should return true when its `int` parameter is a prime number. Otherwise it should return false.

The `Primes` class does not have any kind of internal state that would be represented in the form of instance variables. Any variables that it may need to determine if a number is prime can be declared within the `is-Prime()` method. Thus, its specification, which is shown in Figure 6–20, is very simple:

FIGURE 6–20   The `Primes` class contains just a single instance method.

- Purpose: To determine if a number is prime.
- Public instance method: `isPrime(int)` returns `true` if its parameter is a prime number.

What variables are needed?

The `findPrimes()` Algorithm

The `findPrimes()` method takes a single `int` parameter, N, and will display all of the prime numbers, less than or equal to N, in the applet's `TextArea`. Its algorithm should use a loop to test the numbers between 1 and N and display all the prime numbers in that range. Obviously, this is a counting loop, because you know exactly how many iterations it must make before entering the loop. Also, the task of determining whether an integer is

Counting loop or conditional loop?

prime or not will be farmed out to the Primes object. Thus, this gives us the following algorithm:

```
Display "The following are the primes between 1 and N" in TextArea
for each integer, k, in the range 1 to N
    if k is prime
        display k in the TextArea
```

The isPrime() Algorithm

The isPrime() method should employ a loop to find whether its parameter, N, is a prime. The algorithm in this case should make use of the definition of a prime number—that is, a number divisible only by itself and 1. It could try dividing N by K, where K is $2, 3, 4, 5, \ldots$ and so on up to $N - 1$. If any of these numbers is a divisor of N, then N is not a prime number. If none is a divisor of N, then N is a prime number. Because the number of iterations required for this loop is not known beforehand, it will require a noncounting loop structure.

To test whether N is prime it is necessary to have an entry condition that is the conjunction of two conditions. The loop should iterate while K is less than N, *and* while none of the preceding values of K were divisors of N. In other words, the loop should terminate when a value K is found that evenly divides N. One way to handle this task is to use a local boolean variable as a **flag** that will be raised when a value K is found that divides N:

While or do-while loop?

```
Initialize notDivisibleYet to true
Initialize K to 2
while (notDivisibleYet AND K < N)  {
    if N is divisible by K
        set notDivisibleYet to false
    increment K;
}
```

This is an example of a complex loop bound. It involves the conjunction of both a count bound and a *flag bound*, and it will terminate when *either* bound is reached. Thus, the loop terminates when *either K* equals *N or when N* is divisible by some value of $K < N$. If it terminates with K equal to N, that indicates that N is prime.

Flag bound

Note that for the conjunction *notDivisibleYet AND K < N* to be true, both halves of it must be true. However, for it to be false, either half may be false; it is not necessary that both halves be false. In this case, *either* notDivisibleYet will be false *or* $K \geq N$ will be false. This is an instance of the logic rule known as *DeMorgan's Law*, which can be stated as:

DeMorgan's Law

```
!(P && Q) == !P || !Q
```

where P and Q are simple boolean conditions.

Implementation

The implementation of this program is left to you as a lab (or programming) exercise, but here are some hints and suggestions:

- **Stepwise refinement.** A good first step for writing this program would be to create the TextField and a TextArea components and implement the init() and actionPerformed() methods. The first version of the applet should merely display in the TextArea whatever number the user types into the TextField, without testing for primality.

    Once you have successfully written and tested a simple interface, define the Primes class and write and test the isPrime() method. In order to write this method, you will have to complete the development of the algorithm described in the previous section. Use pseudocode to help you lay out the algorithm. You can use your interface to help you test the method. Have the user input an integer, and then just test whether that integer is prime.

    Once you have a correct isPrime() method, write and test the find-Primes() methods. This last step should be very simple.

- **Preconditions and postconditions.** Use pre- and postconditions in your specification and documentation of the isPrime() and find-Primes() methods. Then use the conditions to help design appropriate test data to verify that your code is correct.

- **Null pointer error.** Beware of **null pointer** errors, which result when you forget to instantiate (create) an object before using it. A null pointer error occurs when you attempt to refer to an object using a reference that has a value of null. When you declare a reference variable, it is given a default value of null. If you forget to instantiate it, you'll get this error. The typical sequence is declare, create, and use, although these don't always happen in the same place in the program. For example, the TextArea display can be declared in the global portion of the program, instantiated in init(), and used in actionPerformed():

Declare, create, use

```
TextArea display;          // Declare a variable
...
display = new TextArea();   // Create an instance (init())
...
display.appendText ("blah");// Use it (actionPerformed())
```

If you forget to instantiate it in init() the use of display in actionPerformed() will cause a null pointer exception.

Optional Refinement

Public key encryption involves the use of composite numbers as well as prime numbers. A challenging extension to this lab would be to let the user type in a composite number and display its prime factorization. Design a method that takes an integer parameter and displays its prime factors in the TextArea. For example, if the user inputs 40, your method should display $40 = 2 * 2 * 2 * 5$.

Repetition Control Structures

Java provides three repetition statements: the for statement, used primarily for counting loops; the while statement, used for conditional loops; and the do-while statement, used for conditional loops that must iterate at least once.

All loop structures must have three elements: an *initializer*, which sets the initial value of the *loop variable*; a *loop entry condition* or *loop boundary condition*, which controls entry (and exit) to (and from) the *loop body*; and an *updater*, a statement that updates the loop variable before the next iteration.

When designing a loop, it is important to analyze the loop structure to make sure that the loop bound will eventually be satisfied. Table 6.2 summarizes the types of loop bound that we have identified. A loop that fails to satisfy its bound will repeat forever and is, therefore, known as an *infinite loop*.

TABLE 6.2 A summary of various loop bounds

Bound	Example
Counting	$k < 100$
Sentinel	*input != 9999*
Flag	*done != true*
Limit	*amount < 0.5*

The For Loop

The for statement has the following syntax:

```
for ( initializer ; loop entry condition ; updater )
    for loop body ;
```

Execution of the for loop begins with the initializer statement. This is usually used to set the initial value of the *loop variable*. Next, the loop entry condition is tested. If it is true, the loop body is executed. If it is false, the loop body is skipped, and control passes beyond the for statement. After each iteration of the loop body, the updater statement is executed, and then the loop entry condition is retested. The following for loop prints the values from 1 to 100.

```
for (int k = 1;  k <= 100; k++ )
    System.out.println(k);
```

The While Loop

The while statement takes the following form:

```
while ( loop entry condition )
    loop body ;
```

Note that unlike the for statement, the while statement does not contain syntax for the initializer and the updater. These must be coded separately. As in the for loop, the loop body can be either a simple statement or a set of statements enclosed within braces.

When a while statement is executed, its loop entry condition is tested *before* the loop body is entered. If it is true, the loop body is executed; otherwise it is skipped and control passes to the next statement beyond the while statement. The loop entry condition is retested after each iteration of the loop body. The following while loop prints the numbers from 1 to 100:

```
int k = 1;                    // Initializer
while (k <= 100) {            // Loop entry condition
    System.out.println(k);
    k++;                      // Updater
}

                              // Postcondition: k > 100
```

The Do-While Loop

The do-while statement has the following general form:

```
do
    loop body ;
while ( loop entry condition ) ;
```

Note, again, that the initializer and the updater statements must be coded separately in the do-while structure.

When a do-while statement is executed, its loop body is executed first. Then its loop entry condition is tested. If it is true, the loop body is executed again. Otherwise control passes to the next statement following the while statement. The do-while statement should be used primarily for loops that require at least one iteration. Here's an example of a do-while loop to print the numbers from 1 to 100.

```
int k = 1;                    // Initializer
do {
    System.out.println(k);
    k++;                      // Updater
} while (k <= 100);          // Loop entry condition
                              // Postcondition: k > 100
```

CHAPTER SUMMARY

Technical Terms

busy waiting	loop body	priming read
compound statement	loop bound	repetition structure
conditional loop	loop entry condition	sentinel bound
counting loop	named constant	unit indexing
do-while statement	nested loop	updater
flag bound	null pointer error	while statement
infinite loop	null statement	zero indexing
initializer	postcondition	
limit bound	precondition	

Summary of Important Points

- A *repetition structure* is a control structure that allows a statement or sequence of statements to be repeated.
- All loop structures involve three elements—an *initializer*, a *loop entry condition* or a *loop boundary condition*, and an *updater*.

- *Structured programming* is the practice of writing programs that are built up from a small set of predefined control structures—the *sequence*, *selection*, *repetition*, and *method-call* structures. An important feature of these structures is that each has a single entry and exit.
- A *precondition* is a condition that must be true before a certain code segment executes. A *postcondition* is a condition that must be true when a certain code segment is finished. Preconditions and postconditions should be used in the design, coding, documentation, and debugging of algorithms and methods.
- The System.exit(int) method can be used to terminate a program in an orderly fashion in case a serious error is detected.

SOLUTION 6.1 Identify the syntax error in the following for loop statements:

SOLUTIONS TO SELF-STUDY EXERCISES

a. Commas are used instead of semicolons in the header.
```
for (int k = 5; k < 100; k++)
    System.out.println(k);
```

b. There shouldn't be 3 semicolons in the header
```
for (int k = 0; k < 12 ; k--)
    System.out.println(k);
```

SOLUTION 6.2 Identify those statements that result in infinite loops:

a. Infinite loop because k is never incremented.

b. Infinite loop because k is always odd and thus never equal to 100.

SOLUTION 6.3 Your sister is learning to count by fours. Write a for loop that prints the following sequence of numbers: 1, 5, 9, 13, 17, 21, 25.

```
for (int k = 1; k <= 25; k = k+4)
    System.out.print(k + " ");
```

SOLUTION 6.4 What value will *j* have when the following loop terminates? *Answer*: *j* will be undefined when the loop terminates. It is a local variable whose scope is limited to the loop body.

```
for (int i = 0; i < 10; i++)
{
    int j;
    j = j + 1;
}
```

SOLUTION 6.5 Write a nested for loop to print the following geometric pattern:

```
#
# #
# # #
# # # #
# # # # #
```

```
for (int row = 1; row <= 5; row++) {    // For each row
    for (int col = 1; col <= row; col++) // Number of columns per row
        System.out.print('#');
    System.out.println();                // New line
} // row
```

SOLUTION 6.6 If *N* is even, divide it by 2. If *N* is odd, subtract 1 and then divide it by 2. This will generate a sequence that is guaranteed to terminate at 0. For example, if *N* is initially 15, then you get the sequence 15, 7, 3, 1, 0. Write a method that implements this sequence. Use a while statement.

```
public static void sub1Div2(int N) {
    while(N != 0) {
        System.out.print(N + " ");
        if (N % 2 == 0)
            N = N / 2;
        else
            N = (N - 1) / 2;
    }
    System.out.println( N );
} // sub1Div2()
```

SOLUTION 6.7 For each of the following problems, decide whether a counting loop structure, a while structure, or a do-while structure should be used, and write a pseudocode algorithm.

• Printing the names of all the visitors to a Web site could use a counting loop because the exact number of visitors is known.

```
for each name in the visitor's log
    print the name
```

• Validating that a user has entered a positive number requires a do-while structure in which you repeatedly read a number and validate it.

```
do
    read a number
    if number is invalid, print error message
while number is invalid
```

• Change all the backslashes (\) in a Windows Web page address, to the slashes (/) used in a Unix Web page address.

```
for each character in the Web page address
    if it is a backslash replace it with slash
```

• Finding the largest in a list of numbers requires a while loop to guard against an empty list.

```
initialize maxMPG to smallest possible number
while there are more cars in the database
    if current car's MPG is greater than maxMPG
        replace maxMPG with it
```

SOLUTION 6.8 Identify the syntax error in the following while structures:

a. ```
int k = 5;
while (k < 100) {
    System.out.println(k);
    k++   << Missing semicolon
}
```

b. ```
int k = 0;
while (k < 12;) {              << Extra semicolon
    System.out.println(k);
    k++;
}
```

SOLUTION 6.9   Determine the output and/or identify the error in each of the following while structures.

a.
```
    int k = 0;
    while (k < 100)
          System.out.println(k);   << Missing the updater in loop body
   Output: infinite loop prints 0 0 0 0 0...
```

b.
```
     while (k < 100) {          << Missing initializer
          System.out.println(k);
          k++;

     }
   Output: unpredictable since k's initial value is not known
```

SOLUTION 6.10   Your younger sister is now learning how to count by sixes. Write a while loop that prints the following sequence of numbers: 0, 6, 12, 18, 24, 30, 36.

```
   int k = 0;                    // Initializer
   while (k <= 36) {             // Loop-entry condition
       System.out.println(k);
       k += 6;                   // Updater
   }
```

SOLUTION 6.11   Identify the syntax error in the following do-while structures:

a.
```
int k = 0;
do while (k < 100) << Misplaced condition
{
     System.out.println(k);
     k++;
}                       << Belongs here
```

b.
```
int k = 0;
do {
     System.out.println(k);
     k++;
} while (k < 12) << Missing semicolon
```

SOLUTION 6.12   Your sister has moved on to counting by sevens. Write a do-while loop that prints the following sequence of numbers: 1, 8, 15, 22, 29, 36, 43.

```
n = 1;                          // Initializer
do {
    System.out.print(n + " ");
    n += 7;                     // Updater
} while (n <= 43);              // Loop entry condition
```

SOLUTION 6.13   Write a method to input and validate pizza sales.

```
public int getAndValidatePizzaPrice() {
    int pizza = 0;
    do {
        System.out.print("Input a pizza price (e.g., 8, 10, or 15) ");
        System.out.print("or 99 to indicate the end of the list >> ");
        String inputString = input.readLine();
        pizza = Integer.parseInt(inputString) ;
        if ((pizza != 99) && (pizza != 8) && (pizza != 10) &&
                    (pizza != 15))
```

```
                System.out.println("Error: you've entered an invalid"
                        + "pizza price\n");     // Error input
         else

                                           // OK input
                System.out.println("You input " + pizza + "\n");
      } while ((pizza != 99) && (pizza != 8) &&
                        (pizza != 10) && (pizza != 15));
      return pizza;
} // getAndValidatePizzaPrice()
```

SOLUTION 6.14 Write a method to input and validate pizza sales using the numbers 1, 2, and 3 to represent different priced pizzas.

```java
public int getAndValidatePizzaPrice() {
    int pizza = 0;
    do {
        System.out.print("Input a 1,2 or 3 to indicate pizza"
                + "price ( 1($8), 2($10), or 3($15) ) ");
        System.out.print("or 0 to indicate the end of the list >> ");
        String inputString  = input.readLine();
        pizza = Integer.parseInt(inputString);
        if ((pizza < 0) || (pizza > 3))
                                           // Error input
            System.out.println("Error: you've entered an invalid"
                                            + "value\n");
        else
            System.out.println("You input " + pizza + "\n"); // OK input
    } while ( (pizza < 0) || (pizza > 3) );
    if (pizza == 1)
        return 8;
    else if (pizza == 2)
        return 10;
    else if (pizza == 3)
        return 15;
    else
        return 0;
} // getAndValidatePizzaPrice()
```

SOLUTION 6.15 Identify the pre- and postconditions on j and k where indicated in the following code segment:

```java
int j = 0; k = 5;
do {
    if (k % 5 == 0) {
                            // Precondition: j <= k
        j += k;
        k--;
    }
    else k *= k;
} while (j <= k);
                        // Postcondition: j > k
```

SOLUTION 6.16 Identify the pre- and postconditions for the following method, which computes x^n for $n >= 0$.

```
// Precondition: N >= 0
// Postcondition: power(x,n) == x to the n
public double power(double x, int n ) {
    double pow = 1;
    for (int k = 1; k <= n; k++)
        pow = pow * x;
    return pow;
} // power()
```

EXERCISE 6.1   Explain the difference between the following pairs of terms:

a. *Counting loop* and *conditional loop.*
b. *For statement* and *while statement.*
c. *While statement* and *do-while statement.*
d. *Zero indexing* and *unit indexing.*
e. *Sentinel bound* and *limit bound.*
f. *Counting bound* and *flag bound.*
g. Loop *initializer* and *updater.*
h. *Named constant* and *literal.*
i. *Compound statement* and *null statement.*

EXERCISE 6.2   Fill in the blank.

a. The process of reading a data item before entering a loop is known as a _____ .

b. A loop that does nothing except iterate is an example of _____ .

c. A loop that contains no body is an example of a _____ statement.

d. A loop whose entry condition is stated as $(k < 100 \; || \; k >= 0)$ would be an example of an _____ loop.

e. A loop that should iterate until the user types in a special value should use a _____ bound.

f. A loop that should iterate until its variable goes from 5 to 100 should use a _____ bound.

g. A loop that should iterate until the difference between two values is less than 0.005 is an example of a _____ bound.

EXERCISE 6.3   Identify the syntax errors in each of the following:

a.
```
for (int k = 0; k < 100; k++)
    System.out.println(k)
```

b.
```
for (int k = 0; k < 100; k++);
    System.out.println(k);
```

c.
```
int k = 0
while  k < 100
{
    System.out.println(k);   k++;
}
```

d.
```
int k = 0;
do
{
    System.out.println(k);   k++;
}
while  k < 100 ;
```

EXERCISES

Note: *For programming exercises,* **first** *draw a UML class diagram describing all classes and their inheritance relationships and/or associations.*

EXERCISE 6.4   Determine the output and/or identify the error in each of the following code segments:

a. ```
for (int k = 1; k == 100; k += 2)
    System.out.println(k);
```

b. ```
int k = 0;
  while (k < 100)
      System.out.println(k);
      k++;
```

c. ```
for (int k = 0; k < 100; k++) ;
    System.out.println(k);
```

**EXERCISE 6.5**   Write pseudocode algorithms for the following activities, paying particular attention to the *initializer, updater,* and *boundary condition* in each case.

a. a softball game
b. a five-question quiz
c. looking up a name in the phone book

**EXERCISE 6.6**   Identify the pre- and postconditions for each of the statements that follow. Assume that all variables are int and have been properly declared.

a.   `int result = x / y;`

b.   `int result = x % y;`

c. ```
int x = 95;
  do
      x /= 2;
  while(x >= 0);
```

EXERCISE 6.7   Write three different loops—a for loop, a while loop, and a do-while loop—to print all the multiples of 10, including 0, up to and including 1,000.

EXERCISE 6.8   Write three different loops—a for loop, a while loop, and a do-while loop—to print the following sequence of numbers: 45, 36, 27, 18, 9, 0, −9, −18, −27, −36, −45.

EXERCISE 6.9   Write three different loops—a for loop, a while loop, and a do-while loop—to print the following ski-jump design:

```
#
# #
# # #
# # # #
# # # # #
# # # # # #
# # # # # # #
```

EXERCISE 6.10   The Straight Downhill Ski Lodge in Gravel Crest, Vermont, gets lots of college students on breaks. The lodge likes to keep track of repeat visitors. Straight Downhill's database includes an integer variable, *visit*, which gives the number of times a guest has stayed at the lodge (1 or more). Write the pseudocode to catch those visitors who have stayed at the lodge at least twice and to send them a special promotional package (pseudocode = send promo). (*Note:* The largest number of stays recorded is eight. The number nine is used as an end-of-data flag.)

EXERCISE 6.11   Modify your pseudocode in the previous exercise. In addition to every guest who has stayed at least twice at the lodge receiving a promotional package, any guest with three or more stays should also get a $40 coupon good for lodging, lifts, or food.

EXERCISE 6.12   Write a method that is passed a single parameter, *N*, and displays all the even numbers from 1 to *N*.

EXERCISE 6.13   Write a method that is passed a single parameter, *N*, that prints all the odd numbers from 1 to *N*.

EXERCISE 6.14   Write a method that is passed a single parameter, *N*, that prints all the numbers divisible by 10 from *N* down to 1.

EXERCISE 6.15   Write a method that is passed two parameters—a `char` *Ch* and an `int` *N*—and prints a string of *N Chs*.

EXERCISE 6.16   Write a method that uses a nested for loop to print the following multiplication table:

```
   1  2  3  4  5  6  7  8  9
1  1
2  2  4
3  3  6  9
4  4  8 12 16
5  5 10 15 20 25
6  6 12 18 24 30 36
7  7 14 21 28 35 42 48
8  8 16 24 32 40 48 56 64
9  9 18 27 36 45 54 63 72 81
```

EXERCISE 6.17   Write a method that uses nested for loops to print the patterns that follow. Your method should use the following statement to print the patterns: `System.out.print('#')`.

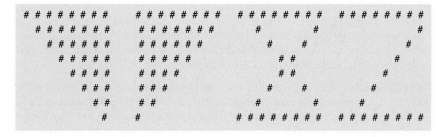

EXERCISE 6.18   Write a program that asks the user for the number of rows and the number of columns in a box of asterisks. Then use nested loops to generate the box.

EXERCISE 6.19   Write a Java application that lets the user input a sequence of consecutive numbers. In other words, the program should let the user keep entering numbers as long as the current number is one greater than the previous number.

EXERCISE 6.20   Write a Java application that lets the user input a sequence of integers terminated by any negative value. The program should then report the largest and smallest values that were entered.

EXERCISE 6.21   How many guesses does it take to guess a secret number between 1 and N? For example, I'm thinking of a number between 1 and 100. I'll tell you whether your guess is too high or too low. Obviously, an intelligent first guess would be 50. If that's too low, an intelligent second guess would be 75. And so on. If we continue to divide the range in half, we'll eventually get down to one number. Because you can divide 100 seven times (50,25,12,6,3,1,0), it will take at most seven guesses to guess a number between 1 and 100. Write a Java applet that lets the user input a positive integer, N, and then reports how many guesses it would take to guess a number between 1 and N.

EXERCISE 6.22   Suppose you determine that the fire extinguisher in your kitchen loses X percent of its foam every day. How long before it drops below a certain threshold (Y percent), at which point it is no longer serviceable? Write a Java applet that lets the user input the values X and Y and then reports how many weeks the fire extinguisher will last.

EXERCISE 6.23   Leibnitz's method for computing π is based on the following convergent series:

$$\frac{\pi}{4} = 1 - \frac{1}{3} + \frac{1}{5} - \frac{1}{7} + \cdots$$

How many iterations does it take to compute π using this series? Write a Java program to find out.

EXERCISE 6.24   Newton's method for calculating the square root of N starts by making a (nonzero) guess at the square root. It then uses the original guess to calculate a new guess, according to the following formula:

```
guess = (( N / guess) + guess) / 2;
```

No matter how wild the original guess is, if we repeat this calculation, the algorithm will eventually find the square root. Write a square root method based on this algorithm. Then write a program to determine how many guesses are required to find the square roots of different numbers. Uses `Math.sqrt()` to determine when to terminate the guessing.

EXERCISE 6.25   Your employer is developing encryption software and wants you to develop a Java applet that will display all of the primes less than N, where N is a number to be entered by the user. In addition to displaying the primes themselves, provide a count of how many there are. Use the method that was developed in this chapter's "Object-Oriented Design" section.

EXERCISE 6.26   Your little sister asks you to help her with her multiplication and you decide to write a Java application that tests her skills. The program will let her input a starting number, such as 5. It will generate multiplication problems ranging from from 5×1 to 5×12. For each problem she will be prompted to enter the correct answer. The program should check her answer and should not let her advance to the next question until the correct answer is given to the current question.

EXERCISE 6.27   Write an application that prompts the user for four values and draws corresponding bar graphs using an ASCII character. For example, if the user entered 15, 12, 9, and 4, the program would draw

```
*******************
************
*********
****
```

EXERCISE 6.28   Revise the application in the previous problem so that the bar charts are displayed vertically. For example, if the user inputs 5, 2, 3, and 4, the program should display

```
**
**          **
**      ** **
** ** ** **
** ** ** **

------------
```

EXERCISE 6.29   The Fibonacci sequence (named after the Italian mathematician Leonardo of Pisa, ca. 1200) consists of the numbers $0, 1, 1, 2, 3, 5, 8, 13, \ldots$ in which each number (except for the first two) is the sum of the two preceding numbers. Write a method `fibonacci(N)` that prints the first N Fibonacci numbers.

EXERCISE 6.30   The Nuclear Regulatory Agency wants you to write a program that will help determine how long certain radioactive substances will take to decay. The program should let the user input two values: a string giving the substance's name and its half-life in years. (A substance's half-life is the number of years required for the disintegration of half of its atoms.) The program should report how many years it will take before there is less than 2 percent of the original number of atoms remaining.

EXERCISE 6.31   Modify the `CarLoan` program so that it calculates a user's car payments for loans of different interest rates and different loan periods. Let the user input the amount of the loan. Have the program output a table of monthly payment schedules.

The next chapter also contains a number of loop exercises.

Photograph courtesy of Lawrence Lawry, PhotoDisc, Inc.

7

Strings and String Processing

OBJECTIVES

After studying this chapter, you will

- Be more familiar with the string data structure.
- Know how to solve problems that involve manipulating strings.
- Be able to use loops in designing string-processing algorithms.
- Have a better understanding of how inheritance can be used in program design.

OUTLINE

7.1   Introduction

> **Inyay isthay apterchay eway illway udystay owhay otay useyay in-gsstray andyay igPay atinLay!** *Translation: In this chapter we will study how to use strings and Pig Latin!*

Remember those Pig Latin games from grade school? In this chapter we will study how to manipulate strings and how to translate normal English words into Pig Latin. To translate *string* into *ingstray*, we first divide it into the prefix *str* and the suffix *ing*. We then concatenate these in reverse order, *ing + str*, and add the new suffix *ay* to the result. This gives *ing + str + ay*, or *ingstray*.

A **data structure** is a collection of data that is organized (structured) in some way. A **string** is a collection of character (char) data. Strings are important data structures in a programming language, and they are used to represent a wide variety of data.

Programmers often have to work with strings. Think of some of the tasks performed by a typical word processor, such as cut, paste, copy, and insert. When you cut and paste text from one part of the document to another, the program has to move one string of text, the cut, from one location in the document and insert it in another.

As we have seen throughout the first few chapters, Strings are used extensively in Java interfaces as the contents of TextFields and other text components, as the values of Labels, as the labels for Buttons, and so on. Moreover, all sorts of I/O operations involve Strings, such as inputting a number either through a TextField or directly from the keyboard.

Strings are also used as a standard way of presenting or displaying objects. One of the key conventions of the Java class hierarchy is that every class inherits the Object.toString() method, which can be used to provide a string representation of any object. For example, Integer.toString() converts an int to a String, so that it can be used in TextFields or Labels.

The main purpose of this chapter is to introduce the details of Java's string-related classes, including the String, StringBuffer, and StringTokenizer classes. These are the important classes for writing string-processing applications. Our goal is to introduce the important String methods and illustrate common string-processing algorithms. We'll learn how to build strings from scratch and from other data types. We'll learn how to find characters and substrings inside bigger strings. We'll learn how to take strings apart and how to rearrange their parts. Finally, we'll learn how to apply these string-processing skills to an interesting encryption problem.

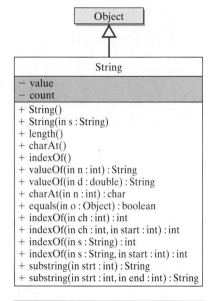

FIGURE 7–1   The java.lang.String class.

Are strings objects?

7.2   String **Basics**

In Java, Strings are considered full-fledged objects. A java.lang.String object is a sequence of characters plus a collection of methods for manipulating strings. The String class (Fig. 7.1) is a direct subclass of Object, and it contains many public methods that can be used to perform useful operations on strings. We will discuss a selection of the more commonly used methods, but for a full listing and description of the String methods see

```
http://java.sun.com/products/jdk/1.3/docs/api/
```

Like other object variables, String variables serve as *references* to their respective objects. However, unlike other Java objects, Strings have certain characteristics in common with the primitive data types. For example, strings can have literals. A **String literal** is a sequence of zero or more characters contained in double quotes—for example, "Socrates" and "" (**empty string**). Similarly, unlike other Java objects, Strings can be used in assignment statements:

```
String s = "hello";
```

7.2.1 Constructing Strings

The String class has many constructors, including the following:

```
public String();                    // Creates an empty string
public String(String initial_value);   // Creates a copy of a string
```

When we create an object using the first constructor, as in

```
String name = new String();
```

Java will create a String object and make name the reference to it (Fig. 7–2). Note that in addition to its literal value, a String object stores a count of how many characters it contains; plus, as for all other objects, a String object contains a bunch of instance methods.

When Java encounters a new literal string in a program, it constructs an object for it. For example, if your program contained the literal "Socrates," Java would create an object for it and treat the literal itself as a reference to the object (Fig. 7–3).

String literals are often used to assign a value to a String variable:

```
String s;              // The value of s is initially null
s = "Socrates";        // s now refers to the "Socrates" object
```

In this case, the reference variable *s* is initially null—that is, it has no referent. However, after the assignment statement, *s* would refer to the literal object "Socrates" that we created in Figure 7–3. Given these two statements together with the preceding declarations, we still have only one object. But now we have two references to it: the literal string "Socrates," and the reference variable *s*.

Assignment statements can also be used as initializers when declaring a String variable:

```
String name1 = "";            // Reference to the empty string
String name2 = "Socrates";    // References to "Socrates"
String name3 = "Socrates";
```

In this case, Java does not construct new String objects. Instead, it simply makes the variables name1, name2, name3 serve as references to the same objects that are referred to by the literal strings "" and "Socrates." This is a direct consequence of Java's policy of creating only one object to serve as

name : String
value = " "
count = 0

FIGURE 7–2   An empty string is a String object with value "" and count 0.

"Socrates" : String
value = "Socrates"
count = 8

FIGURE 7–3   The literal String "Socrates."

String literals

Default value

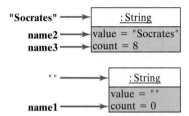

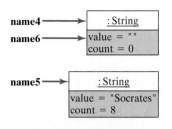

FIGURE 7–4   The variables `name1`, `name2`, `name3` serve as references to the literal `String` objects "Socrates" and "".

name4 ──────► : String
name6 ──────► value = ""
                count = 0

name5 ──────► : String
                value = "Socrates"
                count = 8

FIGURE 7–5   Together with the objects in Figure 7–4, there are now four different `String` objects with eight different references to them, including the literals "Socrates" and "".

String concatenation

Operator overloading

the referent of a literal string, no matter how many occurrences there are of that literal. Thus, these declarations result in no new objects, just new references to existing objects (Fig. 7–4).

Finally, consider the following declarations, which do invoke the `String` constructors:

```
String name4 = new String();          // Creates an object
String name5 = new String("Socrates");
String name6 = name4;
```

In this case, Java creates two new objects and sets `name4` to refer to the first and `name5` to refer to the second. It gives `name4` the empty string as its value, and it gives `name5` "Socrates" as its value. But these two objects must be distinguished from the objects corresponding to the literals ("" and "Socrates") themselves (Fig. 7–5). The declaration of `name6` just creates a second reference to the object referred to by `name4`.

> **JAVA LANGUAGE RULE**   Strings. Java `Strings` are full-fledged objects, but they have some properties in common with primitive types. They can have literal values and they can be used in assignment statements.

> **JAVA LANGUAGE RULE**   String Declaration and Instantiation. Unless a `String()` constructor is called explicitly, no new `String` object is created when declaring a `String` variable and assigning it an initial value.

7.2.2   Concatenating `Strings`

Another way to build a `String` object is to concatenate two other strings:

```
String lastName = "Onassis";
String jackie = new String("Jacqueline " + "Kennedy " + lastName);
```

The second of these statements uses the *concatenation operator*, $+$, to create the `String` "Jacqueline Kennedy Onassis."

> **JAVA LANGUAGE RULE**   String Concatenation. When surrounded on either side by a `String`, the + symbol is used as a binary **concatenation** operator. It has the effect of joining two strings together to form a single string, as in `string1 + string2 ==> string3`.

Using the + symbol as the string concatenation operator is another example of *operator overloading*—using the same operator for two or more different operations.

Note that primitive types are automatically promoted to `Strings` when they are mixed with concatenation operators. Thus, the statement

```
System.out.println("The square root of 25 = " + 5);
```

will print the string "The square root of 25 = 5." The `int` literal 5 will automatically be converted to "5" before the concatenation is done.

SELF-STUDY EXERCISES

EXERCISE 7.1   What will be printed by each of the following segments of code?

a. `String s1 = "silly"; System.out.println(s1);`
b. `String s2 = s1; System.out.println(s2);`
c. `String s3 = new String (s1 + " stuff");    System.out.println(s3);`

EXERCISE 7.2   Write a `String` declaration that satisfies each of the following descriptions:

a. Initialize a `String` variable, *str1*, to the empty string.
b. Instantiate a `String` object, *str2*, and initialize it to the word *stop*.
c. Initialize a `String` variable, *str*, to the concatenation of *str1* and *str2*.

EXERCISE 7.3   Evaluate the following expressions:

```
int M = 5, N = 10;
String s1 = "51", s2 = "75";
```

a. `M + N`   b. `M + s1`   c. `s1 + s2`

EXERCISE 7.4   Draw a picture, similar to Figure 7–5, showing the objects and references that are created by the following declarations:

```
String s1, s2 = "Hello", s3 = "Hello";
String s4 = "hello";
String s5 = new String("Hello");
String s6 = s5;
String s7 = s3;
```

Indexes
0 1 2 3 4 5 6 7
↓ ↓ ↓ ↓ ↓ ↓ ↓ ↓
S o c r a t e s

FIGURE 7–6   The string "Socrates" has eight characters, indexed from 0 to 7. This is an example of *zero indexing*.

7.2.3 **Indexing** Strings

The number of characters in a string is called its *length*. The `String` instance method, `length()`, returns an integer that gives the `String`'s length. For example, consider the following `String` declarations and the corresponding values of the `length()` method for each case:

String length

```
String string1 = "";                 string1.length()  ==> 0
String string2 = "Hello";            string2.length()  ==> 5
String string3 = "World";            string3.length()  ==> 5
String string4 = string2 + " " + string3;  string4.length()  ==> 11
```

The position of a particular character in a string is called its **index**. All `Strings` in Java are **zero indexed**—that is, the index of the first character is zero. For example, in "Socrates," the letter *S* occurs at index 0, the letter *o* occurs at index 1, *r* occurs at index 3, and so on. Thus, the `String` "Socrates" contains eight characters indexed from 0 to 7 (Fig. 7–6). Zero indexing is customary in programming languages. We will see other examples of this when we talk about arrays and vectors.

String index

> **JAVA LANGUAGE RULE**   String Indexing. Strings are indexed starting at 0. The first character in a string is at position 0. However the `String` `length()` method is **unit indexed**—that is, it starts counting at 1.

DEBUGGING TIP: Zero Versus Unit Indexing. Syntax and semantic errors will result if you forget that strings are zero indexed. In a string of N characters, the first character occurs at index 0 and the last at index $N - 1$. In contrast, a string's length is unit indexed.

7.2.4 Converting Data to `String`

The `String.valueOf()` method is a *class method* that is used to convert a value of some primitive type into a `String` object. For example, the expression, `String.valueOf(128)` converts its `int` argument to the `String` "128."

There are different versions of `valueOf()`, each of which has the following type of signature:

```
static public String valueOf(Type);
```

where `Type` stands for any primitive data type, including `boolean`, `char`, `int`, `double`, and so on.

The `valueOf()` method is most useful for initializing `Strings`. Because `valueOf()` is a class method, it can be used as follows to instantiate new `String` objects:

```
String number = new String (String.valueOf(128)); // Creates "128"
String truth = new String (String.valueOf(true)); // Creates "true"
String bee = new String (String.valueOf('B'));    // Creates "B"
String pi = new String(String.valueOf(Math.PI));  // Creates "3.14159"
```

We've already seen that Java automatically promotes primitive type values to `String` where necessary, so why do we need the `valueOf()` methods? For example, we can initialize a `String` as follows:

```
String pi = new String(Math.PI);   // Creates "3.14159"
```

The value of `Math.PI` will automatically be promoted to a `String` value. The point of the `valueOf()` method is twofold. First, it may in fact be the method that the Java compiler relies on to perform string promotions. Second, using it in a statement—even when it is not completely necessary—makes the promotion operations explicit rather than implicit. (Also, see Exercise 7.9.)

SELF-STUDY EXERCISES

EXERCISE 7.5 Evaluate each of the following expressions:

a. `String.valueOf (45)`   c. `String.valueOf ('X')`
b. `String.valueOf (128 - 7)`

EXERCISE 7.6 Write an expression to satisfy each of the following descriptions:

a. Convert the integer value 100 to the string "100".
b. Convert the character 'V' to the string "V".
c. Initialize a new String object to X times Y.

7.3   Finding Things Within a String

The indexOf() and lastIndexOf() methods are instance methods that can be used to find the index position of a character or a substring within a String. There are several versions of each:

```
public int indexOf(int character);
public int indexOf(int character, int startingIndex);
public int indexOf(String string);
public int indexOf(String string, int startingIndex);

public int lastIndexOf(int character);
public int lastIndexOf(int character, int startingIndex);
public int lastIndexOf(String string);
public int lastIndexOf(String string, int startingIndex);
```

The indexOf() method searches from left to right within a String for either a character or a substring. The lastIndexOf() method searches from right to left for a character or substring. To illustrate, suppose we have declared the following Strings:

```
String string1 = "";
String string2 = "Hello";
String string3 = "World";
String string4 = string2 + " " + string3;
```

Recalling that Strings are indexed starting at 0, searching for *o* in the various strings gives the following results:

```
string1.indexOf('o')  ==> -1      string1.lastIndexOf('o')  ==> -1
string2.indexOf('o')  ==>  4      string2.lastIndexOf('o')  ==>  4
string3.indexOf('o')  ==>  1      string3.lastIndexOf('o')  ==>  1
string4.indexOf('o')  ==>  4      string4.lastIndexOf('o')  ==>  7
```

Because string1 is the empty string, "", it does not contain the letter *o*. Therefore, indexOf() returns −1—a value that cannot be a valid index for a String. This convention is followed in indexOf() and lastIndexOf(). Because string2 and string3 each contain only one occurrence of the letter *o*, both indexOf() and lastIndexOf() return the same value when used on these Strings. Because string4 contains two occurrences of *o*, indexOf() and lastIndexOf() return different values in this case.

As Figure 7–7 shows, the first *o* in "Hello World" occurs at index 4, the value returned by indexOf(). The second *o* occurs at index 7, which is the value returned by lastIndexOf().

By default, the single-parameter versions of indexOf() and lastIndexOf() start their searches at their respective (left or right) ends of the string. The two-parameter versions of these methods allow you to specify both the direction and starting point of the search. The second parameter specifies the starting index. Consider these examples:

```
string4.indexOf('o', 5)     ==> 7
string4.lastIndexOf('o', 5) ==> 4
```

If we start searching in both cases at index 5, then indexOf() will miss the *o* that occurs at index 4. The first *o* it finds will be the one at index 7.

Sentinel return value

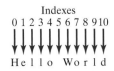

Indexes
0 1 2 3 4 5 6 7 8 9 10

H e l l o   W o r l d

FIGURE 7–7   The indexing of the "Hello World" string.

Similarly, `lastIndexOf()` will miss the *o* that occurs at index 7 and will find the *o* that occurs at index 4.

The `indexOf()` and `lastIndexOf()` methods can also be used to find substrings:

```
string1.indexOf("or")  ==> -1     string1.lastIndexOf("or") ==> -1
string2.indexOf("or")  ==> -1     string2.lastIndexOf("or") ==> -1
string3.indexOf("or")  ==>  1     string3.lastIndexOf("or") ==>  1
string4.indexOf("or")  ==>  7     string4.lastIndexOf("or") ==>  7
```

The substring "or" does not occur in either `string1` or `string2`. It does occur beginning at location 1 in `string3` and beginning at location 7 in `string4`. For this collection of examples, it doesn't matter whether we search from left to right or right to left.

SELF-STUDY EXERCISES

EXERCISE 7.7 Suppose the `String` variable s has been initialized to "mom." Evaluate each of the following expressions:

a. `s.indexOf("m");`   b. `s.indexOf("o");`   c. `s.indexOf("M");`

EXERCISE 7.8 Evaluate the expressions given the `String` declaration `String s1 = "Java, Java, Java";`

a. `s1.length()`   g. `s1.indexOf('a', 5)`
b. `String.valueOf(s1.length())`   h. `s1.lastIndexOf('a', 5)`
c. `s1.indexOf('a')`   i. `s1.indexOf("av", s1.length() - 10)`
d. `s1.lastIndexOf('a')`   j. `s1.lastIndexOf("av",`
e. `s1.indexOf("av")`   `s1.length() - 4)`
f. `s1.lastIndexOf("av")`   k. `s1.indexOf("a", s1.indexOf("va"))`

EXERCISE 7.9 Evaluate the following expression:

```
String tricky = "abcdefg01234567";
tricky.indexOf(String.valueOf( tricky.indexOf("c")));
```

7.4   Example: Keyword Search

One of the most widely used Web browser functions is the search utility. You probably know how it works. You type in a keyword and click on a button, and it returns with a list of Web pages that contain the keyword.

Suppose you were writing a browser in Java. How would you implement this function? Of course, we don't know yet how to read files or Web pages, and we won't cover that until Chapter 14. But, for now, we can write a method that will search a string for all occurrences of a given keyword. That's at least part of the task that the browser's search engine would have to do.

Method design

So we want a method, `keywordSearch()`, that takes two `String` parameters, one for the string that's being searched, and the other representing the keyword. Let's have the method return a `String` that lists the number of occurrences of the keyword, followed by the index of each occurrence. For example, if we asked this method to find all occurrences of *is* in "This is a test," it should return the string "2: 2 5" because there are two occurrences of *is*, one starting at index 2 and the other at index 5 in the string.

The algorithm for this method will require a loop, because we want to know the location of every occurrence of the keyword in the string. One way to do this would be to use the indexOf() method to search for the location of substrings in the string. If it finds the keyword at index *N*, it should record that location and then continue searching for more occurrences starting at index *N* + 1 in the string. It should continue in this way until there are no more occurrences.

Algorithm design

```
Suppose S is our string and K is the keyword.
Initialize a counter variable and result string.
Set P to the indexOf() the first occurrence of K in S.
While (P != -1)
    Increment the counter
    Insert P into the result string
    Set P to the next location of the keyword in S
Insert the count into the result string
Return the result string as a String
```

As this pseudocode shows, the algorithm uses a while loop with a *sentinel bound*. The algorithm terminates when the indexOf() method returns a −1, indicating that there are no more occurrences of the keyword in the string.

Implementation

Translating the pseudocode into Java gives us the method shown in Figure 7–8. Note how string concatenation is used to build the resultStr. Each time an occurrence is found, its location (ptr) is concatenated to the right-hand side of the resultStr. When the loop terminates, the number of occurrences (count) is concatenated to the left-hand side of the resultStr.

Testing and Debugging

What test data should we use for the keywordSearch() method? One important consideration in this case is to test that the method works on strings that contain keyword occurrences at the beginning, middle, and

What test data do we need?

```
/**
 * Pre:  s and keyword are any Strings
 * Post: keywordSearch() returns a String containing the
 *   number of occurrences of keyword in s, followed
 *   by the starting location of each occurrence
 */
public String keywordSearch(String s, String keyword) {
    String resultStr = "";
    int count = 0;
    int ptr = s.indexOf(keyword);
    while (ptr != -1) {
        ++count;
        resultStr = resultStr + ptr + " ";
        ptr = s.indexOf(keyword, ptr + 1);  // Find next occurrence
    }
    resultStr = count + ": " + resultStr;   // Insert the count
    return resultStr;                        // Return as a String
} // keywordSearch()
```

FIGURE 7–8 The keywordSearch() method.

end of the string. These will help verify that the loop will terminate properly. We should also test the method with a string that doesn't contain the keyword. Given these considerations, Table 7.1 shows the tests that were made.

TABLE 7.1 Testing the keywordSearch() method.

Test Performed	Expected Result
keywordSearch("this is a test","is")	2: 2 5
keywordSearch("able was i ere i saw elba","a")	4: 0 6 18 24
keywordSearch("this is a test","taste")	0:

Given this set of tests, the method did produce the expected outcomes. While these tests do not guarantee its correctness, they provide considerable evidence that the algorithm works correctly.

EFFECTIVE DESIGN: Test Data.   In designing test data to check the correctness of a string searching algorithm, it's important to use data that test all possible outcomes.

From the Java Library

java.lang.StringBuffer

http://java.sun.com/products /jdk/1.3/docs/api/

Built-in garbage collection

ONE PROBLEM with the keywordSearch() method is that it is not very efficient. The problem is that a String in Java is a **read-only** object. This means that once it has been instantiated, a String cannot be changed. You can't insert new characters or delete existing characters from it.

> JAVA LANGUAGE RULE   Strings Are Immutable.   Once instantiated, a Java String cannot be altered in any way.

Given this fact, how are we able to build the resultStr in the keyword-Search() method? The answer is that every time we assign a new value to resultStr, Java has to create a new String object. Thus, given the statement

```
resultStr = resultStr + ptr + " ";
```

Java will evaluate the right-hand side, creating a new String object, whose value would be the concatenation of resultStr + ptr + " " (Fig. 7–9a). It would then assign the new object as the referent of resultStr (Fig. 7–9b). This turns the previous referent of resultStr into an **orphan object**—that is, into an object that no longer has any references to it.

The fact that this assignment statement occurs within a loop means that several new objects are created and later garbage collected. Because object creation is a relatively time-consuming and memory-consuming operation, this algorithm is somewhat wasteful of Java's resources.

Of course, except for the inefficiency of doing it this way, Java's garbage collector will automatically reclaim the memory used by the orphaned object, so no real harm is done.

JAVA LANGUAGE RULE | Automatic Garbage Collection. An object that has no reference to it can no longer be used in a program. Therefore, Java will automatically get rid of it. This is known as *garbage collection*.

A more efficient way to write the `keywordSearch()` method would make use of a `StringBuffer` to store and construct the `resultStr`. The `java.lang.StringBuffer` class represents a string of characters. However, unlike the `String` class, a `StringBuffer` can be modified, and it can grow and shrink in length as necessary. As Figure 7–10 shows, the `StringBuffer` class contains several of the same kind of methods as the `String` class, for example, `charAt()` and `length()`. But it also contains methods that allow characters and other types of data to be inserted into a string, such as append(), `insert()`, and `setCharAt()`. Most string-processing algorithms use `StringBuffers` instead of `Strings` as their preferred data structure.

> **PROGRAMMING TIP: StringBuffer.** A `StringBuffer` should be used instead of a `String` for any task that involves modifying a string.

The `StringBuffer` class provides several methods that are useful for string processing. The constructor method, `StringBuffer(String)`, makes it easy to convert a `String` into a `StringBuffer`. Similarly, once you are done processing the buffer, the `toString()` method makes it easy to convert a `StringBuffer` back into a `String`.

The typical way to use a `StringBuffer` is shown in the following revised version of the `keywordSearch()` method:

```java
public String keywordSearch(String s, String keyword) {
    StringBuffer resultStr = new StringBuffer(); // Create StringBuffer
    int count = 0;
    int ptr = s.indexOf(keyword);
    while (ptr != -1) {
        ++count;
        resultStr.append(ptr + " ");  // Insert letters into it
        ptr = s.indexOf(keyword, ptr + 1);
    }
    resultStr.insert(0, count + ": ");
    return resultStr.toString();       // Convert buffer to a String
} // keywordSearch()
```

We declare `resultStr` as a `StringBuffer` instead of a `String`. Then, for each occurrence of a keyword, instead of concatenating the `ptr` and reassigning the `resultStr`, we append() the `ptr` to the `resultStr`. Similarly, after the loop exits, we insert() the count at the front (index 0) of the `resultStr`. Finally, we convert `resultStr` into a `String` by using the `toString()` method before returning the method's result.

One advantage of the `StringBuffer` class is that there are several versions of its `insert()` and `append()` methods. These make it possible to insert any type of data—int, double, Object, and so on—into a `StringBuffer`. The method itself takes care of the type conversion for us.

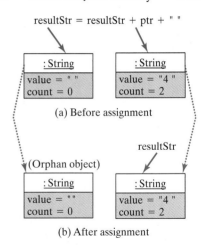

resultStr = resultStr + ptr + " "

(a) Before assignment

(b) After assignment

FIGURE 7–9 Evaluating `resultStr = resultStr + ptr + " "` creates an orphan object that must be garbage collected.

Choosing the appropriate data structure

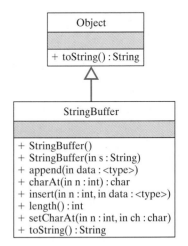

FIGURE 7–10 The `java.lang.StringBuffer` class.

Strings are immutable

To summarize, `String` objects in Java are *immutable*. So when a `String` is "modified," this really means that a new `String` object must be created and the old `String` object must be garbage collected. This is somewhat inefficient, especially if done repeatedly within a loop. To avoid these inefficiencies, use a `StringBuffer` instead of a `String` in such contexts.

7.5 Retrieving Parts of `Strings`

The `charAt(int index)` method is a `String` instance method that can be used to retrieve the character stored at a certain index. The several varieties of the `substring()` method can be used to retrieve a substring of characters from a `String`. These methods are defined as follows:

```
public char charAt(int index)
public String substring(int startIndex)
public String substring(int startIndex, int endIndex)
```

The `charAt()` method returns the character located at the index supplied as its parameter. Thus, `str.charAt(0)` retrieves the first character in `str`, while `str.charAt(str.length()-1)` retrieves the last character.

The `substring()` methods work in a similar way, except that you need to specify both the starting and the ending index of the substring you wish to retrieve. The first version of `substring(int startIndex)` takes a single parameter and returns a `String` consisting of all the characters beginning with `startIndex` and continuing up to the end of the `String`. For example, if the `str` is "HelloWorld", then `str.substring(5)` would return "World" and `str.substring(3)` would return "loWorld":

```
String str = "HelloWorld";
str.substring(5)            ==> "World"
str.substring(3)            ==> "loWorld"
```

The `substring(int, int)` version requires that you specify both the starting and ending index of the substring. Note that the second index always points to the character that is one beyond the last character in the `String` you want to retrieve. For example,

```
//   INDEX:   0123456789
String str = "HelloWorld";
str.substring(5,7)          ==> "Wo"
str.substring(0,5)          ==> "Hello"
str.substring(5, str.length())  ==> "World"
```

Note here that when we want to retrieve "Wo" from `str`, we specify its substring as indexes 5 and 7; the 7 points to the character just beyond "Wo." Similarly, `substring(0,5)`, picks out the first five characters ("Hello"). Note that in the third example the `length()` method is used to specify the substring beginning at index 5 and extending to the end of the string. This is equivalent to `str.substring(5)`:

```
//   INDEX:   0123456789
String str = "HelloWorld";
str.substring(5, str.length())  ==> "World"
str.substring(5)            ==> "World"
```

The fact that the second parameter in substring() refers to the character one beyond the desired substring may seem a bit confusing at first, but it is actually a very useful way to designate a substring. For example, many string-processing problems have to do with retrieving substrings from a *delimited string* of the form "substring1:substring2." In this case, the *delimiter* is the ':'. The following code can be used to retrieve the substring preceding the delimiter:

Delimited strings

```
String str = "substring1:substring2";
int n = str.indexOf(':');
str.substring(0,n)              ==> "substring1"
```

Thus, by making the second index of substring() refer to the character one beyond the last character in the desired substring, we can use indexOf() and substring() together to process delimited strings. Note that it is not necessary to use a temporary variable *n* to store the index of the delimiter, because the two method calls can be nested:

```
String str = "substring1:substring2";
str.substring(0,str.indexOf(':'))       ==> "substring1"
```

DEBUGGING TIP: substring(int p1, int p2). Don't forget that the second parameter in the substring() methods refers to the character just past the last character in the substring. Forgetting this fact can cause an off-by-one error.

SELF-STUDY EXERCISES

EXERCISE 7.10   Given the String declaration

```
String s = "abcdefghijklmnopqrstuvwxyz";
```

evaluate each of the following expressions:

a. s.substring(20)   d. s.substring(23, 25)
b. s.substring(1, 5)   e. s.substring(s.indexOf('x'))
c. s.substring(23)

EXERCISE 7.11   Given the preceding declaration of s, evaluate each of the following expressions:

a. s.substring(20, s.length())
b. s.substring(s.indexOf('b'), s.indexOf('f'))
c. s.substring(s.indexOf("xy"))
d. s.substring(s.indexOf(s.charAt(23)))
e. s.substring(s.length() - 3)

7.6   Example: Processing Names and Passwords

Many computer systems store user names and passwords as delimited strings, such as

```
smith:bg1s5xxx
mccarthy:2ffo900ssi
cho:biff4534ddee4w
```

Algorithm design

Obviously, if the system is going to process passwords, it needs some way to take apart these name-password pairs.

Let's write methods to help perform this task. The first method will be passed a name-password pair and will return the name. The second method will be passed a name-password pair and will return the password. In both cases, the method takes a single `String` parameter and returns a `String` result:

```
String getName(String str);
String getPassword(String str);
```

To solve this problem we can make use of two `String` methods. We use the `indexOf()` method to find the location of the *delimiter*—which is the "`:`"—in the name-password pair and then we use `substring()` to take the substring occurring before or after the delimiter. It may be easier to see this if we take a particular example:

```
INDEX:          10|        20|
INDEX:  012345678901234567890
        jones:b34rdffg12    // (1)
        cho:rtf546          // (2)
```

In the first case, the delimiter occurs at index position 5 in the string. Therefore, to take the name substring, we would use `substring(0,5)`. To take the password substring, we would use `substring(6)`. Of course, in the general case, we would use variables to indicate the position of the delimiter, as in the following methods:

```
public static String getName(String str) {
    int posColon = str.indexOf(':');          // Find the delimiter
    String result = str.substring(0, posColon); // Extract the name
    return result;
}

public static String getPassword(String str) {
    int posColon = str.indexOf(':');          // Find the delimiter
    String result = str.substring(posColon + 1); // Extract the password
    return result;
}
```

Note in both of these cases we have used local variables, `posColon` and `result`, to store the intermediate results of the computation—that is, the index of the "`:`" and the name or password substring.

An alternative way to code these operations would be to use nested method calls to reduce the code to a single line:

```
return str.substring(0, str.indexOf(':'));
```

In this line, the result of `str.indexOf(':')` is passed immediately as the second argument to `str.substring()`. This version dispenses with the need for additional variables. And the result in this case is not unreasonably complicated. But whenever you are faced with a trade-off of this sort—nesting versus additional variables—you should opt for the style that will be easier to read and understand.

EFFECTIVE DESIGN: Nested Method Calls.   Nested method calls are fine as long as there are not too many levels of nesting. The goal should be to produce code that is easy to read and understand.

7.7   Processing Each Character in a String

Many string-processing applications require you to process each character in a string. For example, to encrypt the string "hello" into "jgnnq", we have to go through each letter of the string and change each character to its substitute.

These types of algorithms usually involve a counting loop bounded by the length of the string.

Algorithm: Counting loop

Recall that the length() method determines the number of characters in a String and that strings are zero indexed. This means that the first character is at index 0, and the last character is at index length()-1. Here is an example that prints all of the characters in a String:

```
// Precondition:  str is not null
// Postcondition: the letters in str will have been printed
public void printLetters(String str) {
    for (int k = 0; k < str.length(); k++)    // For each character
        System.out.println(str.charAt(k));    //  Print it
}
```

Note that our loop bound is k < str.length(), since the index of the last character of any String is length()-1. Note also the use of str.charAt(k) to retrieve the *k*th character in str on each iteration of the loop.

Counting bound

Note the use of pre- and postconditions in the method's documentation. The precondition states that str has been properly initialized—that is, it is not null. The postcondition merely states the expected behavior of the method.

7.7.1   Off-by-One Error

A frequent error in coding counter-controlled loops is known as the **off-by-one error**, which can occur in many different ways. For example, if we had coded the loop boundary condition as k <= str.length(), this would cause an off-by-one error, because the last character in str is at location length()-1. This would lead to a Java IndexOutOfBoundsException, which would be reported as soon as the program executed this statement.

Off-by-one error

The only way to avoid off-by-one errors is to check your loop bounds whenever you code a loop. Always make sure you have the loop counter's initial and final values correct.

DEBUGGING TIP: Off-by-One Errors. Loops should be carefully checked to make sure they don't commit an off-by-one error. During program testing, test data should be developed to test the loop bound's initial and final values.

FIGURE 7–11 A method to count the occurrence of a particular character in a string.

```
// Precondition: Neither str nor ch are null
// Postcondition: countchar() == the number of ch in str
public int countChar(String str, char ch) {
    int counter = 0;                        // Initialize a counter
    for (int k = 0; k < str.length(); k++)  // For each character
        if (str.charAt(k) == ch)            //  If it's a ch
            counter++;                      //    count it
    return counter;                         // Return the result
}
```

7.7.2 Example: Counting Characters

As another example of an algorithm that processes each character in a string, consider the problem of computing the frequency of the letters in a given document. Certain text analysis programs perform this type of function.

Method design

The countChar() method will count the number of occurrences of any particular character in a String (Fig. 7–11). This method takes two parameters: a String parameter that stores the string being searched and a char parameter that stores the character being counted.

Algorithm design

It begins by initializing the local variable, counter, to 0. As in the previous example, the for loop here will iterate through each character of the String—from 0 to length()-1. On each iteration a check is made to see if the character in the *k*th position (str.charAt(k)) is the character being counted. If so, counter is incremented. The method ends by returning counter, which, when the method completes, will store an integer representing the number of *ch*'s in str.

7.8 CASE STUDY: Silly CyberPet String Tricks

Many string-processing tasks involve iterating through each character of the string and converting it in some way. We'll use our CyberPet to illustrate these kinds of algorithms.

The last time we left our CyberPet it was just eating and sleeping, although its eating was becoming quite animated! Suppose now we want to give the pet some clever String tricks to perform. These are like card tricks, but they use Strings instead of cards. What they all have in common is that they change the original string into a different string. You might think of these as CyberPet's attempt at a pun!

One way to give our CyberPet this new capability is to create a String-Tricks class. We'll define a bunch of different string tricks and let the CyberPet pull one out of the bag each time the user asks for one. By encapsulating all the tricks in StringTricks, we not only organize them into a single, well-focused class, but we also avoid cluttering up the CyberPet class with too many additional methods.

Problem decomposition

7.8.1 Class Design: StringTricks

What data and methods do we need?

For starters, let's put three tricks (methods) into StringTricks: a method to reverse a string, a method to change each letter of a string to UPPERCASE, and a method to capitalize the first letter of a string. Each of these methods will take a String parameter and return a String result.

In addition to the tricks themselves, let's write a method to get one of the tricks from the repertoire. The getNextTrick() method will decide which trick to perform and then simply invoke it. To help with this task, let's give the StringTricks class a nextTrick variable, which will keep track of the next trick to perform.

Given these considerations, we get the design for the StringTricks class shown in Figure 7–12.

7.8.2 Method Design: getNextTrick()

The getNextTrick() method should take its String parameter and simply pass it to the method whose turn it is, getting back a result string that will be returned to CyberPet. It must also update the nextTrick variable. The algorithm for this method uses a multiway selection structure to choose among the available tricks:

```
/**
 * Pre:  s is any non null string
 * Post: A trick is picked and s is transformed and returned
 *       The nextTrick variable is incremented modulo NTRICKS
 */
public String getNextTrick(String s) {
    String result = new String();        // Stores the result
    if (nextTrick == 0)                   // Do the next trick
        result = reverse(s);
    else if (nextTrick == 1)
        result = capitalize(s);
    else
        result = toUpperCase(s);
    nextTrick = (nextTrick + 1) % NTRICKS; // Update for next time
    return result;
} // getNextTrick()
```

Note how modular arithmetic is used here to increment the nextTrick variable. If NTRICKS is 3, then once nextTrick reaches 2, the expression (nextTrick + 1) % NTRICKS will wrap around to 0. This allows nextTrick to cycle between the values 0, 1,...NTRICKS-1, which are the numbers of the available tricks.

7.8.3 Method Design: reverse()

The reverse() method should use a simple counting loop to reverse the letters in its String parameter. If the loop iterates from the last character to the first, then we can just append each character, left to right, in the result string. As in the other string-manipulation algorithms—for example, keywordSearch()—we should us a StringBuffer to store the method's result:

```
/**
 * Pre:  s is any non null string
 * Post: s is returned in reverse order
 */
public String reverse(String s) {
    StringBuffer result = new StringBuffer();
    for (int k = s.length()-1; k >= 0; k--) {
        result.append(s.charAt(k));
    } //for
    return result.toString();
} // reverse()
```

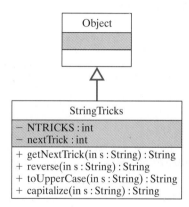

FIGURE 7–12 Design of the StringTricks class.

What control structure do we need?

Modular arithmetic

Algorithm design

Note how the `result` `StringBuffer` is declared at the beginning of the method and then converted back into a `String` at the end of the method.

PROGRAMMING TIP: Changing Each Character in a String.   Algorithms that require you to alter a string should use a `StringBuffer` to store the result.

7.8.4   Method Design: `toUpperCase()`

Algorithm design

The `toUpperCase()` method should use a simple counting loop algorithm to convert each letter in the `String` parameter to uppercase. Recall from Chapter 5 that we wrote the following method to perform this kind of character conversion:

```java
private char toUpperCase (char ch) {
    if ((ch >= 'a') && (ch <= 'z'))
        return (char)(ch - 32);      // Explicit cast required
    return ch;
}
```

Note the use of the cast operation in this method.

Since we'll be performing this kind of conversion repeatedly, we might as well add this method to our class. Note that we declare this method as a `private` utility method because it will not be used outside the class. While we're at it, we might as well add a method to convert characters to lowercase:

```java
private char toLowerCase (char ch) {
    if ((ch >= 'A') && (ch <= 'Z'))
        return (char)(ch + 32);      // Explicit cast required
    return ch;
}
```

Given these utility methods, it is now very simple to write the method to convert a string to uppercase. Like the `reverse()` method, it should use a `StringBuffer` for its result. It should iterate from 0 to `s.length()`-1, using the `charAt()` method to extract each character from the string and convert it to uppercase:

```java
/**
 * Pre:  s is any non NULL string
 * Post: Each letter in s is converted to UPPERCASE
 */
public String toUpperCase(String s) {
    StringBuffer result = new StringBuffer();
    for (int k = 0; k < s.length(); k++) {
        result.append(toUpperCase(s.charAt(k)));
    } //for
    return result.toString();
} // toUpperCase()
```

Note that we have two methods named `toUpperCase()`. This is okay because the methods have different signatures. One method takes a `char` parameter and one takes a `String` parameter. So Java will have no trouble distinguishing them.

7.8.5   **Method Design:** `capitalize()`

The `capitalize()` method should return a `String` whose initial letter is capitalized but whose other letters are lowercase – for example, "Hello". We can use our `toUpperCase(char)` method to capitalize its first letter. Then we can loop through the remaining letters converting each to lowercase:

Algorithm design

```
/**
 * Pre:  s is any non null string
 * Post: s is returned with only its initial letter capitalized
 */
public String capitalize(String s) {
    if (s.length() == 0)                    // Special case: empty string
        return s;
    StringBuffer result = new StringBuffer();
    result.append(toUpperCase(s.charAt(0)));
                                            // Convert the first letter
    for (int k = 1; k < s.length(); k++) { // Convert the rest
        result.append(toLowerCase(s.charAt(k)));
    } //for
    return result.toString();
} // capitalize()
```

The complete implementation of the `StringTricks` class is shown in Figure 7–13.

SELF-STUDY EXERCISES

EXERCISE 7.12   Show the changes necessary to incorporate `StringTricks` into the CyberPet's repertoire. Start by add a `TRICKING` state and a `trick (String)` method. Then add an instance variable for the pet's bag of tricks.

EXERCISE 7.13   Given the changes to `CyberPet` in the previous exercise, modify the `AnimatedCyberPet` applet (Fig. 6–10) so that the user can ask it to do a string trick. Use a `TextField`, with its own `ActionListener`, to input the user's string and to show the altered string.

EXERCISE 7.14   Add a method to the `StringTricks` class that will remove any blanks from a string. It should take a `String` parameter and should return a `String` result.

7.8.6   **Miscellaneous** `String` **Methods**

In addition to the several `String` class methods we have discussed— `valueOf()`, `equals()`, `indexOf()`, `lastIndexOf()`, `charAt()`, `substring()`— Table 7.2 shows some of the other useful methods in the `String` class. Note that because of what we said about the read-only nature of `Strings`, methods such as `toUpperCase()`, `toLowerCase()`, and `trim()` do not change their string. Instead they produce a new string. If you want to use one of these methods to convert a string, you must reassign its result back to the original string:

```
String s = new String("hello world");
s = s.toUpperCase();               // s now equals "HELLO WORLD"
```

FIGURE 7-13 Definition of the StringTricks class, Part I.

```java
public class StringTricks {
    public static final int NTRICKS = 3;
    public static int nextTrick = 0;
    /**
     * Pre:  s is any non null string
     * Post: A trick is picked and s is transformed and returned
     *       The nextTrick variable is incremented modulo NTRICKS
     */
    public String getNextTrick(String s) {
        String result = new String();         // Stores the result
        if (nextTrick == 0)                    // Do the next trick
            result = reverse(s);
        else if (nextTrick == 1)
            result = capitalize(s);
        else
            result = toUpperCase(s);
        nextTrick = (nextTrick + 1) % NTRICKS; // Update for next time
        return result;
    } // getNextTrick()
    /**
     * Pre: ch is any character
     * Post: if ch is between A to Z, it is converted to lower case
     */
    private char toLowerCase (char ch) {
        if ((ch >= 'A') && (ch <= 'Z'))
            return (char)(ch + 32);       // Explicit cast required
        return ch;
    }
    /**
     * Pre: ch is any character
     * Post: if ch is between a to z, it is converted to lower case
     */
    private char toUpperCase (char ch) {
        if ((ch >= 'a') && (ch <= 'z'))
            return (char)(ch - 32);       // Explicit cast required
        return ch;
    }
```

7.9 Comparing Strings

Strings are compared according to their lexicographic order. For the letters of the alphabet, lexicographic order just means alphabetical order. Thus, *a* comes before *b* and *d* comes after *c*. The string "hello" comes before "jello" because *h* comes before *j* in the alphabet.

For Java and other programming languages, the definition of lexicographic order is extended to cover all the characters that make up the character set. We know, for example, that in Java's Unicode character set the uppercase letters come before the lowercase letters (Table 5.11). Therefore, the letter *H* comes before the letter *h* and the letter *Z* comes before the letter *a*.

H precedes h

Lexicographic order can be extended to include strings of characters. Thus, "Hello" precedes "hello" in lexicographic order because its first letter, *H*, precedes the first letter, *h*, in "hello." Similarly, the string "Zero"

```
/**
 * Pre:  s is any non null string
 * Post: s is returned in reverse order
 */
public String reverse(String s) {
    StringBuffer result = new StringBuffer();
    for (int k = s.length() -1; k >= 0; k--) {
        result.append(s.charAt(k));
    } //for
    return result.toString();
} // reverse()
/**
 * Pre:  s is any non null string
 * Post: s is returned with only its initial letter capitalized
 */
public String capitalize(String s) {
    if (s.length() == 0)        // Special case: empty string
        return s;
    StringBuffer result = new StringBuffer();
                                // Convert  first letter
    result.append(toUpperCase(s.charAt(0)));
    for (int k = 1; k < s.length(); k++) { // Convert the rest
        result.append(toLowerCase(s.charAt(k)));
    } //for
    return result.toString();
} // capitalize()
/**
 * Pre:  s is any non NULL string
 * Post: Each letter in s is converted to UPPERCASE
 */
public String toUpperCase(String s) {
    StringBuffer result = new StringBuffer();
    for (int k = 0; k < s.length(); k++) {
        result.append(toUpperCase(s.charAt(k)));
    } //for
    return result.toString();
} // toUpperCase()
} // StringTricks
```

FIGURE 7–13 *(continued)*
StringTricks, Part II.

comes before "aardvark," because *Z* comes before *a*. To determine lexicographic order for strings, we must perform a character-by-character comparison, starting at the first character and proceeding left to right. As an
example, the following strings are arranged in lexicographic order:

```
"" "!" "0" "A" "Andy" "Z" "Zero" "a" "an" "and" "andy" "candy" "zero"
```

We can define **lexicographic order** for strings as follows:

> **JAVA LANGUAGE RULE** Lexicographic Order. For strings *s1* and *s2*, *s1*
> precedes *s2* in lexicographic order if its first character precedes the first
> character of *s2*. If their first characters are equal, then *s1* precedes *s2* if
> its second character precedes the second character of *s2*; and so on. An
> empty string is handled as a special case, preceding all other strings.

TABLE 7.2   Some useful `String` methods applied to the literal string "Perfection."

Method Signature	Example
`boolean endsWith(String suffix)`	`"Perfection".endsWith("tion")` ⇒ true
`boolean startsWith(String prefix)`	`"Perfection".startsWith("Per")` ⇒ true
`boolean startsWith(String prefix, int offset)`	`"Perfection".startsWith("fect",3)` ⇒ true
`String toUpperCase()`	`"Perfection".toUpperCase()` ⇒ "PERFECTION"
`String toLowerCase()`	`"Perfection".toLowerCase()` ⇒ "perfection"
`String trim()`	`"Perfection".trim()` ⇒ "Perfection"

Perhaps a more precise way to define lexicographic order is to define a Java method:

```
public boolean precedes(String s1, String s2) {
    int minlen = Math.min(s1.length(), s2.length()); // Pick shorter length
    for (int k=0; k < minlen; k++) { // For each char in shorter string
        if (s1.charAt(k) != s2.charAt(k)) //   If chars unequal
                                    // return true if s1's char precedes s2's
            return s1.charAt(k) < s2.charAt(k);
    }
    return s1.length() < s2.length();  // If all characters so far are equal
} // precedes()                        // then s1 < s2 if it is shorter than s2
```

Algorithm: Loop bound

This method does a character-by-character comparison of the two strings, proceeding left to right, starting at the first character in both strings. Its for loop uses a counting bound, which starts at *k* equal to zero and counts up to the length of the shorter string. This is an important point in designing this algorithm. If you don't stop iterating when you get past the last character in a string, your program will generate a `StringIndexOutOfBounds` exception. To prevent this error, we need to use the shorter length as the loop bound.

Note that the loop will terminate early if it finds that the respective characters from *s1* and *s2* are unequal. In that case, *s1* precedes *s2* if *s1*'s *k*th character precedes *s2*'s. If the loop terminates normally, that means that all the characters compared were equal. In that case, the shorter string precedes the longer. For example, if the two strings were "alpha" and "alphabet," then the method would return true, because "alpha" is shorter than "alphabet."

SELF-STUDY EXERCISES

EXERCISE 7.15   Arrange the following strings in lexicographic order:

```
zero bath bin alpha Alpha Zero Zeroes a A z Z
```

EXERCISE 7.16   Modify the `precedes()` method so that it will also return true when *s1* and *s2* are equal—for example, when *s1* and *s2* are both "hello".

7.9.1   Object Identity Versus Object Equality

Java provides several methods for comparing `Strings`:

```
public boolean equals(Object anObject); // Overrides Object.equals()
public boolean equalsIgnoreCase(String  anotherString);
public int compareTo(String  anotherString);
```

The first comparison method, `equals()`, overrides the `Object.equals()` method. Two `String`s are equal if they have the exact same letters in the exact same order. Thus, for the following declarations,

```
String s1 = "hello";
String s2 = "Hello";
```

`s1.equals(s2)` is `false`, but `s1.equals("hello")` is `true`.

Equality vs. identity

You have to be careful when using Java's `equals()` method. According to the default definition of `equals()`, defined in the `Object` class, "equals" means "identical." Two `Object`s are equal only if their names are references to the same object.

This is like the old story of the morning star and the evening star, which were thought to be different objects before it was discovered that both were just the planet Venus. After the discovery, it was clear that "the morning star" and "the evening star" and "Venus" were just three different references to one and the same object (Fig. 7–14).

We can create an analogous situation in Java by using the following `Button` definitions:

```
Button b1 = new Button("a");
Button b2 = new Button("a");
Button b3 = b2;
```

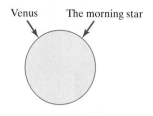

FIGURE 7–14   Venus is the morning star, so "Venus" and "the morning star" are two references to the same object.

Given these three declarations, `b1.equals(b2)` and `b1.equals(b3)` would be `false`, but `b2.equals(b3)` would be `true` because *b2* and *b3* are just two names for the same object (Fig. 7–15). So, in this case, "equals" really means "identical."

Moreover, in Java the equality operator (`==`) is interpreted in the same way as the default `Object.equals()` method. So it really means object identity. Thus, `b1 == b2` and `b1 == b3` would be `false` and `b2 == b3` would be `true`.

Object identity

These points are illustrated in the program shown in Figure 7–16. The program uses methods `isEquals()` and `isIdentical()` to perform the comparisons and print the results. Its output is as follows:

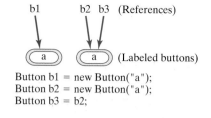

FIGURE 7–15   For most objects, equality means identity. Buttons b2 and b3 are identical (and, hence, equal), but Buttons b1 and b2 are not identical (and, hence, unequal).

```
java.awt.Button[button0,0,0,0x0,invalid,label=a]
   does NOT equal java.awt.Button[button1,0,0,0x0,invalid,label=b]
java.awt.Button[button0,0,0,0x0,invalid,label=a]
   does NOT equal java.awt.Button[button1,0,0,0x0,invalid,label=b]
java.awt.Button[button1,0,0,0x0,invalid,label=b]
   equals java.awt.Button[button1,0,0,0x0,invalid,label=b]
java.awt.Button[button0,0,0,0x0,invalid,label=a]
   is NOT identical to java.awt.Button[button1,0,0,0x0,invalid,label=b]
java.awt.Button[button0,0,0,0x0,invalid,label=a]
   is NOT identical to java.awt.Button[button1,0,0,0x0,invalid,label=b]
java.awt.Button[button1,0,0,0x0,invalid,label=b]
   is identical to java.awt.Button[button1,0,0,0x0,invalid,label=b]
```

```
import java.awt.*;

public class TestEquals {
    static Button b1 = new Button ("a");
    static Button b2 = new Button ("b");
    static Button b3 = b2;

    private static void isEqual(Object o1, Object o2) {
        if (o1.equals(o2))
            System.out.println(o1.toString() + " equals " + o2.toString());
        else
            System.out.println(o1.toString() + " does NOT equal " + o2.toString());
    } // isEqual()

    private static void isIdentical(Object o1, Object o2) {
        if (o1 == o2)
            System.out.println(o1.toString() + " is identical to " + o2.toString());
        else
            System.out.println(o1.toString() + " is NOT identical to " + o2.toString());
    } // isIdentical()

    public static void main(String argv[]) {
        isEqual(b1, b2);         // not equal
        isEqual(b1, b3);         // not equal
        isEqual(b2, b3);         // equal

        isIdentical(b1, b2);     // not identical
        isIdentical(b1, b3);     // not identical
        isIdentical(b2, b3);     // identical
    } // main()
} // TestEquals
```

FIGURE 7–16   The TestEquals program tests Java's default equals() method, which is defined in the Object class.

7.9.2 String **Identity Versus** String **Equality**

Equality vs. identity

In comparing Java Strings, we must be careful to distinguish between object identity and string equality. Thus, consider the following declarations, which create the situation shown in Figure 7–17.

```
String s1 = new String("hello");
String s2 = new String("hello");
String s3 = new String("Hello");
String s4 = s1;                  // s1 and s4 are now identical
String s5 = "hello";
String s6 = "hello";
```

Given these declarations, we would get the following results if we compare the equality of the Strings:

```
s1.equals(s2) ==> true      s1.equalsIgnoreCase(s3) ==> true
s1.equals(s3) ==> false     s1.equals(s5)           ==> true
s1.equals(s4) ==> true      s1.equals(s6)           ==> true
```

and the following results if we compare their identity:

```
s1 == s2  ==> false      s1 == s3  ==> false
s1 == s4  ==> true       s1 == s5  ==> false
s5 == s6  ==> true
```

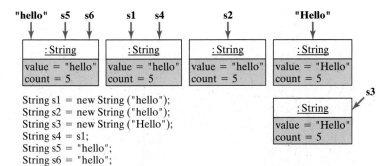

String s1 = new String ("hello");
String s2 = new String ("hello");
String s3 = new String ("Hello");
String s4 = s1;
String s5 = "hello";
String s6 = "hello";

FIGURE 7–17 For String objects, equality and identity are different. Two distinct (nonidentical) String objects are equal if they store the same string value. So s1, s2, s4, s5, and s6 are equal. Strings s1 and s4 are identical, and so are strings s5 and s6.

The only true identities among these Strings are *s1* and *s4*, and *s5* and *s6*. In the case of *s5* and *s6*, both are just references to the literal string, "hello", as we described in Section 7.2. The program in Figure 7–18 illustrates these points. Its output is

```
PROGRAM OUTPUT : :::::::::::::::::::::::::::::::
   hello equals hello
   hello does not equal Hello
   hello equals hello
   hello equals hello
   hello equals hello
   hello is not identical to hello
   hello is not identical to Hello
   hello is identical to hello
   hello is not identical to hello
   hello is identical to hello
END OUTPUT : :::::::::::::::::::::::::::::::::::
```

SELF-STUDY EXERCISES

EXERCISE 7.17 Given the String declarations,

```
String s1 = "java", s2 = "java", s3 = "Java";
String s4 = new String(s2);
String s5 = new String("java");
```

evaluate the following expressions:

a. s1 == s2   d. s1.equals(s3)   g. s2 == s4
b. s1.equals(s2)   e. s2 == s3   h. s1 == s5
c. s1 == s3   f. s2.equals(s4)   i. s4 == s5

EXERCISE 7.18 Why are the variables in TestStringEquals declared static?

EXERCISE 7.19 Given the following declarations,

```
String s1 = "abcdefghijklmnopqrstuvwxyz";
String s2 = "hello world";
```

write Java expressions to carry out each of the following operations:

a. Swap the front and back half of s1 giving a new string.
b. Swap "world" and "hello" in s2 giving a new string.
c. Combine parts of s1 and s2 to create a new string "hello abc".

```java
import java.awt.*;

public class TestStringEquals {
    static String s1 = new String("hello"); // s1 and s2 are equal, not identical
    static String s2 = new String("hello");
    static String s3 = new String("Hello"); // s1 and s3 are not equal
    static String s4 = s1;                   // s1 and s4 are identical
    static String s5 = "hello";              // s1 and s5 are not identical
    static String s6 = "hello";              // s5 and s6 are identical

    private static void testEqual(String str1, String str2) {
        if (str1.equals(str2))
            System.out.println(str1 + " equals " + str2);
        else
            System.out.println(str1 + " does not equal " + str2);
    } // testEqual()

    private static void testIdentical(String str1, String str2) {
        if (str1 == str2)
            System.out.println(str1 + " is identical to " + str2);
        else
            System.out.println(str1 + " is not identical to " + str2);
    } // testIdentical()

    public static void main(String argv[]) {
        testEqual(s1, s2);        // equal
        testEqual(s1, s3);        // not equal
        testEqual(s1, s4);        // equal
        testEqual(s1, s5);        // equal
        testEqual(s5, s6);        // equal

        testIdentical(s1, s2);    // not identical
        testIdentical(s1, s3);    // not identical
        testIdentical(s1, s4);    // identical
        testIdentical(s1, s5);    // not identical
        testIdentical(s5, s6);    // identical
    } // main()
}// TestStringEquals
```

FIGURE 7–18   Program illustrating the difference between string equality and identity.

ONE OF THE most widespread string-processing tasks is that of breaking up a string into its components or **tokens**. For example, when processing a sentence, you may need to break the sentence into its constituent words. When processing a name-password string, such as "boyd:14irXp", you may need to break it into a name and a password.

Java's java.util.StringTokenizer class is specially designed for breaking strings into their tokens (Fig. 7–19). When instantiated with a String parameter, a StringTokenizer breaks the string into *tokens*, using *white space* (blanks, tabs, and line feeds) as *delimiters*. For example, if we instantiated a StringTokenizer as in the code

From the Java Library

java.util. StringTokenizer

 http://java.sun.com/products /jdk/1.3/docs/api/

```
StringTokenizer sTokenizer
  = new StringTokenizer("This is an English sentence.");
```

it would break the string into the following tokens, which would be stored internally in the StringTokenizer in the order shown:

```
This
is
an
English
sentence.
```

Note that the period is part of the last token ("sentence."). This is because punctuation marks are not considered delimiters by default.

If you wanted to include punctuation symbols as delimiters, you could use the second StringTokenizer() constructor, which takes a second String parameter (Fig. 7–19). The second parameter specifies a string of those characters that should be used as delimiters. For example, in the instantiation,

```
StringTokenizer sTokenizer
    = new StringTokenizer("This is an English sentence.", "\b\t\n,;.!");
```

various punctuation symbols (periods, commas, and so on) are included among the delimiters. Note that escape sequences (\b\t\n) are used to specify blanks, tabs, and newlines.

The hasMoreTokens() and nextToken() methods can be used to process a delimited string, one token at a time. The first method returns true as long as more tokens remain; the second gets the next token in the list. For example, here's a code segment that will break a standard URL string into its constituent parts:

```
String url = "http://troy.trincoll.edu/~jjj/index.html";
StringTokenizer sTokenizer = new StringTokenizer( url,":/" );
while (sTokenizer.hasMoreTokens()) {
    System.out.println(sTokenizer.nextToken());
}
```

This code segment will produce the following output:

```
http
troy.trincoll.edu
~jjj
index.html
```

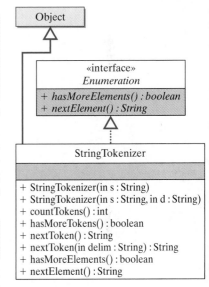

FIGURE 7–19   The java.util.StringTokenizer class.

The only delimiters used in this case were the ":" and "/" symbols. And note that `nextToken()` does not return the empty string between ":" and "/" as a token.

Historical Cryptography

Transposition cipher

Substitution cipher

CRYPTOGRAPHY, the study of secret writing, has had a long and interesting history. Modern-day cryptographic techniques employ sophisticated mathematics to *encrypt* and *decrypt* messages. Today's most secure encryption schemes are safe from attack by even the most powerful computers. Given our widespread dependence on computers and the Internet, secure encryption has become an important application area within computer science. The cryptographic techniques used up through World War II are too simple to serve as the basis for modern-day encryption schemes, but they provide an interesting and accessible introduction to this important area of computer science.

One of the earliest and simplest *ciphers* is the Caesar cipher, used by Julius Caesar during the Gallic wars. According to this scheme, letters of the alphabet are *shifted* by three letters, wrapping around at the end of the alphabet:

```
PlainText: abcdefghijklmnopqrstuvwxyz
CaesarShifted: defghijklmnopqrstuvwxyzabc
```

When encrypting a message, you take each letter of the message and replace it with its corresponding letter from the shifted alphabet. To decrypt a secret message, you perform the operation in reverse—that is, you take the letter from the shifted alphabet and replace it with the corresponding letter from the **plaintext** alphabet. Thus, "hello" would be Caesar encrypted as "khoor."

The Caesar cipher is a **substitution cipher**, because each letter in the plaintext message is replaced with a substitute letter from the **ciphertext** alphabet. A more general form of a substitution cipher uses a *keyword* to create a ciphertext alphabet:

```
PlainText: abcdefghijklmnopqrstuvwxyz
Ciphertext: xylophneabcdfgijkmqrstuvwz
```

In this example, the keyword "xylophone," (with the second *o* removed) is used to set up a substitution alphabet. According to this cipher, the word "hello" would be encrypted as "epddi." Substitution ciphers of this form are found frequently in cryptogram puzzles in the newspapers.

Another type of cipher is known as a **transposition cipher**. In this type of cipher, instead of replacing the letters in a message with substitutes, we rearrange the letters in some methodical way. A simple example would be if we reversed the letters in each word so that "hello" became "olleh." Another technique might rotate the letters of the word by a fixed number of characters, wrapping around to the beginning if necessary. Thus, "hello" would become "lohel," if we shifted each character within the word two places to the right.

OBJECT-ORIENTED DESIGN:
The abstract Cipher Class

Using Inheritance to Define Ciphers

Suppose we wish to design a collection of cipher classes, including a Caesar cipher and a transposition cipher. Because the basic operations used in all forms of encryption are the same, both the `Caesar` class and the `Transpose` class will have methods to `encrypt()` and `decrypt()` messages, where each message is assumed to be a string of words separated by spaces. These methods will take a `String` of words and translate each word using the encoding method that is appropriate for that cipher. Therefore, in addition to `encrypt()` and `decrypt()`, each cipher class will need polymorphic `encode()` and `decode()` methods, which take a single word and encode or decode it according to the rules of that particular cipher.

From a design perspective the `encrypt()` and `decrypt()` methods will be the same for every class: They simply break the message into words and encode or decode each word. However, the `encode()` and `decode()` methods will be different for each different cipher. The `Caesar.encode()` method should replace each letter of a word with its substitute, whereas the `Transpose.encode()` method should rearrange the letters of the word. Given these considerations, how should we design this set of classes?

Because all of the various ciphers will have the same methods, it will be helpful to define a common `Cipher` superclass (Fig. 7–20). `Cipher` will encapsulate those features that the individual cipher classes have in common—the `encrypt()`, `decrypt()`, `encode()`, and `decode()` methods.

Some of these methods can be implemented in the `Cipher` class itself. For example, the `encrypt()` method should take a message in a `String` parameter, encode each word in the message, and return a `String` result. The following method definition will work for any cipher:

Problem decomposition

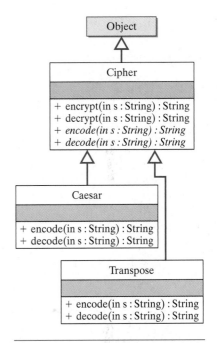

FIGURE 7–20   A hierarchy of cipher classes. The `Cipher` class implements operations common to all ciphers. The `Caesar` and `Transpose` classes implement functions unique to those kinds of ciphers.

```
public String encrypt(String s) {
    StringBuffer result = new StringBuffer("");
    StringTokenizer words = new StringTokenizer(s); // Tokenize s
    while (words.hasMoreTokens()) {                 // Encode each
        result.append(encode(words.nextToken()) + " "); // word in s
    }
    return result.toString();                       // Return result
} // encrypt()
```

This method creates a local `StringBuffer` variable, `result`, and uses `StringTokenizer` to break the original `String` into its component words. It uses the `encode()` method to encode the word, appending the result into `result`. The result is converted back into a `String` and returned as the encrypted translation of *s*, the original message.

If we define `encrypt()` in the superclass, it will be inherited by all of `Cipher`'s subclasses. Thus, if we define `Caesar` and `Transpose` as

Inheritance

```
public class Caesar extends Cipher { ... }
public class Transpose extends Cipher { ... }
```

instances of these classes will be able to use the `encrypt()` method.

Abstract method

On the other hand, the polymorphic encode() method cannot be implemented within Cipher. This is because unlike the encrypt() method, which is the same for every Cipher subclass, the encode() method will be different for every subclass. Fortunately, Java allows us to define a method without implementing it by declaring the method abstract. An abstract method has no body. It is defined by providing its signature followed by a semicolon. Thus, within the Cipher class, we would define encode() and decode() as follows:

```
public abstract String encode(String word); // Abstract method
public abstract String decode(String word); // Abstract method
```

Note here that the semicolon replaces the method's body. This declaration, within the Cipher class, tells the compiler that this method will be implemented within Cipher's subclasses. By defining it as abstract, encode() can be used within the Cipher class, as it was within the encrypt() method earlier.

Rules for Abstract Methods and Classes

Java has the following rules on using abstract methods and classes:

- Any class containing an abstract method must be declared an abstract class.
- An abstract class cannot be instantiated. It must be subclassed.
- A subclass of an abstract class may be instantiated only if it implements *all* of the superclass's abstract methods. A subclass that implements only some of the abstract methods must itself be declared abstract.
- A class may be declared abstract even it contains no abstract methods. It could, for example, contain instance variables that are common to all its subclasses.

We've seen other examples of abstract classes and interfaces. The Action-Listener interface, introduced in Chapter 4, is an example of an abstract interface. It defines but does not implement the actionPerformed() method, which must be implemented in any class that implements the interface. The Image class (see "From the Java Library" in Chapter 4) is an example of an abstract class.

Class Design: Caesar

Figure 7–21 provides the full definition of the Cipher class. The encode() and decode() methods are declared abstract. They are intended to be implemented by Cipher's subclasses.

encode() and decode() are polymorphic

Note that encrypt() and decrypt(), which are implemented in Cipher, invoke encode() and decode(), respectively, which are declared in Cipher but implemented in Cipher's subclasses. The compiler will take care of invoking the appropriate implementation of encode() or decode(), depending on what type of object is involved. For example, if caesar and transpose are Caesar and Transpose objects, respectively, then the following calls to encrypt() will cause their respective encode() methods to be invoked:

```
caesar.encrypt("hello world");      // Invokes caesar.encode()
transpose.encrypt("hello world");   // Invokes transpose.encode()
```

```
import java.util.*;

public abstract class Cipher {

    public String encrypt(String s) {
        StringBuffer result = new StringBuffer("");         // Use a StringBuffer
        StringTokenizer words = new StringTokenizer(s);     // Break s into its words
        while (words.hasMoreTokens()) {                     // For each word in s
            result.append(encode(words.nextToken()) + " "); //   Encode it
        }
        return result.toString();                           // Return the result
    } // encrypt()

    public String decrypt(String s) {
        StringBuffer result = new StringBuffer("");         // Use a StringBuffer
        StringTokenizer words = new StringTokenizer(s);     // Break s into words
        while (words.hasMoreTokens()) {                     // For each word in s
            result.append(decode(words.nextToken()) + " "); //   Decode it
        }
        return result.toString();                           // Return the decryption
    } // decrypt()

    public abstract String encode(String word);             // Abstract methods
    public abstract String decode(String word);
} // Cipher
```

FIGURE 7–21   The abstract Cipher class.

When caesar.encrypt() is called, it will in turn invoke caesar.encode()—
that is, it will call the encode() method implemented in the Caesar class.
When transpose.encrypt() is invoked, it will in turn invoke trans-
pose.encode(). In this way, each object can perform the encoding algorithm appropriate for its type of cipher.

Method polymorphism

Algorithm Design: Shifting Characters

The Caesar class is defined as an extension of Cipher (Fig. 7–22). The only
methods implemented in Caesar are encode() and decode(). The encode()
method takes a String parameter and returns a String result. It takes each
character of its parameter (word.charAt(k)) and performs a Caesar shift on
the character. Note how the shift is done:

```
ch = (char)('a' + (ch -'a'+ 3) % 26);  //  Perform Caesar shift
```

Recall from Chapter 5 that char data in Java are represented as 16-bit integers. This enables us to manipulate characters as numbers. Thus, to shift
a character by 3, we simply add 3 to its integer representation.

For example, suppose that the character (ch) is *h*, which has an ASCII
code of 104 (see Table 5.11). We want to shift it by 3, giving *k*, which has
a code of 107. In this case, we could simply add 3 to 104 to get the desired result. However, suppose that ch was the character *y*, which has an
ASCII code of 121. If we simply add 3 in this case, we get 124, a code that
corresponds to the symbol "—," which is not our desired result. Instead,

Character conversions

```java
public class Caesar extends Cipher {
    /**
     * encode(String word)---iteratively performs a Caesar shift
     * on word where the shift is fixed at 3.
     * Pre:  word != NULL
     * Post: each letter in word has been shifted 3
     */
    public String encode(String word) {
        StringBuffer result = new StringBuffer();   // Initialize a string buffer
        for (int k = 0; k < word.length(); k++) {   // For each character in word
            char ch = word.charAt(k);               //   Get the character
            ch = (char)('a' + (ch -'a'+ 3) % 26);   //   Perform caesar shift
            result.append(ch);                      //   Append it to new string
        }
        return result.toString();                   // Return the result as a string
    } // encode()

    /**
     * decode(String word)---performs a reverse Caesar
     * shift on word where the shift is fixed at 3.
     * Pre:  word != NULL
     * Post: each letter in word has been shifted by 26-3
     */
    public String decode(String word) {
        StringBuffer result = new StringBuffer();       // Initialize a string buffer
        for (int k = 0; k < word.length(); k++) {       // For each character in word
            char ch = word.charAt(k);                   //   Get the character
            ch = (char)('a' + (ch - 'a' + 23) % 26);    //   Perform reverse caesar shift
            result.append(ch);                          //   Append it to new string
        }
        return result.toString();                       // Return the result as a string
    } // decode()
} // Caesar
```

FIGURE 7–22 The Caesar class.

we want the shift in this case to "wrap around" to the beginning of the alphabet, so that y gets shifted into b. In order to accomplish this we need to do some modular arithmetic.

Let's suppose the 26 characters a to z were numbered 0 through 25, so that a corresponds to 0, b to 1, and so on up to z to 25. If we take any number N and divide it (modulo 26), we would get a number between 0 and 25. Suppose, for example, y were numbered 24. Then shifting it by 3 would give us 27, and 27 % 26 would give us 1, which corresponds to b. So, if the a to z were numbered 0 through 25, then we can shift any character within that range using the following formula:

```
(ch + 3) % 26        // Shift by 3 with wraparound
```

To map a character in the range a to z onto the integers 0 to 25, we can simply subtract a from it:

```
'a' - 'a' = 0
'b' - 'a' = 1
```

```
'c' - 'a' = 2
...
'z' - 'a' = 25
```

Finally, to complete the shift operation we simply map the numbers 0 through 25 back to the characters *a* to *z*:

```
(char)('a' + 0) = 'a'
(char)('a' + 1) = 'b'
(char)('a' + 2) = 'c'
...
(char)('a' + 25) = 'z'
```

Note the use here of the cast operator (char) to covert an integer into a char.

To summarize, we can shift any character by 3 if we map it into the range 0 to 25, then add 3 to it mod 26, then map that result back into the range *a* to *z*. Thus, shifting *y* would go as follows:

Modular arithmetic

```
(char)('a' + (ch -'a'+ 3) % 26)      //  Perform Caesar shift
(char)('a' + ('y' - 'a' +3) % 26)    //  on 'y'
(char)(97 + (121 - 97 + 3) % 26)     //  Map 'y' to 0..25
(char)(97 + (27 % 26))               //  Shift by 3, wrapping around
(char)(97 + 1)                       //  Map result back to 'a' to 'z'
(char)(98)                           //  Convert from int to char
'b'
```

Note that in decode() a reverse Caesar shift is done by shifting by 23, which is $26 - 3$. If the original shift is 3, we can reverse that by shifting an additional 23. Together this gives a shift of 26, which will give us back our original string.

Class Design: Transpose

The Transpose class (Fig. 7–23) is structured the same as the Caesar class. It implements both the encode() and decode() methods. The key element here is the transpose operation, which in this case is a simple reversal of the letters in the word. Thus, "hello" becomes "olleh".

This is very easy to do, using the StringBuffer.reverse() method. The decode() method is even simpler, so all you need to do in this case is call encode(). Reversing the reverse of a string gives you back the original string.

Testing and Debugging

Figure 7–24 provides a simple test program for testing Cipher and its subclasses. It creates a Caesar cipher and a Transpose cipher and then encrypts and decrypts the same sentence using each cipher. If you run this program, it will produce the following output:

```
********* Caesar Cipher Encryption *********
PlainText: this is the secret message
Encrypted: wklv lv wkh vhfuhw phvvdjh
Decrypted: this is the secret message

********* Transpose Cipher Encryption *********
PlainText: this is the secret message
Encrypted: siht si eht terces egassem
Decrypted: this is the secret message
```

```
public class Transpose extends Cipher {
    /**
     * encode(String word)---reverses the letters in word
     * Pre:  word != NULL
     * Post: the letters in word have been reversed
     */
    public String encode(String word) {
        StringBuffer result = new StringBuffer(word);// Initialize a string buffer
        return result.reverse().toString();         // Reverse and return it
    } // encode()

    /**
     * decode(String word)---reverses the letters in word by
     *  by just calling encode
     * Pre:  word != NULL
     * Post: the letters in word have been reversed
     */
    public String decode(String word) {
        return encode(word);                        // Just call encode
    } // decode
} // Transpose
```

FIGURE 7–23   The Transpose class.

```
public class TestEncrypt {
    public static void main(String argv[]) {
        Caesar caesar = new Caesar();
        String plain = "this is the secret message";    // Here's the message
        String secret = caesar.encrypt(plain);          // Encrypt the message
        System.out.println(" ********* Caesar Cipher Encryption *********");
        System.out.println("PlainText: " + plain);    // Display the results
        System.out.println("Encrypted: " + secret);
        System.out.println("Decrypted: " + caesar.decrypt(secret)); // Decrypt

        Transpose transpose = new Transpose();
        secret = transpose.encrypt(plain);
        System.out.println("\n ********* Transpose Cipher Encryption *********");
        System.out.println("PlainText: " + plain);    // Display the results
        System.out.println("Encrypted: " + secret);
        System.out.println("Decrypted: " + transpose.decrypt(secret)); // Decrypt
    } // main()
} // end TestEncrypt
```

FIGURE 7–24   The TestEncrypt class.

SELF-STUDY EXERCISES

EXERCISE 7.20   Modify the Caesar class so that it will allow various sized shifts to be used. (*Hint*: Use an instance variable to represent the shift.)

EXERCISE 7.21   Modify Transpose.encode() so that it uses a rotation instead of a reversal. That is, a word like "hello" should be encoded as "ohell" with a rotation of one character.

IN THE LABORATORY: Pig Latin Translation

The purpose of this lab is to use some of the methods of the String class and to employ basic looping structures in solving a programming problem.

- To introduce the String class methods.
- To give practice using simple looping constructs.

Problem Description

Write a Java applet that translates an English sentence or expression into Pig Latin. The rules of Pig Latin are

- If the word begins with a consonant—such as "string," "Latin"—divide the word at the first vowel, swapping the front and back halves and append "ay" to the word—"ingstray," "atinLay."
- If the word begins with a vowel—such as "am," "are," "I"—append "yay" to the word—"amyay," "areyay," "Iyay."
- If the word has no vowels (other than *y*)—such as "my," "thy"—append "yay" to it—"myyay," "thyyay."

GUI Specifications

The Graphical User Interface (GUI) for this applet should contain an input TextField and an output TextArea. The user should be prompted to type a phrase into the TextField and the applet should convert the phrase to Pig Latin and display the result in the TextArea. See Figure 7–25.

Problem Decomposition

One way to decompose this problem is to divide it into two classes: PigLatinApplet, which implements the user interface, and PigLatin, which contains the expertise needed to translate English into Pig Latin (Fig. 7–26). PigLatinApplet should get the input from the user (in a

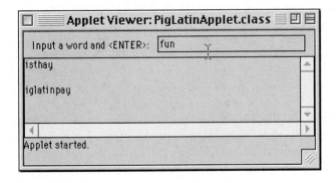

FIGURE 7–25   The user interface for the Pig Latin applet.

FIGURE 7–26 The classes used in the PigLatin program.

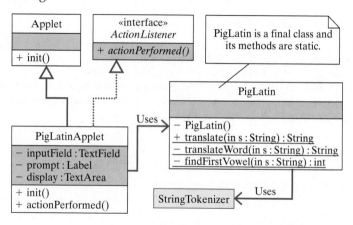

TextField), pass it to PigLatin, which will translate it into Pig Latin, and then display the result in the TextArea.

The Algorithm

The algorithm for this lab will solve the following problem: Given an English sentence or expression—a string of words separated by blanks—translate the string word by word into Pig Latin. For the sake of simplicity, let's leave off all punctuation symbols. The algorithm should go through the string word by word, and for each word, it should translate it into Pig Latin and concatenate it to the result string. As we know, in order to translate a word into Pig Latin, we must find the location of its first vowel and then follow the foregoing translation rules. This suggests the following algorithm, which could be encapsulated into the translate() method:

```
Initialize a result string
For each word in the input string        // String tokenizer task
     translate it into Pig Latin          // translateWord task
     Append it to the result string       // String concatenation task
Return the result string
```

As the comments suggest, this algorithm can be broken up into subtasks. The first subtask is to get each word out of the input string. This is a perfect job for the StringTokenizer class discussed earlier. The second subtask is to translate a single word into Pig Latin. This task is substantial enough to be encapsulated into a separate method, the translateWord() method. Lastly, string concatenation is easily done by using the "+" operator.

To translate a word into Pig Latin, you must find the location of its first vowel (a, e, i, o, or u) and then apply the foregoing rules. If the word begins with a vowel (or doesn't contain a vowel), you simply append "yay" to the end of the word—"able" becomes "ableyay" and "my" becomes "myyay." Otherwise you divide the word into substrings with the first vowel becoming the first letter of the Pig Latin word and any letters preceding it being appended to the end of the word and followed by "ay"—"string" becomes "ing" + "str" + "ay" or "ingstray."

The task of finding the first vowel in a string is also a good candidate for encapsulation into a separate method. It takes an English word as its String parameter and returns an int, giving the index location of the first vowel (Fig. 7–26).

If the word does not contain a vowel—for example, "my"—the method should return 0. For example, `findFirstVowel("hello")` should return 1 as the location of *e*, and `findFirstVowel("able")` should return 0, and `findFirstVowel("my")` should also return 0. The reason for having it return 0 in two different cases is that in both cases you handle the translation in the same way—"able" becomes "ableyay" and "my" becomes "myyay." In other words, according to the Pig Latin rules, there's no difference between a word that begins with a vowel and one that doesn't contain a vowel.

Problem Design: The PigLatin Class

The preceding analysis leads to the design for the `PigLatin` class shown in Figure 7–27. Its main role is to translate English expressions into Pig Latin. One design we could use here is to model `PigLatin` after the `Math` class—that is, as a utility class that provides a useful method but that is not designed to be instantiated at all. The following gives a more detailed specification of the `PigLatin` class:

- Purpose: To translate an English expression into Pig Latin.
- Modifiers: `final`, so it cannot be extended.
- Constructor: `private`, so no instantiation is possible.
- Instance variables: None (no need to store anything).
- Public instance methods: None (no need to have instances).
- Public static method: `translate(String)` translates its `String` parameter into Pig Latin.
- Private static method: `translateWord(String)` translates a single word into PigLatin.
- Private static method: `findFirstVowel(String)` returns the location of the first vowel in its `String` parameter.

As this design suggests, the `PigLatin` class will have only one `public` method but will utilize the `private` methods described previously to help perform its task.

Problem Design: PigLatinApplet

The design of `PigLatinApplet` should be similar to that of other applets we've built (Fig. 7–28). It should contain a `TextField` for user input and a `Label` for prompting the user. Note that its interface (Fig. 7–25) does not contain a `Button`, so the applet's action events will be generated when the user types the Enter key in the `TextField`. (See the "In the Laboratory" section in Chapter 5.)

   `PigLatinApplet` should implement the `ActionListener.actionPer-formed()` method to handle `TextField` actions. When the user types RETURN, `actionPerformed()` should get the input from the `TextField` and pass it to `PigLatin.translate()`, which will return a (Pig Latin) string. The applet should then append the result to the `TextArea`.

   Recall that since we have patterned `PigLatin` after the `Math` class (and `Integer` class), there is no need to instantiate it in order to use its `static` methods. So to translate "Hello World" into Pig Latin, we could simply write

```
System.out.println(PigLatin.translate("Hello World"));
```

PigLatin is a final class and its methods are static.

PigLatin
− PigLatin() + translate(in s : String) : String − translateWord(in s : String) : String − findFirstVowel(in s : String) : int

FIGURE 7–27   The `PigLatin` class has only one public method. Its other methods are utility methods that are hidden from other objects.

PigLatinApplet
− inputField : TextField − prompt : Label − display : TextArea
+ init() + actionPerformed()

FIGURE 7–28   The `PigLatinApplet` class.

The `translate()` method is a *class method*—a `static` method that is associated with the class itself.

Implementation

The implementation of this program is left to you as a lab (or programming) exercise. Remember to use stepwise refinement as you develop your program. Also develop and use appropriate preconditions and postconditions for each of the methods in your program. These will be helpful during design, coding, and testing of your algorithms. For example, the `findFirstVowel()` method would have the following conditions:

```
// findFirstVowel(String s)
// PRE:  s != NULL
// POST: findFirstVowel(s) == 0 If s contains no vowels
//       findFirstVowel(s) == n IF s.charAt(n) is first vowel
```

Optional Refinement

Because it's redundant in Pig Latin to have words like "myyay" that contain "yy," revise your program so that it converts "my" and "why" into "myay" and "whyay" instead of "myyay" and "whyyay." To do this, you could treat English words that end in *y* as a special case in your `translate()` method. Think about what sort of Java expression you would use to determine if a word's last letter is *y*? What `String` method(s) will you need to form this expression?

Java Language Summary

New `String` objects can only be created in two ways. First, a `String` object is created automatically by Java the first time it encounters a *literal string*, such as "Socrates," in a program. Subsequent occurrences of the literal do not cause additional objects to be instantiated. Instead, every occurrence of the literal "Socrates" refers to the same object.

Second, a `String` object is created whenever the `new` operator is used in conjunction with a `String()` constructor—for example, `new String("hello")`. Figure 7–5 provides an illustration of this point.

CHAPTER SUMMARY

Technical Terms

ciphertext	lexicographic order	string literal
concatenation	off-by-one error	substitution cipher
cryptography	orphan object	token
data structure	plaintext	transposition cipher
empty string	read only	unit indexed
index	string	zero indexed

Summary of Important Points

- A String literal is a sequence of 0 or more characters enclosed within double quotation marks. A String object is a sequence of 0 or more characters, plus a variety of class and instance methods and variables.
- The String concatenation operator is the overloaded + symbol; it is used to combine two strings into a single String: "hello" + "world" ==> "helloworld".
- Strings are indexed starting at 0. The indexOf() and lastIndexOf() methods are used for finding the first or last occurrence of a character or substring within a String. The valueOf() methods are used to convert a nonstring into a String. The length() method is used to determine the number of characters in a String. The charAt() method is used to return the single character at a particular index position. The various substring() methods are used to return the substring at particular index positions in a String.
- The overloaded equals() method returns true if two Strings contain the same exact sequence of characters. The == operator, when used on Strings, returns true if two references designate the same String.
- A StringTokenizer is an object that can be used to break a String into a collection of *tokens* separated by *delimiters*. The whitespace characters—tabs, blanks, and newlines—are the default delimiters.
- An abstract class is one that contains one or more abstract methods, which are methods that lack a method body or an implementation. An abstract class can be subclassed but not instantiated.

SOLUTIONS TO SELF-STUDY EXERCISES

SOLUTION 7.1   a. silly   b. silly   c. silly stuff

SOLUTION 7.2

a. String str1 = "";
b. String str2 = new String("stop");
c. String str3 = str1 + str2;

SOLUTION 7.3   a. 15   b. "551"   c. "5175"

SOLUTION 7.4   See Figure 7–29.

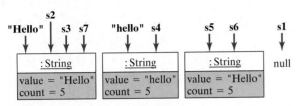

String s1, s2 = "Hello", s3 = "Hello";
String s4 = "hello";
String s5 = new String ("Hello");
String s6 = s5;
String s7 = s3;

FIGURE 7–29 Answer to Exercise 7.4. Note that *s1* is null because it has not been instantiated and has not been assigned a literal value.

SOLUTION 7.5   a. "45"   b. "121"   c. "X"

SOLUTION 7.6

a. String.valueOf(100)
b. String.valueOf('V');
c. String s = new String(String.valueOf(X * Y));

SOLUTION 7.7   a. 0   b. 1   c. −1

SOLUTION 7.8   a. 16   e. 1   i. 7
                    b. "16"   f. 13   j. 7
                    c. 1   g. 7   k. 3
                    d. 15   h. 3

SOLUTION 7.9   Evaluate the following expression:

```
String tricky = "abcdefg01234567";
tricky.indexOf(String.valueOf(tricky.indexOf("c")));
tricky.indexOf(String.valueOf(2));
tricky.indexOf("2");
Answer: 9
```

SOLUTION 7.10   a. "uvwxyz"   c. "xyz"   e. "xyz"
                     b. "bcde"   d. "xy"

SOLUTION 7.11   a. "uvwxyz"   c. "xyz"   e. "xyz"
                     b. "bcde"   d. "xyz"

SOLUTION 7.12   Changes necessary to CyberPet class:

```
public static final int TRICKING = 2;            // New state
private StringTricks tricks = new StringTricks(); // New bag of tricks

public String trick(String s) {                  // New instance method
    petState = TRICKING;
    return tricks.getNextTrick(s);
} // trick()

public String getState() {                // Revised method
    if (petState == EATING)
        return "Eating";
    else if (petState == SLEEPING)
        return "Sleeping";
    else if (petState == TRICKING)        // Here
        return "Tricking";
    else
        return "Error in State";
} // getState()
```

SOLUTION 7.13   Changes required in AnimatedCyberPet applet:

```
private Label nameLabel = new Label(
    "Hi! Type a string into the text field and "
    + "I'll do a trick with it.");                // Revised prompt
private TextField field = new TextField(30);      // New component

// Changes in init() method
  add(field);                                     // Add the new TextField
```

```
    field.addActionListener(this);        // Give it an ActionListener

// Modified ActionPerformed() Method
public void actionPerformed(ActionEvent e) {
    if (e.getSource() == eat)
        pet.eat();
    else if (e.getSource() == sleep)
        pet.sleep();
    else if (e.getSource() == field) { // Perform a trick
                                       // With the string in the TextField
        String s = pet.trick(field.getText());
        field.setText(s);             // Show the result in the TextField
    }
}
```

SOLUTION 7.14   Method to remove all blanks from a string:

```
// Pre: s is a non null string
// Post: s is returned with all its blanks removed
public String removeBlanks(String s) {
  StringBuffer result = new StringBuffer();
  for (int k = 0; k < s.length();  k++)
    if (s.charAt(k) != ' ')         // If this is not a blank
      result.append(s.charAt(k));   //  append it to result
  return result.toString();
}
```

SOLUTION 7.15   A Alpha Z Zero Zeroes a alpha bath bin z zero

SOLUTION 7.16   To modify precedes so that it also returns true when its two string arguments are equal, just change the operator in the final return statement to <=:

```
    if (s1.charAt(k) <= s2.charAt(k) )
        return true;
```

SOLUTION 7.17
a. true   d. false   g. false
b. true   e. false   h. false
c. false   f. true   i. false

SOLUTION 7.18   The variables in TestStringEquals are declared static because they are used in static methods. Whenever you call a method directly from main(), it must be static because main() is static. Remember that static elements are associated with the class, not with its instances. So main() can only use static elements because they don't depend on the existence of instances.

SOLUTION 7.19

a. String s3 = s1.substring(s1.indexOf('n'))
   + s1.substring(0,s1.indexOf('n'));
b. String s4 = s2.substring(6) + " " + s2.substring(0,5);
c. String s5 = s2.substring(0,6) + s1.substring(0,3);

SOLUTION 7.20   Modify the Caesar class so that it will allow various sized shifts to be used.

```
private int shift;                              // Caesar shift
public void setShift(int n) { shift = n;    }
public int getShift()        { return shift; }
// Modification to encode():
ch = (char)('a' + (ch -'a'+ shift) % 26);       //  Perform caesar shift
// Modification to decode():
ch = (char)('a' + (ch -'a'+ (26-shift)) % 26); //  Perform caesar shift
```

SOLUTION 7.21   Modify `Transpose.encode()` so that it uses a rotation instead of a reversal. The operation here is very similar to the shift operation in the Caesar cipher. It uses modular arithmetic to rearrange the letters in the word. For example, suppose the word is "hello". Its letters are indexed from 0 to 4. The following table shows how the expression `((k+2) % 5)` will rearrange the letters as k varies from 0 to 4:

```
k  charAt(k)  (k+2) % 5   charAt((k+2) % 5)
--------------------------------------------
0  'h'           2            'l'
1  'e'           3            'l'
2  'l'           4            'o'
3  'l'           0            'h'
4  'o'           1            'e'
```

```
// Modification to encode():
public String encode(String word) {
    StringBuffer result = new StringBuffer();
    for (int k=0; k < word.length(); k++)
        result.append(word.charAt((k+2) % word.length()));
    return result.toString();
}
```

EXERCISES

Note: *For programming exercises,* **first** *draw a UML class diagram describing all classes and their inheritance relationships and/or associations.*

EXERCISE 7.1   Explain the difference between the following pairs of terms:

a. *Ciphertext* and *plaintext*.
b. *Unit indexing* and *zero indexing*.
c. *Substitution cipher* and *transposition cipher*.
d. *Data structure* and *data type*.
e. `StringBuffer` and `String`.
f. `String` and `StringTokenizer`.
g. *Declaring a variable* and *instantiating a* `String`.
h. *Abstract method* and *stub method*.

EXERCISE 7.2   Fill in the blanks.

a. The fact that the first character in a string has index 0 is known as ＿＿＿＿＿ .
b. A method that contains no body—no implementation—is known as an ＿＿＿＿＿ method.
c. If a class contains methods that have no bodies, the class must be declared ＿＿＿＿＿ .
d. A bunch of characters enclosed within quotes is known as a ＿＿＿＿＿ .
e. A Caesar cipher is an example of a ＿＿＿＿＿ cipher.

EXERCISE 7.3 Given the `String` *str* with the value "to be or not to be that is the question," write Java expressions to extract each of the following substrings:

a. the first "to" in the string

```
ANSI: str.substring(0, 2)
ANS2: (str.indexOf("to"),
       str.indexOf("to") + 2)
```

b. the last "to" in the string

c. the first "be" in the string

d. the last "be" in the string

e. the first four characters in the string

f. the last four characters in the string

Provide two sets of answers. One that uses the actual index numbers of the substrings—for example, the first "to" goes from 0 to 2—and the second that will retrieve the same substring from the following string "it is easy to become what you want to become." (*Hint*: In the second case, use `length()` and indexOf() along with `substring()` in your expressions. If necessary, you may use local variables to store intermediate results. The answer to (a) is provided as an example.)

EXERCISE 7.4 Identify the syntax errors in each of the following, assuming that the `String` s equals "exercise":

a. `s.charAt("hello")`

b. `s.indexOf(10)`

c. `s.substring("er")`

d. `s.lastIndexOf(er)`

e. `s.length`

EXERCISE 7.5 Evaluate each of the following expressions, assuming that the `String` s equals "exercise":

a. `s.charAt(5)`

b. `s.indexOf("er")`

c. `s.substring(5)`

d. `s.lastIndexOf('e')`

e. `s.length()`

EXERCISE 7.6 Write your own `equalsIgnoreCase()` method using only other `String` methods.

EXERCISE 7.7 Write your own `String` equality method without using `String.equals()`. (*Hint*: Modify the `precedes()` method.)

EXERCISE 7.8 Write a method for the `StringTricks` class that takes a `String` argument and returns a `String` result that is the lowercase version of the original string.

EXERCISE 7.9 Implement a method that uses the following variation of the Caesar cipher. The method should take two parameters, a `String` and an `int` N. The result should be a `String` in which the first letter is shifted by N, the second by N + 1, the third by N + 2, and so on. For example, given the string "Hello," and an initial shift of 1, your method should return "Igopt."

EXERCISE 7.10 **Challenge:** Imagine a Caesar cipher that uses the letters of a keyword to determine the shift of each letter in the plaintext. For example, suppose we choose the word "ace" as the keyword. You could also think of "ace" in terms of how many places each of its letters is shifted from the letter *a*. Thus, *a* is shifted by 0, *c* is shifted by 2, and *e* is shifted by 4. So given this keyword, the first letter of the plaintext would be shifted by 0, the second by 2, the third by 4, the fourth by 0, and so on. For example,

```
key:        acea ce a ceacea ceaceac
plaintext:  this is a secret message
shift:      0240 24 0 240240 2402402
ciphertext: tjms jw a uictit oisuegg
```

Write a method to implement this cipher. The method should take two `String` arguments: the string to be encrypted and the keyword.

EXERCISE 7.11   One way to make it more difficult to decipher a secret message is to destroy the word boundaries. For example, consider the following two versions of the same sentence:

```
Plaintext:    This is how we would ordinarily write a sentence.
Blocked text: Thisi showw ewoul dordi naril ywrit easen tence.
```

Write a method that converts its `String` parameter so that letters are written in blocks five characters long.

EXERCISE 7.12   Design and implement an applet that lets the user type a document into a `TextArea` and then provides the following analysis of the document: the number of words in the document, the number of characters in the document, and the percentage of words that have more than six letters.

EXERCISE 7.13   Design and write an applet that searches for single-digit numbers in a text and changes them to their corresponding words. For example, the string "4 score and 7 years ago" would be converted into "four score and seven years ago".

EXERCISE 7.14   A palindrome is a string that is spelled the same way backward and forward. For example, *mom, dad, radar, 727* and *able was i ere i saw elba* are all examples of palindromes. Write a Java applet that lets the user type in a word or phrase and then determines whether the string is a palindrome.

EXERCISE 7.15   Suppose you're writing a maze program and are using a string to store a representation of the maze. Write a method that accepts a `String` parameter and prints a two-dimensional representation of a maze. For example, the maze shown here can be generated from the following string:

```
String: XX_XXXXXXX__XXX_XXXX_XX____XXX_XX_XX_XXX____X____XXXXXXX_X

XX_XXXXXXX
X__XXX_XXX
X_XX____XX
X_XX_XX_XX
X____X____
XXXXXXX_X
```

EXERCISE 7.16   Write a method that takes a delimited string, which stores a name and address, and prints a mailing label. For example, if the string contains "Sam Penn:14 Bridge St.:Hoboken, NJ 01881," the method should print the label shown in the margin.

Sam Penn
14 Bridge St.
Hoboken, NJ 01881

EXERCISE 7.17   Design and implement a `Cipher` subclass to implement the following substitution cipher: Each letter in the alphabet is replaced with a letter from the opposite end of the alphabet: *a* is replaced with *z*, *b* with *y*, and so forth.

EXERCISE 7.18   One way to design a substitution alphabet for a cipher is to use a keyword to construct the alphabet. For example, suppose the keyword is "zebra." You place the keyword at the beginning of the alphabet, and then fill out the other 21 slots with remaining letters, giving the following alphabet:

```
Cipher alphabet:   zebracdfghijklmnopqstuvwxy
Plain alphabet:    abcdefghijklmnopqrstuvwxyz
```

Design and implement an `Alphabet` class for constructing these kinds of substitution alphabets. It should have a single public method that takes a keyword `String` as an argument and returns an alphabet string. Note that an alphabet cannot contain duplicate letters, so repeated letters would have to be removed a keyword like "xylophone."

EXERCISE 7.19   Design and write a `Cipher` subclass for a substitution cipher that uses an alphabet from the `Alphabet` class created in the previous exercise.

EXERCISE 7.20   Design and implement an applet that plays Time Bomb with the user. Here's how the game works. The computer picks a secret word and then prints one asterisk for each letter in the word: * * * * *. The user guesses at the letters in the word. For every correct guess, an asterisk is replaced by a letter: * e * * *. For every incorrect guess, the time bomb's fuse grows shorter. When the fuse disappears, after, say six incorrect guesses, the bomb explodes. Store the secret words in a delimited string and invent your own representation for the time bomb.

EXERCISE 7.21   Challenge: A common string-processing algorithm is the global replace function found in every word processor. Write a method that takes three `String` arguments: a document, a target string, and a replacement string. The method should replace every occurrence of the target string in the document with the replacement string. For example, if the document is "To be or not to be, that is the question" and the target string is "be" and the replacement string is "see," the result should be "To see or not to see, that is the question."

EXERCISE 7.22   Challenge: Design and implement an applet that plays the following game with the user. Let the user pick a letter between *A* and *Z*. Then let the computer guess the secret letter. For every guess the player has to tell the computer whether it's too high or too low. The computer should be able to guess the letter within five guesses. Do you see why?

EXERCISE 7.23   Challenge: Find a partner and concoct your own encryption scheme. Then work separately with one partner writing `encode()` and the other writing `decode()`. Test to see that a message can be encoded and then decoded to yield the original message.

EXERCISE 7.24   Challenge: A *list* is a sequential data structure. Design a `List` class that uses a comma-delimited `String`—such as, "a,b,c,d,12,dog"—to implement a list. Implement the following methods for this class:

```
void addItem( Object o );          // Use Object.toString()
String getItem(int position);
String toString();
void deleteItem(int position);
void deleteItem(String item);
int getPosition(String item);
String getHead();                  // First element
List getTail();                    // All but the first element
int length();                      // Number of items
```

EXERCISE 7.25   Challenge: Use a delimited string to create a `PhoneList` class with an instance method to insert names and phone numbers and a method to look up a phone number given a person's name. Since your class will take care of looking things up, you don't have to worry about keeping the list in alphabetical order. For example, the following string could be used as such a directory:

```
mom:860-192-9876::bill g:654-0987-1234::mary lancelot:123-842-1100
```

Photograph courtesy of Adalberto Rios, PhotoDisc, Inc.

8

Arrays and Array Processing

OBJECTIVES

After studying this chapter, you will

- Know how to use array data structures.
- Be able to solve problems that require collections of data.
- Know how to sort an array of data.
- Be familiar with sequential and binary search algorithms.
- Have a better understanding of inheritance and polymorphism.

OUTLINE

8.1   Introduction

In this chapter we'll learn about arrays. An **array** is a named collection of contiguous storage locations—storage locations that are next to each other—that contain data items of the same type.

Arrays offer a more streamlined way to store data than using individual data items for each variable. You can also work with data stored in arrays more efficiently than with individual variables.

Let's see why. Suppose you want to animate CyberPet. The usual way to do this is to create a sequence of images, each of which shows the pet in a slightly different position. These images can then be loaded into memory. We can give the illusion of motion by displaying each image in turn, with a short delay between one image and the next. The delay should be long enough to allow each separate image to be seen but short enough to blur the transition between one image and the next.

If the number of images is large, it would be inconvenient to create separate variables for each image, because each storage location would require a unique identifier. For example, if our animation used ten images, we would need ten identifiers:

```
Image image1;
Image image2;
 .
 .
Image image10;
```

and to load each image into memory we would need ten `getImage()` statements:

```
image1 = getImage(getDocumentBase(), "image1.gif");
image2 = getImage(getDocumentBase(), "image2.gif");
 .
 .
image10 = getImage(getDocumentBase(), "image10.gif");
```

To display each image for a brief instant, we would need ten `drawImage()` statements. And we would need ten `wait(DELAY)` statements to create a brief delay before the next image is displayed.

```
g.drawImage(image1, 1, 1, this);  wait(DELAY);
g.drawImage(image2, 1, 1, this);  wait(DELAY);
 .
 .
g.drawImage(image10, 1, 1, this);  wait(DELAY);
```

This approach is tedious. Think how much harder it would be if our animation consisted of 100 images or 1,000.

What we need is some way to use a loop to load and display the images, using a loop counter, k, to refer to the kth image on each iteration of the loop. The *array* data structure lets us do that.

Our discussions of arrays begins by showing how to store and retrieve data from one-, two-, and three-dimensional arrays. Among the array-processing algorithms we study are sorting and searching algorithms. Finally, we illustrate how arrays can be used in a variety of applications, including an animation problem, a sorting class, and a card-playing program.

8.2   One-Dimensional Arrays

An array is a named collection of contiguous storage locations that contain data items of the same type. Each element of the array is referred to by its position within the array. If the array is named `arr`, then the elements are named `arr[0]`, `arr[1]`, `arr[2]`, ... `arr[n-1]`, where n gives the number of elements in the array. In Java, as in C, C++, and some other programming languages, the first element of an array has index 0. (This is the same convention we used for `Strings`.)

The array data structure

Zero indexing

Figure 8–1 shows an array named `arr` that contains 15 `int` elements. The syntax for referring to elements of an array is

---

arrayname [*subscript*]

---

where *arrayname* is the name of the array—any valid identifier will do—and **subscript** is the position of the element within the array. As Figure 8–1 shows, the first element in the array has subscript 0, the second has subscript 1, and so on.

An array subscript must be either an integer value or an integer expression. For example, suppose that j and k are integer variables equaling 5 and 7, respectively. Each of the following then would be valid references to elements of the array *arr*:

Subscript expressions

```
arr[4]          Refers to 16
arr[j]          Is arr[5] which refers to 20
arr[j + k]      Is arr[5+7] which is arr[12] which refers to 45
arr[k % j]      Is arr[7%5] which is arr[2] which refers to -1
```

As these examples show, when an expression is used as a subscript, it is evaluated before the reference is made.

It is a syntax error to use a noninteger type as an array subscript. Each of the following expressions would be invalid:

```
arr[5.0]        // 5.0 is a float and can't be an array subscript
arr["5"]        // "5" is a string not an integer
```

For a given array, a valid array subscript must be in the range 0 ... N-1, where N is the number of elements in the array. It is a semantic error to use a subscript whose value is not in this range. This is a run-time error—that is, an error that occurs when the program is running—rather than a syntax error, which can be detected when the program is compiled. For the array `arr`, each of the following would lead to run-time errors:

```
arr[-1]         // Arrays cannot have negative subscripts
arr['5']        // '5' will be promoted to 53, which is out of bounds
arr[15]         // The last element of arr has subscript 14
arr[j*k]        // Since j*k equals 35
```

FIGURE 8–1   An array of 15 integers named `arr`.

Each of these references would lead to an `IndexOutOfBoundsException`, which means that the subscript in each case refers to an element that is not within the *bounds* of the array. (*Exceptions* are covered in detail in Chapter 11.)

> **JAVA LANGUAGE RULE**   Array Subscripts. Array subscripts must be integer values in the range 0 . . . (N-1), where *N* is the number of elements in the array.

> DEBUGGING TIP: Array Subscripts. In developing array algorithms, it's important to design test data that show that array subscripts do not cause run-time errors.

8.2.1   Declaring and Creating Arrays

Are arrays objects?

In Java, arrays are (mostly) treated as objects. They are instantiated with the new operator. They have instance variables (for example, `length`). Array variables are *reference* variables. When arrays are used as parameters, a reference to the array is passed rather than a copy of the entire array. The primary difference between arrays and full-fledged objects is that arrays don't belong to an `Array` class. Thus, arrays don't fit neatly into Java's `Object` hierarchy. They don't inherit any properties from `Object` and they can't be subclassed.

An array contains a number of variables. An *empty* array is one that contains zero variables. As we've seen, the variables contained in an array object are not referenced by name but by their relative position in the array. The variables are called *components*. If an array object has *N* components, then we say that the **array length** is *N*. Each of the components of the array has the same type, which is called the array's *component type*.

Components and elements

A **one-dimensional** array has components that are called the array's **elements**. Their type is the array's **element type**. An array's elements may be of any type, including primitive and reference types. So you can have arrays of `int`, `char`, `boolean`, `String`, `Object`, `Image`, `TextField`, `CyberPet`, and so on.

When declaring a one-dimensional array, you have to indicate both the array's element type and its length. Just as in declaring and creating other kinds of objects, creating an array object requires that we create both a name for the array and then the array itself. The following statements create the array shown in Figure 8–1:

```
int arr[];              // Declare a name for the array
arr = new int[15];      // Create the array itself
```

These two steps can be combined into a single statement as follows:

```
int arr[] = new int[15];
```

In this example, the array's element type is `int` and its `length` is 15. This means that the array contains 15 variables of type `int`, which will be referred to as `arr[0]`, `arr[1]`, . . . `arr[14]`.

8.2.2 Array Allocation

Creating an array, in this case, means allocating 15 storage locations that can store integers. Note that one difference between declaring an array and declaring some other kind of object is that square brackets ([]) are used to indicate that an array type is being declared. The brackets can be attached either to the array's name or to its type, as in the following examples:

```
int arr[];         // The brackets may follow the array's name
int[] arr;         // The brackets may follow the array's type
```

The following example creates an array of five `String`s and then uses a for loop to assign the strings `"hello1"`, `"hello2"`, `"hello3"`, `"hello4"`, and `"hello5"` to the five array locations:

```
String strarr[];                         // Declare a name for the array
strarr = new String[5];                  // Create the array itself
                                         // Assign strings to the array
for (int k = 0; k < strarr.length; k++) // For each array element
    strarr[k] = new String("hello" + (k + 1)); //  Assign it a new string
```

Note that the expression `k < strarr.length` is used to specify the loop bound. Each array has a `length` instance variable, which refers to the number of elements contained in the array. Arrays, like `String`s, are zero indexed, so the last element of the array is always given by its `length-1`. However, unlike for `String`s, where `length()` is an instance method, for arrays, `length` is an instance variable. It would be a syntax error in this example to refer to `strarr.length()`.

length vs. length()

> **DEBUGGING TIP: Array Length.** A common syntax error involves forgetting that for arrays `length` is an instance variable, not an instance method, as it is for `String`s.

In the example, once the array `strarr` is created, a `String` constructor is used to create the five `String`s that are stored in the array. It is important to realize that creating an array to store five `Object`s (as opposed to five primitive data elements) does not also create the `Object`s themselves that will be stored in the array.

When an array of objects is created, the array's elements are references to those objects (Fig. 8–2). Their initial values, like all reference variables, are `null`. So to create and *initialize* the array `strarr`, we need to create *six* objects—the array itself, which is like a container, and then the five `String`s that are stored in `strarr`.

Arrays of objects

One more example will help underscore this point. The following statements create four *new* `Object`s, an array to store three `CyberPet`s plus the three `CyberPet`s themselves:

```
CyberPet pethouse[] = new CyberPet[3]; // Create an array for 3 CyberPets
pethouse[0] = new CyberPet("Socrates");  // Create the first CyberPet
pethouse[1] = new CyberPet("Plato");     // Create the second CyberPet
pethouse[2] = new CyberPet("Aristotle"); // Create the third CyberPet
```

FIGURE 8–2 Creating an array of five `String`s involves six objects, because the array itself is a separate object. In (a), the array variable is declared. In (b), the array is instantiated, creating an array of five `null` references. In (c), the five `String`s are created and assigned to the array.

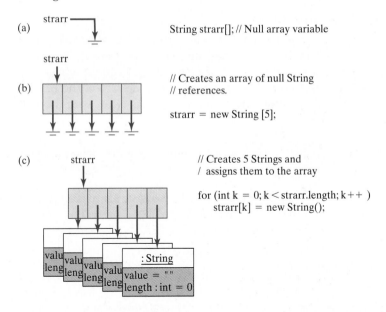

The first statement creates an array named `pethouse` to store three `CyberPets`, and the next three statements create the individual `CyberPets` and assign them to the array (Fig. 8–3). Thus, creating the array and initializing its elements require four `new` statements.

The following sequence of statements would lead to a null pointer exception because the array's elements have not been instantiated:

```
CyberPet pets[] = new CyberPet[3];   // Create an array for 3 CyberPets
System.out.println(pets[0].getName());
```

In this case, `pets[0]` is a null reference, thus causing the exception.

> DEBUGGING TIP: Array Instantiation. Creating a new array does not also create the objects that are stored in the array. They must be instantiated separately. It is a semantic error to refer to an uninstantiated (`null`) array element.

Now that we've assigned the three `CyberPets` to the array, we can refer to them by means of subscripted references. A reference to the `CyberPet` named "Socrates" is now `pethouse[0]`, and a reference to the `CyberPet` named "Plato" is `pethouse[1]`. In other words, to refer to the three individual pets we must refer to their locations within `pethouse`. Of course, we can also use variables, such as loop counters, to refer to a `CyberPet`'s location within `pethouse`. The following for loop invokes each `CyberPet`'s `getState()` method to print out its current state:

```
for (int k = 0; k < pethouse.length; k++)
    System.out.println(pethouse[k].getState());
```

What if the three `CyberPets` already existed before the array was created? In that case, we could just assign their references to the array elements, as in the following example:

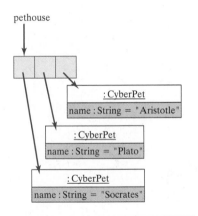

FIGURE 8–3 An array of CyberPets.

```
CyberPet pet1 = new CyberPet("Socrates"); // Existing CyberPets
CyberPet pet2 = new CyberPet("Plato");
CyberPet pet3 = new CyberPet("Aristotle");
CyberPet pets = new CyberPet[3];          // Array
pethouse[0] = pet1;
pethouse[1] = pet2;
pethouse[2] = pet3;
```

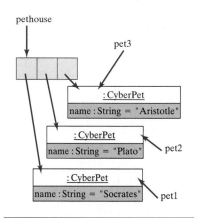

In this case, each of the three CyberPet objects can be referenced by two different references—its variable identifier (such as pet1) and its array location (such as pethouse[0]). For arrays of objects, Java stores just the reference to the object in the array itself, rather than the entire object. This conserves memory, since references require only 4 bytes each whereas each object may require hundreds of bytes (Fig. 8–4).

When an array of N elements is created, the compiler *allocates* storage for N variables of the element's type. In the case of intarr, above, the compiler would allocate storage for 15 ints—60 contiguous bytes of storage, because each int requires 4 bytes (32 bits) of storage. If we declare an array of 20 doubles,

FIGURE 8–4 Arrays of objects store references to the objects, not the objects themselves.

```
double arr[] = new double[20];
```

the compiler will allocate 160 bytes of storage—20 variables of 8 bytes (64 bits) each. In the case of the CyberPet examples and String examples, because these are objects (not primitive types), the compiler will allocate space for N addresses, where N is the length of the array.

How much memory?

SELF-STUDY EXERCISE

EXERCISE 8.1 How much space (in bytes) would be allocated for each of the following?

a. int a[] = new int[5];
b. double b[] = new double[10];
c. char c[] = new char[30];
d. String s[] = new String[10];
e. CyberPet p[] = new CyberPet[5];

8.2.3 Initializing Arrays

Array elements are automatically initialized to default values that depend on the element type: Boolean elements are initialized to false. Integer and real types are initialized to 0. Reference types—that is, arrays of objects—are initialized to null.

Arrays can also be assigned initial values when they are created, although this is feasible only for relatively small arrays. An **array initializer** is written as a list of expressions separated by commas and enclosed by braces. For example, we can declare and initialize the array shown in Figure 8–1 with the following statement:

Array initializer

```
int arr[] = {-2,8,-1,-3,16,20,25,16,16,8,18,19,45,21,-2};
```

Similarly, to create and initialize an array of Strings, we can use the following statement:

```
String strings[] = {"hello", "world", "goodbye", "love"};
```

This example creates and stores four Strings in the array. Subsequently, to refer to "hello", we would use the reference strings[0], and to refer to "love", we would use the reference strings[3]. Note in these examples that when an array declaration contains an initializer, it is not necessary to use new and it is not necessary to specify the number of elements in the array. The number of elements is determined from the number of values in the initializer list.

8.2.4 Assigning and Using Array Values

Array assignment

Array elements can be used in the same way as other variables. The only difference, of course, is that references to the elements are subscripted. For example, the following assignment statements assign values to the elements of two arrays, arr and strings:

```
arr[0] = 5;
arr[5] = 10;
arr[2] = 3;
strings[0] = "who";
strings[1] = "what";
strings[2] = strings[3] = "where";
```

The following loop assigns the first 15 squares—1, 4, 9 . . . —to the array arr:

```
for (int k = 0; k < arr.length; k++)
    arr[k] = (k+1) * (k+1);
```

The following loop prints the values of the array arr:

```
for (int k = 0; k < arr.length; k++)
    System.out.println(arr[k]);
```

SELF-STUDY EXERCISES

EXERCISE 8.2 Declare an array named farr that contains ten floats initialized to the values 1.0, 2.0, . . . , 10.0.

EXERCISE 8.3 Write an expression that prints the first element of farr.

EXERCISE 8.4 Write an assignment statement that assigns 100.0 to the last element in farr.

EXERCISE 8.5 Write a loop to print all of the elements of farr.

8.3 Simple Array Examples

The program in Figure 8–5 creates two arrays of ten elements each and displays their values on the Java console. In this example, the elements of intArr have not been given initial values whereas the elements of realArr have been initialized. Note the use of the integer constant ARRSIZE to store the arrays' size. By using the constant in this way, we do not have to use the literal value 10 anywhere in the program, thereby making it easier to modify the program. If we want to change the size of the array that the program handles, we can just change the value of ARRSIZE. This is an

Maintainability principle

example of the maintainability principle.

```
public class PrintArrays  {
    static final int ARRSIZE = 10;                  // The array's size

    static int intArr[] = new int[ARRSIZE];         // Create the int array
    static double realArr[] = { 1.1, 2.2, 3.3, 4.4,
        5.5, 6.6, 7.7, 8.8, 9.9, 10.10 };           // And a double array

    public static void main(String args[]) {
        System.out.println("Ints \t Reals");        // Print a heading
        for (int k = 0; k < intArr.length; k++) // For each int and double element
            System.out.println( intArr[k] + " \t " + realArr[k]); // Print them
    } // main()
} // PrintArrays
```

FIGURE 8–5   A program that displays two arrays. Its output is shown in Figure 8–6.

EFFECTIVE DESIGN: Symbolic Constants.   Using symbolic constants (final variables) instead of literal values makes the program easier to read and to maintain.

Note the use of the static qualifier throughout the PrintArrays class. This enables us to refer to the array and the other variables from within the main() method. If intArr were not declared static, we would get the compiler error "attempt to make static use of a nonstatic variable." This use of static is justified mainly as a coding convenience rather as a principle of object-oriented design. The only examples we've seen so far in which static elements were a necessary design element were the use of static elements in the Math class—Math.PI and Math.sqrt()—and the use of static final variables in CyberPet—CyberPet.SLEEPING.

For large arrays, it is not always feasible to initialize them in an initializer statement. Consider the problem of initializing an array with the squares of the first 100 integers. Not only would it be tedious to set these values in an initializer statement, it would also be error prone, since it is relatively easy to type in the wrong value for one or more of the squares.

Array initializers

DEBUGGING TIP: Array Initialization. Initializer statements should be used only for relatively small arrays.

The example in Figure 8–7 creates an array of 50 integers and then fills the elements with the values 1, 4, 9, 16, and so on. It then prints the entire array.

This example illustrates a couple of important points about the use of array variables. The array's elements are individual storage locations. In this example, intArr has 50 storage locations. Storing a value in one of these variables is done by an assignment statement:

```
intArr[k] = (k+1) * (k+1);
```

The use of the variable k in this assignment statement allows us to vary the location that is assigned on each iteration of the for loop. Note that in this

Ints	Reals
0	1.1
0	2.2
0	3.3
0	4.4
0	5.5
0	6.6
0	7.7
0	8.8
0	9.9
0	10.1

FIGURE 8–6   Output of the PrintArrays program.

FIGURE 8–7   A program with an array that stores the squares of the first 50 integers. Its output is shown in Figure 8–8.

```
public class Squares {
    static final int ARRSIZE = 50;            // The array's size
    static int intArr[] = new int[ARRSIZE];   // Create an int array

    public static void main(String args[]) {
        for (int k = 0; k < intArr.length; k++)  // Initialize the array
            intArr[k] = (k+1) * (k+1);

        System.out.print("The first 50 squares are"); // Print a heading
        for (int k = 0; k < intArr.length; k++) {     // Print the array
            if (k % 5 == 0)                           // For each 5th square
                System.out.println(" ");             //   print a new line
            System.out.print( intArr[k] + " ");
        } // for
    } // main()
} // Squares
```

Zero vs. unit indexing

example *k* occurs as the array index on the left-hand side of this expression, while *k+1* occurs on the right-hand side as the value to be squared. The reason for this is that arrays are indexed starting at 0 but we want our table of squares to begin with the square of 1. So the square of some number *n+1* will always be stored in the array whose index is one less than the number itself—that is, *n*.

An array's length variable can always be used as a loop bound when iterating through all elements of the array:

```
for (int k = 0; k < intArr.length; k++)
    intArr[k] = (k+1) * (k+1);
```

Off-by-one error

However, it is important to note that the last element in the array is always at location length-1. Attempting to refer to intArr[length] would cause an IndexOutOfBoundsException because no such element exists.

> DEBUGGING TIP: Off-by-One Error. Because of zero indexing, the last element in an array is always length-1. Forgetting this fact can cause an off-by-one error.

```
1 4 9 16 25
36 49 64 81 100
121 144 169 196 225
256 289 324 361 400
441 484 529 576 625
676 729 784 841 900
961 1024 1089 1156 1225
1296 1369 1444 1521 1600
1681 1764 1849 1936 2025
2116 2209 2304 2401 2500
```

FIGURE 8–8   Output of the Squares program.

SELF-STUDY EXERCISE

EXERCISE 8.6   Declare an array of 100 doubles and write a loop to assign the first 100 square roots to its elements. [Use Math.sqrt(double).]

8.4   Example: Testing a Die

Suppose you're writing a computer game that uses the roll of a six-sided die to determine (randomly) which player goes next. Of course, you want the die to be fair. If there are six players, then each player should get a turn approximately one-sixth of the time. If you were using a real die, rather than a computer simulation, this is the behavior you would expect.

8.4.1   Generating Random Numbers

In computer games a special method, called a **random number generator**, is used to generate random numbers, which can then be used to simulate things such as a die or a coin toss. Java's `Math.random()` method is such a method. Each time you call this method, it will generate a random value in the range [0, 1) that is, from 0 to 0.99999999. The value 1.0 is not included in the range. Within this range, the numbers are fairly evenly distributed: If we generated 1,000 values, there would be roughly the same number of values occurring in the interval 0 to 0.1 as in the interval 0.2 to 0.3.

Actually, the numbers generated by `Math.random()` are not truly random. Given the same first number—the same *seed* value—`Math.random()` will generate the same sequence of numbers every time. That's why, strictly speaking, these numbers are called **pseudorandom numbers**. Like *Pseudorandom numbers* truly random numbers, pseudorandom numbers have certain desirable characteristics, such as being uniformly distributed over their given range, but they are generated in a nonrandom way. However, as long as you understand that these numbers are not truly random, we'll refer to them, in most contexts, simply as random numbers.

Random number generators are used in a variety of applications, including simulations and games. For example, a flight simulator would use random numbers to simulate events that occur during flight. Epidemiologists use random numbers to study the spread of a disease. In computer games, random numbers are used to simulate the rolling of dice, flipping of a coin, and a variety of other random or chance events.

`Math.random()` is a method that takes no parameters and generates a `double` value in the range [0.0,1.0):

```
0.0 <= Math.random() < 1.0
```

To illustrate its use, let's use `Math.random()` to simulate a fair coin flip. One way to do this is to multiply `Math.random()` by 2 and convert the result to an `int`:

```
int coinFlip = (int)(Math.random() * 2);    // Heads or tails
```

Multiplying `Math.random()` by 2 will produce a value in the range [0,1.99999). Examples of possible values include 0.0, 0.111, 0.999, 1.001, 1.504, and 1.998. If we convert these values to `int`, we will get 0, 0, 0, 1, 1, 1—that is, three 0's and three 1's. If we let the 0's represent heads and the 1's represent tails, these numbers can be used to represent a coin flip. Thus, assuming that `Math.random()` generates numbers evenly distributed over the range [0,1), we can expect that our "coin flip" will come up heads approximately half the time.

The process of multiplying `Math.random()` by 2 is known as **scaling** and *Scaling factor* takes the following general form:

```
(int)(Math.random() * N)
```

In general, the preceding expression will produce *N* integer values in the range [0,N-1]. *N* is called the *scaling factor*. In the fair coin example, the scaling factor was 2 and two integer values were produced in the range [0,1].

To simulate rolling a die, we would need six values in the range 1 to 6. The following expression will generate six values in the range 0 to 5:

```
int die = (int)(Math.random() * 6);
```

Note the placement of the parentheses in this expression. The entire expression (Math.random() * 6) must be cast into an int, so it is necessary to surround it with parentheses.

Scaling and shifting

If we want to *shift* the values into the range 1 to 6, we can simply add 1 to this expression:

```
int die = 1 + (int)(Math.random() * 6);
```

The variable die now has an equal chance of being set to one of the values 1, 2, 3, 4, 5, or 6, thus simulating the tossing of a fair die. In general, then, the Java expression we use for generating a set of N random integer values in the range M to $M+N-1$ is

```
M + (int)(Math.random() * N)
```

SELF-STUDY EXERCISES

EXERCISE 8.7　Write a Java expression that generates random integers in the range 0 through 10.

EXERCISE 8.8　Write a Java expression that generates random integers in the range 2 through 12.

EXERCISE 8.9　Suppose you are simulating a card game in which you represent cards by two integer values, a suit and a rank. For example, the 2 of clubs has clubs as its suit and 2 as its rank. The ace of diamonds has diamonds as its suit and 14 as its rank. Write Java statements to assign random values to suit and rank.

EXERCISE 8.10　Let's give our CyberPet a mind of its own. Modify CyberPet.eat() and CyberPet.sleep() so that a CyberPet will eat and sleep on command only half the time. [*Hint*: Test the value that random() gives you. If it's above 0.5, have the pet obey the command. Otherwise, have the petulant pet just ignore the command (see Fig. 5–14.)]

8.4.2　The Die-Testing Experiment

Problem statement

Now that we understand how to use Math.random(), let's conduct an experiment to test how good it is—that is, to test how random its values are. To do so, let's create a simple die-tossing simulation that will use Math.random() to simulate a die with six faces. We will repeatedly "toss" the die and count the number of times it comes up 1, 2, 3, 4, 5, and 6. If it's a fair die—if the random number generator produces nicely distributed values—we would expect to get roughly the same number of

Die
+ DIE_LOW : int = 1
+ DIE_HIGH : int = 6
+ FACES : int = DIE_HIGH-DIE_LOW + 1
+ roll() : int

FIGURE 8–9 The Die class.

1's, 2's, 3's, 4's, 5's, and 6's over a period of 1,000 or 10,000 die tosses. That is, the frequencies of the six outcomes should be roughly equal to one-sixth.

As in many of our other programs, this problem breaks down into two classes, one to represent the Die and one to represent the DieExperiment. The DieExperiment class will use an instance of the Die to test the Math.random() method. The Die class is very simple. It just needs a method, roll(), that simulates the rolling of the die (Fig. 8–9).

The roll() method should just return a value between 1 and 6. Thus, the entire Die class can be defined simply as

```java
public class Die {
    public static final int DIE_LOW = 1,
                            DIE_HIGH = 6,
                            FACES = DIE_HIGH-DIE_LOW+1;
    public int roll() {
        return DIE_LOW + (int)(Math.random() * FACES);
    }
}
```

Note the use of class constants (static final variables) to represent the Die's primary characteristics. If we decide to modify this class to represent a 12-sided die, it will be simple to revise this class (see Exercise 8.22).

The DieExperiment is also easy to design. This class has two main tasks: to test the die and to report the results. In order to keep track of the results it will need a six-element int array to store the frequencies obtained for each of the die's faces. This leads to the design shown in Figure 8–10.

The implementation of DieExperiment is shown in Figure 8–11. Note that we use a symbolic constant, NTRIALS, to define the number of trials in the experiment. Note also how we use the static constants defined in the die class to define the array of counters:

DieExperiment
– counter : int[]
– NTRIALS : int = 6000
+ testDie()
+ printResults()
+ main()

FIGURE 8–10 The DieExperiment class.

```java
private int counter[] = new int[Die.FACES+1];
```

We have given the array Die.FACES+1 elements. This will give it seven elements indexed 0 to 6. The reason for this is that we wish to ignore the 0th element and just store test results in locations 1 through 6, which correspond to the numbers of the die's face.

After each die toss, the appropriate counter will be incremented. Because the value of the die will be in the range 1 to 6, we can use the following statement, where die represents the die, to increment the counter that corresponds to the die's face value:

```java
++counter[die.roll()];
```

```
public class DieExperiment {
    private static final int NTRIALS = 6000;        // Number of experimental trials
    private int counter[] = new int[Die.FACES +1];  // Counters

    /**
     * Pre: NTRIALS, the number of trials, is >= 0.
     * Post: the frequencies of NTRIALS die rolls will be recorded in counter[]
     */
    public void testDie() {
        Die die = new Die();                            // Create a die
        for (int k = Die.DIE_LOW; k <= Die.DIE_HIGH; k++)  // Initialize the counters
            counter[k] = 0;
        for ( int k = 0; k < NTRIALS; k++ ) {       // For each trial
            ++counter[die.roll()];                   //   Roll the die and update the counter
        } // for
    }//testDie()

    /**
     * Pre: counter[] array has been initialized
     * Post: the value of each counter is printed
     */
    public void printResults() {
        System.out.println("Out of " + NTRIALS + " die rolls, there were: ");
        for (int k = Die.DIE_LOW; k <= Die.DIE_HIGH; k++)  // Initialize the counters
            System.out.println("\t" + k + "s: " + counter[k]);
    }//printResults()

    public static void main(String args[])  {
        DieExperiment tester = new DieExperiment();
        tester.testDie();
        tester.printResults();
    } // main
} // DieExperiment
```

FIGURE 8–11   Using arrays to store frequencies of die tosses.

Design: The testDie() Method

The testDie() method should create a Die and roll it NTRIALS times, keeping track of the frequencies in the counter array. Before running the test, it should initialize the array elements. A simple counting loop is used for both the initialization task and to run the experiment, but note the difference in the loop bounds used. Here again we see the usefulness of the class constants Die.DIE.LOW and Die.DIE.HIGH. The use of constants here, instead of literal values, would allow us to use this same method to experiment with a 12-sided die:

```
/**
 * Pre: NTRIALS, the number of trials, is >= 0.
 * Post: the frequencies of NTRIALS die rolls will
 *
 *                                be recorded in counter[]
 */
```

```
public void testDie() {
    Die die = new Die();              // Create a die
    for (int k = Die.DIE_LOW; k <= Die.DIE_HIGH; k++)
                                      // Initialize the counters
        counter[k] = 0;
    for ( int k = 0; k < NTRIALS; k++ ) {  // For each trial
        ++counter[die.roll()];        //  Roll the die and update the counter
    } // for
}//testDie()
```

This method assumes that the array of counters is an instance variable of the class. Therefore, there's no need to pass it as a parameter.

Method Design: The `printResults()` Method

After we have run our experiment for a given number of trials, we can print the result by printing the values of each of the NFACES counters. The `printResults()` method uses a simple for loop to print the count of each counter:

Algorithm: counting loop

```
/**
 * Pre: counter[] array has been initialized
 * Post: the value of each counter is printed
 */
public void printResults() {
    System.out.println("Out of " + NTRIALS + " die rolls, there were: ");
                                      // Print the counters
    for (int k = Die.DIE_LOW; k <= Die.DIE_HIGH; k++)
        System.out.println("\t" + k + "s: " + counter[k]);
}//printResults()
```

Note again the use here of symbolic constants instead of literal values. This makes the program more generally useful, easier to read, and easier to modify. The complete source code for this simulation is shown in Figure 8–11. One run of this program on 6,000 trials generated the following output:

```
Out of 6000 die rolls, there were:
  1s: 981  2s: 998  3s: 1024  4s: 956  5s: 1008  6s: 1033
```

As you can see, the results are fairly evenly distributed, with each face coming up approximately one-sixth of the time.

The problem of keeping track of the frequencies of die rolls turns out to be a perfect use for an array. Over all the use of arrays in this example makes the code compact and easy to read and understand. Imagine how difficult this problem would be if we could not use arrays. In that case, we would need six distinct int counters and we would have to refer to each one by name rather than by index, and we would have to use individual assignment statements rather than a for loop to update them. That would surely lead to some tedious code.

EFFECTIVE DESIGN: Representation+Action. Arrays can be processed effectively with counting loops to solve a wide range of problems.

SELF-STUDY EXERCISE

EXERCISE 8.11   It might be argued that one shortcoming with the design of the `DieExperiment` class is that it doesn't let the user vary the number of trials. Describe how you would modify this class to give it this capability.

8.5   CASE STUDY: `CyberPet` Animation

Let's return to the task of making CyberPet move. Our strategy will be to loop through an array of images that depict the CyberPet's actions. We will implement this strategy in an applet whose design is shown in Figure 8–12. The applet uses an array to store the images. We would declare this array as follows, using the constant `NIMAGES` to specify the number of images involved.

```
Image image[] = new Image[NIMAGES]; // Create the array
```

Note again that the preceding statement creates an array to store `Images`, but it does *not* create the images themselves. In order to create an `Image` object for each array location, we use a simple for loop:

```
for (int k = 0; k < image.length; k++)   // Create the images
    image[k] = new Image();              // And store in the array
```

In this example, `Image`'s default constructor is used to create an `Image` for each array element. A *GIF* file is a common type of graphics file format, widely used to represent images on the WWW. (See the section on *Data Compression* for more on GIF files.) Another way to create images for the array would be to read them from GIF files, using the `java.applet.Applet.getImage()` method:

```
for (int k = 0; k < image.length; k++)
    image[k] = getImage(getCodeBase(), "image" + k + ".gif");
```

`getImage()` takes two arguments: the location of the applet (the code base) and the name of the file containing the image. In this example, the file name is constructed by concatenating a base file name (`"image"`) with a number (*k*) and the `".gif"` suffix. This will generate file names such as `"image1.gif"` and `"image2.gif."` Assuming these files are stored in the same directory as the applet (the code base), the images will be loaded into the program and stored in the `image` array.

GIF files

Constructing file names

PROGRAMMING TIP: Image Loading.   Depending on the number and size of the images, the process of loading images may take considerable time. It is good interface design to inform the user whenever this delay will be noticeable.

Algorithm Design: Animation

Once the images are stored in the array, they can be displayed by using Java's `Graphics.drawImage()` method:

```
for (int k = 0; k < image.length; k++) {
    g.drawImage(image[k], 1, 1, this);
    delay(MILLISECS);
}
```

FIGURE 8–12   Design of an applet to illustrate animation.

```
          ┌──────────────┐
          │    Applet     │
          ├──────────────┤
          │              │
          ├──────────────┤
          │              │
          └──────────────┘
                 △
                 │
          ┌──────────────────────────┐
          │         Animate           │
          ├──────────────────────────┤
          │ – NIMAGES : int = 5       │
          │ – MILLISECS : int = 200   │
          │ – image : Image[]         │
          │ – imageN : int            │
          ├──────────────────────────┤
          │ + init()                  │
          │ + paint()                 │
          │ – delay(in n : int)       │
          └──────────────────────────┘
```

FIGURE 8–13 The five images used to animate Spidey.

The drawImage() method takes four arguments. The first is a reference to the image, which in our example is a reference to the *k*th array element. The second and third arguments give the horizontal and vertical coordinates at which the image will be displayed. The last argument provides a reference to the applet in which the image will be displayed.

Drawing images

To illustrate these principles, our applet will create a simple animation of our CyberPet. The animation will cycle through the five images shown in Figure 8–13, which are named "spider1.gif" through "spider5.gif" and stored in the same directory as the applet. The applet loads these images into an array and then repeatedly cycles through the array until the user quits the applet.

The init() method loads the image files into the image array:

```
public void init() {
    showStatus("Loading image files.  Please wait.");
    for (int k = 0; k < image.length; k++)
                        // Read each image from file to array
        image[k] = getImage(getDocumentBase(), "spider" + k + ".gif");
} // init()
```

The paint() method repeatedly displays an image and then delays for MILLISECS milliseconds. This delay is necessary to prevent the images from flashing by so quickly that the illusion of motion is lost. Here's what the code looks like:

```
public void paint(Graphics g) {
    g.drawImage(image[imageN], 1, 1, this); // Draw an image
    imageN = (imageN + 1) % NIMAGES;        // Select the next image
    delay(MILLISECS);                       // Delay for a while
    repaint();                              // Then do it all over again
} // paint()
```

Data Compression

LZW algorithm

THE *Graphical Interchange Format (GIF)* was developed by CompuServe, the commercial online service provider, as a way for transferring digital images over networked computers. GIF files transfer 8-bit digital images—that is, images in which 8 bits are used to represent each pixel. This means that it is limited to images that contain at most $256 = 2^8$ colors.

GIF files are compressed using an algorithm known as Lempel-Ziv-Welch compression, or LZW for short. This is an algorithm that recognizes common string patterns. Instead of representing each separate character in a file, LZW encoding represents each string pattern as a bit pattern. For example, suppose the file consisted of the following sentence, which we depict here as an array of characters, with the array indexes of the first ten characters written above the string:

```
0123456789 // Indexes
the theory is that... // String to compress
```

This sentence can be also represented as follows:

```
the [0,3]ory[3,1]is[3,1][0,2]a[0,1]
```

The first four characters contain no repeats so they are listed verbatim. However, the string "the" repeats the three letters that started at index 0. Instead of repeating "the", we insert the notation [0,3], which means "insert the three characters starting at index 0." The other bracketed expressions perform similar insertions.

Even though this example did not achieve any real compression, significant compression would result if we had a longer file. On average a typical text file is reduced by 50 percent by LZW compression. It is used in common commercial compression programs, such as Stuffit, WinZip, and ZipIt.

It begins by drawing one of the images from the image array. The variable imageN is used to keep track of the current image and is updated after each image is displayed. Note the use of modular arithmetic here:

```
imageN = (imageN + 1) % NIMAGES;
```

If NIMAGES is 5, this statement will cause imageN to take on the values 0 through 4. When imageN equals 4, adding 1 modulo 5 will give 0, thereby causing imageN to wrap around to 0.

Repainting the applet

Recall that the paint() method is called automatically when the applet begins execution. Note the call to repaint() on the last line of paint(). This will cause the cycle of drawing and delaying to be repeated indefinitely.

Delaying the animation

The delay() method is a private method that causes the applet to pause for *n* milliseconds. It causes the applet to sleep for *n* milliseconds. We will discuss how it works when we talk about threads in Chapter 13. The complete Animate.java program is shown in Figure 8–14.

```
import java.applet.Applet;              // Import the applet library
import java.awt.*;                      // Import the GUI components

public class Animate extends Applet {
    private static int NIMAGES = 5;
    private static int MILLISECS = 200;

    private Image image[] = new Image[NIMAGES];
    private int imageN = 0;

    public void init() {
        showStatus("Loading image files.  Please wait.");
        for (int k = 0; k < image.length; k++)     // Read each image from file to array
            image[k] = getImage(getDocumentBase(), "spider" + k + ".gif");
    } // init()

    public void paint(Graphics g) {
        g.drawImage(image[imageN], 1, 1, this);  // Draw an image
        imageN = (imageN + 1) % NIMAGES;         // Select the next image
        delay(MILLISECS);                        // Delay for a while
        repaint();                               // Then do it all over again
    } // paint()

    private void delay(int n) {     // Private helper method
        try {
            Thread.sleep( n );                   // Pause the applet for n milliseconds
        } catch (InterruptedException e) {
            System.out.println(e.toString());
        }
    } // delay()
} // Animate
```

FIGURE 8–14   The Animate applet.

8.6   Array Algorithms: Sorting

Sorting an array is the process of arranging its elements in ascending or descending order. Sorting algorithms are among the most widely used algorithms. Any time large amounts of data are maintained, there is some need to arrange them in a particular order. For example, the telephone company needs to arrange its accounts by the last name of the account holder as well as by phone number.

8.6.1   Bubble Sort

The first sorting algorithm we'll look at is known as **bubble sort**, so named because on each pass through the array the algorithm causes the largest element to "bubble up" toward the "top" of the array, much as the bubbles in a carbonated drink. A second sorting algorithm, **selection sort**, is covered in Section 8.6.3.

Bubble sort requires repeated passes over the unsorted array, but it sorts the elements *in place*, which means that it doesn't require any additional memory to store the sorted elements. In pseudocode, bubble sort can be represented as follows:

```
Bubble sort an array of N elements into ascending order
1. For each of the N-1 passes over the entire array
2.    For each of the N-1 pairs of adjacent elements in the array
3.       If the lower indexed element is greater than the higher
         indexed element
4.          Swap the two elements
```

To see how this works, consider an integer array containing the ages of five friends:

```
21  20  27  24  19
```

For this five-element array, bubble sort will make four passes, comparing each pair of adjacent elements (step 3), swapping elements that are out of order (step 4). Because 21 and 20 are out of order, they are swapped, leading to the following arrangement of the array. The brackets are used to highlight where we are in the trace:

```
[20  21]  27  24  19
```

The next pair of elements, 21 and 27, are in the correct order so the array will remain unchanged. The next pair of elements, 27 and 24, are swapped, giving

```
20  21  [24  27]  19
```

The last pair, 27 and 19, will be swapped, giving

```
20  21  24  [19  27]
```

The result of the first pass over the array is that the largest element, 27, has "bubbled up" to the top of the array. After the second pass through the array, the second largest element, 24, will bubble up to its proper place in the array, giving

```
20  21  19 | 24  27
```

In effect, the numbers to the right of the vertical line are in their proper locations. On the next pass the third largest element will find its proper location giving

```
20  19 | 21  24  27
```

Finally, on the fourth pass, the fourth and fifth largest elements will be arranged in their proper locations. When the algorithm terminates, all of the array elements will have been placed in their proper locations:

```
| 19  20  21  24  27
```

N − 1 passes

Note that for a five-element array, each pass requires that we compare four pairs of adjacent elements. In general, for an N element array, we would have to compare $N - 1$ pairs of adjacent elements on each pass through the array. Also, on each pass one array element will bubble up to its proper location in the sorted array. Thus, to sort an N-element array, bubble sort will make $N - 1$ passes, comparing $N - 1$ adjacent elements on each pass.

The Sort class (Figs. 8–15 and 8–16) provides an implementation of the bubble sort algorithm. Because it takes an int array as a parameter, the bubbleSort() method will sort any array of integers, regardless of the array's length. Note how bracket notation ([]) is used to declare an array parameter. If the brackets were omitted, then arr would be indistinguishable from an ordinary int parameter. Using the brackets indicates that this method takes an array of integers as its parameter.

> **DEBUGGING TIP: Array Parameter.** When declaring an array parameter, it is necessary to use brackets after the array name; otherwise Java will think you're passing a simple data value rather than an array of values.

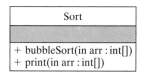

Sort
+ bubbleSort(in arr : int[]) + print(in arr : int[])

FIGURE 8–15 The Sort class illustrates the bubble sort algorithm. *Array parameters*

FIGURE 8–16 The Sort class contains the bubbleSort() method. Note how the method is passed an integer array, which is declared in the main() method.

```
public class Sort {
    /**
     * Goal: Sort the values in arr into ascending order
     * Pre: arr is not null.
     * Post: The values arr[0]...arr[arr.length-1] will be
     *  arranged in ascending order.
     */
    public void bubbleSort(int arr[]) {
        int temp;                            // Temporary variable for swap
        for (int pass = 1; pass < arr.length; pass++)    // For each pass
            for (int pair = 1; pair < arr.length; pair++) // For each pair
                if (arr[pair-1] > arr[pair]) {           //   Compare
                    temp = arr[pair-1];                  //   and swap
                    arr[pair-1] = arr[pair];
                    arr[pair] = temp;
                } // if
    } // bubbleSort()

    public void print(int arr[]) {
        for (int k = 0; k < arr.length; k++)     // For each integer
            System.out.print( arr[k] + " \t ");  //  Print it
        System.out.println();
    } // print()

    public static void main(String args[]) {
        int intArr[] = { 21, 20, 27, 24, 19 };
        Sort sorter = new Sort();
        sorter.print(intArr);
        sorter.bubbleSort(intArr);
        sorter.print(intArr);
    } // main()
} //Sort
```

8.6.2 Algorithm: Swapping Memory Elements

A second important feature of this method is its use of the int variable temp to store one of the two array elements that are being swapped. The need for this variable is a subtlety that beginning programmers frequently

Swapping blunder

overlook, but consider what would happen if `temp` were not used. Suppose that `arr[pair-1]` refers to 4 and `arr[pair]` refers to 2 in the following array:

```
1 4 2 8
```

and suppose in an attempt to swap 4 and 2, we execute the following two assignment statements:

```
arr[pair-1] = arr[pair];
arr[pair] = arr[pair-1];
```

Because the first assignment statement places 2 in the location that was holding 4, both locations will now be holding 2. The 4 will be overwritten and will no longer be available in the second assignment statement. Thus, the result of these two statements is

```
1 2 2 8
```

Swapping algorithm

The proper way to swap the two elements is to use a temporary variable to store the first element while its location is overwritten and then retrieve the stored value from the temporary variable and assign it to the second element:

```
temp = arr[pair-1];       // Save first element in temp
arr[pair-1] = arr[pair];  // Overwrite first with second
arr[pair] = temp;         // Overwrite second from temp (i.e.,first)
```

This code will lead to the result we want—that is, to 4 and 2 being swapped in the array:

```
1 2 4 8
```

In general, the following method implements the swap algorithm for two elements, *el1* and *el2* of an `int` array:

```
/**
 * Goal: Swap el1 and el2 in the int array, arr
 * Pre: arr is not null and el1 and el2 refer to indexes
 *   between 0 and arr.length - 1
 * Post: The values arr[el1] and arr[el2] will be swapped.
 */
void swap(int arr[], int el1, int el2) {
    int temp = arr[el1]; // Assign the first element to temp
    arr[el1] = arr[el2]; // Overwrite first with second
    arr[el2] = temp;     // Overwrite second with temp (i.e., first)
} // swap()
```

PROGRAMMING TIP: Swapping Variables. Whenever you are swapping two memory elements, a temporary variable must be used to store one of the elements while its memory location is being overwritten.

8.6.3 Selection Sort

To illustrate the *selection sort* algorithm, suppose you want to sort a deck of 52 cards. Cards are arranged in order of face value, 2 through 10, jack, queen, king, ace. And suits are arranged according to clubs, diamonds, hearts, and spades, so the first card in the deck will be the two of clubs, and the last card will be the ace of spades.

Selection sort algorithm

Lay the 52 cards out on a table, face up, one card next to the other. Then starting with the first card, look through the deck and find the smallest card (the two of clubs), and exchange it with the card in the first location. Then go through the deck again starting at the second card, find the next smallest card (the three of clubs) and exchange it with the card in the second location. Repeat this process 51 times.

Translating this strategy into pseudocode gives the following algorithm:

```
Selection sort of a deck of 52 cards from small to large
1. For count assigned 1 to 51                    // Outer loop
2.    smallestCard = count
3.    For currentCard assigned count+1 to 52     // Inner loop
4.       If deck[currentCard] < deck[smallestCard]
5.           smallestCard = currentCard
6.    If smallestCard != count                   // You need to swap
7        Swap deck[count] and deck[smallestCard]
```

For a deck of 52 cards, you need to repeat the outer loop 51 times. In other words, you must select the smallest card and insert it in its proper location 51 times. The inner loop takes care of finding the smallest remaining card.

On each iteration of this outer loop, the algorithm assumes that the card specified by the outer loop variable, count, is the smallest card (line 2). (It usually won't be, of course, but we have to start somewhere.)

The inner loop then iterates through the remaining cards (from count+1 to 52) and compares each one with the card that is currently the smallest (lines 4 and 5). Whenever it finds a card that is smaller than the smallest card, it designates it as the smallest card so far (line 5). In effect the smallestCard variable is used to remember where the smallest card is in the deck.

Finally, when the inner loop is finished, the algorithm swaps the smallest card with the card in the location designated by count. Don't forget that in order to swap two memory elements (line 6), you need to use a temporary variable.

The implementation of the selection sort method, as part of the Deck class, is left as a lab exercise or programming assignment.

SELF-STUDY EXERCISES

EXERCISE 8.12   Sort the array, 24 18 90 1 0 85 34 18, by hand using bubble sort. Show the order of the elements after each iteration of the outer loop.

EXERCISE 8.13   Sort the array, 24 18 90 1 0 85 34 18, by hand using selection sort. Show the order of the elements after each iteration of the outer loop.

EXERCISE 8.14   Write a Java code segment to swap two CyberPets, pet1 and pet2.

EXERCISE 8.15 The bubbleSort() in this section will keep passing over the array even if it's already sorted. Modify the algorithm so that it stops when the array is sorted. (*Hint*: Use a boolean variable to keep track of whether a swap was made inside the loop, and check this variable in the loop entry condition.)

8.6.4 Passing Array Parameters

When an array is passed to a method, as in bubbleSort(), only the name of the array should be specified in the method call statement. For example, suppose we have declared an array of integers as follows:

```
int arr[] = { 21, 13, 5, 10, 14, 6, 2 };
```

To sort this array we would use the following method call:

```
bubbleSort(arr); // Correct way to pass an array to a method
```

It would be incorrect to use the following statement as a method call:

```
bubbleSort(arr[]); // Syntax error---brackets aren't allowed
```

DEBUGGING TIP: Passing an Array Argument. A common syntax error is to use brackets when passing an array argument. In passing an array to a method, just use the name of the array. Brackets are only used in the method definition, not in the method call.

Passing a Value and Passing a Reference

Recall from Section 3.5 that when an Object is passed to a method, a copy of the reference to the Object is passed. Because an array is an object, a reference to the array is passed to bubbleSort(), rather than the whole array itself. This is in contrast to how a value of a primitive type is passed. In that case, a copy of the actual value is passed.

JAVA LANGUAGE RULE Primitive Versus Object Parameters. In Java, when a value of a primitive data type—int, double, char, boolean— is passed as a parameter, a copy of the value itself is passed; when a reference to an Object is passed, a copy of the reference is passed.

One implication of this distinction is that when the argument is a primitive type, the original argument cannot be changed within the method, because the method just has a copy of its value. For example, the following method takes a single int parameter *n*, which is incremented within the method:

```
public void add1(int n) {
    System.out.println("n = " + n);
    n = n + 1;
    System.out.println("n = " + n);
}
```

But because *n* is a parameter of primitive type, incrementing it within the method has no effect on its associated argument. Thus, in the following segment the value of *Num*—*n*'s associated argument—will not be affected by what goes on inside the add() method:

Passing a primitive value

```
int Num = 5;
System.out.println("Num = " + Num);
add1(Num);
System.out.println("Num = " + Num);
```

and the output generated by this code segment would be

```
Num = 5
n = 5
n = 6
Num = 5
```

Note that while *n*'s value has changed, *Num*'s value remains unaffected.

The case is much different when we pass a reference to an object. In that case, the method *can* manipulate the object itself. The bubbleSort() method is a good illustration. In the following code segment, the array anArr is printed, then sorted, and then printed again:

Passing an object

```
int anArr[] = { 5, 10, 16, -2, 4, 6, 1 };  // Initialize

for (int k = 0; k < anArr.length; k++)     // Print
    System.out.print(anArr[k] + " ");

System.out.println("");
bubbleSort(anArr);                         // Sort

for (int k = 0; k < anArr.length; k++)     // Print again
    System.out.print(anArr[k] + " ");
```

The output generated by this code would be the following:

```
5 10 16 -2 4 6 1
-2 1 4 5 6 10 16
```

which illustrates that changes within bubbleSort to the array referenced by arr are actually being made to anArr itself. If fact, because bubbleSort() is passed a copy of the reference variable anArr, both arr and anArr are references to the very same object—that is, to the same array (Fig. 8–17).

The justification for passing a reference to an object rather than the entire object itself is a matter of efficiency. A reference uses just 4 bytes of data, whereas an object may use thousands of bytes. It would just be

Method call overhead

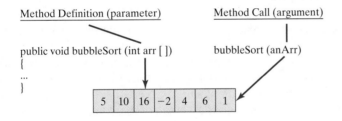

FIGURE 8–17 When an array is passed to a method as an argument, both the array reference itself and the corresponding method parameter are references to the same object.

too inefficient to copy hundreds of bytes each time an object is passed to a method. Instead, the method is passed a reference to the object, thereby giving it access to the object without incurring the expense of copying large amounts of data. Indeed, Java provides no way to pass a copy of an object to a method.

SELF-STUDY EXERCISE

EXERCISE 8.16 Give the values that will be stored in myArr and k AFTER you invoke mystery(myArr, k), where myArr, k and mystery() are declared as follows:

```
int myArr[] = {1,2,3,4,5};
int k = 3;
void mystery(int a[], int m) {
    ++a[m];
    --m;
}
```

8.7 Array Algorithms: Searching

Suppose we have a large array and we need to find one of its elements. We need an algorithm to search the array for a particular value, usually called the *key*. If the elements of the array are not arranged in any particular order, the only way we can be sure to find the key, assuming it is in the array, is to search every element, beginning at the first element, until we find it.

8.7.1 Sequential Search

This approach is known as **sequential search**, because each element of the array will be examined in sequence until the key is found (or the end of the array is reached). A pseudocode description of this algorithm is as follows:

```
1. For each element of the array
2.     If the element equals the key
3.         Return the element's index
4. If the key is not found in the array
5.     Return -1 (to indicate failure)
```

Search
+ sequentialSearch(in arr : int[], in key : int) + binarySearch(in arr : int[], in key : int)

FIGURE 8–18 The Search class.

This algorithm can easily be implemented in a method that searches an integer array, which is passed as the method's parameter. If the key is found in the array, its location is returned. If it is not found, then −1 is returned to indicate failure.

The Search class (Figs. 8–18 and 8–19) provides the Java implementation of the sequentialSearch() method. The method takes two parameters: the array to be searched and the key to be searched for. It uses a for statement to examine each element of the array, checking whether it equals the key or not. If an element that equals the key is found, the method immediately returns that element's index. Note that the last statement in the method will only be reached if no element matching the key is found.

```
public class Search {

    /**
     * Performs a sequential search of an integer array
     * @param arr is the array of integers
     * @param key is the element being searched for
     * @return the key's index is returned if the key is
     *  found otherwise -1 is returned
     * Pre:  arr is not null
     * Post: either -1 or the key's index is returned
     */
    public int sequentialSearch(int arr[], int key) {
        for (int k = 0; k < arr.length; k++)
            if (arr[k] == key)
                return k;
        return -1;            // Failure if this is reached
    } // sequentialSearch()

    /**
     * Performs a binary search of an integer array
     * @param arr is the array of integers
     * @param key is the element being searched for
     * @return the key's index is returned if the key is
     *  found otherwise -1 is returned
     * Pre: arr is an array of int in ascending order
     * Post: -1 or arr[k] where arr[k] == key
     */
    public int binarySearch(int arr[], int key) {
        int low = 0;                        // Initialize bounds
        int high = arr.length - 1;
        while (low <= high) {               // While not done
            int mid = (low + high) / 2;
            if (arr[mid] == key)
                return mid;                 // Success
            else if (arr[mid] < key)
                low = mid + 1;              // Search top half
            else
                high = mid - 1;             // Search bottom half
        }  // while
        return -1;    // Post condition: low > high implies search failed
    } // binarySearch()
}//Search
```

FIGURE 8–19 The Search class contains both a sequentialSearch() and a binarySearch().

EFFECTIVE DESIGN: Sentinel Return Value. Like Java's indexOf() method, the sequentialSearch() returns a sentinel value (−1) to indicate that the key was not found. This is a common design for search methods.

8.7.2 Binary Search

If the elements of an array have been sorted into ascending or descending order, it is not necessary to search sequentially through each element of the array in order to find or not find the key. Instead, the search algorithm can make use of the knowledge that the array is ordered and perform what's known as a **binary search**, a divide-and-conquer algorithm that divides the array in half on each iteration and limits its search to just that half that could contain the key.

To illustrate the binary search, recall the familiar guessing game in which you try to guess a secret number between 1 and 100, being told "too high" or "too low" or "just right" on each guess. A good first guess should be 50. If this is too high, the next guess should be 25, because if 50 is too high the number must be between 1 and 49. If 50 was too low, the next guess should be 75. And so on. After each wrong guess, a good guesser should pick the midpoint of the sublist that would contain the secret number.

How many guesses?

Proceeding in this way, the correct number can be guessed in at most log_2N guesses, because the base-2 logarithm of N is the number of times you can divide N in half. For a list of 100 items, the search should take no more than seven guesses ($2^7 = 128 > 100$). For a list of 1,000 items, a binary search would take at most ten guesses ($2^{10} = 1,024 > 1,000$).

So a binary search is a much more efficient way to search, provided the array's elements are in order. Note that "order" here needn't be numeric order. We could use binary search to look up a word in a dictionary or a name in a phone book.

A pseudocode representation of the binary search is given as follows:

```
TO SEARCH AN ARRAY OF N ELEMENTS IN ASCENDING ORDER

1. Assign 0 low and assign N-1 to high initially
2. As long as low is not greater than high
3.     Assign (low + high) / 2 to mid
4.     If the element at mid equals the key
5.         then return its index
6.     Else if the element at mid is less than the key
7.         then assign mid + 1 to low
8.     Else assign mid - 1 to high
9. If this is reached return -1 to indicate failure
```

Just as with the sequential search algorithm, this algorithm can easily be implemented in a method that searches an integer array that is passed as the method's parameter (Fig. 8–19). If the key is found in the array, its location is returned. If it is not found, then −1 is returned to indicate failure. The method takes two parameters: an integer array to be searched and an integer key to be found. In addition, the local variables low and high are used as *pointers* to the current low and high ends of the array, respectively. Note the loop-entry condition: low <= high. If low ever becomes greater than high, this indicates that key is not contained in the array. In that case, the algorithm returns −1.

Note that as the search progresses, the array is repeatedly cut in half and low and high will be used to point to the low and high index values in that portion of the array that is still being searched. The local variable mid is used to point to the approximate midpoint of the unsearched portion of the array. If the key is determined to be past the midpoint, then low is adjusted to mid+1; if the key occurs before the midpoint, then high is set to mid-1. The updated values of low and high limit the search to the unsearched portion of the original array.

Unlike sequential search, binary search does not have to examine every location in the array to determine that the key is not in the array. The reason, of course, is that the algorithm searches only that part of the array that could contain the key. An example will make this clearer. Suppose the array we are searching is declared as follows:

```
int sortArr[] = { 1,2,3,4,5,6,7,8,9,10,11,12,13,14,15,16,17,18,19,20};
```

And suppose we search for the key −5. Since this key is smaller than any element of the array, the algorithm will repeatedly divide the low end of the array in half until the condition low > high becomes true. We can see this by tracing the values that low, mid, and high will take during the search:

Key	Iteration	Low	High	Mid
-5	0	0	19	9
-5	1	0	8	4
-5	2	0	3	1
-5	3	0	0	0
-5	4	0	-1	Failure

As this trace shows, in order to determine that −5 is not in the array, the algorithm need only examine locations 9, 4, 1, and 0. After checking location 0, the new value for high will become −1, which makes the condition low <= high false. So the search loop will terminate.

The TestSearch class (Figs. 8–20 and 8–21) provides a test program that can be used to test two search methods. It creates an integer array, whose values are in ascending order. It then uses the getInput() method to input an integer from the keyboard and then performs both a sequentialSearch() and a binarySearch() for the number.

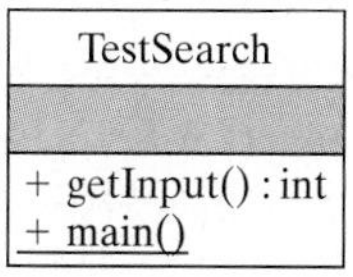

FIGURE 8–20 The TestSearch class.

SELF-STUDY EXERCISE

EXERCISE 8.17   For the array containing the elements 2, 4, 6, and so on up to 28 in that order, draw a trace showing which elements are examined if you search for 21.

```
import java.io.*;

public class TestSearch {

    /**
     * Goal: read an integer from the keyboard and return it
     * @return the the integer read
     * Pre: none
     * Post: the input integer is returned
     */
    public static int getInput() throws IOException {
        BufferedReader input =
            new BufferedReader (new InputStreamReader(System.in));
        String inputString = new String();
        System.out.println("This program searches for values in an array.");
        System.out.print("Input any positive integer (or any negative to quit) : ");
        inputString = input.readLine();
        return Integer.parseInt(inputString);
    } // getInput()

    public static void main(String args[]) throws IOException {
        int intArr[] = { 2,4,6,8,10,12,14,16,18,20,22,24,26,28};
        Search searcher = new Search();
        int key = 0, keyAt = 0;
        key = getInput();
        while (key >= 0) {
            keyAt = searcher.sequentialSearch( intArr, key );
            if (keyAt != -1)
                System.out.println("  Sequential: " + key + " is at intArr[" + keyAt + "]");
            else
                System.out.println("  Sequential: " + key + " is not contained in intArr[]");
            keyAt = searcher.binarySearch(intArr, key);
            if (keyAt != -1)
                System.out.println("  Binary: " + key + " is at intArr[" + keyAt + "]");
            else
                System.out.println("  Binary: " + key + " is not contained in intArr[]");
            key = getInput();
        } // while
    } // main()
} // TestSearch
```

FIGURE 8–21 The TestSearch class.

8.8   Two-Dimensional Arrays

A **two-dimensional array**, an array whose components are themselves arrays, is necessary or useful for certain kinds of problems. For example, suppose you are doing a scientific study in which you have to track the amount of precipitation for every day of the year.

One way to organize these data would be to create a one-dimensional array, consisting of 365 elements:

```
double rainfall[] = new double[365];
```

However, this representation would have a major limitation: It would make it very difficult to calculate the average rainfall within a given month, which happens to be an important part of your study.

Therefore, a better representation for this problem would be to use a two-dimensional array, one dimension for the months and one for the days. The following statement declares the array variable `rainfall` and creates a 12 by 31 array object as its reference:

What data do we need?

```
double rainfall[][] = new double[12][31];
```

Thus, `rainfall` is an *array of arrays*. You can think of the first array as the 12 months required for the problem. And you can think of each month as an array of 31 days. The months will be indexed from 0 to 11, and the days will be indexed from 0 to 30.

The problem with this representation is that when we want to refer to the rainfall for January 5, we would have to use `rainfall[0][4]`. This is awkward and misleading. The problem is that dates—1/5/1999—are unit indexed, while arrays are zero indexed. Because it will be difficult to remember this fact, our representation of the rainfall data may cause us to make errors when we start writing our algorithms.

Choosing an appropriate representation

We can easily remedy this problem by just defining our array to have an extra month and an extra day each month:

```
double rainfall[][] = new double[13][32];
```

This representation creates an array with 13 months, indexed from 0 to 12, with 32 days per month, indexed from 0 to 31. However, we can simply ignore the 0 month and 0 days by using unit indexing in all of the algorithms that process the array. In other words, if we view this array as a two-dimensional table, consisting of 13 rows and 32 columns, we can leave row 0 and column 0 unused (Fig. 8–22).

As Figure 8–22 shows, the very first element of this 416-element array has subscripts (0,0) while the last location has subscripts (12,31). The main advantages of this representation is that the program as a whole will be much easier to read and understand and much less prone to error.

> **EFFECTIVE DESIGN: Readability.**   For some array problems, it is preferable to use unit indexing. This can be done by declaring extra array elements and ignoring those with index 0. This should be done only when it will improve the program's overall readability and robustness.

FIGURE 8–22   A two-dimensional array with 13 rows and 32 columns. To represent 12 months of the year, we can simply ignore row 0 and column 0.

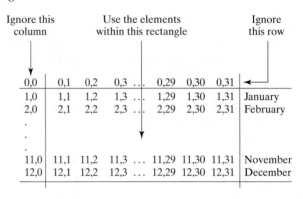

Referring to Elements in a Two-Dimensional Array

In order to refer to an element in a two-dimensional array, you need to use two subscripts. For the `rainfall` array, the first subscript will specify the *month* and the second will specify the *day* within the month. Thus, the following statements assign 1.15 to the `rainfall` element representing January 5, and then print its value:

```
rainfall[1][5] = 1.15;                    // Rainfall for January 5
System.out.println( rainfall[1][5] );
```

Just as in the case of one-dimensional arrays, it is an error to attempt to reference an element that is not in the array. Each of the following examples would cause Java to raise an `IndexOutOfBoundsException`:

```
rainfall[13][32] = 0.15 ;   // No such element
rainfall[11][33] = 1.3;     // No such column
rainfall[14][30] = 0.74;    // No such row
```

SELF-STUDY EXERCISES

EXERCISE 8.18   Declare a two-dimensional array of `int` named `int2d` that contains five rows, each of which contains ten integers.

EXERCISE 8.19   Write a statement that prints the last integer in the third row of the array you created in the previous exercise. Then write an assignment statement that assigns 100 to the last element in the `int2d` array.

Initializing a Two-Dimensional Array

If the initial values of an array's elements are supposed to be zero, there is no need to initialize the elements. Java will do it automatically when you create the array with `new`. However, for many array problems it is necessary to initialize the array elements to some other value. For a two-dimensional array, this would require a nested loop. To illustrate this algorithm, let's use a nested for loop to initialize each element of the `rainfall` array to 0:

```
// Note that both loops are unit indexed.
for (int month = 1; month < rainfall.length; month++)
    for (int day = 1; day < rainfall[month].length; day++)
        rainfall[month][day] = 0.0;
```

Note that both for loops use unit indexing. This is in keeping with our decision to leave month 0 and day 0 unused.

Remember that when you have a nested for loop, the inner loop iterates faster than the outer loop. Thus, for each month, the inner loop will iterate over 31 days. This is equivalent to processing the array as if you were going across each row and then down to the next row in the representation shown in Figure 8–22.

Nested for loops

Note that for a two-dimensional array both dimensions have an associated `length` variable, which is used in this example to specify the upper bound of each for loop. For the `rainfall` array, the first dimension (months) has a length of 13 and the second dimension (days) has a length of 32.

Another way to view the `rainfall` array is to remember that it is an *array of arrays*. The length of the first array, which corresponds to the number (13) of months, is given by `rainfall.length`. The length of each month's array, which corresponds to the number of days (32) in a month, is given by `rainfall[month].length`.

The outer loop of the nested for loop iterates through months 1 through 12. And the inner for loop iterates through days 1 through 31. In this way, $372 = 12 \times 31$ elements of the array are set to 0.0. In Table 8.1 the boldface numbers along the top represent the day subscripts, while the boldface numbers along the left represent the month subscripts.

TABLE 8.1 The initialized `rainfall` array. The unused array elements are shown as dashes.

	0	**1**	**2**	**3**	$\cdots$	**30**	**31**
0	–	–	–	–	$\cdots$	–	–
1	–	0.0	0.0	0.0	$\cdots$	0.0	0.0
2	–	0.0	0.0	0.0	$\cdots$	0.0	0.0
$\vdots$	$\vdots$	$\vdots$	$\vdots$	$\vdots$	$\vdots$	$\vdots$	$\vdots$
10	–	0.0	0.0	0.0	$\cdots$	0.0	0.0
11	–	0.0	0.0	0.0	$\cdots$	0.0	0.0
12	–	0.0	0.0	0.0	$\cdots$	0.0	0.0

SELF-STUDY EXERCISE

EXERCISE 8.20   Write a loop to print all of the elements of `int2d`, which you declared in the exercises in the previous section. Print one row per line with a space between each element on a line.

8.8.1   Two-Dimensional Array Methods

Now that we have figured out how to represent the data for our scientific experiment, let's develop methods to calculate some results. First, we want a method to initialize the array. This method will simply incorporate the nested loop algorithm we developed previously:

```
/**
 * Initializes the rainfall array
 * @param rain is a 2D-array of rainfalls
 * Pre:  rain is non null
 * Post: rain[x][y] == 0 for all x,y in the array
 * Note that the loops use unit indexing.
 */
public void initRain(double rain[][]) {
    for (int month = 1; month < rain.length; month++)
        for (int day = 1; day < rain[month].length; day++)
            rain[month][day] = 0.0;
} // initRain()
```

Array parameters

Note how we declare the parameter for a multidimensional array. In addition to the element type (double), and the name of the parameter (rain), we must also include a set of brackets for *each* dimension of the array.

Note also that we use the parameter name within the method to refer to the array. As with one-dimensional arrays, the parameter is a reference to the array, which means that any changes made to the array within the method will persist when the method is exited.

Method: avgDailyRain()

Algorithm design

One result that our experiment needs is the average daily rainfall. To calculate this result, we would add up all of the rainfalls stored in the 12×31 array and divide by 365. Of course, the array itself contains more than 365 elements. It contains 416 elements, but we're not using the first month of the array, and within some months—those with fewer than 31 days—we're not using some of the day elements. For example, there's no such day as rainfall[2][30], which would represent February 30. However, because we initialized all of the array's elements to 0, the rainfall recorded for the nondays will be 0, which won't affect our overall average.

Method design

The method for calculating average daily rainfall should take our two-dimensional array of double as a parameter, and it should return a double. Its algorithm will use a nested for loop to iterate through the elements of the array, adding each element to a running total. When the loops exits, the total will be divided by 365 and returned:

```
/**
 * Computes average daily rainfall for a year of rainfall data
 * @param rain is a 2D-array of rainfalls
 * @return The sum of rain[x][y] / 356
 * Pre:  rain is non null
 * Post: The sum of rain / 365 is calculated
 * Note that the loops are unit indexed
 */
public double avgDailyRain(double rain[][]) {
    double total = 0;
    for (int month = 1; month < rain.length; month++)
        for (int day = 1; day < rain[month].length; day++)
            total += rain[month][day];
    return total/365;
} // avgDailyRain()
```

Method: `avgRainForMonth()`

One reason we used a two-dimensional array for this problem is so we could calculate the average daily rainfall for a given month. Let's write a method to solve this problem. The algorithm for this method will not require a nested for loop, because we will just iterate through the 31 elements of a given month. So the month subscript will not vary. For example, suppose we are calculating the average for January, which is represented in our array as month 1:

Algorithm design

```
double total = 0;
for (int day = 1; day < rainfall[1].length; day++)
    total = total + rainfall[1][day];
```

Thus, the month subscript is held constant (at 1) while the day subscript iterates from 1 to 31. Of course, in our method we would use a parameter to represent the month, thereby allowing us to calculate the average daily rainfall for any given month.

Method design

Another problem that our method has to deal with is that months don't all have 31 days, so we can't always divide by 31 to compute the monthly average. There are various ways to solve this problem, but perhaps the easiest is to let the number of days for that month be specified as a third parameter. That way the month itself and the number of days for the month are supplied by the user of the method:

Method design: What data do we need?

```
/**
 * Computes average daily rainfall for a given month containing nDays
 * @param rain is a 2D-array of rainfalls
 * @param month is the month of the year, 1 ... 12
 * @param nDays is the number of days in month, 1 ... 31
 * @return The sum of rain[month] / nDays
 * Pre:  1 <= month <= 12 and 1 <= nDays <= 31
 * Post: The sum of rain[month] / nDays is calculated
 */
public double avgRainForMonth(double rain[][], int month, int nDays) {
    double total = 0;
    for (int day = 1; day < rain[month].length; day++)
        total = total + rain[month][day];
    return total/nDays;
} // avgRainForMonth()
```

Given this definition, we can call this method as follows to calculate and print the average daily rainfall for March:

```
System.out.println("March: " + avgRainForMonth(rainfall,3,31));
```

Note that when passing the entire two-dimensional array to the method, we just use the name of the array. We do not follow the name with subscripts.

8.8.2 Passing Part of an Array to a Method

Instead of passing the entire rainfall array to the `avgRainForMonth()` method, we could redesign this method so that it is only passed the particular month that's being averaged. Remember that a two-dimensional

Method design: What data?

array is an array of arrays, so if we pass the month of January, we are passing an array of 32 days. If we use this approach, we need only two parameters: the month, which is array of days, and the number of days in that month:

```
/**
 * Computes average daily rainfall for the given month of rainfall data
 * @param monthRain is a 1D-array of rainfalls
 * @param nDays is the number of days in monthRain
 * @return The sum of monthRain / nDays
 * Pre:  1 <= nDays <= 31
 * Post: The sum of monthRain / nDays is calculated
 */
public double avgRainForMonth(double monthRain[], int nDays) {
    double total = 0;
    for (int day = 1; day < monthRain.length; day++)
        total = total + monthRain[day];
    return total/nDays;
} // avgRainForMonth()
```

Given this definition, we can call it as follows to calculate and print the average daily rainfall for March:

```
System.out.println("March: " + avgRainForMonth(rainfall[3],31));
```

In this case, we're passing an array of double to the method, but in order to reference it, we have to pull it out of the two-dimensional array by giving its *row* subscript as well. Thus, rainfall[3] refers to one month of data in the two-dimensional array. It refers to the month of March. But rainfall[3] is itself a one-dimensional array. Figure 8–23 helps to clarify this point.

It's important to note that deciding whether to use brackets when passing data to a method is not just a matter of whether you are passing an array. It is a matter of what type of data the method parameter specifies. So, whenever you call a method that involves a parameter, you have

Specifying an argument

FIGURE 8–23 Referencing individual elements and array elements in a two-dimensional array.

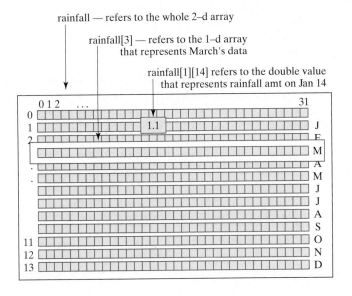

Rainfall
+ initRain(in rain : double[][])
+ avgDailyRain(in rain : double[][]) : double
+ avgDailyRainForMonth(in monthRain : double[], in nDays : int) : double
+ main()

FIGURE 8–24   The Rainfall class.

to look at the method definition to see what kind of data that parameter specifies. Then you must supply an argument that refers to that type of data.

For our two-dimensional rainfall array, we can refer to the entire array as rainfall. We can refer to one of its months as rainfall[j], where *j* is any integer between 1 and 12. And we can refer to any of its elements as rainfall[j][k], where *j* is any integer between 1 and 12, and *k* is any integer between 1 and 31.

> **JAVA LANGUAGE RULE**   Arguments and Parameters. The argument in a method call must match the data type in the method definition. This applies to all parameters, including array parameters.

The Rainfall class (Figs. 8–24 and 8–25) shows how we can test our array algorithms. It creates the rainfall array in the main() method. It then initializes the array and prints out average daily rainfall and average daily rainfall for the month of March. However, note that we have made a slight modification to the initRain() method. Instead of just assigning 0 to each element, we assign a random value between 0 and 2.0:

```
rain[month][day] = Math.random() * 2.0;
```

Generating test data

Using the Math.random() method in this way provides a handy way to generate some realistic test data. In this case, we have scaled the data so that the daily rainfall is between 0 and 2 inches. (Rainfall like this would probably be appropriate for an Amazonian rain forest!) Testing our algorithms with these data provides some indication that our methods are in fact working properly.

> **EFFECTIVE DESIGN: Generating Test Data.**   The Math.random() method can be used to generate numeric test data, when large amounts of data are required. The data can be scaled to fit within the range that the actual data are expected to have.

SELF-STUDY EXERCISES

EXERCISE 8.21   Suppose you're going to keep track of the daily newspaper sales at the local kiosk. Declare a 52 × 7 two-dimensional array of int and initialize each of its elements to 0.

EXERCISE 8.22   Write a method to calculate the average number of newspapers sold per week, using the array you declared in the previous exercise.

```java
public class Rainfall {

    /**
     * Initializes the rainfall array
     * @param rain is a 2D-array of rainfalls
     * Pre:  rain is non null
     * Post: rain[x][y] == 0 for all x,y in the array
     * Note that the loops use unit indexing.
     */
    public void initRain(double rain[][]) {
        for (int month = 1; month < rain.length; month++)
            for (int day = 1; day < rain[month].length; day++)
                rain[month][day] = Math.random() * 2.0;      // Random rainfall
    } // initRain()

    /**
     * Computes average daily rainfall for a year of rainfall data
     * @param rain is a 2D-array of rainfalls
     * @return The sum of rain[x][y] / 356
     * Pre:  rain is non null
     * Post: The sum of rain / 365 is calculated
     * Note that the loops are unit indexed
     */
    public double avgDailyRain(double rain[][]) {
        double total = 0;
        for (int month = 1; month < rain.length; month++)
            for (int day = 1; day < rain[month].length; day++)
                total += rain[month][day];
        return total/365;
    } // avgDailyRain()

    /**
     * Computes average daily rainfall for a given month containing nDays
     * @param monthRain is a 1D-array of rainfalls
     * @param nDays is the number of days in monthRain
     * @return The sum of monthRain / nDays
     * Pre:  1 <= nDays <= 31
     * Post: The sum of monthRain / nDays is calculated
     */
    public double avgRainForMonth(double monthRain[], int nDays) {
        double total = 0;
        for (int day = 1; day < monthRain.length; day++)
            total = total + monthRain[day];
        return total/nDays;
    } // avgRainForMonth()

    public static void main(String args[]) {
        double rainfall[][] = new double[13][32];

        Rainfall data = new Rainfall();
        data.initRain(rainfall);
        System.out.println("The average daily rainfall = "
                            + data.avgDailyRain(rainfall));
        System.out.println("The average daily rainfall for March = "
                            + data.avgRainForMonth(rainfall[3],31));
    } // main()
}//Rainfall
```

FIGURE 8–25 Definition of the Rainfall class.

EXERCISE 8.23 Write a method to calculate the total number of newspapers sold per Sunday, using the array you declared in the previous exercise. Assume that Sunday is the last day of the week.

8.9 Multidimensional Arrays

Java doesn't limit arrays to just two dimensions. For example, suppose we decide to extend our rainfall survey to cover a ten-year period. For each year we now need a two-dimensional array. This results in a three-dimensional array consisting of an array of years, each of which contains an array of months, each of which contains an array of days:

```
final int NYEARS = 10;
final int NMONTHS = 13;
final int NDAYS = 32;
double rainfall[][][] = new double[NYEARS][NMONTHS][NDAYS];
```

Following the design convention of not using the 0 month and 0 days, we end up with a $10 \times 13 \times 32$ array. Note the use of `final` variables to represent the size of each dimension of the array. This helps to make the program more readable.

In Figure 8–26 each year of the rainfall data is represented as a separate page, and on each page there is a two-dimensional table, consisting of 12 rows (1 per month) and 31 columns (1 per day).

You might imagine that our study could be extended to cover rainfall data from a number of different cities. That would result in a four-dimensional array, with the first dimension now being the city. Of course, for this to work, cities would have to be represented by integers, because array subscripts must be integers.

As you might expect, algorithms for processing each element in a three-dimensional table would require a three-level nested loop. For example, the following algorithm would be used to initialize all elements of our three-dimensional rainfall array:

```
for (int year = 0; year < rainfall.length; year++)
    for (int month = 0; month < rainfall[year].length; month++)
        for (int day = 0; day < rainfall[year][month].length; day++)
            rainfall[year][month][day] = 0.0;
```

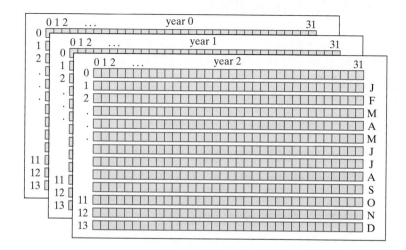

FIGURE 8–26 Three-dimensional data might be viewed as a collection of pages, each of which contains a two-dimensional table.

Note again the proper use of the `length` attribute for each of the three dimensions of the array. In the outer loop, `rainfall.length`, we're referring to the number of years. In the middle loop, `rainfall[year].length`, we're referring to number of months within a given year. In the inner loop, `rainfall[year][month].length`, we're referring to the number of days within a month.

If we added a fourth dimension to our array and wanted to extend this algorithm to initialize it, we would simply embed the three-level loop within another for loop that would iterate over each city.

8.9.1 Array Initializers

It is possible to use an initializer with a **multidimensional array**. For instance, the following examples create several small arrays and initialize their elements:

```
int a[][] = { {1,2,3}, {4,5,6} } ;
char c[][] = { {'a','b'}, {'c','d'} } ;
double d[][][] = { {1.0,2.0,3.0}, {4.0,5.0}, {6.0,7.0,8.0,9.0} } ;
```

The first of these declarations creates a 2×3 array of integers. The second example creates a 2×2 array of characters, and the third example creates an array of `double` consisting of three rows, each of which has a different number of elements. The first row contains three elements, the second contains two elements, and the last row contains four elements. As this last example shows, the rows in a multidimensional array don't all have to have the same length.

Using initializers, as in these examples, is feasible only for relatively small arrays. To see why, just imagine what the initializer expression would be for our three-dimensional `rainfall` array. It would require $4,160 = 10 \times 13 \times 32$ zeroes, separated by commas!

PROGRAMMING TIP: Array Initializers. Initializer (assignment) expressions can be used to assign initial values to relatively small arrays. For larger arrays, an initializer method should be designed.

OBJECT-ORIENTED DESIGN:
Polymorphic Sorting (Optional)

One limitation of the sort routines developed so far is that they only work on one particular type of data. If you've written a bubble sort to sort `int`s, you can't use it to sort `double`s. What would be far more desirable is a **polymorphic sort method**—that is, one method that could sort any kind of data. This is easily done by making use of Java wrapper classes, such as `Integer` and `Double`, together with the `java.lang.Comparable` interface, which is specially designed for this purpose.

The `java.lang.Comparable` Interface

The `java.lang.Comparable` interface consists entirely of the `compareTo()` method:

```
public abstract interface Comparable {
    public int compareTo(Object o);  // Abstract method
}
```

By implementing the `compareTo()` method, a class can impose an ordering on its objects. The `Comparable` interface is implemented by all of Java's wrapper classes—that is, by `Integer`, `Double`, `Float`, `Long`, and so on (Fig. 8–27).

The hierarchy shown in Figure 8–27 exhibits a form of *multiple inheritance*. For example, the `Integer` class is a subclass of `Object` and it implements the `Comparable` interface. Thus, an `Integer` is both an `Object` and a `Comparable`. One implication of this is that an `Integer` can be used in any method that takes either an `Object` parameter or a `Comparable` parameter.

Now let's examine the `compareTo()` method, which takes an `Object` parameter and returns an `int`. The general idea behind `compareTo()` is as follows. An order can be imposed on any two objects *o1* and *o2* by defining `compareTo()` so that it specifies when *o1* is less than or equal to *o2*. For those classes that implement `Comparable`, such as the `Integer` wrapper class, `compareTo()` is defined to be consistent with the following rules:

```
if (o1 < o2)        then o1.compareTo(o2) < 0
if (o1.equals(o2)) then o1.compareTo(o2) == 0
if (o1 > o2)        then o1.compareTo(o2) > 0
```

In other words, if o1 < o2, then o1.compareTo(o2) will return a negative integer. If o1 > o2, then o1.compareTo(o2) will return a positive integer. And if o1 and o2 are equal, then o1.compareTo(o2) will return 0.

For a class that implements `Comparable`, we can use the `compareTo()` method to help sort its elements. The following revised version of the bubble sort method can be used to sort any array of `Comparable` objects—that is, any array of objects whose class implements `Comparable`:

```java
public void sort(Comparable[] arr) {
    Comparable temp;                            // Temporary variable
    for (int pass = 1; pass < arr.length; pass++ )    // For each pass
        for (int pair = 1; pair < arr.length; pair++)     // For each pair
            if (arr[pair].compareTo(arr[pair-1]) < 0) { // If out of order
                temp = arr[pair-1];                 //        swap
                arr[pair-1] = arr[pair];
                arr[pair] = temp;
            } // if
} // sort
```

The primary difference between this method and the original `bubble-Sort()` is that its parameter is an array of `Comparable`. Thus, we can pass it any array whose elements implement `Comparable`, including an array of `Integer` or `Float`, and so on. However, to compare adjacent elements of a `Comparable` array, we must use the `compareTo()` method:

```java
arr[pair].compareTo(arr[pair-1]) < 0
```

Note that our algorithm no longer refers to `int`s, as in the original bubble sort. Indeed, it doesn't mention the *specific* type—`Integer`, `Float`, or whatever—of the objects that it is sorting. It refers only to `Comparable`s, which are any objects whose class implements the `Comparable` interface. Therefore, we can use this method to sort any type of object, as long as it   *Generality principle*

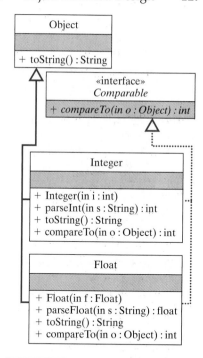

FIGURE 8–27 By implementing the compareTo() method, the Java wrapper classes impose an order on their elements that can be used by a polymorphic sort method to sort them.

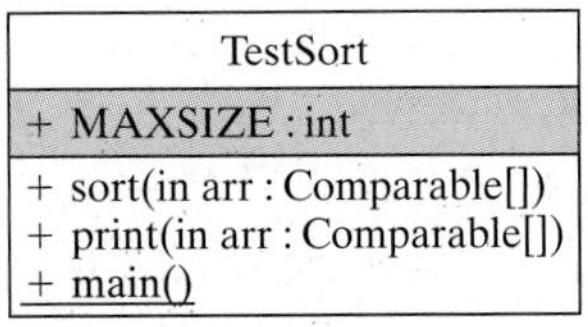

TestSort
+ MAXSIZE : int
+ sort(in arr : Comparable[])
+ print(in arr : Comparable[])
+ main()

FIGURE 8–28 The sort() method in this class can sort any array of Comparable objects—that is, any object that implements the Comparable interface.

implements the Comparable interface. By thus defining the sort method in terms of the superclass (Comparable), we can apply it in general to objects in any of the subclasses (Integers or Floats).

The TestSort class (Fig. 8–28) can be used to illustrate the power of inheritance and polymorphism. It contains three static methods: The sort() method that we just described; a polymorphic print() method, which can be used to print the values of any array of Comparable; and a main() method. As its implementation shows, the main() method creates arrays of Integer and Float and then uses the polymorphic sort() method to sort them (Fig. 8–29). Note how the print() method uses the polymorphic toString() method to print the elements of a Comparable array.

FIGURE 8–29 Implementation of the TestSort class.

```java
public class TestSort {
    public static int MAXSIZE = 25;

    public static void sort(Comparable[] arr) {
        Comparable temp;                              // Temporary variable
        for (int pass = 1; pass < arr.length; pass++)    // For each pass
            for (int pair = 1; pair < arr.length ; pair++) // For each pair
                if (arr[pair].compareTo(arr[pair-1]) < 0) { //   Compare
                    temp = arr[pair-1];                      //   and swap
                    arr[pair-1] = arr[pair];
                    arr[pair] = temp;
                } // if
    } // sort()

    // Print the array 5 per line
    public static void print(Comparable arr[]) {
        for (int k = 0; k < arr.length; k++) {
            if (k % 5 == 0)  System.out.println();        // New row
            System.out.print(arr[k].toString() + "\t");
        }
        System.out.println();
    }

    public static void main(String args[]) {
        Integer iArr[] = new Integer[MAXSIZE]; // The Integer array
        Float fArr[] = new Float[MAXSIZE];    // The Float array

        // Populate each array with randomly generated objects
        for (int k = 0; k < MAXSIZE; k++) {
            iArr[k] = new Integer((int) (Math.random() * 10000));
            fArr[k] = new Float(Math.random() * 10000);
        }

        sort(iArr);       // Sort and print each array
        print(iArr);
        sort(fArr);
        print(fArr);
    } // main()
}
```

This example of polymorphic sorting illustrates once again the great power of inheritance and polymorphism in object-oriented programming. The Integer and Float classes use *class inheritance* to inherit features from the Object class, and they use *interface inheritance* to inherit the compareTo() method from the Comparable class. By implementing versions of the toString() and compareTo() methods that are appropriate for these wrapper classes, Java makes it easier to use Integer and Float objects in a variety of contexts. Taken together, inheritance and polymorphism enable us to design very general algorithms—in this case, a sort() method that can sort any kind of object—and very extensible classes—in this case, any class that implements Java's Comparable interface can arrange its objects in order.

From the Java Library

java.util.Vector

 http://java.sun.com/products /jdk/1.3/docs/api/

THE java.util.Vector class implements an array of objects that can grow in size as needed. One limitation of regular arrays is that their lengths remain fixed. Once the array is full—once every element is used—you can't allocate additional elements.

The Vector class contains methods for storing and retrieving objects, and for accessing objects by their index position within the Vector (Fig. 8–30).

One use for a Vector would be when a program needs to store items, input from the user or a file, without knowing in advance how many items there are. Using a Vector is less efficient than an array in terms of processing speed, but it gives you the flexibility of growing the data structure, as necessary, to meet the storage requirements.

As an illustration of this idea, the program in Figure 8–31 creates a random number of integers and then stores them in a Vector. The Vector, which is declared and instantiated in main(), is initially empty. Integers from 0 to the random bound are then inserted into the Vector. In this case, insertions are done with the addElement() method, which causes the Vector object to insert the element at the next available location, increasing its size, if necessary.

Once all the integers have been inserted, the printVector() method is called. Note that it uses the size() method to determine how many elements the Vector contains. This is similar to using the length() method to determine the number of characters in a String.

Finally, note that a Vector stores objects. It cannot be used to store primitive data values. You cannot store an int in a Vector. Therefore, we need to use the Integer wrapper class to convert ints into Integers before they can be inserted into the Vector. Because you can't just print an Integer, or any other Object, the toString() method is used to print the string representation of the object.

By defining Vector to store Objects, Java's designers have made it as general as it can be and, therefore, as widely useful as can be. See the "In the Laboratory" section of Chapter 11 for some additional comparisons between Vectors and arrays.

Vector
+ Vector()
+ Vector(in size : int)
+ addElement(in o : Object)
+ elementAt(in index : int) : Object
+ insertElementAt(in o : Object, in x : int)
+ indexOf(in o : Object) : int
+ lastIndexOf(in o : Object) : int
+ removeElementAt(in index : int)
+ size() : int

FIGURE 8–30 The java.util.Vector class.

Vectors store objects

FIGURE 8–31 Demonstration of the Vector class. (See also the "In the Laboratory" section of Chapter 11 for another example that uses a Vector.)

```java
import java.util.Vector;

public class VectorDemo {

    public static void printVector(Vector v) {
        for (int k=0; k < v.size(); k++)
            System.out.println(v.elementAt(k).toString());
    } // printVector()

    public static void main(String args[]) {
        Vector vector = new Vector();           // An empty vector

        int bound = (int)(Math.random() * 20);
        for (int k = 0; k < bound; k++ )        // Insert a random
            vector.addElement(new Integer(k));  //  number of Integers
        printVector(vector);                    // Print the elements
    } // main()
}// VectorDemo
```

EFFECTIVE DESIGN: Generality. Defining a data collection, such as an array or a Vector, in terms of the Object class makes it capable of storing and, hence, processing any type of value, including values of the primitive data types. This is because the Object class is the root of the Java class hierarchy.

8.10 CASE STUDY: Simulating a Card Deck

Many computer games—bridge, solitaire, black jack—require a computerized deck of cards, which is an excellent application for an array (Fig. 8–32). A card deck can be represented as a simple array of 52 cards:

```java
Card deck[] = new Card[52];  // 52 cards in a deck
```

where Card is an object that represents an individual playing card. However, given the specialized tasks associated with a card deck, such as shuffling and dealing, a well-designed card-playing application would want to use a Deck class to encapsulate these specialized functions. In that case, the array of Cards that make up the deck would become a private instance variable within the Deck object. Among other benefits, this design would make it easier to have a program that uses multiple decks at one time.

Problem decomposition

8.10.1 Designing a Card class

Data representation

First, let's design the Card class. Each card must have a *suit*—clubs, diamonds, heart, spades—and a *value*—2 through 10, jack, queen, king, and ace. We will represent both suit and value as a function of a Card's *rank*, where rank is an int between 0 (LOW.RANK) and 51 (HIGH.RANK). This will enable us to place the cards in rank order, which is the order found in a new deck of cards:

```
2C 3C ... TC JC QC KC AC 2D 3D ... TD ... AD 2H 3H ... AH 2S ...AS
```

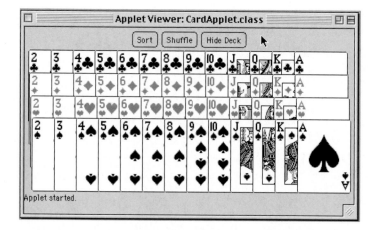

FIGURE 8–32 A deck of cards can be represented as an array of 52 cards.

In this representation, C, D, H, and S stand for clubs, diamonds, hearts, and spades, respectively, and T, J, Q, K, A stand for ten, jack, queen, king, and ace.

Given its rank, a card's suit and value can be computed as

```
suit = rank / 13;      // Gives a number between 0..3
value = 2 + rank % 13;  // Gives a number between 2..14
```

Thus, a Card's suit will be represented as 0 (clubs), 1 (diamonds), 2 (hearts), and 3 (spades), and a Card's value will be a number between 2 and 14, where the numbers from 2 through 9 represent the card with that numeric face value and those with values 10 through 14 represent ten, jack, queen, king, and ace, respectively.

In addition to these basic representational issues, each Card will be associated with a faceImg, a graphical image representing its face. Moreover, it's important that the Card's state be able to keep track of whether it is face up or face down. Therefore, we will use a boolean variable to record this state.

In terms of a Card's functionality, it will require public methods to display itself, to turn itself face up or face down, as well as various access methods to set and get its value or its image. These design specifications are summarized in the UML diagram shown in Figure 8–33.

The implementation of most of the Card class is shown in Figure 8–34. Note how we have defined the constructor method. When a new Card is made, the constructor is passed its rank, which it uses to initialize the Card's suit and value:

```
public Card(int rank) {
    this.rank = rank;
    suit = rank / 13;      // Gives a number between 0 and 3
    value = 2 + rank % 13;  // Gives a number between 2 and 14
    faceUp = true;
} // Card()
```

Thus, rank can be used with simple arithmetic operators to figure out the card's suit and face value. The suit and value are used to figure out the card's representation, but its rank is used to figure out its order within

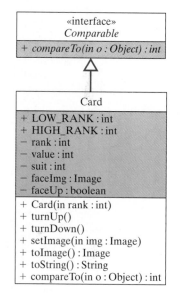

FIGURE 8–33   The Card class represents a playing card. It implements the Comparable interface.

```
import java.awt.*;

public class Card implements Comparable {
    public static final int LOW_RANK = 0,     // Ranks of 52 cards
                            HIGH_RANK = 51;

    private int rank;          // 0..51
    private int value;         // face value 2,3,,,10,11(jack),14(ace)
    private int suit;          // 0=club,1=diamond,2=heart,3=spade

    private Image faceImg;     // Face-up image
    private boolean faceUp;    // True when face-up

    public Card (int rank) {
        this.rank = rank;
        suit = rank / 13;      // Gives a number between 0..3
        value = 2 + rank % 13; // Gives a number between 2..14
        faceUp = true;
    } // constructor

    public void turnUp() {
        faceUp = true;
    }
    public void turnDown() {
        faceUp = false;
    }

    public void setImage (Image img) {
        faceImg = img;
    } // setImage

    public Image toImage() {
        if (faceUp)
            return faceImg;
        else return null;
    }
    /**
     * compareTo() -- from the Comparable interface. This method's
     * implementation is left as an lab exercise.
     */
    public int compareTo(Object o) {
        int oRank = ((Card) o).rank;  // Cast o into a Card reference
        return 0;
    }
    /**
     * toString()  returns a 2 character representation of the card. For
     *    example, "2C" means 2 of clubs, "JD" is jack of diamonds.
     * Algorithm: the instance variables, suit, and value,
     *  are used as indexes into the literal strings that store the correct letters
     */
    public String toString() {
        return "" +  "??23456789TJQKA".charAt(value) + "CDHS".charAt(suit);
    } // toString

} // Card Class
```

FIGURE 8–34 A partial implementation of the Card class. The implementation of compareTo() is left as a lab exercise.

the deck. Having the card's rank will make it easy to sort the deck, so in this case it's convenient to have both representations available.

Note that Card implements the Comparable interface. This means it must implement the compareTo() method, which was discussed in the "Object-Oriented Design" section earlier in this chapter. This will make it easy to sort a deck of Cards, if we store the cards in an array. The implementation of this method is left as a lab exercise.

Note that to compare two cards you must compare their ranks. This makes it necessary to get the rank of the card that is passed as compareTo()'s parameter. Even though compareTo() takes an Object parameter, it is always passed a Card. This is valid because a Card is an Object. But this requires that we cast the parameter into a reference to a Card. Note the syntax of the *cast* operation:

Type casting

```
int oRank = ((Card) o).rank;
```

Because the method's parameter is an Object and not a Card, we use the ((Card) o) operation to cast o into a Card reference *before* we refer to its rank. It would be a syntax error to refer to o.rank because o is not a Card variable.

Note the implementation of the toString() method. This method returns a two-character string that represents a card's suit and value. For example, the two of clubs would be represented as "2C", and the ace of hearts would be "AH". The algorithm that's used here makes two string literals that store the letters used to represent the card's suit ("CDHS") and value ("??23456789TJQKA"). The positions of the letters in the strings correspond to the numeric values of the card's suit and face value, so we can use the instance variables, suit and value, to extract the correct character representation and concatenate them to form the card's representation. This gives the following definition for toString():

Algorithm design

```
public String toString() {
    return "" + "??23456789TJQKA".charAt(suit) + "CDHS".charAt(value);
} // toString
```

For example, the 5 of spades would have suit equal to 3 and value equal to 5. When used in the preceding expression, "5S" would be extracted as the card's string representation. Note the use of the empty string in the concatenation expression. This causes Java to convert the entire expression into a String.

The toImage() method is used to present the Image() associated with the Card. Note that if the Card is face down, this method returns null. In that case, the Deck will display its card back image.

8.10.2   Designing a Deck **class**

Let's now turn to designing the Deck class. This class will need an array to store 52 (NCARDS) Cards. To minimize the amount of manipulation of the array, let's use an int variable to represent the top of the deck. This will always be a value between 0 and NCARDS-1. As cards are dealt, the top can be incremented to point to the next card in the array, wrapping around if necessary:

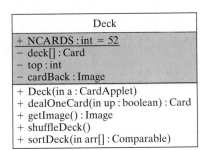

Deck
+ NCARDS : int = 52
– deck[] : Card
– top : int
– cardBack : Image
+ Deck(in a : CardApplet)
+ dealOneCard(in up : boolean) : Card
+ getImage() : Image
+ shuffleDeck()
+ sortDeck(in arr[] : Comparable)

FIGURE 8–35 The Deck class represents a deck of cards. The cards are stored in an array.

```
top = (top + 1) % NCARDS;    // Wrap around to 0 when top == 51
```

In terms of the Deck's functionality, it will need methods to deal a card, shuffle the deck, and sort the deck (into its "new deck" order). This leads to the design shown in Figure 8–35.

Note that the Deck() constructor takes a CardApplet as a parameter. The reason for this is to simplify the task of loading Images to use as the card faces when the Deck is created. As we saw earlier, an easy way to load an Image is to use the Applet.getImage():

```
Image img = getImage(getDocumentBase(), "img.gif");
```

However, the Deck object won't be able to utilize getImage() unless it has a reference to its associated applet. When the applet creates a Deck, it simply passes a reference to itself:

```
Deck deck = new Deck(this);
```

This leads to the following implementation of the Deck() constructor:

```
public Deck(CardApplet a) {
    cardBack = a.cardImage("back");    // Get back of card image
    a.showStatus("Please wait while card images are loading. ");
    for (int k = 0; k < deck.length; k++) {  // Make the cards
        deck[k] = new Card(Card.LOW_RANK + k);
                                        // Get the card's image
        Image img = a.cardImage(deck[k].toString());
        deck[k].setImage(img);
    }
} // Deck()
```

Dot notation

image: = cardImage(s:String) ➜

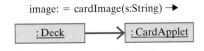

FIGURE 8–36 The applet's cardImage() method takes a string description of a card and returns the corresponding Image to the deck object.

Note how dot notation is used to construct a reference to the applet's methods—for example, a.cardImage(). The applet's cardImage() method takes a string that designates which image to load. It takes arguments such as "back" to represent the back of the card and "2C" to represent the two of clubs. By using this method, we are giving the applet the responsibility for knowing where the images are stored. Figure 8–36 shows a UML depiction of the relationship between the applet and the deck.

The first Image loaded is assigned to cardBack. Then a for loop is used to create 52 Cards, assigning each one its proper rank. Note that each Card must be instantiated with new. Finally, note how the constructor assigns each Card its appropriate Image. To invoke a method or instance variable of an array component, it is necessary to apply the dot operator *after* the array subscript:

```
deck[k].setImage()
deck[k].toString()
```

The reason, of course, is that deck[k] is a reference to a Card.

Let's now turn to the task of dealing the top Card from the Deck. This method is complicated by the fact that cards may be dealt either face up or face down depending on the game situation. Therefore, dealOneCard() requires a boolean parameter to represent face up or face down. The method should then simply return the top Card and update its value for top, since dealing a card will produce a new top card:

```
public Card dealOneCard(boolean faceUp)     {
    Card topCard = deck[top];          // Get the top card
    if (faceUp)      // If face-up deal
        topCard.turnUp();              //  Turn it face up
    else                               // Else
        topCard.turnDown();            //  Turn it face down
    top = (top + 1) % NCARDS;    // top is new top card
    return topCard;    // And deal it
} // dealOneCard()
```

The boolean parameter faceUp will cause dealOneCard() to turn the card up or down depending on whether it is true (up) or false (down). Note the use of a local Card variable here, which is assigned its value from the array, deck[top].

The rest of the implementation of the Deck class is left as laboratory exercise.

IN THE LABORATORY: A Card-Game Applet

The purpose of this lab is to complete a card-playing program using the Card and Deck classes just described. The objectives of this lab are

- To give practice using arrays and array algorithms.
- To give practice using Images.
- To introduce a program that requires manipulation of three separate programmer-defined classes: Card, Deck, and CardApplet.

Problem Description

Write an applet that lets the user shuffle, sort, and display a deck of playing cards. The cards will be represented by the Card class (see Section 8.10.1), and the deck of cards will be represented by the Deck class (see Section 8.10.2). In its completed form the applet will display cards from a set of 53 Images.

However, since it will be too time consuming to load this many images each time you wish to test your program, Card.toString() will be used to represent cards during program development—for example, "2C" (2 of clubs), "JD" (jack of diamonds). After all other methods are developed and tested, the 53 Images will be incorporated into the applet.

GUI Specifications

The Graphical User Interface (GUI) for this applet should contain buttons labeled *Shuffle*, *Sort*, and *Show/Hide Deck*. Shuffling a deck is a matter of rearranging its cards. Sorting a deck will involve putting the deck into its original order, as specified later.

Showing and Hiding the deck should work like a toggle button. If the deck is currently displayed face up, the button should be labeled "Hide Deck," and when it is clicked, it should redisplay the deck face down, and it should toggle its label to "Show Deck." Similarly, if the deck is currently face down, the button should be labeled "Show Deck," and when it is

FIGURE 8–37   The string-based user interface for CardDeckApplet.

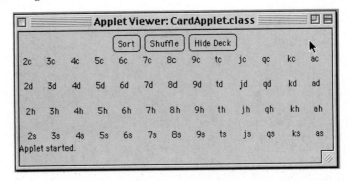

clicked, it should redisplay the deck face up and toggle the button's label to "Hide Deck." (You may wish to use an instance of the ToggleButton class for this button. See Section 4.7.5.)

During program development, the deck should be displayed by painting the String representation of each card on the applet (Fig. 8–37).

You needn't implement the layout shown here, but your layout should be able to display all 52 cards of the deck in some coherent way. To help with this task, the Card.toString() method returns a string representation of the card as "2C" (2 of clubs) or "AS" (ace of spaces). The applet code may have to break this string apart in order to display the card properly.

Problem Decomposition

The problem should be divided into three separate classes: the Card class, most of which was implemented in the previous section, the Deck class, which was designed in the previous section, and the CardApplet class, which we will design and implement from scratch.

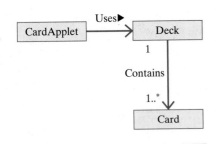

FIGURE 8–38   The CardApplet uses a Deck of 52 Cards.

Figure 8–38 shows the relationship between the objects represented by these classes. The CardApplet serves as the user interface. In addition to the usual GUI objects, it uses a Deck consisting of 52 Cards.

Problem Design: The Deck Class

The design of the Deck class was described in Section 8.10.2, which also included implementations of its constructor method and a method to deal cards. To complete the Deck class you must implement the shuffle() and sort(deck) methods, which were outlined in the specification given in Section 8.10.2. The algorithms for shuffling and sorting the deck are discussed next.

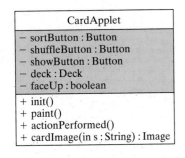

FIGURE 8–39   The CardApplet class.

Problem Design: The CardApplet Class

CardApplet requires instance variables for the three Buttons and the Deck. In addition it will be useful to have a private instance variable to keep track of whether the deck is currently face up or face down. This variable can be reset each time the Show/Hide button is clicked. Its design in summarized in Figure 8–39.

CardApplet must implement three methods: an init() method, where the applet's components are instantiated and added to the applet's interface, a paint() method, which handles the painting of the deck, and an actionPerformed() method, which handles clicks on the three buttons.

- init(): The init() method should simply instantiate the objects used by the applet, including the Deck object.
- actionPerformed(): The actionPerformed() method can simply invoke the appropriate Deck method to sort or shuffle the deck. To toggle between showing and hiding the deck will require the applet to remember what state the deck is in and will require that the Button's label be toggled each time it is clicked. (*Hint*: Here's the place for that boolean variable unless you implement a special ToggleButton.)
- paint(): The entire deck should be repainted or redealt each time the user selects one of the three actions. To display the deck you can repeatedly call Deck.dealOneCard(), which returns the top card on the deck. Once you have a Card, stored in a local variable perhaps, you can invoke either its toString() or toImage() method within the paint() method:

```
g.drawString(tmpCard.toString(), hRef,vRef);
g.drawImage(tmpCard.toImage(), hRef,vRef,this);
```

Note the use of the variables hRef and vRef here to control horizontal and vertical placement of the Card's image or string on the applet. You will have to vary these values after each card is drawn.

Algorithm Design: Shuffling the Deck

Shuffling a deck can be simulated by repeatedly swapping two random cards in the deck, as described in the following pseudocode:

```
For some number of swaps  // 26 swaps or so
    Pick random card1      // Pick two random cards
    Pick random card2
    Swap card1 and card2   // Swap their locations in the deck
```

Algorithm Design: Sorting the Deck

The task of sorting the deck should be very simple, if you understand the discussion of polymorphic sorting in the "Object-Oriented Design" section earlier in this chapter. As we saw in the previous section, the Card class implements the Comparable interface. This means you must complete the implementation of its compareTo() method (Fig. 8–34). Remember that to compare two cards, you must compare their ranks. Once you have implemented compareTo(), you can simply use the polymorphic sort() method described earlier.

Adding Images to the Applet

After you have completed the implementation of CardApplet using Strings to display the cards, you may wish to utilize the card images shown in Figure 8–40. These images can be downloaded from the free-software Web site:

```
http://www.waste.org/~oxymoron/cards
```

They should be stored in the same folder as your applet's class files. Once you have downloaded the images, you must implement code in the applet to display the Card's image instead of its String representation. You must

FIGURE 8–40 The user interface for CardDeckApplet.

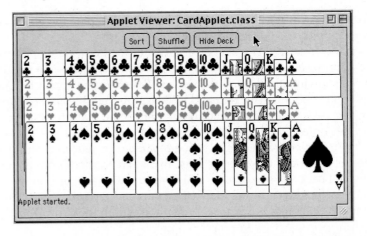

also implement the code in the Deck() constructor that assigns the image to each individual Card. But beware: Loading 53 card images may take a few seconds!

Optional Exercise

Extend your program to play a hand of *Acey-Deucy*. In this game two cards are dealt face up. The player decides either to "hit me!" or "pass!" If the player takes a hit, a third card is dealt. If it falls between the other two cards, the player wins. If not, the player loses. For example, if an ace and a deuce are dealt, and the player draws an ace, the player loses.

You can implement the applet portion of this game with two additional buttons. The first button, call it "Deal," deals a new hand off the top of the deck each time it is clicked. The second button, call it "Hit Me," deals the third card. To implement scorekeeping for this game, it will be necessary to design a method that decides for a given card whether it falls between two other cards. One way to do this is to write a Card method with the following signature:

```
public boolean isBetween(Card c1, Card c2){}
```

This method will return true if the card is between c1 and c2.

Java Language Summary

An **array** is a named collection of contiguous storage locations, each of which stores a data item of the same data type. Each element of an array is referred to by *subscript*—that is, by its position in the array. If the array contains N elements, then its length is N and its indexes are 0, 1, . . . N-1. Array elements are referred to using the following subscript notation:

```
arrayname[subscript]
```

where *arrayname* is any valid identifier, and *subscript* is an integer value in the range 0 to arrayname.length - 1. The array's length instance variable can be used as a bound for loops that process the array.

An *array declaration* provides the name and type of the array. An array instantiation uses the keyword `new` and causes the compiler to allocate memory for the array's elements:

```
int arr[];              // Declare a one-dimensional array variable
arr = new int[15];      // Allocate 15 int locations for it
```

Multidimensional arrays have arrays as their components:

```
int twoDarr[][];           // Declare a two-dimensional array variable
twoDarr = new int[10][15]; // Allocate 150 int locations
```

CHAPTER SUMMARY

Technical Terms

array	multidimensional	random number
array	array	generator
initializer	one-dimensional	scaling
array length	array	selection sort
binary search	polymorphic sort	sequential search
bubble sort	method	sorting
element	pseudorandom	subscript
element type	number	two-dimensional
		array

Summary of Important Points

- An array's values must be initialized by assigning values to each array location. An *initializer* expression may be included as part of the array declaration.
- The `Math.random()` method is used to generate *pseudorandom* numbers, which are useful for simulating chance events such as coin tosses.
- Bubble sort and selection sort are examples of array sorting algorithms. Both algorithms require several passes over the array.
- When an array is passed as a parameter, a reference to the array is passed rather than the entire array itself.
- Swapping two elements of an array, or any two locations in memory, requires the use of a temporary variable.
- Sequential search and binary search are examples of array searching algorithms. Binary search requires that the array be sorted.
- For multidimensional arrays, each dimension of the array has its own `length` variable.

SOLUTIONS TO SELF-STUDY EXERCISES

SOLUTION 8.1 How much space (in bytes) would be allocated for each of the following?

```
a. int a[] = new int[5];          // 5 * 4 = 20 bytes
b. double b[] = new double[10];   // 10 * 8 = 80 bytes
c. char c[] = new char[30];       // 30 * 2  = 60 bytes
d. String s[] = new String[10];   // 10 * 4 (reference) = 40 bytes
e. CyberPet p[] = new CyberPet[5];// 5 * 4 (reference) = 20 bytes
```

SOLUTION 8.2 Declare an array named `farr` that contains 10 `float`s initialized to the values 1.0, 2.0, ... , 10.0.

```
float farr[] = {1.0,2.0,3.0,4.0,5.0,6.0,7.0,8.0,9.0,10.0};
```

SOLUTION 8.3 Write an expression that prints the first element of `farr`.

```
System.out.println(farr[0]);
```

SOLUTION 8.4 Write an assignment statement that assigns 100.0 to the last element in `farr`.

```
farr[farr.length-1] = 100.0;
```

SOLUTION 8.5 Write a loop to print all of the elements of `farr`.

```
for (int j = 0; j < farr.length; j++)
    System.out.println(farr[j]);
```

SOLUTION 8.6 Declare an array of 100 `double`s and write a loop to assign the first 100 square roots to its elements. [Use `Math.sqrt(double)`.]

```
double doubarr[] = new double[100];
for (int k = 0; k < doubarr.length; k++)
    doubarr[k] = Math.sqrt(k+1);
```

SOLUTION 8.7 Write a Java expression that generates random integers in the range 0 to 10.

```
(int)(Math.random() * 11)
```

SOLUTION 8.8 Write an expression that generates random integers in the range 2 through 12.

```
2 + (int)(Math.random() * 11)
```

SOLUTION 8.9 Write expressions to assign random values to a card's suit and rank.

```
int suit = (int)(Math.random() * 4);     // 4 suits: 0,1,2,3
int rank = 2 + (int)(Math.random() * 13); // 13 cards per suit
```

SOLUTION 8.10 Modify `CyberPet`'s `eat()` and `sleep()` methods so half the time the CyberPet will ignore the command.

```
public void eat() {
    if (Math.random() > 0.5) // Approximately half the time
        petState = EATING;
}
public void sleep() {
    if (Math.random() > 0.5) // Approximately half the time
        petState = SLEEPING;
}
```

SOLUTION 8.11   The following changes would be made to the DieExperiment class:

```
private int nTrials = NTRIALS;
public void setTrials(int n) {
    nTrials = n;
}
public int getTrials() {
    return nTrials;
}
```

SOLUTION 8.12   Sort the array, 24 18 90 1 0 85 34 18, by hand using bubble sort. Show the order of the elements after each iteration of the outer loop.

```
24 18 90  1   0  85 34 18 // Initial
18 24  1   0  85 34 18 90 // Pass 1
18  1   0  24 34 18 85 90 // Pass 2
 1  0  18 24 18 34 85 90 // Pass 3
 0  1  18 18 24 34 85 90 // Pass 4
 0  1  18 18 24 34 85 90 // Pass 5
 0  1  18 18 24 34 85 90 // Pass 6
 0  1  18 18 24 34 85 90 // Pass 7
```

SOLUTION 8.13   Sort the array, 24 18 90 1 0 85 34 18, by hand using selection sort. Show the order of the elements after each iteration of the outer loop.

```
24 18 90 1   0   85 34 18 // Initial
 0 18 90 1   24  85 34 18 // Pass 1
 0  1 90 18  24  85 34 18 // Pass 2
 0  1 18 90  24  85 34 18 // Pass 3
 0  1 18 18  24  85 34 90 // Pass 4
 0  1 18 18  24  85 34 90 // Pass 5
 0  1 18 18  24  34 85 90 // Pass 6
 0  1 18 18  24  34 85 90 // Pass 7
```

SOLUTION 8.14   Write a Java code segment to swap two CyberPets, pet1 and pet2.

```
CyberPet tempPet = pet1;
pet1 = pet2;
pet2 = tempPet;
```

SOLUTION 8.15   The preceding version of Bubblesort will keep passing over the array even if it's already sorted. Modify the algorithm so that it stops when the array is sorted. (*Hint*: Use a boolean variable to keep track of whether a swap was made inside the loop. And check this variable in the loop entry condition.)

```
public void bubbleSort(int arr[]) {
    int temp;                 // Temporary variable for swap
    boolean sorted = false; // Initially, assume array is not sorted
                                        // For each pass
    for (int pass = 1; !sorted && pass < arr.length; pass++)
        sorted = true;                  // Assume it's sorted
        for (int pair = 1; pair < arr.length ; pair++ ) // For each pair
            if (arr[pair-1] > arr[pair]) {      //   Compare
                temp = arr[pair-1];             //   And swap
```

```
            arr[pair-1] = arr[pair];
            arr[pair] = temp;
            sorted = false;              // Not yet sorted
        } // if
    } // for pass
} // bubbleSort()
```

SOLUTION 8.16   After mystery(myArr,k) is called myArr will store 1,2,3,5,5 and *k* will store 3.

SOLUTION 8.17   The following trace will result if you search for 21 in 2, 4, 6, 8, 10, 12, 14, 16, 18, 20, 22, 24, 26, 28.;

```
key  iteration  low  high  mid
-------------------------------------
21   0          0    13    6
21   1          7    13    10
21   2          7    9     8
21   3          9    9     9
21   4          10   9     failure
```

SOLUTION 8.18   Declare a two-dimensional array of int named int2d that contains five rows, each of which contains ten integers.

```
int int2d[][] = new int[5][10];
```

SOLUTION 8.19   Write a statement that prints the last integer in the third row of the array you created in the previous exercise. Then write an assignment statement that assigns 100 to the last element in the int2d

```
System.out.println(int2d[2][9]);
int2d[4][9] = 100;
```

SOLUTION 8.20   Write a loop to print all of the elements of int2d, which you declared in the exercises in the previous section. Print one row per line with a space between each element on a line.

```
for (int k = 0; k < int2d.length; k++) {
    for (int j = 0; j < int2d[k].length; j++)
        System.out.print( int2d[k][j] + " ");
    System.out.println();                   // new line
}
```

SOLUTION 8.21   Declare a 52 × 7 two-dimensional array of int and initialize each of its elements to 0.

```
int sales[][] = new int[52][7];
for (int k = 0; k < sales.length; k++)
    for (int j= 0; j < sales[k].length; j++)
        sales[k][j] = 0;
```

SOLUTION 8.22   Write a method to calculate the average number of newspapers sold per week.

```
double avgWeeklySales(int arr[][]) {
    double total = 0;
    for (int k = 0; k < arr.length; k++)
        for (int j= 0; j < arr[k].length; j++)
            total += arr[k][j];
    return total/52;
}
```

SOLUTION 8.23   Write a method to calculate the average number of newspapers sold per Sunday, where Sunday is the last day of the week.

```
double avgSundaySales(int arr[][]) {
    double total = 0;
    for (int k = 0; k < arr.length; k++)
        total += arr[k][6];
    return total/52;
}
```

EXERCISES

Note: *For programming exercises,* **first** *draw a UML class diagram describing all classes and their inheritance relationships and/or associations.*

EXERCISE 8.1   Explain the difference between the following pairs of terms:

a. An *element* and an element *type*.
b. A *subscript* and an *array element*.
c. A *random* number and *pseudorandom* number.
d. A *one-dimensional* array and *two-dimensional* array.
e. An *array* and a *vector*.
f. A *bubble sort* and a *selection sort*.
g. A *binary search* and a *sequential search*.

EXERCISE 8.2   Fill in the blanks.

a. The process of arranging an array's elements into a particular order is known as _____ .
b. One of the preconditions of the binary search method is that the array has to be _____ .
c. An _____ is an object that can store a collection of elements of the same type.
d. An _____ is like an array except that it can grow.
e. For an array, its _____ is represented by an instance variable.
f. An expression that can be used during array instantiation to assign values to the array is known as an _____ .
g. A _____ is an array of arrays.
h. A sort method that can be used to sort different types of data is known as a _____ method.
i. To instantiate an array you have to use the _____ operator.
j. An array of objects stores _____ to the objects.

EXERCISE 8.3   Make each of the following array declarations:

a. A 4 × 4 array of doubles.
b. A 20 × 5 array of Strings.
c. A 3 × 4 array of char initialized to '*';
d. A 2 × 3 × 2 array of boolean initialized to true.
e. A 3 × 3 array of CyberPets.
f. A 2 × 3 array of Strings initialized to "one," "two," and so on.

EXERCISE 8.4   Identify and correct the syntax error in each of the following expressions:

a. int arr = new int[15];
b. int arr[] = new int(15);
c. float arr[] = new [3];
d. float arr[] = new float {1.0,2.0,3.0};
e. int arr[] = {1.1,2.2,3.3};
f. int arr[][] = new double[5][4];
g. int arr[][] = { {1.1,2.2}, {3.3, 1} };

EXERCISE 8.5   Evaluate each of the following expressions, some of which may be erroneous:

```
int arr[] = { 2,4,6,8,10 };
```

a. arr[4]
b. arr[arr.length]
c. arr[arr[0]]
d. arr[arr.length / 2]
e. arr[arr[1]]

f. arr[5 % 2]
g. arr[arr[arr[0]]]
h. arr[5 / 2.0]
i. arr[1 + (int) Math.random()]
j. arr[arr[3] / 2]

EXERCISE 8.6   Evaluate each of the following expressions, some of which may be erroneous:

```
int arr[][] = { {2,4,6},{8,10} };
```

a. arr.length
b. arr[1].length
c. arr[3][0]
d. ++arr[0][0]
e. arr[0] * arr.length

f. arr[0][1]
g. arr[arr.length -1][0]
h. arr[0][3]
i. arr[0][1] * arr.length
j. arr[arr[0][0]][1]

EXERCISE 8.7   What would be printed by the following code segment?

```
int arr[] = { 24, 0, 19, 21, 6, -5, 10, 16};
for (int k = 0; k < arr.length; k += 2)
  System.out.println( arr[k] );
```

EXERCISE 8.8   What would be printed by the following code segment?

```
int arr[][] = { {24, 0, 19}, {21, 6, -5}, {10, 16, 3}, {1, -1, 0} };
for (int j = 0; j < arr.length; j++)
  for (int k = 0; k < arr[j].length; k++)
    System.out.println( arr[j][k] );
```

EXERCISE 8.9   What would be printed by the following code segment?

```
int arr[][] = { {24, 0, 19}, {21, 6, -5}, {10, 16, 3}, {1, -1, 0} };
for (int j = 0; j < arr[0].length; j++)
    for (int k = 0; k < arr.length; k++)
        System.out.println(arr[k][j]);
```

EXERCISE 8.10   What's wrong with the following code segment, which is supposed to swap the values of the int variables, *n1* and *n2*?

```
int temp = n1;
n2 = n1;
n1 = temp;
```

EXERCISE 8.11   What's wrong with the following method, which is supposed to swap the values of its two parameters?

```
public void swapEm(int n1, int n2) {
    int temp = n1;
    n1 = n2;
    n2 = temp;
}
```

EXERCISE 8.12   Declare and initialize an array to store the following two-dimensional table of values:

```
1   2   3   4
5   6   7   8
9  10  11  12
```

EXERCISE 8.13   For the two-dimensional array you created in the previous exercise, write a nested for loop to print the values in the following order: 1 5 9 2 6 10 3 7 11 4 8 12. That is, print the values going down the columns instead of going across the rows.

EXERCISE 8.14   Define an array that would be suitable for storing the following values:

a. The GPAs of 2,000 students.
b. The lengths and widths of 100 rectangles.
c. A week's worth of hourly temperature measurements, stored so that it is easy to calculate the average daily temperature.
d. A board for a tic-tac-toe game.
e. The names and capitals of the 50 states.

EXERCISE 8.15   Write a code segment that will compute the sum of all the elements of an array of int.

EXERCISE 8.16   Write a code segment that will compute the sum of the elements a two-dimensional array of int.

EXERCISE 8.17   Write a method that will compute the average of all the elements of a two-dimensional array of float.

EXERCISE 8.18   Write a method that takes two parameters, an int array and an integer, and returns the location of the last element of the array that is greater than or equal to the second parameter.

EXERCISE 8.19   Write a program that tests whether a 3 × 3 array, input by the user, is a *magic square*. A magic square is an $N \times N$ matrix of numbers in which every number from 1 to N^2 must appear just once, and every row, column, and diagonal must add up to the same total—for example,

```
6 7 2
1 5 9
8 3 4
```

EXERCISE 8.20   Revise the program in the previous exercise so that it allows the user to input the dimensions of the array, up to 4 × 4.

EXERCISE 8.21   Although most dice are six-sided, they also come in other sizes. Write a Java expression that generates random integers for a 12-sided die. The die contains the numbers 1 to 12 on its faces.

EXERCISE 8.22   Revise the `DieExperiment()` program to test the "fairness" of the 12-sided die from the previous exercise.

EXERCISE 8.23   Suppose the 12-sided die from the previous exercise has the numbers 3 through 14 on its faces. Write a Java expression that generates random integers for this die.

EXERCISE 8.24   A *cryptogram* is a message written in secret writing. Suppose you are developing a program to help solve cryptograms. One of the important bits of evidence is to compute the frequencies of the letters in the cryptogram. Write a program that takes a bunch of text as input and displays the relative frequencies of all 26 letters, *a* to *z*. (In English, the *e* is the most frequent letter, with a relative frequency of around 12 percent.)

EXERCISE 8.25   Modify the program from the previous exercise so that it can display the relative frequencies of the 10 most frequent and 10 least frequent letters. Use your program to help you distinguish between messages that were created using a substitution cipher and those that were created using a transposition cipher. What differences in letter frequencies would you expect between transposition and substitution?

EXERCISE 8.26   The *merge sort* algorithm takes two collections of data that have been sorted and merges them together. Write a program that takes two 25-element `int` arrays, sorts them, and then merges them, in order, into one 50-element array.

EXERCISE 8.27   **Challenge:** Design and implement a `BigInteger` class that can add and subtract integers with up to 25 digits. Your class should also include methods for input and output of the numbers. If you're really ambitious, include methods for multiplication and division.

EXERCISE 8.28   **Challenge:** Design a data structure for this problem: As manager of Computer Warehouse, you want to keep track of the dollar amount of purchases made by those clients that have regular accounts. The accounts are numbered from 0, 1, . . . , N. The problem is that you don't know in advance how many purchases each account will have. Some may have one or two purchases. Others may have 50 purchases.

EXERCISE 8.29   An *anagram* is a word made by rearranging the letters of another word. For example, *act* is an anagram of *cat*, and *aegllry* is an anagram of *allergy*. Write a Java program that accepts two words as input and determines if they are anagrams.

EXERCISE 8.30   Challenge: An *anagram dictionary* is a dictionary that organizes words together with their anagrams. Write a program that lets the user enter up to 100 words (in a TextField, say). After each word is entered, the program should display (in a TextArea perhaps) the complete anagram dictionary for the words entered. Use the following sample format for the dictionary. Here the words entered by the user were: *felt, left, cat, act, opt, pot, top.*

```
act:   act cat
eflt:  felt left
opt:   opt pot top
```

EXERCISE 8.31   Acme Trucking Company has hired you to write software to help dispatch its trucks. One important element of this software is knowing the distance between any two cities that it services. Design and implement a Distance class that stores the distances between cities in a two-dimensional array. This class will need some way to map a city name, *Boise*, into an integer that can be used as an array subscript. The class should also contain methods that would make it useful for looking up the distance between two cities. Another useful method would tell the user the closest city to a given city.

EXERCISE 8.32   Write a SlideShowApplet that displays an endless slide show. Use GIF files to store the images that make up the show. Load the images into an array and then repeatedly display an image from the array each time the user clicks on a control button. One modification to this program might be to show the slides in random order. That would make it less boring!

EXERCISE 8.33   Revise CyberPet (Fig. 5–15) so that approximately half the time when commanded to eat or sleep it goes into a NOTHUNGRY or NOTSLEEPY state instead.

Photograph courtesy of Michal Heron, Pearson Education/PH College

9

Graphical User Interfaces

OBJECTIVES

After studying this chapter, you will

- Acquire a familiarity with the Swing component set.
- Understand the relationship between the AWT and Swing.
- Have a better understanding of Java's event model.
- Be able to design and build simple Graphical User Interfaces (GUIs).
- Appreciate how object-oriented design principles were used to extend Java's GUI capabilities.

OUTLINE

9.1   Introduction

As we have seen, a *Graphical User Interface (GUI)* creates a certain way of interacting with a program. It is what gives a program its *look and feel*. A GUI is created from a set of basic components, such as buttons, text fields, labels, and text areas.

In the preceding chapters, we used GUI components from Java's Abstract Windowing Toolkit (AWT). In this chapter we introduce the Swing component set, which extends the AWT in interesting and powerful ways. The Java Foundation Classes (JFC), of which the Swing set is a part, gives software developers the capability to build sophisticated and efficient software written entirely in Java's windowing system rather than relying on the platform's windowing system. Prior to the release of the JFC, this was not possible.

Our focus throughout the chapter will be on designing and building simple GUIs using the Swing classes. The Swing library is so large we will concentrate on a relatively small handful of the basic Swing components. We will try to identify design principles that can be applied to the design of more advanced interfaces.

Because Java's GUI classes provide an excellent example of object-oriented design, we will also try to call attention to some of the important design decisions and principles that have influenced the development of Java's GUI classes in both the AWT and Swing.

From the Java Library

AWT to Swing

www. http://java.sun.com/products /jdk/1.3/docs/api/

WITH THE RELEASE of Java2, also known as Java Development Kit (JDK) 1.2, Java now has two distinct libraries of GUI components. The *Abstract Windowing Toolkit (AWT)* has been part of Java since JDK 1.0. The *Java Foundation Classes (JFC)*, including the *Swing component set*, were originally released with JDK 1.1. Both are included in JDK 1.2 (now renamed Java2).

A Brief History

Although the original version of the AWT was suitable for developing Java applets, it wasn't powerful enough to support full-fledged application development. Programs such as word processors and spreadsheets have GUI requirements that were just too much for the original AWT.

AWT 1.1, which was released with JDK 1.1, improved upon the original version. It was faster, and it provided a better way of handling events. However, despite these improvements, the AWT still did not contain a rich enough set of GUI components to support full-fledged application development. Also, it was still highly dependent on non-Java, native code, so application programs that used the AWT weren't very portable.

Because of these shortcomings, some software developers built their own sets of GUI components. Netscape's *Internet Foundation Classes (IFC)*, which were built upon AWT 1.0 classes, were a vast improvement over the AWT 1.1 classes. Most importantly, the IFC classes were written entirely in Java, which made them much more portable than the AWT classes.

In 1997, Netscape and Sun (JavaSoft) joined forces on the so-called Swing project, whose goal was to develop a sophisticated set of GUI classes written entirely in Java. The results of this effort, the *Java Foundation Classes (JFC)*, including the Swing component set, were released with JDK 2.0.

Like their AWT counterparts, Swing components are GUI controls, such as buttons, frames, and text fields. Because they are rendered entirely by Java code, Swing components make it possible to design GUIs that are truly platform independent. A program that uses Swing components will have the same look and feel on a Mac, Windows, or Unix platform.

The *100% Pure Java* initiative is an industry-wide effort to develop a truly platform-independent programming environment. Such an environment would make it possible to develop programs that could run on all computers. In the present environment, software developers have to spend millions of dollars developing different versions of their products for each different platform.

100% Pure Java

Heavyweight Versus Lightweight Components

AWT components are based on the **peer model**. Every AWT component has a corresponding peer class written in the native system's code. For example, the `java.awt.Button` class has a peer named `java.awt.peer.Button`. The peer class serves as the interface between the Java code and the native windowing system. The methods in the peer class are written in native code. Therefore, AWT components are inherently platform dependent.

The AWT peer model

AWT components are considered *heavyweight* because they depend on the native (peer) system for their drawing and rendering. Every AWT component has an associated component in the native windowing system. This is why a Java button on a Windows platform looks just like a Windows button. In effect, the Java button, via its peer, creates and uses a Windows button. When you change the Java button's label, it must call a method in the peer class that changes the label of the peer button. This interaction between Java and the native windowing system requires a good deal of overhead, thereby affecting the overall efficiency of the system.

A **lightweight component** is one that is written in pure Java. Instead of depending on a native component for its rendering, a lightweight component is drawn and rendered entirely by Java code. One way to build a lightweight component is to extend the abstract `java.awt.Component` class and then override its `paint()` method:

Lightweight components

```java
public class LightWeightButton extends Component {

    public void paint(Graphics g) {
       /* Java code goes here */
    }
}
```

The comment indicates where you would put the commands to draw and paint the button. Because they don't depend on peers in the native windowing system, lightweight components are much more efficient than the regular AWT components.

All Swing components except for the four top-level window classes— the `JApplet`, `JDialog`, `JFrame`, and `JWindow`—are lightweight components. As you can see, Swing components that have corresponding AWT components have names that begin with "J." Figure 9–1 shows the relationship between the AWT `Container` and `Component` classes and the top-level Swing classes.

FIGURE 9–1   Swing classes, part 1: Relationship between the AWT and the top-level Swing windows.

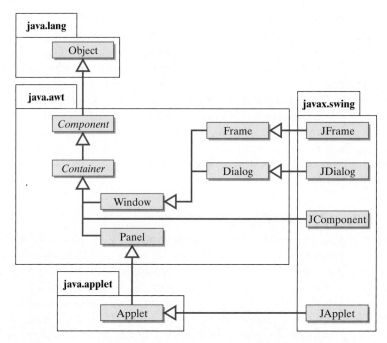

Because these four classes are derived from heavyweight components, they themselves are dependent on the native windowing system. However, note that the abstract JComponent class is derived directly from the Container class. Therefore, it and all of its Swing subclasses are lightweight components (Fig. 9–2).

The Future of the AWT

What's going to happen to the AWT in the future? It is somewhat of a misconception to assume that now that the Swing component set is available, the AWT package will be dropped. However, even if an application or applet uses Swing components (and no AWT component), that will still not break the dependence on the AWT. So despite the introduction of the Swing component set, it is clear that the AWT will remain an essential part of GUI development in Java.

First, Swing's top-level window classes—JApplet, JDialog, JFrame, and JWindow—are defined as extensions to their AWT counterparts. This means that Swing-based GUIs are still dependent on the AWT. Java programs need to have some way to map their windows to the windowing system used on the native (Windows, Solaris, or MacOS) platform. The AWT's top-level windows—Window, Frame, Dialog, and Panel—provide that mapping.

Second, the JComponent class, which is the basis for all Swing components, is derived from java.awt.Container. And there are many more such dependencies. So Swing components are fundamentally based on the AWT.

Finally, all GUI applications and applets use layout managers (java.-awt.FlowLayout), fonts (java.awt.Font), colors (java.awt.Color), and other (noncomponent) classes that are defined in the AWT. So there is no way to design a GUI without using AWT classes.

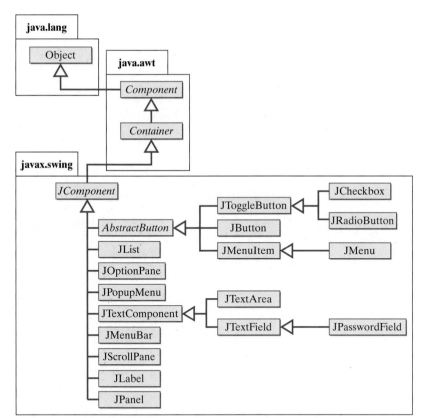

FIGURE 9–2 Swing classes, part 2: Swing components derived from JComponent are lightweight.

The programs presented in this chapter will use Swing components instead of corresponding AWT components. But they will also use layouts and other elements from the AWT. In terms of GUI components alone, Swing provides a replacement for every AWT component, as well as many new components that have no counterpart in the AWT. Although it is possible to mix and match AWT and Swing components in the same application, this is not advisable. Both sets of components use the same event model, so there are no problems on that score. But if you are developing new software in Java, you should use the Swing components. This will allow you to take advantage of the new GUI features that come with Swing, and it will also place your programs squarely on the road to the future. That's the approach we will take in this and subsequent chapters.

PROGRAMMING TIP: Swing Documentation. Complete documentation of the Swing classes is available for downloading or browsing on Sun's Web site at

`http://java.sun.com/products/jdk/1.3/docs/guide/swing/index.html`

SELF-STUDY EXERCISES

EXERCISE 9.1   What would have to be done to make a Swing-based GUI completely platform independent?

EXERCISE 9.2   Why are abstract classes, such as the `Container` and `Component` classes, not dependent on peers in the native windowing system?

9.2   The Swing Component Set

Java's Swing components are defined in a collection of packages named `javax.swing.*`, which is assumed by the code shown in this and subsequent chapters. Swing packages include the following:

```
javax.swing.event.*
javax.swing.plaf.*
javax.swing.text.*
```

The `javax.swing.event` package defines the various Swing events and their listeners. (In the AWT, the AWT events and listeners were defined in `java.awt.event`.)

The `javax.swing.text` package contains the classes for `JTextField` and `JTextComponent`, the Swing classes that replace the AWT's `TextField` and `TextArea` classes. The Swing text components are more complex than their AWT counterparts. For example, one of their important features is the ability to undo changes made to the text they contain. This feature is crucial for building sophisticated word-processing applications.

Look and feel

The `javax.swing.plaf` package contains Swing's look-and-feel classes. The term *plaf* is an acronym for **pluggable look and feel**. It refers to the fact that changing an application's look and feel is a simple matter of "plugging in" a different plaf model. Changing how a program looks does not change what it does.

Swing's platform-independent look and feel is achieved by placing all the code responsible for drawing a component in a separate class from the component itself. For example, in addition to `JButton`, the class that defines the button control, there will be a separate class responsible for drawing the button on the screen. The drawing class will control the button's color, shape, and other characteristics of its appearance.

There are several look-and-feel packages built into Swing. For example, the `javax.swing.plaf.motif` package contains the classes that implement the Motif interface, a common Unix-based interface. These classes know how to draw each component and how to react to mouse, keyboard, and other events associated with these components. The `javax.swing.-plaf.windows` package takes the same responsibility for a Windows 95 style interface.

OBJECT-ORIENTED DESIGN:
Model-View-Controller Architecture

Java's Swing components have been implemented using an object-oriented design known as the **model-view-controller (MVC)** model. Any Swing component can be viewed in terms of three independent aspects: what state it's in (its model), how it looks (its view), and what it does (its controller).

For example, a button's role is to appear on the interface waiting to be clicked. When it is clicked, the button's appearance changes. It looks pushed in or it changes color briefly, and then it changes back to its original (unclicked) appearance. In the MVC model, this aspect of the button is its **view**. If you were designing an interface for a button, you would need visual representations for both the clicked and the unclicked button (as well as other possible states). *View*

When you click a button, its internal state changes from pressed to unpressed. You've also probably seen buttons that were disabled—that is, in a state where they just ignore your clicks. Whether a button is enabled or disabled and whether it is pressed or not are properties of its internal state. All such properties, taken together, constitute the button's **model**. *Model* Of course, a button's view—how it looks—depends on its model. When a button is pressed, it has one appearance, and when it is disabled, it has another.

Because a button's state will change when it is clicked or when it is enabled by the program, some object needs to keep track of these changes. That part of the component is its **controller**. *Controller*

Figure 9–3 shows how the button's model, view, and controller interact with each other. Suppose the user clicks on the button. This action is detected by the controller. Whenever the mouse button is pressed, the controller tells the model to change into the pressed state. The model, in turn, generates an event that is passed to the view. The event tells the view that the button needs to be redrawn to reflect its change in state.

When the mouse button is released, a similar sequence of events occurs. The model is told to change to the unpressed state. It in turn generates an event, handled by the view, which changes the button's appearance.

A change in the button's appearance does not necessarily depend on direct action by the user. For example, the program itself could call a method that disables the button. In this case, the program issues a command

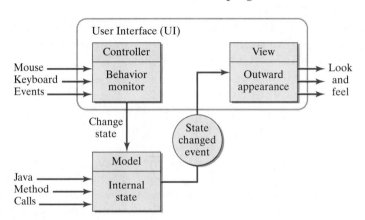

FIGURE 9–3 The model-view-controller architecture.

directly to the model, which in turn generates an event that causes the view to change the object's appearance.

For some Swing components, such as the text components, this three-part model is implemented almost exactly as we just described. For others, such as JButton, one class is used to implement both the view and the controller. The JButton model is defined in the DefaultButtonModel class, and its view and controller are defined in the BasicButtonUI class. The UI acronym stands for User Interface. The point is that for some components, Swing has organized the view and control—the look and the feel—into a single class.

Pluggable Look and Feel

The MVC model uses a clear division of labor to implement a GUI component. The main advantage of this design is the independence between the model, the view, and the controller. If you want to give a button a different look and feel, you can redefine its view and its controller.

By combining the view and controller into a single class, Swing makes it even easier to change a component's look and feel. For example, to design your own look and feel for a JButton, you would define a class that implemented all of the methods in the BasicButtonUI. Of course, this is a job for an experienced software developer.

To set the look and feel within a program, you can use the UIManager.setLookAndFeel() method:

FIGURE 9–4 The same Java application using the Motif, Windows, and Metal look and feel.

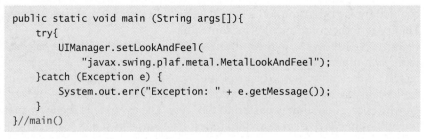

```
public static void main (String args[]){
    try{
        UIManager.setLookAndFeel(
            "javax.swing.plaf.metal.MetalLookAndFeel");
    }catch (Exception e) {
        System.out.err("Exception: " + e.getMessage());
    }
}//main()
```

The *Metal* look and feel is one designed specifically for Java applications, and it is the default. For a Windows look you can use the following argument: "com.sun.java.swing.plaf.windows.WindowsLookAndFeel". Figure 9–4 shows how the same simple application would appear under the three different look-and-feel styles.

SELF-STUDY EXERCISE

EXERCISE 9.3 The MVC architecture is a model of object-oriented design. But if a JButton is really composed of three separate parts, how can we still call it a component? Isn't it really three things?

9.3 The Java Event Model

In Chapter 4, we took a brief look at Java's **event model** as it applied to applets. According to this model, anything that happens while the computer is running is classified as an event. Every keystroke and mouse click, every time a disk is inserted into a disk drive, an event is generated.

When a Java program is running, events generated by the hardware are passed up through the operating system (and through the browser, for applets) to the program. Those events that belong to the program must be handled by the program (refer to Fig. 4–16). For example, if you click on your browser's menu bar, that event will be handled by the browser itself. If you click on a button contained in an applet, that event should be handled by the applet.

9.3.1 Events and Listeners

In Java, whenever something happens within a GUI component, whether an AWT or a Swing component, an event object is generated and passed to the *event listener* that has been registered to handle that component's events. You've seen numerous examples of this process in earlier chapters, but it will be useful to review the details here in terms of a Swing example.

Suppose you create a JButton in an applet:

```
private JButton clickme = new JButton("ClickMe");
```

Whenever the user clicks on the JButton, an ActionEvent will be generated. In order to handle these events, the applet must register the JButton with a listener object that listens for action events. This is usually done in the applet's init() method:

```
public void init() {
    add(clickme);                     // Add clickme to the applet
    clickme.addActionListener(this); // Register it with a listener
}
```

In this case, we have designated the applet itself (this) as an Action-Listener for clickme (Fig. 9–5). A **listener** is any object that implements a *listener interface*, which is one of the interfaces derived from java.util.EventListener. An ActionListener is an object that listens for and receives ActionEvents.

In order to complete the event-handling code, the applet must implement the ActionListener interface. As Figure 9–6 shows, imple-

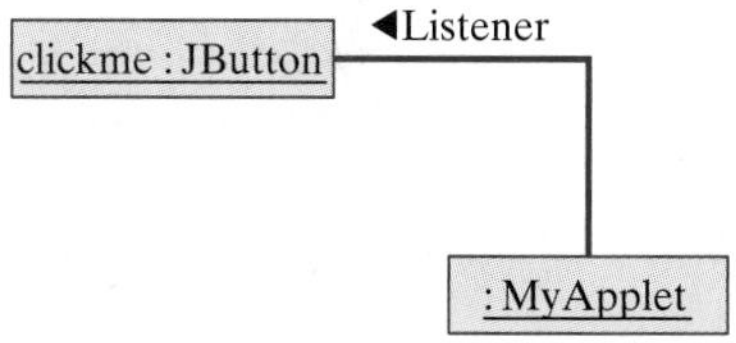

FIGURE 9–5 The applet listens for action events on the JButton.

```
import javax.swing.*;
import java.awt.*;
import java.awt.event.*;
import java.applet.*;

public class MyApplet extends JApplet implements ActionListener {
    private JButton clickme = new JButton("ClickMe");

    public void init() {
        getContentPane().add(clickme);   // Add clickme to the applet
        clickme.addActionListener(this); // Register it with a listener
    } // init()

    public void actionPerformed(ActionEvent e) {
        if (e.getSource() == clickme) {
            showStatus("clickme was clicked");
            System.out.println( e.toString() );
        }
    } // actionPerformed()
} // MyApplet
```

FIGURE 9–6 An applet that handles action events on a JButton.

FIGURE 9–7 A UML sequence diagram showing the sequence of actions and events that take place when a button is clicked.

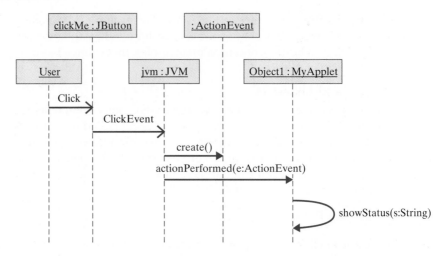

menting an interface is a matter of declaring the interface in the class heading and implementing the methods contained in the interface, in this case the `actionPerformed()` method.

Now that we have implemented the code in Figure 9–6, whenever the user clicks on `clickme`, that action is encapsulated within an `ActionEvent` object and passed to the applet's `actionPerformed()` method (Fig. 9–7). This method contains Java code that will handle the user's action in an appropriate way. For this example, it just prints a message in the applet's status bar and displays a string representation of the event.

The methods used to handle the `ActionEvent` are derived from the `java.util.EventObject` class, the root class for all events (Fig. 9–8). Our example (Fig. 9–6) uses the `getSource()` method to get a reference to the object that generated the event. It also uses the `toString()` method to get a string representation of the event that was generated. Here's what it displays:

EventObject
+ EventObject(in src : Object) + getSource() : Object + toString() : String

FIGURE 9–8 An `EventObject`. The `getSource()` method is used to get the object that caused the event.

```
java.awt.event.ActionEvent[ACTION_PERFORMED,cmd=ClickMe]
  on javax.swing.JButton[,58,5,83x27,
  layout=javax.swing.OverlayLayout]
```

As you can see, the event generated was an `ACTION.PERFORMED` event, in response to the `ClickMe` command. The source of the event was the `JButton`.

9.3.2 Event Classes

Although the event model is the same for both AWT and Swing classes, the Swing package introduces many additional events. Table 9.1 lists the events that are generated by both AWT and Swing components. In the preceding chapters we've written applets that handled `ActionEvents` for `Buttons` and `TextFields`. These same events are generated for the Swing counterparts to these components: `JButton` and `JTextField`.

In viewing Table 9.1, it's important to remember that the classes listed there are arranged in a hierarchy. This will affect the events that a particular object can generate. For example, a `JButton` is a `JComponent` (Fig. 9–2), so in addition to generating `ActionEvents` when the user clicks on it, it can

TABLE 9.1 Java's AWTEvents for each Component type (Original source: David Flanagan, *Java in a Nutshell*, 2d ed., O'Reilly Associates, 1997. Modified for Swing components.)

Components	Events	Description
Button, JButton	ActionEvent	User clicked button
CheckBox, JCheckBox	ItemEvent	User toggled a checkbox
CheckboxMenuItem, JCheckboxMenuItem	ItemEvent	User toggled a checkbox
Choice, JPopupMenu	ItemEvent	User selected a choice
Component, JComponent	ComponentEvent	Component was moved or resized
	FocusEvent	Component acquired or lost focus
	KeyEvent	User typed a key
	MouseEvent	User manipulated the mouse
Container, JContainer	ContainerEvent	Component added/removed from container
List, JList	ActionEvent	User double-clicked a list item
	ItemEvent	User clicked a list item
Menu, JMenu	ActionEvent	User selected menu item
Scrollbar, JScrollbar	AdjustmentEvent	User moved scrollbar
TextComponent, JTextComponent	TextEvent	User edited text
TextField, JTextField	ActionEvent	User typed Enter key
Window, JWindow	WindowEvent	User manipulated window

also generate MouseEvents when the user moves the mouse over it. Similarly, because a JTextField is also a JComponent, it can generate KeyEvents as well as ActionEvents.

Note that the more generic events, such as those that involve moving, focusing, or resizing a component, are associated with the more generic components. For example, the JComponent class contains methods that are used to manage ComponentEvents. Because they are subclasses of JComponent, JButtons and JTextFields can also use these methods. Defining the more generic methods in the JComponent superclass is another example of the effective use of inheritance.

EFFECTIVE DESIGN: Inheritance. The higher a method is defined in the inheritance hierarchy, the broader is its use.

Table 9.2 lists events that are new with the Swing classes. Some of the events apply to new components. For example, JTable and JTree do not have AWT counterparts. Other events provide Swing components with capabilities that are not available in their AWT counterparts. For example, a CaretEvent allows the programmer to have control over mouse clicks that occur within a text component.

Tables 9.1 and 9.2 provide only the barest summary of these classes and Swing components. For further details you should consult the JDK online documentation at

http://java.sun.com/products/jdk/1.3/docs/api/

TABLE 9.2 Some of the events that are newly defined in the Swing library.

Component	Events	Description
JPopupMenu	PopupMenuEvent	User selected a choice
JComponent	AncestorEvent	An event occurred in an ancestor
JList	ListSelectionEvent	User double-clicked a list item
	ListDataEvent	List's contents were changed
JMenu	MenuEvent	User selected menu item
JTextComponent	CaretEvent	Mouse clicked in text
	UndoableEditEvent	An undoable edit has occurred
JTable	TableModelEvent	Items added/removed from table
	TableColumnModelEvent	A table column was moved
JTree	TreeModelEvent	Items added/removed from tree
	TreeSelectionEvent	User selected a tree node
	TreeExpansionEvent	User expanded or collapsed a tree node
JWindow	WindowEvent	User manipulated window

SELF-STUDY EXERCISES

EXERCISE 9.4 Is it possible to register a component with more than one listener?

EXERCISE 9.5 Is it possible for a component to have two different kinds of listeners?

9.4 CASE STUDY: Designing a Basic GUI

What elements make up a basic user interface? If you think about all of the various interfaces you've encountered—and don't just limit yourself to computers—they all have the following elements:

- Some way to provide help/guidance to the user.
- Some way to allow input of information.
- Some way to allow output of information.
- Some way to control the interaction between the user and the device.

Think about the interface on a beverage machine. Printed text on the machine will tell you what choices you have, where to put your money, and what to do if something goes wrong. The coin slot is used to input money. There's often some kind of display to tell you how much money you've inserted. And there's usually a bunch of buttons and levers that let you control the interaction with the machine.

These same kinds of elements make up the basic computer interface. Designing a Graphical User Interface is primarily a process of choosing components that can effectively perform the tasks of input, output, control, and guidance.

EFFECTIVE DESIGN: User Interface. A user interface must effectively perform the tasks of input, output, control, and guidance.

In the programs we designed in the earlier chapters, we used two different kinds of interfaces. In the *command-line* interface, we used printed prompts to inform the user, typed commands for data entry and user control, and printed output to report results. Our applet interfaces used Labels to guide and prompt the user, TextFields and TextAreas as basic input and output devices, and either Buttons or TextFields for user control.

Up to this point, all of our GUIs have taken the form of Java applets. So let's begin by building a basic GUI in the form of a Java application. To keep the example as close as possible to the applet interfaces we've used, we'll build it out of the following Swing components: JLabel, JTextField, JTextArea, and JButton.

9.4.1 The Metric Converter Application

Suppose the coach of the cross-country team asks you to write a Java application that can be used to convert miles to kilometers. The program should let the user input a distance in miles, and it should report the equivalent distance in kilometers.

Before we design the interface for this, let's first define a MetricConverter class that can be used to perform the conversions (Fig. 9–9). For now at least, this class's only task will be to convert miles to kilometers, for which it will use the formula that 1 kilometer equals 0.62 miles:

```java
public class MetricConverter {

    public static double milesToKm(double miles) {
        return miles / 0.62;
    }
}
```

Note that the method takes a double as input and returns a double. Also, by declaring the method static, we make it a class method, so it can be invoked simply by

```java
MetricConverter.milesToKm(10);
```

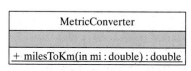

FIGURE 9–9 The MetricConverter class has a single method to convert miles to kilometers.

Choosing the Components

Let's now design a GUI to handle the interaction with the user. First, let's choose Swing components for each of the four interface tasks of input, output, control, and guidance. For each component, it may be useful to refer back to Figure 9–2 to note its location in the Swing hierarchy.

Which components do we need?

- A JLabel is a display area for a short string of text, an image, or both. Its AWT counterpart, the Label, cannot display images. A JLabel does not react to input. Therefore, it is used primarily to display a graphic or small amounts of static text. It is perfectly suited to serve as a prompt, which is what we will use it for in this interface.
- A JTextField is a component that allows editing of a single line of text. It is also identical to its AWT counterpart, the TextField. By using its getText() and setText() methods, a JTextField can be used for either input or output, or both. For this problem, we'll use it to perform the interface's input task.
- A JTextArea is a multiline text area that can be used for either input or output. It is almost identical to the AWT TextArea component. One difference, however, is that a JTextArea does not contain scrollbars by default. For this program, we'll use the JTextArea for displaying the results of conversions. Because it is used solely for output, we'll make it *uneditable* to prevent the user from typing in it.

- Let's use a JButton as our main control for this interface. By implementing the ActionListener interface we will handle the user's action events.

Choosing the Top-Level Window

What top-level window to use?

The next issue we must decide is what kind of top-level window to use for this interface. For applet interfaces, the top-level component would be a JApplet. For Java applications, you would typically use a JFrame as the top-level window. Both of these classes are subclasses of Container, so they are suitable for holding the components that make up the interface (Fig. 9–1).

Also, as we noted earlier, JApplets and JFrames are both examples of heavyweight components, so they both have windows associated with them. To display a JFrame we just have to give it a size and make it visible. Because a frame runs as a stand-alone window, not within a browser context, it should also be able to exit the application when the user closes the frame.

Designing a Layout

How should the components be arranged?

The next step in designing the interface is deciding how to arrange the components so that they will be visually appealing and comprehensible, as well as easy to use.

Figure 9–10 shows a design for the layout. It has the output text area, as the largest component, occupying the center of the JFrame. The prompt, input text field, and control button are arranged in a row above the text area. This is a simple and straightforward layout.

Figure 9–10 also provides a **containment hierarchy**, or a **widget hierarchy**, showing the containment relationships among the various components. Although it may not seem so for this simple layout, the containment hierarchy plays an important role in showing how the various components are grouped together in the interface. For this design, we have a relatively simple hierarchy, with only one level of containment. All of the components are contained directly in the JFrame.

Figure 9–11 shows the design of the Converter class. Let's compare its features to those of a comparable applet. Instead of extending the JApplet class, this program extends the JFrame class. As we just mentioned, a JFrame is a top-level window that can contain GUI components. Also, our program implements the ActionListener interface. This will enable it to

FIGURE 9–10 A design and layout for the Metric Converter GUI. The *containment hierarchy* (also called a *widget hierarchy*) shows the containment relationships among the components.

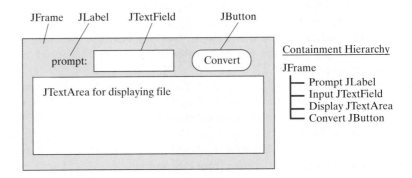

handle action events. The `actionPerformed()` method is exactly the same as it would be for an applet, which underscores the fact that the event model is the same for Swing as it was for the AWT.

Figure 9–12 gives the implementation of the `Converter` class. Note the three packages that are imported. The first contains definitions of the Swing classes, and the other two contain definitions of AWT events and layout managers that are used in the program.

Instead of performing initializations in the `init()` method as we would for an applet, we do all initializing in the constructor. There are two important points to notice about the constructor. First, note that we have set the `JFrame`'s layout to `FlowLayout`. A **layout manager** is the object that is responsible for sizing and arranging the components in a container. A flow layout is the simplest arrangement: The components are arranged left to right in the window, wrapping around to the next "row" if necessary.

Second, note the statements used to set the layout and to add components directly to the `JFrame`. Instead of adding components directly to the `JFrame`, we must add them to its content pane:

```
getContentPane().add(input);
```

A **content pane** is a `JPanel` that serves as the working area of the `JFrame`. It contains all of the frame's components. Java will raise an exception if you attempt to add a component directly to a `JFrame`.

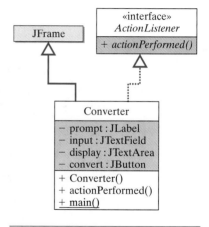

FIGURE 9–11 The `Converter` class is a subclass of `JFrame` and implements the `ActionListener` interface.

> DEBUGGING TIP: A `JFrame` cannot directly contain GUI elements. Instead they must be added to its content pane, which can be retrieved using the `getContentPane()` method.

Unlike their AWT counterparts, `JFrame` and all the other top-level Swing windows have an internal structure made up of several distinct objects that can be manipulated by the program. Because of this structure, GUI elements can be organized into different layers within the window, making possible all sorts of sophisticated layouts. Also, one layer of the structure makes it possible to associate a menu with the frame. Thus, the use of a content pane represents a major advance beyond the functionality available with `java.awt.Frame`.

Finally, note how the `Converter` frame is instantiated, made visible, and eventually exited in the application's `main()` method:

```
public static void main(String args[]) {
    Converter f = new Converter();
    f.setSize(400, 300);
    f.setVisible(true);
    f.addWindowListener(new WindowAdapter() {  // Quit the application
        public void windowClosing(WindowEvent e) {
            System.exit(0);
        }
    });
} // main()
```

```
import javax.swing.*;              // Packages used
import java.awt.*;
import java.awt.event.*;

public class Converter extends JFrame implements ActionListener{

    private JLabel prompt = new JLabel("Distance in miles: ");
    private JTextField input = new JTextField(6);
    private JTextArea display = new JTextArea(10,20);
    private JButton convert = new JButton("Convert!");

    public Converter() {
        getContentPane().setLayout(new FlowLayout());
        getContentPane().add(prompt);
        getContentPane().add(input);
        getContentPane().add(convert);

        getContentPane().add(display);

        display.setLineWrap(true);
        display.setEditable(false);

        convert.addActionListener(this);
    } // Converter()

    public void actionPerformed( ActionEvent e ) {
        double miles = Double.valueOf(input.getText()).doubleValue();
        double km = MetricConverter.milesToKm(miles);
        display.append(miles + " miles equals " + km + " kilometers\n");
    } // actionPerformed()

    public static void main(String args[]) {
        Converter f = new Converter();
        f.setSize(400, 300);
        f.setVisible(true);
        f.addWindowListener(new WindowAdapter() {       // Quit the application
            public void windowClosing(WindowEvent e) {
                System.exit(0);
            }
        });
    } // main()
} // Converter
```

FIGURE 9–12   The Converter class implements a simple GUI interface.

It is necessary to set both the size and visibility of the frame, since these are not set by default. Because we are using a `FlowLayout`, it's especially important to give the frame an appropriate size. Failure to do so may cause the components to be arranged in a confusing way and may even cause some components to not show up at all in the window. These are limitations we will fix when we learn how to use some of the other layout managers.

9.4.2   Inner Classes and Adapter Classes

Note also the code that's used to quit the `Converter` application. The program provides a listener that listens for window closing events. When such an event occurs, it exits the application by calling `System.exit()`.

Inner classes

This syntax used here is an example of an *anonymous inner class*, a language feature that was introduced with JDK 1.1. An inner class is a class defined within another class. The syntax is kind of ugly, because it places the class definition right where a reference to a window listener object would go. In effect what the code is doing is defining a subclass of `WindowAdapter` and creating an instance of it to serve as a listener for window closing events.

Anonymous inner classes provide a useful way of creating classes and objects on the fly to handle just this kind of listener task. The syntax used actually enables us to write one expression that both defines a class and creates an instance of it to listen for window closing events. The new subclass has local scope limited here to the `main()` method. It is anonymous, meaning we aren't even giving it a name, so you can't create other instances of it in the program. Note that the body of the class definition is placed right after the `new` keyword, which takes the place of the argument to the `addWindowListener()` method. For more details on the inner and anonymous classes, see Appendix F.

> **JAVA LANGUAGE RULE**   **Inner Class.** An inner class is a class defined within another class. Inner classes are mostly used to handle a task that supports the work of the containing class.

Adapter class

An *adapter class* is a wrapper class that implements trivial versions of the abstract methods that make up a particular interface. The `WindowAdapter` class implements the methods of the `WindowListener` interface. When you implement an interface, such as `ActionListener`, you must implement all the abstract methods defined in the interface. For `ActionListener`, there's just one method, the `actionPerformed()` method, so we can implement it as part of our applet or frame class. However, the `WindowListener` interface contains seven methods. But we only want to use the `windowClosing()` method in this program, which is the method implemented in the anonymous inner class:

```
public void windowClosing(WindowEvent e) {
    System.exit(0);
}
```

The `WindowAdapter` is defined simply as

```
public abstract class WindowAdapter implements WindowListener {
    public void windowActivated(WindowEvent e) {}
    public void windowClosed(WindowEvent e) {}
    ...
    // Five other window listener methods
}
```

Note that each method is given a trivial implementation ({}). To create a subclass of WindowAdapter, you must implement at least one of its abstract methods.

Another way to manage the application's window closing event is to define a subclass of WindowAdapter:

```
import javax.swing.*;
import java.awt.*;
import java.awt.event.*;
public class WindowCloser extends WindowAdapter {
    public void windowClosing(WindowEvent e) {
        System.exit(0);
    }
}
```

Given this class, we can then place the following statement in Converter's main() method:

```
f.addWindowListener(new WindowCloser());
```

This is somewhat more familiar looking than the inner class construct. If you prefer this way of handling things, you can use it in place of the inner classes in this and other examples.

EFFECTIVE DESIGN: Anonymous Adapter Classes.   Anonymous adapter classes provide a useful way of creating an object to handle one particular kind of event within a program.

9.4.3   GUI Design Critique

Figure 9–13 shows the converter interface. Although our basic GUI design satisfies the demands of input, output, control, and guidance, it has a couple of significant design flaws.

First, it forces the user to manually clear the input field after each conversion. Unless it is important that the user's input value remain displayed until another value is to be input, this is just an inconvenience to the user. In this case, the user's input value is displayed along with the result in the JTextArea, so there's no reason not to clear the input text field:

```
input.setText("");   // Clear the input field
```

EFFECTIVE DESIGN: Reduce the User's Burden.   A GUI should aim to minimize the responsibility placed on the user. In general, the program should do any task that it can do, unless, of course, there is a compelling reason that the user should do the task.

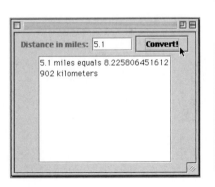

FIGURE 9–13   The first version of the metric converter GUI.

A second problem with our design is that it forces the user to switch between the keyboard (for input) and the mouse (for control). Experienced users will find this annoying. An easy way to fix this problem is to make both the JTextField and the JButton serve as controls. That way, to get the program to do the conversion, the user can just press the Enter key after typing a number into the text field.

To give the interface this type of control, we need only add an ActionListener to the JTextField during the initialization step:

```
input.addActionListener(this);
```

Like its TextField counterpart, a JTextField generates an ActionEvent whenever the Enter key is pressed inside it. We don't even need to modify the actionPerformed() method, since both controls will generate the same action event. This will make it possible for users who prefer the keyboard to carry out all their interactions with the program using just the keyboard.

> **EFFECTIVE DESIGN: User Interface.**   A GUI should aim to minimize the number of different input devices (mouse, keyboard) that the user has to manipulate in order to perform a particular task.

Given that the user can now interact with the interface using just the keyboard, a question arises over whether we should keep the button at all. In this case, it seems justifiable to keep both the button and the text field controls. Some users dislike typing and prefer to use the mouse. Also, having two independent sets of controls is a desirable form of redundancy. You see it frequently in menu-based systems that allow menu items to be selected either by mouse or by special control keys.

> **EFFECTIVE DESIGN: Desirable Redundancy.**   Certain forms of redundancy in an interface, such as two sets of independent controls (mouse and keyboard), make it more flexible or more widely usable.

SELF-STUDY EXERCISES

EXERCISE 9.6   Another deficiency in the converter interface is that it doesn't round off its result, leading sometimes to numbers with 20 or so digits. Develop Java code to fix this problem.

EXERCISE 9.7   Give an example of desirable redundancy in the design of your car.

9.4.4   Extending the Basic GUI: Button Array

Suppose the coach likes our program but complains that some of the folks in the office are terrible typists and would prefer not to have to use the keyboard at all. Is there some way we could modify the interface to accommodate these users?

This gets back to the point we were just making about incorporating redundancy into the interface. One way to satisfy this requirement would

What components do we need?

FIGURE 9–14 A widget hierarchy showing the containment relationships among the components.

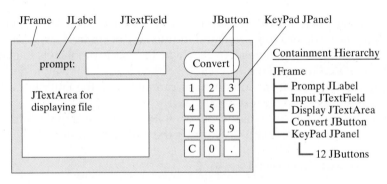

be to implement a numeric keypad for input, similar to a calculator keypad. Regular JButtons can be used as the keypad's keys. As keypad buttons are clicked, their face values—0 through 9—are inserted into the text field. The keypad will also need a button to clear the text field and one to serve as a decimal point.

How should the components be organized?

This new feature will add 12 new JButton components to our interface. Instead of inserting them into the JFrame individually, it will be better to organize them into a separate panel and to insert the entire panel into the frame as a single unit. This will help reduce the complexity of the display, especially if the keypad buttons can be grouped together visually. Instead of having to deal with 16 separate components, the user will see the keypad as a single unit with a unified function. This is an example of the *abstraction principle*, similar to the way we break long strings of numbers (1-888-889-1999) into subgroups to make them easier to remember.

EFFECTIVE DESIGN: Reducing Complexity.   Organizing elements into distinct groups by function helps to reduce the GUI's complexity.

Figure 9–14 shows the revised design for the converter interface. The containment hierarchy shows that the 12 keypad JButtons are contained within a JPanel. In the frame's layout, the entire panel is inserted just after the text area.

Incorporating the keypad into the interface will require several changes in the program's design. Because the keypad has such a clearly defined role, let's make it into a separate object by defining a KeyPad class (Fig. 9–15). The KeyPad will be a subclass of JPanel and will handle its own ActionEvents. A JPanel is a generic container. It is a subclass of Container via the JComponent class (Fig. 9–2). Its main purpose is to contain and organize components that appear together on an interface.

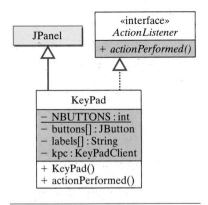

FIGURE 9–15 A KeyPad is a JPanel of JButtons that handles its own action events.

In this case, we will use a JPanel to hold the keypad buttons. As you might expect, to add elements to a JPanel, you use the add() method, which is inherited from Container, just as we did when adding elements to an applet. (Recall that an Applet is also a subclass of Container via the Panel class.)

As a subclass of JPanel, the KeyPad will take care of holding and organizing the JButtons within the visual display. We also need some way to organize and manage the 12 keypad buttons within the program's memory. Clearly, this is a good job for an array. Actually, two arrays would be even better, one for the buttons and one for their labels:

```
private JButton buttons[];
private String labels[] =        // An array of button labels
            { "1","2","3",
              "4","5","6",
              "7","8","9",
              "C","0","." };
```

The `label` array stores the strings that we will use as the buttons' labels. The main advantage of the array is that we can use a loop to instantiate the buttons:

```
buttons = new JButton[NBUTTONS];        // Create the array itself
for(int k = 0; k < buttons.length; k++) {  // For each button
    buttons[k] = new JButton(labels[k]);   //  Create a labeled button
    buttons[k].addActionListener(this);    //  and a listener
    add(buttons[k]);                       //  and add it to the panel
} // for
```

Algorithm design

This code would be placed in the `KeyPad()` constructor. It begins by instantiating the array itself. It then uses a for loop, bounded by the size of the array, to instantiate each individual button and insert it into the array. Note how the loop variable here, *k*, plays a dual role. It serves as the index into both the button array (`buttons`) and the array of strings that serves as the buttons' labels (`labels`). In that way the labels are assigned to the appropriate buttons. Note also how each button is assigned an `ActionListener` and added to the panel:

```
buttons[k].addActionListener(this);   //  Add a listener
add(buttons[k]);                      //  Add button to the panel
```

An important design issue for our `KeyPad` object concerns how it will interact with the `Converter` that contains it. When the user clicks on a keypad button, the key's label has to be displayed in the `Converter`'s text area. But because the text area is private to the converter, the `KeyPad` does not have direct access to it. To address this problem, we will use a Java interface to implement a **callback design**. According to this design, whenever a Key-Pad button is pressed, the `KeyPad` object will call a method in the `Converter` that will display the key's label in the text area.

Callback design

Figure 9–16 provides a summary of the callback design. Note that the association between the `Converter` and the `KeyPad` is bidirectional. This means that each object has a reference to the other and can invoke the other's public methods. This will be effected by having the `Converter` pass a reference to itself when it constructs the `KeyPad`:

```
private KeyPad keypad = new KeyPad(this);
```

Another important design issue is that the `KeyPad` needs to know the name of the callback method and the `Converter` needs to have an implementation of that method. This is a perfect job for an abstract interface:

```
public abstract interface KeyPadClient {
    public void keypressCallback(String s);
}
```

FIGURE 9–16 In a callback design, the `Converter` implements the `KeyPadClient` interface. It passes a reference to itself when it creates the `KeyPad` object. The `KeyPad` object can then invoke the `keypressCallback()` method whenever a keypad button is pressed, and the `Converter` can display the result of the keypress.

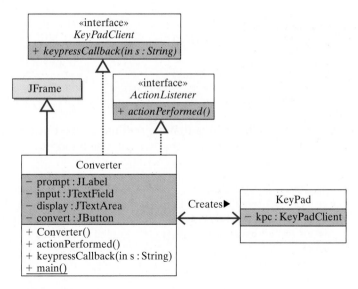

The `KeyPad` can interact with any class that implements the `Key-PadClient` interface. Note that the `KeyPad` has a reference to the `KeyPadClient`, which it will use to invoke the `keypressCallback()` method.

The implementation of `KeyPad` is shown in Figure 9–17. Note that its constructor takes a reference to a `KeyPadClient` and saves it in an instance variable. Its `actionPerformed()` method then passes the key's label to the `KeyPadClient`'s callback method.

Given this design of the `KeyPad`, we need to revise our design of the `Converter` class (Fig. 9–16). The `Converter` will now implement the `KeyPad-Client` interface, which means it must provide an implementation of the `keypressCallback()` method:

```
public void keypressCallback(String s) {
    if (s.equals("C"))
        input.setText("");
    else
        input.setText(input.getText() + s);
}
```

Recall that whenever the `KeyPad` object calls the `keypressCallback()` method, it passes the label of the button that was pressed. The `Converter` object simply appends the key's label to the input text field, just as if the user typed the key in the text field.

The complete implementation of this revised version of the interface is shown in Figure 9–18. The appearance of the interface itself is shown in Figure 9–19.

9.4.5 GUI Design Critique

As Figure 9–19 shows, despite our efforts to group the keypad into a rectangular array, it doesn't appear as a single entity in the interface itself. This is a layout problem. The default layout for our `KeyPad` (which

```java
import java.awt.*;
import java.awt.event.*;
import javax.swing.*;

public class KeyPad extends JPanel implements ActionListener{

    private final static int NBUTTONS = 12;
    private KeyPadClient kpc;        // Owner of the KeyPad
    private JButton buttons[];
    private String labels[] =        // An array of button labels
            { "1","2","3",
              "4","5","6",
              "7","8","9",
              "C","0","." };

    public KeyPad(KeyPadClient kpc) {
        this.kpc = kpc;
        buttons = new JButton[NBUTTONS];            // Create the array itself
        for(int k = 0; k < buttons.length; k++) {   // For each button
            buttons[k] = new JButton(labels[k]);    //   Create a labeled button
            buttons[k].addActionListener(this);     //   and a listener
            add(buttons[k]);                        //   and add it to the panel
        } // for

    }

    public void actionPerformed(ActionEvent e) {
        String keylabel = ((JButton)e.getSource()).getText();
        kpc.keypressCallback(keylabel);
    }
}
```

FIGURE 9–17   The KeyPad object implements a 12-key keypad in a JPanel. It has a reference to the KeyPadClient that contains the keypad.

is a JPanel) is FlowLayout. But a numeric keypad should be arranged into a two-dimensional grid pattern, which is the kind of layout our design called for (Fig. 9–14).

Fortunately, this flaw can easily be fixed by using an appropriate layout manager from the AWT, as we will do in the next version of the program. Indeed, the java.awt.GridLayout is perfectly suited for a two-dimensional keypad layout (Section 9.5.2).

The lesson to be learned from this example is that screen layout is an important element of an effective GUI. If not done well, it can undermine the GUI's effort to guide the user toward the appointed tasks. If done poorly enough, it can even keep the user from doing the task at all.

EFFECTIVE DESIGN: Layout Design.   The appropriate layout and management of GUI elements is an important part of interface design. It contributes to the interface's ability to guide the user's action toward the interface's goals.

```java
import javax.swing.*;        // Packages used
import java.awt.*;
import java.awt.event.*;

public class Converter extends JFrame              // Version 2
                       implements ActionListener, KeyPadClient {

    private JLabel prompt = new JLabel("Distance in miles: ");
    private JTextField input = new JTextField(6);
    private JTextArea display = new JTextArea(10,20);
    private JButton convert = new JButton("Convert!");
    private KeyPad keypad = new KeyPad(this);

    public Converter () {
        getContentPane().setLayout(new FlowLayout());
        getContentPane().add(prompt);
        getContentPane().add(input);
        getContentPane().add(convert);
        getContentPane().add(display);
        getContentPane().add(keypad);
        display.setLineWrap(true);
        display.setEditable(false);

        convert.addActionListener(this);
        input.addActionListener(this);
    } // Converter()

    public void actionPerformed(ActionEvent e) {
        double miles = Double.valueOf(input.getText()).doubleValue();
        double km = MetricConverter.milesToKm(miles);
        display.append(miles + " miles equals " + km + " kilometers\n");
        input.setText("");
    } // actionPerformed()

    public void keypressCallback(String s) {
        if (s.equals("C"))
            input.setText("");
        else
            input.setText(input.getText() + s);
    }

    public static void main(String args[]) {
        Converter f = new Converter();
        f.setSize(400, 300);
        f.setVisible(true);
        f.addWindowListener(new WindowAdapter() {      // Quit the application
            public void windowClosing(WindowEvent e) {
                System.exit(0);
            }
        });
    } // main()
} // Converter
```

FIGURE 9–18   The second version of the Converter class, which implements the GUI shown in Figure 9–19.

FIGURE 9–19   The second version of the metric converter GUI uses a set of keypad buttons for input, but they are not properly arranged.

9.5   Containers and Layout Managers

A Container is a component that can contain other components. Because containers can contain other containers, it is possible to create a hierarchical arrangement of components, as we did in the second version of our Converter interface. In its present form, the hierarchy for Converter consists of a JFrame as the top-level container (Fig. 9–14). Contained within the frame is a KeyPad (subclass of JPanel), which contains 12 JButtons. Most GUIs will have a similar kind of containment hierarchy.

A Container is a relatively simple object whose main task is primarily to hold its components in a particular order. It has methods to add and remove components (Fig. 9–20). As you can see from these methods, a container keeps track of the order of its elements, and it is possible to refer to a component by its index order.

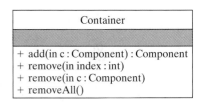

FIGURE 9–20   A Container contains Components.

9.5.1   Layout Managers

The real hard work of organizing and managing the elements within a container is the task of the layout manager. A *layout manager* is an object that manages the layout and organization of its container. Among the tasks it performs are

- To determine the overall size of the container.
- To determine the size of each element in the container.
- To determine the spacing between elements.
- To determine the positioning of the elements.

Although it is possible to manage your own layouts, it is not easy to do. For most applications you are much better off by learning to use one of the AWT's built-in layouts. Table 9.3 gives a brief summary of the available layouts. We will show examples of FlowLayout, GridLayout, and BorderLayout.

Some of the widely used Swing containers have a default layout manager assigned to them (Table 9.4). Note that unlike its Applet counterpart, which had a default FlowLayout, a JApplet has a BorderLayout. This can cause problems if you are converting an AWT-based applet to a Swing-based JApplet. In such cases, it is necessary to override JApplet's default layout by using the setLayout() method.

TABLE 9.3　Some of Java's AWT and Swing layout managers.

Manager	Description
java.awt.BorderLayout	Arranges elements along the north, south, east, west, and in the center of the container.
java.swing.BoxLayout	Arranges elements in a single row or single column.
java.awt.CardLayout	Arranges elements like a stack of cards, with one visible at a time.
java.awt.FlowLayout	Arranges elements left to right across the container.
java.awt.GridBagLayout	Arranges elements in a grid of variably sized cells (complicated).
java.awt.GridLayout	Arranges elements into a two-dimensional grid of equally sized cells.
java.swing.OverlayLayout	Arranges elements on top of each other.

TABLE 9.4　Default layouts for some of the common Swing containers.

Container	Layout Manager
JApplet	BorderLayout (on its content pane)
JBox	BoxLayout
JDialog	BorderLayout (on its content pane)
JFrame	BorderLayout (on its content pane)
JPanel	FlowLayout
JWindow	BorderLayout (on its content pane)

To override the default layout for any of the JApplet, JDialog, JFrame, and JWindow containers, you must remember to use the getContentPane(). The correct statement is

```
getContentPane().setLayout(new FlowLayout());
```

PROGRAMMING TIP: Default Layouts.　When converting an AWT applet to a Swing applet, it is necessary to override the default layout associated with the JApplet's content pane.

DEBUGGING TIP: Content Pane. Attempting to add a component directly to a JApplet or a JFrame will cause an exception. For these top-level containers, components must be added to their content panes.

9.5.2　The GridLayout **Manager**

It is simple to remedy the layout problem that affected the keypad in the most recent version of the Converter program. The problem was caused by the fact that as a subclass of JPanel, the KeyPad uses a default FlowLayout, which causes its buttons to be arranged in a row. A more appropriate layout for a numeric keypad would be a two-dimensional grid, which is exactly the kind of layout supplied by the java.awt.GridLayout. Therefore, to fix this problem, we need only set the keypad's layout to a GridLayout. This takes a single statement, which should be added to the beginning of the KeyPad() constructor:

```
setLayout(new GridLayout(4,3,1,1)); // Arrange in a grid
```

This statement creates a GridLayout object and assigns it as the layout manager for the keypad. It will ensure that the keypad will have four rows and three columns of buttons (Fig. 9–21). The last two arguments in the constructor affect the relative spacing between the rows and the columns. The higher the number, the larger the spacing. As components are added to the keypad, they will automatically be arranged by the manager into a 4 × 3 grid.

Note that for a JPanel, the setLayout() method applies to the panel itself. Unlike the top-level containers, such as JFrame, other containers don't have content panes. The same point would apply when adding components to a JPanel: They are added directly to the panel, not to a content pane. Confusion over this point could be the source of bugs in your programs.

> **DEBUGGING TIP: Content Pane.** Top-level containers, such as JFrame, are the only ones that use a content pane. For other containers, such as JPanel, components are added directly to the container itself.

As its name suggests, the GridLayout layout manager arranges components in a two-dimensional grid. When components are added to the container, the layout manager starts inserting elements into the grid at the first cell in the first row and continues left to right across row 1, then row 2, and so on. If there are not enough components to fill all cells of the grid, the remaining cells are left blank. If an attempt is made to add too many components to the grid, the layout manager will try to extend the grid in some reasonable way in order to accommodate the components. However, despite its effort in such cases, it usually fails to achieve a completely appropriate layout.

> **PROGRAMMING TIP: Grid Layouts.** Make sure the number of components added to a GridLayout is equal to the number of rows times the number of columns.

9.5.3 GUI Design Critique

The layout in Figure 9–21 is much improved. However, there are still some deficiencies. One problem is that the convert button seems to be misplaced. It would seem to make more sense if it were grouped together with the keypad rather than with the input text field.

A more serious problem results from the fact that we are still using a FlowLayout for the program's main window, the JFrame. Among all of Java's layouts, FlowLayout gives you the least amount of control over the arrangement of the components. Also, FlowLayout is most sensitive to changes in the size and shape of its container.

9.5.4 The BorderLayout Manager

One way to fix these problems is to use a BorderLayout to divide the frame into five areas: north, south, east, west, and center, as shown in Figure 9–22. The areas are arranged along the north, south, east, and west edges of the container and at its center. The BorderLayout class contains two constructors:

```
public BorderLayout();
public BorderLayout(int hgap, int vgap);
```

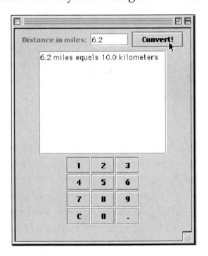

FIGURE 9–21 This version of the metric converter GUI uses a keypad for mouse-based input. It has an attractive overall layout.

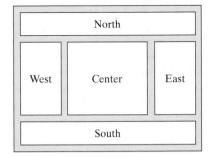

FIGURE 9–22 Arrangement of components in a border layout. The relative size of the areas will vary.

The two parameters in the second version of the constructor allow you to put some spacing between the respective areas.

Components are added to a BorderLayout by using the add(Component, String) method found in the Container class. For example, to set the application window to a border layout and to add the keypad to its east area, we would use the following statements:

```
getContentPane().setLayout(new BorderLayout(2, 2));
getContentPane().add(keypad,"East");
```

In this version of the add() method, the second parameter must be a capitalized String with one of the names, "North," "South," "East," "West," or "Center." The order in which components are added does not matter.

Containment hierarchy

One limitation of the BorderLayout is that only one component can be added to each area. That means that if you want to add several components to an area, you must first enclose them within a JPanel and then add the entire panel to the area. For example, let's create a panel to contain the prompt and the text field and place it at the north edge of the frame:

```
JPanel inputPanel = new JPanel();            // Create the panel
inputPanel.add(prompt);                      // Add the label
inputPanel.add(input);                       // and the text field
getContentPane().add(inputPanel,"North"); // Add the panel to the frame
```

The same point would apply if we want to group the keypad together with the convert button and place them at the east edge. There are several ways these elements could be grouped. In this example, we give the panel a border layout and put the keypad in the center and the convert button at the south edge:

```
JPanel controlPanel = new JPanel(new BorderLayout(0, 0));
controlPanel.add(keypad,"Center");
controlPanel.add(convert, "South");
getContentPane.add(controlPanel,"East"); // Add the panel to the frame
```

Given these details about the BorderLayout, a more appropriate design for the converter application is shown in Figure 9–23. Notice that the border layout for the top-level JFrame uses only the center, north, and east areas. Similarly, the border layout for the control panel uses just the center and south areas.

FIGURE 9–23   A border layout design for the metric converter program. The dotted lines show the panels.

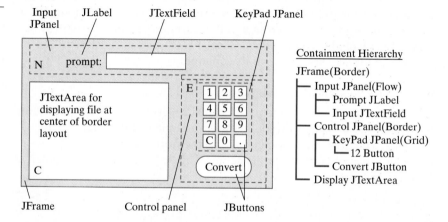

Input JPanel · JLabel · JTextField · KeyPad JPanel

Containment Hierarchy

JFrame(Border)
— Input JPanel(Flow)
  — Prompt JLabel
  — Input JTextField
— Control JPanel(Border)
  — KeyPad JPanel(Grid)
    — 12 Button
  — Convert JButton
— Display JTextArea

JFrame · Control panel · JButtons

In a BorderLayout, when one (or more) border area is not used, then one or more of the other areas will be extended to fill the unused area. For example, if West is not used, then North, South, and Center will extend to the left edge of the Container. If North is not used, then West, East, and Center will extend to the top edge. This is true for all areas except Center. If Center is unused, it is left blank.

Figure 9–24 shows the results we get when we incorporate these changes into the program. The only changes to the program itself occur in the constructor method, which in its revised form is defined as follows:

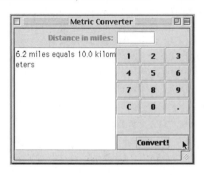

```
public Converter() {
    getContentPane().setLayout(new BorderLayout());
    keypad = new KeyPad(this);

    JPanel inputPanel = new JPanel();              // Input panel
    inputPanel.add(prompt);
    inputPanel.add(input);
    getContentPane().add(inputPanel,"North");

    JPanel controlPanel = new JPanel(new BorderLayout(0, 0));
                                           // Control panel
    controlPanel.add(keypad, "Center");
    controlPanel.add(convert, "South");
    getContentPane().add(controlPanel, "East");

    getContentPane().add(display,"Center");   // Output display
    display.setLineWrap(true);
    display.setEditable(false);

    convert.addActionListener(this);
    input.addActionListener(this);
} // Converter()
```

FIGURE 9–24 The metric converter, showing its appearance when a border design is used.

This layout divides the interface into three main panels, an input panel, display panel, and control panel, and gives each panel its own layout. In addition, the control panel contains the keypad panel within it. Thus, the containment hierarchy for this design is much more complex than for our original design.

SELF-STUDY EXERCISES

EXERCISE 9.8   The border layout for the top window uses the north, center, and east regions. What other combinations of areas might be used for these three components?

EXERCISE 9.9   Why wouldn't a flow layout be appropriate for the control panel?

9.6   Checkboxes, Radio Buttons, and Borders

Suppose you are the software developer for your own software business specializing in computer games. You want to develop an applet-based order form that can be used for ordering software over the Web. At the moment you have three software titles—a chess game, a checkers game, and a crossword puzzle game. The assumption is that the user will choose

Problem statement

one or more of these titles from some kind of menu. The user must also indicate a payment option—either E-cash, credit card, or debit card. These options are mutually exclusive—the user can choose one and only one.

Interface design

Let's design an applet interface for this program. Unlike the previous problem where the input was a numeric value, in this problem the input will be the user's selection from some kind of menu. The result will be the creation of an order. Let's suppose that this part of the task happens behind the scenes—that is, we don't have to worry about creating an actual order. The output the user sees will simply be an acknowledgment that the order was successfully submitted.

What components do we need?

There are several kinds of controls needed for this interface. First, a conventional way to have the users indicate their decisions to make a purchase is to have them click on a Submit button. They should also have the option to cancel the transaction at any time.

In addition to these button controls, a couple of menus must be presented, one for the software titles, and one for the payment options. Swing and AWT libraries provide many options for building menus.

One key requirement for this interface is the mutually exclusive payment options. A conventional way to handle this kind of selection is with a JRadioButton—a button that belongs to a group of mutually exclusive alternatives. Only one button from the group may be selected at one time. The selection of software titles could be handled by a collection of checkboxes. A JCheckbox is a button that can be selected and deselected and that always displays its current state to the user. Using a checkbox will make it obvious to the user exactly what software has been selected.

To complete the design, let's use a JTextArea again to serve as something of a printed order form. It will confirm the user's order and display other messages needed during the transaction.

Given these decisions, we arrive at the design shown in Figure 9–25. In this case, our design uses a JPanel as the main container, instead of using the top window itself. The reason for this decision is that we want to use Swing Borders around the various JPanels to enhance the overall visual appeal of the design. The borders will have titles that help explain the purpose of the various panels.

FIGURE 9–25 A design for an online order form interface.

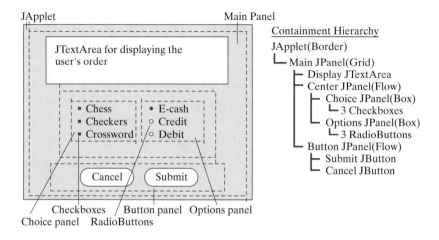

Note that the top-level window in this case is a `JApplet`. By default it will have a border layout. For the main `JPanel` we are using a 3 × 1 `GridLayout`. The components in the main panel are the `JTextArea` and two other `JPanels`. The `GridLayout` will take care of sizing these so they are all of equal size.

What top-level windows do we use?

The center panel, which uses a flow layout, contain panels for the checkboxes and the radio buttons. These elements are grouped within their own panels. Again, we can put a border around them in the final implementation (Fig. 9–26). The button panels use a `BoxLayout`, which we will discuss later. This design leads to the most complex containment hierarchy thus far.

Component layout

Containment hierarchy

9.6.1 Checkbox and Radio Button Arrays

Because we will need three checkboxes, one for each title, and three radio buttons, one for each payment option, it will be useful again to use arrays to store both the buttons and their titles:

What data structures do we need?

```java
private ButtonGroup optGroup = new ButtonGroup();
private JCheckBox titles[] = new JCheckBox[NTITLES];
private JRadioButton options[] = new JRadioButton[NOPTIONS];
private String titleLabels[] =
    {"Chess Master - $59.95", "Checkers Pro - $39.95",
                            "Crossword Maker - $19.95"};
private String optionLabels[] = {"Credit Card", "Debit Card",
                            "E-cash"};
```

Again, the advantage of this design is that it simplifies the instantiation and initialization of the buttons:

```java
for(int k = 0; k < titles.length; k++) {
    titles[k] = new JCheckBox(titleLabels[k]);
    titles[k].addItemListener(this);
    choicePanel.add(titles[k]);
}
```

FIGURE 9–26 Borders around containers help make them stand out more.

The only difference between this array of checkboxes and the keypad array of buttons that we used in the `Converter` program is that checkboxes generate `ItemEvents` instead `ActionEvents`. Therefore, each checkbox must be registered with an `ItemListener` (and, of course, the applet itself must implement the `ItemListener` interface). We'll show how `ItemEvents` are handled later.

The code for instantiating and initializing the radio buttons is almost the same:

```java
for(int k = 0; k < options.length; k++) {
    options[k] = new JRadioButton(optionLabels[k]);
    options[k].addItemListener(this);
    optionPanel.add(options[k]);
    optGroup.add(options[k] );
}
options[0].setSelected(true);    // Set the first button on
```

Radio buttons also generate `ItemEvents`, so they too must be registered with an `ItemListener`. Note that the first button is set on, which represents a default payment option for the user.

FIGURE 9–27   The `ButtonGroup`
object keeps track of each radio
button's state, ensuring that only one
is selected at a time. The
`ItemListener` listens for events on
each button.

The difference between checkboxes and radio buttons is that radio buttons must be added to a `ButtonGroup`—here named `optGroup`—in order to enforce mutual exclusion among them. A `ButtonGroup` is an object whose sole task is to enforce mutual exclusion among its members (Fig. 9–27). Whenever you click on one radio button, the `ButtonGroup` will automatically be notified of this event and will turn off whatever other button was turned on.

Divide and conquer

Note the effective division of labor that's used in Java's design of the various objects that a radio button belongs to. The `optionPanel` is a GUI component (a `JPanel`) that contains the button within the visual interface. Its role is to help manage the graphical aspects of the button's behavior. The `ButtonGroup` is just an `Object`, not a GUI component. Its task is to monitor the button's relationship to the other buttons in the group. Each object has a clearly delineated task.

This division of labor is a key feature of object-oriented design. It is clearly preferable to giving one object too broad a responsibility. For example, a less effective design might have given the task of managing a group of buttons to the `JPanel` that contains them. However, this would lead to all kinds of problems, not least of which is the fact that not everything in the container belongs to the same button group. So a clear division of labor is a much preferable design.

> EFFECTIVE DESIGN: Division of Labor.   In good object-oriented design, objects are specialists (experts) for very narrow, clearly defined tasks. If there's a new task that needs doing, design a new object to do it.

9.6.2   Swing Borders

The Swing `Border` and `BorderFactory` classes can be used to put borders around virtually any GUI element. Using borders is an effective way to make the grouping of components more apparent. Borders can have titles, which enhance the GUI's ability to guide and inform the user. They can also have a wide range of styles and colors, thereby helping to improve the GUI's overall appearance.

A border occupies some space around the edge of a `JComponent`. For the Acme interface, we place titled borders around four of the panels (Fig. 9–26). The border on the main panel serves to identify the company again. The one around the button panel serves to group the two control buttons. The borders around both the checkbox and the radio button menus help to set them apart from other elements of the display and help identify the purpose of the buttons.

Attaching a titled border to a component—in this case to a `JPanel`—is very simple. It takes one statement:

```
choicePanel.setBorder(BorderFactory.createTitledBorder("Titles"));
```

The `setBorder()` method is defined in `JComponent` and inherited by all Swing components. It takes a `Border` argument. In this case, we use the

BorderFactory class to create a border and assign it a title. There are several versions of the static createTitledBorder() method. This version lets us specify the border's title. It uses default values for type of border (etched), the title's position (sitting on the top line), justification (left), and for type and color of the font.

As you would expect, the Border and BorderFactory classes contain methods that let you exert significant control over the border's look and feel. You can even design and create your own custom borders.

9.6.3 The BoxLayout **Manager**

Another simple layout to use is the BoxLayout. This can be associated with any container, and it comes as the default with the Swing Box container. We use it in this example to arrange the checkboxes and radio buttons (Fig. 9–25).

A BoxLayout is like a one-dimensional grid layout. It allows multiple components to be arranged either vertically or horizontally in a row. The layout will not wrap around, as does the FlowLayout. Unlike the GridLayout, the BoxLayout does not force all its components to be the same size. Instead it tries to use each component's preferred width (or height) in arranging them horizontally (or vertically). (Every Swing component has a preferred size that is used by the various layout managers in determining the component's actual size in the interface.) The BoxLayout manager also tries to align its components' heights (for horizontal layouts) or widths (for vertical layouts).

Once again, to set the layout manager for a container you use the setLayout() method:

```
choicePanel.setLayout(new BoxLayout(choicePanel,BoxLayout.Y_AXIS));
```

The BoxLayout() constructor has two parameters. The first is a reference to the container that's being managed, and the second is a constant that determines whether horizontal (*x*-axis) or vertical (*y*-axis) alignment is used.

One very nice feature of the BoxLayout is that it can be used in combinations to imitate the look of the very complicated GridBoxLayout. For example, Figure 9–28 shows an example with two panels (Panel1 and Panel2) arranged horizontally within an outer box (Panel0), each containing four components arranged vertically. The three panels all use the BoxLayout.

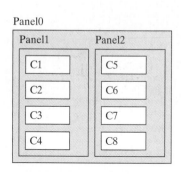

FIGURE 9–28   Complex layouts can be achieved by nesting containers that use the BoxLayout.

9.6.4 The ItemListener **Interface**

ItemEvents are associated with items that make up menus, including JPopupMenus, java.awt.Choice boxes, JCheckboxes, RadioButtons, and other types of menus. Item events are handled by the ItemListener interface, which consists of a single method, the itemStateChanged() method:

```
public void itemStateChanged(ItemEvent e) {
    display.setText("Your order so far (Payment by: ");
    for (int k = 0; k < options.length; k++ )
        if (options[k].isSelected())
            display.append(options[k].getText() + ")\n");
    for (int k = 0; k < titles.length; k++ )
        if (titles[k].isSelected())
            display.append("\t" + titles[k].getText() + "\n");
} // itemStateChanged()
```

This version of the method handles item changes for both the checkbox menu and the radio buttons menu. Two for loops are used. The first iterates through the options menu (radio buttons) to determine what payment option the user has selected. Since only one option can be selected, only one title will be appended to the display. The second loop iterates through the titles menu (checkboxes) and appends each title the user selected to the display. In this way, after every selection, the complete status of the user's order is displayed. The isSelected() method is used to determine if a checkbox or radio button is selected or not.

In this example, we have no real need to identify the item that caused the event. No matter what item the user selected, we want to display the entire state of the order. However, like the ActionEvent class, the ItemEvent class contains methods that can be used to retrieve the item that caused the event:

```
getItem();              // Returns a menu item within a menu
```

The getItem() method is the ItemListener's analogue to the ActionEvent's getSource() method. It enables you to obtain the object that generated the event but returns a representation of the item that was selected or deselected.

9.6.5 The OrderApplet

The design of the OrderApplet is summarized in Figure 9–29 and its complete implementation is given in Figure 9–30. There are several important points to make about this program. First, five JPanels are used to organize the components into logical and visual groupings. This conforms to the design shown in Figure 9–25.

Second, note the use of titled borders around the four internal panels. These help reinforce visually that the components within the border are related by function.

As in other applets, the init() method is used to initialize the interface. This involves setting the layouts for the various containers and filling the containers with their components. Because their initializations are relatively long, the checkboxes and radio buttons are initialized in separate methods, the initChoices() and initOptions() methods, respectively.

Finally, note how the actionPerformed() method creates a mock order form in the display area. This allows the user to review the order before it is submitted. Also note that the algorithm used for submittal requires the user to confirm an order before it is actually submitted. The first time the user clicks on the Submit button, the button's label is changed to "Confirm Order," and the user is prompted in the display area to click the

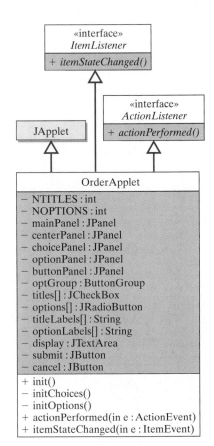

FIGURE 9–29 The OrderApplet makes extensive use of GUI components.

```java
import javax.swing.*;
import javax.swing.border.*;
import java.awt.*;
import java.awt.event.*;

public class OrderApplet extends JApplet implements ItemListener, ActionListener {

    private final int NTITLES = 3, NOPTIONS = 3;

    private JPanel mainPanel = new JPanel(),
                   centerPanel = new JPanel(),
                   choicePanel = new JPanel(),
                   optionPanel = new JPanel(),
                   buttonPanel = new JPanel();

    private ButtonGroup optGroup = new ButtonGroup();
    private JCheckBox titles[] = new JCheckBox[NTITLES];
    private JRadioButton options[] = new JRadioButton[NOPTIONS];
    private String titleLabels[] =
        {"Chess Master - $59.95", "Checkers Pro - $39.95","Crossword Maker - $19.95"};
    private String optionLabels[] = {"Credit Card", "Debit Card", "E-cash"};

    private JTextArea display = new JTextArea(7, 25);
    private JButton submit = new JButton("Submit Order"),
                    cancel = new JButton("Cancel");

    public void init() {
        mainPanel.setBorder(BorderFactory.createTitledBorder("Acme Software Titles"));
        mainPanel.setLayout(new GridLayout(3, 1, 1, 1));
        cancel.addActionListener(this);
        submit.addActionListener(this);
        initChoices();
        initOptions();
        buttonPanel.setBorder( BorderFactory.createTitledBorder("Order Today"));
        buttonPanel.add(cancel);
        buttonPanel.add(submit);
        centerPanel.add(choicePanel);
        centerPanel.add(optionPanel);

        mainPanel.add( display);
        mainPanel.add(centerPanel);
        mainPanel.add( buttonPanel);
        getContentPane().add(mainPanel);
        setSize(400,400);
    } // init()
```

FIGURE 9–30   The OrderApplet class, Part I.

```
    private void initChoices() {
        choicePanel.setBorder(BorderFactory.createTitledBorder("Titles"));
        choicePanel.setLayout(new BoxLayout(choicePanel, BoxLayout.Y_AXIS));

        for (int k = 0; k < titles.length; k++) {
            titles[k] = new JCheckBox(titleLabels[k]);
            titles[k].addItemListener(this);
            choicePanel.add(titles[k]);
        }
    } // initChoices()

    private void initOptions() {
        optionPanel.setBorder(BorderFactory.createTitledBorder("Payment By"));
        optionPanel.setLayout(new BoxLayout(optionPanel, BoxLayout.Y_AXIS));

        for (int k = 0; k < options.length; k++) {
            options[k] = new JRadioButton(optionLabels[k]);
            options[k].addItemListener(this);
            optionPanel.add(options[k]);
            optGroup.add(options[k]);
        }
        options[0].setSelected(true);
    } // initOptions()

    public void itemStateChanged(ItemEvent e) {
        display.setText("Your order so far (Payment by: ");
        for (int k = 0; k < options.length; k++ )
            if (options[k].isSelected())
                display.append(options[k].getText() + ")\n");
        for (int k = 0; k < titles.length; k++ )
            if (titles[k].isSelected())
                display.append("\t" + titles[k].getText() + "\n");
    } // itemStateChanged()

    public void actionPerformed(ActionEvent e){
        String label = submit.getText();
        if (e.getSource() == submit) {
            if (label.equals("Submit Order")) {
                display.append("Thank you. Press 'Confirm' to submit your order!\n");
                submit.setText("Confirm Order");
            } else {
                display.append("Thank you. You will receive your order tomorrow!\n");
                submit.setText("Submit Order");
            }
        } else
            display.setText("Thank you. Maybe we can serve you next time!\n");
    } // actionPerformed()
} // OrderApplet
```

FIGURE 9–30   *(continued)* The OrderApplet class, Part II.

Confirm button to submit the order. This design allows the interface to catch inadvertent button clicks.

A user interface should anticipate potential errors by the user. When an action involves an action that can't be undone—such as placing the order—the program should make sure the user really wants to take that action before carrying it out.

> **EFFECTIVE DESIGN: Anticipate the User.** A well-designed interface should make it difficult for the user to make errors and should make it easy to recover from mistakes when they do happen.

SELF-STUDY EXERCISE

EXERCISE 9.10   What's your favorite interface horror story? The interface needn't be a computer interface.

9.7   Menus and Scroll Panes

Pop-up and pull-down menus allow an application or applet to grow in complexity and functionality without cluttering its interface. Menus are hierarchical in nature. A particular menu is divided into a number of menu items, which can themselves be further subdivided. Menus are very simple to implement in Java.

A JMenuBar is an implementation of a menu bar—a horizontal list of names that appears at the top of a window (Fig. 9–31). Almost all applications have a menu bar. To construct a menu, you add JMenu objects to a JMenuBar. A JMenu is essentially a clickable area on a menu bar that is associated with a JPopupMenu, a small window that pops up and displays the menu's JMenuItems. A menu can also contain JSeparators, which are dividers that can be placed between menu items to organize them into logical groupings.

9.7.1   Adding a Menu Bar to an Application

It is easy to create menus in Swing. The process involves three steps, although they needn't be performed in exactly this order:

1. Create the individual JMenuItems.
2. Create a JMenu and add the JMenuItems to it.
3. Create a JMenuBar and add the JMenus to it.

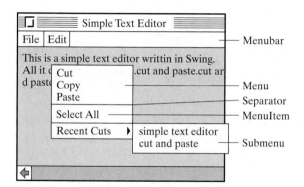

FIGURE 9–31 An application with a menu bar, showing its edit menu, which contains a cascading drop-down menu of recent cuts.

For example, suppose you're building the interface for a text editor. A text editor typically contains at least two standard menus. The file menu is used to create new documents, open and close files, save your document, and so on. The edit menu is used to cut and paste selected text from the document.

Here's how you would create the file menu for this program. First, you create a menu bar and make it the menu bar for the application's JFrame or for the JApplet. This is usually done in the application's constructor or in the applet's init() method:

```
JMenuBar mBar = new JMenuBar();   // Create the menu bar
this.setMenuBar(mBar);            // Set menu bar for this application
```

The next step involves creating and adding menus and menu items to the menu bar. This is also usually done in the constructor or the init() method. If the menu is large, you should break this task up into subtasks and define a method for each subtask.

EFFECTIVE DESIGN: Method Size.   A method that gets longer than 20 to 25 lines is probably trying to do too much and should be divided into separate methods, each with a clearly defined subtask.

Here's the definition of the file menu for our simple text editor:

```
private void initFileMenu() {
    fileMenu = new JMenu("File");   // Create the file menu
    mBar.add(fileMenu);             //   and add it to the menu bar

    openItem = new JMenuItem("Open");   // Open item
    openItem.addActionListener( this );
    openItem.setEnabled(false);
    fileMenu.add(openItem);

    saveItem = new JMenuItem("Save");   // Save item
    saveItem.addActionListener(this);
    saveItem.setEnabled(false);
    fileMenu.add(saveItem);
    fileMenu.addSeparator();            // Logical separator

    quitItem = new JMenuItem("Quit");   // Quit item
    quitItem.addActionListener(this);
    fileMenu.add(quitItem);
} // initFileMenu()
```

The first two statements in the method create the file menu and add it to the menu bar. The rest of the statements create the individual menu items that make up the file menu. Note the use of a *separator* item after the save item. This has the effect of grouping the file-handling items (open and save) into one logical category and distinguishing them from the quit item. A separator is represented as a line in the menu (Fig. 9–31).

EFFECTIVE DESIGN: Logical Design.   In designing interfaces, an effort should be made to use visual cues, such as menu item separators and borders, to group items that are logically related. This will help to orient the user.

Note that each menu item is given an `ActionListener`. As we'll see shortly, action events for menu items are handled the same way as action events for buttons. Finally, note how the `setEnabled()` method is used to disable both the open and save menu items. We don't know how to open and close files yet, so we can't implement these actions now, a deficiency that will be remedied in Chapter 14.

9.7.2   Menu Hierarchies

Menus can be added to other menus to create a hierarchy. For example, the edit menu will include the standard cut, copy, and paste menu items. Some edit menus also contain an "Undo" item, which can be used to undo the last editing operation that was performed. Most editors seem to allow just a single undo. In other words, if you cut a piece of text, you can undo that operation and get that cut back. But if you cut two pieces of text, the first piece is lost forever. That can be a pain, especially if you didn't mean to do the first cut.

So let's add a feature to our editor that will keep track of cuts by storing them in a `Vector`. This function will be like an "Unlimited Undo" operation for cuts. For this example, we won't place any limit on the size of the vector. Every cut the user makes will be inserted at the beginning of the vector. To go along with this feature we need a menu that can grow dynamically during the program. Each time the user makes a cut, the string that was cut will be added to the menu.

This kind of menu should occur within the edit menu, but it will have its own items. So this is a menu within a menu (Fig. 9–31). This is an example of a *cascading* drop-down menu. The edit menu itself drops down from the menu bar, and the recent cuts menu drops down and to the right of where its arrow points. The following method was used to create the edit menu:

```
private void initEditMenu() {
    editMenu = new JMenu("Edit");        // Create the edit menu
    mBar.add(editMenu);                  //   and add it to menu bar

    cutItem = new JMenuItem ("Cut");           // Cut item
    cutItem.addActionListener(this);
    editMenu.add(cutItem);
    copyItem = new JMenuItem("Copy");          // Copy item
    copyItem.addActionListener(this);
    editMenu.add(copyItem);
    pasteItem = new JMenuItem("Paste");        // Paste item
    pasteItem.addActionListener(this);
    editMenu.add(pasteItem);
    editMenu.addSeparator();
    selectItem = new JMenuItem("Select All"); // Select item
    selectItem.addActionListener(this);
    editMenu.add(selectItem);
    editMenu.addSeparator();
    cutsMenu = new JMenu("Recent Cuts");       // Recent cuts submenu
    editMenu.add(cutsMenu);
} // initEditMenu()
```

The main difference between this method and the one used to create the file menu is that here we insert an entire submenu as one of the items in the edit menu. The cutsMenu will be used to hold the strings that are cut from the document. Initially it will be empty.

9.7.3 Handling Menu Actions

Handling JMenuItem actions is no different from handling JButton actions. Whenever the user makes a menu selection, an ActionEvent is generated. Programs that use menus must implement the actionPerformed() method of the ActionListener interface. In the text editor example, there are a total of six enabled menu items, including the recent cuts menu. This translates into a large if-else structure, with each clause handling a single menu item. The following actionPerformed() method is used to handle the menu selections for the text editor:

```java
public void actionPerformed(ActionEvent e) {
    JMenuItem m  = (JMenuItem)e.getSource();      // Get the selected menu item
    if ( m == quitItem ) {                        // Quit
        dispose();
    } else if (m == cutItem) {                    // Cut the selected text
        scratchPad = display.getSelectedText(); // Copy the text to the scratchpad
        display.replaceRange("",                  //   and delete
            display.getSelectionStart(),          //   from the start of the selection
            display.getSelectionEnd());           //   to the end
        addRecentCut(scratchPad);                 // Add the cut text to the cuts menu
    } else if (m == copyItem)                     // Copy the selected text to the scratchpad
        scratchPad = display.getSelectedText();
    } else if (m == pasteItem) {                  // Paste the scratchpad to the document
        display.insert(scratchPad, display.getCaretPosition());    // at the caret position
    } else if ( m == selectItem ) {
        display.selectAll();                      // Select the entire document
    } else {
        JMenuItem item = (JMenuItem)e.getSource();  // Default case is the cutsMenu
        scratchPad = item.getActionCommand();       // Put the cut back in the scratchpad
    }
} // actionPerformed()
```

The method begins by getting the source of the ActionEvent and casting it into a JMenuItem. It then checks each case of the if-else structure. Because the actions taken by this program are fairly short, they are mostly coded within the actionPerformed() method itself. However, for most programs it will be necessary to write a separate method corresponding to each menu item and then call the methods from actionPerformed().

Our text editor's main task is to implement the cut/copy/paste functions. These are very simple to do in Java. The text that's being edited is stored in a JTextArea, which contains instance methods that make it very easy to select, insert, and replace text. To copy a piece of text, the program need only get the text from the JTextArea (getSelectedText()) and assign it to the scratchpad, which is represented as a String. To paste a piece of text, the program inserts the contents of the scratchpad into the JTextArea at the location marked by the *caret*, a cursor-like character in the document that marks the next insertion point.

The structure of this if-else statement is significant. Note how the default case of the if-else is designed. We are using the last else clause as a "catch all" condition to catch and handle selections from the cutsMenu.

All of the other menu items can be referred to by name. However, the menu items in the cutsMenu are just snippets of a string that the user has previously cut from the text, so they can't be referenced by name. Luckily, we don't really need to. For any JMenuItem, the getActionCommand() method returns its text, which in this case is the previously cut text. So we just assign the cut text from the menu to the scratchpad.

Default logic

> **PROGRAMMING TIP: Default Cases.** Although the order of the clauses in an if-else structure is usually not important, the default clause can sometimes be used to handle cases that can't be referenced by name.

Handling Previously Cut Text

The most difficult function in our program is the cut operation. Not only must the selected text be removed from the document and stored in the scratchpad, but it must also be inserted into the vector that is storing all the previous cuts. The addRecentCut() method takes care of this last task. The basic idea here is to take the cut string and insert it at the beginning of the vector, so that cuts will be maintained in a last-in–first-out order. Then the cutsMenu must be completely rebuilt by reading its entries out of the vector, from first to last. That way the most recent cut will appear first in the menu:

Algorithm design

```
private void addRecentCut(String cut) {
    recentCuts.insertElementAt(cut,0);
    cutsMenu.removeAll();
    for (int k = 0; k < recentCuts.size(); k++) {
      JMenuItem item = new JMenuItem((String)recentCuts.elementAt(k));
        cutsMenu.add( item );
        item.addActionListener(this);
    }
} // addRecentCut()
```

The recentCuts Vector stores the cut strings. Note the use of the insert-ElementAt() method to insert strings into the vector and the elementAt() method to get strings from the vector. (You may find it helpful to review the section on vectors in Chapter 8.)

Note also how menu items are removed and inserted in menus. The cutsMenu is reinitialized, using the removeAll() method. Then the for loop iterates through the strings stored in the vector, making new menu items from them, which are then inserted into the cutsMenu. In this way, the cuts-Menu is changed dynamically each time the user cuts a piece of text from the document.

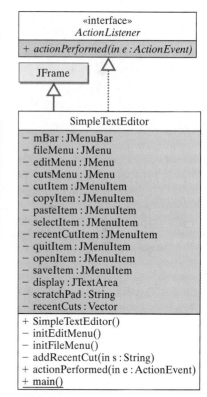

FIGURE 9–32   Design of the SimpleTextEditor.

9.7.4   Adding Scrollbars to a Text Area

The design of the SimpleTextEditor class is summarized in Figure 9–32 and its complete implementation is shown in Figure 9–33. It uses a BorderLayout, with the JTextArea placed at the center. Note how simple it is to add scrollbars to the text area:

Scrollbars

```
this.getContentPane().add(new JScrollPane(display));
```

```java
import javax.swing.*;
import java.awt.*;
import java.awt.event.*;
import java.util.Vector;

public class SimpleTextEditor extends JFrame implements ActionListener{
    private JMenuBar mBar = new JMenuBar();              // Create the menu bar
    private JMenu fileMenu, editMenu, cutsMenu;          // Menu references
    private JMenuItem cutItem, copyItem, pasteItem, selectItem,recentcutItem; // Edit items
    private JMenuItem quitItem, openItem, saveItem;      // File items
    private JTextArea display = new JTextArea();         // Here's where the editing occurs
    private String scratchPad = "";                      // Scratch pad for cut/paste
    private Vector recentCuts = new Vector();

    public SimpleTextEditor() {
        super("Simple Text Editor");      // Set the window title
        this.getContentPane().setLayout(new BorderLayout());
        this.getContentPane().add("Center", display);
        this.getContentPane().add(new JScrollPane(display));
        display.setLineWrap(true);
        this.setJMenuBar(mBar);           // Set this program's menu bar
        initFileMenu();                   // Create the menus
        initEditMenu();
    } // SimpleTextEditer()

    private void initEditMenu() {
        editMenu = new JMenu("Edit");     // Create the edit menu
        mBar.add(editMenu);               //  and add it to menu bar
        cutItem = new JMenuItem ("Cut");          // Cut item
        cutItem.addActionListener(this);
        editMenu.add(cutItem);
        copyItem = new JMenuItem("Copy");         // Copy item
        copyItem.addActionListener(this);
        editMenu.add(copyItem);
        pasteItem = new JMenuItem("Paste");       // Paste item
        pasteItem.addActionListener(this);
        editMenu.add(pasteItem);
        editMenu.addSeparator();
        selectItem = new JMenuItem("Select All"); // Select item
        selectItem.addActionListener(this);
        editMenu.add(selectItem);
        editMenu.addSeparator();
        cutsMenu = new JMenu("Recent Cuts");      // Recent cuts submenu
        editMenu.add(cutsMenu);
    } // initEditMenu()

    private void initFileMenu() {
        fileMenu = new JMenu("File");     // Create the file menu
        mBar.add(fileMenu);               //  and add it to the menu bar
        openItem = new JMenuItem("Open"); // Open item
        openItem.addActionListener( this );
        openItem.setEnabled(false);
        fileMenu.add(openItem);
        saveItem = new JMenuItem("Save"); // Save item
```

FIGURE 9–33   A menu-based `SimpleTextEditor` application, Part I.

```
        saveItem.addActionListener(this);
        saveItem.setEnabled(false);
        fileMenu.add(saveItem);
        fileMenu.addSeparator();        // Logical separator
        quitItem = new JMenuItem("Quit"); // Quit item
        quitItem.addActionListener(this);
        fileMenu.add(quitItem);
    } // initFileMenu()
    public void actionPerformed(ActionEvent e) {
        JMenuItem m = (JMenuItem)e.getSource();   // Get the selected menu item
        if ( m == quitItem ) {                    // Quit
            dispose();
        } else if (m == cutItem) {                // Cut the selected text
            scratchPad = display.getSelectedText(); // Copy the text to the scratchpad
            display.replaceRange("",              //  and delete
                display.getSelectionStart(),      //  from the start of the selection
                display.getSelectionEnd());       //  to the end
            addRecentCut(scratchPad);             // Add the cut text to the cuts menu
        } else if (m == copyItem) {               // Copy the selected text to the scratchpad
            scratchPad = display.getSelectedText();
        } else if (m == pasteItem) {              // Paste the scratchpad to the document
            display.insert(scratchPad, display.getCaretPosition());   // at the caret position
        } else if ( m == selectItem ) {
            display.selectAll();                  // Select the entire document
        } else {
            JMenuItem item = (JMenuItem)e.getSource();  // Default case is the cutsMenu
            scratchPad = item.getActionCommand();       // Put the cut back in the scratchpad
        }
    } // actionPerformed()

    private void addRecentCut(String cut) {
        recentCuts.insertElementAt(cut,0);
        cutsMenu.removeAll();
        for (int k = 0; k < recentCuts.size(); k++) {
            JMenuItem item = new JMenuItem((String)recentCuts.elementAt(k));
            cutsMenu.add( item );
            item.addActionListener(this);
        }
    } // addRecentCut()

    public static void main(String args[]) {
        SimpleTextEditor f = new SimpleTextEditor();
        f.setSize(300, 200);
        f.setVisible(true);
        f.addWindowListener(new WindowAdapter() {   // Quit the application
            public void windowClosing(WindowEvent e) {
                System.exit(0);
            }
        });
    } // main()
} // SimpleTextEditor
```

FIGURE 9–33 *(continued)* The SimpleTextEditor, Part II.

This statement creates a JScrollPane and adds it to the application's container. A JScrollPane is one of Swing's scrollbar classes. Its function is to manage the viewing and scrolling of a scrollable component, such as a JTextArea. A JScrollPane is actually a container. That's why it takes the display as an argument. The display is being added to the JScrollPane.

Just about any Component can be added to a JScrollPane. Once a component is added, the scroll pane will completely manage the scrolling functions for the component. The default constructor used in this example takes a single Component parameter. This refers to the scrollable component, in this case to the JTextArea. Another constructor that you might use takes the following form:

```
public JScrollPane(Component comp, int vsbPolicy, int hsbPolicy);
```

The two integers refer to the vertical and horizontal scrolling policies. These cover properties such as whether the scrollbars are always present or just as needed. The default policy is to attach scrollbars to the component only when needed. Thus, to see the scrollbars in the SimpleText Editor, you would have to shrink the window to the point where all of the text cannot be viewed (Fig. 9–34). Because the text area in this example is wrapping the text, the horizontal scrollbar will never be needed.

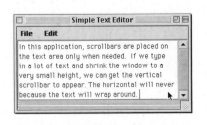

FIGURE 9–34 The scrollbars appear on the text area only when they are needed. In this case, only a vertical scrollbar is necessary.

SELF-STUDY EXERCISES

EXERCISE 9.11 Modify the addRecentCut() method so it limits the cuts stored in the vector to the last ten cuts.

EXERCISE 9.12 Modify the addRecentCut() method so that it doesn't duplicate cuts already stored in the vector. (*Hint*: Use the indexOf(String) method in the Vector class.)

IN THE LABORATORY: The ATM Machine

The purpose of this lab is to use Java GUI components and layouts to design and implement an interface for a bank automatic teller machine (ATM). The interface should be designed so that it may be implemented either as an applet or an application. The objectives are

- To develop from scratch a class that simulates an ATM interface.
- To develop a flexible interface design that will work with either an applet or an application.
- To gain additional practice using arrays.
- To gain additional practice using AWT and Swing components and layouts.

Problem Description

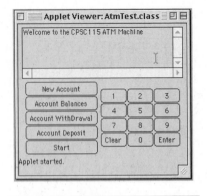

FIGURE 9–35 The user interface for an ATM machine.

Design and implement a Java class that simulates an ATM interface. Your solution should look something like the user interface shown in Figure 9–35. It is not necessary to build complete ATM machine functionality beyond that which is described next—just implement the interface. If you wish, you may design your own layout for the interface, as long as it has the components required in the specification.

CONTEMPORARY COMPUTER interfaces are largely visual and graphical, and many things we use a computer for, such as word processing, still require us to type. Will there come a day when instead of typing a letter or e-mail message, we'll be able to dictate it to our computer? Will computers eventually have the same kind of interface we have—that is, will we someday be able to carry on conversations with our computers? Clearly, a "conversational interface" would require substantial intelligence on the part of the computer. Do computers have any chance of acquiring such intelligence?

The question of machine intelligence or *artificial intelligence (AI)* has been the subject of controversy since the very first computers were developed. In 1950, in an article in the journal *Mind*, Alan Turing proposed the following test to settle the question of whether computers could be intelligent. Suppose you put a person and a computer in another room, and you let a human interrogate both with any kind of question whatsoever. The interrogator could ask them to parse a Shakespearian sonnet, or solve an arithmetic problem, or tell a joke. The computer's task would be to try to fool the interrogator into thinking that it was the human. And the (hidden) human's task would be to try to help the interrogator see that he or she was the human.

Turing argued that someday computers would be able to play this game so well that interrogators would have no better than a 50/50 chance of telling which was which. When that day came, he argued, we would have to conclude that computers were intelligent.

This so-called *Turing test* has been the subject of controversy ever since. Many of the founders of AI and many of its current practitioners believe that computation and human thinking are basically the same kind of process and that eventually computers will develop enough capability that we'll have to call them intelligent. Skeptics argue that even if computers could mimic our intelligence, there's no way they will be self-conscious and, therefore, they can never be truly intelligent. According to the skeptics, merely executing programs, no matter how clever the programs are, will never add up to intelligence.

Computers have made some dramatic strides lately. In 1997, an IBM computer named Deep Blue beat world chess champion Gary Kasparov in a seven-game chess match. In 1998, a computer at Los Alamos National Laboratory proved a mathematical theorem that some of the best mathematicians were unable to prove for the past 40 years.

However, despite these achievements, most observers would agree that computers are not yet capable of passing the Turing test. One area where computers fall short is in natural language understanding. Although computers are good at understanding Java and other computer languages, human languages are still too complex and require too much common sense knowledge for computers to understand them perfectly. Another area where computers still fall somewhat short is in speech recognition. However, just recently an American company demonstrated a telephone that could translate between English and German (as well as some other languages) in real time. The device's only limitation was that its discourse was limited to the travel domain. As computer processing speeds improve, this limitation is expected to be only temporary. Thus, we may be closer than we think to having our "conversational user interface."

Natural language understanding, speech recognition, learning, perception, chess playing, and problem solving are the kinds of problems addressed in AI, one of the major applied areas of computer science. Almost every major research group in AI has a Web site that describes its work. To find some of these, just do a search for "artificial intelligence" and then browse through the links that are found.

Are Computers Intelligent?

GUI Specifications

The Graphical User Interface (GUI) should contain a 4×3 array of buttons that functions as a numeric keypad—you can use the KeyPad class developed earlier—and a second array of buttons to serve as a function pad, representing the various functions one finds on an ATM machine. The GUI should contain a JTextArea that displays the result of clicking one of the buttons. You should feel free to design your own layout for these components.

Designing the ATM Layout

Figure 9–36 provides a sample layout. It consists of a JTextArea that serves as the ATM's display screen. It displays all I/O during an ATM session. The other interface components are the 12 keypad and 5 function JButtons. In this design, the keypad buttons are organized into a KeyPad, which is a JPanel subclass, and the function buttons are organized into a Function-Pad, which is also a JPanel subclass.

Several additional JPanels are used to achieve the overall border layout. There is a main panel (AtmGUI) that contains all of the interface components. It uses a BorderLayout with the machine's display in the center and the keypad and function pad, grouped together into a control panel, at the south edge. The function pad and keypad are arranged as GridLayouts.

Problem Decomposition

One goal of this lab is to develop an ATM interface that can be used as either an applet or a stand-alone application. This suggests that the interface itself should be defined as a separate class that gets instantiated either in an application or an applet. Let's call this the AtmGUI class. As Figure 9–37 shows, the AtmGUI, which is a subclass of JPanel, is contained in the top-level window (either an applet or a frame) and serves as an interface between the AtmMachine itself and the user. The AtmMachine encapsulates the functionality of the actual ATM machine. Its public methods will be used to manage the deposits, withdrawals, and other ATM functions.

FIGURE 9–36 The containment hierarchy for the components used in the ATM machine GUI.

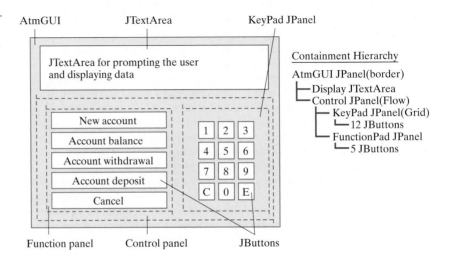

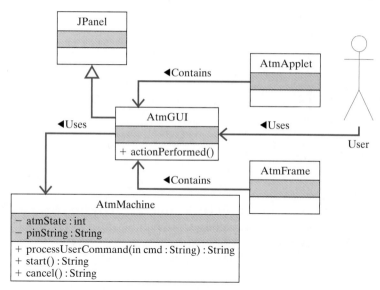

FIGURE 9–37 The main objects involved in the ATM simulator. The same AtmGUI can be used with either an applet or an application.

As a subclass of JPanel, the AtmGUI cannot stand on its own and must, therefore, be added to a top-level window, either a JFrame or a JApplet. This suggests that AtmGUI will need two constructors, one to be used with an application and one with an applet. Each constructor takes a reference to the top-level window (JFrame or JApplet) as a parameter:

```
public AtmGUI(JFrame f) {     // Application constructor from a frame
    createInterface();
    f.getContentPane().add(this); // Add this to the top-level window
    f.pack();
    f.show();
}

public AtmGUI(JApplet app)  { // Applet constructor from an applet
    createInterface();
    app.getContentPane().add(this); // Add this to the top-level window
}
```

Note that each constructor leaves the details of creating the interface to the createInterface() method, which has the following signature:

```
private void createInterface();
```

Then each contructor adds itself to the top-level window's content pane:

```
getContentPane().add(this);
```

By thus encapsulating the GUI elements in a JPanel, which can be added to any kind of top-level window, we achieve a flexible design for our user interface.

Because we have encapsulated the GUI details within the AtmGUI class, the implementation of the top-level windows is quite trivial. The entire applet definition is:

```
import javax.swing.*;
import java.awt.*;
import java.applet.Applet;

public class AtmTest extends JApplet {
    AtmGUI atm;                          // Declare AtmMachine

    public void init() {
        setSize(500,300);
        atm = new AtmGUI(this);          // Create a new atm
    } // init()
} // AtmTest
```

Invoking AtmGUI's constructor in init() will effectively pass control to the new AtmGUI. Note that the applet does not handle any actions directly. All actions are handled by its AtmGUI object.

To create an application that uses AtmGUI is equally simple:

```
import javax.swing.*;
import java.awt.*;

public class AtmApplication extends JFrame {
    public static void main(String args[]) {
        AtmApplication f = new AtmApplication();
        f.setSize(500,300);
        AtmGUI atm = new AtmGUI(f);
    }
}
```

In this case, we first create an AtmApplication (a subclass of JFrame) in main(). We then create an AtmGUI and pass it a reference to the top-level window. This effectively passes control to the AtmGUI, which will handle all of the application's action events.

Problem Design: The AtmGUI Class

Further design details of the AtmGUI class are shown in Figure 9–38. Note that one of its instance variables is a reference to an AtmMachine, which will handle the various ATM functions. The rest of its instance variables are references to GUI elements: a KeyPad, whose design and implementation were discussed in Section 9.4.4; a FunctionPad, whose design can be modeled after the KeyPad; and a JTextArea, which will serve as the main display area. As described in Section 9.4.4, in order for the AtmGUI to use the KeyPad and FunctionPad, it must implement the KeyPadClient interface. In developing your implementation for the function pad, you can use Figure 9–17 as a guide.

Problem Design: The AtmMachine Class

Although our ATM machine will not be fully functional, the only way we can test our AtmGUI is to give the ATM machine some degree of functionality. Therefore, let's design the AtmMachine itself, where the ATM's functionality will reside.

A partial design of the AtmMachine class is shown in Figure 9–37. It contains methods to start() and cancel() an ATM session. It also contains

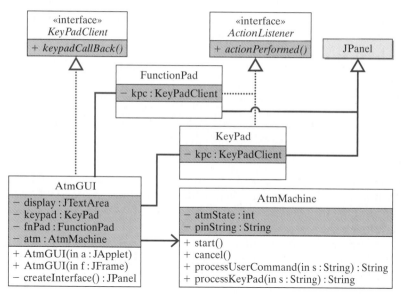

FIGURE 9–38 The AtmGUI serves as a GUI for an AtmMachine. It implements the KeyPadClient interface for its control buttons.

methods processUserCommand() and processKeyPad, which handle all the user input from the GUI. The basic idea is that the AtmGUI will transmit the user's commands—presses on the function pad or keypad—to the Atm-Machine, which will process the command and return a message to the AtmGUI. Note that processUserCommand() takes a String argument (the ATM function) and returns a String result. For example, suppose the user has clicked the GUI's Deposit button. Then the AtmGUI might call the AtmMachine with processUserCommand("Deposit"). For this simulation, the result string returned can just report that the transaction was successful—"Your deposit was accepted."

The UML sequence diagram in Figure 9–39 shows the sequence of actions that takes place whenever the user clicks on one the AtmGUI's function buttons.

Here's how the machine should work. After pressing the Start button, the ATM will prompt you to enter your personal ID number (PIN). If you enter it correctly, you are then allowed to enter one or more transactions. If not, you are given an error message and allowed to reenter it. Once your PIN has been validated, you are allowed to perform one or more transactions—withdrawal, deposit, and so forth. When you are finished, you press the Cancel key to end the session.

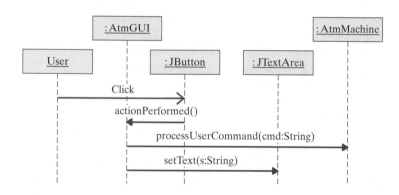

FIGURE 9–39 The AtmGUI passes the user's commands to the AtmMachine, which processes them and returns a result. For our simulation, the AtmGUI just displays the result in the TextArea.

Our partial implementation should be able to distinguish the various phases of the user's interaction with the AtmMachine. One way to implement this is by using an *atmState* variable whose values represent the phases of an ATM transaction. One design might be the following:

```
private static final int INIT_STATE = 0; // State constants
private static final int PIN_STATE = 1;
private static final int GO_STATE = 2;

private int atmState = INIT_STATE;         // State of the atm machine
```

In this design the machine can be in one of three states: an INIT.STATE, which lasts until the user clicks on the Start button; a PIN.STATE, which lasts until the user enters a correct PIN; or a GO.STATE, which lasts until the user cancels the session.

For our partial implementation, the various transactions can be implemented by simply printing a message on the ATM's display. For example, when the AtmMachine receives a "Start" message from the interface, it should base its action on its current state. If the ATM machine is in the INIT.STATE, then it should change into the PIN.STATE and prompt the user for a PIN. If the machine is in any other state, it should do nothing:

```
private String start() {
    if (state == INIT_STATE) {
        state = PIN_STATE;
        return "Please enter your PIN and click on ENTER.\n";
    }
    return "";      // Return empty string to ignore the button
} // start()
```

A similar design can be applied to handle the other functions.

At a minimum your machine should be able to handle two states: INIT.STATE and GO.STATE. It should be able to start and cancel a session. Any button presses that occur during a session, including keypad numbers, can just be "echoed" back to the interface and displayed in the text area. If you are more ambitious, try implementing the PIN.STATE, as described in the next section.

Optional Exercise

The most difficult state transition occurs between the PIN.STATE and the GO.STATE, because it is here that the user's PIN must be checked for validity. What complicates this task is that the keypad must be used to enter the PIN. In the design outlined in Figure 9–37 the ATM machine uses the processKeyPad() method to process keypad actions.

To process the user's PIN, the AtmMachine should maintain an instance variable (pinString), which is initially set to the empty string. As the user enters a PIN, the individual digits can be appended to the String. When the user types the Enter key, signaling that he or she is done entering the PIN, a separate method would then validate the pinString. For testing purposes, it will suffice to develop a simple validity test—for example, a PIN is valid if it contains a value between 1111 and 9999.

Of course, in order to know how to process the keypad, the processKeyPad() method must check the machine's state. There are three possible

TABLE 9.5 The action that the ATM machine takes when a function key is pressed depends on its current state.

State	Key Press	Action
INIT.STATE	Any key	Ignore it
PIN.STATE	Enter	Validate the user's PIN
	A digit key	Mask key and append to PIN
GO.STATE	Enter	Display the key's label
	Digit key	Display the key's label

states, whose actions are identified in Table 9.5. When the machine is in its initial state, all key presses on the keypad are ignored. If the user is in the process of entering a PIN (PIN.STATE), then if the Enter key is pressed, this signals that the user has finished entering the PIN, which should then be validated. If it is valid, the machine should switch into the GO.STATE. Otherwise an error message should be displayed. If a digit key is pressed while the user is entering a PIN, then that digit should be appended to the PIN and displayed as a (*)—that is, masked—in the display.

Finally, when the machine is in GO.STATE, all key presses on the keypad should simply be echoed in the display. Of course, in a full-fledged implementation these key presses would have to be handled in an appropriate, context-sensitive manner. This would require that we expand the number of states to include things like WITHDRAWAL.STATE, and so on.

CHAPTER SUMMARY

Technical Terms

callback design
content pane
containment
  hierarchy
controller
event model
layout manager

lightweight
  component
listener
model
model-view-
  controller
  (MVC)

peer model
pluggable look and
  feel
view
widget hierarchy

Summary of Important Points

- Java now provides two sets of Graphical User Interface (GUI) components, the Abstract Windowing Toolkit (AWT), which was part of Java 1.0 and modified in Java 1.1, and the Swing component set, the GUI part of the Java Foundation Classes (JFC), introduced in JDK 1.1 and now available in JDK 1.2 and later versions (which is also known as Java 2).
- Unlike their AWT counterparts, Swing components are written entirely in Java. This allows programs written in Swing to have a platform-independent look and feel. There are three built-in look-and-feel packages in Swing: a Windows style, a Unix-like Motif style, and a purely Java Metal style.
- Swing components are based on the *model-view-controller (MVC)* architecture, in which the component is divided into three separate objects:

how it looks (*view*), what state it's in (*model*), and what it does (*controller*). The view and controller parts are sometimes combined into a single *user interface* class, which can be changed to create a customized look and feel.

- AWT components are based on the *peer model*, in which every AWT component has a peer in the native windowing system. This model is less efficient and more platform dependent than the MVC model.

- Java's *event model* is based on *event listeners*. When a GUI component is created, it is registered with an appropriate event listener, which takes responsibility for handling the component's events.

- A user interface combines four functions: guidance of the user, input, output, and control.

- The components in a GUI are organized into a *containment hierarchy* rooted at the top-level window. JPanels and other Containers may be used to organize the components into a hierarchy according to function or some other criterion.

- The top-level Swing classes—JApplet, JDialog, JFrame, and JWindow— use a *content pane* as their component container.

- A GUI should minimize the number of input devices the user needs to manipulate, as well as the complexity the user needs to deal with. Certain forms of redundancy—such as two independent but complete sets of controls—are desirable because they make the interface more flexible and more widely applicable.

- A *layout manager* is an object that manages the size and arrangement of the components in a container. The AWT and Swing provide a number of built-in layouts, including flow, border, grid, and box layouts.

- A *radio button* is a toggle button that belongs to a group such that only one button from the group may be selected at the same time. A *checkbox* is a toggle button that always displays its state.

- A well-designed interface should reduce the chance of user error and should make it as easy as possible to recover from errors when they do occur.

SOLUTIONS TO SELF-STUDY EXERCISES

SOLUTION 9.1   The top-level containers—the JApplet, JDialog, JFrame, and JWindow—would have to be implemented completely in Java, thereby breaking their dependence on peer windows in the native windowing environment.

SOLUTION 9.2   Abstract classes cannot be instantiated. They can only be subclassed. Therefore, by definition they cannot have a peer instance. That's what makes them suitable as the foundation for lightweight components.

SOLUTION 9.3   How can a button still be considered a component under the MVC model? This is a good question. The JButton class acts as a wrapper class and hides the model-view-controller details (Fig. 9–40). When you instantiate a JButton, you still get a single instance. Think of it this way. Your body consists of several systems that interact (internally) among themselves, but it's still one body that other bodies interact with as a single object.

SOLUTION 9.4   A component can indeed be registered with more than one listener. For example, the ToggleButton that we defined in Chapter 4 has two listeners. The first is the button itself, which takes care of toggling the button's label. The second is the applet in which the button is used, which takes care of handling whatever action the button is associated with.

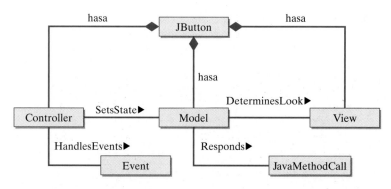

FIGURE 9–40 A `JButton` has internal model-view-controller components that interact with each other to produce the button's overall behavior.

SOLUTION 9.5 Some components can have two different kinds of listeners. For example, imagine a "sticky button" that works like this. When you click and release the button, it causes some action to take place, just like a normal button. When you click and hold the mouse button down, the button "sticks" to the cursor and you can then move it to a new location. This button would need listeners for `ActionEvents`, `MouseEvents`, and `MouseMotionEvents`.

SOLUTION 9.6 To round a double you could use the `Math.round()` method. For example, suppose the number you want to round is d. Then the expression `Math.round(100 * d)/100.0` will round it to two decimal places. Alternatively you could use the `java.text.NumberFormat` class. Both of these approaches were covered in Chapter 5.

SOLUTION 9.7 Many cars today have cruise control as a alternative way to control the accelerator. Push buttons, usually located on the steering wheel, are used to speed up and slow down, so you can drive with your foot or your hand.

SOLUTION 9.8 As an alternative border layout for the top-level window in the `Converter` north-west-center might work. So might center-south-east and center-south-west. What makes these possible is the fact that the layout manager will use up space in any edge area that is not assigned a component.

SOLUTION 9.9 A flow layout would not be appropriate for the control panel because you would have little control of where the `convert` button would be placed relative to the keypad.

SOLUTION 9.10 Interface design disaster: My car uses the same kind of on/off switch for the headlights and the windshield wipers. One is a stem on the left side of the steering wheel, and the other is on a stem on the right side of the steering wheel. On more than one occasion, I've managed to turn off the headlights when I intended to turn on the wipers.

SOLUTION 9.11 Modify the `addRecentCut()` method so it limits the cuts stored in the vector to the last ten cuts. Solution: Check the size of the vector after inserting the cut. If it exceeds ten, remove the last element in the vector.

```java
private void addRecentCut(String cut) {
    recentCuts.insertElementAt(cut, 0);
    if (recentCuts.size() > 10) {           // If more than 10 cuts
        recentCuts.removeElementAt(10);     // remove the oldest one
    }
    cutsMenu.removeAll();
    for (int k = 0; k < recentCuts.size(); k++) {
      JMenuItem item = new JMenuItem((String) recentCuts.elementAt(k));
        cutsMenu.add(item);
        item.addActionListener(this);
    }
} // addRecentCut()
```

SOLUTION 9.12 Modify the `addRecentCut()` method so that it doesn't duplicate cuts stored in the vector. Solution: Use the `indexOf()` method to search for the cut in the vector. If it's already there, don't insert the cut.

```
private void addRecentCut(String cut) {
    if (recentCuts.indexOf(cut) == -1) {      // If not already cut
        recentCuts.insertElementAt(cut,0);
        if (recentCuts.size() > 10) {         // If more than 10 cuts
            recentCuts.removeElementAt(10);   // remove the oldest one
        }
        cutsMenu.removeAll();
        for (int k = 0; k < recentCuts.size(); k++) {
          JMenuItem item = new JMenuItem((String) recentCuts.elementAt(k));
            cutsMenu.add(item);
            item.addActionListener(this);
        }
    } // if not already cut
} // addRecentCut()
```

EXERCISES

Note: *For programming exercises, first draw a UML class diagram describing all classes and their inheritance relationships and/or associations.*

EXERCISE 9.1 Explain the difference between the following pairs of terms:

a. A *model* and a *view*.
b. A *view* and a *controller*.
c. A *lightweight* and *heavyweight* component.
d. A `JButton` and a `Button`.
e. A *layout manager* and a *container*.
f. A *containment hierarchy* and an *inheritance hierarchy*.
g. A *content pane* and a `JFrame`.

EXERCISE 9.2 Fill in the blanks.

a. A GUI component that is written entirely in Java is known as a _____ component.
b. The AWT is not platform independent because it uses the _____ model to implement its GUI components.
c. The visual elements of a GUI are arranged in a _____ .
d. A _____ is an object that takes responsibility for arranging the components in a container.
e. The default layout manager for a `JPanel` is _____ .
f. The default layout manager for a `JApplet` is _____ .

EXERCISE 9.3 Describe in general terms what you would have to do to change the standard look and feel of a Swing `JButton`.

EXERCISE 9.4 Explain the differences between the model-view-controller design of a `JButton` and the design of an AWT `Button`. Why is MVC superior?

EXERCISE 9.5 Suppose you have an applet that contains a `JButton` and a `JLabel`. Each time the button is clicked the applet rearranges the letters in the label. Using Java's event model as a basis, explain the sequence of events that happens in order for this action to take place.

EXERCISE 9.6 Draw a containment hierarchy for the most recent version of the `CyberPetApplet` program.

EXERCISE 9.7   Create a GUI design, similar to the one shown in Figure 9–25, for a program that would be used to buy tickets online for a rock concert.

EXERCISE 9.8   Create a GUI design, similar to the one shown in Figure 9–25, for an online program that would be used to play musical recordings.

EXERCISE 9.9   Design and implement a GUI for the `CDInterest` program (Fig. 5–18). This program should let the user input the interest rate, principal, and period and should accumulate the value of the investment.

EXERCISE 9.10   Design and implement a GUI for the `Temperature` class (Fig. 5–5). One challenge of this design is to find a good way for the user to indicate whether a Fahrenheit or Celsius value is being input. This should also determine the order of the conversion: F to C or C to F.

EXERCISE 9.11   Convert the `CyberPetApplet` to a Swing-based version. The top-level window should be a `JApplet`.

EXERCISE 9.12   The `TextField` class has a `setEchoChar()` method. When the echo character is set, that's the character that will be displayed in the text field as the user types. If it is unset, the text field will just echo the character that the user types. Setting the echo character to "*" is one way to hide sensitive input—for example, while entering a password. Design and implement a `PasswordField` class that *always* hides the user's input. This should be a subclass of `JTextField`.

EXERCISE 9.13   Design an interface for a 16-button integer calculator that supports addition, subtraction, multiplication, and division. Implement the interface so that the label of the button is displayed in the calculator's display—that is, it doesn't actually do the math.

EXERCISE 9.14   **Challenge:** Design and implement a `Calculator` class to go along with the interface you developed in the previous exercise. It should function the same way as a hand calculator except it only handles integers.

EXERCISE 9.15   Modify the `Converter` application so that it can convert in either direction: from miles to kilometers or from kilometers to miles. Use radio buttons in your design to let the user select one or the other alternative.

EXERCISE 9.16   Here's a design problem for you. A biologist needs an interactive program that calculates the average of some field data represented as real numbers. Any real number could be a data value, so you can't use a sentinel value, such as 9999, to indicate the end of the input. Design and implement a suitable interface for this problem.

EXERCISE 9.17   **Challenge:** A dialog box is a window associated with an application that appears only when needed. Dialog boxes have many uses. An error dialog is used to report an error message. A file dialog is used to help the user search for and open a file. Creating a basic error dialog is very simple in Swing. The `JOptionPane` class has class methods that can be used to create the kind of dialog shown in Figure 9–41. Such a dialog box can be created with a single statement:

FIGURE 9–41   A basic `JOptionPane` error dialog.

```
JOptionPane.showMessageDialog(this, "Sorry, your number is out of range.");
```

Convert the `Validate` program (Fig. 6–7) to a GUI interface and use the `JOption-Pane` dialog to report errors.

EXERCISE 9.18   **Challenge:** Design and implement a version of the game *Memory*. In this game you are given a two-dimensional grid of boxes that contains pairs of matching images or strings. The object is to find the matching pairs. When you click on a box, its contents are revealed. You then click on another box. If its contents match the first one, their contents are left visible. If not, the boxes are closed up again. The user should be able to play multiple games without getting the same arrangement every time.

## 10

Graphics and Drawing

OBJECTIVES

After studying this chapter, you will

- Know how to use Java's drawing classes and methods.
- Understand the concept of a graphics context.
- Be able to design scalable drawings.
- Know how to design and implement interfaces.
- Be familiar with handling mouse events.

OUTLINE

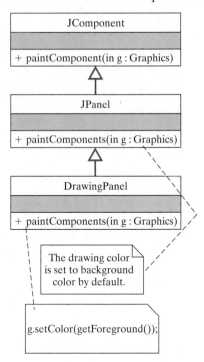

FIGURE 10–1 A JPanel gives you an opaque drawing surface. You must override its `paintComponent()` method in the subclass and set its pen color in order to draw on it.

Transparent or opaque?

What to draw with?

10.1 Introduction

Instead of using predrawn images to display a visual representation of our CyberPet, we could also use Java's drawing and painting methods. In some ways, drawing our own images within the program gives us more flexibility and control. For example, we can scale the drawing to give the impression of movement toward and away from the viewer.

In this chapter, we continue our discussion of Java's GUI elements, this time focusing on its drawing, painting, and mouse-handling functions. All of these elements are part of Java's Abstract Windowing Toolkit (AWT). Most of our attention will be directed toward the java.awt.Graphics class. Except for the issue of choosing an appropriate component class to use as a drawing surface, the Swing component set has had little effect on the way drawing is done in Java.

An important design theme of this chapter is the use of parameters to develop very general methods. An example is in the design of **scalable** drawings—that is, drawings that can easily be made larger or smaller. Another example is drawing scalable text displays that work with different fonts.

After introducing essential details of the relevant AWT classes, we will provide several case studies that illustrate how they can be used effectively.

10.2 The Drawing Surface

In order to draw and paint in a Java program, you need something to draw and paint on. In the Abstract Windowing Toolkit (AWT), a Canvas component is the usual drawing surface. However, Swing does not contain a direct counterpart for this class. Instead, in Swing programs you can either draw directly on the top-level windows—JApplet, JFrame—or on a subclass of JPanel. JPanel is a direct subclass of JComponent.

In order to draw on a JPanel, you have to make a subclass of it and override its paintComponent() method. By default, a JPanel's background color is the same color used for painting (Fig. 10–1). You can't paint with gray on gray. Another possible choice for a drawing surface is to make a subclass of JComponent. The difference between these two alternatives boils down to whether you want a *transparent* or *opaque* drawing surface. A JComponent is always transparent. It will always let its container show through. A JPanel, on the other hand, is transparent by default, but it can be made opaque. We'll see an example of this in the next section.

PROGRAMMING TIP: Drawing Surface. In Swing applications, use a subclass of JComponent if you want a transparent drawing surface. Otherwise use a subclass of JPanel.

10.3 The Graphics Context

Every Java component, including Swing components, has an associated **graphics context**, represented by an object of the java.awt.Graphics class. This is the object you use whenever you want to draw or paint in a program. It contains the drawing methods. However, the Graphics class is abstract, so you can't create a Graphics object directly. You have to get one from a component, such as a JPanel or any subclass of JComponent.

```java
import javax.swing.*;
import java.awt.*;
import java.awt.event.*;

public class DrawingPanel extends JPanel {

public void paintComponent(Graphics g) {
    super.paintComponent(g);            // Make the panel opaque
    g.setColor(getForeground());        // Set g's drawing color
    g.drawString("Hello World", 10, 50);
    g.fillRect(10, 55, 80, 20);
}

public static void main(String args[]) {
    JFrame frame = new JFrame("Drawing Panel");
    DrawingPanel panel = new DrawingPanel();
    frame.getContentPane().add(panel);
    frame.setSize(200, 100);
    frame.setVisible(true);
    frame.addWindowListener(new WindowAdapter() { // Quit program
        public void windowClosing(WindowEvent e) {
            System.exit(0);
        }
    });
} // main()
} // DrawingPanel
```

FIGURE 10–2 Using a JPanel's graphics context to draw "Hello World" and a rectangle.

Figure 10–2 illustrates how this done for a JPanel. This program draws "Hello World" and paints an 80×20 rectangle at location (10,55) of the panel (Fig. 10–3).

The main difference between this Swing program and an AWT drawing program is that for Swing components you override the paintComponent() method, whereas in an AWT program, you override the paint() method. In both cases, Swing and AWT, the graphics object, *g*, is used for both drawing and painting (or filling). It might be useful to compare this program with the HelloWorld applet from Chapter 1 (Fig. 1–9).

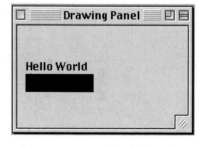

FIGURE 10–3 Using the JFrame's graphics context to draw "Hello World".
Swing vs. AWT

PROGRAMMING TIP: Graphics Object. When drawing on AWT components, you override the paint() method. When drawing on Swing components, you override the paintComponent() method.

The main() method creates a JFrame as the top-level window and then adds an instance of the DrawingPanel to it (Fig. 10–2). Recall that for a top-level Swing container (such as a JFrame), components are added to its *content pane* (getContentPane()) rather than to the container itself.

The content pane

DEBUGGING TIP: Content Pane. It is a semantic error to try to add a component to a top-level Swing window, such as a JApplet or JFrame. Instead you add the component to the window's content pane.

Let's look at the paintComponent() method (Fig. 10–2). This method overrides the JPanel.paintComponent() method. This is the method that will be called automatically whenever its component needs to be re-painted.

The first two lines of the method are used to give the panel a background color (rather than leave it transparent) and to set the drawing color of the Graphics object. The first line calls the superclass (JPanel) method, whose only task is to draw its background.

Opaque JPanel

If you leave these two statements out, the panel will remain transparent, and anything you draw on it will appear on its enclosing frame—on the JFrame. The actual appearance of the panel will depend on the program's look-and-feel default. In the Window's look and feel, putting these statements in or leaving them out won't make any difference, because the JFrame and the JPanel have the same background color. Of course, whether to make the panel transparent or opaque depends on how you are planning to use it in your application.

> **PROGRAMMING TIP: Transparent or Opaque.** To make a subclass of JPanel opaque, you must call JPanel's default paintComponent() method. Otherwise the panel will be transparent by default.

A possible source of frustration could occur if you make the panel opaque (line 1) but forget to set the color of the Graphics object to the panel's default foreground color (line 2). In that case, nothing will appear on the panel, because the Panel.paintComponent() method will have set the color of the Graphics object to the component's *background* color. If you draw on the gray background with a gray pen, nothing will show up. So, if you make the panel opaque, you must always set the color of the Graphics object to something besides the component's background color.

> **DEBUGGING TIP: Setting the Graphics Color.** For opaque JPanels—those that invoke JPanel.paintComponent()—you must set the color of the Graphics object. Otherwise it will be set to the component's background color.

10.3.1   Graphics Color and Component Color

Another possible source of confusion is the difference between the component's colors (foreground and background) and the Graphics object's color. The Graphics object has one color, which is the color it uses for drawing and painting.

What color is the pen and paintbrush?

One helpful way to think about this is to imagine that the graphics object has a pen for drawing and a paintbrush for painting. When you use the g.setColor() method, as we did in the DrawingPanel program, you set the color of both the pen and the paintbrush. Any subsequent drawing or painting by that graphics object will take place in that color.

> **PROGRAMMING TIP: Drawing and Painting.** Drawing refers to making a line drawing. In general, methods named *drawX* [drawRect()] are for drawing. Painting refers to filling a bounded object with color. Methods named *fillX* [fillRect()] are for painting. All painting and drawing are done by a Graphics object in their current pen and paintbrush color.

By contrast, every component has two colors associated with it: a *foreground* and a *background* color. For some components the difference between foreground and background is clear. For a JButton, the button's label is drawn in the foreground color on the button's background color. For a JTextField, the text is drawn in the foreground color, and the text field itself is rendered in the background color. Other components, such as a JPanel, don't use a foreground color. They consist entirely of a background color. For any component, the Component class contains methods to control its colors (Fig. 10–4).

What color is the component?

> DEBUGGING TIP: Setting Colors. A common mistake is to forget that foreground and background apply to the component, not to its associated graphics object.

10.3.2 The Graphics Coordinate System

The graphics context uses a simple coordinate system in which each picture element (**pixel**) is represented by its *x*- and *y*-coordinates. The **origin** of the coordinate system—the point with coordinates (0,0)—is located at the top-left corner of the component. The *x-coordinate* represents the *horizontal* displacement of a point from the origin, and the *y-coordinate* represents its *vertical* displacement. The *x*-coordinate increases from left to right, and the *y*-coordinate increases from top to bottom (Fig. 10–5).

10.3.3 Properties of the Graphics Context

A Graphics object has an internal state that consists of several properties that remain fixed during drawing and painting operations (Table 10.1). One of these is its color, which we have already discussed. Another is the current *font* that is used for drawing text. The *origin* is the point with coordinates (0,0). By default this is set to the component's top-left corner, but it can be *translated* (moved) to any point in the component's coordinate system. The **clip region** is that area of the component where drawing is permitted. By default, the clip region is set to the entire component, but this can be changed.

Component
+ getBackground() : Color
+ getForeground() : Color
+ setBackground(in c : Color)
+ setForeground(in c : Color)

FIGURE 10–4   Methods to control a Component's background and foreground colors.

The graphics state

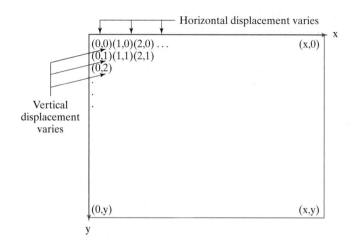

FIGURE 10–5   Java's coordinate system.

TABLE 10.1   Properties of the graphics context.

Property	Description	Default Value
Color	Current drawing color	The `JComponent`'s foreground color
Font	Current text font	The `JComponent`'s font
Drawing mode	Controls the pixel color	New pixels replace old pixels in the same location
Clip region	The drawing region	The entire `JComponent`
Origin	The point with coordinate (0,0)	Top-left pixel of the `JComponent`

Default drawing mode

The default **drawing mode** is to just paint over pixels. For example, if the background is white and the drawing color is black, then in normal mode drawing a pixel will turn it black. However, this too can be changed. One alternative mode is **XORmode**, or *bitwise exclusive or* mode, so named because it matches the logic of the boolean exclusive or operator. In XORmode, an exclusive or is performed on the background and foreground pixels, where the foreground pixel is determined by the pen's color. For black-and-white drawing, Table 10.2 defines what happens. In other words, if the drawing pen is black, then wherever the background is white, the drawing will be black. On the other hand, wherever the background is already black, the drawing will be white. Thus, XOR mode, in this case, will reverse the color of the background. Of course, on a colored background, while a similar effect is obtained, the results aren't so black and white (pun intended!).

XORmode drawing

```
                 Graphics
─────────────────────────────────────────
+ getClip() : Shape
+ getClipBounds() : Rectangle
+ getColor() : Color
+ getFont() : Font
+ getFontMetrics() : FontMetrics
+ setClip(in clip : Shape)
+ setColor(in c : Color)
+ setFont(in f : Font)
+ setPaintMode()
+ setXORMode(in c : Color)
+ translate(in x : int, in y : int)
```

FIGURE 10–6   Some of the main methods of the `Graphics` class.

TABLE 10.2   Java's XORmode drawing rules.

Background Color	Pen Color	Color of Result
White	Black	Black
Black	Black	White

The `java.awt.Graphics` class (Fig. 10–6) contains access methods that allow you to alter the default values of these properties. Examples in the following sections will illustrate how these methods are used.

SELF-STUDY EXERCISES

EXERCISE 10.1   For Figure 10–5, suppose the screen is 200×200. What are the coordinates for the pixel in the bottom-right corner of the screen?

EXERCISE 10.2   Suppose we define the clip region of window with `g.setClip(0,0,100,100)`, and we follow that with a `g.drawString("Hello World",150,150)`. What do you suppose will happen?

EXERCISE 10.3   Describe a problem for which drawing in XORmode would be useful.

10.4   The `Color` Class

RGB colors

Java colors are created from an **RGB value**, which is a collection of three numbers that specify the amounts of red, green, and blue that are mixed together to form the color. The `Color` class provides three constructors, each of which uses a different way of representing a color's RGB value

(Fig. 10–7). In the first constructor, an RGB value is represented as three separate `int`s, one for red, green, and blue, respectively. In this case, each integer represents a value between 0 and 255. The second constructor specifies the RGB value as a single integer, which is constructed as follows:

```
RGB = 65536 * R + 256 * G + B
```

This is the form in which the RGB is actually stored by the `Color` object. The third constructor takes the R, G, and B specifications as three `float` values in the range 0.0 to 1.0, respectively. The closer an R, G, or B value is to 1.0, the more of that hue is mixed into the color.

EFFECTIVE DESIGN: Colors.   Care must be taken in designing programs that use color, because color representation is inherently system dependent. In theory, it is possible to specify $256 \times 256 \times 256 = 16,777,216$ different colors. In practice, however, the number of different colors that can actually be displayed depends on the quality of your system's monitor.

PROGRAMMING TIP: Color Processing.   If your monitor uses only 8 bits to represent each pixel, then it can represent at most $2^8 = 256$ colors. In that case, the operating system decides which 256 (out of 16,277,216) colors to make available. If your program requests a color that is not one of the 256 available colors, the system will choose the closest available color.

Color
+ black : Color
+ blue : Color
+ cyan : Color
+ darkGray : Color
+ gray : Color
+ green : Color
+ lightGray : Color
+ magenta : Color
+ orange : Color
+ pink : Color
+ red : Color
+ white : Color
+ yellow : Color
+ Color(in r : int, in g : int, in b : int)
+ Color(in rgb : int)
+ Color(in r : float, in g : float, in b : float)
+ brighter() : Color
+ darker() : Color
+ equals(in o : Object) : boolean
+ getBlue() : int
+ getGreen() : int
+ getRGB() : int
+ getRed() : int
+ toString() : String

FIGURE 10–7   The `Color` class.

In addition to the three constructors described earlier, the `Color` class defines a number of standard colors as class constants (Fig. 10–7). These can be used directly to define new `Color` objects as follows:

```
Color color1 = Color.red;
Color color2 = Color.magenta;
```

If you wish to define a custom color, you can specify the individual R, G, and B components of your color.

RGB colors

PROGRAMMING TIP: Creating Custom Colors.   The primary colors—red, green, and blue—are represented by giving two of the other three R, G, B components a value of zero. A color whose green and blue components are both 0 will be some shade of red.

PROGRAMMING TIP: Creating Shades of Gray.   The RGB mixture (255,255,255) can be used to create pure white, while (0,0,0) is used to specify black. Shades of gray are colors whose RGB components have equal values. Thus, (128,128,128) is the specification for `Color.gray`, while (192,192,192) represents a lighter shade and (140,140,140) a darker shade of gray.

The `Color` class also provides several instance methods for modifying colors (Fig. 10–7). The various `get()` methods enable you to retrieve a `Color`'s individual RGB value. The `brighter()` and `darker()` methods enable you to start with a standard color and darken or lighten it:

```
Color red = Color.red;              // Pure red
Color brightRed = red.brighter();   // Brighter red
Color darkRed = red.darker();       // Darker red
```

SELF-STUDY EXERCISES

EXERCISE 10.4 Describe what will happen if you pick a color in Java that can't be displayed on your monitor.

EXERCISE 10.5 Design question: Why are the built-in colors defined as class constants?

EXERCISE 10.6 Although technically millions of colors are possible, most are minor shade or brightness variants indistinguishable by the human eye. Which three colors do color monitors "mix" to make all the rest, whether dozens or "millions"?

10.4.1 Example: The `ColorPicker` Applet

To illustrate how to use the methods of the `Color` class, consider the `ColorPicker` applet, whose interface is shown in Figure 10–8. This applet lets you experiment with the various RGB ratios. It provides three labeled `JTextFields` for the R, G, and B values that make up a color. When a return is typed in any text field, a new `Color` object is made with the three input values and then displayed on a separate `JPanel` located in the center of the applet.

The new color is displayed in various formats. First, it is displayed using the `Color.toString()` method, which just displays the integer values of the color's RGB components. Next, the color is used to paint a colored rectangle and draw a colored string. Finally, the color is brightened and darkened, and these new colors are displayed as both a rectangle and a string.

FIGURE 10–8 Output from the `ColorPicker` program.

The applet's border interface is divided into two separate panels: a controls `JPanel`, which contains the input text fields, and a canvas `JPanel`, which is responsible for all the drawing and painting (Fig. 10–9). Although it is possible to draw directly on a `JApplet`, a more flexible interface can be created by using a separate `JPanel`, within the applet window, for drawing. That's the purpose of the `Canvas` class, which is described later.

EFFECTIVE DESIGN: Drawing Interface Design. If a drawing program uses controls and other components, it is best to use a separate panel for the drawing area. That way the program's layout can be managed by a layout manager.

Note how the applet's layout is created in the `init()` and `initControls()` methods. Once again, because a `JApplet` is a top-level Swing container, the panels must be added to its content pane. Note how the `BorderFactory` class is used to create borders around each of the panels. This helps to improve the applet's overall appearance, while dividing the interface into logical regions at the same time.

```java
import javax.swing.*;
import java.awt.*;
import java.awt.event.*;

public class ColorPicker extends JApplet implements ActionListener {
    private JTextField redIn, greenIn, blueIn;
    private JLabel R = new JLabel("R:"),
                   G = new JLabel("G:"),
                   B = new JLabel("B:");
    private JPanel controls = new JPanel();
    private Canvas canvas = new Canvas();

    public void init() {
        initControls();
        getContentPane().add(controls, "North");
        getContentPane().add(canvas, "Center");
        canvas.setBorder(BorderFactory.createTitledBorder("The Color Display"));
        getContentPane().setBackground(Color.white);
        setSize(250,150);
    } // init()

    private void initControls() {
        redIn = new JTextField("128", 4);      // Create 3 input textfields
        greenIn = new JTextField("128", 4);
        blueIn = new JTextField("128", 4);
        redIn.addActionListener(this);         // Give them listeners
        greenIn.addActionListener(this);
        blueIn.addActionListener(this);
        controls.setLayout( new FlowLayout());
        controls.setBorder(BorderFactory.createTitledBorder("Type in values for RGB"));
        controls.add(R);
        controls.add(redIn);       // Add prompts and textfields
        controls.add(G);
        controls.add(greenIn);
        controls.add(B);
        controls.add(blueIn);
    } // initControls()

    public void actionPerformed(ActionEvent e) {
        int r = Integer.parseInt(redIn.getText());    // Get user's inputs
        int g = Integer.parseInt(greenIn.getText());
        int b = Integer.parseInt(blueIn.getText());
        canvas.setColor(new Color(r, g, b));          // Reset the canvas's color
        repaint();                                    // Repaint the applet
    } // actionPerformed()
} // ColorPicker
```

FIGURE 10–9   The ColorPicker program allows you to experiment with the
RGB ratios of the various colors.

```java
import javax.swing.*;
import java.awt.*;

public class Canvas extends JPanel {
    private final int HREF = 40, VREF = 55;       // Reference points
    private final int WIDTH = 40, HEIGHT = 50;    // Rectangle dimensions
    private final int HGAP = 70,  VGAP = 60;      // Spacing constants

    private Color color = Color.gray;
    public void setColor(Color c) {
        color = c;
    }

    public void paintComponent(Graphics g) {
        super.paintComponent(g);                              // Make the panel opaque
        g.setColor(color);                                    // Set the pen's color
        g.drawString(color.toString(), HREF, VREF-15 );       // Draw the color's RGB's
        g.fillRect(HREF, VREF, WIDTH, HEIGHT);                // Color a rectangle
        g.drawString("color", HREF, VREF + VGAP);
        g.setColor(color.brighter());                         // Brighten the color
        g.fillRect(HREF + HGAP, VREF, WIDTH, HEIGHT);
        g.drawString("brighter", HREF + HGAP, VREF + VGAP);
        g.setColor(color.darker());                           // Darken the color
        g.fillRect(HREF + HGAP * 2, VREF, WIDTH, HEIGHT);
        g.drawString("darker", HREF + HGAP * 2, VREF + VGAP);
    } // paintComponent()
} // Canvas
```

FIGURE 10–10   The Canvas class is a JPanel subclass that can be used for drawing on an applet.

Each time the user types a return in one of the JTextFields, the action-Performed() method retrieves the three RGB values from the JTextFields and uses them to create a new Color. It uses the color to set the canvas's color.

The canvas JPanel takes care of all the drawing (Fig. 10–10). This class has the same basic design as the DrawingFrame class we defined earlier. It extends JPanel and overrides the paintComponent() method, which is the method where all the drawing takes place.

10.4.2   Painting Components

Repainting rules

It's important to understand how Java's event handling works in this program. As you know, an applet is repainted automatically whenever it is moved, or resized, or made visible again after being hidden. This is done by calling the applet's paint() method. A program can also force an applet to repaint itself by explicitly calling repaint(), as we have done in this case. But this applet doesn't contain a paint() method.

Repainting protocol

So how is this applet painted? The answer is that it is repainted as part of Java's default event handling. The reason the applet does not contain a paint() method is because it doesn't do any painting of its own. That task is handled by the canvas object. However, as a subclass of Container, a JApplet invokes the Container.paint() method. The default behavior of

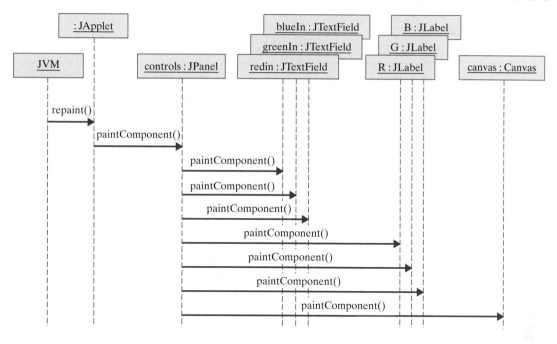

FIGURE 10–11   When it is repainted, a container, such as an applet or a panel, repaints all of its components.

this method is to paint all the components contained in the container. It does this by calling their respective paint methods.

When a top-level window receives an event that requires it to repaint itself, it sends a "repaint" message to each of its contained components. Figure 10–11 illustrates how this process works for the ColorPicker applet. Whenever the applet is repainted, all of the text fields and labels are repainted, and the canvas is repainted. Because the canvas is a JPanel, it is repainted by calling its paintComponent() method. Thus, every time the user types a return key in one of the text fields, the actionPerformed() method repaints the JApplet, which in turn repaints all of the components that it contains. If the components are containers themselves, then all of their components will be repainted.

> **PROGRAMMING TIP: Automatic Repainting.** Whenever a container, such as an a JApplet, JFrame, or JPanel, is repainted, all of its contained components are repainted.

SELF-STUDY EXERCISES

EXERCISE 10.7   For each of the following expressions, predict what color would be produced:

a. new Color(255,10,10)   b. new Color(0,255,20)   c. new Color(10,15,255)

EXERCISE 10.8   Explain what would happen if you remove the repaint() method call from the ColorPicker's actionPerformed() method.

EXERCISE 10.9   What's the difference between the JApplet's paint() method and the JPanel's paintComponent method?

OBJECT-ORIENTED DESIGN:
Reference Constants

Note how the constants—the `final int` variables—are used in the Canvas class to simplify the layout of the drawing area (Fig. 10–10). HREF and VREF serve as reference points. All of the drawing takes place relative to these two values. Also, the horizontal and vertical spacing is defined in terms of the HGAP and VGAP constants. This enables you to develop simple formulas for aligning and spacing the output. For example, the three strings

```
color        brighter       darker
```

are printed, horizontally spaced, on the same line, by using the following three statements:

```
g.drawString("color", HREF, VREF + VGAP);
g.drawString("brighter", HREF + HGAP, VREF + VGAP);
g.drawString("darker", HREF + HGAP * 2, VREF + VGAP);
```

Note the use of the formula HREF + HGAP * k (where k ranges from 0 to 2) to produce the desired spacing. Similarly, note the use of the WIDTH and HEIGHT constants to specify the size of the colored rectangles:

```
g.fillRect(HREF, VREF, WIDTH, HEIGHT);
g.fillRect(HREF + HGAP, VREF, WIDTH, HEIGHT);
g.fillRect(HREF + HGAP * 2, VREF, WIDTH, HEIGHT);
```

Here again HREF, VREF, and HGAP are used to control the spacing of the rectangles.

Symbolic constants

The main advantage of using constants in this way is that the program is easier to develop and maintain. By using symbolic constants in the code, you can easily try different values until you get the right layout. To change the size of horizontal spacing of the elements, you need only edit one value in the program—the constant definition—no matter how often that value is used. Also, it is easy to incorporate new elements into the scheme, making the program easier to maintain over time. In this case, because the reference points and sizes of the components don't change, we are able to use constants. In subsequent examples we will use variables and method parameters to achieve results that are even more general.

EFFECTIVE DESIGN: Use symbolic constants—that is, `final` variables—in place of literal values to make your code more general. It will be easier both to develop and to maintain.

SELF-STUDY EXERCISES

EXERCISE 10.10 Write a method to display a sequence of 20 small 3×3 rectangles horizontally across the screen starting at XREF, VREF, with a space of HGAP between each pair of rectangles. This should be a void method and should take a Graphics parameter.

EXERCISE 10.11 Write a method to display a sequence of 20 small 3 × 3 rectangles diagonally across the screen starting at XREF, VREF, with a horizontal and vertical space of HGAP and VGAP between each pair of rectangles. This should be a void method and should take a Graphics parameter.

THE java.awt.Point class (Fig. 10–12) represents a point in the Graphics coordinate system. As you can see, the Point class makes it possible to manipulate *x*- and *y*-coordinates as a single entity. It also makes it possible to break a point up into its *x*- and *y*-coordinates. Note that a Point's *x*- and *y*-coordinates are defined as public instance variables. This makes it possible to refer to them, using the following convenient syntax:

```
Point p = new Point(100, 50);
System.out.println("x = " + p.x + " y = " + p.y);
```

The main justification for making *x* and *y* public is that it is more efficient to access them directly than being forced to use getX() and getY() methods. Method calls require more processing overhead than direct access and efficiency is an important factor in drawing three-dimensional graphics.

EFFECTIVE DESIGN: Public Instance Variables. Although instance variables should usually be declared private, there are situations, such as when efficiency is of paramount importance, when you are justified in making them public.

The java.awt.Dimension class (Fig. 10–13) represents the size (width and height) of a component. A Dimension makes it possible to manipulate an object's width and height as a single entity. Because height and width are public instance variables, the following syntax can be used to refer to a component's dimensions:

```
Dimension d = new Dimension(100, 50);
System.out.println("width = " + d.width + " height = " + d.height);
```

Note the redundancy built into the Dimension class. For example, in addition to being able to set a Dimension's instance variables directly, public access methods are provided. Also, by defining more than one version of some access methods, the class achieves a higher level of flexibility. The same can be said for providing several different constructors, including a copy constructor. Finally, note how it overrides the equals() and toString() methods. These are all examples of good object-oriented design.

EFFECTIVE DESIGN: Redundancy. Redundancy is often a desirable characteristic of object design. It makes the object easier to use and more widely applicable.

EFFECTIVE DESIGN: Overriding Generic Methods. All classes that are designed for widespread use, especially library classes, should override the Object class's toString() and equals() methods.

From the Java Library

Points **and** Dimensions

www. http://java.sun.com/products /jdk/1.3/docs/api/

Point
+ x : int
+ y : int
+ Point()
+ Point(in p : Point)
+ Point(in x : int, in y : int)
+ equals(in o : Object) : boolean
+ getLocation() : Point
+ setLocation(in p : Point)
+ setLocation(in x : int, in y : int)

FIGURE 10–12   The Point class.

Dimension
+ height : int
+ width : int
+ Dimension()
+ Dimension(in d : Dimension)
+ Dimension(in width : int, in height : int)
+ equals(in o : Object) : boolean
+ getSize() : Dimension
+ setSize(in d : Dimension)
+ setSize(in width : int, in height : int)
+ toString() : String

FIGURE 10–13   The Dimension class.

SELF-STUDY EXERCISES

EXERCISE 10.12   Write a method that takes two parameters, a Graphics object and a Point p, and draws a sequence of 20 small 3 × 3 rectangles horizontally across the screen starting at p.x, p.y, with a space of HGAP between each pair of rectangles.

EXERCISE 10.13   Suppose you have a JPanel whose dimensions are represented by Dimension d. Write an expression to calculate its area.

10.5   Painting and Drawing Lines and Shapes

Drawing and painting shapes

In addition to the fillRect() method, which we used in the ColorPicker program, Java's java.awt.Graphics class (Fig. 10–14) contains a good assortment of methods that are used for drawing and painting lines and shapes. The methods categorized as drawing methods are used to draw lines, arcs, and various kinds of shapes, including ovals, rectangles, and *n*-sided polygons. The methods categorized as filling methods are used to fill bounded regions, such as ovals, rectangles, and polygons, with a color.

As we've seen, the conventional way to draw or paint in color is first to set the context's color and then to use one of these methods. For example, the following statements will draw a red rectangle and a red oval:

```
g.setColor(Color.red);         // Set the drawing color to red
g.drawRect(10, 50, 100, 50);   // A 100 x 50 rectangle at location 10,50
g.drawOval(150, 50, 100, 50);  // An oval inscribed in a 100 x 50 rectangle
```

Both drawRect() and drawOval() take the same parameters, the *x*- and *y*-coordinates where the shape should be located, and the shape's *length* and *width*. In the case of drawRect(), the coordinates refer to the rectangle's top-left corner. In the case of drawOval(), they refer to the top-left corner and the length and width of an invisible rectangle within which the oval is inscribed. You can also use these methods to draw squares and circles, which are just special cases of rectangle and oval.

FIGURE 10–14   Some of the methods of the Graphics class.

Graphics
+ draw3DRect(in x : int, in y : int, in w : int, in h : int, in raised : boolean)
+ drawArc(in x : int, in y : int, in w : int, in h : int, in startAngle : int, in arcAngle : int)
+ drawLine(in x1 : int, in y1 : int, in x2 : int, in y2 : int)
+ drawOval(in x : int, in y : int, in w : int, in h : int)
+ drawPolygon(in xPoints : int[], in yPoints : int[], in nPoints : int)
+ drawPolygon(in p : Polygon)
+ drawPolyline(in xPoints : int[], in yPoints : int[], in nPoints : int)
+ drawRect(in x : int, in y : int, in w : int, in h : int)
+ drawRoundRect(in x : int, in y : int, in w : int, in h : int, in arcW : int, in arcH : int)
+ clearRect(in x : int, in y : int, in w : int, in h : int)
+ fill3DRect(in x : int, in y : int, in w : int, in h : int, in raised : boolean)
+ fillArc(in x : int, in y : int, in w : int, in h : int, in startAngle : int, in arcAngle : int)
+ fillOval(in x : int, in y : int, in w : int, in h : int)
+ fillPolygon(in xPoints : int[], in yPoints : int[], in nPoints : int)
+ fillPolygon(in p : Polygon)
+ fillRect(in x : int, in y : int, in w : int, in h : int)
+ fillRoundRect(in x : int, in y : int, in w : int, in h : int, in arcW : int, in arcH : int)

In both cases the outline of the shapes would be red. The inside of the shapes would be transparent—that is, they would have the color of the container's background. The following statements draw the same shapes but fill the shapes with color:

```
g.setColor(Color.red);       // Set the drawing color to red
g.fillRect(10, 50, 100, 50); // A 100 x 50 rectangle at location 10,50
g.fillOval(150, 50, 100, 50); // An oval inscribed in a 100 x 50 rectangle
```

SELF-STUDY EXERCISES

EXERCISE 10.14   Use drawRect() to draw an 80 × 40 rectangle, and place the top left of the rectangle at coordinates (0,20).

EXERCISE 10.15   Write the Java code to inscribe a yellow oval in the rectangle you drew in the previous exercise.

10.6   Example: The ShapeDemo Applet

The ShapeDemo applet (Fig. 10–15) illustrates the use of the various drawing and painting commands. The program shows two kinds of shapes: drawn shapes (top) and filled shapes (bottom). It shows examples of ovals, 3-D rectangles, and rounded rectangles.

Note how this program (Fig. 10–16) is designed. Unlike the ColorPicker applet, this applet does not contain components, such as text fields or buttons. It just does drawing. Therefore, the drawing can be done directly on its top-level container—the JApplet. This means that the drawing will be done by the applet's paint() method rather than the paintComponent() method used by JComponents. The paintComponent() method only applies to subclasses of JComponent. (You may want to review the Swing hierarchy diagram in Figure 9–1.)

Problem decomposition

> DEBUGGING TIP: Painting AWT and Swing Components. A possible source of confusion concerns which paint method to use for a component. Swing JComponents use paintComponent(). AWT components and top-level Swing windows, JApplet and JFrame, which are subclasses of java.awt.Component, use the paint() method.

The drawLine() method is used to draw a line separating the two types of shapes (Fig. 10–16). Note again how symbolic constants are used to

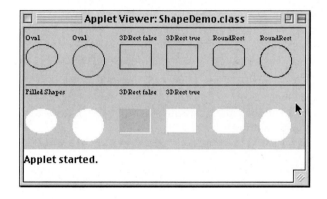

FIGURE 10–15 Output from the ShapeDemo program. A "RoundRect" is a rectangle with rounded corners. Note that if you set the parameters correctly, you can make it into a circle. A "3DRect" is a rectangle that has a 3-D appearance. Two examples are shown.

```java
import java.awt.*;
import javax.swing.*;

public class ShapeDemo extends JApplet {
    public final int NFIGS = 5;        // Number of shapes
    public final int HREF = 2;         // Horizontal reference
    public final int VREF = 20;        // Vertical reference
    public final int WIDTH = 40;       // Width of figure
    public final int HGT = 20;         // Height of figure
    public final int HGAP = 20;        // H gap between figures
    public final int VGAP = 20;        // V gap between figures

    public void paint( Graphics g ) {
        setSize((NFIGS +1) * (WIDTH + HGAP), 3 * (HGT + HGAP));
        setBackground(Color.lightGray);
        g.setFont(new Font("Serif", Font.PLAIN, 9));
        int fontHgt = g.getFontMetrics().getHeight();
        g.drawString("Oval", HREF, VREF - 5 );
        g.drawOval(HREF, VREF, WIDTH, HGT);
        g.drawString("Oval", HREF + (WIDTH + HGAP), VREF - 5);
        g.drawOval(HREF + (WIDTH + HGAP), VREF, WIDTH, WIDTH);
        g.drawString("3DRect false", HREF + 2 * (WIDTH + HGAP), VREF - 5);
        g.draw3DRect(HREF + 2 * (WIDTH + HGAP), VREF, WIDTH, HGT, false);
        g.drawString("3DRect true", HREF + 3 * (WIDTH + HGAP), VREF - 5);
        g.draw3DRect(HREF + 3 * (WIDTH + HGAP), VREF, WIDTH, HGT, true);
        g.drawString("RoundRect", HREF + 4 * (WIDTH + HGAP), VREF - 5);
        g.drawRoundRect(HREF + 4 * (WIDTH + HGAP), VREF, WIDTH, HGT, WIDTH/2, HGT/2);
        g.drawString("RoundRect", HREF +5 * (WIDTH + HGAP), VREF - 5);
        g.drawRoundRect(HREF + 5 * (WIDTH + HGAP), VREF, WIDTH, WIDTH, WIDTH, WIDTH);

        g.drawLine(HREF, VREF + HGT + VGAP, HREF + (NFIGS + 1) * (WIDTH + HGAP ), VREF + HGT + VGAP);

        g.drawString("Filled Shapes", HREF, VREF + HGT + VGAP + fontHgt );
        g.drawString("3DRect false", HREF + 2 * (WIDTH + HGAP), VREF + HGT + VGAP + fontHgt);
        g.drawString("3DRect true", HREF + 3 * (WIDTH + HGAP),  VREF + HGT + VGAP + fontHgt);
        g.setColor(Color.white);
        g.fillOval(HREF ,VREF + 2 *  HGT + VGAP, WIDTH, HGT);
        g.fillOval(HREF + (WIDTH + HGAP), VREF + 2 *  HGT + VGAP, WIDTH, WIDTH);
        g.fill3DRect(HREF + 2 * (WIDTH + HGAP), VREF + 2 * HGT + VGAP, WIDTH, HGT, false);
        g.fill3DRect(HREF + 3 * (WIDTH + HGAP), VREF + 2 * HGT + VGAP, WIDTH, HGT, true);
        g.fillRoundRect(HREF + 4 * (WIDTH + HGAP), VREF + 2 * HGT + VGAP, WIDTH, HGT, WIDTH/2, HGT/2);
        g.fillRoundRect(HREF + 5 * (WIDTH + HGAP), VREF + 2 * HGT + VGAP, WIDTH, WIDTH, WIDTH, WIDTH);
    } // paint()
} // ShapeDemo
```

FIGURE 10–16   The `ShapeDemo` class illustrates the use of the `Graphics` class's basic drawing and painting methods.

specify the locations, spacing, and sizes of the shapes. Even the size of the applet screen is calculated as a function of these constant values:

Setting a container's size

```
setSize((NFIGS +1) * (WIDTH + HGAP), 3 * (HGT + VGAP));
```

This formula says that the horizontal dimension of the screen is calculated by assuming that each shape is given a horizontal space equal to its WIDTH plus the horizontal gap between shapes, HGAP. The horizontal dimension of the screen is then calculated as the number of shapes, NFIGS+1, times each shape's allotted horizontal space. The "+1" adds a little extra space. The vertical dimension of the screen is calculated as three times the sum of the height of each shape, HGT, plus the vertical spacing between each shape, VGAP.

Algorithm design

The program's output (Fig. 10–15) shows the difference between drawn and filled shapes of the same dimensions. The drawn shapes are transparent, while the filled shapes are colored (white). The 3-D shapes were drawn by the following commands:

```
g.draw3DRect(HREF + 2 * (WIDTH + HGAP), VREF, WIDTH, HGT, false);
g.draw3DRect(HREF + 3 * (WIDTH + HGAP), VREF, WIDTH, HGT, true);
g.fill3DRect(HREF + 2 * (WIDTH + HGAP),
                     VREF + 2 * HGT + VGAP, WIDTH, HGT, false);
g.fill3DRect(HREF + 3 * (WIDTH + HGAP),
                     VREF + 2 * HGT + VGAP, WIDTH, HGT, true);
```

The boolean argument in these methods determines the rectangle's color scheme. When false, the main part of the rectangle is drawn in the current pen color, and the outline (bottom, right sides) consists of an alternate color. When false, these colors are reversed.

Note also the use of the rounded rectangle shapes, which can be used to draw shapes ranging from a circle to a rectangle with rounded corners. The statements used to produce these shapes are

```
g.drawRoundRect(HREF + 4 * (WIDTH + HGAP),
                   VREF, WIDTH, HGT, WIDTH/2, HGT/2);
g.drawRoundRect(HREF + 5 * (WIDTH + HGAP),
                   VREF, WIDTH, WIDTH, WIDTH, WIDTH);
g.fillRoundRect(HREF + 4 * (WIDTH + HGAP),
                   VREF + 2 * HGT + VGAP, WIDTH, HGT, WIDTH/2, HGT/2);
g.fillRoundRect(HREF + 5 * (WIDTH + HGAP),
                   VREF + 2 * HGT + VGAP, WIDTH, WIDTH, WIDTH, WIDTH);
```

The last two parameters in each of these methods are used to specify the width and the height of the arc that defines the shape's corners. As the program illustrates, the larger the arc, the more rounded the corners. When using these kinds of shapes in your program, the best strategy is to experiment with different values until you get the desired appearance. Again, however, the use of symbolic constants, instead of literal values, makes the program easier to develop and modify. In this case, it also helps to clarify the relationship between the arcs and the dimensions of the enclosing rectangles.

Rounded rectangles

SELF-STUDY EXERCISES

EXERCISE 10.16   What kind of shape would be drawn by the following statement?

```
g.drawRoundRect(XREF, VREF, 50, 50, 50, 50);
```

EXERCISE 10.17   Write a statement using the `drawRoundRect()` method to draw a circle with diameter D, inside of the rectangle located at XREF, YREF.

10.7   Graphing Equations

No discussion of graphics would be complete without an illustration of how to use the drawing commands to graph equations. For mathematical and scientific graphs, it is necessary to use the **Cartesian coordinate system**. As you know, in Cartesian coordinates, the origin (0,0) is located in the center of the graph and is intersected by the x- and y-axes. Obviously, graphing lines and equations on the Cartesian plane would be made much easier if we could move the drawing frame's origin to the center of the frame. Fortunately, this is very simple to do using the `Graphics.translate()` method.

Translating the origin

For example, assuming the size of the frame is 400×400, we can place the origin at the center with the following statement:

```
g.translate(200, 200); // Move origin to the center
```

This statement will move the origin 200 pixels to the right and 200 pixels down from its present (top-left corner) location. Of course, this will not, by itself, give us a Cartesian coordinate system, because the vertical coordinates will still grow from small to large as you move downward from the origin. In Cartesian coordinates, the y-coordinates decrease as you move downward, so in graphing equations, we will have to make this adjustment in our programs.

DEBUGGING TIP: Moving the Origin. The parameters in the `translate()` method specify the horizontal and vertical displacement by which the origin should be moved. They do not specify the coordinates of the new location.

DEBUGGING TIP: Your graphs will come out upside down if you forget to reorient them to account for the fact that in Java's coordinate system the y-axis grows in the downward direction.

Once you translate the origin, any subsequent references to coordinates will now assume that the origin is at (200,200). For example, the following statement,

```
g.fillOval(0, 0, 2, 2);
```

will draw an oval inscribed within a 2×2 rectangle whose upper-left corner is at the very center of the screen.

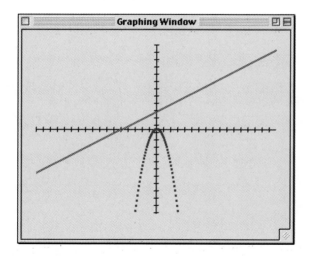

FIGURE 10–17 Graphing mathematical or scientific equations.

SELF-STUDY EXERCISE

EXERCISE 10.18 Suppose you have a 200 × 200 JPanel. Relative to its default origin, in which (0,0) is at the top-left corner of the panel, where would the origin be after the following statements are executed?

```
g.translate(50, 200);
g.translate(-10, -150);
```

10.7.1 Example: The Graph Program

Translating the origin in this way makes it very simple to develop programs to draw mathematical or scientific graphs (Fig. 10–17). The Graph application, described in this section, provides an illustration of the basic techniques. The Graph class is a subclass of JPanel (Fig. 10–18). This means that all the drawing for this application will be done in the paintComponent() method, although it contains three private methods, drawXYAxes() and graphLine(), and graphQuadratic(), that help break up the drawing task. The Graph's initial size will be set in its constructor. Note that class constants, WIDTH and HEIGHT, are used to set the initial size of the top-level window.

Problem decomposition

The implementation of the Graph class is shown in Figure 10–19. The main() method creates a top-level window for the application JFrame and

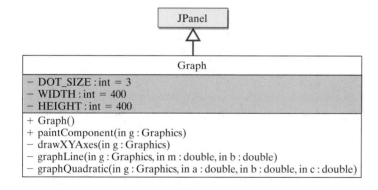

FIGURE 10–18 The Graph class.

```java
import java.awt.*;
import javax.swing.*;
import java.awt.event.*;

public class Graph extends JPanel {
    private final int WIDTH = 400, HEIGHT = 400; // Default width and height
    private final int DOT_SIZE = 3;

    public Graph () {
        setSize(WIDTH,HEIGHT);
    }

    public void paintComponent(Graphics g) {
        Dimension size = this.getSize();
        g.setColor(getBackground());                        // Clear the drawing area
        g.setClip(0, 0, size.width, size.height);
        g.fillRect(0, 0, size.width, size.height);
        g.setClip(20, 20, size.width - 40, size.height - 40);   // Reset the clip region
        g.translate(size.width / 2, size.height / 2);       // Place origin at middle
        g.setColor(Color.black);
        drawXYAxes(g);                                      // Draw the X and Y axes
        graphLine(g, 0.5, 25.2);                            // Graph y = 0.5x + 25.2
        graphQuadratic(g, -0.125, 0, 0 );                   // Graph 4y = -x^2
    } // paintComponent()

    private void drawXYAxes(Graphics g) {
        Dimension size = this.getSize();            // Get the panel's size
        int hBound = size.width / 2;                // Use it to set the bounds
        int vBound = size.height / 2;
        int tic = size.width / 100;

        g.drawLine(-hBound,0,hBound,0);             // Draw X-axis
        for (int k = -hBound; k <= hBound; k+=10)
            g.drawLine(k, tic, k, -tic);
        g.drawLine(0, vBound, 0, -vBound);          // Draw Y-axis
        for (int k = -vBound; k <= vBound; k+=10)
            g.drawLine(-tic, k, +tic, k);
    } // drawXYAxes()

    private void graphLine(Graphics g, double m, double b) {
        Dimension size = this.getSize();            // Get the panel's size
        int hBound = size.width / 2;                // Use it to set the bounds
        g.setColor( Color.red );
        for (int x = -hBound; x <= hBound; x++) {   // For each pixel on x axis
            int y = (int)(m * x + b );
            y = -y;                                 // Reverse y coordinate (Cartesian)
            g.drawLine(x, y, x+1, y+1);             // Draw a point
        }
    } // graphLine()

    private void graphQuadratic( Graphics g, double a, double b, double c ) {
        Dimension size = this.getSize();                // Get the panel's size
        int hBound = size.width/2;                      // Use it to set the bounds
```

FIGURE 10–19   The `Graph` application illustrates how to draw mathematical and scientific graphs (Part I).

```
        g.setColor(Color.red);
        for (int x = -hBound; x <= hBound; x++) {      // For each pixel on x axis
            int y = (int)(a * x * x + b * x + c);
            y = -y;                                      // Reverse y coordinate (cartesian)
            g.fillOval(x-1, y-1, DOT_SIZE, DOT_SIZE);    // Draw a point
        }
    } // graphQuadratic()

    public static void main(String args[]) {
        JFrame f = new JFrame("Graphing Window");
        Graph graph = new Graph();
        f.getContentPane().add(graph);
        f.setSize(graph.getSize().width, graph.getSize().height);
        f.setVisible(true);
        f.addWindowListener(new WindowAdapter() {        // Quit the application
            public void windowClosing(WindowEvent e) {
                System.exit(0);
            }
        });
    } // main()
}// Graph
```

FIGURE 10–19   *(continued)* Graph, Part II.

then adds the Graph to the window. All of the drawing in the application is handled by the paintComponent() method. Remember that this method will be called automatically each time the application's window is resized, so we want to design an algorithm that will produce an appropriately sized graph, no matter how big the window is.

Algorithm design

To accomplish this goal, we will make the location and size of the graph dependent on the size of its panel. The paintComponent() method begins by getting the JPanel's current size and stores it in a local Dimension variable:

What data do we need?

```
Dimension size = this.getSize();
```

The size is used to calculate the clip region, and to calculate the location of the panel's center, which is used by the translate() method to relocate the origin:

Centering the origin

```
g.translate(size.width/2, size.height/2);   // Place origin at middle
```

Thus, no matter what size the window is, the graph's origin will be located at the center. Note that it is necessary to clear the panel each time paintComponent() is called (Fig. 10–19). Otherwise, the old version of the graph would remain visible in the resized panel. This is another possible source of confusion between drawing on AWT and Swing components. When an AWT method is updated, because it has been resized or moved, its background is cleared. When a Swing JComponent is updated, its background is not cleared. This is an appropriate design, because JComponents can be transparent.

Clearing the panel

> DEBUGGING TIP: Clearing a Component. AWT components have their backgrounds cleared whenever they are updated, but Swing JCompo-nents are not automatically cleared.

In order to improve the appearance of the graph, the panel's clip region is set to an area 20 pixels inside of its borders:

```
g.setClip(20, 20, size.width - 40, size.height - 40);
```

Clipping the drawing

This will prevent the drawing commands from drawing right up to the panel's edges. In this case, it is important that the clip region be set *before* moving the origin, because it's much easier to specify the clip region when the top-left corner (the default origin) is used as a reference point.

Given now that the origin is at the center of the frame, the drawXYAxes() method draws the graph's axes (Fig. 10–19). Note again how the JPanel's size is used to calculate the horizontal and vertical bounds of the axes and the size of their tic marks. The axes themselves are just lines:

Drawing the axes

```
g.drawLine(-hBound,0,hBound,0)
```

but a for loop is used to draw their tic marks (Fig. 10–17). The tic marks are placed every 10 pixels (no matter what size the window is). However, note that the tic variable is defined as size.width/100, so that it will always be proportional to the size of the graph itself. You should experiment to test how well it scales when you resize its window.

Finally, given the ability to place the origin at the center of the frame, it is quite simple to design methods to graph equations. Two examples are shown in Figure 10–19. The graphLine() method graphs a linear equation, given its **slope-intercept** representation. In slope-intercept form, the equation of a line is given by

$$y = mx + b$$

Graphing a line

where m represents the line's slope and b represents its y-intercept. The graphLine() method takes m and b as parameters and then uses the foregoing equation to determine the line's coordinates. A for loop is used to calculate the y-coordinate for each x on the graph. Note the statement used to reverse y's sign to translate the graph for the Cartesian plane. Note again the use of the panel's size to determine the bounds of the graph.

Similarly, the graphQuadratic() method graphs a quadratic equation using the same basic approach (Fig. 10–19). A quadratic equation takes the following form:

$$y = ax^2 + bx + c$$

Graphing a parabola

The method takes the coefficients a, b, and c as parameters. It uses a for loop to calculate the curve's coordinates. As you can see from Figure 10–17, the equation used in the sample program yields a parabola.

> EFFECTIVE DESIGN: Relative Locations. Graphing equations is simplified by making the graph's origin be the origin of the graphics context. Then all points can be plotted relative to the origin.

SELF-STUDY EXERCISE

EXERCISE 10.19   What would be the consequences of forgetting to set the Graph object's size in its constructor method?

10.8   Drawing Bar Charts and Pie Charts

The origin of the Graphics context can be relocated repeatedly. This is particularly handy if you want to draw more than one graph on the frame. To illustrate this, let's design a bar chart and a pie chart and place them on the same drawing panel. As Figure 10–20 illustrates, we will implement the charts as separate methods in the ChartDemo class. The charts will be scaled to the size of the drawing panel's WIDTH and HEIGHT.

Suppose you want to display your company's sales data for the most recent quarter. There are five sellers and your boss wants a bar chart comparing each seller's sales for the past two quarters. She also wants a pie chart of this quarter's sales, broken up by each seller's percentage of total sales. And she wants it all in dazzling shades of gray!

Suppose that the data for this program are stored in arrays:

```java
private double quarter1[] = {1099.85, 2105.86, 3105.25, 987.20, 5000.45};
private double quarter2[] = {2199.85, 3105.86, 2805.25, 1500.20, 6250.95};
```

The bar chart should compare quarter1 and quarter2 sales for each seller, and the pie chart should compare each seller's quarter2 sales.

10.8.1   Scaling the Bar Chart

A bar chart, or **histogram**, consists of plain old rectangles of a fixed width but of varying heights. The rectangle's height illustrates the *relative* size of the quantity being graphed. In this case, the height of a bar will represent the seller's total sales for the quarter. You can't use the actual quantity because it might be greater than the size of the window. For example, the sales quantities might be numbers like 5,000, but we can't draw rectangles that are 5,000 pixels in height. Therefore, the height of each bar must be *scaled* to guarantee that it fits within the screen.

One way to scale the bars would be to base their size on a predetermined maximum sales amount. For example, suppose we know that the maximum sales for a quarter will be no more than $10,000. We can then decide to represent this quantity by a certain size bar. For example, let's say a bar that is 75 percent of the frame's height will represent $10,000. If the frame is 400 pixels in height, then the maximum sales amount will be represented by a rectangle of 300 pixels. Amounts smaller than the maximum will be represented proportionally (Fig. 10–21). This analysis suggests that we want to declare the following constants:

```java
                               // Initial Width and Height
public static final int WIDTH = 400, HEIGHT = 300;
private final int NSELLERS = 5;
private final int MAXSALES = 6000; // Max quarter sales amount
private final double SCALE = 0.75; // % of height used for max sales amount
```

The WIDTH and HEIGHT are used to set the panel's initial size (Fig. 10–22). The other constants are used to control the size of the bar chart.

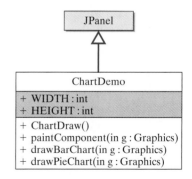

FIGURE 10–20   Basic features of the ChartDemo class, which contains methods to draw a bar chart and a pie chart.

Scaling a shape

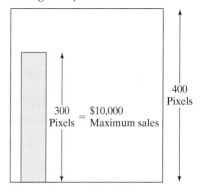

$$\frac{300\ \text{Pixels}}{} = \frac{\$10,000}{\text{Maximum sales}}$$

400 Pixels

FIGURE 10–21   Scaling a bar in a histogram.

```java
import java.awt.*;
import javax.swing.*;
import java.awt.event.*;
public class ChartDemo extends JPanel {

    public static final int WIDTH = 400, HEIGHT = 300; // Initial Width and Height
    private final int NSELLERS = 5;
    private final int MAXSALES = 6000;          // Max quarter sales amount
    private final double SCALE = 0.75;          // % of height used for maximum sales

    private double quarter1[] = {1099.85, 2105.86, 3105.25, 987.20, 5000.45};
    private double quarter2[] = {2199.85, 3105.86, 2805.25, 1500.20, 6250.95};

    public ChartDemo() {
        setSize(WIDTH, HEIGHT);
    }

    public void paintComponent( Graphics g ) {
        Dimension size = this.getSize();
        g.setColor(getBackground());
        g.fillRect(0, 0, size.width, size.height);              // Clear the panel
        g.translate(size.height / 20, size.height - size.height / 20); // Move origin to bottom left
        drawBarChart(g);
        int pieSize = Math.min(size.width, size.height) / 3;
        int barWidth = size.width / 40;
        g.translate(NSELLERS * 4 * barWidth, -pieSize);         // Move origin right and up
        drawPieChart(g, pieSize);
    } // paintComponent()

    public void drawBarChart(Graphics g) {
        Dimension size = this.getSize();
        int maxBar = (int)(SCALE * size.height);        // Size of tallest bar in histogram
        int barWidth = size.width / 40;                 // Width of bars
        int hGap = size.width / 60;                     // Gap between bars
        g.drawLine(0, 0, NSELLERS * (2 * barWidth + hGap), 0); // Draw the x-axis

        int href = 0;
        for (int k = 0; k < NSELLERS; k++ ) {           // For each seller
            int hgt = (int)(maxBar * quarter1[k] / MAXSALES); // Height of quarter1 sales
            g.setColor(Color.black);
            g.drawString( k+1 + "", href + 5, 13);      // Label the chart
            g.fillRect(href, -hgt, barWidth, hgt);
            hgt = (int)(maxBar * quarter2[k] / MAXSALES); // Height of quarter2 sales
            href += barWidth;                           // Move reference point
            g.setColor(Color.darkGray);                 // Use 2nd color
            g.fillRect(href, -hgt, barWidth, hgt);
            href += barWidth + hGap;                    // Move reference pt
        } // for
    } // drawBarChart()
```

FIGURE 10–22 ChartDemo illustrates how to draw bar charts and pie charts (Part I).

```
        private double total(double sales[]) {
            double sum = 0;
            for (int k = 0; k < NSELLERS; k++)
                sum += sales[k];
            return sum;
        } // total()

        public void drawPieChart(Graphics g, int pieSize) {
            double sumq2 = (int)total(quarter2);              // Compute total sales for qtr
            int rgb = 0;
            Color color = null;
            int startAngle = 0;
            for (int k = 0; k < NSELLERS; k++) {              // For each seller
                color = new Color(rgb, rgb, rgb);             // For grays r = g = b
                g.setColor(color);
                rgb += 32;                                    // Lighten the color
                double percent = quarter2[k] / sumq2;         // Percentage sales
                int currAngle = (int)Math.round(360 * percent); // Scale to 360 degrees
                g.fillArc(0, 0, pieSize, pieSize, startAngle, currAngle); // Draw pie slice
                startAngle += currAngle;                      // Advance start angle
            } //for
        } // drawPieChart()

        public static void main(String args[]) {
            JFrame f = new JFrame("Chart Window");
            ChartDemo chart = new ChartDemo();
            f.getContentPane().add(chart);
            f.setSize( chart.WIDTH, chart.HEIGHT );
            f.setVisible(true);
            f.addWindowListener(new WindowAdapter() {     // Quit the application
                public void windowClosing(WindowEvent e) {
                    System.exit(0);
                }
            });
        } //main()
} // ChartDemo
```

FIGURE 10–22   *(continued)* ChartDemo, Part II.

Given these quantities, each rectangle in the bar chart can be drawn relative to the size of the panel:

```
                            // Size of biggest bar in histogram
int maxBar = (int)(SCALE * size.height);
int barWidth = size.width / 40;             // Width of bar
                        // Height of quarter1 sales
int hgt = (int)(maxBar * quarter1[k] / MAXSALES);
g.fillRect(href, -hgt, barWidth, hgt);      // Draw the bar
```

This example calculates the rectangle's height for the quarter 1 sales of the *k*th seller. The height of the rectangle is proportional to the seller's quarterly sales as they compare to MAXSALES.

The drawBarChart() method, from the ChartDemo program (Fig. 10–22), draws the entire bar chart. There are several points worth noting about this method. First, the method assumes that the bar chart's origin is at its lower-left corner. The method begins by recalculating the chart's

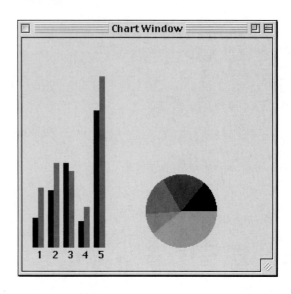

dimensions—the maxBar, barWidth, and hGap. It then draws a single horizontal line to represent the chart's *x*-axis.

Algorithm design

The drawing of the bar chart itself is handled by a for loop, which iterates through NSELLERS. For each seller, it displays a black rectangle for the quarter1 sales, and a darkGray rectangle for the quarter2 sales. Note how the color is changed within the loop, and note also how the horizontal reference point for the rectangle's location, href, is recalculated after each rectangle is drawn. Here is where we use the constant and variable quantities that we described earlier. Finally, note the statement used to paint the rectangle itself:

```
g.fillRect(href, -hgt, barWidth, hgt);
```

Given the relocated origin, the value (href,-hgt) gives the coordinates for the rectangle's top-left corner, and barWidth and hgt represent the rectangle's width and height, respectively. Figure 10–23 shows how the bar chart would appear when you run the ChartDemo program.

EFFECTIVE DESIGN: Scalability. Variables representing its location and dimensions should be used to generalize a figure's design. In addition to making the figure itself *scalable*, this strategy helps to simplify both its development and its maintainability.

10.8.2 Drawing Arcs

To draw a pie chart we will use the fillArc() method, which takes the following parameters:

```
fillArc(int x, int y, int width, int hgt, int startAngle, int arcAngle );
```

Like many other shapes, arcs are drawn within a bounding rectangle, whose top-left corner is specified by *x* and *y*, and whose width and height are specified by width and hgt. The arc itself is drawn starting at the startAngle and turning through arcAngle degrees.

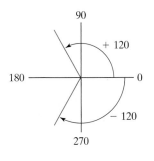

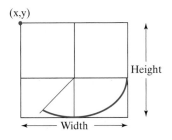

FIGURE 10–24 To draw or fill an arc, you must specify its bounding rectangle plus the starting angle of the arc and its size in degrees.

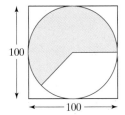

To Draw the Pie Chart
g.setColor(Color.blue);
g.fillArc(0,0,100,100,0,225);
g.setColor(Color.white);
g.fillArc(0,0,100,100,225,135);

The angles used by arcs are measured in degrees and use the coordinate system shown in Figure 10–24. Positive arcs sweep in a counterclockwise direction. Negative arcs sweep in a clockwise direction. The sample pie chart shown in Figure 10–24 was drawn with the following statements:

```
g.setColor(Color.blue);
g.fillArc(0, 0, 100, 100, 0, 225);
g.setColor(Color.white);
g.fillArc(0, 0, 100, 100, 225, 135);
```

The first pie segment has a starting angle of 0 and an arc of 225 degrees. The second segment starts where the first one left off (225 degrees) and has an arc of 135 degrees. These two segments take the entire 360 degrees of the pie (225 + 135 = 360).

Note that because the entire pie chart is contained within a bounding rectangle, the first four parameters are the same for every segment in the chart. The segments of the pie chart depend only on the values of the startAngle and arcAngle parameter. By adjusting these two parameters, we can draw all the segments of the pie chart, going in a counterclockwise direction.

Starting and reference angle

PROGRAMMING TIP: Drawing Arcs. When using fillArc(x,y,w, h,startAngle,arcAngle) to draw pie chart segments, the startAngle for each new pie segment is calculated as the sum of the previous startAngle plus the previous arcAngle. By using variables to represent these two angles, you can use a loop to draw any pie chart.

Drawing a Pie Chart

Given this background, let's design our pie chart. Again, we want to design it so that its size is proportional to the frame's size. Since a pie chart is round, we'll want an enclosing rectangle that is square—one that

Algorithm design

has the same width and height. Let's use the frame's smaller dimension to calculate the size of the pie chart:

```
int pieSize = Math.min(width, height) / 3;
```

According to this formula, the pie chart will always be approximately one-third the size of the smaller of the panel's two dimensions. Now let's position the pie chart on the frame by once again moving the origin. This time we want to move it to the right of the bar chart. Of course, the distance we move it depends on the size of the bar chart, which can be calculated as NSELLERS * 4 * barWidth:

```
                              // Move origin right and up
g.translate(NSELLERS * 4 * barWidth,-pieSize);
```

The reason we have to move the origin up by -pieSize is because the arcs we draw will be contained within a rectangle specified by its top-left corner.

Pie chart algorithm

We want to draw a pie chart showing each seller's proportion of the total quarter2 sales. If one seller sold one-third of total sales, his or her section should represent one-third of the pie chart, or 120 degrees. In order to represent a seller's percentage of total sales, we must calculate total sales for the entire quarter. This is done by the total() method. So to calculate each segment of the pie, we have to calculate the seller's percentage of total sales and then scale that value to 360 degrees. This will represent the size of the angle of that pie segment:

```
                              // Compute total sales for qtr
double sumq2 = (int)total(quarter2);
double percent = quarter2[k] / sumq2;   // Percentage sales
                              // Scale to 360 degrees
int currAngle = (int)Math.round(360 * percent);
                              // Draw pie slice
g.fillArc(0, 0, pieSize, pieSize, startAngle, currAngle);
```

Note that this algorithm uses the quarter2 sales for the *k*th seller. Thus, we can use a for loop to draw one pie segment for each seller. On each iteration of the for loop two things must change: the starting angle and the color of the pie segment. Assuming that the starting angle starts at 0, we can update it as follows on each iteration of the loop:

```
startAngle += currAngle;            // Advance the start angle
```

That is, on each iteration the starting angle simply advances in the counterclockwise direction.

Color iterations

To modify the drawing color for each pie segment, we can make use of the fact that all shades of gray have equal values for their red, green, and blue components. So one way to manage the pie chart's colors is to start with black and then increase the RGB values by a constant amount on each iteration of the loop. Thus, assuming that rgb is initialized to 0, we use the following statements within the loop:

```
color = new Color(rgb, rgb, rgb);   // For grays r = g = b
g.setColor(color);                  // Set the drawing color
rgb += 32;                          // Lighten color for next time
```

Because R = G = B, we can use one variable for all three color components, and we can simply increase its value on each iteration of the loop. The remaining details of the `drawPieChart()` method are shown in the listing of ChartDemo in Figure 10–22.

> **PROGRAMMING TIP**: Extensibility.   By using constants and variables to serve as reference points, simple algorithms can be developed to create a more general and more extensible program.

SELF-STUDY EXERCISES

EXERCISE 10.20   What do you suppose would happen if you reversed the order of the `setSize()` and `setVisible()` statements in the `main()` method in ChartDemo?

EXERCISE 10.21   What purpose does the empty string serve in this expression: `g.drawString(k+1 + "", href+5, 13)`?

10.9   Handling Text in a Graphics Context

In order to create attractive interfaces, it is often necessary to be able to select and control the font that is used. Even a simple drawing task, such as being able to center a component's label, requires that we know the font's dimensions and be able to manipulate them. In this section, we learn how to work with Java's fonts and font control methods.

Each graphics context has an associated `Font` and `FontMetrics` object, and the `Graphics` class (Fig. 10–25) provides several methods to access them. A `FontMetrics` is an object that encapsulates important data about a font, such as its height and width. Java assigns a default font to each `Graphics` object. This is the font used by the `drawString()` method. The particular font used is system dependent, but to override the default one can simply invoke the `setFont()` method:

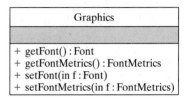

FIGURE 10–25   Methods to access the `Font` and `FontMetrics` objects associated with each `Graphics` context.

```
g.setFont(new Font("TimesRoman", Font.ITALIC, 12));
```

In this case, the `Font()` constructor is used to specify a 12-point, italicized, *TimesRoman* font. Once the font is set, it will be used in all subsequent drawings.

10.9.1   The `Font` and `FontMetrics` Classes

The `Font` class (Fig. 10–26) provides a platform-independent representation of an individual font. A font is distinguished by its name, size, and style, and the `Font` class includes `protected` instance variables for these properties, as well as a constructor method that allows these three characteristics to be specified.

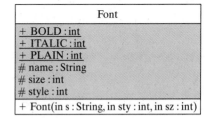

FIGURE 10–26   The `Font` class.

In Java 1.1 and later versions, the supported font names include Serif, SansSerif, Monospaced, Dialog, and DialogInput. And the supported styles include `PLAIN`, `BOLD`, `ITALIC`, and `BOLD+ITALIC`. These names and styles are platform independent. When used in a program, they are mapped to real fonts available in the host system. If the host system does not have an exact match for the specified font, it will supply a substitute. For example, if you specify a 48-point, italic, Monospaced font,

```
import java.awt.*;
import javax.swing.*;

public class FontNames extends JApplet {

    public void paint(Graphics g) {

        // Get the font names available in this graphics environment
        GraphicsEnvironment ge = GraphicsEnvironment.getLocalGraphicsEnvironment();
        String[] fonts = ge.getAvailableFontFamilyNames();

        // Display hello world and font's name in the first 10 fonts
        int vRef = 30;
        int vGap = 15;
        g.drawString("The first 10 fonts on this system are: ", 30, vRef);
        for (int k = 0; k < 10; k++) {
            vRef += vGap;
            g.setFont(new Font(fonts[k], Font.PLAIN, 12));
            g.drawString("Hello World! (" + fonts[k] + ")", 30, vRef);
        }
    } // paint()
} // FontNames
```

FIGURE 10–27   The FontNames applet.

```
Font myFont = new Font("Monospaced", Font.ITALIC, 48);
```

the system may map this to a 24-point, italic Courier font, if that's the largest fixed-spaced font available.

10.9.2   Example: The FontNames Applet

The FontNames applet (Fig. 10–27) demonstrates the use of Font class methods. The applet consists of a paint() method, which uses java.awt.GraphicsEnvironment's getAvailableFontFamilyNames() method to retrieve an array of the names of the fonts available on this system. It then draws "Hello World" plus the font's name for the first ten fonts (Fig. 10–28). Each font is displayed in PLAIN style and 12-point size. Note that this list begins with the standard Java fonts. However, the list doesn't specify what sizes and styles are available in each of these fonts. Even if a host system has the SansSerif font, it may not have the particular size requested. In that case, the system will supply a substitute.

The Font() constructor used in this example is designed to work with any set of arguments. Thus, if you supply the name of a font that is not available, the system will supply a default font as a substitute. For example, on my system, specifying a nonexistent font named Random,

```
g.setFont(new Font("Random", Font.ITALIC, 12) );
g.drawString("Hello World! (random, italic, 12)", 30, 45);
```

produces the same font used as the mapping for Dialog and DialogInput.

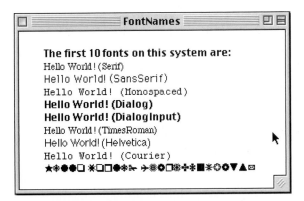

FIGURE 10–28   The names and appearance of the first ten fonts on my Macintosh. The first line is the system font. Note that some fonts with different names appear to be the same.

> **EFFECTIVE DESIGN: Font Portability.**   The fact that Font() will produce a font for virtually any set of arguments is important in ensuring that a Java program will run on any platform. This is another example of how Java has been designed for portability.

The FontNames example uses the setFont() method to set the font associated with the graphics context. All AWT and JFC components have an associated font, which can be accessed using the Component.setFont() and Component.getFont() methods. For example, the following code could be used to override a Button's font:

```
Button b = new Button("Label");
b.setFont(new Font("Times", Font.ITALIC, 14));
```

If 14-point, italic, Times font is not available on the host system, a substitute will be supplied.

SELF-STUDY EXERCISE

EXERCISE 10.22   In the FontNames applet, why is the paint() method used instead of the paintComponent() method?

10.9.3   Font Metrics

To illustrate how to use the FontMetrics class, let's write a "Hello World" application that centers its message both horizontally and vertically in its window. The message should be centered regardless of the size of the application window. Thus, we will have to position the text relative to the window size, which is something we learned in positioning geometric shapes. The message should also be centered no matter what font is used. This will require us to know certain characteristics of the font itself, such as the height and width of its characters, whether the characters have a fixed or variable width, and so on. In order to get access to these properties, we will use the FontMetrics class.

Figure 10–29 illustrates the various properties that are associated with a font. The **baseline** of a font refers to the line on which the bottom of most characters occurs. When drawing a string, the *x*- and *y*-coordinates determine the baseline of the string's first character. Thus, in

```
g.drawString("Hello World", 10, 40);
```

the bottom left of the *H* in "Hello World" would be located at (10, 40).

Problem statement

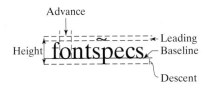

FIGURE 10–29   An illustration of the various font measurements.

FontMetrics
font : Font
FontMetrics(in font : Font)
+ charWidth(in ch : int) : int
+ charWidth(in ch : char) : int
+ getAscent() : int
+ getDescent() : int
+ getFont() : Font
+ getHeight() : int
+ getLeading() : int
+ getMaxAdvance() : int
+ getMaxDescent() : int
+ stringWidth() : int

FIGURE 10–30 The FontMetrics class.

Algorithm design: Generality

Centering text

All characters ascend some distance above the baseline. This is known as the character's **ascent**. Some characters, such as *y*, may extend below the baseline, into what's known as the *descent*. Each font has a *maximum descent*. Similarly, some characters, such as accent characters, may extend above the *maximum ascent* into a space known as the *leading*.

The *height* of a font is defined as the sum (in pixels) of the ascent, descent, and leading values. The height is a property of the font itself rather than of any individual character. Except for fixed-width fonts, in which the width of all characters is the same, the characters that make up a font have varying widths. The width of an individual character is known as its *advance*.

The FontMetrics class (Fig. 10–30) provides methods for accessing a font's properties. These can be useful to control the layout of text on a GUI. For example, when drawing multiple lines of text, the getHeight() method is useful for determining how much space should be left between lines. When drawing character by character, the charWidth() method can be used to determine how much space must be left between characters. Alternatively, the stringWidth() method can be used to determine the number of pixels required to draw the entire string.

10.9.4   Example: Centering a Line of Text

Given this background, let's take on the task of centering a message in an application window. In order for this application to work for any font, we must take care not to base its design on characteristics of the particular font that we happen to be using. To underscore this point, let's design it to work for a font named Random, which, as we noted earlier, will be mapped to some font by the system on which the application is run. In other words, we will let the system pick a font for this application's message. An interesting experiment would be to run the application on different platforms to see what fonts are chosen.

The only method we need for this application is the paint() method. Let's begin by setting the font used by the graphics context to a random font. To get the characteristics of this font, we create a FontMetrics object and get the font metrics for the font we just created:

```
g.setFont(new Font("Random", Font.BOLD, 24));
FontMetrics metrics = g.getFontMetrics();
```

The next step is to determine the JFrame's dimensions using the getSize() method, and then to use its width and height to calculate the *x*- and *y*-coordinates for the string.

In order to center the string horizontally, we need to know its width, which is supplied by the metrics object. If the JFrame is d.width pixels wide, then the following expression subtracts the width of the string from the width of the JFrame and then divides the leftover space in half:

```
                    // Calculate coordinates
int x = (d.width - metrics.stringWidth(str)) / 2;
```

Similarly, the following expression adds the height of the string to the height of the JFrame and divides the leftover space in half:

```
int y = (d.height + metrics.getHeight()) / 2;
```

```
import java.awt.*;
import javax.swing.*;

public class CenterText extends JFrame {
                            // Print hello world! in center of frame
public void paint(Graphics g) {
    String str = "Hello World!";
    g.setFont(new Font("Random", Font.PLAIN, 24));   // Create a random font
    FontMetrics metrics = g.getFontMetrics();        //  And get its metrics

    Dimension d = getSize();                          // Get the frame's size
                // Clear the frame
    g.setColor(getBackground());
    g.fillRect(0,0,d.width,d.height);
    g.setColor(Color.black);
    int x = (d.width - metrics.stringWidth(str)) / 2; // Calculate coordinates
    int y = (d.height + metrics.getHeight()) / 2;

    g.drawString( str, x, y );                        // Draw the string
} // paint()

public static void main(String args[]) {
    CenterText ct = new CenterText();
    ct.setSize(400,400);
    ct.setVisible(true);
}
} // CenterText
```

FIGURE 10–31   The CenterText application.

FIGURE 10–32   The CenterText application keeps its message centered no matter how its window is resized.

Taken together, these calculations give the coordinates for the lower left pixel of the first character in "Hello World!" The only remaining task is to draw the string (Fig. 10–31). Because the paint() method is called automatically whenever the JFrame is resized, this application, whose output is shown in Figure 10–32, will recenter its message whenever it is resized by the user.

PROGRAMMING TIP: Generality.   By using a component's size and font as the determining factors, you can center text on virtually any component. These values are available via the component's getFont() and getSize() methods.

SELF-STUDY EXERCISE

EXERCISE 10.23   Modify the FontNames application so that for each of the first ten fonts, a random font size is chosen between 10 and 24 point. Use the `FontMetrics.height` value to provide the appropriate spacing for each line of output. Also modify the algorithm so that each line of output is horizontally centered.

10.10   CASE STUDY: Interactive Drawing

In all of our drawing examples so far, the drawing has been done by the program. What if we want to enable the user to draw? In order to support drawing by the user, or interactive drawing, we need to learn how to control the mouse. As you would expect, mouse control is exerted by handling the various kinds of mouse-related events that can occur.

10.10.1   Handling Mouse Events

There are two types of mouse events: **mouse events** and **mouse motion events**. Each type is handled by its own listener interface. The MouseMotionListener handles mouse events that involve motion (Fig. 10–33). The mouse is said to be "dragged" if it is moved while one of its buttons is held down. It is "moved" when it is moved without holding any button down.

The MouseListener interface (Fig. 10–34) handles mouse events. As the names of the methods suggest, mouse events occur when the mouse is clicked and when the mouse enters or exits a GUI component. The `mousePressed()` and `mouseReleased()` methods are called when the user has pressed and released one of the mouse buttons. The `mouseClicked()` method is called when the user has pressed and released a mouse button without any intervening mouse drag—that is, the pressing and releasing of the button occurred while the mouse was at the same location.

Obviously, a mouse clicked and mouse released event can be generated by the same user action. We will see examples that help us decide which event is significant within a given context.

10.10.2   An Interactive Painting Program

To illustrate how both interfaces are used, let's develop a simple interactive painting application. You've probably used this type of program. It lets the user draw letters or pictures by dragging the mouse within a drawing area. Our simple version will let the user (1) draw within a drawing region by dragging the mouse, and (2) clear the drawing area by clicking within a certain area of the screen.

10.10.3   GUI Design

In order to define the drawing area, we can draw a large red square on the screen. When the user drags the mouse within this area, the program will paint a dot at the mouse's current location. In order to make the drawing area stand out from the rest of the screen, let's indent it by 10 or 20 pixels from the edge of the screen.

One way to indicate the "clear screen" action is to have the user click within a rectangular area that's located in the frame's top-left corner. To help define this area, let's fill this rectangle with red. Finally, to help orient the user, let's draw a string at the very bottom of the screen, outside the drawing area, which gives some simple directions. Figure 10–35 shows the details of this GUI design.

«interface»
MouseMotionListener
+ *mouseDragged(in e : MouseEvent)*
+ *mouseMoved(in e : MouseEvent)*

FIGURE 10–33   The MouseMotionListener interface.

«interface»
MouseListener
+ *mouseClicked(in e : MouseEvent)*
+ *mouseEntered(in e : MouseEvent)*
+ *mouseExited(in e : MouseEvent)*
+ *mousePressed(in e : MouseEvent)*
+ *mouseReleased(in e : MouseEvent)*

FIGURE 10–34   The MouseListener interface.

Problem statement

Mouse-based user control

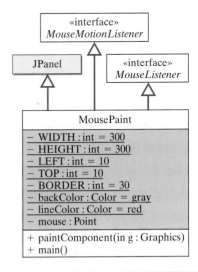

10.10.4   Problem Decomposition: The MousePaint Class

This program is simple enough to implement with a single class, the MousePaint class (Fig. 10–36). As in our other application, this class should be a subclass of JPanel. An instance of this class will be added to the application's top-level JFrame. Because it will handle mouse events, this class must implement both the MouseListener and MouseMotionListener interfaces. In fact, designing these interface methods will be one of the main challenges in developing this program.

What classes do we need?

The main thing we'll have to keep track of in this program is the location of the mouse. That's how we'll decide what the user wants to do. If the user clicks on the mouse while it is at the top left of the rectangle, the program should clear the drawing area. If the user drags the mouse within the drawing area, the program should draw. We'll need a Point object to keep track of the mouse's coordinates.

What data do we need?

There are a couple of things that won't change during this program. One constant is the color of the rectangles that define the drawing area and the clear area. A second constant is the color used for drawing. These should be defined as final variables and placed at the beginning of the program, so that they can easily be changed if you decide to change the color scheme. Another thing that won't change is the location of the clear rectangle. Therefore, let's use constants to define its location. Even if the user changes the window's size, the location of this rectangle will remain fixed.

10.10.5   Algorithm: Handling Mouse Events

Because this JPanel implements both the MouseListener and MouseMotion-Listener interfaces, it must implement a total of seven methods. However, most of the methods won't really be used, so their bodies can be left empty. Which methods are these?

FIGURE 10–36   The overall design of the MousePaint program.

What methods do we need?

First, with respect to the mouse's motion, we only care about when the user drags the mouse, so we only need to implement the `mouseDragged()` method from the `MouseMotionListener` interface. Second, with respect to the other mouse actions, we only care about when the user clicks within the "clear" rectangle. To handle this event, we only need to implement the `mouseClicked()` method from the `MouseListener` interface. That means we can leave the bodies empty for the following five methods:

```
public void mouseEntered(MouseEvent e) { } // These five interface
public void mouseExited(MouseEvent e)  { } //  methods are not used
public void mousePressed(MouseEvent e) { } //  but must be defined
public void mouseReleased(MouseEvent e){ } //  anyway
public void mouseMoved(MouseEvent e)   { }
```

Method design?

Let's now design the `mouseClicked()` and `mouseDragged()` methods. What should these methods do? Actually, their tasks are quite simple. All they need to do is keep track of the mouse's location and repaint the screen every time one of these events occurs. The `paintComponent()` method can handle the decision as to where the mouse was clicked and dragged. If it was clicked within the "clear" rectangle, then the drawing area should be cleared. If it was dragged within the drawing area, the drawing should be shown.

The mouse's coordinates are stored as part of the `MouseEvent` whenever an event occurs. The `getPoint()` method can be used to retrieve them:

```
public void mouseDragged(MouseEvent e) {   // When the mouse is dragged
    mouse = e.getPoint();                   //  get its coordinates
    repaint();
}

public void mouseClicked(MouseEvent e) {   // When mouse is clicked
    mouse = e.getPoint();                   //  get its coordinates
    repaint();
}
```

As you can see, the implementations for both of these methods are the same: Just record the mouse's location and repaint the panel.

10.10.6   Algorithm: The `paintComponent()` Method

The `paintComponent()` method creates the layout for the user interface and handles all of the drawing and clearing actions. First, `paintComponent()` gets the `JPanel`'s dimensions. It then uses these values to draw the interface, including the instructions to the user:

```
Dimension d = getSize();
g.setColor(lineColor);
g.fillRect(0, 0, LEFT, TOP);             // The clear rectangle
                                         // The drawing area
g.drawRect(LEFT, TOP, d.width - BORDER, d.height - BORDER);
g.drawString("Drag to draw; Click the red rectangle to clear.",
                                LEFT, d.height - 5);
g.setColor(Color.black);                 // Set drawing color
```

Note that the "clear" rectangle is located at the top left of the screen. Its location is not dependent on the panel's size. However, the drawing area rectangle and the instructions at the very bottom of the screen are based on the panel's dimensions. Note that a fixed BORDER is used around the drawing area.

Once the fixed part of the interface is drawn, the paintComponent() method can handle any drawing or clearing that needs to be done:

```
if ((mouse.x > LEFT) && (mouse.x < LEFT + d.width - BORDER)
                    && (mouse.y > TOP)
                    && (mouse.y < TOP + d.height - BORDER))
    g.fillRect(mouse.x, mouse.y, 3, 3);

                    // If clicked at top left clear the drawing
if ((mouse.x < LEFT) && (mouse.y < TOP))
    g.clearRect(LEFT + 1, TOP + 1, d.width - BORDER - 1,
                                d.height - BORDER - 1);
```

Note the expressions used in these conditions. They depend on the panel's dimensions, as stored in d.width and d.height, as well as the mouse's current coordinates, as stored in mouse.x and mouse.y. The first if statement checks whether the mouse is in the drawing area. If so, it draws a small, 3×3 rectangle at the current location. This is the drawing action. It takes place when the user drags the mouse.

The mouse's location determines the program's action

The second if statement checks whether the mouse is in the "clear" rectangle. If so, it clears a rectangular area that is 1 pixel smaller all around than the drawing area itself. The complete implementation of MousePaint is shown in Figure 10–37.

```
import javax.swing.*;
import java.awt.*;
import java.awt.event.*;

public class MousePaint extends JPanel implements MouseListener,
                                            MouseMotionListener {

    private static final int WIDTH = 300, HEIGHT = 300; // Initial size
    private static final int LEFT = 10;                 // Reference points
    private static final int TOP = 10;
    private static final int BORDER = 30;

    private static final Color backColor = Color.gray;  // Background color
    private static final Color lineColor = Color.red;   // Outline color

    private Point mouse = new Point();                   // Mouse's current location
    public MousePaint() {
        addMouseMotionListener(this);    // Add mouse and mouse motion listeners
        addMouseListener(this);
        setSize(WIDTH, HEIGHT);
    } // MousePaint()
```

FIGURE 10–37 The MousePaint application, Part I.

```
    public void paintComponent(Graphics g) {
        Dimension d = getSize();
        g.setColor(lineColor);
        g.fillRect(0, 0, LEFT, TOP);                          // The clear rectangle
        g.drawRect(LEFT, TOP, d.width - BORDER, d.height - BORDER); // The drawing area
        g.drawString("Drag to draw; Click the red rectangle to clear.", LEFT, d.height - 5);
        g.setColor(Color.black);                              // Set drawing color

                // If the mouse is within the drawing area, draw a dot
        if ((mouse.x > LEFT) && (mouse.x < LEFT + d.width - BORDER)
                    && (mouse.y > TOP) && (mouse.y < TOP + d.height - BORDER))
            g.fillRect(mouse.x, mouse.y, 3, 3);

                // If the mouse is clicked at top left corner clear the drawing
        if ((mouse.x < LEFT) && (mouse.y < TOP))
            g.clearRect(LEFT + 1, TOP + 1, d.width - BORDER - 1, d.height - BORDER - 1);
    } // paintComponent()

/* Mouse Handling Interfaces:   MouseMotionListener and MouseListener */

    public void mouseDragged(MouseEvent e) {  // When the mouse is dragged (mouse motion listener)
        mouse = e.getPoint();                 //  get its coordinates
        repaint();
    }

    public void mouseClicked(MouseEvent e) {  // When mouse is clicked (mouse listener)
        mouse = e.getPoint();                 //  get its coordinates
        repaint();
    }
    public void mouseEntered(MouseEvent e) { } // These five interface methods are not used
    public void mouseExited(MouseEvent e)  { } //  but must be defined.
    public void mousePressed(MouseEvent e) { }
    public void mouseReleased(MouseEvent e){ }
    public void mouseMoved(MouseEvent e)   { }

    public static void main(String args[]) {
        JFrame f = new JFrame("Drawing Window");  // Create the top-level window
        MousePaint mp = new MousePaint();         // And give it a drawing panel
        f.getContentPane().add(mp);
        f.setSize(mp.WIDTH, mp.HEIGHT);
        f.setVisible(true);
        f.addWindowListener(new WindowAdapter() {     // Quit the application
            public void windowClosing(WindowEvent e) {
                System.exit(0);
            }
        });
    } // main()
} // MousePaint
```

FIGURE 10–37 *(continued)* MousePaint, Part II.

DEBUGGING TIP: Swing Versus AWT. If a JApplet or JFrame is used as a drawing canvas, it would be necessary to override Java's default definition of the update() method. Because JApplet and JFrame are subclasses of the AWT Component class, the update() method would be called automatically after each mouse event, and it would clear the window. The following implementation will do the trick:

```
public void update(){}
```

OBJECT-ORIENTED DESIGN:
The Scalable CyberPet

The various drawing examples that we have looked at have illustrated the importance of using reference points and reference values to orient and organize the drawing. Thus, in the ColorPicker and ShapeDemo examples, we used constants and variables to serve as the reference points and dimensions of the various objects that were displayed. In the Graph and Chart-Demo programs, in addition to using constants and variables to design the layout, we changed the location of the origin to help simplify the calculation of the graphs and charts. Also, by making the layout dependent on the dimensions of the main screen, we were able to scale the size of the graphs and charts to the size of the screen. Thus, the examples illustrate an important principle that applies not only to designing drawings, but also more broadly to designing any object or method.

EFFECTIVE DESIGN: Generality and Extensibility. Objects and methods should be designed to be as general and as extensible as possible.

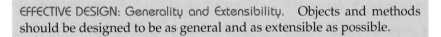

To underscore this point, let's design a version of our CyberPet that permits members of its subclasses to be drawn in a variety of ways at a wide range of scales. In other words, we want a design that will easily allow a CyberDog or a CyberCat to be drawn. Moreover, we want to draw the object, not just display a canned image of the object.

As we have seen in studying the Java class hierarchy, one of the best ways to design extensible objects is to use interfaces. An **interface** defines the methods that a class of objects can perform. Thus, the listener interfaces define the various kinds of events that an object can handle. If we follow this approach, then the best way to design a CyberPet that can be drawn and scaled in an endless variety of ways is to define interfaces for these drawing and scaling actions. CyberPet subclasses can then implement the interfaces to suit their unique circumstances.

Programmer-defined interfaces

An interface is more appropriate here than an abstract class, which we used in designing the Cipher classes in Chapter 7. An abstract class is appropriate when there's a certain amount of basic behavior that should be inherited by its subclasses. Thus, the Caesar and Transpose subclasses of Cipher both implemented the abstract encode() and decode() methods but inherited the encrypt() and decrypt() methods from Cipher. In this case, however, there's no way to inherit drawing behavior. Each type of pet will have to have its own drawing and scaling routines. That's why we want to use an interface.

EFFECTIVE DESIGN: Interfaces Versus Abstract Classes. An interface should be used to implement a set of well-defined behaviors. An abstract superclass should be used when its subclasses must all inherit some shared behavior or state.

Thus, to define a `CyberPet` that can be drawn, we'll define a `Drawable` interface. To define a `CyberPet` that can change size, we'll define a `Scalable` interface. Once we define these interfaces, they can be attached to (implemented by) any class of objects. For example, if we needed a button that would change its size depending on the size of its frame, we could define a scalable button as

```
public class ScalableButton extends Button implements Scalable ;
```

A `Drawable` *Interface*

What methods do we need?

In some sense, defining a `Drawable` interface is a matter of defining what it means to draw an object. The `Drawable` interface must define, but not implement, those methods that would be used to draw an object. Most of the shapes that we have drawn have used either draw or fill methods to represent the object. For example, we used `drawRect()`, `fillRect()`, `drawOval()`, and `fillOval()`. Therefore, let's conclude that in order to draw any object, you must implement either a draw method, a fill method, or both. This gives us the following definition for `Drawable`:

```
import java.awt.*;

/**
 *   The Drawable interface defines two methods used for drawing
 *    graphical objects, the draw() and fill() methods.
 */
public interface Drawable {
    public abstract void draw(Graphics g);
    public abstract void fill(Graphics g);
} // Drawable
```

Note that both methods take a reference to a graphics context, which will usually be the context of the applet or application within which the drawing is done. Note also that no coordinates are supplied as parameters. This assumes that an object that implements this interface knows its own location, so, when a drawable `CyberPet` is created, we will have to give it location variables.

A `Scalable` *Interface*

The `Scalable` interface is just as simple to define. By *scalable* we mean that an object can be enlarged or reduced in size without affecting its overall proportions. Thus, if the `CyberPet`'s head is approximately one-third the height of its whole body, it should retain these proportions when it is enlarged or reduced.

What methods do we need?

We could have a method to enlarge and a method to reduce. Both of these methods would require some kind of parameter to indicate the amount of enlargement or reduction. For example, we might want to enlarge by doubling or tripling the size, or reduce by halving the size. A good candidate for the type of this parameter would be `double`, as that would provide the most flexibility in terms of scaling an object.

If we define both enlarge and reduce, what will be meant by `enlarge (0.5)` and `enlarge(1.5)`? Or by `reduce(0.5)` or `reduce(1.5)`? These seem somewhat confusing, because enlarging by 0.5 suggests reducing the size of the object. Therefore, let's dispense with these method names and just use a single method, `scale()`, to either reduce or enlarge an object:

```
/**
 *  The Scalable interface defines the scale() method, which
 *   is used to resize graphical objects.
 */
import java.awt.*;

public interface Scalable {
    public abstract void scale(double ratio);
}//Scalable
```

Thus, `scale(0.5)` will mean to cut the size in half, and `scale(1.5)` will mean to increase the size by 50 percent.

The `DrawableCyberPet` Class

To create a drawable, scalable CyberPet, we will define a subclass of the `CyberPet` class defined in Figure 5–14. You may want to consult that definition now. This class will implement both the `Drawable` and `Scalable` interfaces. Also, as we noted, the drawable pet will need to have a location and a size. This leads to the preliminary design shown in Figure 10–38. Note that the class's instance variables, `size` and `location`, are declared `protected`. This makes it possible for subclasses of `DrawablePet` to inherit them.

There are two basic reference variables used in this design. The `size` variable refers to the vertical radius of the head. All of the other dimensions of the pet's body will be defined as a factor of this one variable. The `location` variable will refer to the top-left corner of the rectangle enclosing

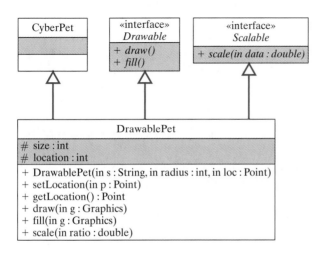

FIGURE 10–38 Design of the `DrawablePet` class.

the head. In addition to the instance variables, we've defined a constructor method and two public access methods for getting and setting the pet's location.

EFFECTIVE DESIGN: Multiple Inheritance. Java interfaces provide a limited and controlled form of **multiple inheritance**. A class that extends a superclass and implements one or more interfaces inherits methods from all of those sources. Because interfaces cannot contain instance variables, they cannot conflict with any of the superclass's state variables.

Multiple inheritance

Multiple inheritance is a mechanism that allows a class to inherit elements from two or more unrelated superclasses. For example, if class A and class B are not related—neither is a subclass of the other—multiple inheritance would occur if class C could extend both A and B. Languages such as C++ support full-fledged multiple inheritance. In C++, unlike in Java, a subclass can inherit not only methods but also instance variables from two or more unrelated superclasses. This can sometimes cause problems if the instance variables conflict in some way. For example, suppose both A and B have an instance variable named size. This could pose all kinds of potential problems for class C. Java avoids these kinds of problems by only allowing multiple inheritance of methods (via interfaces). Many language designers think that this restricted form of multiple inheritance is a good feature of the language.

Drawing the CyberPet

Let's now design an image that looks something like a spider. Before you can write methods to draw a figure, you need to do some planning. Figure 10–39 shows our plan for the drawing.

FIGURE 10–39 A plan for the drawing of the spider. The variable r in this plan corresponds to the size variable in the program.

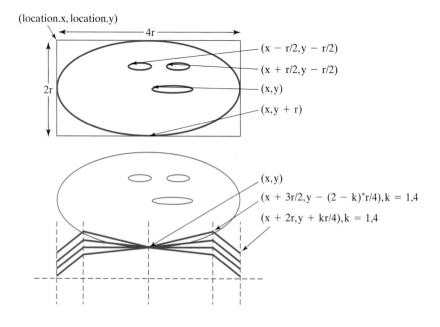

The spider's head is an oval whose width is four times the `size` variable and whose height is twice the `size` variable. The `location` variable defines the top-left corner of its enclosing rectangle. This is the point that will be used to draw the outline of the head.

Design: Find a good reference point

To draw the spider's face, it will be easier if we use the center of the oval *(x,y)* as a reference point. It is easier to position the eyes at certain displacement above and to the left and right of *(x,y)* than it would be with respect to `location`. Also, it is important that the size and location of the eyes be computed as a factor of the `size` variable rather than as some absolute value. This will enable the `CyberPet`'s face to scale properly when it is resized. Because all the facial components are determined relative to *(x,y)*, we can easily design a `drawFace(x,y)`, where (x,y) is the location of the center of the face.

Similarly, note how the legs are designed. All eight legs start at a common point located at (`location.x + 2r`, `location.y + 2r`)—relative to the spider's overall location. However, rather than use the `location` variable as their reference point, the legs will be much easier to draw if we use their common starting point as the reference. Let's call this point *(x,y)*, but note that it is not the same *(x,y)* that we used as the reference point for the face. We can do this because we will use separate methods, each with their local *(x,y)* reference point, to draw the face and the legs. Thus, we can define a method, `drawJointedLegs(x,y)`, where (x,y) defines the starting point of all eight legs. Everything within the method will be measured relative to this point.

Design: Pick a suitable reference point

Each leg contains a knee joint, so we will need two `drawLine()` statements of the following form to draw each leg:

```
g.drawLine(x, y, x1, y1);
g.drawLine(x1, y1, x2, y2);
```

How can we calculate the three points, (x,y), (x1,y1), and (x2,y2)? Let's break this problem up into two parts: the horizontal (*x*) and the vertical (*y*) coordinates for each leg. Because the left and right sets of legs are symmetrical, we'll limit our discussion to the right set.

Use symmetry to simplify things

For the horizontal coordinates, note in Figure 10–39 that all the knee joints have the same *x*-coordinate, and all the leg ends have the same *x*-coordinate. The joints are displaced by $\frac{3}{2}$ of a radius to the right of the reference point, *(x,y)*, and the leg ends are displaced by two radii to the right of the reference point. If *r* represents the radius, we get the following equations for the *x*-coordinates of the right legs:

```
x1 = x + 3r/2
x2 = x + 2r
```

TABLE 10.3 Values used to calculate the spider's legs. The values represent the *displacements* of the *y*-coordinate from leg's *(x,y)* reference point.

Leg	Knee joint	End of Leg
1	-r/4	r/4
2	0	2r/4
3	r/4	3r/4
4	r/2	r

For the vertical coordinates, we want to find a similar regularity. Notice that the *y*-coordinates of the legs are evenly spaced. Thus, we can represent the *y*-coordinates by some proportion of *r* from the reference point *(x,y)*. If you measure the distance between the legs, you'll find that they are separated by *r/4*. However, notice that the knee joint for the first leg is above the reference point by *r/4*, while the end of its leg is below the reference point by *r/4*.

Look for regularities

This suggests that the values shown in Table 10.3 can be used for the displacements of the *y*-coordinates from the reference point *(x,y)*. So, the *y*-coordinate of the first leg's knee joint will be $y - r/4$ and the *y*-coordinate of the end of that leg will be $y + r/4$. Note that as you move down the rows of the table, you are just adding $r/4$ to the value in the previous row.

Assuming that *k* is the leg number, the preceding table of values leads to the following formulas for the *y*-coordinates of the knee joint and end of leg:

```
y2 = y - (2 - k) * size / 4  // Knee joint
y3 = y + k       * size / 4  // End of leg
```

Because we can easily express these formulas in terms of *k*, we will be able to use a for loop to draw the legs.

 EFFECTIVE DESIGN: Exploiting Regularities. To simplify drawing of complex figures, it is helpful to look for symmetries and other regularities that can be incorporated into the design. These serve to make the design more general and more extensible.

The Drawing Methods

Our design considerations translate easily into the drawing methods shown in Figure 10–40. There are several points to note about the program.

```java
import java.awt.*;

public class DrawablePet extends CyberPet implements Drawable, Scalable {

    protected int size = 30;    // Default size = vertical radius of head
    protected Point location;   // Top-left corner of head
    protected Color color;

    public DrawablePet(String s, int radius, Point loc, Color c) {
        super(s);
        size = radius;
        location = loc;
        color = c;
    } // DrawablePet

    public void setLocation(Point p) {
        location = p;
    }
    public Point getLocation() {
        return location;
    }

    public void draw(Graphics g){
        g.drawOval(location.x, location.y, 4 * size, 2 * size);        // Draw the head
        drawFace(g, location.x + 2 * size, location.y + size);
        drawJointedLegs(g, location.x + 2 * size, location.y + 2 * size, size / 12);
    } // draw()
```

FIGURE 10–40   The DrawablePet class, Part I.

```
    // x,y gives center of the head
    private void drawFace(Graphics g, int x, int y) {
        g.drawOval(x, y, size, size / 2);                        //Mouth
        g.drawOval(x - size / 2, y - size / 2, size / 2, size / 3); //Eye
        g.drawOval(x + size / 2, y - size / 2, size / 2, size / 3); //Eye
    } // drawFace()

    private void drawJointedLegs(Graphics g, int x, int y, int lineWidth) {
        int x1 = x - 2 * size;
        int x2 = x - 3 * size / 2;
        int x3 = x + 3 * size / 2;
        int x4 = x + 2 * size;
        for (int j = 0; j < lineWidth; j++) {   // Loop to control width of legs
            for (int k = 1; k <= 4; k++) {       // Draw 4 left, right pairs of legs
                int y2 = y - (2 - k) * size / 4;
                int y3 = y + k * size / 4;
                g.drawLine(x, y, x2, y2);                   //Left leg
                g.drawLine(x2, y2, x1, y3);
                g.drawLine(x, y, x3, y2);                   //Right leg
                g.drawLine(x3, y2, x4, y3);
            }
            y++;                                 // Redraw line 1 pixel off to give width
        }
    } // drawJointedLegs()

    public void fill(Graphics g) {
        g.setColor( color );
        g.fillOval(location.x, location.y, 4 * size, 2 * size);
        fillFace(g, location.x + 2 * size, location.y + size);
    } // fill()

    private void fillFace(Graphics g, int x, int y) {
        g.setColor(Color.white);
        g.fillOval(x, y, size, size / 2);                        //Mouth
        g.fillOval(x - size / 2, y - size / 2, size / 2, size / 3); //Eye
        g.fillOval(x + size / 2, y - size / 2, size / 2, size / 3); //Eye
        g.setColor(Color.black);
    } // fillFace()

    public void scale( double ratio ){
        size = (int) (size * ratio);
    } // scale()
} // DrawablePet
```

FIGURE 10–40   *(continued)* DrawablePet, Part II.

Method decomposition

Recall that in order to implement the Drawable interface, we just implement the draw() method. If you look at that method, you will see that the drawing task has been broken down into three subtasks: drawing the head, drawing the face, and drawing the legs. The first subtask is handled by simply drawing an oval for the outline of the head at (location.x, location.y). The second is encapsulated in the drawFace() method, which uses the center of the head as its reference point. The third is encapsulated in the drawJointedLegs() method, which uses the base of the legs as its reference point. We saw earlier how the use of reference points simplifies the design of the drawing. In the same way, the use of parameters simplifies the design of the corresponding methods.

In terms of the details of the methods, the drawFace() method simply draws three ovals for the mouth and the two eyes. The mouth is one-half the size variable, whereas the eyes are one-third of size. So all of the facial features are proportional to size.

Loops can exploit regularities

As we described earlier, the drawJointedLegs() method uses the reference point (x,y) and the size to position and proportion the legs. Note the use of the for loop to draw the four legs. The only new feature added here is that a second for loop is used to give some width to the legs. Instead of using a single, one-pixel line for each leg, we draw several lines for each leg, each one displaced by one pixel in its y-coordinate:

```
for (int j = 0; j < lineWidth; j++) {   // Loop to control width of legs
    ...                 // Draw the four legs
    y++;                // Move the y-coordinate down by 1 pixel
}
```

As all other dimensions of our drawing, the width of the legs must also be made proportional to the size of the figure. Thus, when we call the drawJointedLegs() method, we pass it size/12 as the lineWidth argument. The smaller the spider, the skinnier its legs will be!

The implementation of the fill() method and the corresponding fillFace() method are nearly identical to draw() and drawFace(). The major difference is that the fill methods use the fillOval() method instead of drawOval(). They also set the graphic context's color, based on the pet's color scheme.

Finally, in order to implement the Scalable interface, we must implement the scale() method. Given the way we've designed our drawing methods, this method need only change the pet's size variable by the desired ratio:

```
public void scale( double ratio ){
    size = (int)(size * ratio);
}
```

EFFECTIVE DESIGN: Scalability. A scalable object is one whose dimensions are defined relative to one or more variables. By changing the value of the variables, you change the dimensions of the the object.

```
import java.awt.*;
import javax.swing.*;

public class DrawablePetApplet extends JApplet {

    private DrawablePet pet;

    public void init() {
        setSize(400,400);
    }

    public void paint(Graphics g) {
        pet = new DrawablePet("Spidey", 60, new Point(50,10), Color.green);
        pet.sleep();
        pet.setLocation(new Point(50, 10));
        pet.draw(g);
        pet.fill(g);
        pet.scale(0.5);
        pet.eat();
        pet.setLocation(new Point(100, 200));
        pet.draw(g);
        pet.scale(0.5);
        pet.setLocation(new Point(300, 200));
        pet.draw(g);
    }
} // DrawablePetApplet.java
```

FIGURE 10–41   An applet to display the scalable CyberPet.

Testing the DrawablePet

To test DrawablePet we need only draw several images at different locations and different scales, which is what the applet in Figure 10–41 does. The program's output can be seen in Figure 10–42.

One important feature of the applet is that a new DrawablePet is created in the paint() method rather than in init(). This leads to a better visual effect when the applet's window is repainted. Unless you create a new pet each time, the drawings will be reduced each time—because of the pet.scale(0.5) statements—until they are too small to see. That's the bad news. The good news is that no matter how small they get, DrawablePets maintain their proportions!

SELF-STUDY EXERCISE

EXERCISE 10.24   Modify the DrawablePet.drawFace() method so that the spider's eyes are closed a bit more when it is sleeping.

IN THE LABORATORY: The SelfPortrait Class

The purpose of this lab is to gain some hands-on experience with the design and drawing techniques discussed in this chapter. Your main task will be to design and draw a self-portrait. The objectives of the lab are

FIGURE 10–42 Output from the DrawablePet program.

FIGURE 10–43 Self-portrait of the author.

- To design a portrait of yourself that uses reference points in the same way they were used in the DrawablePet example.
- To define a SelfPortrait class that implements the Drawable and Scalable interfaces and draws your self-portrait.

Problem Description

Design a portrait of yourself that contains at least the following elements: a head, a face with eyes, nose, and mouth, a hat, some hair, and a torso wearing a sweater with your school's letter on it. A sample figure is shown in Figure 10–43. Your design for the portrait should make careful use of reference points the way we did in the DrawablePet example. Once you have developed a satisfactory design, define a SelfPortrait class and implement the Drawable and Scalable interfaces for it.

Problem Decomposition

This problem breaks down into four classes and interfaces (Fig. 10–44):

- The SelfPortrait class will contain the implementation of the Drawable and Scalable interfaces. It will be responsible for drawing the portrait.
- The Drawable interface was defined earlier and should be incorporated into your project.
- The Scalable interface was defined earlier and should be incorporated into your project.
- The PortraitApplet or PortraitFrame, neither of which is shown here, should contain the main program. It should create instances of Self-Portrait and test that they work correctly.

The SelfPortrait Class

As in the DrawablePet example, this class will need instance variables to define its size, color, and any other features that make up its internal state.

There should be an appropriate collection of public access methods for these variables—for example, the getSize() and setSize() methods.

In addition to the draw(), fill, and scale() methods, this class should contain methods to draw the major features of your portrait—for example, the face, torso, hat, and so on. Each of these methods should take a set of *x* and *y* parameters that serve as a *reference point* for that particular portion of the drawing.

Algorithm Development and Testing

Because the "correctness" of this program depends on how it looks, it is very important to develop it in a stepwise fashion. Even the most careful design on paper may not look the way you want it to when you incorporate it into your program. Also, if you get just one coordinate wrong in the program, it's very easy to end up with a completely indecipherable mess.

Therefore, test each method, line by line and statement by statement, as you develop it. For example, in drawing the face, write the code needed to draw the outline and test it. Write the code needed to draw the mouth and test it. And so on. As you add each new facial feature, run your code and see whether it looks the way you had planned it.

Documentation

Be sure to provide appropriate documentation of your final program according to the document specifications described in Appendix A.

FIGURE 10–44 Overall design of the SelfPortrait class.

CHAPTER SUMMARY

Technical Terms

ascent	histogram	pixel
baseline	interface	RGB value
Cartesian coordinates	mouse events	scalable
clip region	mouse motion events	slope-intercept form
drawing mode	multiple inheritance	XORmode
graphics context	origin	

Summary of Important Points

- Every Java component has an associated *graphics context*, an instance of the Graphics class, which provides the drawing methods used on that object.
- In Java's coordinate system, the *origin* (0,0) is located in the top left corner. Each *pixel* of the screen has an *x*- and *y-coordinate*. The *x*-coordinates increase in value from left to right and the *y*-coordinates increase in value from top to bottom. This is different from the *Cartesian coordinate* system, which you used in mathematics.
- Every graphics context has certain properties that remain fixed during drawing. These are the context's *origin, color, font, drawing mode,* and *clip region*. The Graphics object has methods that can be used to change these properties.

- Colors in Java are represented as a combination of the three primary colors, red, green, and blue (RGB). The *RGB value* for a color can be specified in its constructor. There are 13 predefined colors in the Color class, which also contains methods to brighten and darken a given color.
- A *symbolic constant* is a variable specified as final so its value cannot be changed during a program. Constants should be used to define reference points and dimensions whose values are not expected to change during drawing or painting. This is an example of the *generality principle*.
- Drawn shapes are transparent while filled shapes are colored in the current color of the graphics context. The Graphics class contains methods for drawing and filling a variety of shapes, including arcs, ovals, rectangles, lines, and polygons.
- Graphing equations is made easier by translating the default origin of the graphics context to the graph's origin, using the Graphics.translate() method, and then drawing the graph relative to the origin. Remember, however, that the *y*-axis is reversed in Java's coordinate system.
- The fillArc() method is useful for creating pie charts, which are also made simpler by translating the origin to the reference point needed for the fillArc() method.
- In order to make your drawings *scalable*, it is important to define all locations and dimensions in the drawing relative to some fixed reference point. A good way to do this is to make the reference point a parameter of the drawing method.
- The FontMetrics class is used to obtain the specific dimensions of the the various Fonts. It is useful when you wish to center text. Fonts are inherently platform dependent. For maximum portability, it is best to use default fonts.
- You can make your drawings scalable within a frame by designing their dimensions relative to the frame size.
- The MouseListener and MouseMotionListener interfaces must be implemented in any class that purports to handle mouse events. The former interface handles mouse clicks, while the latter handles mouse motion, including dragging.

SOLUTIONS TO SELF-STUDY EXERCISES

SOLUTION 10.1 The bottom-right corner would have coordinates (199,199).

SOLUTION 10.2 If the clip region is defined from (0,0) to (100,100) and the drawing is done starting at (150,150), nothing will show up because it is outside the clip region.

SOLUTION 10.3 One use of XORmode is when you want to draw a string that will span two differently colored backgrounds; for example, imagine two adjacent areas, one black and one white. If you draw a black string across both areas in XORmode, it will show up white on black and black on white.

SOLUTION 10.4 If you pick a color not supported by your monitor, Java will pick the closest color that your monitor can display.

SOLUTION 10.5   The built-in colors are defined as class constants so they can be used even when no Color instance is defined.

SOLUTION 10.6   All colors are made by mixing red, green, and blue.

SOLUTION 10.7   Each of the three color expressions is dominated by one of the three RGB values, so the resulting colors will be a shade of the primary color in each case: a shade of red (a), a shade of green (b), and a shade of blue (c).

SOLUTION 10.8   If you remove the repaint() method call from ColorPicker's actionPerformed() method, the canvas panel will never change in response to the user's actions.

SOLUTION 10.9   The JApplet's paint() method is called automatically to paint AWT components and their subclasses, of which JApplet is one. The paint-Component() method is called automatically to paint Swing JComponents and members of their subclasses.

SOLUTION 10.10

```
// A method to draw 20 3 x 3 horizontal
//   rectangles starting at HREF,VREF:

public void drawHRects(Graphics g) {
    int href = HREF;
    for (int k = 0; k < 20; k++) {
        g.drawRect(href, VREF, 3, 3);
        href += HGAP;
    }
}
```

SOLUTION 10.11

```
// A method to draw 20 3 x 3 diagonally
//   rectangles starting at HREF,VREF:

public void drawDiagonalRects(Graphics g) {
    int href = HREF;
    int vref = VREF;
    for (int k = 0; k < 20; k++) {
        g.drawRect(href, vref, 3, 3);
        href += HGAP;
        vref += VGAP;
    }
}
```

SOLUTION 10.12

```
// A method to draw 20 3 x 3 rectangles horizontal
//   starting at point p with a gap of HGAP.
public void drawHRects(Graphics g, Point p) {
    int href = p.x;
    for (int k = 0; k < 20; k++) {
        g.drawRect(href, p.y, 3, 3);
        href += HGAP;
    }
}
```

SOLUTION 10.13   The area of a JPanel with Dimension d is given by d.width * d.height.

SOLUTION 10.14   An 80×40 rectangle at (0,20): g.drawRect(0,20,80,40).

SOLUTION 10.15   To inscribe a yellow oval inside an 80×40 rectangle at (0,20): g.fillOval(0,20,80,40).

SOLUTION 10.16   The shape drawn by g.drawRoundRect(XREF,VREF, 50,50,50,50) would turn out to be a circle with diameter 50.

SOLUTION 10.17   A circle with diameter D, inside a rectangle located at XREF,YREF, can be drawn by g.drawRoundRect(XREF,YREF,D,D,D,D).

SOLUTION 10.18   After translating the origin from (0,0) by first (50,200) and then by $(-10,-150)$ would place it finally at (40,50) relative to the default origin.

SOLUTION 10.19   If you forget to set the Graph object's size in the constructor, this will affect the size of the top-level window, which by default will be 0.

SOLUTION 10.20   If you reverse the setSize() and setVisible() statements in ChartDemo.main() the window will not be properly sized. It should be sized before it is made visible.

SOLUTION 10.21   In the expression g.drawString(k+1 + "" href+5, 13) the empty string forces the + operator to be interpreted as string concatenation rather than addition. It forces k+1 to be promoted to a String.

SOLUTION 10.22   The paint() method is used in FontNames because the drawing is done on a JApplet, which is not a subclass of JComponent.

SOLUTION 10.23   The algorithm for varying the vertical line space according to the height of the font is as follows:

```
public void paint( Graphics g ) {
    String[] fonts = Toolkit.getDefaultToolkit().getFontList();
    FontMetrics metric = g.getFontMetrics();
    int fontHgt = metric.getHeight();
    int vRef = 30;
    int vGap = 2;
    g.drawString("The first 10 fonts on this system are: ", 30, vRef);
    for (int k = 0; k < 10; k++) {
        vRef += fontHgt + vGap; // Use font hgt to set vertical ref
        int fontSize = (int)(10 +  Math.random() * 15);
        g.setFont( new Font (fonts[k], Font.PLAIN, fontSize) );
        g.drawString( "Hello World! (" + fonts[k] + ")", 30, vRef );
        metric = g.getFontMetrics();   // Get font's metrics
        fontHgt = metric.getHeight();  // And its height
    }
}
```

SOLUTION 10.24

```
private void drawFace(Graphics g, int x, int y ) {
    if (state != SLEEPING) {
        g.drawOval(x, y, size, size / 2);                            //mouth
        g.drawOval(x - size / 2, y - size / 2, size / 2, size / 3); //eye
        g.drawOval(x + size / 2, y - size / 2, size / 2, size / 3); //eye
    } else {
        g.drawOval(x, y, size, size / 8);                            //mouth
        g.drawOval(x - size / 2, y - size / 2, size / 2, size / 8); //eye
        g.drawOval(x + size / 2, y - size / 2, size / 2, size / 8); //eye
    }
}
```

EXERCISE 10.1   Explain the difference between the following pairs of terms:

a. *Drawing* and *painting.*
b. *Cartesian coordinates* and *Java coordinates.*
c. An *RGB value* and a *color.*
d. A *graphics context* and a *component.*
e. *Background* and *foreground* colors.
f. An *interface* and a *class.*
g. *XORmode* and *normal mode* drawing.
h. The paint() and paintComponent() methods.
i. A *mouse event* and a *mouse motion event.*
j. A public and a protected element.
k. A private and a protected element.
l. A Font and a FontMetrics object.
m. A Dimension and a Point object.

EXERCISE 10.2   As we have discussed, when a window is reopened or resized, it is necessary to repaint it. Explain how Java uses knowledge of the window's *containment hierarchy* to repaint the window.

EXERCISE 10.3   Java interfaces give Java a limited form of *multiple inheritance.* Explain.

EXERCISE 10.4   Fill in the blanks.

a. Components that are subclassed from JComponent should use the _____ method to do their drawing.

b. A JApplet or JFrame should use the _____ method to do its drawing.

c. When a _____ component is updated, its background is not automatically cleared.

d. When a _____ component is updated, its background is automatically cleared.

e. When the mouse is clicked, this event should be handled by methods of the _____ interface.

f. When the mouse is dragged, this event should be handled by methods of the _____ interface.

EXERCISE 10.5   Write Java statements to implement the following tasks (where necessary, use *g* as a reference to the graphics context):

a. Move the default origin to a point that's displaced 50 pixels to the right and 100 pixels above the origin's current location.
b. Draw a 50 × 100 blue rectangle at location (10,10).
c. Paint a 50 × 100 magenta oval at location (100,10).
d. Paint a red circle with diameter 100 at location (200,10).
e. Draw a 50 × 100 3-D yellow rectangle at location (10,200).
f. Paint a white 50 × 100 rounded rectangle at location (100,200).
g. Paint an black 50 × 100 rounded rectangle at location (100,200).
h. Set a JPanel's size to 400 × 300.
i. Set a JPanel's foreground color to yellow and its background color to blue.

EXERCISE 10.6   Write a method that takes an array of Points and paints a 3 × 3 rectangle at each point. This should be a void method and should also take a Graphics parameter.

EXERCISES

Note: *For programming exercises,* **first** *draw a UML class diagram describing all classes and their inheritance relationships and/or associations.*

EXERCISE 10.7 One `Graphics` method that was not demonstrated in the chapter was the `drawPolygon()` method. For parameters this method takes two `int` arrays representing the *x*- and *y*-coordinates of the polygon's points. A third `int` parameter gives the number of points in the polygon. Here's an example of how this can be used:

```
int xcoords[] = {100, 50, 70, 130, 100};
int ycoords[] = {100, 150, 200, 200, 100};
g.drawPolygon(xcoords, ycoords, xcoords.length);
```

Use graph paper and a pencil to design a hexagon (six-sided figure) and an octagon (eight-sided figure). Then use `drawPolygon()` to draw their shapes in an application.

EXERCISE 10.8 Use the `drawPolygon()` and corresponding `fillPolygon()` method to draw the three-dimensional object shown in Figure 10–45. (*Hint*: Each face can be viewed as a polygon or a rectangle.)

EXERCISE 10.9 Write a method to draw a bull's-eye. This method can make good use of `g.setXORMode(Color.black)`. Here's how the method should work. Draw the outer circle of the bull's-eye. Then draw a slightly smaller circle within it, and then a slightly smaller circle within that. And so on. The method should take a `Graphics` parameter as well as parameters for the bull's-eye's location and diameter.

EXERCISE 10.10 Write a method that takes an array of `Points` and draws a line between each pair of consecutive points. This should be a `void` method and should also take a `Graphics` parameter.

EXERCISE 10.11 Design and implement a Java applet or application that draws a colored pie chart representing the relative numbers of As, Bs, Cs, Ds, and Fs in a fictitious computer science course. Allow the numbers of each grade to be input by the user.

EXERCISE 10.12 Design and implement an applet or application that draws a histogram representing the relative numbers of As, Bs, Cs, Ds, and Fs in a fictitious computer science course. Allow the numbers of each grade to be input by the user.

EXERCISE 10.13 Design and implement an applet or application that displays a multiline message in various fonts and sizes input by the user. Let the user choose from among a fixed selection of fonts, sizes, and styles.

EXERCISE 10.14 Modify the `Graph` program so the user can enter the coordinates of the linear or quadratic equations to be graphed.

EXERCISE 10.15 Design and implement a Java applet or application that draws and paints a scalable logo for a fictitious company.

EXERCISE 10.16 Design and implement an applet or application that plays the following game with the user. Draw a shape or an image on the screen and invite the user to click on it. Every time the user clicks on it, move the shape to an new random location.

EXERCISE 10.17 Modify the program in the previous exercise so that the shape moves whenever the user moves the mouse to within a certain distance of the shape.

FIGURE 10–45 Use polygons to draw this figure.

EXERCISE 10.18   Challenge: Design and implement an applet or application that plays the following game with the user. Place a puck at a random location on the screen and paint a goal in some other location. Invite the user to move the puck into the goal. Have the user's mouse-controlled stick exert a repulsive force on the image. The puck always moves away from the stick on an imaginary line originating at the stick and intersecting the puck. When the user gets the puck in the goal, draw a happy face on the screen.

EXERCISE 10.19   Create a `DrawableRectangle` subclass of the `Rectangle` class (defined in Chapter 1) that implements the `Drawable` and `Scalable` interfaces.

EXERCISE 10.20   Challenge: Add the ability to handle mouse operations to the `DrawableRectangle` class defined in the previous exercise. In other words, it should implement `MouseListener` and `MouseMotionListener`. These handlers should enable a user to pick up and move a rectangle to a new location.

EXERCISE 10.21   Challenge: Design and implement your own `Polygon` class, using an array of `Point` as the primary data structure. Use the `Drawable` interface.

EXERCISE 10.22   Challenge: Design and implement a class that creates and renders three-dimensional cubes of varying size. The class should contain a constructor that takes three parameters: length, width, and height. It should contain access methods for the cube's location, size, and color. Use the `Drawable` and `Scalable` interfaces in your design.

Photograph courtesy of Adam Crowley, PhotoDisc, Inc.

11

Exceptions: When Things Go Wrong

OBJECTIVES

After studying this chapter, you will

- Understand Java's exception-handling mechanisms.
- Be able to use the Java `try/catch` statement.
- Know how to design effective exception handlers.
- Be able to design your own `Exception` subclasses.
- Appreciate the importance that exception handling plays in program design.
- Understand the computational overhead of exception handling.

OUTLINE

11.1   Introduction

Mistakes happen. Making mistakes is the norm rather than the exception. This is not to say that we make mistakes more often than we get it right. It is to say that (almost) nothing we do or build is ever perfectly correct, least of all computer software. No matter how well designed a program is, there is always the chance that some kind of error will arise during its execution.

Exception

An **exception** is an erroneous or anomalous condition that arises while a program is running. Examples of such conditions would include attempting to divide by 0 (arithmetic exception), reading a decimal value when an integer is expected (number format exception), attempting to write to a file that doesn't exist (I/O exception), or referring to a nonexistent character in a string (index out of bounds exception). The list of potential errors and anomalies is endless.

A well-designed program should include code to guard against errors and other exceptional conditions when they arise. This code should be incorporated into the program from the very first stages of its development. That way it can help identify problems during development. In Java, the preferred way of handling such conditions is to use *exception handling*, a divide-and-conquer approach that separates a program's normal code from its error-handling code.

This chapter describes Java's exception handling features. We begin by contrasting the traditional way of handling errors within a program with Java's default exception-handling mechanism. We show how exceptions are raised (thrown) and handled (caught) within a program and identify the rules that apply to different kinds of exceptions. We then focus on some of the key design issues that govern when, where, and how to use exceptions in your programs. As a lesson in when not to use exceptions, the lab project for this chapter focuses on the computational costs of exception handling. It shows that because exceptions require a relatively high computational overhead, they should not be used to handle routine processing tasks. Instead they should be used to deal with truly exceptional circumstances.

11.2   Handling Exceptional Conditions

Figure 11–1 shows a method that computes the average of the first N integers, an admittedly contrived example. We use it mainly to illustrate the basic concepts involved in exception handling. As its precondition suggests, the avgFirstN() method expects that N will be greater than 0. If N

FIGURE 11–1   Bad design. No attempt is made to guard against a divide-by-zero error.

```
/**
 * Precondition:  N > 0
 * Postcondition: avgFirstN() equals the average of (1+2+...+N)
 */
public double avgFirstN(int N) {
    int sum = 0;
    for (int k = 1; k <= N; k++)
        sum += k;
    return sum/N;          // What if N is 0?
} // avgFirstN()
```

```
/**
 * Precondition:  N > 0
 * Postcondition: avgFirstN() equals the average of (1+2+...+N)
 */
public double avgFirstN(int N) {
    int sum = 0;
    if (N <= 0) {
      System.out.println("ERROR avgFirstN: N <= 0. Program terminating.");
      System.exit(0);
    }
    for (int k = 1; k <= N; k++)
        sum += k;
    return sum/N;            // What if N is 0?
} // avgFirstN()
```

FIGURE 11–2 One way to handle a divide-by-zero error might be to terminate the program, assuming it's the kind of program that can be safely aborted. This version does not use exceptions.

happens to be 0, an error will occur in the expression sum/N, because you cannot divide an integer by 0.

11.2.1 Traditional Error Handling

Obviously, this method should not simply ignore the possibility that N might be 0. Figure 11–2 shows a revised version of the method, which includes code that takes action if the method's precondition fails. Because there is no way to compute an average of 0 elements, the revised method decides to abort the program. Aborting the program appears to be a better alternative than returning 0 or some other default value (like -1) as the method's result and thereby allowing an erroneous value to propagate throughout the program. That would just compound the error.

Divide-by-zero error

> EFFECTIVE DESIGN: Unfixable Error.   If an unfixable error is detected, it is far better to terminate the program abnormally than to allow the error to propagate throughout the program.

The revised avgFirstN() method takes the traditional approach to error handling: Error-handling code is built right into the algorithm. If N happens to be 0 when avgFirstN() is called, the following output will be generated:

```
ERROR avgFirstN: N <= 0. Program terminating.
```

11.2.2 Java's Default Exception Handling

To help detect and handle common runtime errors, Java's creators incorporated an exception-handling model into the language itself. In the case of our divide-by-zero error, the Java Virtual Machine (JVM) would detect the error and abort the program. To see this, consider the program in Figure 11–3. Note that the avgFirstN() method is passed an argument of 0 in

FIGURE 11–3 Note that there are two public classes defined in this figure, which would be saved in separate Java files.

```java
public class CalcAverage {

    public double avgFirstN(int N) {
        int sum = 0;
        for (int k = 1; k <= N; k++)
            sum += k;
        return sum/N;          // What if N is 0?
    } // avgFirstN()
}//CalcAverage

public class CalcAvgTest {
    public static void main(String args[]) {
        CalcAverage ca = new CalcAverage();
        System.out.println( "AVG + " + ca.avgFirstN(0) );
    }//main
}//CalcAvgTest
```

the `CalcAvgTest.main()`. When the JVM detects the error, it will abort the program and print the following message:

```
Exception in thread "main" java.lang.ArithmeticException: / by zero
        at CalcAverage.avgFirstN(Compiled Code)
        at CalcAvgTest.main(CalcAvgTest.java:5)
```

The error message describes the error and provides a trace of the method calls, from last to first, that led to the error. This trace shows that the error occurred in the `CalcAverage.avgFirstN()` method, which was called by the `CalcAvgTest.main()` method.

As this example suggests, Java's default exception handling is able to detect and handle certain kinds of errors and exceptional conditions. In the next section, we will identify what kinds of conditions are handled by the JVM.

11.3 Java's Exception Hierarchy

The Java class library contains a number of predefined exceptions, some of which are shown in Figure 11–4. The most general type of exception, `java.lang.Exception`, is located in the `java.lang` package, but most of its subclasses are contained in other packages. Some of the various `IOException` classes are contained in the `java.io` package, while others are contained in the `java.net` package. In general, exception classes are placed in the package that contains the methods that throw those exceptions.

Exception hierarchy

Each of the classes in Figure 11–4 identifies a particular type of exception, and each is a subclass of the `Exception` class. Obviously a subclass defines a more specific exception than its superclass. Thus, both `ArrayIndexOutOfBoundsException` and `StringIndexOutOfBoundsException` are more specific than `IndexOutOfBoundsException`.

Table 11.1 gives a brief summary of some of the most important exceptions. You've undoubtedly encountered some of these exceptions, because they are thrown by methods we have used repeatedly in programming examples. Table 11.2 summarizes the exceptions raised by some of the methods we've used most frequently.

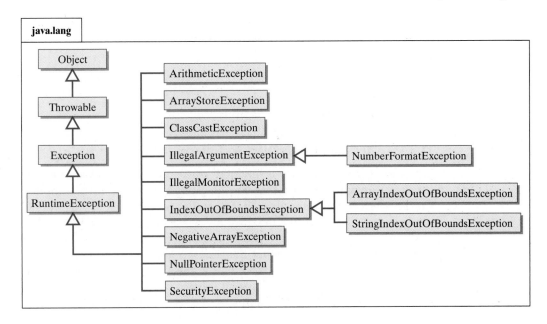

FIGURE 11–4   Part of Java's exception hierarchy. All subclasses of
RuntimeException are known as *unchecked* exceptions. Java programs are not
required to catch these exceptions.

TABLE 11.1   Some of Java's important exceptions.

Class	Description
ArithmeticException	Division by zero or some other kind of arithmetic problem
ArrayIndexOutOfBoundsException	An array index is less than zero or greater than or equal to the array's length
FileNotFoundException	Reference to a file that cannot be found
IllegalArgumentException	Calling a method with an improper argument
IndexOutOfBoundsException	An array or string index is out of bounds
NullPointerException	Reference to an object that has not been instantiated
NumberFormatException	Use of an illegal number format, such as when calling a method
StringIndexOutOfBoundsException	A String index is less than zero or greater than or equal to the String's length

TABLE 11.2   Some of Java's important exceptions by method.

Class	Method	Exception Raised	Description
Double	valueOf(String)	NumberFormatException	The String is not a double
Integer	parseInt(String)	NumberFormatException	The String is not a int
String	String(String)	NullPointerException	The String is null
	indexOf(String)	NullPointerException	The String is null
	lastIndexOf(String)	NullPointerException	The String is null
	charAt(int)	StringIndexOutOfBoundsException	The int is not a valid index
	substring(int)	StringIndexOutOfBoundsException	The int is not a valid index
	substring(int,int)	StringIndexOutOfBoundsException	An int is not a valid index

SELF-STUDY EXERCISE

EXERCISE 11.1 What type of exception would be thrown for the following statements?

a. `Integer.parseInt("26.2");`
b. `String s; s.indexOf('a');`
c. `String s = "hello"; s.charAt(5);`

11.3.1 Checked and Unchecked Exceptions

Checked exceptions

Java's exception hierarchy is divided into two types of exceptions. A **checked exception** is one that can be analyzed by the Java compiler. Checked exceptions are thrown by methods such as the `Buffered-Reader.readLine()` method, in which there is a substantial likelihood that something might go wrong. When the compiler encounters one of these method calls, it checks whether the program either handles or declares the exception. Compile-time checking for these exceptions is designed to reduce the number of exceptions that are not properly handled within a program. This is an attempt to improve the security of Java programs.

> **JAVA LANGUAGE RULE** Checked Exceptions. A checked exception, such as an IOException, must either be handled or declared within the program.

The throws *Clause*

The IOException, which we encountered in Chapter 5, is a checked exception. If you look back at Figure 5–6, you will see that its main() method called the BufferedInput.readLine()) method, which is a method that can throw an IOException:

```java
public static void main(String argv[]) throws IOException {
    BufferedReader input = new BufferedReader
            (new InputStreamReader(System.in));
    String inputString = input.readLine();    // May throw IOException
}
```

By qualifying the main() method with the expression throws IOException, we declare that we are using a method, readLine(), that might throw an exception. The Java compiler knows that readLine() is a method that can throw an IOException. If we omitted the throws declaration, the compiler would generate a syntax error. An alternative approach would be to *catch* the IOException within the main() method. We will see examples of this approach later in this and subsequent chapters.

Throwing an exception

In general, any method that contains an expression that may throw a checked exception must declare the exception. However, because one method can call another method, this can get a little tricky. If a method calls another method that contains an expression that might throw an unchecked exception, then both methods must have a throws clause. For example, consider the following program:

```
import java.io.*;
public class Example {
    BufferedReader input = new BufferedReader
            (new InputStreamReader(System.in));
    public void doRead() throws IOException {
      String inputString = input.readLine();    // May throw IOException
    }
    public static void main(String argv[]) throws IOException {
        Example ex = new Example();
        ex.doRead();
    }
}
```

In this case, the doRead() method contains a readLine() expression, which might throw an IOException. Therefore, the doRead() method must declare that it throws IOException. However, because doRead() is called by main(), the main() method must also declare the IOException.

> **JAVA LANGUAGE RULE** Where to Use throws. Unless a checked exception, such as an IOException, is caught and handled by a method, it must be declared with a throws clause within the method and within any method that calls that method.

Unchecked Exceptions

An **unchecked exception** is any exception belonging to a subclass of RuntimeException (Fig. 11–4). Unchecked exceptions are not checked by the compiler. The possibility that some statement or expression will lead to an ArithmeticException or NullPointerException is extremely difficult to detect at compile time. The designers of Java decided that forcing programmers to declare such exceptions would not significantly improve the correctness of Java programs.

Therefore, unchecked exceptions do not have to be handled within a program. And they do not have to be declared in a throws clause. As shown in the foregoing example of the divide-by-zero exception, unchecked exceptions are handled by Java's default exception handlers, unless your program takes specific steps to handle them directly. As we will see in Section 11.5, in many cases leaving the handling of such exceptions up to Java may be the best course of action.

Runtime (unchecked) exceptions

> **JAVA LANGUAGE RULE** Unchecked Exceptions. An unchecked exception—one belonging to some subclass of RunTimeException—does not have to be caught within your program.

11.3.2 The Exception Class

The java.lang.Exception class itself is very simple, consisting of just two constructor methods. (See Figure 11–5.) The Throwable class, from which Exception is derived, is the root class of Java's exception and error hierarchy. It contains definitions for the getMessage() and printStackTrace()

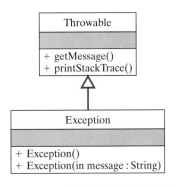

FIGURE 11–5 The java.lang.Exception class.

methods, which are two methods that we will use frequently in our error-handling routines.

SELF-STUDY EXERCISE

EXERCISE 11.2 Which of the following are examples of *unchecked* exceptions?

a. IOException
b. IndexOutOfBoundsException
c. NullPointerException
d. ClassNotFoundException
e. NumberFormatException

11.4   Handling Exceptions Within a Program

This section will describe how to handle exceptions within the program rather than leaving them to be handled by the JVM.

11.4.1   Trying, Throwing, and Catching an Exception

Pulling the program's fire alarm

In Java, errors and other abnormal conditions are handled by throwing and catching exceptions. When an error or an exceptional condition is detected, you can **throw an exception** as a way of signaling the abnormal condition. This is like pulling the fire alarm. When an exception is thrown, an **exception handler** will **catch the exception** and deal with it (Fig. 11–6).

If we go back to our avgFirstN() example, the typical way of handling this error in Java would be to *throw* an exception in the avgFirstN() method and *catch* it in the calling method. Of course, the calling method could be in the same object or it could belong to some other object. In the latter case, the detection of the error is separated from its handling. This division of labor opens up a wide range of possibilities. For example, a program could dedicate a single object to serve as the handler for all its exceptions. The object would be sort of like the program's fire department.

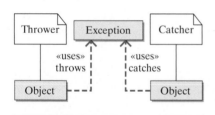

FIGURE 11–6   Exception handling. When an exception occurs, an object will throw an Exception. The exception handler, possibly the same object, will catch it.

To illustrate Java's try/throw/catch mechanism, let's revisit the CalcAvgTest program. The version shown in Figure 11–7 mimics the way Java's default exception handler works. If a divide-by-zero error occurs in the avgFirstN() method, an ArithmeticException is thrown. The exception is caught by the catch clause in the CalcAvgTest.main() method.

Let's go through this example step by step. The first thing to notice is that when the divide-by-zero error is detected, the CalcAverage.avgFirstN() method will throw an exception:

```
if (N <= 0)
    throw new ArithmeticException("ERROR: Can't average 0 elements");
```

Note the syntax of the throw statement. It creates a new ArithmeticException object and passes it a message that describes the error. This message becomes part of the exception's internal state. It can be retrieved using the getMessage() method, which is inherited from the Throwable class (Fig. 11–4).

```
public class CalcAverage {
    /**
     * Precondition:  N > 0
     * Postcondition: avgFirstN() equals the average of (1+2+...+N)
     */
    public double avgFirstN(int N) {
        int sum = 0;
        if (N <= 0)
            throw new ArithmeticException("ERROR: Can't average 0 elements");
        for (int k = 1; k <= N; k++)
            sum += k;
        return sum/N;            // What if N is 0?
    } // avgFirstN()
} // CalcAverage

public class CalcAvgTest {
    public static void main(String args[]) {
        try {
            CalcAverage ca = new CalcAverage();
            System.out.println( "AVG + " + ca.avgFirstN(0));
        }
        catch (ArithmeticException e) {          // Exception Handler
            System.out.println(e.getMessage());
            e.printStackTrace();
            System.exit(0);
        }
    }//main
}// CalcAvgTest
```

FIGURE 11–7   In this version, if an `ArithmeticException` is thrown in `CalcAverage.avgFirstN()`, it would be handled by the catch clause in `CalcAvgTest.main()`.

When a `throw` statement is executed, the JVM interrupts the normal execution of the program and searches for an exception handler. We will describe the details of this search shortly. In this case, the exception handler is the `catch` clause contained in the `CalcAvgTest.main()` method:

```
catch (ArithmeticException e) {          // Exception Handler
    System.out.println(e.getMessage());
    e.printStackTrace();
    System.exit(0);
}
```

When an `ArithmeticException` is thrown, the statements within this `catch` clause are executed. The first statement uses the `getMessage()` method to print a copy of the error message. The second statement uses the `printStackTrace()` method, which is defined in `Throwable` and inherited by all `Exceptions`, to print a trace of the method calls leading up to the exception. The last statement causes the program to terminate.

When we run this program, the following output will be generated as a result of the divide-by-zero error:

```
ERROR: Can't average 0 elements
java.lang.ArithmeticException: ERROR: Can't average 0 elements
    at java.lang.Throwable.fillInStackTrace(Native Method)
    at java.lang.Throwable.<init>(Throwable.java:94)
    at java.lang.Exception.<init>(Exception.java:42)
    at java.lang.RuntimeException.<init>(RuntimeException.java:47)
    at java.lang.ArithmeticException.<init>(ArithmeticException.java:43)
    at CalcAverage.avgFirstN(Compiled Code)
    at CalcAvgTest.main(CalcAvgTest.java:5)
```

Thus, as in the previous example of Java's default exception handler, our exception handler also prints out a description of the error and a trace of the method calls that led up to the error. However, in this example, we are directly handling the exception rather than leaving it up to Java's default exception handler. Of course, this example is intended mainly for illustrative purposes. It would make little sense to write our own exception handler if it does nothing more than mimic Java's default handler.

EFFECTIVE DESIGN: Using an Exception. Unless your program's handling of an exception is significantly different from Java's default handling of it, the program should just rely on the default.

Finally, note that the catch clause is associated with a try block. The handling of exceptions in Java takes place in two parts: First, we *try* to execute some statements, which may or may not lead to an exception. These are the statements contained within the try clause:

```
try {
    CalcAverage ca = new CalcAverage();
    System.out.println( "AVG + " + ca.avgFirstN(0));
}
```

Second, we provide one or more catch clauses to handle particular types of exceptions. In this case, we are only handling ArithmeticExceptions.

Responding to the fire alarm

As we said earlier, throwing an exception is like pulling a fire alarm. The throw occurs somewhere within the scope of the try block. The "fire department" in this case is the code contained in the catch clause that immediately follows the try block. This is the exception handler for this particular exception. There's something like a game of catch going on here: Some method within the try block throws an Exception object, which is caught and handled by the catch block located in some other object (Fig. 11–8).

11.4.2 Separating Error Checking from Error Handling

Divide and conquer

As we see in the CalcAvgTest example, an important difference between Java's exception handling and more traditional approaches is that error handling can be separated from the normal flow of execution within a program. The CalcAverage.avgFirstN() method still *checks* for the error and it still throws ArithmeticException if *N* does not satisfy the method's precondition. But it does not contain code for handling the exception. The exception-handling code is located in the CalcAvgTest class.

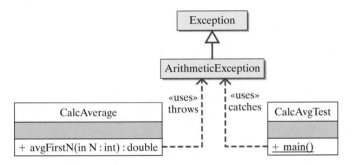

FIGURE 11–8 Playing catch: In this design, the `ArithmeticException` is thrown by the `CalcAverage.avg-FirstN()` method and caught by the catch clause within `CalcAvgTest.main()` method.

Thus, the `CalcAvgTest` program creates a clear separation between the normal algorithm and the exception-handling code. One advantage of this design is that the normal algorithm is uncluttered by error-handling code and, therefore, easier to read.

Another advantage is that the program's response to errors has been organized into one central location. By locating the exception handler in `CalcAvgTest.main()`, one exception handler can be used to handle other errors of that type. For example, this catch clause could handle *all* `Arith-meticExceptions` that get thrown in the program. Its use of `printStack-Trace()` will identify exactly where the exception occurred. In fact, because a Java application starts in the `main()` method, encapsulating all of a program's executable statements within a single `try` block in the `main()` method will effectively handle all the exceptions that occur within a program.

EFFECTIVE DESIGN: Normal Versus Exceptional Code. A key element of Java's exception-handling mechanism is that the exception handler—the catch block—is distinct from the code that throws the exception—the try block. The try block contains the normal algorithm. The catch block contains code for handling exceptional conditions.

11.4.3 Syntax and Semantics of Try/Throw/Catch

A **try block** begins with the keyword `try` followed by a block of code enclosed within curly braces. A *catch clause* or **catch block** consists of the keyword `catch`, followed by a parameter declaration that identifies the type of `Exception` being caught, followed by a collection of statements enclosed within curly braces. These are the statements that handle the exception by taking appropriate action.

The try block

The catch block

Once an exception is thrown, control is transferred out of the try block to an appropriate catch block. Control does not return to the try block.

JAVA LANGUAGE RULE Try Block Control. If an exception is thrown, the try block is exited and control does not return to it.

The complete syntax of the `try/catch` statement is summarized in Figure 11–9. The try block is meant to include a statement or statements that might throw an exception. The catch blocks—there can be one or more—are meant to handle exceptions that are thrown in the try block. A catch

FIGURE 11–9 Java's
try/throw/catch/finally
mechanism.

```
try {
    // Block of statements
    // At least one of which may throw an exception

    if ( /* Some condition obtains */ )
        throw new ExceptionName();

} catch (ExceptionName ParameterName) {
    // Block of statements to be executed
    // If the ExceptionName exception is thrown in try
} catch (ExceptionName2 ParameterName) {
    // Block of statements to be executed
    // If the ExceptionName2 exception is thrown in try

...  // Possibly other catch clauses

} finally {
    // Optional block of statements that is executed
    // Whether an exception is thrown or not
}
```

block will handle any exception that matches its parameter class, including subclasses of that class. The **finally block** is optional. It will always be executed whether an exception is thrown or not.

Normal flow of execution

The statements in the try block are part of the program's normal flow of execution. By encapsulating a group of statements within a try block, you thereby indicate that one or more exceptions may be thrown by those statements, and that you intend to catch them. In effect, you are *trying* a block of code with the possibility that something might go wrong.

Exceptional flow of execution

If an exception is thrown within a try block, Java exits the block and transfers control to the first catch block that matches the particular kind of exception that was thrown. Exceptions are thrown by using the throw statement, which takes the following general form:

```
throw new ExceptionClassName(OptionalMessageString);
```

The keyword throw is followed by the instantiation of an object of the ExceptionClassName class. This is done the same way we instantiate any object in Java: by using the new operator and invoking one of the exception's constructor methods. Some of the constructors take an OptionalMessageString, which is the message that gets returned by the exception's getMessage() method.

A catch block has the following general form:

```
catch (ExceptionClassName ParameterName) {
    // Exception handling statements
}
```

A catch block is very much like a method definition. It contains a parameter, which specifies the class of exception that is handled by that block.

The *ParameterName* can be any valid identifier, but it is customary to use e as the catch block parameter. The parameter's scope is limited to the catch block, and it is used to refer to the caught exception.

The *ExceptionClassName* must be one of the classes in Java's exception hierarchy (see Fig. 11–4). A thrown exception will match any parameter of its own class or any of its superclasses. Thus, if an ArithmeticException is thrown, it will match both an ArithmeticException parameter and an Exception parameter, because ArithmeticException is a subclass of Exception.

Exceptions are objects

Note that there can be multiple catch clauses associated with a given try block, and the order with which they are arranged is important. A thrown exception will be caught by the first catch clause it matches. Therefore, catch clauses should be arranged in order from most specific to most general. (See the exception hierarchy in Fig. 11–4.) If a more general catch clause precedes a more specific one, it will prevent the more specific one from executing. In effect, the more specific clause will be hidden by the more general one. You might as well just not have the more specific clause at all.

Arranging catch *clauses*

To illustrate how to arrange catch clauses, suppose an ArithmeticException is thrown in the following try/catch statement:

```
try {
    // Suppose an ArithmeticException is thrown here
} catch (ArithmeticException e) {
    System.out.println("ERROR: " + e.getMessage() );
    e.printStackTrace();
    System.exit(1);
} catch (Exception e) {
    System.out.println("ERROR: " + e.getMessage() );
}
```

In this case, the exception would be handled by the more specific ArithmeticException block. On the other hand, if some other kind of exception is raised, it will be caught by the second catch clause. The Exception class will match any exception that is thrown. Therefore, it should always occur last in a sequence of catch clauses.

Which handler to use?

> **PROGRAMMING TIP: Arranging Catch Clauses.** Catch clauses should be arranged from most specific to most general. The Exception clause should always be the last in the sequence.

11.4.4 Restrictions on the try/catch/finally Statement

There are several important restrictions that apply to Java's exception-handling mechanism. We'll describe these in more detail later.

- A try block must be immediately followed by one or more catch clauses and a catch clause may only follow a try block.
- A throw statement is used to throw both **checked** and **unchecked** exceptions, where unchecked exceptions are those belonging to RuntimeException or its subclasses. Unchecked exceptions need not be caught by the program.

• A throw statement must be contained within the dynamic scope of a try block, and the type of Exception thrown must match at least one of the try block's catch clauses. Or the throw statement must be contained within a method or constructor that has a throws clause for the type of thrown Exception.

JAVA LANGUAGE RULE Try/Catch Syntax. A try block must be followed immediately—with no intervening code—by one or more catch blocks. A catch block can only be preceded by a try block or by another catch block. You may not place intervening code between catch blocks.

11.4.5 Dynamic Versus Static Scoping

How does Java know that it should execute the catch clause in CalcAvg-Test.main() when an exception is thrown in avgFirstN()? Also, doesn't the latest version of avgFirstN() (Fig. 11–7) violate the restriction that a throw statement must occur within a try block?

An exception can only be thrown within a *dynamically enclosing* try block. This means that the throw statement must fall within the **dynamic scope** of an enclosing try block. Let's see what this means.

Dynamic scope

Dynamic scoping refers to the way a program is executed. For example, in CalcAverage (Fig. 11–7), the avgFirstN() method is called from within the try block located in CalcAvgTest.main(). Thus, it falls within the dynamic scope of that try block.

Static scope

Dynamic scope must be contrasted with **static scope**, which we've used previously to define the scope of parameters and local variables (Fig. 11–10). Static scoping refers to the way a program is written. A statement or variable occurs within the scope of a block if its text is actually written within that block. For example, consider the definition of MyClass (Fig. 11–11). The variable X occurs within the (static) scope of method1(), and the variable Y occurs within the (static) scope of method2().

FIGURE 11–10 Dynamic versus static scoping. Static scoping refers to how the program is written. Look at its definitions. Dynamic scoping refers to how the program executes. Look at what it actually does.

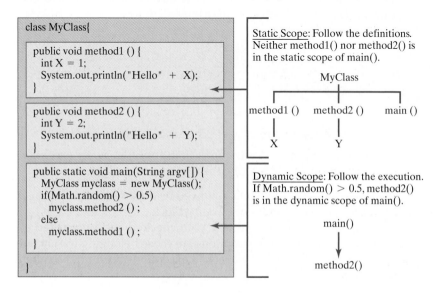

```
public class MyClass {
    public void method1() {
        int X = 1;
        System.out.println("Hello" + X);
    }
    public void method2() {
        int Y = 2;
        System.out.println("Hello" + Y);
    }
    public static void main( String argv[] ) {
        MyClass myclass = new MyClass();
        if (Math.random() > 0.5)
            myclass.method2();
        else
            myclass.method1();
    }
} // MyClass
```

FIGURE 11–11   An example of dynamic versus static scoping.

A method's parameters and local variables occur within its static scope. Also, in the `MyClass` definition, the `System.out.println()` statements occur within the static scope of `method1()` and `method2()`, respectively. In general, static scoping refers to where a variable is declared or where a statement is located. Static scoping can be completely determined by just reading the program.

Dynamic scoping can only be determined by running the program. You can't necessarily determine it by reading the program. For example, in `MyClass` the order in which its statements are executed depends on the result of `Math.random()`. Suppose that when `random()` is executed it returns the value 0.99. In that case, `main()` will call `method2()`, which will call `System.out.println()`, which will print "Hello2." In that case, the statement `System.out.println("Hello" + Y)` has the following dynamic scope:

```
main()
    method2()
        System.out.println("Hello" + Y);
```

It occurs within the (dynamic) scope of `method2()`, which is within the (dynamic) scope of `main()`. On the other hand, if the result of `random()` had been 0.10, that particular `println()` statement wouldn't have been executed at all. Thus, to determine the dynamic scope of a particular statement, you must trace the program's execution. In fact, this is what the `printStackTrace()` method does. It prints a trace of a statement's dynamic scope.

11.4.6   Exception Propagation: Searching for a Catch Block

When an exception is thrown, Java uses both static and dynamic scoping to find a catch clause to handle it. Java knows how the program is defined—after all, it compiled it. This defines the static scope of its methods. Java also places a record of every method call the program makes on a method call stack. A **method call stack** is a data structure that behaves like a stack of dishes in the cafeteria. For each method call, a *method call block* is

Method call stack

FIGURE 11–12 The method call stack for the Propagate program. The curved arrows give a trace of the method calls leading to the program's present state.

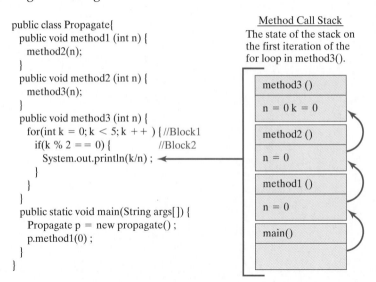

Method Call Stack
The state of the stack on the first iteration of the for loop in method3().

```
public class Propagate{
    public void method1 (int n) {
        method2(n);
    }
    public void method2 (int n) {
        method3(n);
    }
    public void method3 (int n) {
        for(int k = 0; k < 5; k ++ ) { //Block1
            if(k % 2 == 0) {              //Block2
                System.out.println(k/n) ;
            }
        }
    }
    public static void main(String args[]) {
        Propagate p = new propagate() ;
        p.method1(0) ;
    }
}
```

placed on top of the stack (like a dish), and when a particular method call returns, its block is removed from the top of the stack (Fig. 11–12).

An important feature of the method call stack is that the current executing method is always represented by the top block on the method call stack. If an exception happens during that method call, you can trace backward through the method calls, if necessary, to find an exception handler for that exception. In Figure 11–12, you can visualize this back trace as a matter of reversing the direction of the curved arrows.

In order to find a matching catch block for an exception, Java uses its knowledge of the program's static and dynamic scope to perform a **method stack trace**. The basic idea is that Java traces backward through the program until it finds an appropriate catch clause. The trace begins within the block that threw the exception. Of course, one block can be nested (statically) within another block. If the exception is not caught by the block in which it is thrown, Java searches the enclosing block. This is static scoping. If it is not caught within the enclosing block, Java searches the next higher enclosing block, and so on. This is still static scoping.

Method stack trace

If the exception is not caught at all within the method in which it was thrown, Java uses the method call stack (Fig. 11–12) to search backward through the method calls that were made leading up to the exception. This is dynamic scoping. In the case of our CalcAvgTest() example (Fig. 11–7), Java would search backward to the CalcAvgTest.main() method, which is where avgFirstN() was called, and it would find the catch clause there for handling ArithmeticExceptions. It would, therefore, execute that catch clause.

SELF-STUDY EXERCISES

EXERCISE 11.3 Suppose a program throws an ArrayIndexOutOfBounds-Exception. Using the exception hierarchy in Figure 11–4, determine which of the following catch clauses could handle that exception.

a. catch (RunTimeException e)
b. catch (StringIndexOutOfBoundsException e)
c. catch (IndexOutOfBoundsException e)

d. catch (Exception e)

e. catch (ArrayStoreException e)

EXERCISE 11.4 In the program that follows suppose that the first time random() is called it returns 0.98, and the second time it is called it returns 0.44. What output would be printed by the program?

```
class MyClass2 {
    public void method1(double X) {
        if (X > 0.95)
            throw new ArithmeticException(X + " is out of range");
        System.out.println("Hello " + X);
    }
    public void method2(double Y) {
        if (Y > 0.5)
            throw new ArithmeticException(Y + " is out of range");
        System.out.println("Hello " + Y);
    }
    public static void main(String argv[]) {
        MyClass2 myclass = new MyClass2();
        try {
            myclass.method1(Math.random());
            myclass.method2(Math.random());
        } catch (ArithmeticException e) {
            System.out.println(e.getMessage());
        }
    } // main()
} // MyClass2
```

EXERCISE 11.5 For the values returned by random() in the previous exercise, show what would be output if printStackTrace() were called in addition to printing an error message.

EXERCISE 11.6 In the MyClass2 program, suppose that the first time random() is called it returns 0.44, and the second time it is called it returns 0.98. What output would be printed by the program?

EXERCISE 11.7 For the values returned by random() in the previous exercise, show what would be output if printStackTrace() were called instead of printing an error message.

EXERCISE 11.8 Find the divide-by-zero error in the following program, and then show what stack trace would be printed by the program:

```
public class BadDivide {
    public void method1 (int n) {
        method2(100, n);
    }
    public void method2 (int n, int d) {
        System.out.println(n / d);
    }
    public static void main(String args[]) {
        BadDivide bd = new BadDivide();
        for (int k = 0; k < 5; k++)
            bd.method1(k);
    }
}
```

EXERCISE 11.9 Modify `method2()` so that it handles the divide-by-zero exception itself, instead of letting Java handle it. Have it print an error message and a stack trace.

EXERCISE 11.10 What would be printed by the following code segment if `someValue` equals 1000?

```java
int M = someValue;
try {
    System.out.println("Entering try block");
    if (M > 100)
        throw new Exception(M + " is too large");
    System.out.println("Exiting try block");
} catch (Exception e) {
    System.out.println("ERROR: " + e.getMessage());
}
```

EXERCISE 11.11 What would be printed by the code segment in the preceding question if `someValue` equals 50?

EXERCISE 11.12 Write a `try/catch` block that throws an `Exception` if the value of variable `X` is less than zero. The exception should be an instance of `Exception` and, when it is caught, the message returned by `getMessage()` should be "ERROR: Negative value in X coordinate."

11.5 Error Handling and Robust Program Design

An important element of program design is to develop appropriate ways of handling erroneous and exceptional conditions. As we have seen, the JVM will catch any unchecked exceptions that are not caught by the program itself. For your own (private) programs, the best design may simply be to use Java's default exception handling. The program will terminate when an exception is thrown, and then you can debug the error and recompile the program.

On the other hand, this strategy would be inappropriate for commercial software, which cannot be fixed by its users. A well-designed commercial program should contain exception handlers for those truly exceptional conditions that may arise.

In general there are three ways to handle an exceptional condition that isn't already handled by Java (Table 11.3). If the exceptional condition cannot be fixed, the program should be terminated, with an appropriate error message. Second, if the exceptional condition can be fixed without invali-

Let Java do it?

What action should we take?

TABLE 11.3 Exception-handling strategies.

Kind of Exception	Kind of Program	Action to Be Taken
Caught by Java		Let Java handle it
Fixable condition		Fix the error and resume execution
Unfixable condition	Stoppable	Report the error and terminate the program
Unfixable condition	Not stoppable	Report the error and resume processing

dating the program, then it should be remedied and the program's normal execution should be resumed. Third, if the exception cannot be fixed, but the program cannot be terminated, the exceptional condition should be reported or logged in some way, and the program should be resumed.

EFFECTIVE DESIGN: Handling Exceptions.   There are three general ways to handle exceptions: (1) Report the exception and terminate the program; (2) fix the exceptional condition and resume normal execution; and (3) report the exception to a log and resume execution.

11.5.1   Print a Message and Terminate

Our divide-by-zero example is a clear case where the exception is best handled by terminating the program. In fact this particular error is best left to Java's default exception handling. There is simply no way to satisfy the postcondition of the avgFirstN() method when *N* is 0. This type of error often calls attention to a design flaw in the program's logic that should be caught during program development. The throwing of the exception helps identify the design flaw.

Program development

EFFECTIVE DESIGN: Exceptions and Program Development.   Java's built-in exception handling helps identify design flaws during program development. Your own use of exceptions should follow this approach.

Similar problems can (and often do) arise in connection with errors that are not caught by Java. For example, suppose your program receives an erroneous input value, whose use would invalidate the calculation it is making. This won't be caught by Java. But it should be caught by your program, and an appropriate alternative here is to report the error and terminate the program. Fixing this type of error may involve adding routines to validate the input data before they are used in the calculation.

Don't spread bad data!

In short, rather than allowing an erroneous result to propagate throughout the program, it is best to terminate the program.

EFFECTIVE DESIGN: Report and Terminate.   If an exceptional condition is serious enough to affect the correctness or integrity of the program, then unless the error can be fixed or unless the program cannot reasonably be terminated, it is better to report the error and terminate the program rather than allowing the program to continue running with an erroneous value.

11.5.2   Log the Error and Resume

Of course, the advice to stop the program assumes that the program can *be* terminated reasonably. Some programs—such as programs that monitor the space shuttle or programs that control a nuclear magnetic resonance (NMR) machine—cannot (and should not) be terminated because of such an error.

Such *failsafe* programs are designed to run without termination. For these programs, the exception should be reported in whatever manner

Failsafe programs

Programs that can't be stopped

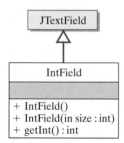

FIGURE 11–13   An `IntField` is a `JTextField` that accepts only integers.

is most appropriate, but the program should continue running. If the exceptional condition invalidates the program's computations, then the exception handler should make it clear that the results are tainted.

Other programs—such as programs that analyze a large transaction database—should be designed to continue processing after catching such errors. For example, suppose the program is one that a large airline runs, once a day, to analyze the ticketing transactions that took place. This kind of program might use exceptions to identify erroneous transactions or transactions that involve invalid data of some sort. Clearly, there's no question here of fixing the error. And because there are bound to be many errors of this kind in the database, it is not reasonable to stop the program. This kind of program shouldn't stop until it has finished processing all of the exceptions. So an appropriate action for this kind of program is to log the exceptions into some kind of file and continue processing the transactions.

Suppose a divide-by-zero error happened in one of these programs. In that case, you would override Java's default exception handling to ensure that the program is *not* terminated. More generally, it's important that these types of programs be designed to catch and report such exceptions. This type of exception handling should be built right into the program's design.

EFFECTIVE DESIGN: Report and Resume.   If an unfixable exception arises in a program that cannot be terminated reasonably, the exception should be reported and the program should continue executing.

11.5.3   Fix the Error and Resume

Problem statement

As an example of a problem that can be fixed, consider the task of inputting an integer into a text field. As you have probably experienced, if the program is expecting an integer and you attempt to input something beside an integer, this will generate a `NumberFormatException` and the program will terminate. For example, if you attempt to input "$55" when prompted to input an integer dollar amount, this will generate an exception when the `Integer.parseInt()` method is invoked. The input string cannot be parsed into a valid `int`. However, this is the kind of error that can be fixed.

Problem decomposition

Let's design a special `IntField` that functions like a normal text field but accepts only integers. If the user enters a value that generates a `NumberFormatException`, an error message should be printed and the user should be invited to try again. As Figure 11–13 shows, we want this special field to be a subclass of `JTextField` and to inherit the basic `JTextField` functionality. It should have the same kind of constructors that a normal `JTextField` has. This suggests the definition shown in Figure 11–14.

What constructors do we need?

Note that the constructor methods use `super` to call the `JTextField` constructor. For now, these two constructors should suffice. However, later we will introduce a third constructor that allows us to associate a bound with the `IntField`.

What methods do we need?

Our `IntField` class needs a method that can return its contents. This method should work like `JTextField.getText()`, but it should return a valid integer. The `getInt()` method takes no parameters and will return an `int`, assuming that a valid integer is typed into the `IntField`. If the

```
import javax.swing.*;

public class IntField extends JTextField {
    public IntField () {
        super();
    }
    public IntField (int size) {
        super(size);
    }
    public int getInt() throws NumberFormatException {
        return Integer.parseInt(getText());
    } // getInt()
} // IntField
```

FIGURE 11–14 A NumberFormatException might be thrown by the Integer.parseInt() method in IntField.getInt().

user types "$55," a NumberFormatException will be thrown by the Integer.parseInt() method. Note that getInt() declares that it throws this exception. This is not necessary because a NumberFormatException is not a checked exception, but it makes the code clearer.

Where and how should this exception be handled? The exception cannot easily be handled within the getInt() method. This method has to return an integer value. If the user types in a noninteger, there's no way to return a valid value. Therefore, it's better just to throw the exception to the calling method, where it can be handled more easily.

In a GUI application or applet, the calling method is likely to be an actionPerformed() method, such as the following:

```
public void actionPerformed(ActionEvent e) {
    try {
        userInt = intField.getInt();
        message = "You input " + userInt + " Thank you.";
    } catch (NumberFormatException ex) {
        JOptionPane.showMessageDialog(this,
            "The input must be an integer.  Please reenter.");
    } finally {
        repaint();
    }
} // actionPerformed()
```

The call to getInt() is embedded in a try/catch block. This leads to the design summarized in Figure 11–15. The IntField throws an exception that is caught by the applet, which then displays an error message.

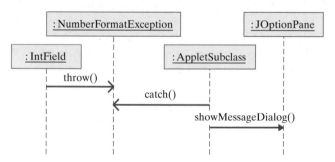

FIGURE 11–15 If the user types a noninteger into an IntField, it will throw a NumberFormatException. The applet will display an error message in a JOptionPane (a dialog window).

FIGURE 11–16   This exception
handler opens a dialog box to display
an error message.

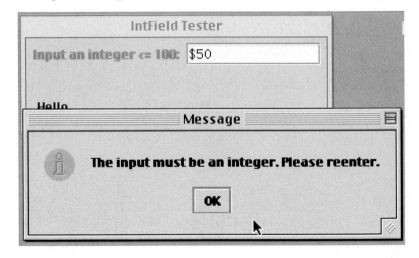

If the user inputs a valid integer, the program will report a message
that displays the value. A more real-world example would do something
more interesting with the value. On the other hand, if the user types an
erroneous value, the program will pop up the dialog box shown in Figure 11–16. (See the "From the Library" section of this chapter for more
on dialog boxes.) When the user clicks the OK button, the program will
resume normal execution, so when an exception is raised, the input value
is not used, and no harm is done by an erroneous value. The user can
try again to input a valid integer. Note that the finally clause repaints the
GUI. In this case, repainting would display the appropriate message on
the applet or application.

Defensive design: Anticipating an
exception

This is an example of defensive design. We anticipate a possible input
error and take steps to ensure that a bad value is not propagated throughout the program.

EFFECTIVE DESIGN: Defensive Design.   Well-designed code should anticipate potential problems, especially potential input problems. Effective use of exceptions can help with this task.

Admittedly, the sense in which the error here is "fixed" is simply that
the user's original input is ignored and reentered. This is a legitimate
and simple course of action for this particular situation. It is far preferable to ignoring the exception. If the program does not handle this exception itself, Java will catch it and will print a stack trace and terminate the
program. That would not be a very user-friendly interface!

Anticipating exceptions

Clearly this is the type of exceptional condition that should be
anticipated during program design. If this happens to be a program designed exclusively for your own use, then clearly this type of exception
handling may be unnecessary. But if the program is meant to be used
by others, it is important that the program be able to handle user input
without crashing.

> **EFFECTIVE DESIGN: Fixing an Exception.**   If a method can handle an exception effectively, it should handle it locally. This is both clearer and more efficient.

> **EFFECTIVE DESIGN: Library Exception Handling.**   Many of Java's library classes do not handle their own exceptions. The thinking behind this design is that the user of the class is in a better position to handle the exception in a way that's appropriate to the application.

11.5.4   To Fix or Not to Fix

Let's now consider a problem where it is less clear whether an exception can be successfully fixed "on the fly." Suppose you have a program that contains an array of `Strings`, which is initially created with just two elements.

```
String list[] = new String[2];
```

If an attempt is made to add more than two elements to the array, an `ArrayIndexOutOfBoundsException` will be raised. This exception can be handled by extending the size of the array and inserting the element. Then the program's normal execution can be resumed.

Let's design a method that will insert a string into the array. Suppose that this is intended to be a `private` method that will only be used within the program. Also, let's suppose that the program maintains a variable, `count`, that keeps track of how many values have been stored in the array. Therefore, it will not be necessary to pass the array as a parameter. So, this will be a `void` method with one parameter, the `String` to be inserted:

Problem statement

```
private void insertString(String str) {
    list[count] = str;     // Might throw ArrayIndexOutOfBoundsException
    ++count;
}
```

The comment notes where an exception might be thrown.

Can we handle this exception? When this exception is raised, we could create a new array with one more element than the current array. We could copy the old array into the new array and then insert the `String` in the new location. Finally, we could set the variable `list`, the array reference, so that it points to the new array. Thus, we could use the following `try/catch` block to handle this exception:

Algorithm design

```
private void insertString(String str) {
    try {
        list[count] = str;
    } catch (ArrayIndexOutOfBoundsException e) {
        String newList[] = new String[list.length+1];// Create a new array
        for (int k = 0; k < list.length; k++)        // Copy old to new
            newList[k] = list[k];
        newList[count] = str;        // Insert item into new
        list = newList;              // Make old point to new
    } finally {                      // Since the exception is now fixed
        count++;                     // Increase the count
    }
} // insertString()
```

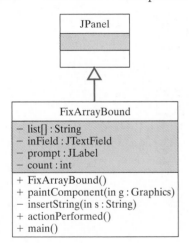

FIGURE 11–17 The `FixArrayBound` class uses exception handling to extend the size of an array each time a new element is inserted.

The effect of the `catch` clause is to create a new array, still referred to as `list`, but containing one more element than the original array.

Note the use of the `finally` clause here. For this problem it's important that we increment `count` in the `finally` clause. This is the only way to guarantee that `count` is incremented exactly once whenever an element is assigned to the array.

The design of the `FixArrayBound` class is shown in Figure 11–17. It provides a simple GUI interface that enables you to test the `insertString()` method. This program has a standard Swing interface. A `JFrame` is used as the top-level window. The program's components are contained within a `JPanel` that's added to the `JFrame` in the `main()` method.

Each time the user types a string into the text field, the `actionPerformed()` method calls the `insertString()` method to add the string to the array. On each user action, the `JPanel` is repainted. The `paintComponent()` method simply clears the panel and then displays the array's elements (Fig. 11–18).

> **DEBUGGING TIP: Clearing the JPanel.** Swing components, such as `JPanel`, do not automatically clear their backgrounds, so this must be done explicitly in the `paintComponent()` method.

The complete implementation of `FixArrayBound` is given in Figure 11–19. This example illustrates how an exception *can* be handled successfully and the program's normal flow of control resumed. However, the question is whether such an exception *should* be handled this way.

Poor program design

Unfortunately, this is not a well-designed program. The array's initial size is way too small for the program's intended use. Therefore, the fact that these exceptions arise at all is the result of poor design. In general, exceptions should *not* be used as a remedy for poor design.

> **EFFECTIVE DESIGN: Truly Exceptional Conditions.** A well-designed program should use exception handling to deal with truly exceptional conditions, not to process conditions that arise under normal or expected circumstances.

Proper array usage

For a program that uses an array, the size of the array should be chosen so that it can store all the objects required by the program. If the program is some kind of failsafe program, which cannot afford to crash, then something like the foregoing approach might be justified, provided this type of exception occurs very rarely. Even in that case it would be better to generate a message that alerts the program's user that this condition has occurred. The alert will indicate a need to modify the program's memory requirements and restart the program.

FIGURE 11–18 The strings displayed are stored in an array that is extended each time a new string is entered.

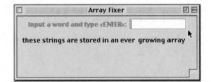

```java
import java.awt.*;
import java.awt.event.*;
import javax.swing.*;

public class FixArrayBound extends JPanel implements ActionListener  {
    public static final int WIDTH = 350, HEIGHT = 100;

    private JTextField inField = new JTextField(10);
    private JLabel prompt = new JLabel("Input a word and type <ENTER>: ");
    private String list[] = new String[2];         // Initially list has 2 elements
    private int count = 0;

    public  FixArrayBound() {
        inField.addActionListener(this);
        add(prompt);
        add(inField);
        setSize(WIDTH, HEIGHT);
    } // FixArrayBound()

    public void paintComponent(Graphics g) {
        g.setColor(getBackground());              // Clear the background
        g.fillRect(0, 0, WIDTH, HEIGHT);
        g.setColor(getForeground());
        String tempS = "";
        for (int k = 0; k < list.length; k++)
            tempS = tempS +  list[k] + " ";
        g.drawString(tempS, 10, 50);
    } // paintComponent

    private void insertString(String str) {
        try {
            list[count] = str;
        } catch (ArrayIndexOutOfBoundsException e) {
            String newList[] = new String[list.length+1]; // Create a new array
            for (int k = 0; k < list.length; k++)         // Copy old to new
                newList[k] = list[k];
                newList[count] = str;        // Insert item into new
                list = newList;              // Make old point to new
        } finally {                          // Since the exception is now fixed
            count++;                         // Increase the count
        }
    } // insertString()

    public void actionPerformed(ActionEvent evt) {
        insertString(inField.getText());
        inField.setText("");
        repaint();
    } // actionPerformed()
```

FIGURE 11–19 FixArrayBound increases the size of the array when a ArrayIndexOutOfBoundsException is raised.

```
    public static void main( String args[] ) {
        JFrame f = new JFrame("Array Fixer");
        FixArrayBound panel = new FixArrayBound();
        f.getContentPane().add(panel);
        f.setSize(panel.WIDTH, panel.HEIGHT);
        f.setVisible(true);
        f.addWindowListener(new WindowAdapter() {        // Quit the application
            public void windowClosing(WindowEvent e) {
                System.exit(0);
            }
        });
    } // main()
} // FixArrayBound
```

FIGURE 11–19   *(continued)* `FixArrayBound` increases the size of the array when a `ArrayIndexOutOfBoundsException` is raised.

Choosing the correct data structure

If it is not known in advance how many objects will be stored in an array, a better design would be to make use of the `java.util.Vector` class (see "From the Java Library" in Chapter 8). Vectors are designed to grow as necessary as new objects are inserted. In some ways the exception-handling code in our example mimics the behavior of a vector. However, the `Vector` class makes use of efficient algorithms for extending its size. By contrast, exception-handling code is very inefficient. Because exceptions force the system into an abnormal mode of execution, it takes considerably longer to handle an exception than it would to use a `Vector` for this type of application. (See "In the Laboratory" in this chapter.)

> **EFFECTIVE DESIGN: Appropriate Data Structure.**   A major component of problem solving is choosing the best way to represent the data. A vector should be used as an array structure whenever the size of the array will grow and shrink dynamically during the program's execution.

SELF-STUDY EXERCISE

EXERCISE 11.13   For each of the following exceptions, determine whether it can be handled in such a way that the program can be resumed or whether the program should be terminated:

a. A computer game program detects a problem with one of its GUI elements and throws a `NullPointerException`.
b. A factory assembly-line control program determines that an important control value has become negative and generates an `Arithmetic-Exception`.
c. A company's Web-based order form detects that its user has entered an invalid `String` and throws a `SecurityException`.

11.6   Creating and Throwing Your Own Exceptions

Like other Java classes, the `Exception` class can be extended to handle cases that are not already covered by Java's built-in exceptions. Exceptions that you define will be handled the same way by the Java interpreter, but you will have to `throw` them yourself.

For example, Figure 11–20 shows the design of an exception that can be used for validating that an integer is less than or equal to a certain maximum value. It would be coded as follows:

```
/**
 *  IntOutOfRangeException reports an exception when an
 *     integer exceeds its bound.
 */
public class IntOutOfRangeException extends Exception {

    public IntOutOfRangeException (int Bound) {
        super("The input value exceeds the bound " + Bound);
    }
}
```

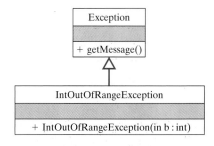

FIGURE 11–20   The IntOutOfRange exception.

The class extends Exception and consists entirely of a constructor method that merely calls the superclass constructor. The argument passed to the superclass constructor is the message that will be returned by getMessage() when an instance of this exception is created.

Now let's consider an example where this new exception will be thrown. Suppose we wish to constrain the IntField class that we developed previously (Fig. 11–14) so that it will only accept numbers that are less than a certain bound. First, let's modify IntField so that its bound can be set when an instance is created. We want its bound to be an instance variable, with some initial value, and we want to provide a constructor that can be used to override the default (Fig. 11–21). This leads to the following revision of IntField:

Inheriting functionality

```
public class IntField extends JTextField {
    private int bound = Integer.MAX_VALUE;

    public IntField(int size, int max) {
        super(size);
        bound = max;
    }
    // The rest of the class is unchanged for now
} // IntField
```

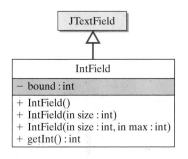

FIGURE 11–21   The revised IntField class contains a bound on the size of the numbers that should be input.

Our new constructor has the signature IntField(int,int), which doesn't duplicate any of JTextField's constructors. This is good. In extending a class, we want to be careful about the effect our definitions have on the original methods in the superclass. Superclass methods should be overridden by design, not by accident. If a method is redefined inadvertently, it may not function as expected by users of the subclass.

EFFECTIVE DESIGN: Extending a Class.   When extending a class, care must taken to ensure that the superclass's methods are not inadvertently overridden. A superclass method should only be overridden by design, not by accident.

Note how we have handled the problem of setting the default value of the bound. Integer.MAX.VALUE is a class constant that sets the maximum value for the int type. It's an appropriate value to use, because any valid

FIGURE 11–22 The revised
`IntField` class containing the revised
`getInt()` method.

```java
import javax.swing.*;

public class IntField extends JTextField {
    private int bound = Integer.MAX_VALUE;

    public IntField (int size) {
        super(size);
    }

    public IntField(int size, int max) {
        super(size);
        bound = max;
    }

    public int getInt() throws NumberFormatException,
                              IntOutOfRangeException {
        int num = Integer.parseInt(getText());
        if (num > bound)
            throw new IntOutOfRangeException(bound);
        return num;
    } // getInt()

} // IntField
```

int that the user types should be less than or equal to MAX.VALUE. Given these changes to `IntField`, let's now incorporate our new exception into its `getInt()` method (Fig. 11–22).

This new version of `getInt()` throws an exception if the integer input by the user is greater than the `IntField`'s bound. Here again, it is difficult to handle this exception appropriately in this method. The method would either have to return an erroneous value—because it must return something—or it must terminate. Neither is an acceptable alternative. It is far better to throw the exception to the calling method.

The `IntFieldTester` class (Fig. 11–23) has the design and functionality shown in Figure 11–15. It provides a simple GUI interface to test the `IntField` class. It prompts the user to type in an integer that is less than 100, and then it echoes the user's input. Note how the exception is handled in the `actionPerformed()` method. If an exception is thrown in `IntField.getInt()`, the `actionPerformed()` method pops up an error dialog. The erroneous input is not used. Instead the user is given another chance to enter a valid integer.

SELF-STUDY EXERCISES

EXERCISE 11.14   Define a new `Exception` named `FieldIsEmptyException`, which is meant to be thrown if the user forgets to enter a value into a `IntField`.

EXERCISE 11.15   Modify the `IntField.getInt()` method so that it throws and catches the `FieldIsEmptyException`.

```
import java.awt.*;
import java.awt.event.*;
import javax.swing.*;

public class IntFieldTester extends JPanel implements ActionListener  {
    public static final int WIDTH = 300, HEIGHT = 300;

    private JLabel prompt = new JLabel("Input an integer <= 100: ");
    private IntField intField = new IntField(12, 100);
    private int userInt;
    private String message = "Hello";

    public IntFieldTester() {
        add(prompt);
        intField.addActionListener(this);
        add(intField);
        setSize(WIDTH, HEIGHT);
    } // IntFieldTester()

    public void paintComponent( Graphics g ) {
        g.setColor(getBackground());            // Clear the panel
        g.fillRect(0, 0, WIDTH, HEIGHT);
        g.setColor(getForeground());
        g.drawString(message, 10, 70);
    } // paintComponent()

    public void actionPerformed(ActionEvent evt) {
        try {
            userInt = intField.getInt();
            message = "You input " + userInt + " Thank you.";
        } catch (NumberFormatException e) {
            JOptionPane.showMessageDialog(this,
                "The input must be an integer.  Please reenter.");
        } catch (IntOutOfRangeException e) {
            JOptionPane.showMessageDialog(this, e.getMessage());
        } finally {
            repaint();
        }
    } // actionPerformed()

    public static void main(String args[]) {
        JFrame f = new JFrame("IntField Tester");
        IntFieldTester panel = new IntFieldTester();
        f.getContentPane().add(panel);
        f.setSize(panel.WIDTH, panel.HEIGHT);
        f.setVisible(true);
        f.addWindowListener(new WindowAdapter() {       // Quit the application
            public void windowClosing(WindowEvent e) {
                System.exit(0);
            }
        });
    } // main()
} // IntFieldTester
```

FIGURE 11–23   An application that uses an `IntField` object to input integers.

From the Java Library

`javax.swing.JOptionPane`

http://java.sun.com/products/jdk/1.3/docs/api/

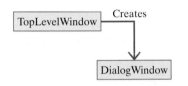

FIGURE 11–24 A dialog window cannot stand alone. It must be created by a top-level window.

Modal and nonmodal dialogs

A dialog box is a window that can be opened by a program to communicate in some way with the user. Dialog boxes come in many varieties and have many uses in a GUI environment. You've undoubtedly encountered them when using your own computer.

For example, a *file dialog* is opened whenever you want to open or save a file. It provides an interface that lets you name the file and helps you search through the computer's directory structure to find a file.

A *warning dialog* or **error dialog** is opened whenever a program needs to notify or warn you that some kind of error occurred. It usually presents an error message and an OK button that you click to dismiss the dialog.

Dialogs are easy to create and use in Java. The Swing component set provides several different kinds of basic dialogs that can be incorporated into your program with one or two lines of code. For example, the `IntFieldTester` class makes use of a simple message dialog to report an input error to the user. This dialog was created by the following code segment in the program (see Figure 11–23):

```
catch (NumberFormatException e) {
    JOptionPane.showMessageDialog(this,
        "The input must be an integer.  Please reenter.");
}
```

This method call displays the window shown in Figure 11–16. It contains the error message and an OK button that is used to close the window. The `showMessageDialog()` method is a `static` method of the `javax.swing.JOptionPane` class. This class provides a collection of similar methods for creating and displaying basic dialog boxes.

A dialog differs from other kinds of top-level windows—such as `JApplet` and `JFrame`—in that it is associated with another window (Fig. 11–24). The first parameter in this version of the `showMessageDialog()` method is a reference to the dialog's parent window. The second parameter is a `String` representing the message.

The basic message dialog used in this example is known as a **modal dialog**. This means that once it's been displayed, you can't do anything else until you click the OK button and dismiss the dialog. It's also possible to create *nonmodal* dialogs. These can stay around on the screen while you move on to other tasks.

Note that the dialog box also contains an *icon* that symbolizes the purpose of the message (Fig. 11–25). The icon is representative of the dialog's message type. Among the basic types available in `JOptionPane` are the following:

```
JOptionPane.PLAIN_MESSAGE
JOptionPane.INFORMATIONAL_MESSAGE      // Default
JOptionPane.WARNING_MESSAGE
JOptionPane.QUESTION_MESSAGE
JOptionPane.ERROR_MESSAGE
```

To set the dialog to anything other than the default (informational) type, you can use the following version of `showMessageDialog()`:

```
showMessageDialog(Component comp, Object message,
                  String title, int msgType);
```

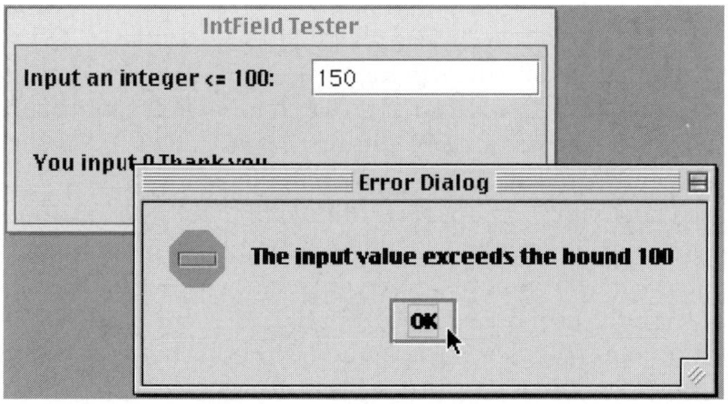

FIGURE 11–25   An error dialog.

The first parameter is a reference to the parent window. The second is the message string. The third is a string used as the dialog window's title, and the fourth is one of the five dialog types. For example, we can change our dialog to an error dialog with the following statement:

```
catch (IntOutOfRangeException e) {
    JOptionPane.showMessageDialog(this,
            e.getMessage(),
            "Error dialog",
            JOptionPane.ERROR_MESSAGE);
}
```

This would produce the dialog shown in Figure 11–25.

The other kinds of basic dialogs provided by the `JOptionPane` class are listed in Table 11.4. All of the dialogs listed there can be created with a line or two of code. In addition to these, it's also possible to create sophisticated dialogs that can be as customized as any other GUI interface you can build in Java.

Basic Swing dialogs

TABLE 11.4   Basic dialogs provided by `JOptionPane`.

Dialog	Description
Message Dialog	Presents a simple error or informational message
Confirm Dialog	Prompts the user to confirm a particular action
Option Dialog	Lets the user choose from a couple of options
Input Dialog	Prompts and inputs a string

IN THE LABORATORY:
Measuring Exception Overhead

The purpose of this lab is to design an experiment to measure the amount of computational overhead required by Java's exception-handling mechanism. The lesson of this experiment will be that exceptions should only be used to handle truly exceptional situations, not as a means of solving the problem at hand. The objectives of this lab are

- To implement `try/catch` statements.
- To develop and test appropriate design strategies for handling `Exceptions`.
- To demonstrate the inefficiency of using exception handling as a means of normal program control.

Introduction

Exception processing overhead

Each time an exception is thrown, the Java Virtual Machine must suspend normal execution of the program and search for and execute an exception handler. All of this takes time. How much overhead does Java exception handling expend? That's the question you will be addressing in this lab.

Suppose you are writing an application that must store a variable number of objects in memory. You don't know for certain how many objects will be stored. You want to test three different ways of solving this problem. One way will use an array of 0 (initial) elements and will grow the array each time a new element is to be inserted. This approach will use the algorithm designed in the `FixArrayBound` program to expand the array as needed. Therefore, this approach will generate one exception on each insertion.

The second way will utilize an array with *N* (initial) elements. No exceptions should be thrown for this approach, because the array is always the correct size.

The third approach will use a vector to store the objects. The `java.-util.Vector` class is specifically designed for the problem of storing objects in an array that can expand in size as needed.

Problem Description

Problem specification

Write a Java application that will test the relative efficiency of the three approaches just described. The application should prompt the user to input the number, *N*, of objects to be stored in the array. It should then insert *N* objects into each of the three structures described—a 0-element array, an *N*-element array, and a `Vector`—and it should measure how long each approach takes.

Once you have correctly implemented and tested your application program, perform at least 10 trials, using different values for *N*. Obtain data for the following three situations:

- Milliseconds required to insert *N* items into a vector.
- Milliseconds required to insert *N* items into an array of *N* elements.
- Milliseconds required to insert *N* items into an array of 0 elements.

You should observe a considerable difference between these three times. Note that the third case represents the situation in which *N* exceptions will be generated, one for each insertion.

Analyzing the results

Create a table and a graph of your results, and try to calculate the amount of *overhead* time, in milliseconds, that the system uses to process a single exception in this case. The overhead is the amount of time the system requires in order to process the exception. By comparing cases two and three, you should be able to get a pretty good estimate for this value.

You should also see a significant difference between the time required to store the objects in a `Vector` and the time required to store the objects in an array of *N* elements. Use this difference to estimate the amount of overhead required to implement a Java `Vector`. As you might expect, it is more efficient to store values in an array that is large enough to hold values than it is to store them in a vector that must dynamically change its size on each insertion.

Problem Decomposition

An appropriate design for this problem should make use of some of the classes we designed in this chapter. The IntField class will be useful for inputting *N*, the number of objects used in each run of the experiment. The IntOutOfRangeException class is used by IntField.getInt(), so it should be included in your project. Finally, the main class, call it ExceptionExperiment, should be a frame-based application. It should present a simple GUI and be responsible for running the various experiments. This leads to the following breakdown:

What classes should we use?

- ExceptionExperiment—a subclass of JFrame that serves as the main program for this application.
- IntField—a subclass of JTextField that serves as the main input element for this application (Fig. 11–22).
- IntOutOfRangeException—a subclass of Extension, this class was developed and tested previously.

GUI Design

The GUI for this application should be kept simple. It uses a JFrame as the main container. Remember that the default layout for JFrames is BorderLayout. Along the north border, you should place a control panel that consists of a simple prompt and the IntField. In the center of the frame you should place a JTextArea that will be used to display the results of the experiments.

The application should run the experiments each time the user inputs a valid number in the IntField. Remember that IntField.getInt() returns 0 if the user types a value that is out of range. The output from each experiment should look something like the following:

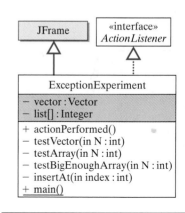

FIGURE 11–26   Design of the ExceptionExperiment class.

```
100 Integers were inserted into
    Vector in 4 milliseconds
    array of 0 elements in 53 milliseconds
    array of 100 elements in 1 milliseconds
1000 Integers were inserted into
    Vector in 37 milliseconds
    array of 0 elements in 1225 milliseconds
    array of 1000 elements in 8 milliseconds
```

As you can see from these results, which were taken from an actual run, there is a significant time difference among the three approaches.

Importing from the Java Library

This project will require several classes from the Java class library, including the java.util.Vector class and the java.awt.* and java.awt.event.* packages.

Designing the ExceptionExperiment Class

ExceptionExperiment should contain two private instance variables, a Vector and an array (Fig. 11–26). In terms of this experiment's objectives, it doesn't matter what types of objects are stored in these fields. However, the same type of object should be stored in both structures. Integer objects

What data structures do we need?

would be a good choice, because it is easy to generate N different Integer objects using a for loop. For example, the following statement can be used to generate *N* integers for a Vector:

```
vector = new Vector(0);
for (int k = 0; k < N; k++)
    vector.addElement(new Integer(k));
```

The Vector and the array can be instantiated anew for each experiment. An example of this will be given next. All other variables can be declared, as needed, within the class's methods.

Algorithm Design

The algorithm for this program can be decomposed into the following methods:

- actionPerformed()—This method will get the value of *N* from the int-Field() and then run the three experiments.
- testVector(int N)—This method will perform *N* insertions into the Vector and will report the number of milliseconds required. The code required to insert *N* Integers into a Vector, *vector*, is as follows:

```
vector = new Vector(0);            // Instantiate the Vector, vector
for (int k = 0; k < N; k++)        // For n iterations
    vector.addElement(new Integer(k)); // Insert a new integer into vector
```

- testArray(int N)—This method will perform *N* insertions into

```
list = new Integer[0];
```

In this case, we are using an array of Integers. This is the method in which the ArrayIndexOutOfBoundsExceptions will be thrown.

- testBigEnoughArray(int N)—This method will perform *N* insertions into an array of *N* elements and will report the number of milliseconds required. The difference between this method and the previous one is that in this case the array is instantiated with an initial size of *N*, so that no exceptions will be generated as the *N* items are inserted.
- insertAt(int k)—This method will be called by both testBigEnough-Array() and testArray() to insert an item into the array at index *k*. It should be a simple variant of the insertString() method that was designed in Section 11.4.4.

It is important for the experiment that the same method be used to do the insertions in both arrays. That way the only difference in the time taken will be due to the exceptions raised.

One modification that you'll want to make to the insertString() method is that you can drop its finally clause. The variable k will be passed into the method as a parameter and will be incremented by the calling method. A loop such as the following can be used in both testArray() and testBigEnoughArray():

```
for (int k = 0; k < N; k++)
    insertAt(k);
```

- `main()`—Finally, the `main()` method for this application will simply create an instance of the application:

```
public static void main(String args[]) {
    ExceptionExperiment et = new ExceptionExperiment();
    et.show();
} // main()
```

Timing an Operation

Timing an operation in Java is easy. To time an operation you can just call `System.currentTimeMillis()` before and after the operation and then compute the difference in the two values:

```
long startTime = System.currentTimeMillis();
for (k = 0; k < size; k++)
    insertAt(k);
long currentTime = System.currentTimeMillis();
System.out.println("Elapsed time = " + (currentTime - startTime));
```

In this case, we are computing the time it takes to insert *size* items into the array.

Testing Your Algorithm

When testing your program, it is important to make sure that it is successfully inserting the elements into the appropriate structures. Therefore, during program development, you want to use a `for` loop to display the array and the `Vector` after the items have been inserted. For example, something like the following code should be used to verify that the objects are actually installed in the array:

```
// Display the array contents
for (int j = 0; j < size; j++)
    System.out.println(list[j]);
```

This part of the program should be deleted or commented out during the running of the experiments themselves.

Reporting Your Results

Use your experimental results to answer the following questions:

- On average, how many milliseconds does it take to handle a thrown exception on your system?
- On average, how much longer does it take to insert an element into a vector as opposed to a (suitably sized) array?
- Why does it take longer to insert something into a vector than into an array?
- Because a `Vector` requires more overhead than an array, why would you ever use a `Vector`? That is, describe an application problem where you can't use a "big enough" array.

Optional Exercise

Java would not use a loop to copy one array into another as we have done in the FixArrayBound program. Instead it would use the java.lang.-System.arraycopy() method:

```
public static void arraycopy(Object src, int srcP, Object dest,
                                      int destP, int len);
```

For example, to copy all the elements of array1 into array2 you could use the following statement:

```
arraycopy(array1, 0, array2, 0, array1.length);
```

Modify your experiment to make use of this method, which is the method used by the Vector class when it needs to resize. This will give a measure of the overhead caused by exception throwing.

Java Language Summary

The try/catch/finally statement has the following syntax:

```
try {
    // Block of statements
    // At least one of which may throw an exception

    if ( /* Some condition obtains */ )
        throw new ExceptionName();
} catch (ExceptionName ParameterName) {
    // Block of statements to be executed
    // If the ExceptionName exception is thrown in try
}
..
} catch (ExceptionName2 ParameterName) {
    // Block of statements to be executed
    // If the ExceptionName2 exception is thrown in try
} finally {
    // Optional block of statements that is executed
    // Whether an exception is thrown or not
}
```

The try block is meant to include a statement or statements that might throw an exception. The catch blocks—there can be one or more—are meant to handle exceptions that are thrown in the try block. A catch block will handle any exception that matches its parameter class, including subclasses of that class. The finally block is optional. It will be executed whether an exception is thrown or not. If an exception is thrown in the try block, the try block is exited permanently.

The throw statement inside the try block is there to illustrate how throw can be used. You will usually not see a throw statement in a try block, because most throws are done from within Java library methods, which are called from a try block.

Technical Terms   CHAPTER SUMMARY

catch block   exception   static scope
catch an exception   exception handler   throw an exception
checked exception   finally block   try block
dialog box   method call stack   unchecked exception
dynamic scope   method stack trace
error dialog   modal dialog

Summary of Important Points

- In Java, when an error or exceptional condition occurs, you `throw` an `Exception`, which is caught by special code known as an *exception handler*. A `throw` statement—`throw new Exception()`—is used to throw an exception.
- A *try block* is a block of statements containing one or more statements that may throw an exception. Embedding a statement in a try block indicates your awareness that it might throw an exception and your intention to handle the exception.
- Java distinguishes between *checked* and *unchecked* exceptions. Checked exceptions must either be caught by the method in which they occur or you must declare that the method containing that statement `throws` the exception.
- The unchecked exceptions are those that belong to subclasses of `RuntimeException`. If they are left uncaught, they will be handled by Java's default exception handlers.
- A *catch block* is a block of statements that handles the exceptions that match its parameter. A catch block can only follow a try block, and there may be more than one catch block for each try block.
- The `try`/`catch` syntax allows you to separate the normal parts of an algorithm from special code meant to handle errors and exceptional conditions.
- A *method stack trace* is a trace of the method calls that have led to the execution of a particular statement in the program. The `Exception.print-StackTrace()` method can be called by exception handlers to print a trace of exactly how the program reached the statement that threw the exception.
- *Static scoping* refers to how the text of the program is arranged. If a variable is declared within a method or a block, its static scope is confined to that method or block.
- *Dynamic scoping* refers to how the program is executed. A statement is within the dynamic scope of a method or block, if it is called from that method or block, or if it is called by some other method that was called from that method or block.
- When searching for a catch block to handle an exception thrown by a statement, Java searches upward through the statement's static scope and backward through its dynamic scope until it finds a matching catch block. If none is found, the Java Virtual Machine will handle the exception itself by printing an error message and a method stack trace.

- Many Java library methods throw exceptions when an error occurs. These throw statements do not appear in the program. For example, Java's integer division operator will throw an ArithmeticException if an attempt is made to divide by zero.
- Generally, there are four ways to handle an exception: (1) Let Java handle it; (2) fix the problem that led to the exception and resume the program; (3) report the problem and resume the program; and (4) print an error message and terminate the program. Most erroneous conditions reported by exceptions are difficult or impossible to fix.
- A finally statement is an optional part of a try/catch block. Statements contained in a finally block will be executed whether an exception is raised or not.
- A well-designed program should use exception handling to deal with truly exceptional conditions, not as a means of normal program control.
- User-defined exceptions can be defined by extending the Exception class or one of its subclasses.

SOLUTIONS TO SELF-STUDY EXERCISES

SOLUTION 11.1

a. `Integer.parseInt("26.2");`   ==> NumberFormatException
b. `String s; s.indexOf('a');`   ==> NullPointerException
c. `String s = "hello"; s.charAt(5);` ==> StringIndexOutOfBoundsException

SOLUTION 11.2 The unchecked exceptions are IndexOutOfBoundsException, NumberFormatException, and NullPointerException, because these are subclasses of RuntimeException. The others are checked exceptions.

SOLUTION 11.3 An ArrayIndexOutOfBoundsException could be handled by the handlers in a, c, or d, because their classes are all superclasses of ArrayIndexOutOfBoundsException.

SOLUTION 11.4 If Math.random() in MyClass2 returns 0.98 and then 0.44, the program will generate the following output:

```
0.98 is out of range
```

Note that because the out-of-range error occurs in method1(), method2() is not called at all.

SOLUTION 11.5 If Math.random() in MyClass2 returns 0.98 and then 0.44, the following stack trace would be printed:

```
java.lang.ArithmeticException: 0.98 is out of range
    at MyClass2.method1(MyClass2.java:3)
    at MyClass2.main(MyClass2.java:15)
```

SOLUTION 11.6 If Math.random() in MyClass2 returns 0.44 and then 0.98, the program will generate the following output:

```
Hello 0.44
0.98 is out of range
```

SOLUTION 11.7   If `Math.random()` in `MyClass2` returns 0.44 and then 0.98, the following stack trace would be printed:

```
java.lang.ArithmeticException: 0.98 is out of range
    at MyClass2.method2(MyClass2.java:8)
    at MyClass2.main(MyClass2.java:16)
```

SOLUTION 11.8   The divide-by-zero error in `BadDivide` occurs in the expression `n/d` in `Method2()`. It would generate the following stack trace:

```
java.lang.ArithmeticException: divide by zero
    at BadDivide.method2(BadDivide.java:7)
    at BadDivide.method1(BadDivide.java:3)
    at BadDivide.main(BadDivide.java:13)
```

SOLUTION 11.9   The following version of `BadDivide.method2()` will handle the divide-by-zero error itself:

```java
public void method2 (int n, int d) {
    try {
        System.out.println(n / d);
    } catch (ArithmeticException e) {
        System.out.println(e.getMessage());
        e.printStackTrace();
        System.exit(0);
    }
}
```

SOLUTION 11.10   If `someValue` equals 1000, the code segment will print

```
Entering try block
ERROR: 1000 is too large
```

SOLUTION 11.11   If `someValue` equals 50, the code segment will print

```
Entering try block
Exiting try block
```

SOLUTION 11.12

```java
try {
    if (X < 0)
        throw new Exception("ERROR: Negative value in X coordinate");
} catch (Exception e) {
    System.out.println( e.getMessage() );
}
```

SOLUTION 11.13

a. It depends. This is a computer game, so one way to handle this problem would be to generate a message into a log file and resume the game. If the GUI element is crucial to the game, it's hard to see how it could be successfully handled.
b. It depends. You would have to decide whether it would be more harmful or dangerous to continue production than not.
c. The program could report the security violation to the user and to the system manager and then keep accepting user input.

SOLUTION 11.14

```java
public class FieldIsEmptyException extends Exception {

    public FieldIsEmptyException () {
        super("The input field is empty ");
    }
}
```

SOLUTION 11.15

```java
public int getInt() {
    int num = 0;
    try {
        String data = getText();
        if (data.equals(""))
            throw new FieldIsEmptyException();
        num = Integer.parseInt( getText() );
        if (num > bound)
            throw new IntOutOfRangeException(bound);
    } catch (FieldIsEmptyException e) {
        System.out.println("Error: " + e.getMessage() );
    } catch (NumberFormatException e) {
        System.out.println("Error: You must input an integer.
                                          Please try again.");
    } catch (IntOutOfRangeException e) {
        System.out.println(e.getMessage());
        return 0;
    }
    return num;
}
```

EXERCISES

Note: For programming exercises, **first** *draw a UML class diagram describing all classes and their inheritance relationships and/or associations.*

EXERCISE 11.1   Explain the difference between the following pairs of terms:

a. *Throwing an exception* and *catching an exception.*
b. *Try block* and *catch block.*
c. *Catch block* and *finally block.*
d. *Try block* and *finally block.*
e. *Dynamic scope* and *static scope.*
f. *Dialog box* and *top-level window.*
g. *Checked* and *unchecked* exception.
h. *Method stack* and *method call.*

EXERCISE 11.2   Fill in the blanks.

a. _____ an exception is Java's way of signaling that some kind of abnormal situation has occurred.

b. The only place that an exception can be thrown in a Java program is within a _____ .

c. The block of statements placed within a catch block are generally known as an _____ .

d. To determine a statement's _____ scope, you have to trace the program's execution.

e. To determine a statement's _____ scope, you can just read its definition.

f. When a method is called, a representation of the method call is placed on the _____ .

g. The root of Java's exception hierarchy is the _____ class.

h. A _____ exception must be either caught or declared within the method in which it might be thrown.

i. An _____ exception may be left up to Java to handle.

EXERCISE 11.3   Compare and contrast the four different ways of handling exceptions within a program.

EXERCISE 11.4   Suppose you have a program that asks the user to input a string of no more than five letters. Describe the steps you'd need to take in order to design a StringTooLongException to handle cases where the user types in too many characters.

EXERCISE 11.5   Exceptions require more computational overhead than normal processing. Explain.

EXERCISE 11.6   Suppose the following ExerciseExample program is currently executing the if statement in method2():

```java
public class ExerciseExample {
    public void method1(int M) {
        try {
            System.out.println("Entering try block");
            method2( M );
            System.out.println("Exiting try block");
        } catch (Exception e) {
            System.out.println("ERROR: " + e.getMessage());
        }
    } // method1()

    public void method2(int M) {
        if (M > 100)
            throw new ArithmeticException(M + " is too large");
    }

    public static void main(String argv[]) {
        ExerciseExample ex = new ExerciseExample();
        ex.method1(500);
    }
} // ExerciseExample
```

Draw a picture of the *method call stack* that represents this situation.

EXERCISE 11.7   Repeat the previous exercise for the situation where the program is currently executing the second println() statement in method1().

EXERCISE 11.8   Draw a hierarchy chart that represents the static scoping relationships among the elements of the ExerciseExample program.

EXERCISE 11.9   What would be printed by the ExerciseExample program when it is run?

EXERCISE 11.10   What would be printed by the ExerciseExample program, if the statement in its main method were changed to ex.method1(5)?

EXERCISE 11.11 Consider again the ExerciseExample program. If the exception thrown were Exception rather than ArithmeticException, explain why we would get the following error message: java.lang.Exception must be caught, or it must be declared. . . .

EXERCISE 11.12 Write a try/catch block that throws an Exception if the value of variable X is less than zero. The exception should be an instance of Exception and, when it is caught, the message returned by getMessage() should be "ERROR: Negative value in X coordinate."

EXERCISE 11.13 Look at the IntFieldTester program (Fig. 11–23) and the IntField class definition (Fig. 11–22). Suppose the user inputs a value that's greater than 100. Show what the method call stack would look like when the IntField.getInt() method is executing the num > bound expression.

EXERCISE 11.14 As a continuation of the previous exercise, show what the program's output would be if the user input a value greater than 100.

EXERCISE 11.15 As a continuation of the previous exercise, modify the IntOutOfRangeException handler so that it prints the message call stack. Then show what it would print.

EXERCISE 11.16 Define a subclass of RuntimeException named InvalidPasswordException, which contains two constructors. The first constructor takes no parameters and an exception thrown with this constructor should return "ERROR: invalid password" when its getMessage() is invoked. The second constructor takes a single String parameter. Exceptions thrown with this constructor should return the constructor's argument when getMessage() is invoked.

EXERCISE 11.17 Extend the IntField class so that it will constrain the integer JTextField to an int between both a lower and upper bound. In other words, it should throw an exception if the user types in a value lower than the lower bound or greater than the upper bound.

EXERCISE 11.18 Modify the ColorPicker program presented in the last chapter so that its JTextFields will restrict user inputs to values between 0 and 255. Use the extended IntField class that you defined in the previous exercise.

EXERCISE 11.19 Design Issue: One of the preconditions for the bubbleSort() method (Fig. 8–16) is that its array parameter not be null. Of course, this precondition would fail if the array were passed a null array reference. In that case, Java would throw a NullPointerException and terminate the program. Is this an appropriate way to handle that exception?

EXERCISE 11.20 With respect to the previous exercise, suppose you decide that it is more appropriate to handle the NullPointerException by presenting an error dialog. Modify the method to accommodate this behavior.

EXERCISE 11.21 Design Issue: Another possible way to design the sequentialSearch() method (Fig. 8–19) would be to have it throw an exception when its key is not found in the array. Is this a good design? Explain.

EXERCISE 11.22 **CyberPet Problem:** One of the CyberPet constructors takes an integer parameter to specify the CyberPet's state. If an erroneous value (for example, −1 or 100) is passed to the constructor, that will invalidate the CyberPet's state, which will cause all kinds of problems for the simulation. Design an appropriate Exception and a handler to fix this problem and incorporate it into the CyberPet class.

EXERCISE 11.23   CyberPet Challenge: One of the problems with the animated CyberPet applet (Fig. 8–14) is that if the image files are missing from the applet's directory, the applet will continue to run but no images will show up. First, convert the applet from an AWT program to a Swing program. Then design and implement a way to use exceptions to handle this problem. What kind of exception will you throw? Where and how will you detect it? If an exception is thrown, open an error dialog and inform the user.

Photograph courtesy of Jim Wehtje, PhotoDisc, Inc.

12

Recursive Problem Solving

OBJECTIVES

After studying this chapter, you will

- Understand the concept of recursion.
- Know how to use recursive programming techniques.
- Have a better appreciation of recursion as a problem-solving technique.

OUTLINE

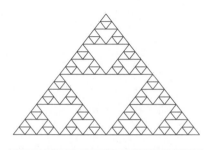

FIGURE 12–1 The Sierpinski gasket.

12.1 Introduction

The pattern in Figure 12–1 is known as the Sierpinski gasket. Its overall shape is that of an equilateral triangle. But notice how inside the outer triangle there are three smaller triangles that are similar to the overall pattern. And inside each of those are three even smaller triangles, and so on. The Sierpinski gasket is known as a *fractal* because when you divide it up, you end up with a smaller version of the overall pattern. The overall gasket pattern is repeated over and over, at smaller and smaller scales, throughout the figure.

How would you draw this pattern? If you try to use some kind of nested loop structure, you'll find that it is very challenging. It can be done using loops, but it isn't easy. On the other hand, if you use an approach known as *recursion*, this problem is much easier to solve. It's a little bit like the representation issue we discussed in Chapter 5. Your ability to solve a problem often depends on how you represent the problem. Recursion gives you another way to approach problems that involve repetition, such as the problem of drawing the Sierpinski gasket.

The main goal of this chapter is to introduce recursion as both a problem-solving technique and as alternative to loops (Chapter 6) for implementing repetition. We begin with the notion of a *recursive definition*, a concept used widely in mathematics and computer science. We then introduce the idea of a *recursive method*, which is the way recursion is used in a program. These ideas are illustrated by means of a number of examples.

Recursion is a topic that is taken up in considerable detail in upper-level computer science courses, so our goal here is mainly to introduce the concept and give you some idea of its power as a problem-solving approach. Because our discussion is introductory, the examples we've chosen are very simple. One risk in using simple examples is that you might be tempted to think that recursion is only good for "toy problems." Nothing could be further from the truth. Recursion is often used for some of the most difficult algorithms. Some of the exercises at the end of the chapter provide examples of challenging problems.

12.1.1 Recursion as Repetition

A **recursive method** is a method that calls itself. An **iterative method** is a method that uses a loop to repeat an action. In one sense, *recursion* is an alternative to the iterative (looping) control structures we studied in Chapter 6. In this sense, recursion is just another way to repeat an action.

Iterative method

For example, consider the following iterative method for saying "Hello" N times:

```java
public void hello(int N)  {
    for (int k = 0; k < N; k++)
        System.out.println("Hello");
} // hello()
```

Recursive method

A recursive version of this method would be defined as follows:

```java
public void hello(int N)  {
    if (N > 0) {
        System.out.println("Hello");
        hello(N - 1);                      // Recursive call
} // hello()
```

This method is recursive because it calls itself, when N is greater than 0. However, note that when it calls itself, it passes $N - 1$ as the value for its parameter. If this method is initially called with N equal to 5, here's a trace of what happens. Indentation is used to indicate each time the method calls itself:

```
hello(5)
    Print "Hello"
    hello(4)
        Print "Hello"
        hello(3)
            Print "Hello"
            hello(2)
                Print "Hello"
                hello(1)
                    Print "Hello"
                    hello(0)
```

Thus, "Hello" will be printed five times, just as it would be in the iterative version of this method.

So, in one sense, recursion is just an alternative to iteration. In fact, there are some programming languages, such as the original versions of LISP and PROLOG, that do not have loop structures. In these languages, *all* repetition is done by recursion. On the other hand, if a language contains loop structures, it can do without recursion. Anything that can be done iteratively can be done recursively, and vice versa.

Moreover, it is much less efficient to call a method five times than to repeat a for loop five times. Method calls take up more memory than loops and involve more **computational overhead**—for such tasks as passing parameters, allocating storage for the method's local variables, and returning the method's results. Therefore, because of its reliance on repeated method calls, recursion is usually less efficient than iteration as a way to code a particular algorithm.

Computational overhead

> **EFFECTIVE DESIGN: Efficiency.** Iterative algorithms and methods are generally more efficient than recursive algorithms that do the same thing.

SELF-STUDY EXERCISES

EXERCISE 12.1 What would be printed if we call the following method with the expression mystery(0)?

```
public void mystery(int N) {
    System.out.println(N);
    if (N <= 5)
        mystery(N + 1);
} // mystery()
```

What about mystery(100)?

EXERCISE 12.2 What would be printed if we call the following method with the expression mystery(5)?

```
public void mystery(int N) {
    System.out.println(N);
    if (N <= 5)
        mystery(N - 1);
} // mystery()
```

12.1.2 Recursion as a Problem-Solving Approach

Given that recursion is not really necessary (if a programming language has loops) and not more efficient than loops, why is it so important? The answer is that, in a broader sense, recursion is an effective approach to problem solving. It is a way of viewing a problem. And it is mostly in this sense that we want to study recursion.

Recursion is based on two key problem-solving concepts: *divide and conquer* and **self-similarity**. In recursive problem solving we use the divide-and-conquer strategy repeatedly to break a big problem into a sequence of smaller and smaller problems until we arrive at a problem that is practically trivial to solve.

Subproblems

What allows us to create this series of subproblems is that each subproblem is similar to the original problem—that is, each subproblem is just a smaller version of the original problem. Look again at the task of saying "Hello" *N* times. Solving this task involves solving the similar task of saying "Hello" *N* − 1 times, which can be divided into the similar task of saying "Hello" *N* − 2 times. And so on.

Self-similarity

The ability to see a problem as being composed of smaller, self-similar problems is at the heart of the recursive approach. And although you may not have thought about this before, a surprising number of programming problems have this self-similarity characteristic. Let's illustrate these ideas with some simple examples.

PROGRAMMING TIP: Divide and Conquer. Many programming problems can be solved by dividing them into smaller, simpler problems. For recursive solutions, finding the key to the subproblem often holds the solution to the original problem.

12.2 Recursive Definition

One place you may have already seen recursion is in mathematics. A *recursive definition* in mathematics is one that defines the *n*th case of a concept in terms of the (*n* − 1)st case plus some kind of boundary condition.

12.2.1 Factorial: *N*!

For example, consider the problem of calculating the factorial of *n*—that is, *n*! for $n \geq 0$. As you may recall, *n*! is calculated as follows:

```
n! = n * (n-1) * (n-2) * ... * 1, for n > 0
```

In addition, 0! is defined as 1. Let's now look at some examples for different values of *n*:

```
4! = 4 * 3 * 2 * 1 = 24
3! = 3 * 2 * 1 = 6
2! = 2 * 1 = 2
1! = 1
0! = 1
```

As these examples suggest, *n*! can always be calculated in terms of (*n* − 1)! This relationship may be clearer if we rewrite the foregoing calculations as follows:

```
4! = 4 * 3 * 2 * 1 = 4 * 3! = 24
3! = 3 * 2 * 1     = 3 * 2! = 6
2! = 2 * 1         = 2 * 1! = 2
1!                 = 1 * 0! = 1
0!                 = 1
```

The only case in which we can't calculate $n!$ in terms of $(n-1)!$ is when n is 0. Otherwise, in each case we see that

```
n! = n * (n-1)!
```

This leads to the following recursive definition:

```
n! = 1          if n = 0    // Boundary (or base) case
n! = n * (n-1)! if n > 0    // Recursive case
```

A **recursive definition** consists of two parts: a recursive part in which the nth value is defined in terms of the $(n-1)$st value, and a nonrecursive, boundary case, which defines a limiting condition. Note that if we had omitted the base case, the recursion would have continued to $(-1)!$ and $(-2)!$ and so on.

DEBUGGING TIP: Bounding the Repetition. An infinite repetition will result if a recursive definition is not properly bounded.

The recursive case uses divide and conquer to break the problem into a smaller problem, but the smaller problem is just a smaller version of the original problem. This combination of self-similarity and divide and conquer is what characterizes recursion. The base case is used to stop or limit the recursion.

EFFECTIVE DESIGN: Recursive Definition. For recursive algorithms and definitions, the **base case** serves as the bound for the algorithm. The **recursive case** defines the nth case in terms of the $(n-1)$st case.

12.2.2 Drawing a Nested Pattern

As another example, consider the problem of drawing the nested boxes pattern in Figure 12–2. The self-similarity occurs in the fact that for this pattern, its parts resemble the whole. The basic shape involved is a square, which is repeated over and over at an ever-smaller scale. A recursive definition for this pattern would be

```
Base case:      if side < 5 do nothing
Recursive case: if side >= 5
                draw a square
                decrease the side and draw a smaller
                        pattern inside the square
```

This definition uses the length of the square's side to help define the pattern. If the length of the side is greater than or equal to 5, draw a square with dimensions *side* × *side*. Then decrease the length of the side and draw a smaller version of the pattern inside that square. In this case, the *side*

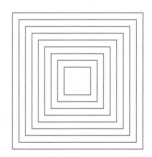

FIGURE 12–2   The nested squares pattern.

Self-similarity

Smaller subpattern

The side as a parameter

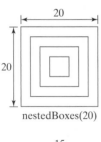

nestedBoxes(20)

nestedBoxes(15)

nestedBoxes(10)

nestedBoxes(5)

FIGURE 12–3 A trace of the nested boxes definition starting with a side of 20 and decreasing the side by 5 each time.

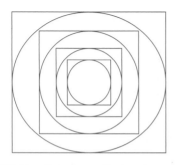

FIGURE 12–4 Write a recursive definition for this pattern.

variable will decrease at each level of the drawing. When the length of the side becomes less than 5, the recursion stops. Thus, the length of the side serves as the limit or bound for this algorithm.

You should note that the length of the side functions here like a parameter in a method definition: It provides essential information for the definition, just as a method parameter provides essential data to the method. Indeed, this is exactly the role that parameters play in recursive methods. They provide essential information that determines the method's behavior.

Figure 12–3 illustrates how we would apply the definition. Suppose the side starts out at 20 and decreases by 5 at each level of recursion. Note that as you move from top to bottom across the four patterns, each pattern contains the one below it. So a nestedBoxes(20) can be drawn by drawing a 20×20 square and then drawing a nestedBoxes(15) pattern inside it. Similarly, a nestedBoxes(15) can be drawn by drawing a 15×15 square and then drawing a nestedBoxes(10) pattern inside it. And so on.

These examples illustrate the power of recursion as a problem-solving technique for problems that involve repetition. Like the iterative (looping) control structures we studied in Chapter 6, recursion is used to implement repetition within a bound. For recursive algorithms, the bound is defined by the base case, whereas for loops, the bound is defined by the loop's entry condition. In either case, repetition stops when the bound is reached.

> DEBUGGING TIP: Infinite Recursion. An unbounded or incorrectly bounded recursive algorithm will lead to infinite repetition. Care must be taken to get the bound right.

SELF-STUDY EXERCISES

EXERCISE 12.3 You can calculate 2^n by multiplying 2 by itself n times. For example, 2^3 is $2 \times 2 \times 2$. Note also that $2^0 = 1$. Given these facts, write a recursive definition for 2^n, for $n \geq 0$.

EXERCISE 12.4 Generalize your solution to the previous exercise by giving a recursive definition for x^n, where x and n are both integers ≥ 0.

EXERCISE 12.5 Is the recursive definition given earlier for the nested boxes equivalent to the following recursive definition? Explain.

```
Draw a square.          // in every case
If side > 5
    draw a smaller nested boxes inside the square
```

In this case, the base case (*side* $<= 5$) is implicit.

EXERCISE 12.6 Write a recursive definition for the recursive pattern shown in Figure 12–4.

12.3 Recursive String Methods

A **recursive method** is a method that calls itself. Like recursive definitions, recursive methods are designed around the divide-and-conquer and self-similarity principles. Defining a recursive method involves very much the same kind of analysis we used in designing recursive definitions. We identify a self-similar subproblem of the original problem plus one or more limiting cases.

```
/**
 * printString() prints each character of the string s
 * Pre: s is initialized (non-null)
 * Post: none
 */
public void printString(String s) {
    if (s.length() == 0)
        return;                        // Base case: do nothing
    else {
        System.out.print(s.charAt(0)); // Recursive case: print head
        printString(s.substring(1));   // Print tail of the string
    }
} // printString()
```

FIGURE 12–5   The recursive printString() method.

The idea of a method calling itself seems a bit strange at first. It's perhaps best understood in terms of a clone or a copy. When a method calls itself, it really calls a copy of itself, one that has a slightly different internal state. Usually the difference in state is the result of a difference in the invoked method's parameters.

How can a method call itself?

12.3.1 Printing a String

To illustrate the concept of a recursive method, let's define a recursive method for printing a string. This is not intended to be a practical method—we already have the println() method for printing strings. But pretend for a moment that you only have a version of println() that works for characters, and your task is to write a version that can be used to print an entire string of characters.

A little terminology will help us describe the algorithm. Let's call the first letter of a string the *head* of the string, and let's refer to all the remaining letters in the string as the *tail* of the string. Then the problem of printing a string can be solved using a **head-and-tail algorithm**, which consists of two parts: printing the head of the string and recursively printing its tail. The limiting case here is when a string has no characters in it. It's trivial to print the empty string—just don't do anything! This leads to the method definition shown in Figure 12–5.

Head-and-tail algorithm

The base case here provides a limit and bounds the recursion when the length of s is 0—that is, when the string is empty. The recursive case solves the problem of printing s by solving the smaller, self-similar problem of printing a substring of s. Note that the recursive case makes progress toward the limit. On each recursion, the tail will get smaller and smaller until it becomes the empty string.

EFFECTIVE DESIGN: Recursive Progress. In a recursive algorithm, each recursive call must make progress toward the bound, or base case.

Let's now revisit the notion of a method calling itself. Obviously this is what happens in the recursive case, but what does it mean—what actions does this lead to in the program? Each recursive call to a method is really a

Recursive call

call to a *copy* of that method, and each copy has a slightly different internal state. We can define printString()'s internal state completely in terms of its recursion parameter, *s*, the string that's being printed. A **recursion parameter** is a parameter whose value is used to control the progress of the recursion. In this case, if *s* differs in each copy, then so will s.substring(1) and s.charAt(0).

EFFECTIVE DESIGN: Recursion and Parameters.   Recursive methods use a *recursion parameter* to distinguish between self-similar instances of the method call. The parameter controls the progress of the recursion toward its bound.

Self-similar instances

Figure 12–6 illustrates the sequence of recursive method calls and the output that results when printString("hello") is invoked. Each box represents a separate instance of the printString() method, with its own internal state. In this illustration its state is represented by its parameter, s. Because each instance has a different parameter, the behavior of each will be slightly different, so each box also shows the character that will be printed by that instance (s.charAt(0)), and the string that will be passed on to the next instance (s.substring(1)).

DEBUGGING TIP: Off-by-One Error. The expressions s.charAt(0) and s.substring(1) will generate exceptions if *s* is the empty string.

The arrows represent the method calls and returns. Note that the first return that's executed is the one in the base case. Each instance of the method must wait for the instance it called to return before it can return. That's why the instances "pile up" in a cascade-like structure. The arrowless lines trace the order in which the output is produced.

Each instance of printString() is similar to the next in that each will print a character and pass on a substring, but each performs its duties on a different string. Note how the string, the recursion parameter in this case, gets smaller in each instance of printString(). This represents progress toward the method's base case s.length() == 0. When the empty string is passed as an argument, the recursion will stop. If the method does not make progress toward its bound in this way, the result will be an infinite recursion.

Progress toward the bound

EFFECTIVE DESIGN: Bounding the Recursion.   For recursive algorithms, the *recursion parameter* is used to express the algorithm's bound or *base case*. In order for the algorithm to terminate, each recursive call should make progress toward the bound.

Self-similarity

Note also the order in which things are done in this method. First s.charAt(0) is printed, and then s.substring(1) is passed to printString() in the recursion. This is a typical structure for a *head-and-tail algorithm*. What makes this work is that the tail is a smaller, self-similar version of the original structure.

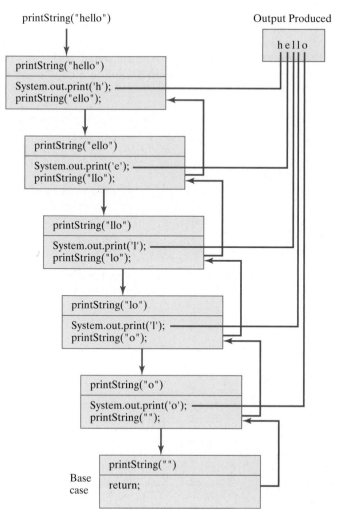

printString("hello")

Output Produced

FIGURE 12–6 A recursive method call invokes a copy of the method, each with a slightly different internal state. As this is done repeatedly, a stack of method calls is created.

EFFECTIVE DESIGN: Head-and-Tail Algorithm.   Many recursive solutions involve breaking a sequential structure, such as a string or an array, into its *head* and *tail*. An operation is performed on the head, and the algorithm recurses on the tail.

SELF-STUDY EXERCISE

EXERCISE 12.7   What would be printed by the following version of the printString2() method, if it is called with printString2("hello")?

```java
public void printString2(String s)  {
    if (s.length() == 1)
      System.out.print(s.charAt(0));              // Base case:
    else {
      System.out.print(s.charAt(s.length() - 1)); // Print last char
      printString2(s.substring(0, s.length() - 1));
                                                  // Print rest of string

    }
} // printString2()
```

12.3.2   Printing the String Backward

What do you suppose would happen if we reversed the order of the statements in the `printString()` method? That is, what if the recursive call came before `s.charAt(0)` is printed, as in the following method:

```
/**
 * printReverse() prints each character s in reverse order
 * Pre: s is initialized (non-null)
 * Post: none
 */
public void printReverse(String s) {
    if (s.length() > 0) {                    // Recursive case:
        printReverse(s.substring(1));        //   Print tail of the string
        System.out.print(s.charAt(0));       //   Then print the first char
    }
} // printReverse()
```

As its name suggests, this method will print the string in reverse order. The trace in Figure 12–7 shows how this works. Before `printReverse("hello")`

FIGURE 12–7   A trace of `printReverse(s)`, which prints its string argument in reverse order.

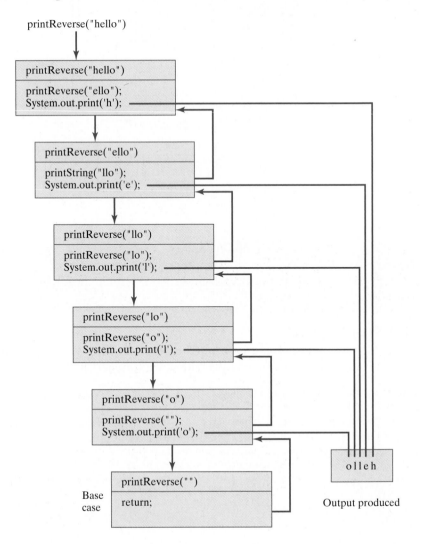

can print *h*, it calls printReverse("ello") and must wait for that call to complete its execution and return. But printReverse("ello") calls print-Reverse("llo") and so must wait for that call to complete its execution and return.

This process continues until printReverse("") is called. While the base case is executing, the other five instances of printReverse() must each wait for the instance that they called to complete its execution. It is only after the base case returns, that printReverse("o") can print its first character and return. So the letter *o* will be printed first. After printReverse("o") has returned, then printReverse("lo") can print its first character. So the letter *l* will be printed next, and so on, until the original call to printRe-verse("hello") is completed and returns. Thus, the string will get printed in reverse order.

Note that the method call and return structure in this example follows a **last-in–first-out (LIFO) protocol**. That is, the last method called is always the first method to return. This is the protocol used by all method calls, recursive or otherwise.

Last-in–first-out protocol

> **JAVA LANGUAGE RULE** LIFO. Procedure call and return in Java, and all other programming languages, uses a last-in-first-out protocol.

For example, compare the order in which things happen in Figure 12–7 with the method stack trace in Figure 11–12. The only real difference between the two figures is that here the method stack is represented as growing downward, whereas in Figure 11–12 it grows upward. As each method call is made, a representation of the method call is placed on the **method call stack**. When a method returns, its block is removed from the top of the stack. The only difference between recursive and nonrecursive method calls is that recursive methods call instances of the same method definition. Of course, as we've seen, the instances are all slightly different from each other.

Method call stack

SELF-STUDY EXERCISES

EXERCISE 12.8 Write a recursive method called countDown() that takes a single int parameter, $N \geq 0$, and prints a countdown, such as "5, 4, 3, 2, 1, blastoff." In this case, the method would be called with countDown(5).

EXERCISE 12.9 Revise the method in the previous exercise so that when it's called with countDown(10), it will print "10 8 6 4 2 blastoff"; if it's called with countDown(9), it prints "9 7 5 3 1 blastoff."

12.3.3 Counting Characters in a String

Suppose you're writing an encryption program and you need to count the frequencies of the letters of the alphabet. Let's write a recursive method for this task.

Problem statement

This method will have two parameters: a String to store the string that will be processed and a char to store the target character—the one we want to count. The method should return an int, representing the number of occurrences of the target character in the string:

```
// Goal: count the occurrences of ch in s
public int countChar(String s, char ch) {
    ...
}
```

FIGURE 12–8   The recursive
countChar() method.

```
/**
 * Pre:  s is a non-null String, ch is any character
 * Post: countblanks() == the number of occurrences of ch in str
 */
public int countChar(String s, char ch) {
    if (s.length() == 0)                        // Base case: empty string
        return 0;
    else if (s.charAt(0) == ch)                 // Recursive case 1
        return 1 + countChar(s.substring(1), ch); // Head equals ch
    else                                        // Recursive case 2
        return 0 + countChar(s.substring(1), ch); // Head is not the ch
} // countChar()
```

Here again our analysis must identify a recursive step that breaks the problem into smaller, self-similar versions of itself, plus a base case or limiting case that defines the end of the recursive process. Because the empty string will contain no target characters, we can use it as our base case. So, if it is passed the empty string, countChar() should just return 0 as its result.

Base case

Recursive case

For the recursive case we can divide the string into its head and tail. If the head is the target character, then the number of occurrences in the string is (1 + the number of occurrences in its tail). If the head of the string is not the target character, then the number of occurrences is (0 + the number of occurrences in its tail). Of course, we'll use recursion to calculate the number of occurrences in the tail.

This analysis leads to the recursive method shown in Figure 12–8. Note that for both recursive cases the same recursive call is used. In both cases we pass the tail of the original string, plus the target character. Note also how the return statement is evaluated:

```
return 1 + countChar(s.substring(1),ch);   // Head equals ch
```

Evaluation order is crucial

Before the method can return a value, it must receive the result of calling countChar(s.substring(1),ch) and add it to 1. Only then can a result be returned to the calling method. This leads to the following evaluation sequence for countChar("dad",'d'):

```
countChar("dad",'d');
1 + countChar("ad",'d');
1 + 0 + countChar("d",'d');
1 + 0 + 1 + countChar("",'d');
1 + 0 + 1 + 0 = 2                // Final result
```

In this way, the final result of calling countChar("dad",'d') is built up recursively by adding together the partial results from each separate instance of countChar(). The evaluation process is also shown graphically in Figure 12–9.

DEBUGGING TIP: Return Type. A common error with nonvoid recursive algorithms is forgetting to make sure that those return statements that contain a recursive call yield the correct data type.

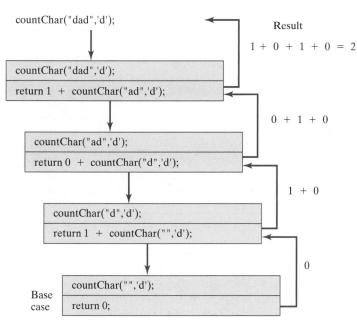

FIGURE 12–9 A trace of
`countChar("dad", 'd')`, which
returns the value 2.

SELF-STUDY EXERCISE

EXERCISE 12.10 Here's a numerical problem. Write a recursive method
to compute the sum of 1 to *N*, given *N* as a parameter.

12.3.4 Translating a String

A widely used string-processing task is to convert one string into another
string by replacing one character with a substitute throughout the string.
For example, suppose we want to convert a Unix path name, which uses
the forward slash "/" to separate one part of the path from another, into a
Windows path name, which uses the backslash character "\" as a separator. For example, we want a method that can translate the following two
strings into one another: *Problem statement*

```
/unix_system/myfolder/java
\Windows_system\myfolder\java
```

Thus, we want a method that takes three parameters: a `String`, on
which the conversion will be performed, and two `char` variables, the first
being the original character in the string and the second being its substi-   *Method design*
tute. The precondition for this method is simply that each of these three
parameters has been properly initialized with a value. The postcondition
is that all occurrences of the first character have been replaced by the
second character.

As in our previous string-processing methods, the limiting case in this   *Head-and-tail algorithm*
problem is the empty string, and the recursive case will divide the string
into its head and its tail. If the head is the character we want to replace,
we concatenate its substitute with the result we obtain by recursively
converting its tail.

FIGURE 12–10 The convert() method replaces one character with another in a string.

```
/**
 * Pre:  str, ch1, ch2 have been initialized
 * Post: the result contains a ch2 everywhere that ch1 had occurred
 *       in str
 */
public static String convert(String str, char ch1, char ch2) {
    if (str.length() == 0)              // Base case: empty string
        return str;
    else if (str.charAt(0) == ch1)    // Recursive 1: ch1 at head
        return ch2 + convert(str.substring(1), ch1, ch2); // Replace it
    else                               // Recursive 2: ch1 not at head
        return str.charAt(0) + convert(str.substring(1), ch1, ch2);
} // convert()
```

This analysis leads to the definition shown in Figure 12–10. This method has more or less the same head and tail structure as the preceding example. The difference is that here the operation we perform on the head of the string is concatenation rather than addition.

The base case is still the case in which str is the empty string. The first recursive case occurs when the character being replaced is the head of str. In that case, its substitute (ch2) is concatenated with the result of converting the rest of the string and returned as the result. The second recursive case occurs when the head of the string is *not* the character being replaced. In this case, the head of the string is simply concatenated with the result of converting the rest of the string. Figure 12–11 shows an example of its execution.

FIGURE 12–11 A trace of convert("bad",'d','m'), which returns "bam."

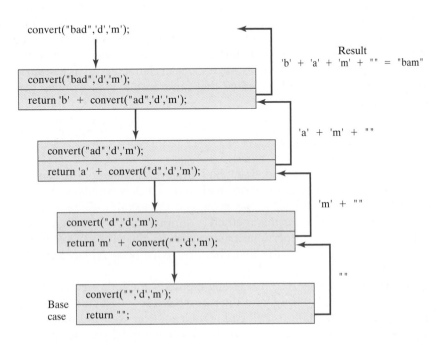

SELF-STUDY EXERCISE

EXERCISE 12.11 Write a recursive method that changes each blank within a string into two consecutive blanks, leaving the rest of the string unchanged.

12.4 Recursive Array Processing

Like strings, arrays also have a recursive structure. Just as each substring of a string is similar to the string as a whole, each portion of an array is similar to the array as a whole. Similarly, just as a string can be divided into a head and a tail, an array can be divided into its *head*, the first element, and its *tail*, the rest of its elements (Fig. 12–12). Because the tail of an array is itself an array, it satisfies the self-similarity principle. Therefore, arrays have all the appropriate characteristics that make them excellent candidates for recursive processing.

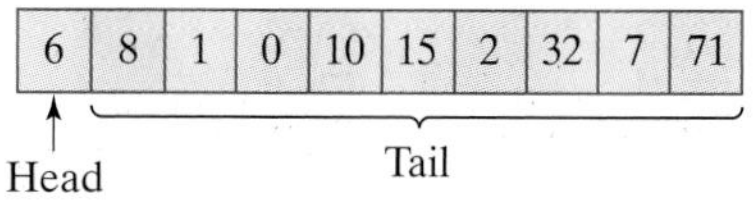

12.4.1 Recursive Sequential Search

Let's start by developing a recursive version of the sequential search algorithm that we discussed in Chapter 8. Recall that the sequential search method takes two parameters: the array being searched and the *key*, or target value, being searched for. If the key is found in the array, the method returns its index. If the key is not found, the method returns −1, thereby indicating that the key was not contained in the array. So the iterative version of this method has the following general form:

FIGURE 12–12 An array of int is a recursive structure whose tail is similar to the array as a whole.

Method design

```
/**
 * Performs a sequential search of an integer array
 * @param arr is the array of integers
 * @param key is the element being searched for
 * @return the key's index is returned if the key is
 *   found otherwise -1 is returned
 * Pre:  arr is not null
 * Post: either -1 or the key's index is returned
 */
public int sequentialSearch(int arr[], int key) {
    return -1;           // failure if this is reached
}
```

If we divide the array into its head and tail, then one way to describe a recursive search algorithm is as follows:

```
If the array is empty, return -1
If the head of the array matches the key, return its index
If the head of the array doesn't match the key,
   return the result of searching the tail of the array
```

This algorithm clearly resembles the approach we used in recursive string processing: Perform some operation on the head of the array and recurse on the tail of the array.

The challenge in developing this algorithm is not so much knowing what to do but knowing how to represent concepts like the head and tail of the array. For strings, we had methods such as s.charAt(0) to represent the head of the string and s.substring(1) to represent the string's tail.

How do we represent head and tail?

FIGURE 12–13   A parameter, *head*, can represent the head of some portion of the array.

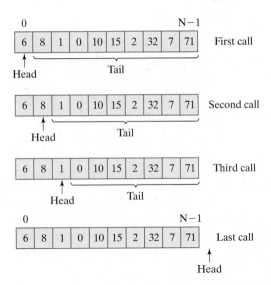

For an array named arr, the expression arr[0] represents the head of the array. Unfortunately, we have no method comparable to the substring() method for strings that lets us represent the tail of the array.

To help us out of this dilemma, we can use an integer parameter to represent the head of the array. Let's have the int parameter, *head*, represent the current head of the array (Fig. 12–13). Then *head* + 1 represents the start of the tail, and arr.length-1 represents the end of the tail. Our method will always be passed a reference to the whole array, but it will restrict the search to the portion of the array starting at *head*. If we let *head* vary from 0 to arr.length on each recursive call, the method will recurse through the array in head/tail fashion, searching for the key. The method will stop when head = arr.length.

> PROGRAMMING TIP: Subarray Parameter.   For methods that take an array argument, an int parameter can be used to designate the portion of the array that should be processed in the method.

This leads to the definition for recursive search shown in Figure 12–14. Note that the recursive search method takes three parameters: the array to be searched, arr, the key being sought, and an integer head that gives the starting location for the search. The algorithm is bounded when head = arr.length. In effect, this is like saying the recursion should stop when we have reached a tail that contains 0 elements. This underscores the point we made earlier about the importance of parameters in designing recursive methods. Here the *head* parameter serves as the **recursion parameter**. It controls the progress of the recursion.

Recursion parameter

Note also that for the search algorithm we need two base cases. One represents the successful case, where the key is found in the array. The other represents the unsuccessful case, which comes about after we have looked at every possible head in the array and not found the key. This case will arise through exhaustion—that is, when we have exhausted all possible locations for the key.

```
/**
 * search(arr,head,key)---Recursively search arr for key
 *  starting at head
 * Pre:  arr != null and 0 <= head <= arr.length
 * Post: if arr[k] == key for some k,  0 <= k < arr.length, return k
 *       else return -1
 */
private int search(int arr[], int head, int key)  {
    if (head == arr.length)      // Base case: empty list - failure
        return -1;
    else if (arr[head] == key)   // Base case: key found---success
        return head;
    else                         // Recursive case: search the tail
        return search(arr, head + 1, key);
}
```

FIGURE 12–14 The recursive search method takes three parameters. The *head* parameter points to the beginning of that portion of the array that is being searched.

DEBUGGING TIP: Recursive Search. For the recursive search method to work properly, it must be called with the correct value for the *head* parameter.

12.4.2   Information Hiding

Note that in order to use the search() method, you would have to know that you must supply a value of 0 as the argument for the *head* parameter. This is not only awkward but also impractical. After all, if we want to search an array, we just want to pass two arguments, the array and the key we're searching for. It's unreasonable to expect users of a method to know that they also have to pass 0 as the head in order to get the recursion started. This design is also prone to error, because it's quite easy for a mistake to be made when the method is called.

Design issue

For this reason, it is customary to provide a nonrecursive interface to the recursive method. The interface hides the fact that a recursive algorithm is being used, but this is exactly the kind of implementation detail that should be hidden from the user. A more appropriate design would make the recursive method a `private` method that's called by the public method, as shown Figure 12–15 and implemented in the `Searcher` class (Fig. 12–16).

Hide implementation details

EFFECTIVE DESIGN: Information Hiding. Unnecessary implementation details, such as whether a method uses a recursive or iterative algorithm, should be hidden within the class. Users of a class or method should be shown only those details that they need to know.

Searcher
+ search(in arr[] : int, in key : int) : int
− search(in arr[] : int, in head : int, in key : int) : int

FIGURE 12–15 The public search() method serves as an interface to the private recursive method, search(). Note that the methods have different signatures.

```
public class Searcher {
    /**
     *  search(arr,key) -- searches arr for key.
     * Pre:  arr != null and 0 <= head <= arr.length
     * Post: if arr[k] == key for some k,  0 <= k < arr.length, return k
     *       else return -1
     */
    public int search(int arr[], int key) {
        return search(arr, 0, key);        // Call recursive search to do the work
    }


    /**
     * search(arr, head, key) -- Recursively search arr for key
     *  starting at head
     * Pre:  arr != null and 0 <= head <= arr.length
     * Post: if arr[k] == key for some k,  0 <= k < arr.length, return k
     *       else return -1
     */
    private int search(int arr[], int head, int key)  {
        if (head == arr.length)     // Base case: empty list - failure
            return -1;
        else if (arr[head] == key)  // Base case: key found -- success
            return head;
        else                        // Recursive case: search the tail
            return search(arr, head + 1, key);
    } // search()

    public static void main(String args[]) {
        int numbers[] = {0, 2, 4, 6, 8, 10, 12, 14, 16, 18};
        Searcher searcher = new Searcher();
        for (int k = 0; k <= 20; k++) {
            int result = searcher.search(numbers, k);
            if (result != -1)
                System.out.println(k + " found at " + result);
            else
                System.out.println(k + " is not in the array ");
        } // for
    } // main()
} // Searcher
```

FIGURE 12–16   The Searcher class illustrates the principle of information hiding. Its public search() method calls the private, recursive search() method to perform the search. It, thus, hides the fact that it is using a recursive algorithm.

SELF-STUDY EXERCISE

EXERCISE 12.12   Write a `main()` method for the `Searcher` class to conduct the following test of `search()`. Create an `int` array of ten elements, initialize its elements to the even numbers from 0 to 18, and then use a for loop to search the array for each of the numbers from 0 to 20.

12.4.3   Recursive Selection Sort

The *selection sort* algorithm was described in Chapter 8. It goes as follows. Suppose you have a deck of 52 cards. Lay them out on a table, face up, one card next to the other. Then starting at the last card look through the deck, from last to first, find the largest card and exchange it with the last card. Then go through the deck again starting at the next to the last card, find the next largest card, and exchange it with the next to the last card. Then go to the next card, and so on. If you repeat this process 51 times, the deck will be completely sorted.

Sorting a deck of cards

> DEBUGGING TIP: Off-by-One Error. Sorting algorithms are particularly susceptible to an off-by-one error. To sort an array with N elements, you generally need to make $N - 1$ passes.

Let's design a recursive version of this algorithm. The algorithm we just described is like a head-and-tail algorithm in reverse, where the *last* card in the deck is like the head, and the cards before it are like the tail. After each pass or recursion, the last card will be in its proper location, and the cards before it will represent the unsorted portion of the deck. If we use parameter to represent *last*, then at each level of the recursion, it will be moved one card to the left.

Figure 12–17 illustrates this process for an array of integers. The base case is reached when the *last* parameter is pointing to the first element in the array. An array with one element in it is sorted. It needs no rearranging. The recursive case involves searching an ever-smaller portion of the array. This is represented in our design by moving *last* down one element to the left.

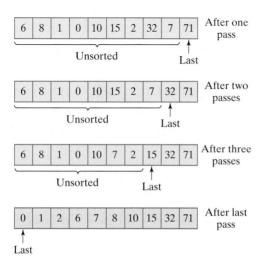

FIGURE 12–17   Selection sort: Using a head-and-tail algorithm in reverse to sort an integer array.

FIGURE 12–18 The selection-
Sort() method uses the findMax()
and swap() methods to help it sort an
array.

```
/**
 * selectionSort(arr,last) -- Recursively sort arr starting at last
 * Pre:  arr != null and 0 <= last < arr.length
 * Post: arr will be arranged so that arr[j] <= arr[k], for any j < k
 */
private void selectionSort(int arr[], int last) {
    if (last > 0) {
        int maxLoc = findMax (arr, last);    // Find the largest
        swap(arr, last, maxLoc);             // Swap it with last
        selectionSort(arr, last - 1);        // Move down the array
    }
} // selectionSort()
```

Figure 12–18 provides a partial implementation of selection sort for an
array of int. In this definition, the array is one parameter. The second parameter, int last, defines that portion of the array, from right to left, that
is yet to be sorted. On the first call to this method, *last* will be arr.length
− 1. On the second, it will be arr.length − 2, and so on. When *last* gets
to be 0, the array will be sorted. Thus, in terms of the card deck analogy,
last represents the last card in the unsorted portion of the deck.

Task decomposition

Note how simply the selectionSort() method can be coded. Of course,
this is because we have used separate methods to handle the tasks of finding the largest element and swapping the last element and the largest.
This not only makes sense in terms of the divide-and-conquer principle,
but we also already defined a swap() method in Chapter 8. So this is a
good example of reusing code:

```
/**
 * swap(arr0, el1 el2) swaps el1 and el2 in the arrary, arr
 * Pre: arr is non null, 0 <= el1 < arr.length, 0 <= el2 < arr.length
 * Post: el1 is located where el2 was located in arr and vice versa
 */
private void swap(int arr[], int el1, int el2)  {
    int temp = arr[el1]; //   Assign the first element to temp
    arr[el1] = arr[el2]; //   Overwrite first with second
    arr[el2] = temp;     //   Overwrite second with temp (i.e., first)
} // swap()
```

The definition of the findMax() method is left as a self-study exercise.

PROGRAMMING TIP: Method Decomposition.   A task can be simplified
by breaking it up into simpler subtasks, especially if you already have
methods for solving one or more of the subtasks.

SELF-STUDY EXERCISES

EXERCISE 12.13   As in the case of the search() method, we need to provide a public interface to the recursive selectionSort() method, so that
the user can just sort an array by calling sort(arr), where arr is the name
of the array to be sorted. Define the sort() method.

EXERCISE 12.14 Define an iterative version of the findMax(arr,N) method that is used in selectionSort(). Its goal is to return the location (index) of the largest integer between arr[0] and arr[N].

12.5 Example: Drawing (Recursive) Fractals

A *fractal* is a geometric shape that exhibits a recursive structure. When it is divided into parts, each part is a smaller version of the whole. Fractal patterns occur throughout nature. If you look at a graph of the Dow Jones Industrial Average (DJIA) over the past year, the graph for each day is similar to the graph of each month, which is similar to the graph of each year, and so on. Each part is a reduced-scale version of the whole. If you look at a coastline from an airplane, the shape of each part of the coastline, no matter how small the scale, resembles the shape of the whole coastline. If you look at a tree, each branch of the tree is similar in shape to the whole tree.

So, fractal patterns are all around us. Because of their self-similarity and divisibility, fractals are well suited for recursive programming. Drawing recursive patterns is also an excellent way to illustrate how to use parameters to create generality in method design. In this section, we will develop two simple patterns and incorporate them into an applet.

12.5.1 Nested Squares

Earlier in this chapter, we developed a recursive definition for drawing a nested squares pattern (Fig. 12–2). Now let's develop a recursive method that actually draws the pattern. For this pattern, the base case is the drawing of the square. The recursive case, if more divisions are desired, is the drawing of smaller patterns within the square:

```
Draw a square.
If more divisions are desired
    draw a smaller version of the pattern within the square.
```

An important consideration for this algorithm is to specify precisely what we mean by "if more divisions are desired." In other words, how exactly do we control the recursion? In our earlier definition of the pattern, we used the length of the side to control the algorithm. When *side* $\geq$ 5, we recursed.

Another more general way to do this is to describe the fractal structure in terms of its *levels*. For nested squares, the level-zero pattern would be just the basic square shape (Fig. 12–19). A level-one pattern would be the basic square shape plus an inner square, and so on. The higher the level, the more subdividing we do. Therefore, one way to control the recursion is to use a *level* parameter as the *recursion parameter*—as the parameter that controls the recursion:

```
Draw a square.
If the level is greater than 0,
    draw a smaller version of the pattern within the square.
```

What other parameters will we need for this method? If we're going to draw a rectangle, we'll need parameters for its *x*- and *y*-coordinates. This is a perfect job for a Point object. We'll also need a parameter for the length

Level 0

Level 1

Level 4

FIGURE 12–19 Levels 0, 1, and 4 of the nested squares pattern.

How should we represent the problem?

Levels of recursion

Method design

```
/**
 * drawBoxes()---recursively draws a pattern of nested squares
 *   with loc as the top left corner of outer square and side
 *   being the length square's side.
 * level (>= 0) is the recursion paramenter (base case: level  0)
 * delta is used to adjust the length of the side.
 */
private void drawBoxes(Graphics g, int level, Point loc, int side, int delta) {
    g.drawRect(loc.x, loc.y, side, side );
    if (level > 0) {
        Point newLoc = new Point( loc.x + delta, loc.y + delta);
        drawBoxes(g, level - 1, newLoc, side - 2 * delta, delta);
    }
} // drawBoxes()
```

FIGURE 12–20   The `drawBoxes()` method.

of sides of the square. Another issue we need to decide is how much the length of the sides should change at each level. Should length change by a fixed amount, by a fixed ratio, or by some other factor? In order to allow this kind of flexibility, let's use another parameter for this value.

These design considerations suggest the method shown in Figure 12–20. Note that we must also provide a `Graphics` parameter so the method can use the `drawRect()` method to draw the square. As we decided, the `level` parameter controls the recursion. Note that its value is decreased by 1 in the recursive call. This will ensure that `level` will eventually reach 0, and recursion will stop.

Finally, note the use of the `delta` parameter. In this case it is used to change the length of the sides by a fixed amount, 2 * `delta`, at each level. It is also used to calculate the *x*- and *y*-coordinates for the location of the next level of boxes *(loc.x + delta, loc.y + delta)*. But `delta`'s value remains constant through all the levels. This will lead to a pattern where the "gap" between nested squares is constant.

> **EFFECTIVE DESIGN: Levels of Recursion.**   Many recursive algorithms use a *level* parameter as the recursion parameter.

SELF-STUDY EXERCISES

EXERCISE 12.15   Trace through the `drawBoxes()` method and draw the level-four and level-five versions of the nested boxes pattern. Assume that the initial values for `side` and `delta` are 100 and 5, respectively, and the initial coordinates for `loc` are (20,20).

EXERCISE 12.16   The pattern shown in Figure 12–21 can be drawn by using `delta` as a fixed ratio of the length of the side, for example, 10 percent. Modify the `drawBoxes()` method to use `delta` in this way.

EXERCISE 12.17   Write an iterative version of the `drawBoxes()` method. (*Hint*: On each iteration, you must change the *x*- and *y*-coordinates of the square's location and the length of its side.)

FIGURE 12–21   This version of nested boxes can be drawn by using `delta` as a fixed percentage of the length of the side.

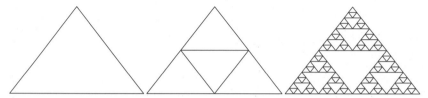

12.5.2   The Sierpinski Gasket

Let's return now to the *Sierpinski gasket* pattern that we introduced at the start of this chapter. This is a much more interesting fractal pattern (Fig. 12–22). The overall shape of the pattern is that of a triangle, but notice how the outer triangle is divided into three smaller triangles. Then each of those triangles are divided into three smaller triangles. If you continue this process of dividing and shrinking, you get the level-seven pattern shown here.

Let's develop a recursive method to draw this pattern. If we follow the same strategy we used in the nested squares example, we get the following algorithm:

```
Base case:        draw a triangle.
Recursive Case:   if more divisions are desired,
                      draw three smaller gaskets within the triangle.
```

For this pattern the base case is the drawing of the basic triangle. The recursive cases, if more divisions are desired, are the drawing of smaller gaskets within the triangle. Again we will use a `level` parameter to control the depth of the recursion. The higher the level, the more divisions will be drawn.

If we're going to draw a triangle shape, we need the coordinates of its three vertices—that is, an *x*- and *y*-coordinate for each vertex. This is a perfect job for a `Point` object. Taken together these design considerations suggest the method definition shown in Figure 12–23.

What other parameters do we need?

As we described earlier, we use the `level` parameter as the recursion parameter for this method. It controls the recursion. Note that each of the three recursive calls decreases the `level` by 1. This will ensure that eventually `level` will equal 0, and recursion will stop.

Levels of recursion

Note also how the three pairs of coordinates are used. Drawing a triangle is simple. Just draw three lines from (`p1.x`,`p1.y`) to (`p2.x`,`p2.y`), from (`p2.x`,`p2.y`) to (`p3.x`,`p3.y`), and from (`p3.x`,`p3.y`) back to (`p1.x`, `p1.y`). The most complicated part of the method is calculating the vertices for the three inner gaskets. If you look at Figure 12–22 again, you'll notice that each of the inner triangles uses one of the vertices of the main triangle, plus the *midpoints* of the two adjacent sides. Thus, the triangle on the "left" uses the left vertex (`p1.x`,`p1.y`), and the midpoints of the other two lines from (`p1.x`,`p1.y`) to (`p2.x`,`p2.y`) and from (`p1.x`,`p1.y`) to (`p3.x`,`p3.y`). As you may remember from high school math, the formula for computing the midpoint of the line segment $(x1, y1)$ to $(x2, y2)$ is

Midpoint of a line

```
( (x1 + x2) / 2, (y1 + y2) / 2 )
```

```
/**
 * drawGasket()---recursively draws the Sierpinski gasket
 *   pattern, with points p1, p2, p3, representing the vertices
 *   of its enclosing triangle.
 * level (>= 0) is the recursion paramenter (base case: level  0)
 */
private void drawGasket(Graphics g, int lev, Point p1, Point p2, Point p3) {
    g.drawLine(p1.x, p1.y, p2.x, p2.y);                // Draw a triangle
    g.drawLine(p2.x, p2.y, p3.x, p3.y);
    g.drawLine(p3.x, p3.y, p1.x, p1.y);
    if (lev > 0) {            // If more divisions desired, draw 3 smaller gaskets
        Point midP1P2 = new Point( (p1.x + p2.x) / 2, (p1.y + p2.y) / 2 );
        Point midP1P3 = new Point( (p1.x + p3.x) / 2, (p1.y + p3.y) / 2 );
        Point midP2P3 = new Point( (p2.x + p3.x) / 2, (p2.y + p3.y) / 2 );
        drawGasket(g, lev - 1, p1, midP1P2, midP1P3);
        drawGasket(g, lev - 1, p2, midP1P2, midP2P3);
        drawGasket(g, lev - 1, p3, midP1P3, midP2P3);
    }
} // drawGasket()
```

FIGURE 12–23 The drawGasket() method.

This formula is used repeatedly to calculate the vertices of the three smaller gaskets.

OBJECT-ORIENTED DESIGN: Tail Recursion

Although the drawBoxes() method is relatively simple to convert into an iterative version (see Self-Study Exercise 12.17), the same cannot be said for the drawGasket() method. It is clearly a case where the recursive approach makes the problem easier to solve.

One difference between drawBoxes() and drawGasket() is that draw-Boxes() is an example of a tail-recursive method. A method is **tail recursive** if all of its recursive calls occur as the last action performed in the method. You have to be a bit careful about this definition. The recursive call in a tail-recursive method has to be the last *executed* statement. It needn't be the last statement appearing in the method's definition.

For example, the following method will print "Hello" *N* times. This method is tail recursive even though its last statement is not a recursive call:

Tail recursion

```
public void printHello(int N) {
    if (N > 1) {
        System.out.println("Hello");
        printHello(N - 1); // This will be the last executed statement
    } else
        System.out.println("Hello");
} // printHello()
```

This method is tail recursive because the last statement that will be executed, in its recursive cases, is the recursive call.

A tail-recursive method is relatively easy to convert into an iterative method. The basic idea is to make the recursion parameter into a loop variable, taking care to make sure the bounds are equivalent. Thus, the following iterative method will print "Hello" *N* times:

```java
public void printHelloIterative(int N) {
    for (int k = N; k > 0; k--)
        System.out.println("Hello");
}
```

In this case, we use the parameter *N* to set the initial value of the loop variable, *k*, and we decrement *k* on each iteration. This is equivalent to what happens when we decrement the recursion parameter in the recursive call.

EFFECTIVE DESIGN: Tail Recursion. Tail-recursive algorithms are relatively simple to convert into iterative algorithms that do the same thing.

As you can see, recursive methods that are not tail recursive are much more complex. Just compare the drawGasket() and drawBoxes() methods. Yet it is precisely for these nontail-recursive algorithms that recursion turns out to be most useful. As you might expect, if you can't give a simple tail-recursive solution to a problem, the problem probably doesn't have a simple iterative solution either. Thus, the problems where we most need recursion are those where we can't give a simple tail-recursive or a simple iterative solution. And there are a lot of such problems, especially when you get into nonlinear data structures such as trees and graphs.

To gain some appreciation for this complexity, consider how difficult it would be to draw the Sierpinski gasket using an iterative approach. We could start by developing an outer for loop to account for the different levels in the pattern:

```java
for (int k = level; k > 0; k--) {
    drawGasket(g, lev - 1, p1, midP1P2, midP1P3);
    drawGasket(g, lev - 1, p2, midP1P2, midP2P3);
    drawGasket(g, lev - 1, p3, midP1P3, midP2P3);
}
```

But now each of the method calls within the body of this loop would have to be replaced by very complex loops. That would be a daunting task. So the lesson to be drawn from this observation is that recursion is most useful as a problem-solving technique for problems that don't yield to a simple iterative solution.

EFFECTIVE DESIGN: Recursion or Iteration. If you have difficulty designing an iterative solution to a problem, try developing a recursive solution to it.

SELF-STUDY EXERCISES

EXERCISE 12.18 Trace the drawGasket() method for levels two and three. Pick your own values for the three vertices.

EXERCISE 12.19 Is the printReverse() method, discussed earlier, tail recursive? Explain.

EXERCISE 12.20 Is the `countChar()` method, discussed earlier, tail recursive? Explain.

OBJECT-ORIENTED DESIGN: Recursion or Iteration?

As we mentioned at the outset of this chapter, recursive algorithms require more computational overhead than iterative algorithms. We're now in a good position, perhaps, to appreciate why this is so.

A recursive algorithm incurs two kinds of overhead that are not incurred by an iterative algorithm: memory and CPU time. Both of these are direct results of the fact that recursive algorithms do a lot of method calling.

Method call overhead

As we saw in our various traces, each time a method is called, a representation of the method call is placed on the *method call stack*. These representations often take the form of a *block* of memory locations, which can be quite large. The block must contain space for the method's local variables, including its parameters. Also, unless the method is `void`, the block must contain space for the method's return value. In addition it must contain a reference to the calling method, so it will know where to go when it is done. Figure 12–24 shows what the method call block would look like for the `search()` method.

Memory overhead

CPU overhead

In addition to the memory required, a method call also requires extra CPU time. Each time a method is called, Java must create a method call block, copy the method call arguments to the parameters in the block, create initial values for any local variables that are used by the method, and fill in the return address of the calling method. All of this takes time, and in the case of a recursive method, these steps are repeated at each level of the recursion.

Compare these memory and CPU requirements with what normally transpires for an iterative algorithm—an algorithm involving a loop. The loop structure usually occurs entirely within a method, so it doesn't incur either the memory or CPU overhead involved in recursion. Therefore, iterative algorithms are generally more efficient than recursive algorithms. One useful guideline, then, is when runtime performance and efficiency are of prime importance, you should use iteration instead of recursion.

FIGURE 12–24 A more detailed picture of the method call stack, showing two method blocks for `search()` after two levels of recursion.

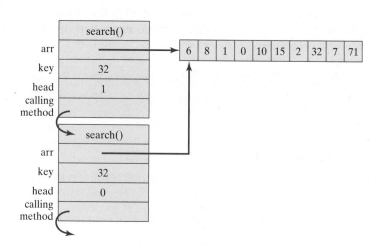

EFFECTIVE DESIGN: Iteration or Recursion.   Use an iterative algorithm instead of a recursive algorithm whenever efficiency and memory usage are important design factors.

On the other hand, for many problems, recursive algorithms are much easier to design than the corresponding iterative algorithms. We tried to illustrate this point in our development of the Sierpinski gasket algorithm, but there are many other examples that we could have used. Given that programmer and designer time is the most expensive resource involved in software development, a recursive solution may be easier to develop and maintain than a corresponding iterative solution. And given the great cost of software development, a less efficient solution that is easier to develop, easier to understand, and easier to maintain may be preferable to a highly efficient algorithm that's difficult to understand. For some problems then, such as the Sierpinski gasket, a recursive algorithm may provide the best solution.

Efficiency of development

Exploring the Mandelbrot Set

THE MANDELBROT set is one of the most fascinating fractals. It is named after its discover, Benoit Mandelbrot, an IBM mathematician. The Mandelbrot set itself is the black, heart-shaped image in the picture. What makes the Mandelbrot set so interesting is that with the help of a Java applet you can explore the set as if you were taking a trip through outer space.

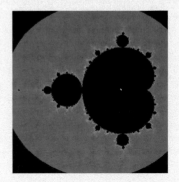

The most interesting regions to explore are those just along the boundary of the set. For example, notice that the boundary contains numerous circular shapes, each of which is itself studded with circular shapes. This is an example of the scaled self-similarity that we found to be so prevalent in recursive structures. By continually expanding the regions around the boundary, you'll find an infinite recursion of fascinating images and shapes. In some regions of the set you'll even find miniature replications of the set itself.

The Mandelbrot set is generated by an *iterated function system*. The mathematics underlying this fascinating object is quite accessible, and there are a number of online tutorials that explain how the set is generated and how the pictures are produced. Many of the Mandelbrot and fractal Web sites contain excellent Java applets that let you explore the Mandelbrot set as well as related sets.

An excellent place to start your exploration would be David Joyce's award-winning Web site,

```
http://aleph0.clarku.edu/djoyce/julia/wwwrefs.html
```

which contains references to a number of other good sites. For a tutorial on how the various Java programs work, see

```
http://storm.shodor.org/mteach/
```

> **EFFECTIVE DESIGN: Keep It Simple.**   When all other factors are equal, choose the algorithm (recursive or iterative) that is easiest to understand, develop, and maintain.

Optimizing compiler

One final point that's worth making is that some *optimizing* compilers are able to convert recursive methods into iterative methods when they compile the program. The algorithms for doing this are well known. They are often subjects for study in a data structures course, so we won't go into them here. The resulting runtime programs will be just as efficient, in CPU time and memory, as if you had written iterative methods. The point is that if you have such a compiler, you really get the best of both worlds. You get the advantage of using recursion as a problem-solving and software development approach, and the compiler takes care of producing an efficient object program.

From the Java Library

javax.swign.JComboBox

http://java.sun.com/products /jdk/1.3/docs/api/

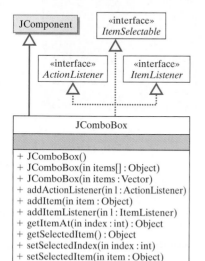

FIGURE 12–25   A JComboBox responds to action events and item events.

A JComboBox is a Swing component that combines a text field and a drop-down list (Fig. 12–25). It lets the user either type in a selection or choose a selection from a list that appears when the user requests it. (A JComboBox's drop-down behavior is somewhat similar to a java.awt.Choice box.)

A JComboBox can be used to represent a *drop-down menu*. When the user clicks on a JComboBox, a list of options drops down, and the user can select a particular option that is stored in the box's internal state (Fig. 12–26). The list of options associated with a JComboBox can be built beforehand and inserted into the component in a constructor, or items can be inserted one at a time by repeatedly using its addItem() method.

As Figure 12–25 shows, either an array or a vector of items can be passed to a constructor method to initialize the box's menu. The items stored in a JComboBox box are references to Objects, most commonly Strings that represent the name of the menu item. They are stored in the (zero indexed) order in which they are added. The addItem() method is used to add an individual Object to a JComboBox. By default, the first item added to a JComboBox will be the *selected* item until the user selects another item.

When the user makes a selection in a JComboBox, the item selected can be gotten either by its reference (getSelectedItem()) or by its position within the menu (getSelectedIndex()). There are also methods to setSelectedItem() and setSelectedIndex() that let you select an individual item either by its reference or its position. The addItemListener() method is used to designate some object as the listener for the ItemEvents that are generated whenever the user selects a menu option. Alternatively, the addActionListener() method lets you handle action events, such as when the user types a value into the box.

A JComboBox *Example*

As a simple example, let's design an applet interface that can be used to display the fractal patterns we developed earlier. This program will also be used in this chapter's lab, where you will develop some additional fractal drawings. We want an interface that lets the user select from among the available patterns—we'll use the Sierpinski gasket and nested boxes for starters. In addition, the user should also be able to select different levels for the drawings, from 0 to 9. We want to present these options in two menus, with one JComboBox for each menu.

The first step is to declare and instantiate the JComboBoxes as instance variables:

```
private String items[] = {"Sierpinski Gasket","Nested Boxes"};
private JComboBox patterns = new JComboBox(items);
private JComboBox levels = new JComboBox();
```

Note that in this case we pass the constructor for the patterns menu an entire array of items. If we hadn't done it this way, we would add individual items to the combo box in the applet's init() method. In fact that's how we'll initialize the levels menu:

```
for (int k=0; k < 10; k++)          // Add 10 levels
    levels.addItem(k + "" );
levels.setSelectedItem("4");        // Select level 4 as default
```

This loop would be placed in the applet's init() method. It adds strings representing levels 0 to 9 to the menu and initializes the box so that level four is showing as the default option.

Our next step is to designate the applet as the ItemListener for both menus—that is, the applet is named as the object that will handle the events that occur in the JComboBoxes. Then we add the JComboBox component to the applet's window:

```
controls.add(levels);             // Control panel for menus
controls.add(patterns);
getContentPane().add(controls, "North"); // Add the controls
getContentPane().add(canvas, "Center");  // And the drawing panel
levels.addItemListener(this);  // Register the menus with a listener
patterns.addItemListener(this);
```

Note that we use a separate controls panel (a JPanel) for the two menus and a canvas panel (another JPanel) for the drawings.

The next step is to implement the itemStateChanged() method to handle the user's selections. Whenever the user selects an item from a JComboBox menu, an ItemEvent is generated (Fig. 12–27). In order to handle these events, the applet must implement the ItemListener interface, which consists of the single method itemStateChanged(). This method is

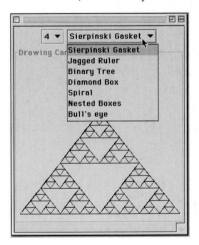

FIGURE 12–26 Using a JComboBox box.

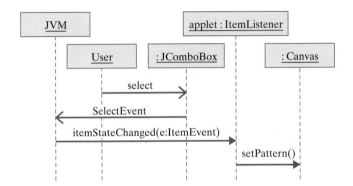

FIGURE 12–27 This UML sequence diagram shows the interaction between the various objects included in the action of selecting an item from a JComboBox.

invoked automatically whenever the user selects an item from one of the JComboBoxes:

```
public void itemStateChanged(ItemEvent e) {
    canvas.setPattern(patterns.getSelectedIndex(),
                                    levels.getSelectedIndex());
    repaint();
}
```

The itemStateChanged() method has the same general form as the actionPerformed() method, except that its parameter is an ItemEvent. For this example, the program uses the getSelectedIndex() method to get the selected pattern and the selected level by their respective item numbers within the menus. It then passes these values along to the canvas object, which takes care of the drawing (Fig. 12–27). Finally, the method invokes the repaint() method. Because the applet is a container, this will cause all of its components to be repainted as well. The complete implementation for the applet is given in Figure 12–28.

```
import java.awt.*;
import javax.swing.*;
import java.awt.event.*;

public class RecursivePatterns extends JApplet implements ItemListener {
    private String choices[] = {"Sierpinski Gasket", "Nested Boxes"};
    private JComboBox patterns = new JComboBox(choices);     // Pattern choices
    private JComboBox levels = new JComboBox();              // Level choices
    private Canvas canvas = new Canvas();                    // Drawing panel
    private JPanel controls = new JPanel();

    public void init() {
        for (int k=0; k < 10; k++)                          // Add 10 levels
            levels.addItem(k + "" );
        patterns.setSelectedItem(choices[0]);    // Initialize the menus
        levels.setSelectedItem("4");

        canvas.setBorder(BorderFactory.createTitledBorder("Drawing Canvas"));
        controls.add(levels);                        // Control panel for menus
        controls.add(patterns);
        getContentPane().add(controls,"North");    // Add the controls
        getContentPane().add(canvas,"Center");     // And the drawing panel
        levels.addItemListener( this );    // Register the menus with a listener
        patterns.addItemListener( this );
        setSize(canvas.WIDTH,canvas.HEIGHT+controls.getSize().width);
    } // init()

    public void itemStateChanged(ItemEvent e) {
        canvas.setPattern(patterns.getSelectedIndex(), levels.getSelectedIndex());
        repaint();                                   // Repaint the applet
    } // itemStateChanged()
} // RecursivePatterns
```

FIGURE 12–28   The RecursivePatterns applet.

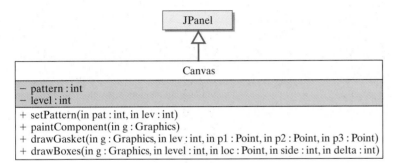

FIGURE 12–29   Design of a drawing
Canvas class.

The actual drawing of the fractal patterns is handled by the canvas JPanel component, whose design is shown in Figure 12–29 and whose implementation is given in Figure 12–30. All of the drawing is done in the paintComponent() method. Because the canvas is contained within the applet, the paintComponent() method is called automatically whenever the applet repaints itself. Notice how the switch statement uses the pattern that the user chose to call the corresponding drawing method. You can see from this switch statement that a JComboBox's items are *zero indexed*.

Zero indexing

```java
import javax.swing.*;
import java.awt.*;

public class Canvas extends JPanel {
    private static final int GASKET = 0, BOXES = 1;
    public static final int WIDTH=400, HEIGHT=400;
    private final int HBOX=10, VBOX=50, BOXSIDE=200, BOXDELTA=10;
    private final Point gasketP1 = new Point(10, 280);   // Initial gasket points
    private final Point gasketP2 = new Point(290, 280);
    private final Point gasketP3 = new Point(150, 110);
    private int pattern = 0 ;                             // Current pattern
    private int level = 4;                                // Current level

    public Canvas() {
        setSize(WIDTH, HEIGHT);
    }

    public void setPattern(int pat, int lev) {
        pattern = pat;
        level = lev;
    }
```

FIGURE 12–30   The Canvas class is a drawing panel, Part I.

```java
public void paintComponent(Graphics g) {
    g.setColor(getBackground());      // Redraw the panel's background
    g.drawRect(0, 0, WIDTH, HEIGHT);
    g.setColor(getForeground());
    switch (pattern) {
    case GASKET:
        drawGasket(g, level, gasketP1, gasketP2, gasketP3 );
        break;
    case BOXES:
        drawBoxes(g, level, new Point(HBOX, VBOX), BOXSIDE, BOXDELTA );
        break;
    } // switch
} // paintComponent()


/**
 * drawGasket()---recursively draws the Sierpinski gasket
 * pattern, with points p1, p2, p3, representing the vertices
 * of its enclosing triangle.
 * level (>= 0) is the recursion paramenter (base case: level  0)
 */
private void drawGasket(Graphics g, int lev, Point p1, Point p2, Point p3) {
    g.drawLine(p1.x, p1.y, p2.x, p2.y);            // Draw a triangle
    g.drawLine(p2.x, p2.y, p3.x, p3.y);
    g.drawLine(p3.x, p3.y, p1.x, p1.y);
    if (lev > 0) {          // If more divisions desired, draw 3 smaller gaskets
        Point midP1P2 = new Point( (p1.x + p2.x) / 2, (p1.y + p2.y) / 2 );
        Point midP1P3 = new Point( (p1.x + p3.x) / 2, (p1.y + p3.y) / 2 );
        Point midP2P3 = new Point( (p2.x + p3.x) / 2, (p2.y + p3.y) / 2 );
        drawGasket(g, lev - 1, p1, midP1P2, midP1P3);
        drawGasket(g, lev - 1, p2, midP1P2, midP2P3);
        drawGasket(g, lev - 1, p3, midP1P3, midP2P3);
    }
} // drawGasket()


/**
 * drawBoxes()---recursively draws a pattern of nested squares
 * with loc as the top left corner of outer square and side
 * being the length square's side.
 * level (>= 0) is the recursion paramenter (base case: level  0)
 * delta is used to adjust the length of the side.
 */
private void drawBoxes(Graphics g, int level, Point loc, int side, int delta) {
    g.drawRect(loc.x, loc.y, side, side );
    if (level > 0) {
        Point newLoc = new Point( loc.x + delta, loc.y + delta);
        drawBoxes(g, level - 1, newLoc, side - 2 * delta, delta);
    }
} // drawBoxes()
} // Canvas
```

FIGURE 12–30   *(continued)* The Canvas class, Part II.

IN THE LABORATORY: The RecursivePatterns Applet

The purpose of this lab is to gain some some hands-on experience with designing and implementing recursive algorithms. You will develop an applet that draws fractal patterns, similar to the nested boxes and Sierpinski graphics patterns developed earlier in the chapter. The objectives of this lab are

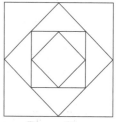

DiamondBox

- To design and implement recursive graphics algorithms.
- To build a menu-driven applet interface that uses a JComboBox.
- To gain an appreciation for the importance of recursion as a problem-solving technique.

Problem Description

Develop methods to draw the fractal patterns shown in Figure 12–31. Each pattern should be developed as a separate recursive method. Here are some design suggestions:

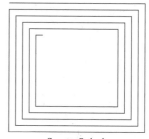

SquareSpiral

- **DiamondBoxes.** Like the Sierpinski gasket, the nested diamond pattern uses the midpoints of the line segments at one level to determine the vertices of the diamond pattern at the next level. The diamond shape can be drawn using g.drawLine(). Unlike the Sierpinski gasket, however, it is tail recursive.
- **SquareSpiral.** The challenge in this pattern is to identify the basic pattern that gets repeated, on a smaller scale, at each level. The pattern itself can be drawn using only the g.drawLine() method.
- **Bull's-eye.** The bull's-eye pattern is an excellent place to use *XORmode*. If you paint a large circle, and then paint a smaller one inside it in XORmode, the inside circle will be in the opposite color.

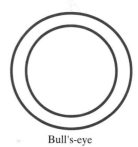

Bull's-eye

FIGURE 12–31 All three patterns are shown at level four.

GUI Design

You can adapt the RecursivePatterns and Canvas classes for use in this project. The drawing methods themselves should be added to the Canvas class. As you incorporate each new pattern into the program, you must add an item for it in the patterns menu in RecursivePatterns. You must also add a constant for it in the Canvas class and you must add a case for it to the switch statement in the Canvas.paintComponent() method.

Note the utility of the menus for this program. One lists the available patterns, and the other lists the available drawing levels. This is a convenient way for the user to indicate which pattern to draw. It also constrains the number of levels that can be drawn. This helps prevent the creation of a "runaway algorithm" in case the user enters a large value for the level. If the user accidentally typed in 100, for example, the program would either crash or run for a very long time.

> **EFFECTIVE DESIGN: Menus.** Because they constrain the user's choices to a fixed set of options, the use of menus for certain kinds of input reduces the chance of input errors.

CHAPTER SUMMARY

Technical Terms

base case	iterative method	recursive case
computational overhead	last-in-first-out (LIFO)	recursive definition recursive method
head-and-tail algorithm	method call stack recursion parameter	self-similarity tail recursive

Summary of Important Points

- A *recursive definition* is one that defines the *n*th case of a concept in terms of the $(n-1)$st case plus a limiting condition. It is based on the idea of breaking a problem up into smaller, self-similar problems.
- A *recursive method* is one that calls itself. It is usually defined in terms of a *base case* or limiting case, which stops the recursive process, and a recursive case, which breaks the method into a smaller, self-similar copy of itself. A *recursion parameter* is generally used to control the recursion.
- An iterative algorithm is one that uses some kind of loop as its control structure. Any algorithm that can be done iteratively can also be done recursively, and vice versa.
- Because method calling is relatively costly both in terms of memory used and CPU time involved, a recursive algorithm is generally less efficient than an iterative one that does the same thing.
- In designing recursive algorithms, the *base case* defines a limit. Each level of recursion should make progress toward the limit, and the algorithm should eventually reach the limit. The limit is usually expressed in terms of the *recursion parameter*.
- A recursive method is *tail recursive* if and only if each of its recursive calls is the last action executed by the method.
- A Swing JComboBox component is used to represent a GUI drop-down menu.

SOLUTIONS TO SELF-STUDY EXERCISES

SOLUTION 12.1   The output produced by mystery(0) would be 0 1 2 3 4 5 6. The output produced by mystery(100) would be 100.

SOLUTION 12.2   The output produced by mystery(5) would be: 5 4 3, and so on. In other words, this is an infinite recursion.

SOLUTION 12.3

```
Definition: twoToN(N), N >= 0
  1, if N == 0                    // Base case
  2 * twoToN(N - 1),  N > 0       // Recursive case
```

SOLUTION 12.4   The function x^n is known as the power function:

```
Definition: power(X,N), N >= 0
  1, if N == 0                    // Base case
  X * power(X, N - 1),  N > 0     // Recursive case
```

SOLUTION 12.5 Yes, the two definitions for nested boxes are equivalent. Suppose the square starts out with a side of 20. The definition given in the exercise will also draw squares with sides 20, 15, 10, 5.

SOLUTION 12.6 A recursive definition for the pattern in Figure 12–4:

```
Draw a square with side, s.
Inscribe a circle with diameter, s.
If s > 5,
    Draw a smaller version of the same pattern.  // Recursive case
```

SOLUTION 12.7 The printString2("hello") method will print: "olleh."

SOLUTION 12.8 A definition for countDown():

```
/** countDown(N) recursively prints a countdown beginning at N
 *   and ending at 1
 * @param N >= 1
 * Base case: N == 0
 */
void countDown(int N) {
    if (N == 0)                          // Base case
        System.out.println("blastoff");
    else {
        System.out.print(N + ", ");      // Recursive case
        countDown(N - 1);
    }
} // countDown()
```

SOLUTION 12.9 A revised definition for countDown():

```
/** countDown(N) recursively prints a countdown beginning at N,
 *   counting every other number, 10 8 6 ... and ending at "blastoff"
 * @param N >= 1
 * Base case: N <= 0
 */
void countDown(int N) {
    if (N <= 0)                          // Base case
        System.out.println("blastoff");
    else {
        System.out.print(N + ", ");  // Recursive case
        countDown(N - 2 );
    }
} // countDown()
```

SOLUTION 12.10 A method to sum the numbers from 1 to N.

```
int sum(int N) {
    if (N == 0)
        return 0;
    else
        return N + sum(N-1);
}
```

SOLUTION 12.11 A method to change each blank within a string to two blanks.

```
String addBlanks(String s) {
    if (s.length() == 0)
        return "";
    else if (s.charAt(0) == ' ')
        return ' ' + s.charAt(0) + addBlanks(s.substring(1));
    else
        return s.charAt(0) + addBlanks(s.substring(1));
}
```

SOLUTION 12.12

```
public static void main(String args[]) {
    int numbers[] = {0, 2, 4, 6, 8, 10, 12, 14, 16, 18};
    Searcher searcher = new Searcher();
    for (int k = 0; k <= 20; k++) {
        int result = searcher.search(numbers, k);
        if (result != -1)
            System.out.println(k + " found at " + result);
        else
            System.out.println(k + " is not in the array ");
    }
} // main()
```

SOLUTION 12.13 The sort() method is used as a public interface to the recursive selectionSort() method:

```
/** sort(arr) sorts the int array, arr
 *  Pre: arr is not null
 *  Post: arr will be arranged so that arr[j] <= arr[k] for any j < k
 */
public void sort(int arr[]) {
    selectionSort(arr, arr.length - 1);
            // Just call the recursive method
}
```

SOLUTION 12.14 An iterative version of findMax():

```
/** findMax (arr,N) returns the index of the largest
 *  value between arr[0] and arr[N], N >= 0.
 *  Pre: 0 <= N <= arr.length -1
 *  Post: arr[findMax()] >= arr[k] for any k between 0 and N.
 */
private int findMax(int arr[], int N) {
    int maxSoFar = 0;
    for (int k = 0; k <= N; k++)
        if (arr[k] > arr[maxSoFar])
            maxSoFar = k;
    return maxSoFar;
} // findMax()
```

Level 4

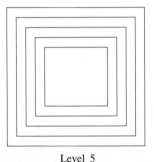

Level 5

FIGURE 12–32 Levels four and five of the nested boxes pattern.

SOLUTION 12.15 Levels four and five of the nested boxes pattern are shown in Figure 12–32.

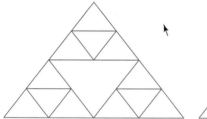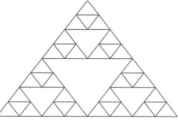

FIGURE 12–33 Levels two and three of the Sierpinski gasket.

SOLUTION 12.16 The following method will reduce the length of the side by delta percent at each level of recursion. The spacing between the boxes will vary by a constantly decreasing amount.

```
private void  drawBoxes(Graphics g, int level, Point loc,
                        int side, int delta) {
    g.drawRect(loc.x, loc.y, side, side );
    if (level > 0) {
        int deltaside = side * delta / 100; // Treat delta as a percent
        Point newLoc = new Point(loc.x + deltaside, loc.y + deltaside);
        drawBoxes(g, level - 1, newLoc, side - 2 * deltaside, delta);
    }
} // drawBoxes()
```

SOLUTION 12.17

```
private void drawBoxesIterative(Graphics g, int level, Point loc,
                                int side, int delta) {
    for (int k = level; k >= 0; k--) {
        g.drawRect(loc.x, loc.y, side, side );  // Draw a square
        loc.x += delta;                         // Calculate new location
        loc.y += delta;
        side -= 2 * delta;                      // Calculate new side length
    }
} // drawBoxes()
```

SOLUTION 12.18 The level two and three gaskets are shown in Figure 12–33.

SOLUTION 12.19 The printReverse() method is not tail recursive because in that method the recursive call is not the last statement executed.

SOLUTION 12.20 The countChar() method is tail recursive. The recursive calls are not the last statements in the method definition. However, each of the recursive calls would be the last statement executed by the method.

EXERCISE 12.1 Explain the difference between the following pairs of terms:

a. *Iteration* and *recursion*.
b. *Recursive method* and *recursive definition*.
c. *Base case* and *recursive case*.
d. *Head* and *tail*.
e. *Tail* and *nontail* recursive.

EXERCISE 12.2 Describe how the *method call stack* is used during a method call and return.

EXERCISES

Note: *For programming exercises,* **first** *draw a UML class diagram describing all classes and their inheritance relationships and/or associations.*

EXERCISE 12.3 Why is a recursive algorithm generally less efficient than an iterative algorithm?

EXERCISE 12.4 A tree, such as a maple tree or pine tree, has a recursive structure. Describe how a tree's structure displays *self-similarity* and *divisibility*.

EXERCISE 12.5 Write a recursive method to print each element of an array of double.

EXERCISE 12.6 Write a recursive method to print each element of an array of double from the last to the first element.

EXERCISE 12.7 Write a recursive method that will concatenate the elements of an array of String into a single String delimited by blanks.

EXERCISE 12.8 Write a recursive method that is passed a single int parameter, $N \geq 0$, and prints all the odd numbers between 1 and N.

EXERCISE 12.9 Write a recursive method that takes a single int parameter $N \geq 0$ and prints the sequence of even numbers between N down to 0.

EXERCISE 12.10 Write a recursive method that takes a single int parameter $N \geq 0$ and prints the multiples of 10 between 0 and N.

EXERCISE 12.11 Write a recursive method to print the following geometric pattern:

```
#
# #
# # #
# # # #
# # # # #
```

EXERCISE 12.12 Write recursive methods to print each of the following patterns.

```
# # # # # # #      # # # # # # #
 # # # # # #       # # # # # #
  # # # # #        # # # # #
   # # # #         # # # #
    # # #          # # #
     # #           # #
      #            #
```

EXERCISE 12.13 Write a recursive method to print all multiples of M up to $M * N$.

EXERCISE 12.14 Write a recursive method to compute the sum of grades stored in an array.

EXERCISE 12.15 Write a recursive method to count the occurrences of a substring within a string.

EXERCISE 12.16 Write a recursive method to remove the HTML tags from a string.

EXERCISE 12.17 Implement a recursive version of the Caesar.decode() method from Chapter 7.

EXERCISE 12.18   The Fibonacci sequence (named after the Italian mathematician Leonardo of Pisa, ca. 1200) consists of the numbers 0,1,1,2,3,5,8,13,... in which each number (except for the first two) is the sum of the two preceding numbers. Write a recursive method `fibonacci(N)` that prints the first *N* Fibonacci numbers.

EXERCISE 12.19   Write a recursive method to rotate a `String` by *N* characters to the right. For example, `rotateR("hello", 3)` should return "llohe."

EXERCISE 12.20   Write a recursive method to rotate a `String` by *N* characters to the left. For example, `rotateL("hello", 3)` should return "lohel."

EXERCISE 12.21   Write a recursive method to convert a `String` representing a binary number to its decimal equivalent. For example, `binTodecimal("101011")` should return the `int` value 43.

EXERCISE 12.22   A palindrome is a string that is equal to its reverse—"mom," "i," "radar" and "able was i ere i saw elba." Write a recursive `boolean` method that determines whether its `String` parameter is a palindrome.

EXERCISE 12.23   Challenge: Incorporate a `drawBinaryTree()` method into the `RecursivePatterns` program. A level-one binary tree has two branches. At each subsequent level, two smaller branches are grown from the endpoints of every existing branch. The geometry is easier if you use 45-degree angles for the branches. Figure 12–34 shows a level-four binary tree drawn upside down.

EXERCISE 12.24   Challenge: Towers of Hanoi. According to legend, some Buddhist monks were given the task of moving 64 golden disks from one diamond needle to another needle, using a third needle as a backup. To begin with, the disks were stacked one on top of the other from largest to smallest (Fig. 12–35). The rules were that only one disk can be moved at a time and that a larger disk can never go on top of a smaller one. The end of the world was supposed to occur when the monks finished the task!

Write a recursive method, `move(int N, char A, char B, char C)`, that will print out directions the monks can use to solve the towers of Hanoi problem. For example, here's what it should output for the three-disk case, `move(3, "A", "B", "C")`:

```
Move 1 disk from A to B.
Move 1 disk from A to C.
Move 1 disk from B to C.
Move 1 disk from A to B.
Move 1 disk from C to A.
Move 1 disk from C to B.
Move 1 disk from A to B.
```

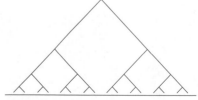

FIGURE 12–34   A level-four binary tree pattern.

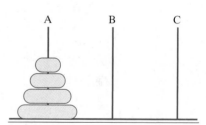

FIGURE 12–35   The towers of Hanoi problem. Move all the disks from needle A to needle B. Only one disk can be moved at a time, and a larger disk can never go on top of a smaller one.

Photograph courtesy of Nell Deer, PhotoDisc, Inc.

13

Threads and Concurrent Programming

OBJECTIVES

After studying this chapter, you will

- Understand the concept of a thread.
- Know how to design and write multithreaded programs.
- Be able to use the `Thread` class and the `Runnable` interface.
- Understand the life cycle of a thread.
- Know how to synchronize threads.
- Appreciate the use of inheritance in threaded applications.

OUTLINE

13.1   Introduction

This chapter concerns doing more than one thing at a time. Doing more than one thing at once is commonplace in our everyday lives. For example, let's say your breakfast today consists of cereal, toast, and a cup of java. You have to do three things at once to have breakfast: eat cereal, eat toast, and drink coffee.

Actually, you do these things "at the same time" by alternating among them: You take a spoonful of cereal, then a bite of toast, and then sip some coffee. Then you have another bite of toast, or another spoonful of cereal, more coffee, and so on, until breakfast is finished. If the phone rings while you're having breakfast, you will probably answer it—and continue to have breakfast, or at least to sip the coffee. This means you're doing even more "at the same time."

Everyday life is full of examples where we do more than one task at the same time.

The computer programs we have written so far have performed one task at a time. But there are plenty of applications where a program needs to do several things at once, or **concurrently**. For example, if you wrote an Internet chat program, it would let several users take part in a discussion group. The program would have to read messages from several users at the same time and broadcast them to the other participants in the group. The reading and broadcasting tasks would have to take place concurrently.

In Java, concurrent programming is handled by threads, as we will now see.

13.2   What Is a Thread?

A **thread** (or a *thread of execution* or a *thread of control*) is a single sequence of executable statements within a program. For Java applications, the flow of control begins at the first statement in `main()` and continues sequentially through the statements of the program. For Java applets, the flow of control begins with the first statement in `init()`. Loops within a program cause a certain block of statements to be repeated. If-else structures cause certain statements to be selected and others to be skipped. Method calls cause the flow of execution to jump to another part of the program, from which it returns after the method's statements are executed. Thus, within a single thread, you can trace the sequential flow of execution from one statement to the next.

Visualizing a thread

One way to visualize a thread is to imagine that you could make a list of the program's statements as they were executed by the computer's central processing unit (CPU). Thus, for a particular execution of a program with loops, method calls, and selection statements, you could list each instruction that was executed, beginning at the first, and continuing until the program stopped, as a single sequence of executed statements. That's a thread!

Now imagine that we break a program up into two or more independent threads. Each thread will have its own sequence of instructions. Within a single thread, the statements are executed one after the other, as usual. However, by alternately executing the statements from one thread and another, the computer can run several threads *concurrently*. Even though the CPU executes one instruction at at time, it can run multiple threads concurrently by rapidly alternating among them. The main advantage of concurrency is that it allows the computer to do more than one task at a time. For example, the CPU could alternate between downloading an image from the Internet and running a spreadsheet calculation. This is the same way you ate toast and cereal and drank coffee in our earlier breakfast example. From our perspective, it might look as if the computer had several CPUs working in parallel, but that's just the illusion created by an effective scheduling of the threads.

> **JAVA LANGUAGE RULE** JVM Threads. The Java Virtual Machine (JVM) is itself an example of a multithreaded program. JVM threads perform tasks that are essential to the successful execution of Java programs.

> **JAVA LANGUAGE RULE** Garbage Collector Thread. One of the JVM threads, the *garbage collector thread*, automatically reclaims memory taken up by objects that are not used in your programs. This happens at the same time that the JVM is interpreting your program.

13.2.1 Concurrent Execution of Threads

The technique of concurrently executing several tasks within a program is known as **multitasking**. A *task* in this sense is a computer operation of some sort, such as reading or saving a file, compiling a program, or displaying an image on the screen. Multitasking requires the use of a separate thread for each of the tasks. The methods available in the Java Thread class make it possible (and quite simple) to implement **multithreaded** programs.

Multitasking

Most computers, including personal computers, are *sequential* machines that consist of a single CPU, which is capable of executing one machine instruction at a time. In contrast, *parallel computers* are made up of multiple CPUs working in tandem.

Today's personal computers, running at clock speeds over 1 gigahertz—1 *gigahertz* equals 1 billion cycles per second—are capable of executing millions of machine instructions per second. Despite its great speed, however, a single CPU can process only one instruction at a time.

Each CPU uses a **fetch-execute cycle** to retrieve the next instruction from memory and execute it. Since CPUs can execute only one instruction at a time, multithreaded programs are made possible by dividing up the CPU's time and sharing it among the threads. The CPU's schedule is managed by a *scheduling algorithm* that is under the control of the operating system and the Java Virtual Machine (JVM). The choice of a scheduling algorithm is dependent on the platform, with thread scheduling handled differently on Unix, Windows, and Macintosh systems.

One common scheduling technique is known as **time slicing**, in which each thread alternatively gets a slice of the CPU's time. For example, suppose we have a program that consists of two threads. Using this technique, the system would give each thread a small **quantum** of CPU time—say, one thousandth of a second (one *millisecond*)—to execute its instructions. When its quantum expired, the thread would be *preempted* and the

CPUs are sequential

Time slicing

FIGURE 13–1   Each thread gets a slice of the CPU's time.

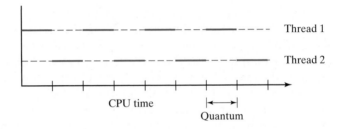

other thread would be given a chance to run. The algorithm would then alternate in this **round-robin** fashion between one thread and the other (Fig. 13–1). During each millisecond on a 300-megahertz CPU, a thread can execute 300,000 machine instructions. (One **megahertz** equals 1 million cycles per second.) Thus, within each second of real time, each thread will receive 500 time slices and will be able to execute something like 150 million machine instructions.

Priority scheduling

Under **priority scheduling**, threads of higher priority are allowed to run to completion before lower-priority threads are given a chance. An example of a high-priority thread would be processing keyboard input or any other kind of interactive input from the user. If such tasks were given low priority, users would experience noticeable delays in their interaction, which would be quite unacceptable.

The only way a high-priority thread can be preempted is if a thread of still higher priority becomes available to run. In many cases, higher-priority threads are those that can complete their task within a couple of milliseconds, so they can be allowed to run to completion without starving the lower-priority threads. An example would be processing a user's keystroke, a task that can begin as soon as the key is struck and can be completed very quickly.

> **JAVA LANGUAGE RULE** Thread Support. Depending on the hardware platform, Java threads may be supported by assigning different threads to different processors, by time slicing a single processor, or by time slicing many hardware processors.

13.2.2   Multithreaded Numbers

Let's consider a simple example of a threaded program. Suppose we give each individual thread a unique ID number, and each time it runs, it just repeatedly prints its ID. For example, when the thread with ID 1 runs, the output produced would just be a sequence of 1's: 111111.

As shown in Figure 13–2, the NumberThread class is defined as a subclass of Thread and overrides the run() method. As the following definition shows, the constructor takes a single parameter that is used to set the thread's ID number. In the run() method, the thread simply executes a loop that prints its own number ten times:

FIGURE 13–2   The NumberThread class overrides the inherited run() method.

```
public class NumberThread extends Thread {

    int num;

    public NumberThread(int n) {
        num = n;
    }
}
```

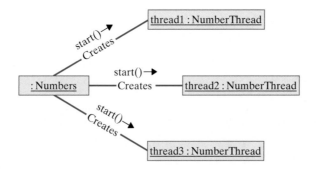

```
    public void run() {
        for (int k=0; k < 10; k++) {
            System.out.print(num);
        } //for
    } // run()
} // NumberThread
```

A Thread subclass

Now let's define another class whose task will be to create a bunch of `NumberThreads` and get them all running at the same time (Fig. 13–3). For each `NumberThread`, we want to call its constructor and then `start()` it:

```
public class Numbers {

    public static void main(String args[]) {
        NumberThread number1, number2, number3, number4, number5; // 5 threads

    // Create and start each thread
        number1 = new NumberThread(1); number1.start();
        number2 = new NumberThread(2); number2.start();
        number3 = new NumberThread(3); number3.start();
        number4 = new NumberThread(4); number4.start();
        number5 = new NumberThread(5); number5.start();
    } // main()
} // Numbers
```

When a thread is `start()`ed, it automatically calls its `run()` method. The output generated by this version of the `Numbers` application is as follows:

Starting a thread

```
111111111122222222223333333333344444444445555555555
```

From this output, it appears that the individual threads were run in the order in which they were created. As it turned out in this case, each thread was able to run to completion before the next thread started running.

What if we increase the number of iterations that each thread performs? Will each thread still run to completion? The following output was generated for 200 iterations per thread:

```
1111111111111111111111111111111111111111111111111111111111111
1111111111111111111111111111111111111111111111111111111111111
11111111111111111111111111111111111111111111111111111111112222222
22222222222222222222222222222222222222222222222222222222222222222
22222222222222222222222222222222222222222222222222222222222222222
```

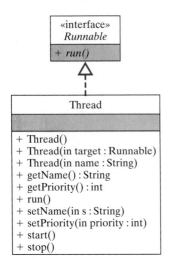

FIGURE 13–4   The `java.lang.Thread` class.

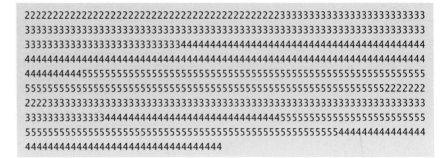

```
22222222222222222222222222222222222222222222222333333333333333333333333
33333333333333333333333333333333333333333333333333333333333333333333333
33333333333333333333333333344444444444444444444444444444444444444444444
44444444444444444444444444444444444444444444444444444444444444444444444
4444444444455555555555555555555555555555555555555555555555555555555555
55555555555555555555555555555555555555555555555555555555555552222222
2222333333333333333333333333333333333333333333333333333333333333333333
3333333333333344444444444444444444444444444445555555555555555555555555
55555555555555555555555555555555555555555555555555555554444444444444444
44444444444444444444444444444444444
```

Note that in this case only thread 1 managed to run to completion. Threads 2, 3, 4, and 5 did not. As this example illustrates, the order and timing of a thread's execution are highly unpredictable. This example also serves to illustrate one way of creating a multithreaded program:

- Create a subclass of the `Thread` class.
- Within the subclass, implement a method with the signature `void run()` that contains the statements to be executed by that thread.
- Create several instances of the subclass and start each thread by invoking the `start()` method on each instance.

JAVA LANGUAGE RULE   Thread Creation. One way to create a thread in Java is to define a subclass of `Thread` and override the default `run()` method.

From the Java Library

java.lang.Thread

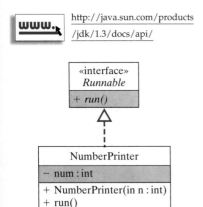

FIGURE 13–5   Any object that implements the `Runnable` interface can be run as a separate thread.

THE `java.lang.Thread` class contains the public methods shown in Figure 13–4 (a partial list). Note that `Thread` implements the `Runnable` interface, which consists simply of the `run()` method.

Another way to create a thread is to create a `Thread` instance and pass it a `Runnable` object that will become its body. A `Runnable` object is any object that implements the `Runnable` interface—that is, any object that implements the `run()` method (Fig. 13–5). The following example provides an alternative way to implement the `NumberThread` program:

```java
public class NumberPrinter implements Runnable {
    int num;

    public NumberPrinter(int n) {
        num = n;
    }

    public void run() {
        for (int k=0; k < 10; k++)
            System.out.print(num);
    } // run()
} // NumberPrinter
```

Given this definition, we would then pass instances of this class to the individual threads as we create them:

```
public class Numbers {

    public static void main(String args[]) {

        Thread number1, number2, number3, number4, number5; // 5 threads
        // Create and start each thread
        number1 = new Thread(new NumberPrinter(1)); number1.start();
        number2 = new Thread(new NumberPrinter(2)); number2.start();
        number3 = new Thread(new NumberPrinter(3)); number3.start();
        number4 = new Thread(new NumberPrinter(4)); number4.start();
        number5 = new Thread(new NumberPrinter(5)); number5.start();
    } // main()
} // Numbers
```

The NumberPrinter class implements Runnable by defining exactly the same run() that was used previously in the NumberThread class. We then pass instances of NumberPrinter when we create the individual threads. Doing things this way gives exactly the same output as earlier. This example serves to illustrate another way of creating a multithreaded program:

- Implement the Runnable interface for an existing class by implementing the void run() method, which contains the statements to be executed by that thread.
- Create several Thread instances by first creating instances of the Runnable class and passing each instance as an argument to the Thread() constructor.
- For each thread instance, start it by invoking the start() method on it.

> **JAVA LANGUAGE RULE** Thread Creation. A thread can be created by passing a Runnable object to a new Thread instance. The object's run() method will be invoked automatically as soon as the thread's start() method is called.

> **EFFECTIVE DESIGN: Converting a Class to a Thread.** Using the Runnable interface to create threads enables you to turn an existing class into a thread. For most applications, using the Runnable interface is preferable to redefining the class as a Thread subclass.

SELF-STUDY EXERCISE

EXERCISE 13.1 Use the Runnable interface to convert the following class into a thread. You want the thread to print all the odd numbers up to its bound:

```
public class PrintOdds {
    private int bound;
    public PrintOdds(int b) {
        bound = b;
    }

    public void print() {
        if (int k = 1; k < bound; k+=2)
            System.out.println(k);
    }
} // PrintOdds
```

Controlling threads

Thread Control

The various methods in the Thread class (Fig. 13–4) can be used to exert some control over a thread's execution. The start() and stop() methods play the obvious roles of starting and stopping a thread. These methods will sometimes be called automatically. For example, an applet is treated as a thread by the browser, or appletviewer, which is responsible for starting and stopping it.

As we saw in the NumberThread example, the run() method encapsulates the thread's basic algorithm. It is usually not called directly. Instead, it is called by the thread's start() method, which handles any system-dependent initialization tasks before calling run().

Thread Priority

The setPriority(int) method lets you set a thread's priority to an integer value between Thread.MIN.PRIORITY and Thread.MAX.PRIORITY, the bounds defined as constants in the Thread class. Using setPriority() gives you some control over a thread's execution. In general, higher-priority threads get to run before, and longer than, lower-priority threads.

> **JAVA LANGUAGE RULE** Preemption. A higher-priority thread that wants to run will *preempt* any threads of lower priority.

To see how setPriority() works, suppose we change NumberThread's constructor to the following:

```
public NumberThread(int n) {
    num = n;
    setPriority(n);
}
```

Thread priority

In this case, each thread sets its priority to its ID number. So, thread five will have priority five, a higher priority than all the other threads. Suppose we now run 2 million iterations of each of these threads. Because 2 million iterations will take a long time if we print the thread's ID on each iteration, let's modify the run() method, so that the ID is printed every 1 million iterations:

```
for (int k = 0; k < 10; k++)
    if (k % 1000000 == 0)
        System.out.print(num);
```

Given this modification, we get the following output when we run Numbers:

```
5544332211
```

It appears from this output that the threads ran to completion in priority order. Thus, thread five completed 2 million iterations before thread four started to run, and so on. This shows that, on my system at least, the Java Virtual Machine (JVM) supports priority scheduling.

PROGRAMMING TIP: Platform Dependence. Thread implementation in Java is platform dependent. Adequate testing is necessary to ensure that a program will perform correctly on a given platform.

EFFECTIVE DESIGN: Thread Coordination. One way to coordinate the behavior of two threads is to give one thread higher priority than another.

DEBUGGING TIP: Starvation. A high-priority thread that never gives up the CPU can starve lower-priority threads.

Forcing Threads to Sleep

The `Thread.sleep()` and `Thread.yield()` methods also provide some control over a thread's behavior. When executed by a thread, the `yield()` method causes the thread to yield the CPU, allowing the thread scheduler to choose another thread. The `sleep()` method causes the thread to yield and not to be scheduled until a certain amount of real time has passed.

Sleep vs. yield

> **JAVA LANGUAGE RULE** Sleep Versus Yield. Both the `yield()` and `sleep()` methods yield the CPU, but the `sleep()` method keeps the thread from being rescheduled for a fixed amount of real time.

The `sleep()` method can halt a running thread for a given number of milliseconds, allowing other waiting threads to run. The `sleep()` method throws an `InterruptedException`, which is a checked exception. This means that the `sleep()` call must be embedded within a `try/catch` block or the method it's in must throw an `InterruptedException`. Try/catch blocks were covered in Chapter 11.

```
try {
    sleep(100);
} catch (InterruptedException e) {
    System.out.println(e.getMessage());
}
```

For example, consider the following version of the `NumberPrinter.run()`:

```
public void run() {
    for (int k=0; k < 10; k++) {
        try {
            Thread.sleep((long)(Math.random() * 1000));
        } catch (InterruptedException e) {
            System.out.println(e.getMessage());
        }
        System.out.print(num);
    } // for
} // run()
```

In this example, each thread is forced to sleep for a random number of milliseconds between 0 and 1,000. When a thread sleeps, it gives up the CPU, which allows one of the other waiting threads to run. As you would expect, the output we get from this example will reflect the randomness in the amount of time that each thread sleeps:

```
14522314532143154232152423541243235415523113435451
```

As we will see, the `sleep()` method provides a rudimentary form of thread synchronization, in which one thread yields control to another.

SELF-STUDY EXERCISES

EXERCISE 13.2   What happens if you run five `NumberThreads` of equal priority through 2 million iterations each? Run this experiment and note the output. Don't print after every iteration! What sort of scheduling algorithm (round-robin, priority scheduling, or something else) was used to schedule threads of equal priority on your system?

EXERCISE 13.3   Try the following experiment and note the output. Let each thread sleep for 50 milliseconds (rather than a random number of milliseconds). How does this affect the scheduling of the threads? To make things easier to see, print each thread's ID after every 100,000 iterations.

EXERCISE 13.4   The purpose of the Java garbage collector is to recapture memory that was used by objects that are no longer being used by your program. Should its thread have higher or lower priority than your program?

The Asynchronous Nature of Threaded Programs

Threads are **asynchronous**. This means that the order of execution and the timing of a set of threads are sporadic and unpredictable, at least from the programmer's point of view. Threads are executed under the control of the scheduling algorithm used by the operating system and the Java Virtual Machine. In general, unless threads are explicitly synchronized, it is impossible for the programmer to predict when and for how long an

Thread preemptions are unpredictable

individual thread will run. In some systems, under some circumstances, a thread may run to completion before any other thread can run. In other systems, or under different circumstances, a thread may run for a short time and then be suspended while another thread runs. Of course, when a thread is preempted by the system, its state is saved so that its execution can be resumed without losing any information.

   One implication of a thread's asynchronicity is that it is not generally possible to determine where in its source code an individual thread might be preempted. You can't even assume that a thread will be able to complete a Java arithmetic operation once it has started it. For example, suppose a thread had to execute the following operation:

```
int N = 5 + 3;
```

An arithmetic operation can be interrupted

This operation computes the sum of 5 and 3 and assigns the result to N. It would be tempting to think that once the thread started this operation, it would be able to complete it, but that is not necessarily so. You have to remember that Java code is compiled into a rudimentary bytecode, which is translated still further into the computer's machine language. In machine language, this operation would break down into something like the following three steps:

```
Fetch 5 from memory and store it in register A.
Add 3 to register A.
Assign the value in register A to N.
```

Although none of the individual machine instructions can be preempted, the thread could be preempted between any two machine instructions. The point is that not even a single Java language instruction can be assumed to be indivisible or unpreemptible. Therefore, it is impossible to make any assumptions about when a particular thread will run and when it will give up the CPU. This suggests the following important principle of multithreaded programs:

Threads are asynchronous

JAVA LANGUAGE RULE Asynchronous Thread Principle. Unless they are explicitly prioritized or synchronized, threads behave in a completely *asynchronous* fashion.

PROGRAMMING TIP: Thread Timing.   Unless they are explicitly synchronized, your program cannot make any assumptions about when, or in what order, individual threads will execute, or where a thread might be interrupted or preempted during its execution.

As we will see, this principle plays a large role in the design of multithreaded programs.

13.3   Thread States and Life Cycle

Each thread has a **life cycle** that consists of several different states, which are summarized in Figure 13–6 and Table 13.1. Thread states are represented by labeled ovals, and the transitions between states are represented by labeled arrows. Much of a thread's life cycle is under the control of the operating system and the Java Virtual Machine. Those transitions represented by method names—such as start(), stop(), wait(), sleep(), notify()—can be controlled by the program. Of these methods, the stop() method has been deprecated in JDK 1.2 because it is inherently unsafe to stop a thread in the middle of its execution. Other transitions—such as *dispatch, I/O request, I/O done, time expired, done sleeping*—are under the control of the CPU scheduler. When first created a thread is in the ready state, which means that it is ready to run. In the ready state, a thread is waiting, perhaps with other threads, in the **ready queue**, for its turn on the CPU. A **queue** is like a waiting line. When the CPU becomes available, the first thread in the ready queue will be **dispatched**—that is, it will be given the CPU. It will then be in the running state.

Ready, running, and sleeping

Controlling a thread

The ready queue

Transitions between the ready and running states happen under the control of the CPU scheduler, a fundamental part of the Java runtime system.

CPU scheduler

FIGURE 13–6 A depiction of a thread's life cycle.

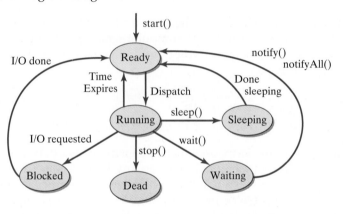

TABLE 13.1 A summary of the different thread states.

State	Description
Ready	The thread is ready to run and waiting for the CPU.
Running	The thread is executing on the CPU.
Waiting	The thread is waiting for some event to happen.
Sleeping	The thread has been told to sleep for a time.
Blocked	The thread is waiting for I/O to finish.
Dead	The thread is terminated.

The job of scheduling a bunch of threads in a fair and efficient manner is a little like sharing a single bicycle among several children. Children who are ready to ride the bike wait in line for their turn. The grown up (scheduler) lets the first child (thread) ride for a period of time before the bike is taken away and given to the next child in line. In round-robin scheduling, each child (thread) gets an equal amount of time on the bike (CPU).

When a thread calls the sleep() method, it voluntarily gives up the CPU, and when the sleep period is over, it goes back into the ready queue. This would be like one of the children deciding to rest for a moment during his or her turn. When the rest was over, the child would get back in line.

Threads can give up the CPU

When a thread calls the wait() method, it voluntarily gives up the CPU, but this time it won't be ready to run again until it is notified by some other thread.

This would be like one child giving his or her turn to another child. When the second child's turn is up, it would notify the first child, who would then get back in line.

Threads block on I/O operations

The system also manages transitions between the **blocked** and ready states. A thread is put into a blocked state when it does some kind of I/O operation. I/O devices, such as disk drives, modems, and keyboards, are very slow compared to the CPU. Therefore, I/O operations are handled by separate processors known as *controllers*. For example, when a thread wants to read data from a disk drive, the system will give this task to the disk controller, telling it where to place the data. Because the thread can't do anything until the data are read, it is blocked, and another thread is allowed to run. When the disk controller completes the I/O operation, the blocked thread is unblocked and placed back in the ready queue.

In terms of the bicycle analogy, blocking a thread would be like giving the bicycle to another child when the rider has to stop to tie his or her shoe. Instead of letting the bicycle just sit there, we let another child ride it. When the shoe is tied, the child is ready to ride again and goes back into the ready line. Letting other threads run while one thread is waiting for an I/O operation to complete improves the overall utilization of the CPU.

SELF-STUDY EXERCISE

EXERCISE 13.5   Round-robin scheduling isn't always the best idea. Sometimes *priority scheduling* leads to a better system. Can you think of ways that priority scheduling—higher-priority threads go to the head of the line—can be used to improve the responsiveness of an interactive program?

13.4   Using Threads to Improve Interface Responsiveness

One good use for a *multithreaded* program is to help make a more responsive user interface. In a single-threaded program, if the program is executing statements in a long (perhaps even infinite) loop, it will remain unresponsive to the user's actions until the loop is exited. Any action events that take place while the program is looping will be postponed until the loop is finished. Thus, the user will experience a noticeable and sometimes frustrating delay between the time an action is initiated and the time it is actually handled by the program.

13.4.1   Single-Threaded Design

It's always a good idea that the interface be responsive to user input, but sometimes it is crucial to an application. For example, suppose a program is being used in a psychometric experiment that measures how quickly the user responds to a certain stimulus presented by the program. Obviously, for this kind of application, the program should take action as soon as the user clicks on a button to indicate a response to the stimulus.

Problem Statement

A psychologist is conducting a psychometric experiment to measure user response to a visual cue and asks you to create the following program. The program should have two buttons. When the Draw button is clicked, the program begins drawing thousands of black dots at random locations within a rectangular region of the screen (Fig. 13–7). After a random time interval, the program begins drawing red dots. This change corresponds to the presentation of the stimulus. As soon as the stimulus is presented the user is supposed to click on a Clear button, which clears the drawing area. To provide a measure of the user's reaction time, the program should report how many red dots were drawn before the user clicked the Clear button.

FIGURE 13–7   Random dots are drawn until the user clicks the Clear button.

Problem specification

FIGURE 13–8 GUI design for the dot-drawing applet.

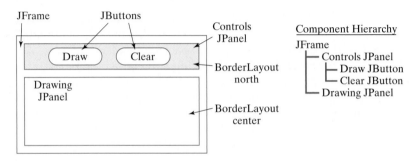

GUI design

Figure 13–8 shows a GUI design for this program's applet interface. It contains a control JPanel that contains the two JButtons. The dots are drawn on a JPanel, which is positioned in the center of a BorderLayout design.

Problem Decomposition

Interface class and drawing class

This program should be decomposed into two classes, an applet to handle the user interface and a drawing class to manage the drawing. The main features of its classes are as follows:

- RandomDotApplet Class: This class manages the user interface, responding to user actions by calling methods of the Dotty class (Fig. 13–9).
- Dotty Class: This class contains draw() and clear() methods for drawing on the applet's drawing panel.

RandomDotApplet
+ NDOTS : int = 10000
− dotty : Dotty
− controls : JPanel
− canvas : JPanel
− draw : JButton
− clear : JButton
+ init()
+ actionPerformed(in e : ActionEvent)

FIGURE 13–9 The RandomDotApplet provides a standard applet interface.

The RandomDotApplet *Class*

The implementation of RandomDotApplet is shown in Figure 13–10. The applet arranges the control and drawing panels in a BorderLayout and listens for action events on its JButtons. When the user clicks the Draw button, the applet's actionPerformed() method will create a new Dotty instance and call its draw() method:

```
dotty = new Dotty(canvas, NDOTS);
dotty.draw();
```

Note that Dotty is passed a reference to the drawing canvas as well as the number of dots to be drawn. When the user clicks the Clear button, the applet should call the dotty.clear() method. Of course, the important question is, how responsive will the applet be to the user's action?

The Dotty *Class*

The purpose of the Dotty class (Fig. 13–11) will be to draw the dots and to report how many red dots were drawn before the canvas was cleared. Because it will be passed a reference to the drawing panel and the number of dots to draw, the Dotty class will need instance variables to store these two values. It will also need a variable to keep track of how many dots

What data do we need?

```
import java.awt.*;
import javax.swing.*;        // Import Swing classes
import java.awt.event.*;

public class RandomDotApplet extends JApplet implements ActionListener  {
    public final int NDOTS = 10000;

    private Dotty dotty;                           // The drawing class
    private JPanel controls = new JPanel();
    private JPanel canvas = new JPanel();
    private JButton draw = new JButton("Draw");
    private JButton clear = new JButton("Clear");

    public void init() {
        getContentPane().setLayout(new BorderLayout());
        draw.addActionListener(this);
        clear.addActionListener(this);
        controls.add(draw);
        controls.add(clear);
        canvas.setBorder(BorderFactory.createTitledBorder("Drawing Canvas"));
        getContentPane().add("North", controls);
        getContentPane().add("Center", canvas);
        getContentPane().setSize(400, 400);
    } // init()

    public void actionPerformed(ActionEvent e) {
        if (e.getSource() == draw) {
            dotty = new Dotty(canvas, NDOTS);
            dotty.draw();
        } else {
            dotty.clear();
        }
    } // actionPerformed()
} // RandomDotApplet
```

FIGURE 13–10   The RandomDotApplet class.

were drawn. Finally, since it will be drawing within a fixed rectangle on the panel, the reference coordinates and dimensions of the drawing area are declared as class constants.

The Dotty() constructor method will be passed a reference to a drawing panel as well as the number of dots to be drawn and will merely assign these parameters to its instance variables. In addition to its constructor method, the Dotty class will have public draw() and clear() methods, which will be called from the applet. The draw() method will use a loop to draw random dots. The clear() will clear the canvas and report the number of dots drawn.

Dotty
+ HREF : int final = 20
+ VREF : int final = 20
+ LEN : int final = 200
– canvas : JPanel
– nDots : int
– nDrawn : int
– firstRed : int = 0
+ Dotty(in canv : JPanel, in n : int)
+ draw()
+ clear()

FIGURE 13–11   The Dotty manages the drawing actions.

The complete implementation of Dotty is shown in Figure 13–12. Note how its draw() method is designed:

```
public void draw() {
    Graphics g = canvas.getGraphics();
    for (nDrawn = 0; nDrawn < nDots; nDrawn++) {
        int x = HREF + (int)(Math.random() * LEN);
        int y = VREF + (int)(Math.random() * LEN);
        g.fillOval(x, y, 3, 3);                    // Draw a dot

        if (Math.random() < 0.001 && firstRed == 0) {
            g.setColor(Color.red);                 // Change color to red
            firstRed = nDrawn;
        }
    } //for
} // draw()
```

```
import java.awt.*;
import javax.swing.*;    // Import Swing classes

public class Dotty {
    private static final int HREF = 20, VREF = 20, LEN = 200; // Coordinates

    private JPanel canvas;
    private int nDots;        // Number of dots to draw
    private int nDrawn;       // Number of dots drawn
    private int firstRed = 0;   // Number of the first red dot

    public Dotty(JPanel canv, int dots) {
        canvas = canv;
        nDots = dots;
    }

    public void draw() {
        Graphics g = canvas.getGraphics();
        for (nDrawn = 0; nDrawn < nDots; nDrawn++) {
            int x = HREF + (int)(Math.random() * LEN);
            int y = VREF + (int)(Math.random() * LEN);
            g.fillOval(x, y, 3, 3);                    // Draw a dot

            if ((Math.random() < 0.001) && (firstRed == 0)) {
                g.setColor(Color.red);                 // Change color to red
                firstRed = nDrawn;
            }
        } //for
    } // draw()

    public void clear() {                        // Clear screen and report result
        Graphics g = canvas.getGraphics();
        g.setColor(canvas.getBackground());
        g.fillRect(HREF, VREF, LEN + 3, LEN + 3);
        System.out.println("Number of dots drawn since first red = " + (nDrawn-firstRed));
    } // clear()
} // Dotty
```

FIGURE 13–12   The Dotty class, single-threaded version.

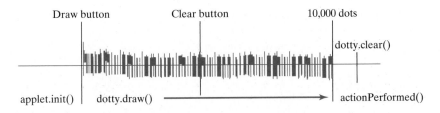

FIGURE 13–13 A single-threaded execution of random dot drawing.

The drawing loop is bounded by the number of dots to be drawn. On each iteration the draw() method picks a random location within the rectangle defined by the coordinates (HREF,VREF) and (HREF+LEN, VREF+LEN), and draws a dot there. On each iteration it also generates a random number. If the random number is less than 0.001, it changes the drawing color to red and keeps track of the number of dots drawn up to that point.

Drawing algorithm

The problem with this design is that as long as the draw() method is executing, the program will be unable to respond to the applet's Clear button. In a single-threaded design, both the applet and dotty are combined into a single thread of execution (Fig. 13–13). When the user clicks on the Draw button, the applet's actionPerformed() method is invoked. It then invokes Dotty's draw() method, which must run to completion before anything else can be done. If the user clicks on the Clear button, while the dots are being drawn, the applet won't be able to get to this until all the dots are drawn.

Single-threaded design: Waiting for the loop to end

If you run this program with nDots set to 10,000, the program will not clear the drawing panel until all 10,000 dots are drawn, no matter when the Clear button is pressed. Therefore, the values reported for the user's reaction time will be wrong. Obviously, since it is so unresponsive to user input, this design completely fails to satisfy the program's specifications.

> **JAVA LANGUAGE RULE** Single-Threaded Loop. In a single-threaded design, a loop that requires lots of iterations will completely dominate the CPU during its execution, forcing other tasks, including user I/O tasks, to wait.

SELF-STUDY EXERCISE

EXERCISE 13.6 Suppose the Java Virtual Machine (JVM) was single threaded and your program got stuck in an infinite loop. Would you be able to break out of the loop by typing some special command (such as Control-C) from the keyboard?

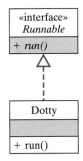

13.4.2 Multithreaded Drawing: The Dotty Thread

One way to remedy this problem is to create a second thread (in addition to the applet itself) to do the drawing. The drawing thread will be responsible just for drawing, while the applet thread will be responsible for handling user actions in the interface. The trick to making the user interface more responsive will be to interrupt the drawing thread periodically so that the applet thread has a chance to handle any events that have taken place.

Multithreaded design: Interrupt the drawing loop

As Figure 13–14 illustrates, the easiest way to convert Dotty into a thread is to have it implement the Runnable interface:

```
public class Dotty implements Runnable {

    // Everything else remains the same

    public void run() {
        draw();
    }
}
```

This version of Dotty will perform the same task as before except that it will now run as a separate thread of execution. Note that its run() method just calls the draw() method that we defined in the previous version. When the Dotty thread is started by the RandomDotApplet, we will have a multithreaded program.

However, just because this program has two threads doesn't necessarily mean that it will be any more responsive to the user. There's no guarantee that the drawing thread will stop as soon as the Clear button is clicked. On *Thread control* most systems, if both threads have equal priority, the applet thread won't run until the drawing thread finishes drawing all *N* dots.

DEBUGGING TIP: Thread Control. Just breaking a program into two separate threads won't necessarily give you the desired performance. It may be necessary to *coordinate* the threads.

Therefore, we have to modify our design in order to guarantee that the applet thread will get a chance to handle the user's actions. One good way to do this is to have Dotty sleep for a short instance after it draws *Using* sleep() *to interrupt the* each dot. When a thread sleeps, any other threads that are waiting their *drawing* turn will get a chance to run. If the applet thread is waiting to handle the user's click on Clear, it will now be able to call Dotty's clear() method.

The new version of draw() is shown in Figure 13–15. In this version of draw(), the thread sleeps for 1 millisecond on each iteration of the loop. This will make it possible for the applet to run on every iteration, so it will handle user actions immediately.

Another necessary change is that once the clear() method is called, the Dotty thread should stop running (drawing). The correct way to stop a thread is to use some variable whose value will cause the run loop (or in this case the drawing loop) to exit, so the new version of Dotty uses the boolean variable isCleared to control when drawing is stopped. Note that the variable is initialized to false and then set to true in the clear() method. The for loop in draw() will exit when isCleared becomes true. This causes the draw() method to return, which causes the run() method to return, which causes the thread to stop in an orderly fashion.

EFFECTIVE DESIGN: Threaded Applets. Designing a multithreaded applet involves creating a secondary thread that will run concurrently with the applet thread. The applet thread handles the user interface, while the secondary thread performs CPU-intensive calculations.

```java
import java.awt.*;
import javax.swing.*;        // Import Swing classes

public class Dotty implements Runnable {
    private static final int HREF = 20, VREF = 20, LEN = 200; // Coordinates

    private JPanel canvas;
    private int nDots;                   // Number of dots to draw
    private int nDrawn;                  // Number of dots drawn
    private int firstRed = 0;            // Number of the first red dot
    private boolean isCleared = false;   // The panel has been cleared

    public void run() {
        draw();
    }

    public Dotty(JPanel canv, int dots) {
        canvas = canv;
        nDots = dots;
    }

    public void draw() {
        Graphics g = canvas.getGraphics();

        for (nDrawn = 0; !isCleared && nDrawn < nDots; nDrawn++) {
            int x = HREF + (int)(Math.random() * LEN);
            int y = VREF + (int)(Math.random() * LEN);
            g.fillOval(x, y, 3, 3);          // Draw a dot

            if (Math.random() < 0.001 && firstRed == 0) {
                g.setColor(Color.red);       // Change color to red
                firstRed = nDrawn;
            }

            try {
                Thread.sleep(1);             // Sleep for an instant
            } catch (InterruptedException e) {
                System.out.println(e.getMessage());
            }

        } //for
    } // draw()

    public void clear() {
        isCleared = true;
        Graphics g = canvas.getGraphics();
        g.setColor( canvas.getBackground() );
        g.fillRect(HREF,VREF,LEN+3,LEN+3);
        System.out.println("Number of dots drawn since first red = " + (nDrawn-firstRed) );
    } // clear()
} // Dotty
```

FIGURE 13–15 By implementing the Runnable interface, this version of Dotty can run as a separate thread.

> PROGRAMMING TIP: Threading an Applet. To create a second thread within an applet requires three steps: (1) Define the secondary thread to implement the `Runnable` interface, (2) override its `run()` method, and (3) incorporate some mechanism, such as a `sleep()` state, into the thread's run algorithm so that the applet thread will have a chance to run periodically.

Modifications to `RandomDotApplet`

We don't need to make many changes in `RandomDotApplet` to get it to work with the new version of `Dotty`. The primary change comes in the `action-Performed()` method. In the original version of this method, each time the Draw button was clicked, we created a `dotty` instance and then called its `draw()` method. In the revised version we must create a new `Thread` and pass it an instance of `Dotty`, which will then run as a separate thread.

Starting the drawing thread

```java
public void actionPerformed(ActionEvent e) {
    if (e.getSource() == draw) {
        dotty = new Dotty(canvas, NDOTS);
        dottyThread = new Thread(dotty);
        dottyThread.start();
    } else {
        dotty.clear();
    }
} // actionPerformed()
```

Note that in addition to a reference to `dotty` we also have a reference to a `Thread` named `dottyThread`. This additional variable must be declared within the applet.

Recall that when you call the `start()` method, it automatically calls the thread's `run()` method. When `dottyThread` starts to run, it will immediately call the `draw()` method and start drawing dots. After each dot is drawn, `dottyThread` will sleep for an instant.

Notice how the applet stops the drawing thread. Recall that in the new version, `Dotty.clear()` will set the `isCleared` variable, which will cause the drawing loop to terminate. Once again, this is the proper way to stop a thread. Thus, as soon as the user clicks the Clear button, the `Dotty` thread will stop drawing and report its result.

> DEBUGGING TIP: Stopping a Thread. The best way to stop a thread is to use a `boolean` control variable whose value can be set to true or false to exit the `run()` loop.

13.4.3   Advantages of Multithreaded Design

By creating a separate thread for `Dotty`, we have turned a single-threaded program into a multithreaded program. One thread, the applet, handles the user interface. The second thread handles the drawing task. By forcing the drawing to sleep on each iteration, we guarantee that the applet thread will remain responsive to the user's actions. Figure 13–16 illustrates the difference between the single- and multithreaded designs. Note that the

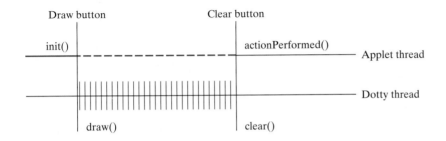

applet thread starts and stops the drawing thread, and the applet thread executes `dotty.clear()`. The drawing thread simply executes its `draw()` method. In the single-threaded version, all of these actions are done by one thread.

Divide and conquer!

The trade-off involved in this design is that it will take somewhat longer to draw *N* random dots, since `dottyThread.draw()` will sleep for an instant on each iteration. But the extra time is hardly noticeable. Thus, by breaking the program into two separate threads of control, one to handle the drawing task and one to handle the user interface, the result is a much more responsive program.

Trade-off: speed vs. responsiveness

> EFFECTIVE DESIGN: Responsive Interfaces.   In order to give a program a more responsive user interface, divide it into separate threads of control. Let one thread handle interactive tasks, such as user input, and let the second thread handle CPU-intensive computations.

SELF-STUDY EXERCISES

EXERCISE 13.7   Someone might argue that because the Java Virtual Machine uses a round-robin scheduling algorithm, it's redundant to use the `sleep()` method, since the applet thread will get its chance to run. What's wrong with this argument in terms of interface responsiveness?

EXERCISE 13.8   Instead of sleeping on each iteration, another way to make the interface more responsive would be to set the threaded `Dotty`'s priority to a low number, such as 1. Make this change, and experiment with its effect on the program's responsiveness. Is it more or less responsive than sleeping on each iteration? Why?

13.5 CASE STUDY: Cooperating Threads

For some applications it is necessary to synchronize and coordinate the behavior of threads to enable them to carry out a cooperative task. Many cooperative applications are based on the **producer/consumer model**. According to this model, two threads cooperate at producing and consuming a particular resource or piece of data. The producer thread creates some message or result, and the consumer thread reads or uses the result. Obviously, the consumer has to wait for a result to be produced, and the producer has to take care not to overwrite a result that hasn't yet been consumed.

One application for this model would be to control the display of data that is read by your browser. As information arrives from the Internet,

Producer and consumer threads

it is written to a buffer by the producer thread. A separate consumer thread reads information from the buffer and displays it in your browser window. Obviously the two threads must be carefully synchronized. There are many other coordination problems that would fit into the producer/consumer model.

13.5.1 Problem Statement

Simulating a waiting line

To illustrate how to address the sorts of problems that can arise when you try to synchronize threads, let's consider a simple application in which several threads use a shared resource. You're familiar with those take-a-number devices that are used in bakeries to manage a waiting line. Customers take a number when they arrive, and the clerk announces who's next by looking at the device. As customers are called, the clerk increments the "next customer" counter by one.

Obviously, there are potential coordination problems here. The device must keep proper count and can't skip customers. Nor can it give the same number to two different customers. Nor can it allow the clerk to serve nonexistent customers.

Our task is to build a multithreaded simulation that uses a model of a take-a-number device to coordinate the behavior of customers and a (single) clerk in a bakery waiting line. To help illustrate the various issues involved in trying to coordinate threads, we will develop more than one version of the program.

Problem Decomposition

What classes do we need?

This simulation will use four classes of objects. The TakeANumber object will serve as a model of a take-a-number device. This is the resource that will be shared by the threads. It is not a thread itself. The Customer class, a subclass of Thread, will model the behavior of a customer who arrives on line and takes a number from the TakeANumber device. There will be several Customer threads created that then compete for a space in line. The Clerk thread, which simulates the behavior of the store clerk, should use the TakeANumber device to determine who the next customer is and should serve that customer. Finally, there will be a main program that will have the task of creating and starting the various threads. Let's call this the Bakery class. This gives us the following list of classes:

- Bakery—responsible for creating the threads and starting the simulation.
- TakeANumber—represents the gadget that keeps track of the next customer to be served.
- Clerk—will use the TakeANumber to determine the next customer and will serve the customer.
- Customer—represents the customers who will use the TakeANumber to take their place in line.

Figure 13–17 provides a UML representation of the interactions among the objects.

13.5.2 Design: The TakeANumber Class

The TakeANumber class must keep track of two things: which customer will be served next, and which waiting number the next customer will be given. This suggests that it should have at least two public methods:

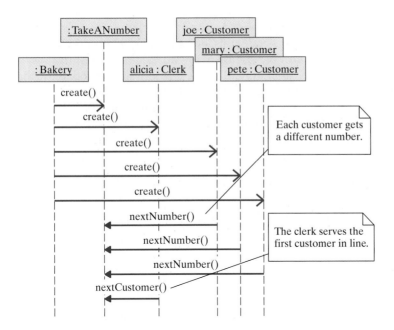

FIGURE 13–17 The Bakery creates the Customer and Clerk threads and the TakeANumber gadget. Then Customers request and receive waiting numbers and the Clerk requests and receives the number of the next customer to serve.

nextNumber(), which will be used by customers to get their waiting numbers, and nextCustomer(), which will be used by the clerk to determine who should be served (Fig. 13–18). Each of these methods will simply retrieve the values of the instance variables, next and serving, which keep track of these two values. As part of the object's state, these variables should be private.

How should we make this TakeANumber object accessible to all of the other objects—that is, to all of the customers and to the clerk? The easiest way to do that is to have the main program pass a reference to the TakeANumber when it constructs the Customers and the Clerk. They can each store the reference as an instance variable. In this way, all the objects in the simulation can share a TakeANumber object as a common resource. Our design considerations lead to the definition of the TakeANumber class shown in Figure 13–19.

TakeANumber
− next : int
− serving : int
+ nextNumber() : int
+ nextCustomer() : int

FIGURE 13–18 The TakeANumber object keeps track of numbers and customers.

Passing a reference to a shared object

```
class TakeANumber {
    private int next = 0;      // Next place in line
    private int serving = 0;   // Next customer to serve

    public synchronized int nextNumber() {
        next = next + 1;
        return next;
    } // nextNumber()

    public int nextCustomer() {
        ++serving;
        return serving;
    } // nextCustomer()

} // TakeANumber
```

FIGURE 13–19 Definition of the TakeANumber class, Version 1.

Synchronized methods

Note that the `nextNumber()` method is declared `synchronized`. As we will discuss in more detail, this ensures that only one customer at a time can take a number. Once a thread begins executing a synchronized method, no other thread can execute that method until the first thread finishes. This is important because otherwise several `Customers` could call the `nextNumber` method at the same time. It's important that the customer threads have mutually exclusive access to the `TakeANumber` object. This form of **mutual exclusion** is important for the correctness of the simulation.

SELF-STUDY EXERCISE

EXERCISE 13.9   What is the analogue to mutual exclusion in the real-world example of the bakery situation?

13.5.3   Java Monitors and Mutual Exclusion

The monitor concept

An object that contains `synchronized` methods has a **monitor** associated with it. A monitor is a widely used synchronization mechanism that ensures that only one thread at a time can execute a `synchronized` method. When a `synchronized` method is called, a **lock** is acquired on that object. For example, if one of the `Customer` threads calls `nextNumber()`, a lock will be placed on that `TakeANumber` object. While an object is *locked*, no other `synchronized` method can run in that object. Other threads must wait for the lock to be released before they can execute a `synchronized` method.

Mutually exclusive access to a shared object

While one `Customer` is executing `nextNumber()`, all other `Customers` will be forced to wait until the first `Customer` is finished. When the synchronized method is exited, the lock on the object is released, allowing other `Customer` threads to access their `synchronized` methods. In effect, a synchronized method can be used to guarantee mutually exclusive access to the `TakeANumber` object among the competing customers.

JAVA LANGUAGE RULE   `synchronized`. Once a thread begins to execute a `synchronized` method in an object, the object is *locked* so that no other thread can gain access to that object's synchronized methods.

EFFECTIVE DESIGN: Synchronization.   In order to restrict access of a method or set of methods to one object at a time (*mutual exclusion*), declare the methods `synchronized`.

One cautionary note here is that although a synchronized method blocks access to other synchronized methods, it does not block access to nonsynchronized methods. This could cause potential problems. We will return to this issue in the next part of our case study when we discuss the testing of our program.

13.5.4 The Customer Class

A Customer thread should model the behavior of taking a number from the TakeANumber gadget. For the sake of this simulation, let's suppose that after taking a number, the customer just prints it out. This will serve as a simple model of "waiting on line." What about the Customer's state? To help distinguish one customer from another, let's give each customer a unique ID number starting at 10001, which will be set in the constructor method. Also, as we noted earlier, each Customer needs a reference to the TakeANumber object, which is passed as a constructor parameter (Fig. 13–20). This leads to the definition of Customer shown in Figure 13–21. Note that before taking a number the customer sleeps for a random interval of up to 1,000 milliseconds. This will introduce a bit of randomness into the simulation.

Another important feature of this definition is the use of the static variable number to assign each customer a unique ID number. Remember that a static variable belongs to the class itself, not to its instances. Therefore, each Customer that is created can share this variable. By incrementing it and assigning its new value as the Customer's ID, we guarantee that each customer has a unique ID number.

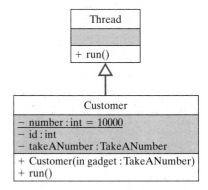

FIGURE 13–20 The Customer thread.

Static (class) variables

> **JAVA LANGUAGE RULE** Static (Class) Variables. Static variables are associated with the class itself and not with its instances.

> **EFFECTIVE DESIGN: Unique IDs.** Static variables are often used to assign a unique ID number or a unique initial value to each instance of a class.

```java
public class Customer extends Thread {

    private static int number = 10000;   // Initial ID number
    private int id;
    private TakeANumber takeANumber;

    public Customer( TakeANumber gadget ) {
        id = ++number;
        takeANumber = gadget;
    }

    public void run() {
        try {
            sleep( (int)(Math.random() * 1000 ) );
            System.out.println("Customer " + id + " takes ticket "
                                + takeANumber.nextNumber());
        } catch (InterruptedException e) {
            System.out.println("Exception " + e.getMessage());
        }
    } // run()
} // Customer
```

FIGURE 13–21 Definition of the Customer class, Version 1.

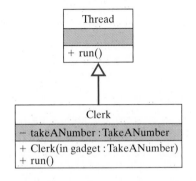

FIGURE 13–22 The Clerk thread.

FIGURE 13–23 Definition of Clerk, Version 1.

13.5.5 The Clerk Class

The Clerk thread should simulate the behavior of serving the next customer in line, so the Clerk thread will repeatedly access TakeANumber.-nextCustomer() and then serve that customer. For the sake of this simulation, we'll just print a message to indicate which customer is being served. Because there's only one clerk in this simulation, the only variable in its internal state will be a reference to the TakeANumber object (Fig. 13–22). In addition to the constructor, all we really need to define for this class is the run() method. This leads to the definition of Clerk shown in Figure 13–23. In this case, the sleep() method is necessary to allow the Customer threads to run. The Clerk will sit in an infinite loop serving the next customer on each iteration.

```java
public class Clerk extends Thread {
    private TakeANumber takeANumber;

    public Clerk(TakeANumber gadget) {
        takeANumber = gadget;
    }

    public void run() {
        while (true) {
            try {
                sleep( (int)(Math.random() * 50));
                System.out.println("Clerk serving ticket " +
                                        takeANumber.nextCustomer());
            } catch (InterruptedException e) {
                System.out.println("Exception " + e.getMessage() );
            }
        } //while
    } //run()
} // Clerk
```

13.5.6 The Bakery Class

The main program

Finally, Bakery is the simplest class to design. It contains the main() method, which gets the whole simulation started. As we said, its role will be to create one Clerk thread and several Customer threads, and get them all started (Fig. 13–24). Notice that the Customers and the Clerk are each passed a reference to the shared TakeANumber gadget.

Problem: Nonexistent Customers

Testing and debugging

Now that we have designed and implemented the classes, let's run several experiments to test that everything works as intended. Except for the synchronized nextNumber() method, we've made little attempt to make sure that the Customer and Clerk threads will work together cooperatively, without violating the real-world constraints that should be satisfied by the simulation. If we run the simulation as it is presently coded, it will generate five customers and the clerk will serve all of them. But we get something like the following output:

```
public class Bakery {
    public static void main(String args[]) {
        System.out.println( "Starting clerk and customer threads" );
        TakeANumber numberGadget = new TakeANumber();
        Clerk clerk = new Clerk(numberGadget);
        clerk.start();
        for (int k = 0; k < 5; k++) {
            Customer customer = new Customer(numberGadget);
            customer.start();
        }
    } // main()
} // Bakery
```

FIGURE 13–24 Definition of the Bakery class.

```
Starting clerk and customer threads
  Clerk serving ticket 1
  Clerk serving ticket 2
  Clerk serving ticket 3
  Clerk serving ticket 4
  Clerk serving ticket 5
Customer 10004 takes ticket 1
Customer 10002 takes ticket 2
  Clerk serving ticket 6
Customer 10005 takes ticket 3
  Clerk serving ticket 7
  Clerk serving ticket 8
  Clerk serving ticket 9
  Clerk serving ticket 10
Customer 10001 takes ticket 4
Customer 10003 takes ticket 5
```

Obviously, our current solution violates an important real-world constraint: You can't serve customers before they enter the line! How can we ensure that the clerk doesn't serve a customer unless there's actually a customer waiting?

Problem: The clerk thread doesn't wait for customer threads

The wrong way to address this issue would be to increase the amount of sleeping that the Clerk does between serving customers. Indeed, this would allow more customer threads to run, so it might appear to have the desired effect, but it doesn't truly address the main problem: A clerk cannot serve a customer if no customer is waiting.

The correct way to solve this problem is to have the clerk check that there are customers waiting before taking the next customer. One way to model this would be to add a customerWaiting() method to our TakeANumber object. This method would return true whenever next is greater than serving. That will correspond to the real-world situation in which the clerk can see customers waiting in line. We can make the following modification to Clerk.run():

The clerk checks the line

```
public void run() {
    while (true) {
        try {
            sleep((int)(Math.random() * 50));
            if (takeANumber.customerWaiting())
```
(continues on next page)

```
                        System.out.println("Clerk serving ticket "
                                            + takeANumber.nextCustomer());
            } catch (InterruptedException e) {
                System.out.println("Exception " + e.getMessage() );
            }
        } // while
    } // run()
```

TakeANumber
− next : int
− serving : int
+ nextNumber() : int
+ nextCustomer() : int
+ customerWaiting() : boolean

FIGURE 13–25 The revised TakeANumber class.

And we add the following method to TakeANumber (Fig. 13–25):

```
public boolean customerWaiting() {
    return next > serving;
}
```

In other words, the Clerk won't serve a customer unless there are customers waiting—that is, unless next is greater than serving. Given these changes, we get the following type of output when we run the simulation:

```
Starting clerk and customer threads
Customer 10003 takes ticket 1
  Clerk serving ticket 1
Customer 10005 takes ticket 2
  Clerk serving ticket 2
Customer 10001 takes ticket 3
  Clerk serving ticket 3
Customer 10004 takes ticket 4
  Clerk serving ticket 4
Customer 10002 takes ticket 5
  Clerk serving ticket 5
```

This example illustrates that in designing applications that involve cooperating threads the algorithm used must ensure the proper cooperation and coordination among the threads.

EFFECTIVE DESIGN: Thread Coordination. When two or more threads must behave cooperatively, their interaction must be carefully coordinated by the algorithm.

13.5.7 Problem: Critical Sections

It is easy to forget that thread behavior is asynchronous. You can't predict when a thread might be interrupted or might have to give up the CPU to another thread. In designing applications that involve cooperating threads, it's important that the design incorporates features to guard against problems caused by asynchronicity. To illustrate this problem, consider the following statement from the Customer.run() method:

Thread interruptions are unpredictable

```
System.out.println("Customer " + id + " takes ticket "
                                    + takeANumber.nextNumber());
```

Even though this is a single Java statement, it breaks up into several Java bytecode statements. A Customer thread could certainly be interrupted between getting the next number back from TakeANumber and printing it out. We can simulate this by breaking the println() into two statements and putting a sleep() in their midst:

```
public void run() {
    try {
        int myturn = takeANumber.nextNumber();
        sleep( (int)(Math.random() * 1000 ) );
      System.out.println("Customer " + id + " takes ticket " + myturn);
    } catch (InterruptedException e) {
        System.out.println("Exception " + e.getMessage());
    }
} // run()
```

If this change is made in the simulation, you might get the following output:

```
Starting clerk and customer threads
  Clerk serving ticket 1
  Clerk serving ticket 2
  Clerk serving ticket 3
Customer 10004 takes ticket 4
  Clerk serving ticket 4
  Clerk serving ticket 5
Customer 10001 takes ticket 1
Customer 10002 takes ticket 2
Customer 10003 takes ticket 3
Customer 10005 takes ticket 5
```

Because the Customer threads are now interrupted in between taking a number and reporting their number, it looks as if they are being served in the wrong order. Actually, they are being served in the correct order. It's their reporting of their numbers that is wrong!

The problem here is that the Customer.run() method is being interrupted in such a way that it invalidates the simulation's output. A method that displays the simulation's state should be designed so that once a thread begins reporting its state, that thread will be allowed to finish reporting before another thread can start reporting its state. Accurate reporting of a thread's state is a critical element of the simulation's overall integrity. *Problem: An interrupt in a critical section*

A **critical section** is any section of a thread that should not be interrupted during its execution. In the bakery simulation, all of the statements that report the simulation's progress are critical sections. Even though the chances are small that a thread will be interrupted in the midst of a println() statement, the faithful reporting of the simulation's state should not be left to chance. Therefore, we must design an algorithm that prevents the interruption of critical sections.

Creating a Critical Section

The correct way to address this problem is to treat the reporting of the customer's state as a critical section. As we saw earlier when we discussed the concept of a monitor, a synchronized method within a shared object ensures that once a thread starts the method, it will be allowed to finish it before any other thread can start it. Therefore, one way out of this dilemma is to redesign the nextNumber() and nextCustomer() methods in *Making a critical section uninterruptible*

```
public class TakeANumber {
    private int next = 0;      // Next place in line
    private int serving = 0;   // Next customer to serve

    public synchronized int nextNumber(int custId) {
        next = next + 1;
        System.out.println( "Customer " + custId + " takes ticket " + next );
        return next;
    }

    public synchronized int nextCustomer() {
        ++serving;
        System.out.println("  Clerk serving ticket " + serving );
        return serving;
    }

    public synchronized boolean customerWaiting() {
        return next > serving;
    }
} // TakeANumber
```

FIGURE 13–26 Definition of the TakeANumber class, Version 2.

the TakeANumber class so that they report which customer receives a ticket and which customer is being served (Fig. 13–26). In this version all of the methods are synchronized, so all the actions of the TakeANumber object are treated as critical sections.

Note (Fig. 13–26) that the reporting of both the next number and the next customer to be served are now handled by TakeANumber. Because the methods that handle these actions are synchronized, they cannot be interrupted by any threads involved in the simulation. This guarantees that the simulation's output will faithfully report the simulation's state.

Given these changes to TakeANumber, we must remove the println() statements from the run() methods in Customer:

```
public void run() {
    try {
        sleep((int)(Math.random() * 2000));
        takeANumber.nextNumber(id);
    } catch (InterruptedException e) {
        System.out.println("Exception: " + e.getMessage() );
    }
} // run()
```

and from the run() method in Clerk:

```
public void run() {
    while (true) {
        try {
            sleep( (int)(Math.random() * 1000));
            if (takeANumber.customerWaiting())
                takeANumber.nextCustomer();
```
(continues on next page)

```
            } catch (InterruptedException e) {
                System.out.println("Exception: " + e.getMessage());
            }
        } // while
    } // run()
```

Rather than printing their numbers, these methods now just call the appropriate methods in TakeANumber. Given these design changes, our simulation now produces the following correct output:

```
Starting clerk and customer threads
Customer 10001 takes ticket 1
  Clerk serving ticket 1
Customer 10003 takes ticket 2
Customer 10002 takes ticket 3
  Clerk serving ticket 2
Customer 10005 takes ticket 4
Customer 10004 takes ticket 5
  Clerk serving ticket 3
  Clerk serving ticket 4
  Clerk serving ticket 5
```

The lesson to be learned from this is that in designing multithreaded programs, it is important to assume that if a thread can be interrupted at a certain point, it will be interrupted at that point. The fact that an interrupt is unlikely to occur is no substitute for the use of a critical section. This is something like "Murphy's Law of Thread Coordination."

Preventing undesirable interrupts

EFFECTIVE DESIGN: The Thread Coordination Principle. Use critical sections to coordinate the behavior of cooperating threads. By designating certain methods as synchronized, you can ensure their mutually exclusive access. Once a thread starts a synchronized method, no other thread will be able to execute the method until the first thread is finished.

In a multithreaded application, the classes and methods should be designed so that undesirable interrupts will not affect the correctness of the algorithm.

PROGRAMMING TIP: Critical Sections. Java's monitor mechanism will ensure that while one thread is executing a synchronized method, no other threads can gain access to it. Even if the first thread is interrupted, when it resumes execution again it will be allowed to finish the synchronized method before other threads can access synchronized methods in that object.

SELF-STUDY EXERCISE

EXERCISE 13.10   Given the changes we've described, the bakery simulation should now run correctly regardless of how slow or fast the Customer and Clerk threads run. Verify this by placing different-sized sleep intervals in their run() methods. (*Note*: You don't want to put a sleep() in the synchronized methods because that would undermine the whole purpose of making them synchronized in the first place.)

13.5.8   Using `wait`/`notify` to Coordinate Threads

The examples in the previous sections were designed to illustrate the issues of thread asynchronicity and the principles of mutual exclusion and critical sections. Through the careful design of the algorithm and the appropriate use of the `synchronized` qualifier, we have managed to design a program that correctly coordinates the behavior of the `Customers` and `Clerk` in this bakery simulation.

The Busy-Waiting Problem

Busy waiting

One problem with our current design of the Bakery algorithm is that it uses **busy waiting** on the part of the `Clerk` thread. This is wasteful of CPU time, and we should modify the algorithm.

As it is presently designed, the `Clerk` thread sits in a loop that repeatedly checks if there's a customer to serve:

```
public void run() {
    while (true) {
        try {
            sleep( (int)(Math.random() * 1000));
            if (takeANumber.customerWaiting())
                takeANumber.nextCustomer();
        } catch (InterruptedException e) {
            System.out.println("Exception: " + e.getMessage());
        }
    } // while
} // run()
```

A far better solution would be to force the `Clerk` thread to wait until a customer arrives without using the CPU. Under this design, as soon as a `Customer` becomes available, the `Clerk` thread can be notified and enabled to run. Note that this description views the customer/clerk relationship as one-half of the producer/consumer relationship. The customer's taking of a number *produces* a customer in line that must be served (that is, *consumed*) by the clerk.

Producer/consumer

This is only half the producer/consumer relationship because we haven't placed any constraint on the size of the waiting line. There's no real limit to how many customers can be produced. If we did limit the line size, customers might be forced to wait before taking a number if, say, the tickets ran out, or the bakery filled up. In that case, customers would have to wait until the line resource became available and we would have a full-fledged producer/consumer relationship.

The `wait`/`notify` *Mechanism*

So, let's use Java's `wait`/`notify` mechanism to eliminate busy waiting from our simulation. As noted in Figure 13–6, the `wait()` method puts a thread into a waiting state, and `notify()` takes a thread out of waiting and places it back in the ready queue. To use these methods in this program we need to modify the `nextNumber()` and `nextCustomer()` methods. When the `Clerk` calls the `nextCustomer()` method, if there is no customer in line, the `Clerk` should be made to `wait()`:

```
public synchronized int nextCustomer() {
    try {
        while (next <= serving)
            wait();
    } catch(InterruptedException e) {
        System.out.println("Exception: " + e.getMessage());
    } finally {
        ++serving;
        System.out.println("  Clerk serving ticket " + serving);
        return serving;
    }
}
```

Note that the Clerk still checks whether there are customers waiting. If there are none, the Clerk calls the wait() method. This removes the Clerk from the CPU until some other thread notifies it, at which point it will be ready to run again. When it runs again, it should check that there is in fact a customer waiting before proceeding. That's why we use a while loop here. In effect, the Clerk will wait until there's a customer to serve. But this is not busy waiting because the Clerk thread loses the CPU and must be notified each time a customer becomes available.

A waiting thread gives up the CPU

When and how will the Clerk be notified? Clearly, the Clerk should be notified as soon as a customer takes a number. Therefore, we put a notify() in the nextNumber() method, the method called by each Customer as it gets in line:

```
public synchronized int nextNumber( int custId) {
    next = next + 1;
    System.out.println("Customer " + custId + " takes ticket " + next);
    notify();
    return next;
}
```

Thus, as soon as a Customer thread executes the nextNumber() method, the Clerk will be notified and allowed to proceed.

What happens if more than one Customer has executed a wait()? In that case, the JVM will maintain a queue of waiting Customer threads. Then, each time a notify() is executed, the JVM will take the first Customer out of the queue and allow it to proceed.

If we use this model of thread coordination, we no longer need to test customerWaiting() in the Clerk.run() method. It is to be tested in the TakeANumber.nextCustomer(). Thus, the Clerk.run() can be simplified to

```
public void run() {
    while (true) {
        try {
            sleep((int)(Math.random() * 1000));
            takeANumber.nextCustomer();
        } catch (InterruptedException e) {
            System.out.println("Exception: " + e.getMessage() );
        }
    } // while
} // run()
```

The Clerk thread may be forced to wait when it calls the nextCustomer method.

Because we no longer need the customerWaiting() method, we end up with the new definition of TakeANumber shown in Figures 13–27 and 13–28. Given this version of the program, the following kind of output will be generated:

TakeANumber
− next : int
− serving : int
+ nextNumber() : int<<synchronized>>
+ nextCustomer() : int<<synchronized>>

FIGURE 13–27 In the final design of TakeANumber, its methods are synchronized.

```
Starting clerk and customer threads
Customer 10004 takes ticket 1
Customer 10002 takes ticket 2
  Clerk serving ticket 1
  Clerk serving ticket 2
Customer 10005 takes ticket 3
Customer 10003 takes ticket 4
  Clerk serving ticket 3
Customer 10001 takes ticket 5
  Clerk serving ticket 4
  Clerk serving ticket 5
  Clerk waiting
```

```java
public class TakeANumber {

    private int next = 0;
    private int serving = 0;

    public synchronized int nextNumber(int custId) {
        next = next + 1;
        System.out.println( "Customer " + custId + " takes ticket " + next );
        notify();
        return next;
    } // nextNumber()

    public synchronized int nextCustomer() {
        try {
            while (next <= serving)  {
                System.out.println(" Clerk waiting ");
                wait();
            }
        } catch(InterruptedException e) {
            System.out.println("Exception " + e.getMessage() );
        } finally {
            ++serving;
            System.out.println(" Clerk serving ticket " + serving );
            return serving;
        }
    } // nextCustomer()
} // TakeANumber
```

FIGURE 13–28 The TakeANumber class, Version 3.

PROGRAMMING TIP: Busy Waiting.   Java's wait/notify mechanism can be used effectively to eliminate busy waiting from a multithreaded application.

EFFECTIVE DESIGN: Producer/Consumer.   The producer/consumer model is a useful design for coordinating the wait/notify interaction.

SELF-STUDY EXERCISE

EXERCISE 13.11   An interesting experiment to try is to make the Clerk a little slower by making it sleep for up to 2,000 milliseconds. Take a guess at what would happen if you ran this experiment. Then run the experiment and observe the results.

The wait/notify *Mechanism*

There are a number of important restrictions that must be observed when using the wait/notify mechanism:

Wait/notify go into synchronized methods

- Both wait() and notify() are methods of the Object class, not the Thread class. This enables them to lock objects, which is the essential feature of Java's monitor mechanism.
- A wait() method can be used within a synchronized method. The method doesn't have to be part of a Thread.
- You can only use wait() and notify() within synchronized methods. If you use them in other methods, you will cause an IllegalMonitorStateException with the message "current thread not owner."
- When a wait() [or a sleep()] is used within a synchronized method, the lock on that object is released, allowing other methods access to the object's synchronized methods.

DEBUGGING TIP: Wait/Notify. It's easy to forget that the wait() and notify() methods can only be used within synchronized methods.

13.6   CASE STUDY: The Spider and Fly Threads

Another good use for threads is to simulate the behavior of two independent entities in an application. Let's design a Java applet that simulates the interaction between two or more CyberPets. One CyberPet will be the spider that we introduced in Chapter 2. In addition to eating and sleeping, however, this version will also be able to dream big dreams and will be able to catch buzzing flies as well as flies already trapped in its web.

Problem statement

The second type of CyberPet will be a fly, which, for this simulation, will buzz around just outside the reach of the spider's web. In its frustration, the spider begins wishing that it was a frog so that it could capture the fly with its sticky tongue. And, lo and behold, in its dream state the spider magically transforms into a frog and captures the buzzing fly (Fig. 13–29). To see how this all looks, you may wish to run the demo program at

```
http://starbase.trincoll.edu/~jjjava/cyberpet/
```

FIGURE 13–29 The Spider and the fly.

13.6.1 Problem Decomposition

What objects do we need?

For this simulation, we want to represent the spider and the fly as separate classes: Spider and Fly. It will also be necessary that Spider and Fly be independent threads (Fig. 13–30). A third class, an applet, will provide a GUI interface, displaying the animated images of the characters, and will also serve as their intermediary. There will be no direct interaction between the Spider and the Fly. The applet will make it possible for the Spider to "see" the Fly and eat the Fly by reporting the Fly's location to the Spider whenever it "looks at" the fly (Fig. 13–31). It will also enable the spider to "eat" the fly by telling the fly to "die" whenever the spider "eats" it. In order to refer to the applet, both Spider and Fly will need references to it.

One possible design is to define Fly and Spider as Thread subclasses. However, this design presents certain problems. Because a class can have only one immediate superclass, if Fly and Spider are Threads, they can't also be CyberPets.

A better design would be to define Spider and Fly as subclasses of CyberPet and have each of them implement the Runnable interface (Fig. 13–32). This design uses a limited form of *multiple inheritance*. As subclasses of CyberPet, both Spider and Fly inherit their shared characteristics, such as the state variable, the eat() and sleep() methods, and so on. But as Runnable objects, they inherit the basic characteristics of a thread. This leads to the following basic definitions:

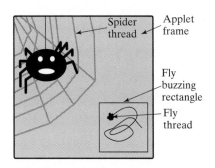

FIGURE 13–30 Design of the GUI for the spidey/fly applet.

```
public class Fly extends CyberPet implements Runnable { ... }
public class Spider extends CyberPet implements Runnable { ... }
```

FIGURE 13–31 This UML diagram shows the communication model used by the Spider/Fly simulation. The applet mediates all interactions between the Spider and the Fly, which have no direct association.

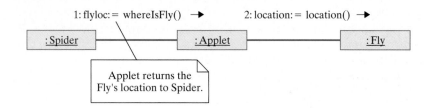

Given this class hierarchy (Fig. 13–32), to make Spiders and Flys into independent threads, we need only define their respective run() methods.

> EFFECTIVE DESIGN: Multiple Inheritance.   Java interfaces provide a limited form of multiple inheritance, because they allow a class to inherit methods from more than one superclass.

13.6.2 The Revised CyberPet Class

Given our design of Spider as a subclass of CyberPet, we have to make several design changes in the CyberPet class (Figs. 13–33 and 13–34).

First, the CyberPet's internal state has been expanded to include the DREAMING, DEAD, and FLYING states as possible state values. As in previous versions of CyberPet, these are defined as class constants. Second, the state variables, state and name, must now be declared protected, instead of private, so they can be inherited by the Spider and Fly subclasses.

Finally, the other major change is that we have removed all but the minimal functionality from the various public methods that define the CyberPet's behavior. For example, the eat() method in this version simply changes CyberPet's state to EATING:

```java
public void eat() {
    state = EATING;
}
```

In previous versions of this class the eat(), sleep(), think(), and dream() methods also displayed images of the CyberPet's current state. That part of a CyberPet's functionality must now be handled by its subclasses—by Spider and Fly—so the images will be appropriate to the type of CyberPet. Although the default versions of these methods will suffice for the Fly class, we have to override them in the Spider class. For example,

```java
public void sleep() {
    Graphics g = applet.getGraphics();
    int choice = (int)(Math.random() * 3);
    if (choice == 2)                     // i.e., 1 in 3 chance
        g.drawImage(image[NOT_SLEEPY_IMG], 20, 100, applet);
    else {
        state = SLEEPING;
        g.drawImage(image[SLEEPING_IMG], 20, 100, applet);
    }
} // sleep()
```

Note how the reference to the applet enables the Spider to use the applet's Graphics object to do the drawing. Also, as in previous versions of Cyber-Pet, the Spider sometimes sleeps and sometimes doesn't when it is told to sleep. This functionality is now defined in the Spider class, as a Spider behavior, not in the CyberPet class, as a behavior that is common to all CyberPets.

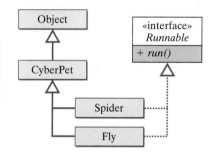

FIGURE 13–32   Hierarchy of the classes used in the Spider/Fly simulation.

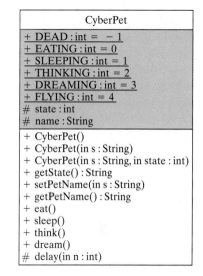

FIGURE 13–33   To serve as a superclass, the CyberPet's state and name variables must be declared protected (#).

Referring to a shared object

FIGURE 13–34   The revised
CyberPet class.

```java
public class CyberPet {
    protected int state;
    protected String name;
    public static final int DEAD = -1;
    public static final int EATING = 0;
    public static final int SLEEPING = 1;
    public static final int THINKING = 2;
    public static final int DREAMING = 3;
    public static final int FLYING = 4;      // For flying cyberpets

    public CyberPet ( ) {
        state = EATING;
        name = "no name";
    }

    public CyberPet (String str) {
        name = str;
        state = EATING;
    }

    public CyberPet (String str, int inState) {
        state = inState;
        name = str;
    }

    public String getState() {
        if (state == EATING)
            return "Eating";
        else if (state == SLEEPING)
            return "Sleeping";
        else if (state == THINKING)
            return "Thinking";
        else if (state == DREAMING)
            return "Dreaming";
        return "Error in State";
    } // getState()

    public void setPetName(String name) { this.name = name;   }
    public String getPetName()          { return name;        }

    // The next four methods can be overridden in subclasses

    public void eat()                   { state = EATING;   }
    public void sleep()                 { state = SLEEPING; }
    public void think()                 { state = THINKING; }
    public void dream()                 { state = DREAMING; }

    protected void delay(int N) {        // delay for N milliseconds
      try {
          Thread.sleep(N);
      } catch (InterruptedException e) {
          System.out.println(e.toString());
      }
    } // delay()
} // CyberPet
```

EFFECTIVE DESIGN: Inheritance. The higher you place methods and variables in an inheritance hierarchy, the more broadly they can be shared. Features that should be shared by subclasses should be defined in their superclass. Those that make a particular subclass unique should be defined in the particular subclass.

13.6.3 The Fly Thread

The Fly thread is simple to design, because the Fly's only action will be to buzz around just outside the reach of the spider's web. Its overall design is summarized in Figure 13–35. There are several important features of our design. First, note the collection of constants used to define a rectangle within which the fly's image will move to simulate "buzzing around." The applet attribute will provide a reference to the GUI where the fly's image will be drawn. This reference will be passed in the constructor method. Note also the specialized methods that define the fly's behavior: buzzaround(), die(), and getLocation(). The getLocation() method will be called by the applet to determine where the fly is so that it can pass this information on to the spider. The die() method will be called by the applet whenever the spider successfully eats the fly. Finally, note the run() method, which implements the Runnable interface. This method will repeatedly call buzzaround() as long as the fly is alive.

Let's now describe the details of this design. We define a collection of class constants to demarcate the fly's buzzing area. These are the minimum and maximum values of the fly's *x*- and *y*-coordinates on the display:

```
private static final int XMIN = 225;
private static final int XMAX = 300;
private static final int YMIN = 245;
private static final int YMAX = 305;
private static final int SIDE = 5;          // Size of fly rectangle
private static final int MAX_RANGE = 15;  // Max and min change of location
private static final int MIN_DELTA = -10;
```

Next the Fly's state will be amplified to include its location. In addition to the variables it inherits from CyberPet, a Fly needs instance variables to keep track of its current location on the applet window:

```
private CyberPetApplet applet; // Reference to the simulation's interface
private Point location;        // The fly's coordinates within the applet
```

The Fly() constructor method can be defined as follows:

```
public Fly (CyberPetApplet app) {
    applet = app;
    location = new Point(XMAX, YMAX);  // Starting location
    state = FLYING;
}
```

Thus, when a Fly is constructed, it is given a reference to the applet where its image will be displayed and an initial location within the applet.

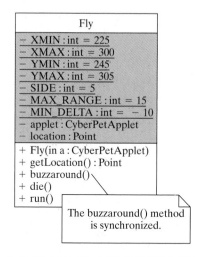

FIGURE 13–35   Design of the Fly class.

What data does Fly *need?*

Next let's design the `Fly`'s `buzzaround()` method. Suppose the buzzing fly will be represented by a colored rectangle drawn directly onto the applet. The animation can be carried out by a three-step algorithm:

1. Erase the current image of the fly.
2. Move the fly to a new location.
3. Draw the fly at the new location.

Simulating random motion

To simulate the fly's random motion, the new coordinates for its location will be generated randomly. Finally, we will use if-else statements to ensure that the random locations we generate stay within the boundaries of its buzzing rectangle (Fig. 13–30). These design considerations lead to the definition of the `buzzaround()` method shown in Figure 13–36. Note there that because this method changes the fly's state, we want to define it as a critical method. Hence, we declare it to be `synchronized`. This will ensure that it can't be interrupted by the spider.

Animation

PROGRAMMING TIP: Animation.   Animation can be implemented by repeatedly drawing, erasing, and moving an image. A delay may be necessary between these steps to achieve the desired appearance.

Thread Communication

What methods do we need?

In order to simulate the `Spider` eating the `Fly`, the `Spider` will need to know the `Fly`'s location. This is the purpose of the `Fly`'s `getLocation()` method:

```
public Point getLocation() {
    return location;
}
```

Since `Fly`s will occasionally get eaten, we need a method to simulate this:

```
public synchronized void die() {
    state = DEAD;
}
```

The `die()` method simply sets the `Fly`'s state to DEAD. Given the foregoing definitions, the `Fly`'s run algorithm is very simple to define. The fly will simply `buzzaround()` until it is DEAD:

```
public void run() {
    while (state != DEAD) {
        buzzaround();
        delay(125);
    }//while
} // run()
```

Delaying the animation

Note the use of the `delay(N)` method to make the `Fly`'s buzzing seem more realistic. This method was defined in the `CyberPet` class, so that it can be used to provide a delay for both the `Spider` and the `Fly`. It simply calls the `Thread.sleep()` method.

```java
import java.awt.*; // Import the GUI components

public class Fly extends CyberPet implements Runnable {

    // The image is 283 x 210 and its top left edge
    // is at (20,100). We want the fly to buzz around
    // just outside the spider's web.
    private static final int XMIN = 225;
    private static final int XMAX = 300;
    private static final int YMIN = 245;
    private static final int YMAX = 305;
    private static final int SIDE = 5;          // Size of fly rectangle
    private static final int MAX_RANGE = 15;  // Max and min change of location
    private static final int MIN_DELTA = -10;

    private CyberPetApplet applet;   // Reference to the simulation's interface
    private Point location;          // The fly's coordinates within the applet
    public Fly (CyberPetApplet app) {
        applet = app;
        location = new Point(XMAX, YMAX); // Starting Location
        state = FLYING;
    }

    public Point getLocation() {
        return location;
    }

    public synchronized void buzzaround() {
        state = FLYING;
        Graphics g = applet.getGraphics();
                                    // Erase current image
        g.setColor(Color.white);
        g.fillRect(location.x, location.y, SIDE, SIDE);
                                    // Calculate new location
        int dx = (int)(MIN_DELTA +  Math.random() * MAX_RANGE);
        int dy = (int)(MIN_DELTA + Math.random() * MAX_RANGE);

        if (location.x + dx >= XMIN)  location.x = location.x + dx;
        else                          location.x = XMIN;
        if (location.y + dy >= YMIN)  location.y = location.y + dy;
        else                          location.y = YMIN;
        if (location.x + dx <= XMAX)  location.x = location.x + dx;
        else                          location.x = XMAX;
        if (location.y + dy <= YMAX)  location.y = location.y + dy;
        else                          location.y = YMAX;
                                    // Draw new image at new location
        g.setColor(Color.red);
        g.fillRect(location.x, location.y, SIDE, SIDE);
    } // buzzaround()

    public synchronized void die() {
        state = DEAD;
    }
```

FIGURE 13–36   The Fly class.

```
    public void run() {
        while (state != DEAD) {
            buzzaround();
            delay(125);
        }//while
    } // run()
} // Fly
```

FIGURE 13–36   *(continued)* The `Fly` class.

13.6.4   The Spider Thread

The `Spider` thread should behave more or less the same as in its previous incarnation as `CyberPet` (Fig. 13–37). It should respond to eat and sleep commands issued through the applet, but it should occasionally (randomly) ignore the commands. It should decide autonomously when it wants to eat, sleep, or think. Also, for this simulation, it should contain a fourth state, DREAMING, during which it will magically transform into a frog and catch the buzzing fly. Since dreaming is a state that might well apply to other kinds of `CyberPets`, let's define it in `CyberPet`, thereby making it inheritable by all `CyberPets`. (Maybe someday `Flys` will learn to dream!)

Simulating the spider

The `Spider`'s run method should generate one of four possible actions and then simply take that action:

```
public void run() {
    while (true) {
        int choice = (int)(Math.random() * 4);
        if (choice == 0)
            autoeat();
        else if (choice == 1)
            autosleep();
        else if (choice == 2)
            think();
        else
            dream();
        delay(5000);
    } //while
} // run()
```

FIGURE 13–37   Design of the `Spider` class. Note that it overrides `CyberPet`'s `eat()`, `sleep()`, `dream()`, and `think()` methods. Its `run()` method will coordinate its various behaviors.

Spider
applet : CyberPetApplet # image[] : Image − flyLocation : Point
+ Spider(in name : String, in a : CyberPetApplet) + getImages() + eat() − autoeat() + sleep() − autosleep() + think() + dream() + run()

The `dream()` method is synchronized.

On each iteration of its infinite loop, the Spider alternates randomly between eating, sleeping, thinking, and dreaming. The Math.random() method is used to ensure that each activity is done approximately one-fourth of the time. To make the animation more realistic looking, the Spider delays for a relatively long interval—up to 5,000 milliseconds—on each iteration.

As noted earlier, the Spider will occasionally eat the Fly. This will happen in the dream() method. (See the definition of this method in Fig. 13–38.) The basic script for the dream is that the Spider first wishes it could be a frog, and then it magically transforms into one and catches the fly with its sticky tongue.

The transformation to a frog is done by changing the images that are displayed on the applet. A sequence of three images is used with appropriate delays. The first image shows the spider wishing it were a frog. The second shows a frog. And the third shows a happy frog saying "yum, yum," after just having eaten the Fly.

Eating the buzzing fly is simulated by drawing a line from the frog's tongue to the Fly's current location. Note how the applet is used as an intermediary object here to get the Fly's location:

Spider/fly interaction

```
flyLocation = applet.getFlyLocation();      // Look at the fly
```

As soon as the line is drawn, the Fly thread must stop and the Fly must disappear. Stopping the Fly thread is done by calling applet.eatFly(), which in turn calls Fly's die() method, which causes the fly thread to exit:

```
public void eatFly() {
    pest.die();
}
```

Making the Fly disappear from the screen is done by displaying the image of the happy frog. Then, after a suitable delay, the applet.newFly() method is invoked, which causes a new buzzing fly to be created:

```
public void newFly() {
    pest = new Fly(this);
    new Thread(pest).start();
}
```

It's important to note that the reason the Fly disappears from the display is twofold: First, since it is DEAD, it no longer buzzes around redrawing itself at a new location. In fact, it exits its run() method, which kills that thread instance. Second, the Spider displays a new image. This causes the lingering image of the Fly to disappear. Of course, this happens so quickly, that it gives a reasonably convincing animation of a frog eating the fly. The complete implementation of the Spider class is shown in Figure 13–38.

```java
import java.awt.*;                          // Import the GUI components

public class Spider extends CyberPet implements Runnable {
    protected int nImageFiles = 13;
    protected String imageFileName = "spiderweb";
    protected Image image[] = new Image[nImageFiles];

    protected CyberPetApplet applet ;        // Spider's interface
    static int currentImg = 0;

    private static final int SLEEPING_IMG = 5;
    private static final int NOT_HUNGRY_IMG = 6;
    private static final int NOT_SLEEPY_IMG = 7;
    private static final int LIKE_FLY = 8;
    private static final int NO_ESCAPE = 9;
    private static final int DREAMING_IMG = 10;
    private static final int FROG = 11;
    private static final int HAPPY_FROG = 12;

    private static final int FROG_X = 60;
    private static final int FROG_Y = 125;

    private Point flyLocation;

    public Spider(String name, CyberPetApplet app) {
        super(name);                         // Construct a CyberPet
        applet = app;
    }

    public void getImages() {
        Graphics g = applet.getGraphics();
        for (int k = 0; k < nImageFiles; k++) {
            image[k] = applet.getImage(applet.getDocumentBase(),imageFileName + (k+1) + ".gif");
            g.drawImage(image[k],20,100,applet);
        }
    } // getImages()

    public synchronized void dream() {
        state = DREAMING;
        applet.updateStateField();
        Graphics g = applet.getGraphics();              // Draw dreaming image
        g.drawImage(image[DREAMING_IMG], 20, 100, applet);
        delay(5000);
        g.drawImage(image[FROG], 20, 100, applet);  // Transform to a frog
        delay(5000);
        flyLocation = applet.getFlyLocation();          // Look at the fly
        g.setColor( Color.pink);
        g.drawLine(FROG_X, FROG_Y, flyLocation.x, flyLocation.y);  // Eat the fly
        g.drawLine(FROG_X + 1, FROG_Y + 1, flyLocation.x + 1, flyLocation.y + 1);
        g.drawLine(FROG_X + 2, FROG_Y + 2, flyLocation.x + 1, flyLocation.y + 1);
        g.drawLine(FROG_X + 3, FROG_Y + 3, flyLocation.x + 1, flyLocation.y + 1);
        applet.eatFly();
        delay(250);
        g.drawImage(image[HAPPY_FROG], 20, 100, applet);
        delay(5000);
        applet.newFly();
    } // dream()
```

FIGURE 13–38   The Spider class, Part I.

```
    public void eat() {
        Graphics g = applet.getGraphics();
        int choice = (int) ( Math.random() * 3 );
        if ( choice == 2 )             // i.e., 1 in 3 chance
            g.drawImage(image[NOT_HUNGRY_IMG], 20, 100, applet);
        else {
            state = EATING;
            for (int k = 0;   k < SLEEPING_IMG; k++) {
                g.drawImage(image[k], 20, 100, applet);
                delay(200) ;
            }
        } // else
    } // eat()

    private void autoeat() {
        Graphics g = applet.getGraphics();
        state = EATING;
        applet.updateStateField();
        for (int k = 0;   k < SLEEPING_IMG; k++) {
            g.drawImage(image[k], 20, 100, applet);
            delay(200) ;
        }
    } // autoeat()

    public void sleep() {
        Graphics g = applet.getGraphics();
        int choice = (int)(Math.random() * 3);
        if (choice == 2)                   // i.e., 1 in 3 chance
            g.drawImage(image[NOT_SLEEPY_IMG], 20, 100, applet);
        else {
            state = SLEEPING;
            g.drawImage(image[SLEEPING_IMG], 20, 100, applet);
        }
    } // sleep()

    private void autosleep() {
        Graphics g = applet.getGraphics();
        state = SLEEPING;
        applet.updateStateField();
        g.drawImage(image[SLEEPING_IMG], 20, 100, applet);
    } // autosleep()

    public void think() {
        state = THINKING;
        applet.updateStateField();
        Graphics g = applet.getGraphics();
        int choice = (int)(Math.random() * 2);
        if (choice == 1)                   // i.e., 1 in 2 chance
            g.drawImage(image[NO_ESCAPE], 20, 100, applet);
        else {
            g.drawImage(image[LIKE_FLY], 20, 100, applet);
        }
    } // think()

    public void run() {
        while (true) {
            int choice = (int)(Math.random() * 4);
            if (choice == 0)      autoeat();
            else if (choice == 1) autosleep();
            else if (choice == 2) think();
            else                  dream();
            delay(5000);
        }//while
    } // run()
} // Spider
```

FIGURE 13–38 (*continued*) The Spider class, Part II.

13.6.5 The CyberPetApplet Class

The applet serves as an intermediary

The final component of the simulation is the applet class, which is shown in its entirety in Figure 13–39. The applet is where we instantiate the Spider and Fly objects and start their independent threads:

```
private Spider spidey = new Spider ("Spidey", this);  // Create a Pet
private Fly pest = new Fly(this);                      //  and a Fly
...
new Thread(spidey).start();      // Start spidey thread (in init())
new Thread(pest).start();        // Start the fly thread (in init())
...
```

The only other changes required from previous incarnations of this applet are the public methods used to coordinate the interaction between the Spider and the Fly:

```
public void eatFly() {
    pest.die();
}
public void newFly() {
    pest = new Fly(this);
    new Thread(pest).start();
}
public Point getFlyLocation() {
    return pest.getLocation();
}
```

As we discussed, these methods are invoked from the Spider and Fly threads and serve to mediate the interaction between these two, otherwise independent threads.

OBJECT-ORIENTED DESIGN:
Inheritance and Polymorphism

The spider and fly simulation provides a good example of how the object-oriented principles of inheritance and polymorphism contribute to the design of extensible code. First, we've used inheritance in our design by defining Spider and Fly as subclasses of CyberPet. This required several fairly minimal changes to CyberPet itself—such as changing its private instance variables to protected and defining some new static, final class constants. The largest change was that the public methods that define a CyberPet's actions—eat() and sleep()—were given simple, default implementations in CyberPet, with the intention that they would be overridden, if necessary, in Spider and CyberPet subclasses. This way, different kinds of CyberPet could implement these actions in ways that were appropriate.

Using inheritance to share methods

One advantage of this design is that it allows us to locate shared methods and variables within the superclass. Thus, the getState() and delay() methods are shared by all subclasses of CyberPet. The default versions of eat(), sleep(), and so on are also available to all subclasses.

Other advantages of this design are its generality and extensibility. We can easily add Dog, Cat, and other subclasses to the CyberPet hierarchy and give them distinguishing characteristics. Each new subclass will inherit the functionality now defined in the CyberPet class.

```java
import java.awt.*;                              // Import the GUI components
import java.awt.event.*;                        // Import event classes
import javax.swing.*;                           // Import Swing classes

public class CyberPetApplet extends JApplet implements ActionListener {
    private Spider spidey = new Spider ("Spidey", this);  // Create a Pet
    private Fly pest = new Fly(this);                     // and a Fly
                                                          // GUI Components
    private JLabel nameLabel = new JLabel("Hi.  I'm "
                            + spidey.getPetName() +  " and I'm");
    private JTextField stateField = new JTextField(8);
    private JButton eatButton = new JButton("Eat!");
    private JButton sleepButton = new JButton("Sleep!");
    private JPanel controls = new JPanel();

    public void init() {
        eatButton.addActionListener(this);      // Initialize the interface
        sleepButton.addActionListener(this);
        controls.add(nameLabel);
        controls.add(stateField);
        controls.add(eatButton);
        controls.add(sleepButton);
        controls.setBorder(BorderFactory.createTitledBorder("Controls"));
        this.getContentPane().add(controls, "North");
        this.setSize(425,350);

        stateField.setText(spidey.getState()); // Init spidey's state
        showStatus("Loading image files");      //  and loads its images
        spidey.getImages();

        new Thread(spidey).start();      // Start spidey thread
        new Thread(pest).start();        // Start the fly thread
    } // init()

    public void eatFly() {
        pest.die();
    }
    public void newFly() {
        pest = new Fly(this);
        new Thread(pest).start();
    }
    public Point getFlyLocation() {
        return pest.getLocation();
    }
    public void updateStateField() {
        stateField.setText( spidey.getState() ); // Display state
    }
    public void actionPerformed (ActionEvent evt) {
        if (evt.getSource() == eatButton)   // If eatButton clicked
            spidey.eat();                   //       tell spidey to eat
        else                                // If sleepButton clicked
            spidey.sleep();                 //       tell spidey to sleep
        updateStateField();                 // Display state
    } // actionPerformed()
} // CyberPetApplet
```

FIGURE 13–39 The CyberPetApplet class.

The use of polymorphism in this example occurs in the way that a thread's run() method is implemented. Within the runnable interface, the run() method is defined as an abstract method—that is, a method without a body. By implementing run() in each of our CyberPet subclasses, we are creating a polymorphic method—that is, a method that behaves differently depending upon the object that executes it. This is seen most clearly in the fact that nowhere in our program do we actually call our thread's run() method directly. Instead we run a thread by invoking its start() method. As you would expect, the Thread.start() method invokes run():

```
public synchronized void start() {
  // Do some system-related stuff
  run();
}
```

Using polymorphism to extend built-in functionality

Because Java's thread system depends for its implementation on features of the particular operating system platform, it is necessary to incorporate all threads into a preexisting system. This is done by the start() method before the thread's run() method is invoked. The run() method itself is inherently polymorphic, because you *have* to override it.

IN THE LABORATORY:
The Spider, the Fly, and the Bee

The main purpose of this lab is to extend the spider/fly animation so that it incorporates a buzzing bee, as a third independent CyberPet thread. This is not hard, but it requires that you understand the concepts of *inheritance* and threads, as they were discussed in this chapter. The objectives of the lab are

- To define a Bee subclass of CyberPet.
- To incorporate a Bee instance into the spider/fly animation.
- To understand appropriate uses of inheritance in object-oriented design.

Problem Description

Define a Bee class as a subclass of CyberPet. A Bee is very similar to a Fly. For example, both fly around in the same rectangular area of the display. However, a Bee has the following differences:

- Bees are magenta, whereas Flys are red.
- Bees are bigger than Flys.
- New Bees start from a different location than Flys.
- Bees make a beep-beep sound when they die.

Object-Oriented Design

What objects do we need?

There are different ways to design the Bee class. You could define Bee as a direct subclass of CyberPet. According to this design, the Bee class would be very similar, in its details, to the Fly subclass. Thus, you could simply copy the Fly class and then modify some of its details and save it as the Bee class.

This cut-and-paste approach is probably the poorest design alternative with the least flexibility and the most redundancy. For example, both the Bee and Fly class will have almost identical declarations and method definitions. Why should all the CyberPet subclasses that fly around have to duplicate the buzzaround() code? Surely this is not a good example of code reuse.

Alternatively, you could define Bee as a subclass of Fly. This model would require that you make certain changes to Fly before extending it. For example, instead of defining the Fly's size as a class constant, you would want to make it a variable that can be set in both the Fly and Bee constructors. You'd want to make similar changes to accommodate their differences in color and initial location. Also, you would want to redesign the buzzaround() method, so that it will work for both Bees and Flys.

According to this model, a Bee is a kind of Fly. An important advantage of this model is that it could easily be extended to define, say, a Wasp. And it cuts down on the amount of redundant code. For example, all subclasses of Fly could use its buzzaround() method. This model would also be easier to maintain. If there's a change in the design of buzzaround(), it needs to be made only once and it will be inherited by all Fly subclasses.

A third model would define an abstract class, FlyingInsect, and make both Fly and Bee its direct subclasses (Fig. 13–40). This abstract class would implement those methods common to all flying insects, leaving as abstract those methods that distinguish one type of flying insect from another. For example, because all flying insects will buzz around, it would be useful to implement the buzzaround() method in the FlyingInsect class. For most subclasses, this method could be used as is. *Using an* abstract *class*

Similarly, because all flying insects eventually die, it would be useful to implement the die() method in FlyingInsect. However, suppose that all flying insects make some kind of distinct noise when they die, ranging from the Bee's beep-beep to the Wasp's peep, and so on. The Fly's silence, of course, could be treated as a special case, or we could modify it and make it beep when it dies. One way to design this feature would be to define an abstract lastGasp() method, which is called in die(), but implemented in the subclasses. That way it can be given an implementation that is appropriate to that particular subclass. *The* lastGasp() *method is polymorphic*

This is the most economical and most extensible design. It gets the most mileage from code reuse. And, to define a new subclass of FlyingInsect, you need only implement its lastGasp() method and distinguish its color and size. Let's adopt this design for this project.

The FlyingInsect Class

The FlyingInsect class will now absorb most of the constants, variables, and methods that were previously defined in the Fly class. Here's a list of things that should be incorporated into the definition of FlyingInsect (Fig. 13–40):

- In order to allow FlyingInsects to have different colors, sizes, and starting locations, it will be necessary to use variables rather than class constants for these values.
- In addition to the constructor that was defined in the Fly class, you should define a constructor that allows a FlyingInsect's color, size, and initial location to be set. An appropriate signature for this method would be

```
FlyingInsect (CyberPetApplet app, Color col, int siz, Point loc);
```

FIGURE 13–40 Hierarchy of classes for this lab.

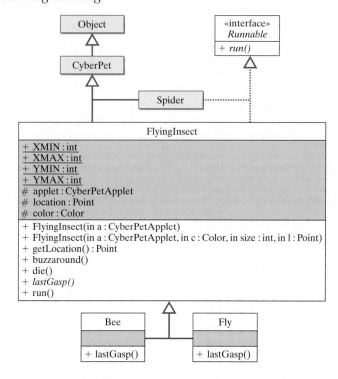

- The getLocation() and run() methods can be adopted from the previous version of Fly.
- Modify the implementations of the buzzaround() and die() methods so they will work with any FlyingInsect subclass. For example, buzzaround() should display the right color and size of the insect. And die() must call the lastGasp() method.
- Define the abstract method lastGasp(). Its implementation will be left up to the subclasses.

The Fly and Bee Classes

The revised Fly class will now be a subclass of FlyingInsect. To illustrate how simple this class becomes, we provide its full definition in Figure 13–41. Note how it uses the super keyword to call FlyingInsect's constructor method. Note also how the Toolkit.beep() method is used to generate a sound during the lastGasp() method. The Bee class will be a simple variant of this definition.

FIGURE 13–41 Definition of the Fly class.

```java
import java.awt.*;    // IMPORT the GUI components

public class Fly extends FlyingInsect implements Runnable{

    public Fly ( CyberPetApplet app ) {
        super(app);
    }

    public void lastGasp(){
        Toolkit.getDefaultToolkit().beep();
    }
} // Fly
```

The `CyberPetApplet` Class

To incorporate a second buzzing insect into the simulation, several changes must be made to the applet class. First, you need to create a `Bee` instance in the applet and `start()` it running. The most interesting design issue here is how the applet will serve as an intermediary now that there are two buzzing insects. This will require changes to the following methods:

The applet as intermediary object

- `getFlyLocation()`: Which fly's location should be returned by this method, the `Bee`'s or the `Fly`'s? One way to "finesse" this issue would be to return one or the other at random. You could use `Math.random()` and if its value is greater than 0.5, you could return `Fly`'s location; otherwise, you return `Bee`'s location. Because the frog will eat the insect whose location is returned, it will be necessary to remember which insect was picked. Therefore, you'll want to create an instance variable of type `CyberPet` and assign it a reference to either the `Bee` or the `Fly`, depending on which one was picked:

```
currentPest = (Bee) bee;
```

  Note the use of the cast operator, `(Bee)`, to convert a `Bee` reference into (a more general) `CyberPet` reference.
- `eatFly()`: The change to this method should just make use of the `currentPest` reference to decide which insect should die.
- `newFly()`: Similarly, if you killed the `Bee` during `eatFly()`, you should make a new `Bee` in this method, again making use of `currentPest`.

Resources

In order to animate your simulation, you will need the same set of images that was used in `CyberPet` animation in this chapter. These are available on the course Web site.

CHAPTER SUMMARY

Technical Terms

asynchronous	monitor	queue
blocked	multitasking	ready queue
busy waiting	multithreaded	round-robin
concurrent	mutual exclusion	scheduling
critical section	priority scheduling	thread
dispatched	producer/consumer	thread life cycle
fetch-execute cycle	model	time slicing
lock	quantum	

Summary of Important Points

- *Multitasking* is the technique of executing several tasks at the same time within a single program. In Java we give each task a separate *thread of execution*, thus resulting in a *multithreaded* program.
- A *sequential* computer with a single *central processing unit (CPU)* can execute only one machine instruction at a time. A *parallel* computer uses multiple CPUs operating simultaneously to execute more than one instruction at a time.

- Each CPU uses a *fetch-execute cycle* to retrieve the next machine instruction from memory and execute it. The cycle is under the control of the CPU's internal clock, which typically runs at several hundred *megahertz*—where 1 megahertz (MHz) is 1 million cycles per second.
- *Time slicing* is the technique whereby several threads can share a single CPU over a given time period. Each thread is given a small slice of the CPU's time under the control of some kind of scheduling algorithm.
- In *round-robin scheduling*, each thread is given an equal slice of time, in a first-come–first-served order. In *priority scheduling*, higher-priority threads are allowed to run before lower-priority threads are run.
- There are generally two ways of creating threads in a program. One is to create a subclass of `Thread` and implement a `run()` method. The other is to create a `Thread` instance and pass it a `Runnable` object—that is, an object that implements `run()`.
- The `sleep()` method removes a thread from the CPU for a determinate length of time, giving other threads a chance to run.
- The `setPriorty()` method sets a thread's priority. Higher-priority threads have more and longer access to the CPU.
- Threads are *asynchronous*. Their timing and duration on the CPU are highly sporadic and unpredictable. In designing threaded programs, you must be careful not to base your algorithm on any assumptions about the threads' timing.
- To improve the responsiveness of interactive programs, you could give compute-intensive tasks, such as drawing lots of dots, to a lower-priority thread or to a thread that sleeps periodically.
- A thread's life cycle consists of ready, running, waiting, sleeping, and blocked states. Threads start in the ready state and are dispatched to the CPU by the scheduler, an operating system program. If a thread performs an I/O operation, it blocks until the I/O is completed. If it voluntarily sleeps, it gives up the CPU.
- According to the *producer/consumer* model, two threads share a resource, one serving to produce the resource and the other to consume the resource. Their cooperation must be carefully synchronized.
- An object that contains `synchronized` methods is known as a *monitor*. Such objects ensure that only one thread at a time can execute a synchronized method. The object is *locked* until the thread completes the method or voluntarily sleeps. This is one way to ensure mutually exclusive access to a resource by a collection of cooperating threads.
- The `synchronized` qualifier can also be used to designate a method as a *critical section*, whose execution should not be preempted by one of the other cooperating threads.
- In designing multithreaded programs it is useful to assume that if a thread *can* be interrupted at a certain point, it *will* be interrupted there. Thread coordination should never be left to chance.
- One way of coordinating two or more cooperating threads is to use the `wait/notify` combination. One thread waits for a resource to be available, and the other thread notifies when a resource becomes available.
- In the spider/fly example, inheritance is used to implement the shared elements of the `Spider` and `Fly` classes. By implementing the runnable interface, both `Spider` and `Fly` can be implemented as independent threads. Each can provide its own implementation of the `run()` method.

SOLUTION 13.1

```java
public class PrintOdds implements Runnable {
  private int bound;
  public PrintOdds(int b) {
   bound = b;
  }

  public void print() {
    if (int k = 1; k < bound; k+=2)
      System.out.println(k);
  }

  public void run() {
    print();
  }
}
```

SOLUTION 13.2   On my system the experiment yielded the following output, if each thread printed its number after every 100,000 iterations:

```
1111111222222221111111133333333222222221111111133333333
2222224444444443333333444444455555555544444455555555555555
```

This suggests that round-robin scheduling is being used.

SOLUTION 13.3   If each thread is given 50 milliseconds of sleep on each iteration, they tend to run in the order in which they were created:

```
123451234512345...
```

SOLUTION 13.4   The garbage collector runs whenever the available memory drops below a certain threshold. It must have higher priority than the application, since the application won't be able to run if it runs out of memory.

SOLUTION 13.5   To improve the responsiveness of an interactive program, the system could give a high priority to the threads that interact with the user and a low priority to those that perform noninteractive computations, such as number crunching.

SOLUTION 13.6   If the JVM were single threaded, it wouldn't be possible to break out of an infinite loop, because the program's loop would completely consume the CPU's attention.

SOLUTION 13.7   If round-robin scheduling is used, each thread will be get a portion of the CPU's time, so the applet thread will eventually get its turn. But you don't know how long it will be before the applet gets its turn, so there may still be an unacceptably long wait before the user's actions are handled. Thus, to *guarantee* responsiveness, it is better to have the drawing thread sleep on every iteration.

SOLUTION 13.8   If Dotty's priority is set to 1, a low value, this does improve the responsiveness of the interface, but it is significantly less responsive than using a sleep() on each iteration.

SOLUTION 13.9   In a real bakery only one customer at a time can take a number. The take-a-number gadget "enforces" mutual exclusion by virtue of its design: There's room for only one hand to grab the ticket and there's only one ticket per number. If two customers got "bakery rage" and managed to grab the same ticket, it would rip in half and neither would benefit.

SOLUTION 13.10   One experiment to run would be to make the clerk's performance very slow by using large sleep intervals. If the algorithm is correct, this should not affect the order in which customers are served. Another experiment would be to force the clerk to work fast but the customers to work slowly. This should still not affect the order in which the customers are served.

SOLUTION 13.11   You should observe that the waiting line builds up as customers enter the bakery, but the clerk should still serve the customers in the correct order.

EXERCISES

Note: *For programming exercises,* **first** *draw a UML class diagram describing all classes and their inheritance relationships and/or associations.*

EXERCISE 13.1   Explain the difference between the following pairs of terms:
a. *Blocked* and *ready*.
b. *Priority* and *round-robin* scheduling.
c. *Producer* and *consumer*.
d. *Monitor* and *lock*.
e. *Concurrent* and *time slicing*.
f. *Mutual exclusion* and *critical section*.
g. *Busy* and *nonbusy* waiting.

EXERCISE 13.2   Fill in the blanks.

a. _____ happens when a CPU's time is divided among several different threads.
b. A method that should not be interrupted during its execution is known as a _____ .
c. The scheduling algorithm in which each thread gets an equal portion of the CPU's time is known as _____ .
d. The scheduling algorithm in which some threads can preempt other threads is known as _____.
e. A _____ is a mechanism that enforces mutually exclusive access to a synchronized method.
f. A thread that performs an I/O operation may be forced into the _____ state until the operation is completed.

EXERCISE 13.3   Describe the concept of *time slicing* as it applies to CPU scheduling.

EXERCISE 13.4   What's the difference in the way concurrent threads would be implemented on a computer with several processors and on a computer with a single processor?

EXERCISE 13.5   Why are threads put into the *blocked* state when they perform an I/O operation?

EXERCISE 13.6   What's the difference between a thread in the sleep state and a thread in the ready state?

EXERCISE 13.7   **Deadlock** is a situation that occurs when one thread is holding a resource that another thread is waiting for, while the other thread is holding a resource that the first thread is waiting for. Describe how deadlock can occur at a four-way intersection with cars entering from each branch. How can it be avoided?

EXERCISE 13.8   **Starvation** can occur if one thread is repeatedly preempted by other threads. Describe how starvation can occur at a four-way intersection and how it can be avoided.

EXERCISE 13.9   Use the `Runnable` interface to define a thread that repeatedly generates random numbers in the interval 2 through 12.

EXERCISE 13.10   Use the `Runnable` interface to convert `CyberPet` into a thread. For its `run()` method, have the `CyberPet` alternate endlessly among eating, sleeping, and thinking.

EXERCISE 13.11   Create a version of the `Bakery` program that uses two clerks to serve customers.

EXERCISE 13.12   Modify the `Numbers` program so that the user can interactively create `NumberThreads` and assign them a priority. Modify the `NumberThreads` so that they print their numbers indefinitely (rather than for a fixed number of iterations). Then experiment with the system by observing the effect of introducing threads with the same, lower, or higher priority. How do the threads behave when they all have the same priority? What happens when you introduce a higher-priority thread into the mix? What happens when you introduce a lower-priority thread into the mix?

EXERCISE 13.13   Create a bouncing ball simulation in which a single ball (thread) bounces up and down in a vertical line. The ball should bounce off the bottom and top of the enclosing frame.

EXERCISE 13.14   Modify the simulation in the previous exercise so that more than one ball can be introduced. Allow the user to introduce new balls into the simulation by pressing the space bar or clicking the mouse.

EXERCISE 13.15   Modify your solution to the previous problem by having the balls bounce off the wall at a random angle.

EXERCISE 13.16   **Challenge:** One type of producer/consumer problem is the *reader/writer* problem. Create a subclass of `JTextField` that can be shared by threads, one of which writes a random number to the text field, and the other of which reads the value in the text field. Coordinate the two threads so that the overall effect of the program will be that it will print the values from 0 to 100 in the proper order. In other words, the reader thread shouldn't read a value from the text field until there's a value to be read. The writer thread shouldn't write a value to the text field until the reader has read the previous value.

EXERCISE 13.17   **Challenge:** Create a streaming banner thread that moves a simple message across a panel. The message should repeatedly enter at the left edge of the panel and exit from the right edge. Design the banner as a subclass of `JPanel` and have it implement the `Runnable` interface. That way it can be added to any user interface. One of its constructors should take a `String` argument that lets the user set the banner's message.

EXERCISE 13.18   **Challenge:** Create a slide show applet, which repeatedly cycles through an array of images. The displaying of the images should be a separate thread. The applet thread should handle the user interface. Give the user some controls that let it pause, stop, start, speed up, and slow down the images.

EXERCISE 13.19   **Challenge:** Create a horse race simulation, using separate threads for each of the horses. The horses should race horizontally across the screen, with each horse having a different vertical coordinate. If you don't have good horse images to use, just make each horse a colored polygon or some other shape. Have the horses implement the `Drawable` interface, which we introduced in Chapter 10.

EXERCISE 13.20   **Challenge:** The game of Pong was the rage in the 1970s. It consists of a ball that moves within a rectangular region, as in a previous exercise, and a single paddle, which is located at the right boundary, which can be moved up and down by the user. When the ball hits the paddle, it bounces off at a random angle. When it hits the wall, it just reverses direction. The ball should be one thread and the user interface (and paddle) should be the other.

EXERCISE 13.21   **Challenge:** Create a multithreaded digital clock application. One thread should keep time in an endless while loop. The other thread should be responsible for updating the screen each second.

Photograph courtesy of Nick Koudis, PhotoDisc, Inc.

14

Files, Streams, and Input/Output Techniques

OBJECTIVES

After studying this chapter, you will

- Be able to read and write text files.
- Know how to read and write binary files.
- Understand the use of `InputStreams` and `OutputStreams`.
- Be able to design methods for performing input and output.
- Know how to use the `File` class.
- Be able to use the `JFileChooser` class.

OUTLINE

14.1   Introduction

Input refers to *reading* information or data from some external source into a running program. Up to this point in the book, whenever our programs have input data, they have come from the keyboard or from a `JTextField` in a GUI interface. These external sources are *transitory* in that they exist only while the program is running. `JTextFields` reside in the computer's primary memory in an area that is temporarily assigned to the program that created them. They cease to exist when the program stops running.

Output refers to *writing* information or data from the running program to some external destination. Up to this point, whenever our programs have produced output, it has been sent to the Java console, to a text area, or to some other GUI component. All of these destinations are transitory, in the sense that they too reside in the computer's primary memory and exist only so long as the program is running.

A *file* is a collection of data that's stored on a disk or on some other relatively permanent storage medium. A file's existence does not depend on a running program. In this chapter, we will learn how to create files and how to perform input and output operations on their data.

14.2   Streams and Files

I/O streams

All input and output (I/O) in Java, whether it be file I/O or I/O involving the keyboard and the screen, is accomplished through the use of streams. A **stream** is an object that delivers information to and from another object. A stream is like a pipe or a conduit that connects a source of information and its destination. In Java, three streams, `System.out`, `System.in`, and `System.err`, are automatically created and ready for use when a program begins. We have routinely used `System.out` and `System.in` (Fig. 14–1).

`System.out` connects your program (source) to the screen (destination). More generally, `System.out` is an **output stream** that connects a program to the *standard output device*. When you perform a `System.out.println()` statement, information flows from the program through `System.out` to the screen. Similarly, `System.in` usually connects the keyboard (source) to the running program (destination). As an **input stream**, it connects a *standard input device* to a running program. When you perform a `System.in.read()` operation, information flows from the keyboard through `System.in` to the program.

System.in and System.out streams

FIGURE 14–1   A stream serves like a pipe through which data flow.

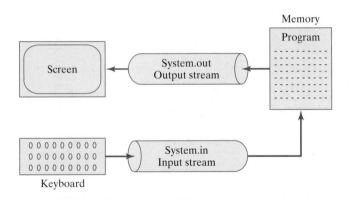

14.2.1 The Data Hierarchy

What flows through a Java stream, and what is stored in a file, is information or data. All data are comprised of binary digits or *bits*. A bit is simply a 0 or a 1, or rather the electronic states that correspond to these values. A bit is the smallest unit of data.

However, it would be tedious if a program had to work with data in units as small as bits. Therefore, most operations involve various-sized aggregates of data such as an 8-bit byte, a 16-bit short, a 16-bit char, a 32-bit int, a 64-bit long, a 32-bit float, or a 64-bit double. As we know, these are Java's primitive numeric types. In addition to these aggregates, we can group together a sequence of char to form a String.

It is also possible to group data of different types into objects. A **record**, which corresponds closely to a Java object, can have **fields** that contain different types of data. For example, a student record might contain fields for the student's name and address (Strings), expected year of graduation (int), and current grade point average (double). Collections of these records are typically grouped into **files**. For example, your registrar's office may have a separate file for each of its graduating classes. These are typically organized into a collection of related files, which is called a **database**.

Taken together, the different kinds of data that are processed by a computer or stored in a file can be organized into a **data hierarchy** (Figure 14–2).

It's important to recognize that while we, the programmers, may group data into various types of abstract entities, the information flowing through an input or output stream is just a sequence of bits. There are no natural boundaries that mark where one byte (or one int or one record) ends and the next one begins. Therefore, it will be up to us to provide the boundaries as we process the data.

14.2.2 Binary Files and Text Files

There are two types of files in Java: binary files and text files. Both kinds store data as a sequence of bits—that is, a sequence of 0's and 1's. Thus, the difference between the two types of files lies in the way they are interpreted by the programs that read and write them. A **binary file** is processed as a sequence of bytes, whereas a **text file** is processed as a sequence of characters.

Text editors and other programs that process text files interpret the file's sequence of bits as a sequence of characters—that is, as a string. Your Java source programs (*.java) are text files, and so are the HTML files that populate the World Wide Web. The big advantage of text files is their portability. Because their data are represented in the ASCII code (Table 5.11), they can be read and written by just about any text-processing program. Thus, a text file created by a program on a Windows/Intel computer can be read by a Macintosh program.

In non-Java environments, data in binary files are stored as bytes, and the representation used varies from computer to computer. Binary data stored in a file have the same representation as binary data stored in the computer's memory. Thus, binary data are not very portable. A binary file of integers created on a Macintosh cannot be read by a Windows/Intel program.

The data hierarchy

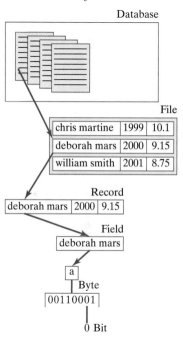

FIGURE 14–2   The data hierarchy.

Text files are portable

Binary files are platform dependent

One reason for the lack of portability is that each type of computer uses its own definition for how an integer is defined. On some systems it may be 16 bits, and on others it may be 32 bits, so even if you know that a Macintosh binary file contains integers, that still won't make it readable by Windows/Intel programs. Another problem is that even if two computers use the same number of bits to represent an integer, they may use different representation schemes. Thus, on some computers, 10000101 is used as the 8-bit representation of the number 133, whereas on other computers, the reverse, 10100001, is used to represent 133.

The good news for us is that Java's designers have made its binary files **platform independent** by carefully defining the exact size and representation that must be used for integers and all other primitive types. Thus, binary files created by Java programs can be interpreted by Java programs on any platform.

> **JAVA LANGUAGE RULE** Platform Independence. Java binary files are platform independent. They can be interpreted by any computer that supports Java.

14.2.3 Input and Output Streams

I/O streams

Java has a wide variety of streams for performing I/O. They are defined in the `java.io` package, which must be imported by any program that does I/O. They are generally organized into a hierarchy (Fig. 14–3). We will cover only a small portion of the hierarchy. Generally speaking, binary files are processed by subclasses of `InputStream` and `OutputStream`. Text files are processed by subclasses of `Reader` and `Writer`, both of which are streams, despite their names. Table 14.1 gives a brief description of the most commonly used input and output streams.

`InputStream` and `OutputStream` are abstract classes that serve as the root classes for reading and writing binary data. Their most commonly used subclasses are `DataInputStream` and `DataOutputStream`, which are used for processing `String` data and data of any of Java's primitive types—`char`, `boolean`, `int`, `double`, and so on. The analogues of these classes for processing text data are the `Reader` and `Writer` classes, which serve as the root classes for all text I/O.

> PROGRAMMING TIP: Choosing a Stream. In choosing an appropriate stream for an I/O operation, `DataInputStreams` and `DataOutputStreams` are normally used for binary I/O. `Reader` and `Writer` streams are normally used for text I/O.

The various subclasses of these root classes perform various specialized I/O operations. Thus, `FileInputStream` and `FileOutputStream` are used for performing binary input and output on files. The `PrintStream` class contains methods for outputting various primitive data—integers, floats, and so forth—as text. The `System.out` stream, one of the most widely used output streams, is an object of this type. The `PrintStream` class has been deprecated in JDK 1.2 and has been superseded by the `PrintWriter`

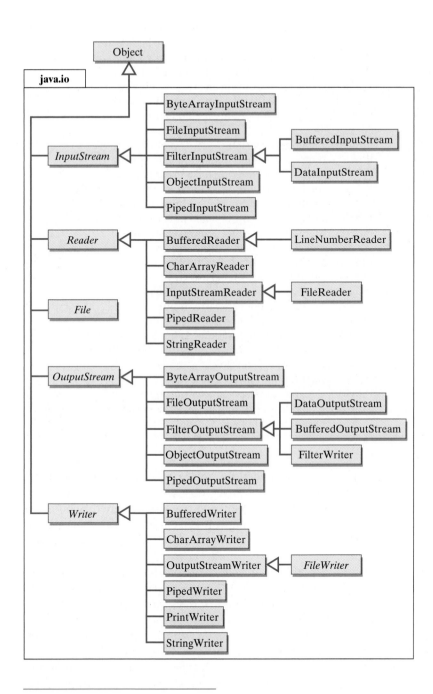

FIGURE 14–3   Java's stream hierarchy.

TABLE 14.1 Description of some of Java's important stream classes.

Class	Description
InputStream	Abstract root class of all binary input streams
FileInputStream	Provides methods for reading bytes from a binary file
FilterInputStream	Provides methods required to filter data in various ways
BufferedInputStream	Provides input data buffering for reading large files
ByteArrayInputStream	Provides methods for reading an array as if it were a stream
DataInputStream	Provides methods for reading Java's primitive data types
PipedInputStream	Provides methods for reading piped data from another thread
OutputStream	Abstract root class of all binary output streams
FileOutputStream	Provides methods for writing bytes to a binary file
FilterOutputStream	Provides methods required to filter data in various ways
BufferedOutputStream	Provides output data buffering for writing large files
ByteArrayOutputStream	Provides methods for writing an array as if it were a stream
DataOutputStream	Provides methods for writing Java's primitive data types
PipedOutputStream	Provides methods for writing piped data to another thread
PrintStream	Provides methods for writing primitive data as text
Reader	Abstract root class for all text input streams
BufferedReader	Provides buffering for character input streams
CharArrayReader	Provides input operations on char arrays
FileReader	Provides methods for character input on files
FilterReader	Provides methods to filter character input
StringReader	Provides input operations on Strings
Writer	Abstract root class for all text output streams
BufferedWriter	Provides buffering for character output streams
CharArrayWriter	Provides output operations to char arrays
FileWriter	Provides methods for output to text files
FilterWriter	Provides methods to filter character output
PrintWriter	Provides methods for printing binary data as characters
StringWriter	Provides output operations to Strings

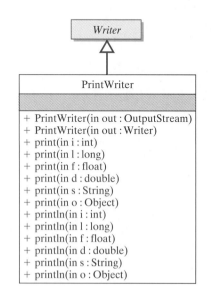

FIGURE 14–4 `PrintWriter` methods print data of various types.

class (Fig. 14–3), which is designed to support platform independence and internationalized I/O.

The various methods defined in `PrintWriter` are designed to output a particular type of primitive data (Fig. 14–4). As you would expect, there is both a `print()` and `println()` method for each kind of data that one wishes to output.

Filtering refers to performing operations on data while they are being input or output. Methods in the `FilterInputStream` and `FilterReader` classes can be used to filter binary and text data during input. Methods in the `FilterOutputStream` and `FilterWriter` can be used to filter output data. These classes serve as the root classes for various filtering subclasses. They can also be subclassed to perform customized data filtering.

One type of filtering is **buffering**, which is provided by several buffered streams, including `BufferedInputStream` and `BufferedReader`, for performing binary and text input, and `BufferedOutputStream` and `BufferedWriter`, for buffered output operations. A **buffer** is a relatively large region of memory used to temporarily store data while they are being input or output. When buffering is used, rather than reading one byte at a time from the relatively slow input device, the program will transfer a large number of bytes into the buffer and then transfer these to the program as each read operation is performed. The transfer from the buffer to the program's memory is very fast.

Similarly, when buffering is used during output, rather than writing one byte at a time (or one integer or one float), data are transferred directly to the buffer and then written to the disk when the buffer fills up or when the flush() method is called.

> PROGRAMMING TIP: Buffering.   Buffered streams can be used to improve a program's overall efficiency by reducing the amount of time it spends accessing relatively slow input or output devices.

You can also define your own data filtering subclasses to perform customized filtering. For example, suppose you want to add line numbers to a text editor's printed output. To perform this task, you could define a FilterWriter subclass and override its write() methods to perform the desired filtering operation. Similarly, to remove the line numbers from such a file during input, you could define a FilterReader subclass. In that case, you would override its read() methods to suit your own purposes.

Buffering

Filtering data

The various piped streams consist of methods used to transfer data between threads rather than files. A *pipe* is simply a type of communication channel between two threads. Once a pipe has been established, methods of the PipedInputStream and PipedOutputStream classes can be used to perform binary I/O between the two threads. Similarly, methods of the PipedReader and PipedWriter classes can be used for text I/O between two threads.

There are several classes that provide I/O-like operations on various internal memory structures. Thus, ByteArrayInputStream and ByteArrayOutputStream and CharArrayReader and CharArrayWriter are classes that take input from or send output to arrays in the program's memory. Methods in these classes may be useful for performing various operations on data during input or output. For example, suppose a program reads an entire line of integer data from a binary file into a ByteArray. It might then transform the data by, say, computing the remainder modulo N of each value. These transformed data can then be read by the program by treating the byte array as an input stream. A similar example would apply for some kind of output transformation.

The StringReader and StringWriter classes provide methods for treating Strings and StringBuffers as I/O streams. These methods are sometimes useful for performing certain data conversions.

> PROGRAMMING TIP: Integer/String Conversion.   An integer can be converted to a String by writing it to a StringBuffer, which can then be output as an entire line of text. StringReader methods can be used to read integer data from an ordinary String object.

14.3   CASE STUDY: Reading and Writing Text Files

Suppose you are writing a simple text editor, as we will be doing in the laboratory project for this chapter. One of the subtasks of this project is to be able to read and write data to and from a text file. Thus, let's develop a set of methods to perform I/O on text files. To help us test our methods, we'll write a frame-based application.

GUI design

The GUI for this application will contain a JTextArea, where text file data may be input and displayed, and a JTextField, where the user can enter the file's name. It will also contain two JButtons, one for reading a file into the JTextArea, and the other for writing the data in the JTextArea into a file (Fig. 14–5). Note that even this simple interface will let the user create new files and rename existing files.

FIGURE 14–5   The GUI design for a program that reads and writes text files.

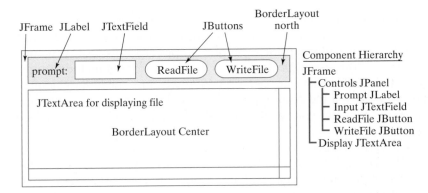

14.3.1   Text File Format

The end-of-file character

A text file consists of a sequence of characters divided into zero or more lines and ending with a special **end-of-file character**. When you open a new file in a text editor, it contains zero lines and zero characters. After typing a single character, it would contain one character and one line. The following would be an example of a file with four lines of text:

```
one\ntwo\nthree\nfour\n\eof
```

Note the use of the end-of-line character, \n, to mark the end of each line, and the use of the end-of-file character, \eof, to mark the end of the file. As we'll see, the I/O methods for text files use these special characters to control reading and writing loops. Thus, when the file is read by appropriate Java methods, such as the BufferedReader.readLine() and Buffered-Reader.read() methods, one or more characters will be read until either an end-of-line or end-of-file character is encountered. When a line of characters is written using println(), the end-of-line character is appended to the characters themselves.

14.3.2   Writing to a Text File

Let's see how to write to a text file. In this program we write the entire contents of the JTextArea() to the text file. In general, writing data to a file requires three steps:

1. Connect an output stream to the file.
2. Write text data into the stream, possibly using a loop.
3. Close the stream.

As Figure 14–1 shows, connecting a stream to a file is like doing a bit of plumbing. The first step is to connect an output stream to the file. The output stream serves as a conduit between the program and a named file. It opens the file and gets it ready to accept data from the program. If the file already exists, then opening the file will destroy any data it previously contained. If the file doesn't yet exist, then it will be created from scratch.

Output stream

Once the file is open, the next step is to write the text to the stream, which passes it on to the file. This step may require a loop that outputs one line of data on each iteration. Finally, once all the data have been written to the file, the stream should be closed. This also has the effect of closing the file itself.

> **EFFECTIVE DESIGN: Writing a File.**   Writing data to a file requires a three-step algorithm: (1) Connect an output stream to the file, (2) write the data, and (3) close the file.

Code Reuse: Designing an Output Method

Now let's see how these three steps are done in Java. Suppose the text we want to write is contained in a JTextArea. Thus, we want a method that will write the contents of a JTextArea to a named file.

What output stream should we use for the task of writing a String to a named file? To decide this, we need to use the information in Figure 14–3 and Table 14.1. As we pointed out earlier, because we're writing a text file, we would use a Writer subclass. But which subclass should we use? The only way to decide this is to consult the Java API documentation at

Choosing an output stream

http://java.sun.com/products/jdk/1.3/docs/api/

to see what methods are available in the various subclasses. For I/O operations you want to consult the classes in the java.io package. Ideally, we would like to be able to create an output stream just given the name of the file, and we would like to be able to write a String to the file.

One likely candidate is the FileWriter class (Fig. 14–6). Its name and description (Table 14.1) suggest that it's designed for writing text files. And indeed it contains the kind of constructor we need—that is, one that takes the file name as a parameter. Note that by taking a boolean parameter, the second constructor allows us to append data to a file rather than rewrite the entire file, which is the default case.

However, FileWriter doesn't define a write() method. This doesn't necessarily mean that it doesn't contain such a method. It might have inherited one from its superclasses, OutputStreamWriter and Writer. Indeed, the Writer class contains a method, write(), whose signature suggests that it is ideally suited for our task (Fig. 14–6).

Inheritance

Having decided on a FileWriter stream, the rest of the task of designing our method is simply a matter of using FileWriter methods in an appropriate way:

FIGURE 14–6 To find the right I/O method, it is sometimes necessary to search the Java class hierarchy. This is easy to do with the online documentation.

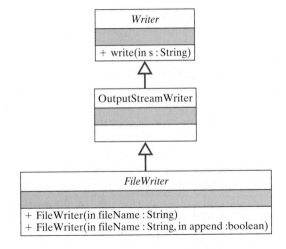

```
private void writeTextFile(JTextArea display, String fileName) {
                        // Create stream & open file
    FileWriter outStream = new FileWriter(fileName);
                        //  Write the entire display text
    outStream.write(display.getText());
    outStream.close();   //  Close the output stream
}
```

We use the `FileWriter()` constructor to create an output stream to the file whose name is stored in `fileName`. In this case, the task of writing data to the file is handled by a single `write()` statement, which writes the entire contents of the `JTextArea` in one operation.

Finally, once we have finished writing the data, we `close()` the output stream. This also has the effect of closing the file. The overall effect of this method is that the text contained in `display` has been output to a file, named `fileName`, which is stored on the disk.

PROGRAMMING TIP: Closing a File. Even though Java will close any files and streams left open when a program terminates normally, it is good programming practice to close the file yourself with a `close()` statement. It also reduces the chances of damaging the file if the program terminates abnormally.

Because so many different things can go wrong during an I/O operation, most I/O operations generate some kind of *checked exception*. Therefore, it is necessary to embed them within a `try/catch` statement. In this example, the `FileWriter()` constructor, the `write()` method, and the `close()` method may each throw an `IOException`. Therefore, the entire body of this method should be embedded within a `try/catch` block that catches the `IOException` (Fig. 14–7).

14.3.3   Code Reuse: Designing Text File Output

The `writeTextFile()` method provides a simple example of how to write data to a text file. More importantly, its development illustrates the kinds of choices necessary to design effective I/O methods. Two important design questions we asked and answered were

```
private void writeTextFile(JTextArea display, String fileName) {
    try {
        FileWriter outStream
            = new FileWriter (fileName);
        outStream.write (display.getText());
        outStream.close();
    } catch (IOException e) {
        display.setText("IOERROR: " + e.getMessage() + "\n");
        e.printStackTrace();
    }
} // writeTextFile()
```

FIGURE 14–7   A method to write a text file.

- What methods do we need to perform the desired task?
- What streams contain the desired methods?

As in so many other examples we've considered, designing a method to perform a task is often a matter of finding the appropriate methods in the Java class hierarchy.

Method design

EFFECTIVE DESIGN: Code Reuse.   Developing effective I/O routines is primarily a matter of choosing the right library methods. Start by asking yourself, "What methods do I need?" and then find a stream class that contains the appropriate methods.

As you might expect, there is more than one way to write data to a text file. Suppose we decided that writing text to a file is like printing data to System.out. And suppose we chose to use a PrintWriter object as our first candidate for an output stream (Fig. 14–3 and Table 14.1). This class (Fig. 14–4) contains a wide range of print() methods for writing different types of data as text. So it has exactly the kind of method we need: print(String). However, this stream does not contain a constructor method that allows us to create a stream from the name of a file. Its constructors require either a Writer object or an OutputStream object.

This means that we can use a PrintWriter to print to a file, but only if we can first construct either an OutputStream or a Writer object to the file. So we must go back to searching Figure 14–3 and Table 14.1 for an appropriate candidate. Fortunately, the FileOutputStream class (Fig. 14–8) has just the constructors we want. We now have an alternative way of coding the writeTextFile() method, this time using a combination of PrintWriter and FileOutputStream:

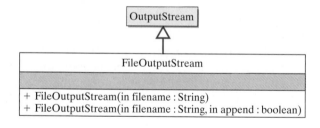

FIGURE 14–8   The FileOutputStream class.

```
PrintWriter outStream =    // Create an output stream
                           // And open the file
   new PrintWriter(new FileOutputStream(fileName));
                              // Write the entire display text
outStream.print ( display.getText() );
outStream.close();           // Close the output stream
```

Note how the output stream is created in this case. First, we create a `File-OutputStream` using the file name as its argument. Then we create a `PrintWriter` using the `FileOutputStream` as its argument. The reason we can do this is because the `PrintWriter()` constructor takes a `FileOutputStream` parameter. This is what makes the connection possible.

Parameter agreement

To use the plumbing analogy again, this is like connecting two sections of pipe between the program and the file. The data will flow from the program through `PrintWriter`, through the `OutputStream`, to the file. Of course, you can't just arbitrarily connect one stream to another. They have to "fit together," which means that their parameters have to match.

EFFECTIVE DESIGN: Stream/Stream Connections.   Two different kinds of streams can be connected if a constructor for one stream takes the second kind of stream as a parameter. This is often an effective way to create the kind of object you need to perform an I/O task.

http://java.sun.com/products/jdk/1.3/docs/api/

The important lesson here is that we found what we wanted by searching through the `java.io.*` hierarchy. This same approach can be used to help you to design I/O methods for other tasks.

SELF-STUDY EXERCISE

EXERCISE 14.1   Is it possible to perform output to a text file using a `Print-Writer` and a `FileWriter` stream in combination? If so, write the Java code.

14.3.4   Reading from a Text File

Let's now look at the problem of inputting data from a text file. In general, there are three steps to reading data from a file:

1. Connect an input stream to the file.
2. Read the text data using a loop.
3. Close the stream.

As Figure 14–9 shows, the input stream serves as a kind of pipe between the file and the program. The first step is to connect an input stream to the file. Of course, in order to read a file, the file must exist. The input stream serves as a conduit between the program and the named file. It opens the file and gets it ready for reading. Once the file is open, the next step is to read the file's data. This will usually require a loop that reads data until the end of the file is reached. Finally, once all the data are read, the stream should be closed.

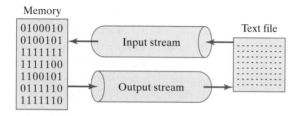

FIGURE 14–9 A stream serves as a pipe through which data flow.

EFFECTIVE DESIGN: Reading data from a file requires a three-step algorithm: (1) Connect an input stream to the file, (2) read the data, and (3) close the file.

Now let's see how these three steps are done in Java. Suppose that we want to put the file's data into a JTextArea. Thus, we want a method that will be given the name of a file and a reference to a JTextArea, and it will read the data from the file into the JTextArea.

What input stream should we use for this task? Here again we need to use the information in Figure 14–3 and Table 14.1. Because we're reading a text file, we should use a Reader subclass. A good candidate is the File-Reader, whose name and description suggest that it might contain useful methods.

Choosing an input stream

What methods do we need? As in the previous example, we need a constructor method that connects an input stream to a file, given the name of the file. And, ideally, we'd like to have a method that will read one line at a time from the text file. The FileReader class (Fig. 14–10) has the right kind of constructor. However, it contains no readLine() methods itself (Fig. 14–10). Searching upward through its superclasses, we find that InputStreamReader, its immediate parent class, has a method that reads ints:

What methods should we use?

```
public int read() throws IOException();
```

This method turns out to be an override of the read() method defined in the Reader class, the root class for text file input streams. Thus, there are no readLine() methods in the Reader branch of the hierarchy.

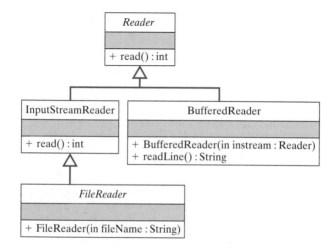

FIGURE 14–10 FileReader's superclasses contain read() methods but no readLine() methods.

One class that does contain a `readLine()` method is `BufferedReader` (Fig. 14–10). Can we somehow use it? Fortunately, the answer is yes. `BufferedReader`'s constructor takes a `Reader` object as a parameter. But a `FileReader` *is* a `Reader`—that is, it is a descendant of the `Reader` class. So, to use our plumbing analogy again, to build an input stream to the file, we can join together a `BufferedReader` and a `FileReader`

```
BufferedReader inStream
    = new BufferedReader(new FileReader(fileName));
```

Given this sort of connection to the file, the program can use `Buffered-Reader.readLine()` to read one line at a time from the file.

So we have a method that reads one line at a time. Now we need an algorithm that will read the entire file. Of course, this will involve a loop, and the key will be to make sure we get the loop's termination condition correct. An important fact about `readLine()` is that it will return `null` as its value when it reaches the end of the file. Recall that text files have a special end-of-file character. When `readLine()` encounters this character, it will return `null`. Therefore, we can specify the following `while` loop:

Using the end-of-file character

```
String line = inStream.readLine();
while (line != null) {
    display.append(line + "\n");
    line = inStream.readLine();
}
```

We begin (outside the loop) by attempting to read a line from the file. If the file happens to be empty (which it might be), then `line` will be set to `null`; otherwise it will contain the `String` that was read. In this case, we append the line to a `JTextArea`. Note that `readLine()` *does not* return the end-of-line character with its return value. That's why we add a \n before we append the line to the `JTextArea`.

PROGRAMMING TIP: End of Line.   Remember that `readLine()` does not return the end-of-line character, \n, as part of the text it returns. If you want to print the text on separate lines, you must append \n.

The last statement in the body of the loop attempts to read the next line from the input stream. If the end of file has been reached, this attempt will return `null` and the loop will terminate. Otherwise, the loop will continue reading and displaying lines until the end of file is reached. Taken together these various design decisions lead to the definition for `readTextFile()` shown in Figure 14–11.

IOException

Note that we must catch both the `IOException`, thrown by `readLine()` and `close()`, and the `FileNotFoundException`, thrown by the `FileReader()` constructor. It's important to see that the read loop has the following form:

```
try to read one line of data and store it in line    // Loop initializer
while ( line is not null ) {                          // Loop entry condition
    process the data
    try to read one line of data and store it in line  // Loop updater
}
```

```
private void readTextFile(JTextArea display, String fileName) {
    try {
        BufferedReader inStream                          // Create and
            = new BufferedReader (new FileReader(fileName));// Open the stream
        String line = inStream.readLine();               // Read one line
        while (line != null) {                           // While more text
            display.append(line + "\n");                 // Display a line
            line = inStream.readLine();                  // Read next line
        }
        inStream.close();                                // Close the stream
    } catch (FileNotFoundException e) {
        display.setText("IOERROR: File NOT Found: " + fileName + "\n");
        e.printStackTrace();
    } catch ( IOException e ) {
        display.setText("IOERROR: " + e.getMessage() + "\n");
        e.printStackTrace();
    }
} // readTextFile()
```

FIGURE 14–11   A method for a text file.

When it attempts to read the *end-of-file* character, readLine() will return
null.

EFFECTIVE DESIGN: Reading Text.   In reading text files, the readLine()
method will return null when it tries to read the end-of-file character.
This provides a convenient way of testing for the end of file.

EFFECTIVE DESIGN: Reading an Empty File.   Loops designed for reading
text files are designed to work even if the file is empty. Therefore, the
loop should attempt to read a line *before* testing the loop-entry condition. If the initial read returns null, that means the file is empty and the
loop body will be skipped.

SELF-STUDY EXERCISE

EXERCISE 14.2   What's wrong with the following loop for reading a text
file and printing its output on the screen?

```
String line = null;
do {
    line = inStream.readLine();
    System.out.println ( line );
} while (line != null);
```

14.3.5 Code Reuse: Designing Text File Input

Our last example used `BufferedReader.readLine()` to read an entire line from the file in one operation. But this isn't the only way to do things. For example, we could have used the `FileReader` stream directly if we were willing to do without the `readLine()` method. Let's design an algorithm that will work in this case.

As we saw earlier, if you use a `FileReader` stream, then you must use the `InputStreamReader.read()` method. This method reads bytes from an input stream and translates them into Java Unicode characters. The `read()` method, for example, returns a single Unicode character as an `int`:

```
public int read() throws IOException();
```

Of course, we can always convert this to a `char` and concatenate it to a `JTextArea`, as the following algorithm illustrates:

```
int ch = inStream.read(); // Initializer: try to read the next character
while (ch != -1) { // Loop-entry-condition: while more characters to read
    display.append((char)ch + ""); // Append the character
    ch = inStream.read();   // Updater: try to read the next character
}
```

Although the details are different, the structure of this loop is the same as if we were reading one line at a time.

The loop variable in this case is an `int` because `InputStreamReader.-read()` returns the next character as an `int`, or it returns −1 if it encounters *Data conversion* the `end-of-file` character. Because `ch` is an `int`, we must convert it to a `char` and then to a `String` in order to `append()` it to the display.

A loop to read data from a file has the following basic form:

```
try to read data into a variable       // Loop initializer
while ( read was successful ) {         // Loop entry condition
    process the data
    try to read data into a variable    // Loop updater
}
```

EFFECTIVE DESIGN: Read Loop Structure. The `read()` and `readLine()` methods have different ways to indicate when a read attempt fails. This will affect how the loop-entry condition is specified, but the structure of the read loop is the same.

PROGRAMMING TIP: Read Versus Readline. Unless it is necessary to manipulate each character in the text file, reading a line at a time is more efficient and, therefore, preferable.

Reusing existing code   It is worth noting again the point we made earlier: Designing effective I/O routines is largely a matter of searching the `java.io` package for appropriate classes and methods. The methods we've developed can serve as suitable models for a wide variety of text I/O tasks, but if you find that they aren't suitable for a particular task, you can design your own method.

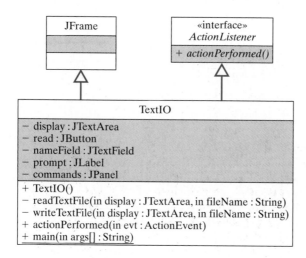

FIGURE 14–12 The TextIO class.

Just find the stream classes that contain methods you can use to perform the desired task. The basic reading and writing algorithms will be pretty much the same no matter which particular read or write method you use.

SELF-STUDY EXERCISE

EXERCISE 14.3   What's wrong with the following loop for reading a text file and printing its output on the screen?

```
int ch;
do {
    ch = inStream.read();
    System.out.print((char)ch);
} while (ch != -1) {
```

14.3.6 The TextIO Application

Given the text I/O methods we wrote in the previous sections, we can now specify the overall design of our TextIO class (Fig. 14–12). In order to complete this application, we need only set up its GUI and write its action-Performed() method. Given that we have defined methods to handle the text I/O, the actionPerformed() method is quite short:

```
public void actionPerformed(ActionEvent evt) {
    String fileName = nameField.getText();
    if (evt.getSource()  == read) {
        display.setText("");
        readTextFile(display, fileName);
    }
    else writeTextFile(display, fileName);
} // actionPerformed()
```

Setting up the GUI for this application is straightforward. The details are shown in Figure 14–14, and Figure 14–13 shows how the finished product looks.

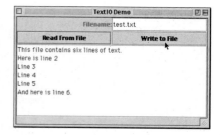

FIGURE 14–13   An application that performs simple text I/O.

```java
import javax.swing.*;          // Swing components
import java.awt.*;
import java.io.*;
import java.awt.event.*;

public class TextIO extends JFrame implements ActionListener{
    private JTextArea display = new JTextArea();
    private JButton read = new JButton("Read From File"),
                    write = new JButton("Write to File");
    private JTextField nameField = new JTextField(20);
    private JLabel prompt = new JLabel("Filename:",JLabel.RIGHT);
    private JPanel commands = new JPanel();

    public TextIO() {                        // Constructor
        super("TextIO Demo");                // Set window title
        read.addActionListener(this);
        write.addActionListener(this);
        commands.setLayout( new GridLayout(2,2,1,1));  // Control panel
        commands.add(prompt);
        commands.add(nameField);
        commands.add(read);
        commands.add(write);
        display.setLineWrap(true);
        this.getContentPane().setLayout(new BorderLayout());
        this.getContentPane().add("North", commands);
        this.getContentPane().add( new JScrollPane(display));
        this.getContentPane().add("Center", display);
    } // TextIO

    private void readTextFile(JTextArea display, String fileName) {
        try {
            BufferedReader inStream                      // Create and
                = new BufferedReader (new FileReader(fileName));//Open the stream
            String line = inStream.readLine();           // Read one line
            while (line != null) {                       // While more text
                display.append(line + "\n");             // Display a line
                line = inStream.readLine();              // Read next line
            }
            inStream.close();                            // Close the stream
        } catch (FileNotFoundException e) {
            display.setText("IOERROR: File NOT Found: " + fileName + "\n");
            e.printStackTrace();
        } catch (IOException e) {
            display.setText("IOERROR: " + e.getMessage() + "\n");
            e.printStackTrace();
        }
    } // readTextFile
```

FIGURE 14–14　Part I of the TextIO class.

```
        private void writeTextFile(JTextArea display, String fileName) {
            try {
                FileWriter outStream = new FileWriter (fileName);
                outStream.write (display.getText());
                outStream.close();
            } catch (IOException e) {
                display.setText("IOERROR: " + e.getMessage() + "\n");
                e.printStackTrace();
            }
        } // writeTextFile()

        public void actionPerformed(ActionEvent evt) {
            String fileName = nameField.getText();
            if (evt.getSource()  == read) {
                display.setText("");
                readTextFile(display, fileName);
            }
            else writeTextFile(display, fileName);
        } // actionPerformed()

        public static void main(String args[]) {
            TextIO tio = new TextIO();
            tio.setSize(400, 200);
            tio.setVisible(true);
            tio.addWindowListener(new WindowAdapter() {        // Quit the application
                public void windowClosing(WindowEvent e) {
                    System.exit(0);
                }
            });
        } // main()
}//TextIO
```

FIGURE 14–14   (*continued*) The TextIO class, Part II.

14.4   The File Class

As we've seen, an attempt to create a FileReader stream may throw a FileNotFoundException. The only way this can happen is if the user has provided a name for a file that doesn't exist or that isn't located where its name says it should be located. Is there any way we can detect these kinds of errors before attempting to read the file?

The java.io.File class provides methods that we can use for this task. The File class provides a representation of the computer's file and directory information in a platform-independent manner. As you know, a **file** is a collection of data, whereas a **directory** is a collection of files. (Actually, a directory is a file that stores its files' names and attributes, not the files themselves.)

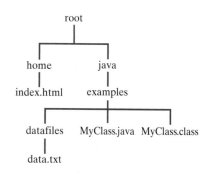

FIGURE 14–15   A simple hierarchy of directories and files.

14.4.1   Names and Paths

File systems are organized into a hierarchy. A **path** is a description of a file's location in the hierarchy. For example, consider the hierarchy of files in Figure 14–15. Assume that your Java program is named MyClass.class.

The file hierarchy

When a program is running, the program's directory is considered the `current directory`. Any files located in the current directory can be referred to by name alone—for example, `MyClass.java`. To refer to a file located in a subdirectory of the current directory, you would provide the name of the subdirectory and the file: `datafiles/data.txt`. In this case, we are assuming a Unix file system, so we are using the `/` as the separator between the name of the directory (`datafiles`) and the name of the file (`data.txt`).

When a file is specified in relation to the current directory, this is called a **relative path name**. Alternatively, a file can be specified by its **absolute path name**. This would be a name whose path starts at the root directory of the file system. For example,

```
/root/java/examples/datafiles/data.txt
```

would be the absolute path name for the file named `data.txt` on a Unix system. When you supply the name of a file to one of the stream constructors, you are actually providing a *path* name. If the path consists of just a name, such as `data.txt`, Java assumes that the file is located in the same directory as the program itself.

14.4.2   Validating File Names

The `File` class (Fig. 14–16) provides platform-independent methods for dealing with files and directories. It contains methods that list the contents of directories, determine a file's attributes, and rename and delete files. Note the several `static` constants provided. These allow path names to be specified in a platform-independent way. For example, on a Unix system, the `File.separator` character will be the `/` and on a Windows system it will be the `\`, `backslash`. `File.separator` will be initialized to the appropriate separator for the particular system being used.

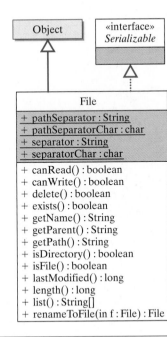

FIGURE 14–16   The `java.io.File` class.

Method design

> PROGRAMMING TIP: File Separators.   To make your programs platform independent, use the `File.separator` constant instead of a literal value whenever you are specifying a path name.

As an example of how you might use some of `File`'s methods, let's write a method that tests whether the file name entered by the user is the name of a valid, readable file.

A file may be unreadable for a number of reasons. It may be owned by another user and readable only by that user. Or it may be designated as not readable by its owner. We'll pass the method the name of the file (a `String`), and the method will return `true` if a readable file with that name exists. Otherwise the method will throw an exception and return `false`:

```
private boolean isReadableFile(String fileName) {
    try {
        File file = new File(fileName);
        if (!file.exists())
            throw (new FileNotFoundException("No such File:" + fileName));
        if (!file.canRead())
            throw (new IOException("File not readable: " + fileName));
        return true;
```

(continues on next page)

```
        } catch (FileNotFoundException e) {
            System.out.println("IOERROR: File NOT Found: " + fileName + "\n");
            return false;
        } catch (IOException e) {
            System.out.println("IOERROR: " + e.getMessage() + "\n");
            return false;
        }
    } // isReadableFile
```

The method simply creates a `File` instance and uses its `exists()` and `can-Read()` methods to check whether its name is valid. If either condition fails, an exception is thrown. The method handles its own exceptions, printing an error message and returning false in each case.

Before attempting to write data to a file, we might want to check that the file has been given an appropriate name. For example, if the user leaves the file name blank, we should not write data to the file. Also, a file might be designated as unwriteable in order to protect it from being inadvertently overwritten. We should check that the file is writeable before attempting to write to it:

```
private boolean isWriteableFile(String fileName) {
    try {
        File file = new File (fileName);
        if (fileName.length() == 0)
            throw (new IOException("Invalid file name: " + fileName));
        if (file.exists() && !file.canWrite())
            throw (new IOException("IOERROR: File not writeable: "
                                                    + fileName));
        return true;
    } catch (IOException e) {
        display.setText("IOERROR: " + e.getMessage() + "\n");
        return false;
    }
} // isWriteableFile()
```

The first check in this code tests that the user has not forgotten to provide a name for the output file. It is unlikely that the user wants to name the file with the empty string. We use the `exists()` method to test whether the user is attempting to write to an existing file. If so, we use the `canWrite()` method to test whether the file is writeable. Both kinds of errors result in `IOExceptions`.

SELF-STUDY EXERCISE

EXERCISE 14.4   The other methods of the `File` class are just as easy to use. Write a method that takes the name of file as its single parameter and prints the following information about the file: its absolute path, its length, and whether it is a directory or a file.

14.5   Example: Reading and Writing Binary Files

Although text files are extremely useful and widespread, they can't be used (and shouldn't be used) for every data-processing application. For example, your college's administrative data system undoubtedly uses files to store student records. Because your student record contains a variety of different types of data—Strings, ints, doubles—it cannot be processed as text. Similarly, a company's inventory files, which include data of a wide variety of types, cannot be processed as text. Files such as these must be processed as binary data.

Suppose you are asked to write an application that involves the use of a company's employee records. Recall that a **record** is a structure that combines different types of data into a single entity. It's like an object with no methods, just instance variables.

A binary file is a sequence of bytes. Unlike a text file, which is terminated by a special end-of-file marker, a binary file consists of nothing but data. A binary file doesn't have an end-of-file character because any such character would be indistinguishable from a binary datum.

> DEBUGGING TIP: End of Binary File. Because a binary file does not have an end-of-file character, it would be an error to use the same loop-entry conditions we used in the loops we designed for reading text files.

Generally speaking, the steps involved in reading and writing binary files are the same as for text files:

1. Connect a stream to the file.
2. Read or write the data, possibly using a loop.
3. Close the stream.

The difference between text and binary file I/O resides in the Java streams that we use.

14.5.1   Writing Binary Data

Generating binary data

Let's begin by designing a method that will output employee data to a binary file. As the developer of this program, one thing you'll have to do is build some sample data files. These can't easily be built by hand—remember you can't use a text editor to create them—so you'll want to develop a method that can generate some random data of the sort your application will have to process.

> EFFECTIVE DESIGN: I/O Design.   When designing file I/O applications, it is good to design the input and the output methods together. This is especially important for binary I/O.

The first thing we need to know is exactly what the data look like. Let's assume that each record contains three individual pieces of data—the employee's name, age, and pay rate. For example, the data in a file containing four records might look like this, once the data are interpreted:

```
Name0 24 15.06
Name1 25 5.09
Name2 40 11.45
Name3 52 9.25
```

As you can see, these data look as if they were randomly generated, but they resemble the real data in the important respects: They are of the right type—String, int, double—and have typical values. Of course, when these

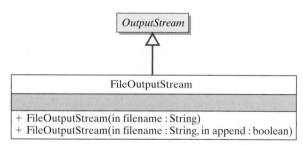

FIGURE 14–17   The `FileOutputStream` class.

data are stored in the file, or in the program's memory, they just look like one long string of 0's and 1's.

Our approach to designing this output method will be the same as the approach we used in designing methods for text I/O. That is, we start with two questions:

- What stream classes should I use?
- What methods can I use?

And we find the answers to these by searching through the java.io package (Fig. 14–3 and Table 14.1).

Because we are performing binary output, we need to use some subclass of OutputStream. Because we're outputting to a file, one likely candidate is FileOutputStream (Fig. 14–17). This class has the right kind of constructors, but it only contains write() methods for writing ints and bytes. We need to be able to write Strings and doubles as well as ints. These kinds of methods are found in DataOutputStream (Fig. 14–18), which contains a write() method for each different type of data. As you can see, there's one method for each primitive type. However, note that the writeChar() takes an int parameter, which indicates that the character is written in binary format rather than as a ASCII or Unicode character. Although you can't tell by just reading its method signature, the writeChars(String) method also writes its data in binary format rather than as a sequence of characters. This is the main difference between these write() methods and the ones defined in the Writer branch of Java's I/O hierarchy.

We've now found the classes and methods we need. To construct a stream to use in writing employee records, we want to join together a DataOutputStream and a FileOutputStream. The DataOutputStream gives us the output methods we need, and the FileOutputStream lets us use the file's name to create the stream:

```
DataOutputStream outStream
      = new DataOutputStream(new FileOutputStream (fileName));
```

The program will write data to the DataOutputStream, which will pass them through the FileOutputStream to the file itself. That settles the first question.

To develop the output algorithm, we need some kind of loop that involves calls to the appropriate methods. In this case, because we are generating random data, we can use a simple for loop to generate, say, five records of employee data. We need one write() statement for each of the elements in the employee record: the name (String), age (int), and pay rate (double):

Choosing an output stream

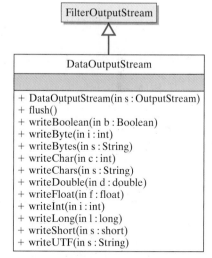

FIGURE 14–18   The java.io.DataOutputStream class contains methods for writing all types of data.

```
for (int k = 0; k < 5; k++) {              // Output 5 data records
    outStream.writeUTF("Name" + k);              // Name
    outStream.writeInt((int)(20 + Math.random() * 25)); // Random age
    outStream.writeDouble(Math.random() * 500); // Random payrate
}
```

Within the loop body we have one output statement for each data element in the record. The names of the methods reflect the type of data they write. Thus, we use `writeInt()` to write an `int` and `writeDouble()` to write a `double`. But why do we use `writeUTF` to write the employee's name, a `String`?

The Unicode Text Format (UTF)

There is no `DataOutputStream.writeString()` method. Instead `Strings` are written using the `writeUTF()` method. **UTF** stands for *Unicode Text Format*. It is a coding scheme for Java's Unicode character set. Recall that Java uses the Unicode character set instead of the ASCII set. As a 16-bit code, Unicode can represent 8-bit ASCII characters plus a huge variety of Asian and other international characters. However, Unicode is not a very efficient coding scheme if you aren't writing an international program. If your program just uses the standard ASCII characters, which can be stored in 1 byte, you would be wasting 1 byte per character if you stored them as straight Unicode characters. Therefore, for efficiency purposes, Java uses the more efficient UTF format. UTF encoding can still represent all of the Unicode characters, but it provides a more efficient way of representing the ASCII subset.

ASCII vs. Unicode

It's now time to combine these separate elements into a single method (Fig. 14–19). The `writeRecords()` method takes a single `String` parameter that specifies the name of the file. This is a `void` method. It will output data to a file, but it will not return anything to the calling method. The method follows the standard output algorithm: Create an output stream, write the data, close the stream. Note also that the method includes a `try/catch` block to handle any `IOExceptions` that may be thrown.

```java
private void writeRecords( String fileName )  {
    try {
        DataOutputStream outStream
            = new DataOutputStream(new FileOutputStream(fileName)); // Open stream
        for (int k = 0; k < 5; k++) {                       // Output 5 data records
            String name = "Name" + k;
            outStream.writeUTF("Name" + k);                        // Name
            outStream.writeInt((int)(20 + Math.random() * 25));    // Age
            outStream.writeDouble(5.00 + Math.random() * 10);      // Payrate
        } // for
        outStream.close();                                  // Close the stream
    } catch (IOException e) {
        display.setText("IOERROR: " + e.getMessage() + "\n");
    }
} // writeRecords()
```

FIGURE 14–19 A method to write a binary file consisting of five randomly constructed records.

14.5.2   Reading Binary Data

The steps involved in reading data from a binary file are the same as for reading data from a text file: Create an input stream and open the file, read the data, close the file. The main difference lies in the way you check for the end-of-file marker in a binary file.

Let's design a method to read the binary data that were output by the `writeRecords()` method. We'll call this method `readRecords()`. It too will consist of a single `String` parameter, which provides the name of the file to be read. And it too will be a void method. It will just display the data on `System.out`.

What stream classes should we use, and what methods should we use? For binary input, we need an `InputStream` subclass (Fig. 14–3 and Table 14.1). As you've probably come to expect, the `FileInputStream` class contains constructors that let us create a stream from a file name (Fig. 14–20). However, it does not contain useful `read()` methods. Fortunately, the `DataInputStream` class contains the input counterparts of the methods we found in `DataOutputStream` (Fig. 14–21). Therefore, our input stream for this method will be a combination of `DataInputStream` and `FileInputStream`:

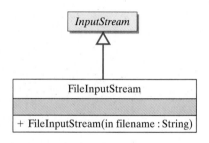

FIGURE 14–20   The `java.io.File-InputStream` class.

Choosing an input stream

```
DataInputStream inStream
    = new DataInputStream(new FileInputStream(file));
```

Now that we have identified the classes and methods we'll use to read the data, the most important remaining issue is designing a read loop that will terminate correctly. Unlike text files, binary files do not contain a special end-of-file marker. Therefore, the read methods can't see anything in the file that tells them they're at the end of the file. Instead, when a binary read method attempts to read past the end of the file, an end-of-file exception `EOFException` is thrown. Thus, the binary loop is coded as an infinite loop that's exited when the `EOFException` is raised:

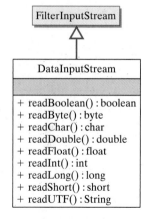

```
try {
    while (true) {                          // Infinite loop
        String name = inStream.readUTF();      // Read a record
        int age = inStream.readInt();
        double pay = inStream.readDouble();
        display.append(name + "    " + age + "    " + pay + "\n");
    } // while
} catch (EOFException e) {}                 // Until EOF exception
```

The read loop is embedded within a `try/catch` statement. Note that the catch clause for the `EOFException` does nothing. Recall that when an exception is thrown in a `try` block, the block is exited for good, which is precisely the action we want to take. That's why we needn't do anything when we catch the `EOFException`. We have to catch the exception; otherwise Java will catch it and terminate the program. This is one example of an expected exception.

FIGURE 14–21   The `java.io.Data-InputStream` class contains methods for reading all types of data.

An expected exception

EFFECTIVE DESIGN: `EOFException`.   An attempt to read past the end of a binary file will cause an `EOFException` to be thrown. Catching this exception is the standard way of terminating a binary input loop.

```
private void readRecords( String fileName ) {
    try {
        DataInputStream inStream
          = new DataInputStream(new FileInputStream(fileName)); // Open stream
        display.setText("Name    Age Pay\n");
        try {
            while (true) {                          // Infinite loop
                String name = inStream.readUTF();       // Read a record
                int age = inStream.readInt();
                double pay = inStream.readDouble();
                display.append(name + "    " + age + "    " + pay + "\n");
            } // while
        } catch (EOFException e) {                  // Until EOF exception
        } finally {
            inStream.close();                          // Close the stream
        }
    } catch (FileNotFoundException e) {
        display.setText("IOERROR: File NOT Found: " + fileName + "\n");
    } catch (IOException e) {
        display.setText("IOERROR: " + e.getMessage() + "\n");
    }
} // readRecords()
```

FIGURE 14–22   A method for reading binary data.

Note also the read() statements within the loop are mirror opposites of the write() statements in the method that created the data. This will generally be true for binary I/O routines: The statements that read data from a file should "match" those that wrote the data in the first place.

EFFECTIVE DESIGN: Matching Input to Output.   The statements used to read binary data should match those that wrote the data. If a writeX() method were used to write the data, a readX() should be used to read it.

To complete the method, the only remaining task is to close() the stream after the data are read. The complete definition is shown in Figure 14–22.

It's important that a close() statement be placed after the catch EOF-Exception clause. If it were placed in the try block, it would never get executed. Note also that the entire method is embedded in an outer try block that catches the IOException, thrown by the various read() methods, and the FileNotFoundException, thrown by the FileInputStream() constructor. These enlarge the method, but it is nicely self-contained.

PROGRAMMING TIP: The finally Block.   In coding a binary read loop, the try block is exited as soon as the EOFException is raised. Therefore, the close() statement must be placed in the finally clause, which is executed after the catch clause.

EFFECTIVE DESIGN: Nested Try/Catch.   Nested try blocks must be used to perform binary I/O correctly. The outer block encapsulates statements that throw IOExceptions. The inner block encapsulates the read loop and catches the EOFException. No particular action need be taken when the EOFException is caught.

SELF-STUDY EXERCISE

EXERCISE 14.5   Identify the error in the following method, which is supposed to read a binary file of ints from a DataInputStream:

```java
public void readIntegers(DataInputStream inStream) {
    try {
        while (true) {
            int num = inStream.readInt();
            System.out.println(num);
        }
        inStream.close();
    } catch (EOFException e) {
    } catch (IOException e) {
    }
} // readIntegers
```

14.5.3   The BinaryIO Application

Given the methods we wrote in the previous section, we can now specify the overall design of the BinaryIO class (Fig. 14–23). The program sets up the same interface we used in the text file example (Fig. 14–24). It allows the user to specify the name of a data file to read or write. One button allows the user to write random employee records to a binary file, and the other allows the user to display the contents of a file in a JTextArea. The BinaryIO program in Figure 14–25 incorporates both readRecords() and writeRecords() into a complete Java program.

14.5.4   Abstracting Data from Files

It's important to recognize that the method to read a binary file must exactly match the method that wrote the binary file in the relative order in which the write and read statements are placed. If the file contains records that consist of a String followed by an int followed by a double, then they must be written by a sequence consisting of

```java
writeUTF();
writeInt():
writeDouble();
```

And they must thereafter be read by a sequence consisting of

```java
readUTF();
readInt():
readDouble();
```

Attempting to do otherwise would make it impossible to interpret the data in the file.

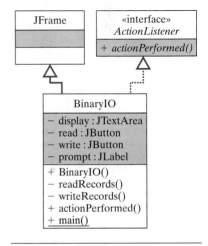

FIGURE 14–23   Design of the BinaryIO class.

FIGURE 14–24   A program to read and write binary files.

```java
import javax.swing.*;        // Swing components
import java.awt.*;
import java.io.*;
import java.awt.event.*;

public class BinaryIO extends JFrame implements ActionListener{
    private JTextArea display = new JTextArea();
    private JButton read = new JButton("Read Records From File"),
                    write = new JButton("Generate Random Records");
    private JTextField nameField = new JTextField(10);
    private JLabel prompt = new JLabel("Filename:", JLabel.RIGHT);
    private JPanel commands = new JPanel();

    public BinaryIO() {
        super("BinaryIO Demo");                    // Set window title
        read.addActionListener(this);
        write.addActionListener(this);
        commands.setLayout(new GridLayout(2,2,1,1)); // Control panel
        commands.add(prompt);
        commands.add(nameField);
        commands.add(read);
        commands.add(write);
        display.setLineWrap(true);
        this.getContentPane().setLayout(new BorderLayout () );
        this.getContentPane().add("North", commands);
        this.getContentPane().add( new JScrollPane(display));
        this.getContentPane().add("Center", display);
    } // BinaryIO()

    public void actionPerformed(ActionEvent evt) {
        String fileName = nameField.getText();
        if (evt.getSource()  == read)
            readRecords(fileName);
        else
            writeRecords(fileName);
    } // actionPerformed()

    private void readRecords( String fileName ) {
        try {
            DataInputStream inStream
                = new DataInputStream(new FileInputStream(fileName)); // Open stream
            display.setText("Name   Age Pay\n");
            try {
                while (true) {                              // Infinite loop
                    String name = inStream.readUTF();        // Read a record
                    int age = inStream.readInt();
                    double pay = inStream.readDouble();
                    display.append(name + "    " + age + "    " + pay + "\n");
                } // while
            } catch (EOFException e) {                  // Until EOF exception
            } finally {
                inStream.close();                           // Close the stream
            }
        } catch (FileNotFoundException e) {
            display.setText("IOERROR: File NOT Found: " + fileName + "\n");
        } catch (IOException e) {
            display.setText("IOERROR: " + e.getMessage() + "\n");
        }
    } // readRecords()
```

FIGURE 14–25   Part I of the BinaryIO class, which illustrates simple input and output from a binary file.

```
    private void writeRecords( String fileName )  {
        try {
            DataOutputStream outStream
                = new DataOutputStream(new FileOutputStream(fileName)); // Open stream
            for (int k = 0; k < 5; k++) {                    // Output 5 data records
                String name = "Name" + k;
                outStream.writeUTF("Name" + k);                      // Name
                outStream.writeInt((int)(20 + Math.random() * 25));  // Age
                outStream.writeDouble(5.00 + Math.random() * 10);    // Payrate
            } // for
            outStream.close();                              // Close the stream
        } catch (IOException e) {
            display.setText("IOERROR: " + e.getMessage() + "\n");
        }
    } // writeRecords()

    public static void main(String args[]) {
        BinaryIO bio = new BinaryIO();
        bio.setSize(400, 200);
        bio.setVisible(true);
        bio.addWindowListener(new WindowAdapter() {      // Quit the application
            public void windowClosing(WindowEvent e) {
                System.exit(0);
            }
        });
    } // main()
} // BinaryIO
```

FIGURE 14–25   (*continued*) The `BinaryIO` class, Part II.

This point should make it evident why (non-Java) binary files are not portable whereas text files are. With text files, each character consists of 8 bits, and each 8-bit chunk can be interpreted as an ASCII character. So even though a text file consists of a long sequence of 0's and 1's, we know how to find the boundaries between each character. That's why any text editor can read a text file, no matter what program created it.

Portability

On the other hand, binary files are also just a long sequence of 0's and 1's, but we can't tell where one data element begins and another one ends. For example, the 64-bit sequence

```
0101001100110010010101001100110000010100110011001011010100110011 00
```

could represent two 32-bit `int`s or two 32-bit `float`s or one 64-bit `double` or four 16-bit `char`s or a single `String` of 8 ASCII characters. We can't tell what data we have unless we know exactly how the data were written.

DEBUGGING TIP: Interpreting Binary Data. The fact that you can read the data in a binary file is no guarantee that you are interpreting it correctly. To interpret it correctly, you must read it the same way it was written.

EFFECTIVE DESIGN: Data Abstraction. Binary data are "raw." They have no inherent structure. It is only the programs that read and write the data that provide them with structure. A string of 64 0's and 1's can be interpreted as two ints or one long or even as some kind of object, so an int, long or an object is an abstraction imposed upon the data by the program.

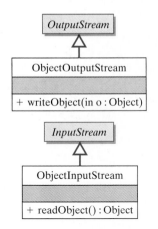

FIGURE 14–26 Classes used for performing I/O on objects.

Object serialization

14.6 Object Serialization: Reading and Writing Objects

The examples in the previous sections showed how to do I/O operations on simple binary data or text. The java.io package also provides methods for reading and writing objects, a process known as **object serialization**. Objects can be *serialized* using the ObjectOutputStream class, and they can be *deserialized* using the ObjectInputStream class (Fig. 14–26). Despite the complexity of the serialization/deserialization processes, the methods in these classes make the task just as easy as reading and writing primitive data.

To illustrate object serialization, let's begin by defining a Student class (Fig. 14–27). In order to serialize an object, it must be a member of a class that implements the Serializable interface. The Serializable interface is a *marker interface*, an interface that doesn't define any methods or constants but just serves to designate whether an object can be serialized or not.

The Student class contains its own I/O methods, readFromFile() and writeToFile(). This is an appropriate object-oriented design. The Student class encapsulates all the relevant information needed to read and write its data.

EFFECTIVE DESIGN: I/O Design. If an object is going to be input and output to and from files, it should define its own I/O methods. An object contains all the relevant information needed to perform I/O correctly.

Note the definition of the writeToFile() method, which performs the output task. This method's FileOutputStream parameter is used to create an ObjectOutputStream, whose writeObject() method is used to write the object into the file. To output a Student object, we merely invoke the writeObject() method. This method writes out the current values of all the object's public and private fields. In this case, the method would write a String for the object's name, an int for the object's year, and a double for the object's gpa.

Although our example doesn't require it, the writeObject() method can also handle fields that refer to other objects. For example, suppose our Student object contained a field for courses that contained a reference to an array of objects, each of which described a course the student has taken. In that case, the writeObject() method would recursively serialize the array and all its objects (assuming they are serializable). Thus, when a complex object is serialized, the result would be a complex structure that contains all the data linked to that root object.

Object deserialization

Object deserialization, as shown in the readFromFile() method, is simply the reverse of the serialization process. The readObject() method

```java
import java.io.*;

public class Student implements Serializable {
    private String name;
    private int year;
    private double gpa;

    public Student() {}

    public Student (String nameIn, int yr, double gpaIn) {
        name = nameIn;
        year = yr;
        gpa = gpaIn;
    }

    public void writeToFile(FileOutputStream outStream)
                                    throws IOException{
        ObjectOutputStream ooStream = new ObjectOutputStream(outStream);
        ooStream.writeObject(this);
        ooStream.flush();
    } // writeToFile()

    public void readFromFile(FileInputStream inStream)
                    throws IOException, ClassNotFoundException {
        ObjectInputStream oiStream = new ObjectInputStream(inStream);
        Student s = (Student)oiStream.readObject();
        this.name = s.name;
        this.year = s.year;
        this.gpa = s.gpa;
    } // readFromFile()

    public String toString() {
        return name + "\t" + year + "\t" + gpa;
    }
} // Student
```

FIGURE 14–27   The *serializable* Student class.

reads one serialized object from the ObjectInputStream. Its result type is Object, so it is necessary to cast the result into the proper type. In our example we use a local Student variable to store the object as it is input. We then copy each field of the local object to this object.

Note that the readFromFile() method throws both the IOException and ClassNotFoundException. An IOException will be generated if the file you are attempting to read does not contain serialized objects of the right type. Objects that can be input by readObject() are those that were output by writeObject(). Thus, just as in the case of binary I/O, it is best to design an object's input and output routines together so that they are compatible. The ClassNotFoundException will be thrown if the Student class cannot be found. This is needed to determine how to deserialize the object.

PROGRAMMING TIP: Object Serialization.   Java's serialization classes, `ObjectOutputStream` and `ObjectInputStream`, should be used whenever an object needs to be input or output from a stream.

14.6.1   The `ObjectIO` Class

Given the `Student` class, let's now write a user interface that can read and write `Student` objects. We can use the same interface we used in the `BinaryIO` program. The only things we need to change are the `write-Records()` and `readRecords()` methods. Everything else about this program will be exactly the same as in `BinaryIO`.

Figure 14–28 provides the full implementation of the `ObjectIO` class. Note that the `writeRecords()` method will still write five random records

```java
import javax.swing.*;           // Swing components
import java.awt.*;
import java.io.*;
import java.awt.event.*;

public class ObjectIO extends JFrame implements ActionListener{
    private JTextArea display = new JTextArea();
    private JButton read = new JButton("Read From File"),
                 write = new JButton("Write to File");
    private JTextField nameField = new JTextField(10);
    private JLabel prompt = new JLabel("Filename:",JLabel.RIGHT);
    private JPanel commands = new JPanel();

    public ObjectIO () {
        super("ObjectIO Demo");                      // Set window title
        read.addActionListener(this);
        write.addActionListener(this);
        commands.setLayout( new GridLayout(2,2,1,1)); // Control panel
        commands.add(prompt);
        commands.add(nameField);
        commands.add(read);
        commands.add(write);
        display.setLineWrap(true);
        this.getContentPane().setLayout(new BorderLayout () );
        this.getContentPane().add("North",commands);
        this.getContentPane().add( new JScrollPane(display));
        this.getContentPane().add("Center", display);
    } // ObjectIO

    public void actionPerformed(ActionEvent evt) {
        String fileName = nameField.getText();
        if (evt.getSource() == read)
            readRecords(fileName);
        else
            writeRecords(fileName);
    } // actionPerformed()
```

FIGURE 14–28   Part I of the `ObjectIO` class, which provides an interface to reading and writing files of `Students`.

```
    private void readRecords(String fileName) {
        try {
            FileInputStream inStream = new FileInputStream(fileName);  // Open a stream
            display.setText("Name\tYear\tGPA\n");
            try {
                while (true) {                         // Infinite loop
                    Student student = new Student();        // Create a student instance
                    student.readFromFile(inStream);         //  and have it read an object
                    display.append(student.toString() +  "\n"); //  and display it
                }
            } catch (IOException e) {                   // Until IOException
            }
            inStream.close();                           // Close the stream
        } catch (FileNotFoundException e) {
            display.append("IOERROR: File NOT Found: " + fileName + "\n");
        } catch (IOException e) {
            display.append("IOERROR: " + e.getMessage() + "\n");
        } catch (ClassNotFoundException e) {
            display.append("ERROR: Class NOT found " + e.getMessage() + "\n");
        }
    } // readRecords()

    private void writeRecords(String fileName) {
        try {
            FileOutputStream outStream = new FileOutputStream( fileName ); // Open a stream
            for (int k = 0; k < 5 ; k++) {             // Generate 5 random objects
                String name = "name" + k;                  // Name
                int year = (int)(2000 + Math.random() * 4);   // Class year
                double gpa = Math.random() * 12;           // GPA
                Student student = new Student(name, year, gpa); // Create the object
                display.append("Output: " + student.toString() +  "\n"); //  and display it
                student.writeToFile(outStream) ;           //  and tell it to write data
            } //for
            outStream.close();
        } catch (IOException e) {
            display.append("IOERROR: " + e.getMessage() + "\n");
        }
    } // writeRecords()

    public static void main(String args[]) {
        ObjectIO io = new ObjectIO();
        io.setSize( 400,200);
        io.setVisible(true);
        io.addWindowListener(new WindowAdapter() {  // Quit the application
            public void windowClosing(WindowEvent e) {
                System.exit(0);
            }
        });
    } // main()
} // ObjectIO
```

FIGURE 14–28   (*continued*) The ObjectIO class, Part II.

to the data file. The difference in this case is that we will call the `Student.writeToFile()` method to take care of the actual output operations. The revised algorithm will create a new `Student` object, using randomly generated data for its name, year, and GPA and then invoke its `writeToFile()` to output its data. Note how a `FileOutputStream` is created and passed to the `Student.writeToFile()` method.

The `readRecords()` method (Fig. 14–28) will read data from a file containing serialized `Student` objects. To do so, it first creates a `Student` object and then invokes its `readFromFile()` method, passing it a `FileInputStream`. Note how the `FileInputStream` is created, and note that unlike in `BinaryIO`, the inner try block is exited by an `IOException` rather than an `EOFException`.

SELF-STUDY EXERCISE

EXERCISE 14.6   Given the following definition, would a binary file consisting of several `SomeObjects` be readable by either the `BinaryIO` or the `ObjectIO` programs?

```
public class SomeObject {
    private String str;
    private short n1;
    private short n2;
    private long  n3;
}
```

Explain.

From the Java Library

`javax.swing.JFileChooser`

http://java.sun.com/products/jdk/1.3/docs/api/

THE `javax.swing.JFileChooser` class is a useful class for dealing with files and directories in a GUI environment. You are probably already familiar with `JFileChoosers`, although you may not have known them by that name. A `JFileChooser` provides a dialog box that enables the user to select a file and a directory when opening or saving a file. Figure 14–29 shows an example.

A `JFileChooser` is designed primarily to be used in conjunction with menu-based programs. The `JFileChooser` class (Fig. 14–30) contains methods that support the *Open File* and *Save As* menu options. We've used `JMenus` and `JDialogs` in Chapter 9, so you should already be familiar with their general functioning.

FIGURE 14–29   The *Open File* dialog window.

The laboratory for this chapter will involve writing a simple text-editing program using a JFileChooser to help manage files, so in this section we just provide the basics for how to use a JFileChooser.

A JFileChooser is not itself the dialog window but rather the object that manages the dialog. After creating a JFileChooser instance, its showOpen-Dialog() or showSaveDialog() methods are used to open a dialog window. Note that these methods require a Component parameter. This is usually a JFrame or a JApplet. Thus, JFileChoosers can be used only in GUI applications and applets.

To illustrate how to use a JFileChooser, let's consider the case where the user has selected the *Open File* menu item. In this case, we want to present an "Open File" dialog:

```
JFileChooser chooser = new JFileChooser();
int result = chooser.showOpenDialog(this);

if (result == JFileChooser.APPROVE_OPTION) {
    File file = chooser.getSelectedFile();
    String fileName = file.getName();
    display.setText("You selected " + fileName);
} else
    display.setText("You cancelled the file dialog");
```

We begin by creating a JFileChooser and then telling it to showOpenDia-log(). If we were saving a file, rather than opening one, we would tell it to showSaveDialog(). In either case, a dialog window will pop up on the screen. The dialog assists the user in navigating through the file system and selecting a file (Fig. 14–29).

The dialog contains two buttons, one labeled Open and the other labeled Cancel. If the user selects a file, that choice will correspond to the APPROVE_OPTION. If the user cancels the dialog, that will correspond to the CANCEL_OPTION. After opening a dialog, the code should check which option resulted. In this case, if the user opened a file, the code gets a reference to the file and then simply uses that to print the file's path name.

Opening a file

Using Command-Line Arguments

File dialogs are useful for GUI applications. However, what if your application uses a *command-line* interface, as in many Unix systems? One way to handle file specifications would be to allow the user to input them as **command-line arguments**. Command-line arguments are strings, separated by blank spaces, that follow the name of the application program on the command line. For example, suppose you had a FileCopy application that copies one file to another. One way to specify the names of the two files would be

Command-line arguments

```
java FileCopy file.txt newfile.txt
```

In this case, file.txt is the original file and newfile.txt is a copy that will be made by the program. They both serve as command-line arguments to the FileCopy program. These arguments are passed to the main() (by the system) as an array of String. As you know, every main() method takes

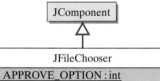

FIGURE 14–30   The javax.-swing.JFileChooser class.

an array of String as a parameter. The purpose of this array is to store the command-line arguments where they can be accessed by the program.

For example, in FileCopy, suppose main()'s parameter is named args[]. Given the foregoing command line, the following array would be passed to CopyFile:

```
file.txt newfile.txt
```

That is, the first array element, args[0], contains the first command-line argument, file.txt, and the second array element, args[1], contains the second command-line argument, newfile.txt. If there were additional arguments, they would be contained in args[2], args[3], and so on.

In order to use the command-line arguments in your program, you must extract them from args and then pass them to the I/O methods. For example, suppose the copy program is named FileCopy and it contains a public fileCopy() method, which takes the name of the source and destination files as String parameters. The following main() could be used:

```
public static void main(String args[]) {
    FileCopy fc = new FileCopy();
    if (args.length >= 2)
        fc.fileCopy(args[0], args[1]);
    else {
        System.out.println("Usage: java FileCopy srcFile destFile");
        System.exit(1);
    }
} // main()
```

Note that before accessing the args array we check that it contains at least two elements. If not, the user has forgotten to supply the correct number of arguments. In that case, an error message should be printed and the program should terminate.

SELF-STUDY EXERCISE

EXERCISE 14.7   Write the fileCopy() method used in the preceding example. To be as general as possible you should treat file copying as a binary I/O task. Use DataInputStream and DataOutputStream and the readByte() and writeByte() methods in your solution.

IN THE LABORATORY: The TextEdit Program

The main purpose of this lab is to develop a simple text-editing application with a GUI interface. The program will let the user create and edit text files that can then be saved, renamed, or reedited. In terms of programming techniques, this lab will provide practice in designing code that uses Files and Streams. The objectives are

- To develop a text-editing application by extending the SimpleText-Editor editing application developed in Figure 9–33.
- To develop appropriate I/O routines using Java's stream hierarchy.
- To develop an appropriate GUI that makes use of Java's JFileChooser and JMenu classes.

Databases and Personal Privacy

DURING A typical day we all come in contact with lots of electronic databases that store information about us. If you use a supermarket discount card, every purchase you make is logged against your name in the supermarket's database. When you use your bank card at the ATM machine, your financial transaction is logged against your account. When you charge gasoline or buy dinner, those transactions are logged against your credit card account. If you visit the doctor or dentist, a detailed record of your visit is transmitted to your medical insurance company's database. If you receive a college loan, detailed financial information about you is entered into several different credit service bureaus. And so on.

Should we be worried about how this information is used? Many privacy advocates say yes. With the computerization of medical records, phone records, financial transactions, driving records, and many other records, there is an enormous amount of personal information held in databases. At the same time, there are pressures from a number of sources for access to this information. Law enforcement agencies want to use this information to monitor individuals. Corporations want to use it to help them market their products. Political organizations want to use it to help them market their candidates.

Recently there has been pressure from government and industry in the United States to use the social security number (SSN) as a unique identifier. Such an identifier would make it easy to match personal information across different databases. Right now the only thing your bank records, medical records, and supermarket records may have in common is your name, which is not a unique identifier. If all online databases were based on your SSN, it would be much simpler to create a complete profile. While this might improve services and reduce fraud and crime, it might also pose a significant threat to our privacy.

The creation and use of online databases serve many useful purposes. They help fight crime and reduce the cost of doing business. They help improve government and commercial services that we have come to depend on. On the other hand, the databases can be and have been misused. They can be used by unauthorized individuals or agencies or in unauthorized ways. When they contain inaccurate information, they can cause personal inconvenience or even harm.

There are a number of organizations that have sprung up to address the privacy issues raised by online databases. If you're interested in learning more about this issue, a good place to start would be the Web site maintained by the Electronic Privacy Information Center (EPIC) at

`http://www.epic.org/`

Problem specification

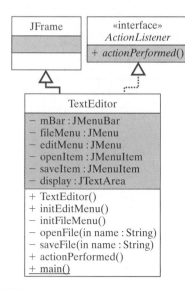

FIGURE 14–31   The TextEditor class.

Problem Description

Write a Java GUI application that implements a simple *text editor*. The application should enable the user to open and save existing text files and to create and save new files. It should enable the user to edit a file's text data by cutting, copying, and pasting the text or by simply typing in new text. Your implementation should make use of the techniques, methods, and classes that were introduced in this chapter.

Object-Oriented Design

An appropriate design for this problem would define a single class, let's call it TextEditor, which will implement both the file handling and edit functions of the application (Fig. 14–31). This should be a Java application rather than an applet because Java applets are restricted for security reasons from performing most types of file I/O. Because the program will perform file I/O, it must import the java.io.* package. The following is an appropriate outline for the TextEditor class:

```
import javax.swing.*;
import java.awt.*;
import java.awt.event.*;
import java.io.*;

public class TextEdit extends JFrame implements ActionListener {

    public void actionPerformed(ActionEvent e) { }
}
```

EFFECTIVE DESIGN: Applications Versus Applets.   Programs that perform file I/O should be designed as Java applications, not applets. Applets have too many security restrictions to permit their effective use for file I/O.

An appropriate GUI interface for a text editor will make use of Java menus, which were discussed in Chapter 9. And an appropriate approach to designing and coding this application would extend the program shown in Figure 9–33, which provides a suitable framework for a menu-based, editing application. The program in Figure 9–33 implements an *Edit* menu, which supports copying, cutting, and pasting of the text in the application's JTextArea. An appropriate extension of that program will involve the following additions and modifications:

- Modify and rename the quitMenu so that it becomes a full-fledged file-Menu. As such it should contain menu items for the *Open, Save, Save As, Quit* functions.
- Modify the actionPerformed() method to incorporate the code needed to implement the new menu items.
- Design and write a method named openFile(String), which takes a single String parameter, representing the full path name for a file. This method should create a BufferedReader input stream to the file that was named as its parameter. It should then read the entire contents of the file into the program's JTextArea. (See Figures 14–14 and 14–25 for ideas on how to design this method.)

- Design and write a method named saveFile(String), which takes a single String parameter, representing the full path name for a file. This method should create a FileWriter output stream to the file that was named as its parameter. It should then write the entire contents of the JTextArea to the file. (See Figures 14–14 and 14–25 for ideas on how to design this method.)

Algorithm Design

The algorithms used in the methods of this application are simple variations of the algorithms used in the programs shown in Figures 14–14 and 14–25. You should be able to modify and adapt that code to suit the requirements of this application.

Testing and Using the Text Editor

As always, you should use the stepwise refinement approach to implement your application. The individual steps should correspond pretty closely to the individual items listed in the previous section.

Despite its simplicity, this text editor has quite a wide range of functionality. It could easily be useful as an editor for creating Java programs, HTML files, or other simple editing tasks. To convince yourself of its usefulness, once you have completed the implementation, use the program to carry out each of the following tasks:

- Create from scratch a new file named file1.txt on your computer's desktop.
- Open file1.txt and make several editing changes to it, and save it as file2.txt on your computer's desktop.
- Create from scratch a new file named file3.txt and save it on your computer's desktop.
- Merge the contents of file1.txt and file3.txt into a new file named file4.txt. (*Hint*: Copy the contents of one file onto the clipboard before opening the other file.)

CHAPTER SUMMARY

Technical Terms

absolute path name	end-of-file character	platform
binary file	field	independence
buffer	file	record
buffering	filtering	relative path name
command-line	input stream	stream
argument	object serialization	text file
database	output stream	Unicode Text Format
data hierarchy	path	(UTF)
directory		

Summary of Important Points

- A *file* is a collection of data stored on a disk. A *stream* is an object that delivers data to and from other objects. An InputStream is a stream that delivers data to a program from an external source—such as the keyboard or a file. System.in is an example of an InputStream. An OutputStream is a stream that delivers data from a program to an external destination—such as the screen or a file. System.out is an example of an OutputStream.

- Data can be viewed as a hierarchy. From highest to lowest, a *database* is a collection of files. A *file* is a collection of records. A *record* is a collection of fields. A *field* is a collection of bytes. A *byte* is a collection of 8 bits. A *bit* is one binary digit, either 0 or 1.

- A *binary file* is a sequence of 0's and 1's that is interpreted as a sequence of bytes. A *text file* is a sequence of 0's and 1's that is interpreted as a sequence of characters. A text file can be read by any text editor. A binary file cannot. InputStream and OutputStream are abstract classes that serve as the root classes for reading and writing binary data. Reader and Writer serve as root classes for text I/O.

- *Buffering* is a technique in which a *buffer*, a temporary region of memory, is used to store data while they are being input or output.

- A text file contains a sequence of characters divided into lines by the \n character and ending with a special *end-of-file* character.

- The standard algorithm for performing I/O on a file consists of three steps: (1) Open a stream to the file, (2) perform the I/O, and (3) close the stream.

- Designing effective I/O routines proceeds by answering two questions: (1) What streams should I use to perform the I/O? (2) What methods should I use to do the reading or writing?

- To prevent damage to files when a program terminates abnormally, streams should be closed when they are no longer needed.

- Most I/O operations generate an IOException that should be caught in the I/O methods.

- Text input uses a different technique to determine when the end of a file has been reached. Text input methods return null or -1 when they attempt to read the special end-of-file character. Binary files don't contain an end-of-file character, so binary read methods throw an EOFException when they attempt to read past the end of the file.

- The java.io.File class provides methods that enable a program to interact with a file system. Its methods can be used to check a file's attributes, including its name, directory, and path.

- Streams can be joined together if necessary to perform I/O. For example, a DataOutputStream and a FileOutputStream can be joined to perform output to a binary file.

- A binary file is "raw" in the sense that it contains no markers within it that allow you to tell where one data element ends and another begins. The interpretation of binary data is up to the program that reads or writes the file.

- Object serialization is the process of writing an object to an output stream. Object deserialization is the reverse process of reading a serialized object from an input stream. These processes use the java.io.-ObjectOutputStream and java.io.ObjectInputStream classes.

- The JFileChooser class provides a dialog box that enables the user to select a file and directory when opening or saving a file.

SOLUTIONS TO SELF-STUDY EXERCISES

SOLUTION 14.1   Because FileWriter contains a constructor that takes a file name argument, FileWriter(String), it can be used with PrintWriter to do output to a text file:

```
PrintWriter outStream =              // Create an output stream
   new PrintWriter(new FileWriter(fileName)); // And open the file
outStream.print (display.getText());// Write the entire display text
outStream.close();                   // Close the output stream
```

SOLUTION 14.2   This loop doesn't worry about the possibility that the file might be empty. If the file is empty, it will print a null line. The test line != null, should come right after the readLine(), as it does in the while loop.

SOLUTION 14.3   This loop won't work on an empty text file. In that case, ch would be set to −1, and the attempt to cast it into a char would cause an error.

SOLUTION 14.4

```
public void getFileAttributes(String fileName) {
    File file = new File (fileName);
    System.out.println(filename);
    System.out.println("absolute path:" + file.getAbsolutePath());
    System.out.println("length:" + file.length());
    if (file.isDirectory())
        System.out.println("Directory");
    else
        System.out.println("Not a Directory");
} // getFileAttributes()
```

SOLUTION 14.5   The inStream.close() statement is misplaced in read-Integers(). By placing it inside the same try/catch block as the read loop, it will get skipped and the stream will not be closed. The EOFException should be caught in a separate try/catch block from other exceptions, and it should just cause the read loop to exit.

SOLUTION 14.6   Yes, a binary file containing several SomeObjects would be "readable" by the BinaryIO program because the program will read a String followed by 64 bytes. However, BinaryIO would misinterpret the data, because it will assume that n1 and n2 together comprise a single int, and n3 (64 bits) will be interpreted as a double. A file of SomeObjects could not be read by the ObjectIO program, because SomeObject does not implement the Serializable interface.

SOLUTION 14.7

```java
public void fileCopy(String src, String dest) {
    try {
        DataInputStream inStream
            = new DataInputStream(new FileInputStream(src));
        DataOutputStream outStream
            = new DataOutputStream(new FileOutputStream(dest));
        try {
            while (true) {
                byte data = inStream.readByte();
                outStream.writeByte(data);
            } // while
        } catch (EOFException e) {
        } finally {
            inStream.close();
            outStream.close();
        }
    } catch (IOException e) {
        System.out.println("IOERROR: " + e.getMessage());
    }
} // fileCopy()
```

EXERCISES

Note: *For programming exercises,* **first** *draw a UML class diagram describing all classes and their inheritance relationships and/or associations.*

EXERCISE 14.1   Explain the difference between each of the following pairs of terms:

a. `System.in` and `System.out`.
b. *File* and *directory*.
c. *Buffering* and *filtering*.
d. *Absolute* and *relative path name*.
e. *Input stream* and *output stream*.
f. *File* and *database*.
g. *Record* and *field*.
h. *Binary file* and *text file*.
i. *Directory* and *database*.

EXERCISE 14.2   Fill in the blanks.

a. Unlike text files, binary files do not have a special _____ character.

b. In Java, the `String` array parameter in the `main()` method is used for

_____ .

c. _____ files are portable and platform independent.

d. A _____ file created on one computer can't be read by another computer.

EXERCISE 14.3   Arrange the following kinds of data into their correct hierarchical relationships: `bit`, `field`, `byte`, `record`, `database`, `file`, `String`, `char`.

EXERCISE 14.4   In what different ways can the following string of 32 bits be interpreted?

```
00010101111000110100000110011110
```

EXERCISE 14.5   When reading a binary file, why is it necessary to use an infinite loop that's exited only when an exception occurs?

EXERCISE 14.6   Is it possible to have a text file with 10 characters and 0 lines? Explain.

EXERCISE 14.7   In reading a file, why is it necessary to attempt to read from the file before entering the read loop?

EXERCISE 14.8   When designing binary I/O, why is it especially important to design the input and output routines together?

EXERCISE 14.9   What's the difference between ASCII code and UTF code?

EXERCISE 14.10   Could the following string of bits possibly be a Java object?

```
000101110001111010101010000111001000100
110100100101010010101001000001000000111
```

Explain.

EXERCISE 14.11   Write a method, which could be added to the TextIO program, that reads a text file and prints all lines containing a certain word. This should be a void method that takes two parameters: the name of the file and the word to search for. Lines not containing the word should not be printed.

EXERCISE 14.12   Write a program that reads a text file and reports the number of characters and lines contained in the file.

EXERCISE 14.13   Modify the program in the previous exercise so that it also counts the numbers of words in the file. (*Hint*: The StringTokenizer class might be useful for this task.)

EXERCISE 14.14   Modify the ObjectIO program so that it allows the user to designate a file and then input Student data with the help of a GUI. As the user inputs data, each record should be written to the file.

EXERCISE 14.15   Write a program that will read a file of ints into memory, sort them in ascending order, and output the sorted data to a second file.

EXERCISE 14.16   Write a program that will read two files of ints, which are already sorted into ascending order, and merge their data. For example, if one file contains 1, 3, 5, 7, 9, and the other contains 2, 4, 6, 8, 10, then the merged file should contain 1, 2, 3, 4, 5, 6, 7, 8, 9, 10.

EXERCISE 14.17   Suppose you have file of data for a geological survey, such that each record consists of a longitude, a latitude, and an amount of rainfall, all represented by doubles. Write a method to read this file's data and print them on the screen, one record per line. The method should be void and it should take the name of the file as its only parameter.

EXERCISE 14.18   Suppose you have the same data as in the previous exercise. Write a method that will generate 1,000 records of random data and write them to a file. The method should be void and should take the file's name as its parameter. Assume that longitudes have values in the range $+/-$ 0 to 180 degrees, latitudes have values in the range $+/-$ 0 to 90 degrees, and rainfalls have values in the range 0 to 20 inches.

EXERCISE 14.19   Design and write a file copy program that will work for either text files or binary files. The program should prompt the user for the names of each file and copy the data from the source file into the destination file. It should not overwrite an existing file, however. (*Hint*: Read and write the file as a file of byte.)

EXERCISE 14.20   Design a class, similar to `Student`, to represent an `Address`, consisting of street, city, state, and zip code. This class should contain its own `readFromFile()` and `writeToFile()` methods.

EXERCISE 14.21   Using the class designed in the previous exercise, modify the `Student` class so that it contains an `Address` field. Modify the `ObjectIO` program to accommodate this new definition of `Student` and test your program.

EXERCISE 14.22   Write a program called `Directory`, which provides a listing of a directory. This program should use an optional command-line argument, so that it will have the following command line:

```
java Directory [ dirName ]
```

The brackets here indicate that `dirName` is an optional argument. If no `dirName` is given, the program should print a directory listing of the current directory. If a directory name is given, it should print a listing of that directory. The listing should contain the following information: the full path name of the directory, and then for each file, the file name, length, and last modified date, and a read/write code. The read/write code should be an *r* if the file is readable and a *w* if the file is writeable, in that order. Use a "-" to indicate not readable or not writeable. For example, a file that is readable but not writable will have the code *r*-. Here's an example listing:

```
Listing for directory: myfiles
   name         length modified   code
   index.html   548    129098     rw
   index.gif    78     129190     rw
   me.html      682    128001     r-
   private.txt  1001   129000     --
```

Note that the `File.lastModified()` returns a `long`, which gives the modification time of the file. This number can't easily be converted into a date, so just report its value.

EXERCISE 14.23   **Challenge:** In Unix systems there's a program named `grep` that can be used to list the lines in a text file that contain a certain string. It has the following command line:

```
grep "search string" filename
```

Write a Java version of this program.

EXERCISE 14.24   **Challenge:** Write the following command-line program in Java. The program's name is `Copy` and its purpose is to copy one file into another. So its command line will be as follows:

```
java Copy filename1 filename2
```

Both `filename1` and `filename2` must exist or the program should throw a `FileNotFoundException`. Although `filename1` must be the name of a file (not a directory), `filename2` may be either a file or a directory. If `filename2` is a file, then the program should copy `filename1` to `filename2`. If `filename2` is a directory, then the program should simply copy `filename1` into `filename2`. That is, it should create a new file with the name `filename1` inside the `filename2` directory, copy the old file to the new file, and then delete the old file.

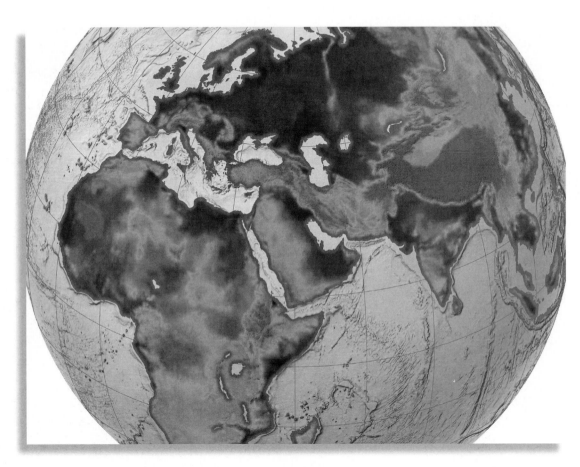

Photograph courtesy of Cartesla, PhotoDisc, Inc.

15

Sockets and Networking

OBJECTIVES

After studying this chapter, you will

- Understand some basic facts about networks.
- Know how to use Java's URL class to download network resources from an applet or application.
- Be able to design networking applications, using the client/server model.
- Understand how to use Java's Socket and ServerSocket classes.

OUTLINE

15.1   Introduction

Suppose you want to turn CyberPet into an Internet pet? For example, can we get it to retrieve stock quotes for us from an Internet stock quote server?

One of the key strengths of Java is the support it provides for the Internet and client/server programming. In the previous chapter, we saw how to make Java programs transfer information to and from external files. Although files are external to the programs that process them, they are still located on the same computer. In this chapter, we learn how to transfer information to and from files that reside on a network. This enables programs to communicate with programs running on other computers. With networking, we can communicate with computers anywhere in the world. With networking, we can "train" CyberPet to fetch our Internet newspaper for us!

15.2   An Overview of Networks

Networking is a broad and complex topic. In a typical computer science curriculum, it is covered in one or more upper-level courses. Nevertheless, in this chapter you can learn enough about networking to be able to use network resources and to design simple Java networking applications.

15.2.1   Network Size and Topology

Computer networks come in a variety of sizes and shapes. A *local area network (LAN)* is usually a privately owned network located within a single office or a single organization. Your campus network would be an example of a LAN. A *wide area network (WAN)* spans a wide geographical distance like a country or a continent. It may use a combination of public, private, and leased communication devices. Some of the large commercial networks, such as MCI and Sprint, are examples of WANs.

The computers that make up a network can be arranged in a variety of *topologies*, or shapes, some of the most common of which are shown in Figures 15–1 and 15–2. As you would expect, different topologies use different techniques for transmitting information from computer to computer.

Network topology

FIGURE 15–1   Star, bus, and ring topologies.

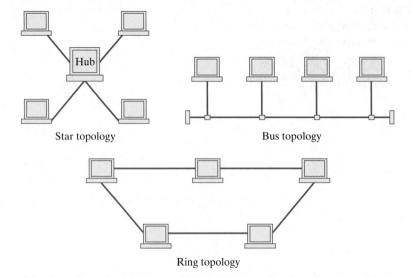

Star topology

Bus topology

Ring topology

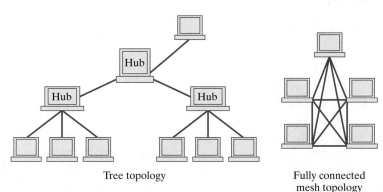

FIGURE 15–2 Tree and fully connected mesh topologies.

Tree topology

Fully connected
mesh topology

In a star network (Fig. 15–1), a central computer functions as a hub, with every other computer in the network connected to the hub. Each computer can communicate with the others but only through the hub. The bus topology doesn't have a hub computer. Instead, each node looks at each message sent on the bus to find those that are addressed to it. In sending a message, a node waits until the bus is free and then transmits the message.

A ring network (Fig. 15–1) also has no host, and the computers are connected in a loop, through which they exchange information. The tree topology (Fig. 15–2) is organized into a hierarchy, with each level (trunk of the tree, major branch of the tree) controlled by a hub. The fully connected mesh network directly connects all points to all points, eliminating the "middleman." Here there is no need to go through one or more other computers in order to communicate with a particular computer in the network.

Network topologies differ quite a bit in the expense of the wiring they require, their efficiency, their susceptibility to failure, and the types of protocols they use. These differences are beyond the scope of this chapter.

15.2.2 Internets

An **internet** (lowercase *i*) is a collection of two or more distinct networks, joined by devices called **routers** (Fig. 15–3). An internet is like a meeting of the United Nations. Each country sends a delegation, all of whose mem-

An internet vs. the Internet

FIGURE 15–3 An internet is a collection of distinct networks joined together by routers.

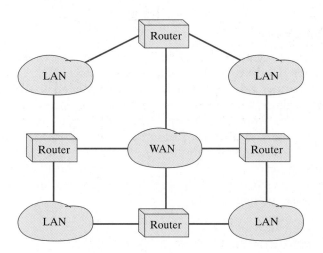

bers speak that country's language. A national delegation is like a single computer network. Language interpreters take on the task of translating one language to another so that any two delegations, say, the United States and China, can communicate. The routers play a similar translation role within an internet. The UN conference, composed of communicating delegations from all the different countries of the world, is like a worldwide internet.

The United Nations is an apt analogy for the **Internet** (uppercase *I*), which is an example of a particular worldwide internet. Internets, in the generic sense, shouldn't be confused with the Internet. It's quite likely that your campus LAN is itself composed of several, smaller networks, each of which uses its own "language."

SELF-STUDY EXERCISES

EXERCISE 15.1 In a network of ten computers, which topology would require the most cables?

EXERCISE 15.2 Which topology would be most resistant to having one of its computers crash?

EXERCISE 15.3 Which topology would be least resistant to having one of its computers crash?

15.2.3   Network Protocols

Network protocols

A **protocol** is a set of rules that governs the communication of information. For example, the **World Wide Web** is based on the **HyperText Transfer Protocol (HTTP)**. HTTP describes how information is to be exchanged between a Web browser, such as Internet Explorer or Netscape Navigator, and a Web server, which stores an individual's or company's Web pages. Web pages are encoded in the *HyperText Markup Language (HTML)*. Among other things, the HTTP protocol is able to interpret HTML pages.

Similarly, the *Simple Mail Transfer Protocol (SMTP)* is a set of rules that governs the transfer of *e-mail*. And the *File Transfer Protocol (FTP)* is the protocol that governs the transfer of files across the Internet.

Application Protocols

These three examples—HTTP, SMTP, and FTP—are examples of application protocols. They are relatively high-level protocols that support and govern a particular network application, such as e-mail or WWW access. Among the things they govern are how one addresses different computers on the network. For example, the HTTP protocol specifies Web addresses by using a **Uniform Resource Locator (URL)**. A URL specifies three necessary bits of information: the method used to transfer information (e.g., HTTP or FTP), the address of the host computer (e.g., www.prenhall.com), and the path describing where the file is located on the host (/morelli/index.html):

```
METHOD://HOST/PATH
HTTP://www.prenhall.com/morelli/index.html
```

Similarly, an e-mail address is specified by the SMTP protocol to consist of a local mailbox address (`George.W.Bush`) followed by the address of the computer (`mail.whitehouse.gov`):

```
LOCAL_MAILBOX@COMPUTER
George.W.Bush@mail.whitehouse.gov
```

Another good example of an application protocol is the Internet's *Domain Name System (DNS)*, which is the system that governs how names, such as `whitehouse.gov` and `troy.trincoll.edu`, can be translated into numeric addresses. In the DNS, each host computer on the Internet is identified with a unique host name—for example, `mail`, `troy`—which is usually made up by the network administrator whose job it is to manage an organization's network. The DNS divides the entire Internet into a hierarchy of *domains* and *subdomains*. The generic domains are names like `com`, `edu`, and `mil`, which refer to the type of organization— commercial, educational, and military, respectively. In addition to these there are country domains, such as `fr`, `au`, and `nz`, for France, Australia, and New Zealand. Finally, individuals and organizations can buy their own **domain names**, such as `whitehouse`, `microsoft`, and `trincoll`.

Internet domain names

What makes the whole system work is that certain computers within the network are designated as DNS servers. It is their role to translate names such as `troy.trincoll.edu` to numeric addresses whenever they are requested to do so by clients such as the SMTP or the HTTP server. Also, the DNS servers must communicate among themselves to make sure that their databases of names and addresses are up-to-date.

SELF-STUDY EXERCISE

EXERCISE 15.4   What's the URL of the Web server at Prentice Hall? Identify its component parts—host name, domain name, Internet domain.

15.2.4   Client/Server Applications

The HTTP, FTP, SMTP, and DNS protocols are examples of **client/server protocols**, and the applications they support are examples of client/server applications. In general, a client/server application is one in which the task at hand has been divided into two subtasks, one performed by the **client** and one performed by the **server** (Fig. 15–4).

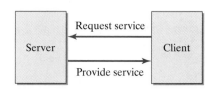

For example, in the HTTP case, the Web browser plays the role of a client by requesting a Web page from a Web (HTTP) server. A Web server is just a computer that runs HTTP software—a program that implements the HTTP protocol. For e-mail, the program you use to read your e-mail— Eudora, Pine, or Outlook—is an e-mail client. It requests certain services, such as send mail or get mail, from an e-mail (SMTP) server, which is simply a computer that runs SMTP software. In the FTP case, to transfer a program from one computer to another, you would use an FTP client, such as Fetch. Finally, in the DNS case, the DNS servers handle requests for name to address translations that come from HTTP, FTP, and SMTP servers, acting in this case like clients.

FIGURE 15–4   Client/server application.

E-mail client/server

So we can say that a client/server application is one that observes the following protocol:

```
Server: Set up a service on a particular host computer.
Client: Contact the server and request the service.
Server: Accept a request from a client and provide the service.
```

As these examples illustrate, many Internet applications are designed as client/server applications.

 EFFECTIVE DESIGN: Divide and Conquer. The client/server protocol is an example of the effective use of the divide-and-conquer strategy.

Application level: Provide services. (HTTP, SMTP, DNS)

Transport layer: Deliver packets; error recovery. (TCP, UDP)

Network layer: Move packets; provide internetworking. (IP)

Physical and data link layers: Transmit bits over a medium from one address to another. (ETHERNET)

FIGURE 15–5   Levels of network protocols.

Packet transfer

Disparate protocols

The Internet protocol

SELF-STUDY EXERCISE

EXERCISE 15.5   Lots of our everyday interactions fit into the client/server model. Suppose you are the client in the following services:
- Buying a piece of software at a bookstore.
- Buying a piece of software over the phone.
- Buying a piece of software over the Internet.
Identify the server and then describe the basic protocol.

15.2.5   Lower Level Network Protocols

Modern computer networks, such as the Internet, are organized into a number of levels of software and hardware. Each level has its own collection of protocols (Fig. 15–5).

The application level, which contains the HTTP, FTP, SMTP, and DNS protocols, is the highest level. Underlying the application-level protocols are various *transmission protocols,* such as the *Transfer Control Protocol (TCP)* and the *User Datagram Protocol (UDP).* These protocols govern the transfer of large blocks of information, or **packets**, between networked computers. All of the applications we mentioned—WWW, e-mail, and file transfer— involve data transmission and, therefore, rely on one or more of the transmission protocols.

At the very lowest end of this hierarchy of protocols are those that govern the transmission of bits or electronic pulses over wires and those that govern the delivery of data from node to node. Most of these protocols are built right into the hardware—the wires, connectors, transmission devices—that networks use. On top of these are protocols, such as the **ethernet protocol** and *token ring protocol*, that govern the delivery of packets of information on a local area network. These too may be built right into the network hardware.

As you might expect, these lower level protocols are vastly different from each other. An ethernet network cannot talk directly to a token ring network. How can we connect such disparate networks together? Think again of our United Nations analogy. How do we get French-speaking networks to communicate with English-speaking networks? The answer supplied by the Internet is to use the **Internetworking Protocol (IP)**, which governs the task of translating one network protocol to a common format (Fig. 15–6).

To push the UN analogy a bit further, the Internet's IP is like a universal language built into the routers that transmit data between disparate networks. On one end of a transmission, a router takes a French packet of information, received from one of the delegates in its network. The router

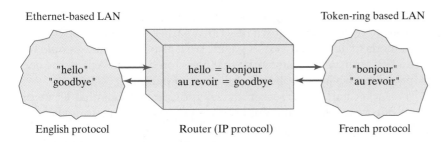

Ethernet-based LAN   Token-ring based LAN

English protocol   Router (IP protocol)   French protocol

FIGURE 15–6   Routers between individual networks use the IP protocol to translate one network protocol to another.

translates the French packet into an IP packet, which it then sends on through the network to its destination. When the IP packet gets close to its destination, another router takes it and translates it into an English packet before sending it on to its destination on its network.

15.2.6   The java.net **Package**

As we have seen, networks are glued together by a vast array of protocols. Most of these protocols are implemented in software that runs on general-purpose computers. You can install software on your personal computer to turn it into a Web server, an FTP server, or an e-mail server. Some of the lower level protocols are implemented in software that runs on special-purpose computers, the routers. Still other protocols, such as the ethernet protocol, are implemented directly in hardware.

Fortunately, we don't have to worry about the details of even the highest level protocols in order to write client/server applications in Java. The java.net (Fig. 15–7) package supplies a powerful and easy-to-use set of classes that supports network programming.

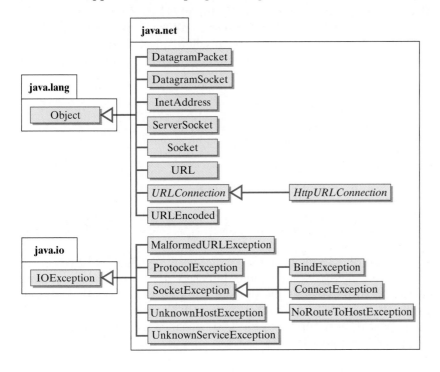

FIGURE 15–7   The java.net package.

java.net.*

The `java.net.URL` class provides a representation of the Internet's Uniform Resource Locator that we described earlier. We'll show how to use its methods to download WWW pages. We'll also look at an example that uses a URL and an input stream so that files stored on the Web can be used as input files to a Java applet or application program.

The `Socket` and `ServerSocket` classes provide methods that let us develop our own networking applications. They enable us to make a direct connection to an Internet host, and read and write data through `InputStreams` and `OutputStreams`. As we will see, this is no more difficult than reading and writing data to and from files. The `DatagramPacket` and `DatagramSocket` classes provide support for even lower level networking applications, based on Internet packets.

15.3   Using Network Resources from an Applet

Problem statement

Suppose you want to write an applet that will automatically display a slide show consisting of images or documents that you've prepared and stored on your Web site. Perhaps you can use such an applet to give people who visit your site a tour of your campus (Fig. 15–8). Or perhaps a company might use such an applet to advertise its products. In addition to making the slide show available through its main Web site, you can imagine it running continuously on a computer kiosk in the company's lobby.

FIGURE 15–8   An applet that continuously displays slides downloaded from the Web.

In order to solve this problem we have to be able to download and display Web resources. As you know, Web resources are multimedia. That is, they could be documents, images, sounds, video clips, and so on. All Web resources are specified in terms of their Uniform Resource Locators (URLs). Thus, to download an image (or an HTML file or audio clip), we usually type its URL into a Web browser. We want our program to know beforehand the URLs of the images it will display, so there won't be any need for inputting the URL. We want to implement something like the following algorithm:

Specifying Web resources

```
repeat forever
    Generate the URL for the next slide.
    Use the URL to download the image or document.
    Display the image or document.
```

A URL specification is just a `String`, such as,

```
http://starbase.trincoll.edu:80/~jjjava/slideshow/slide1.gif
```

which describes how to retrieve the resource. First, it specifies the protocol or method that should be used to download the resource (`http`). Next, it provides the domain name of the server that runs the protocol and the port number where the service is running (`starbase.trincoll.edu:80`). Next, the URL specifies the resource's file name (`~jjjava/slideshow/slide1.gif`).

GIVEN SUCH a URL specification, how can we download its associated resource? Are there Java classes that can help us solve this problem? Fortunately, there are. First, the `java.net.URL` class contains methods to help retrieve the resource associated with a particular URL (Fig. 15–9). The URL class represents a Uniform Resource Locator. The `URL()` constructor shown here (there are thers) takes a URL specification as a `String`, and assuming it specifies a valid URL, it creates a URL object. If the URL specification is invalid, a `MalformedURLException` is thrown. A URL might be invalid if the protocol were left off or if it is not a oknown protocol. The following simple code creates a URL for the home page of our companion Web site:

```
URL url;
try {
    url = new URL("http://www.prenhall.com:80/morelli/index.html");
} catch (MalformedURLException e) {
    System.out.println("Malformed URL: " + url.toString()) ;
}
```

Note how we catch the `MalformedURLException` when we create a new URL.

Once we have a valid URL instance, it can be used to download the data or object associated with it. There are different ways to do this. The `open-Connection()` method creates a `URLConnection`, which can then be used to download the resource. You would only use this method if your application required extensive control over the download process. A much simpler approach would use the `openStream()` method. This method will open an `InputStream`, which you can then use to read the associated URL data the same way you would read a file. This method is especially useful for writing Java applications (rather than applets). As you might guess, downloading Web resources is particularly easy from a Java applet. So let's search around for other methods that we can use.

Code Reuse: The `java.applet.Applet` Class

The `java.applet.Applet` class itself contains several useful methods for downloading and displaying Web resources. These methods are inherited by `javax.swing.JApplet`:

```
public class Applet extends Panel {
    public AppletContext getAppletContext();
    public AudioClip getAudioClip(URL url);
    public Image getImage(URL url);
    public void play(URL url);
    public void showStatus(String msg);
}
```

As you see, both the `getImage()` and `getAudioClip()` methods use a URL to download a resource. An `AudioClip` is a sound file encoded in AU format, a special type of encoding for sound files. The `getImage()` method can return files in either GIF or JPEG format, two popular image file formats. The `play()` method does the downloading and playing of an audio file in one easy step. For example, to download and play an audio clip within an applet requires just two lines of code:

From the Java Library

java.net.URL

 http://java.sun.com/products/jdk/1.3/docs/api/

URL
+ URL(in urlSpec : String) + openConnection() : URLConnection + openStream() : InputStream

FIGURE 15–9   The `java.net.URL` class.

URLs and streams

```
URL url;
try {
    url = new URL("http://starbase.trincoll.edu/~jjjava/slideshow/sound.au");
    play(url);
} catch (MalformedURLException e) {
    System.out.println("Malformed URL: " + url.toString()) ;
}
```

Similarly, to download (and store a reference to) an image is just as simple:

```
URL url;
try {
    url = new URL("http://starbase.trincoll.edu/~jjjava/slideshow/slide0.gif") ;
    imgRef = getImage(url);
} catch (MalformedURLException e) {
    System.out.println( "Malformed URL: " + url.toString()) ;
}
```

What methods can we use?

So, it looks as if we've found the methods we need to implement our slide show applet. We'll use the URL() constructor to create a URL from a String, and we'll use the Applet.getImage(URL) method to retrieve the images from the Web.

15.4   The Slide Show Applet
Problem Specification
Let's suppose our slide show will repeatedly display a set of images named "slide0.gif," "slide1.gif," and "slide2.gif." Suppose these images are stored on a Web site on starbase.trincoll.edu and are stored in a directory named /~jjjava/slideshow. This means our program will have to load the following three URLs:

```
http://starbase.trincoll.edu/~jjjava/slideshow/slide0.gif
http://starbase.trincoll.edu/~jjjava/slideshow/slide1.gif
http://starbase.trincoll.edu/~jjjava/slideshow/slide2.gif
```

We want our show to cycle endlessly through these images, leaving around 5 seconds between each slide.

User Interface Design
The user interface for this applet doesn't contain any GUI components. It just needs to display an image every 5 seconds. It can use a simple paint() method to display an image each time it is repainted:

```
public void paint(Graphics g) {
    if (currentImage != null)
        g.drawImage(currentImage, 10, 10, this);
}
```

The assumption here is that the currentImage instance variable will be set initially to null. Each time an image is downloaded, it will be set to refer to that image. Because paint() is called before the applet starts downloading the images, it is necessary to guard against attempting to draw a null image, which would lead to an exception.

Problem Decomposition

One problem we face with this applet is getting it to pause between each slide. One way to do this is to set up a loop that does nothing for around 5 seconds:

```
for (int k = 0; k < 1000000; k++ ) ;// Busy waiting
```

However, this isn't a very good solution. As we saw in Chapter 13, this is a form of **busy waiting** that monopolizes the CPU, making it very difficult to break out of the loop. Another problem with this loop is we don't really know how many iterations to do to approximate 5 seconds of idleness.

A much better design would be to use a separate timer thread, which can `sleep()` for 5 seconds between each slide. So our program will have two classes: one to download and display the slides and one to serve as a timer (Figs. 15–10 and 15–11).

- `SlideShowApplet`—This `JApplet` subclass will take care of downloading and displaying the images and starting the timer thread.
- `Timer`—This class will implement the `Runnable` interface so it can run as a separate thread. It will repeatedly sleep for 5 seconds and then tell the applet to display the next side.

> EFFECTIVE DESIGN: Busy Waiting.   Instead of busy waiting, a thread that sleeps for a brief period on each iteration is a better way to introduce a delay into an algorithm.

15.4.1   The `SlideShowApplet` class

What should we do with the images we download? Should we repeatedly download and display them, or should we just download them once and store them in memory? The second of these alternatives seems more efficient. If an image has already been downloaded, it would be wasteful to download it again.

> EFFECTIVE DESIGN: Network Traffic.   In general, a design that minimizes network traffic is preferable.

So we'll need an array to store the images. Our slide show will then consist of retrieving the next image from the array and displaying it. To help us with this task, let's use a `nextImg` variable as an array index to keep track of the next image. Even though it isn't absolutely necessary, we could use a third variable here, `currentImage`, to keep track of the current image to be displayed. Thus, our applet needs the following instance variables:

```
private static final int NIMGS = 3;
private Image[] slide = new Image[NIMGS];
private Image currentImage = null;
private int nextImg = 0;
```

Given these variables, let's now write a method to take care of choosing the next slide. Recall that the `paint()` method takes care of displaying currentImage, so all this method needs to do is to update both currentImage and nextImg. This method should be designed so that it can be called by

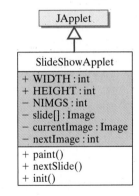

FIGURE 15–10   The `SlideShow-Applet` downloads and displays the images.

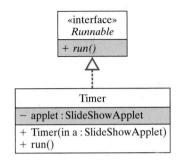

FIGURE 15–11   The `Timer` class delays the applet thread between each slide.

What data do we need?

Method design

the `Timer` thread whenever it is time to display the next slide. So it should be a `public` method. It can be a `void` method with no parameters, because the applet already contains all the information needed to display the next slide. Thus, there's no need for information to be passed back and forth between `Timer` and this method:

```java
public void nextSlide() {
    currentImage = slide[nextImg];
    nextImg = (nextImg + 1) % NIMGS;
    repaint();
}// nextSlide()
```

The method's algorithm is very simple. It sets `currentImage` to whatever `slide` is designated by `nextImg` and it then updates `nextImg`'s value. Note here the use of modular arithmetic to compute the value of `nextImg`. Given that `NIMGS` is 3, this algorithm will cause `nextImg` to take on the repeating sequence of values 0, 1, 2, 0, 1, 2, and so forth. Finally, the method calls `repaint()` to display the image.

PROGRAMMING TIP: Modular Arithmetic. Modular arithmetic (x % N) is useful for cycling repeatedly through the values 0, 1, ..., N-1, 0, 1,...,N-1.

The applet's `init()` method will have two tasks:

- Download and store the images in `slide[]`.
- Start the `Timer` thread.

As we discussed, downloading Web resources requires the use of the `getImage()` method. Here we just place these method calls in a loop:

```java
for (int k=0; k < NIMGS; k++)
    slide[k] = getImage(getCodeBase(), "gifs/demo" + k + ".gif");
```

Note here how we convert the loop variable *k* into a `String` and concatenate it right into the URL specification. This allows us to have URLs containing "slide0.gif," "slide1.gif," and "slide2.gif." This makes our program easily extensible should we later decide to add more slides to the show. Note also the use of the class constant `NIMGS` as the loop bound. This too adds to the program's extensibility.

PROGRAMMING TIP: Concatenation. Concatenating an integer value (k) with a string lets you create file names of the form `file1.gif`, `file2.gif`, and so on.

The task of starting the `Timer` thread involves creating an instance of the `Timer` class and calling its `start()` method:

```java
Thread timer = new Thread(new Timer(this));
timer.start();
```

Note that Timer is passed a reference to this applet. This enables Timer to call the applet's nextSlide() method every 5 seconds. This programming technique is known as *callback* and the nextSlide() method is an example of a **callback method** (Fig. 15–12).

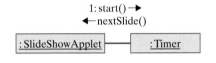

> PROGRAMMING TIP: Callback. Communication between two objects can often be handled using a callback technique. One object is passed a reference to the other object. The first object uses the reference to call one of the public methods of the other object.

FIGURE 15–12 Timer uses the nextSlide() method to *call back* the applet to remind it to switch to the next slide.

This completes our design and development of SlideShowApplet, which is shown in Figure 15–13.

```java
import java.awt.*;
import javax.swing.*;
import java.net.*;

public class SlideShowApplet extends JApplet  {
    public static final int WIDTH=300, HEIGHT=200;
    private static final int NIMGS = 3;
    private Image[] slide = new Image[NIMGS];
    private Image currentImage = null;
    private int nextImg = 0;

    public void paint(Graphics g) {
        g.setColor(getBackground());
        g.fillRect(0, 0, WIDTH, HEIGHT);
        if (currentImage != null)
            g.drawImage(currentImage, 10, 10, this);
    }//paint()

    public void nextSlide() {
        currentImage = slide[nextImg];
        nextImg = (nextImg + 1) % NIMGS;
        repaint();
    }// nextSlide()

    public void init() {
        for (int k=0; k < NIMGS; k++)
            slide[k] = getImage(getCodeBase(), "gifs/demo" + k + ".gif");

        Thread timer = new Thread(new Timer(this));
        timer.start();
        setSize( WIDTH, HEIGHT );
    }// init()
}// SlideShowApplet
```

FIGURE 15–13 The SlideShowApplet class.

15.4.2   The Timer Class

The timer thread

The Timer class is a subclass of Thread, which means it must implement the run() method. Recall that we never directly call a thread's run() method. Instead we call its start() method, which automatically calls run(). This particular thread has a very simple and singular function. It should call the SlideShowApplet.nextSlide() method and then sleep for 5 seconds. So its main algorithm will be

```
while (true) {
    applet.nextSlide();
    sleep( 5000 );
}
```

However, recall that Thread.sleep() throws the InterruptedException. This means that we'll have to embed this while loop in a try/catch block.

Note also that in order to call the applet's nextSlide() method, we need a reference to the SlideShowApplet, so we need to give it such a reference as an instance variable, as well as a constructor that allows the applet to pass Timer a reference to itself.

Given these design decisions, the complete implementation of Timer is shown in Figure 15–14. To see how it works, download it from the *Java, Java, Java* Web site and run it.

SELF-STUDY EXERCISE

EXERCISE 15.6 Describe the design changes you would make to SlideShowApplet if you wanted to play a soundtrack along with your slides. Assume that the sounds are stored in a sequence of files, "sound0.au," sound1.au," and so forth, on your Web site.

FIGURE 15–14   The Timer class.

```
public class Timer implements Runnable {
    private SlideShowApplet applet;

    public Timer( SlideShowApplet app ) {
        applet = app;
    }

    public void run() {
        try {
            while ( true ) {
                applet.nextSlide();
                Thread.sleep( 5000 );
            }
        } catch (InterruptedException e) {
            System.out.println(e.getMessage());
        }
    }// run()
}// Timer
```

15.5 Using Network Resources from an Application

The `SlideShowApplet` illustrates the ease of downloading Web resources from an applet. However, applets have limited use in this regard, because they come with rather severe security restrictions that would make them a poor choice for most networking applications (see Section 15.8). For example, applets cannot save files that they download, because they cannot access the host computer's file system. Similarly, an applet can only download files from the same host from which it was downloaded. This wouldn't be a problem for the slide show applet, since we can simply store the slides in the same directory as the applet itself. So, we want to learn how to download Web resources from a Java application. The next example illustrates a solution to this problem.

Applet restrictions

Problem Specification

Suppose a realtor asks you to write a Java application that will let its customers view pictures and descriptions of homes from its online database. The application should allow the customer to select a home and should then display both an image of the home and a text description of its features, such as square footage, asking price, and so on.

Problem statement

Suppose that the database of image and text files is kept at a fixed location on the Web, but the names of the files themselves may change. This will enable the company to change the database as it sells the homes. As input to this program the company will provide a text file that contains the names of the files for the current selection of homes. To simplify matters, both image and text files have the same name but different extensions—for example, `ranch.txt` and `ranch.gif`. The data file will store just the names of the files, one per line, giving it the following format:

```
beautifulCape
handsomeRanch
lovelyColonial
```

15.5.1 Downloading a Text File from the Web

This application requires us to solve three new problems:

1. How do we download a text file of names and use them as menu items?
2. How do we download a text file and display it in a `JTextArea`?
3. How do we download and display an image file?

The third problem is very similar to the problem we solved in `SlideShowApplet`, but here we can't use the `Applet.getImage()` method. However, as we shall see, we can find a Java library method to perform this task for us.

Therefore, the most challenging part of this program is the task of downloading a Web file and using its data in the program. For this program we must make use of two types of data downloaded from the Web. The first will be the names of the image and document files. We'll want to read these names and use them as menu items that the user can select. Second, once the user has selected a house to view, we must download and display an image and a text description of the house. Downloading

Understanding the problem

the text is basically the same as downloading the file of names. The only difference is that we need to display this text in a JTextArea. Downloading the image file can be handled in more or less the same way that it was handled in the SlideShowApplet— by using a special Java method to download and display the image file.

Clearly the problems of downloading a file from the Web and reading a file from the disk are quite similar. Recall that for reading disk files, we used *streams* to handle the I/O operations. The various InputStream and OutputStream classes contained the read() and write() methods needed for I/O. The situation is exactly the same for downloading Web files.

Recall that the URL class contains the openStream() method, which opens an InputStream to the resource associated with the URL. Once the stream has been opened, you can read data from the stream just as if it were coming from a file. The program doesn't care whether the data are coming from a file on the Internet or a file on the disk. It just reads data from the stream. So, to download a data file from the Internet, regardless of whether it's a text file, image file, audio file, or whatever, you would use the following general algorithm:

File download algorithm

```
URL url;
InputStream data;
try {
    url = new URL(fileURL);              // Create a URL
    data = url.openStream();             // Open a stream to the URL
  // READ THE FILE INTO MEMORY          // Read the data
    data.close();                        // Close the stream
} catch (MalformedURLException e) {      // May be thrown by URL()
    System.out.println(e.getMessage());
} catch( IOException e ) {       // May be thrown by read or close
    System.out.println(e.getMessage());
}
```

The algorithm consists of four basic steps:

- Create a URL instance.
- Open an InputStream to it.
- Read the data.
- Close the stream.

Step 3 of this algorithm—read the data—involves many lines of code and has, therefore, been left as a subtask suitable for encapsulation within a method.

Reading the Data

Text or binary data?

As we saw in the previous chapter, the algorithm for step 3 will depend on the file's data. If it's a text file, we would like to read one line at a time, storing the input in a String. If it's an image or an audio file, we would read one byte at a time.

What library methods can we use?

Because our data are contained in a text file, we want to read one line at a time. The BufferedReader class contains a readLine() method that returns either a String storing the line or the value null when it reaches the end of file. The following method shows how you would read a text file into the program's JTextArea, which is named display:

```
private void readTextIntoDisplay(URL url) throws IOException {
    BufferedReader data
        = new BufferedReader(new InputStreamReader(url.openStream()));

    display.setText("");              // Reset the text area
    String line = data.readLine();
    while (line != null)  {           // Read each line
        display.append(line + "\n");  // And add it to the display
        line = data.readLine();
    }
    data.close();
}// readTextIntoDisplay()
```

The method is passed the file's URL and it uses the URL.openStream()
method to open the input stream. Note that the method throws
IOException, which means that any I/O exceptions that get raised will be
handled by the calling method.

I/O exceptions

In this example, the input algorithm reads each line of the file and adds
it to the display. For our real estate application, the same basic algorithm
can be used to read the names of the data files and store them in a menu
that can be used to make selections. For example, if we use a JComboBox
menu named homeChoice, we would simply add each line to it:

```
String line = data.readLine();
while (line != null) {
    homeChoice.addItem(line);
    line = data.readLine();
}
```

15.5.2   Code Reuse: The java.awt.Toolkit Class

How do we read and display an image file? Recall that in the SlideShow-
Applet we were able to find the Applet.getImage() method to retrieve an
image from the Web. Is there a similar method that we could use for applications? Fortunately, there is. It's located in the java.awt.Toolkit class
(Fig. 15–15).

The Toolkit class implements various platform-dependent methods
to support the Java GUI Components. The getDefaultToolkit() method is
used to retrieve the toolkit that's being used by a particular platform. To
use a Toolkit method, you must first retrieve the default kit and then use it
as reference to the method you wish to use. For example, to use the beep()
method, which causes an audible beep to be emitted, you would type,

Toolkit
+ getDefaultToolkit() : Toolkit
+ beep()
+ getImage(in filename : String) : Image
+ getImage(in url : URL) : Image

FIGURE 15–15   The java.awt.-
Toolkit class contains useful
methods for downloading sounds
and images.

```
Toolkit.getDefaultToolkit().beep();
```

The beep() method might be useful as an alternative to a printed error
message when the user mistypes something during input.

The getImage(String) and getImage(URL) method inputs an image from
a disk file and from a URL, respectively. The use of Toolkit.getImage()
will greatly simplify the task of downloading and displaying an image.
Without it, we could easily manage downloading the image file, but how
would we convert it into an Image object that could be used by the program? With this method, our task is simplified to

```
Image currentImage = Toolkit.getDefaultToolkit().getImage(url);
```

FIGURE 15–16 User interface design for the real estate application.

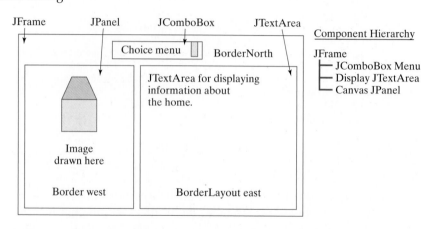

15.5.3 The RealEstateViewer Application

Now that we have figured out how to download and use Web resources in an application, let's design our RealEstateViewer application.

Interface Design

The interface for this application is very important. It should provide some means to display a text file and an image. The text file can be displayed in a JTextArea, and the image can be drawn on a JPanel.

In terms of the controls, the customer should be allowed to select a home to view from a menu of options. Because the program will have the list of available homes, it can provide the options in a JComboBox pull-down menu.

In terms of an appropriate layout, we want to make sure that the controls, the image, and JTextArea all have their own region of the application's window. This suggests a BorderLayout, which is the default layout for a JFrame. We can put the JComboBox menu at the "North" border, and the image and text on the "West" and "East" borders, respectively. Figure 15–16 summarizes these various design decisions.

Problem Decomposition: RealEstateViewer

The task of downloading and displaying information from the Internet is best handled by two separate classes: one to perform the downloading and user interface tasks and the other to take care of displaying the image.

The task of downloading the image and text files from the Web can be handled by the program's main class, the RealEstateViewer, which will also handle the user interface (Fig. 15–17). As the application's top-level window, RealEstateViewer will be a subclass of JFrame. Because its controls will include a JComboBox, it must implement the itemStateChanged() method of the ItemListener interface.

What components and other instance variables will we need for this class? According to our interface design, it will need a JComboBox, a JTextArea, and the ImagePanel. Because it will be downloading images, it will need an Image variable.

In terms of constants used by this application, the URL string for the data file should be defined as a constant. Also, because all the images and data files will start with the same prefix,

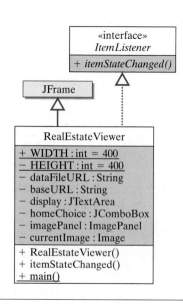

FIGURE 15–17 The RealEstate-Viewer class defines the user interface.

What classes do we need?

What data do we need?

```java
import java.awt.*;
import java.awt.event.*;
import java.net.*;
import java.io.*;
import javax.swing.*;

public class RealEstateViewer extends JFrame implements ItemListener {
    public static final int WIDTH=400,HEIGHT=200;
    private final String dataFileURL = "http://troy.trincoll.edu/~jjjava/homes/homes.txt";
    private final String baseURL = "http://troy.trincoll.edu/~jjjava/homes/";
    private JTextArea display = new JTextArea(20,20);
    private JComboBox homeChoice = new JComboBox();
    private ImagePanel imagePanel = new ImagePanel(this);
    public Image currentImage = null;

    public RealEstateViewer () {}                        // Constructor
    public void itemStateChanged( ItemEvent evt ) { }   // ItemListener

    public static void main(String args[]) {
        RealEstateViewer viewer = new RealEstateViewer();
        viewer.setSize(viewer.WIDTH,viewer.HEIGHT);
        viewer.setVisible(true);
        viewer.addWindowListener(new WindowAdapter() {  // Quit the application
            public void windowClosing(WindowEvent e) {
                System.exit(0);
            }
        });
    }// main()
}// RealEstateViewer
```

FIGURE 15–18   The `RealEstateViewer`, Version 1.

```
http://troy.trincoll.edu/~jjjava/homes/
```

we should make this a constant in the program. These preliminary decisions lead to the initial version of `RealEstateViewer` shown in Figure 15–18. Note that the `main()` method merely creates an instance of the application and shows it. Note also that the `currentImage` variable is declared `public`. This will let the `ImagePanel` have direct access to `currentImage` whenever it needs to display a new image.

The `ImagePanel` Class

We'll use a second class, the `ImagePanel`, to handle the displaying of the image (Figs. 15–19 and 15–20). The reason we use a separate class for this task is that we want the image to appear in its own panel (which appears on the West border of the main window). Besides its constructor, the only method needed in this class is the `paintComponent()` method. This method will be called automatically whenever the main window is repainted. Its task is simply to get the current image from its parent frame and display it. Note that a reference to the parent frame is passed to the object in its constructor.

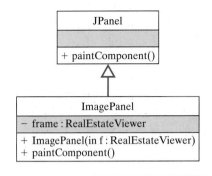

FIGURE 15–19   An overview of the `ImagePanel` class.

FIGURE 15–20   The `ImagePanel` class.

```
import javax.swing.*;
import java.awt.*;

public class ImagePanel extends JPanel {

    private RealEstateViewer frame;

    public ImagePanel(RealEstateViewer parent) {
        frame = parent;
    }

    public void paintComponent(Graphics g) {
        if (frame.currentImage != null)
            g.drawImage(frame.currentImage, 0, 0, this);
    }
}// ImagePanel
```

Method Decomposition

The stub methods listed in the initial version of `RealEstateViewer` (Fig. 15–18) outline the main tasks required by the application. Some of these methods are very simple and even trivial to implement. Others should be broken up into subtasks.

The constructor method should be responsible for creating the user interface, most of which will involve the routine tasks of registering a listener for the `homeChoice` menu and setting up an appropriate layout that implements the design we developed for the user interface:

```
public RealEstateViewer () {
    super("Home Viewer Application");    // Set the window title
    homeChoice.addItemListener( this);
    this.getContentPane().add("North",homeChoice);
    this.getContentPane().add("East",display);
    this.getContentPane().add("Center",imagePanel);
    display.setLineWrap(true);
    initHomeChoices();                   // Set up the choice box
    showCurrentSelection();              // Display the current home
}
```

Note the last two statements of the method. The first sets up the `JComboBox` by reading its contents from a file stored in the company's database. Because that task will require several statements, we define it as a separate method, `initHomeChoices()`, and defer its development for now. Similarly, the task of displaying the current menu choice has been organized into the `showCurrentSelection()` method, whose development we also defer for now.

ItemListener

The `itemStateChanged()` method is called automatically when the user selects a home from the `JComboBox` menu. Its task is to download and display information about the current menu selection. So it can simply call the `showCurrentSelection()` method:

```
public void itemStateChanged(ItemEvent evt) {
    showCurrentSelection();
}
```

Downloading the Menu Items

Recall that according to our specification, the real estate firm stores its current listing of homes in a text file, one home per line. The initHome-Choices() method downloads the text and uses its contents to set up the items in the homeChoice JComboBox menu:

```java
private void initHomeChoices() {
    try {
        URL url = new URL(dataFileURL);
        BufferedReader data = new BufferedReader(
                         new InputStreamReader(url.openStream()));
        String line = data.readLine();
        while (line != null) {
            homeChoice.addItem(line);
            line = data.readLine();
        }
        data.close();
    } catch (MalformedURLException e) {
        System.out.println( "ERROR: " + e.getMessage()) ;
    } catch (IOException e) {
        System.out.println( "ERROR: " + e.getMessage()) ;
    }
}// initHomeChoices()
```

It uses the algorithm we developed earlier for downloading a text file. Each line of the text file represents a menu item, so, as each line is read, readLine(data), it is added to the JComboBox menu.

Downloading and Displaying Home Information

The showCurrentSelection() method is responsible for downloading and displaying images and text files whenever the user selects a home to view. Recall that our specification called for using the name of the menu item as a basis for constructing the name of its corresponding text file and image file. Therefore, the basic algorithm we need is

- Get the user's home choice.
- Create a URL for the associated text file.
- Download and display the associated text file.
- Create a URL for the associated GIF file.
- Download and display the image.

Because downloading a text document requires stream processing, we should handle that in a separate method. The task of downloading an image file is also a good candidate for a separate method. Both of these methods will use a URL, so we can leave that task up to showCurrent-Selection() itself. The showCurrentSelection() method will create the URLs and then invoke the appropriate methods to download and display the resources:

Method decomposition

```java
private void showCurrentSelection() {// throws IOException {
    URL url = null;
                              // Get user's choice
    String choice = homeChoice.getSelectedItem().toString();
    try {                              (continues on next page)
```

FIGURE 15–21 The RealEstate-Viewer program downloads images and documents over the Web.

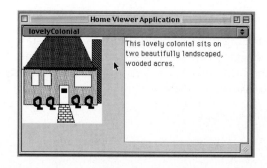

```
            url = new URL(baseURL + choice + ".txt") ;// Create url
                                    // Download and display text file
            readTextIntoDisplay(url);
            url = new URL(baseURL + choice + ".gif"); // Create url
                                    // Download image
            currentImage = Toolkit.getDefaultToolkit().getImage(url);
            Toolkit.getDefaultToolkit().beep();         // Alert the user
            repaint();
        } catch (MalformedURLException e) {
            System.out.println( "ERROR: " + e.getMessage()) ;
        } catch (IOException e) {
            System.out.println("ERROR: " + e.getMessage()) ;
        }
    } // showCurrentSelection()
```

Note that we have also elected to handle both the MalformedURLException and IOException in this method. The advantage of this design is that it separates exception handling from the normal algorithm and organizes it into one method. Finally, note how string concatenation is used to build the URL specifications, each of which consists of three parts: the baseURL, the user's choice, and the file extension.

The task of reading the text file and displaying its contents has been encapsulated into the readTextIntoDisplay() method. This private utility method performs a standard file-reading algorithm using the read-Line() method that we developed earlier. Figure 15–21 provides a view of the program's appearance as it is displaying information to a user. Figure 15–22 provides the complete implementation of this program.

15.5.4   Reusing Code

As in other examples we have developed, our discovery and use of the Toolkit.getImage() method and other classes from the Java class library illustrate an important principle of object-oriented programming.

EFFECTIVE DESIGN: Code Reuse.   Before writing code to perform a particular task, search the available libraries to see if there is already code that performs that task.

An important step in designing object-oriented programs is making appropriate use of existing classes and methods. In some cases, you want to directly instantiate a class and use its methods to perform the desired

```java
import java.awt.*;
import java.awt.event.*;
import java.net.*;
import java.io.*;
import javax.swing.*;

public class RealEstateViewer extends JFrame implements ItemListener {
    public static final int WIDTH=400,HEIGHT=200;
    private final String dataFileURL = "http://troy.trincoll.edu/~jjjava/homes/homes.txt";
    private final String baseURL = "http://troy.trincoll.edu/~jjjava/homes/";
    private JTextArea display = new JTextArea(20,20);
    private JComboBox homeChoice = new JComboBox();
    private ImagePanel imagePanel = new ImagePanel(this);
    public Image currentImage = null;

    public RealEstateViewer () {
        super("Home Viewer Application");       // Set the window title
        homeChoice.addItemListener( this);
        this.getContentPane().add("North",homeChoice);
        this.getContentPane().add("East",display);
        this.getContentPane().add("Center",imagePanel);
        display.setLineWrap(true);
        initHomeChoices();                      // Set up the choice box
        showCurrentSelection();                 // Display the current home
    }

    private void initHomeChoices() {
        try {
            URL url = new URL(dataFileURL);
            BufferedReader data = new BufferedReader(new InputStreamReader(url.openStream()));
            String line = data.readLine();
            while (line != null) {
                homeChoice.addItem(line);
                line = data.readLine();
            } data.close();
        } catch (MalformedURLException e) {
            System.out.println( "ERROR: " + e.getMessage()) ;
        } catch (IOException e) {
            System.out.println( "ERROR: " + e.getMessage()) ;
        }
    }// initHomeChoices()
```

FIGURE 15–22   The RealEstateViewer class, Part I.

```java
    private void readTextIntoDisplay(URL url) throws IOException {
        BufferedReader data
            = new BufferedReader(new InputStreamReader(url.openStream()));

        display.setText("");                    // Reset the text area
        String line = data.readLine();
        while (line != null)  {                 // Read each line
            display.append(line + "\n");        // And add it to the display
            line = data.readLine();
        } data.close();
    }// readTextIntoDisplay()

    private void showCurrentSelection() {// throws IOException {
        URL url = null;
        String choice = homeChoice.getSelectedItem().toString();      // Get user's choice
        try {
            url = new URL(baseURL + choice + ".txt") ;                // Create URL
            readTextIntoDisplay(url);                                 // Download and display text file
            url = new URL(baseURL + choice + ".gif");                 // Create URL
            currentImage = Toolkit.getDefaultToolkit().getImage(url);// Download image
            Toolkit.getDefaultToolkit().beep();                       // Alert the user
            repaint();
        } catch (MalformedURLException e) {
            System.out.println( "ERROR: " + e.getMessage()) ;
        } catch (IOException e) {
            System.out.println("ERROR: " + e.getMessage()) ;
        }
    }// showCurrentSelection()

    public void itemStateChanged(ItemEvent evt) {
        showCurrentSelection();
    }

    public static void main(String args[]) {
        RealEstateViewer viewer = new RealEstateViewer();
        viewer.setSize(viewer.WIDTH,viewer.HEIGHT);
        viewer.setVisible(true);
        viewer.addWindowListener(new WindowAdapter() {        // Quit the application
            public void windowClosing(WindowEvent e) {
                System.exit(0);
            }
        });
    }// main()
}// RealEstateViewer
```

FIGURE 15–22   *(continued)* `RealEstateViewer`, Part II.

tasks. In other cases, it is necessary to create a subclass (inheritance) or implement an interface (inheritance) in order to gain access to the methods you need.

Of course, knowing what classes exist in the libraries is something that comes with experience. There's no way that a novice Java programmer would know about, say, the `Toolkit.getImage()` method. However, one skill or habit of mind that you should try to develop is always to ask yourself the question: "Is there a method that will do what I'm trying to do here?" That question should be the first question on your search through the libraries and reference books.

```
http://java.sun.com/products/jdk/1.3/docs/api/
```

15.6   Client/Server Communication via Sockets

As we said earlier, many networking applications are based on the client/server model. According to this model, a task is viewed as a service that can be requested by clients and handled by servers. In this section, we develop a simple client/server framework based on a socket connection between the client and the server.

A **socket** is a simple communication channel through which two programs communicate over a network. A socket supports two-way communication between a client and a server, using a well-established protocol. The protocol simply prescribes rules and behavior that both the server and client must follow in order to establish two-way communication.

According to this protocol, a server program creates a socket at a certain port and waits until a client requests a connection. A **port** is a particular address or entry point on the host computer, which typically has hundreds of potential ports. It is usually represented as a simple integer value. For example, the standard port for an HTTP (Web) server is 80. Once the connection is established, the server creates input and output streams to the socket and begins sending messages to and receiving messages from the client. Either the client or the server can close the connection, but it's usually done by the client.

Sockets and ports

> DEBUGGING TIP: Reserved Port Numbers. Port numbers below 1024 are reserved for system use and should not be used by an application program.

To help clarify this protocol, think of some service performed by a human using a telephone connection. The "server" waits for the phone to ring. When it rings, the server picks it up and begins communicating with the client. A socket, combined together with input and output streams, is something like a two-way phone connection.

Client/server protocol

From the client's side, the protocol goes as follows. The client creates a socket and attempts to make a connection to the server. The client has to know the server's URL and the port at which the service exists. Once a connection has been established, the client creates input and output streams to the socket and begins exchanging messages with the server. The client can close the connection when the service is completed.

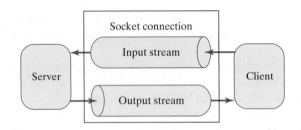

Think again of the telephone analogy. A human client picks up the
phone and dials the number of a particular service. This is analogous to
the client program creating a socket and making a connection to a server.
Once the service agent answers the phone, two-way communication between the client and the server can begin.

Figure 15–23 provides a view of the client/server connection. Note that
a socket has two channels. Once a connection has been established between a client and a server, a single two-way channel exists between them.
The client's output stream is connected to the server's input stream. The
server's output stream is connected to the client's input stream.

Sockets and channels

PROGRAMMING TIP: Socket Streams.   Each socket has two streams, one
for input and one for output.

15.6.1 The Server Protocol

Let's now see how a client/server application would be coded in Java. The
template in Figure 15–24 shows the code that is necessary on the server
side. The first step the server takes is to create a `ServerSocket`. The first
argument to the `ServerSocket()` method is the port at which the service
will reside. The second argument specifies the number of clients that can
be backlogged, waiting on the server, before a client will be refused service. If more than one client at a time should request service, Java would
establish and manage a waiting list, turning away clients when the list is
full.

Waiting for client requests

The next step is to wait for a client request. The `accept()` method will
block until a connection is established. The Java system is responsible for
waking the server up when a client request is received.

FIGURE 15–24   Template for the
server protocol.

```
Socket socket;          // Reference to the socket
ServerSocket port;      // The port where the server will listen
try {
    port = new ServerSocket(10001, 5); // Create a port
    socket = port.accept();            // Wait for the client to call

// Communicate with the client

    socket.close();
} catch (IOException e) {
    e.printStackTrace();
}
```

Once a connection is established, the server can begin communicating with the client. As we have suggested, a socket connection is like a two-way telephone conversation. Both the client and server can "talk" back and forth to each other. The details of this step are not shown here. As we will see, the two-way conversation is managed by connecting both an input and an output stream to the socket.

Once the conversation between client and server is finished—once the server has delivered the requested service—the server can close the connection by calling close(). Thus, there are four steps involved on the server side:

- Create a ServerSocket and establish a port number.
- Listen for and accept a connection from a client.
- Converse with the client.
- Close the socket.

What distinguishes the server from the client is that the server establishes the port and accepts the connection.

15.6.2   The Client Protocol

The client protocol (Fig. 15–25) is just as easy to implement. Indeed, on the client side there are three steps involved. The first step is to request a connection to the server. This is done in the Socket() constructor by supplying the server's URL and port number. Once the connection is established, the client can carry out two-way communication with the server. This step is not shown here. Finally, when the client is finished, it can simply close() the connection. Thus, from the client side, the protocol involves just three steps:

Initiating a request

- Open a socket connection to the server, given its address.
- Converse with the server.
- Close the connection.

What distinguishes the client from the server is that the client initiates the two-way connection by requesting the service.

```
Socket connection;        // Reference to the socket
try {                     // Request a connection
    connection = new Socket("troy.cs.trincoll.edu", 10001);

    // Carry on a two-way communication

    connection.close();   // Close the socket
} catch (IOException e ) {
    e.printStackTrace();
}
```

FIGURE 15–25 Template for the client protocol.

15.6.3   A Two-Way Stream Connection

Now that we have seen how to establish a socket connection between a client and server, let's look at the actual two-way communication that takes place. Because this part of the process will be exactly the same

Output routine

for both client and server, we develop a single set of methods, write-ToSocket() and readFromSocket(), that may be called by either.

The writeToSocket() method takes two parameters, the Socket and a String, which will be sent to the process on the other end of the socket:

```
protected void writeToSocket(Socket sock, String str) throws IOException {
    oStream = sock.getOutputStream();
    for (int k = 0; k < str.length(); k++)
        oStream.write(str.charAt(k));
}// writeToSocke()
```

If writeToSocket() is called by the server, then the string will be sent to the client. If it is called by the client, the string will be sent to the server.

Protected methods

The method is declared protected because we will define it in a super-class so that it can be inherited and used by both the client and server classes. Note also that the method declares that it throws an IOException. Because there's no way to fix an IOException, we'll just let this exception be handled elsewhere, rather than handling it within the method.

In order to write to a socket we need only get the socket's OutputStream and then write to it. For this example, oStream is an instance variable of the client/server superclass. We use the Socket.getOutputStream() method to get a reference to the socket's output stream. Note that we are not creating a new output stream here. We are just getting a reference to an existing stream, which was created when the socket connection was accepted. Note also that we do not close the output stream before exiting the method. This is important. If you close the stream, you will lose the ability to communicate through the socket.

JAVA LANGUAGE RULE   Socket Streams. When a socket is created, it automatically creates its own streams. To use one you just need to get a reference to it.

DEBUGGING TIP: Socket Streams. After writing to or reading from a socket I/O stream, do not close the stream. That would make the socket unusable for subsequent I/O.

Given the reference to the socket's output stream, we simply write each character of the string using the OutputStream.write() method. This method writes a single byte. Therefore, the input stream, on the other side of the socket, must read bytes and convert them back into characters.

EFFECTIVE DESIGN: Designing a Protocol.   In designing two-way communication between a client and a server, you are designing a protocol that each side must use. Failure to design and implement a clear protocol will cause the communication to break down.

Input routine

The readFromSocket() method takes a Socket parameter and returns a String:

```
protected String readFromSocket(Socket sock) throws IOException {
    iStream = sock.getInputStream();
    String str="";
    char c;
    while ( ( c = (char) iStream.read() ) != '\n')
        str = str + c + "";
    return str;
}
```

It uses the `Socket.getInputStream()` method to obtain a reference to the socket's input stream, which has already been created. So here again it is important that you don't close the stream in this method. A socket's input and output streams will be closed automatically when the socket connection itself is closed.

The `InputStream.read()` method reads a single byte at a time from the input stream until an end-of-line character is received. For this particular application, the client and server will both read and write one line of characters at a time. Note the use of the cast operator (`char`) in the `read()` statement. Because `byte`s are being read, they must be converted to `char` before they can be compared to the end-of-line character or concatenated to the `String`. When the read loop encounters an end-of-line character, it terminates and returns the `String` that was input.

> **DEBUGGING TIP: Bytes and Chars.** It is a syntax error to compare a byte and a char. One must be converted to the other using an explicit cast operator.

15.7 CASE STUDY: Generic Client/Server Classes

Suppose your boss asks you to set up generic client/server classes that can be used to implement a number of related client/server applications. One application that the company has in mind is a query service, in which *Problem statement* the client would send a query string to the server, and the server would interpret the string and return a string that provides the answer. For example, the client might send the query "Hours of service," and the client would respond with the company's business hours.

Another application the company wants will have the client fill out an order form and transmit it as a string to the server. The server will interpret the order, fill it, and return a receipt, including instructions as to when the customer will receive the order.

All of the applications to be supported by this generic client/server will communicate via strings, so something very much like the `readFromSocket()` and `writeToSocket()` methods can be used for their communication. Of course, you want to design classes so they can be easily extended to support byte-oriented, two-way communications, should that type of service become needed.

In order to test the generic models, we will subclass them to create a simple echo service. This service will echo back to the client any message *The echo service* that the server receives. For example, we'll have the client accept keyboard input from the user and then send the user's input to the server and simply report what the server returns. The following shows the output generated by a typical client session:

```
CLIENT: connected to 'troy.cs.trincoll.edu'
SERVER: Hello, how may I help you?
CLIENT: type a line or 'goodbye' to quit
INPUT: hello
SERVER: You said 'hello'
INPUT: this is fun
SERVER: You said 'this is fun'
INPUT: java java java
SERVER: You said 'java java java'
INPUT: goodbye
SERVER: Goodbye
CLIENT: connection closed
```

On the server side, the client's message will be read from the input stream and then simply echoed back (with some additional characters attached) through the output stream. The server doesn't display a trace of its activity other than to report when connections are established and closed. We will code the server in an infinite loop so that it will accept connections from a (potentially) endless stream of clients. In fact, most servers are coded in this way. They are designed to run forever and must be restarted whenever the host that they are running needs to be rebooted. The output from a typical server session is as follows:

```
Echo server at troy.cs.trincoll.edu/157.252.16.21 waiting for connections
Accepted a connection from troy.cs.trincoll.edu/157.252.16.21
Closed the connection

Accepted a connection from troy.cs.trincoll.edu/157.252.16.21
Closed the connection
```

EFFECTIVE DESIGN: Infinite Loop.   A server is an application that's designed to run in an infinite loop. The loop should be exited only when some kind of exception occurs.

15.7.1   Object-Oriented Design

A suitable solution for this project will make extensive use of object-oriented design principles. We want Server and Client classes that can easily be subclassed to support a wide variety of services. The solution should make appropriate use of *inheritance* and *polymorphism* in its design. Perhaps the best way to develop our generic class is first to design the echo service, as a typical example, and then generalize it.

The Threaded Root Subclass: ClientServer

One lesson we can draw at the outset is that both clients and servers use basically the same socket I/O methods. Thus, as we've seen, the readFromSocket() and writeToSocket() methods could be used by both clients and servers. Because we want all clients and servers to inherit these methods, they must be placed in a common superclass. Let's name this the ClientServer class.

Where should we place this class in the Java hierarchy? Should it be a direct subclass of Object, or should it extend some other class that would give it appropriate functionality? One feature that would make our clients and servers more useful is if they were independent threads. That way they could be instantiated as part of another object and given the subtask of communicating on behalf of that object. For example, if we give our CyberPet a Client object, the CyberPet could use it to communicate with a server.

Therefore, let's define the ClientServer class as a subclass of Thread (Fig. 15–26). Recall from Chapter 13 that the typical way to derive functionality from a Thread subclass is to override the run() method. The run() method will be a good place to implement the client and server protocols. Because they are different, we'll define run() in both the Client and Server subclasses.

For now, the only methods contained in ClientServer (Fig. 15–27) are the two I/O methods we designed. The only modification we have made to the methods occurs in the writeToSocket() method, where we have added code to make sure that any strings written to the socket are terminated with an end-of-line character.

This is an important enhancement, because the read loop in the readFromSocket() method expects to receive an end-of-line character. Rather than rely on those who implement specific clients to guarantee that their strings end with \n, our design takes care of this problem for them. This

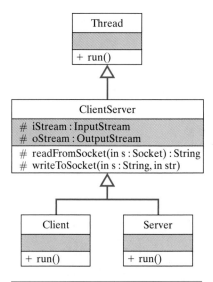

FIGURE 15–26   Overall design of a client/server application.

```java
import java.io.*;
import java.net.*;

public class ClientServer extends Thread {

    protected InputStream iStream;          // Instance variables
    protected OutputStream oStream;

    protected String readFromSocket(Socket sock) throws IOException {
        iStream = sock.getInputStream();
        String str="";
        char c;
        while (  ( c = (char) iStream.read() ) != '\n')
            str = str + c + "";
            return str;
    }

    protected void writeToSocket(Socket sock, String str) throws IOException {
        oStream = sock.getOutputStream();
        if (str.charAt( str.length() - 1 ) != '\n')
            str = str + '\n';
        for (int k = 0; k < str.length() ; k++)
            oStream.write(str.charAt(k));
    }// writeToSocket()
}// ClientServer
```

FIGURE 15–27   The ClientServer class serves as the superclass for client/server applications.

ensures that every communication that takes place between one of our clients and servers will be line oriented.

> EFFECTIVE DESIGN: Defensive Design. Code that performs I/O, whether it be across the network or otherwise, should be designed to anticipate and remedy common errors. This will lead to more robust programs.

15.7.2 The EchoServer Class

Let's now develop a design for the echo server. This class will be a subclass of ClientServer (Fig. 15–28). As we saw in discussing the server protocol, one task that echo server will do is create a ServerSocket and establish a port number for its service. Then it will wait for a Socket connection, and once a connection is accepted, it will then communicate with the client. This suggests that our server needs at least two instance variables. It also suggests that the task of creating a ServerSocket would be an appropriate action for its constructor method. This leads to the following initial definition:

What data do we need?

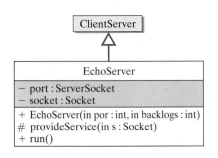

FIGURE 15–28 Design of the EchoServer class.

```
import java.net.*;
import java.io.*;

public class EchoServer extends ClientServer {

    private ServerSocket port;
    private Socket socket;

    public EchoServer(int portNum, int nBacklog)  {
        try {
            port = new ServerSocket (portNum, nBacklog);
        } catch (IOException e) {
            e.printStackTrace();
        }
    }

    public void run() { }  // Stub method
}// EchoServer
```

Note that the constructor method catches the IOException. Note also that we have included a stub version of run(), which we want to define in this class.

Once EchoServer has set up a port, it should issue the port.accept() method and wait for a client to connect. This part of the server protocol belongs in the run() method. Most servers are designed to run in an infinite loop. That is, they don't just handle one request and then quit. Instead, once started (usually by the system), they repeatedly handle requests until deliberately stopped by the system. This leads to the following run algorithm:

The server algorithm

```
public void run() {
    try {
        System.out.println("Echo server at "
                            + InetAddress.getLocalHost()
                            + " waiting for connections ");
        while(true) {
            socket = port.accept();
            System.out.println("Accepted a connection from "
                                + socket.getInetAddress());
            provideService(socket);
            socket.close();
            System.out.println("Closed the connection\n");
        }
    } catch (IOException e) {
        e.printStackTrace();
    }
}// run()
```

Note that for simplicity we are printing the server's status messages on System.out. Ordinarily these should go to a log file. Note also that the details of the actual service algorithm are hidden in the provideService() method.

As described earlier, the provideService() method consists of writing a greeting to the client and then repeatedly reading a string from the input stream and echoing it back to the client via the output stream. This is easily done using the writeToSocket() and readFromSocket() methods we developed. The implementation of this method is shown, along with the complete implementation of EchoServer, in Figure 15–29.

The protocol used by EchoServer.provideService() starts by saying "hello" and loops until the client says "goodbye." When the client says "goodbye," the server responds with "goodbye." In all other cases it responds with "You said X," where X is the string that was received from the client. Note the use of the toLowerCase() method to convert client messages to lowercase. This simplifies the task of checking for "goodbye."

EFFECTIVE DESIGN: Defensive Design. Converting I/O to lowercase helps to minimize miscommunication between a client and server and leads to a more robust protocol.

This completes the design of the EchoServer. We have deliberately designed it in a way that will make it easy to convert into a generic server. Hence, we have the motivation for using provideService() as the name of the method that provides the echo service. In order to turn EchoServer into a generic Server class, we can simply make provideService() an abstract method, leaving its implementation to the Server subclasses. We'll discuss the details of this change later.

Designing for extensibility

EFFECTIVE DESIGN: Encapsulation. Encapsulating a portion of the algorithm into a separate method makes it easy to change the algorithm by overriding the method.

FIGURE 15–29 The service provided by EchoServer is simply to echo the client's message.

```java
import java.net.*;
import java.io.*;

public class EchoServer extends ClientServer {

    private ServerSocket port;
    private Socket socket;

    public EchoServer( int portNum, int nBacklog)  {
        try {
            port = new ServerSocket (portNum, nBacklog);
        } catch (IOException e) {
            e.printStackTrace();
        }
    }

    public void run() {
        try {
            System.out.println("Echo server at "
                            + InetAddress.getLocalHost()
                            + " waiting for connections ");
            while(true) {
                socket = port.accept();
                System.out.println("Accepted a connection from "
                            + socket.getInetAddress());
                provideService(socket);
                socket.close();
                System.out.println("Closed the connection\n");
            }
        } catch (IOException e) {
            e.printStackTrace();
        }
    }// run()

    protected void provideService (Socket socket) {
        String str="";
        try {
            writeToSocket(socket, "Hello, how may I help you?\n");
            do {
                str = readFromSocket(socket);
                if (str.toLowerCase().equals("goodbye"))
                    writeToSocket(socket, "Goodbye\n");
                else
                    writeToSocket( socket, "You said '" + str + "'\n");
            } while (!str.toLowerCase().equals("goodbye"));
        } catch (IOException e) {
            e.printStackTrace();
        }
    }// provideServer()

    public static void main(String args[]) {
        EchoServer server = new EchoServer(10001,3);
        server.start();
    }// main()
}// EchoServer
```

15.7.3 The EchoClient Class

The EchoClient class is just as easy to design (Fig. 15–30). It too will be a subclass of ClientServer. It needs an instance variable for the Socket that it will use, and its constructor should be responsible for opening a socket connection to a particular server and port. The main part of its protocol should be placed in the run() method. Its initial definition is as follows:

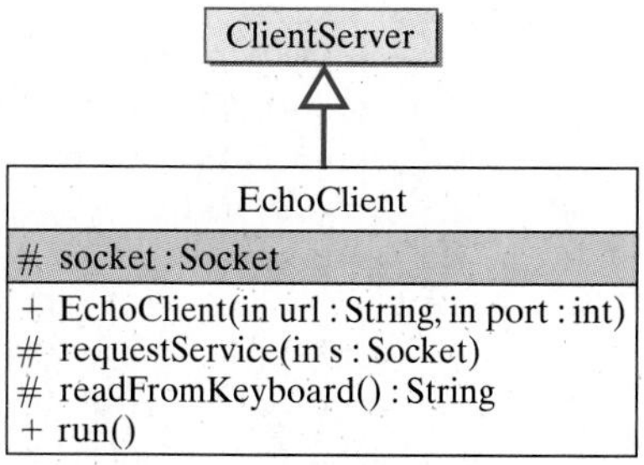

```java
import java.net.*;
import java.io.*;

public class EchoClient extends ClientServer {

    protected Socket socket;

    public EchoClient(String url, int port) {
        try {
            socket = new Socket(url, port);
            System.out.println("CLIENT: connected to "
                             + url + ":" + port);
        } catch (Exception e) {
            e.printStackTrace();
            System.exit(1);
        }
    }// EchoClient()

    public void run() { }// Stub method
}// EchoClient
```

FIGURE 15–30 Design of the EchoClient class.

The constructor method takes two parameters that specify the URL and port number of the echo server. By making these parameters, instead of hard coding them within the method, we give the client the flexibility to connect to servers on a variety of hosts.

As with other clients, EchoClient's run() method will consist of requesting some kind of service from the server. Our initial design called for EchoClient to repeatedly input a line from the user, send the line to the server, and then display the server's response. Thus, for this particular client, the service requested consists of the following algorithm:

The client algorithm

```
Wait for the server to say "hello".
Repeat
    Prompt and get and line of input from the user.
    Send the user's line to the server.
    Read the server's response.
    Display the response to the user.
until the user types "goodbye"
```

With an eye toward eventually turning EchoClient into a generic client, let's encapsulate this procedure into a requestService() method, which we can simply call from the run() method. This method will take a Socket parameter and perform all the I/O for this particular client:

```
protected void requestService(Socket socket) throws IOException {
    String servStr = readFromSocket(socket);                    // Check for "Hello"
    System.out.println("SERVER: " + servStr);                   // Report the server's response
    System.out.println("CLIENT: type a line or 'goodbye' to quit"); // Prompt the user
    if (servStr.substring(0,5).equals("Hello")) {
        String userStr = "";
        do {
            userStr = readFromKeyboard();                       // Get input from user
            writeToSocket(socket, userStr + "\n");              // Send it to server
            servStr = readFromSocket(socket);                  // Read the server's response
            System.out.println("SERVER: " + servStr);          // Report the server's response
        } while (!userStr.toLowerCase().equals("goodbye"));    // Until user says 'goodbye'
    }
} // requestService()
```

Although this method involves several lines, they should all be familiar to you. Each time the client reads a message from the socket, it prints it on System.out. The first message it reads should start with the substring "Hello". This is part of its protocol with the client. Note how the substring() method is used to test for this. After the initial greeting from the server, the client begins reading user input from the keyboard, writing it to the socket, then reading the server's response, and displaying it on System.out.

Note that the task of reading user input from the keyboard has been made into a separate method, which is one we've used before:

```
protected String readFromKeyboard( ) throws IOException {
    BufferedReader input = new BufferedReader(
                            new InputStreamReader(System.in));
    System.out.print("INPUT: ");
    String line = input.readLine();
    return line;
}// readFromKeyboard()
```

The only method remaining to be defined is the run(), which is shown together with the complete definition of EchoClient in Figure 15–31. The run() method can simply call the requestService() method. When control returns from the requestService() method, run() closes the socket connection. Because requestService() may throw an IOException, the entire method must be embedded within a try/catch block that catches that exception.

Testing the Echo Service

Both EchoServer and EchoClient contain main() methods (Figs. 15–29 and 15–31). In order to test the programs, you would run the server on one computer and the client on another computer. (Actually they can both be run on the same computer, although they wouldn't know this and would still access each other through a socket connection.)

The EchoServer must be started first, so that its service will be available when the client starts running. It must pick a port number. In this case it picks 10001. The only constraint on its choice is that it cannot use one of the privileged port numbers—those below 1024—and it cannot use a port that's already in use.

```java
import java.net.*;
import java.io.*;

public class EchoClient extends ClientServer {

    protected Socket socket;

    public EchoClient(String url, int port) {
        try {
            socket = new Socket(url, port);
            System.out.println("CLIENT: connected to " + url + ":" + port);
        } catch (Exception e) {
            e.printStackTrace();
            System.exit(1);
        }
    }// EchoClient()

    public void run() {
        try {
            requestService(socket);
            socket.close();
            System.out.println("CLIENT: connection closed");
        } catch (IOException e) {
            System.out.println(e.getMessage());
            e.printStackTrace();
        }
    }// run()

    protected void requestService(Socket socket) throws IOException {
        String servStr = readFromSocket(socket);          // Check for "Hello"
        System.out.println("SERVER: " + servStr);         // Report the server's response
        System.out.println("CLIENT: type a line or 'goodbye' to quit");// Prompt the user
        if (servStr.substring(0,5).equals("Hello")) {
            String userStr = "";
            do {
                userStr = readFromKeyboard();                  // Get input from user
                writeToSocket(socket, userStr + "\n");         // Send it to server
                servStr = readFromSocket(socket);              // Read the server's response
                System.out.println("SERVER: " + servStr);      // Report the server's response
            } while (!userStr.toLowerCase().equals("goodbye"));// Until user says 'goodbye'
        }
    }// requestService()

    protected String readFromKeyboard( ) throws IOException {
        BufferedReader input = new BufferedReader(new InputStreamReader(System.in));
        System.out.print("INPUT: ");
        String line = input.readLine();
        return line;
    }// readFromKeyboard()

    public static void main(String args[]) {
        EchoClient client = new EchoClient("troy.trincoll.edu",10001);
        client.start();
    }// main()
}// EchoClient
```

FIGURE 15–31   The EchoClient class prompts the user for a string and then sends it to the EchoServer, which simply echoes it back.

```
public static void main(String args[]) {
    EchoServer server = new EchoServer(10001,3);
    server.start();
}// main()
```

When an `EchoClient` is created, it must be given the server's URL (`troy.-trincoll.edu`) and the port that the service is using:

```
public static void main(String args[]) {
    EchoClient client = new EchoClient("troy.trincoll.edu",10001);
    client.start();
}// main()
```

As they are presently coded, you will have to modify both `EchoServer` and `EchoClient` to provide the correct URL and port for your environment. In testing this program, you may wish to experiment by trying to introduce various errors into the code and observing the results. When you run the service, you should observe something like the following output on the client side:

```
CLIENT: connected to troy.trincoll.edu:10001
SERVER: Hello, how may I help you?
CLIENT: type a line or 'goodbye' to quit
INPUT: this is a test
SERVER: You said 'this is a test'
INPUT: goodbye
SERVER: Goodbye
CLIENT: connection closed
```

15.7.4   Abstracting the Generic Server

This completes the design and testing of the generic echo service. It is based on a common root class, `ClientServer`, a subclass of `Thread`. Both `EchoServer` and `EchoClient` extend the root class, and each implements its own version of `run()`. How can we turn this design into one that can be used to support a wide range of services?

Designing for extensibility

The answer lies in being able to distinguish what is common to all servers and clients and what is particular to the echo service and client. Clearly, the general server and client protocols, as defined here in their respective `run()` methods, is something that all servers and clients have in common. What differs from one application to another is the particular service provided and requested, as detailed in their respective `provideService()` and `requestService()` methods.

Abstract service methods

Therefore, the way to generalize this application is to define the `run()` method in the generic `Server` and `Client` classes. The overall design of the echo service will now consist of five classes organized into the hierarchy shown in Figure 15–32. At the root of the hierarchy is the `ClientServer` class, which contains nothing but I/O methods used by both clients and servers. The abstract `Server` and `Client` classes contain implementations of the `Thread.run()` method, which defines the basic protocols for servers and clients, respectively. The details of the particular service are encoded in the `provideService()` and `requestService()` methods. Because the `run()`

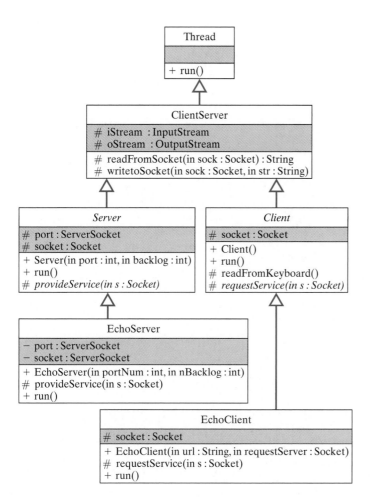

FIGURE 15–32 Class hierarchy for a generic client/server application.

methods defined in Client and Server call provideService() and request-Service(), respectively, these methods must be declared as abstract methods in the Server and Client classes. Any class that contains an abstract method must itself be declared abstract. These design decisions lead to the definition of Server shown in Figure 15–33. Note that provideService() is left unimplemented. Servers such as EchoServer can implement provideService() in a way that is appropriate for that particular service.

EFFECTIVE DESIGN: Polymorphism. Defining a method as abstract within a superclass, and implementing it in various ways in subclasses, is an example of polymorphism. Polymorphism is a powerful object-oriented design technique.

Given the abstract definition of the Server class, defining a new service is simply a matter of extending Server and implementing provideService(), as the new definition of EchoServer illustrates (Fig. 15–34). Note that EchoServer contains a main() method. This will enable us to test it, but this would be omitted if EchoServer were to be used as part of another application.

Extensibility

```
import java.net.*;
import java.io.*;

public abstract class Server extends ClientServer {

    protected ServerSocket port;
    protected Socket socket;

    public Server(int portNum, int nBacklog)  {
        try {
            port = new ServerSocket (portNum, nBacklog);
        } catch (IOException e) {
            e.printStackTrace();
        }
    }// Server()

    public void run() {
        try {
            System.out.println("Server at " + InetAddress.getLocalHost()
                                    + " waiting for connections ");

            while (true) {
                socket = port.accept();
                System.out.println("Accepted a connection from "
                                + socket.getInetAddress());
                provideService(socket);
                socket.close();
                System.out.println("Closed the connection\n");
            }// while
        } catch (IOException e) {
            e.printStackTrace();
        }
    }// run()

  // Implemented in subclass
    protected abstract void provideService(Socket socket);

}// Server
```

FIGURE 15–33   The abstract Server class.

```
import java.net.*;
import java.io.*;

public class EchoServer extends Server {

    public EchoServer(int port, int backlog) {
        super(port,backlog);
    }

    protected void provideService (Socket socket) {
        String str="";
        try {
            writeToSocket(socket, "Hello, how may I help you?\n");
            do {
                str = readFromSocket(socket);
                if (str.toLowerCase().equals("goodbye"))
                    writeToSocket(socket, "Goodbye\n");
                else
                    writeToSocket(socket, "You said '" + str + "'\n");
            } while (!str.toLowerCase().equals("goodbye"));
        } catch (IOException e) {
            e.printStackTrace();
        }
    }// provideService()

    public static void main(String args[]) {
        EchoServer server = new EchoServer(10001,5);
        server.start();
    }// main()
}// EchoServer
```

FIGURE 15–34 The EchoServer class.

The same points apply to the relationship between the abstract Client class (Fig. 15–35) and its extension in EchoClient (Fig. 15–36). The requestService() method is called by Client.run(). It is implemented in EchoClient. In this way, any number of clients can be derived from Client by simply implementing their own requestService() method. Note that we have left the readFromKeyboard() method in the Client class. This is a useful, general method that can be used by a large variety of clients, so it is best if they don't have to redefine it themselves.

Creating new clients

> **EFFECTIVE DESIGN: Inheritance.** By placing as much functionality as possible into a generic client/server superclass, you can simplify the creation of new services. This is an effective use of Java's inheritance mechanism.

SELF-STUDY EXERCISE

EXERCISE 15.7 The design of the client/server hierarchy makes it easy to create a new service by extending both the Server and Client classes. Describe how you would implement the scramble service using this model. The scramble service is useful for people trying to solve the daily scramble puzzles given in many newspapers. Given a string of letters, the scramble service will return a string containing all possible permutations of the letter. For example, given "cat," the scramble service will return "act atc cat cta tac tca."

```
import java.net.*;
import java.io.*;

public abstract class Client extends ClientServer {

    protected Socket socket;

    public Client(String url, int port) {
        try {
            socket = new Socket(url,port);
            System.out.println("CLIENT: connected to " + url + ":" + port);
        } catch (Exception e) {
            e.printStackTrace();
            System.exit(1);
        }
    }// Client()

    public void run() {
        try {
            requestService(socket);
            socket.close();
            System.out.println("CLIENT: connection closed");
        } catch (IOException e) {
            System.out.println(e.getMessage());
            e.printStackTrace();
        }
    }// run()

    protected abstract void requestService(Socket socket) throws IOException;

    protected String readFromKeyboard() throws IOException {
        BufferedReader input = new BufferedReader
                                (new InputStreamReader(System.in));
        System.out.print("INPUT: ");
        String line = input.readLine();
        return line;
    }// readFromKeyboard()
}// Client
```

FIGURE 15–35   The abstract Client class.

```
import java.net.*;
import java.io.*;

public class EchoClient extends Client {

    public EchoClient( String url, int port ) {
        super(url,port);
    }

    protected void requestService(Socket socket) throws IOException {
        String servStr = readFromSocket(socket);            // Check for "Hello"
        System.out.println("SERVER: " + servStr);           // Report the server's response
        System.out.println("CLIENT: type a line or 'goodbye' to quit");// Prompt the user
        if ( servStr.substring(0,5).equals("Hello") ) {
            String userStr = "";
            do {
                userStr = readFromKeyboard();               // Get input from user
                writeToSocket(socket, userStr + "\n");       // Send it to server
                servStr = readFromSocket(socket);            // Read the server's response
                System.out.println("SERVER: " + servStr);   // Report the server's response
            } while(!userStr.toLowerCase().equals("goodbye")); // Until user says 'goodbye'
        }
    }// requestService()

    public static void main(String args[]) {
        EchoClient client = new EchoClient("troy.trincoll.edu", 10001);
        client.start();
    }// main()
}// EchoClient
```

FIGURE 15–36 The derived EchoClient class.

15.7.5 Testing the Echo Service

Testing the revised version of the echo service will be no different than for the original version. The service will work exactly the same way as in the original version, even though we have given it a different implementation. The advantage of our new design is not in its functionality but in the fact that it can be easily extended to create other services.

To test the service, you want to run both EchoServer and EchoClient at the same time and preferably on different computers. As they are presently coded, you will have to modify both EchoServer and EchoClient to provide the correct URL and port for your environment.

SELF-STUDY EXERCISE

EXERCISE 15.8 Describe what happens when each of the following errors is introduced into the EchoClient or EchoServer programs:
- Specify the wrong host name when running EchoClient.
- Specify the wrong port number when running EchoClient.
- Remove the reference to \n in the writeToSocket() call in request-Service().

15.8   Java Network Security Restrictions

One of the most attractive features of Java is that extensive effort has been made to make it a *secure* language. This is especially important for a language that makes it so easy to implement networking applications. After all, nobody wants to download a Java applet that proceeds to erase the hard disk. Such an applet might be written by a cyberterrorist, deliberately aiming to cause severe damage, or it might be written by a cyberdoofus, who inadvertently writes code that does severe damage.

Code verification

What are some of Java's techniques for guarding against either deliberately or inadvertently insecure code? One level of security is Java's *byte-code verification* process, which the Java Virtual Machine performs on any "untrusted" code that it receives. Java checks every class that it loads into memory to make sure it doesn't contain illegal or insecure code. Another line of defense is the so-called **sandbox security model**, which refers to the practice of restricting the kinds of things that certain programs can do.

Limited privileges

For example, the "sandbox" environment made available to Java applets restricts them from having any access whatsoever to the local file system.

Another restriction imposed on applets is to limit their networking capabilities. For example, a Java applet cannot create a network connection to any computer except the one from which its code was downloaded.

Limited network access

Also, a Java applet cannot listen for, or accept, connections on privileged ports—those numbered 1024 or lower. Together, these two restrictions severely limit the kinds of client/server programs that can be built as applets.

Java sets aside certain locations as repositories for **trusted code**. For example, the Java class libraries would be placed in such a location, as would the directories where your Java programs are stored. Any class loaded from some other directory is considered *untrusted*. By this definition, applets downloaded over the Internet would be considered untrusted code.

Trusted code

In addition to the foregoing restrictions for applets, which apply to all untrusted code, Java defines a number of other limitations:

- Untrusted code cannot make use of certain system facilities, such as `System.exit()` and classes in the `java.security` package.
- Untrusted code cannot make use of certain AWT methods, such as methods that access the system clipboard. Another AWT restriction is that any window created by untrusted code must display a message informing the user that it is untrusted. You may have seen such messages on windows opened from applets.
- Untrusted code is limited in the kinds of threads it can create.

New security enhancements introduced in JDK 1.2 are based on the concepts of "permission" and "policy." Code is assigned "permissions" based on the security policy currently in effect. Each permission specifies the type of access allowed for a particular resource (such as "read" and "write" access to a specified file or directory, or "connect" access to a given host and port). The policy that controls permissions can be initialized from an external configurable policy file. Unless a permission is explicitly granted to code, it cannot access the resource that is guarded by that permission. These new enhancements offer a more fine-grained and extensible approach to security for both applets and applications.

As this brief overview illustrates, the Java Virtual Machine is designed with security as one of its primary issues. This doesn't guarantee 100 percent security, but it is a big improvement over some of the languages and systems that preceded Java. Moreover, security is an ongoing concern of the Java development process. Flaws in the existing security system are fixed very quickly. Advanced methods are constantly being developed and incorporated into the system. One such enhancement is the use of encryption to guarantee the integrity of classes transferred over the network.

IN THE LABORATORY: The Internet CyberPet

The purpose of this lab is to develop a stock quote service by extending the client/server model developed in the generic client/server example. As the interface to this service, the client will use our familiar CyberPet interface. The objectives of this lab are

- To extend the Server and Client class to define a new client/server application.
- To write a method that reads a file of stock quotes.
- To incorporate the client object within a CyberPet object.

Problem Description

Design and implement a stock quote service by extending the client/server model developed in the generic client/server. The stockmarket quotes will be stored in a tab-delimited text file that is accessible to the server—for example, in the directory of the server itself. The service works as follows: The client prompts the user for the stock's symbol. It then sends the symbol, as a query, to the quote server. The quote server looks up the stock in the file and returns, as a single line, the stock symbol, name, and current price. If the server can't find the stock, it should return a line that reports ERROR: Stock not found. The client should report this error as Sorry, the stock you requested cannot be found. Please make sure your symbol is correct and try again.

Stock quote service

The quote file stores the stock data as tab-delimited text, with one stock per line. That is, there is a tab character, \t, between each field in the line:

```
AppleC      Apple Computer    45.0
Cisco       Cisco Systems     103.58
Intel       Intel             129.25
MCSFT       Microsoft         150.50
Netscpe     Netscape          63.87
SunMic      Sun Microsystems  89.75
```

User Interface

The Graphical User Interface (GUI) should contain a JTextField into which the user can enter the stock's symbol and a JTextArea where the client can report the stock quotes. It is not necessary to clear the JTextArea after every quote. For example, Figure 15–37 shows an appropriate design for a simple client interface.

Privacy and the Internet

IN 1999 the Intel Corporation was awarded an "Orwell Award" by the London-based privacy advocacy group, Privacy International. The awards recognize government or private groups that have done the most to invade personal privacy in the United States. The award was announced at a "Big Brother Awards" ceremony, scheduled to coincide with the fiftieth anniversary of the publication of George Orwell's classic novel, *1984*.

Intel was cited for its controversial Pentium III chip, which includes a Processor Serial Number (PSN). According to Intel, the purpose of the PSN was to help identify and authenticate users in electronic commerce and other Internet applications. Its intended goal was to make the Internet more secure and reliable as a medium for business and commerce. Privacy advocates worried that the PSN, which can be accessed remotely across the Internet, would be used by mass marketers and others to link users' Internet transactions and further encroach on their privacy.

In some ways the PSN would function like a universal *cookie*. As you may know, a cookie is an identifier that's placed on your PC by a remote Web site. It helps the Web site identify you in future transactions so that it can customize its services to you. Browsers are programmed to ask your permission before storing cookies on your system. However, most browsers allow you to give blanket permission, after which any Web site can simply store cookies on your system without your necessarily being aware of it. One problem with cookies is that they differ in format and content from site to site. However, representatives of the marketing industry have been pushing for standardization of cookies so that consumer information can be more easily shared.

In addition to viewing it as a potential threat to consumer privacy, Intel's PSN also came under criticism from computer security professionals who believed that the software designed to access the PSN would not be completely protected from hackers intent on forging the PSN.

Even through Intel descontinued its plans for the PSN, the Intel/PSN controversy serves to illustrate the basic tension that exists between two conflicting needs: the need to ensure that commerce and financial transactions can be performed securely, and the need to guard the consumer's right to privacy. While this particular controversy may pass, it will undoubtedly be followed by similar issues. If you are interested in this and related issues, a good place to start your search would be by visiting the Electronic Freedom Foundation (EFF) Web site at

http://www.eff.org/

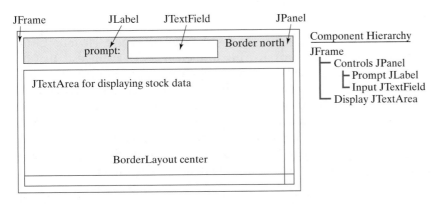

Component Hierarchy

JFrame
├─ Controls JPanel
│   ├─ Prompt JLabel
│   └─ Input JTextField
└─ Display JTextArea

FIGURE 15–37 A GUI design for the stock quote application.

Designing the Stock Quote Service

It is important that the user interface for this application be kept distinct from the client itself. That will make it possible for the client part of the service to be attached to other interfaces—for example, a CyberPet interface.

Problem Decomposition

Our goal is to develop a client/server application to provide stock quotes. Given that we want the interface to be kept separate from the client, this suggests that we need three separate classes:

- StockServer will supply stock quotes.
- StockClient will request stock quotes on behalf of the user.
- ClientInterface will get the user input and pass it along to the Stock-Client object.

Design: StockServer

The StockServer class should be derived from the generic Server class (Fig. 15–38). You should use the EchoServer (Fig. 15–34) as a model. What's new in StockServer is that it has to be able to read stock data from a file in order to supply answers to the queries it will receive. One strategy that the server could use is to read the entire file of quotes into some sort of memory structure when it starts up and then just look them up from there as needed. However, because it's important that the stock quotes be up-to-date, it's probably a better idea to search the quote file itself each time a query is received.

One method that the StockServer must implement is the provide-Service() method. Once a proper connection is established with the client, this method should carry out something like the following algorithm:

- Read a stock symbol from the client [readFromSocket()].
- Look up the symbol's record in stock file.
- Write a reply to the client using writeToSocket().

What methods does the StockServer need, in addition to provide-Service()? Steps 1 and 3 of the preceding algorithm should be simple method calls. However, step 2 will require several statements and possibly even additional methods. Therefore, let's design a method, named getQuoteBySymbol(), to handle this task.

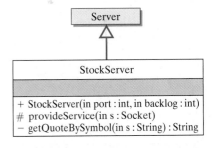

FIGURE 15–38 The StockServer should be able to read stock data from a file.

What methods do we need?

The `getQuoteBySymbol()` Method

According to our specification, the server should receive a symbol string from the client and return a string to the client. This suggests that the `getQuoteBySymbol()` method should take a `String` parameter, the stock symbol, and return a `String` result, the complete stock quote, as described in the specification. Because this method will be used only within this class, it should be declared `private`.

Algorithm design

In terms of an algorithm for this method, have we already solved the problem of reading data from a text file? Yes. The following algorithm from Chapter 14 can easily be adapted to read the stock file:

```
BufferedReader inStream =              // Create an input stream
    new BufferedReader (new FileReader(fileName)); // And open the file
String line = inStream.readLine();// Read one line
while (line != null) {                 // As long as there are more lines
    display.append(line + "\n");       //  Display the current line
    line = inStream.readLine();        //  Read the next line
}
inStream.close();                      // Close the input stream
```

What sort of adaptations will we need to make? One change is that it may not be necessary to read every line of the file. If we find the stock we're searching for before the end of the file, we can just execute a `return` statement, thereby exiting the `while` loop before the end of file. Some of the other design questions you should think about in designing this method are

- How will you break apart the input line into the individual fields? (*Hint*: Use the `StringTokenizer` class.)
- What if the symbol passed by the client is in uppercase, but the stock symbol in the file is lowercase?
- How will you handle the case where the stock is not found in the file?

```
        Client
          △
      StockClient
──────────────────────────
+ getQuote(in symbol : String) : String
# requestService(in s : Socket)
```

FIGURE 15–39 The `StockClient` class implements a stub version of `requestService()`.

Service duration?

The `StockClient` Class

The `StockClient` class should be derived from `Client` (Fig. 15–35). Therefore, it must implement the `requestService()` method. What's new in this class is that we want to separate its communication functions from its interface functions (Fig. 15–39). Recall that `EchoClient` used a method named `readFromKeyBoard()` to get the user's query. We want `StockClient` to get its input—a stock symbol—from the interface. Another difference is that `StockClient` should respond to the user's initiatives rather than simply run through a loop that prompts the user on each iteration. How can these changes be done?

Another design issue for `StockClient` concerns how long it should keep open the connection. The user will initiate queries, so it would not be good design to keep the connection open if the user hasn't even requested a stock quote. To do so would prevent other clients from accessing the server. A better strategy would be to create a new `StockClient` each time the user initiates a query, have the client make one query, and then say goodbye.

It looks as if we don't want our StockClient to run() in a loop at all. To prevent this we just won't call its start() method. Instead, we want to be able to call a method (from the interface class) that causes the StockClient to send a query to the StockServer. Thus, we need a public method that takes a String parameter, a stock symbol, and returns a String, the stock quote. An appropriate algorithm for the getQuote() method would be

Algorithm design

```
public String getQuote( String symbol ) {
    String replyStr = "";
  // write the symbol to the socket
  // read the server's reply
  // say "goodbye" to the server
    return replyStr;
}
```

Given this design for getQuote(), each time the user initiates a query through the interface, the interface class would execute something like the following code:

```
StockClient sc = new StockClient( host, port );
String result = sc.getQuote( symbol );
```

What about the requestService() method? How would our design make use of it? It looks as if we don't even need to use this method, so we can just implement it as a stub method—that is, we can leave its body empty. In other words, this subclass of client will not use the run() or the requestService() methods.

Design: Client/Server Communication

In designing a client/server application, you must take care that both the server and the client know each other's protocol. For example, after the connection is made, will the server say "hello" rather than just waiting for a query from the client? If so, then the client must read the "hello" before sending a query. Similarly, how will the client indicate that it is done? The server must be aware of how the client says "goodbye" so that it can close the connection. The important point is that both the client and server must agree upon the protocol they will use for communication. Otherwise communication will inevitably break down.

Protocol design

Design: ClientInterface

Develop a simple frame-based interface to test your client. This class should implement the GUI described earlier.

Debugging and Testing

Testing a client/server application presents a real challenge because there are so many different kinds of things that can go wrong. That's why it is especially important to develop your application in stages using stepwise refinement. Here's a stepwise development plan that you might wish to follow:

Stepwise refinement

- Test that StockServer successfully waits for a connection.
- Test that StockServer can find a symbol in the data file.
- Test that StockClient successfully makes a connection to StockServer.

- Test that StockServer and StockClient can successfully communicate an appropriate "hello" and "goodbye" protocol.
- Test that StockClient can send an appropriately formatted query to StockServer.
- Test that StockServer returns the correct result.

One advantage of using a tab-delimited text file instead of a binary file is that you can easily type in some test data.

The Stock Quoting CyberPet (Optional)

Once you have successfully tested the stock quote service using the simple frame-based interface, incorporate a StockClient into a CyberPet interface. There are a number of interesting ways you might do this:

- Have CyberPet give up eating, sleeping, or thinking in favor of making stock quotes!
- Have CyberPet make autonomous recommendations based on the stock quotes—"Apple Computer is currently 60.5. You should buy some."
- Create your own images for a CyberStockPet and make stock quoting its only activity.

CHAPTER SUMMARY

Technical Terms

busy waiting	internet	sandbox security
callback method	Internet	model
client	Internetworking	server
client/server	Protocol (IP)	socket
protocols	packet	trusted code
domain name	port	Uniform Resource
ethernet protocol	protocol	Locator (URL)
HyperText Transfer	router	World Wide Web
Protocol (HTTP)		(WWW)

Summary of Important Points

- An *internet* is a collection of two or more distinct networks joined by *routers*, which have the task of translating one network's language to the other's. The *Internet* is an internet that uses the *Internet Protocol (IP)* as the translation medium.
- A *protocol* is a set of rules that controls the transfer of information between two computers in a network. The *HyperText Transfer Protocol (HTTP)* governs information exchange on the World Wide Web (WWW). The *Simple Mail Transfer Protocol* controls mail service on the Internet. The *File Transfer Protocol (FTP)* controls the transfer of files between Internet computers. The *Domain Name System (DNS)* governs the use of names on the Internet.

- A *client/server* application is one that divides its task between a client, which requests service, and a server, which provides service. Many Internet applications and protocols are based on the client/server model.
- Lower-level protocols, such as the *ethernet protocol* and *token ring protocol*, govern the transmission of data between computers on a single network. The *Internet Protocol (IP)* translates between such protocols.
- A *Uniform Resource Locator (URL)* is a standard way of specifying addresses on the Internet. It consists of several parts separated by slashes and colons: METHOD://HOST:PORT/PATH/FILE. The `java.net.URL` class is used to represent URLs.
- Files of text or data (images, audio files) on the Internet or Web can be downloaded using the same `InputStreams` and `OutputStreams` as files located on a disk. To read or write a resource located on a network, you need to connect its URL to an input or output stream.
- The `java.awt.Toolkit` class contains useful methods for downloading `Images` into an application.
- A *socket* is a two-way communication channel between two running programs on a network. The `java.net.Socket` class can be used to set up communication channels for client/server applications. The *server* process listens at a socket for requests from a client. The *client* process requests service from a server listening at a particular socket. Once a connection exists between client and server, input and output streams are used to read and write data over the socket.

SOLUTIONS TO SELF-STUDY EXERCISES

SOLUTION 15.1 The fully connected mesh topology requires the most cables.

SOLUTION 15.2 The fully connected mesh topology would have the most potential to use alternate routes if one of the host computers crashed.

SOLUTION 15.3 The star topology would be rendered completely useless if its central hub crashed.

SOLUTION 15.4 Prentice Hall's Web server is located at

```
http://www.prenhall.com
```

The protocol is `http`. The host computer is named www. Prentice Hall's domain name is `prenhall`, and it is part of the `com` (commercial) Internet domain.

SOLUTION 15.5
- For buying a piece of software at a bookstore, the server would be the sales clerk. The protocol would be to select the software from off the shelf, bring it to the checkout counter, give the sales clerk the money, and get a receipt.
- For buying a piece of software over the phone, the server would be the telephone sales clerk. The protocol would be to select from a catalog, provide the sales clerk with your credit card information, and say goodbye.
- For buying a piece of software over the Internet, the server would be the computer that handles the transaction. The protocol would be to select the item from a Web-based form, provide the form with personal and payment information, and click on the Buy button.

SOLUTION 15.6 To play sounds along with slides in the SlideShowApplet, you would make the following modifications to the code:

```
private URL soundURL[] = new URL[NIMGS];
```

Declare an array of URLs to store the URLs of the audio files you want to play.
Assign URLs to the array at the same time you input the images:

```
for (int k=0; k < NIMGS; k++) {
  url = new URL( "http://starbase.trincoll.edu/~jjjava/slide"
                      + k + ".gif" ) ;
  slide[k] = getImage( url );
  soundURL[k] = new URL("http://starbase.trincoll.edu/~jjjava/sound"
                      + k + ".au");
}
```

Each time an image is displayed in paint(), play the corresponding sound by using the URL from the array:

```
public void paint(Graphics g) {
    if (currentImage != null) {
        g.drawImage(currentImage,10,10,this);
        play( soundURL[currentImage] );
    }
}
```

SOLUTION 15.7 The scramble service would be implemented by defining two new classes: The ScrambleServer class is a subclass of Server, and the ScrambleClient class is a subclass of Client. The ScrambleClient would implement the requestService() method and the ScrambleServer would implement the provideService() method.

SOLUTION 15.8
- If you specify the wrong host name or port, you will get the following exception: java.net.ConnectException: Connection refused.
- If you leave off the \n in the writeToSocket() call, nothing will go wrong because the writeToSocket() method will catch this error and add the end-of-line character to the string before sending it to the server. The server reads lines from the client, so every communication must end with \n or the protocol will break down.

EXERCISES

Note: *For programming exercises,* **first** *draw a UML class diagram describing all classes and their inheritance relationships and/or associations.*

EXERCISE 15.1 Explain the difference between each of the following pairs of terms:
a. *Stream* and *socket.*
b. *Internet* and *internet.*
c. *Domain name* and *port.*
d. *Client* and *server.*
e. *Ethernet* and *Internet.*
f. *URL* and *domain name.*

EXERCISE 15.2 What is a *protocol*? Give one or two examples of protocols that are used on the Internet.

EXERCISE 15.3 What service is managed by the HTTP protocol?

EXERCISE 15.4 Give examples of client applications that use the HTTP protocol.

EXERCISE 15.5 Why is it important that applets be limited in terms of their network and file system access? Describe the various networking restrictions that apply to Java applets.

EXERCISE 15.6 What does the `Internet Protocol` do? Describe how it would be used to join together an ethernet and a token ring network.

EXERCISE 15.7 Describe one or two circumstances under which a `ConnectException` would be thrown.

EXERCISE 15.8 Modify the `SlideShowApplet` so that it plays an audio file along with each slide.

EXERCISE 15.9 Design and implement a Java applet that downloads a random substitution cryptogram and provides an interface that helps the user try to solve the cryptogram. The interface should enable the user to substitute an arbitrary letter for the letters in the cryptogram. The cryptogram files should be stored in the same directory as the applet itself.

EXERCISE 15.10 Design and implement a Java application that displays a random message (or a random joke) each time the user clicks a `GetMessage` button. The messages should be stored in a set of files in the same directory as the applet itself. Each time the button is clicked, the applet should download one of the message files.

EXERCISE 15.11 Write a client/server application of the message or joke service described in the previous exercise. Your implementation should extend the `Server` and `Client` classes.

EXERCISE 15.12 Write an implementation of the scramble service. Given a word, the scramble service will return a string containing all possible permutations of the letters in the word. For example, given "man," the scramble service will return "amn, anm, man, mna, nam, nma." Use the `Server` and `Client` classes in your design. (See the Self-Study Exercises for a description of the design.)

EXERCISE 15.13 **Challenge:** Design a Nim server that plays a two-person game of Nim. There are many versions of Nim but here's a simple one. The game starts with 21 sticks being thrown on the table. The players take turns picking up sticks. On each turn the player must pick one, two, or three sticks. The player who picks up the last stick wins the game. The server should start the game and then let the client have the first move. The server should also announce who won the game. (The server should be a good sport and shouldn't gloat too much when it wins!)

EXERCISE 15.14 **Challenge:** Modify the previous program so that the client and server can negotiate the rules of the game, including how many sticks, how many pick ups per turn, and who goes first.

EXERCISE 15.15 **Challenge:** Design a CyberPet protocol and use it to establish a two-way conversation between two CyberPets. One pet will have to play the role of the server and the other the role of the client. Use the protocol to let two CyberPets carry on a simple exchange of information—what their favorite food is.

EXERCISE 15.16 **Challenge:** CyberPets need a registry to help them select food gifts for each other. Design and implement a registry service. The service should let a CyberPet register itself by giving its name and its favorite food. A CyberPet can also request the server to tell it another CyberPet's favorite food. Design a client program that acts as an interface to the registry server.

Photograph courtesy of Andrew Olney, Tony Stone Images.

16

Data Structures: Lists, Stacks, and Queues

OBJECTIVES

After studying this chapter, you will

- Understand the concept of a dynamic data structure.
- Be able to create and use dynamic data structures such as linked lists.
- Grasp the concept of an Abstract Data Type (ADT).
- Understand the stack and queue ADTs.
- Know how to use inheritance to define extensible data structures.

OUTLINE

16.1   Introduction

A **data structure** is a construct used to organize information to make it easy and efficient to access and process. An *array* is an example of a data structure in which all of the data are of the same type or class and in which individual elements are accessed by their position (index or subscript) within the structure. An array is an example of a **static structure**, because its size is fixed for the duration of the program's execution. (This is a different meaning of *static* than the Java keyword `static`.)

A **vector** is another example of a data structure. Like an array, individual vector elements are accessed by their position. However, unlike arrays, a vector is an example of a **dynamic structure**—that is, one that can grow and shrink during a program's execution.

These are only two of the many data structures developed by computer scientists. For more advanced problems, it is often necessary to develop specialized structures to store and manipulate information. Some of these structures—linked lists, stacks, queues—have become classic objects of study in computer science. This chapter describes how to implement a linked list and how to use inheritance to extend the list to implement the stack and queue structures.

16.2   The Linked List Data Structure

Static vs. dynamic

As we said, a *static* data structure is one whose size is fixed during a program's execution—its memory is allocated at compile time—while a *dynamic* structure is one that can grow and shrink as needed. In this section, we will develop a dynamic list structure. A **list** is a data structure whose elements are arranged in a linear sequence. There is a first element in the list, a second element, and so on. Lists are quite general and have a broad range of applications. Depending on how elements are inserted and removed from a list, they can be used for a range of specialized purposes.

16.2.1   Using References to Link Objects

Referring to objects

As you know from earlier chapters, when you create an object using the `new` operator you get back a **reference** to the object, which you can assign to a reference variable. In the following example, *b* is a reference to a `JButton`:

```
JButton b = new JButton();
```

We have defined many classes that contained references to other objects:

```
public class CyberPet {
    private String name;
}
```

In this example, `name` is a reference to a `String` object.

A **linked list** is a list in which a collection of nodes are linked together by references from one node to the next. To make a linked list, we will

Self-referential objects

define a class of self-referential objects. A **self-referential object** is one that contains a reference to an object of the same class. The convention is to name these objects `Nodes`:

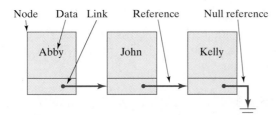

FIGURE 16–1 A linked list of Nodes terminated by a null link.

```
public class Node {
    private String name;
    private Node next;
}
```

In addition to the reference to a String object, each Node object contains a reference to another Node object. The next variable is often called a **link** because it is used to link together two Node objects. For example, Figure 16–1 provides an illustration of a linked list of Nodes.

Linking objects together

By assigning references to the next variables in each Node, we can chain together arbitrarily long lists of objects. Therefore, we will want to add methods to our Node class that enable us to manipulate a Node's next variable (Fig. 16–2). By assigning it a reference to another Node, we can link two Nodes together. By retrieving its value, we can find the next Node in the list.

JAVA LANGUAGE RULE	Self-Referential Object. A *self-referential object* is one that contains an instance variable that refers to an object of the same class.

In addition to the link variable, each Node stores some data. In this example, the data is a single String. But there's no real limit to the amount and type of data that can be stored in a linked list. Therefore, in addition to methods that manipulate a Node's link, we will also want methods to manipulate its data. These points suggest the following basic design for a Node:

Node
− data : Object
− next : Node
+ Node(in o : Object)
+ setData(in o : Object)
+ getData() : Object
+ setNext(in link : Node)
+ getNext() : Node

FIGURE 16–2 The Node class.

```
public class Node {
    private Object data;
    private Node next;

    public Node(Object obj);          // Constructor

    public void setData(Object obj);  // Data access
    public Object getData();

    public void setNext(Node link);   // Link access
    public Node getNext();
} // Node
```

Note that we have defined the Node's data in the most general possible way: as a reference to an Object. Because the Object class is the root of Java's entire class hierarchy, an Object can encompass any kind of data. By using Java's wrapper classes, such as Integer and Double, a Node's data can even include primitive data.

Divide and conquer

The important point is that regardless of its type of data, a Node will have data access methods and link access methods. The data access methods differ, depending on the type of data, but the link access methods will generally be the same.

> **EFFECTIVE DESIGN: Link Versus Data.** Making a clear distinction between an object's data and those elements used to manipulate the object is an example of the divide-and-conquer principle.

SELF-STUDY EXERCISES

EXERCISE 16.1   Write a statement to create a new Node whose data consist of the String "Hello."

EXERCISE 16.2   Write a statement to create a new Node whose data consist of the CyberPet named "Socrates."

16.2.2   Example: The Dynamic Phone List

Let's define a PhoneListNode class that can be used to implement a phone list (Fig. 16–3). This definition will be a straightforward specialization of the generic Node list defined in the previous section. Each element of the phone list will consist simply of a person's name and phone number. These will be the node's data and can be stored in two String variables. To

Accessing a list's data

access these data, we will provide a constructor and a basic set of access methods. Thus, we have the definition shown in Figure 16–4.

The constructor and data access methods should be familiar to you. Note that the constructor sets the initial value of next to null, which means that it refers to no object.

> **DEBUGGING TIP: Null Reference.** A common programming error is the attempt to use a null reference to refer to an object. This usually means the reference has not been successfully initialized.

Manipulating a list's nodes

Let's discuss the details of the link access methods—the setNext() and getNext() methods—which are also quite simple to implement. Because this is a PhoneListNode, these methods take PhoneListNode as a parameter and return type, respectively. Given a reference to a PhoneListNode, the setNext() method simply assigns it to next. The getNext() method simply returns the value of its next link.

FIGURE 16–3   Design of the PhoneListNode class.

PhoneListNode
− name : String
− phone : String
− next : PhoneListNode
+ PhoneListNode(in name : String, in phone : String)
+ setData(in name : String, in phone : String)
+ getName() : String
+ getData() : String
+ toString() : String
+ setNext(in next : PhoneListNode)
+ getNext() : PhoneListNode

```
public class PhoneListNode {
    private String name;
    private String phone;
    private PhoneListNode next;

    public PhoneListNode(String s1, String s2) {
        name = s1;
        phone = s2;
        next = null;
    } // PhoneListNode()

    public void setData(String s1, String s2) {
        name = s1;
        phone = s2;
    } // setData()

    public String getName() {
        return name;
    } // getName()

    public String getData() {
        return name + " " + phone;
    } // getData()

    public String toString() {
        return name + " " + phone;
    } // toString()

    public void setNext(PhoneListNode nextPtr) {
        next = nextPtr;
    } // setNext()

    public PhoneListNode getNext() {
        return next;
    } // getNext()
} // PhoneListNode
```

FIGURE 16–4   The PhoneListNode class.

Let's now see how we would use these methods to construct a list. The following statements create three nodes:

```
PhoneListNode node1 = new PhoneListNode("Roger M", "090-997-2918");
PhoneListNode node2 = new PhoneListNode("Jane M", "090-997-1987");
PhoneListNode node3 = new PhoneListNode("Stacy K", "090-997-9188");
```

The next two statements chain the nodes together into the list shown in Figure 16–5:

```
node1.setNext(node2);
node2.setNext(node3);
```

If we wanted to add a fourth node to the end of this list, we could use the following statements:

```
PhoneListNode node4 = new PhoneListNode("gary g","201-119-8765");
node3.setNext(node4);
```

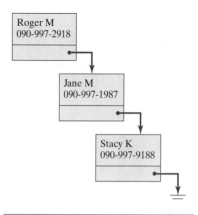

FIGURE 16–5   The phone list: a linked list of nodes, each of which contains a person's name and phone number.

Although this example illustrates the basic technique for inserting nodes at the end of the list, it depends too much on our knowledge of the list. In order to be truly useful we will have to develop a more general set of methods to create and manipulate a list of nodes.

EFFECTIVE DESIGN: Generality.   In a well-designed list data structure, you should be able to manipulate its elements without knowing anything about its data.

SELF-STUDY EXERCISE

EXERCISE 16.3   Suppose you know that nodeptr is a reference to the last element of a linked list of PhoneListNodes. Create a new element for "Bill C" with phone number "111-202-3331" and link it into the end of the list.

16.2.3   Manipulating the Phone List

In addition to the Nodes that make a list, we must define a class containing methods to manipulate the list. This class will include the insert, access, and remove methods. It must also contain a reference to the list itself. This leads to the basic design shown in Figure 16–6. Because this is a list of PhoneListNodes, we need a PhoneListNode reference to point to the list, which is the purpose of the head variable.

A preliminary coding of the PhoneList class is shown in Figure 16–7. As you can see there, when a new PhoneList instance is constructed, head is initialized to null, meaning the list is initially empty. Since we will frequently want to test whether the list is empty, we define the boolean isEmpty() method for that purpose. As you can see, its definition says that a list is empty when the reference to the head of this list is null.

PhoneList
– head : PhoneListNode
+ PhoneList() + isEmpty() : boolean + insert(in node : PhoneListNode) + getPhone(in name : String) : String + remove(in name : String)

FIGURE 16–6   The PhoneList class has a reference to the first node of the list (head) and methods to insert, remove, and look up information.

An empty list

PROGRAMMING TIP: The null Reference.   A null reference is useful for defining limit cases, such as an empty list or an uninstantiated object.

FIGURE 16–7   A preliminary version of the PhoneList class.

```
public class PhoneList {
    private PhoneListNode head;

    public PhoneList() {
        head = null;          // Start with empty list
    }
    public boolean isEmpty() {  // Defines an empty list
        return head == null;
    }
    public void insert(PhoneListNode node) { }
    public String getPhone(String name) { }
    public String remove(String name) { }
    public void print() { }
} // PhoneList
```

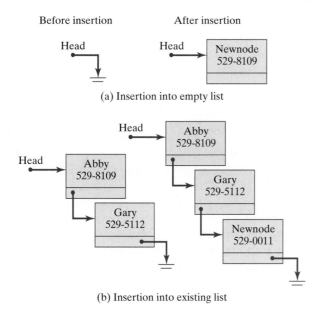

Before insertion   After insertion

(a) Insertion into empty list

(b) Insertion into existing list

FIGURE 16–8   Two cases. (a) The list is empty before the insertion, which takes place at head. (b) The list is not empty, so the insertion takes place at the end of the list.

Inserting Nodes into a List

The insert() method will have the task of inserting new PhoneListNodes into the list. There are a number of ways to do this. The node could be inserted at the beginning or at the end of the list, or in alphabetical order, or possibly in other ways. As we'll see, it is easiest to insert a new node at the head of the list. But for this example, let's develop a method that inserts the node at the end of the list.

There are two cases we need to worry about for this algorithm. First, if the list is empty, we can insert the node by simply setting head to point to the node [Figure 16–8(a)]. Second, if the list is not empty, we must **traverse** down the links of the list until we find the last node and insert the new node after it [Figure 16–8(b)]. In this case, we want to set the next variable of the last node to point to the new node. This gives us the following algorithm:

Insertion algorithm

```
public void insert(PhoneListNode newNode) {
    if (isEmpty())
        head = newNode;                   // Insert at head of list
    else {
        PhoneListNode current = head;     // Start traversal at head
        while (current.getNext() != null)// While not at the last node
            current = current.getNext();  //   go to the next node
        current.setNext( newNode );       // Do the insertion
    }
} // insert()
```

Recall that when nodes are linked together, their next variables are non-null. So when a node's next variable is null, that indicates the end of the list—there's no next node. Thus, our algorithm begins by checking if the list is empty. If so, we assign head the reference to newNode, the PhoneListNode that's being inserted.

Traversing a list

If the list is not empty, then we need to find the last node. In order to traverse the list, we will need a temporary variable, current, which will always point to the current node. It's important to understand the while loop used here:

```
PhoneListNode current = head;        // Initializer
while (current.getNext() != null)    // Entry condition
    current = current.getNext();     // Updater
```

The loop variable, current, is initialized by setting it to point to the head of the list. The entry condition tests whether the next link, leading out of current, is null (Fig. 16–9). That is, when the link coming out of a node is null, then that node is the last node in the list [Figure 16–9(c)]. Inside the while loop, the update expression simply assigns the next node to current. In that way, current will point to each successive node until the last node is found. It's very important that the loop exits when current.getNext() is null—that is, when the next pointer of the current node is null. That way current is pointing to the last node and can be used to set its next variable to the node being inserted [Figure 16–9(d)]. Thus, after the loop is exited, current still points to the last node. At that point, the setNext() method is used to link newNode into the list as the new last node.

Loop-exit condition

DEBUGGING TIP: List Traversal. A common error in designing list-traversal algorithms is an erroneous loop-entry or loop-exit condition. One way to avoid this error is to hand trace your algorithm to make sure your code is correct.

FIGURE 16–9 The temporary variable current is used to traverse the list to find its end.

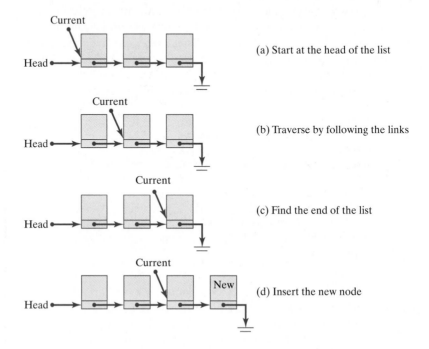

(a) Start at the head of the list

(b) Traverse by following the links

(c) Find the end of the list

(d) Insert the new node

Printing the Nodes of a List

The print() method also uses a traversal strategy to print the data from each node of the list. Here again it is necessary to test whether the list is empty. If so, we must print an error message. (This would be a good place to throw a programmer-defined exception, such as an EmptyList-Exception.) If the list is not empty, then we use a temporary variable to traverse the list, printing each node's data along the way:

List traversal

```
public void print() {
    if (isEmpty())
        System.out.println("Phone list is empty");
    PhoneListNode current = head;              // Start traversal at head
    while (current != null) {                  // While not at end of list
        System.out.println( current.toString() ); //  print node's data
        current = current.getNext();           //  go to the next node
    }
} // print()
```

Note the differences between this while loop and the one used in the insert() method. In this case, we exit the loop when current becomes null; there's no action to be taken after the loop is exited. The printing takes place within the loop. Thus, in this case, the entry condition, (current != null), signifies that the task has been completed.

PROGRAMMING TIP: Terminating a Traversal.   In designing list-traversal algorithms where the reference, *p*, points to the nodes in the list, if you need to refer to the last node in the list after the traversal loop exits, then your exit condition should be p.getNext() == null. If you have finished processing the nodes when the loop exits, your exit condition should be p == null.

Looking up a Node in a List

The traversal strategy must also be used to look up someone's phone number in the PhoneList. Here again we start at the head of the list and traverse down the next links until we find the node containing the desired phone number. This method takes the name of the person as a parameter. There are three cases to worry about: (1) The list is empty; (2) the normal case where the person named is found in the list; and (3) the person named is not in the list. Because the method returns a String, we can return error messages in the first and third cases:

List traversal

```
public String getPhone(String name) {
    if (isEmpty())                            // Case 1: empty list
        return "Phone list is empty";
    else {
        PhoneListNode current = head;
        while ((current.getNext() != null) && (!current.getName().equals(name)))
            current = current.getNext();
        if (current.getName().equals(name))   // Case 2: found the name
            return current.getData();
        else                                  // Case 3: no such person
            return ("Sorry.  No entry for " + name);
    }
} // getPhone()
```

Compound exit condition

Note the while loop in this case. As in the `insert()` method, when the loop exits, we need a reference to the `current` node, so we can print its phone number [`current.getData()`]. But here there are three ways to exit the loop: (1) We reach the end of the list without finding the named person; (2) we find the named person in the interior of the list; or (3) we find the named person in the last node of the list. In any case, after the loop is exited, it is necessary to test whether the name was found or not. Then appropriate action can be taken.

SELF-STUDY EXERCISE

EXERCISE 16.4   What if the exit condition for the while loop in `getPhone()` were stated as

```
((current.getNext() != null) || (!current.getName().equals(name)))
```

Removing a Node from a List

Node-removal algorithm

By far the most difficult task is that of removing a node from a list. In the `PhoneList` we use the person's name to identify the node, and we return a `String`, which can be used to report either success or failure. There are four cases to worry about in designing this algorithm: (1) The list is empty, (2) the first node is being removed, (3) some other node is being removed, and (4) the named person is not in the list. The same traversal strategy we used in `getPhone()` is used here, with the same basic while loop for cases 3 and 4.

As Figure 16–10 shows, the first two cases are easily handled. If the list is empty, we just return an error message. We use `current` as the traversal variable. If the named node is the first node, we simply need to set `head` to `current.getNext()`, which has the effect of making `head` point to the

```
public String remove(String name) { // Remove an entry by name
    if (isEmpty())                           // Case 1: empty list
        return "Phone list is empty";
    PhoneListNode current = head;
    PhoneListNode previous = null;
    if (current.getName().equals(name)) {        // Case 2: remove first node
        head = current.getNext();
        return "Removed " + current.toString() ;
    }
    while ((current.getNext() != null) && (!current.getName().equals(name)))  {
        previous = current;
        current = current.getNext();
    }
    if (current.getName().equals(name)) {        // Case 3: remove named node
        previous.setNext(current.getNext());
        return "Removed " + current.toString();
    } else
        return ("Sorry.  No entry for " + name); // Case 4: node not found
} // remove()
```

FIGURE 16–10   The `remove()` method.

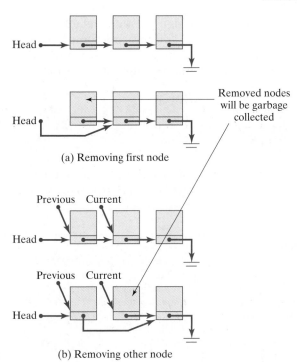

FIGURE 16–11   Removing different nodes from a linked list.

(a) Removing first node

(b) Removing other node

Removed nodes
will be garbage
collected

second node in the list [Figure 16–11(a)]. Once the node is cut out from the chain of links, there will be no further reference to it. In this case, Java will recapture the memory it uses when it does garbage collection.

> **JAVA LANGUAGE RULE**   Garbage Collection. Java's garbage collector handles the disposal of unused objects automatically. This helps to simplify linked-list applications. In languages such as C++ the programmer would have to *dispose* of the memory occupied by the deleted node.

In order to remove some other node besides the first, two traversal variables are needed: previous and current. And they proceed in tandem down the list, with previous always pointing to the node just before the current node. The reason, of course, is that to remove the current node, you need to adjust the link pointing to it contained in the previous node [Figure 16–11(b)]. That is, the new value of previous.next will be the current value of current.next. We use the getNext() and setNext() methods to effect this change:

Tandem traversal

```
previous.setNext(current.getNext());
```

Testing the List

In developing list-processing programs, it is very important to design good test data. As we have seen, the insertion and removal operations each involves several distinct cases. Proper testing of these methods would ideally test every possible case. Of course, there are often so many combinations of list operations that exhaustive testing may not be feasible.

Designing test data

At the very least you should design test data that test each of the different conditions identified in your algorithms. For example, in testing removals from a list, you should test all four cases that we discussed. In testing insertions or lookups, you should test all three cases that were identified.

EFFECTIVE DESIGN: Test Data.   Test data for validating list-processing algorithms should (at least) test each of the cases identified in each of the removal and insertion methods.

The `main()` program in Figure 16–12 illustrates the kinds of tests that should be performed. This method could be incorporated directly into the `PhoneList` class, or it could be made part of a separate class.

FIGURE 16–12   A `main()` method containing a set of tests for the `PhoneList` class.

```java
public static void main(String argv[]) {
                              // Create list and insert some nodes
    PhoneList list = new PhoneList();
    list.insert( new PhoneListNode("Roger M", "997-0020"));
    list.insert( new PhoneListNode("Roger W", "997-0086"));
    list.insert( new PhoneListNode("Rich P", "997-0010"));
    list.insert( new PhoneListNode("Jane M", "997-2101"));
    list.insert( new PhoneListNode("Stacy K", "997-2517"));

                              // Test whether insertions worked
    System.out.println( "Phone Directory" );
    list.print();
                              // Test whether lookups work
    System.out.println("Looking up numbers by name");
    System.out.println(list.getPhone("Roger M"));
    System.out.println(list.getPhone("Rich P"));
    System.out.println(list.getPhone("Stacy K"));
    System.out.println(list.getPhone("Mary P"));
    System.out.println(list.remove("Rich P"));

    System.out.println("Phone Directory");
    list.print();
              // Test removals, printing list after each removal
    System.out.println(list.remove("Roger M"));
    System.out.println("Phone Directory");
    list.print();
    System.out.println(list.remove("Stacy K"));
    System.out.println("Phone Directory");
    list.print();
    System.out.println(list.remove("Jane M"));
    System.out.println("Phone Directory");
    list.print();
    System.out.println(list.remove("Jane M"));
    System.out.println("Phone Directory");
    list.print();
    System.out.println(list.remove("Roger W"));
    System.out.println("Phone Directory");
    list.print();
    System.out.println(list.remove("Roger W"));
    System.out.println("Phone Directory");
    list.print();
} // main()
```

SELF-STUDY EXERCISES

EXERCISE 16.5 Trace through the `main()` method line by line and predict its output.

EXERCISE 16.6 Design a test of `PhoneList` that shows that new elements can be inserted into a list after some or all of its previous nodes have been removed.

OBJECT-ORIENTED DESIGN:
The List Abstract Data Type (ADT)

The `PhoneList` example from the previous section illustrates the basic concepts of the linked list. Keep in mind that there are other implementations that could have been described. For example, some linked lists use a reference to both the first and last elements of the list. Some lists use nodes that have two pointers, one to the next node and one to the previous node. This enables traversals in two directions: front to back and back to front. So the example we showed was intended mainly to illustrate the basic techniques involved in list processing.

Also, the `PhoneList` example is limited to a particular type of data— *A generic list structure* namely, a `PhoneListNode`. Let's develop a more general linked list class and a more general node class that can be used to store and process lists of any kind of data.

An **Abstract Data Type (ADT)** involves two components: the data that are being stored and manipulated and the methods and operations that can be performed on those data. For example, an `int` is an ADT. The data are the integral whole values ranging from some `MININT` to some `MAXINT`. The operations are the various integer operations: addition, subtraction, multiplication, and division. These operations prescribe the ways that `int`s can be used. There are no other ways to manipulate integers.

Moreover, in designing an ADT, it's important to hide the implementa- *Information hiding* tion of the operations from the users of the operations. Thus, our programs have used all of these integer operations on `int`s, but we have no real idea how they are implemented—that is, what exact algorithm they use.

Objects can be easily designed as ADTs, because we can easily distinguish an object's use from its implementation. Thus, the `private` parts of an object—its instance variables and private methods—are hidden from the user while the object's interface—its `public` methods—are available. As with the integer operators, the object's public methods prescribe just how the object can be used.

So let's design a list ADT. We want it to be able to store any kind of data, and we want to prescribe the operations that can be performed on *Design specifications* those data—the insert, delete, and so on. Also, we want to design the ADT so that it can be easily extended to create more specialized kinds of lists.

The `Node` *Class*

EFFECTIVE DESIGN: Generalizing a Type. An effective strategy for designing a list abstract data type is to start with a specific list and generalize it. The result should be a more abstract version of the original list.

Node
− data : Object
− next : Node
+ Node(in o : Object)
+ setData(in o : Object)
+ getData() : Object
+ setNext(in link : Node)
+ getNext() : Node
+ toString() : String

FIGURE 16–13 The Node class is a generalization of the PhoneListNode class.

Our approach will be to generalize the classes we created in the Phone-List example. Thus, the PhoneListNode will become a generic Node that can store any kind of data (Fig. 16–13). Some of the changes are merely name changes. Thus, wherever we had PhoneListNode, we now have just Node. The link access methods have not changed significantly. What has changed is that instead of instance variables for the name, phone number, and so on, we now have just a single data reference to an Object. This is as general as you can get, because, as we pointed out earlier, data can refer to any object whatsoever, even to primitive data.

The implementation of the Node class is shown in Figure 16–14. Note that the data access methods, getData() and setData(), use references to Object for their parameter and return type. Note also how we've defined the toString() method. It just invokes data.toString(). Because toString() is defined in Object, every type of data will have this method. And because toString() is frequently overridden in defining new objects, it is very useful here.

FIGURE 16–14 The Node class is a more abstract version of the Phone-ListNode class.

```
public class Node {
    private Object data;          // Stores any kind of data
    private Node next;

    public Node(Object obj) {  // Constructor
        data = obj;
        next = null;
    }                                // Data access methods
    public void setData(Object obj) {
        data = obj;
    }
    public Object getData() {
        return data;
    }
    public String toString() {
        return data.toString();
    }                                // Link access methods
    public void setNext( Node nextPtr ) {
        next = nextPtr;
    }
    public Node getNext() {
        return next;
    }
} // Node
```

List
− head : Node
+ List()
+ isEmpty() : boolean
+ print()
+ insertAtFront(in o : Object)
+ insertAtRear(in o : Object)
+ removeFirst() : Object
+ removeLast() : Object

FIGURE 16–15 The List class contains a pointer to the head of the list and public methods to insert and remove objects from both the front and rear of the list.

The List Class

Let's now generalize the PhoneList class (Fig. 16–15). The List class will still contain a reference to the head of the list, which will now be a list of Nodes. It will still define its constructor, its isEmpty() method, and its print() method in the same way as in the PhoneList.

However, in designing a generic List class, we want to design some new methods, particularly because we want to use this class as the basis for more specialized lists. The PhoneList.insert() method was used to insert nodes at the end of a list. In addition to this method, let's design a method that inserts at the head of the list. Also, PhoneList had a method to remove nodes by name. However, now that we have generalized our data, we don't know if the list's Objects have a name field, so we'll scrap this method in favor of two new methods that remove a node from the beginning or end of the list, respectively.

We already know the basic strategies for implementing these new methods, which are shown in the definition in Figure 16–16. We have renamed the insertAtRear() method, which otherwise is very similar to the PhoneList.insert() method. The key change is that now its parameter must be an Object, because we want to be able to insert any kind of object into our list. At the same time, our list consists of Nodes, so we have to use the Object to create a Node in our insert methods:

```
head = new Node(obj);
```

Recall that the Node constructor takes an Object argument and simply assigns it to the data reference. So when we insert an Object into the list, we make a new Node and set its data variable to point to that Object. Note that we check if the list is empty *before* traversing to the last node.

The new insertAtFront() method (Fig. 16–16) is very simple to implement, as no traversal of the list is necessary. You simply need to create a new Node with the Object as its data element and then link the new node into the head of the list:

```
Node newnode = new Node(obj);
newnode.setNext(head);
head = newnode;
```

See Figure 16–8a for a graphical representation of this type of insertion.

The new removeFirst() method is also quite simple to implement. In this case, you want to return a reference to the Object that's stored in the first node. But you also want to adjust head so that it points to whatever the previous head.next was pointing to before the removal. This requires the use of a temporary variable, as shown in the method.

The new removeLast() method is a bit more complicated, but no more so than the PhoneList.remove() method. It handles three cases: (1) the empty list case, (2) the singleton list, and (3) all other lists. If the list is empty, it merely returns null. Obviously, it shouldn't even be called in this case. In designing subclasses of List we will first invoke isEmpty() before attempting to remove a node.

If the list contains a single node, we treat it as a special case and simply set head to null, thus resulting in an empty list. In the typical case, case 3, we traverse the list to find the last node, using again the strategy of maintaining both a previous and a current pointer. When we find the last node, we must adjust previous.next so that it no longer points to it.

Testing the List ADT

Testing the list ADT follows the same strategy used in the PhoneList example. However, one of the things we want to test is that we can indeed create lists of heterogeneous types—lists that include Integers mixed with Floats, mixed with CyberPets, and so on. The main() method in Figure 16–17 illustrates this feature.

Heterogeneous lists

The list we create here involves various types of data. The Phone-Record class is a scaled-down version of the PhoneListNode we used in the

```java
public class List {
    private Node head;

    public List() {
        head = null;
    }

    public boolean isEmpty() {
        return head == null;
    }

    public void print() {
        if (isEmpty())
            System.out.println("List is empty");
        Node current = head;
        while (current != null) {
            System.out.println(current.toString());
            current = current.getNext();
        }
    } // print()

    public void insertAtFront(Object obj) {
        Node newnode =  new Node(obj);
        newnode.setNext(head);
        head = newnode;
    }

    public void insertAtRear(Object obj) {
        if (isEmpty())
            head = new Node(obj);
        else {
            Node current = head;                        // Start at head of list
            while (current.getNext() != null)           // Find the end of the list
                current = current.getNext();
            current.setNext(new Node(obj));  // Create and insert the newNode
        }
    } // insertAtRear()

    public Object removeFirst() {
        if (isEmpty())                    // Empty List
            return null;
        Node first = head;
        head = head.getNext();
        return first.getData();
    } // removeFirst()
```

FIGURE 16–16   The List ADT.

```
      public Object removeLast() {
          if (isEmpty())  // empty list
              return null;
          Node current = head;
          if (current.getNext() == null) {      // Singleton list
              head = null;
              return current.getData();
          }

          Node previous = null;                 // All other cases
          while (current.getNext() != null) {
              previous = current;
              current = current.getNext();
          }
          previous.setNext(null);
          return current.getData();
      } // removeLast()
} // List
```

FIGURE 16–16 *(continued)* The List ADT.

previous example (Fig. 16–18). Its definition is shown in Figure 16–19. Note in main() how we use an Object reference to remove objects from the list. We use the Object.toString() method to display the object that was removed.

EFFECTIVE DESIGN: The List ADT. One advantage of defining a List ADT is that it let's you avoid having to write the relatively difficult list-processing algorithms each time you need a list structure.

```
public static void main( String argv[] ) {
                  // Create list and insert heterogeneous nodes
      List list = new List();
      list.insertAtFront(new PhoneRecord("Roger M", "997-0020"));
      list.insertAtFront(new Integer(8647));
      list.insertAtFront(new String("Hello World"));
      list.insertAtRear(new PhoneRecord("Jane M", "997-2101"));
      list.insertAtRear(new PhoneRecord("Stacy K", "997-2517"));

                  // Print the list
      System.out.println("Generic List");
      list.print();
                  // Remove objects and print resulting list
      Object o;
      o = list.removeLast();
      System.out.println(" Removed " + o.toString());
      System.out.println("Generic List:");
      list.print();
      o = list.removeLast();
      System.out.println(" Removed " + o.toString());
      System.out.println("Generic List:");
      list.print();
      o = list.removeFirst();
      System.out.println(" Removed " +o.toString());
      System.out.println("Generic List:");
      list.print();
} // main()
```

FIGURE 16–17 A series of tests for the List ADT.

FIGURE 16–18 The PhoneRecord class stores data for a phone directory.

PhoneRecord
− name : String − phone : String
+ PhoneRecord(in name : String, in phone : String) + toString() : String + getName() : String + getPhone() : String

FIGURE 16–19 A PhoneRecord class.

```java
public class PhoneRecord {
    private String name;
    private String phone;

    public PhoneRecord(String s1, String s2) {
        name = s1;
        phone = s2;
    }
    public String toString() {
        return name + " " + phone;
    }
    public String getName( ) {
        return name;
    }
    public String getPhone( ) {
        return phone;
    }
} // PhoneRecord
```

SELF-STUDY EXERCISES

EXERCISE 16.7 Trace through the main() method line by line and predict its output.

EXERCISE 16.8 Design a test of the List program that shows that it is possible to insert new elements into a list after some or all of its previous nodes have been removed.

16.3 The Stack ADT

Stack operations

A **stack** is a special type of list that limits insertions and removals to the front of the list. Therefore, it enforces **last-in–first-out (LIFO)** behavior on the list. Think of a stack of dishes at the salad bar. When you put a dish on the stack, it goes onto the top of the stack. When you remove a dish from the stack, it comes from the top of the stack. These operations are conventionally called **push**, for insert, and **pop**, for remove, respectively (Fig. 16–20). Thus, the stack ADT stores a list of data and supports the following operations:

- Push—inserts an object onto the top of the stack.
- Pop—removes the top object from the stack.
- Empty—returns true if the stack is empty.
- Peek—retrieves the top object without removing it.

Stack applications

Stacks are useful for a number of important computing tasks. For example, during program execution, method call and return happens in

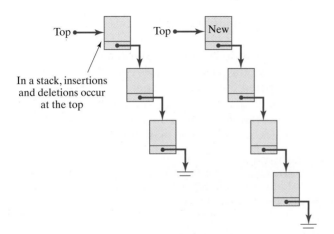

FIGURE 16–20 A stack is a list that permits insertions and removals only at its top.

a LIFO fashion. The last method called is the first method exited. Therefore, a stack—sometimes called the run time stack—is used to manage method calls during program execution. When a method is called, an activation block is created, which includes the method's parameters, local variables, and return address. The activation block is pushed onto the stack. When that method call returns, the return address is retrieved from the activation block and the whole block is popped off the stack. The `Exception.printStackTrace()` method makes use of the run time stack to print a trace of the method calls that led up to an exception.

16.3.1 The `Stack` Class

Given our very general definition of `List` and `Node`, it is practically trivial to define the stack ADT as a subclass of `List` (Fig. 16–21). As a subclass of `List`, a `Stack` will inherit all of the public and protected methods defined in `List`. Therefore, we can simply use the `insertAtFront()` and `removeFirst()` methods for the push and pop operations, respectively (Fig. 16–22). Because the `isEmpty()` method is defined in `List`, there's no need to override it in `Stack`. In effect, the `push()` and `pop()` methods merely rename the `insertAtFront()` and `removeFirst()` methods. Note that the `Stack()` constructor calls the superclass constructor. This is necessary so that the list can be initialized.

Do we have to make any changes to the `List` class in order to use it this way? Yes. We want to change the declaration of head from `private` to `protected`, so it can be accessed in the `Stack` class. And we want to declare

List
head : Node
+ List() # isEmpty() : boolean # print() # insertAtFront(in o : Object) # insertAtRear(in o : Object) # removeFirst() : Object # removeLast() : Object

Stack
+ Stack() + push(in o : Object) + pop() : Object + peek() : Object

FIGURE 16–21 As a subclass of `List`, a `Stack` inherits all of its public (+) and protected (#) elements. Therefore, `push()` can be defined in terms of `insertAtFront()` and `pop()` can be defined in terms of `removeFirst()`.

FIGURE 16–22 The Stack ADT.

```
public class Stack extends List {
    public Stack() {
        super();            // Initialize the list
    }
    public void push( Object obj ) {
        insertAtFront( obj );
    }
    public Object pop() {
        return removeFirst();
    }
} // Stack
```

List's public access methods, such as insertAtFront() and removeFirst(), as protected.

That will allow them to be used in Stack, and in any classes that extend List, but not by other classes. This is essential. Unless we do this we haven't really restricted the stack operations to push and pop and, therefore, we haven't really defined a stack ADT. Remember, an ADT defines the data and the operations on the data. A stack ADT must restrict access to the data to just the push and pop operations.

> **JAVA LANGUAGE RULE** Protected Elements. An object's protected elements are hidden from all other objects except instances of the same class or its subclasses.

> **EFFECTIVE DESIGN: Information Hiding.** Use the private and protected qualifiers to hide an ADT's implementation details from other objects. Use public to define the ADT's interface.

SELF-STUDY EXERCISE

EXERCISE 16.9 Define the peek() method for the Stack class. It should take no parameters and return an Object. It should return the Object on the top of the stack.

16.3.2 Testing the Stack Class

Reversing a string

A stack can be used to reverse the letters in a String. The algorithm is this: Starting at the front of the String, push each letter onto the stack until you reach the end of the String. Then pop letters off the stack and concatenate them, left to right, into another String, until the stack is empty (Fig. 16–23).

Note that because our Nodes store Objects, we must convert each char into a Character, using the wrapper class. Note also that we can use the toString() method to convert from Object to String as we are popping the stack.

FIGURE 16–23 A method to test the Stack ADT, which is used here to reverse a String of letters.

```java
public static void main( String argv[] ) {
    Stack stack = new Stack();
    String string = "Hello this is a test string";

    System.out.println("String: " + string);
    for (int k = 0; k < string.length(); k++)
        stack.push(new Character( string.charAt(k)));

    Object o = null;
    String reversed = "";
    while (!stack.isEmpty()) {
        o  = stack.pop();
        reversed = reversed + o.toString();
    }
    System.out.println("Reversed String: " + reversed);
} // main()
```

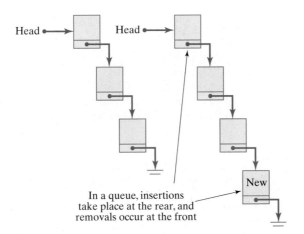

In a queue, insertions take place at the rear, and removals occur at the front

16.4 The Queue ADT

A **queue** is a special type of list that limits insertions to the rear and removals from the front of the list. Therefore, it enforces **first-in–first-out (FIFO)** behavior on the list. Think of the waiting line at the salad bar. You enter the line at the rear and you leave the line at the front. These operations are conventionally called **enqueue**, for insert, and **dequeue**, for remove, respectively (Fig. 16–24). Thus, the queue ADT stores a list of data and supports the following operations:

- Enqueue—insert an object onto the rear of the list.
- Dequeue—remove the object at the front of the list.
- Empty—return true if the queue is empty.

Queues are useful for a number of computing tasks. For example, the ready, waiting, and blocked queues used by the CPU scheduler all use a FIFO protocol. Queues are also useful in implementing certain kinds of simulations. For example, the waiting line at a bank or a bakery can be modeled using a queue.

16.4.1 The Queue Class

The Queue class is also trivial to derive from List (Fig. 16–25). Here we just restrict operations to the insertAtRear() and removeFirst() methods (Fig. 16–26). To test the methods of this class we replace the push() and pop() operations of the last example to enqueue() and dequeue(), respectively

List
head : Node
+ List() # isEmpty() : boolean # print() # insertAtFront(in o : Object) # insertAtRear(in o : Object) # removeFirst() : Object # removeLast() : Object

Queue
+ Queue() + enqueue(in o : Object) + dequeue() : Object

FIGURE 16–25 The Queue's enqueue() and dequeue() methods can use the List's insertAtRear() and removeFirst() methods, respectively.

FIGURE 16–26 The Queue ADT.

```
public class Queue extends List {
    public Queue() {
        super();          // Initialize the list
    }
    public void enqueue(Object obj) {
        insertAtRear( obj );
    }
    public Object dequeue() {
        return removeFirst();
    }
}// Queue
```

FIGURE 16–27   A method to test the Queue ADT. Letters inserted in a queue come out in the same order they went in.

```java
public static void main(String argv[]) {
    Queue queue = new Queue();
    String string = "Hello this is a test string";
    System.out.println("String: " + string);
    for (int k = 0; k < string.length(); k++)
        queue.enqueue( new Character(string.charAt(k)));
    System.out.println("The current queue:");
    queue.print();

    Object o = null;
    System.out.println("Dequeuing:");
    while (!queue.isEmpty()) {
        o = queue.dequeue();
        System.out.print( o.toString() );
    }
} // main()
```

(Fig. 16–27). In this case, the letters of the test string will come out of the queue in the same order they went in—FIFO.

SELF-STUDY EXERCISE

EXERCISE 16.10   Define a peekLast() method for the Queue class. It should take no parameters and return an Object. It should return a reference to the Object stored in the last Node of the list without removing it.

EFFECTIVE DESIGN: ADTs.   ADTs encapsulate and manage the difficult tasks involved in manipulating the data structure. But because of their extensibility, they can be used in a wide range of applications.

From the Java Library

`java.util.Stack`

http://java.sun.com/products /jdk/1.3/docs/api/

THE JAVA CLASS LIBRARY contains implementations of some of the abstract data types that we discussed earlier. The Java utility package, java.util.*, contains a Stack class, implemented as a subclass of the java.util.Vector class. It contains the methods shown in Figure 16–28. For the most part, its methods provide the same functionality as the methods we developed.

The java.util.LinkedList is an implementation of a linked list (Fig. 16–29). Like our implementation, it contains methods that can easily be used to define the standard stack and queue methods. Many of

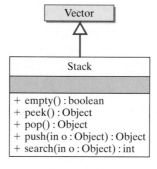

FIGURE 16–28   The java.util.-Stack class is a subclass of Vector.

the standard list-processing methods are defined as part of the List interface.

The advantage of defining list operations as an interface is that they can be attached to a wide range of sequential structures. For example, you could define a stack or a queue class that stored its objects in an array rather than a linked list. By implementing the List interface, this design would still function the same way as the class we defined or as Java's java.util.Stack class.

> EFFECTIVE DESIGN: Code Reuse. Given the relative difficulty of writing correct and efficient list-processing algorithms, applications that depend on lists should make use of library classes whenever possible.

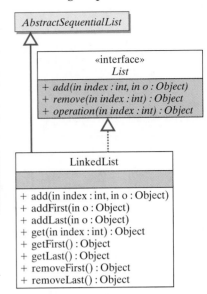

FIGURE 16–29 The java.util.LinkedList class (partial) implements the List interface.

IN THE LABORATORY: Capital Gains

Problem Statement

Suppose your accountant asks you to write a program that will help him calculate the capital gain or loss for a stock account. As you may know, accountants have two ways of accounting for such transactions: *LIFO accounting* and *FIFO accounting*.

In LIFO accounting, the order of buys and sells are taken in a last-in–first-out manner—as if they were stored in a stack. In FIFO accounting, the order of buys and sells are taken in a last-in–first-out manner—as if they were stored in a queue.

For example, suppose you bought 100 shares of a particular stock in each of the months of January, February, and May, for prices of $10, $15, $3, respectively. And suppose you sold 100 shares in March when the price per share was $20. So you presently hold 200 shares of the stock. In calculating your gain or loss you wouldn't count those shares.

If you use FIFO accounting, your capital gain or loss would be calculated by using the March transaction as income. You would match it against the expense of the 100 shares you bought in January. Your total capital gain would be calculated as $100 \times 20 - 100 \times 10 = 1,000$. So you would have a gain of $1,000.

FIFO accounting

If you use LIFO accounting, your capital gain or loss would be calculated by using your March transaction as income again. But this time it would be matched against the 100 shares you bought in May. Using this form of accounting your total capital gain would be calculated as $100 \times 20 - 100 \times 3 = 1,700$. So you would have a gain of $1,700.

LIFO accounting

Of course, if you're interested in minimizing your tax liability, you would want to use FIFO accounting in this case. According to that method, you made less money.

Specifications

Design and write a Java application that lets the user input a sequence of stock transactions, either purchases or sales, and then calculates the capital gain or loss using both LIFO and FIFO accounting. The user should be

Problem statement

The LISP Language

ONE OF the very earliest computer languages, and the one that's most often associated with artificial intelligence (AI), is LISP, which stands for *LISt Processor*. The earliest (pure) versions of LISP had no control structures and the only data structure they contained were the list structure. Repetition in the language was done by recursion.

Lists are used for everything in LISP, including LISP programs themselves. LISP's unique syntax is very simple. A LISP program consists of symbols, such as *5* and *x*, and lists of symbols, such as *(5)*, *(1 2 3 4 5)*, and *((this 5) (that 10))*, where a list is simply anything enclosed within parentheses. The null list is represented by *()*.

Programs in LISP are like mathematical functions. For example, here's a definition of a function to compute the square of two numbers:

```
(define (square x) (* x x) )
```

The expression *(square x)* is a list giving the name of the function and its parameter. The expression *(* x x)* gives the body of the function. LISP uses *prefix notation* in which *(* x x)* is equivalent to *(x * x)* in Java's *infix notation*. To run this program, you would simply input an expression like *(square 25)* to the LISP interpreter, and it would evaluate it to 625.

LISP provides three basic list operators. The expression *(car x)* returns the first element of the (nonempty) list x. The expression *(cdr x)* returns the tail of the list *x*. Finally, *(cons z x)* constructs a list by making *z* the head of the list and *x* its tail. For example, if *x* is the list *(1 3 5)*, then *(car x)* is 1, *(cdr x)* is *(3 5)*, and *(cons 7 x)* is *(7 1 3 5)*.

Given these basic list operators, it is practically trivial to define a stack in LISP:

```
(define (push x stack) (cons x stack))
(define (pop stack) (setf stack (cdr stack)) (car stack))
```

The push operation creates a new stack by forming the *cons* of the element *x* and the previous version of the stack. The pop operation returns the *car* of the stack but first changes the stack (using setf) to the tail of the original stack.

These simple examples show that you can do an awful lot of computation using just a simple list structure. The success of LISP, particularly its success as an AI language, shows the great power and generality inherent in recursion and lists. LISP has been used to build programs for human learning, natural language processing, chess playing, human vision processing, and a wide range of other applications.

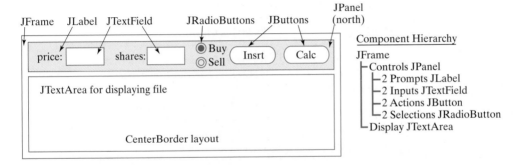

FIGURE 16–30   GUI design for the accounting application.

able to input several transactions and then press a button to process the transactions and compare the results of the two accounting methods. After one batch of transactions is processed, the user should be able to input another batch.

GUI Design

For each transaction, the user has to enter three items of data: the price of the stock, the number of shares, and whether the transaction is a sale or a purchase. JTextFields can be used for inputting the price and number of shares. A good way to input the type of transaction would be to use a set of JRadioButtons, since the transaction must be either a purchase or a sale.

User interface

What controls are needed for this application? The user will be taking two kinds of actions: entering data for a transaction, and asking the program to do the accounting for the current set of transactions. This suggests two JButton controls: an Insert Transaction button and a Calculate button.

In terms of the program's layout, we can use a JFrame for the top-level window. As we have done in other programs, we can place a control panel, containing the buttons and text fields at the top border of the window, and a JTextField at the center. This suggests the layout shown in Figure 16–30.

Problem Decomposition

In addition to the GUI components used in the interface, this project requires several objects to help with the computation. First, we'll need a JFrame object to serve as the top-level window and handle the user interface tasks.

What objects do we need?

The transactions that the user inputs should be represented as individual objects of the Transaction class. We also need an Accountant object to serve as the accountant expert. This object will do all the accounting tasks for the application.

The Accountant object will need Queues and Stacks to store the stock transactions. Because these objects depend for their definition on the List and Node classes, our project must also include definitions for these two classes. Table 16.1 gives the list of classes needed for this project. Figures 16–31 and 16–32 provide UML diagrams for the classes involved in this project.

Accountant
− buyQueue : Queue
− sellQueue : Queue
− buyStack : Stack
− sellStack : Stack
+ Accountant()
+ insert()
+ lifoAccounting() : double
+ fifoAccounting() : double

FIGURE 16–31   Design of the Accountant class.

TABLE 16.1   The classes needed for the Accountant project.

Class	Task Description
AccountantFrame	Top-level window; user interface
Accountant	FIFO/LIFO accounting expert
Transaction	Stock transaction object
Queue	FIFO queue of transactions
Stack	LIFO stack of transactions
List	Superclass of Queue and Stack
Node	Data element of List

FIGURE 16–32   Design of the Transaction class.

Transaction
– BUY : boolean = true
– SELL : boolean = false
– pricePerShare : double
– nShares : double
– type : boolean
+ Transaction(in price : double, in shares : double, in type : boolean)
+ toString() : String
+ getValue() : double

The Transaction Class

What data do we need?

Each Transaction contains three pieces of data: the price of the stock, the number of shares, and whether it is a purchase or sale transaction (Fig. 16–32). So these elements will have to be defined as instance variables. The constructor method for this class should let the user pass the values for these variables when a Transaction is instantiated.

What methods do we need?

In terms of the methods needed for this class, it's always useful to have a toString() method. This lets you display the object's value, which can be useful during program development as well as part of the program's output. It will also be convenient if each transaction would calculate its total value. This is done by multiplying the number of shares by the price per share. If the transaction is a sale, the transaction amount would be positive (income). If the transaction is a purchase, the amount would be negative (an expense). These design decisions lead to the following initial definition of the Transaction class:

A transaction's value

```java
public class Transaction {
    public static final boolean BUY = true, SELL=false;
    public double pricePerShare;
    public double nShares;
    public boolean transType;      // Buy or sell

    public Transaction(double price, double shares, boolean type) {}
    public String toString() {}
    public double getValue() {}
}
```

The Accountant Class

The Accountant class is responsible for calculating capital gains and losses using the FIFO and LIFO accounting methods (Fig. 16–32). How will this be done?

Capital gains (or losses) are triggered by the sale of stock, because a sale transaction generates income. Each sale of X shares of stock must be balanced against a corresponding purchase of X shares. (To simplify this algorithm, let's assume that all purchases and sales happen in blocks of X shares.)

The accounting algorithm

For a given sales transaction, the difference between the FIFO and LIFO models lies in how they choose the matching purchase transaction. FIFO chooses by starting at the first purchase made. LIFO chooses by starting at the last purchase made. For example, the following algorithm calculates capital gains using FIFO accounting:

```
// Algorithm for FIFO calculation of capital gain
  Set capital gain to zero.
  For each sale transaction in the Sales Queue
      Add the amount of the sale transaction to capital gain.
      Get the next purchase in the Purchases Queue.
      Add the amount of the purchase transaction to capital gain.
```

Note that the algorithm uses two queues, one to store the sales and the second to store the purchases. One important condition for this problem is that the length of the sales queue must always be less than or equal to the length of the purchases queue. You can't sell stock that you don't have.

What data do we need?

A similar algorithm for the LIFO calculation would use two stacks to store purchases and sales, respectively. Given these considerations we have the following initial definition of the Accountant class:

```
public class Accountant {
    private Queue buyQueue, sellQueue;
    private Stack buyStack, sellStack;

    public Accountant() { }
    public void insert (Transaction trans) { }// Insert a transaction.
    public double lifoAccounting() { }       // Return capital gain(loss)
    public double fifoAccounting() { }       // Return capital gain(loss)
}
```

The constructor should create instances of the four data structures. The insert() method should insert one transaction record into the queues and stacks. In order to be able to compare FIFO and LIFO accounting, it will be necessary to insert the transaction in two lists, either in the two sell structures, if it's a sale, or in the two buy structures, if it's a purchase. Finally, the lifoAccounting() and fifoAccounting() methods are responsible for calculating capital gain or loss.

What methods do we need?

The AccountantFrame Class

The AccountantFrame class is responsible for managing the user interface. Figure 16–30 shows a design for the interface. JRadioButtons are used to designate the transaction as a purchase or sale. Remember that radio buttons must be added to a ButtonGroup object, which will manage their mutual selection.

The AccountantFrame must implement the ActionListener interface. The way it should work is that the user should input the transaction data and then click on the Insert button. This will cause the transaction to be

FIGURE 16–33   An example
calculation of capital gains.

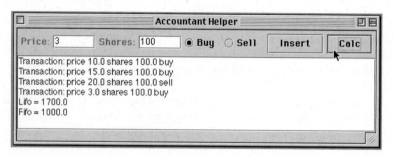

inserted in the Accountant object. After entering several transactions—
remember there must always be more purchases than sales—the user
will click on the Calculate button. At this point the program will print
a comparison of the two accounting methods in the display area.

Figure 16–33 shows a sample calculation. You can use the data shown
there to test your own program.

CHAPTER SUMMARY

Technical Terms

Abstract Data Type (ADT)	last-in–first-out (LIFO)	reference
data structure	link	self-referential object
dequeue	list	stack
dynamic structure	linked list	static structure
enqueue	pop	traverse
first-in–first-out (FIFO)	push	vector
	queue	

Summary of Important Points

- A *data structure* is a construct used to organize data and make them
  more efficient to process. An array is an example of a *static structure*,
  since its size does not change during a program's execution. A vector is
  an example of a *dynamic structure*, one whose size can grow and shrink
  during a program's execution.
- A *linked list* is a linear structure in which the individual nodes of the list
  are joined together by references. A *reference* is a variable that refers to
  an object. Each node in the list has a *link* variable that refers to another
  node. An object that can refer to the same kind of object is said to be
  self-referential.
- The Node class is an example of a self-referential class. It contains a link
  variable that refers to a Node. By assigning references to the link variable, Nodes can be chained together into a linked list. In addition to their
  link variables, Nodes contain data variables, which should be accessible
  through public methods.
- Depending on the use of a linked list, nodes can be inserted at various
  locations in the list: at the head, the end, or in the middle of the list.

- Traversal algorithms must be used to access the elements of a singly linked list. To traverse a list you start at the first node and follow the links of the chain until you reach the desired node.
- Depending on the application, nodes can be removed from the front, rear, or middle of a linked list. Except for the front node, traversal algorithms are used to locate the desired node.
- In developing list algorithms, it is important to test them thoroughly. Ideally, you should test every possible combination of insertions and removals that the list can support. Practically, you should test every independent case of insertions and removals that the list supports.
- An *Abstract Data Type (ADT)* is a concept that combines two elements: a collection of data, and the operations that can be performed on the data. For the list ADT, the data are the values (Objects or ints) contained in the nodes that make up the list, and the operations are insertion, removal, and tests of whether the list is empty.
- In designing an ADT, it's important to provide a public interface that can be used to access the ADT's data. The ADT's implementation details should not matter to the user and should, therefore, be hidden. A Java class definition, with its public and private aspects, is perfectly suited to implement an ADT.
- A *stack* is a list that allows insertions and removals only at the front of the list. A stack insertion is called a *push* and a removal is called a *pop*. The first element in a stack is usually called the top of the stack. The Stack ADT can easily be defined as a subclass of List. Stacks are used for managing the method call and return in most programming languages.
- A *queue* is a list that only allows insertions at the rear and removals from the front of a list. A queue insertion is called *enqueue*, and a removal is called *dequeue*. The Queue ADT can easily be defined as a subclass of List. Queues are used for managing the various lists used by the CPU scheduler—such as the ready, waiting, and blocked queues.

SOLUTIONS TO SELF-STUDY EXERCISES

SOLUTION 16.1

```
Node node = new Node(new String("Hello"));
```

SOLUTION 16.2

```
Node node = new Node(new CyberPet("Socrates"));
```

SOLUTION 16.3

```
PhoneListNode newNode = new PhoneListNode("Bill C", "111-202-3331");
nodeptr.setNext(newNode);
```

SOLUTION 16.4 The following condition is too general. It will cause the loop to exit as soon as a nonnull node is encountered, whether or not the node matches the one being sought.

```
((current.getNext() != null)||(!current. getName().equals(name)))
```

SOLUTION 16.5 The `PhoneList` program will generate the following output, which has been edited slightly to improve its readability:

```
Phone Directory
---------------
Roger M 997-0020        Roger W 997-0086        Rich P  997-0010
Jane M  997-2101        Stacy K 997-2517
Looking up numbers by name
  Roger M 997-0020
  Rich P 997-0010
  Stacy K 997-2517
  Sorry. No entry for Mary P
Removed Rich P  997-0010
Phone Directory
---------------
Roger M 997-0020        Roger W 997-0086        Jane M  997-2101
Stacy K 997-2517
Removed Roger M 997-0020
Phone Directory
---------------
Roger W 997-0086        Jane M  997-2101        Stacy K 997-2517
Removed Stacy K 997-2517
Phone Directory
---------------
Roger W 997-0086        Jane M  997-2101
Removed Jane M  997-2101
Phone Directory
---------------
Roger W 997-0086
Sorry. No entry for Jane M
Phone Directory
---------------
Roger W 997-0086
Removed Roger W 997-0086
Phone Directory
---------------
Phone list is empty
```

SOLUTION 16.6 Executing the following method calls will test whether it is possible to insert items into a list after items have been removed:

```java
    // Create and insert some nodes
PhoneList list = new PhoneList();
list.insert(new PhoneListNode("Roger M", "997-0020"));
list.insert(new PhoneListNode("Roger W", "997-0086"));
System.out.println(list.remove("Roger M") );
list.insert(new PhoneListNode("Rich P", "997-0010"));
System.out.println(list.remove("Roger W"));
list.insert(new PhoneListNode("Jane M", "997-2101"));
list.insert(new PhoneListNode("Stacy K", "997-2517"));
System.out.println(list.remove("Jane M"));
System.out.println(list.remove("Stacy K"));
list.print();
    // List should be empty
```

SOLUTION 16.7   The List ADT program will produce the following output:

```
Generic List
---------------
Hello World
8647
Roger M 997-0020
Jane M 997-2101
Stacy K 997-2517
 Removed Stacy K 997-2517
Generic List:
Hello World
8647
Roger M 997-0020
Jane M 997-2101
 Removed Jane M 997-2101
Generic List:
Hello World
8647
Roger M 997-0020
 Removed Hello World
Generic List:
8647
Roger M 997-0020
```

SOLUTION 16.8   Executing the following method calls will test whether it is possible to insert items into a List after items have been removed:

```
    // Create and insert some nodes
List list = new List();
list.insertAtFront(new PhoneRecord("Roger M", "997-0020"));
list.insertAtFront(new PhoneRecord("Roger W", "997-0086"));
System.out.println("Current List Elements");
list.print();
Object o = list.removeLast();    // Remove last element
list.insertAtFront(o);           // Insert at the front of the list
System.out.println("Current List Elements");
list.print();
o = list.removeFirst();
System.out.println("Removed " + o.toString());
o = list.removeFirst();
System.out.println("Removed " + o.toString());
list.insertAtRear(o);
System.out.println("Current List Elements");
list.print();                    // List should have one element
```

SOLUTION 16.9   The peek() method should just return the first node without deleting it:

```
public Object peek() {
    return head;
}
```

SOLUTION 16.10   The peekLast() method can be modeled after the List.removeLast() method:

```
public Object peekLast() {
    if (isEmpty())
        return null;
    else {
        Node current = head;               // Start at head of list
        while (current.getNext() != null)// Find the end of the list
            current = current.getNext();
        return  current;                   // Return last node
    }
} // peekLast()
```

EXERCISES

Note: *For programming exercises,* **first** *draw a UML class diagram describing all classes and their inheritance relationships and/or associations.*

EXERCISE 16.1   Explain the difference between each of the following pairs of terms:

a. *Stack* and *queue*.

b. *Static structure* and *dynamic structure*.

c. *Data structure* and *Abstract Data Type*.

d. *Push* and *pop*.

e. *Enqueue* and *dequeue*.

f. *Linked list* and *node*.

EXERCISE 16.2   Fill in the blanks.

a. An *Abstract Data Type* consists of two main parts: _____ and _____ .

b. An object that contains a variable that refers to an object of the same class is a _____ .

c. One application for a _____ is to manage the method call and returns in a computer program.

d. One application for a _____ is to balance the parentheses in an arithmetic expression.

e. A _____ operation is one that starts at the beginning of a list and processes each element.

f. A vector is an example of a _____ data structure.

g. An array is an example of a _____ data structure.

h. By default the initial value of a reference variable is _____ .

EXERCISE 16.3   Add a removeAt() method to the List class to return the object at a certain index location in the list. This method should take an int parameter, specifying the object's position in the list, and it should return an Object.

EXERCISE 16.4   Add an insertAt() method to the List class that will insert an object at a certain position in the list. This method should take two parameters, the Object to be inserted, and an int to designate where to insert it. It should return a boolean to indicate whether the insertion was successful.

EXERCISE 16.5   Add a removeAll() method to the List class. This void method should remove all the members of the list.

EXERCISE 16.6   Write an int method named size() that returns the number of elements in a List.

EXERCISE 16.7   Write an boolean method named contains(Object o) that returns true if its Object parameter is contained in the list.

EXERCISE 16.8   The *head* of a list is the first element in the list. The *tail* of a list consists of all the elements except the head. Write a method named tail() that returns a reference to the tail of the list. Its return value should be Node.

EXERCISE 16.9   Write a program that uses the List ADT to store a list of 100 random floating-point numbers. Write methods to calculate the average of the numbers.

EXERCISE 16.10   Write a program that uses the List ADT to store a list of Student records, using a variation of the Student class defined in Chapter 14. Write a method to calculate the average grade point average for all students in the list.

EXERCISE 16.11   Write a program that creates a copy of a List. It is necessary to copy each node of the list. This will require that you create new nodes that are copies of the nodes in the original list. To simplify this task, define a copy constructor for your node class and then use that to make copies of each node of the list.

EXERCISE 16.12   Write a program that uses a Stack ADT to determine if a string is a palindrome—spelled the same way backward and forward.

EXERCISE 16.13   Design and write a program that uses a Stack to determine whether a parenthesized expression is well formed. Such an expression is well formed only if there is a closing parenthesis for each opening parenthesis.

EXERCISE 16.14   Design and write a program that uses Stacks to determine whether an expression involving both parentheses and square brackets is well formed.

EXERCISE 16.15   Write a program that links two lists together, appending the second list to the end of the first list.

EXERCISE 16.16   Design a Stack class that uses a Vector instead of a linked list to store its elements. This is the way Java's Stack class is defined.

EXERCISE 16.17   Design a Queue class that uses a Vector instead of a linked list to store its elements.

EXERCISE 16.18   **Challenge:** Design a List class, similar in functionality to the one we designed in this chapter, that uses an *array* to store the list's elements. Set it up so that the middle of the array is where the first element is put. That way you can still insert at both the front and rear of the list. One limitation of this approach is that, unlike a linked list, an array has a fixed size. Allow the user to set the initial size of the array in a constructor, but if the array becomes full, don't allow any further insertions.

EXERCISE 16.19   **Challenge:** Add a method to the program in the previous exercise that lets the user increase the size of the array used to store the list. You may want to review the "In the Laboratory" section of Chapter 11.

EXERCISE 16.20   **Challenge:** Recursion is a useful technique for list processing. Write recursive versions of the print() method and the lookup-by-name method for the PhoneList. (*Hint*: The base case in processing a list is the empty list. The recursive case should handle the head of the list and then recurse on the tail of the list. The tail of the list is everything but the first element.)

EXERCISE 16.21   **Challenge:** Design an OrderedList class. An ordered list is one that keeps its elements in order. For example, if it's an ordered list of integers, then the first integer is less than or equal to the second, the second is less than or equal to the third, and so on. If it's an ordered list of employees, then perhaps the employees are stored in order according to their social security numbers. The OrderedList class should contain an insert(Object o) method that inserts its object in the proper order. One major challenge in this project is designing your class so that it will work for any kind of object. (*Hint:* Define an Orderable interface that defines an abstract precedes() method. Then define a subclass of Node that implements Orderable. This will let you compare any two Nodes to see which one comes before the other.)

APPENDIX A
Coding Conventions

This appendix covers various aspects of programming style and coding conventions. It follows the conventions suggested in the Java Language Specification (http://java.sun.com/docs/books/jls/), which is summarized on Sun's Java Web site (http://java.sun.com/docs/). The conventions have been modified somewhat to fit the needs of an academic programming course. For further details see

http://java.sun.com/docs/codeconv/index.html

Coding conventions improve the readability and maintainability of the code. Because maintenance is often done by programmers who did not have a hand in designing or writing the original code, it is important that the code follow certain conventions. For a typical piece of commercial software, much more time and expense are invested in maintaining the code than in creating the code.

Comments

Java recognizes two types of comments: *C-style* comments use the same syntax found in C and C++. They are delimited by /* ... */ and //. The first set of delimiters is used to delimit a multiline comment. The Java compiler will ignore all text that occurs between /* and */. The second set of delimiters is used for a single-line comment. Java will ignore all the code on the rest of the line following a double slash (//). C-style comments are called *implementation comments* and are mainly used to describe the implementation of your code.

Documentation comments are particular to Java. They are delimited by /** ... */. These are used mainly to describe the specification or design of the code rather than its implementation. When a file containing documentation comments is processed by the *javadoc* tool that comes with the Java Development Kit (JDK), the documentation comments will be incorporated into an HTML document. This is how online documentation has been created for the Java library classes.

Implementation Commenting Guidelines

Implementation (C-style) comments should be used to provide an overview of the code and to provide information that is not easily discernible from the code itself. They should not be used as a substitute for poorly written or poorly designed code.

In general, comments should be used to improve the readability of the code. Of course, readability depends on the intended audience. Code that's easily readable by an expert programmer may be completely inde-cipherable to a novice. Our commenting guidelines are aimed at someone who is just learning to program in Java.

Block Comments

A *block comment* or *comment block* is a multiline comment that is used to describe files, methods, data structures, and algorithms:

```
/*
 * Multiline comment block
 */
```

Single-Line Comments

A single-line comment can be delimited either by // or by /* ... */. The // is also used to *comment out* a line of code that you want to skip during a particular run. The following example illustrates these uses:

```
/* Single line comment */
System.out.println("Hello");          // End of line comment
// System.out.println("Goodbye");
```

Note that the third line is commented out and would be ignored by the Java compiler.

In this text, we generally use slashes for single-line and end-of-line comments. And we frequently use end-of-line comments to serve as a running commentary on the code itself. These types of comments serve a pedagogical purpose—to teach you how the code works. In a "pro-duction environment" it would be unusual to find this kind of running commentary.

Java Documentation Comments

Java's online documentation has been generated by the javadoc tool that comes with the Java Development Kit (JDK). To conserve space, we use documentation comments only sparingly in the programs listed in this textbook itself. However, javadoc comments are used more extensively to document the online source code that accompanies the textbook.

Documentation comments are placed before classes, interfaces, con-structors, methods, and fields. They generally take the following form:

```
/**
 * The Example class blah blah
 * @author J. Programmer
 */
public class Example { ...
```

Note how the class definition is aligned with the beginning of the com-ment. Javadoc comments use special tags, such as *author* and *param*, to identify certain elements of the documentation. For details on javadoc, see

```
http://java.sun.com/products/jdk/1.3/docs/tooldocs/tools.html
```

Indentation and White Space

The use of indentation and white space helps to improve the readability of the program. *White space* refers to the use of blank lines and blank space in a program. It should be used to separate one program element from another, with the goal being to draw attention to the important elements of the program.

- Use a blank line to separate method definitions and to separate a class's instance variables from its methods.
- Use blank spaces within expressions and statements to enhance their readability.
- Be consistent in the way you use white space in your program.

Code should be indented in a way that shows the logical structure of the program. You should use a consistent number of spaces as the size of the indentation tab. The Java Language Specification recommends four spaces.

In general, indentation should represent the *contained in* relationships within the program. For example, a class definition contains declarations for instance variables and definitions of methods. The declarations and definitions should be indented by the same amount throughout the class definition. The statements contained in the body of a method definition should be indented:

```java
public void instanceMethod() {
    System.out.println("Hello");
    return;
}
```

An if statement contains an if clause and an else clause, which should be indented:

```java
if (condition)
    System.out.println("If part");    // If clause
else
    System.out.println("Else part"); // Else clause
```

The statements contained in the body of a loop should be indented:

```java
for (int k = 0; k < 100; k++) {
    System.out.println("Hello " + 'k'); // Loop body
}
```

Finally, indentation should be used whenever a statement or expression is too long to fit on a single line. Generally, lines should be no longer than 80 characters.

Naming Conventions

The choice of identifiers for various elements within a program can help improve the readability of the program. Identifiers should be descriptive of the element's purpose. The name of class should be descriptive of the class's role or function. The name of a method should be descriptive of what the method does.

The way names are spelled can also help improve a program's readability. Table A.1 summarizes the various conventions recommended by the Java Language Specification and followed by professional Java programmers.

TABLE A.1   Naming rules for Java identifiers.

Identifier Type	Naming Rule	Example
Class	Nouns in mixed case with the first letter of each internal word capitalized.	CyberPet TextField
Interfaces	Same as class names. Many interface names end with the suffix *able*.	Drawable ActionListener
Method	Verbs in mixed case with the first letter in lowercase and the first letter of internal words capitalized.	actionPerformed() sleep() insertAtFront()
Instance Variables	Same as method names. The name should be descriptive of how the variable is used.	maxWidth isVisible
Constants	Constants should be written in uppercase with internal words separated by _.	MAX_LENGTH XREF
Loop Variables	Temporary variables, such as loop variables, may have single character names: i, j, k.	int k; int i;

Use of Braces

Curly braces { } are used to mark the beginning and end of a block of code. They are used to demarcate a class body, a method body, or simply to combine a sequence of statements into a single code block. There are two conventional ways to align braces and we have used both in the text. The opening and closing brace may be aligned in the same column with the enclosed statements indented:

```
public void sayHello()
{
    System.out.println("Hello");
}
```

This is the style that's used in the first part of the book, because it's easier for someone just learning the syntax to check that the braces match up.

Alternatively, the opening brace may be put at the end of the line where the code block begins, with the closing brace aligned under the beginning of the line where the code block begins:

```
public void sayHello() {
    System.out.println("Hello");
}
```

This is the style that's used in the last two parts of the book, and it seems the style preferred by professional Java programmers.

Sometimes even with proper indentation, it it difficult to tell which closing brace goes with which opening brace. In those cases, you should put an end-of-line comment to indicate what the brace closes:

```
public void sayHello() {
    for (int k=0; k < 10; k++) {
        System.out.println("Hello");
    }//for loop
}// sayHello()
```

File Names and Layout

Java source files should have the .java suffix, and Java bytecode files should have the .class suffix.

A Java source file can only contain a single public class. Private classes and interfaces associated with a public class can be included in the same file.

Source File Organization Layout

All source files should begin with a comment block that contains important identifying information about the program, such as the name of the file, author, date, copyright information, and a brief description of the classes in the file. In the professional software world, the details of this "boilerplate" comment will vary from one software house to another. For the purposes of an academic computing course, the following type of comment block would be appropriate:

```
/*
 * Filename: Example.java
 * Author: J. Programmer
 * Date:   April, 20 1999
 * Description: This program illustrates basic coding conventions.
 */
```

The beginning comment block should be followed by any package and import statements used by the program:

```
package java.mypackage;
import java.awt.*;
```

The *package* statement should only be used if the code in the file belongs to the package. None of the examples in this book use the package statement. The *import* statement allows you to use abbreviated names to refer to the library classes used in your program. For example, in a program that imports java.awt.* we can refer to the java.awt.Button class as simply Button. If the import statement were omitted, we would have to use the fully qualified name.

The import statements should be followed by the class definitions contained in the file. Figure A–1 illustrates how a simple Java source file should be formatted and documented.

Statements

Declarations

There are two kinds of declaration statements: field declarations, which include a class's instance variables, and local variable declarations.

- Put one statement per line, possibly followed by an end-of-line comment if the declaration needs explanation.
- Initialize local variables when they are declared. Instance variables are given default initializations by Java.
- Place variable declarations at the beginning of code blocks in which they are used rather than interspersing them throughout the code block.

```
/*
 * Filename: Example.java
 * Author: J. Programmer
 * Date:  April, 20 1999
 * Description: This program illustrates basic coding conventions.
 */

import java.awt.*;

/**
 * The Example class is an example of a simple class definition.
 *
 * @author J. Programmer
 */
public class Example {

    /** Doc comment for instance variable, var1 */
    public int var1;

    /**
     * Constructor method documentat comment describes
     *   what the constructor does.
     */
    public Example () {
    // ... method implementation goes here
    }

    /**
     *  An instanceMethod() documentation comment describes
     *   what the method does.
     *  @param N is a parameter than ....
     *  @return This method returns blah blah
     */
    public int instanceMethod( int N ) {
    // ... method implementation goes here
    }
}// Example
```

FIGURE A–1 A sample Java source file.

The following class definition illustrates these points:

```
public class Example {
    private int size = 0;          // Window length and width
    private int area = 0;          // Window's current area

    public void myMethod() {
        int mouseX = 0;            // Beginning of method block

        if (condition) {
            int mouseY = 0;        // Beginning of if block
        ...
        }
    }// myMethod()
}// Example
```

Executable Statements

Simple statements, such as assignment statements, should be written one per line and should be aligned with the other statements in the block. Compound statements are those that contain other statements. Examples would include if statements, for statements, while statements, and do-while statements. Compound statements should use braces and appropriate indentation to highlight the statement's structure. Here are some examples of how to code several kinds of compound statements:

```
if (condition) {           // A simple if statement
    statement1;
    statement2;
}
if (condition1) {          // An if-else statement
    statement1;
} else if (condition2) {
    statement2;
    statement3;
} else {
    statement4;
    statement5;
}
for (initializer; entry-condition; updater) { // For statement
    statement1;
    statement2;
}
while (condition) {         // While statement
    statement1;
    statement2;
}
do {                       // Do-while statement
    statement1;
    statement2;
} while (condition);
```

Preconditions and Postconditions

A good way to design and document loops and methods is to specify their preconditions and postconditions. A *precondition* is a condition that must be true before the method (or loop) starts. A *postcondition* is a condition that must be true after the method (or loop) completes. Although the conditions can be represented formally—using boolean expressions—this is not necessary. It suffices to give a clear and concise statement of the essential facts before and after the method (or loop).

Chapter 6 introduces the use of preconditions and postconditions and Chapters 6 through 8 provide numerous examples of how to use them. It may be helpful to reread some of those examples and model your documentation after the examples shown there.

Sample Programs

For specific examples of well-documented programs used in the text, see the online source code that is available on the accompanying Web site at

```
http://www.prenhall.com/morelli
```

APPENDIX B
The Java Development Kit

The Java Development Kit (JDK), which is now officially known as the Java™ 2 Software Development Kit (J2SDK), version 1.3, is a set of command-line tools for developing Java programs. It is available for free in versions for Microsoft Windows (95, 98, NT, 2000), Linux, and Solaris (Sun Microsystems). Download information and documentation are available for the entire range of products associated with the Java™ 2 Platform, Standard Edition (J2SE) at

```
http://java.sun.com/j2se/
```

This appendix summarizes some of the primary tools available in the JDK. For more detailed information you should consult Sun's Web site.

Table B.1 provides a summary of some of the JDK tools.

TABLE B.1 Tools included in the Java Development Kit.

Tool Name	Description
javac	Java compiler. Translates source code into bytecode.
java	Java interpreter. Translates and executes bytecode.
javadoc	Java documentation generator. Creates HTML pages from documentation comments embedded in Java programs.
appletviewer	Appletviewer. Used instead of a browser to run Java applets.
jar	Java archive manager. Manages Java archive (JAR) files.
jdb	Java debugger. Used to find bugs in a program.
javap	Java disassembler. Translates bytecode into Java source code.

Sun Microsystems provides detailed directions on how to install J2SDK on various systems, including how to set the system's PATH and CLASSPATH variables. For example, Windows users should consult:

```
http://java.sun.com/j2se/1.3/install-windows.html
```

The Java Compiler: `javac`

The Java compiler (`javac`) translates Java source files into Java bytecode. A Java source file must have the `.java` extension. The `javac` compiler will create a bytecode file with the same name but with the `.class` extension. The `javac` command takes the following form:

javac   [*options*]   *sourcefiles*   [*files*]

The brackets in this expression indicate optional parts of the command. Thus, *options* is an optional list of command-line options (including the

-classpath option), and *files* is an optional list of files, each of which contains a list of Java source files. The *files* option would be used if you were compiling a very large collection of files, too large to list each file individually on the command line.

Most of the time you would simply list the *sourcefiles* you are compiling immediately after the word javac, as in the following example:

```
javac MyAppletClass.java MyHelperClass.java
```

Given this command, javac will read class definitions contained in MyAppletClass.java and MyHelperClass.java in the current working directory and translate them into bytecode files named MyAppletClass.class and MyHelperClass.class.

If a Java source file contains inner classes, these would be compiled into separate class files. For example, if MyAppletClass.java contained an inner class named Inner, javac would compile the code for the inner class into a file named MyAppletClass$Inner.class.

If you are writing a program that involves several classes, it is not necessary to list each individual class on the command line. You must list the main class—that is, the class where execution will begin. The compiler will perform a search for all the other classes used in the main class. For example, if MyAppletClass uses an instance of MyHelperClass, you can compile both classes with the following command:

```
javac MyAppletClass.java
```

In this case, javac will perform a search for the definition of MyHelperClass.

How Java Searches for Class Definitions

When compiling a file, javac needs a definition for every class or interface that's used in the source file. For example, if you are creating a subclass of java.applet.Applet, javac will need definitions for all of Applet's superclasses, including Panel, Container, and Component. The definitions for these classes are contained in the java.awt package. Here's how javac will search for these classes.

The Classpath

Javac will first search among its library files for definitions of classes, such as Applet and Panel. Next, javac will search among the files and directories listed on the user's *class path*. The class path is a system variable that lists all the user directories and files that should be searched when compiling a user's program. J2SDK no longer requires a class path variable. The class path can be set either by using the environment variable CLASSPATH or by using the -classpath option when invoking javac. By default, J2SDK will check in the current working directory for user classes. It doesn't require that the CLASSPATH variable be set. If this variable **is** set, it must include the current directory. The preferred way to set the classpath is by using -classpath option. For example,

```
javac -classpath ../source:. MyApplet.java
```

will tell javac to search in both the current directory (.) and in the ../source directory for user source files. Because the details for setting the CLASSPATH variable are system dependent, it's best to consult the online installation documentation to see exactly how this is done on your system.

During a successful search, javac may find a source file, a class file, or both. If it finds a class file but not source file, javac will use the class file. This would be the case for Java library code. If javac finds a source file but not a class file, it will compile the source and use the resulting class file. This would be the case for the first compilation of one of your source programs. If javac finds both a source and a class file, it determines whether the class file is up-to-date. If so, it uses it. If not, it compiles the source and uses the resulting class file. This would be the case for all subsequent compilations of one of your source programs.

As noted earlier, if your application or applet uses several source files, you need only provide javac with the name of the main application or applet file. It will find and compile all the source files, as long as they are located in a directory that's listed in the class path.

The Java Interpreter: java

The java interpreter launches a Java application. This command takes one of the following forms:

```
java        [ options ]    classname    [ argument ... ]
java        [ options ]    -jar         file.jar        [ argument ... ]
```

If the first form is used, java starts a Java runtime environment. It then loads the specified *classname* and runs that class's main() method, which must be declared as follows:

```
public static void main(String args[])
```

The String parameter args[] is an array of strings, which is used to pass any *argument*s listed on the command line. Command-line arguments are optional.

If the second form of the java command is used, java will load the classes and resources from the specified *Java archive (JAR)*. In this case, the special -jar option flag must be specified. The **options** can also include many other command-line options, including the -classpath option.

The appletviewer

The appletviewer tool lets you run Java applets without using a Web browser. This command takes the following form:

```
appletviewer    [ threads flag ]    [ options ]    url ...
```

The optional *threads flag* tells Java which of the various threading options to use. This is system dependent. For details on this feature and the command line *options*, refer to Sun's Web site.

The appletviewer will connect to one or more HTML documents specified by their *Uniform Resource Locators (URLs)*. It will display each applet referenced in those documents in a separate window. Some example commands would be

```
appletviewer http://www.domain.edu/~account/myapplet.html
appletviewer myapplet.html
```

In the first case, the document's full path name is given. In the second case, since no host computer is mentioned, `appletviewer` will assume that the applet is located on the local host and will search the class path for `myapplet.html`.

Once `appletviewer` retrieves the HTML document, it will find the applet by looking for either the `object`, `embed`, or `applet` tags within the document. The `appletviewer` ignores all other HTML tags. It just runs the applet. If it cannot find one of these tags, the appletviewer will do nothing. If it does locate an applet, it starts a runtime environment, loads the applet, and then runs the applet's `init()` method. The applet's `init()` must have the following method signature:

```
public void init()
```

The `applet` Tag

The `applet` tag is the original HTML 3.2 tag used for embedding applets within an HTML document. If this tag is used, the applet will be run by the browser, using the browser's own implementation of the Java Runtime Environment (JRE).

Note, however, that if your applet uses the latest Java language features and the browser is not using the latest version of JRE, the applet may not run correctly. For example, this might happen if your applet makes use of Swing features that are not yet supported in the browser's implementation of the JRE. In that case, your applet won't run under that browser.

To ensure that the applet runs with the latest version of the JRE—the one provided by Sun Microsystems—you can also use the `object` or the `embed` tags. These tags are used to load the appropriate version of the JRE into the browser as a *plugin* module. A plugin is a helper program that extends the browser's functionality.

The `applet` tag takes the following form:

```
<applet
    code="yourAppletClass.class"
    object="serializedObjectOrJavaBean"
    codebase="classFileDirectory"
    width="pixelWidth"
    height="pixelHeight"
>
    <param name="..." value="...">
    ...
    alternate-text
</applet>
```

You would use only the `code` or `object` attribute, not both. For the programs in this book, you should always use the `code` tag. The `code` tag specifies where the program will begin execution—that is, in the applet class.

The optional `codebase` attribute is used to specify a relative path to the applet. It may be omitted if the applet's class file is in the same directory as the HTML document.

The `width` and `height` attributes specify the initial dimensions of the applet's window. The values specified in the applet tag can be overridden in the applet itself by using the `setSize()` method, which the applet inherits from the `java.awt.Component` class.

The `param` tags are used to specify arguments that can be retrieved when the applet starts running (usually in the applet's `init()` method). The methods for retrieving parameters are defined in the `java.applet.Applet` class.

Finally, the `alternative-text` portion of the applet tag provides text that would be displayed on the Web page if the appletviewer or browser is unable to locate the applet.

Here's a simple example of an applet tag:

```
<applet
    code="HelloWorldApplet.class"
    codebase="classfiles"
    width="200"
    height="200"
>

    <param name="author" value="Java Java Java">
    <param name="date" value="May 1999">

    Sorry, your browser does not seem to be able to
    locate the HelloWorldApplet.
</applet>
```

In this case, the applet's code is stored in a file name `HelloWorld-Applet.class`, which is stored in the `classfiles` subdirectory—that is, a subdirectory of the directory containing the HTML file. The applet's window will be 200×200 pixels. And the applet is passed the name of the program's author and date it was written. Finally, if the applet cannot be located, the "Sorry ..." message will be displayed instead.

The `object` Tag

The `object` tag is the HTML 4.0 tag for embedding applets and multimedia objects in an HTML document. It is also an Internet Explorer (IE) 4.x extension to HTML. It allows IE to run a Java applet using the latest JRE plugin from Sun. The `object` tag takes the following form:

```
<object
    classid="name of the plugin program"
    codebase="url for the plugin program"
    width="pixelWidth"
    height="pixelHeight"
>

    <param name="code" value="yourClass.class">
    <param name="codebase" value="classFileDirectory">

    ...
    alternate-text
</object>
```

Note that parameters are used to specify your applet's code and codebase. In effect, these are parameters to the plugin module. An example tag that corresponds to the `applet` tag for the `HelloWorldApplet` might be as follows:

```
<object
    classid="clsid:8AD9C840-044E-11D1-B3E9-00805F499D93"
    codebase="http://java.sun.com/products/plugin/1.1/
                        jinstall-11-win32.cab#Version=1,1,0,0"
    width="200"
    height="200"
>
    <param name="code" value="HelloWorldApplet.class">
    <param name="codebase" value="classfiles">
    <param name="author" value="Java Java Java">
    <param name="date" value="May 1999">

    Sorry, your browser does not seem to be able to
    locate the HelloWorldApplet.
</object>
```

For further details on how to use the object tag, see Sun's plugin site at

```
http://java.sun.com/products/plugin/1.3/docs/tags.html
```

The embed Tag

The embed tag is Netscape's version of the applet and object tags. It is included as an extension to HTML 3.2. It can be used to allow a Netscape 4.x browser to run a Java applet using the latest Java plugin from Sun. It takes the following form:

```
<embed
    type="Type of program"
    code="yourAppletClass.class"
    codebase="classFileDirectory"
    pluginspage="location of plugin file on the web"
    width="pixelWidth"
    height="pixelHeight"
>
    <noembed>
    Alternative text
    </noembed>
</embed>
```

The type and pluginspage attributes are not used by the appletviewer, but they are necessary for browsers. They would just be ignored by the appletviewer.

For example, an embed tag for HelloWorldApplet would be as follows:

```
<EMBED
    type="application/x-java-applet;version=1.1"
    width="200"
    height="200"
    code="HelloWorldApplet.class"
    codebase="classfiles"
    pluginspage="http://java.sun.com/products/plugin/
                        1.1/plugin-install.html">

    <NOEMBED>
        Sorry.  This page won't be able to run this applet.
    </NOEMBED>
</EMBED>
```

It is possible to combine the `applet`, `embed`, and `object` tags in the same HTML file. And Sun even provides a program to convert HTML files so they will work with the correct Java plugin no matter what browser runs the applet. For details, see Sun's plugin page:

```
http://java.sun.com/products/plugin/1.3/docs/htmlconv_01.html
```

The Java Archiver `jar` Tool

The `jar` tool can be used to combine multiple files into a single JAR archive file. Although the `jar` tool is a general-purpose archiving and compression tool, it was designed mainly to facilitate the packaging of Java applets and applications into a single file.

The main justification for combining files into a single archive and compressing the archive is to improve download time. The `jar` command takes the following format:

jar   [*options*] destination-file   input-file   [input-files]

For an example of its usage, let's use it to archive the files involved in the `AnimatedCyberPet` example in Chapter 6. This is an applet that uses several images to animate the pet. We want to allow users to download the applet via a browser. To improve download times we want to combine all the `.class` files and the `.gif` files into a single jar file. Here's a list of the files we want to archive:

```
AnimatedCyberPet.class
CyberPet.class
eatImage.gif
eat2Image.gif
happyImage.gif
sleepImage.gif
```

The command we use is as follows:

```
jar cf animated.jar *.class *.gif
```

In this case, the `cf` options specify that we are creating a jar file named `animated.jar` that will consist of all the files having the `.class` and `.gif` suffixes.

Once we have created the jar file, we need to specify it in the `applet` tag. For example, the HTML file for the animated pet applet now becomes

```
<html>
    <head><title>CyberPet Applet</title></head>
    <body>
    <applet
        archive="animated.jar"
        code="AnimatedCyberPet.class"
        width=350 height=350
    >
        <parameter name="author" value="Java Java Java">
        <parameter name="date" value="February 1999">
    </applet>
    </body>
</html>
```

When specified in this way, the browser will take care of downloading the archive file and extracting the individual files needed by the applet. Note that the code attribute must still designate the file where the program will start execution.

The Java Documentation Tool: javadoc

The javadoc tool parses the declarations and documentation comments in a Java source file and generates a set of HTML pages that describes the following elements: public and protected classes, inner classes, interfaces, constructors, methods, and fields.

The javadoc tool can be used on a single file or an entire package of files. Recall that a Java documentation comment is one that begins with /** and ends with */. These are the comments that are parsed by javadoc.

The javadoc tool has many features, and it is possible to use Java *doclets* to customize your documentation. For full details on using the tool, it is best to consult Sun's Web site. To illustrate how it might be used, let's just look at a simple example.

The FirstApplet program from Chapter 1 contains documentation comments. It was processed using the following command:

```
javadoc FirstApplet.java
```

javadoc generated the following HTML documents:

```
FirstApplet.html        -The main documentation file
allclasses-frame.html  -Names and links to all the classes used in
                         FirstApplet
overview-tree.html      -A tree showing FirstApplet's place
                         in the class hierarchy
packages.html           -Details on the packages used in FirstApplet
index.html              -Top-level HTML document for
                         FirstApplet documentation
index-all.html          -Summary of all methods and variables in
                         FirstApplet
```

To see how the documentation appears, review the FirstApplet.java source file and the documentation it generated. Both are available at

```
http://www.prenhall.com/morelli/
```

APPENDIX C
The ASCII and Unicode Character Sets

Java uses version 2.0 of the Unicode character set for representing character data. The Unicode set represents each character as a 16-bit unsigned integer. It can, therefore, represent $2^{16} = 65{,}536$ different characters. This enables Unicode to represent characters from not only English but also a wide range of international languages. For details about Unicode, see

```
http://www.unicode.org
```

Unicode supersedes the ASCII character set (American Standard Code for Information Interchange). The ASCII code represents each character as a 7-bit or 8-bit unsigned integer. A 7-bit code can represent only $2^7 = 128$ characters. In order to make Unicode backward compatible with ASCII, the first 128 characters of Unicode have the same integer representation as the ASCII characters.

Table C.1 shows the integer representations for the *printable* subset of ASCII characters. The characters with codes 0 through 31 and code 127 are *nonprintable* characters, many of which are associated with keys on a standard keyboard. For example, the delete key is represented by 127, the backspace by 8, and the return key by 13.

TABLE C.1   ASCII codes for the printable characters.

Code	32	33	34	35	36	37	38	39	40	41	42	43	44	45	46	47
Char	SP	!	"	#	$	%	&	'	(	)	*	+	,	-	.	/

Code	48	49	50	51	52	53	54	55	56	57
Char	0	1	2	3	4	5	6	7	8	9

Code	58	59	60	61	62	63	64
Char	:	;	<	=	>	?	@

Code	65	66	67	68	69	70	71	72	73	74	75	76	77
Char	A	B	C	D	E	F	G	H	I	J	K	L	M

Code	78	79	80	81	82	83	84	85	86	87	88	89	90
Char	N	O	P	Q	R	S	T	U	V	W	X	Y	Z

Code	91	92	93	94	95	96
Char	[	\	]	^	_	`

Code	97	98	99	100	101	102	103	104	105	106	107	108	109
Char	a	b	c	d	e	f	g	h	i	j	k	l	m

Code	110	111	112	113	114	115	116	117	118	119	120	121	122
Char	n	o	p	q	r	s	t	u	v	w	x	y	z

Code	123	124	125	126
Char	{	|	}	~

APPENDIX D

Java Keywords

The words shown in Table D.1 are reserved for use as Java *keywords* and cannot be used as identifiers. The keywords const and goto, which are C++ keywords, are not actually used in Java. They were included mainly to enable better error messages to be generated when they are mistakenly used in a Java program.

The words true, false, and null may look like keywords but are technically considered *literals*. They also cannot be used as identifiers.

TABLE D.1 The Java keywords cannot be used as names for identifiers.

abstract	default	if	private	throw
boolean	do	implements	protected	throws
break	double	import	public	transient
byte	else	instanceof	return	try
case	extends	int	short	void
catch	final	interface	static	volatile
char	finally	long	super	while
class	float	native	switch	
const	for	new	synchronized	
continue	goto	package	this	

APPENDIX E
Operator Precedence Hierarchy

Table E.1 summarizes the precedence and associativity relationships for Java operators. Within a single expression, an operator of order m would be evaluated before an operator of order n if $m < n$. Operators having the same order are evaluated according to their association order. For example, the expression

```
25 + 5 * 2 + 3
```

would be evaluated in the order shown by the following parenthesized expression:

```
(25 + (5 * 2)) + 3   ==> (25 + 10) + 3 ==> 35 + 3  ==> 38
```

In other words, because * has higher precedence than +, the multiplication operation is done before either of the addition operations. And because addition associates from left to right, addition operations are performed from left to right.

Most operators associate from left to right, but note that assignment operators associate from right to left. For example, consider the following code segment:

```
int i, j, k;
i = j = k = 100;      // Equivalent to i = (j = (k = 100));
```

TABLE E.1 Java operator precedence and associativity table.

Order	Operator	Operation	Association
0	( )	*Parentheses*	
1	++ -- .	*Postincrement, Postdecrement, Dot Operator*	*L to R*
2	++ -- + - !	*Preincrement, Predecrement, Unary plus, Unary minus, Boolean NOT*	*R to L*
3	(type) new	*Type Cast, Object Instantiation*	*R to L*
4	* / %	*Multiplication, Division, Modulus*	*L to R*
5	+ - +	*Addition, Subtraction, String Concatenation*	*L to R*
6	< > <= >=	*Relational Operators*	*L to R*
7	== !=	*Equality Operators*	*L to R*
8	^	*Boolean XOR*	*L to R*
9	&&	*Boolean AND*	*L to R*
10	||	*Boolean OR*	*L to R*
11	= += -= *= /= %=	*Assignment Operators*	*R to L*

In this case, each variable will be assigned 100 as its value. But it's important that this expression be evaluated from right to left. First, k is assigned 100. Then its value is assigned to j. And finally j's value is assigned to i.

For expressions containing mixed operators, it's always a good idea to use parentheses to clarify the order of evaluation. This will also help avoid subtle syntax and semantic errors.

APPENDIX F
Advanced Language Features

●————————————

This appendix describes basic features of some advanced elements of the Java language. As for many language features, there are details and subtleties involved in using these features that are not covered here. For further details, you should consult Sun's online references or other references for a more comprehensive description.

Inner Classes

Inner classes were introduced in Java 1.1. This features lets you define a class as part of another class, just as fields and methods are defined within classes. Inner classes can be used to support the work of the class in which they are contained.

Java defines four types of inner classes. A *nested top-level* class or interface is a *static* member of an enclosing top-level class or interface. Such classes are considered top-level classes by Java.

A *member class* is a nonstatic inner class. It is not a top-level class. As a full-fledged member of its containing class, a member class can refer to the fields and methods of the containing class, even the `private` fields and methods. Just as you would expect for the other instance fields and methods of a class, all instances of a member class are associated with an instance of the enclosing class.

A *local class* is an inner class that's defined within a block of Java code, such as within a method or within the body of a loop. Local classes have local scope—they can only be used within the block in which they are defined. Local classes can refer to the methods and variables of their enclosing classes. They are used mostly to implement *adapters*, which are used to handle events.

When Java compiles a file containing a named inner class, it creates separate class files for them with names that include the nesting class as a qualifier. For example, if you define an inner class named `Metric` inside a top-level class named `Converter`, the compiler will create a class file named `Converter$Metric.class` for the inner class. If you wanted to access the inner class from some other class (besides `Converter`), you would use a qualified name: `Converter.Metric`.

An *anonymous class* is a local class whose definition and use are combined into a single expression. Rather than defining the class in one statement and using it in another, both operations are combined into a single expression. Anonymous classes are intended for one-time use. Therefore, they don't contain constructors. Their bytecode files are given names like `ConverterFrame$1.class`.

```java
public class Converter {
    private static final double INCH_PER_METER = 39.37;
    private final double LBS_PER_KG = 2.2;

    public static class Distance {          // Nested Top-level class
        public double metersToInches(double meters) {
            return meters * INCH_PER_METER;
        }
    }// Metric

    public class Weight {                    // Member class
        public double kgsToPounds(double kg) {
            return kg * LBS_PER_KG;
        }
    }//Weight
}//Converter

public class ConverterUser {

    public static void main(String args[]) {
        Converter.Distance distance = new Converter.Distance();
        Converter converter = new Converter();
        Converter.Weight weight = converter.new Weight();

        System.out.println( "5 m = " + distance.metersToInches(5) + " in");
        System.out.println( "5 kg = " + weight.kgsToPounds(5) + " lbs");
    }
}// ConverterUser
```

FIGURE F–1   A Java application containing a top-level nested class.

Nested Top-Level Versus Member Classes

The Converter class (Figure F–1) shows the differences between a nested top-level class and a member class. The program is a somewhat contrived example that performs various kinds of metric conversions. The outer Converter class serves as a container for the inner classes, Distance and Weight, which perform specific conversions.

The Distance class is declared static, so it is a top-level class. It is contained in the Converter class itself. Note the syntax used in ConverterUser.main() to create an instance of the Distance class:

```java
Converter.Distance distance = new Converter.Distance();
```

A fully qualified name is used to refer to the static inner class via its containing class.

The `Weight` class is not declared `static`. It is, therefore, associated with *instances* of the `Converter` class. Note the syntax used to create an instance of the `Weight` class:

```
Converter converter = new Converter();
Converter.Weight weight = converter.new Weight();
```

Before you can create an instance of `Weight`, you have to declare an instance of `Converter`. In this example, we have used two statements to create the `weight` object, which requires using the temporary variable, converter, as a reference to the `Converter` object. We could also have done this with a single statement by using the following syntax:

```
Converter.Weight weight = new Converter().new Weight();
```

Note that in either case the qualified name `Converter.Weight` must be used to access the inner class from the `ConverterUser` class.

There are a couple of other noteworthy features in this example. First, an inner top-level class is really just a programming convenience. It behaves just like any other top-level class in Java. One restriction on top-level inner classes is that they can only be contained within other top-level classes, although they can be nested one within the other. For example, we could nest additional converter classes within the `Distance` class. Java provides special syntax for referring to such nested classes.

Unlike a top-level class, a member class is nested within an instance of its containing class. Because of this, it can refer to instance variables (`LBS_PER_KG`) and instance methods of its containing class, even to those declared `private`. By contrast, a top-level inner class can only refer to class variables (`INCH_PER_METER`)—that is, to variables that are declared `static`. So you would use a member class if it were necessary to refer to instances of the containing class.

There are many other subtle points associated with member classes, including special language syntax that can be used to refer to nested member classes and rules that govern inheritance and scope of member classes. For these details you should consult the *Java Language Specification*, which can be accessed online at

```
http://java.sun.com/docs/books/jls/html/index.html
```

www.

Local and Anonymous Inner Classes

As we have seen, Java's event-handling model uses predefined interfaces, such as the `ActionListener` interface, to handle events. When a separate class is defined to implement an interface, it is sometimes called an *adapter* class. Rather than defining adapter classes as top-level classes, it is often more convenient to define them as local or anonymous classes. In the `ConverterFrame` class (Fig. F–2) a local class is used to create an `ActionEvent` handler for the application's two buttons.

```java
import javax.swing.*;
import java.awt.*;
import java.awt.event.*;

public class ConverterFrame extends JFrame {

    private Converter converter = new Converter();        // Reference to app
    private JTextField inField = new JTextField(8);
    private JTextField outField = new JTextField(8);
    private JButton metersToInch;
    private JButton kgsToLbs;

    public ConverterFrame() {
        metersToInch = createJButton("Meters To Inches");
        kgsToLbs = createJButton("Kilos To Pounds");

        getContentPane().setLayout( new FlowLayout() );
        getContentPane().add(inField);
        getContentPane().add(outField);
        getContentPane().add(metersToInch);
        getContentPane().add(kgsToLbs);
    }

    private JButton createJButton(String s) {        // A method to create a JButton
        JButton jbutton = new JButton(s);

        class ButtonListener implements ActionListener { // Local class

            public void actionPerformed(ActionEvent e) {
                double inValue = Double.valueOf(inField.getText()).doubleValue();
                JButton button = (JButton) e.getSource();
                if (button.getText().equals("Meters To Inches"))
                    outField.setText(""+ converter.new Distance().metersToInches(inValue));
                else
                    outField.setText(""+ converter.new Weight().kgsToPounds(inValue));
            }
        }// ButtonListener

        ActionListener listener = new ButtonListener();// Create a listener
        jbutton.addActionListener(listener);                // Register buttons with listener
        return jbutton;
    }// createJButton()

    public static void main(String args[]) {
        ConverterFrame frame = new ConverterFrame();
        frame.setSize(200,200);
        frame.setVisible(true);
    }// main()
}// ConverterFrame
```

FIGURE F–2   The use of a local class as an `ActionListener` adapter.

The key feature of the `ConverterFrame` program is the `createJButton()` method. This method is used instead of the `JButton()` constructor to create buttons and to create action listeners for the buttons:

```java
private JButton createJButton(String s) {     // A method to create a JButton
    JButton jbutton = new JButton(s);

    class ButtonListener implements ActionListener { // Local class

        public void actionPerformed(ActionEvent e) {
            double inValue = Double.valueOf(inField.getText()).doubleValue();
            JButton button = (JButton) e.getSource();
            if (button.getText().equals("Meters To Inches"))
                outField.setText(""+ converter.new Distance().metersToInches(inValue));
            else
                outField.setText(""+ converter.new Weight().kgsToPounds(inValue));
        }
    }// ButtonListener

    ActionListener listener = new ButtonListener();// Create a listener
    jbutton.addActionListener(listener);          // Register buttons with listener
    return jbutton;
}// createJButton()
```

The `createJButton()` method takes a single `String` parameter for the button's label. It begins by instantiating a new `JButton`, a reference to which is passed back as the method's return value. After creating an instance button, a local inner class named `ButtonListener` is defined.

The local class merely implements the `ActionListener` interface by defining the `actionPerformed` method. Note how `actionPerformed()` uses the containing class's converter variable to acquire access to the meters-ToInches() and kgsToPounds() methods, which are inner class methods of the `Converter` class (Fig. F–1). A local class can use instance variables, such as converter, that are defined in its containing class.

After defining the local inner class, the `createJButton()` method creates an instance of the class (listener) and registers it as the button's action listener. When a separate object is created to serve as listener in this way, it is called an *adapter*. It implements a listener interface and thereby serves as adapter between the event and the object that generated the event. Any action events that occur on any buttons created with this method will be handled by this adapter. In other words, for any buttons created by the createJButton() method, a listener object is created and assigned as the button's event listener. By using local classes, the code for doing this is much more compact and efficient.

Local classes have some important restrictions. Although an instance of a local class can use fields and methods defined within the class itself or inherited from its superclasses, it cannot use local variables and parameters defined within its scope unless these are declared final. The reason for this restriction is that final variables receive special handling by the Java compiler. Because the compiler knows that the variable's value won't change, it can replace uses of the variable with their values at compile time.

Anonymous Inner Classes

An anonymous inner class is just a local class without a name. Instead of using two separate statements to define and instantiate the local class, Java provides syntax that let's you do it in one expression. The following code illustrates how this is done:

```java
private JButton createJButton(String s) {// A method to create a JButton
    JButton jbutton = new JButton(s);

    jbutton.addActionListener( new  ActionListener() {      // Anonymous class
        public void actionPerformed(ActionEvent e) {
            double inValue = Double.valueOf(inField.getText()).doubleValue();
            JButton button = (JButton) e.getSource();
            if (button.getLabel().equals("Meters To Inches"))
                outField.setText("" + converter.new Distance().metersToInches(inValue));
            else
                outField.setText("" + converter.new Weight().kgsToPounds(inValue));
        }// actionPerformed()
    });
    return jbutton;
}// createJButton()
```

Note that the body of the class definition is put right after the new operator. The result is that we still create an instance of the adapter object, but we define it on the fly. If the name following new is a class name, Java will define the anonymous class as a subclass of the named class. If the name following new is an interface, the anonymous class will implement the interface. In this example, the anonymous class is an implementation of the ActionListener interface.

Local and anonymous classes provide an elegant and convenient way to implement adapter classes that are intended to be used once and have relatively short and simple implementations. The choice of local versus anonymous should largely depend on whether you need more than one instance of the class. If so, or if it's important that the class have a name for some other reason (readability), then you should use a local class. Otherwise, use an anonymous class. As in all design decisions of this nature, you should use whichever approach or style makes your code more readable and more understandable.

APPENDIX G
Java and UML Resources

Reference Books

- Kim Topley, *Java Foundation Classes*, Prentice Hall, 1998. Part of the Prentice Hall core series, this book provides a comprehensive introduction to the JFC, especially the Swing components.
- David Flanagan, *Java in a Nutshell*, 2d ed., O'Reilly and Associates 1997. Part of the O'Reilly Java series, this book provides a concise desktop reference to Java and the API.
- James Gosling, Bill Joy, and Guy Steele, *The Java Language Specification*, Addison-Wesley, 1996. This book, which is part of Addison-Wesley's Java Series, provides a detailed description of the Java language. An online version is available at

`http://java.sun.com/docs/books/jls`

- Martin Fowler, with Kendall Scott, *UML Distilled*, 2d ed., Addison-Wesley, 2000. This book, which is part of Addison-Wesley's Object Technology Series, provides a concise introduction to UML.

Online References

- `http://www.omg.org/` and `http://www.rational.com/` are two of the key Web sites for information on UML.
- `http://java.sun.com` is one of Sun Microsystems' Java Web sites. From this link you can find information about Java documentation, products, demonstrations, and links to other interesting Java sites.
- `http://java.sun.com/products/jdk/1.3/docs/` is the root page for all documentation on version 1.3 of the Java Development Kit.
- `http://java.sun.com/products/jdk/1.3/docs/api/index.html` is the root page for all documentation on the application programming interface, including detailed and up-to-date specifications for all classes in all API packages.
- `http://java.sun.com/products/jdk/1.3/docs/guide/awt/index.html` is the root page for all documentation pertaining to the Abstract Window Toolkit. It is complete and up-to-date.
- `http://java.sun.com/products/jdk/1.3/docs/guide/swing/index.html` provides detailed documentation about the Swing component set.
- `http://java.sun.com/docs/codeconv/index.html` provides a description of coding conventions suggested by the *Java Language Specification* and followed by the Java programming community. (These are summarized in Appendix A.)

- `http://java.sun.com/tutorial` provides an online Java tutorial.
- `http://softwaredev.earthweb.com/java/` is an extensive online Java resource center. This site includes reference information, free downloads, lots of demonstration programs, discussion groups, a glossary, and a directory to other Java sites.
- `http://www.javaworld.com` is the online version of *Java World* magazine.
- `news:comp.lang.java` is the Java online newsgroup.
- `www.JARS.com` is another Gamelan site that provides reviews and ratings of the best Java applets.

Subject Index

End User License Agreements

Sun Microsystems, Inc.

Binary Code License Agreement

READ THE TERMS OF THIS AGREEMENT AND ANY PROVIDED SUPPLEMENTAL LICENSE TERMS (COLLEC-TIVELY "AGREEMENT") CAREFULLY BEFORE OPENING THE SOFTWARE MEDIA PACKAGE. BY OPENING THE SOFTWARE MEDIA PACKAGE, YOU AGREE TO THE TERMS OF THIS AGREEMENT. IF YOU ARE ACCESSING THE SOFTWARE ELECTRONICALLY, INDICATE YOUR ACCEPTANCE OF THESE TERMS BY SELECTING THE "ACCEPT" BUTTON AT THE END OF THIS AGREEMENT. IF YOU DO NOT AGREE TO ALL THESE TERMS, PROMPTLY RETURN THE UNUSED SOFTWARE TO YOUR PLACE OF PURCHASE FOR A REFUND OR, IF THE SOFTWARE IS ACCESSED ELECTRONICALLY, SELECT THE "DECLINE" BUTTON AT THE END OF THIS AGREEMENT.

1. LICENSE TO USE. Sun grants you a non-exclusive and non-transferable license for the internal use only of the accompanying software and documentation and any error corrections provided by Sun (collectively "Software"), by the number of users and the class of computer hardware for which the corresponding fee has been paid.

2. RESTRICTIONS. Software is confidential and copyrighted. Title to Software and all associated intellectual property rights is retained by Sun and/or its licensors. Except as specifically authorized in any Supplemental License Terms, you may not make copies of Software, other than a single copy of Software for archival purposes. Unless enforcement is prohibited by applicable law, you may not modify, decompile, or reverse engineer Software. You acknowledge that Software is not designed, licensed or intended for use in the design, construction, operation or maintenance of any nuclear facility. Sun disclaims any express or implied warranty of fitness for such uses. No right, title or interest in or to any trademark, service mark, logo or trade name of Sun or its licensors is granted under this Agreement.

3. LIMITED WARRANTY. Sun warrants to you that for a period of ninety (90) days from the date of purchase, as evidenced by a copy of the receipt, the media on which Software is furnished (if any) will be free of defects in materials and workmanship under normal use. Except for the foregoing, Software is provided "AS IS". Your exclusive remedy and Sun's entire liability under this limited warranty will be at Sun's option to replace Software media or refund the fee paid for Software.

4. DISCLAIMER OF WARRANTY. UNLESS SPECIFIED IN THIS AGREEMENT, ALL EXPRESS OR IMPLIED CONDITIONS, REPRE-SENTATIONS AND WARRANTIES, INCLUDING ANY IMPLIED WARRANTY OF MERCHANTABILITY, FITNESS FOR A PARTIC-ULAR PURPOSE OR NON-INFRINGEMENT ARE DISCLAIMED, EXCEPT TO THE EXTENT THAT THESE DISCLAIMERS ARE HELD TO BE LEGALLY INVALID.

5. LIMITATION OF LIABILITY. TO THE EXTENT NOT PROHIBITED BY LAW, IN NO EVENT WILL SUN OR ITS LICENSORS BE LIABLE FOR ANY LOST REVENUE, PROFIT OR DATA, OR FOR SPECIAL, INDIRECT, CONSEQUENTIAL, INCIDENTAL OR PUNITIVE DAMAGES, HOWEVER CAUSED REGARDLESS OF THE THEORY OF LIABILITY, ARISING OUT OF OR RELATED TO THE USE OF OR INABILITY TO USE SOFTWARE, EVEN IF SUN HAS BEEN ADVISED OF THE POSSIBILITY OF SUCH DAMAGES. In no event will Sun's liability to you, whether in contract, tort (including negligence), or otherwise, exceed the amount paid by you for Software under this Agreement. The foregoing limitations will apply even if the above stated warranty fails of its essential purpose.

6. Termination. This Agreement is effective until terminated. You may terminate this Agreement at any time by destroying all copies of Software. This Agreement will terminate immediately without notice from Sun if you fail to comply with any provision of this Agreement. Upon Termination, you must destroy all copies of Software.

7. Export Regulations. All Software and technical data delivered under this Agreement are subject to US export control laws and may be subject to export or import regulations in other countries. You agree to comply strictly with all such laws and regulations and acknowledge that you have the responsibility to obtain such licenses to export, re-export, or import as may be required after delivery to you.

8. U.S. Government Restricted Rights. If Software is being acquired by or on behalf of the U.S. Government or by a U.S. Government prime contractor or subcontractor (at any tier), then the Government's rights in Software and accompanying documentation will be only as set forth in this Agreement; this is in accordance with 48 CFR 227.7201 through 227.7202-4 (for Department of Defense (DOD) acquisitions) and with 48 CFR 2.101 and 12.212 (for non-DOD acquisitions).

9. Governing Law. Any action related to this Agreement will be governed by California law and controlling U.S. federal law. No choice of law rules of any jurisdiction will apply.

10. Severability. If any provision of this Agreement is held to be unenforceable, this Agreement will remain in effect with the provision omitted, unless omission would frustrate the intent of the parties, in which case this Agreement will immediately terminate.

11. Integration. This Agreement is the entire agreement between you and Sun relating to its subject matter. It supersedes all prior or contemporaneous oral or written communications, proposals, representations and warranties and prevails over any conflicting or additional terms of any quote, order, acknowledgment, or other communication between the parties relating to its subject matter during the term of this Agreement. No modification of this Agreement will be binding, unless in writing and signed by an authorized representative of each party.

Java™ 2 Software Development Kit (J2SDK), Standard Edition, Version 1.3

SUPPLEMENTAL LICENSE TERMS

These supplemental license terms ("Supplemental Terms") add to or modify the terms of the Binary Code License Agreement (collectively, the "Agreement"). Capitalized terms not defined in these Supplemental Terms shall have the same meanings ascribed to them in the

Agreement. These Supplemental Terms shall supersede any inconsistent or conflicting terms in the Agreement, or in any license contained within the Software.

1. Software Internal Use and Development License Grant. Subject to the terms and conditions of this Agreement, including, but not limited to Section 4 (Java™ Technology Restrictions) of these Supplemental Terms, Sun grants you a non-exclusive, non-transferable, limited license to reproduce internally and use internally the binary form of the Software complete and unmodified for the sole purpose of designing, developing and testing your Java applets and applications intended to run on the Java platform ("Programs").

2. License to Distribute Software. Subject to the terms and conditions of this Agreement, including, but not limited to Section 4 (Java™ Technology Restrictions) of these Supplemental Terms, Sun grants you a non-exclusive, non-transferable, limited license to reproduce and distribute the Software in binary code form only, provided that (i) you distribute the Software complete and unmodified and only bundled as part of, and for the sole purpose of running, your Programs, (ii) the Programs add significant and primary functionality to the Software, (iii) you do not distribute additional software intended to replace any component(s) of the Software, (iv) you do not remove or alter any proprietary legends or notices contained in the Software, (v) you only distribute the Software subject to a license agreement that protects Sun's interests consistent with the terms contained in this Agreement, and (vi) you agree to defend and indemnify Sun and its licensors from and against any damages, costs, liabilities, settlement amounts and/or expenses (including attorneys' fees) incurred in connection with any claim, lawsuit or action by any third party that arises or results from the use or distribution of any and all Programs and/or Software.

3. License to Distribute Redistributables. Subject to the terms and conditions of this Agreement, including but not limited to Section 4 (Java Technology Restrictions) of these Supplemental Terms, Sun grants you a non-exclusive, non-transferable, limited license to reproduce and distribute the binary form of those files specifically identified as redistributable in the Software "README" file ("Redistributables") provided that: (i) you distribute the Redistributables complete and unmodified (unless otherwise specified in the applicable README file), and only bundled as part of Programs, (ii) you do not distribute additional software intended to supersede any component(s) of the Redistributables, (iii) you do not remove or alter any proprietary legends or notices contained in or on the Redistributables, (iv) you only distribute the Redistributables pursuant to a license agreement that protects Sun's interests consistent with the terms contained in the Agreement, and (v) you agree to defend and indemnify Sun and its licensors from and against any damages, costs, liabilities, settlement amounts and/or expenses (including attorneys' fees) incurred in connection with any claim, lawsuit or action by any third party that arises or results from the use or distribution of any and all Programs and/or Software.

4. Java Technology Restrictions. You may not modify the Java Platform Interface ("JPI", identified as classes contained within the "java" package or any subpackages of the "java" package), by creating additional classes within the JPI or otherwise causing the addition to or modification of the classes in the JPI. In the event that you create an additional class and associated API(s) which (i) extends the functionality of the Java platform, and (ii) is exposed to third party software developers for the purpose of developing additional software which invokes such additional API, you must promptly publish broadly an accurate specification for such API for free use by all developers. You may not create, or authorize your licensees to create, additional classes, interfaces, or subpackages that are in any way identified as "java", "javax", "sun" or similar convention as specified by Sun in any naming convention designation.

5. Trademarks and Logos. You acknowledge and agree as between you and Sun that Sun owns the SUN, SOLARIS, JAVA, JINI, FORTE, STAROFFICE, STARPORTAL and iPLANET trademarks and all SUN, SOLARIS, JAVA, JINI, FORTE, STAROFFICE, STARPORTAL and iPLANET-related trademarks, service marks, logos and other brand designations ("Sun Marks"), and you agree to comply with the Sun Trademark and Logo Usage Requirements currently located at http://www.sun.com/policies/trademarks. Any use you make of the Sun Marks inures to Sun's benefit.

6. Source Code. Software may contain source code that is provided solely for reference purposes pursuant to the terms of this Agreement. Source code may not be redistributed unless expressly provided for in this Agreement.

7. Termination for Infringement. Either party may terminate this Agreement immediately should any Software become, or in either party's opinion be likely to become, the subject of a claim of infringement of any intellectual property right.

For inquiries please contact: Sun Microsystems, Inc. 901 San Antonio Road, Palo Alto, California 94303 (LFI#83838/Form ID#011801)

Forte™ For Java™, Release 3.0, Community Edition

SUPPLEMENTAL LICENSE TERMS

These supplemental license terms ("Supplemental Terms") add to or modify the terms of the Binary Code License Agreement (collectively, the "Agreement"). Capitalized terms not defined in these Supplemental Terms shall have the same meanings ascribed to them in the Agreement. These Supplemental Terms shall supersede any inconsistent or conflicting terms in the Agreement, or in any license contained within the Software.

1. Software Internal Use and Development License Grant. Subject to the terms and conditions of this Agreement, including, but not limited to Section 4 (Java™ Technology Restrictions) of these Supplemental Terms, Sun grants you a non-exclusive, non-transferable, limited license to reproduce internally and use internally the binary form of the Software complete and unmodified for the sole purpose of designing, developing and testing your Java applets and applications intended to run on the Java platform ("Programs").

2. License to Distribute Software. Subject to the terms and conditions of this Agreement, including, but not limited to Section 4 (Java™ Technology Restrictions) of these Supplemental Terms, Sun grants you a non-exclusive, non-transferable, limited license to reproduce and distribute the Software in binary code form only, provided that (i) you distribute the Software complete and unmodified and only bundled as part of, and for the sole purpose of running, your Programs, (ii) the Programs add significant and primary functionality to the Software, (iii) you do not distribute additional software intended to replace any component(s) of the Software, (iv) for a particular version of the Java platform, any executable output generated by a compiler that is contained in the Software must (a) only be compiled from source code that conforms to the corresponding version of the OEM Java Language Specification; (b) be in the class file format defined by the corresponding version of the OEM Java Virtual Machine Specification; and (c) execute properly on a reference runtime, as specified by Sun, associated with such version of the Java platform, (v) you do not remove or alter any proprietary legends

or notices contained in the Software, (v) you only distribute the Software subject to a license agreement that protects Sun's interests consistent with the terms contained in this Agreement, and (vi) you agree to defend and indemnify Sun and its licensors from and against any damages, costs, liabilities, settlement amounts and/or expenses (including attorneys' fees) incurred in connection with any claim, lawsuit or action by any third party that arises or results from the use or distribution of any and all Programs and/or Software.

3. License to Distribute Redistributables. Subject to the terms and conditions of this Agreement, including but not limited to Section 4 (Java Technology Restrictions) of these Supplemental Terms, Sun grants you a non-exclusive, non-transferable, limited license to reproduce and distribute the binary form of those files specifically identified as redistributable in the Software "RELEASE NOTES" file ("Redistributables") provided that: (i) you distribute the Redistributables complete and unmodified (unless otherwise specified in the applicable RELEASE NOTES file), and only bundled as part of Programs, (ii) you do not distribute additional software intended to supersede any component(s) of the Redistributables, (iii) you do not remove or alter any proprietary legends or notices contained in or on the Redistributables, (iv) for a particular version of the Java platform, any executable output generated by a compiler that is contained in the Software must (a) only be compiled from source code that conforms to the corresponding version of the OEM Java Language Specification; (b) be in the class file format defined by the corresponding version of the OEM Java Virtual Machine Specification; and (c) execute properly on a reference runtime, as specified by Sun, associated with such version of the Java platform, (v) you only distribute the Redistributables pursuant to a license agreement that protects Sun's interests consistent with the terms contained in the Agreement, and (v) you agree to defend and indemnify Sun and its licensors from and against any damages, costs, liabilities, settlement amounts and/or expenses (including attorneys' fees) incurred in connection with any claim, lawsuit or action by any third party that arises or results from the use or distribution of any and all Programs and/or Software.

4. Java Technology Restrictions. You may not modify the Java Platform Interface ("JPI", identified as classes contained within the "java" package or any subpackages of the "java" package), by creating additional classes within the JPI or otherwise causing the addition to or modification of the classes in the JPI. In the event that you create an additional class and associated API(s) which (i) extends the functionality of the Java platform, and (ii) is exposed to third party software developers for the purpose of developing additional software which invokes such additional API, you must promptly publish broadly an accurate specification for such API for free use by all developers. You may not create, or authorize your licensees to create, additional classes, interfaces, or subpackages that are in any way identified as "java", "javax", "sun" or similar convention as specified by Sun in any naming convention designation.

5. Java Runtime Availability. Refer to the appropriate version of the Java Runtime Environment binary code license (currently located at http://www.java.sun.com/jdk/index.html) for the availability of runtime code which may be distributed with Java applets and applications.

6. Trademarks and Logos. You acknowledge and agree as between you and Sun that Sun owns the SUN, SOLARIS, JAVA, JINI, FORTE, and iPLANET trademarks and all SUN, SOLARIS, JAVA, JINI, FORTE, and iPLANET-related trademarks, service marks, logos and other brand designations ("Sun Marks"), and you agree to comply with the Sun Trademark and Logo Usage Requirements currently located at http://www.sun.com/policies/trademarks. Any use you make of the Sun Marks inures to Sun's benefit.

7. Source Code. Software may contain source code that is provided solely for reference purposes pursuant to the terms of this Agreement. Source code may not be redistributed unless expressly provided for in this Agreement.

8. Termination for Infringement. Either party may terminate this Agreement immediately should any Software become, or in either party's opinion be likely to become, the subject of a claim of infringement of any intellectual property right.

For inquiries please contact: Sun Microsystems, Inc. 901 San Antonio Road, Palo Alto, California 94303 (LFI#91205/Form ID#011801)

Prentice Hall License Agreement and Limited Warranty

READ THE FOLLOWING TERMS AND CONDITIONS CAREFULLY BEFORE OPENING THIS SOFTWARE PACKAGE. THIS LEGAL DOCUMENT IS AN AGREEMENT BETWEEN YOU AND PRENTICE-HALL, INC. (THE "COMPANY"). BY OPENING THIS SEALED SOFTWARE PACKAGE, YOU ARE AGREEING TO BE BOUND BY THESE TERMS AND CONDITIONS. IF YOU DO NOT AGREE WITH THESE TERMS AND CONDITIONS, DO NOT OPEN THE SOFTWARE PACKAGE. PROMPTLY RETURN THE UNOPENED SOFTWARE PACKAGE AND ALL ACCOMPANYING ITEMS TO THE PLACE YOU OBTAINED THEM FOR A FULL REFUND OF ANY SUMS YOU HAVE PAID.

1. GRANT OF LICENSE: In consideration of your purchase of this book, and your agreement to abide by the terms and conditions of this Agreement, the Company grants to you a nonexclusive right to use and display the copy of the enclosed software program (hereinafter the "SOFTWARE") on a single computer (i.e., with a single CPU) at a single location so long as you comply with the terms of this Agreement. The Company reserves all rights not expressly granted to you under this Agreement.

2. OWNERSHIP OF SOFTWARE: You own only the magnetic or physical media (the enclosed media) on which the SOFTWARE is recorded or fixed, but the Company and the software developers retain all the rights, title, and ownership to the SOFTWARE recorded on the original media copy(ies) and all subsequent copies of the SOFTWARE, regardless of the form or media on which the original or other copies may exist. This license is not a sale of the original SOFTWARE or any copy to you.

3. COPY RESTRICTIONS: This SOFTWARE and the accompanying printed materials and user manual (the "Documentation") are the subject of copyright. The individual programs on the media are copyrighted by the authors of each program. Some of the programs on the media include separate licensing agreements. If you intend to use one of these programs, you must read and follow its accompanying license agreement. You may not copy the Documentation or the SOFTWARE, except that you may make a single copy of the SOFTWARE for backup or archival purposes only. You may be held legally responsible for any copying or copyright infringement which is caused or encouraged by your failure to abide by the terms of this restriction.

4. USE RESTRICTIONS: You may not network the SOFTWARE or otherwise use it on more than one computer or computer terminal at the same time. You may physically transfer the SOFTWARE from one computer to another provided that the SOFTWARE is used

on only one computer at a time. You may not distribute copies of the SOFTWARE or Documentation to others. You may not reverse engineer, disassemble, decompile, modify, adapt, translate, or create derivative works based on the SOFTWARE or the Documentation without the prior written consent of the Company.

5. TRANSFER RESTRICTIONS: The enclosed SOFTWARE is licensed only to you and may not be transferred to any one else without the prior written consent of the Company. Any unauthorized transfer of the SOFTWARE shall result in the immediate termination of this Agreement.

6. TERMINATION: This license is effective until terminated. This license will terminate automatically without notice from the Company and become null and void if you fail to comply with any provisions or limitations of this license. Upon termination, you shall destroy the Documentation and all copies of the SOFTWARE. All provisions of this Agreement as to warranties, limitation of liability, remedies or damages, and our ownership rights shall survive termination.

7. MISCELLANEOUS: This Agreement shall be construed in accordance with the laws of the United States of America and the State of New York and shall benefit the Company, its affiliates, and assignees.

8. LIMITED WARRANTY AND DISCLAIMER OF WARRANTY: The Company warrants that the SOFTWARE, when properly used in accordance with the Documentation, will operate in substantial conformity with the description of the SOFTWARE set forth in the Documentation. The Company does not warrant that the SOFTWARE will meet your requirements or that the operation of the SOFTWARE will be uninterrupted or error-free. The Company warrants that the media on which the SOFTWARE is delivered shall be free from defects in materials and workmanship under normal use for a period of thirty (30) days from the date of your purchase. Your only remedy and the Company's only obligation under these limited warranties is, at the Company's option, return of the warranted item for a refund of any amounts paid by you or replacement of the item. Any replacement of SOFTWARE or media under the warranties shall not extend the original warranty period. The limited warranty set forth above shall not apply to any SOFTWARE which the Company determines in good faith has been subject to misuse, neglect, improper installation, repair, alteration, or damage by you. EXCEPT FOR THE EXPRESSED WARRANTIES SET FORTH ABOVE, THE COMPANY DISCLAIMS ALL WARRANTIES, EXPRESS OR IMPLIED, INCLUDING WITHOUT LIMITATION, THE IMPLIED WARRANTIES OF MERCHANTABILITY AND FITNESS FOR A PARTICULAR PURPOSE. EXCEPT FOR THE EXPRESS WARRANTY SET FORTH ABOVE, THE COMPANY DOES NOT WARRANT, GUARANTEE, OR MAKE ANY REPRESENTATION REGARDING THE USE OR THE RESULTS OF THE USE OF THE SOFTWARE IN TERMS OF ITS CORRECTNESS, ACCURACY, RELIABILITY, CURRENTNESS, OR OTHERWISE.

IN NO EVENT, SHALL THE COMPANY OR ITS EMPLOYEES, AGENTS, SUPPLIERS, OR CONTRACTORS BE LIABLE FOR ANY INCIDENTAL, INDIRECT, SPECIAL, OR CONSEQUENTIAL DAMAGES ARISING OUT OF OR IN CONNECTION WITH THE LICENSE GRANTED UNDER THIS AGREEMENT, OR FOR LOSS OF USE, LOSS OF DATA, LOSS OF INCOME OR PROFIT, OR OTHER LOSSES, SUSTAINED AS A RESULT OF INJURY TO ANY PERSON, OR LOSS OF OR DAMAGE TO PROPERTY, OR CLAIMS OF THIRD PARTIES, EVEN IF THE COMPANY OR AN AUTHORIZED REPRESENTATIVE OF THE COMPANY HAS BEEN ADVISED OF THE POSSIBILITY OF SUCH DAMAGES. IN NO EVENT SHALL LIABILITY OF THE COMPANY FOR DAMAGES WITH RESPECT TO THE SOFTWARE EXCEED THE AMOUNTS ACTUALLY PAID BY YOU, IF ANY, FOR THE SOFTWARE.

SOME JURISDICTIONS DO NOT ALLOW THE LIMITATION OF IMPLIED WARRANTIES OR LIABILITY FOR INCIDENTAL, INDIRECT, SPECIAL, OR CONSEQUENTIAL DAMAGES, SO THE ABOVE LIMITATIONS MAY NOT ALWAYS APPLY. THE WARRANTIES IN THIS AGREEMENT GIVE YOU SPECIFIC LEGAL RIGHTS AND YOU MAY ALSO HAVE OTHER RIGHTS WHICH VARY IN ACCORDANCE WITH LOCAL LAW.

Acknowledgment

YOU ACKNOWLEDGE THAT YOU HAVE READ THIS AGREEMENT, UNDERSTAND IT, AND AGREE TO BE BOUND BY ITS TERMS AND CONDITIONS. YOU ALSO AGREE THAT THIS AGREEMENT IS THE COMPLETE AND EXCLUSIVE STATEMENT OF THE AGREEMENT BETWEEN YOU AND THE COMPANY AND SUPERSEDES ALL PROPOSALS OR PRIOR AGREEMENTS, ORAL, OR WRITTEN, AND ANY OTHER COMMUNICATIONS BETWEEN YOU AND THE COMPANY OR ANY REPRESENTATIVE OF THE COMPANY RELATING TO THE SUBJECT MATTER OF THIS AGREEMENT.

Should you have any questions concerning this Agreement or if you wish to contact the Company for any reason, please contact in writing at the address below.

Robin Short
Prentice Hall PTR
One Lake Street
Upper Saddle River, New Jersey 07458